International borders as of 1937
ESTONIA
LATVIA
Riga
Baltic Sea
Dünaberg
Krottingen
LITHUANIA
Kowno
Wilna
EAST PRUSSIA (GER.)
Hochwald
Danzig
Augustow
Grodno
Graudenz
Wolfsschanze
Minsk
Moscow
U. S. S. R.
Kursk
Prokhorovka
Teterewino
Belgorod
Alexandrowka
Ljubotin
Kharkov
Federowka
Smijew
Stanitschnoje
Jefremowka
Staroverowka
Donets R.
romberg
Soldau
Bialystok
taren
Plock
Warsaw
POLAND
Kutno
Lodz
Tomassow
Bug R.
Kielce
Lublin
Oppeln
Vistula R.
Pripyat
Krasnoborki
Sabolot
Radomyshl
Pekartschina
Kiev
Tortschin
Zhitomir
Przemysl
hwitz
Krakau
Jaroslaw
Dnieper R.
Pivd. Buh R.
Taganrog
Rostov
Mariupol
VAKIA
Dniester R.
Greigova
Cherson
Budapest
HUNGARY
ya
ROMANIA
Black Sea
Danube R.
GOSLAVIA
BULG.
ALBANIA
GREECE
Larissa
onian Sea
Athens
NETH.
Venlo
Düsseldorf
Antwerp
GERMANY
Rhine R.
Hasselt
Cologne
Brussels
Maastricht
Düren
Weilwerwist
Altenkirchen
Aachen
Bonn
BELGIUM
Meuse R.
Rheinbach
Huy
Liege
Bad Münstereifel
Charleroi
La Gleize
Malmedy
Blankenheim
Koblenz
Ligneuville
Losheim
Petit Thier
Thirimont
Marienfels
St. Vith
Prüm
Mosel R.
Bastogne
Lutrebois
LUX.
Osweiler
Colmar-Berg
FRANCE
Trier
0 40 miles
0 40 kilometers
Luxembourg City

PEIPER'S LAST GAMBLE

PEIPER'S LAST GAMBLE

HITLER'S PANZER SPEARHEAD IN THE BATTLE OF THE BULGE 1944

BY
DANNY S. PARKER

FRONTLINE
BOOKS

First published in Great Britain in 2024
by Frontline Books
An imprint of
Pen & Sword Books Ltd
Yorkshire - Philadelphia

ISBN 978 1 03611 897 6

A CIP catalogue record for this book is available from the British Library

Typeset by Lapiz Digital
Printed and bound in the UK by CPI Group (UK) Ltd, Croydon, CR0 4YY.

Printed on paper from a sustainable source by
CPI Group (UK) Ltd, Croydon, CR0 4YY

Pen & Sword Books Limited incorporates the imprints of Archaeology, Atlas, Aviation, Battleground, Digital, Discovery, Family History, Fiction, History, Local, Local History, Maritime, Military, Military Classics, Politics, Select, Transport, True Crime, Air World, Claymore Press, Frontline Publishing, Leo Cooper, Remember When, Seaforth Publishing, The Praetorian Press, Wharncliffe Books, Wharncliffe Local History, Wharncliffe Transport, Wharncliffe True Crime and White Owl.

For a complete list of Pen & Sword titles please contact
PEN & SWORD BOOKS LTD
47 Church Street, Barnsley, South Yorkshire, S70 2AS, England
E-mail: enquiries@pen-and-sword.co.uk
Website: www.pen-and-sword.co.uk
or
PEN & SWORD BOOKS
1950 Lawrence Rd, Havertown, PA 19083, USA
E-mail: uspen-and-sword@casematepublishers.com

For Ann, Jens
and Will Cavanagh

CONTENTS

ACKNOWLEDGMENTS

Historical research spanning three decades depends on many institutions and individuals. I'll apologise at the outset: it is a massive work, reporting from over a hundred interviews and thousands of archival pages consulted. Still, I must honor those who have entrusted their stories to me. And the archival finds I've made will be lost if I don't give them to you now.

The late William C.C. Cavanagh roamed around through the Ardennes with me for many weeks in the 1980s and 1990s to interview many civilian witnesses while they were still living. Will also knew the Ardennes battlefield like the back of his hand (he lived in Faymonville) and his insights into engagements, terrain and the battle itself now are in full bloom in this account. I remain deeply grateful to his memory, but also to his wife Denise and daughter Fiona.

I was greatly assisted by Dr Jens Westemeier, whose Ph.D. dissertation on Peiper at the University of Potsdam towers over supposition and myth. While we have approached our subject differently, Jens was instrumental in making many contacts and interviews and was always helpful. Indeed, we did ten years of research in parallel and developed a friendship over that time.

One person to whom I owe an exceptionally heavy debt is my very professional Austrian interpreter, Helmut Thiess. More than a professor with interest in languages, Helmut became a close friend, only to die tragically in the midst of the long research. Helmut performed a very difficult job in assisting me in three trips to Germany with many interviews as well as the translation of hundreds of pages of key documents relative to my story. I miss his warm wit and wise counsel and like to think he would be proud of what he helped me to create.

Neill Thomson, an expert on Jochen Peiper, was always enthusiastic in assisting with various documents and matters important to the puzzle. In Holland, Mike Smeets was helpful with the many titbits and interviews he has collected over the years. In Germany, Col Eckart Klink provided important access to his father's papers containing important correspondence with Jochen Peiper. *Quick* journalist Harvey T. Rowe kindly shared documents from his own research.

At the U.S. National Archives, I had much help. Richard Boylan and the late John E. Taylor have been instrumental in helping me over a decade to wade through the mountain of documents and papers dealing with the

Malmedy trial, Peiper and the many records involved. Jim Kelling and Niels Cordes assisted with long hours reviewing microfilm. Spending many weeks in Washington, I am indebted to the Tabard Inn – my home away from home.

Thanks to the late John Toland and his daughter Tamiko for making all of his private papers and taped interviews available to me at both the Franklin D. Roosevelt Library and the Library of Congress. In Hyde Park, I was ably assisted by Karen Burtis and at the Library of Congress I had assistance from Ronald E. Cogan, Jeff Flannery and Bryan Cornell. Linda Wheeler guided me through the NSDAP Hauptarchiv at the Hoover Institution at Stanford University, where we unearthed critical letters that Peiper wrote to Himmler's mistress during wartime. We located the originals at the BA-Koblenz.

In the United Kingdom, I had the considerable assistance of Vivienne Bales and Bruno Derrick at the Public Records Office at Kew Gardens. In York, the late Charles Whiting made a number of documents and letters available to me from his association with the Peiper and was kind enough to cover his recollections at his home in York. Similarly, Gen. Michael Reynolds, the late author of his own important account, *The Devil's Adjutant*, always lent a hand.

The late John S.D. Eisenhower graciously made available his personal papers at the Eisenhower library as well as agreed to a pleasurable afternoon interview covering his father's remembrances of those days. At the Eisenhower Library in Abilene, Kansas, James Leyerzapf helped me wade through the collections there. At the *Bundesarchiv-Koblenz* I was guided through important personal papers by Gregor Pickro and photographic collections by Frau Ruhl. Similar help was rendered by Dr Günther Montfort and Carina Notzke at the *Bundesarchiv-Freiburg*.

Before his passing, Burton Ellis made all of his personal papers and documents available for the work. Similarly from the Malmedy trial defense, Willis Everett III made similar material available from his late father's papers. Of particular note also must be Dr James Weingartner at the University of Southern Illinois, the author of a seminal work on the trial: *Crossroads of Death*. Jim has always shared from the Everett Papers and other resources.

I made a special effort to speak to present each side of the story. As such, there is certain to be material in the book that will affront both camps. I remain unapologetic; the story of this personality has long suffered from biased coverage. I approached the story with as much objectivity as I could muster. In Germany, many faced me with openness even when our views did not match. While a number of veterans were hesitant to speak, others were forthcoming: Hans Siptrott, Arndt Fischer, Rolf Reiser, Paul Fröhlich, Erhard Gührs, Fritz Kosmehl, Ralf Tiemann and Manfred Thorn. Werner Ackermann consented to three extensive interviews concerning his experiences in the tank regiment of the Leibstandarte and particularly over key insights relative to the Malmedy incident and post-war cover-up. I acknowledge several unmentioned who were willing to speak only on condition of anonymity. Appreciation also to the late Hubert Meyer for access to the previously secret HIAG archives at BA-MA Freiburg. Hans Weber and Timm Hassler, both experts on the Ardennes and Kampfgruppe Peiper, checked important details.

Within the project, I benefitted from helpful readers: Ann Hamilton Shields and Erik Wuite, who helped review the writing with critical comment throughout. During my last ten years of work, Ann really became the project research assistant in Germany and contributed hundreds of selfless hours. Lisa Kramer and Josephine Moore helped with early editing. Gene Thorp professionally rendered the maps for the new book. I appreciate my literary agent Katherine Fausset with Curtis Brown, who has always helped in a conscientious manner. I appreciate her long patience. Thankful, also to Martin Mace and Lisa Hoosan at Frontline who were co-operative in taking on the massive capstone to the Peiper quadrilogy.

At home, my family cheerily endured years of work with Peiper and the war. That means a lot.

Danny S. Parker
Cocoa Beach, January 2024

PROLOGUE – A NEW DUNKIRK

What was this forest savage, rough and stern,
Which in the very thought renews the fear.
So bitter it is, death is little more.

— Dante, *Inferno*, Canto I

In the Second World War, the self-styled leader of Nazi Germany, Adolf Hitler, saw his plans of European conquest falter in late 1944, both in Russia and in France. Hitler's Third Reich seemed to teeter near its end. Still, as his Western and Eastern foes paused in their advance to crush Germany that autumn, Hitler wondered: might there be a final chance to reverse the course of the failing war?

"Joachim" Peiper, a Waffen SS officer, was one of the most celebrated heroes of Hitler's armies. A long-time adjutant of Heinrich Himmler, the head of the SS, and completely dedicated to the Nazi cause, Peiper had fought in every major campaign. Yet, as with Hitler's wartime aims, this SS warrior was now ailing from the German military's devastation in summer 1944. After vanquishing Hitler's armies in Normandy, the Allied forces were now poised on the German border to end Hitler's Third Reich. 'We shall win this war,' Peiper had remarked wryly to a comrade while under furious Allied bombardment in France, 'just like the last one.' Ailing from a combination of battle fatigue and hepatitis, he was evacuated to a field hospital and then back Germany in August 1944.

In the autumn, leaves of Upper Bavaria in 1944 shifted yellow and gold as Peiper, with facial tones to match, ebbed in the *Haus Bayern* in Lake Tegern. Formerly the hotel had been a resort of holiday delight. The historic place, owned up until the First World War by the Grand Duchesse of Coburg and frequented by Russian dukes, was now a military infirmary, as were almost all of the hotels in the area.[1] Here, Bavarian oldsters took the cure while basking in the idyllic view of the glacial blue waters of Lake Tegern. Now the grand old hotel, high on the hill at 23 Neureuthstrasse, served as an improvised hospital for the flood of scarred and wounded soldiers returning for front-line duty in Hitler's beleaguered Reich.

Wounds had little to do with Peiper's suffering. The few shrapnel splinters Peiper took to his right thigh at Normandy on 2 August 1944 healed quickly. The rumour circulated widely within the 1st SS Panzer Division, the Leibstandarte Adolf Hitler, that Jochen Peiper collapsed from a heart attack just before the near suicidal advance towards Avranches.[2] Others said jaundice and nerves had weakened him to the point of breakdown.[3] Excessive use of Pervitin? That he suffered from hepatitis was sure, but rumours suggested worse. To those who visited, the tough SS Lt. colonel seemed near the end of his resources.

The military hospital where Peiper was sequestered was not far from his home. The posh dining room in SS Reserve Hospital 501 was ironically breathtaking – from its ornate, white-framed casement windows the ailing soldiers could see clear across Lake Tegern towards Rottach Egern. There lived his wife Sigurd and her three children, able to pay periodic visits to Papi nearby. There was Elke, now a little girl of 4 years old, Hinrich the boy toddler, and Silke, born just the previous summer. Although Sigurd was happy to see her man – the fabled war hero and the SS Reichsführer's former adjutant – she could see that his continuing maladies were worsening. Elke remembered her father's strangely yellow skin with a child's innocent fascination.

The SS colonel's skin had a sickly ochre cast from jaundice and three years of front-line combat. Too many days of coffee and cigarettes followed by nights of fighting and frustration. His nerves were shot. His physician at the hospital confided to Sigurd that her husband was at his mental breaking point. The cumulative wounds taking Peiper away from Normandy impacted more his mind than his body. *Nervenzusammenbruch* was the whisper among the old panzer hands – 'Just a little more and the cable could break without warning.'[4] The signs of *Kriegsneurose* were there – the shakes, a detached stare, and fitful sleep. During the early autumn officers and men from the Leibstandarte visited Peiper frequently.[5] Though he seemed less spirited, he was heartened to learn that his division was being rebuilt once more. He intended to return.

From his bed Peiper learned that the Leibstandarte had first concentrated around Siegburg and was earnestly now rebuilt near Minden. Replacements flooded into the skeletal regiments, even if they were not the Waffen SS material of old. The requirements for athleticism, flawless teeth, and a towering physique had long since been ignored. Autumn's infusion of SS manhood included ethnic Germans from Rumania, Hungary, and the Balkans. And those who were German were now often less-than-enthusiastic draftees pulled from the shrinking *Kriegsmarine* or – worse – the impotent Luftwaffe. Peiper himself referred to these derisively as those 'bastards from Paris'.[6]

While Jochen Peiper recuperated from Normandy's disasters, his nation's troubled leader was also convalescing. The assassination attempt in July transformed Hitler into a physical wreck. His left arm trembled, he was now hard of hearing, and in August he had a terrible head cold. It was with these physical ailments and his deepening quandary following the disasters of the summer of 1944 that the idea for the grand stroke in Ardennes was born. In Russia an entire army group was swallowed up, and in the West the Allies stormed out of Normandy and raced for the German border. And yet even as his armies ran for their lives on these last days of August, Hitler showed flashes of his old defiance. 'We will continue this fight at all costs,' he railed, 'until, as Frederick the Great said, one of our damned enemies becomes too exhausted to continue the fight.'[7]

Now Hitler might as well have been among the guileless German public whom his propaganda minister manipulated. For, like those he led, Hitler enthusiastically embraced Propaganda Minister, Josef Goebbels' mantra of new miracle weapons – *Wunderwaffen* – although he himself was aware that none of them were really available. True, the new Sturmgewehr MP 44 assault rifle was a masterpiece of ingenuity and mass production – an infantry weapon finally available to the infantry masses, one that delivered the accuracy of a rifle along with the devastating automatic fire of a submachine gun.[8] Yet how would they train the green conscripts who would shoulder the new assault rifle? The Messerschmitt Me-262 jet aircraft were certainly revolutionary, but the nascent technology suffered teething troubles and they were not available in numbers that could change the air equation.[9] Similarly, watching the V-2 rocket spout flame and bolt beyond the far reaches of the atmosphere had initially buoyed Hitler's hopes, but in the final months of 1944 the 5,000 missiles he needed to wage a wanton vengeance campaign on England simply were not there.[10] And the one factor that would truly change the war – German atomic bomb research – crept along at a leaden pace. In 1942 Hitler learned that such a weapon might be possible, but it remained years off.

Through the intrigue of Allied counter-espionage and the dreamy uncertainties of Werner Heisenberg's calculations and his atomic bomb programme, the Allied nightmare vision of a German nuclear weapon loomed a question mark. Erich Schumann, the physics professor in charge of Hitler's weapons research, wrote in 1944 that he had discovered a method that used hollow charges to generate the extremely high temperatures (millions of degrees centigrade) and pressures necessary to trigger nuclear fusion. Some said that Kurt Diebner, a rival of Heisenberg, might manage a test of a crude weapon based on these principles in early 1945. Were atomic weapons possible?[11]

With time an imperative; the need for a delay in the war's trajectory churned in Hitler's mind. Just maybe … Indeed, Himmler had said as much to Jochen Peiper earlier that autumn. If the war dragged on for much longer, a revolutionary super bomb would be unleashed to end the conflict. Hitler needed to hang on for a further six months, though, before this weapon was available to settle the score.[12] In July 1944 the head of Himmler's *Ahnenerbe* (an SS ancestral heritage think-tank), Wolfram Sievers, confided to SS anthropologist Ernst Schaefer about a new 'secret weapon which would decide the outcome of the war'.

Peiper knew Schaefer well as an SS adventurer-cum-Indiana-Jones type. Schaefer learned from Sievers that 'enormous quantities of energy would be released from the disintegration of atoms' from the new weapon, and it would result in 'earthquake like explosions'.[13] Such claims were making the rounds. 'Just hold out until Christmas and then everything is saved,' declared a regimental commander in the 2nd Panzer Division. 'The secret weapon that destroys everything within 750 metres is already in mass production.' For any opportunity to buy time, Hitler needed a great blow against the western alliance, a decisive strike. It would take something of that magnitude to delay the war for the *Geheimwaffen* – the secret weapons.

For a time the Führer remained bedridden, lethargic, and uncharacteristically indecisive. But after thwarting the bold Allied airborne landings at Arnhem in mid-September, it might be that his western armies could hold on to a defensive line roughly along the German border. Seeing himself as a beleaguered modern-day Frederick the Great, he looked for some bold counterattack that would change his fortunes in the West. Even as early as 19 August he had commanded his internal military staff to consider a bold counter-stroke in the West in November, when Allied air power could not operate, insisting that twenty-five new divisions be delivered to that front in the next two months.[14] Splitting the Allied alliance was key, he wagered, but that would require a shattering blow. The recent Allied capture of the great port of Antwerp now pushed the worried German leader toward a tantalising target. Seizing Antwerp would be a devastating setback to the Allied war effort.

In the days that followed, Hitler's closest general, Genobst Alfred Jodl, was called to his sickbed, bringing along a map on his request.[15] To Jodl, Hitler seemed to have shaken his lethargy, even if he was still in pyjamas. His stenographer noted that the 'bomb which had meant death and severe injuries for many of his staff' had left Hitler convinced of his divine providence.[16] His language was animated as he stammered vigorously about the need to 'advance against the flank and rear of the Allies at a time still to be decided and to bring about a fundamental change in the situation in the West'.

As he drew a crayon line on the map, Hitler told Jodl of another intuitive flash. He would strike a shattering blow against the Allies from the Ardennes – that magical Belgian border land that some said was Shakespeare's 'Forest of Arden'. The blast would take the Allies by surprise – just as done in 1940 – but this time with the objective of Antwerp.[17] Jodl made a rough sketch on the map, listening as Hitler emphasized a proviso that the new SS 'Sixth Panzer Army be formed under Oberstgruppenführer Josef "Sepp" Dietrich, who is to be charged with its reconstitution'. Gen. Hasso von Manteuffel would command of the 5th Panzer Army to camouflage the move. *A full SS army under old Dietrich.*[18] SS officer Otto Günsche, Hitler's personal adjutant, recalled:

> Why did he attack when the Russians were approaching from the east? … Hitler always pointed out the possibility of peace with the west. The war could not be won militarily. Hitler knew it. He knew he couldn't speak with Churchill and Roosevelt politically the way things stood. He proposed to attack the west with all possible military forces. Then he could achieve political success through military success – to break the western alliance and split the U.S. and Britain.[19]

Hitler saw the Ardennes as his decisive field – a place to crystallise smouldering differences among the Western Allies, allowing him to broker a separate peace.[20] Although Hitler was ready to entrust him with the prime effort, Sepp Dietrich was hardly up to the task, either in experience or in motivation. Normandy had sapped his enthusiasm. 'After hard fighting of 64 days duration,' Dietrich would later recall, 'the invasion front collapsed and the German troops, although delaying the enemy, had to fall back to the Westwall.'

> ... the German people were at the end of their strength. Only the 'figure-jugglers' and the inventors of God's miracle weapons had the vigour to end the war.[21]

Hitler's household military staff would learn of the German leader's desperate plan only days later on 16 September at his East Prussian headquarters near Rastenburg. It was a grey Sunday afternoon in that dismal pine forest when Werner Kreipe, the new Luftwaffe liaison, attended the usual meeting of Hitler and his generals at OKW in the bunker complex. Kreipe dutifully recorded the proceedings – as uninspiring as they were. Word from the fighting fronts detailed a dizzying series of German reversals.

Genobst Jodl, standing before his glum audience, groped for something optimistic. One teasing titbit involved a handful of SS panzer troops from Das Reich, the 2nd SS Panzer Division, audaciously throwing back a much larger American attack force attempting to punch their way out of the Ardennes into the German Eifel. Jodl quickly moved from the other disasters to describe this minor affair, but at the word 'Ardennes', Hitler bolted to his feet as if receiving an electric shock. He moved to the gigantic situation map – the Ardennes. That romantic land of the French – Wallonian castles, verdure, and swift-flowing tree-lined streams. It was also the place where his 1940 gamble had precipitated the collapse of the French Republic. 'I will attack,' he said, sweeping his hand across the unrolled map, 'from here out of the Ardennes with the objective Antwerp!'

The audience at *Wolfsschanze* reeled. Everywhere the German army was retreating; Antwerp was over a hundred miles away from the front. The means for a stand on the German border – much less a grand offensive – seemed whimsical. Yet on that day Hitler saw sudden inspiration. His brainwave would reverse the course of the war – or so he said. 'Führer's decision, counter-attack out the Ardennes, objective Antwerp,' Kreipe recorded tersely in his diary, 'Slice through between the British and the Americans – a new Dunkirk!'[22]

The German leader believed that the Allies would hold the Ardennes lightly before their push into Germany north and south of that notoriously difficult terrain. The Führer was so confident in his bold ploy that he ordered file records drawn from the dazzling 1940 Blitzkrieg that swept the same region. 'A single breakthrough on the Western Front!' he crowed to his incredulous armaments minister. 'You'll see!'

> It will lead to collapse and panic among the Americans. We'll drive right through their middle and take Antwerp. Then they have lost their supply port. And a tremendous pocket will encircle the entire English army, with hundreds of thousands of prisoners, as we used to do in Russia![23]

Inevitably, the subject of the air cover arose. In 1940, the Luftwaffe had been instrumental in the German victory. The offensive would be launched in the winter, Hitler opined. 'In bad flying weather,' Hitler argued pointedly, 'the enemy air force won't be flying either.' It was a thinly veiled reference to the impotence of Hermann Göring's air force. Hitler declared the attack would begin in November. But just in case, he had another request, which Werner Kreipe tersely jotted in his notebook. 'Hitler demands one thousand five hundred fighters by November 1st.'

The chiefs of staff of the German high command reached back to a time-honored tradition stretching back to Helmuth von Moltke, the Elder who planned German military operations before the Great War. Hitler ordered his generals to study alternative offensive plans and submit them along with operational details covering his pet operation. This was done. The five alternatives drawn up meticulously by Jodl's staff officers were dismissed as lacking in imagination. Instead, Hitler guided their thinking back to the Ardennes.[24] A combined plan submitted to the German leader on 11 October proposed the broad outlines: an attack by two panzer armies and one regular army moving out from the German Eifel between Monschau and Echternach, sweeping across the Meuse river in a lightning advance through the Ardennes. The rapier-like thrust would bypass Brussels and reach Antwerp within a week.[25]

For his part, Jodl and the *Wehrmachtführungsstab* (Armed Forces Operations Staff) would mastermind the operational details and locate combat forces. Meanwhile, Genobst Wilhelm Keitel, nominally powerful head of OKW, was assigned to secure the necessary fuel and ammunition.[26] Even such mundane details remained top secret, with all communication exchanged by courier. And all those brought in on the plan had to sign a statement saying that, should word leak out, failure would be punishable by firing squad.

Adolf Hitler vigorously pursued any way out for his crumbling empire, as recorded by his fawning diary keeper, Dr Percy Schramm.[27] Hitler continually lectured that reaching Antwerp would depend on a slashing advance from the German border to seize bridges across the formidable Meuse river. *Die Maas* – in German – was that magnificent water course sweeping its winding way through a series of precipitous defiles all the way from the French frontier at Givet, past fortress-hilled Dinant and Namur, to that large industrial city of Liège astride the big river. The gorges were numerous, with a height often over 90m, and the river itself over 80m wide, running both swift and deep. Bridges were few.

Given the limitations, Hitler knew he would need panzer leaders capable of a Blitzkrieg advance of classic proportions and perhaps one that took advantage of the hours of darkness. Peiper and the Leibstandarte were already on his mind – the man who had punched through Russian lines in the dead of night to save the 320th Division; the man who had seized Kharkov to press on to Belgorod, and the man whose dedicated tank regiment had slashed into the Russians at Kursk and at Mortain in Normandy – even if turned back.

These were the kind of men who would lead his final great gamble. Perhaps he could stack the deck by inserting some battle-tried shenanigans to catch the cocky Americans off guard. By spreading confusion in the wake of a planned panzer wedge, the Ardennes would be his new Rossbach and Leuthen. And to deliver such an audacious victory? SS Obersturmbannführer Jochen Peiper.

Chapter 1

'HOLD THE REINS LOOSE'

The whole art of war consists of guessing what is on the other side of the hill.

The Duke of Wellington

In the late autumn of 1944, weighty details of Adolf Hitler's final great military gamble piled up against his ambition. Even with great effort, the timing of the attack slipped to late November. That was the earliest time that the German leader expected to be able to assemble effective reserves, not the least of which was an SS tank army with which he fervently desired to lead his offensive. He also needed time to accumulate 17,500 cubic metres of fuel – a difficult task given the Allied aerial torment of that industry.[1] Most vital, Hitler's armies must have poor flying weather under which to attack. That large exception to 1940 glared at the Führer and his generals as they ran map exercises. Without this air cover, the Allied air forces would strafe their troops, bomb their tanks, and destroy supply lines:

> The only thing which is not in our favor this time is the air situation. That is why we are now forced to take advantage of the bad winter weather. The air situation forces us to do so.[2]

Just as in 1940, the question also arose over whether the panzer or infantry forces should lead the attack. In the May 1940 campaign it was decided to use both infantry and tank forces simultaneously, even though at that time Genflm. Erich von Manstein worried that his mobile units might arrive on the Meuse too exhausted to force the river crossing. Four years later Hitler, the First World War infantry corporal, had his own ideas. On 18 November 1944, he decreed that the first attack wave, wherever possible, was to consist mainly of infantry forces with assault guns to preserve the effectiveness of the waiting armor.[3] Doubts persisted among Hitler's staff. Jochen Peiper had definite opinions. Inexperienced teenage infantry or lackadaisical ex-air force men to effect a breakthrough? 'Wastes too much time,' Peiper sneered, complaining that those advocating this knew nothing of modern battle.

The need for poor flying weather produced a suggestion from Dr Oskar Schuster, Hitler's staff meteorologist. The target date should be 25 November as historically, low-pressure cyclones with poor flying weather dominated Western Europe at that time of year. Yet with flagging fuel deliveries and delayed reinforcement arrivals, it became clear that 25 November was impossible for O-Tag. It was then that Dr Werner Schwerdtfeger at the Luftwaffe's Central Weather Group received a call. Even though Schwerdtfeger was considered a meteorological prodigy, the request flabbergasted him. He was asked to identify a five-day period in the month of December west of the Rhine and in South England and the Ardennes where fog or low clouds would continuously cover the region and inhibit flying. Moreover, the young meteorologist was told he must give at least a two-day warning of the forecast. Then, on 11 December, he hastily contacted OKW with news: poor flying weather was about to begin around 15 December, he claimed, and 'the Allies cannot bomb or use visual air support for the next seven days'.[4] Hitler immediately affixed the starting date for the offensive as 16 December.

'Watch on the Rhine' included an elaborate cover plan: the Germans leaked that a large armored reserve was being accumulated to protect the southern entrance to the industrial Ruhr. A lengthy series of instructions followed, all to bolster the credibility of the fake operation. Movements were to be night only in the Eifel area opposite the Ardennes, whereas daylight unloading of troops was to be done in the Cologne area. The troop assembly areas were carefully staged a distance north and south of the breakthrough zone so as to not disclose the true intent of the movements. Camouflage officers were authorised to exact severe punishment on troops not properly observing security protocols. Reconnaissance and artillery registration were expressly forbidden. More obvious moves, such as headquarters and armor units, were to be done only at the last minute, with supply depots carefully dispersed by forest roads.[5] Of greatest importance were orders forbidding wireless transmissions. Without radio traffic, evidence vanished of the build-up from Gen. Dwight D. Eisenhower's 'most secret source' ULTRA – the secret British intelligence decoding system.

In the sudden vacuum, conventional American intelligence became convinced that Genflm. Gerd von Rundstedt had taken over leadership of the German armed forces.[6] Hitler had not been heard publicly since the day of the failed attempt on his life on 20 July 1944. Was he dead, wounded, or insane?[7] Some speculated that von Rundstedt held the military reins, while Himmler played the remaining political cards. One radio dispatch suggested Hitler's late autumn leadership on the Eastern Front demanded some display that the Führer was still alive and in charge, lest flagging morale there plummet even further.[8]

For the most part the Allies fell for the German ruse, mostly because it was what the commanders expected. Their top-secret intelligence weapon, ULTRA, had always forewarned of major impending enemy operations; no one suspected that the Germans might have caught on. So heavily had the Allies come to rely on ULTRA that the intelligence officers such as Brig. Gen. Edwin L. Sibert, with the U.S. 12th Army Group, took the absence of direct evidence of a German attack as proof that one was not in the offing.

The fact was that the Germans had come to suspect that they had a security problem. Rather than blaming the fallibility of their coding machine, a typewriter-like apparatus called Enigma, Hitler suspected internal leaks among his untrustworthy generals. The far-reaching conspiracy associated with the attempt on his life on 20 July 1944 did little to alter that perception.

Even more, the German *Abwehr* had increasing awareness that Enigma had been penetrated. The 'leak' came from the indiscretion of a staff member of Prince Bernhard of The Netherlands. The American intelligence service, the OSS, had long been concerned about the ability of the C-in-C of Dutch Forces to choose trustworthy associates. Their caution was warranted, for the prince selected a certain Mr Lindemans as his confidential agent.

What Bernhard did not know was that 27-year old Christiaan Antoniius Lindemans was a dangerous and shrewd double agent who had been working for the German Abwehr since 1943.[9] By November 1944, SHAEF intelligence had found him out, but not before he had infiltrated the British sector of the Normandy beachhead the previous summer. In September he was able to get back to German intelligence at Driebergen the astounding claim that the Allies had *broken* Enigma. His other intelligence – that the English were about to stage a major airborne operation to seize a bridge across the Rhine – came true when the British began parachuting into Arnhem a week later.

The German signals security chiefs had already begun to suspect the confidence of their radio transmissions. All this seems to have filtered up to OKW. Although it was true that use of radio would need to go on for simple military expediency, ULTRA or not, the Germans endeavoured to make greater use of their field telephones as they retired to the natural safety behind their border. In late 1944 a new ciphering machine was manufactured, but use of Enigma continued – it was simply not possible to produce enough updated machines quickly enough. Perhaps with this in mind, Hitler, when setting the ground rules for the planning of his surprise offensive, dictated that none of the orders related to the operation be sent over wireless.

To throw off Allied intelligence types, a fake defensive operation with the name *Abwehrschlacht im Westen* (Defensive Battle in the West) was floated on to the airwaves. The hoax suggested the German armored reserves were to be used as the Allies threatened the Rhine crossing. The Allied intelligence chiefs took the bait. This was precisely what their intelligence officers suspected, and their own prejudice aided the enemy misdirection. Meanwhile, extraordinary security cloaked the real intentions.

The closest the Allies came to the secret was in a message decrypted from the Japanese. On 15 November 1944, the Japanese ambassador Baron Hiroshi Oshima, met over lunch with Foreign Minister Joachim von Ribbentrop in Berlin. Oshima cabled the Japanese emperor the following day that, 'Hitler had promised him a German attack in the West,' not realising that the messages

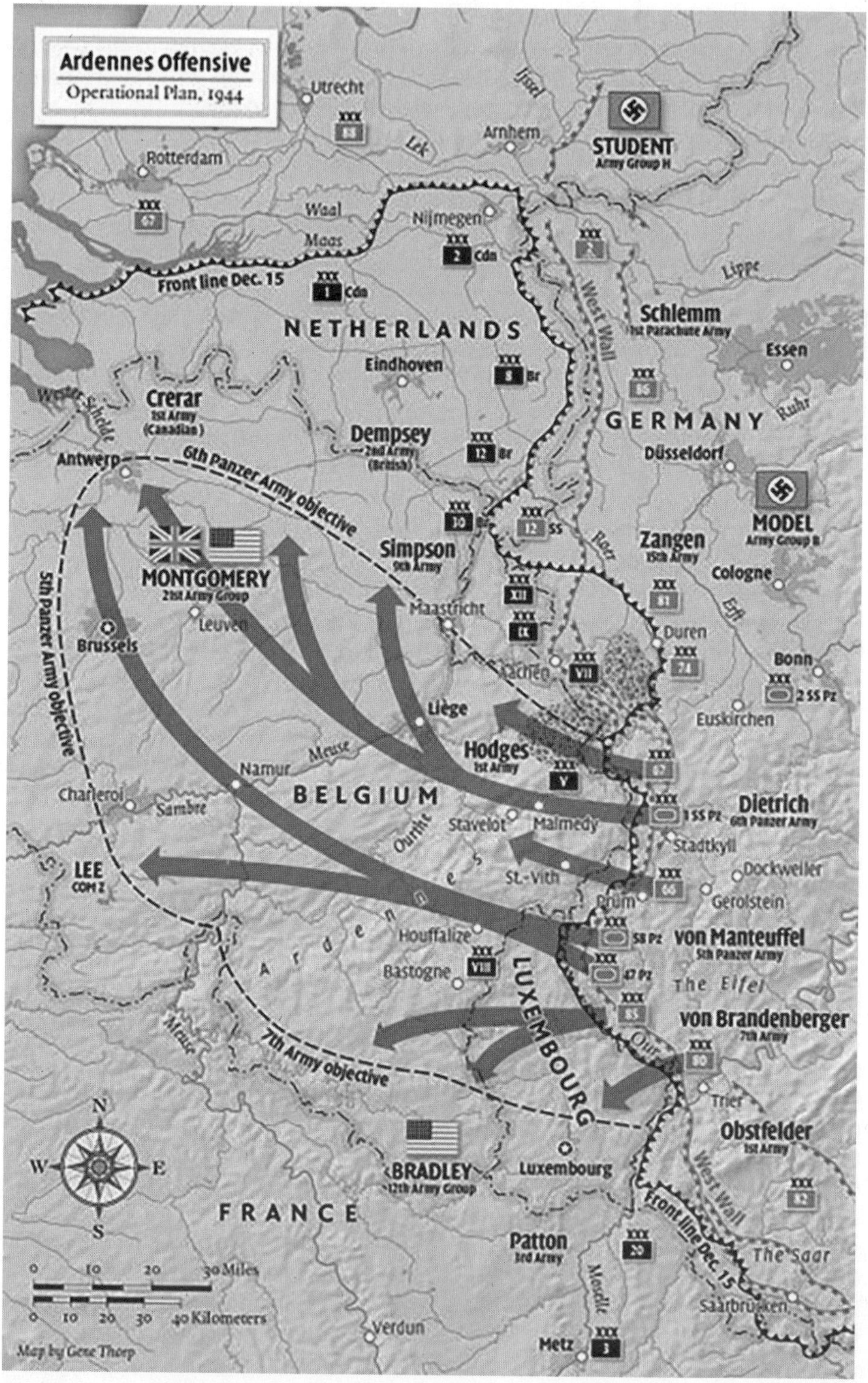

Ardennes Offensive
Operational Plan, 1944
Utrecht
Rotterdam
Arnhem
STUDENT
Army Group H
Waal
Maas
Nijmegen
2 Cdn
Front line Dec. 15
1 Cdn
NETHERLANDS
Schlemm
1st Parachute Army
Essen
Eindhoven
8 Br
West Wall
Crerar
1st Army (Canadian)
Dempsey
2nd Army (British)
12 Br
GERMANY
Ruhr
Düsseldorf
Antwerp
6th Panzer Army objective
30 Br
12 SS
MODEL
Army Group B
Zangen
15th Army
Simpson
9th Army
MONTGOMERY
21st Army Group
Cologne
Maastricht
Leuven
Brussels
Duren
Bonn
2 SS Pz
Euskirchen
5th Panzer Army objective
Liège
Hodges
1st Army
Meuse
Namur
BELGIUM
Dietrich
6th Panzer Army
1 SS Pz
Charleroi
Sambre
Stavelot
Malmedy
Stadtkyll
Ourthe
LEE
COM Z
St.-Vith
Dockweiler
Prüm
Gerolstein
Houffalize
58 Pz
von Manteuffel
5th Panzer Army
Ardennes
47 Pz
Bastogne
LUXEMBOURG
The Eifel
von Brandenberger
7th Army
Our
7th Army objective
Trier
Obstfelder
1st Army
N
W
E
S
BRADLEY
12th Army Group
Luxembourg
FRANCE
West Wall
Patton
3rd Army
Front line Dec. 15
The Saar
Moselle
0 10 20 30 Miles
0 10 20 30 40 Kilometers
Saarbrücken
Verdun
Metz
Map by Gene Thorp

were straight away moving onto the ULTRA decrypt list.[10] Unwittingly, Oshima clouded the intelligence with his own doubts as to the German foreign minister's trustworthiness: 'In view of Ribbentrop's record … this can be recorded as one of the instances in which truth from the mouth of a liar reaches the highest pinnacle of deceptiveness.'

Despite that fact that Gen. Bradley appeared to have discerned a German attack in the West, he did not know where it would come. Indeed, the Allies expected a German response as they attacked towards the Roer River) or a limited spoiling attack. But this was not worrisome enough to stop their plans. 'At that moment,' Bradley wrote after the war, 'nothing less than an unequivocal indication of impending attack in the Ardennes could have induced me to quit the winter offensive … It was a calculated risk.'[11]

The Germans, he believed, would have to be crazy to launch a full-scale attack through the Ardennes. Besides, they had no fuel. Allied intelligence was confident that cold, calculating von Rundstedt was in charge. Moreover, although the Germans had come through the Ardennes in 1870 as well as 1914 and again in 1940, it was not suited to mobile warfare – most of Gen. Heinz Guderian's brilliant fighting in May 1940 had come *after* the Germans crossed the Meuse river.[12]

Nonetheless, Hitler's generals and field marshals informed directly of the operation found it difficult to fathom. As a military object, Antwerp, they warned, was far too distant upon which to stake Germany's last strategic reserve.[13] The group enlisted the energetic diminutive general, Hasso von Manteuffel, who, in leading the 5th Panzer Army, always seemed to have Hitler's ear. The group of generals and field marshals personally met with Hitler on 2 December, although haughty old von Rundstedt again sent his adjutant, Siegfried Westphal. At the meeting, von Manteuffel, who enjoyed contract bridge, made a convincing case for his 'Little Slam' – card game parlance for a modest operation to entrap the U.S. 1st Army east of the Meuse river. When the notion of the 'Small Solution' fell flat with Hitler, von Manteuffel raised a litany of objections.

In particular, von Manteuffel described a personal reconnaissance along the Ardennes front to a rapt Hitler. It was useless to use an artillery preparation on the Americans that first morning, the aristocratic panzer general told Hitler – it would only wake them up. Better to let them sleep while his *Stosstruppen* crossed the Our River in rubber boats. When they awoke, his grenadiers would already be upon them. Then, too, he said the inexperienced Volksgrenadier infantry would be too slow to effect a swift breakthrough – better to use the panzer troops.

Meanwhile, Sepp Dietrich, in charge of the 6th Panzer Army, sat motionless and silent at the table. He would keep the artillery barrage. Von Manteuffel didn't even believe Dietrich was qualified to lead a division – an unexpressed opinion shared by Peiper himself.[14] When Westphal drove back to his OB West Ziegenberg headquarters and recounted the unchanged plan, von Rundstedt fumed, 'saying all the officers at OKW [Hitler's headquarters] were idiots'.[15]

The concentration of troops, armor, and aircraft to the east in the German Eifel continued at a frenzied pace at the end of November. 'There will be absolutely no change in the present intentions,' Hitler declared. On 2 December, the Luftwaffe chief of staff, Gen. Karl Koller, cabled Hitler's optimistic assessment:

> Allied losses high, reserves largely committed, supply difficult, front thinly occupied at point of attack. In spite of German difficulties, full plan to be put into operation on Hitler's orders. Hitler agrees with C. in C. West that it should be possible to seize Meuse crossings on first day … O-tag to be 10 December 44.[16]

Tardy fuel deliveries and late arrival of rocket brigades and heavy tanks kept delaying the schedule. Then a final date: 16 December. On 10 December, Hitler moved to his OKW headquarters to Bad Nauheim in the Taunus hills near Frankfurt to be nearby von Rundstedt and OB West. 'These are the most dramatic days of my life,' he told his attending doctor. 'We've *got* to win a great victory!'[17] Hitler's convoy of cars arrived at the Eagle's Nest at 6.30 a.m. on the 11th. 'This will be the great blow that must succeed … If it does not succeed I no longer see any possibility for ending the war well.'[18] It would be the *Grosser Entschluss* – the 'total decision'.

Genobst Alfred Jodl, the head of Hitler's staff, pointed out that the distance from the German border near Hallschlag to Ombret-Rawsa on the glittering Meuse – Peiper's objective – was just over a hundred kilometers. Such a dash could be done in a single day. Indeed, Peiper had done that frequently in Russia at Belgorod. With any luck, Jodl told Hitler, Peiper's SS vanguard would arrive at the Meuse the first evening.[19] Were there other men Hitler could depend on?

In fact, the Leibstandarte leadership was diluted. Sepp Dietrich had been promoted to lead an entire new panzer army. SS leader Fritz Witt had been killed near Caen in June, and SS Brigf. Teddi Wisch was so badly wounded in his harrowing escape from the Falaise pocket that he could not have fought again even if he had not been taken captive. Word was that SS Obf.Wilhelm Mohnke would get the new command of the Leibstandarte. He was an old-timer, having been one of the original 117 members of the Leibstandarte-SS Adolf Hitler (LAH) and the most senior available leader within the I SS Panzer Corps.[20] He had lost a foot on the first day of the Greek campaign and had also been potentially implicated in atrocities against Allied POWs in Wormhoudt, France, in 1940 and more recently in Normandy. Yet for a leadership position in the Waffen SS, that seemed to matter less than the Knight's Cross he was awarded on 11 July 1944 and his penchant for ferocious battle with zero quarter for the enemy.

For his part, Peiper did not see eye to eye with Mohnke, whom he saw as an opiate-addicted street brawler. Peiper had his own preference to become commander of the Leibstandarte: the tall and coolly collected SS Standartenführer Albert Frey. Frey was a personal friend.[21] Even Frey, however, was still incapacitated by terrible facial wounds suffered in Normandy near Garcelles from shell splinters on 20 July. How could Peiper influence things from his hospital bed in Tegernsee? Nonetheless, the cool days with rest and good food gradually brought him back. The jaundice looked better, and the doctor gave him leave to visit the family, but that was soon followed by a trip to visit the nearby SS officer candidate school at Bad Tölz. On 7 October he was released to meet up with Heinrich Himmler, who was returning from visiting Both Himmler and Peiper called on Hedwig Potthast, his mistress, and her children in the Obersalzberg. After celebrating Himmler's birthday that Saturday, Peiper would make his way back to the Leibstandarte.[22]

While Peiper remained focused on loyalty and the fight, his old superior, Sepp Dietrich, had lost his fire. Promoted to leadership well beyond his means, the avuncular SS general was now drinking heavily – and there was plenty of reason.[23] The prospect of defeat and military disgrace seemed less ominous than Hitler and Himmler's dark secret. Indeed, Dietrich had confided in Genlt Hans Speidel, chief of staff to Erwin Rommel, in the summer of 1944 'that Hitler's policy and his methods of waging war would lead to catastrophe.'[24] Even if Hitler was not aware of Dietrich's ebbing will, he was fully cognisant of his limitations as military commander.[25] Thus, the German leader personally saw to it that a capable army officer was assigned. As in Normandy, this would be Genmaj. Fritz Krämer, now endowed with the rank of SS Brigadeführer.

Krämer was charged with actually directing the main offensive effort. Looking over the terrain, Krämer worried that Hitler's time schedule was unrealistic. To fathom the prospects, Krämer personally drove to the bivouac area of the Leibstandarte near Eüskirchen just west on Bonn, to speak with Joachim Peiper.

Krämer was pleased to see Peiper leading the 1st SS Panzer Regiment. Peiper was renowned as *the* expert in rapid night-time armored advance. 'Could a tank column advance 80 kilometers in a single night in the Eifel?,' he asked Peiper. The SS panzer leader was not one to speculate. He personally ordered one of his more experienced tankers, Hans Hennecke, to drive a Panther that distance on the night of 11 December.[26] The next day Peiper wistfully informed Krämer that a single tank could do it, but whether it could be accomplished by an entire column in enemy territory and over icy roads was very different question. Peiper suspected a big night attack.

On 13 December, Peiper's suspicions were verified when SS Gruppenführer Hermann Priess, the commander of I SS Panzer Corps, informed the SS colonel of the true nature of his tank regiment's sojourn in the Eifel. He would be the lead spearhead – attacking into the Losheim Gap in the Ardennes before racing to the Meuse river south of Liège. Seizing those bridgeheads would be the springboard for the second phase, where the armored mass would punch on towards Antwerp.

Knowing the SS Lt Colonel - Obersturmbannführer - was an avid horseman, Krämer encouraged a gallop. 'Drive fast,' he told Peiper, and 'hold the reins loose.'[27] Get a single tank across the Meuse river, Krämer said, scaling back expectations. That was all he would ask.

The Allies had their own justifications to find an end to the war. By the end of summer 1944, even if the Roosevelt administration had known for years, the American public was slowly realising the scope of the racial genocide practised under Himmler's direction.[28] The discovery of the Majdanek concentration camp in Lublin, Poland, electrified the world. That horrible place was a combination labor and extermination camp. Due to the sudden advance of the Russians in the Lublin area, the SS had been unable to destroy the incriminating evidence. A Polish and Soviet joint commission began investigating the grim findings, inviting shocked foreign journalists to tour the site in late August. A stunned *New York Times* reporter described Majdanek as 'the most terrible place on the face of the earth', baring an altogether horrific tale of the camp and its victims – gas chambers, ovens to incinerate victims, unused cans of Zyklon B gas, and a warehouse piled with the shoes of 400,000 victims. Hell was served up at the American breakfast table.[29]

Yet another ugly side of war emerged within Germany. Peiper's reconstituted panzer regiment trained in bombed-out Düren. 'We scraped civilian bodies off the walls,' he recalled. 'When I saw this, I could easily have castrated the people who did that with a broken bottle.'[30] That the German cities were being utterly destroyed was beyond question. A U.S. intelligence agent for the Office of Strategic Services (OSS) forwarded the following report on the German capital that appeared on President Roosevelt's desk on 20 March 1944:

> The destruction in Berlin is enormous, but it is extraordinary to observe the fatalism with which the inhabitants accept the new situation. Thousands of people live in ruins, in cellars and temporary shelters. At the beginning of the bombardment, there were many complaints. Now it seems the population is somewhat used to them …[31]

It was with perhaps that motivation that Peiper's training regime did not let up that autumn. He remained keen on night exercises:

> During training he occasionally intervened with extraordinarily severe orders. For instance he would ask a company to march all night from 7 p.m. until 7 a.m, more than 50 kilometers. Afterwards, he would ask with a smile: 'How was the march?'[32]

Predictably, not all the soldiers under his command were happy. One who knew him well from Russia and Normandy recounted,

> I learned to know him as a man who in action exceeded all others in tactical success, who engaged himself and others recklessly, who severely and pitilessly punished the weakness of individuals, and who was hard and pitiless towards the enemy. One could admire him for his success, but then fear the thought of having him as an adversary.[33]

On Himmler's birthday on 7 October 1944, the Reichsführer SS toured and extravagantly praised the rebuilding Waffen SS panzer divisions in western

Germany. Peiper was just re-joining his division. 'Like our fathers we want to be loyal,' said Himmler, 'loyal to the Führer, whom the Lord God sent us, loyal to the Reich which unites all Germans over the centuries.'[34] In speaking vengefully of the nation's enemies, Himmler was mindful of the treatment his SS had meted out to conquered peoples as he addressed the newly assembled Volkssturm:

> We have learned from the very mouths of our enemies what we can expect, the destruction of our country, the clearance of our woods, the dissolution of our economy, the annihilation of our towns, the burning down of our villages and the extermination [*Ausrottung*] of our peoples.[35]

Himmler enjoined the Waffen SS to fight hard in the decisive battles that would soon come. Later he stopped by his home in the Obersalzberg to visit his devoted mistress, Hedwig Potthast, and his two children from that relationship. He had just legalised his paternity of the boy, Helge, on 12 September. On this grey day he spent the entire day at home, playing the role of the benevolent father.[36] Meanwhile, Himmler's brother, Gebhard, visited his famous brother to hear him express fanciful desires for what would be done after the war: excavation of old Viking villages to provide historical context for Nazi culture and the development of herbal medicines used in the Middle Ages on the theory that this was a science of pure Germanic origin. In addition, Heinrich expressed his intention to create a '*Staats-Schutz-Korps*' or 'State Security Corps' from the hand-picked ranks of the SS.[37]

Himmler's perceived loyalty in the wake of the failed assassination plot against Hitler the previous summer saw the Reichsführer SS assigned ever greater responsibilities. With Hitler conspicuously absent from the public eye since the assassination attempt, Willi Frischauer in the London *Daily Herald* now wondered if Himmler might soon eclipse his superior:

> Hitler, even if he is alive and sane, can no longer rule Germany without Himmler … For almost six months they have lived without Hitler. Whether he is … in his mysterious Field H.Q. or on his way to Japan in a submarine, it makes little difference to them. Hitler is no longer indispensable.[38]

That autumn, the German armed forces newspaper, *Nachrichten für Die Truppe*, ran an article mockingly titled 'Heil Himmler!' Although it did much to embarrass Peiper's old boss, there was no arguing with Himmler's ascent.[39] That September Himmler was made chief of the replacement army and put in charge of resuscitating the defenses at the German border.[40] His first move was to make sure the wave of desertion sweeping the Western Front was checked. He issued a punishing edict: any deserters would be sentencing their families to concentration camps.[41]

Himmler planned to quickly raise a new army of forty *Volksgrenadier* – people's infantry divisions. Copiously equipped with the new fully automatic assault rifles and speedily trained, they would serve as the infantry mass for

Hitler's plans to change the course of the war. Most veteran German soldiers, such as Jochen Peiper, with their long experience, were deeply distrustful of such cannon fodder. Although bearing old infantry division numbers, most of these new divisions had only a handful of veterans. Some of those were ailing, convalescent, or Luftwaffe draftees, so they had next to no experience. Never mind: although they were untested, these new infantry divisions had not yet known defeat.

Jochen Peiper, the SS officer, was anything if not devoted; he insisted on returning to his command. In early October 1944 Peiper was given convalescent leave from the hospital. Yet instead of resting in Rottach-Egern at his private home as his doctors had recommended, he immediately made his way to the Leibstandarte headquarters in the green picturesque hills near Lübbecke after visiting Himmler in Bad Tolz. 'My well-known insubordination,' he christened his impetuosity. He had arrived by 13 October 1944 to find his 1st SS Panzer Regiment then reorganising in Rahden in the green hills of Westphalian Germany.[42] SS Maj. Werner Poetschke, had managed the panzer regiment since Peiper's departure and would continue to do so in the training around Wietzendorf. Peiper would remain in the area around Rahden with the SPW battalion, the 9th Panzer Pioneer Company, and elements of the extended panzer regiment.[43]

Unknown to Peiper, Hitler and his generals were planning for how he might fight again. On the morning of 22 October, Hitler's right-hand general, Alfred Jodl, strode into Hitler's East Prussian headquarters with a revised version of the Ardennes operation. Hitler reviewed the pen-marked maps at the *Wolfsschanze* and pronounced himself pleased. Fishing for an appropriate moniker, Hitler code-named his new offensive after an old nationalistic song – '*Wacht am Rhein*,' or 'Watch on the Rhine'. He further took the opportunity to bring his field marshals, von Rundstedt and Walther Model, in on the plan.

Never mind that the failed airborne operation at Arnhem was a spectacular British disaster and something of a comeuppance for Field Marshal Bernard L Montgomery. The Allied generals were fighting among themselves, as they reached German soil. On 10 September 1944, Heinrich Himmler appeared at an air raid shelter in Frankenberger in Aachen, telling everyone present that this important city on the western reaches of the Reich – the capital of the empire created by Charlemagne – must never fall into American hands.[44] In contrast to Himmler's notion, American shells rained on the city over the following weeks and, by 13 October, the 246th Volkgrenadier Division was embroiled in a losing house-to-house battle. In spite of counterattacks by motley groups of Leibstandarte veterans and trainees of uneven morale on 12 and 14 October – Kampfgruppe Diefenthal and SS Battalion Rink – the American advance proved unstoppable.[45] On Wednesday, 18 October, Aachen fell to the U.S. 1st Infantry Division. It was on that inauspicious note that ego-minded chiefs of staff – Genlt Siegfried Westphal (OB West) and the petulant Genlt Hans Krebs (Heeresgruppe B) – arrived at the Wolfsschanze for a requested meeting with Hitler.[46]

Both staff officers steeled themselves for a tongue lashing. Instead, both men were surprised when, upon arriving, they were asked to immediately sign an affidavit swearing them to secrecy regarding a new shadowy plan. If word got out, both would be shot. While von Rundstedt had instructed Westphal to demand more troops for the Westwall from Hitler, he was further surprised when Genobst Jodl handed them a long list of new troops, units, and equipment that were to arrive on the Western Front. For the defense, they wondered. No, Hitler lectured: *Wacht am Rhein* was to be a great offensive, 'a decisive turning point in the Campaign in the West and possibly even of the entire war'.[47] The briefing went on for hours; Aachen wasn't mentioned, which was just as well, as Hitler had recently reminded Jodl that the defense of the city should be 'a shining example … of the ruggedness with which we would fight for our Fatherland'.[48] Hitler's monologue went on for over an hour.

Their heads loaded up with copious detail, both generals dutifully reported back to their superiors. Genflm. Karl Gerd von Rundstedt, now 70 years old and having been called out of retirement in 1940, had experienced so many quarrels with Hitler during the war that he had grown apathetic.[49] 'I was staggered,' von Rundstedt complained.

When the aging field marshal settled down, he informed Gen. Westphal that there might be a silver lining. 'I am glad we are to receive more forces in the West. Before the beginning of this ordained offensive, much water will have flowed down the Rhine.' Patton was attacking towards Metz; Von Rundstedt wanted to form a stable front with a large panzer reserve, similar to what he had attempted in Normandy. 'From a preliminary glance I can say that the distant objective of Antwerp cannot be reached with the forces available … The entire planning of this offensive strikes me as failing to meet the demand of reality.'[50]

Even Genflm. Model, whom everyone knew as an insanely hard-driving Nazi fanatic, was doubtful. 'This plan doesn't have a damned leg to stand on!'[51] Yet Jodl and Hitler had a ready answer for the nay-sayers: 'The Ardennes undertaking was an operation of the most extreme daring – there was no question of that …'

> But we were in a desperate situation, and the only way to save was by a desperate decision. By remaining on the defensive, we could not hope to escape the evil fate hanging over us. By fighting, rather than waiting, we might save something … we had to risk everything.[52]

On that day Hitler did not know the negative reaction when Krebs and Westphal returned. Instead, there was other excitement – the Russians were so close to the *Wolfsschanze* that it had become a moving day, lest Hitler's headquarters come in range of big Russian guns. Later that afternoon of te 22 October, Hitler invited into his quarters a tall SS officer – a man Peiper knew well. It was SS Ostubaf. Otto Skorzeny, the Führer's champion of SS-commando derring-do.

The tall Austrian was conducted to a small room in the bunker with stale air. Skorzeny was impressed that Hitler seemed calm and composed. Having snatched Mussolini from his captors in September 1943, Skorzeny had recently succeeded at another daring exploit – the kidnapping of Admiral Horthy's son and the seat of the Hungarian government. With Hungary's defection from the Axis side at least temporarily averted Hitler promoted him on the spot. 'From now on you are an Obersturmbannführer of the Waffen SS, and I am awarding you the German Cross in Gold.' Skorzeny produced the requisite Hitlerian genuflections. When Skorzeny rose to go, the German leader motioned for him to stay. Soon he conducted him to an adjoining room. On the wall hung a huge map of the entire Western Front.

'I have something to tell you,' Hitler began, 'The world thinks Germany is finished, with only the day and hour of the funeral to be announced. I am going to show how mistaken they are. The corpse will rise and hurl itself in fury in the West. Then we will see!' Hitler took Skorzeny over to a wall map and pointed to the front line along the German border. There they were, where they had been in 1940. Hitler gleamed; soon be like 1940 again. 'In December Germany will launch a great offensive which will decide the destiny of our country.'

Hitler pointed to the Ardennes. No one, he said, could now foresee that Germany might launch a second attack in the same sector. A sharp chisel blow into the seam of the American armies in the Ardennes. It was the vulnerable place where France had been shattered and split asunder in 1940 and the British were forced to evacuate the continent in three weeks. Hitler tapped his finger on Antwerp. If his great gamble out of the Ardennes could reach that Belgian port, both the British and Americans would be hopelessly isolated. A second Dunkirk in winter?

Skorzeny looked on thoughtfully, but said little. Hitler could see his guest's doubt and continued enthusiastically. There would be 6,000 artillery pieces and many heavy tanks – masses of the new King Tigers and a super heavy *Jagdtiger* mounting a 128mm gun. And most important of all, there would be brand-new jet aircraft – 2,000 of them. All this was being hoarded for the operation. 'Now, Skorzeny,' he began, 'I will very likely entrust you with the most important mission of your career as a soldier. One of the most difficult tasks within the framework of the offensive will be your assignment. There are several bridges between the cities of Liège and Namur on the Meuse river. Your commandos will capture one or more of these bridges before they can be destroyed. I have decided that this can be accomplished more quickly and with lighter losses if your men wear American uniforms.'[53] Another fantastic *ruse de guerre*.

Skorzeny was taken aback by the suggestion, but Hitler prattled on about how his men could make mischief and chaos around American front lines while wearing U.S. Army olive drab and not be considered spies so long as they didn't fire their sidearms. That seemed ludicrous too, but Hitler was on a roll. 'I know the Americans used this tactic in the vicinity of Aachen. Some of the commandos will remain camouflaged to mislead the enemy and spread the confusion … It will be code-named Operation Greif.' That was the mythical animal that was half lion and half eagle – a fine name – but there were many hanging questions. 'There's no time to build up an English-speaking unit,' Skorzeny protested. 'I'll have to improvise.' Ushering Skorzeny to a more detailed briefing with Gen. Jodl, Hitler assured the scar-faced SS officer that he would be provided with a large batch of English-speaking German soldiers, American uniforms, trucks, captured tanks, and weapons. 'I know time is very short,' Hitler nodded, 'but I can count on you to do the impossible.'[54] Skorzeny was getting a headache.

Amazingly, on 26 October, just days after Hitler had vetted him with sweeping powers, Skorzeny received a printed notice being distributed all over the Western Front. On the top was printed 'SECRET COMMANDO OPERATIONS'. 'The Führer has ordered the formation of a special fighting unit of approximately two battalion strength for use on the Western Front.' The notice went on to request English-speaking officers and men from all services of the Wehrmacht. They were to report for duty to Friedenthal by 10 November for a special operation under Dienststelle Skorzeny. Skorzeny was flabbergasted at the bone-headed notice – signed by Keitel. Such a document would surely reach Allied intelligence.[55] He demanded to see Hitler.

Skorzeny contacted SS orderly Hermann Fegelein, in Hitler's office. Skorzeny 'protested violently'.[56] Through Fegelein he informed Hitler that *Operation Greif* must be abandoned, as the element of surprise was already lost. Hitler agreed that the leak was unfortunate, but he persuaded Skorzeny (now given the cover name of *Solar*) to continue with plans for the operation anyway.[57] For Skorzeny, with the formation of the fake panzer brigade, now designated *Rabenhügel*, the entire operation veered off course – an espionage version of the Keystone Cops.

Not all was amateurish, however. Leonard 'Bud' Bornemann of the 602nd Tank Destroyer Battalion had been taken captive in September 1944 during Operation Market Garden and was held at Stalag III-C in Alt-Drewitz in Western Poland that autumn. In late November, Bornemann puzzled over a new development. Several German soldiers in neatly pressed uniforms visited Bornemann and fellow prisoners in their hut, seemingly intent on speaking English. At first the Americans thought the Germans were after intelligence. But these guys wanted to know nothing other than what life had been like in the States. After a day of pointless conversation, the English-yakking Germans came back for a second afternoon shooting the breeze. Several asked Bornemann about the quality of their English. Bornemann remained clueless. *Good English,* the St Louis native thought, *but most had heavy accents.*[58] Sure enough. Some of the language-challenged commando trainees, such as Oberschuetze Josef Kania, leaned on others with a superior command of English at Grafenwöhr where Skorzeny was training.

Gruppe Einheit Stielau, trained by Oblt Lothar Stielau, would comprise two dozen jeep loads of commandos with expert English and espionage experience. To his amazement, Kania learned that a Feldwebel Goetz from Einheit Stielau was to 'fill the role of a U.S. Colonel and to participate directly in the "Eisenhower Aktion".'[59] Like the capture of Miklos Horthy or Benito Mussolini, Skorzeny would kidnap or kill the head of Allied forces in the west. At first, Kania was dubious, but he noted that Goetz and another assistant received special attention from the barber at Grafenwöhr. American officers had distinctive haircuts.

Goetz also showed Kania how to open a pack of cigarettes American style and taught him the most popular swear words and how to use them. 'Goddammit!' appeared to fit just about every situation. Skorzeny himself later claimed that a week after the publication of the 'secret order' the first volunteers arrived at Friedenthal. English skills? Most could just say yes and no. Reviewing the rabble, Skorzeny 'struck a new level of despondency. I wanted to consign the whole thing to the devil.'[60]

Jochen Peiper was similarly despondent, When he arrived that autumn in Rhaden to examine his new panzer command, he was shocked. Many new personnel were *completely* green. Not only were there only a few tanks just now arriving, but there were new tank crewmen who had never even been inside one. There were replacement tank drivers who only had a licence from driving a few hours' around Berlin and gunners who had never fired a tank cannon.[61] His old experienced officers informed him that enforced radio silence and a deplorable fuel situation meant that realistic tank exercises and manoeuvre co-ordination were impossible. Moreover, the local civilian population in the green farms and pastures along the Weser River north of Minden would not take well to training with live ammunition.[62] Besides, they didn't have much.

Young Werner Ackermann was an experienced hand among the recruits in his Panzer IV that autumn. Even though only an enlisted man, an SS Sturmmann, he was a skilled driver; indeed, he was an instructor at the panzer school, nearly losing his leg to a bad driver the previous year. The lack of fuel was particularly maddening, as training drivers was Ackermann's speciality.[63] Training inside the confining panzer interior was critical, Ackermann knew, to co-ordinate five men into an effective fighting force. Inside the tank, everyone, regardless of rank, was '*Du*' rather than the more formal '*Sie*' – even for officers. That helped ease stress, particularly when the hatches were closed – the sign for entering serious battle. It was then that the acrid odours from cigarettes and the powder fog from firing the main cannon added to the tension. Some of the new ones complained of claustrophobia and the foul odour, but Ackermann told them this was nothing compared to being under air attack – that was worst. Winter was another challenge; the inside of the steel panzer was frigid, particularly near the front hatches, where the air entered. The forward driver and the radio man had gloves and leather clothing to protect from frost and numbness.

Outside the tank everyone reverted back to '*Sie*' for their superiors. Most of the time the talk was of home and better foods than the simple beef and barley stew being served by the field kitchen. And real coffee rather than tea or the ersatz brew being provided. Although the men invariably spoke about women, some said that was on the decline, as the army was now salting their food with 'soda', (saltpeter), to calm them down. Still, meeting women at the local *Wirtshaus* was ever popular. Ackermann remembered that all the women were treated in a 'friendly and respectful manner'. Having recovered from a penetrating head wound in Russia, Ackermann firmly appreciated the fairer sex: nurses had saved his life. He never forgot it.

Strangely, that autumn, without fuel, much of training devolved into marching. It was for morale as much as anything. Marching about Rahden each morning, they sang all the old songs – '*Das Panzer Lied*', the 'Westerwald Lied', and such.[64] Was there any panache left for being a panzer man? Yet even without the driving Ackermann would have desired, there were still important eccentricities of the Panzer IV to bring to the attention of the green recruits. Turning the turret 40 degrees off center in battle was dangerous; if the tank were hit, it would block the hatch for egress of the driver or the radioman. Many men who were unaware of that issue had already perished in Russia. And for the commander, it was important to try to turn the tank within 12 degrees or so to face the main gun directly at the enemy so as to not expose the thinner metal sides to attack. Then, too, everyone had to be trained on the arduous technique of manually cranking the turret when the electric turning mechanism failed.

Off duty, most of the men smoked and drank. To pass the time during evenings, some played poker or *Mau/Mau*. Often the men had no money, so they played for pistols. But the problems with excessive drinking were greater for the officers than the enlisted men, as the older veterans had become accustomed to higher-proof alcohol in Russia. Some even crossed the line and drank on duty. But Ackermann knew intimately of the problems of drinking; heck, he'd be an NCO had he not been busted at Putlos for celebrating his tank crew's test performance at an all-afternoon drink-a-thon. Still, his superiors recognised Ackermann was an expert in training drivers on the Panzer IV.

Peiper was well aware of the drinking trouble with the old panzer hands. When Peiper first arrived, there was a little welcome party. Peiper had encouraged the wives of some of his officers to join them in Rahden and looked to bring up morale. SS Sturmmann Horst Schumann, from his old tank crew, was there, just before going to Nuremberg for leadership school. Schumann managed to bang out some old war romance tunes on a tired piano in the *Wirtshaus* – 'Come back to me, I'm waiting for you'.[65] But even that was a bit much for Peiper. Halfway through the recital, Peiper asked him politely if he wasn't tired – a clue to stop the beer, music and revelry.

That autumn Peiper was working his body back into health through vigorous sessions of handball and preening his mind with night-time reading on historical subjects. Officers under him had other ideas. SS-Ost. Benoni Junker with the 6. Panzer Kompanie was one of the big party animals – now seemingly depressed about everything. 'Sixth year of war,' he jotted in his diary on 1 September, 'my situation is crappy, but at least I am still here.' Three days later he was assigned to transfer sixteen tanks to the 116th Panzer Division near Hasselt. Yet Junker was so drunk that he passed out, only to be awakened when American anti-tank guns ambushed the column. Nearly every tank was destroyed, and Genlt Gerhard von Schwerin, in charge of the army division, ordered Junker investigated. He narrowly avoided a court martial. 'Big manure,' Junker dutifully wrote in his diary.[66]

Werner Ackermann, in the 6th Panzer Company since July 1944, found Benoni Junker 'very disappointing'. However, Ackermann did find him humane and thoughtful in a unit that seemed overpopulated with National Socialist fanatics and rowdies. Still, as someone to lead men into mortal combat, his leadership left a lot to be desired. 'Junker was an officer's club, officer,' Ackermann recalled. 'He was totally wonderful in the barracks and in drilling and the parade.' In battle 'he was often missing or on the bottle'.[67]

With time on their hands, some were missing at morning roll call, having got totally drunk in a *Wirsthaus*. Peiper wasn't around; 'blue hour' became a daily event. Indeed, August Tonk and Werner Sternebeck, SS men in the 6th Panzer Company, had got into a schnapps-induced fist fight in a *Wirtshaus* that saw them under arrest for fourteen days.[68] Returning to the scene, like Himmler, Peiper had little tolerance for excessive drinking.[69] Sternebeck took it in his stride, proud of his flamboyance. How else could he be a hard-drinking horseman with such appeal to the ladies? Indeed, it was rumoured that the swashbuckling Sternebeck sometimes led his tank platoon into battle with a raised lance. Some said he had wined and dined the wife of a senior official in Berlin. Peiper prescribed punishment: Sternebeck would lead the panzer at the point of the next big attack as part of the *Himmelfahrtskommando* – frequently a death sentence.[70] All the others in the point platoon were under punishment as well.[71]

Drinking was hardly the only problem. To Peiper, the recently minted SS infantry troopers that would fight alongside his tanks seemed even more pathetic. Many had been soldiers for only four to six weeks, and instead of receiving rudimentary basic training, they had been used instead to clean away debris in bombed-out Cologne. They knew little about co-ordinated assault or how to secure a village once his tanks had punched through.

The replacements were mostly Hitler Jugend members from the Berlin area keen on enthusiasm but short on experience. Since 1943, often replacements for enlisted men were ex-Luftwaffe or despised rear-echelon types – *Etappenhengst*. Peiper saw them as the worst.[72] They were soft and – he complained to his superiors – 'not the best *Menschenmaterial*'.[73]

Chapter 2

A FOREST DARK

I found myself within a forest dark, for the straightforward pathway had been lost. Ah me! How hard a thing is to say, what was this forest savage, rough, and stern, which in the very thought renews the fear. So bitter is it, death is little more …

Dante

On 6 December, SS Obergruppenführer Willi Bittrich, commander of the II SS Panzer Corps, representing Sepp Dietrich, presented the 6th Panzer Army attack plan in a map exercise at Brühl, Germany. Field Marshal Model and Krebs, his chief of staff, were present, along with Hermann Priess of I SS Panzer Corps as well as all the divisional commanders in the 6th Panzer Army. Model had a reputation. He was known to the troops as *der Katastrophengeneral* because of his talent for turning up at the front just in time to stave off total collapse. The Ardennes would further test his mettle. Wilhelm Mohnke, in charge of the 1st SS Panzer Division, was there as they unveiled the plan. The scheme emphasized the need for a rapid advance on the Meuse river if there was to be any chance of reaching Antwerp and changing the war's direction.

Mohnke even unveiled a wild-eyed new tank tactic. If the tank assault showed any signs of slowing, powerful searchlights would be brought up at night and flicked on to blind the *Amis* so the assault could regain momentum.[1] To Peiper, the tank night fighter, the plan must have sounded crazy: searchlights and a pre-dawn artillery barrage would just wake everyone. These were obviously desk fighters. On 10 December the formal orders were forwarded to the army:

> On O-Tag, after a strong artillery preparation, 6th Panzer Army will break through the enemy front on both sides of Hollerath, and will relentlessly thrust across the Maas toward Antwerp. For this purpose Sixth Panzer Army will make full use of its motorized forces and will disregard the protection of its flanks. I SS Panzer Corps will start its attack at 0600 on O-Tag and will break through

> the enemy positions in the sector Monschau–Udenbreth–Losheim with 12th SS Panzer Division on the right and the 1st SS Panzer Division on the left. They will cross the Meuse in the Liège–Huy sector. According to developments in the situation, the mission of the corps will be to deploy itself to relentlessly pierce toward Antwerp by making full use of its motorized elements, or make them available for the defense of the right flank along the Albert Canal.

And then the attack orders became very specific for Hermann Priess and I SS Panzer Corps:

> Carefully selected advance detachments, led by particularly daring commanders will advance rapidly and capture the bridges in the Meuse sector before the enemy can destroy them.[2]

Daring commanders ... could only refer to Jochen Peiper and his ilk. In the mind of most SS leaders, he was the king of the Blitzkrieg advance, the destructive night-time behind-enemy-line romp and the champion of contemptuous derring-do in the face of any enemy. Peiper's command was famous: the *Lötlampen Abteilung* – the Blowtorch Battalion.

At that time a massive concentration of the German forces was being completed by rail. To protect Hitler's great secret, the German High Command had applied a strict schedule that would cover the assembly and concentration of forces for the great blow. The Leibstandarte, like the others, was only moved up in the last few weeks, arriving in the assembly area around Meckenheim on 20 November in some sixty trains. The attached Tiger battalion arrived in another ten trains by 9 December.[3] The march and motorized movement to the front was yet to be accomplished, but as the frontier was approached, the security regulation and camouflage officers became insistent.

Although Peiper didn't yet know it, Sepp Dietrich and the 6th Panzer Army would be the main attack force for the bid to wrest Antwerp from the Allies and change the course of the war. And the main spearhead for Dietrich's army: Jochen Peiper and his 'blowtorch battalion' – now the full panzer regiment of the Leibstandarte Division. As befitted the *Schwerpunkt* – the offensive center of gravity – the 6th Panzer was by far the strongest of the three German armies, containing five Volksgrenadier divisions – a false titular for poorly trained, green infantry – but bolstered by the elite SS panzer divisions.

Including support elements, the army totalled over 140,000 men, 1,025 pieces of corps artillery, and some 642 tanks and assault guns.[4] Of this force, on 10 December Peiper's tank regiment of the 1st SS Panzer Division could count thirty-four Mk IVs and thirty-seven Panthers – a far cry from the established tank strength for a panzer regiment in late 1944. To make of up for the armored deficiency, Heinz von Westernhagen's *Heavy* SS Panzer Battalion 501 was attached with a further forty-five heavy Tigers II – although only thirty were combat ready on the indicated date. The division could field a further twenty-two Jagdpanzer IV hunting tanks in SS Panzerjäger Battalion 1 that would fight with the other battlegroups.

Meanwhile, back at the alpine idyll of Rottach-Egern, Sigurd Peiper continued to worry about her husband, Jochen. Sigurd was apologising in a letter to her friend and Himmler's mistress, Hedwig Potthast, for attempting to intercede on Jochen's behalf:

Rottach, 11 December 1944

My Dear Häschen:
I did not have time until today to thank you heartily for your letter of November 25. During the last weeks, things went crazily. The children, one after the other, have had chicken pox. Right now Silke has it. As such, a harmless children's disease, but for Mami always a few sleepless nights and you know how difficult that it is to keep children in bed. On top of that, I had to drag myself around with the flu and spend a few days in bed. But now things are going rather well again. I would like to thank you especially heartily for your open and honest letter. Häschen, I already regret having written at all. You must not think that I bared my heart to you in order for you to talk with K.H. [König Heinrich – referring to Heinrich Himmler] about that. It is not in me to want to do 'career adjustments' for my husband. He fortunately does not need that. I must concur with the considerations of K.H. Jochen in a staff position would be intolerable in the end. There really is no work there, because his talents are really in the military leadership area. During my visits with Jochen, I observed repeatedly how his men and officers love him, how he influences them, inspires, and electrifies them, and how immensely Jochen enjoys them.

You know my Jochen's mission: guide young people and turn them into leaders. But only very few know what it means to live through three years of such intensive front-line duty. When the comrades get together at night to relax, then Jochen sits and reads books not of military matters in order not to become one-sided in his judgement and knowledge. I really admire his endurance and ambition, but I hope you will understand that I am worried about him. Because I know how worn out he is and it would really be high time to get an area of work where he could also consider his health, because his experience and skills will no longer be of use to anybody if he takes a bullet.

He is totally at the end of his nerves and no longer up to the demands of the front line. The physician treating Jochen here has put a particular fear into me. He said that people who participate so intensively in everything and who store up within themselves all of it are subject to an especially heavy load on their nervous system. One could compare it with a wire that can take a certain load under a certain pressure but then tears apart. And that would have unimaginable consequences, which do not always manifest themselves in jaundice.

But things will happen as they should and we cannot change anything anyway. It is also difficult to report all that by letter. Häschen, one is always egotistical and so am I in this respect: I worry about my happiness and I am afraid that one day there will be a terrible bang. But enough of that. Let us continue to have faith in our lucky star …

To you and your children many loving and heartfelt greetings.

I am Your Sigurd[5]

As Peiper's wife penned her letter, Adolf Hitler moved to his new *Adlerhorst* headquarters, nestled in the wooded Taunus Hills near Bad Nauheim. At 5 p.m.

on 10 December he had departed Berlin by fast train on the *Führersonderzug Brandenburg* and steamed west through the night. As their destination was over a four-hour drive from disembarkation at the Kloster Arnsburg station, his group did not arrive at the snow-bound headquarters until 8 a.m. the following morning.

Adlerhorst was a massive network of camouflaged concrete bunkers and barracks constructed there earlier in the war for *Operation Seelöwe*, the anticipated invasion of England in 1940. As that campaign never came to pass, the hastily outfitted complex would now be used to co-ordinate Hitler's last great military gamble of the war.[6] Although they had procured Hitler's required horse-hair mattress and night table for his walnut-panelled bedroom there, the place was hardly ready as a command center. 'Here we have been dumped into a badly prepared quarters,' the Reich's secretary, Martin Bormann, complained after a sleepless night in transit. 'Our tele-printers are unsuitably installed, no tele-printer cables are connected, neither are there typewriter desks nor shelves set up in the tiny room where my typists must work.'[7]

Adlerhorst was situated strategically. Genflm. Gerd von Rundstedt was ensconced in stately accommodation in Schloss Ziegenberg, a mile and a half down a winding road.[8] There, in Ziegenberg castle, which Goethe had once visited, Hitler addressed his assembled generals on 11 December. Obst Wilhelm Viebig would command one of the Volksgrenadier divisions that would open the way for the SS tank columns. Viebig had seen Hitler earlier in war, but was hardly prepared for the 1944 version. 'When he came out, I was terribly shocked,' he noted. Hitler teetered as he entered the room, appearing supported by SS Gen. Gottlob Berger and Genflm. Wilhelm Keitel on either side. 'He looked old and shrunken with unsightly red blotches on his face … worn out … but then after he had spoken for an hour life came back. Then his eyes were shining.'

'How can a man have the ambition to be a leader of an army if he won't listen to advice?' Hitler railed rhetorically. 'And I say, you military people are the prophets of doom.'[9] Soon he was rapping on a map. 'This battle will decide the war.'

The *alter Kämpfer*, Sepp Dietrich was also among the assembled. 'He gave a long speech and said we had to do something,' Dietrich recalled. At the end of the speech Dietrich stood in line to have a brief moment to speak with the German leader personally, 'I told Hitler that I wasn't ready to attack with my army and that we lacked the ammunition or fuel to carry it out successfully.' The Führer dismissed Dietrich's worry, telling him that he would have all he needed and motioned for the next person in line.[10] Dietrich grumbled all the same:

> All he wants me to do is cross a river, capture Brussels, and then go and take Antwerp! All this in the worst time of year through the Ardennes where the snow is waist deep and there isn't room to deploy four tanks abreast, let alone a panzer division! Where it doesn't get light until 8 and it's dark again at four and with re-formed divisions made up chiefly of kids and sick old men – and all this at Christmas![11]

Peiper's old towering comrade from the days fighting in 1941 near Rostov, Heinrich Springer, now working as an SS orderly officer for Field Marshal Model, was among those there:

> Everyone knew why they were being brought together. Hitler was going to explain this last big offensive and try to get everyone's enthusiasm up. We needed to be as strong as possible. Hitler stood before us, but his main talk was not about objectives, tactics, and other military questions. Rather, it was more like a long history lesson – he spoke about the Battle of Leuthen on 4 February 1757 and Frederick the Great's victory. Hitler appeared calm, collected, and did not seem agitated. His gestures were lively and enthusiastic, but he spoke clearly and calmly. At the end of the long lecture on history, he got around to talking about the Ardennes Offensive. The goal would be the destruction of the American and British forces by a sudden thrust to Antwerp. It would be another big encirclement battle that would turn the tide of the war. Even today, I remember his final words to us: 'Gentlemen, if we do not achieve the decisive breakthrough from Liège to Antwerp, we will face a bloody fate in this war. Time is not on our side. This is our last final chance to alter the fortunes of the war.'[12]

Peiper was not at the address, nor did he know of the coming operation. Yet he suspected it – and was concerned more with brave battle, regardless of the assignment given. SS Lt Erich Rumpf, who had been with the engineer company of the tank regiment, remained impressed with Peiper, who reminded everyone of his personal motto from the Zarah Leander song:

> A bad reputation has its commitments ... He explained orally to us and underlined that expressly. It was clear that for me that where the situation became more difficult when we had prisoners, the commander would never think for a second to shoot his prisoners ... In this context, every order from the commander has to be understood ... Peiper had a personal talk with me and underscored that I had a special responsibility that no SPW was to be left back without orders and I was to be responsible that the company stayed together because it was decisive for the battle group that the few infantry that were together should remain with us ... It was the last briefing he gave me that morning.[13]

Rumpf went on to say:

> You can admire him [Peiper] if you are with him, but if you have him as an enemy you will learn to fear him. He loves to give dramatic orders. He likes especially his officers who follow his way. His special favorites were Wolff, Preuss, and Paul Guhl, who fought with him in the SPW battalion. He is responsible for the merciless fight that took place in the East, and that merciless fight was brought back to the west. His orders were not the main thing; everyone in his unit knows that the commander will agree with the merciless fight. Those who fought in this way, he would praise and point out to the other men. Also, during the training, he made tough orders.[14]

How did favored Preuss feel about his superior? 'He was from Berlin,' the SS Hauptsturmführer said. 'He was very arrogant.'[15]

In the nights leading up to mid-December, the SS panzer division threaded ever deeper into the Blankenheimer Wald. They were concentrating for the big one.[16] Karl Wortmann remembered:

> Somewhere around the 13th of December, we were surprised by the transfer of our Regiment south-west in the direction of the Eifel. Close to this area lay the front. Our Panzer and trucks drove like mad. During the day we observed the firing of V-weapons from not far away. The nights were so beastly cold that we gathered shrubs and brush to serve as our camp at night, and used rugs and tent straps as blankets. Of course we couldn't sleep due to the cold. In some locations we were allowed a small campfire to help warm us. We talked about memories of our earlier war days. Soon everyone was talking about the fact that this time, again, we had a significant mission coming up.[17]

On Thursday, 14 December, the new commander of the Leibstandarte, SS-Oberführer Wilhelm Mohnke, called together a briefing at a forester's house in the thickly wooded hills around Tondorf. The meeting was scheduled to begin at 11 a.m. sharp, but Peiper arrived late, as the roads leading to the headquarters were jammed with vehicles and traffic – an annoying portent of things to come. Peiper was already in a foul mood but was caught up on the mission briefing by the divisional chief of staff, SS Obersturmbannführer Dietrich Ziemssen.[18] Present were his experienced regimental commanders – Hansen, Sandig, Knittel, and Peiper. Otto Skorzeny was invited too, and he brought along officers masquerading as Americans who would operate in with Peiper's forces. Mohnke told the men that the upcoming operation was very risky but of vital importance.

The 1st SS Panzer Division would be committed in three strong battle groups along assigned panzer rolling roads (Rollbahn). The three northern roads, designated A through C, were assigned to the 12th SS Panzer Division, which would advance on the right flank of the Leibstandarte through the Elsenborn area to Malmedy and then to Spa and Theux before reaching the Meuse on both sides of Liège. The southernmost road, Rollbahn E, would be travelled by Kampfgruppe Hansen, including SS Panzergrenadier Regiment 1, the SS Panzerjäger Battalion, and a battalion of artillery. Their assigned route of advance would take them through Krewinkel–Manderfeld–Recht–Trois-Ponts, Werbomont, and Hamoir, reaching the Meuse at Huy. Following in Hansen's wake, Kampfgruppe Knittel, the reinforced reconnaissance battalion, would veer into the open to take the lead on the sparse road network. He would lead the division quickly to the Meuse.

The main effort would come on Rollbahn D. Here, Kampfgruppe Peiper, with most of the division's tanks and self-propelled elements, would thrust forward from Blankenheim to Büllingen–Stavelot–Harze and reach the Meuse at Amay just north of Huy. Kampfgruppe Sandig, led by SS Ostbf. Rudi Sandig, with SS Panzer Grenadier Regiment 2 and artillery and engineering elements,

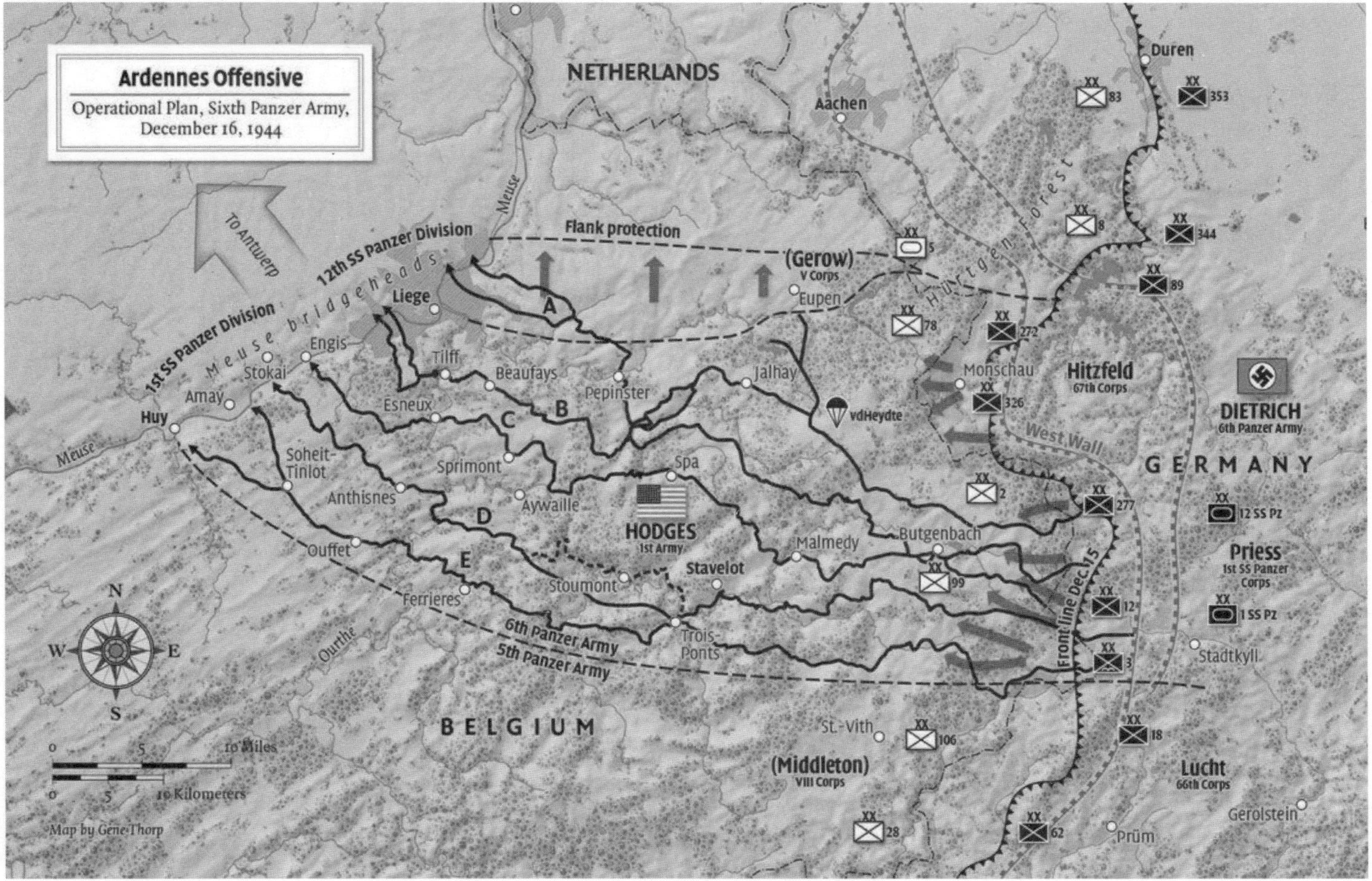
Ardennes Offensive
Operational Plan, Sixth Panzer Army, December 16, 1944
NETHERLANDS
GERMANY
BELGIUM
Flank protection
To Antwerp
12th SS Panzer Division
1st SS Panzer Division
Meuse bridgeheads
Meuse
Ourthe
Hürtgen Forest
West Wall
Front line Dec 15
6th Panzer Army
5th Panzer Army
(Gerow)
V Corps
HODGES
1st Army
(Middleton)
VIII Corps
Hitzfeld
67th Corps
DIETRICH
6th Panzer Army
Priess
1st SS Panzer Corps
Lucht
66th Corps
vdHeydte
12 SS Pz
1 SS Pz
Duren
Aachen
Eupen
Monschau
Liege
Huy
Amay
Stokai
Engis
Tilff
Beaufays
Pepinster
Jalhay
Esneux
Soheit-Tinlot
Sprimont
Spa
Anthisnes
Aywaille
Butgenbach
Malmedy
Ouffet
Stavelot
Stoumont
Ferrieres
Trois-Ponts
Stadtkyll
St.-Vith
Gerolstein
Prüm
A
B
C
D
E
N
S
E
W
10 Miles
10 Kilometers
Map by Gene Thorp

would come behind Peiper, followed by Mohnke and the divisional staff. 'Bridges on the Meuse will be taken in undamaged condition by ruthless and rapid penetration. This will be accomplished by specially organized forward detachments under the command of suitable officers.'

Each of the SS panzer divisions would have a proven SS tank leader in charge of forging a rapid advance.[19] In particular, great hopes were pinned that the advance elements of Battlegroup Peiper might reach the Huy bridgehead across the canyon-like Meuse river gorge the first night of the advance. To Skorzeny, Mohnke's exhortations rung naive and were better suited to the 'young impressionable recruits' that the SS general had been lecturing to during his autumn effort to rehabilitate the Leibstandarte and imbue new recruits with the requisite Nazi fanaticism. Then, too, Skorzeny was still smarting from his difficulty getting the Luftwaffe to provide aerial photographs of the Meuse bridges he was to seize.[20] Yet Mohnke made it clear that Peiper's speed of advance was critical, telling him that the battle 'has to be fought with special brutality and without humane inhibitions'. Mohnke paused and glared at Peiper. 'One should remember the victims of the bombing terror!' Mohnke said that the 'Führer had spoken excellently – for three full hours and expressed complete confidence in victory.'[21]

> My division commander again emphasized to me the prime importance of my task, again telling me of the need for a very rapid breakthrough, the necessity that every man commit himself relentlessly ... He quoted several sentences from the conference with the Führer in Bad Nauheim in which he again expressed his confidence in the Leibstandarte.[22]

Hitler said they were to fight 'fanatically'. But Peiper paid scant attention. 'I did not read the material given to me at the Division Command Post because I was in a hurry and I also was in a bad mood, because I disagreed with the entire preparation for the undertaking which looked highly defective to me.'

> I returned on the same day to my command post, which was located in a forester's house inside the Blankenheim woods. First, I ordered my adjutant to call a commander's meeting for the same day at 1600 hours. This left me about two hours, which I used to study the material ... The very first impression of the terrain I got, with the aid of maps, reassured my opinion that this was a desperate undertaking. I can remember that in this material, among other things, was an order from the Sixth Panzer Army, with the contents that considering the desperate situation of the German people, a wave of terror and fright should precede our troops ... the German soldier should in this offensive recall the innumerable German victims of the bombing terror ... Enemy resistance had to be broken by terror.[23]

Hstuf. Oskar Klingelhöfer with the 7th Panzer Company remembered other details that were less flattering to the tank regiment commander. 'All scruples and humane feelings shall be thrown overboard ... With reference to prisoners of war, I remember distinctly that Peiper himself made this comment: "Situations can arise in which no prisoners of war will be made."'[24] Werner Poetschke was also at Peiper's briefing, providing even stronger language on the same topic. Both men repeatedly used the word 'terror', with Peiper emphasizing that the enemy should become so afraid as to run rather than fight.[25]

However, when matters moved on to operational considerations, both panzer leaders examined their assigned panzer rolling road closely. Peiper wilted. Panzer Rollbahn – hardly! 'We were to advance over roads that were not roads,' he later said. The whole escapade elevated wishful thinking – 'trying to repeat the success of 1940, now to be attempted again under completely different weather conditions'.[26] Peiper looked with envy at one of the routes assigned to the Hitler Jugend Panzer Division and Kampfgruppe Kuhlmann. Route C travelled over main roads, whereas the route assigned to him seemed pathetic – thin stretches of tarmac though thickly wooded hills, with some stretches unpaved and like the muddy trails he knew well from Russia.

'I immediately pointed out that these roads were not for tanks, but for bicycles,' Peiper scowled with dismay. Those roads were so narrow in places that a Tiger or even a Panther might not even fit, and where they were not paved, the rolling roads would likely dissolve into muddy tracks.[27] In the Schnee Eifel, with its thick forest, how would they deploy such armored beasts off the road? He knew enough of that from Russia. His blood pressure rose further when he realised that those at the meeting were ignoring him. 'They wouldn't even discuss it. They said it was the Führer's orders.'[28] To his men, Peiper pulled no punches. 'I explained that we had to make an attack in a terrain unsuitable for tanks, that the only chance of success depended upon speed, surprise, and relentless commitment of personnel and materiel.'

During the meeting Peiper detailed his composition of a lead panzer command with Poetschke's 1st Panzer Battalion – with tanks, SPWs, artillery guns, and engineers – 'composed in such a manner that it should be suitable … to solve all coming problems. This group should advance without regard and not pay attention to unimportant enemy goals nor booty, nor prisoners of war.'[29] The last statement would haunt him. Yet none of the old panzer hands at the meeting could have hardly been encouraged by his prognosis: 'owing to the unfavorable terrain, [the first panzer group] would likely be rubbed out … the task of this group should be finished if only one Panzer Mk IV were to reach the Meuse'. If that happened – which he fully expected – he planned to move up the heavy Tigers to deal with the opposition. 'The 1st Battalion received a very desperate task which I very clearly explained to the officers.' There was to be no concern for the flanks and no pause in the advance, he explained to Poetschke, nor any concern with losses:

> You will go ahead at high speed on the assigned road. Your task will be fulfilled after you have been blown up. The one that will take over after you is the tank right behind you. If shooting has to be done, it will be done while moving. There will be no stopping for anything. No booty is to be taken, no confiscated enemy

> vehicles are to be examined ... It is not the job of the spearhead to worry about prisoners of war. It is the job of the infantry following ... Armed civilians will be treated as partisans.[30]

Rather than a pep talk, Peiper's briefing developed a bitter outline as he went along. Less shooting would be good, given the transportation situation; reinforcement could not be counted on. Then, too, he could only promise that they would start with their gasoline tanks topped off. Further supply seemed exceedingly uncertain – a big concern given his fuel-thirsty Panthers and Tigers.[31] They would need to depend on captured fuel, although he noted grimly that, based 'on my experience, that would likely not be possible'.

Peiper spent nearly two hours poring over details – particularly the composition of his 25km-long march order. So narrow were the roads, there could be no question of modifying it once battle was joined. The lighter Mk IVs – his quarter horses – would be located in the *Spitze*, or spearhead. The heavier Panthers would advance with Diefenthal's grenadiers just behind. And the big, slow Tigers – the cold bloods – would be located to the rear. He would locate himself in the center of the advance column – the *Vorhut* – with Werner Poetschke leading the critical point assault.

On the following day, 15 December, Peiper received orders to go to still another briefing at I SS Panzer Corps. There he again found Wilhelm Mohnke, but this time with SS commando Otto Skorzeny present as well as the various regimental Leibstandarte commanders. Everyone learned about the Skorzeny operation and Panzer Brigade ISO, but first they had to endure speeches from SS leaders above Peiper. Mohnke launched into a repetitive monologue, with phrases liberally lifted from Hitler's speech at Bad Nauheim three days before.

> The Führer said that the impending battle must be won by all means. The decisive hour of the German people had arrived and it was to be or not to be. We would have to fight hard and recklessly. The Führer said furthermore that we would have to act with brutality and show no humane inhibitions ... a wave of terror and fight should precede us and the enemy's resistance had to be broken by terror.[32]

Skorzeny sat impassively. 'Old hares as we were,' he recalled, 'we only half-listened to Mohnke, who had steadily grown red in the face with the effort.'[33] Neither did Hermann Priess: 'I considered the speech of the Führer as propaganda,' he said, 'and did not conclude from it that the fighting methods on the Western Front should be changed.' Nevertheless, Priess indicated that the order of the day of the 6th Panzer Army may have been open to interpretation:

> I transmitted the part of the field order which concerned the divisions to the respective units under my command to be read to all the troops. I remember that these two orders said we had to push ruthlessly to the Maas, that every man had

> to give his best and that terror would be met with terror … I interpreted those remarks concerning ruthlessness, use of terror, etc. as propaganda, as I did the speech of the Führer at Bad Nauheim.[34]

That the invective carried further than the Leibstandarte was echoed in an order to the 12th SS Panzer Division's 3rd Panzer Company in mid-December. In Himmeldorf, near Steuss, the division commander, Hugo Kraas, a former member of the Leibstandarte, addressed his panzer commanders under him, among them Rudolf Sauer under Hstuf. Kurt Brodel's 3rd Company:

> This coming offensive is of great importance and can eventually be decisive for the fate of the German people. Furthermore, he said – and I can remember it distinctly, 'that in this offensive, he does not want to see any prisoners of war'.[35]

Peiper claimed later to have tuned the entire thing out, recalling it merely as 'a patriotic appeal for the hearts of German men'. He was rather more interested in the Skorzeny mission, which they were told had been especially requested by Hitler and 'had the goal to precede our advance with a wave of panic and confusion'.[36] SS Obersturmbannführer Willi Hardieck and Kampfgruppe Z of the Panzer Brigade ISO would be attached to Peiper to follow in the wake of his unit until after they had broken through the enemy front. Peiper's spearhead, and that of 12th SS Panzer Division, was expected to pass south of the Hohes Venn plateau by midnight on 17 December; six hours later, Skorzeny's forces would overtake and fan out before the tank spearheads and capture the Meuse bridgeheads ahead of the *Panzerblitz*.[37]

At least the Skorzeny commandos would be expected to fight in the rhythm expected by Peiper. Before the commandos had left Grafenwöhr just prior to the operation, they had been addressed by the fanatical Gauleiter of Franconia, Karl von Holz. 'When you start this offensive, shoot everything that comes before your weapons,' the zealous Nazi district official told them. 'Shoot every American soldier; shoot every civilian. Remember only the dead can no longer harm us. Take prisoners only of deserters, for these can be interrogated profitably.'[38] The fake American soldiers under Einheit Grabowski knew their Knight's Cross-bearing commander fully endorsed that view. 'Shoot all colored prisoners on sight, because they stink,' Obstlt Josef Grabowski told his men, adding that he would personally shoot any American captives coming under his control 'with a cold smile' – *mit einem kuehlen Laecheln*.

There were other concerns. Peiper worried about the confusion created in front of him by a group of German commandos dressed as Americans:

> It was possible that he would take prisoners that I would later meet, and since it was our habit to let prisoners of war stand on the side of the road unguarded, the danger existed that if I were to approach, I would consider them an able enemy and so my point might open fire on them. I therefore asked Hardieck what to do with prisoners, and Hardieck told me we were to operate exactly like the British

> Commandos [at Dieppe] – if we were to be caught, we will be finished; we don't give any mercy either.[39]

Before Peiper's meeting on the 15th with Hardieck ended, Peiper had a heart-to-heart with SS Ostubaf. Rudi Sandig, who would lead the SS Panzer Grenadier Regiment 2 that would follow in his wake. 'I told him in detail,' Peiper later recalled, 'that it was very important that I not get separated from my column, since the danger of my point being surrounded was always present, and I told him that the prisoners and the booty which I would leave behind should not be reported as his own successes.'[40]

Peiper headed back to his command post, calling a final meeting to brief his battalion commanders on their mission and what would be expected. He further asked them to brief their subordinate commanders, down to company level, the evening prior to the attack. And what transpired in the briefing?

Sturmmann Werner Löhman, a tank driver in the 7th Company, later testified that on the evening prior to the big attack Oberscharführer Hans Siptrott gathered his platoon. 'We are now starting an attack against the Americans,' he said with great seriousness. 'The enemy has to be afraid of us once more. For that reason we will fight in the old SS spirit. No prisoners will be taken. This is a new order.'[41] Of course, what Löhman said would later be denied. But the real issue was the many other German enlisted men and even officers who claimed the same.

That night Peiper had a meeting to brief his battalion and company commanders in the small hall at the Blankenheim Forester's house. The man who often served as Werner Sternebeck's orderly was there. 'Model has commanded that our panzers must roll!' Peiper told them all.[42] The situation for Germany was desperate beyond belief. *'Alles in die Waagschale werfen'* – throw everything you have into the pan!

The panzer units would be attacking in wooded terrain, and due to the lack of reconnaissance and the ever-present danger of ambush, the tank commanders were told that they must hold themselves chest high out of the top of each panzer to watch out for trouble. 'That wasn't too reassuring,' SS officer Arndt Fischer noted. More troubling, when the meeting let out at 9 p.m., prisoners remained a question.[43] Arndt Fischer would recall about the meeting that 'at the time Stubaf. Poetschke spoke about that we should not take any prisoners where the military situation absolutely required it. Poetschke also declared that this was a secret order.' Did that discussion come up? A multitude of statements of company commanders would affirm it, although Arndt Fischer would later vehemently deny his own handwritten statement.[44]

But the holes in the dam kept breaking open. SS Lt Hans Hennecke, one of Peiper's trusted tank commanders, contradicted Fischer's denial in a parallel statement. 'Obstuf. Peiper gave orders before the attack started – to fight a hard, cruel and disregarding fight because this was the last possibility to win,' Hennecke would later tell his first interrogators. He would claim to recall, almost word for word, what Peiper had told his company commanders in December:

> In the coming operation, the regiment will have the duty to attack recklessly. No consideration will be paid to man or machine. The coming mission will be the last chance to win the war. Therefore, we will attack like a storm wind [*Sturmwind*]. The enemy must become totally crazed with fear that the SS is coming. That is our obligation.[45]

Was it true that when Peiper's panzer regiment was leading a spearhead attack that they would typically shoot prisoners rather than bother with detaining them? 'Yes, it is a fact,' Hennecke admitted. 'One cannot deny it.'[46] Friedrich Christ, who would lead the 2nd Company of Panthers in the coming offensive, was heard vividly by Rttf. Georg Bunder with his 3rd Platoon on the evening of 15 December. According to Bunder, Christ coyly left the matter vague: 'We are not placing any value on the taking of prisoners of war.[47] Yet that declaration smacked of inside language within the Leibstandarte. Why otherwise mention prisoners at all?

Predictably as well, Peiper's own orderly, SS Hstuf. Gerhard Nueske, claimed no wrong-doing. At Peiper's command post, he was charged with making certain that the order of march was observed and operational directives were issued. 'I myself typed up the division order for the Ardennes Offensive utilising the corps order,' Nueske would later contend. 'In addition, I knew Sepp Dietrich's order of the day. None of these orders contained anything extraordinary.'[48] The big emphasis was that Kampfgruppe Peiper should advance rapidly without regard to its flanks.

In any case, in the morning, the great attack would come. Peiper could only balance Heinrich Himmler's old admonition. 'The word *impossible*,' the Reichsführer SS was fond of saying, 'must never be heard in the SS.' Yet Peiper, his former adjutant, could only shake his head: *Wacht am Rhein* was, he opined, 'a hopeless operation'.[49] How could it work? 'We freely expressed our negative opinion about the plan, but did not protest the inevitable.'[50]

Another old panzer hand with the Tigers, Werner Wendt, with the SS Heavy Panzer Battalion 501 said it best: '*Die Lage ist hoffnungslos, aber nicht ernst*' – The situation is hopeless, but not serious. His unit had been on the Russian front since it was first equipped with the heavy tanks, but was surprised in November 1944 when his battalion received 45 brand-new King Tigers.[51] Now, even though assigned to Peiper, he remained frustrated by weeks of paltry fuel and ammunition supply to train green drivers and his own specialty – gunnery. It was true that he had once shot down seventeen Soviet tanks in a single day in Russia, but this was a different crew with Königstiger Nr. 133. Inside a tank, a gunner needed not only an able loader but also a driver who would put his gun in the right spot and a radio man who could quickly survey the situation to the platoon front.

On the night of 13 December they had moved by rail from Cologne to detrain in Engelgau, just north of Tondorf. The battalion commander, SS Obstuf. Heinz von Westernhagen, set up shop nearby, while his tankers worked feverishly in the pre-dawn to move the Tigers under the thick conifers that lined the road to Blankenheim. If protected from Allied airborne eyes, the steel tanks covered with pine boughs were no protection against the cold, and coffee could only be brewed at night. No movement at all was authorised during the day. On the evening of 15 December their company commander briefed them on the mission, and they were surprised to hear of a big attack with far-flung objectives. Even more unsettling was the news that German troops disguised as Americans would be mixed in with their forces.[52] Indeed, the paratroopers from 5th Company of 12th Fallschirmjäger Regiment z.B.V. (*zur besonderen Verwendung*: for special employment) from that unit would ride on their Tigers to provide Peiper extra infantry support.[53]

Like Wendt, SS Obersturmführer Eberhard Kosch, the adjutant for the SS Panzer Artillery Regiment 1, was pleasantly surprised that autumn by how quickly the division was materially rebuilt. Indeed, although they had called their unit panzer artillery for two years, self-propelled artillery pieces were in short supply. At least the division would have a group of self-propelled 105mm Bison infantry guns and a couple of other self-propelled panzer artillery weapons – Wespe and Hummel.[54] Yet they felt fortunate to at least have the gun batteries up to strength. The rapid re-equipment was worrying, as 'every soldier knew something big was up'.

What little fuel they had for the new towed equipment was used for training exercises that involved manoeuvres in mountainous terrain. The rumour mill flourished. When they transferred to Siegburg in November, the rumour grew that they would go to Switzerland. After another mountain fire exercise, Kosch ventured to his superior that perhaps they would go to the Eifel. 'Man, that is crazy!' he said. 'What could we do in the Eifel?' He waved his hand in dismissal. 'If one vehicle stops, the entire division would be stuck!'[55]

The first days of December found the division moving stealthily across the Rhine to Euskirchen and then the Eifel by night. Slowly they moved down roads 'crawling with vehicles, tanks and artillery pieces'. At sunrise everyone looked for cover. 'If you didn't have your vehicle camouflaged, you were punished then and there.' Not all elements were on hand, and some of the grenadiers under SS Staf. Max Hansen with the SS Panzer Grenadier Regiment 1 marched 30km through the snow-dusted Eifel the last night before the attack to reach the border jump-off point near Ormont.[56] By 14 December the artillery regiment found itself in Blankenheim on the fringe of the Eifel. The next day Kosch and the other *Bumskopf* (literally 'boom heads') set up the batteries carefully and quietly between the pines and forest trails.

Meanwhile, the nearby self-propelled flak tank company was also ordered to move from their comfy farmhouse near Weilerswist and headed towards Blankenheim. Karl Wortmann was a gunner on one of the quad 20mm guns mounted on a Mk IV chassis, but even though his commanding officer had told him that big things would soon be expected, he was dismayed at the materiel situation. Their company was supposed to have sixteen flak panzers, but possessed only half that number. In fact, rather than the 3.7cm gun that he preferred, his panzer had the 20mm variety. Worse than that, the company arrived in the forest near Losheim to find there were no quarters, and Wortmann slept in the open cold, learning that his flak panzer would be committed with the SPWs of Georg Preuss's 10th Company, II Panzer Grenadier Battalion. As they moved to the forest, it was cold, and the steel hull of the flak panzer offered no sanctuary. Even though tempting the ire of the camouflage officers roaming the German front, Wortmann built a small fire just so he and his crew could warm their hands.[57]

SS Hscha. Jochen Thiele commanded the 12th Company, of Josef Diefenthal's III Battalion, of the armored infantry that would accompany Peiper. Aware of Peiper and Diefenthal's chemistry, Thiele sought to impart his SPW-mounted grenadiers with the right National Socialist attitude. 'The offensive, which is imminent, will decide the fate of the whole German nation,' Anton Motzheim heard him implore the audience in Dorweiler. 'Think of it, that American gangsters have made our cities into piles of rubble, millions of women and children killed … If you think about all of that, then you know what you, as SS men, have to do in case you capture American soldiers.'[58]

Just like the orders for the surprise winter offensive, such an order, or *Befehl*, would not be written down. A hardened SS NCO, SS Hscha. Heinz Hendel, conveyed much the same message to SPW panzer grenadiers of his 2nd platoon of the 11th Company the night before the attack. 'Men, you have heard the speech of the company commander,' Hendel said, evoking SS Lt Heinz Tomhardt's message. 'It is necessary that we fight ruthlessly in this offensive. All that comes before our barrels will be shot. Prisoners of war will be shot. In his offensive, plenty of "*Rabatz*" [ruckus] will be made, and all that shows itself in the streets and in the windows will be shot.'[59] From the perspective of the Leibstandarte, the surprise attack would be conducted with special savagery only known before in the East. Now, the *Amis* in the West would know it too.

Chapter 3

THE SECRET

Weather: Generally foggy to misty in the morning. Visibility too low for air activity over the Ardennes. Sunrise 0829. Sunset 1645.

Forecast for 16 December 1944, U.S. First Army

Could Hitler's secret offensive code-named Wacht am Rhein be kept from Allied intelligence operatives? Although the German army strictly obeyed Hitler's orders, his Luftwaffe continued its lax policy of radio transmissions. Meanwhile, ULTRA listened in. ULTRA was the Allied codebreaking system using the world's first electro-mechanical computers in Bletchley Park, Buckinghamshire, England. Contrary to some post-war assessments, ULTRA was anything but quiet. Some forty to fifty decrypt messages were received from the European theatre each day. ULTRA decrypts were filled with communiqués regarding extensive rail and road movements to the Eifel region, consisting of units such as the artillery batteries of Eberhard Kosch with the Panzer Artillery Regiment.

The Allies eavesdropped on plans of the German high command to rebuild the Leibstandarte. On 5 October, SS operations headquarters signaled OKH that four SS panzer divisions (1st, 2nd, 9th, and 12th SS) and the 2nd Panzer Division and Panzer Lehr would be built up to full armored strength in coming weeks – at least 134 tanks each, with heavy armor attached.[1]

Not only were heavy weapons to be made fully available, but offensive-minded training would be pursued vigorously. Heavily armed armored cars and half-tracks were to be delivered. ULTRA eavesdroppers pondered with their superiors the purpose of such a potent enemy attack force. On 10 November the director general of transport complained that the 2nd SS Panzer Division had fallen thirty-six hours behind schedule in its rail movement. For the Allied intelligence observers, a large question loomed: what movement was so important that an SS armored unit had to adhere to a strict schedule? Yet in contrast to that worrisome question was the fact that the enemy now had a *Magen Battalion*, which was composed of conscripts with stomach ulcers who could only eat white bread. What better evidence that the Wehrmacht was scraping the bottom of the barrel?[2]

Beginning in the last week of November, the Luftwaffe urgently issued a series of daily orders. The orders called for top-priority aerial reconnaissance of portions of the Northern Ardennes by the swift Ar 234B jet aircraft of Detachment Sperling. The intercepts called for photographic images of the bridge crossings over the Meuse river from Liège to Givet, spelling out the Germans' intent to determine the status of the bridges and the locations of Allied supply and troop concentrations.[3] Why all this attention on this idle sector? Then came a curious development on 10 December: an intercept related the observation by II Jagdkorps that 'SS units are maintaining radio silence.' When this ULTRA was relayed to Gen. Patton, he immediately suspected trouble; his own army usually went silent on the airwaves just before a big attack. An even more provocative event arrived on the next rash of ULTRA intercepts just after noon on 16 December: the air force liaison, *Flivo*, with the I SS Panzer Corps, reported radio silence was over. His reported location was even more telling – he was broadcasting from Blankenheim, immediately east of the Eifel and just before the entrance to the Losheim Gap in the Ardennes.[4] On the following morning, the Luftwaffe fighter group in the west, II Jagdkorps, indicated their intention to support the 5th and 6th Panzer Armies.

Conventional battlefield intelligence mushroomed. Aerial reconnaissance for Hodges' First Army was the responsibility of Col George W. Peck's 67th Tactical Reconnaissance Group (TRG) of the IX Tactical Air Command (TAC) for the northern reaches. In spite of dreadful weather, the sightings by 'Peck's Bad Boys' widened eyes each time they were able to take a look. On the last day of November the pilots spied heavy rail traffic along the Euskirchen–Münstereifel railway, with twenty flat cars loaded with uncovered Tiger tanks. At about the same time, a reliable German prisoner from the 81st Machine Gun Battalion was interrogated; he had seen elements of the 6th Panzer Army north of Senne and opposite the Ardennes. He claimed to have seen many 'Tiger tanks with new trainloads arriving every two or three days with sixty tanks at a time'.[5] Suspicious?

On the ground, at locations from the Schnee Eifel to Diekirch, Luxembourg, American soldiers noted the sounds of tank treads, and a few frightened civilians reported large collections of German bridging equipment and heavy weapons just across the Our River. And on 11 December a seized German prisoner of the beleaguered 272nd Volksgrenadier Division claimed to have seen panzer troops of the SS Hitler Jugend Division coming to relieve them near Bergstein. Another claimed to have seen German paratroopers – sage veterans from Crete – now equipped to jump again.

Even more curious, on 9 December came a report from the VIII Corps G-2 (U.S. Army intelligence officer) forwarded to higher headquarters that a 1st SS Panzer Division forward gunnery observer had been captured right on the edge of the Ardennes front. Surprisingly, the POW was captured by GIs in a patrol against the sector held by the 2nd Battalion, 991st Regiment of the

277th Volksgrenadier Division, and he insisted that the artillery regiment of the SS Panzer Division Leibstandarte Adolf Hitler on 5 December was moving towards the sector east of Wahlerscheid – right across from the U.S. 2nd Infantry Division.[6] Similar evidence came from V Corps on the same day. When Pvt. Hans Rothenburger, an Alsatian deserter from 3rd Fallschirmjäger Division, eagerly crossed over to American lines on 9 December, he revealed to his interrogators the 'persistent rumour' was that they would soon be relieved by SS Division Leibstandarte.[7]

Yet the V Corps intelligence officers brushed all this aside, noting that other captured prisoners in the same vicinity whined about poor equipment, limited ammunition, and a lack of food. Rothenburger had admitted that few in his replacement company knew how to properly handle their weapons. But SS tank troops on the front? 'Believed unlikely', came the retort – a reflection of the December crystal ball from Allied intelligence mavens.[8] The VIII Corps report was ignored altogether. As if to underscore complacency, the day before the German offensive, the Allied Supreme Headquarters G-3 operations officer, Maj. J.F.M. Whitely, in a briefing to his air commanders dismissed the Ardennes with 'nothing to report'.[9]

Others were not so satisfied. By 13 December Maj. Gen. Kenneth Strong, the British head of Allied intelligence for the Supreme Command, was increasingly disturbed by enemy radio silence. He went so far as to warn Gen. Dwight D. Eisenhower, the Supreme Commander, as well as Gen. Omar Bradley, of the 12th Army Group, of the possibility of an enemy spoiling attack in the Ardennes. 'The enemy's hand is dealt for a showdown before Christmas,' he warned.[10] Eisenhower, who had experienced the cunning of his cornered enemy in North Africa, was mindful of the possibility of a 'nasty little Kasserine' and asked Strong to have a word with Bradley. Maj. Gen. Strong motored down to Luxembourg City to visit with Bradley and his G-2, or intelligence officer, Maj. Gen. Edwin Sibert.

A graduate of the same 1915 West Point class that had produced Eisenhower, Gen. Omar Bradley was called the 'infantryman's general'. The 12th Army Group commander had a reputation for being stubborn, informal, and clear-headed. Those in his headquarters reflected their boss: his intelligence people were immediately inclined to dismiss the possibility of a major German attack, pointing to the continuing dirge of ULTRA decrypted enemy reports describing the poverty of troops, weapons, and, most of all, fuel. They argued that even if the enemy did try something big, they hardly had enough petrol to sustain a drive of more than 120 to 150 miles. Both considered Strong something of a doomsayer, which was of course part and parcel of the pessimism expected from a British G-2. Nevertheless, Strong drafted a top-secret memo to all Army groups on 14 December. He warned of the possibility of a 'German relieving attack' through the Ardennes. Montgomery denounced his counsel.

Others in the Allied camp needed less convincing. Foremost among these was Col Benjamin A. 'Monk' Dickson. A strapping Philadelphian in Lt Gen. Courtney Hodges' First Army headquarters, Dickson looked to be the thinking type: moustachioed, well read, and quick witted. Although a West Point graduate and a participant in the First World War, he was not the average Army officer type. Academically inclined, after returning from Europe Dickson chose further education over the Army. He studied at MIT to become an engineer and then travelled abroad as something of a *bon vivant*, soon becoming proficient in both French and German.

That capability became his destiny. And when he was called into the army in 1940 in the intelligence arm, he tended to surround himself with like minds, what some called Dickson's 'backroom boys'. Whereas the term 'battlefield intelligence' remained an oxymoron – the unending brunt of Army jokes – Dickson and his outfit were among the most experienced.[11] Yet that winter he found himself effectively blacklisted within Eisenhower's intelligence community. Dickson admitted to being a confirmed pessimist – a survival habit learned in North Africa after being chased around Tunisia by Erwin Rommel's tanks.[12] And even after annoying his commanders during the summer at Normandy – warning about enemy capabilities, secret weapons and the Luftwaffe – the breathless victories at summer's end appeared to change him. Even worrying about enemy operatives gone dark, he described his G-2 mission with zeal:

> The welcome to the American troops by the majority of the Belgians is sincere. The Germanophile elements have not yet recovered from the shock of the German defeat and the surprise of seeing the First American Army roll through Belgium six weeks after the breakthrough at St-Lô. We are, for the moment, psychologically wrapped in the armor of invincibility, and the legends of American inventiveness and power enhance our reputation. From a psychological viewpoint, we hold all the aces at the moment.[13]

Even with his misgivings, Dickson had relaxed. His late-autumn quarters reflected a changed mood. Gone was the mud and tents; now he was housed comfortably in the fashionable Hotel Britannique five minutes off the main square in Spa. There, they could go to the outdoor casino terrace, take a curative mineral bath, or throw back a few cocktails at Zebra, the officers' lounge.[14] Besides, their most secret source, the ULTRA codebreaking system, was nearly silent. Perhaps the Germans were finished.

Yet as November drew to a close, the intelligence winds shifted in Dickson's mind. By the end of the first week in December 1944, the G-2 officer became totally obsessed with the idea that the enemy was planning a major operation – an idea that began to ferment as he put together puzzle pieces fed to him by Lt Col Adolph G. Rosengarten Jr, his cerebral liaison for the ULTRA communiqués[15] More than just an aide to assist with the top-secret ULTRA, Rosengarten was something of puzzle-solving sleuth.

One weird clue was the enemy recruitment of English-speaking soldiers into a unit associated with Otto Skorzeny. That was worrisome enough, but then came the sharp uptick in the morale of prisoners being culled from patrols on the Ardennes front. Finally, the new signals being baldly dispatched by the Luftwaffe piqued Rosengarten – even if he was inclined to doubt his own interpretation. Yet Dickson had more experience and was soon forecasting a major German counteroffensive while other Allied G-2s saw a doddering enemy on the verge of collapse.[16] Dickson's new crusade made him unpopular with Eisenhower and Bradley.[17]

Nevertheless, on 10 December Dickson puzzled over the relocation of the mysterious missing enemy armored reserve, the SS-laden 6th Panzer Army, along with other troubling intelligence. The following day, two prisoners of the 246th Volksgrenadier Division told of seeing SS men in company strength from the 1st SS 'Adolf Hitler' Panzer Division on 4 December in Zülpich – only 40km from Monschau.[18] 'It is plain that the strategy and defense of the Reich is based on the exhaustion of our offensive to be followed by an all-out counterattack armor between the Roer and the Urft, supported by every weapon he can bring to bear.'

> The enemy is capable of a concentrated counterattack with air, armor, infantry and secret weapons at a selected focal point at a time of his own choosing ... He has brought up and continues to bring up army and corps artillery formations and to build up his fighter and fighter-bomber strength on the Western Front ... A captured order for a comb out of selected personnel speaking the American dialect to report to HQ Skorzeny at Friedenthal, near Oranienburg by 1 November, obviously presages special operations for sabotage, attacks on CPs (command posts) and other vital installations by infiltrated or parachuted specialists. An extremely intelligent PW whose other observations check exactly with established facts, stated that every means possible is being gathered for the coming all-out counteroffensive. It is notable that morale among PWs freshly captured ... recently achieved a new high ... Indications to date point to the location of this focal point as being between Roermond and Schleiden.[19]

In Dickson's mind, only the 'focal point' was in doubt. Here his information was dated. 'His armored reserve is believed to be quartered in houses and barns along the railroads, generally in a semi-circle from Dusseldorf to Koblenz with Köln as a center point.' Schleiden was just east of Monschau in the Ardennes, and even as he wrote the intelligence, Sepp Dietrich's infantry and artillery were threading through that zone on their way to the jump-off points for *Wacht am Rhein*.

For the blinded Allied intelligence officers, the 6th Panzer Army, including the elite SS divisions and the Leibstandarte, was the tail of the donkey – find it and you could divine the enemy's intentions. Yet, denied such information by stealthy enemy night movement and thickly clouded skies, Dickson cleverly used clues to unravel German preparations. What of the sudden German halt in their robot bombardment of London and Antwerp? 'The suspension of V-1 fire from Baumholder area and the Bonn sites,' his intelligence read, 'is believed to be based on the use of his railroads for the bringing up of new Volksgrenadier divisions west of the Rhine and for the build-up of the necessary artillery and supplies necessary to support his all-out counterattack.'

Then, on 14 December, Dickson was informed of a frightened Luxembourg woman, Elise Delé, who had seen 'many vehicles, pontoons and boats and other river crossing equipment coming from the direction of Bitburg!'[20] This set off a cascade of chain reaction of intelligence ciphers in Dickson's head. 'It's the Ardennes!' he blurted as he smacked the situation map unfurled on the wall in the First Army briefing room. Gen. Hodges and his right-hand man, Gen. William B. Kean, were both in the room in Spa, Belgium, but Hodges later claimed to have missed Dickson's exclamation.[21] At least one other man, Capt. William Cox, with the First Army G-1 section, who was keeping track of telltale signs of German armored movements on another big map in Spa, concluded the same thing, but he only shared this point of view to Col Peter C. Haines over supper.[22] Otherwise, the U.S. First Army staff seemed oblivious, while Hodges himself was suffering a severe head cold and worried that their attack was bogging down. 'I was terribly tired that night,' he remembered.[23]

Hodges' lack of faith in Monk Dickson's brashness was hardly new. Although pessimism came naturally to any intelligence officer (a G-2's motto: 'Regardless of what happens, there is always someone who said it would …'), even Dickson's peers saw him as a less than trustworthy oracle. His detractors felt him to be an extroverted and exaggerating alarmist. An anonymous member of the Office of Strategic Services in Luxembourg City had penned a caption below a mocking portrait of Hitler that hung in the Sibert's office. 'He fools some of the people some of the time, but he fools Dickson all of the time.'[24]

On 15 December, Eisenhower and SHAEF had told Sibert to rein Dickson in – he was scaring people needlessly. The British 21st Army Group agreed. 'The enemy,' read an intelligence summary to be released on 16 December, 'is at present fighting a defensive campaign on all fronts … He is incapable of launching major offensive operations.'[25] That same day Field Marshal Montgomery cabled Eisenhower to see if he could take leave to England the following week. Monty set off by plane to play a bit of golf with the Welsh professional, Dai Rees.

Back in Washington, D.C., mid-December found the city struggling with a heavy early snowfall that crippled Maryland traffic and left pedestrians braving icy streets. War-related conservation was in full bloom. The National Christmas Tree would again not be illuminated, and petrol rationing left cars and taxis marooned on the Capitol City streets. Most service stations posted 'No Gas', signs and motorists suffered long lines. Meanwhile, newspaper editorials decried flaring tempers from the domestic cigarette shortage, as ration coupon counterfeiters were jailed.[26] The supply of red meat was rationed as well.

Back home the war remained the main news story, but most headlines described what readers wanted to see: swashbuckling General George Patton pushing into the Saar. Still, there was the grim reality. Each day brought lists of Washingtonians killed overseas and a grim report that American casualties since D-Day now exceeded a quarter of a million. The selective service announced tightening regulations on the draft of men aged 26 through 37, but the Ardennes and even the entire First Army remained nearly anonymous.

The missing American manpower overseas left a shortage of volunteer Santas and men with experience in driving snow ploughs. Coming back to Washington after a three-week vacation at the 'Little White House' in Warm Springs, Georgia, President Franklin D. Roosevelt concerned himself with the war – Eisenhower's infantry replacement situation seemed particularly dire – but he did not seem discouraged.[27] His wife, Eleanor, meanwhile, was reading *What to Do with Germany*, by Louis Nizer and telling her husband that unconditional surrender of Hitler's Germany would do little. The real work was to transform its youth, now enthusiastically obsessed with fascism.[28]

Indeed, even in the sixth year of war, the youth of Germany were on the march. Signs soon appeared before front-line units in the Ardennes. The assistant commander of the 106th Division, Brig. Gen. Herbert T. Perrin, witnessed a disturbing event on 12 December. The 106th was the newly installed greenhorn infantry division taking over the cold but quiet positions on the Schnee Eifel along the Westwall. Perrin would later relate that on the first night they were in line after taking over for the 2nd Infantry Division, a patrol captured a Russian prisoner who claimed that five German divisions were about to attack the 106th.[29] No reaction came from the top; regardless of what the 106th G-2 reported, its credibility was lacking. They were too green.

Yet three days later, on Friday, 15 December, the U.S. 106th issued an even more worrisome report, this one concerning the interrogation of a deserter from the 18th Volksgrenadier Division just across from the Losheim Gap. A German infantryman had more clout. While he confirmed that the division was largely made up of inexperienced Luftwaffe and Navy conscripts, he told how his trainees had been copiously equipped with machine pistols and trained in night fighting. There would be a large-scale attack against the Americans before Christmas, he told interrogators. And then he related a rumour of an outrageous new secret weapon, which likely helped the U.S. 1st Army to ignore the warning just like the first.[30]

Monk Dickson wasn't around to see these intelligence reports. His wolf cry: 'It's the Ardennes!' earned him a long-delayed leave to Paris. Meanwhile, Bradley and his optimist G-2, Gen. Sibert, were inclined to dismiss the entire mass of spotty intelligence. The German army was like a staggering wounded man, ready to collapse: 'With continuing Allied pressure in the south and in the north,' recited Sibert's G-2 estimate of 12 December, 'the [enemy] breaking point may develop suddenly and without warning.'[31] 'A breakthrough by the Third and Seventh U.S. armies could easily develop similarly [to Normandy] into a disastrous 'end run'. The Germans could fall apart at any time with the Allies marching to Berlin to pick up the pieces.

Given that, Dickson's warning seemed preposterous, and besides, he had used G-2 data from 'a sensitive source', almost certainly referring to the top-secret ULTRA decrypts – any mention of which was forbidden in the Allied intelligence arena. Maj. Gen. Kenneth Strong, with Eisenhower's SHAEF intelligence headquarters, called Sibert in Luxembourg and told him to contact Dickson and 'set him straight'. But when Sibert phoned him, he found that Dickson was already on leave. Sibert was relieved; he had already tussled with Dickson about his 'alarmist' Intelligence Estimate 37. Besides, 'Dickson was an old hand' at intelligence, and such an old dog was unlikely to change his ways.[32]

On 16 December 1944 Company B of the veteran 612th Tank Destroyer Battalion had been moved from its attachment to the veteran 2nd Infantry Division to the largely untested 99th Infantry Division.[33] More than that, they would shortly be ordered from their bivouac near Sourbrodt to Honsfeld, Belgium, closer to the fighting front. Their seventy-day mission overlooking the enemy pillboxes on the Westwall that autumn at the German border was a time of muddy trenches and unrelenting misery. Most of the battalion hands were tough farm boys from the Deep South. Their battalion commander, Col Willis A. Hedden, was an old cavalryman from Dahlonega, Georgia, an area in the south-eastern United States where Jeb Stuart's hard-riding confederates were still embraced by military types. But Hedden had experience; he had fought with tanks in the First World War. Leading in cavalry boots and wielding a swagger stick, Hedden gave the TD outfit an oversized character. Even though they were saddled with the unenviable towed 3in guns, few units in the U.S. Army had more pride.[34] 'We would have jumped on anything that God put in front of us,' one veteran remembered. 'We could thread a needle with those guns.'[35]

On Thursday, 14 December, while the American intelligence seers argued enemy intentions, on the other side of the Belgian–German border Jochen Peiper met with 36-year-old Genmaj. Gerhard Engel with the 12th Volksgrenadier Division. Peiper and Engel were better acquainted than would seem likely for a regular army and Waffen SS officer in December 1944. Like Peiper, Engel had connections. 'He knew everybody in the regime,' said one of his regimental commanders. 'We were equipped with more weapons than we knew what to do with.'[36] During the triumphal dash across Poland in September 1939, Peiper and Engel had been together with Hitler in the *Frontkolonne* – (Hitler's personal convoy) in the wake of the advance.

Engel had also served as Hitler's personal army adjutant from 1938 until March 1943, when he transferred to a field command in Russia. There he developed a reputation as being brave and bold, but also arrogant and prone to throw his weight around. Obst Rudolf von Gersdorff, on the Staff of the German Seventh Army, often joked that if Engel couldn't be found, he was likely 'on the phone to Hitler'.[37] Engel knew at least some of the dark secrets of the Reich. When he had asked Himmler to go along on an inspection of a concentration camp, Himmler answered that, as policy, army adjutants were not authorised to see these places.[38] To Peiper, however, Engel was someone from Hitler's inner circle, and that implied trust:

> On the afternoon of 14 December 1944, I drove over to confer with the commander of the 12th Volksgrenadier Division who was supposed to crack the initial line. We developed a joint plan … He said that he had a very heavy artillery concentration ready to destroy the American front-line positions. He then said that they would attack with two regiments … Genmaj. Engel explained that he hoped to make the

> initial penetration and reach Losheim by 0700 hours. I then asked Genmaj. Engel to clear the road of mines in the area around Losheim.[39]

Engel was in charge of the best infantry division in the 6th Panzer Army – a superlative that meant little in 1944. Recruited in the area around Mecklenburg before the war, the 12th Infantry Division had a long and proud history. The unit had been almost totally destroyed in Russia in the summer of 1944, but had been hastily reconstituted to fight admirably in the costly autumn battles for Aachen, Emperor Charlemagne's old capital. Even so, the bestowed honorific title of Volksgrenadier rang hollow in December 1944; many of his 14,800 troops were green. Fully a quarter of his replacements were still trickling into the assembly area around Kronenburg in the forty-eight hours leading up to O-Tag.[40] The only positive was Engel's nucleus of well-trained NCOs and officers.

On the eve of the great attack, Gen. Jodl dispatched Hitler's last instructions to Genflm. Model with Heeresgruppe B. While brimming with confidence, they emphatically warned against any resurrection of the Small Solution. 'Any turning of the panzer formations east of the Meuse river to the north is expressly forbidden …'

> The final decisions have been made … everything points to victory. The magnitude and scope of which … depends entirely on the handling of the operation; … if … these basic principles for the conduct of operations are adhered to … a major victory is assured.[41]

Genflm. Model felt himself obliged to respond, even late that evening of 15 December. At 2230 hours he cabled Hitler's headquarters with a message marked 'for immediate delivery to the Führer'. Model reiterated that 'the objective of the army group remains fixed on Antwerp. … However, a timely and sufficient delivery of fuel remains decisive for the successful outcome of the operation … At this time, supply, in spite of all efforts, remains insufficient.'[42]

That Friday, 15 December, at *Adlerhorst* the office hummed with activity even while Hitler slept. SS Adjutant Hermann Fegelein rousted Reichsleiter Martin Bormann at daybreak to take a two-hour power walk through the wooded rolling hills. Fegelein talked constantly as they hiked, but the thickset Bormann was out of shape, with a paunchy gut pushing out beyond his Reichsleiter belt buckle. He stumbled back to *Adlerhorst* winded and sore, hastening to make ready as he and Fegelein were to meet 'Uncle H.H.' for lunch. Almost never late, Himmler arrived promptly for the midday meal at 2 p.m. After their repast, SS Reichsführer and Fegelein worked together for two more hours, but Bormann was called away. Hitler was not up until 11.45 a.m., but upon rising he called the Reischsleiter to accompany him for a short stroll with his Alsatian dog, Blondi. As they walked, Hitler spoke glowingly about *Wacht am Rhein*, but Bormann seemed preoccupied.[43]

Returning to the bunker, Hitler had lunch with his secretaries before the 3 p.m. situation meeting with Himmler and Siegfried Westphal, Genflm. von

Rundstedt's snobbish chief of staff. Himmler had arrived the day before from Schloss Kransberg, an old German castle complex in the south, by car to join his Führer just before the big attack. Hitler enthusiastically related the good omens. There was no special news from the enemy side, he told Himmler – it looked like the great secret was secure.

For his part, Himmler assured Hitler of his Waffen SS armored divisions. They would strike quickly to the Meuse; indeed, his former adjutant, Jochen Peiper, would lead the main Leibstandarte spearhead. Afterwards, at 5.30 p.m., Himmler and Hitler had tea with infantry General Walther Buhle, Genflm. von Rundstedt, Reichsleiter Bormann, and Genobst Jodl while the Führer's doctor fretted about his patient's 'great emotional crisis regarding the coming offensive'.[44] There were the usual injections of vitamins, glucose and liver extract. At least the German leader wasn't then needing powerful injections of Eukodal and methamphetamine.

Hitler looked forward to the nightly war report on 15 December. The German leader was optimistic – even jaunty – as he ate his simple vegetarian meal with his secretaries. Later he moved back to the situation room at 1.10 a.m. to go over last-minute preparations with Obst von Nicolaus von Below and his army adjutant, Maj. Willi Johannmeyer. The evening tea did not begin until 2.20 a.m. Later he bent the ear of his foreign minister's liaison officer, Walther Hewel, likely discussing what opportunities a German victory might present. The small talk went on until the early morning hours, leaving his audience exhausted.

Hitler plodded to his bunkerised quarters to fall asleep at 5 a.m., only a half-hour before 2,000 artillery guns were to open up on the unsuspecting U.S. troops in the Ardennes. Just down the road at von Rundstedt's headquarters, the officer in charge of the OB West war diary jotted a final entry. 'Tomorrow's big attack brings the beginning of a new chapter in the Campaign in the West.'[45] Near the front, even the new Leibstandarte recruits were talking of 'reaching Paris by Christmas and living on abandoned *Ami* supplies en route'.[46] In the Eifel that evening came an exhortative from Sepp Dietrich himself:

> Soldiers of the 6th Panzer Army!
> We stand before the greatest decision of the war. The Führer has given us a particularly important mission. We have the mission of quickly attacking across the Meuse river without looking right or left. With us, other formations of the Army and Luftwaffe will destroy the enemy forces standing on German soil. The homeland is working day and night for us, our highest duty is to protect them. I expect every soldier will commit himself to be the first to reach the Meuse![47]

Feldwebel Karl Laun would be supporting Kampfgruppe Peiper as part of the Luftwaffe's 84th Flak Sturm Battalion to provide protection from Allied aircraft. The Austrian youth knew little about the mission other than they had moved from Grevenbroich, and now, for days they had been 'hiding in this thicket of the Eifel'. The men asked their commander what a flak battalion could possibly do here in the woods. On the evening of 15 December, their commander, Maj. von Sacken, gathered them in Dahlem for a briefing:

> Tomorrow is *Der Tag*. Remember the 16th of December as the turning point of the war. Germany's fate for the next hundred years will be in the balance. Thousands of airplanes – German planes – will appear in the skies. Burst from thousands of artillery pieces will pave the way for our infantry. ... Even German soldiers in American uniforms will participate in the fight.[48]

Idle talk? There were so many promises, but they had seen tanks and artillery pieces lining up. Enlisted SS panzer driver Werner Ackermann recalled gathering with the crew members of Panzer 635 the night before the attack.[49] Under the pine trees lining the road from Schmidtheim, their young crew of five, along with twenty other panzer men of the 6th Company, kindled a blazing campfire to take away the cold.[50] The platoon tank men held out their hands to gather warmth and pondered what the next day would bring. There were already plenty of rumours about the concentration of tanks and big guns they had seen in the past days moving up to the west German border alongside their Panzer IVs. Before the fire, the bows of the pines glowed orange, with popping sparks swirling up into the dark sky.

Presently, the 3rd platoon commander, SS Oscha. August Wien, appeared. Ackermann did not particularly like his superior. Wien was 'vain and a total fanatic,' he said.[51] To the possibility of battle, he liked to nod his head, chuckling, and 'tap his throat with his fingers to show how he needed a Knight's Cross'. Like Sternebeck, Wien always seemed in search of more medals. 'He showed up around the fire and told us "there was an order to not take prisoners."'[52]

> Oscha. Wien assembled his platoon and made a speech. He mentioned in this speech that we were now starting a big offensive in which we would be supported by Volksgrenadier Divisions, paratrooper units, much artillery and multi-barrelled rocket launchers as well as the German air force and secret weapons. In the first place, it would be important to surprise the enemy and disregarding losses, to kill everybody who comes before our barrels. The day has now come when we will avenge our relatives who died in the Fatherland through enemy bombs. Above all, we had to fight in the spirit of the old SS.[53]

'Wien gave the speech,' Ackermann said in an interview many years later. 'He did not specifically call for us to shoot prisoners, but the rowdies in the group appeared to interpret it that way.' Wien passed out map cards with clear directions for our march. There were red lines to the left side. Wien said part of the 6th Panzer Company would go on that route.

By the time Wien left with his macabre instructions, Ackermann noted that another tank leader, August Tonk, had joined them.[54] Ackermann viewed Tonk as a buddy – a congenial older comrade. 'When he arrived that night before the attack, there was instantly a good mood.' Tonk liked to regale the youths with tales of his past. 'We were a lot younger than him and we liked his stories.'

Tonk was an adventurer and joined the Leibstandarte in the mid-1930s. He liked to go to pubs and taverns. In one story, Tonk got quite inebriated and ended up in a drunken brawl. He shattered an empty bottle over a man's head and the man collapsed to the floor, unmoving. Tonk assumed he'd killed the man and staggered out of the pub, leaving Hamburg during the night and signing on as a shipman. This escape was complete as the ship travelled to Morocco, where he somehow ended up married to 14-year-old Moroccan girl.

Hans Siptrott, with the 7th Panzer Company, had known Tonk since the early days. 'He was a wild one,' Siptrott remembered. At Sennelager training ground he was known as a hard drinker. 'We knew he had been in Spain,' Siptrott joked, 'but no one was sure which side he had been on.'[55] Tonk spun more yarns through the night. He was in Morocco when the Spanish Civil War erupted, and Tonk, the mercenary galoot, left Morocco with other Hitler enthusiasts to help fascist Franco. There Tonk came in contact with the Condor Legion from Germany. As the Hamburg native told it, the war in Spain was another exciting swashbuckling adventure. He proudly showed his Silver Spanish Cross with Swords.

Although appreciating any levity after Wien's grim news, SS-Sturmmann Werner Ackermann, the driver for Mk IV Panzer 635, worried about the next morning. He had first trained as a mechanic before becoming a driver, and knew his panzer was in bad shape. The 12-cylinder Maybach engine had run poorly in the preceding days as it toiled up to the Westwall; the batteries were weak. At least fuel had been delivered and his tank filled up in the forest at Blankenheim. His panzer carried a standard full load of 700 liters of fuel, as well as a barrel with 200 liters more strapped on the hull. With the first enemy contact the barrels were thrown away, and for good reason. Troubling was that his tank's commander, SS Uscha. Heinz Phillip, was an ex-Luftwaffe officer with no experience in battle. 'He didn't know anything,' Ackermann said. At least two men in the Panzer 635 crew, Braun and Köhler, had some experience.

Nor did things look particularly rosy in the sister 7th Panzer Company. SS Uscha. Hans Siptrott, in charge of the 3rd platoon of the 7th Panzer Company, was not inspired by his new company commander, Oskar Klingelhöfer. Siptrott had a great deal more experience than his arrogant new chief. Over his long career, 'Spitz' Siptrott amassed 680 combat days – nearly two years of heavy fighting in which he reputedly was knocked out in his tank eleven times. Peiper repeatedly praised Siptrott for his courage in desperate tank battles stretching from Kharkov to Prochorowka to Tilly in Normandy.[56] Hans Siptrott was a fighting legend in the Waffen SS world.

Even though Siptrott was an SS Hauptschaführer – a panzer master sergeant – he was still not an officer. Even for a seasoned *Kämpfer*, the schism between officer and NCO in the Waffen SS ran deep. Klingelhöfer was an SS captain. It was Klingelhöfer who had ordered Siptrott's platoon of five tanks to park their Mk IV/H panzers deep in the Blankenheimer Forest off the road. When some of his tanks mired down under the pine boughs, Siptrott scowled, 'Why did you chase us into these woods?' Klingelhöfer barely batted an eye: 'We're preparing for an attack action.' Siptrott shook his head. 'He's put us into a swamp!' Here was another haughty panzer officer with only *Landser* – ordinary German soldier – experience.[57]

Inside his own tank, Siptrott saw more trouble. His assistant gunner, who joined his crew in Bliesheim, was SS Strm. Georg Fleps, a temperamental 22-year-old Rumanian farmhand who had a bad reputation. He was a hothead and unpredictable. Fleps, an ethnic German, had been conscripted into the Leibstandarte after being released from the Rumanian army in May 1943. From the outset, Fleps seemed star-crossed in the fighting in Russia and Normandy; each 7th Company tank crew he joined seemed to get knocked out, with everyone in the crew killed or seriously wounded.[58] Superstitious SS tankers were wary, but here he was, in the 3rd platoon leader's own Panzer Mk IV: Nr. 731. But such were the tank replacements in 1944. Siptrott woke his crew for the pre-attack briefing.

Another old hand, SS Ostf. Eberhard Kosch, with the panzer artillery regiment, heard the spirited order with the rest. So this was it? The Eifel: to blast through with a stopover at the Meuse. The gun barrels canted upwards, with the tanks of the Leibstandarte crowding the nearby roads. In Schmidtheimer Wald the heavy tanks were parked under conifers and camouflaged with pine boughs. Even tank tracks were carefully brushed away. Due to the security measures, big campfires were now *verboten* and the air in the Eifel was cold and damp. Gunners huddled under blankets, teeth chattering in the winter mists.

At one point, as the artillery commanders carefully sited their guns, the panzer regiment commander pulled up in a *Kübelwagen* and squeaked to a stop. Jochen Peiper got out and walked into the makeshift artillery regiment command post. The SS Lt Col looked fatigued.[59] Even so, he briefly engaged Kosch's superior, SS Obersturmbannführer Franz Steineck, in twilight conversation. Steineck was an old-timer. When Peiper had been evacuated from the debacle in Normandy and Theodor Wisch, the earlier Leibstandarte commander, was wounded in Falaise, Steineck had briefly commanded the tattered remnants of the Leibstandarte.

Over the last six months the division had been rebuilt completely once more. A new offensive? The old warriors were fatalistic: *Besser ein Ende mit Schrecken als eine Schrecken ohne Ende – better a frightful end, than fright without end.* The cold December fog curled into the dark forest. Steineck assured Peiper that Hauptsturmführer Ludwig Kalischko's two self-propelled guns of II Battalion and eighteen 10.5cm towed howitzers would support him. First they would carry out SS Gruppenführer Walter Staudinger's hurricane artillery bombardment of the American front line at 5.35 a.m. Peiper continued to condemn this as a stupid idea.

Peiper's concern remained: Would Kalischko be ready to advance with him at daybreak? Assuming the 12th Volksgrenadier Division breached the American line, Peiper's tanks would fall in at 7 a.m. He intended to go fast and far, reaching the Meuse before daybreak on the second day.[60] He would need that towed artillery when he reached the big river. Presently, the SS colonel seemed satisfied and headed for his staff car. Its engine coughed to life. As Jochen Peiper drove off into the fog, the SS artillery officer bid him farewell. 'Have a good trip,' he waved. 'See you in America!'[61]

Chapter 4

WACHT AM RHEIN

So long as blood shall warm our veins,
While for the sword one hand remains,
One arm to bear a gun – no more
Shall foot of foeman tread thy shore!
Der Fatherland, no fear be thine,
Firm stands thy guard along the Rhine.[1]

At midnight on 16 December 1944 the curtain rose on a day that would reveal Adolf Hitler's final great bid for victory in the Second World War. For Jochen Peiper, the debut of the Ardennes Offensive began inauspiciously. Upon learning of the great offensive, it reminded him of the failed big attacks of the past: lots of artillery, a predictable groping infantry assault, followed by the tanks. Hadn't *Operation Zitadelle* in Russia taught these paper generals anything? Peiper argued at length with Sepp Dietrich, his army commander. Let him blast through the line after midnight the night before.[2] By the time the *Amis* woke up, he would be 80km closer to the Meuse – just like Russia.

No. Dietrich seemed nervous about the question and said his hands were tied. They had to go with the artillery preparation; they were to wait for the infantry to open the *Panzer Rollbahnen* – the tank rolling roads – for the Leibstandarte and Hitler Jugend (the 12th SS Panzer Division) and the whole show could not begin until just before dawn. So muzzled, Peiper could only jockey his tanks and half-tracks into position and wait. He headed for the command post of the 12th Volksgrenadier Division that would spring him loose at dawn.

During the preceding nights both Waffen SS and regular German Army assault forces crept stealthily into their final positions in the deep wintry recesses of the Blankenheimer Wald. The German border with Belgium was just 20km away. Under inky black skies, camouflaged trucks rolled unsteadily forward, the path poorly illuminated by blackout lights. Panzers rumbled ahead, covered in pine boughs with their tracks clanking over road-spread straw to muffle the clattering din. Soon they parked under spreading firs on either side of the Reichstrasse 51 that would soon take them from Schmidtheim into Belgium and beyond. Stopping for the night, the tank crews warmed themselves, huddling around small fires to temper the cold and preparing mattresses of brushwood. Rolf Ehrhardt was the driver for #701 – the personal tank of Oskar Klingelhöfer in charge of the 7th Panzer Company. 'We spent the freezing hours exchanging ideas about the forthcoming operation.'[3]

> There was absolute secrecy about this ... After returning from the mission briefing in the nearby forester's house, Hstuf. Klingelhöfer called the platoon leaders into the company office and gave the attack orders to them ... The platoon leaders informed their crews. Thereafter Klingelhöfer and I walked up and down the edge of the forest for a short while ... At that occasion I sensed in him some optimism which I hadn't seen in a long time. The length of the war had left some marks on him too.

Not in recent Germany military memory had there been so many tanks and weapons. Artillery guns and rockets seemed to bristle under every tree. Rumours abounded that they would soon attack with the help of 'thousands of jet planes' or with new secret weapons of immense power. 'Hopeful and certain, we went into battle,' said one SS trooper. One commander told them they would all be in Paris by Christmas.[4] SS tank gunner Oskar Mauer and the 2nd Panzer Company were so enthusiastic that the men spontaneously broke into the old panzer songs before their commander, Friedrich Christ, showed up to review them.[5]

Other jaded veterans were less impressed. Having fought with the Tigers for two long years in Russia and Normandy, SS Uscha. Werner Wendt welcomed his chief's orders to be quiet because that meant a chance for shut-eye. Jürgen Wessel, the 1st Company commander of the Tigers, had briefed them the night before Blankenheim with the strange news. 'We were told we had to be careful since we would have Skorzeny's people running around.' Germans in American uniforms? Wendt hoped none of the new gunners would mistakenly shoot them down. What a crazy idea. Even so, he was soon dreaming. 'You learned to sleep when you could.'[6]

Meanwhile, in his headquarters in the Blankenheim forester's hut under the ice-crusted conifers, Jochen Peiper caught a few winks. Peiper awoke and had coffee and a cigarette before dispatching messages to his immediate staff. Soon he had on his panzer uniform, covered improbably by an Italian flying suit, but studded by his dangling oak-leaved iron cross. Shoeing on matching Italian *Alpini* boots, he was ready to give a quick update to his staff.

Peiper had made other last-minute arrangements: he had sent his regular adjutant, Hans Gruhle, to make sure the rear supply columns were ready to move. In Gruhle's place he appointed SS Untersturmführer Arndt Fischer (normally with Werner Poetschke) to serve as his adjutant in the coming battle. Peiper and Gruhle were not on good terms. Some said that was because Gruhle was a paper warrior – 'when the guns fired, the iron in their hearts turned into lead in their pants'.

Arndt Fischer, however, was an eager panzer man with a distinct ideological edge. A native of Waltersdorf, near Zittau, Fischer had volunteered for the SS Totenkopfverbände in 1939, with assignments to the concentration camps at Buchenwald and Oranienburg until being transferred to Poland. Later he attended Waffen SS officers school at Braunschweig in early 1943 and joined the Leibstandarte Adolf Hitler as a panzer officer with the I Battalion right after Kursk.[7] It was in that capacity that Fischer met Peiper when the latter joined the tanks in November 1943. Although Fischer had not been pleased at first to have Peiper lead the tanks – 'they could not be led like cavalry' – he gained a grudging respect after the new tank leader adjusted to armor: 'powerful, but a bit clumsy'. Peiper had first tried to lead the tanks like fast horses, but after stunning losses he tempered his audacity. 'In the course of the war, I became one of his friends,' Fischer said of Peiper. 'He gave perhaps the impression of being arrogant. He was only 28 years old. But if one is to lead men in battle, one must be confident.'[8]

But no one could accuse Fischer of cowardice – he had been shot twice during the mad fighting in Normandy. And on 15 December, Peiper had simply informed Fischer: 'At the beginning of the attack you are the acting adjutant and will go with me.' Peiper told him that absolute radio silence was critical, but he was short on details. Secrecy was key, said Fischer:

> All messages were carried by messenger. There was a meeting on the afternoon of the 15th. The time of the attack was given as X plus one hour. But even then, we did not know when X would be. This was not mentioned since it was top secret. At the meeting we discussed the march order and routes and who was following whom and their destination.[9]

With Peiper there, Fischer learned formally of *Wacht am Rhein*. 'At 4 a.m. we were told about the operation. One hour was necessary to warm up the tanks.' He and the other panzer battalion officers had heard about the operation through unofficial channels for a while. The sand box exercises two weeks earlier had included a detailed model of the terrain leading up to the Meuse river, and the attack orders merely confirmed what they had seen with that model. But Fischer remembered the critical decision point that they had repeated several times. 'Would Skorzeny be able to race ahead to seize the bridges?'[10] A key question.

While Fischer was warming up the 700hp Maybach engine of Panther #152 and readying the cannon-packing iron ox to do battle, his replacement, Rolf Reiser, was stuck in an endless snarl of traffic.[11] While with the divisional troops at Rahden on 14 December, he received a telephone call the day before to proceed to the panzer regiment immediately to replace Fischer as Poetschke's adjutant. Yet when night fell on 15 December, Reiser was still making his way along the crowded roads towards Blankenheim, puttering forward on a motorcycle with a sidecar. Not only was traffic a problem, but the motorcycle's transmission gave out, and Reiser hitchhiked on a divisional supply truck. Before dawn, he was still waiting in a traffic jam.[12]

Like the tanks, the heavily gunned *Schützenpanzerwagen* (SPW) of Uscha. Anton 'Toni' Motzheim stood lined up in traffic near Blankenheim, waiting for something to move. SS Hscha. Jochen Thiele, the head of the K.W.K. platoon, with its heavy cannon, came by while everyone waited expectantly for the column to budge. 'Motzheim, we have reached this stage,' he called out, slapping his underling Motzheim on the back. 'Be with your whole heart in this undertaking. Prisoners won't be taken in this attack. All will be bumped off. Do you understand?'[13]

Until the night of 15 December, Peiper's command post was in the Blankenheim forest house. However, in the hours before the start of the offensive, Peiper moved to the Kaiserhaus on the Route 51. From there, he would try to make sure his combat elements were in proper march order to press rapidly along Rollbahn D. It was still gloomy when Jochen Peiper emerged from the forester's house, surprised by elements of Skorzeny's strangely adorned armored Trojan Horse panzer brigade jockeying for position on the Route 51. There were three Sherman tanks on the road, along with two crudely converted olive-drab Panthers aiming to look like M-10 tank destroyers – all joining the other vehicles of his assembling tank regiment. Next came American jeeps with German commandos in their midst. Would they be shot by accident?

Never mind, Peiper zoomed off to Hallschlag to the headquarters of General Gerhard Engel's 12th Volksgrenadier Division. Soon he arrived at the bunker command post in the dragon's teeth, 2km east of the border. Engel's troops were to open up the path for his waiting steel battle wagons.

Feldwebel Heinz Rohde commanded one of the Skorzeny's twenty-odd jeep teams designed to lead the spearheads and sow panic in the American rear.[14] The *Einheit Stielau* teams, under the command of English linguistics trainer Oblt Lothar Stielau, had three missions: (1) radio reconnaissance from behind enemy lines, (2) serve as special 'guides' for the tank spearheads, and (3) sabotage.[15] The latter mission entailed destroying or seizing enemy depots, cutting communications lines, and thwarting American bridge demolition efforts. But among the many commandos training with Rohde there were whispers about a secret fourth mission: a special long-range Skorzeny espionage team aiming to assassinate Eisenhower.[16]

For Heinz Rohde, cloak-and-dagger themes seemed distant in misty Münstereifel that morning. Although his jeep would serve as a 'special' guide for one of the tank spearheads, he saw only problems. Three guides would ride in their jeep, but only Rohde, disguised as Sgt Morris Woodahl, spoke English well. His father had lived in Woodstock, New York, and his accent was much better than other jeep leaders, who often had a distinctly British twang. To finish out the subterfuge, he now had a pressed American uniform, complete with papers in his breast pocket attesting to Oklahoma roots – and even a photograph of his pretty curly-haired girl, Eloyse from Tulsa. The others in his jeep had satisfactory ID papers too, but little ability with English. 'A few minutes before zero-hour, we gave our comrades a goodbye handshake and got into our jeeps, each of which had taken up position behind its giant panzer,' Rohde recalled. 'The commander of our armored combat steeds ... had already inspected our small group when it arrived with repeated head shakes, but without any special question.'[17]

At exactly 5.15 a.m. a hellish artillery fire exploded overhead, landing just to the west. When it ended, the big panzer in front of Rohde creaked forward 50m, after which he was waved ahead. Beyond was no-man's-land. So encouraged, their jeep driver pressed hard on the accelerator, and in minutes they found themselves scooting past a burning American truck in the woods, awkwardly peeling off their paratrooper fatigues to reveal American uniforms. Driving west, they joined other U.S. traffic fleeing in the same direction. Presently, they were confronted by a knot of American infantrymen manhandling an anti-tank gun on to the road. A U.S. MP, with his white-banded helmet, attempted to flag them down to help. In urgent tones, Rohde pressed his driver. 'Faster!' There were no shots, just a look of bewilderment as they sped pass. Breaking into the open on a muddy fire trail in the woods, Rohde closed his eyes in relief. Splattered with mud, they were on their way to the Meuse river.

In the pre-dawn hours of 16 December Peiper's battlegroup eased out on the crowded road from Schmidtheim. From the start there was a shortage of road space. Kampfgruppe Peiper consisted of some 4,800 men and 800 vehicles, including 117 tanks, 8 Flak panzers, and 149 half-tracks. Such a tank force needed an expansive road network to deploy, a problem in the forested Ardennes. Indeed, if laid end to end, Peiper's parent 1st SS Panzer Division had more offensive road stock than there were roads. Only two panzer rolling roads, or *Rollbahnen,* were assigned, and on both Rollbahn D and E, entire regiments were echeloned to the rear of attacking columns.

Peiper organized his column into a platoon-sized *Spitze,* or spearhead, under Werner Sternebeck, the vanguard panzer column under Werner Poetschke, and he with the main body of the battlegroup.[18] The result was a long, serpentine column stretching almost 24km. Another battlegroup consisting of the reinforced SS Panzer Grenadier Regiment 2 under SS Ostbf. Rudi Sandig was to follow Peiper closely.[19] And Gustav Knittel, with the panzer reconnaissance battalion, was to fan out on whatever road they could find that was free of the enemy. Kampfgruppe Hansen was moving nearby too. Pavement was at a premium: an entire SS panzer division, the 9th SS Panzer 'Hohenstaufen', waited behind the Leibstandarte to be committed as soon as Kampfgruppe Peiper and Kampfgruppe Kuhlmann with 12th SS Panzer Division had reached the heights of the Hohes Venn midway to the Meuse river. An improvised last-minute German parachute operation, under Obst Friedrich von der Heydte, would land there at a strategic crossroads at Baraque Michel to stall any American reinforcements attempting to block Peiper or Kuhlmann.

Peiper was hardly focused on forces waiting behind him, for he intended to be first. And for the panzer leader who would lead the charge for the Meuse river, roads and bridges were a chief worry. His panzers would be forced to stay on the narrow, winding tracks that ran up and down the rugged forested hills of the Ardennes or, alternately, meandered along steep ravines that followed ancient river beds, the roads hugging the stream banks with thick stands of conifers on either side. Fields of fire were limited to forest hide-and-seek, with great tactical potential for ambushes and sacrificial road blocks. It was hardly a place to deploy a tank regiment, and Peiper's aims were clearly focused on getting his panzers out of the Ardennes and to the wide fields beyond the Meuse river as swiftly as possible. There, he might at last use his less mobile Tigers, where their 88mm guns could dominate an open battlefield, as had been so convincingly demonstrated by Michael Wittmann at Villers Bocage in Normandy. The value of the steel monsters had been proven in Russia before that, and, more recently, by an Army Tiger unit on the Roer Plain near Puffendorf in November 1944.[20]

But in contrast to the Hollywood vision of the SS vanguard tank leader in the movie *Battle of the Bulge*, the real version of Colonel Hessler, Jochen Peiper, had little use for the lumbering Tiger tanks in the swift battles he anticipated.[21] He preferred the faster, more nimble Mk IV and Mk V Panthers that could get more kilometers per liter of fuel and were more apt to find secondary bridges in the Ardennes that might support their weight. Besides, the 24-ton Mk IVs could meet a U.S. M4 Sherman on equal terms. At the distances expected in the Ardennes, where rounding a curve meant tank gunnery resembling a high-noon gunfight, the key was getting off the first shot. The 45-ton Panthers, a medium battle-tested tank, were more than an equal for any Allied tank. The slower 70-ton Tigers under Rudolf von Westernhagen would bring up the rear. Peiper had organized his march column immediately after his meeting with divisional commander Wilhelm Mohnke on 12 December:

> I sat down and decided how to organize my own combat team. I decided my column would be about 25 km long, and the vehicles would travel at maximum speed. It was impossible for the vehicles in the rear to overtake those in the front because of the bad roads. Therefore, all combat elements had to be placed in the front of the column. In order to provide maximum speed and power, I decided that my armored half-tracks would proceed as fast as possible until they met resistance, and then the tanks would come up and destroy the resistance, following which the half-tracks would again advance. I expected that if all went well I would need only Mark IVs and Panthers to proceed through the mountains and reach the Meuse river with one panzer company. Then, I would move up the heavy Tiger tanks later.[22]

As had been the case for Peiper's swashbuckling night-time tank exploits behind enemy lines in Russia, bridges would be key. It was with that concern that Peiper assigned two companies of panzer pioneers just behind his tank spearhead. Another big problem was that the heavy bridging equipment that would carry his tanks was only available at corps level. The man who would lead Peiper's panzer assault was panzer commander non-grata SS Ostuf. Werner Sternebeck. Under punishment again for his usual offences of drinking and women, Sternebeck rubbed Peiper the wrong way. Nevertheless, the horse-loving Berliner took over Panzer #614, designated as the commander's vehicle in the attack. 'He was personally brave, quiet and not a braggart,' one of the panzer veterans recalled. 'But for the regimental commander, this was seen as a weakness.'[23]

Peiper liked the officers under him obedient but brash and headstrong – types like Werner Wolff and Georg Preuss. Werner Sternebeck fitted all that, but was assigned to the dreaded *Spitze*. It seems he refused orders for a reckless advance in Normandy, so now as punishment he was on the point.[24] Yet others who knew Sternebeck doubted whether the assignment to the dangerous *Spitze* bothered him at all. 'He was totally crazy to earn a Knight's Cross,' remembered one.[25]

In any case, all the thirty-odd bad boys of the *Spitze* were seen by Peiper as misfits – now condemned to lead the head of the dragon, a suicide-like assignment one was unlikely to survive. That was how Peiper and Poetschke weeded out those who didn't toe the Waffen SS company line – at least the narrow vision as they saw it. SS Sturmmann Gerhard Walla had been Poetschke's driver, but a minor infraction had landed him the duty – meted out by Peiper himself – of being the *Spitze* messenger. He drove a thin-skinned amphibious *Schwimmwagen*.[26] Others were in a similar fix. One, Valentin Bersin, was a terrible *Rabauke* – a rowdy – and always in trouble, but his wild battlefield temerity suited Peiper just fine. He was exceedingly brave and somehow lucky in battle.[27] Accordingly, Sternebeck assigned Bersin to command the lead Panther. What were the chances of coming through unscathed?

Another primitive type, old fighter SS Sergeant August Tonk, had been in the German Condor Legion before the war, fighting for Franco in Spain and the Kriegsmarine before that. How did others in the panzer regiment see him? 'A real hot rod,' said one. In addition to a penchant for drinking, Tonk was fond of showing up in a turban rather than an officer's cap, or lining his uniformed collar with gaudy silks. 'It looks ridiculous to show up at the front like that,' Peiper complained. 'Look at this band on your arm [Leibstandarte Adolf Hitler]. You can't behave in this fashion.' Yet Tonk somehow saw himself as superior to even Peiper. And predictably found himself assigned to the point.[28] There he would celebrate his 33rd birthday on 16 December 1944, leading a steel battle wagon in one of Sternebeck's dirty dozen. Even so, many observant old hands in the Leibstandarte did not approve of Werner Sternebeck's punishment. Even if he had romanced the wrong women in Berlin and was prone to hysterical front-line antics, the man was brave to a fault – and Peiper knew that. In any case, Sternebeck's panzer *Spitze* full of misfits would be the first ones out.[29] They waited on the road for the artillery barrage to begin, the road already lined hull-to-hull with tanks, half-tracks, and trucks.

Still ringing in Peiper's ears was the final rave from Wilhelm Mohnke. 'My combat team in the center was to have the decisive role in the offensive,' Peiper recalled. 'I was not to bother about my flanks, but was to drive rapidly to the Meuse river, making full use of the element of surprise ...'[30]

> I had a conference of my own commanders, plus Skorzeny's deputy [SS Ostuf. Willi Hardieck] … I explained the plan and its importance, that there were three main spearheads and that, of course, my combat team would be the first to reach the Meuse river.

Peiper and Poetschke's orders to Sternebeck were equally clear: break through the American lines in concert with the Skorzeny commandos and the reconnaissance battalion Kampfgruppe Knittel to dash forward and seize the first bridge over the Amblève river at Ligneuville. The vanguard, 10th SS Panzer Grenadier Company under Georg Preuss, would follow immediately behind to provide infantry support. Yet Peiper still stewed about the Skorzeny commandos dressed like Americans in their midst. More detailed identification procedures were hammered out, but Peiper feared the worst. 'As it is well known, the field of vision one has in a tank is very poor and one is forced to shoot at practically every living thing, by way of preventative measures,' Peiper would later testify. 'I wanted to make sure we would not be accidently shooting prisoners of war moving to the rear.'

> Hardieck [in charge of a Skorzeny combat team], told me that he wouldn't bother with prisoners of war … If they would actually be wearing American uniforms they certainly would be senseless to approach the Americans by shooting at them … He also implied to me that, of course, they wouldn't expect any mercy if they would fall into the hands of the enemy.[31]

Meanwhile, SS Gruf. Hermann Priess, in charge of the I SS Panzer Corps, savoured the attack plan, thinking the unsuspecting Americans might be fully swallowed up. 'Individual sections of the enemy's main front line were to be bypassed,' he recalled. 'It was believed that the tactic of cutting off enemy strongpoints and continuing our advance – which had proved so successful in the East – would be relatively unknown to the Americans.'[32]

In the early morning before the attack, Peiper more closely questioned Willi Hardieck about the *Operation Greif* mission and his Kampfgruppe Z. 'Hardieck explained that his group would try to overtake the leading panzers as soon as possible and would infiltrate and create confusion among the American troops, drop off fake MPs to misdirect traffic, seize command posts and a bridge over the Meuse river at either Huy or Ombret Rawsa.' They then discussed provisions to keep the commandos from being fired on.[33]

> The actual plan of attack was to take place in three phases. First of all, the infantry would be put in to break through the front, break through the American lines. Following that, my armored division would be put into action in order to break through the main combat territory of the opponent. After I had done away with the last remnants of opposition of the enemy, the fighting unit of Hardieck, which was back in my marching column, would then catch up and take leave of us and go on ahead with the following mission: to go as far as the Meuse with the greatest possible speed and to take possession of one or more bridges and keep those bridges until we arrived.[34]

The SS colonel issued orders against looting. 'We could not afford to lose time,' he concluded. The biggest worry was waiting during the offensive for the infantry to open a hole through which he could advance. That wasn't the way he had done it in Russia. There, the answer was to attack at 2 a.m. in the morning – no artillery, no nothing to announce a raging storm that blew like a blowtorch through enemy lines. But now, not only would a big artillery preparation squander the element of surprise, but he would have to depend on the German infantry to open the holes for his tanks, preserving the strength of the panzer divisions for the advance past the Meuse river. How crazy, he thought. He had seen these *Volksgrenadiers*.[35] They'd be lucky to open their mess kits.

Still, Peiper took some comfort that the enemy across from him was short on experience as well. The 32km-long American line was mainly composed of the U.S. 99th Infantry Division (Maj. Gen. Walter E. Lauer) to the north from Monschau to the railway just north of Lanzerath. The light force of the U.S. 14th Armored Cavalry Group was positioned just to the south of Peiper's march route in the so-called Losheim Gap.

The 99th Division was relatively untested, having arrived on the continent in November 1944 and brought by the U.S. First Army to the quiet Ardennes sector to gain some experience. The Germans may not well know the American dispositions, but they were fully aware that the 'the Battle Babies' division was green too. Yet the 99th was one of the ASTP – Army Specialized Training Programme – divisions, which consisted of serious young soldiers of high aptitude who had been recruited as future officers, and were only now committed as an infantry division because of shortages of riflemen in late 1944. In spite of Peiper's high-handed disregard – 'it was a pity to have wasted so much artillery on them' – the 99th Infantry Division was to stymie Peiper's plan to reach the Meuse right from the very start.[36]

At the same time as the German Ardennes offensive began, the Americans were launching an assault of their own. The plan was for the veteran U.S. 2nd Infantry Division to advance through the lines of the 99th Infantry, capturing the German positions along the Westwall near Dreiborn as a part of the greater American plan to seize the Roer River dams. But concentrating American strength for that attack (which had begun on 13 December), meant the 99th Division was left covering an extended front. The American lines were so thin that only the 394th Infantry Regiment under Col Don Riley was aligned across from Peiper. There, they held a 7km sector that stretched from 2nd Battalion's Neuhof in the north – in the zone of the 12th SS Panzer Division attack – to the 1st Battalion's border crossroads hamlet of Losheimergraben. The American infantry line lay entirely in the thick timber belt of the Forst Gerolstein alongside the International Highway. Directly across from the 12th Volksgrenadier Division, opening the path for Peiper, was the 1st Battalion of the 394th Regiment in Losheimergraben, with the 3rd Battalion in reserve at Buchholz railway station just a kilometer to the west.

Yet in the Losheim Gap – a locale where the Eifel Forest was not so thick and the valleys cut not so deep – the American defense was weak. This was even stranger because the Losheim Gap had been a historical sally point of German invasion into Belgium; indeed, a straight line drawn between Berlin and Paris exactly bisects that region. It was here that the clopping jangle of the Kaiser's horse cavalry of 1914 was replaced by the clanking grind of the panzers of Gen. Erwin Rommel's 7th Panzer Division in 1940.[37] In this critical locale, the 18th Squadron of Col Mark Devin's lightly armored 14th Cavalry Group patrolled the southern reaches of the Gap near the border villages of Krewinkel, Weckerath, and Manderfeld. A gap of about 3km existed between the 394th Regiment and the light tanks and scout cars of the 18th Squadron of the Cavalry Group. The gap was the U.S. V Corps and VIII Corps boundary.

Well aware of this lapse, Gen. Lauer posted the tiny eighteen-man I&R (Intelligence and Reconnaissance) Platoon of the 394th Infantry Regiment on a small knoll just west of the village of Lanzerath overlooking the road that headed west toward Bucholz Station. Lt Lyle Bouck's platoon would soon face an entire division, the 3rd Fallschirmjäger Division. On 13 December, the U.S. First Army intelligence termed the German 3rd Fallschirmjäger as 'the best division encountered on the Western Front', even if that was a dated evaluation. Bouck's platoon was up against a tenacious foe in this mismatch of power.

Most of the Germans were volunteers ranging from 18 to 21 years of age, with experience on various fronts as an elite troop. The prisoners taken in Normandy were typically fanatical National Socialists: proud, arrogant, and security minded. '*Ein Fallschirmjäger – der stirbt im Loch,*' their commander Genlt Schimpf had grimly forecast of their lot – 'A paratrooper – he dies in his foxhole.'[38] Yet, the division identified on the First Army front near Düren that December bore little resemblance to that proud formation in Normandy.

Formed in France in October 1943, the 3rd Fallschirmjaeger had battled through the disaster of the Falaise–Argentan Gap in the summer of 1944, suffering heavy losses in the attempted breakthrough near Chambois. Their number of dead was only exceeded by the Leibstandarte Adolf Hitler itself. When a group of officers who had broken out of encirclement learned that Gen. Richard Schimpf was severely wounded and still in the pocket, they formed a marauding band to retrieve him. The division was rehabilitated in Holland in the late fall of 1944 under the leadership of Genmaj. Walther Wadehn, but this time the replacements included a large number of Luftwaffe ground personnel with limited combat experience. Wadehn lacked Schimpf's elan and was more comfortable flying a Heinkel 111 than he was leading an infantry division. It was telling that even Wadehn's chief of staff had to be replaced before the Ardennes operation due to complete inexperience with ground combat.

Moreover, even while pulling back to the Westwall in August, remnants of the division were activated for the next month to plug breaches in the line. The ensuing battle for Mons virtually destroyed the remnants. An attempt was made in October and early November to hurriedly resuscitate the division in the area around Enschede, Holland, but results remained deficient. Indeed, many of the men now fighting as common infantry had hoped at the time of their induction to enter careers as pilots or mechanics in the Luftwaffe. Officer and NCO replacements had similar inexperience; it was not unusual to see a former observer in a fighter squadron now assigned to duty as a battalion commanding officer.[39] Morale plunged.

Typically, the paratrooper forces could count on superior equipment and replacements, but this did not extend to the 3rd Fallschimjäger in late 1944. The reconstituted unit had a ration strength of 12,252 men at the beginning of December, but then was in serious fighting before Dueren the first week of the month.[40] It had no assault guns or motorised section assigned, and was even missing the equivalent of an entire regiment (parts of the 5th and 8th Fallschirmjäger were still marching), when it was committed in the Ardennes. Moreover, elements of the 5th Fallschirmjäger Regiment arrived so late and in such an exhausted state from an extended road march that it was not immediately deployed.

The main attack was carried forward by the 9th Fallschirmjäger Regiment with 1,710 men.[41] And even the 9th was still missing a substantial number of heavy weapons.[42] Moreover, morale in Wadehn's division was short of the expectations of an SS icon like Jochen Peiper. Many straggling paratroopers were not with the division; an engineer platoon of the division, designated as a reserve, celebrated an early Christmas away from the front in Weiden on the day of the attack. Tapping a keg of birthday beer at a Gasthaus near Aachener Strasse was more vital.[43]

Only the Fallschimjäger Regiment a was fully available for the attack on 16 December. Although this lone regiment was supposedly motorised, the regulation vehicles were missing, necessitating a 32km march from Kronenburg to Hallschlag for the paratroopers. Weapons and munitions were hauled on hand carts and even in baby carriages. The outlook for the average paratrooper was hardly favorable:

> On 15 December, in the afternoon, we were ordered to move out. I was issued a machine gun, MP 44. However, when I checked the weapon, I discovered the firing pin, which was irreplaceable, was missing. The 2nd Battalion's adjutant replied to my inquiry about a replacement. He told me to wait until someone was killed in action near me and then to take theirs. What comfort that was, as it indicated we were headed for terrible action.[44]

Just after 5 a.m. the men of the 1st Company, 9th Fallschimjäger Regiment gathered in a semicircle under the pines opposite Hill 574. Something big was in the air. Earlier that night they were surprised to see artillery pieces lined up on either side of the road as they marched through Stadtkyll. They even passed a group of German-speaking soldiers in American uniforms gathered around a Sherman tank along the road. How odd. Teeth chattered; it was still early, dark, and cold. Feldwebel (Sgt) Vincent Kuhlbach, an old battle horse from Italy and Normandy, received a large Manila envelope from headquarters. Under the light of a shielded torch, Kuhlbach opened the envelope and pulled out a map and some printed matter. The eighty men edged a little closer, urging Kuhlbach to tell them of the contents.[45] He read by the firelight; it was a general order of the day from venerable old Genflm. Gerd von Rundstedt:

> Soldiers of the Western Front!
> Your decisive hour has arrived! Strong offensive armies are assembled today against the Anglo-Americans. I need not tell you more. You all feel it: *Es geht ums Ganze!* – We gamble everything![46]

At 5.30 a.m. the front thundered to life with the planned artillery barrage of the 620 artillery pieces and rocket launchers in Dietrich's 6th Panzer Army. For Kuhlbach, the artillery barrage was 'very impressive and unlike anything we had experienced before'. Morale soared. 'The morning was dark and foggy,' remembered, Hans Zeplien, the commander of the Panzerfaust-armed anti-tank company of the 12th Volksgrenadier Division. 'All of us were awake. We left our pillbox to witness the bombardment in an open-air performance … We had heard rumours of new and war-deciding weapons.'[47]

With the first gust of artillery gunfire heard at Schmidtheim, Peiper's new adjutant, Arndt Fischer, coaxed his Panther out of the assembly area. Further ahead, some of the tanks of the 6th and 7th Companies were already on the R51 highway.[48] The artillery impressed SS Ustuf. Rolf Ehrhardt, Oskar Klingelhöfer's tank driver for #701 (Mk IV):

> During the night to 16 December all of us slept little. When we were woken in time before hour X, it did not take much effort. General excitement and the cold weather made that easy. Again, I stood with Klingelhöfer at the edge of the forest and we waited for the beginning of the fire storm of 6,000 [sic] cannon. Minutes came and passed. Everything remained quiet. Then, suddenly after a few minutes delay, a single medium-calibre cannon, about 1 kilometer distant, fired a few rounds. I could not suppress a critical observation, because the information from Klingelhöfer had sounded quite different from this. The company commander himself was rather annoyed.[49]

SS Sturmmann Reinhold Kyriss in Panzer #722 had a similar reaction. 'Expectations were great … During the night the V-1 robot bombs were roving overhead.' To pass the late hours, he hummed a few bars from 'Sweetheart Goodbye'. Then it was morning. 'The artillery fire was supposedly to be enormous,' he recalled. 'But the artillery was not much after all that.'[50]

Yet, at other places the fire was heavy. For Belgian civilians, who thought the war was over with the ejection of the Germans the previous autumn, the artillery cannonade was an unpleasant surprise. 'A hellish spectacle,' remembered a farmer in Manderfeld, horrified to see nearby American artillery pieces preparing to flee. 'Tomorrow the Germans will be here,' one called out.[51] Local farmers took to the roads. Matthias Goenen in Merlscheid had been living with GIs all autumn, first with the U.S. 2nd Infantry Division and now the 14th Cavalry Group:

> I awoke at about 0500 in the morning and went to the toilet. At the time I was on the other side of the courtyard. On my way back, as I crossed half of the yard, I saw hundreds of flashes illuminating the sky and heard a terrifying rumble. The sky was so clear that I could see like in daylight. I will never forget that breathtaking sight. Soon I heard the deafening scream of rocket launchers and the first shells passed overhead. I ran back to the house and everyone was in the cellar crying and praying. When the fire died down, we left the cellar and from the living room window, I could see the GIs running towards their dugouts. In the distance I could see fires in Berterath, Afst, and Krewinkel. It was now getting light and GIs came back and chased us towards Manderfeld. They were very nervous.[52]

Günther Holz with the 12th Volksgrenadier Panzerjäger Battalion was posted by the front:

> The earth seemed to break open. A hurricane of iron and fire went down into the enemy positions with a deafening noise. The drumfire was incessant. We old soldiers had seen many a heavy barrage, but never before had we seen one like this ... Then the fire suddenly stopped ... The searchlights lit up, and the field before the attack was lit like day.[53]

Meanwhile, on the American side the artillery shelling, though frightening – the new replacements on the rest front had never experienced anything like it – did surprisingly little damage. Given that army field telephone lines were merely strung out on the ground, many crossroads would have fifty wires strung out across them. Many phone lines were shot out, with disruptions in traffic and supply. Still, casualties were surprisingly light. And just as SS Gruf. Walter Staudinger, the SS Panzer Corps artillery leader, had worried, without reconnaissance or artillery observation most of the German artillery rounds fell on unoccupied crossroads or on vacant positions – 'more squandered ammunition' that simply put the enemy on alert.[54] Even the fire that momentarily straddled American positions some 4 to 7km deep inside the woodlands had done little damage.

Like other GIs in the rainy Ardennes, the U.S. 99th Division infantry had taken advantage of the quiet sector to construct winterised log huts or at least log roofing for foxholes. With the 2nd Division attacking north towards Dreiborn, Maj. Gen. Leonard T. 'Gee' Gerow of the V Corps had warned everyone to expect an enemy reaction. A southern general from Roanoke, Virginia, it was Gerow who had led American forces on to Omaha Beach. Gerow was a natural-born worrier.[55] Divisional intelligence had located only two horse-drawn artillery pieces opposite the men of the 99th. There was a particularly sharp moment of shelling in a bombardment that roared on for an hour and five minutes in the sector of the 3rd Battalion, 394th Infantry. 'They sure worked those horses to death,' Maj. George A. Clayton announced sarcastically at headquarters in Bucholz Station.[56]

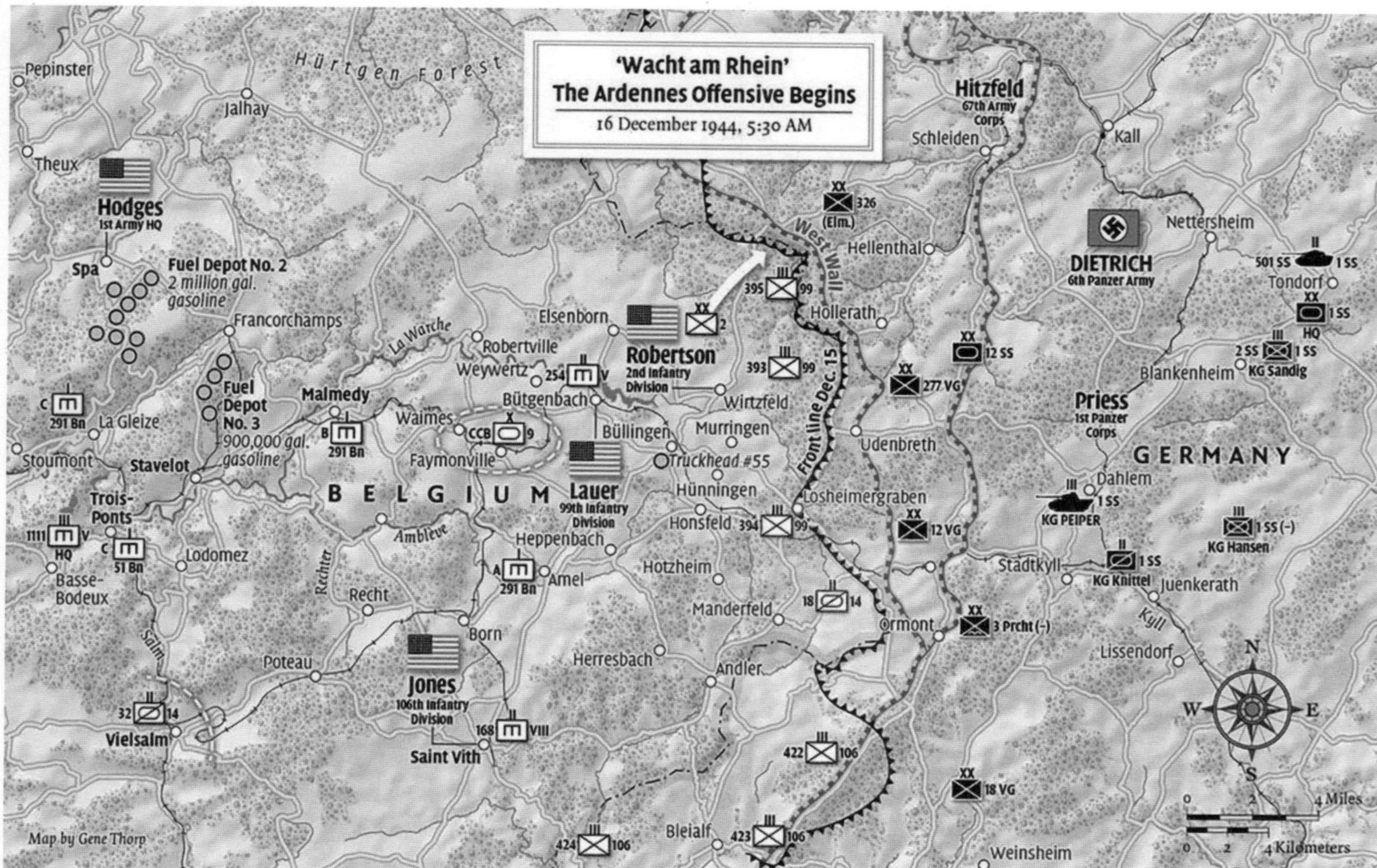

'Wacht am Rhein'
The Ardennes Offensive Begins
16 December 1944, 5:30 AM
Hürtgen Forest
Pepinster
Jalhay
Theux
Hodges
1st Army HQ
Spa
Fuel Depot No. 2
2 million gal. gasoline
Francorchamps
Fuel Depot No. 3
900,000 gal. gasoline
La Gleize
Stoumont
Stavelot
Trois-Ponts
Malmedy
Lodomez
Basse-Bodeux
Salm
Vielsalm
Poteau
Recht
Rechter
Amblève
Born
Jones
106th Infantry Division
Saint Vith
Waimes
Faymonville
CCB
Robertville
Weywertz
La Warche
Bütgenbach
Elsenborn
Robertson
2nd Infantry Division
Lauer
99th Infantry Division
BELGIUM
Heppenbach
Amel
Büllingen
Murringen
Wirtzfeld
Truckhead #55
Hünningen
Honsfeld
Hotzheim
Manderfeld
Herresbach
Andler
Bleialf
Losheimergraben
Front line Dec. 15
West Wall
Hollerath
Hellenthal
Schleiden
Hitzfeld
67th Army Corps
Udenbreth
Ormont
Kall
Nettersheim
DIETRICH
6th Panzer Army
Blankenheim
Priess
1st Panzer Corps
GERMANY
Dahlem
KG PEIPER
Stadtkyll
KG Knittel
Juenkerath
Kyll
Lissendorf
Weinsheim
Tondorf
KG Sandig
KG Hansen
501 SS
1 SS
2 SS
1 SS (-)
12 SS
277 VG
12 VG
3 Prcht (-)
18 VG
326 (Elm.)
291 Bn
51 Bn
1111
HQ
168
VIII
254
395
393
394
99
422
423
424
106
18
14
32
9
2
N
E
S
W
0 2 4 Miles
0 2 4 Kilometers
Map by Gene Thorp

At 6 a.m. the German pounding ceased, and powerful searchlights of the III Flak Corps flicked on, bouncing their beams off low-hanging clouds to 'spread a milky light over no-man's-land'.[57] As if on cue, squad after squad of grey-clad German infantry advanced out of the fog of the Eifel as V-1 jet-propelled robot bombs howled overhead, just clearing the treetops.[58] The German armies were advancing along a 180km front.

At first news seemed to hint at a new German blitzkrieg – this time in winter. Early reports coming into the I SS Panzer Corps at 7.30 a.m. told of a rapid infantry advance seizing U.S. outposts with scarcely any resistance.[59] The Americans seemed totally surprised. With communications disrupted from the artillery barrage and radios jammed by a loud racket of German march music, most sectors in front of Peiper's battlegroup believed they were experiencing an isolated patrol action. But after at first huddling in foxholes and wooden huts, the American infantry soon recovered from their surprise to fight back. It was nearly an hour after their signaled advance that the German infantry made contact with their enemy,

With the end of the uneven artillery bombast, Peiper's tankers revved up their engines. The panzer commanders in their black uniforms braced themselves in the round cupola hatch of their giant steel monsters. The radios crackled, but no word arrived. Unlike Jochen Peiper's typical midnight rampage forward in Russia, no message came telling them to zoom ahead. Instead, in the gloomy half-light at 8 a.m., Peiper's tanks were snarled in traffic on the Blankenheim–Scheid road. 'The set-up of my combat groups started on the 16th at about 6 a.m.,' Peiper remembered. 'By noon they had all been organized.'[60] Organized, but not moving.

When the artillery cannonade began, big, strapping SS Unterscharführer Karl Wortmann was still slumbering fitfully in his cold flak panzer. There he was near the head of battlegroup Peiper on the Losheim–Hallschlag road:

> Early in the morning on 16 December, the offensive began before daylight. We had been sitting in our panzers the whole night. None of us could sleep that night, but we had been dozing. Suddenly we were awakened by artillery fire along the whole front line. Despite all the preparation fire, our Kampfgruppe, led by Peiper, didn't manage to advance very far on the morning of 16 December. Our advance march route was so crammed with vehicles that it was almost impossible for us to move forward.[61]

For the grenadiers hauling *Panzerfaust* anti-tank rockets, seeing the German tanks just behind them 'was an unusual sight'.

> At dawn, and despite the fog, we notice German panzer units moving on a forest road leading along our pillboxes in a parallel position to the front line. These were medium and heavy tanks on a slow movement, and then stopping all over again even though neither obstacles nor resistance was noticed. This stopping and starting went on all morning and still in the afternoon, we saw them through the fog in a waiting position.[62]

In the meantime, SS-Ostbf. Otto Skorzeny, the audacious SS commando, was simply trying to find out what was going on. Although his three combat teams had assembled as planned, they had not succeeded in reaching the head of the German assault columns. To penetrate the fog and uncertainty, Skorzeny set off from his command post in Schmidtheim towards Losheim:

> The endless rows of vehicles moved in stop and go tempo, covering barely a hundred metres at a time. It was a wretched sight and I couldn't imagine that it was really necessary to move all these huge columns. I'd just got out on to the main road as we stopped again for a long time. I turned around and drove back to Schmidtheim and then continued along on almost impassable side roads to Dahlem. It was the same picture there: backed up vehicles and hardly a movement forwards. There was nothing left to do but get out and walk. I walked slowly towards Stadtkyll … The traffic had come to a complete standstill in the steep valley bends around Stadtkyll. It was even difficult for me to get through here on foot.[63]

In Losheim that afternoon, Skorzeny met with three of his jeep teams. If traffic was bad, their spirits seemed upbeat. 'Go to the south of the front and try to get through. Spread rumours and look for open roads for our three panzer spearheads to reach the Meuse river,' he instructed.[64] The teams set off, and Skorzeny returned glumly to Schmidtheim. Then a shock came when he regained radio contact with his command: 'Obersturmbannführer Hardieck has been killed!' Hardieck's command car had driven over a mine. There was nothing to do but dispatch his chief of staff, SS Hstuf. Adrian von Foelkersam, to take over.

At the I SS Panzer Corps HQ, also at Schmidtheim, Skorzeny eavesdropped on incoming reports. They 'didn't sound too good,' he decided. The barrage, he learned, hadn't done much damage to the American forces doggedly defending Losheimergraben. As of mid-morning the airwaves only told of heavy fighting. 'The complete breakthrough along the entire front that we were hoping for hasn't been achieved,' recalled Skorzeny. And there was no sense putting his three battlegroups on the road because the entire Eifel south of Blankenheim was one big parking lot. 'I'll wait 24 hours,' Skorzeny announced to Fritz Krämer. In a personal meeting with Hitler weeks before, Skorzeny got approval to not commit his combat forces until the SS tank spearheads had broken into the open beyond the Hohes Venn.[65]

Attired in a U.S. uniform in an American command car, Skorzeny vowed to Krämer that he would personally smuggle himself into an American column to snatch Jochen Peiper's Meuse river bridge. Otto Skorzeny hoped his audacious bridge capture would come at night – the darker, the better. The crudely disguised 'American' tanks under his command? 'They might fool very young American troops, seeing them from very far away – and at night.'[66]

Chapter 5

ROLLBAHN D

I immediately pointed out that these roads were not for tanks, but for bicycles.[1]

When the artillery barrage thundered overhead that morning of 16 December at the start of the Ardennes Offensive, Jochen Peiper chaffed impatiently at the command post of Genmaj. Gerhard Engel's 12th Volksgrenadier Division. He would 'observe his attack in order to estimate the proper moment for launching my own push'. Both leaders had high expectations: they had jointly planned the infantry assault just two days earlier. As befitted the tactical abilities of the unevenly trained Volksgrenadier conscripts under Engel's command, the script was simple – a brash infantry charge on both sides of hard-surfaced Panzer Rolling Road C (Rollbahn C) that led towards Losheimergraben, then north to Honsfeld and then to Büllingen.

Knowing the main hard-surfaced road would be defended stoutly, the reinforced Grenadier Regiment 48 would advance through the woods just to the north of the highway and the Füsilier Regiment 27 would go south to seize the secondary road. The hope was that Engel's more experienced grenadiers would sweep the surprised and shell-shocked U.S. 394th Infantry Regiment of the 99th Infantry Division out of the way by seven o'clock that morning. The key was the seizure of the village of Losheimergraben near the German–Belgian border. That done, a push along the rail line that would throw open Rollbahnen C and D. Engel's response to Peiper's request for a rapid penetration was to have the most experienced commander, Obstlt Wilhelm Osterhold, launch his men forward *before* the artillery barrage. With luck, they would pounce and seize the Losheimergraben crossroads before the Americans knew what was happening.

At 4 a.m. Osterhold, a veteran of all war campaigns since Poland, quietly moved the men of his 1st Battalion ahead from Frauenkron through the darkness to pause just short of the assault line. At first, the foot advance of Maj. Siegfried Moldenhauer's I Battalion groped slowly through the dark conifer forest, delayed by tree barriers, barbed wire, and a thick ground fog that sharply reduced visibility in the early morning gloom. Some platoons got lost in muddy trails leading towards the Losheimergraben crossroads. Still, many marched well; about half a kilometer from Frauenkron, Moldenhauer had his men take a knee under the pines at the edge of the forest just east of the American positions. He remained frustrated they were allowed no reconnaissance to learn the positions of the Americans ahead. Yet Moldenhauer's men were mostly unobserved.

In the pre-dawn darkness before any artillery fire, U.S. Army Staff Sgt Nick Machnick Jr, of B Company I Battalion, 394th Regiment, spied shadowy forms – German patrols – before his outpost north of Losheim. Machnick called up his immediate superior, a captain, and shouted for mortar fire on his own positions and artillery fire on the Siegfried Line to the east. The captain hesitated: 'Sergeant, you are dreaming,' the voice on the field telephone snapped. 'Go back to sleep.'[2] *Was he drunk?* Machnick protested and cursed; he was not seeing things. The night near his outpost seemed to be crawling with Germans. Permission to pull back? 'This is an outpost,' he protested, 'and not a place to fight.' His request was denied just minutes before he heard booming artillery. 'At first, I thought it was ours.' The shelling seemed to be falling a mile to the west.

At 5.30 a.m. thundering artillery gunfire spouted from German positions just to the rear, but Osterhold, a veteran of many an artillery *Feuerwalze* in Russia, was dismayed at all this distant shelling – it was not hitting the enemy just before him. 'The damned artillery is falling too far away,' complained Osterhold to his lead battalion commander. 'This fire plan must have been drawn up in Berlin!'[3]

Even so, some of the 'distant fire' was falling on American positions behind the forward foxhole line at the Losheimergraben crossroads. To Pvt. Lloyd E. Long, rudely awakened in a log hut, the German *Nebelwerfer* rocket artillery 'sounded like wolves howling. The *screeming meemies* came in, hitting the trees and blowing off their tops, splattering shrapnel all around.'[4] Shocked by the shelling, he and a buddy jumped out from their log hut to dive into nearby foxholes. Sgt Machinick was in trouble at his forward outpost a mile to the south-east. 'While the barrage was in progress, the Germans were all over our positions and yelling for us to come out with our hands up. I came out to see that my men were already POWs.'[5]

Ostensibly, Rollbahn C was assigned for the 12th SS Panzer Regiment and Kampfgruppe Kuhlmann, and the primary route for Rollbahn D went from Losheim to Losheimergraben, but then turned north-west to Honsfeld.[6] Interest in helping Engel break through beyond Losheimergraben confirmed that Peiper would have no hesitation in pre-empting that hard-surfaced road to Büllingen for his own tanks if his sister division were delayed. Peiper knew that the assigned routes were suggestions and not fixed.[7] Beyond that, his divisional commander, SS-Obf. Wilhelm Mohnke, had made clear in an earlier briefing that large stores of American petrol were located in Büllingen, and Peiper knew that the tortuous road in the Ardennes – not to speak of idling in traffic jams – would burn fuel at twice the rate than they had on the Russian flat lands. 'The tanks only had enough gas for approximately 50 miles of operation – approximately one half of the basic load and without any reserve.'[8] He would need that American fuel.

Peiper knew SS-Stbf. Herbert Kuhlmann well; they had long been competing panzer leaders in the Leibstandarte. It had been Kuhlmann who had presided over the disastrous advance of the 1st SS Panzer Regiment in Normandy near Argentan when Peiper was out due to ill health.[9] And although he was now the tank regiment commander for the Hitler Jugend Division, even his own men doubted his aggressive vigour in the sixth year of the war.[10] Peiper *knew* his own unit would be first and aimed to advance over the hard-surfaced N32 from Losheim to Honsfeld. From there, he could bolt through the American line and be halfway to the Meuse by the time the Americans knew what was happening.[11]

At 2 p.m. that Saturday, Peiper was still drumming his fingers at Engel's bunker command post along the Dragon's Teeth near Hallschlag. He waited expectantly for word that the Volksgrenadiers had finally broken through. Between 9 and 10 a.m. Fusilier Regiment 27 reported seizing the village of Losheim and advancing on either side of the railway, only to find the railway overpass still blown where it crossed the N32.[12]

Similarly, Oberstlt Wilhelm Osterhold's Grenadier Regiment 48 succeeded in reaching the Gerolstein Forest without encountering resistance, but then they stalled against surprisingly sharp resistance from the U.S. 99th Infantry Division before the strategic crossroads at Losheimergraben. They had counted on these green American soldiers to break. '*Es war zum Kotzen*' – It made you sick – Peiper recalled. 'Time was running out fast. Soon all surprise would be gone and I was sitting on my ass in Engel's headquarters.'[13]

By the official timeline drawn up by Genmaj. Fritz Krämer, Dietrich's chief of staff, the big breakthrough was to have taken place by 7 a.m. On the contrary, mid-morning messages coming in from the front showed Engel's infantry was not advancing as hoped. 'The roads were poor,' Peiper surmised, 'and the infantry had to bypass numerous nests of resistance which caused considerable trouble after they had been bypassed … There were numerous mines on the roads also.'[14]

Marching west to emerge from the wooded draws at Bucholz Rail Station, Füsilier Regiment 27 first surprised Company L, 394th Infantry as they were emerging to line up for breakfast at 7 a.m. 1st Lt Neil Brown, in charge of L company, and 1st Sgt Elmer P. Klug were inside the rail station. Klug had set up a schedule so that each platoon would queue up at the chow line. Yet peering down the railway, he spied forty men marching out of the fog. 'Klug,' he said, 'First Platoon is coming in early for their breakfast. What the hell is going on?' Klug drew up alongside the window and squinted into the grey mist. 'First Platoon my ass,' the barrel-chested sergeant snarled, grabbing for his carbine. 'Those are Germans.' Klug charged outside and boldly ordered the column to halt. A German voice barked a surprised response, and Klug shouldered his weapon and dropped the leader with a single shot from 70m.

With that, two German columns scattered, after which Klug turned and ran as well. By then, the men in the chow line scrambled for their rifles as artillery fire exploded all about the station. An exchange of sporadic gunfire grew steadily. Grenadiers were scurrying for cover in abandoned railcars by the station in a see-saw battle that would rage on for hours. At the end of the day the Germans were stalled and even repulsed.[15] Still, the ferocity of the assault shook the Americans. Col Riley, with the 394th, ordered four platoons from the Maj. Norman Moore's 3rd Battalion to lend a hand at Losheimergraben. Unfortunately, that left only a few dozen men to cover the parallel Bucholz–Honsfeld road. Americans there were caught by the rapidity of the German assault, but they didn't surrender. Peiper's idea of a rapid coup failed.

Still, rifles were no good against tanks. Seeing himself nearly surrounded and confronted by steel monsters, Richard A. Render hid in a culvert at Buchholz Station, listening as the German armor and trucks clattered overhead. Hiding for hours, after dark he fell asleep. The following morning he was spotted by a German grenadier stopping to urinate by the culvert. '*Raus! Raus!*' Render spent the rest of the war as a POW.[16]

Meanwhile, just half a mile to the east came the main effort, the 48th Grenadier Regiment's assault under Obstlt Wilhelm Osterhold that was to open the big highway for Peiper by seizing Losheimergraben. Blocking their way was the 1st Battalion of the U.S. 394th Infantry Regiment, which was defending a foxhole line some 1,200m east of the fortified customs houses at the border crossroads at Losheimergraben. While the artillery barrage hammered on, Osterhold's forces threaded their way through the forest belt, delayed at first by mines and trip wires just in front of the American positions.[17] Near Bucholz Station Maj. Siegfried Moldenhauer stumbled on the hastily abandoned Company B kitchen area, surprised to find it stocked with frozen turkeys and even bottles of Coca-Cola – something he had never tasted. He opened his first bottle of soda pop near an abandoned kitchen truck, took a generous swig, then spat it out. A terrible taste, he thought. 'But if the Americans can afford to send frozen turkeys and soft drinks over to Europe,' he mumbled, 'then surely the war is lost!'[18]

While Moldenhauer dismissed his first encounter with American epicure, he hastened to assemble his battalion to launch an assault on the enemy foxhole line not far away. Yet the Volksgrenadiers were so enthusiastic to cut the trip wires that they severed Osterhold's phone communication to his own divisional artillery at a critical moment. A sharp barrage was pending, right before his grenadiers advanced to hit the enemy the corps guns had missed. And although Moldenhauer normally would have a hand-powered radio set – here co-ordinating with artillery batteries of the Leibstandarte – the radio was not at hand.[19] The confusion proved deadly; the artillery barrage from German guns – which had been falling to the rear – suddenly dropped right among his assembling 1st Battalion. 'Our own artillery showered our 1st Battalion with about 500 rounds from heavy calibres. The results were devastating.'[20] The 1st Battalion was totally disorganized, with terrible casualties from the tree bursts. Not even five yards from where Osterhold hugged the ground, the I Battalion commander, Maj. Siegfried Moldenhauer, was severely wounded.

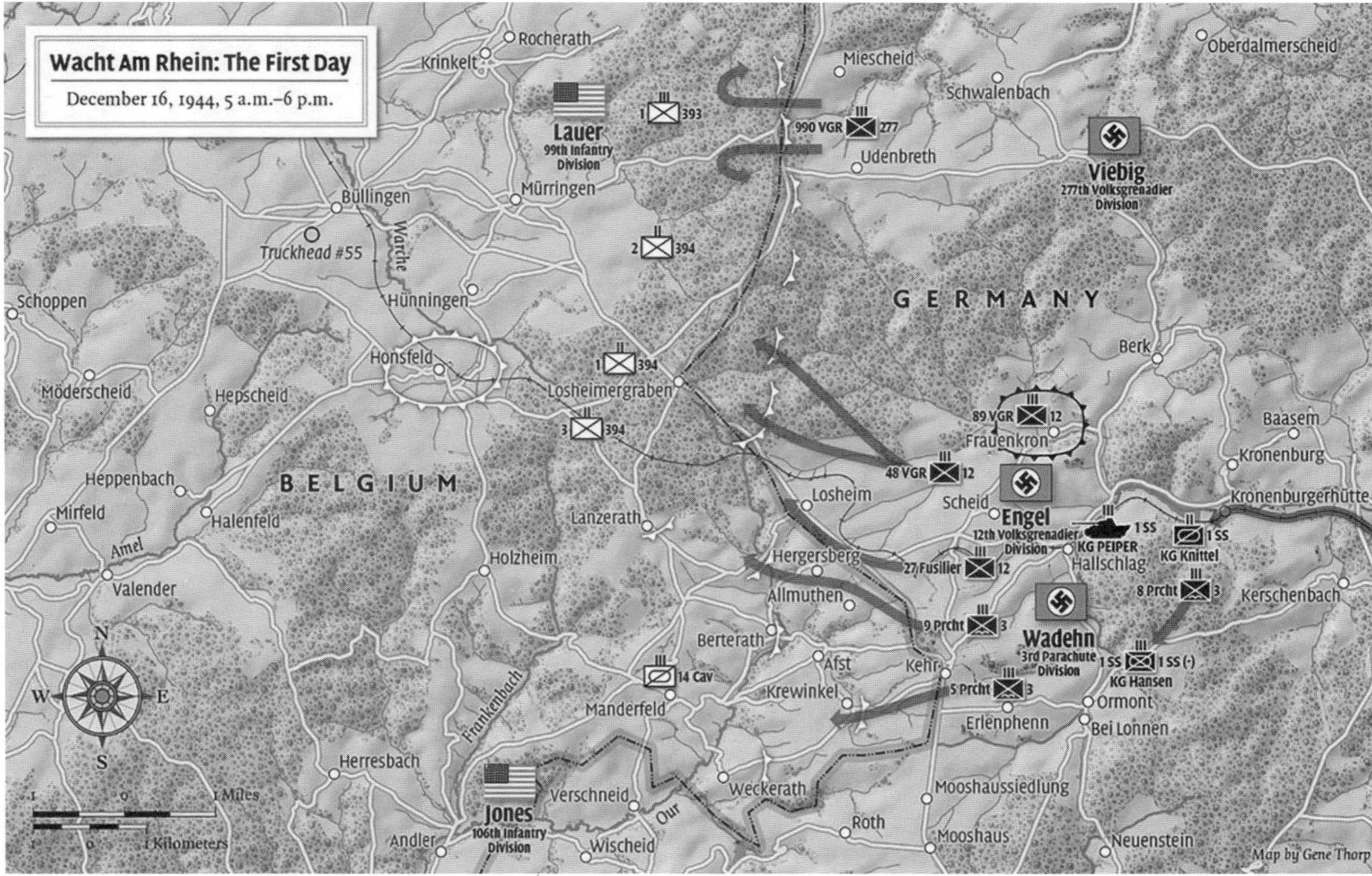
Wacht Am Rhein: The First Day
December 16, 1944, 5 a.m.–6 p.m.
Rocherath
Krinkelt
Lauer
99th Infantry Division
1 393
990 VGR 277
Miescheid
Schwalenbach
Oberdalmerscheid
Udenbreth
Viebig
277th Volksgrenadier Division
Büllingen
Mürringen
Warche
Truckhead #55
2 394
Schoppen
Hünningen
GERMANY
Honsfeld
1 394
Losheimergraben
Berk
Möderscheid
Hepscheid
3 394
89 VGR 12
Frauenkron
Baasem
Kronenburg
48 VGR 12
Heppenbach
BELGIUM
Losheim
Scheid
Engel
12th Volksgrenadier Division
Kronenburgerhütte
Mirfeld
Halenfeld
Lanzerath
1 SS
KG PEIPER
KG Knittel
Amel
Valender
Holzheim
Hergersberg
27 Fusilier 12
Hallschlag
8 Prcht 3
Kerschenbach
Allmuthen
9 Prcht 3
Wadehn
3rd Parachute Division
N
W
E
S
Berterath
Afst
Kehr
1 SS
1 SS (-)
KG Hansen
14 Cav
Krewinkel
5 Prcht 3
Ormont
Manderfeld
Erlenphenn
Bei Lonnen
Frankenbach
Herresbach
Weckerath
Mooshaussiedlung
Verschneid
1 Miles
Our
Roth
Jones
106th Infantry Division
Andler
1 Kilometers
Wischeid
Mooshaus
Neuenstein
Map by Gene Thorp

With more time lost, Osterhold ordered his 2nd Battalion to lead the assault. Yet the march of Maj Gerhard Kruse's assault companies from the rear took more time. But when they stuck, the impact was decisive. By noon the German assault had collapsed the B Company foxhole line and forced them back towards the customs houses, with sixty American casualties and many more captured. A bitter gunfight continued for the rest of the day. Nightfall found the Americans still holding on grimly to the intersection, but by then with fewer than twenty men, still fighting from cellars and foxholes only 20 yards from the enemy.

It would not be until noon on 17 December that the Losheimergraben crossroads could be taken after the stubborn American outpost there ran out of ammunition. It was this heroic defense of the U.S. 99th Division that would throw a monkey wrench into Peiper's anticipated dash westward.[21] 'If our own infantry had broken through by 0700 as planned,' Peiper lamented, 'I think we might have reached the Meuse in one day.'[22]

But there was no breakthrough. By 3 p.m. Peiper was still pacing impatiently at General Engel's field headquarters. There, in a command bunker just northwest of Hallschlag in the Westwall, he saw that the infantry advance was a slog, not a breakthrough. Peiper left on foot, determined to get something going, only to discover the road between Scheid and Hallschlag was one vast river of stalled vehicles. Arriving, he was greeted with the next instalment of unwelcome news, this time from the Leibstandarte chief of staff, SS-Obsbf. Rudi Lehmann. 'Two train loads of gasoline, urgently needed for the offensive, had not arrived,' Peiper recalled.

> Orders were issued to all the units to supply themselves with captured gasoline … Our intelligence officer had a situation map purporting to show supply installations. We believed from that map that we could capture gasoline at Büllingen and Stavelot.[23]

With no other choice, Peiper signaled his troops forward and mounted his own Panther. On the radio he ordered his column to proceed. 'I fell out with my group at 1600 hours,' Peiper remembered. But in joining his command, he learned that Werner Sternebeck's lead Panzer IVH was still crawling towards Hallschlag at that hour.[24] Even the enlisted men felt it:

> When it became known that there was going to be a long-distance attack to Antwerp, the feeling we had was 'We are going to show them!' But then the first disappointment was that we couldn't go. We didn't advance at all! We had orders to advance, but we just stood in traffic. It was the most unfavorable terrain for a tank.[25]

The Tiger battalion was also ensnarled. 'We just sat there. We didn't go anywhere,' remembered a veteran of the heavy tanks. 'There was a huge column on the road, so we waited all day to get into action. We didn't fire a single round that first day.'[26] Immediately behind the Tigers was Feldwebel

Karl Laun with the Luftwaffe 84th Flak Battalion. They waited for the offensive to begin, assigned to the very rear of the Kampfgruppe Peiper:

> Last night, the platoon leaders received their march orders, but march orders notwithstanding, H-Hour (0500) still finds us lying fitfully in an air raid shelter ... No special concentration of aeroplanes, a few solitary artillery missions, otherwise nothing new on the Western Front ... Something must have gone haywire. Finally at 1700 we see Kampfgruppe Peiper approaching. My platoon and I stand at a street crossing west of Dahlem ready to join the convoy. The Königstigers present an imposing picture, as they thunder past us, their exhaust pipes aglow.[27]

How would Peiper get his spearhead tanks ahead, much less the Tigers? 'I ordered my vehicles to push through rapidly,' he recalled, 'and to run down anything in the road ruthlessly.' *Anything* meant *anything* – vehicle, man, or horse.

Strm. Werner Ackermann in Panzer 635 was among those attempting to advance that afternoon as Peiper had ordered. There were traffic jams. Even though he was an experienced Panzer IV driver, Ackermann found the hilly and icy roads slippery and treacherous. However, even he was surprised that late afternoon to find horse-drawn artillery on the panzer rolling road ahead – it was a total *Stau- traffic jam*. Visible through his driver's slit was a 15cm gun towed by six bucking horses, now stalled, with gun and beasts marooned in the middle of the road.

> We had orders to force them off the road, but I knew horses from my father's farm and I couldn't do that. One I really liked as a boy was called Emma. These horses, on the road to Hallschlag, were afraid and nervous. As a farm boy from Landstein, I felt sorry for them. So I got out of the tank and I calmed them down and when they went on, I encouraged them, 'Go Emma!' And they pulled the artillery gun ahead and out of the way.[28]

Soon after that, Ackermann's panzer moved on ahead, but the Maybach engine he had worried about the day before was now coughing and sputtering. Their 25-ton war machine steadily lost power, and they fell further and further back in the tank column. Soon they were holding up the column's progress – never a good thing. A few kilometers down the road the tank engine threatened to quit altogether and Ackermann pulled off the highway to await for a repair crew.

More trouble: Peiper soon learned that the 12th Volksgrenadier Division engineers were unable to repair the Scheid rail bridge overpass over which Rollbahn D was to pass.

> There was a blown bridge in 'no-man's-land' south-east of Losheim. The bridge had been blown by the Germans in their previous retreat [earlier that autumn] ... Another delay occurred when either Corps or Army ordered the [12th Volksgrenadier] Division Artillery to move up farther ... Since the Division

> Artillery was a horse-drawn artillery regiment, it clogged up the roads. This was a completely idiotic idea, in as much as the regiment did no firing. From 1400 to 1900 [hrs], I went down to the bridge to regulate traffic and tried to restore order. The bridge would not be ready until 1930.[29]

'The Polish cavalry had not been able to stop us in 1939,' Peiper would later relate to comrades, 'and our own horses were not going to stop me in 1944.'[30] Still, Peiper found it nearly impossible get his troops moving, as 'the traffic on the road proved to be chaotic'.

> Bad road conditions and an immense number of vehicles were compressed in this area with Skorzeny's group, which apparently had not very much training ... For one walking on foot, it was almost impossible to walk down the road to the so-called 'no-man's land' between the German and American positions. There was a bridge which had previously been blown up. Because of the road jams, the engineers who were supposed to repair the bridge could not get through. And ... the entire artillery of the 12th Volksgrenadier Division had to change positions to the front. Since the artillery of this division was horse-drawn, there was a terrible heap of King Tiger tanks on the road with four-legged mules. I, myself, and my commanders were standing on this road to regulate traffic and since the bridge was not completed on time, I had to have a detour built.[31]

Peiper seethed: an ineffective artillery barrage squandering surprise, the inane decision to lead the attack with green infantry, and now divisional commanders ordering horse-drawn artillery on to the panzer rolling roads blocked by bridges blown by friendly engineers weeks before. It was now twilight. 'I could only start off twelve hours late,' he carped – all that time frittered away.[32] If he had it to do over again, he would 'put a general at each street corner to regulate traffic'. 'There were two good reasons for such a move,' Peiper said sarcastically, 'and one of them was not traffic control.'[33]

Angered once more, Peiper ordered his entire panzer column to leave the road and crash down across a nearby slope across a dirt trail, grind across the rail line to the north-west, and regain the Reichstrasse 421 on the other side. 'I finally found a detour around the bridge – a deep cut in the terrain – and reached Losheim.' It wasn't a brilliant move, but time was the deeper wound. It was 7.30 p.m and pitch black.

At the border town came an unwelcome radio message from a reconnaissance patrol ahead that still another bridge – the railway bridge on the Route 265 – was out just ahead. Without engineers one the scene, more time would slip away. And then disappointing word came from I SS Panzer Corps that the Americans were still fighting north of Losheimergraben.[34] But there was one positive development: the 3rd Fallschirmjäger Division had broken through American lines near Lanzerath, but they also reported heavy resistance in the woods near Büllingen. 'I was then told to drive to Lanzerath, where I should meet up with elements of a parachute regiment of the 3rd Fallschirmjäger Division.' Peiper had only scorn for the Luftwaffe.[35]

In spite of the obstacles, the artillery barrage was impressive when it began that Saturday morning. 'It was 530 hours when the ghostly Ardennes front started spitting fire,' remembered one Luftwaffe-officer-cum-Fallschirmjäger, 'Field artillery, howitzers, and rocket launchers opened a display of fire that made so much light that flashlights were not needed for reading maps.' The 9th Fallschirmjäger Regiment's commander, Obst Helmuth von Hoffmann, was unmoved by the artillery display. The commander of the 15th Pioneer Company, Ludwig Havighorst, was even horrified, for a squad of his men had pushed so rapidly in the wake of the artillery fire that all were wounded or killed by a round that fell short. 'Havighorst,' Hoffmann said, placing his hand on his shoulder, 'the Führer must find a way to end this war!'[36]

Regardless of qualms in its leadership, the 3rd Fallschirmjäger Division shuffled from Hergersberg towards the villages of Manderfeld and Berterath in the Losheim Gap on the morning of 16 December. These places were defended as a series of strongpoints by the 18th Cavalry Squadron of the U.S. 14th Armored Cavalry Group. To make matters worse for Col Mark Devine's thinly stretched troops, the edge of Gen. Hasso von Manteuffel's 5th Panzer Army's blow to the south would also squarely face the Americans in the Losheim Gap with a Volksgrenadier Regiment of the 18th Volksgrenadier Division and Sturmgeschutz Brigade 244 – a veteran unit from the Russian front.

Lt Carl Johnson was with the 3rd Platoon of the 820th TD Battalion in Berterath right on the front line in the Losheim Gap. He and his men had been brought to the Ardennes in mid-November and were told that this was a rest area – even if it was uninviting: grey, cold, and damp. The only Germans they had seen were changing guards on the Westwall line (Americans called it the Siegfried Line) just a kilometer away, also known as 'Home Guard' units – old men. 'They won't shoot at you,' the departing 2nd Infantry Division chided, 'if you don't shoot at them.'[37] Yet in the last week the night had become more active; the enemy seemed intent on throwing grenades at anything that moved. Johnson got an order on the night of 15 December for payback. He took three men and probed half a mile to see if they could catch some of their tormentors on patrol. 'It was so quiet, you could hear a mouse sneeze,' he recalled. But no Germans were found. Johnson came back and tried to get some sleep.

> It was about 5 a.m., and hell broke loose – the artillery started coming. We were bracketed, and it started falling all around us. We were in a farm house on the side of a hill. One of our men panicked and ran out into an open stairwell and fell to his death. We put mattresses on the cellar window and sat out the barrage … I started counting heads, and we were missing our cook. He was so scared, he couldn't move. I brought him downstairs. When the barrage ended, we were very surprised to see several Germans standing in the curve of the road about 400 feet away. We fired a few 3in rounds from our guns and they disappeared. After that we decided it was best to get out of there. When we went to start our half-tracks, they wouldn't start, so we left the guns and the half-tracks. We had about fifty-four men and made a run for it to the jeeps. We got up with Captain Nash about two or three miles down the road. There was mass confusion. 'What

> the hell is going on?' We dropped back about four to five miles further back down the road.[38]

On the German side, early reports from the paratroopers to Peiper's left told of walking into a minefield off the National Highway west of Ormont.[39] Others were tangled in barbed wire or delayed by trees felled over the roads. Ludwig Havighorst's command immediately helped remove the minefields as he and his men advanced into sporadic enemy resistance near Hullscheid. Threading through the obstacles, some of the paratroopers arrived in Merlscheid, unaware that the Americans were ahead. 'In the evening of 16 December, we arrived at the first objective of the attack,' remembered the engineer company commander. 'The Americans had fled head over heels. They left everything behind. The food was still standing on the tables.'[40] Still, once the Americans recovered from their surprise, Platoon A of the 820th TD Battalion fought their way out of encirclement and inflicted heavy losses on the German paratroopers.[41]

At Krewinkel and Afst, the Luftwaffe troops displayed extraordinary tactical ineptitude, boldly approaching the American positions of Troop A and C of the cavalry in a four-column march as if on a Sunday parade. Waiting to the last moment, the American defenders cut loose with automatic fire on the paratroopers at a 20m range. The stream of bullets inflicted terrible losses on the paratroopers; by noon Troop C had only two men down from wounds, whereas GIs estimated that there were clumps of 375 slain German infantry before them.[42] That was doubtless an exaggeration, but still an indication of terrible losses.

Nevertheless, the pressure of the 18th Volksgrenadier Division and its attached assault gun brigade had been too much for Col Damon's 18th Cavalry Squadron, who began to pull back from the Losheim Gap to a line stretching from Holzheim to Andler that afternoon after an unsuccessful counterattack of the 32nd Squadron from Manderfeld.[43] The woods to the south now seemed to be crawling with an infiltrating enemy of SS troopers (Kampfgruppe Hansen) of fanatic determination – 'soldiers who had been hopped up.'[44] Capt. Benson, the Group surgeon, 'indicated that they [appeared to have] been treated with some Benzedrine derivative'. In any case, the SS troopers were surging ahead alongside German '*Landser*' infantry and paratroopers.

Lt Robert Reppa of Troop A, having lost contact with headquarters by enemy-jammed radio communications, decided to pull out from Holzheim to Honsfeld, where he hoped his strongly embattled command would be out of harm's way.[45] Indeed, hours earlier, Troop A of the 18th Cavalry Squadron had surrendered in the village of Roth – ninety-five men captured in one go. By nightfall the 14th Cavalry Group was disintegrating as a cohesive fighting force.

As a result, Wadehn's paratroopers marched into the vacuum, filtering into the villages of Berterath–Merlscheid before pressing on towards Lanzerath. Bypassed, the Americans at the villages of Roth and Kobscheid capitulated that afternoon.

Located on the north side of the Losheim Gap, the tiny village of Lanzerath was part of the German-speaking sector of Belgium. And although the Treaty of Vienna had created that country in 1830, the residents of this area thought of themselves first and foremost as German. Indeed, there were 60,000 individuals in the eastern reaches of Belgium east of Malmedy who spoke only a few words of French (and this remains so even today). Allegiances were confused during the war, and many of the young men of that zone had been drafted into the German Army.

Sixteen-year-old Adolf Schür was one of these young men, drafted into Hitler's legions as a *Flakhelfer* but then sent back home given his small stature. Many young Belgian farm boys like Schür – men who considered themselves German – had supported Hitler's rule during the war. Schür only came to doubt the regime as troubling rumours came to light and his brother-in-law was killed in Russia.[46] Schür also liked the Americans – they had taught him a few English swear words that, when repeated back, caused the GIs to laugh uproariously. At the same time, while Schür thought they were friendly, they also seemed to be suspicious of him. That was understandable; all the locals spoke German. In his own home Schür even had a picture of his father on the mantle from the First World War showing the elder Schür wearing the Kaiser's garb.

When the paratroopers swarmed into Lanzerath that morning – flooding the tiny village of twenty-three houses and a church – they did so without awareness of the Americans backed up against the forest on the hill just above of town. In fact, the hamlet had first been occupied for some weeks by several towed 3in anti-tank guns of the 2nd Platoon, Company A of the 820th TD Battalion under Lt John Arculeer and a small party of C Battery, 371st FA Battalion. The TD men had been staying at the house of Susanne 'Sanny' Schür, who was Adolf Schür's cousin. Although the Americans had dug out a machine gun position in her garden that autumn, they were very friendly. The children got chocolate and forbidden coffee. Sanny played cribbage with a young man from Chicago, keeping score in her diary. Even more, Sanny was 25 years old and pretty. Her father, the village cobbler, knew the world of deprived soldiers. Sanny slept between her mother and father. They all woke with a start that morning. 'There was a devil of a sound – artillery fire. We ran from our bed to the cellar.'[47] Sanny had a similar story:

> On the morning of the 16th I can remember the artillery fire began in the early morning. We went down to the cellar. The Americans were above. They were part of a tank destroyer unit. We were sleeping in the basement when the artillery fire began. We had a big potato bin with loads of potatoes in it, and they put the mattresses on the potatoes. When the artillery fire stopped, the Americans took off in a big hurry. Some of them left their weapons – pistols and pistol belts. My father said to me, 'Something is wrong when soldiers leave their weapons!'
>
> They went upstairs, and when they looked up the back towards Losheim, they could see these fresh holes in the snow from where shells had fallen. There were hundreds of them. We could hear lots of noise – gunfire and shelling. About

> 7 or 7.30, when it began to get light, my father wanted some coffee, so he sent me off to light a fire. I came up and lit the fire. My parents stayed downstairs. Then my parents came up after I had made the coffee between 7.30 and 8 a.m. I heard a door open somewhere out here, and it was somebody trying to get into the barn. And they slipped on the steps trying to get in the barn and they were cursing. 'This is where the pigs have been living!' – *Da haben die Schweinehunde gehaust!* It was a German paratrooper. There was a telephone the Americans had left here in the stable, and the Germans came in and were angry and threw it out.[48]

Sanny Schür was petrified. Sanny and her parents spoke the local Belgian hill country German *Plattdeutsch* at home. Seeing the German soldiers' rage, Schür's father addressed his wife in French: '*Le Boche sole la.*' – The Germans are there. They had lived through the long occupation of this part of Belgium since 1940. The local arm of the German gestapo, the *Staatliche Kriminalpolizei,* was active in Malmedy and Büllingen.[49] When the Germans were out of earshot, he turned to both. 'The war,' he whispered. 'Now, the whole thing is starting again!'[50]

The observation post for the artillery observers was in the top floor of a Lanzerath house occupied by Anna Christen and Agnes Dahm. The observers' job was to watch Losheim to the east and bring down artillery fire if anything happened. Yet, like everyone else, the German attack caught them unaware. When the morning artillery blast began, Lt Warren P. Springer, T/5 Peter A. Gacki, T/5 Billy S. Queen, T/4 Willard J. Wibben, and the others were shaken awake in the darkness by sudden explosions. Rushing to a window, the trained observers were shocked by what they saw. Out to the east, Losheim 'was lit up like a Christmas tree', as flames belched from distant German cannon.[51] The hits seemed to be scattered all over, but some fell nearby. One round shook the house, digging out a crater in the backyard. Even worse was what Springer saw when he turned high-power binoculars to the east after the artillery blasts faded. 'Holy Christ!' he blurted. 'Germans! Lots of them. Heading straight for us!'[52] They were marching up the road. Springer scrambled down the stairs and outside to find the last of the tank destroyer half-tracks hastily pulling out into the street. There was a German column advancing up the road, the men told Springer. Springer and the rest fled the house, with Gacki thrusting a Christmas package into Anna Christen's hands. The men piled into their vehicles – they were getting the hell out.[53] They sped off north towards Honsfeld.

They had only gone a short distance when Lt Springer stopped to speak with a young American lieutenant, Lyle Bouck, of the I&R Platoon of the 394th Infantry Regiment on the ridge above the town. Could they provide artillery support, Bouck wanted to know? 'I guess we stayed too long,' remembered Gacki. 'Very shortly, we were cut off and involved in "Bouck's Last Stand".'

Bouck had no intention of becoming another George Armstrong Custer, but his defense amounted to a sophisticated ambush. Although totally outnumbered, Bouck's field of fire and his platoon's weapons handling were excellent. As the Germans marched down the road in front of their positions, Bouck ordered his men to hold their fire until the main body of the enemy came. Over a hundred German paratroopers passed before their gunsights when Bouck spied three men walking behind the vanguard – the leaders. Bouck ordered his men to draw a bead on them.

Just then, a blonde girl of about 13 suddenly ran from a house just a bit further up the road. Approaching the three Germans, she pointed. Up on the hill, Bouck hesitated, lest the girl be gunned down. 'Hold your fire!'[54] At that moment the Germans yelled something too and immediately the entire column seemed to dive for the ditches. Young Adolf Schür was watching the entire scene from his family's barn just across from the Café Palm, which offered a view of Bouck's hilltop position. The girl was a neighbour's child, Tina Scholzen.[55] 'Goddamn,' he muttered. Would she be killed? Unconsciously he whispered other curse words the American soldiers had taught him: 'Mother fucker! Son of a bitch!'[56] Soon she was back inside her house.

Meanwhile, Springer's gunfire just then upon the Germans narrowed Bouck's options, as firing on the platoon's positions began. He and the rest of the artillerymen, knowing the lethality of shot and shell, instinctively jumped and crawled into the covered foxholes of the I&R platoon. Disciplined and undaunted by the enemy numbers, Bouck and his small party repulsed three separate German frontal assaults on his positions as paratrooper casualties mounted.[57]

By the end of the day the 9th FJ Regiment would count thirty-three killed and 113 wounded – most of these in unexpectedly severe fighting in Lanzerath.[58] 'After a hard battle, our first battalion took Lanzerath,' remembered one German veteran, 'and we stopped there.'[59] Not only was it a hard battle, but so serious were the losses to the 1st Battalion that a temporary mass grave for some thirty German paratroopers was dug across from the Café Palm.[60] In the final assault, Bouck and his men ran out of ammunition. The paratroopers, now stunned by their losses, moved to outflank Bouck's positions. Adolf Schür was with his father and brother watching from the barn:

> There was a thick fog when the shelling stopped. My father said, 'What's going on?' Nobody knew the Americans were gone. Everything was quiet. We could see from the kitchen. The Americans always carried their weapons under their arms. But coming out of the fog, we saw these men coming up the road with their weapons on their chests. We knew they were Germans. As they got closer, we could see they were German paratroopers. When we realised they were Germans, and they came into the village, we couldn't be unfriendly to them … All the German troops were on foot. The Germans came up the road, and some went up past the lane by their house. Then all of a sudden we could hear rat-tat-tat – a machine gun firing. We didn't know the Americans were on the hill above town. There was a hell of a racket. My father told me, 'Come into the barn [on the north side of the house],' he said. 'Come and see the war. Now, you can see what war is really like.'
>
> We could see the Germans attack up the hill. The first attack lasted about half an hour. A lot of Germans were getting shot; it was bloody and terrible. Many of the wounded were yelling. They attacked several times. Eventually, the Germans came down with prisoners. We buried some of the German men by the schoolyard. There were not forty [dead], but more may have been wounded.

> Later, eventually a group of maybe 20 Americans prisoners came down, and things got quiet again. The Germans made the American prisoners carry the German wounded.'[61]

Meanwhile, stymied before Losheimergraben to the east, Peiper threaded his tanks south-west to avoid the roadblock. Turning his column around in the darkness with the poorly trained tank drivers made for a chaos. Even worse, in trying to feel their way south out of Losheim to Hüllscheid, his lead Panther #122, under Uscha. Valentin Bersin, hit a mine and stopped with a thud:

> In the evening of 16 December it was already dark when I arrived at approximately 1700 hours in Losheim. Losheim had already been taken by troops of the 12th Volksgrenadier Division at that time. A terrible traffic jam was in the town itself. It was an exceptionally dark night, and the town was under American artillery fire … Contrary to my original orders, according to which I was supposed to proceed along the main highway, I here received an order to take a route via Lanzerath. Leaving town and proceeding towards Lanzerath was very difficult since we had to pass through mine fields which were not cleared. They were mainly mines which were old and snowed under and for which we had to uncover with our armored vehicles … To the best of my recollection, I lost about three tanks and five half-tracks on the way from Losheim to Lanzerath … I received a radio order from either division or corps … according to which a regiment of the 3rd Fallschirmjäger Division had got held up in Lanzerath.[62]

Peiper and his adjutant, SS-Ustuf. Arndt Fischer, got out of their tanks to look at the predicament before Sternebeck's point team. The mined road ahead was a mess. Rudolf Dörr and the panzer engineers were not far away, but Peiper fumed.[63] Rather than halt and waste more precious time, he ordered his armor to speed on ahead and clear the mines with their own tracks. 'As the time factor was more important than some armored vehicles,' he would later recall, 'I decided to detonate the mines by rolling over them.'[64] Less than half a kilometer west, one more Mk V, that of SS Uscha. 'Willi' Bahrend, was lost when they hit German mines as they clanked through Hüllscheid. SS-Ostuf. Erich Rumpf's engineers would later completely clear that minefield, but Sternebeck continued with the advance, and the rest of the tanks followed. SS Ostuf. Benoni Junker, the 6th Panzer Company SS leader who fancied himself a poet, noted Peiper's moody determination that morning reminded him of lines from Tennyson's 'Charge of the Light Brigade'.[65]

The other three divisional assault columns had run into similar troubles.[66] To the south, SS Kampfgruppe Hansen with SS Panzergrenadier Regiment 1 started off from Ormont with Jagpanzer IVs in the lead, already delayed for hours by minefields and terrible roads. The same could be said for Schnelle Gruppe Knittel; the 'Fast Group' moniker already seemed ridiculous, for Knittel had waited for hours on the road between Glaadt and Stadkyll. The road was choked with every conceivable German vehicle – whether powered by motor or hoof. Even worse was the situation for Kampfgruppe Sandig with

SS Panzergrenadier Regiment 2. Their wait for road space on Peiper's Rollbahn D meant they had scarcely moved from their assembly point in Tondorf. Otto Skorzeny, with his three commando battle groups – Kampfgruppe X, Y, and Z, were all stuck in traffic too. Every plan was out the window.

The only good thing was that Peiper learned that his prolonged delays allowed the lumbering King Tigers of SS Heavy Panzer Battalion 501 to catch up with his advance elements. Karl Laun was just behind them with the flak battalion. 'We reach Stadtkyll, and the first American PW s are marched past my vehicle. They look dead tired; most have probably marched a hell of a long way. The battery comes to a halt, and I try to catch a few winks, but the doodle-bug or as the population calls it, 'the Eifel terror' always rudely awakens me. Like a cyclops it ranges through the night – truly a heinous weapon.'[67]

Sternebeck was now the point tank, grinding ahead on the road. Yet north-west of Merlscheid, within half a kilometer of Lanzerath, Sternebeck heard a dull roar and felt his Panzer IVH buckle and lurch. He had hit a mine for sure. Although his Panzer #614 could be repaired – one track was totally inoperable – he did not have time to consider the options. Frustrated, the *Spitze* leader then moved over to Mk IV #612 of SS Ustuf. Karl-Heinz Asmussen, disheartened to lose most of his strength.[68] 'Our two Panthers, supposed to be heavy battering rams,' Sternebeck brooded, 'were put out of action without even having any contact with the enemy.'[69] And now he had lost his own tank. Yet Sternebeck was not one to consider a halt; he knew Peiper would not tolerate it. He was, after all, in the punishment platoon at the point. 'Expect to be blown up,' Peiper said. 'Then you have done your duty.'

By midnight on 16 December Peiper and his battle group had negotiated the darkened, narrow road to reach the hilltop village of Lanzerath. By radio, I SS Panzer Corps had advised Peiper that although the paratroop regiment had broken through the initial main line of resistance, their infantry reported that they had been repulsed three times in attempts to head beyond Lanzerath towards Honsfeld. Peiper could not know it, but the message from corps almost certainly referred to the valiant defense being displayed by Lt Lyle Bouck and the I&R platoon, which had bloodily repulsed the Fallschirmjäger Regiment 9.[70] 'I received orders to take over this [parachute] regiment and to attack.'[71] Silence prevailed when Peiper arrived at the little Belgian border town. 'Not a single shot rang out,' he recalled.

As he strode into the Café Scholzen, which was now the temporary headquarters for the paratroopers, Peiper found it strangely calm and quiet – only the squeals of his tanks closing up interrupted the fading hours of 16 December.[72] Inside Peiper found a mixture of dozing unshaven German paratroopers and American captives. Many were wounded, some groaning, others snoring. For Peiper, it was a pathetic scene, stinking of sweat, blood, and a pall from ersatz cigarettes. The Americans there were survivors of the I&R platoon of the 394th Regiment who had been captured at the end of the fight. One of them was Lt Lyle Bouck. who was holding Pvt. William J. Tsakanikis, whose face had been nearly shot off, his blood soaking Bouck's tunic. In one corner a German snored; across the room a badly wounded paratrooper periodically shouted, 'Panzerfaust! Panzerfaust!' in pitiful delirium.[73] The Americans were sprawled out under a cuckoo clock whose bird finally emerged to chime midnight. It was now 17 December 1944, Bouck realised – his 21st birthday – a hell of a way to become a man.

Upon meeting Oberst Hoffmann (Fallschirmjäger Regiment 9) in Lanzerath, Peiper's disdain for the *Hermann Göring Spende* rose again. Everyone 'seemed to have gone to bed rather than waging war'.[74] Peiper was disgusted. It was now the middle of the night – the best time for a Peiper-style gallop behind enemy lines. Hoffmann outranked him, but Peiper scowled.[75] The SS officer demanded to know why the paratroopers had halted.[76] Peiper unfurled an oversized map with awkward folds. Peiper solved the situation by holding the sheet against the wall across from the tavern bar, then stabbing the corners with two bayonets. Voices rose. Peiper didn't believe there had been much fighting in Lanzerath.[77] Hoffmann reported strong enemy resistance ahead. 'I asked him for all the information that he had on the enemy situation,' Peiper recalled:

> His answer was that the woods were heavily fortified and that scattered fire from prepared pillboxes plus mines in the road were holding up his advance. He told me that it was impossible to attack under these circumstances. I asked him if he had personally reconnoitred the American positions in the woods, and he replied that he had received the information from a Captain in his battalion. I called the Captain and he said he had not personally seen the American forces, but it had been 'reported to him'. At this point, I became very angry and ordered the parachute regiment to give me one battalion, and I would lead the breakthrough.[78]

'I ordered him to get one battalion ready for attack along the road from Lanzerath to Honsfeld. They were to be used only as defense for the flanks and close combat for my troops.'[79] Peiper thought the paratroop leader a desk warmer from the '*Luftfahrtministerium*'. He ordered the I Battalion of Hoffmann's regiment be temporarily attached to his battle group, riding on the outside of his tanks. The II Battalion/Fallschirmjäger Regiment 9 under Maj. Siegfried Taubert would protect Peiper's flanks.[80] Hoffmann had his own version:

> After Lanzerath had been taken and cleared on the evening of 16 December, it was my opinion that the woods west of the town were full of enemy forces ... Without prior briefing of the regiment, Peiper and his battle group appeared and demanded we make room for him and to let one battalion mount his tanks, which he would take along as long as he needed them.

Col von Hoffmann refused and made it clear that Peiper would be hampering the continued attack of the regiment.[81] Arndt Fischer waited in his Panther tank while the argument went on inside the Café Scholzen. When Peiper returned, he was still cursing. 'These Luftwaffe officers are cowardly Schwein,' he scowled. He told Fischer they would be getting some paratroopers to mount their tanks. He was to prepare to move out.[82] Lyle Bouck was wounded:

> Sometime after that there was the sound of a lot of motors outside and a group of SS officers – I could see their SS tunics with the lightning bolts. One of the smaller guys, who was Peiper, was really excited. He had a cap on and was obviously in charge. He was talking. Sak and I were on one side of the room and they were on the other. They moved over to this wall, and there was a bureau there with a drawer, and they were looking at it [the map] with lanterns and it kept falling off the bureau. There was a lot of cursing by this guy, and he got two big knives or bayonets and stabbed it with them on the wall and put the lanterns on either side so they could study it. Slape and Milosovitch were in the corner. Then paratroop officers come in, and the SS man all of a sudden is ordering them out. There were about three different groups that came in, and there were heated conversations. Peiper seemed pissed off. He and three other guys were with him. There was a lot of stomping and pounding fists and lots of shouting and pointing.[83]

Peiper railed on the incompetence of the paratroopers, and Baron von Hoffmann bellowed back. The road ahead was mined, he said. Eventually Peiper did convince him to allow Taubert's battalion to go along; they immediately mounted his tanks in the darkness. 'You do your job,' Hoffmann said turning away, 'and I do mine.' Peiper set off into the darkness with Taubert's paratroopers climbing on to the decks of his tanks. Hoffmann boasted to a fellow officer: 'I don't let these people give me orders!'[84]

After midnight Peiper now set about rearranging his *Spitze*, frustrated by the delay to round up the impressed parachute battalion of Maj. Siegfried Taubert. 'We lost a lot of time,' Peiper remembered. 'Because it was completely dark, the paratroopers who were sleeping all over in houses could not be located right away and the regrouping of my spearhead took some time in the darkness and the narrow village road.'[85] As Peiper finally organized it, two Panthers would take the lead, followed by a platoon from 10th Company / SS Panzer Grenadier Regiment 2 under SS Hauptsturmführer Georg Preuss, with two flak panzers under SS Obersturmführer Vögler.

The borrowed paratroopers would ride on his tanks to provide infantry support as they penetrated the forest ahead. They would then advance at the greatest possible speed, moving north to pick up Rollbahn D at Honsfeld. Still, the infantry assault would not be all that fast, as many of the paratroopers would have to march alongside.[86] Nevertheless, Peiper's eyes were firmly set many kilometers beyond. Once he smashed whatever was in those woods, his tank spearheads would race for the Meuse river.

Chapter 6

THE ARDENNES

The Ardennes is impenetrable.[1]

On the evening of 16 December 1944, the Belgian town of Spa was 30km away from Jochen Peiper's attack in the dark woods at Lanzerath, close to the German border. Spa was home to the U.S. First Army headquarters of Gen. Courtney H. Hodges. For the most part, the Allied commanders spent 16 December in a state of unknowing. Hodges was no exception. 'It looked like a spoiling attack,' he would later recall. 'I was apprehensive – our attack was bogging down – but not particularly worried. I was terribly tired that night.'[2]

Strange things were going on, as Gen. Hodges would have readily admitted. The newly arrived Maj. Gen. Alan W. Jones, in charge of the new and totally green 106th Infantry Division, had rung up with news that large enemy shells were falling about his headquarters in the Sankt Josef's Kloster all the way back at St Vith. Although Jones had been in the army for thirty years, this was his first combat action. Jones had expressed some apprehension to the departing U.S. 2nd Infantry Division with whom he was replacing. His two regiments were on the other side of the Our River on the Westwall in Germany. He did not know the huge shells were coming from the behemoth 240mm rail gun of the Heeresgruppe B's Eisenbahn Artillery Batallion 725, firing from a siding some 20km away in Niederprüm, Even worse: Jones told Hodges that every one of this regiments and front-line battalions were under artillery fire or ground assault.

To the north, Col Mark Devine was in Manderfeld, with a single squadron of the 14th Cavalry Group, screening the Losheim Gap between the 106th and 99th Division. His surprised outposts soon sent word that ghostly enemy columns were bypassing them in the murky early morning fog. In the hamlet of Roth, Capt. Stanley E. Porsché with Troop A reported a desperate situation by 8.30 a.m.: 'Tiger tank 75 yards from CP,' he called out on the field telephone over the din of explosions, 'belting us with direct fire.'[3]

Maj. Gen. Jones in St Vith was stunned. His division had just moved into line five days earlier; the 106th did not even have much of their promised ammunition on hand and his troops were short on winter clothing. Now his two marooned regiments out on the Schnee Eifel reported mortar bombs and hissing rockets falling all around their frozen foxhole line. By afternoon, Jones was reporting that the police in the town were uneasy, and the civilians – particularly the German-speaking informers – were starting to flee.[4] Soon the roads were jammed with a civilian stampede – everyone for themselves.

In fact, at this moment 250,000 German troops and some 717 tanks and assault guns with over 2,600 artillery pieces were launching the largest offensive in the west since 1940. Such an attack seemed absolutely impossible, and rather than worry about a comeback of the German Army, Allied brass were pondering the fate of band leader Glenn Miller that night. Miller's AAF band had given a hotly anticipated performance on Thursday, 14 December at the Bedford Corn Exchange in England. There were other big names present – David Niven and Humphrey Bogart – and the place had been jammed with American airmen. Miller and his band ran through the whole gamut of swing tunes, bringing the crowd to its feet. But the next day, Miller left in a light plane for Paris, where his band was already waiting. He was never heard from again.

There were also only nine shopping days left before Christmas, and the attention of many homesick troops turned back to the States, when they heard Bing Crosby sing his 'White Christmas'. The infectious optimism had risen all the way up to the intelligence staffs. After all, weren't the Allies decoding secret German radio transmissions as they sent them? Time and again, this greatest Allied secret of the war had revealed German intentions to the top SHAEF brass. Moreover, the intel had *never* been wrong. So when reports began flooding into the S-2 catacombs about German attacks everywhere in the Ardennes, the news was met with astonished disbelief. In the meantime, the ULTRA codebreakers were busy decrypting a sudden tirade of German radio traffic. As always, it would be hours or even days before it could be decoded, translated, and enciphered for transmission to the select few Allied commanders 'in the know'.

The Allies were so convinced in late autumn of 1944 that their enemy was beaten that the senior commanders were obsessed with their own operations to end this tiresome war. The terrible ground battles of autumn – Aachen, Hurtgen Forest, Lorraine – had all been grinding, costly encounters reminiscent of the bloodletting in the First World War. The conventional wisdom was that the Germans were now sapped and ripe for destruction. In mid-December Bradley's 12th Army Group was poised for two powerful assaults on the Siegfried Line. One was an attack by the U.S. First Army to push out of the northern reaches of the Ardennes to thrust towards the Roer River dams as prelude to advance to the lower Rhine river, the gateway to Germany.

The southern blow would be landed by the pistol-packing Third Army commander, Gen. George S. Patton. His effort would breach the Siegfried Line near Saarburg and then push towards the Palatinate and the south-western corner of the German Rhineland. The Germans would be clamped between the two giant pincers and pinned with their backs up against the Rhine. Allied intelligence knew that the Germans were building up a reserve, so a counterattack seemed likely. The general opinion, supported by intercepted German radio transmissions, was that the Germans would hit the First Army as it moved towards the Roer River dams, which controlled the flood stage of that river.

The U.S. First Army made its headquarters in the High Belgian Ardennes in the town of Spa. Long known for the curative powers of its mineral waters, Spa was the watering hole from which all such places took their name. At 58 years old, Lt Gen. Courtney Hicks Hodges was an aging and serious commander who knew war. Along with 'Big Bill' Simpson leading the Ninth Army, he had chased Pancho Villa through Mexico in 1916. Possessing a 'courtly manner' – he always dressed immaculately and demanded the same from his staff – Eisenhower quipped that his major fault was that, 'God gave him a face that always looked pessimistic.'[5] Unlike most senior American commanders other than Patton, Hodges had considerable combat experience as a machine gunner in the deadly Meuse–Argonne battles of the Great War. To others he was 'a sound commander who never fought over land where he could be outmanoeuvred'.[6]

Confronted with war's grimness, Hodges saw the Ardennes as a gift horse. The region was a resort area, and he intended to make the best of it for himself and his men 'within the limits of propriety'. He and his staff settled into comfortable accommodation on the second floor of the famous Hôtel Britannique. Steeped in history, it was in the hotel that Ludendorff had directed the Kaiser's legions in the Great War. And it was also the place, in 1918, where von Hindenburg was forced to inform his superiors that the First World War was lost. Now the hotel casino suffered drab metal U.S. Army field desks spread out on the richly carpeted floors under fine crystal chandeliers. The autumn had been comfortable; the quarters were cosy with the trappings of the good life. Even though Hodges would often keep late hours, he was fond of a nip before bed. Occasionally, he would enjoy the mineral baths for which Spa was famous.

Like many commanders, after the difficult years of Sicily, Normandy, and now the Hürtgen, Hodges thought the great conflict was in its waning phases – something he eagerly encouraged. An avid hunter, he looked forward to the end of the war. 'I want to get the hell away,' he confided in his driver, S/Sgt William Spratt, 'where the only sound of shooting is me shooting ducks.'[7]

The autumn days at Spa settled into a routine, with the First Army band even pumping out marching tunes for the town folk on Sundays. On 20 November, the mayor – *le bourgmestre* – of Spa, Monsieur Jos. Léonard, invited the entire town to join the First Army in celebrating an American Thanksgiving.[8] To prepare the traditional turkey, Hodges even had a Belgian chef assist his own cook, T/3 Luigi Bosi. On Thursday, 25 November, American flags seemed to float from each house in town. It was all very civil.

The situation three weeks later at Spa on the morning of Saturday, 16 December seemed shaky but hardly dire. A chain smoker, Hodges awoke that morning to a pounding head cold. To break the fog, his waiter, T/5 Jim DeCesare, brought several cups of black coffee. The sullen commander of the First Army was just sitting down to breakfast when word arrived of an enemy attack in the Losheim Gap. Another report was even more disconcerting: '28th Infantry Division reports the heaviest artillery fire ever received.' Gen. Elwood 'Pete' Quesada, in charge of the IX Tactical Air Command, and Gen. Bradley joined Hodges for breakfast.

After their repast, the men were met by Monsieur Auguste Francotte, the famous gun manufacturer, who was to fit the avid shooters with brand-new shotguns he had brought from Liège.[9] No one suspected that the Germans were blasting a colossal artillery barrage and tank-led infantry attack on the thinly manned U.S. line not 50km away. Hodges could hear the dull thunder of the artillery to the east. In the meantime, huge 280mm shells were falling in Rötgen, Eupen, and Malmedy.[10] As the generals were being measured for the stock and drop of their new hunting weapons, aides kept intruding with messages. Each note told the stodgy American commander of more attacks at the front, some as far south as the Luxembourg village of Echternach. Hodges remained nonplussed; the U.S. 2nd Infantry Division had been attacking for the Wahlerscheid crossroads and had expected some sort of counterattack response from the Germans. That's what they always did.

Meanwhile, Gen. Omar Bradley hustled off to meet with Eisenhower at Versailles. Later messages from the front assuaged some of the alarm from the earlier reports; at 4.15 p.m. the 28th Division, reported intense shelling and said the situation was 'well at hand'. Later on the 16th, as Hodges was getting to bed, disturbing news arrived from the Ninth Army. German air transports, the notice said, were in flight to locations near First Army from German airfields near Paderborn. And there had been mad minutes at the end of the day when U.S. anti-aircraft units between Verviers and Spa were buzzed by a low-flying Me- 262 jet randomly shooting up the roads and zipping around faster than American AA guns could swivel.[11] The guards were doubled at the gatehouse, given the unusual warning to be on the alert for enemy parachutists. No one got much sleep at the Hôtel Britannique that night.

And the worst news of the worst: Marlene Dietrich was cancelled. Gen. Omar Bradley, the head of the U.S. 12th Army Group normally posted in Luxembourg City at the Hotel Alpha, had been using his staff car for the past few days to escort the sultry German-born actress around the front. Dietrich appeared in a series of morale-building appearances across the Ardennes front, There were rumours she had taken up with Gen. Patton, who had given her the code name *Legs*.[12] Was it true? During the day she visited lucky wounded in the hospitals; during evenings she was the star of the USO travelling road show.

Even if Bradley was amused by Dietrich's continuous bitching about the food and accommodation, the entire shindig had been wildly popular. The movie siren gave GIs lipstick autographs wherever she went, while taking medicinal Calvados brandy to preserve her voice in the damp cold. Even if *Captain* Dietrich's act was strictly vaudeville (she played a saw), there were the sequined gowns and those nylon-graced gams – insured for a million bucks. On a rainy Thursday on 14 December she played for Troy Middleton's VIII Corps headquarters in Bastogne. The following night she was in Diekirch to entertain the whooping infantry of the 28th Infantry Division. Of course she sang 'Lili Marlene' – the haunting wartime anthem:

> Resting in a billet just behind the line,
> Even though we're parted, your lips are close to mine.
> You wait where that lantern gently gleams.
> Your sweet face seems to haunt my dreams.
> My Lili of the lamplight.

On Saturday, 16 December the actress was to make a hotly anticipated appearance at a U.S.O. show in the village of Honsfeld. Indeed, men of Lyle Bouck's I&R platoon of the 394th Regiment were set to attend – until cancellation after vague reports of 'something up there'.[13]

So, rather than escorting Dietrich, Bradley and his intelligence officer, Edwin Siebert, tried to make sense of confusing intelligence. Their focus was a big situation wall map. Where previously there had been precious little note of the enemy in the Ardennes, now there were little German flags all over the map.

The Supreme Headquarters of the Allied Expeditionary Forces (SHAEF) was headquartered at Versailles. The Trianon Palace – with its timeless buildings, ornate décor, and sculptured courtyards – made the Allied headquarters a distinctly fashionable setting. The weather on 16 December was bitterly cold, and the Parisian skies were grey and overcast. Still, this was an important day on Ike's social calendar. The supreme commander, Gen. Eisenhower, was receiving a promotion to five-star general – the U.S. Army's highest rank. Eisenhower was up at 6 a.m. for a breakfast of sausage topped with hominy grits.

At the end of the meal Ike received a note from Fldm. Bernard Montgomery, requesting holiday leave and reminding him that he owed him five pounds on a bet made fourteen months earlier, that the war would be over by Christmas. 'I'll pay,' Eisenhower grumbled to an aide, 'but not before Christmas.'[14] Later Eisenhower and Gen. Walter Bedell Smith, his chief of staff and SHAEF office manager, followed along to the Louis XIV chapel at Versailles. There they attended the wedding of Eisenhower's personal aide, Sgt Michael J. 'Mickey' McKeogh, to a petite bespectacled lady from the Women's Army Corps, Sgt Pearlie Hargrave. After the ceremony, all the attendees went to Eisenhower's quarters at Saint-Germain for champagne. Everyone was in high spirits.[15]

For American correspondents covering the war news on the front from the Hotel Scribe, the ninth day before Christmas in the City of Light presented a grand opportunity to guzzle French wines against a backdrop of posh Napoleonic furnishings. Even so, many complained that the famous 'Le Muses' bar had no whisky. Part of the problem: black marketeers in the Montmartre District.[16]

Not all was light in Paris, though. While Eisenhower celebrated the festivities, his chief intelligence officer learned of a troubling development. Gen. Strong received a message reporting an enemy attack during the predawn hours on the First U.S. Army front. Strong kept his composure, although alarmed that several participating enemy divisions had been identified. Allied intelligence was still blind: because of icy fog and low clouds covering the enemy front, the Supreme Command lacked aerial reconnaissance for the last few days.

That afternoon Gen. Strong and a group of top generals met with Ike in his map room at 2 p.m. to discuss the latest.[17] Fldm. Montgomery, in charge of the 21st Army Group, was not present, as he was on the golf course at Eindhoven with the Welsh professional Dai Rees.[18] Eisenhower's generals had gathered to discuss the critical shortage of infantry replacements.

The six officers listened attentively around a large table as Eisenhower discussed his continued intention to remain relatively idle in certain sectors like the Ardennes, meanwhile gathering the forces to capture the Roer River dams. At that moment Brig. Edward Gen. Edward C. Betts interrupted and called Strong away. He had an urgent message. Gen. Strong knew Betts as an otherwise steady and calm subject, but he looked nervous and rattled. The news from the Ardennes was serious, Betts began. There had been a continuing series of dangerously violent attacks with a *massive* artillery barrage. 'Situation obscure,' read one report. 'Regimental command posts under attack.' More enemy units had been identified, including some strategically important panzer divisions, and there had been German penetrations at five points in the Ardennes.[19] Strong returned to the meeting with the news.

Meanwhile, Fldm. Montgomery and Dai Rees had just played a few holes of golf, when a plane landed. A messenger jumped out and sprinted to the fairway. There was 'a hell of a row' from the enemy in the 12th Army Group in the Ardennes.[20] Montgomery chucked the game and headed back to his command post. Soon he was on his way in a Rolls-Royce command car motoring through the murk to Eisenhower's Versailles headquarters.

After Montgomery arrived, the Allied commanders crowded around a map that Betts had marked up with the identified attacking enemy before the Ardennes. Bradley had just returned from Paris. Bradley said he had two divisions in reserve to respond to the development. He urged that the 10th Armored be moved up from the south and the 7th Armored down from the north.

While Bradley was away, the generals had already noted that the Germans identified outnumbered the U.S. forces, all of which were either tired or green, along the 'ghost front' in the Ardennes. Strong ventured that the Germans might try to thrust west across the Meuse to reach Brussels, cutting off much of the U.S. First Army from its supply base. Eisenhower nodded worriedly, but Bradley was sceptical as he returned to the agitated group. This was a spoiling attack, he opined, designed to draw Allied attention away from the Roer River offensive or Patton's coming attack into Germany from the Saar. Gen. Strong disagreed. Most had only known the *Germans* in retreat – Africa, Italy, France.

They did not know, as did Strong, the terror of 1940 and the ferocity of their opponent on the attack. 'He who has not fought the Germans,' went the British adage, 'does not know war.'

After the meeting Lt Gen. Everett S. Hughes and the other generals joined Eisenhower for a celebratory dinner for Ike's promotion to five-star Army rank. Ike enjoyed his favorite food – a big plate of oysters – and Hughes pulled out a bottle of Highland Piper Scotch. In Eisenhower's entourage there was no more highly prized gift . Everyone quaffed some of the spirits, and a few lit cigars, basking in the afterglow. But their reverie was interrupted once more with news from the Ardennes. Fragmentary reports reaching Versailles identified a number of German divisions involved in the operation. Bradley, who had elected to stay with Eisenhower to await developments, spoke with Sibert in Luxembourg City. His G-2 intelligence officer seemed strangely unperturbed; the attacks would soon peter out for want of supply, he ventured.

At 11 p.m. Sibert entered an appraisal into his G-2 journal that would long haunt him: 'The sudden attacks and seemingly overwhelming array of six enemy divisions … should not be misinterpreted,' he opined, believing these actions to be a spoiling attack designed to forestall the planned upcoming Allied offensives. 'The quality of the divisions involved … and the apparent lack of long-range objectives would seem to limit the enemy threat.' He discounted rumours that German tanks had been sighted 'miles behind the Allied lines' and took solace in the fact that no SS divisions from the Sixth Panzer Army had been sighted.[21] But Bradley, on hearing of the enemy numbers, decided to leave immediately for Luxembourg City.

On the other side of the fence, Hitler's *Adlerhorst* headquarters near Bad Nauheim bustled on the morning after the start of the great offensive with tapping teletype machines, jangling phones and messengers coming and going. Hitler was not there. The German leader was still asleep, having stayed up until 5 a.m. to ring up his various commanders and remind them of their duty for a supreme effort to pursue *Wacht am Rhein*. When he was awakened at 11.30 a.m. the news was good. 'I told the Führer on the first day of the attack that complete surprise had been achieved,' Jodl would later recall.[22] When his doctor, Theodor Morrell, arrived at noon, he found his patient with high blood pressure and a permanent tremor in his left hand. 'Great emotional crisis because of the offensive!'[23]

On 13 December, at the Ziegenberg command post, Dr Schuster, the young director of the Luftwaffe Weather Service, had forecast an extended period of poor weather and fog. But meteorology was still a notoriously inexact science. Jodl jauntily announced that Schuster had been right: the weather was still overcast and thick with mist.[24] Hitler invited Schuster to accompany him on his daily walk.

And for once the tables seemed turned. On 17 December, the Germans were supporting the attack with the greatest numbers of air sorties since D-Day. Göring strutted into Hitler's Western Front Eagle's Nest headquarters with aplomb. Even when the mists cleared to allow limited air operations, the Allied air forces found the Germans aloft in sufficient numbers to keep the tactical wings of the U.S. Ninth Air Force more than busy. The mood at the cloister-like Führer bunker was upbeat. Hitler and his aides took a quick stroll above ground at the compound. 'We can hear the artillery fire from the front,' recorded his stenographer, Karl Thöt:

> As [Ewald] Reynitz and I went in the afternoon around 1500 hours to the situation meeting, a sizable number of German fighter aircraft passed overhead. Major [Herbert] Büchs, recovering from the obvious inferiority of the German Luftwaffe at this sight, turned to all who enthusiastically saw our fighters roaring across and looked up: 'Now let anyone speak up against the German Luftwaffe!' Hardly had those words been said, an air raid alarm was sounded. The surprise was so great that everybody broke out in loud and hearty laughter. As it turned out, they had been German fighters, indeed, which had scrambled from the Frankfurt area in response to an enemy air raid.
>
> As we approached the situation room, the Führer had already arrived, contrary to his custom. It was clearly visible how the first good news about our offensive occupied his mind. Already before the situation meeting, Reich Press Chief Dr [Otto] Dietrich said: 'Well, now you are finally getting something pleasant and joyful to write again. That proved to be true. Today, on the whole day the air is full with German aircraft flying over us to the West.'[25]

Although the thousand-man parachute jump to protect Peiper's right flank did not take place, it was rescheduled for the following night. This was much to the chagrin of commander Baron Friedrich August von der Heydte, who had tried to have it cancelled. By Sunday at 3 a.m. the first German night-time parachute operation of the war floated in silken canopies down over the Ardennes. 'Jump at Mont Rigi,' the report droned laconically. '*Operation Stösser* is said to be a success.'[26] When Hitler retired in the early morning hours, the news continued to trend favorable. 'The attack completely surprised the opponent,' went the final evening report, 'and gained ground quickly all around … The attack against the entire front is being continued on into the night.'[27]

Back at Lanzerath, Belgium, Jochen Peiper looked to make good on that aim. At 4 a.m. Kampfgruppe Peiper's column moved out of Lanzerath and headed north. Peiper was just behind the head of the column in his Mk V Panther.[28] 'The forest offered neither resistance,' he scowled, 'nor were there any mines.'[29]

So long was the tail of Kampfgruppe Peiper that the German tanks and vehicles moved through Lanzerath all day as they headed north. Sanny Schür and her teenage cousin Adolf ventured out of their houses to watch. 'We knew we were German again when we saw those tanks coming!' the young boy remembered. 'There seemed like many more than a hundred … it was endless.' They saw Lyle Bouck and the American prisoners at the Café Scholzen marched off to the east into captivity.[30]

> It was lunchtime. There were tanks all over the place. American prisoners passed through; maybe a hundred coming down the road. There were also two civilians with them; I didn't think anything of it at the time. But then I heard two sharp shots. I was in the house. Later on when I heard that two people had been shot in the barn I realised what I had heard. There were a group of soldiers in the house and the barn and sometime later a man came in through the barn with blood all over him. He came to our door. He came in and he sat on a box in the front of our house and was bleeding badly. We knew the man – it was Peter Mueller.[31]

Peter Mueller had been hiding in a cellar in Honsfeld with his nephew Johann Brodel when the Germans came. Neither of the two Belgians wanted to be anywhere nearby because the Germans would try to force them in the army – or worse. They had come down from Honsfeld with the other American prisoners and had been trying to escape. Mueller had protested to the Germans that he had nothing to do with the Americans; he had just been in the cellar to get away from the fighting. But the Germans didn't believe him, and shot him and his nephew near the Schür's tin-roofed barn. Young Brodel had been shot right through the neck. He died instantly.

Amazingly, the two bullets that passed through Mueller's upper neck had not killed the Belgian farmer. After crawling across the road, he managed to reach the kitchen door of the Schür home and knocked for help. Opening the door, the Schürs came upon a ghastly sight – a groaning man covered in blood. They hauled him inside, Adolf's mother treating Mueller's wound with a bandage after wiping away the blood. Soon the bleeding slowed. Suddenly a German SS man was at the door and barged his way inside. 'The German was complaining loudly,' Adolf remembered. 'He wanted to finish off the man.' A photograph of Christolf Schür always hung on the wall of their home, showing Adolf's grandfather in a First World War uniform.

Now the SS man was wanting to take Mueller outside – a certain end. Christolf Schür boldly thrust out his chest. 'He was a German soldier in World War I, like me,' he bellowed pointing to the photograph. 'I'm glad he didn't live to see this …' He motioned to Mueller, who was still bleeding in the chair. 'He is just a dumb farmer,' Schür said. 'Leave him alone. We never hurt anyone like this in that war.' The SS man finally left.[32]

To young Adolf Schür, the German column seemed to snake through Lanzerath for days. Some of the German soldiers looked war weary and hungry, but the majority appeared eager to fight. He listened to one as he left town. 'We'll push them back to the English Channel,' he called out to another. 'Soon,' he crowed, 'we'll be on the heights above Liège!'[33]

That would be true if Peiper had anything to do with it. By 4 a.m. he, Poetschke, and Fischer had finally reorganized their battlegroup, mounting each tank with a dozen or so paratroopers of Maj. Siegfried Taubert's II/ Fallschirmjäger Regiment 9.[34] Those who could not straddle the big tanks would walk alongside on foot, using their assault weapons to protect Peiper's armor as they moved into Hoffmann's 'enemy-infested' woods north of Lanzerath.

Yet Peiper was not about to timidly approach what others saw as an inevitable ambush. His mood? 'Very angry'. The Meuse was still far away, and for Peiper, accustomed to cavalry-like panzer rides behind enemy lines through the darkness, 16 December had been a disaster. Yet now it was after midnight – the smallest of Sunday hours and Peiper time. With paratroopers clinging to their decks, his tanks surged ahead.[35]

Chapter 7

HONSFELD

Fight because you don't know how to die quietly.

Nora Sakovic

If frustrated by the dawdling pace of the first day of the attack, Jochen Peiper looked to change the gait. His tank column slashed out from Lanzerath at 4 a.m. in the pre-dawn darkness on 17 December. With paratroopers riding atop with weapons drawn, his tanks ground over the wood-lined trail into the dense Schirr Busch Forest. Each moment, they were expecting the worst. 'In our tanks we always had great fear of being ambushed in the woods,' remembered one experienced panzer man.[1] The tank leaders chirped at each other over the radio while paratroopers nervously marched ahead, holding out white handkerchiefs to keep the tanks from driving off the narrow road.

There was not a single shot as they pushed further into the woods. The only excitement was fleeting; a few American soldiers running away towards Buchholz railway station.[2] Soon, the flak panzers following the tanks came under fire from American guns from K Company of the 3rd Battalion of the 394th Infantry Regiment. But the Germans suffered no damage, and after the response – a blaze of armor-mounted automatic fire, the GIs bugged out. 'I proceeded to attack with my tanks,' Peiper recalled, 'supported by motorised infantry and infantry on foot, towards the forest. Contrary to reports received from the parachute troops, the forest was free of enemy troops. The forest was under a severe artillery barrage …'[3]

> We moved through the woods towards Honsfeld without encountering any opposition. Approximately one battalion of paratroopers provided flank protection on either side of the road and the tanks moved through the woods. During the night some interdiction fire fell in the woods; however, none of it was effective … It was daylight, about 0500 or 0600 [sic, likely around 7 a.m.] when the column reached Honsfeld. The occupants of the town were taken completely by surprise. The march was conducted under normal blackout conditions, with

> guides leading each tank holding a white handkerchief for identification, and flanking infantry on either side to protect the tanks from ambush.[4]

Honsfeld, a village of 300 Belgian souls, was just a few gear shifts up the road. As SS leader Georg Preuss drew near its houses – many with American vehicles parked under the eaves – he ordered his SPWs to open fire. Peiper was just behind:

> An American reconnaissance unit was stationed at Honsfeld. The vehicles were standing in front of all the doors of all the houses in town and there were plenty of weapons around, particularly tank destroyers, but the troops were not at their weapons or their vehicles, but were in the houses asleep. For that reason there was hardly any fighting at all. The first moving spearhead at the point of which 1st Lt Preuss was driving merely shot at some groups of houses for preventative reasons and the town was passed without any serious resistance. At that time I was with the point. My own command group, which was in march in the convoy behind the group of Poetschke, had remained behind and I myself decided to personally remain with the point in order to be able to take action rapidly, to be able to encourage the troops out front and in order to be able to evaluate the results of the reconnaissance performed by the units of Knittel and Hardieck (Skorzeny), both which were to pass by me.[5]

But after seeing Skorzeny in the pre-attack meetings and receiving the seemingly endless reminders about the codes to protect against friendly fire on the commandos in their American garb, Peiper lost sight of them. 'They might as well have stayed home,' Peiper groused, 'as they were never near the head of the column where they planned to be.'[6]

Young 16-year-old Andreas Peter Schroeder was one of the eight civilians left in the town, to tend the cows. The Americans there felt slightly ill at ease. Located in the German-speaking section of Belgium, Honsfeld was considered to be part of the Reich during the war. 'When we were at school,' he remembered, 'there was no praying – it was "*Heil Hitler!*"'[7]

After the Germans lost the First World War, French became the official language in Honsfeld once more, but not even lip service was paid. Schroeder's father had fought long years for Germany in that war. Although he did learn French, at home everyone spoke German. Still, after the conquest of 1940, the area was officially designated as part of Hitler's domain. 'The linguistic situation here was crazy,' Andre said. 'You can't make a Belgian out of German. We were more German than Belgian.' Indeed, Andre's young age was the only reason he was not in Hitler's army. All four of his brothers were fighting for the Wehrmacht, and one had been already killed in Caen with the 12th SS Panzer Division.

After the Americans liberated the region during their advance in September 1944, the civilians close to the fighting zone at the German border were evacuated. Left in town were only eight individuals, including the priest, Henri Signon, and the burgomeister, Hubert Fickers. Andre was needed.

Honsfeld was a poor Belgian farming village, and everyone there depended on the cattle. Tending to the beasts was important – without them one did not eat. Never having seen foreigners, Schroeder was scared of the Americans – at least at first:

> The Germans during the war had made the local Belgians believe, through propaganda, that when the Americans came here, they would kill everybody and that they were all blacks. And when they got there in September, I was surprised to find that most of them were white just like us. The Americans who were here were okay; they gave us chocolate, cheese, and other rations. We got our first pineapple – we didn't know what it was ... An American officer came after I had been there by myself for a few days and said, 'You're a young boy, and you can't stay here by yourself.' They brought me into Honsfeld, and I stayed at the burgomeister's house by the school. There were a few rounds of artillery fire that landed here on 16 December, but not many. Lots of Americans with tanks and trucks were here, and they started falling back and we wanted to know why ... We were scared ...[8]

By 4 a.m. Honsfeld was asleep – even Andre Schroeder and the edgy U.S. soldiers. The German paratroopers facing them were shocked by the GI nonchalance. 'In the morning of 17 December 1944, we mounted the tanks of Jochen Peiper,' one remembered. 'The thundering attack proceeded. We wheeled into Honsfeld at daybreak. The Americans were still in their beds. We took many prisoners without fighting.'[9]

It was true. At 4.30 a.m. Sternebeck reported his armored *Spitze* – now just four tanks and two half-tracks – sped into the outskirts of the darkened streets of Honsfeld, with the snoozing American soldiers unaware. Few noticed the German arrival given the extent of U.S. Army traffic headed in the same direction. Sternebeck stopped at one point to check out an American reconnaissance vehicle parked in the road, thinking it was one of Skorzeny's fake tanks. He pulled back hastily to find its owners were American and snoring noisily.[10] Rather than rousing their enemy, Sternebeck resumed his saddle and sped off into the darkness. Soon he was on the radio to Peiper. The town was undefended, he reported.[11]

With darkness and fog, the entrance to Honsfeld was screened by the 1st Recon platoon of the 801st Tank Destroyer Battalion with its towed 3in guns. Just after midnight an officer with the U.S. 18th Cavalry Squadron had called up section leader Sgt James Gallagher to tell him he would bring his light tanks past his position that morning – friendlies. It was a prudent precaution, as all through that autumn, friendly fire in the Ardennes 'rest area' had been more dangerous than enemy weapons. At 5.15 a.m. a column of tanks approached the little outpost.

When Gallagher and his aide went downstairs to investigate, the sky was pitch black. He walked towards the dark shape of the lead tank. '18th Cav?' he piped up. Without warning, Gallagher was slammed over the head by a rifle butt and sent sprawling to the ground. Although his companion escaped amid a flurry of gun shots, the section leader was soon conveyed to a German interrogator who spoke clear English. 'You are completely surrounded by infantry and armor,' he boasted. It was useless for any of his troops to do anything but surrender.[12] Gallagher was stunned. When questioned, he just mumbled: name, rank, and serial number.

1st Lt Bob Reppa, with Troop A of the 32nd Cavalry Squadron, had sought sanctuary in Honsfeld. Knowing he was close to the front, he had dispatched Sgt George Creel with the 3rd platoon in a wheeled armored car to the southernmost house in Honsfeld before bedding down for the night at the Red Cross headquarters. Creel would stand guard outside. Should anything strange happen – the day had been plenty weird already – Reppa said to alert him. Early evening brought nothing special. Reppa dozed off. Meanwhile, in the turret of the M-8 armored car at the end of town, Creel too fought off sleep. Every few minutes a vehicle or two would approach with 'cat's eye' blackout headlights, but invariably they turned out to be more Americans pulling back from the debacle in the Losheim Gap.

It was close to 5 a.m. when an American vehicle passed by, only to have another approaching just a minute behind it. In the darkness, Creel doubted what he saw and rubbed his eyes. There, in the middle of the road, was a man motioning with a flashlight 'the biggest damned tank I've ever seen'. At first, Creel planned to fire, but the trailer attached to his M-8 blocked his field of fire. He instinctively crouched as the behemoth passed – so close that he saw the German cross on the side.[13] Hell, he only had a 37mm gun anyway. Moments after it passed, someone else started firing up ahead. With the German tanks ahead distracted, he jumped off and ran off to warn Reppa. He found himself in 'a wild scramble' with other GIs similarly surprised at the south-east edge of town.

'Those don't sound like ours,' Reppa said to Sgt William Lovelock. Lovelock dashed to the door and eased it open. In the darkness, a shell burst illuminated the street outside. Revealed in the flash outside were enormous tanks and half-tracks. 'They *are* German,' Lovelock whispered, closing the door. Just then Sgt Creel appeared at the entrance. Reppa was dismayed. 'Why didn't you shoot at these tanks?' Creel explained that he had not been warned by anyone further back.[14]

The shooting Creel had heard was the reaction as the German tanks reached the small stream that ran south of Honsfeld. On the north side of the creek was a scattered line of American infantry organized by an American captain in charge of the 99th Infantry Division rest center. Greeting the German tanks with scattered rifle fire only served to shake the beehive. Punishing return fire blazed out of the guns from German flak wagons with 20mm and 37mm rounds. The American skirmish line bolted. The fleeing infantry ran past two towed 3in guns of the third platoon of A Company, 801 TD Battalion, and sprinted down the street where two platoons of sleeping gunners of the 612th TD Battalion were bedded down in houses.

Meanwhile, the 801 TD Battalion and its attached 2nd Recon platoon were in deep trouble. At 7.45 a.m. the TD men were confronted by two Panther tanks with heavily armed enemy infantry clinging to their decks. Attempting to manhandle TD guns into place, the American soldiers were sprayed with machine gun fire. A quick radio call to battalion headquarters told more bad news: the town was crawling with Germans, and the recon platoon should make their way west as best they could.[15] Although losing most of their guns, the crews scurried ahead to reach the north-east edge of Honsfeld. Using the railway cut there, they made their way to the hillside west of Hünningen, where a surviving section of the battalion was located. Peiper's battlegroup pushed through the town:

> It is incredible, the Americans in the village slept so deeply that they did not hear us. Their presence is confirmed by some reconnaissance vehicles parked along the houses, with their parking lights on. Honsfeld is one big mud hole. The paratroopers, who had dismounted and had to go through the mud, were not to be envied. Our group passed through the village without fighting. The surprise apparently was so complete that the Americans only later thought of fighting back, which then, however, was intensive.[16]

Pvt. Jim Foley of the 394th Regiment was one of the hundred-odd American GIs determined to enjoy his time off at Camp Maxley, the 99th Infantry Division rest camp at the Saal Eifelerhof Gasthaus in Honsfeld. Even if Marlene Dietrich's appearance was cancelled because of the shelling hours before, things had settled down once again in Honsfeld. That Saturday night Foley and a private enjoyed a movie in the rec hall, even if there was no sound, but the highlight had been a hot shower and early sleep. At 10 p.m. 'stuff' started falling.

> We didn't think much of it. After all, they told us it was just a heavy patrol action – what a patrol! Then a shell blew the hell out of the improvised shower room across the street. Booch was getting plenty worried and so was I, but I wasn't going to get out of that sleeping bag until they blew me out. About 2 a.m. we heard vehicles in the street. That didn't worry us, but what did worry us was the fact that they were going the wrong way! Still, we stayed in the sack until about 5 a.m. We heard some heavy vehicles in the street. But before I got a chance to look out, I hear a shot outside, and Wooten, that big jerk from G Company, came running into our room. All he had on were his long johns, and he looked funny as hell. He said, 'One of those silly damned guards of ours just took a shot at me when I stepped out to take a piss.' … It was so dark outside, he couldn't see a damned thing. I once again piled into the sack until I heard Kraut voices in the street. This was quite confusing to say the least … I stuck my head outside and had a time to see a few of our recon cars across the street all knocked out and three Kraut tanks which were very much intact. Then some bastard opened up with a burp gun on me, so I got my ass inside in a hurry.[17]

For a time, Foley and his comrades thought about attempting to break out. 'I sat on the floor with my .45 calibre, which couldn't hit a B-29 at ten paces, and waited.' A few minutes later a sergeant appeared who ordered the surrender of the entire rest camp.

> There were a few minutes of horrible confusion, and then we were all lined up outside with a bunch of stupid 'Supermen' screaming like crazy at us. I hated to give up like that. We didn't have so much as a BAR [Browning Automatic Rifle] in the entire group. If we had started shooting, they would have slaughtered us like a bunch of cattle.

Belgian civilians, such as Andre Schroeder, were equally surprised:

> Early the next morning, when we peeked out the door before light, there were lots of German vehicles on the road. There were no light or lamps outside, there was no electricity, but I could plainly see that there were Germans all about. The road passed right in front of their house … We were lucky no Americans were in our house, but most of them in the other houses were asleep … An SS man said that they were fighting for Adolf Hitler; to us they seemed to be fighting to get the American rations. The Germans came inside, and they wanted to get warm. Some of these SS guys were very arrogant and you didn't talk to them.[18]

Many of the 612th TD Battalion were sleeping.[19] On the afternoon of 16 December word had come to the 612th TD battalion to depart Sourbrodt, Belgium, and head to Honsfeld. Yet Pvt. William 'W.T.' Hawkins, with the battalion, was worried. As they moved east towards the front that night, all the Army traffic seemed to be streaming west. None of the MPs could tell him what was up. Swigs of the whisky ration didn't give him any comfort.[20]

When they arrived at the north-west end of Honsfeld it was 4 a.m. Captain John Kennedy kept mumbling, 'I think we're in the wrong place,' and Lt Baysek admitted that he didn't even have a map. Kennedy sent everyone to bed down for the night, billeting part of 2nd platoon in a house a little further into the village, while locating 1st platoon in a three-storey stone building on the western exit of town.'[21]

The men assigned to the first platoon were settling down in a dwelling on the right side of the road, and the 2nd platoon was in another house across the way. They were positioned at the critical junction of the Büllingen–Heppenbach Road at a corner known to locals as '*Am Borren*'. Pvt. Francis Hayes, in the same house as Hawkins, was unnerved. His best friend was his driver and the mail orderly for B company, T/5 Edward L. Stegall. From Humboldt, Tennessee, Stegall was a short, likeable guy with a dark complexion. Some said he was part Indian. He helped stamp out homesickness by handling the mail and often strummed country tunes on his guitar. Hayes asked what Stegall thought of the latest move?

> Somehow this thing didn't feel right to me. I had a gut feeling that something was not right. That was the only time I had a feeling that the army was getting into trouble. It was cold, and we were ordered to move early in the night. I was a recon NCO, and I was supposed to stay with Capt. Kennedy. 'You and Stegall put Lt Gribbin in your jeep and tail the column,' he told me. We had been ordered to leave Sourbrodt to move to Honsfeld. It was dark when we left. We were told

> that the 99th has this area secured, but this is a recreation area, and you have two or three days there. Enjoy it and rest up. Capt. Kennedy came with us and dropped us off in Honsfeld; he continued on and left us three there ...[22]

The 1st platoon was surprised to find an older Belgian man and his nephew in their assigned house. Michael M. Papendick, the company interpreter, learned that Peter Mueller and Johann Brodel were very nervous. They had left Manderfeld to escape the Germans the day before, when Brodel had refused to help the new arrivals. Both men feared being accused of being enemy collaborators – why weren't they in the German Army?[23]

Meanwhile, the Germans were at the south end of Honsfeld. After scaring the daylights out of Sgt Creel of the 32nd Cavalry and setting he and others to wild flight, Kampfgruppe Peiper rushed forward on the road until they reached the house where men from 2nd platoon of B Company, 612th TD Battalion, under Sgt Charles W. Townsend, were bedded down. Townsend was pulling the first watch. 'It must have been 4 a.m. and very dark when I saw a tank, followed by a group of men go by ... I couldn't make out any markings. I tried to contact the company headquarters, but all channels on the radio were jammed.'[24] It was quiet now, and Townsend sent off a messenger to seek help. He never came back. S/Sgt Ralph J. 'Frenchy' LeBlanc was with him:[25]

> Just about daybreak I was awakened by machine gunfire going through the window of the house. I was on the second floor. There was plaster falling and glass breaking. I thought there was a drunken GI outside, and I went to the window. I looked out, and there was a guy outside the window, just below, and he was not in a GI uniform! The road outside was full of German tanks and troop carriers. Just about then [Vernon G.] 'Red' Winfree came up halfway up the stairs, 'Frenchy,' he yelled, 'we got to get out of here! We are surrounded!' He yelled for us to come downstairs. I was ready since I had slept with my clothes on. I yelled for Charlie Sisco to come on down, and I took a loaded grease gun. When I got downstairs, Sergeant Charles Townsend told me, 'Put the damned gun down. We gotta surrender, and we gotta make a decision real quick.' They had already thrown a grenade inside, and Pvt. Parmer Gunter had been killed. Charlie Sisco, who was behind me, never got out either.[26]

Townsend had sent out a second messenger, who was captured and yelled back at the house that if they didn't surrender, the Germans would execute him. LeBlanc continued:

> We gathered in the kitchen, and there was one guy who had a Red Cross arm band and helmet, and we thought if we let him go out first, they would take us. I put my gun on the table, fully loaded. There was only one German outside when we came out of the house with our hands up. The road outside was jammed with German tanks and trucks full of infantry. 'Man, we've really had it,' I thought, 'we could have never held off this.' We were marched across the street and lined up against a building there. This was the main drag, and all the tanks were

> going by us. There was a U.S. recon car across the street. The men in that vehicle were dead, and there was a German inside it, swinging the barrel around on the 50-calibre machine gun, firing into a vacant lot and just recklessly firing it. There was one guy, a paratrooper – I could tell from his clothing – and he searched us for weapons. When he came to me, he hit my pockets, and I had a clip of ammo in the chest pocket. He was going to hit me across the face with it, but then he just threw it across the ground. He continued on down the line. There must have been about ten of us. Then we were marched alongside the road east out through town. There were still GIs in some of the houses; we could see them ducking back inside the houses … As we marched out through town, we went out passing the front line, and all the American soldiers who were there were dead.

In the early morning, with small arms fire popping off all over, more groggy Americans soldiers stumbled from their beds. Pvt. Elmer Haynes was a good ol' boy from Murfreesboro, Tennessee. They made their beds in the second storey of a stone house known to locals as the *Haus Krütz* around 4 a.m. With the rest of the 1st Platoon, they had gone to sleep knowing that Honsfeld was the divisional rest area.[27] They didn't even bother unlimbering their towed anti-tank guns. 'It's safe here. You guys just pull in and park.'[28] There had been sporadic artillery fire the day before; just more misery from an enemy who had shelled them periodically for the last seventy-three wretched days in Winterspelt.

The battalion always kept guards, but Haynes was surprised when Pvt. Robert 'R.B.' Taylor came in just after everyone had gone to sleep. 'Haynes!' he yelled, 'a German reconnaissance unit just came right through here at 25–30mph and didn't even slow down!' Taylor had just seen Peiper's *Panzerspitze* under Werner Sternebeck. 'There were about four or five vehicles.' Haynes woke Lt William Baysek. 'You think R.B. is just imagining things?' he asked. Soon neither man needed convincing. Both could hear the rumble of tanks groaning in the morning quiet. 'Lieutenant, that sounds like them now!' Haynes was on the ground floor and ran out to his gun. His driver helped him uncouple the piece from its half-track hitch.[29] Pvt George Block:

> We took our rifle butt and lifted the slats of the blinds, and you could see Germans crawling all over. 'What do you think about that?' I asked the guy rooming with me. 'Well, we sure don't have uniforms in our outfit like that.' Germans didn't seem to know we were there. Then our people started firing. George Polk was my gunner, and we got downstairs and tried to set up our guns. We had a lot of small arms fire and some mortar rounds. We unhooked the guns off the half-tracks, and somebody else helped me, and we split the trails and lined it up so that it would come right back in the hall of this house from the recoil.[30]

S/Sgt Billy Wilson of the recon company was in the same house:

> First thing we knew, tanks were coming though in convoy. We thought they were our tanks at first, and then two enlisted men from the 18th Cavalry came into the house and old us their CP had just been overrun, and about that time enemy

infantrymen came down the road behind the tanks. We had a .50-calibre and .30-calibre machine gun and opened up on them with that and with the small arms the men had … We pinned some of them down and killed some others.[31]

The Americans took to sniping at the German infantry passing by the windows. Some of the enemy were wounded – or at least sent scurrying for cover. Over a period of two hours the American prospects degenerated as the Germans brought up heavy weapons and methodically surrounded the houses where the Americans fired. For the enemy, any Americans who kept firing were 'snipers' – to be treated without mercy upon capture. Rainer Bender was one of the German paratroopers laying siege:

Elements of the 5th Company, 9th Regiment mounted on King Tigers of the Waffen SS drove into Honsfeld on the morning of the 17th. The place was filled with parked jeeps and American half-tracks. We captured quite a number of prisoners without meeting much resistance. The Americans were coming out of the houses and looking very frightened, lifting their arms and surrendering … There was only one major farm building that offered resistance, and we received orders to attack this building. The area around the building was flat, with some fruit trees and a small hedge. We moved towards the farm when suddenly we received heavy fire. Everybody was trying to seek cover behind the trees or the hedge. The ground was mostly frozen, and we couldn't dig in! We were sitting in a goldfish bowl! An Oberjäger was hit in the mouth. I was hit by a shell fragment in the lower lip. A number of my comrades were killed or seriously wounded. Our first aid comrades came forward under the banner of the Red Cross to give aid to the wounded. When one medic reached a wounded man, he was killed by a single shot … Anger was rising.[32]

While Bender and his comrade went back to get rifle grenades, the German troops took to blasting the Americans out of the houses. Pvt Elmer Haynes remembered:

I only had part of my crew. All happened fast; it was barely getting daylight. From the house, my gun was the only one pointing towards this right turn. I could not see the tanks until they came around this building and had to come around this turn. I was firing across this kerb. It was only about 50 yards. I saw the first one come around. I let the second and third one come around. I fired towards the gun turret. I ripped the track off. When I hit the first one, the turret was smashed, and the gun barrel dropped to the pavement and caught fire. I then went back to the first one and hit it in the turret and then the one in the middle and hit it too. All of them sat there in the street and burned. We fired one more round as the Germans boiled out the tanks. No firing in return. I could see them trying to move their gun around to get at me, but they turned broadside to me.

After that, there was a short lull, I heard this artillery shell, and I ran into this house for protection. I hollered, 'It's coming in after us.' A shell landed by the rock wall, and I got shrapnel in my left leg. Others were killed. I went on inside, and I had shrapnel in the calf of my leg, and I bandaged my leg with sulfonamide powder.

I went upstairs in the house. Hayes was across the street in another house. I was in the last house on the right. There was nothing between this house and the road. I went upstairs and I was by myself. Just as I walked in the room, I heard a shell. I fell flat on my face. A terrific explosion blew in the wall and shrapnel tore the room apart. I was almost knocked out from the concussion. When I got up I had some minor cuts from flying plaster. I was covered with plaster dust. When I got downstairs, I heard Lt [William] Baysek out in the street. 'All of my men have been killed or wounded. I am ordering all you men to surrender.' I came out in the street, and Baysek told us to put our hands over our head.

There were about twenty-five of us in the street. This German tank came in from behind us from the other direction from where the tanks were knocked out. The tank stopped and opened fire with this machine gun on us … I was on the other side. I fell down immediately on my stomach with my head to one side so I could see it. He fired back and forth on the road as long as he could see anyone moving. When he decided all were dead, he turned his tank around and went back from where he had come from.[33]

Billy Wilson remembered that not only was his surrendering group fired upon, but those of Sgt Devers Bryant across the way were as well. 'I saw two men walk out of the house across the street with a white flag in their hand,' he said. 'They were about four or five yards from the house, and they were shot.'[34] Wilson went immediately to Lt Laurens B. Grandy, who had ordered everyone in their own house to give up. 'I don't think it is any use to surrender,' he said, shaking his head. 'We'll be killed anyway.' He saw two men shot down.

Who had shot the surrendering men? That would only come out in a trial months later, but Ernst Koehler with the SS 1st Panzer Company described seeing the shooting of Americans coming out from a house near Honsfeld with a white flag, a described scene uncannily similar to what happened with the 612th TD Battalion. The shooter, said Koehler, was company chief SS Ostuf. Karl Kremser.[35] For George Block, it was a desperate moment:

Then somebody called out for us to surrender. I came out behind Lt Baysek in the house. They waited until we came out to shoot. They motioned for us to come on. One of the guys came out with white flag on a stick. Everybody had their hands held high. When we got out in front of the lead tank, everybody was coming out on to the highway. The man on top of the tank dropped inside, and the machine gun started and just sprayed the road. I jumped in a ditch. The ones they didn't kill with the guns they drove over with tanks. Later, the others came out. I saw Thomas who was killed there. He and I walked out hand in hand, and he was killed while I fell into the ditch unhurt.[36]

As the Americans in the house yelled '*Kamerad*' and then were marched outside, holding a white handkerchief on a 3ft stick, they were fired upon by a tank just down the road.[37] Sgt Morris Woodall:

We had a big TD gun and got it set up in position and fired and hit one German tank. We shot at the Germans until I guess we shot all our ammunition. Germans

> had already blown up our jeeps and guns. Pvt. Dock Albritton of Arcadia, Florida, was ahead of me wearing a long overcoat. They started shooting at us, and we ran behind a building. Germans called for us to stop shooting. 'Dock, are you hit?' I looked over. 'Well, Dock, you got holes in both sides of that jacket.'
>
> We came out with our hands up. They took our helmets, took our stocking cap, and left us with a helmet liner. Took our overshoes and overcoats. All I had left was a pair of OD pants, an Eisenhower jacket, and a green shirt. Then this German made me lock my hands over my head and stuck a rifle on my shoulder and walked behind me with the rifle leaning on my shoulder. As we walked, the American planes were bombing and strafing. One came down and strafed and bullets came within two feet of me and the German – it knocked dirt over both of us. The plane pulled up when he saw my hands over my head. Another plane came over and wiggled his wings and they left. This German lieutenant walked out on the porch; they walked in the house and went down into the cellar and went down into the stairs, and he called out for them to surrender. He threw a grenade by me and it exploded, but I was not hurt. 'I told them they might just as well come on out – the Germans were all over.' He marched us all out. I remember that as they were marched outside several American soldiers were shot when they came out of a house with a white flag on a stick. They were shot by a tank down the road, which opened up with a machine gun.[38]

Pvt. Charles O. Huttoe had remained in the house with a second group of prisoners who only came out after a German soldier yelled for the firing to stop and then escorted them out of the house.[39] Billy Wilson recalled:

> We all single filed out of the house and stood up facing the house about four yards from it with our hands over our heads, and one German corporal got out of a half-track and walked up to the front of the rank and just raised his burp gun and shot two men at the end of the line on my left … He hit Private Mann and Pvt. John Crowell, who were the first two on the end of the line … I heard Crowell scream and saw him fall.[40]

Wilson wasn't going to wait for the shots to reach his end of the line. He turned and sprinted away, dashing into a field and running as fast as his feet would carry him. Bullets trailed him. Wilson ran north-east over a mile until he reached the lines of the U.S. 99th Infantry Division south of the village of Berg. Who fired the shots?

On 28 February 1946, in the eventual U.S. Army investigation of the incident at Honsfeld, SS Uscha. Anton Motzheim, with the 12th Company, 3rd Panzergrenadier Battalion of Kampfgruppe Peiper, described a scenario squaring eerily with Wilson's description, replete with a detailed map that exactly described the positions of the 612th TD Battalion and even located the two knocked-out German flak panzers just before their positions:

> On the morning of 17 December 1944, between 8 and 9 o'clock, I drove through the village, which I believe was Honsfeld … I reached two knocked-out American anti-tank guns knocked out on [the] right and the left side of the road, as indicated

in my sketch. When my vehicle halted abreast of the American A.T. gun, which was on the right side of the road, I jumped off the vehicle with my machine pistol in my hand … As soon as I was on the ground I noticed an American soldier jumping up … The American soldier was facing me, hands extended to the side, and I assumed he wanted to surrender. I was about 5–8 metres from the American, and as far as I know, he did not have any weapons … I fired a burst of about 3–4 shots from my machine pistol. And he slumped in a lifeless manner to the ground.[41]

Just behind the flak panzers in the line of march was the 3rd Panzer Pioneer Company under SS-Ostuf. Franz Sievers. When the SPW of Joachim Hoffmann passed by the destroyed American anti-tank guns, he saw eight Americans standing by a large house, with their hands overhead and covered by those bearing weapons in the SPW of SS Uscha. Max Beutner (the 2nd Platoon leader) and Ernst Goldschmidt. Similar to Motzheim's diagram, the maps of Siegfried Jackel, Gustav Neve, Joachim Hoffmann, and Gustav Sprenger corroborated Hoffmann's description.[42] Jackel claimed he had seen these same men shot by the side of the road.

We were shooting at prisoners near Honsfeld … We heard the shots before we reached the curve on the road where it turns to the right. [There] I saw prisoners of war who had just been shot. It was in this town where the artillery [*sic*, anti-tank] pieces were, and I saw dead men, and in front of them was the crew of Beutner's SPW … [SS Strm. Gerhardt] Schlingmann and [SS Uscha. Edgar] Dickmann stood right in front of a pile of the dead. [Pionier Willi] Hanke and [SS Rttf. Max] Hammerer were standing in the rear part of the SPW with rifles. Goldschmidt was standing on the bench of the SPW, holding his machine pistol. Beutner was standing on the hood of the SPW with a machine pistol.[43]

Not knowing what he faced, W.T. Hawkins was shocked to find himself in combat armed only with a German Walther P-38 pistol.[44] Sgt Francis Hayes prepared to fire back:

I was in the third storey of a house with Stegall, Hawkins, Lt Gribbin. Big Lt William Baysek was downstairs. I was sleeping. Suddenly there was bunch of jabbering outside. I woke up with a start; it was German voices. I don't think the Germans knew we were there anymore than we knew they were coming. I looked outside, and it was just getting daylight. I saw several German vehicles passing by out there. 'Lord,' I said to Stegall, 'we're sure enough in for something here!' Only a few vehicles had come through, and then there was a lull before more came. 'Let's go down there and get our guns!' We grabbed some ammunition and our carbines. There was bunch of folks in the house – the regular platoon was there. We had our guns sitting down around the house, still hooked to the half-track. Stegall and myself went downstairs and took a .30-calibre off a jeep when the commotion started and brought it back up to the floor. Cpl Haynes got his gun unhooked from the half-track in the front yard and turned it towards the noise coming up the road. But he had no chance to dig it in. Bryant had his gun

> limbered too and was firing. I heard them fire while I was looking out the side window. I could see the German infantry coming though the apple orchard, and we started firing with carbines. We laid a lot of them down. Stegall and myself were firing, and they were firing back. I never got wounded, but a piece of brick hit me in the forehead and I began to bleed. They were about 100 yards away. There were others of our people at the other windows, and there was a lot of shooting going on from the house. We could see the Germans dropping in the orchard, but they stepped up their response and their numbers were increasing.
>
> Then it became evident that we were outgunned and outmanned. That tank column looked five miles long. It was looking like the Alamo. Suddenly we heard Gribbin yell from the floor below us, 'Only thing we can do is surrender.' I thought, 'We're in a hell of a mess!' There was no way we could have held out. We stopped firing, and we went downstairs. I smashed my carbine to pieces.[45]

The German tank shells were slowly turning their stone house of refuge into smoking rubble. Machine gun fire was crashing through the windows. Hawkins:

> Some of our men got two of our towed guns unhitched from our half-tracks and into action and knocked out two of the German lead tanks. The enemy tank fire was destroying the house we were in, so our senior officer ordered us to surrender by first destroying our personal weapons. Lt Gribbins then put a white flag on a stick and led us out of the house on to the road. As we were marching down the road with our hands over our heads … the tanks going by opened up with machine guns. The guys started dropping to the ground or scattered into the woods. I stayed in the ditch with my face in the mud, scared to death … An officer finally got the firing stopped. As soon as the firing let up, the Germans began rounding us up again. Two or three of the men who were killed were writhing a few feet of me at the time they fell. Lt Gribbins was not hit and, as I later found out, he got to a shed and hid out, eventually getting back to our company four or five days later. Also, two enlisted men of the 2nd platoon across the road from us played dead and did not move when they were checked by the Germans. Both these men were wounded and lay in the snow until around 11 p.m. that night, then got up and away after the German troops had gone to sleep.[46]

Hayes described the same scene:

> Everybody put their hands up and lined up at the door. Just as we got out the door, the first bunch had already gone out the door, and a machine gun on a German tank fired into the first group that had come out of the house. We were right there. We could see them falling just outside the door. That group of men had their hands up. Milliner was one of the first group. We backed up from the door and went inside. I thought, 'Well, they're going to kill us all. We've had it.' [There was only four people of our whole group that got away.] That didn't last a second or two, and they told us to come on out. Lt [William Baysek] told us, 'Well, we might as well go on out.' We came out. They did not fire on us, but I could see several bodies lying in the road. I saw Milliner in the road; he was

> shot. He recognized me and yelled something. He was shot in the legs and he was crawling. Then a tank swerved towards him and just ran over him. I can still hear him screaming yet … I saw this with my own eyes.
>
> We walked out the house on to a narrow street, and we could see the tanks lined up its whole length. The Germans were young and looked very tough. They were mean; you got the impression that they were out to kill you. We turned south down the street … Stegall and myself were together, walking alongside those tanks. There was a shot and he fell. I reached for him; he was dead when he hit the ground. I thought he had been hit in the back or stomach, but he died instantly.[47]

Sgt John M. Dluski also witnessed Edward Stegall's fate.[48]

> At about 1100 hours on the same day, we were passing a column of tanks, which had stopped on the road on which we were going in the opposite direction. All at once as we passed one of the tanks, I hear a voice in perfect English call out, 'Hey you.' I immediately turned my face to the left in the direction of the voice, and as I did, I saw an SS man standing in the turret of the tank shoot T/5 Stegall in the middle of the head with a revolver … I was not more than five feet away from the man who fired the shot … I saw Stegall fall backwards to the ground with blood spurting from his forehead. We were forced to keep moving, and consequently I could not stop to render any aid.[49]

Sgt Devers E. 'Deb' Bryant was set up in the first platoon house as a guard that night. Right after daylight he heard noise up the road. Running to the window, he gasped. 'The Germans are breaking through!' But none of his sleeping crew believed him. 'Come look for yourself!' he said. 'The Germans were all over – infantry, tanks everything.'[50]

T/5 Charles L. Morris and Pvt. Ronayne G. White saw 1st Lt Richard Chandler attempt to surrender members of his 2nd Platoon to a German panzer only to have the tank open fire on the Americans with raised hands. Several of the men were hit, including Chandler and Pvt. William Bradley. Others dashed to the house while White and Morris watched in horror. Scared witless, both scrambled from the opposite side of the house to dive into a wood pile by a pig stye. 'We could hear our men out in the roadway calling for help, and I could hear them groaning.' Somehow, White and Morris made their way out of Honsfeld by darkness the following day.[51]

Others fought back. Under attack with the first platoon, Sgt Orville Johns and Corp. James Franya sprinted from their besieged house towards their half-track to turn its machine gun at the enemy. Emerging from the door, the two men were blasted down by machine gunfire from tanks in the street. Pvt. Edward F. Dunn howled with rage watching his buddies cut down in the yard. He ran out of the house, firing his M-1 carbine wildly at the tanks. Dunn, was shot, and his body and the other two crumpled onto the street until German tankers calmly ran over them.[52]

Sgt Clinton Patrick had sent his squad out from their house to surrender under the white flag with the others. There was shooting everywhere, but when Patrick emerged, he was faced with a horrifying sight. Several of his squad had been shot down by a tank that had already passed by. Yet after emerging from the house and being taken prisoner, Patrick and another soldier were ordered to carry a wounded SS officer to a German aid station. On the way, they had to step over the bodies of 612th soldiers who had been killed. Patrick was so angered to see his dead comrades lining the road with hands extended over their heads that the burly Texan slowly strangled the wounded German before he finally laid him down at the German aid station.[53] The three medics assigned to B Company remained. 'When we marched off, our medics were kept behind,' Francis Hayes would recall. 'We never saw them again.'

Bryant and the others who survived the fusillade watched as men across the street came up on Lt Gribbins' improvised flag. Francis Hayes was among the group. 'Some of the men were already standing in front of the tanks with their hands over their heads. One tank fired [with a machine gun] just as I got to the steps and knocked down five men. A friend of mine [Pvt. James Milliner] had both legs shot out from under him. As he was calling for help, the tank swerved to the left and ran over him. It went right by me and kept going.'[54] From across the way, Devers Bryant saw the same thing, as James Milliner was wounded and then savagely crushed by a German tank – a gruesome incident also witnessed by Pvt. Andrew S. Pratz.[55]

Seeing this brutal execution of those who tried to surrender, Devers Bryant and his men ran back into the house near them. 'But a tank stuck its gun in a window and the crew started hollering '*Raus!*' We had run to the basement, but German soldiers came in and marched us out to line up.' By then, Lt Gribbin and Lt Basek had led out the rest of the 1st Platoon. About one hundred men were assembled and joined Bryant's men, who were standing with their hands up. 'They went down the line taking gas masks, overshoes, watches and rings …'[56] Pvt. William 'Toby' Littlejohn:

> We walked up into the street with our hands up, and they lined us up … We just stood there in the ranks for quite a while, and then German tanks came by, and some of those Germans on those tanks fired into some of our guys, and then we jumped into the ditch for cover. The Germans who had been with us before rousted us back out.[57]

'You know war is hell,' Devers Bryant concluded wearily fifty years later.[58]

That much was evident to everyone in the town. Seventeen-year-old Walter Fickers had stayed behind with Erna Collas in Honsfeld to help milk the cows. Fickers thought the Americans still in town were playful, even if they didn't fully trust him or the other German-speaking civilians. On the night of 16 December he didn't sleep. He too was worried that the Germans might accuse him of being a deserter. Why wasn't he fighting instead of milking cows?

> The Germans were passing in columns with their vehicles through the night of the 16th before morning. The tanks passed through the village in the direction

> of Büllingen in the dark. At 6–7 that morning the Germans infantry came up, and there was a gun in front of our house. All these American prisoners in the street at 2 p.m. I cried, 'Those are Americans in the street going by with their hands up, not Germans!' They were behind the road down there. We could see everything. At Honsfeld on the 17th there were 250 Americans, and all them – they were prisoners in the village. From where we lived, they could see the whole village … The first deaths came from some German guards. I saw seven men up against a wall and shot. After I saw that, I hid.[59]

Andre Schroeder was the other boy tending the cows:

> On the 17th, after the Germans came, I still had to go to the seven or eight stables I looked after and take care of the cows. I went to one house on the outskirts of town that day, and there were seven or eight dead Americans in the yard.[60]

They looked like they had been executed. Later Schroeder overheard two Germans talking. 'We found seven Americans sleeping in bed,' they told him. 'And so we took them out of bed and we shot them.' It later turned out that the Americans who had been shot were some of the GIs he had got to know over the ten days or so before. 'They were good guys … killed [still] wearing their long-john underwear.'

When he saw them lying on the ground by the dwelling next to the red brick house, Schroeder was sickened. He returned home to the basement of the burgomeister, Hubert Fickers. The Collas girls were there. Andre spoke to Fickers: 'They've killed some American guys at a house.'[61]

With the battle now largely over, hungry members of Kampfgruppe Peiper commenced to scour Honsfeld for food. Father Henri Signon now faced German SS troopers demanding coffee and something to eat. His home was ransacked, and that Sunday afternoon the Germans invaded the local chapel. Several paraded about in the sacred vestments as sacramental wine was gulped down. As the priest recoiled at the scene, an artillery shell suddenly exploded on a tree outside the thick-walled building, showering deadly shrapnel through the chapel window. One of those desecrating the chapel was killed instantly, another had an arm shorn off.[62]

Andre Schroeder hid in the basement all morning, but later came out and met some of the Waffen SS troops. Moving through the village, he saw bodies of seven Americans soldiers bunched up oddly by an anti-tank gun in front of the home of Joseph Collas. Seeing bodies scattered amid a scene of intense combat was not unusual, but later that night an SS man boasted proudly that he had been present when they were shot down.[63] There was one more terrible episode in Honsfeld. Along with Andre and Walter Fickers, young Erna Collas and her sister helped look after the cows.

> On the night the German attack began, Erna Collas was with us in the basement at the burgomeister's house. On the 17th or 18th, the Germans came in and asked us, 'What is the way to Heppenbach?' [Schroeder] He and a friend were sleeping

> at the back of the cellar. She was sleeping by the door of the cellar. She said to me and my friend, 'Stay there, I will show them.' She seemed young; she wasn't like a 17-year-old today. She was pretty … There were two SS men. It was around 8–10 in the morning. This was a few days later. This was a few days after the Germans first came to town. And she disappeared with them and was never seen alive again. Later that day the burgomeister asked me, 'Where is Erna Collas?' 'I don't know,' and I told him, and we never knew that year. She was found in a foxhole hidden between here and Büllingen in the spring. There were a few branches over her. Someone had tried to hide what they did … The whole village was shocked.[64]

When Honsfeld was recaptured later in January 1945, two prisoners of war from the Einsatz Brigade 999, Pvts Max Drechsner and Wolfgang Weinfurtner, were interrogated:

> I heard from a comrade that there were bodies lying by the cemetery. I went over to check on it and saw from the position that they could not have died a natural death. So I walked over to a farmer and inquired about it. The farmer told us that he saw the SS shoot these prisoners with the explanation that they could not use any PWs. The farmer lives about 10 minutes from the cemetery … People were too scared to talk about it.[65]

In retrospect, it is difficult to determine which of the soldiers of the 612th TD were murdered on 17 December rather than killed in action. In the official U.S. Army history, Hugh Cole claimed, 'Irrefutable evidence shows that nineteen unarmed Americans were shot down in Honsfeld and fifty at Büllingen.'[66] However, the author's investigation shows that while this figure is inflated, American soldiers who had surrendered were, in fact, shot down in Honsfeld.[67] The total number of American soldiers of the 612th TD Battalion who died in Honsfeld on 17 December was twenty-two. At least seven of these, according to witnesses, had not surrendered, but rather were killed in combat. Attempting to conclusively categorise the other fifteen is difficult. It is possible, however, to establish that T/5 Edward L. Stegall was killed after surrendering, as there are multiple witnesses. Pvt. James M. Milliner was seen shot as well, and crushed by a tank while still alive – a horrific sight seen by Devers Bryant and several others. S/Sgt Morris Woodall of Cross City, Florida, claimed to have seen four Americans shot down in Honsfeld after coming out under a white flag – undoubtedly the same incident described by others. He conclusively identified Pfc. Cecil Mann and Pfc. John E. Cowell as victims.[68]

Both Ronayne White and Charles Morris agreed that Pvt. William Bradley from Sgt Bryant's gun team had been among those they saw executed while attempting to surrender. Further, George Block was able to identify T/5 Robert H. Thomas – Sgt Fayne Haynes' driver – as one of those killed during the attempt at surrender. Two of the three medics of the battalion who were carried off by Kampfgruppe Peiper on that day have never been found and must be assumed to have perished at an unknown time and place.[69]

All told, we can establish with relative certainty that at least six American soldiers were shot down in cold blood after surrendering in Honsfeld on 17 December 1944, not including the two medics who were impressed into medical service with the Leibstandarte Adolf Hitler and never seen again.[70] The likely number of prisoners who were shot is higher – particularly given the testimony of civilians Andre Schroeder and Walter Fickers.[71] However, the shootings were not widespread. On three different occasions, veterans of the 612th described how a German officer 'prevented them from being killed by hot heads'.[72]

Moving beyond Honsfeld, Kampfgruppe Peiper quelled remaining resistance. One Königstiger that rumbled along took four hits without damage, but sent clinging paratroopers of the 5th Fallschirmjäger Company running for cover.[73] When Peiper reached Honsfeld in his Panther 001, the bulk of II/ Fallschirmjäger Regiment 9 were jumping off to find warm accommodation in the village. However, once the Americans were awake, the paratroopers proved much more vulnerable than the steel panzers they rode. The I battalion lost fifteen men killed or wounded, and the 2nd Battalion lost thirty-eight more.[74] 'The Americans tried in particular to shoot the paratroopers riding the tanks,' Vince Kuhlbach remembered.[75] Yet by noon, American resistance ended.

In the meeting engagement, the 612th destroyed two 3.7cm *Möbelwagen* ('furniture vans') German flak wagons in Honsfeld.[76] However, the third flak tank, a Wirbelwind, cut down the men manning the guns.[77] In the first flak vehicle the 25-year-old company leader, SS-Obersturmführer Karl-Heinz Vögler, was wounded, as was SS Hscha. Paul Schröder, one of the platoon leaders riding on the second Möbelwagen.[78] Peiper, the leader of the German column, passed through the village before dawn:

> We drove through the forest to the town of Honsfeld. That is where we had the next surprise. We were way behind our schedule. The Americans were soundly asleep. Anti-tank guns stood at the entrance to the town, no men with them. The Americans sat all over in the houses and snored. We roared through rapidly and with the machine guns fired into the houses to introduce ourselves. And they came out from everywhere, like crazy … We had to stop briefly because pulling through the forest we had been stretched out pretty much. And there was that paratrooper major, a Major Taubert, I remember well, because his father was an SS Obergruppenführer; this is how he introduced himself. He wanted to depart from my unit. I asked, why? 'You are assigned to me. You are coming along.' 'No,' he said. 'I must not go any further.' There I said, 'Kiss my ass, you will stay.' And that was quite funny, because one company of them that rode along with us, because they liked it with us … And we drove on. This moment of surprise made me realise that we had quite some success – despite the difficulties in the beginning … the Americans were surprisingly not prepared for anything … That continued, because near Honsfeld was an airstrip on which some seven or eight aircraft stood with propellers turning. We set them on fire with high-power explosives. They did not get to take off.[79]

The German paratroopers counted 180 American prisoners, with much war booty – fifteen anti-tank guns, fifty reconnaissance vehicles, and eighty trucks from the hapless 32nd Cavalry Squadron.[80] The American 612th TD battalion alone lost nine guns, four officers, and 130 men killed, taken prisoner, or missing in action.[81] The German paratroopers celebrated, doling out captured food, drinks, and cigarettes to passing Königstiger crews.

The tail end of Peiper's column included the 84th Flak Sturm Battalion. Luftwaffe Sgt Karl Laun was shocked to come across the bodies of the Americans shot dead in Honsfeld beside their abandoned anti-tank guns. He dutifully recorded in his diary:

> We drive on, accompanied by the constant pounding of American artillery … Past an abandoned flak position, we advance in the direction of Honsfeld. Stretched on the road lie the first Landser [soldier] victims. They obviously died a horrible death – a silent accusation of those war criminals. The brass knows they better give us a pep talk.[82]

If Honsfeld had been a comparatively easy victory, when Peiper's Panther drove out of town, he realised he had little fuel sloshing in his 730-liter fuel tank. Over the hilly Ardennes roads, his Panthers were burning 7 liters of *Benzin* for every muddy kilometer.

Beyond Honsfeld, Peiper sent Preuss's panzer grenadiers to scout the way. They reported that the assigned road west towards Hepscheid–Möderscheid was reminiscent of Russia: one gummy mess. There *was* the well-paved road to the north through Büllingen. Yet that route was part of Rollbahn C and assigned to Kampfgruppe Kuhlmann of the 12th SS Panzer Division.

Standing outside his tank, Peiper listened carefully to any battle noise from the north. From long years in Russia, Peiper's trained battle ear told him Herbert Kuhlmann was nowhere near. Peiper ordered his column to drive hard north via Rollbahn C. He would push as quickly as he could to Büllingen. If he could capture the store of American petrol there, that might be enough to get his fuel-thirsty tanks most of the way to the Meuse.

Chapter 8

INTO THE STORM WIND

Whether it storms or snows, whether the sun smiles on us,
the day blazing hot or icy-cold the night,
Dusted are our faces, but cheerful is our mind,
our Panzer roars into the storm wind ...[1]

While focused on punching beyond Honsfeld and seizing enemy fuel, Peiper knew he was newly vulnerable in the daylight advance beyond the town. Now on the second day of the attack, total surprise would soon be gone. What if Allied eyes in the air observed Kampfgruppe Peiper's thin serpentine armored penetration behind American lines? He knew that answer from Normandy.

Alerted to the pandemonium at Honsfeld, the U.S. 99th Division ordered the available Company B of the 254th Engineer Combat Battalion to assume defensive positions to the south and east of Büllingen. The urgency of that mission was underlined when, in the middle of the night, a sergeant and 1st lieutenant of a TD outfit showed up at the battalion headquarters. They had just escaped capture in Honsfeld a short distance down the road and counted twelve enemy tanks, with more coming. They were asked the location of their command post. 'I'm mobile,' the officer explained. 'The Germans are out there,' he ventured nervously, and not far away.

The action before Büllingen was a confused mess – both because of the rapid and chaotic deployment of the American blocking force and because Preuss, with the vanguard group of panzer grenadiers of the 10th Company, was now in the lead. Werner Sternebeck's panzer followed immediately behind Preuss, a decision Peiper had made back at Lanzerath in light of the tanks' severely limited vision in night assaults. In the darkness, the *Spitze* arriving first in Büllingen mistakenly took the right road at the fork at entrance to the village, while Preuss kept to the main road, leaving Preuss in the lead.

Nevertheless, by 6 a.m. the 254th Engineer Combat Battalion's B and C Companies reported themselves astride the main Büllingen–Honsfeld road.

B company was about 400m south of the airstrips, while C company was assigned to defend the aircraft. The point of Kampfgruppe Peiper was now Sternebeck's Panzer *Spitze* followed by the vanguard unit of Georg Preuss and the 10th SS Panzer Grenadier Company – an assignment that Preuss likened to a 'suicide mission'. Preuss himself was one of Peiper's favorites, although he was not well liked by his peers. Subordinates looked at him as 'an egotist' at best, and others sarcastically referred to him as *Scheiss Preusse* – Shit Preuss.[2] Even those who favored him called him *Schweinehund,* a bastard.[3]

Peiper now occupied a spot in the convoy just behind the vanguard units.[4] Just north of Honsfeld, the panzer grenadiers scouting a route for Peiper, ran squarely into a company of the 254th Engineer Battalion that seemed to be waiting. 'Right after we left Honsfeld,' remembered one of the paratroopers with Peiper, 'we met strong American resistance. Heavy fighting caused many wounded and dead on both sides.'[5]

Well aware of the questionable nature of his assigned route from Honsfeld, Peiper had sent Preuss and his more fleet-footed SPWs to scout the westward road to Heppenbach. Soon came the report that the 'road' was, in fact, a muddy track, and Preuss turned back rather than risk getting stuck in the quagmire. If an SPW was sinking, then the heavier Panther would certainly founder to its deck. Recalled Peiper:

> On account of the obviously poor road conditions I decided to go by way of Büllingen. Büllingen itself was assigned to the Division Hitler Youth [12th SS Panzer Division] by operational order. Since I heard the noise of combat, which was due to the Division Hitler Youth comparatively far to the rear and up north-east, I thought it might be possible to pass through the town of Büllingen without causing a traffic jam … I continued along the main road to Büllingen. There was an aerodrome on the left side a short distance outside of Büllingen. About 12–13 American liaison planes were standing at that airdrome, the propellers were moving and the machines were ready for take-off. The crews of these planes were apparently also taken completely by surprise; they hid in the hedgerows which surrounded the aerodrome and opened fire on us … The vehicles in the point thereupon proceeded to strafe the hedgerows with machine gun and artillery fire and in that manner destroyed all the aeroplanes.[6]

Peiper and his point were now beyond Honsfeld, where they paused briefly for the slower vehicles to fill in. Peiper was on the move in Panther #001, driven by Otto Becker, and now headed toward Büllingen.[7] But just short of the airfield south of Büllingen, Peiper's Panther sputtered to a stop – engine troubles.[8] In the hilly Ardennes terrain, the radio had hardly been working anyway. Wilhelm Nusshag was the radioman in the regimental commander's tank. Peiper took the cue to change vehicles. Nusshag was not surprised. 'Peiper didn't like to ride in tanks,' he suggested. 'He preferred to go in an amphibian car.'[9] So Peiper briefly climbed atop the Mk V of Werner Poetschke to confirm that priorities for the advance were clear before leaving Nusshag's regimental communications umbrella: take Rollbahn C to Büllingen and not Rollbahn D to Heppenbach.[10] That done, Peiper switched to the command SPW of his old comrade Jupp Diefenthal, now leading Peiper's old III Battalion, SS Panzergrenadier Regiment 2. After all, the SPW was still the mount on which he felt most comfortable, and Diefenthal was his old comrade from all the way back in France 1940. Soon Peiper was bouncing along towards Büllingen in Diefenthal's SPW with Paul Zwigart, his favorite driver, at the wheel. 'At that time I was with the spearhead – with the point. My own command group which was to march behind the group of Poetschke now remained way behind and I decided to personally remain with the point in order to be able to take action more rapidly, to be able to encourage the troops out front and to be able to evaluate the results of reconnaissance.'[11]

With the wrong turn in Büllingen, Werner Sternebeck was just ahead of the half-tracks from Preuss's 10th Company. Earlier that morning around 6 a.m., Sternebeck had been surprised by a column of vehicles heading his way as the tank point moved out of Honsfeld. Thinking quickly, Sternebeck signaled with a flashlight for the column to stop. By the time the American driver got out of his vehicle, they were prisoners. An American supply column of eight trucks was captured without a single round fired.

Büllingen was another gloomy border town, larger than Honsfeld. Normally the population was around two thousand, but now there were just a few diehard farmers and a smattering of American soldiers. Büllingen was also the service center for troops supporting the U.S. 2nd Infantry and 99th Divisions. Men from two service batteries of the 99th Division's field artillery worked at a telephone communications center in the basement of the village post office. Soldiers from the observation battalions were spread out in houses there, along with the 2nd Division's quartermaster company. The quartermasters managed a large cache of petrol near Spa in readiness for the upcoming U.S. Army offensive towards the Roer Dams. In spite of artillery fire the previous day, word of anything serious had been lost that Sunday morning. Many of the men were just coming out of the houses for breakfast.

As Kampfgruppe Peiper rushed towards Büllingen at 7 a.m., Sternebeck's tank spearhead, with Diefenthal's half-tracks and Peiper in his personal command car, came upon an airstrip with a dozen Piper Cub observation planes for the 99th Infantry Division. Somehow the ground crews had got frenzied word to the pilots. 'Krauts! – big breakthrough!' Several of the L-4 planes were able to buzz off just before Peiper's tanks arrived. Off to the right were other planes of the 2nd Infantry Division who were not able to reach their planes; instead the 2nd Infantry called down artillery fire on their own aircraft about to be seized before making a break for it on foot. Sternebeck's armored platoon blasted the planes but found themselves chastised over radio by Peiper: forget the booty and get moving rapidly towards Büllingen![12] Twelve American spotter planes were destroyed.[13]

It was just south of Büllingen that Georg Preuss and the 10th SS Panzer Grenadier Company ran up against Company B of the 254th Engineer Combat Battalion.[14] 'The Germans are coming!' one man yelled as many men grabbed weapons and ran off to the south. Company C frantically dug foxholes just south of the airstrips near the town, and Company B deployed further south of their backstop. Until that morning, shooting had been confined to hunting deer in the Ardennes Forest to supplement their unimaginative rations. But the ominous approach of German armor made it clear: this morning was altogether different.

The first sign of trouble for the Americans had come earlier in the darkness at 6 a.m., when blue, white, and red flares suddenly erupted over their positions. Soon, tracked vehicles could be heard from the south in the night, along with barking German shouts. As the sound drew closer, the Company B's lieutenant ordered his men to cut loose with everything they had. Machine gun, rifle fire, and grenades punished the German infantry swarming from the tank and six half-tracks before them. The German grenadiers got within 14m of their positions before pulling back. The attack resumed twenty minutes later, with the German infantry flanking the American positions. Still, the enemy was thrown back a second time. But ten minutes later numerous German tanks arrived, pelting the American positions with direct fire and crushing two machine gun positions as the tanks ran over the foxhole line. One German tank was hit, but the American engineers were now overrun.[15] By 7 a.m. Companies B and C pulled out, withdrawing to the north while Peiper's forces followed quickly on their heels, intent on seizing fuel and making a rapid advance.

At about that time Capt. James W. Cobb of the Service Battery of the 924th Field Artillery Battalion in Büllingen, directed a hastily armed platoon to improvise a roadblock at the south entrance into town. The unlucky men were Sgt Grant Yager and Pvts Arthur Romaker and Santos Maldanado. They set up their ambush just behind a small rise covered by Pvt. Bernard Pappel Jr, who manned a .30-calibre machine gun. Besides a single bazooka and a machine gun, their little team only had carbines and a few hand grenades.

The men were not fully ready at 7.40 a.m. when a German tank crested the rise and rattled towards them before they could even react. It was Werner Sternebeck's *Spitze.* Recovering from their surprise, the Americans hastily ran and crouched with Yager to the cover of a hedge by the left side of the road. Soon Yager had a bazooka perched on his shoulder, but thirty seconds later another German tank approached. Firing over open sites from behind the hedge, Yager now loosed a rocket at Panzer #725, under SS Scha. Horst Rempel, from less than a hundred feet away. The round hit the tank with a loud flash and explosion; the wounded beast spun around in the road. Werner Sternebeck came up behind, watching in horror as the surviving German crew attempted to escape the stricken tank. Yager cut down two of the fleeing Germans before his carbine jammed. Then Bernie Pappel showered the steel hulk with his machine gun – the entire crew was killed. By this time the Germans pulled up a half-track teeming with panzer grenadiers. They soon laid down a blistering volume of automatic fire. Pappel was wounded in the arm and leg, and soon the little roadblock was surrounded.

There was no choice but surrender. Within minutes the Germans were moving again. The Germans did allow Yager and Romaker to give Pappel first aid, but soon a complaining SS leader arrived. 'A German officer in a cream-colored jacket approached me, talking fast in German and poking me with his pistol. I couldn't understand him, and apparently he spoke no English. He walked away, leaving me standing by the half-track, and in a few minutes the column moved on. They made the three of us sit on the hood of the German half-track.' A cream-colored jacket? Who, other than Josef Diefenthal, could that be?

T/4 Preston H. Davis was also taken captive at the roadblock, as were fifty-seven of the sixty-nine men in Yager's battery. Yager then saw the SS leader approach Romaker and motion him to leave the wounded man. 'I then saw the German officer go up to where Private Pappel lay.' The German in a cream-colored jacket motioned to another German with him, who then approached Pappel. 'He shot and killed him with his pistol,' Yager recalled. Yager had turned, so he did not see the shots, but Romaker did. 'My God!' he exclaimed. 'They shot Pappel in the head!'[16]

Immediately after the clash with Grant Yager, Sternebeck was roaring ahead to Büllingen. At 8 a.m. the tiny six-vehicle *Panzerspitze* zoomed off to the east fork of the main road, missing the main American blocking position of Company B's 254th, which was south and west of the town. Waiting for nothing, Sternebeck soon clattered down the streets of Büllingen, completely surprising T/Sgt Edward Vickstrom and the headquarters section of the 254th:

> The battalion command post was established in the town proper of Büllingen early in the morning of 17 December. We couldn't dig strategically located foxholes in town, so most of us headquarters types took up defensive positions in buildings; several of us in a main street hay loft ... I heard the sound of tanks. Not knowing if they were friendly or hostile, I worked my way back carefully to Büllingen's main street. Exactly at the same time I cautiously peered around the corner of a building, two Panzer Mk IV tanks came roaring out of a side street from the Honsfeld direction some 50 feet away from me, turned right away from me, and as they traversed the main street at high speed, the lead tank pumped two rounds into the buildings ahead of it. Being cut off from Battalion HQ, alone and armed only with a .30-calibre carbine, I figured this was no place to be for the expected mounted infantry support behind the tanks. So I quickly dashed across the street and worked my way cautiously through town.

It was daylight by the time Vickstrom reached the north part of town.[17]

Evidence that Sternebeck entered Büllingen on the east side of town comes from the account of Sgt Roger D. Phillips of Company C of the 254th Battalion, whose men had been ordered to pull back to Honsfeld after the beating taken by Company B between 6 and 7 a.m. Doing so, they were surprised to find themselves made captive by a half dozen tanks and half-tracks that approached Büllingen on the road just before the railway tracks:

> We were on a forest march, but not fast enough when these [enemy] tanks and half-tracks came at us from behind ... As we saw the German column coming up behind, we ran off to the east side of the road, but had no cover to conceal us. We encountered small arms fire from the half-tracks, but our M-1s didn't slow them down. Only minutes before, the 644th tank destroyers had set up on the main

> street north of us in Wirtzfeld and knocked out four of the tanks. The remaining tanks and half-tracks turned around and headed back down the hill to Büllingen. We were practically helpless, so Lt Anderson, our platoon commander, gave the order for all of us to throw down our weapons and hold our hands up.[18]

The Germans made Phillips and the others line up by the railway overpass on the east side of town. Philips looked at his watch. It was 8.40 a.m. After losing still another tank and crew, Sternebeck was taking no further chances. 'Driving wildly and firing from all weapons,' the rest of his armored point charged into the town.[19] 'The enemy was totally confused,' Sternebeck remembered, 'and offered no organized resistance.'

Meanwhile, the 644th TD Battalion posted at Elsenborn sent out a reconnaissance platoon to find out whether the enemy was near Büllingen as reported. They got more than they bargained for: the eight-man section under Sgt Ed Patterson was shot to pieces as they approached the town at 10 a.m. An M-8 armored car and two jeeps were lost, the occupants scattering to the surrounding buildings. Patterson managed to crawl into the basement of the Hotel Rauw, using a walkie-talkie to give hourly counts of the German armor streaming through the town. Even so, by the next day, the entire platoon would be taken prisoner – a situation repeated all over town.[20]

On the other side, Georg Preuss had taken serious losses in Büllingen – first from fighting the engineer companies attempting to bar his way and then from GIs shooting downward into the SPWs from second-storey windows in Büllingen. Preuss lost two platoon leaders – SS Hscha. Rudi Knobloch, who was wounded, and SS Oscha. Gustav Otto, who was shot through the head. 'The *Amis* fired down out of the houses into our open SPWs,' said Preuss, 'and I had to get us out of the town as quickly as possible.'[21]

The main phalanx of tanks of Kampfgruppe Peiper arrived behind the spearhead. Soon Peiper himself was in Büllingen, clattering along with Jupp Diefenthal in his half-track. Peiper later claimed that civilians in the town were 'shooting from the windows rather regularly' when he collected sixty American prisoners there and ordered Diefenthal to have them sent with their trucks to the rear. 'We captured an American fuel dump and refuelled as rapidly as possible. American soldiers were working in that fuel dump also,' he recalled sarcastically, 'and they were of great help in refueling.'[22]

In fact, the SS leader may have been confused by American soldiers in bedclothes firing against his battle group out of windows in Büllingen. Arnold Betcher was nearby with the U.S. 2nd Quartermaster Company and narrowly avoided capture:

> We moved into Büllingen on the 16th of December and on the morning of 17 December, we were ready to go after more supplies when a company of infantry came running through town. I ran out, myself, and asked what was going on and the officer in charge said, 'German tanks are coming and we can't hold them!' Some of our men and trucks with fuel were in a creamery in town and we sent a jeep to warn them. Some of those guys jumped in the back of a truck and took off

> with the German tanks not far behind … Some of our people who were left behind were captured. The trucks were loaded with 5-gallon gas cans. There were at least six German tanks and two armored half-tracks loaded with troops … One of the tanks pulled up firing on the trucks and people leaving … We picked up about 20 stragglers, but somehow got back to Elsenborn.[23]

Not all were so lucky. Fifty Americans were captured near the market square on the south-west side of town and were forced to refuel German tanks at gunpoint. The 5,000-gallon fuel dump was located on the road on the west end of town, 600m from the church by the cattle market.[24] One of the men captured later complained that, when his filling obligations were done, the Germans placed him on a tank so it would not get fired on. The other prisoners were collected near the church at the north end of town. Peiper:

> At that time, the American artillery proceeded to put the town under heavy fire, which speeded up our very rapid movements even more. The vehicles left Büllingen at full speed in the order in which they refuelled and left the town along the road going to the south-west. At this road fork [about 3km from Büllingen], I ordered a short break in order to make it possible that the column which had broken up, could close up again … At this fork, one or two American ambulances came down the road from the north. They were sent back along this road which we had come [as prisoners] without delay.[25]

Pfc. Roger Foehringer, with the 924th Field Artillery Service Battalion, was totally surprised by Peiper's advance into the town. Only eleven men out of eighty-two managed to escape being killed or captured:

> I was captured at the south edge of town with about six other guys, two of which were cooks. We were firing out of the top windows of a farmhouse when the Krauts had enough of that. They swung a tank over to the house we were in and told us to come out or they would blow us up! We were searched immediately and taken down the road to Honsfeld, passing a solid line of traffic with half-tracks with men yelling at us. When I was brought into Honsfeld, we were made to walk over GIs' bodies that were smashed into the ground.[26]

The main group of Kampfgruppe Peiper reached Büllingen at 11 a.m. Rolf Ehrhardt described his war in Panzer #701 just behind Sternebeck's *Panzerspitze.*

> Now we are proceeding towards Büllingen. Before that, we pass an American field airstrip on which a few high-wing monoplanes are parked. Apparently reconnaissance aircraft. What to do? Keep driving. An intersection in the town, stop. The commanding officer [Hstuf. Oskar Klingelhöfer] jumps off the vehicle, checks the closing up by the other vehicles, talks to the platoon leaders, and tries to orient himself. While I check the driving gears of our vehicle, the other crew members check the surrounding terrain. In the meantime, it has become day and we sit in our places. We were ordered to be ready for radio traffic. Suddenly, from the direction of Bütgenbach an American ambulance comes towards us

> at quite some speed and fully unaware. I jump out of my seat and hang on a rope. In my haste I had forgotten to take off my throat microphone. With a jerk I free myself and run towards the ambulance, which in the meantime has come to a halt. Thunderstruck, driver and assistant driver raise their arms. I make it clear to them that they should drive, one of them sitting on a fender, towards Honsfeld. Barely had the heroes left, when a GMC three-axle truck comes in view, from the direction of Büllingen. But he clearly grasps the situation faster, backs up quickly, and disappears. My pistol does not seem to have impressed him and our cannon was not ready.
>
> I run carelessly after the disappeared GMC to the curve by myself in order to determine that he is gone for good. At the right side of the curve is a pharmacy. In the window of the upper floor stands an elderly man who suddenly caused me to laugh. He wore a nightcap, as I know them from Wilhelm Busch pictures. He motions to me to be careful. Doing so he points downwards to the front door. Only then do I notice an olive green tent standing between the large firs in the front yard. I got really woozy, as I looked in and three sleepy-eyed *Amis* peeled themselves out of their sleeping bags. The warriors stand in front of me in their underpants. Fortunately, my loader Peter Mühlbach had followed me. At the same time I saw a stack of gasoline cans in a small rack right across. With arms and legs I make it clear to my three *Amis* to bring the cans to the side of the road. Supervised by Peter, they immediately start their 'work detail' transporting cans, while I run back. I reported to the CO about the possibility to tank up and drive up with my vehicle. We succeed in filling up with several cans; a few more are loaded on to the vehicle. The same is done, with more or less success, with additional tanks of our company. In the meantime, the order arrived to assemble towards Bütgenbach. At the same time, American guns from Elsenborn report with less friendly morning greetings. The crew of the GMC that got away certainly woke up their comrades. The iron content of the air is increasing and we are not unhappy to be able to leave the road to Bütgenbach.[27]

The American artillery now zeroed in on Kampfgruppe Peiper as they passed through Büllingen. As mounting blows of artillery fire began to slam into the town, the German tanks quickly took on fuel and then raced away to find roads capable of bearing tanks.[28] This fire was so chaotic that the organization of the battle group became confused once again. Preuss and his panzer grenadiers headed off over the poor cattle trails to the west of Büllingen, while the heavy panzers sought paved roads.

From Büllingen, the armor left the highway for narrow roads that were sometimes just muddy field tracks in the area of Schoppen, Faymonville, Ondenval, and Thirimont. Further behind, a large part of Peiper's column was strung out for miles on the miserable roads. A telling commentary on this section of Rollbahn D was the progress of the Blitzkrieg advance: Peiper's progress from Büllingen to Thirimont averaged just 7 km/h, hardly like 1940.[29] With each mired wheel and tank track, the vehicles following them piled up. Franz Sievers, with the 3rd Panzer Pioneer Company, was stuck in traffic jams:

> At about 1600 hours on the 16th of December in the afternoon I fell back with my SPW and I had a substitute SPW sent for [me] from the Second Platoon, from

> the group of Bode. On the 16th, I had a radio installed into this tank. Since it was not possible in the evening to drive ahead since the road was completely jammed. So on the morning of the 17th of December at around eight o'clock I came to Losheim by detours over fields and roads. I arrived in Losheim at about 10 o'clock. Then I went ahead and arrived in Lanzerath. Before Lanzerath, I came upon the wrecking [*sic*, recovery] unit of the panzer regiment who were trying to get the road clear because of the 16th December some tanks had hit mines. Since the road was cut off there I had to wait about one hour. I was asked by an officer there to look around and see if there were any more mines in this spot where the tanks were standing and I used my messengers of my company who picked up two mines. Then I sent on from Lanzerath to the station at Bucholz. I arrived there at approximately twelve o'clock. I was alone in my SPW … I caught up with the column on the evening of the 17th of December in the vicinity of Stavelot.[30]

Despite the confusion on the outskirts of Büllingen, resistance seemed to evaporate when Peiper and his combat team pierced into the town. The Americans woke up to find the streets teeming with German armor. Capt. Ralph G. Hill Jr was one of the many who hid out in the stout Belgian farm buildings. Since last autumn, Hill had been assigned as a liaison to the Belgian locals just north of the Losheim Gap.[31] Once American units arrived, it was Hill who handled the evacuation of ten thousand locals from the war zone. He had left only a few hundred farmers in the tiny towns and villages to attend to livestock and milk the cows. It was not enough. The 99th Division commander, Gen. Walter Lauer ordered Hill to get rid of 'these thousands of bellowing cows' keeping his men up all night. Hill organized a dozen slaughtering stations and sent beef back to Bütgenbach in supply trucks for use by the rear. To co-ordinate the operation, Hill had set up a communications center in the old post office in Büllingen, where he found himself on the morning of 16 December. Soon, the artillery barrage began.

Peiper, meanwhile, was out of radio contact with division headquarters. The radio in his headquarters tank had barely worked from the beginning, and he sent back his trusty messenger, Karl Paul Fröhlich, to get the latest word from the division commander, Mohnke, at Schmidtheim. Although the 24-year-old Fröhlich managed to reach the divisional command post, he found the roads completely jammed with dense traffic when he tried to return. He ditched his *Schwimmwagen* and hitched a ride atop one of Peiper's flak tanks, an arrangement that ended in Honsfeld when the flak tank was blasted by the American anti-tank guns in that village.

Even after the gun was destroyed and its crew overcome, the traffic jam remained, and Fröhlich continued by foot to deliver the message. He found Peiper in Büllingen still aboard Diefenthal's SPW. Out of breath, Fröhlich handed over the orders. Peiper took a quick look. 'Not important,' he said, folding up the paper, 'but thank you very much.'[32] Peiper invited Fröhlich aboard their vehicle. The exhausted SS marathon man boarded Diefenthal's SPW, and the loaded SPW was soon slithering along the gummy roads between Möderscheid and Ondenval.

With Peiper changing from his command tank to Diefenthal's SPW, Sternebeck was out of radio contact, and the fog of war closed in once more as he pushed forward at 8 a.m. 'Confusion apparently got to us too,' Sternebeck remembered. Until that time he had been navigated over the radio by Werner Poetschke, who was guiding him by map. Sternebeck's intent was to drive south-west towards Möderscheid and Amel. The tangle of roads in the Belgian town was confusing enough, but in Büllingen, static consumed the radio waves. 'In the town we got totally lost and proceeded north towards Wirtzfeld rather than west.'[33]

Alert tank destroyers of the 644 TD Battalion attached to the U.S. 2nd Infantry Division were lying in wait for Sternebeck's wrong turn. One kilometer north of Büllingen, where Sternebeck's *Spitze* nosed around the corner, they ambushed the lead Panzer IV, #631, of August Wien. His tank was blasted by anti-tank fire, killing Wien instantly when the commander's cupola was torn away.[34] The radio crackled. 'We could not locate the enemy,' Sternebeck said, 'but with radio contact re-established, we were ordered to return.' Realising his error, Sternebeck wheeled about and raced back through the town to head west. He detoured west, but this time in the direction of Dom Bütgenbach.

Peiper tried in vain to find Sternebeck's spearhead. Perhaps they had been destroyed? At that time, hobbling from a foot injury, SS Obstuf. Benoni Junker came up to order Panzer #615 to take the lead and advance out of the confusion and artillery fire in Büllingen.[35] SS Rttf. Peter Kasparek made the same wrong turn as Sternebeck had, heading north rather than west. Kasparek, in #615, took the lead, with the Mk IV of SS Uscha. Heinz Fremdling (#613) following along with two half-tracks. Even if an error, the German move led to momentary panic among the American defenders, as the move towards Wirtzfeld would have cut off supply and manoeuvre for the bulk of the U.S. 2nd Infantry Division that was attacking up near Dreiborn. The American V Corps under Gen. Gerow were acutely aware of the danger and rushed the available company of the 644th Tank Destroyer Battalion down south to halt the Germans.

Lt Owen McDermott, of Company C of the 644th TD Battalion, hastily set up an ambush just outside of Wirzfeld on the reverse side of a slope leading into town. As soon as the first tank came into his sights, he ordered his M-10 TDs to open fire. Alerted by crashing shells, the German tanks returned the opening volley. Even so, all the panzers were quickly hit and destroyed. Most of the crew of Panzer #615 was taken captive at 7.30 a.m., minus Fremdling in #613 who was killed.[36] Now Georg Preuss, leading his 10th Panzer Grenadier Company, also made a wrong turn as he headed west.

> The driver of the point vehicle, 1st Lt Preuss, at that point lost contact with the rest of the column for the reason that he continued along the road which I had originally ordered him to go along to the south-west. But since down there in the next town, there was another bridge – and these were points of particular danger for us – I decided at this road fork to choose the road to Möderscheid through the forest – particularly since this saved time and was a short cut and took us away in an unexpected direction.[37]

It was about 10.15 a.m. when two P-47 fighter-bomber squadrons of the U.S. 366th Fighter Group struck Kampfgruppe Peiper. Unfortunately the bombing and strafing near Büllingen did more imagined than real damage.[38] The American pilots were agog as they watched hundreds of enemy vehicles scatter as they strafed the column. 'From K-912035 to K-930025, a hundred plus vehicles and fifty tanks are bumper to bumper for four miles along the roads and going north-west,' reported one pilot.[39] Then, a flock of Messerschmitt Bf 109 fighters dropped out of the clouds to challenge the American Thunderbolts.[40] Luftwaffe Feldwebel Karl Laun was with the 84th Flak Sturm Battalion assigned to provide aerial protection:

> There they are already, those Thunderbolts and Lightnings. Their flying order is perfect – those Katzenjammer kids, diving in and out of formation and generally indulging in gymnastic horseplay. They are always there where there is something interesting to dive on. Now, the first wave of Thunderbolts starts diving on us. Our quadruple flak platoon opens up and succeeds in setting the last plane on fire. However, our positions here along the highway are so unfortunate that a series of prematurely bursting flak shells makes seven of our men candidates for the *Verwundeten* medal. Instead of the advertised thousand planes, approximately fifty Messerschmitts and Focke Wulfs arrive, who are evidently very reluctant to enter into dogfights. One can easily sense it from down here how they wriggle and turn to get out of the *Jabos'* field of vision ... the proportion of planes shot down is 3:1 in favor of the U.S.[41]

The advance was further delayed, but little physical damage had been done, and under Peiper's orders, the German column resumed the drive west.

On the morning of 17 December the 3rd platoon of the 47th Field Hospital at Bütgenbach occupied the battered four-storey schoolhouse, too busy tending to the wounded streaming in to think about looming danger.[42] Nurse Ruth Nance was more concerned with her badly injured patients than anything except the V-1 buzz bombs. 'They were the only thing that frightened me. When they stopped they dropped and everybody ducked.' All through the night of 16 December they heard jeeps and trucks driving past their facility, curious as to why the traffic seemed to be moving away from the front. 'We knew there was a battle going on,' recalled Capt. Claude M. Warren. 'We knew we were only a few miles from the front, but most of us thought it was a joke.'[43] Nurse Nance saw worrisome signs: whereas the 99th Division troops had been heading to the front two days prior in neat columns, now they were fleeing back as if a in rabble. 'I had a foreboding feeling.'[44]

Nance had been with the field hospitals since Normandy. 'We took no ambulatory patients,' she remembered. 'Most of those admitted had horrible wounds, and it was obviously a terrible place.' At midnight the hospital admitted a young GI with both legs shot off. Capt. Warren struggled all night to save the boy's life. 'You never got used to seeing people die,' Nance said.

Capt. Warren was dead tired. The surgeon took off his bloody smock and went down to eat a cold breakfast before turning over responsibility to the next team and going to bed. At this moment he heard small arms fire down the road. Everyone in the hospital ran out. 'Jeeps were racing by, each one loaded to the gills.' After a brief lull, a Belgian boy pedalled a bicycle furiously towards them, screaming and pointing downward. He had been shot in the foot, but the real casualty was everyone's nerves. Some of the doctors panicked. Just then an Army radar truck came careening around a sharp bend in the road going so fast that it crashed into the ditch. Warren ran out across the slushy ground. 'How does it look up front?' the doctor asked.

'Rough,' the soldier said, getting out of the truck. 'Got out just in time.' And then he eyed the doctor. 'What are *you* doing here?'

'We are running a hospital.' The captain looked annoyed.

'You mean you are running a hospital out here?' he said. 'You had better get yourself some guns, or you will be operating on *Heines*. Büllingen is full of 'em.'

With that, platoon commander Maj. John W. Henderson decided to evacuate his nurses and the incapacitated wounded to Waimes. Still, he and Warren remained incredulous – there was a lull in the noise. Then, at 8 a.m., a lieutenant colonel surgeon from the 2nd Division ran into the hospital so out of breath that he could hardly speak. 'Get everybody out of here and damned quick!' he yelled. 'The Germans are just down the road!' Most of the remaining staff ran off, flagging down any vehicle they could to take them west to the other field hospital at Waimes. But two doctors, Maj. John Peyton and Capt. Hollis Brainard, couldn't find a ride and found themselves cowering in the ditch when the enemy approached.

At 9.40 a.m. Werner Sternebeck drove up to the village of Dom Bütgenbach with Peiper's tank spearhead – now just four vehicles. There, he ran into the few stragglers of the 47th Field Hospital left behind, who offered to surrender. Sternebeck wasn't interested and drove on. He, in his own Panzer IV and together with the tank of SS Hauptscharführer August Tonk and the two SPWs loaded with grenadiers from 9th Panzer Pioneer Company, linked up with Peiper at the crossroads north-east of Amblève, near Hill 616. His orders were to race to Ligneuville and the vital bridge beyond.

A forward aid station run by another platoon of the 47th Field Hospital was not far away, at the schoolhouse in Waimes. That morning the surgeons, nurses, and orderlies listened with anxiety to the rumble of gunfire from the front – now seemingly close. By mid-morning incoming patients flooded the hospital, fleeing from the facility Sternebeck had overrun at Bütgenbach. While the Waimes aide station was to remain open, the stunned section from Bütgenbach was to pull back. Ruth Nance was disturbed. 'We left everything,' she remembered. 'Lt Margarte Kuntz was not even allowed to get her coat. It was the first time I was scared.'[45]

By late morning the medium tanks of Christ's 2nd Panzer Company were driving north towards Büllingen. SS Ustuf. Willi Kritzler's Panther #232 and SS Ustuf. Walter Puplik's #235 (likely the same tanks seen by Sain) were first bombed and then knocked out by gunfire from the direction of Hünningen –

towed guns of the 801 TD Battalion with clear fields of fire.[46] Walter Köbler was the loader in Panther #221 under SS Hscha. Knappich:

> On the 17th [of] December 1944 … the 2nd Company was about to reach a village [Büllingen], when two tanks of the third platoon were shot down by an anti-tank cannon hidden in a wood to the right side of the road at a distance of about a 1,000 metres. As we were just in a depression, we stopped and thus were out of range of the cannon, which was destroyed by the units following us.[47]

Another Panther, #213, was hit by a bomb from a P-47, killing the driver but otherwise only temporarily disabling the vehicle. Soon the American fighter-bombers were gone and the American towed guns were destroyed or sent packing to Mürringen.

With the Americans reeling, Peiper surged ahead. Following Möderscheid, the *Spitze* continued towards Schoppen. They didn't know it, but the tank column had been sighted by Sgt William H. Smith of Company A of the 291st Engineer Combat Battalion. He had been dispatched mid-morning to find the target of the U.S. air attacks, German troops just beyond their command post in a schoolhouse in the little Ardennes village of Ambève. There, Cpl Alfred C. Schommer, a radio operator, had just received a strange message from another radio man – uncoded and affronting all security: *Imminent Danger: Retire to Previous Position*. The unknown radio operator, Schommer thought, 'had found a jug and was imbibing'.[48] But just then, at 10.30 a.m., Sgt Smith appeared at the door with his report, breathless and wide-eyed. 'A whole column of German tanks is up there and headed in this direction,' Smith told his company commander. 'If we don't get out of here fast, we're not going to get out at all!'[49] However, their trucks were almost out of gas from a previous move. A driver was dispatched to fetch jerricans from Malmedy, and he returned half an hour later – after getting shot at by the enemy. With that, the platoon from Company A left in near panic, all personnel clinging to a single GMC with only enough fuel to rush out of town.

In spite of their gains, the German progress barely resembled the fabled Blitzkrieg. The roads were boggy and narrow; their intention to race ahead slowed to a muddy crawl. Even so, Sternebeck sensed he was now behind enemy lines. There was no further contact with the Americans, with the only delay being the roads. For nearly two hours they motored along, out of contact with both the enemy and their own headquarters. Beyond Schoppen was Ondenval and then Thirimont. They reached the later village around noon – miles behind enemy lines, dashing about with only two tanks and a couple of half-tracks. At Thirimont, Sternebeck turned north towards the Baugnez crossroads. By now, between the bad radio reception and Sternebeck's swift two-tank advance, Peiper had lost communication with him. Diefenthal himself was irate: Where was his vanguard 10th Company? Where was Georg Preuss, who should be just ahead of him? Efforts to raise his company chief on the 10-watt transmitter were unsuccessful.

Preuss, it seems, was lost in the woods. With their commander missing, the 10th Company panzer grenadiers tried a shortcut from Thirimont directly to Ligneuville. The problem was the road: a torturous trail before curving down to cross a little Ardennes rivulet, the Ru de Fagnes, with no bridge – just a muddy track across a culvert. Between noon and three o'clock, a 29-year-old farmer from Thirimont, Alphonse Grosjean, saw the SPWs bog down:

> When the battle started, rumour spread that the Germans were coming back. The day that the tank column entered the village on 17 December, I decided to leave. I picked up a bag and my bicycle and left Thirimont. I took a little dirt road that runs through the fields and eventually joins up with the road from Baugnez to Ligneuville. From Thirimont, I went downhill, passing across a little stream, *le Ru des Fagnes*, and began to go up the other hill when I heard a big roar of big engines behind me. I quickly pushed my bicycle into the forest and hid to see what was going on. I then spotted a column of about ten vehicles coming down from Thirimont. Instead of taking the dirt road, they took off cross country, and several vehicles got bogged down in the mud. From there I could see the crews waving and shouting. I was scared and I didn't know what to do, so I hid and spent the night there.[50]

Part of the problem was a lack of leadership, for Preuss himself was not with his command. Advancing past Büllingen, his leading SPW had taken Peiper's original advance route to the south, whereas Preuss alone followed the planned route. Alas, he soon found himself mixed in behind a fleeing U.S. truck column that fired on his vehicle. Being a single SPW, he ordered his driver, Kolhles, to head off the road into a thicket of fir trees – afraid the enemy column might overpower him. Parking deep in the woods, Preuss cautiously spent the entire afternoon of 17 December in the forest belt 3km west of Büllingen and north of Hepscheid. Later he came upon an American aviator and took him prisoner in the woods nearby; then, on Preuss's orders, the aviator was shot.[51] All the while during this dubious intrigue, Preuss was missing from those he was to command.[52]

Meanwhile, other columns of the Leibstandarte Adolf Hitler had shaken loose. In particular, the 1st SS Panzer Reconnaissance Battalion south of Peiper had burst into the open near Holzheim. The intention was to either reinforce Peiper or continue on with Rollbahn E – albeit not without another murderous incident similar to what had happened in Honsfeld. On 17 December eleven black men from the support company of the fleeing U.S. 333rd Field Artillery Battalion were captured and brutally executed by German forces just south of Heppenbach near Wereth, Belgium.[53] The battalion had been routed from their positions to the east, with a small contingent becoming lost in the thick forest north of Herresbach. Lost, hungry, and cold that Sunday, the black artillery men had approached the home of Matthias Langer in Wereth intent on surrendering. Learning there were no Germans there, the men were invited inside. Meanwhile, a party of four SS men arrived in the village in a *Schwimmwagen*.[54] An SS sergeant accosted villager Maria Martes with a loud '*Heil Hitler!*' asking about the black soldiers. She pointed to the home of Mathias Langer, who later described the events:

> On Sunday, December 17th 1944, eleven Negro American soldiers came to my house at 4 p.m. They came on foot, with their hands up bearing a white flag. Apparently they believed that there were Germans already in town. They had two rifles, but made no effort to use them. When they found out there were no Germans present, they stayed about a half hour or an hour and ate food which I gave them. Then four or five Germans came in a reconnaissance car looking for the Negroes who ran outside and put up their hands. The Germans searched the Negroes, took off their helmets and made them sit on the ground which was extremely cold and wet for about an hour until dark. After it became dark, the men were lined up in the street and made to run in front of the vehicle carrying the German soldiers. Neither I nor any members of my family ever saw the Negro soldiers alive again. The next day they were found dead about 800 metres from my house.[55]

Langer and his neighbors heard shots in the dark pre-dawn but did not dare go out to investigate. The following day they found the pitifully smashed bodies just north of the village in a cattle lane by the road. When the remains were later examined in February 1945, it was discovered that Pvt. William Pritchett had broken legs – as if he had been run down by the German amphibious car before being stabbed and clubbed to death. Most of the men had been both shot and smashed over the head or bayoneted – some speared through the chest or eyes.

Those responsible for the execution were likely from of the 3rd Company of Kampfgruppe Knittel, under SS Ostuf. Hans-Martin Leidreiter. Ominously, nearly a quarter of Leidreiter's troopers had been transferred to the 3rd SS-PzAA1 in October of 1944 from the SS Ausbildungs und Ersatz Battalion Totenkopf in Poland.[56] That formation had a dreadful reputation, having been a smaller unit alongside the SS Dirlewanger and Kaminski Brigades in the Warsaw. Those units had waged a murderous campaign of indescribable brutality against the Polish resistance fighters in the Warsaw uprising in August 1944.

Knittel left a bloody path of killings and mayhem in their wake wherever their SS troopers went. Yet Peiper hardly concerned himself. His eyes remained fixed on the mission – 'Lead from the front' was another of his favorite mottos. After the capture of U.S. Lt Col John Ray just outside Waimes, Peiper learned that General Timberlake had set up the headquarters of the 49th AA Artillery Brigade at Ligneuville. The AA Artillery unit was tasked with shooting down the V-1 buzz bombs headed for Liège. Attempting to seize the fleeting opportunity, Peiper ordered his *Panzerspitze* to push ahead as quickly as possible. At the time his position was about five minutes behind Sternebeck in Diefenthal's half-track, just before main body of the tank troop following. Just ahead of Peiper was panzer battalion commander Werner Poetschke in

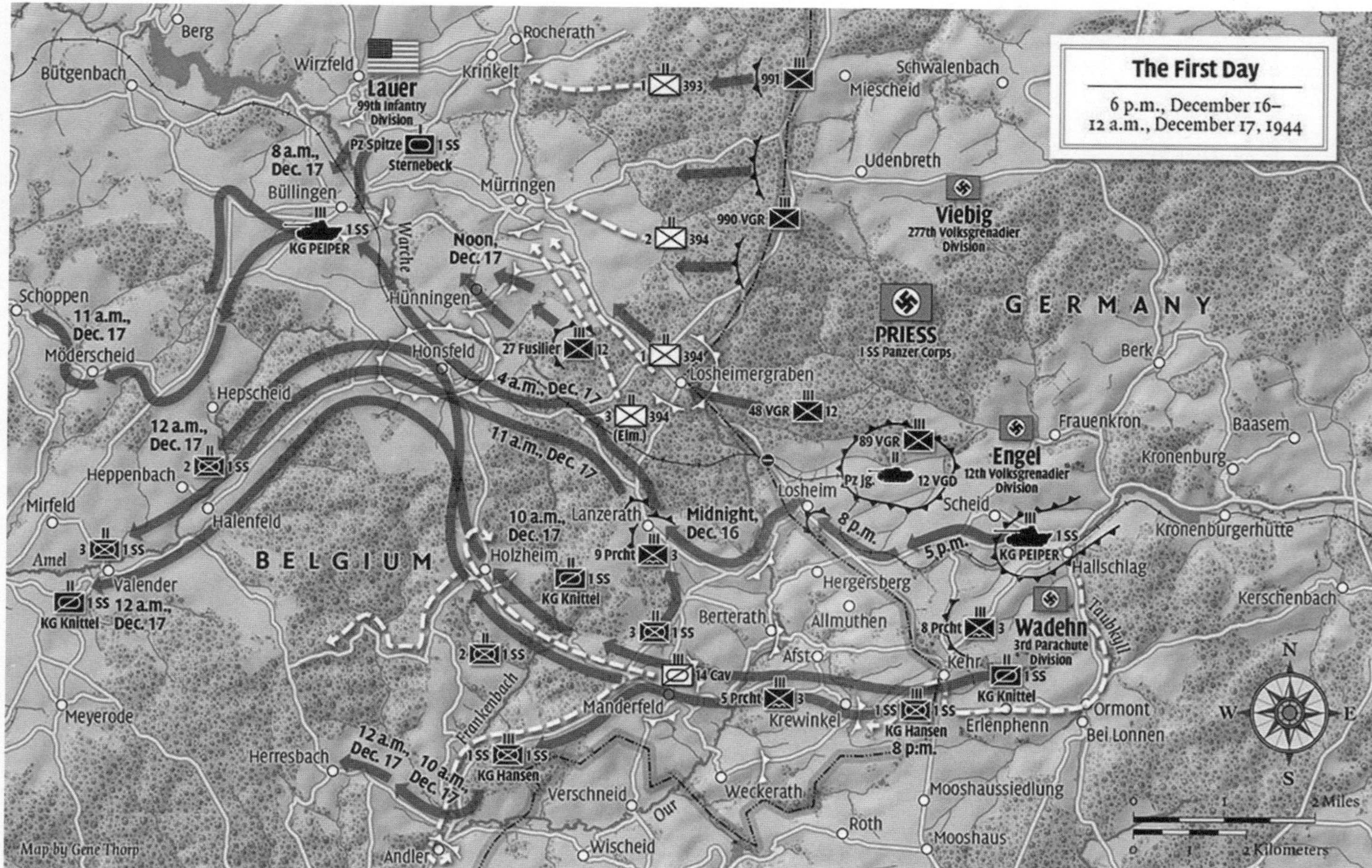
The First Day
6 p.m., December 16–
12 a.m., December 17, 1944
GERMANY
BELGIUM
Lauer
99th Infantry Division
Viebig
277th Volksgrenadier Division
PRIESS
1 SS Panzer Corps
Engel
12th Volksgrenadier Division
Wadehn
3rd Parachute Division
KG PEIPER
KG Knittel
KG Hansen
Pz Spitze
Sternebeck
8 a.m., Dec. 17
Noon, Dec. 17
11 a.m., Dec. 17
4 a.m., Dec. 17
12 a.m., Dec. 17
10 a.m., Dec. 17
Midnight, Dec. 16
5 p.m.
8 p.m.
27 Fusilier
990 VGR
48 VGR
89 VGR
12 VGD
Pz Jg.
9 Prcht
8 Prcht
5 Prcht
14 Cav
(Elm.)
Bütgenbach
Berg
Wirzfeld
Rocherath
Krinkelt
Schwalenbach
Miescheid
Udenbreth
Mürringen
Büllingen
Warche
Hünningen
Honsfeld
Schoppen
Möderscheid
Hepscheid
Heppenbach
Mirfeld
Amel
Valender
Halenfeld
Losheimergraben
Losheim
Lanzerath
Holzheim
Berk
Frauenkron
Baasem
Kronenburg
Kronenburgerhütte
Scheid
Hallschlag
Hergersberg
Allmuthen
Berterath
Afst
Kehr
Taubkyll
Kerschenbach
Manderfeld
Krewinkel
Erlenphenn
Ormont
Bei Lonnen
Frankenbach
Meyerode
Herresbach
Verschneid
Weckerath
Mooshaussiedlung
Roth
Mooshaus
Our
Wischeid
Andler
N
E
S
W
2 Miles
2 Kilometers
Map by Gene Thorp

Panther #151 and Arndt Fischer in #152 as well as the other SPWs supporting the panzer battalion.

'From Moderscheid, we went to Schoppen and then to Ondenval,' Peiper recalled. 'All along the road, the American vehicles kept joining our column.'[57] Strangely, that was true. Having just left the tiny hamlet of Schoppen, Peiper's troops suddenly confronted four American jeeps that appeared on the reverse side of a hill. These unlucky eleven Americans were from the reconnaissance company of the U.S. 32nd Armored Regiment, 3rd Armored Division.[58] The path-finding jeeps were sent that morning from Stolberg, Germany, with a mission to hurry down to St Vith. In the thick soupy fog, they passed through a captured section of the German Westwall border fortifications in the north, with its 'Dragon's Teeth' – concrete tank obstacles.

In one of the jeeps was Lt Lloyd Iames with his driver, Cpl James I. Cummings of Durant, Oklahoma. Sgt Vernon Anderson, the radio operator, was huddled in the backseat. It was cold. 'Where are we going?' Cummings asked Iames. The lieutenant told him they were scouting roads for the advance of the combat elements of the 3rd Armored Division. Neither Cummings nor his jeep mates had any premonition of trouble. 'Our job wasn't to fight,' he recalled. 'Binoculars and radio were the most important parts of our unit.'[59] 'There is nothing to worry about,' Iames told him. 'We won't be contacting the enemy.' Just the same, Cummings cradled a Thompson submachine gun in his lap as they headed south. But all that was forgotten when U.S. fighter-bombers zoomed out of breaks in the murky skies, bombing and strafing. The planes seemed to be hitting something just behind them. Cummings turned to Anderson and remarked, 'Boy, something is wrong here …'

> We went through the town of Waimes and we went a short distance and made a right turn and were going south. We went for a ways and went through some woods and then we started down a little hill with grade over a curve into a little valley. There were tall shrubs on the sides of the road and as we drove down into it, the Germans jumped up out of the bushes and started screaming … It reminded me of cowboys and Indians. But that was it for us; we were surrounded and put up our hands …
>
> It scared the hell out of us – we didn't have a chance … There was a tank up there with its muzzle pointing right down the road. They lined us up there and started to question us. They wanted to know what our unit was, our mission. There was one German officer. To this day, I do believe it was Peiper. He was well dressed, clean shaven, well-built guy. He spoke to Lt McDermott and when McDermott gave him a smart answer, the German said, 'You know I was educated in the U.S. in Boston.' Then he told Lt McDermott. 'At about 11.30 on Sunday morning, we will be in Paris.' Then, McDermott said back to him, 'If you are in Paris, you'll be behind a barbed wire fence.' McDermott was worrying me – he was going to get us all shot! The German officer stepped in front of me. 'What unit are you with?' I gave name, rank, and serial number. 'You are a good soldier.' 'Get on your vehicles,' he said. 'I know you are recon, if you go back here with me, we will show you what we have.' There was a big tank and a half-track of infantry right by us. We travelled down the road toward the south

> and they were just bumper to bumper. We had seen enough and turned around. Wendt and Iames ended up riding on a tank.[60]

Cpl Walter Wendt, a German-speaking native of Appleton, Wisconsin, was the field interpreter of the scout section of the 32nd Armored Regiment. The situation was touchy:

> When we were captured, we were out of our jeeps in a group. Then the German who was leading his column approached us and asked us, 'Is there anyone among you who can speak German?' He spoke in German and I could understand, but I did not answer although I was the only one who could. He just snickered and walked to his command car.[61]

There were tense moments, as Wendt's jeep mired in the mud and the German guard in his vehicle threatened to shoot him if he didn't get it moving. With adrenaline, Wendt and the others got the jeep back on the road. Cummings continues:

> When we got back to the front of the column, they started moving again. For some reason, I was in the jeep by myself. Originally in my jeep was Iames and Sgt Anderson. We went quite a distance with the German column. When we stopped, they put Bill Barron on my jeep and a German kid to drive it along with Sgt Anderson. We went a short distance and stopped again and they put a major and a Lt Col on that jeep. It was really loaded down. The Lt Col was from some other unit. One of the others was named [Seymour] Green.[62]

By noon Kampfgruppe Peiper, with its American recon jeep section, reached the Belgian village of Thirimont. But before that, they ran into another American jeep that nearly collided with their column. It was carrying a lieutenant colonel. Peiper was interested:

> I, myself, was riding in the vehicle of Diefenthal most of the time, and part of the time also in the tank of Poetschke … Major Poetschke was in charge of the point group … I left Diefenthal's vehicle for a short time between Ondenval and Thirimont because a jeep was standing along there with a driver next to it and since I had nothing to do at the moment and was very much interested in the tactical situation around Malmedy I questioned the driver about this briefly. The man had orders to repair a telephone line along our road and was able to tell me that the American troops had to give up Malmedy and were retreating in a westerly and south-westerly direction.[63]

Not only had Peiper captured four American jeeps of the 3rd Armored, but he had also snared Lt Col John Ray. Ray was a West Point ordnance officer who had served his cadet years with Omar Bradley. In 1944, Ray was dedicated to the U.S. Army, but before the war admitted he had more interest in polo and girlfriends than artillery.[64] All changed when Ray lost a brother at Midway. He arrived with American forces in Europe in late 1942, aiming to kick the Germans out of North Africa. Reality differed. 'Rommel took care of us, instead,' he said. He was captured and made a German prisoner while on reconnaissance after the Battle of Kasserine Pass in April 1943. But the fortunes of war changed quickly in Africa, and in June it was the Germans who surrendered to him.

After joining the logistics branch with the U.S. First Army for the invasion, Lt Col Ray found a chaotic logistics situation in autumn 1944. Now, however, everything paled with the desperate straits posed by the enemy counteroffensive. Ammunition Supply Point 126 had some 200 tons of shells strung out along 3km on the shoulders of the hard-surfaced road leading out of Waimes. It was clearly in the enemy path; Gen. Timberlake was in Ligneuville and out of radio contact with headquarters, as the Germans were jamming the airwaves. Someone needed to warn the general.[65] Lt Col Ray remembered:

> On December 16th, Col Medaris called me to his office. I drove to his headquarters in Spa that night. In his office he told me, 'We have a very serious situation out to our front.' His office was in Spa. I drove there by jeep that night. He informed me that I was to advise ordnance unit commanders of the danger that they faced from the attack that had just been launched in the last few hours. I suppose the reason he called me was because Ammunition Supply Points are not very mobile. You can use all kinds of Ft. Leavenworth language, but they are not very fleet footed. There were huge numbers and quantities of ordnance. Col Medaris wanted me to take a jeep to warn a number of installations and ammunition supply points and some quartermaster installations … They wanted me to go because army HQ was out of communications …
>
> I immediately phoned Roger, my kid brother, who was with G-2 in First Army, and told him I was to go out at daybreak and do this reconnaissance and warn everybody. 'Roger,' I asked him, 'Come and have breakfast with me, I want to see you before you go.' I left at about 7 a.m.[66] I had to get a jeep from the motor pool. I can't remember the driver's name, but it wasn't my regular driver. 'Pyree' [*sic*] sticks in my mind.[67] I had breakfast with Roger and I took off my West Point ring and I told him, 'Take care of this until I get back.' I knew what I was going to do was dangerous.
>
> We took off. Before I got to my first place to inform or warn, I was stopped by rifle fire. I don't recall what the location was or where I was sent.[68] I would have had notes made by myself and unit locations on paper on where I was going. I may have been going to see General Timberlake … Typically, I would write notes to myself for something like this; I can't remember where my notes were. We weren't concerned with records or anything you understand – it was a 'shit storm' – a mess – believe that. It was just the driver and me in the jeep on a road and we motored along. I would have given him directions on where to go. We were stopped by rifle fire somewhere near Malmedy. It happened suddenly. I took a bullet through the leaf on my helmet. We jumped into the ditch and the jeep tipped over. Within no more than a minute, there were two German enlisted men on top of us. They took charge of our tipped-over jeep and they got it started and got it on the road. I was put in the back seat. There was a German driver and another German in the other seat. We drove a short distance, not more than two miles, and I realised that I had blood on my face. There was no pain, but there

> was a lot of blood. My memory is a bit hazy after this point; I can't remember whether other vehicles were with us or whether my driver was along.[69]

Around noon they reached Thirimont and arrived at the village center by 12.30. From there, the armored group marched north to the N23 highway that ran from Waimes to Ligneuville. While Peiper determined he could get little information out of groggy Lt Col John Ray, the papers in Ray's possession told an important story.

> Büllingen was taken against medium resistance. The only unpleasant thing was the increasing artillery fire from the northern direction. We happened to come across a small American fuel dump and were able to refuel in a hurry under concentrated artillery barrages. Upon leaving Grosbois, north of Thirimont, my spearhead – perhaps three tanks and as many half-tracks – detected to their left an American convoy heading south on the Malmedy–St Vith road. When they opened up, I was a few hundred yards further to the rear riding in a U.S. jeep and questioning a U.S. Lt Colonel who had bumped into us. I learned that Ligneuville accommodated a higher U.S. headquarters and that nobody expected us … I therefore dashed to the leading tanks.[70]

Peiper had never captured an American general. A loud crack interrupted this anticipation. There was a great boom ahead. Peiper knew the sound – his tank guns were firing.

Chapter 9

'EVERYTHING HAS CHANGED ...'

The fleeting opportunity can be decisive. One must be able to exploit the moment and seize territory which is otherwise unconquerable for weeks or months.[1]

Far away from the cold and misty Ardennes where Peiper's tanks were racing westward, Adolf Hitler eagerly followed the offensive progress. From his *Adlerhorst* headquarters, deep in the snow-dusted Taunus Hills, Hitler took his cold afternoon walk. How close were the panzer spearheads to the Meuse?[2] What about Peiper? A quick check produced a terse report from Heeresgruppe B: the division was west of Hallschlag, Germany, but Peiper was further on: 'Advance unit of the 1st SS Panzer Division at Lanzerath,' the communiqué read. 'Unconfirmed reports of further penetrations.'[3]

That was enough for Hitler. In the morning hours of 17 December, he rang up Gen. d. Pztrp. Hermann Balck, commander of German forces south of the Ardennes. Hitler could scarcely contain himself. He told Balck how swiftly *Wacht am Rhein* was moving along. Reports filtering back from the haze and fog of war in the Ardennes seemed to harken to the old days of 1940 – Hitler's forces had achieved total surprise. Did he know that Kampfgruppe Peiper in Dietrich's army had penetrated 20km behind enemy lines? 'Balck! Balck!' Hitler shouted over the phone. 'Everything has changed in the West. Success – complete success is in our grasp!'[4]

Early Sunday morning, reports of clashes throughout the Ardennes now poured in to Allied Supreme Commander Dwight Eisenhower's Supreme Headquarters, Allied Expeditionary Force (SHAEF) headquarters at Versailles west of Paris. News of Peiper's slashing attack chattered on the teletype. 'As of 0625 hours, enemy tanks had penetrated our lines and reached Honsfeld,' signaled the V Corps intelligence officer, 'and thirty tanks were moving in the Lanzerath area.'[5] G-2 officers now identified both the 1st SS and 12th SS Panzer

Divisions operating in the north and splitting the seam between the U.S. V and VIII Corps. So baffling was the situation that afternoon that Gen. Omar Bradley, learning that the weather had grounded all air traffic, ventured north from Luxembourg City by command car to meet Eisenhower. Lt Col Chester B. Hansen captured the mood at Ike's headquarters:

> The crisis that developed yesterday with the fourteen-division counterattack of the Germans on our lightly held sector was reflected in the office of General Ike when I met Brad there that morning. The general did not look worried, but he was tired. Last night, he and Ike cracked a bottle of champagne to mark Ike's fifth star. Hughes brought the champagne in from Paris with him. Then, they played five rubbers of bridge, and got to bed about twelve o'clock in the morning. General Bradley admitted, however, that he had not slept well. He lay awake, thinking of the problem posed by the German attack. While it is threatening, it is not yet critical. The main force is aimed toward Liège in an effort to cut off our supply line.[6]

The next morning, 17 December, Bradley awoke early in the handsome stone villa at Saint-Germain-en-Laye that Eisenhower provided for him as quarters. But the palatial setting could cheer up no one that day. The weather was terrible as word arrived that the Germans were plopping parachutists behind American lines. Orders went out to Gen. Pete Quesada of the IX Tactical Air Command to somehow get some fighters and recon planes up to see what was going on. Bradley grumbled at the morning SHAEF situation map. 'This is Rundstedt's all-out attack.' It didn't seem as bad as Tunisia – at least not yet. By phone Bradley briefly argued with Gen. George Patton of the Third Army about the advisability of sending the 10th Armored Division north. Rank prevailed and Patton acquiesced.

Bradley was now smarting from the warning his own G-2 had ignored from Monk Dickson and First Army. But Bradley was unapologetic. 'Like most G-2s he was often a pessimist,' he would later write, 'Had I gone on guard every time Dickson, or any other G-2 called wolf, we would never have taken any of the riskier moves.' But now, alarmed that the front might collapse, General Bradley hastened back to his headquarters at the Hotel Alfa in Luxembourg City. With him was Lt Col Hansen in his drab-green Cadillac command car. For the first time since Normandy, they were escorted by a machine gun jeep.

As Bradley's entourage motored from Verdun, everyone along the road seemed spooked, dashing inside houses or away from windows. Crossing the misty French border into the Ardennes, Bradley pointed to a huge American flag suspended from the roof of a modest farmhouse. 'I hope he doesn't have to take that down,' he motioned.[7] The cottage disappeared into the gloom as they drove on. Would they have to consider pulling their troops back from Luxembourg? Hansen wanted to know. 'I will never move backward with a headquarters,' Bradley said sternly, 'There is too much prestige at stake.'

As Peiper surged through Honsfeld and Büllingen, another of Hitler's *Wacht am Rhein* brainstorms blossomed in the night sky just north of his tank route. *Operation Stösser*, with a reinforced battalion of parachutists, was launched in an attempt to block the roads in before Peiper's path that might otherwise hold up progress of Dietrich's 6th Panzer Army. Just before midnight on 16–17 December, Obstlt von der Heydte gave his men a final inspection at Paderborn airfield. The Baron was not only from an aristocratic family, but devoutly Catholic. In the inky darkness, a priest summoned from Oerlinghausen blessed both men and the aircraft. They would need it, as Kampfgruppe von der Heydte was poorly trained. The inexperienced pilots were least inspiring of all.[8]

Now, in the whipping airstream, the Baron clutched his right arm in a splint and threw himself into the night. His special triangular parachute opened, but the fierce crosswind caused it to oscillate wildly. The colored incendiary flares marking the drop zone swirled beneath his feet off to one side. Even with all his jump experience, von der Heydte struck the ground with such force that he was nearly knocked out. Soon he got his bearings and rose from the marshy grass. Above him was an angry sky filled with roaring planes, searchlights, machine guns, and anti-aircraft fire. Already he could tell there were too few billowing parachutes wafting down above him. By 3.30 a.m. the German planes were gone and the shooting racket faded. He seemed to be alone in the cold marsh. Orienting by compass, he headed off to the crossroads just to the north.

Von der Heydte arrived at the dark Mont Rigi intersection to confront a dire reality. There, in the night, he met four nervous enlisted German parachutists and a sergeant with a badly sprained ankle.[9] A few minutes later another twenty men arrived, but nothing like the numbers that were supposed to have dropped near Baraque Michel. A brisk wind whipped along the marshy ground. Keenly aware of the inexperienced pilots, the Baron suspected most of his paratroopers never made it to the drop zone.[10]

Von der Heydte continued to collect parachute stragglers by the road. Even with gloomy light on the morning of 17 December, a thick, wafting mist limited visibility as the clueless airborne troops hunkered down in the ditches by the bog. So confusing was the scene that the Americans passing through along the road assumed the human shapes were other GIs.

> At the anticipated rendezvous, a road fork north of Mont Rigi, only twenty-five men had turned up by 0600 hours; by 0800 hours approximately 100 men had assembled. American personnel carriers and tanks, passing very close to us, almost incessantly, did not bother about us and did not prevent the unit from assembling ... When I stood on the highway, American soldiers shouted jokes at me from trucks passing by![11]

Instead of blocking the Americans driving down the road, the German paratroopers hid in the woods by the ditches and watched tank columns of the 7th Armored Division pass without engaging. Contrary to plans, they were unable to call long-range artillery fire to stop the parade of American reinforcements passing by. Ostuf. Harald Etterich and his SS Hitler-Jugend radio operator had survived the jump with von der Heydte, but their radio itself was *kaputt*.

Not far to the south, Jochen Peiper was threading to the west, expecting to push into the unimpeded enemy rear. Instead, he found himself cutting west with a stream of American reinforcements moving down from the north. Von der Heydte's thousand parachutists had failed to still them. 'These men were not the same as those at Crete,' Peiper would comment wryly.[12]

The calibre of the U.S. air force on the Allied side contrasted with the disorganized Luftwaffe parachutists now on the ground below. In spite of the murky skies over the Ardennes on 17 December, the U.S. 365th Fighter Group, the 'Hell Hawks', were assigned that Sunday to fly support missions for the 8th and 78th Infantry Divisions in the quiescent area of Monschau and Düren. They knew nothing of the enemy counteroffensive. The first flight, with thirteen P-47s under Capt. John H. Slinde, took off at 10.41 a.m. with a 500lb bomb slung under each wing. However, arriving over the front, the controller announced he had no specific targets and asked the pilots to take a look around since German attacks had been reported to the south. Maj. John W. Motzenbecker descended for a dangerous treetop-level search. What he saw shocked him: the roads to the south of Monschau were clogged with trucks, infantry, and tanks.

Motzenbecker had spied Kampfgruppe Peiper; even the side roads were jammed with traffic. As he gawked at the sight below, a chunk of flak tore through one of his wings. The surprised pilot called his liaison with the U.S. V Corps: 'There's a hell of a big convoy heading into our lines just south of Monschau,' he told the controller. 'They fired at me. Could that be us, or is it the enemy?' 'That,' the controller called back, 'is the enemy!' Motzenbecker hadn't seen anything like it since the massive German retreat across the Seine River the previous August. He took his squadron in for a strafing run. By the time they arrived the enemy column had dispersed into the woods and fog.[13]

Nor was the German air force quiet. With daylight on 17 December, Luftwaffe air activity suddenly erupted to a level not seen by Allied observers since D-Day. The skies were partially clear and Bf 109s zipped across the foggy landscape, strafing at random behind Allied lines. 'All day long, the drone of planes throbbed to the crash of artillery,' remembered reporter Iris Carpenter, in Spa. 'The sky overhead got so full of vapour trails, it looked as if people had spent the day ice skating over it.' And on that same afternoon a jet-powered Me 262 roared just above treetop level across the front south of Verviers, Belgium. American artillery observers were agog, watching the roaring jet randomly strafing everything in sight.[14] Everyone took to the ditches.

Meanwhile, back at Hitler's headquarters, the German leader awoke on 17 December to the anticipated news: his armies were on the move. Moreover, his morning briefing from Heeresgruppe B had a bright new nugget. 'Panzergruppe from the 1st SS Panzer Division,' went the morning report, 'penetrated all the way from the Forsthaus at Buchholz and is now breaking through at Honsfeld.'

That was Kampfgruppe Peiper. An intercepted American message from von Rundstedt's radio intelligence service delighted Hitler.

'We are surrounded. What should we do? ... We can't find a way to get our guns out!'

'Blow up your guns,' came the answer. 'We are retreating six miles to build a new front.'[15]

Resistance evaporated. Although no one knew what had happened to Georg Preuss, when Werner Sternebeck was last heard from he and the tank spearhead reported nothing ahead but open road.

From further on came a report from Feldwebel Heinz Rohde, who was passing himself off as Sgt Morris Woodahl. Rohde headed one of the three Skorzeny commando jeep teams assigned to Peiper. In the inky darkness, Rohde watched American searchlights illuminate a wide span across the Meuse river just 300m away. While Peiper was racing toward Büllingen, Rohde whispered into the radio that his team had reached the prime spearhead's Meuse bridgehead at Huy. But Rohde was worried. The bridge was jammed with two-way traffic and the place was crawling with *Amis*.[16] They had already shaken off a challenge by some MPs along with an American officer who was looking to give them orders. Even with a perfect subterfuge and a good command of GI slang, they couldn't stay there long.

Joachim Peiper didn't intend to make them wait. Ahead, Peiper could hear the booming of panzer guns as they fired on an enemy column. To his trained ear, the shooting sounded one-sided, with the enemy hardly responding. The entire tank column, including their SPW, stuttered to a stop. What was the hold-up? Peiper did not have access to a strong radio in Diefenthal's vehicle – just an Fu.5 10-watt transmitter. He needed to contact Werner Poetschke, who was in charge of the battering ram of the tank battalion just ahead. There must be no delay. Peiper ordered driver Paul Zwigart to drive off the shoulder of the road and pass the stalled vehicles ahead. *Top speed.*

Soon they were springing ahead, using Peiper's rank to curse anyone out of the way. In the seat of his favored *Schützenpanzerwagen* with hard-riding comrade Jupp Diefenthal, Peiper intended to charge across the Meuse within twenty-four hours.

Chapter 10

THE BLOWTORCH BATTALION

One should remember the victims of the bombing terror![1]

Square-jawed, with a stern face, piercing blue eyes and a cleft chin, Werner Poetschke was a fearsome character within the clutch of Jochen Peiper's extraordinarily rugged SS Panzer regiment officers. Even though long on tank leadership with the Leibstandarte Adolf Hitler, Poetschke was a hothead, volatile and unpredictable. Poetschke's conduct in battle demanded absolute dedication from subordinates, and anything less than total obedience was punished severely. For the enemy there was only contempt. 'My backside would shake whenever I was around him,' an enlisted man remembered.[2]

Born in Brussels in 1914, Poetschke had grown up, like Peiper, in Berlin. At the time the Ardennes operation, 30-year-old SS Sturmbannführer Poetschke's rank was just under that of Peiper's. Of course, in the Waffen SS, that was *all* the difference. They were both SS officers, but there was officially no question as to who was in charge – at least nominally. On the surface, Peiper and Poetschke got on well enough, but underneath friction brewed.

Jochen Peiper was the snobbish, well-connected adjutant of Heinrich Himmler. But it wasn't just his poster boy hero status that was contemptible to the old tank hands. Peiper was often away from the front – particularly, it seemed, when the going got rough. Why was he always ill – and then being sent home to recuperate? Was it just the endless cigarettes, coffee, and insomnia-laced escapades? In truth, Peiper's experience leading the tank regiment in action was limited. In January 1944, he had overseen the at-times brilliant, but ultimately destructive commitment of the tank regiment in Russia. Later in August, after months away in Normandy, he suffered 'a heart attack' just before the suicidal blitz toward Avranches.[3] Poetschke had survived that death ride. Then, too, Peiper continued to ally himself closely with his old SPW battalion, now under Jupp Diefenthal. Whispered complaints said that most of his recommendations for medals were going to the SPW troopers rather than the panzer men. That SPW unit was his old command, and old allegiances remained strong.

Werner Poetschke, however, held the reins fast and knew the tanks. He was the epitome of the tough nihilistic SS warrior. No one would accuse the SS leader of lack of nerve, but even his superiors felt that his bravery emanated from cruel courage. While Peiper seemed Prussian and reserved, Poetschke would emote things that most felt were better left unspoken. Somewhere deep inside there seemed to be a boiling temper, so much that his subordinates greatly feared him. He tolerated no breach of loyalty or response to orders, or even simple omissions of proper dress or salute.[4] Just a minor slip might produce extreme repercussions. And Poetschke was unstable – the smallest thing could set him off. One stumble meant an offender might end up on the point of the next bold attack – a misstep that could easily mean death. Yet, Poetschke had a Janus-like aspect to his character and at times was amicable – not only fighting and training hard, but joining other regiment officers in cathartic Wirsthaus drinking binges in the autumn of 1944.

Poetschke's early career evaluations were unusual. From 1935 to 1937 he had been with the Leibstandarte, where Peiper came to know him. Yet within the troop, he was a loner and not well liked, a man known to have a cruel streak who made few friends. Perhaps reflecting his low popularity, Poetschke spent two years as an SS 2nd lieutenant when promotions should have come sooner. He received the Iron Cross 1st Class in Poland and in 1940 was cited for extraordinary bravery during the French campaign, where his reconnaissance troop found an unblown bridge across the Meuse–Waal canal. There, he had charged boldly across the span, firing wildly from a motorcycle, and shortly afterward brought back a huddle of prisoners. Capture of the bridge was decisive, and soon thereafter he had single-handedly taken out an entire enemy motorcycle unit and six anti-tank cannon near the French hamlet of Dissen.

Such a feat would generally have earned the Knight's Cross, yet Poetschke was only recommended for a long-overdue promotion.[5] His evaluation later that autumn was poor. 'He is a very uneven character,' wrote a superior. 'Again and again he does things his own way and without authority. While at times he does extraordinary things with the reconnaissance troops, at other turns he launches off into wild escapades with unclear messages and without any result. He has his own arbitrary rules and makes no friends or comrades … He misses the necessary experience of how to treat his men.' What did it mean in the Leibstandarte Adolf Hitler when an evaluation said that a leader did not know 'how to treat his men?' Poetschke's behavior was so cruel and abusive that he was transferred from the Leibstandarte to the SS Das Reich.

Poetschke's extreme behavior followed him to his next assignment. Although the SS leader had earned the German Cross in Gold for wanton daredevilry in Russia during the summer invasion of 1941, it became clear that, in Das Reich, too, he was unwanted. In April 1943 he transferred back from Das Reich to the Leibstandarte – a highly unusual move. Even so, Poetschke's evaluations turned more favorable under Peiper's tutelage. Was it because Peiper relished wild ones like Werner Wolff and Georg Preuss? Or was it Poetschke's death wish bravery? Even the man's frivolity was unpredictable. 'I never knew which Poetschke I would encounter,' one said.[6]

In the winter battles of early 1944, Poetschke was wounded three times as a new tank commander in fierce fighting. These actions culminated in his nomination for a Knight's Cross for the SS man, earned in the brutal combat near Davidkowce on the first day of April 1944. There – while Peiper was recovering at home – Poetschke fought off a massive Russian assault with two Panthers and forty grenadiers followed by a counterattack so reckless and savage that the surviving enemy fled in panic. No quarter was given; for 156 enemy dead there were only two prisoners. Yet Poetschke's contempt was not only reserved for the enemy. His abuse of subordinates was underscored in 1944 when he was investigated by a military court for 'unnecessarily severe punishment of his men' in actions at Kharkov. In the Waffen SS such a charge,could mean death.[7]

How did Peiper see him? 'He had arguments with Poetschke,' a subordinate, SS Rttf. Günther Boese, confessed, 'because he was too strict with his men.'[8] Boese was in the staff company of the 1st SS Panzer Battalion those weeks before the Ardennes Operation. 'An excellent soldier,' the Berliner would later confide, 'but a son of a bitch of the very first order due to his behavior ... He knew no consideration of his men and drove them into slaughter.' According to Boese, he frequently forced his men ahead at pistol point and often threatened enlisted men for even the smallest infractions. Boese himself was punished for being AWOL from Berlin even with a written excuse. No matter, the condemned would now join Ostuf. Erich Rumpf's engineer company of the panzer regiment which 'had become a punishment platoon – a *Strafzug*'. Now, Boese could dig for mines under fire.[9]

Poetschke had zero patience with potentially hostile civilians. According to SS Rttf. Boese, during the retreat in Russia between Korostenka and Zhitomir in early February 1944, Poetschke ordered two natives he suspected as partisans shot on the spot. In August 1944, during the retreat from Normandy in the area of Ranes near Argentan, Poetschke executed a Frenchman found carrying a rifle. Poetschke encouraged a ruthless reaction from those under him to any resistance from local civilians. As the Americans approached Paris that August, Ustuf. Hans Hennecke was suddenly fired upon from several upper windows while driving through the city in an SPW. Instead of returning the fire, Hennecke supposedly swivelled an MG-42 and shot at pedestrians lining the Parisian street. Rttf. Boese witnessed the incident from a following SPW and told how Hennecke boasted of the incident to Poetschke. Rembering the incident, both men laughed.[10]

Now Werner Poetschke was leading Peiper's 1st Panzer Battalion in the Ardennes. On the morning of the second day of the German offensive Poetschke possessed orders to blast their way rapidly to the Meuse river without restraint. Indeed, no delay could be tolerated – nothing was to hold them up. Peiper was famous for a roaming cavalry-like style of warfare; it 'was an everyday event'.[11] Peiper said: 'In the course of many other breakthroughs we really had nothing to do with prisoners of war … We were driving at great speed and firing from all barrels. We penetrated the soft spots of the enemy like an arrow and the infantry which followed collected the prisoners of war.' How did Peiper view his mission?

> During the Ardennes Offensive, I was not only the regimental CO, but also the commanding officer of a very strong armored combat command. I received a very important mission and was bearing a very severe responsibility, particularly for the reason that I did not have hardly any communications from higher headquarters from the first day to the last. I never received any order, but had to invent my own …
>
> I did not have the slightest idea where our main line of resistance would be. For that reason, the prisoner of war responsibility was a particularly severe one in the course of this mission. My tasks were of a purely tactical nature and I myself considered it my first duty to be present at the point at all times in order to speed matters up and in order to attempt to achieve some surprises in spite of the great delays of time which occurred at the beginning. In that connection, it must be also said that it certainly was not my task to personally care for prisoners of war … We had a pretty large bunch of prisoners and I felt that these represented a very great burden to me …
>
> During the whole mission prisoners did not interest me at any time. In the meeting of my commanders and officers in Blankenheim, I expressly told them that I was not a bit interested in prisoners of war and that the only important matter, as far as we were concerned, was to break through fanatically at maximum speed and that anything which in the course of our breakthrough would remain lying in the ditches, be it prisoners of war or material or tools of war, they would later be picked up by the infantry following us.[12]

The point of Peiper's battlegroup reached the Baugnez crossroads by 1 p.m. on the 17th and the middle of the column arrived thirty minutes later.[13] Peiper said he was between Ondenval and Thirimont on an American jeep interrogating a captured American lieutenant colonel. Alas, the regimental commander was out of radio contact:

> About this time, I suddenly heard my cannon and machine guns open fire. I therefore, realised that the point had hit the main road from Malmedy to Petit-Thier and, since at that moment I was alone with the jeep driver, I drove off to the point in the jeep. The column was behind me since the piece of road between this road fork and Moderscheid was exceptionally difficult. About one kilometer east of the town of Baugnez, I met my armored spearhead. About five tanks and the same number of half-tracks were standing in front of me and they were shooting with all their weapons at their disposal … at a range of about 500 metres … At that time myself, I saw an American truck convoy … The column attempted to break down in a southerly direction at great speed.[14]

Minutes before, Werner Sternebeck and August Tonk in the *Spitze* ran into the Americans of the 285th Field Artillery Observation Battalion, shooting up the trucks and motoring past startled Americans soldiers.[15] The mere sight of the long-gunned hulking panzers sent American hands reaching in surrender. Sternebeck hardly paused:

> As I stopped for observation, on the road from Thirimont north-west, some 800–1,200 metres east of the 'Baugnez' road intersection, I saw a motor vehicle column (285th Field Artillery Observation Battalion) going through the intersection in a southerly direction. The armored spearhead opened fire (explosive shells) against the moving column, which had been about 200–300 metres south of the intersection. Some motor vehicles burned immediately, the vehicles closing up and driving into each other. The crews jumped off and looked for cover. This was the moment we advanced on the Waimes–Baugnez road immediately before the intersection. Even before arriving at the intersection, the dismounted crews fired on us with machine guns and rifles. We, in turn, returned the fire with our on-board machine guns and attacked the standing column at high speed. As my point tank had approached the column to within 60–70 metres, the Americans got out of the ditch and the terrain, raised their arms, and surrendered. We approached the column slowly, and with arm motions I made the enemy soldiers understand they were to march to the rear toward the intersection. I announced by radio to the armored group that we had made enemy contact with an exchange of fire, and the result. Again, I was told to proceed to Engelsdorf [Ligneuville] without delay. There was a time interval of about ten minutes between the armored spearhead and the vanguard, in which the commander's squad [Diefenthal and Peiper's SPW] marched.[16]

August Tonk, driving just behind Sternebeck in Panzer #623, was beset by a battlefield question: what to do with all these prisoners? As they moved ahead the American soldiers jumped from the now-stationary trucks into the ditches. The spearhead now had only two tanks – weak indeed! In the meantime, Sternebeck did not even stop at the crossroads, but sped along, painfully aware that he was alone. The other tanks had not come with him; the SPWs of Dörr and Wemmel, originally assigned to the point, were now behind, having been briefly delayed after leaving Büllingen.[17] Other than Tonk, he only had a half-track load of 2nd squad engineers under Rttf. Karl Ohlrogge in his wake.[18] Right away, Sternebeck was on the radio. 'August, follow up!'[19]

Later, Sternebeck would claim that he had seen a German man at the crossroads who guarded the prisoners when he left.[20] That was likely the hapless enlisted SS messenger, Gerhard Walla. He also remembered that Tonk, behind him, had turned over the Americans to the following advance guard panzer element just behind him. An SS Unterscharführer named Manfred Thorn was driving the lead tank of the advance guard – the *Vorhut*.[21]

Indeed the only other element along with Sternebeck's tiny *Spitze* was the *Schwimmwagen* of SS enlisted man messenger Gerhard Walla. When Walla pulled around the corner at the crossroads a few moments later, he was greeted with a gust of gunfire from the American column. Instinctively, he swerved. His *Schwimmer* lurched into the ditch; a front tire of his amphibious jeep was smashed and twisted. He crawled in the ditch behind his jeep. Sternebeck was somewhere ahead, he thought. Luckily, the lumbering advance of August

Tonk's tank down the road now seemed to soon quiet further resistance from the enemy column. Walla crawled out of the ditch only to find that the tanks were gone. Now, just some SPWs were passing by. He was all alone with the dozens of Americans crawling out of their trucks and jeeps. They had their hands over their heads, but were milling about. Walla felt uneasy, but sidled up to the café to be greeted by its owner, Adele Bodarwe, who had something for him. It was a welcome bottle of schnapps.[22] 'I had no orders to deal with prisoners,' Walla recalled, 'We left each other alone!' Soon, however, additional German tanks drew near to his uneasy outpost.

Walla had been trying to extricate his *Schwimmwagen* from the muddy ditch. Sternebeck and Tonk were gone and for long minutes, Walla had been sitting warily by the American prisoners at the crossroads. He couldn't speak English, but he tried to make it clear to them that they should wait for the main part of the battle group. As much for distraction as anything else, he went to the café for refreshment. Afterward, Walla sat uncomfortably on the hood of his damaged amphibious car, weapon in hand. Two Panther tanks approached. One stopped by the café, its steel cupola popping up to reveal Werner Poetschke. Another big tank, commanded by Arndt Fischer, pulled out into the road to his left. Walla didn't notice, but just before Fischer's departure, Diefenthal's SPW bearing Peiper drove up.

It was the panzer battalion vanguard – the main body. Peiper himself was now close to the point of Poetschke's tank spearhead, not far from the road intersection from Thirimont to Waimes. 'About five tanks and about the same number of half-tracks were standing in front of me and they were shooting with all weapons … in a south-westerly direction at a range of about 500 metres … At that time I myself saw the American truck convoy. It might have been 1300 hours.'[23]

> I gave an order to cease fire several times, since I was annoyed at having my armored spearhead held up, in view of the fact that we had lost so much time already. Furthermore, I was annoyed at having these beautiful trucks, which we needed so badly, all shot up. It might have taken two more minutes until I was understood everywhere. I, thereupon, loudly ordered them to continue to drive on at great speed.

SS Uscha. Erich Maute, a medic in the SPW of Rudolf Dörr, was supposed to be right up with Werner Sternebeck and the *Spitze*, but had fallen behind in the artillery chaos on the streets of Büllingen.[24] Instead, his SPW and one other were now sandwiched between the *Spitze* – which was just two tanks, a half-track loaded with pioneers, and an amphibious jeep – and the main body of the tank spearhead. Behind them were Mk IV tanks – the 7th Panzer Company.

After they stopped, Maute pulled out his rifle and joined in pelting the American trucks with gunfire. As he and the others banged away, Maute noted some SPWs including those of Ustuf. Günther Hering and Erich Rumpf wriggled by them to move ahead on the crowded road. In the backseat of one of the half-tracks was Jochen Peiper. Peiper drove up to the tank of

Werner Poetschke just before the crossroads. Through him, he could finally communicate by radio:

> I then mounted the vehicle of Major Poetschke and ordered him to send a radio message to the Division, since I did not have any communications of my own. He was to report that the enemy was leaving Malmedy and was retreating to the south and south-west, and that we had reached the main road south of Malmedy … I then mounted Diefenthal's vehicle (an SPW) and followed the vehicles we had already proceeded to move to the crossroads. The road [leading south of Malmedy] between the crossroads at the beginning of the forest was pretty well blocked by the American vehicles. And a Panther was right in front of me and it was pushing the shot American vehicles into the ditches by alternately moving to the left and the right. I myself, with the vehicles, followed at a speed no faster than walking. At that time I saw a large number of Americans.[25]

Peiper's memory of his encounter with Poetschke was muted. In truth, when he reached the crossroads, his temper likely boiled like fire. By then, Poetschke had already reached Baugnez with his own Panther #151, although evidently damaging his tank in some fashion. When his adjutant, Arndt Fischer, in Panzer #152 arrived just behind him, he saw that a Panther already by the café had track damage, from perhaps trying to take the turn too sharply or some other ill-advised manoeuvre. Just then Peiper showed up in Diefenthal's SPW, 'springing up out of its cab to shout to the commander of the Panther'.[26] Only then did Fischer, with a tanker's typical slit-vision myopia, likely realise that the Panther belonged to his commander – Werner Poetschke.

Werner Sternebeck and August Tonk had already passed by the American column, now showing signs of having been pummelled by shot and shell. Some of the GMC trucks looked like pepper pots. Where was the *Spitze* now? And here again, the tanks of the vanguard 7th Company were shooting again. Peiper yelled for that the shooting to stop.

Poetschke and Fischer had parked their tanks at the crossroads. The only other German there was SS Rttf. Gerhard Walla in an amphibious *Schwimmwagen* – the sole remaining throwback of the Sternebeck party. Peiper had driven past the six Mk IV tanks of the lead elements of the 7th Panzer Company that had been firing like mad into the American column. The first rounds had been fired from Panzer #734 at the head column.[27] It was the first tank – the Mark IV was commanded by SS Uscha. Horst Pilarzek, and driven by SS Uscha. Manfred Thorn.

Normally, Panzer #702 under SS Uscha. Heinz Schraeder would have been in the lead of the company with #701 under SS Hstuf. Oskar Klingelhöfer following right behind – it was never standard procedure for the company commander to occupy the lead tank.[28] But Schraeder had been slowed by the gooey road leading out of Thirimont. Siptrott, the 3rd platoon commander, had also been delayed. Seeking a shortcut, most of the tanks had tested the muddy rut that led off to Ligneuville directly from Thirimont. All the tanks turned back. The lead of the entire spearhead fell to Pilarzek's Panzer #734 driven by Uscha. Manfred Thorn:

> In Thirimont, I found Hans Siptrott with the 3rd platoon in front of me. In the meantime, Siptrott, my platoon leader, had been ordered to take the lead because Sternebeck was missing. Siptrott took over the lead and I followed. In Thirimont we turned left by the church and should have driven through the forest in the direction of Engelsdorf. The 10th Company drove through the forest but became bogged down in the forest road. Siptrott gave that approach a try. But his tank tracks and wheels were so full of mud that he had to unhook it and clean it up. I drove to where Hans Siptrott had stopped in the forest and asked him what the trouble was. Hans told me, 'You take over the *Spitze*.' He was busy with his tank track, which was going to take some time. So, in taking over the *Spitze*, I received the order to drive in the direction of Bagatelle. Everything came over the radio from the Company Chief [Oskar Klingelhöfer]. 'Go from Thirimont to Bagatelle.'

At the point where trees line both sides of the road, there are three fir trees still standing today, about 500m before Bagatelle on the right-hand side of the road. At this point, Pilarzek became nervous.[29] 'There are the Americans, Manfred!' he called down. 'What should we do?' If that seemed uncharacteristic for a panzer man, Pilarzek was short on experience, having just come from another unit. 'Okay, I'll take over,' Thorn agreed, 'but you stay where you are and I'll drive.' Pilarzek nodded as Thorn continued. Pilarzek could see a long column of American vehicles – trucks – approaching on the road they were facing to the west. This was the main road from Malmedy. Thorn barked at the gunner, Werner Löhmann. 'Explosive shells at 900 metres … Fire when ready!'[30] The tank shook as each 75mm shell burst from the muzzle.

Thorn could hear Klingelhöfer's tank #701 firing, too. Driven by Rolf Ehrhardt, it was just behind him. Even further back in the column, Hans Siptrott in #731 hustled to catch up and join the firing. 'Shortly before coming to the main road, I saw the American vehicles in the distance,' he recalled, 'and fired two rounds with my cannon on them.'[31] In seconds, both the first and second trucks positioned nearly several hundred yards south of the crossroads had been broadsided. One was burning. The entire American column halted. 'We stopped firing,' Thorn added, 'I continued my driving faster than before to get to the intersection as rapidly as possible. When I came to the main road, I saw five SPWs of our troops coming from Waimes.[32] They waited for me to pass.'

> As I was driving to the crossroads from Bagatelle, I received the orders from Peiper over the radio to cease firing at the column for the simple reason that this would warn the American officers who might be in Engelsdorf. Peiper had drawn up close behind us. He wanted to get his hands on those trucks as well. I headed from Bagatelle in the direction of the Café Bodarwe. I drove up to the café, at which point the stopped American column was about 500 metres long. Many of the Americans were still in their vehicles – particularly those in the rear part of the column. We had only destroyed the first two trucks. So, I stopped in the middle of the crossing.[33]

Drawing up beside the café, Thorn saw Americans soldiers still sitting in their trucks with a jeep facing the village of Engelsdorf, the German name for

Ligneuville. He motioned for the men in the trucks to surrender. A minute went by. A big Panther pulled up alongside parallel to Thorn's Panzer IV. Dejected American prisoners were dismounting their trucks and lining up in front of the café. Out of the turret popped Werner Poetschke. 'Drive as quickly as you can in the direction of Engelsdorf,' he called out to Thorn, 'and make contact with Sternebeck.'[34] With that, Thorn suddenly realised that he wasn't the first vehicle in the assault. Glancing about, it was obvious that other trucks had been shot up in addition to those he had just fired upon. Where was the missing *Spitze*? 'There were vehicles everywhere and some of the engines of the American trucks were still running.' Thorn obediently drove off to the south, clanking by more Americans treading back toward the crossroads.

Some SPWs pulled next to the trucks and Thorn watched the men eagerly pilfering from each. They were all low on food. As his Panzer IVH rolled past the long line of American vehicles, Thorn and his crew decided to get theirs, too. One American truck seemed to brimmed with provisions. Manfred slowed down and sent radioman Willi Richter to get what he could – cigarettes, food, and chocolate. He only saw American soldiers lying in the ditches.

Just behind Thorn's panzer was the tank of company chief Oskar Klingelhöfer driven by Rolf Ehrhardt. The tank company had fired five or six shots at the trucks before Peiper screamed for everyone to stop. As Ehrhardt approached the crossroads behind Pilarzek, he saw Americans standing by the path near the café. 'At the crossing before Engelsdorf [Baugnez], I saw a total of twenty-five to thirty-five prisoners with raised hands who stood partly by the trees immediately before the right of the field and partly to the left at the first house following the crossing [the café]. A few of our infantrymen were with them.' Ehrhardt pulled up beside the panzer battalion leader's Panther at the crossroads.

'Poetschke's car [sic, panzer] stood about 30–50 metres from the house [café]. Poetschke himself, pistol in hand, stood at the near side of the car. I remember the pistol so well, as he pointed with it to my car. We stopped short and Poetschke gave us the order to drive on after we received cigarettes from his crew.'[35] Meanwhile, Panzer #702 under Heinz Schraeder clanked past to follow behind Thorn and Pilarzek as Klingelhöfer briefly dismounted to talk over things with Poetschke.[36] Ehrhardt could not hear what Poetschke told the panzer leader, but the result sent them packing. Soon, Klingelhöfer was also on his way pressing behind the other two company tanks ahead of him.

By far the strangest element in the column of Kampfgruppe Peiper as they approached the crossroads were four U.S. jeeps driven by captured members of the U.S. 32nd Armored Regiment's recon company. The Germans had earlier seized their weapons and forced them to drive along in the column, and Cpl Edward Bojarski and several other American captives – nine enlisted men and two officers – were now an unwilling element of the German battle group. From his vantage point in the middle of the German column, Bojarski remembered the German tanks in front of him belting a U.S. truck column coming from the north with direct fire. The contest was uneven. The column of green trucks lurched to a stop and bewildered GIs immediately began piling out. 'The

Germans were gathering our soldiers at the head of the column … The column was going slow.' It was a winter traffic jam, the Wisconsin man thought. With that, the Germans made Bojarski, Zach, and the others get out of their jeeps and join the other captives who were being assembled at the crossroads.[37]

Back at the café, the dense traffic of the Kampfgruppe Peiper slowly snarled toward the crossroads. Shortly after Poetschke stopped, the point SPW of the 11th Company arrived with some infantry. Driver SS Rttf. Arvid Freimuth wheeled up as the point vehicle of Diefenthal's panzer grenadiers. His SPW was commanded by SS Hscha. Heinz Hendel in charge of the 2nd platoon. Just to his front, he spied two Mk V Panthers pulled off by the long column of American olive-drab trucks jumbled by the roadside. He did not know it, but these were the tanks of Poetschke and Fischer.

Although Freimuth remained obediently at the wheel of his armored troop carrier, Hendel ordered the rest of the infantry out from behind the 14mm steel sides. Two more SPWs arrived, with their occupants quickly disarming the surrendering Americans. They were motioned back toward the crossroads. Freimuth watched as prisoners materialised from the long column of trucks that stretched south toward Ligneuville. American soldiers emerged groggily from the vehicles, hands held high. The German infantry had orders to recruit the American drivers and the assistant drivers, but none could first resist pilfering the goodies. The Americans had real cigarettes, not that ersatz tobacco that now plagued the Reich. Watches, rings, and chocolate, too, were welcome spoils of war. Minutes passed.

Just then, Joseph Diefenthal's Sdfkz 251/3 Ausf D. radio command half-track roared forward. Driver Paul Zwigart screeched to a stop, the vehicle's rear whip antenna waving in the air. There was Jochen Peiper and Jupp Diefenthal, too, in his tan flyer's jacket. Peiper stood up across from two pine bough-covered Panther tanks and several other SPWs, whose commanders emerged and rose up from behind the steel skirts and tank cupolas. Freimuth didn't recognise them immediately, but one of the tankers was Werner Poetschke and the other was his adjutant, Arndt Fischer. Diefenthal stood with the tank regimental commander at his side. Peiper raised one hand. 'He gave us a bawling out,' Freimuth remembered. His SPW was only 5 metres behind Peiper's vehicle.[38]

Hans Assenmacher, a Rhinelander from Oberhausen, recalled the same scene from inside Peiper's SPW. Assenmacher, the radio operator, had been sitting beside Diefenthal's driver, Paul Zwigart, as they bumped along on the muddy road from Thirimont. Passing through a copse of heavy pine woods north of that town, they soon approached the crossroads. Diefenthal and Peiper conferred in the gloomy light sitting across from each other on the blanket-covered metal benches behind Zwigart, who was wearing his good-luck driver's ski-cap. Then, the sound of shooting blared through the headphones that covered Assenmacher's ears. The column slowed to a crawl some 150m before the Baugnez crossroads. Curious, Assenmacher stood up in the armored half-track. From there he could see that ahead a column of American trucks had run into the first tanks of Kampfgruppe Peiper.

As Assenmacher recalled, there was a lot of firing, most of it German. Some of the American trucks were peppered with bullet holes and clearly ruined. Even distracted by the radio, he could tell that Peiper was angry. Still, even with some tanks taking a short cut across the meadow for the other side of the crossroads, the column snarled to a stop. Jupp Diefenthal suddenly rose from his seat beside Peiper, jumped off the SPW, and trotted off toward the crossroads. At Peiper's behest, Assenmacher had been striving to establish contact with SS-Ostuf. Georg Preuss, the commander of the 10th Company, missing since they had left the Belgian village of Büllingen hours before. Where was Preuss and the panzer grenadiers? And for that matter, where was the *Panzerspitze* and Werner Sternebeck?

As they started moving once more, Assenmacher tried again without success to raise them on the powerful 30-watt *Friedrich* transmitter as they started moving again, slushing their way through the muddy ditch alongside the stalled column. Ahead, the sounds of shooting continued. Presently, Peiper's SPW drew close to Werner Poetschke's tank near the crossroads. He was barking out orders even before they stopped. Jupp Diefenthal, who was now back in the saddle, could see that Peiper was displeased. 'Stop this firing!' he insisted, 'We need these trucks for our supply system.'[39] American prisoners were still milling about and being assembled just south of the crossroads – another annoyance. Soon Peiper and the SPW continued on. Had Peiper told Poetschke anything about the prisoners? There was the brief slip on that subject by Paul Zwigart to a fellow prisoner later in the summer of 1945.[40] Otherwise none of the witnesses would say anything more: an SS *omertà*.

Whatever the contents of that fateful conversation, in moments, Diefenthal's *Funkpanzerwagen* SPW passed the crossroads and turned off toward Ligneuville (Engelsdorf in German), gliding past abandoned U.S. artillery observer trucks. A sign floated by on their right; Malmedy was only a few kilometers away, and would provide a lot better road route to the Meuse than the trail-like Rollbahn D. 'Let's make an excursion to Malmedy,' Diefenthal motioned to Peiper. 'Too bad we can't do that,' Peiper responded, 'we have orders to the contrary.'[41] Even if Herbert Kuhlmann (12th SS Panzer Division) was nowhere to be seen, Panzer Rollbahn C passing through Malmedy was assigned to his other SS tank group.[42] Peiper moved his hands to the sides of his eyes with the palms facing inward. In boyish mocking contempt for superiors, Peiper simulated the blinkers on a horse's bridle. Narrow vision – they would stay on the bad roads that went to Ligneuville and then double back north to Stavelot, taking the long way around.

That possibility vetoed, Diefenthal's HQ half-track had only gone a short distance when Zwigart wheeled behind another SPW that had pulled off to the right side of the road. Still clad in headphones, Assenmacher, fiddling with the radio, could hear Peiper bellowing at the German soldiers standing next to the SPW. Peiper waved his hand back in the direction of the crossroads behind them. Assenmacher cocked his head up from the radio set and pulled the headphones from one ear, thinking that Peiper wanted his attention.

'Of which company are you?' Peiper snapped.[43] It was clear he was addressing the German soldiers lolling about. '*Nine Panzer Pioneer*,' answered one. 'What is the matter with you?' Peiper flared, 'Why are you still standing here?' 'We had a link-pin break,' was the response. 'Get that fixed,' Peiper shot back without hesitation, 'and drive on as fast as possible.'

Diefenthal sat in the SPW across from Peiper, Freimuth recalled. Diefenthal sported a yellow leather jacket with fur lining and a visored cap. Peiper was arrayed in a dark submariner's fur-lined jacket with a front zipper, his *Ritterkreuz* dangling from his collar. Their SPW pulled up to the left behind him as a number of other SPWs had collected by the crossroads. The infantry from the vehicles were searching the prisoners and assembling them in the field. Several other Mark IV tanks arrived on the scene, but Peiper was impatient. Even as Freimuth and his crew hastily departed to follow behind Arndt Fischer's Panther, Peiper was standing in the SPW, still yelling. Freimuth recalled his exact words. 'Goddamn it!' Peiper cursed. 'What kind of business is it to stop here for hours?' Peiper turned to the tank commanders scornfully. 'The little that is to be done here,' he continued, 'the men in the rear will do!'[44] Just then the radio crackled. 'Fischer proceed!' The Panther of Arndt Fischer lurched ahead with Diefenthal's SPW pulling in just behind.

They had been at the intersection for scarcely five minutes, but Assenmacher claimed to have been too busy tweaking the radio to notice the American prisoners assembling nearby. Yet as they waited there Diefenthal had suddenly appeared and jumped on board. Peiper's flash of anger seemed to fade. Even though he knew there may be an American general in Ligneuville, Peiper also expected some resistance there, and wanted thick armor and a big gun ahead of his thin-skinned half-track. He waved his arm forward, signalling Arndt Fischer's Panther and a couple of other tanks to throttle up toward Ligneuville ahead of him.

Another short delay came along the curvy road that sloped downhill to Ligneuville. In spite of Peiper's admonitions about time lost to looting, even he couldn't resist when they discovered an abandoned American jeep loaded with booty. Zwigart screeched the *Schützenpanzerwagen* to a stop. Assenmacher poked around the drab-green vehicle, soon emerging with spoils. Diefenthal reached for a pack of Camel cigarettes, but Peiper satisfied himself with a fistful of the GI square-shaped K-ration biscuits. Just at that moment, came a distant spasm of machine gun fire. The sound echoed from the direction of the crossroads – clearly the staccato rip of an MG-42. Peiper raised his arm and motioned everybody forward. As they roared off, Hans Assenmacher could still hear the sound of firing behind them.[45]

Paul Zwigart was unhappy. Although Diefenthal thought the youth was a good driver, Zwigart's nerves were shot since being buried by Allied bombs in Normandy. For his part, Zwigart found Diefenthal, who took over the 3rd Battalion in August 1944, harsh and unrelenting. Now, as Diefenthal's command vehicle driver, he seemed to always find himself at the front and in harm's way. Peiper was better, but things always seemed on edge. 'He was always in a hurry.'[46] But now Zwigart wrenched the big, black steering wheel to put their SPW back on the road. He was soon drafting behind the hulk of Fischer's big Mk V Panther tank.

Back by the crossroads, Poetschke's Panther had suffered damage when he used it as a battering ram to push American trucks off the road. It remained behind just across from the Café Bodarwe, its muzzle pointing into the field where the American prisoners were gathering. The verbal thrashing from Peiper left Werner Poetschke fuming. He dismounted his Panther and walked down among the American prisoners skulking back toward the crossroads. 'Chauffeur? Chauffeur?' he called out.[47] It was the best English he could muster to recruit American drivers. For the most part, the American artillery observer GIs ignored him.

Walla was understandably focused on Poetschke. Before the punishment assignment with the *Panzerspitze,* the enlisted man had been with the staff company of the 1st Panzer Battalion. Now, Poetschke was speaking to him – an intimidating prospect as Walla's *Schwimmwagen* was still stuck in the ditch. It smacked of incompetence. Other tanks and vehicles passed by. Walla quickly explained his situation. Even if his vehicle was hopelessly marooned in mud, at least he was guarding these prisoners. He could report that Werner Sternebeck and the *Spitze* were somewhere ahead. Seemingly satisfied, Poetschke told him to wait around until SS Ostuf. Rumpf appeared with help to get his vehicle out of the ditch. 'What about the prisoners?' Walla asked. 'We don't bother with them,' Poetschke responded. 'The infantry will come.'[48] Yet Reinhard Maier, the I Panzer Battalion communications operator heard the same question from Walla, but related a very different answer from Poetschke. 'What to do with the prisoners?' 'Kill them!'[49]

In the panzer column just behind Peiper and Diefenthal were the SPWs from the 9th Panzer Pioneer Company and similar vehicles from the 3rd Panzer Pioneer Company.[50] The blond-haired leader of the 9th Panzer Pioneer was 23-year-old SS-Ostuf. Erich Rumpf. Born to a miner's family in Bleicherode am Harz, Rumpf had fought a long time with the Leibstandarte – often in a role that brought him into contact with the unsavory underbelly of the Waffen SS. Even though sympathisers later claimed they were 'soldiers like any others', their enemies claimed otherwise. At a young age, Rumpf had been with the Hitler Jugend and joined the Waffen SS in September 1939. He graduated as an SS leader and was assigned the Leibstandarte on 30 January 1942.[51] Rumpf was a convinced SS leader. 'We were adherents to National Socialism,' his wife would later write, 'because we did not know anything else … but there was war, and war is brutal.'[52]

From France to Russia and back again, Rumpf fought with the Leibstandarte on nearly every front, eventually moving to the thankless leadership position of Peiper's disciplinary platoon. That group was filled with the worst types.[53] There was the bestial campaign in Russia – a behavioral justification that Rumpf was only too willing to invoke. Yet in Werner Poetschke, Erich Rumpf seemed to meet his match. He incited the worst type of behavior – or at least said some Rumpf-sympathetic subordinates after the war. Others painted a less charitable picture of Rumpf himself. They said he talked the same killing game as Poetschke.

Indeed, in a meeting of his unit at the end of November 1944, a radio operator in one of Rumpf's SPWs, SS Private Walter Fransee, recounted a speech made by Rumpf on the first floor of a school building in Eckdorf, Germany. 'The reputation of the SS has to precede kilometers ahead of us.' Rumpf told his audience, 'In this connection, he also said that no prisoners were to be taken.'[54] Yet for Fransee, such exhortations were hardly new; this type of warfare matched other horrific experiences in the East. A vividly disturbing memory, he said, took place at the end of February 1943 when a Russian village near Kharkov – supposedly harbouring partisans – was ruthlessly burned down on the orders of Kurt 'Panzer' Meyer.[55]

Fransee recalled other horrors at Ziglerowka and Utgatschi. Meyer was not the only Waffen SS commander right out of Joseph Conrad's *Heart of Darkness*. Of Jochen Peiper's command, Fransee said, 'Ever since, his battalion has been called the *Lötlampenabteilung* and has a burning blowtorch as its symbol.' The implication was clear. Hardly a smear, that moniker was an SS epithet of honor.[56]

Chapter 11

AT THE CROSSROADS

Take up the bodies; such a sight as this
Becomes the field, but here shows much amiss
Go, bid the soldiers shoot.[1]

In early December 1944, during sand table exercises with Jochen Peiper and Werner Poetschke at Weilerwist, Germany, the SS leaders there emphasised 'that the rules of warfare which up to then had been followed in the West would not be strictly adhered to'. Even more, in a later meeting with Peiper in mid-December, Erich Rumpf was advised that in the coming operation, 'the situation can arise when prisoners of war have to be shot and if necessary the resistance has to be broken by terror'. While Rumpf, the head of the 9th Panzer Pioneer company, was reading this order, Jochen Peiper entered the room. Peiper glanced at the paper and then repeated his sardonic epithet, 'Also, a bad reputation has its commitments.'[2] It was one of Peiper's long-standing mottos, the adoption of a suggestive refrain from heart-throb singer Zarah Leander.[3] With his penal squad, Rumpf always drew the dirtiest jobs.

At the head of the German armored column, just behind Sternebeck who was further on, Jochen Peiper and Diefenthal in their SPW ran across some Americans being escorted back to the crossroads after being taken captive. The German officer laughed. 'It's a long way to Tipperary boys!' he shouted in English as captive American soldiers, Al Valenzi and Bill Merriken, marched north with their hands up. They had been greeted by Jochen Peiper.[4]

Back at the crossroads on 17 December 1944, Poetschke got his Panther tank operating and then clattered down the road after Fischer and the others in the vanguard. Just before he left, Panzer #602 under Uscha. Wrabetz came by the crossroads, seeing the American prisoners still standing with their hands up. His loader, Rttf. Michael Mundt, recalled seeing some civilians by the café as well as Diefenthal and Peiper in an SPW. They had been parked by a tank across from the assembled Americans. Stubf. Poetschke was on foot, and he ordered them to hurry south.[5] Mundt motored partway to Ligneuville, when the communications SPW of the headquarters company of the 1st Panzer Battalion of the 1st SS Panzer Regiment drove up. SS Rottenführer Reinhard Maier, the half-track driver, was stunned by the conversation he overheard that followed:

> At about 1300 hours on 17 December 1944, his [Maier's] SPW was about 1 kilometer past the field in which the massacre occurred. He parked on the road behind the Mk V (Panther) in which SS Sturmbannführer Poetschke was riding. Witnesses saw forty to fifty American POWs being led back to the rear [from the field]. After about twenty minutes, a messenger arrived from the rear from the 9th Panzer Pioneer Company that had been detailed to assemble the prisoners and asked Stubf. Poetschke what to do with the prisoners. Poetschke, in his presence, said: 'Shoot them.'[6]

Although no record remains, the messenger seems to have returned to deliver the news to Erich Rumpf.[7] Eventually, it became common knowledge in the panzer regiment that Poetschke ordered the crossroads shootings.[8] Rumpf was parked just before the intersection across from the café. Ten metres further back was the 1st platoon SPW of Uscha. Günther Hering.[9]

> We stood there awhile when Obstuf. Rumpf motioned for us to come to him. At that time he stood in front of a house [café] which stood directly at the corner of the right-hand side of the street … We had not yet arrived when he shouted to us to get our weapons and follow him right away. He led us – the whole crew of the SPW of Oscha. Wedeleit – to a pasture which was immediately south of the house. We stood on the north side of this pasture next to the street. On this pasture approximately ninety American prisoners were standing with their hands raised … The prisoners had no arms [weapons] and stood there quietly … Immediately thereafter Ostuf. Rumpf gave us the following order after we arrived: 'Bump the prisoners off.' … Thereupon we opened fire on the prisoners of war and at the same time, from the machine guns of the tanks and SPWs that also stood on the street at this pasture.[10]

Willi von Chamier and the others of a nearby SPW had moved before the prisoners on foot, only to find a line of SPWs and tanks already across from the prisoners. On orders, von Chamier said he personally fired half a dozen shots with a carbine:

> We returned to our SPWs and mounted after the prisoners had fallen to the ground. Only Haas remained in the pasture and I saw from our SPW Haas walking once more among the prisoners and shooting the prisoners lying on the ground. One case I remember especially clearly, namely one of those lying on the ground and believed to be dead, raised himself halfway up. He pointed to the rear part of his body which gave me the impression that he was wounded there. Haas also shot this man dead with his machine pistol. After the shooting was over, we received an order from Ostuf. Rumpf to proceed on our march.[11]

Walter Fransee, the radio operator in Hering's SPW, also saw Hering himself join in firing at a kneeling prisoner. These were a small group who came out of the woods with their hands up approaching their SPW to surrender. When he was 8m away, Hering blasted the man in the chest with a full magazine of machine pistol rounds. That done, he then casually handed the empty magazine to Fransee to reload.[12]

Had Rumpf been responsible for the orders to shoot? His underlings, Dörr, Rieder, and von Chamier said so. Moreover, many saw him at the place of the massacre.[13] Indeed, two witnesses said Rumpf personally fired his own pistol into the prisoners. And in his own long-winded statement to investigators, he admitted that he was at the crossroads when the massacre took place, but said the thought of seeing the prisoners shot was mentally too much. In a tortured alibi, Rumpf said he hid in an American truck, stuffing his pockets with American K-rations.[14]

Rumpf described how his line of SPWs stopped short of the crossroads, but he observed some other SPWs and a Mk IV tank lined up across from the café. Rumpf said that he volunteered Dörr's men, only to have them return minutes later. 'This man tells me that I should shoot prisoners of war!' Dörr protested. His men began returning back from the field just as two Mk V tanks, including that of Hans Hennecke, drove up to the crossroads and paused in front of the café.[15]

> All of this happened before the shooting started. After I talked to Oscha. Dörr, I went to an American truck as I did not want to watch the shooting that was about to take place. During this time my SPWs totalling four or five stood on the road directly before the crossing. Some other SPWs and panzers drove slowly around the corner. After I stood at the truck for about one or two minutes while the men unloaded 'K' rations, the firing at the prisoners of war standing next to the house began, which I could hear but not see. A great number of weapons were fired; machine guns, rifles, and pistols. This shooting lasted about one-half minute or a little less. Immediately following it, some single shots were fired. Three minutes after the big shooting was over I left the American truck and went to my SPW. I shouted to my men, 'Let's go – we move out!' About a minute later we drove off in the direction toward Engelsdorf.[16]

Peering through the grey mist, not only had Erich Rumpf and his men seen their own SPWs at the north end of the crossroads, but they also observed other camouflaged German half-tracks mixed among the tanks of the 7th Panzer Company. These were the vehicles of the SS Uscha. Max Beutner's 2nd platoon of the 3rd Panzer Pioneer Company carrying bridging equipment and arriving early on the scene – about the same time that Rumpf stopped just short of the crossroads. Straightaway, he took over guard of the prisoners with one or two half-tracks of the 11th Company. As Peiper had emphasised that everyone keep moving, the job of guarding the prisoners was a shifting responsibility – and one that Werner Poetschke looked to end swiftly.

Two of Beutner's Sdkfz. 251/7 SPWs arrived laden with grenadiers bristling with automatic weapons sticking above their siding of steel bridging equipment. They pulled off to the right side of the road before the assembling prisoners. SS man Joachim Hoffmann and the armored half-track of Sepp Witkowski and its crew of twelve had arrived at the Baugnez crossroads after 1 p.m. Just before they reached the intersection, they passed three SPWs of Erich Rumpf parked on the right side of the road. Turning left and continuing on, they found the SPW of Max Beutner, with its three-gun 1.5cm 'Drilling' AA guns already trained on a group of a hundred Americans standing in the field. Ahead, he claimed to have seen the assault bridge SPW of Friedel Bode, driven by Herbert Losenski. As Hoffman moved up to pass his platoon leader on the right, Beutner called out to him. 'After I had pulled the SPW to a stop, he told us to get the machine guns ready and that the men should get ready to "Bump off the prisoners."'[17]

That deadly preparation took some time; the weapons were not loaded nor sited properly to allow them to fire to the right. Minutes passed as machine guns were moved and belts of ammunition were prepared. 'Bump them off! Bump them off!' Hoffmann claimed someone was shouting and Gustav Neve remembered that it was Beutner himself who egged them on: 'Bump them off – all of them!'[18] Machine gunner Heinz Stickel in the same SPW recalled seeing sixty odd Americans standing in the meadow across from him just before direct orders from SPW leader Witkowski to shoot into them.[19]

'As far as I remember,' Hoffmann wrote, 'the first shots were from Beutner's SPW.' After that everyone joined in the firing. After the deadly fusillade ended, Beutner ordered everyone into the field to administer mercy shots to the Americans still alive. Hoffmann admitted having participated in those grim proceedings. Hoffmann recalled that there was a line of tanks slowly passing behind them as Beutner stood in the road and ordered everyone to fire. A lot was going on. Like Sprenger, Hoffmann said that he had seen Jupp Diefenthal and Erich Rumpf at the crossroads. Both were congregated around a Panther some distance north of the prisoners – the tank of Werner Poetschke. That all happened just minutes before the shooting took place.[20] No evidence placed them elsewhere.

Deepening the moral bog of the 3rd Panzer Pioneer Company, SS men Gustav Neve, Siegfried Jaekel, and Heinz Stickel gave accounts corroborating Hoffmann. They were all in the same SPW directly across from the American prisoners.[21, 22, 23] Based on their multiple accounts, the SPW of Max Beutner was the first vehicle on the scene after Sternebeck's *Spitze* disappeared. As driver Joachim Hoffmann approached, Max Beutner stood in the middle of the road, his hand stretched out and signalling them to halt. The prisoners were to be shot, Beutner informed Sepp Witkowski – a conversation witnessed by a number in this half-track. He ordered them to move just a bit further on and park across from the prisoners so as to not block his field of fire. Obediently, they complied.

Soon afterward, Beutner was seen conversing with some officers by a Panther who had been located north of the field. Erich Rumpf was among them.[24] Presently, another SPW belonging to SS Uscha. Gerhard Schumacher of the 11th Panzer Grenadier Company happened on the scene. Without hesitating, Beutner ordered Schumacher to load his stubby 75mm assault cannon and prepare to blow the prisoners off the field. Schumacher turned his SPW so it was directly facing the assembling group of Americans. Even though personally horrified, SS Grenadier Heinz Friedrich noted that, 'Uscha. Schumacher seemed delighted at the chance to shoot these prisoners ... he rubbed his hands together calling out "*Masche, masche!*"' It was the infectious bad-boy expression of their leader, Georg Preuss. Even so, Schumacher's crew could not depress the short, stubby 7.5cm cannon from the road to train it upon the increasingly uneasy Americans in the field.[25] Beutner waved Schumacher on, Friedrichs overhearing him remark that the next tank 'would take care of the job'.

Meanwhile, Jaekel and other crew members just south of Beutner's SPW prepared Witkowski's automatic weapons for the execution salvo that was to come.[26] Belts of ammunition were loaded swiftly and machine guns sited so they could fire off the right-hand side of the SPW hulls. At the same time, a line of Mk IV tanks from the 7th Panzer Company were making their approach. Just as Beutner had flagged down the SPWs of Dörr and Schumacher moments before, he was now attempting to halt oncoming tanks. Several of the machines managed to slip by, and Beutner quickly signaled Panzer #731, which was approaching across the field to the east. On the road behind it paraded a line of Panzer IVs.

Sprenger and Oettinger's armored personnel carriers were just arriving when the shooting began. Marcel Boltz, the Alsatian machine gunner in Sprenger's SPW, claimed to hear a gust of machine gun fire just before he reached the crossroads. Ahead of him was the SPW of Max Beutner, the platoon leader. A short way up the line Friedel Bode and Sepp Witkowski drove their own carriers. If he turned around, he could see the SPW driven by Hans Oettinger.[27] 'We will start firing!'[28] Beutner shouted before a brief pause. 'Shoot!' Grenadier Siegfried Jaekel's yelled a split second before the crack of pistol shots shattered the air. Goldschmidt in Beutner's SPW opened fire. As if on cue, everyone with a weapon immediately joined.[29]

Not long before Max Beutner and Erich Rumpf tried to locate help to do-in the prisoners, the 7th Panzer Company began to snake by the half-tracks that had pulled off the road. The grinding traffic was constant. Sternebeck and Tonk with the *Spitze* were now far ahead. Behind them had been Pilzarek's #734 driven by Manfred Thorn with Schraeder's #702 and then Klingelhöfer's #701 driven by Rolf Ehrhardt just behind him. The crews of these three tanks (734, 702, and 701) had passed by while Rumpf and Beutner sized up the assembling prisoners. Unluckily for the crew, the next panzer approaching Beutner's position was #731 under Peiper's old panzer hand from Russia, SS Oscha. Hans Siptrott.

Immediately behind Siptrott was Clotten's Panzer #723. The tank had got mired near Thirimont in the same muck that had immobilised Hans Siptrott. With effort, both Mk IVs were freed to resume their advance. As the tanks had lost their place in the march formation – Panzer #734 under Horst Pilarzek was in the lead – together, they took a shortcut north of Thirimont, cutting across the hedgerow-lined pasture before the Baugnez crossroads. Intending to resume their place in the line, both regained the road just south of the café and across from the American prisoners assembling there. Panzer leader Hans Siptrott:

> Approximately sixty American prisoners of war, with hands raised over their heads, were standing on the right-hand side of the shed in the field … On the right-hand side of the road, exactly opposite them, were two or three SPWs – I believe there were three. I passed the SPWs at 15–20 kilometers per hour. There I took notice as a commander of one of the SPWs waved at me. I stopped and this commander approached me and said: 'Turn your gun around and shoot into them.' I answered him, 'I don't have enough ammunition for such a thing.' I did not know this above-named commander. I believe that the SPW belonged to the 9th Pioneer Company because the SPW standing nearest to me was equipped with bridging equipment …[30] During the time I was talking to the commander of the SPW, Sturmmann Fleps was sitting in the loader's slit. When I turned around, I saw that Fleps, who apparently was eager to shoot, had a pistol in his hand. Because Hstuf. Klingelhöfer had made a speech to the platoon leaders telling us that we should not take any prisoners, I permitted Fleps to shoot … I said to Fleps, 'Shoot!' As far as I can remember, he fired two shots, one immediately after the other. Right after that, or almost simultaneously, the SPW standing nearest to me started shooting … Hardly more than a minute after the shooting started, I gave orders to resume march.[31]

The key player in Panzer #731 was SS enlisted man Georg Fleps:

> Just past the intersection on the right side which leads to Engelsdorf, I saw many Americans standing in the field with their hands up … At this time I was assistant gunner in my tank, which was #731 … Up ahead of us was a Mk V tank. Behind us drove SS-Oscha. Clotten with his tank … On the right side of the street opposite the group of captured Americans stood an SPW with its machine gun pointed at the Americans. As we approached the SPW, the commander gave us a signal with his hand to stop.[32] He said to Siptrott: 'We have received orders from up ahead to bump off the Americans. Everything must go quickly. Every vehicle is needed up ahead. Help us with this and make it go fast.' Siptrott said at first, 'I do not have much ammunition.' Then the commander said something else to Siptrott whereupon Siptrott, who saw that I already had my pistol in hand, gave me the order to shoot. I then fired a shot at one of the Americans standing in the front row and I saw him fall over. … As far as I know, this shot of mine was the first one shot at the Americans. Immediately afterward, the SPW behind us (we had driven up a little) began to fire with its machine gun at the prisoners. At that, Siptrott remarked, 'These wretched dogs.'[33] When the machine gun on the SPW ceased firing, a single American was still standing up straight. I pointed my pistol at him and fired. Watching my shots, I saw him fall … Just as we drove away, the machine guns commenced firing again.[34]

Roman Clotten in Panzer #723 was grinding forward just behind Siptrott. Prior to the events, he spied a long line of American trucks seemingly guarded by a lone Mk V Panther tank that stood stationary at the crossroads just to his rear. He didn't know whose tank it was, but considering his position near the point, he surmised that it must be the vehicle of Poetschke, or Fischer his adjutant who had been just ahead of them in the line of march.[35]

> We reached the crossing, and without stopping, made a sharp turn to the left. As I was turning the corner where the road makes this left curve, I saw on the right-hand side, in a field next to the road, American PWs standing ... They were standing very close together. In front of the PWs, with their backs to the road, stood a few SS men who wore grey uniforms from which I concluded they were not members of the tank crews, but that they belonged to the two SPWs which I saw standing there. The two SPWs were standing in the field in front of the house [café]. I remember that the SPW people who were guarding the prisoners had begun the firing. This happened just as I was turning slowly with my tank into the road. How many shots were fired, I cannot say any longer. In any case the Americans fell to the ground like lightning ... Until the start of the shooting, the Americans stood there with their arms raised and I saw none of them try to escape or show an aggressive attitude, or else give any cause for being shot at ... All guards, about eight in number, who were standing in the field shot into the prisoners. Two or three of them did not return to their SPWs right away, but continued firing at these Americans lying on the ground ... There I saw how some of the wounded twitched and still moved.[36]

If self-serving, Clotten claimed not to have shot at the prisoners, but was unsure about the other tanks. Clotten said he had watched all the machine guns on the SPWs fire as well as three or so who shot into the mass of Americans with machine pistols. He observed two men – one of whom he recognised as Obersturmführer Erich Rumpf – leave his position just south of the prisoners and walk briskly toward his tank, out of the line of fire. Clotten's vehicle rumbled along slowly at a walking pace as he saw the prisoners felled by gunfire.

Although anxious to get away from the disturbing scene, Clotten was forced to halt about 20m from the spot where the prisoners were lying. There, SS Oscha. Siptrott in #731 was stopped in front of him, standing tall in his turret. At the moment he halted, his gunner, SS Strm. Hermann Bock, grabbed the tank's machine pistol, rose to the deck, and began blasting away. The din was deafening, but there was a similar racket to his rear. Out of the corner of his eye Clotten thought he saw the tank of Oscha. Erich Dubbert behind his own along with two SPWs. Dubbert, too, was firing into the prisoners with a machine pistol.[37] Bock then fired once more. 'Stop!' Clotten shouted. 'This makes no sense. They are dead anyhow.'[38] Besides, there was hardly any more ammunition for their inferior Italian machine pistol.

About 20m ahead of Clotten's tank was Siptrott's Mk IV. Further ahead of Siptrott's panzer was another Mk IV – of which he couldn't be sure.[39] Behind Dubbert's tank was one or two SPWs parked across from the prisoners as they had approached. Behind the SPWs stood the tank of SS-Oscha. Koch – a sketch he later produced prior to trial, showing there were two other SPWs parked by the café on the corner as well as a mysterious Mk V Panther standing near the crossroads. Clotten couldn't be certain, but thought it was the tank of either the leader of the 1st Panzer Battalion, Werner Poetschke, or his adjutant, Arndt Fischer.

Who could have given the orders for the shooting? 'The general belief is that it could have been Poetschke,' Clotten claimed. 'Nobody seems to believe that Peiper gave the order because it is contrary to his nature – everybody believes that is impossible.'[40]

Nearly the last in the line of 7th Company tanks was Panzer #711 under Heinz Rehagel. Sturmmann Hans Joachim Piper (not Peiper) was the gun loader in that tank.[41] He, too, had seen the prisoners in the field and watched as Koch in Panzer #712 just ahead of them fired at those prisoners. Rehagel came back to his tank and spoke briefly to an officer from his turret and soon joined in the firing on the Americans, who were now lying in the field.

Who fired the first shots at Baugnez? In the official U.S. Army account, it was Georg Fleps who fired the first pistol rounds from the south end of the field. However, the accounts of many American survivors claimed that the initial gunfire came from one of the half-tracks parked closer to the north end of the field. Siegfried Jaekel and Joachim Hoffmann said that the first shots came from Max Beutner's half-track right across from the prisoners.

Indeed, several accounts indicate that both Beutner and SS Ostuf. Erich Rumpf looked to recruit passers-by for the execution detail and that both SS men gave appropriate orders. Corroborating testimony came from Heinz Friedrich, Rudolf Dörr, and Hans Siptrott. Whether he fired the first shots, Max Rieder and Willi von Chamier claimed that Erich Rumpf issued orders and joined the initial firing with a pistol. While the statements claiming that Beutner and Rumpf fired at the crossroads were later repudiated, it is significant that neither Hans Siptrott nor Georg Fleps himself ever denied that Fleps had fired early shots at the Americans. Indeed, their statements said a spate of automatic fire followed that event.[42] The Carinthian radio operator in Panzer #731, Strm. Otto Arnold, later claimed after the shooting that his tank commander, Hans Siptrott, 'blamed the rifleman Fleps heavily and abused him in very strong terms and said he would report this incident to his superior officer'.[43] In an interview with the author, Siptrott gave his version, still peeved with Fleps fifty years later:

> I drove across and I came out in my tank below the crossroads. The Americans were not shooting at us. In the middle of the field the Americans were standing and my loader [Fleps] must have seen them as they tried to escape into the forest. He fired two rounds at them before we continued driving on. I kicked him in the backbone. I told him, 'Why are you firing?' I kicked him, because I didn't know why he shot – I was surprised. And we continued driving on. I was sitting on top of the tank looking out and Fleps was the loader and popped out of the loader's hatch. He was out of the hatch to his waist [shows how Fleps stood and how he reached from the commander's hatch with his leg to kick him]. I kicked him in the backbone and hit my shin bone and hurt myself.[44]

When asked what came next, Hans Siptrott was decidedly reserved:

Q: So, the Americans tried to run away and Fleps shot at them?
A: Fleps shot at them with a pistol from 300–400 metres away.
Q: I want to point out in the testimony which you gave soon after the incident, you said 30–40 metres, which agrees with what Fleps himself claimed ... You don't remember any other shooting that occurred while you were present?
A: Afterward, rounds were fired because they tried to run away.
Q: A lot of firing?
A: Yes. We got out of there.
Q: But you continued on your way down into Engelsdorf?
A: Yes.
Q: So, rounds were being fired at the Americans as you were leaving?
A: Yes ...

While it is very possible that Fleps fired the first shot, it is almost certain that this was joined or even led by Max Beutner and Erich Rumpf firing pistol rounds just before all of the SPWs commenced with machine guns. As astutely pointed out by researcher, John Bauserman, over half of the U.S. Army survivors' accounts said the first pistol shots came from a half-track (or command vehicle), while the vehicle from which Fleps fired was Hans Siptrott's Mk IV panzer located somewhat to the south of the mass of prisoners.[45]

This seeming contradiction begs the question: when people are threatened with bullets, will they remember accurately the type of vehicle occupied by their assailant?[46] And particularly if all the various vehicles present would fire almost immediately after the first shots? The likely Occam's razor explanation is that the first shots were fired by Fleps, but that Rumpf and perhaps Beutner were pointing pistols at the same time the shots rang out. Their added salvos to the fusillade would make it appear as if the first shots came from the direction one was looking. And while the official U.S. Army account and Siptrott's statement at Schwäbisch Hall, where those suspected of involvement of the Malmedy massacre were questioned, would seem to indicate that Fleps fired the first shots, one often overlooked testimony differed markedly.

This was the recollection of tank gunner Werner Löhmann, the gunner in Pilarzek's Panzer #734, who testified at the Malmedy trial that when he was in Wanne later during the offensive Fleps told him about his actions at Baugnez during idle conversation. As Fleps had related it, two SPWs with MG 42s had fired on the prisoners on orders. 'Upon that I pulled my pistol and fired several shots into them, too.'[47] True? At the time the massacre took place, at least two SPWs were certainly positioned across from the prisoners: that of Beutner himself, also the vehicle of Sepp Witkowski and most likely also the SPW of Friedel Bode. No one in Beutner's SPW would talk at Schwäbisch Hall or later; one suspects they had good reasons.

However, those in the Sepp Witkowski's SPW were more forthcoming. Crew members Siegfried Jaekel and Joachim Hoffmann indicated that early shots came from Beutner's SPW.[48] Finally, Max Rieder, within the 9th Panzer Pioneer Company recalled that after being ordered by SS Obstuf. Erich Rumpf to shoot the prisoners, he pulled his rifle out of his SPW and then went back to the field where the prisoners were standing with their hands up. There, he found Rumpf already south of the café in front of the prisoners with a pistol in hand. 'Our company commander, Obstuf. Rumpf shot into the prisoners with his pistol.'[49]

Regardless of who started it, according to all accounts, when the firing began – just pistol shots – everyone joined in. Thus, it may have been very difficult for any observers to determine who fired the first shots. Everything happened very fast. Siegfried Jaekel:

> Then came Beutner's command to fire. My recollection is that the first firing I heard was pistol fire from Beutner's SPW … We fired approximately seventy-five rounds from the front machine gun. As soon as the first firing began, all the American prisoners who were in the field fell to the ground. Then I went to the rear machine gun, loaded it, and started shooting [again] into the American prisoners. It was during the time that I was firing the rear machine gun on our SPW that Sprenger's SPW pulled up on the right-hand side behind my SPW. I saw Sturmmann Boltz firing the machine gun from Sprenger's SPW.[50]

German witnesses estimated that the initial blast of automatic fire went on for two to four minutes. Even with that question answered, others remained. Who killed the Americans lying wounded or feigning death in the field? Based on multiple witnesses' testimony, members of both the 3rd Panzer Pioneer Company and the 9th Pioneer Company moved into the field to finish off anyone who was still living. When Gustav Sprenger's SPW pulled up, Marcel Boltz fired a volley of machine gun fire into the prisoners sprawled on the ground, but for the most part the heavy volume of fire had ceased. Sprenger said he saw fifty to eighty Americans in the field, just shot down. 'When I stopped in front of the pasture where the American soldiers lay in the field, they were still twisting and turning in their own blood and at least those nearest the road were moaning and groaning in pain.' Sprenger noticed that a group of officers and men were already in the field applying the *coup de grace*. Coming from the group who had been standing by the Panther, Max Beutner approached him with an gruesome command: 'Go and shoot those who are still alive.'[51]

Sprenger then dismounted his SPW with its commander and another grenadier. All three used pistols or machine pistols to dispatch any prisoners who were still living – Sprenger himself fired off a thirty-two-round magazine into five Americans who looked to still be alive. 'I aimed mostly for the chest of those I fired at.' Sprenger claimed he had no doubt that each man he shot was killed.[52] He deeply regretted what he had done, he later said aloud before his U.S. Army judges, but explained those were his orders. In the Waffen SS, an order was *more* than an order.

Clearly, some of the 9th Panzer Pioneer Company also participated. At the Malmedy trial both Walter Fransee and Paul Buth testified in court that both

Günther Hering and Helmuth Haas under Erich Rumpf had administered mercy shots – in one case to kill an American who begged for his life on his knees.[53] And perhaps worst of all was Hubert Huber of the 6th Panzer Company whom numerous witnesses saw stop and get off his Mk IV tank at the crossroads where he 'finished up the Americans who were still showing signs of life'.[54] Several described how Huber had kicked the prone bodies to find one American soldier still alive at the north end of the field while his tank crew looked on.[55] Huber then forced the man to take off his overshoes and took his watch. Then, with his pistol, he shot the man in the head at point-blank range.[56]

How did Waffen SS veterans later judge those who shot at the crossroads? One who passed by the scene was repulsed. 'Look at this,' Hans Knospe said to a comrade as his SPW passed the field littered with American dead, 'there's been some dirty business here.'[57] The decades-old memory of another anonymous SS veteran tanker was less condemnatory:

> I cannot say that the ones who shot the Americans were murderers. You know that in any army there are pigs. There are some who have fast fingers. Luckily, I was not there.[58]

Jochen Peiper admitted having been at the crossroads just minutes before the event, but his memory after fifteen years was focused on irony:[59]

> North of Thirimont, my spearhead (perhaps three tanks and as many half-tracks) detected to their left an American convoy heading south on the Malmedy–St Vith road. When they opened up, I was a few hundred yards further to the rear riding in a U.S. jeep and questioning an American lieutenant colonel who had bumped into us. I learned that Ligneuville accommodated a higher U.S. headquarters and that nobody expected us in that region. I therefore dashed to the leading tanks and had them cease fire and proceed without delay. Perhaps it was still possible to surprise Ligneuville too despite the battle noise raised at so inconvenient a moment.
>
> When we reached the crossroads and swung south, the passage was partly blocked by crashed and burning trucks. In the road ditch and the adjoining field were quite a number of U.S. soldiers (perhaps sixty, I guess). Apart from those killed and wounded by our heavy fire at so short a distance, were practically three groups to be distinguished: one was coming back up to the road with their hands clasped behind their helmets and surrendering. We thumbed them back as it was the task of the infantry following later to collect what we had left along the route of advance.
>
> [A second group] lay close to the road and played dead. I distinctly remember some of our half-track soldiers making a joke to give them a 'warning shot across the bow', whereupon they jumped to their feet and came to the road, too, while everybody was roaring with laughter. The third group, last but not least, played dead, too, but was closer to the nearby forest. These soldiers imperceptibly tried to slowly approach the edge of the woods by crawling now and then. Some shots were wasted on them. The spearhead then proceeded toward Ligneuville while

> the POWs, on their own account and more or less unguarded, assembled near the crossroads and were captured after a short skirmish.

Jochen Peiper would later write to historian John Toland about the deadly events that came next. 'There exists more than one version on what has happened later at the crossroads,' he told the American author in 1959, 'but nobody really knows, nor do I.'[60]

Chapter 12

LIGNEUVILLE

You can ask anything of me, but time.[1]

Napoleon Bonaparte

While Jochen Peiper's battle group shot a group of American prisoners at the Baugnez crossroads – an episode that would dog the SS leader for the rest of his life – U.S. Brig. Gen. Edward Timberlake was just sitting down to lunch in Ligneuville, Belgium. It was not just any lunch. Timberlake, in charge of the 49th AAA Brigade, made his headquarters in the sumptuous Hôtel du Moulin in Ligneuville, four curving kilometers away from Baugnez.

Timberlake did not know that just east of the Belgian border in the German Eifel, Luftwaffe Flak Regiment 155 (W) was preparing to launch wave after wave of jet-powered missiles officially known as the Fieseler 103 flying bomb. Designated by Hitler himself as the *Vergeltungswaffe* 1 – Vengeance Weapon 1 – the world's first pilotless flying bomb had been blasting London and Belgium all autumn. The British called them 'Doodlebugs', but the average GI knew these annoying enemy weapons as V-1s, or 'buzz bombs', for the infernal growl of their Argus pulse-jet in flight. But whatever the name, the V-1s were inspiring for the beleaguered German *Landsers* on the ground, and equally worrisome to the Allies.[2] If not intercepted, the flying bombs could be deadly, suddenly sputtering to a stop, and plunging out of the sky to explode their 1-ton warhead in Spa, Verviers, or Liège.

That autumn, Timberlake's multi-battalion belt of anti-aircraft guns had been charged with shooting down the stream of V-1s as they buzzed over the northern Ardennes on their way to their targets. 'We Keep Them Falling' was the unit's motto.[3] Still, more than a thousand of the flying bombs survived the gauntlet to reach Liège, killing a like number of civilians and damaging 97 per cent of the buildings in the city.[4]

Stocky and with prematurely greying hair, Timberlake was one of the youngest American generals in command in Europe, but some said he was not the brightest. At a news conference in Britain before deployment in France,

Timberlake had been asked, point blank, if he was, indeed, the third from the last in his graduating class at West Point. When Timberlake nodded, the reporter asked if he would care to comment. 'Well,' said Timberlake stoically, 'I was a lot smarter than those other two guys.'[5]

After the invasion there was precious little for the anti-aircraft gun units to do in France other than following behind the advance of Patton and Bradley. Blasted into submission by the Allied air forces, Hermann Göring's Luftwaffe was almost completely absent over French skies. Timberlake stayed with the assigned mission anyway, but did it his way. In September, his AA gun battalions set up to protect the Meuse river crossings in Belgium and by 30 October were ordered to advance to the German border to protect the U.S. First Army as it prepared a plunge into Germany toward the Roer Dams.[6] Their soft assignment did not go unnoticed by ordinary GIs. At a time when infantry riflemen were critically short, there were 52,000 American boys under General Timberlake assigned to shoot down a seldom-seen German air force. Meanwhile, Timberlake set up his quarters in one posh location or another: the blue-blood castle at Signy-le-Petit, Belgium, the expansive Château de Namur, and now Ligneuville's Hôtel du Moulin.

The quest for the good life filtered down: some of the gunners took advantage of the less-than-pressing anti-aircraft assignment to got into trouble in Paris. Pfc. Everett N. 'Jim' Longson had first been with the 49th AAA Brig. when his superior ordered him to head to Paris and the Champs-Élysées – ostensibly to look for women. But when Longson's superior emerged the next morning, their jeep was gone – stolen by the blooming black market. Longson was busted to private and sent to Gen. Timberlake in Ligneuville. 'It was the best thing that ever happened to me,' Longson remembered.[7] Being on the German border, the assignment sounded worrisome. Yet, arriving at Ligneuville, Longson was smart enough to spot a good thing. The front lines to the east were static and extraordinarily quiet. Then, too, the heavily forested region seemed to lack offensive potential for either side. Ligneuville was a rest area.

Although Ligneuville was nominally part of Belgium, it had only been so since the First World War, and most of the inhabitants were German or of German heritage. Indeed, most referred to the town by its German name, Engelsdorf, rather than by the French name of Ligneuville. At first the GIs of Timberlake's command were hesitant about the few hundred locals, and went around armed, but fears soon melted with the local hospitality. The elderly proprietor of the hotel, Peter Rupp, prided himself on first-class accommodation and *haute cuisine*, even in wartime. True, there were no tourists or gastronomic weekends anymore, but Rupp had his standards. His was an exclusive summer resort destination where one could imbibe the finest wines and hunt for wild boar, deer, or fish for trout in the clear Amblève. After being wined and comfortably stuffed, the good general could sleep on down pillows.

Timberlake and his staff soon met local 'hunters' who turned out to be members of the Belgian resistance. With no Germans to expel that autumn, Some of the quartered American soldiers were soon shooting game to supplement the chef's table. Still, Timberlake and his officers were amazed at what Peter Rupp, his wife, and their servants Bertha, Therese, and Maria could do with GI victuals as supplemented by the trout so easily caught in the Amblève river.[8] Within a few weeks, the entire command was spoiled by the comfort, food, and friendly townspeople. Then at Thanksgiving, Herr Rupp went all out: he prepared a turkey dinner for everyone as if back home. Here was a general and his staff, living like a king in posh quarters while front-line men crouched in wet foxholes 15 miles east.[9]

If not quite as fashionable as the Hôtel du Moulin, 26-year-old Jim Longson's quarters on the upper floor of the Hôtel des Ardennes were only slightly worse. Right across the street was a little local store. Over time, he became friends with the family who ran it and particularly with little 12-year-old Julie Bastin and her 10-year-old sister, Thèrése. As Christmas approached, Longson – a Massachusetts boy – was homesick. And he was sad, too; he had married just before shipping out and was forlorn far away from his bride. But on 6 December, St Nicolas Day, Jim was invited to a little holiday party at the Bastin home up the hill. He brought some cake and candy he had been hoarding and soon was the American hero.

Unusually tall with close-cropped hair, Joseph Bastin was the fatherly head of the household. He was responsible for maintaining the electric generator for the village between their house and the Hôtel du Moulin. He also hauled milk with a horse and cart, and during the war brought German wounded back from the German border. Although multilingual, Joseph was no German sympathiser.[10] All of the family became Jim's friends and he was soon living in a room at their house. During the day, he worked on Timberlake's staff on the first floor of the hotel as a typist and teletype operator in the S-1 section.

Other days, during leave, Longson hunted rabbits to help supplement the Bastin family diet. Young Julie Bastin even taught Longson French and he taught her a little English and a song or two. Longson was typing for Timberlake during the day, but when it turned 5 p.m. he was off duty and headed up the hill. There were small gatherings every night and the neighbourhood kids came by to dance to a few scratchy phonograph records. Every day – and sometimes at night – they would hear the growl of a V-1 buzz bomb overhead and Longson would listen carefully. So long as you could hear the robotic beasts, he didn't worry, but if the buzzing pulse-jet suddenly went silent, everyone ducked.[11] On Saturday, 2 December, one ploughed into the nearby Belgian village of Heppenbach and severely wounded seven American soldiers.[12] Then on 7 December, without explanation, the annoying procession of buzz bombs overhead suddenly ceased.[13]

More than the parties of the Belgian locals, Longson was touched by the innocent, young Julie Bastin and her sister. Julie and Jimmy became pals. She tagged along wherever he went as though she was his younger Belgian sister. They took photos with the uncle's borrowed camera and Jim took young Julie along on a jeep trip to Verviers, where he bought her a first Coca-Cola. It was the first time she had been more than 6 miles from home. Soon 'Jimmy' became part of the Bastin family as he was invited into their home each evening. After supper there would be music, talk, and radio around the fire. And at the end of the night she would mimic the ditty he had taught. 'You are my sunshine' she would sing with a lilting French accent, 'you make me happy when clouds are grey'. A tear came that second week in December and he felt like he was somehow home. Far away in Belgium, this was his Christmas.

Then came, Saturday, 16 December. Sleeping soundly in his room at the Bastin house, Longson was awakened by the booming of distant thunder. To be sure, these were shells going off at a distance, but closer than he had ever heard before. When he left the Bastin home that morning for the command post at the Hotel Rupp there was now again a steady skyward march of V-1 buzz bombs roaring overhead, snarling their way toward Liège.[14] Word came, too, that a V-2 rocket hit on Antwerp the previous afternoon had killed over five hundred people.[15] 'What's going on?' Longson worried.

A foreboding atmosphere confronted him at the office on the first floor of the hotel that morning. Disturbing reports were coming in from neighbouring units to the east – particularly on the front of the untried U.S. 106th Infantry Division. The 14th Tank Battalion of Combat Command B (CCB) of the 9th Armored Division had been located a mile north-west of Ligneuville. 'All through the day we had been hearing heavy firing to the east,' Capt. Cecil Roberts of the tank battalion remembered about the artillery firing on the 16th; 'most of us thought it was in connection with the attack on the Roer Dams.'[16] Yet by 2.04 p.m. came the report that a powerful enemy counterattack with tanks had seized the village of Auw just off to the east.[17] Before dawn on 17 December, battalion commander Col Leonard E. Engeman had been ordered to move the tanks to St Vith as soon as possible, as an enemy counterattack was under way. Only its maintenance section and the supply trains remained. The fifty tanks were rumbling off to St Vith and whatever trouble lay there.[18]

Gen. Timberlake remained dubious, but ordered his gun battalions to move fire-control equipment and the top-secret 'Pozit' ammunition to the safety of rear areas. Even though headquarters insisted their headquarters stay put, most of the 450 anti-aircraft men were pulling out. At 5 p.m. when Longson went off as usual to visit his Belgian friends on the hill, he found the Bastin family worried; there were bad rumours. Longson returned to the Hôtel des Ardennes at 11 p.m.

Longson had no sooner crawled into his bed at the hotel than a runner came: report to the CP at the Hôtel du Moulin right away. The town felt spooky as he walked the 100 yards that separated the hotels. In front of the hotel, General Timberlake had ordered a 30-calibre machine gun set up in the road by the church. Longson and another GI were told to train the gun on the N-23 coming down north from Malmedy. It was eerie that night, and Longson worried about what the heck he would do with that machine gun if a German tank appeared out of the inky darkness. Luckily nothing happened; there was only mysterious booming gunfire in the distance. At daylight, some trucks and a couple of tanks appeared, but they were friends from the 9th Armored. A quick cup of coffee at the Hôtel du Moulin and he found the grateful American mess officer, Capt. Guy R. Sperry, speaking to the hotel proprietor. 'Mr. Rupp,' he began, 'we have to leave. There's nothing to be worried about, we'll be back in three or four days.'[19]

Working the headquarters teletype on the Sunday morning of 17 December, Longson became aware of more bad news. An enemy armored column had evidently broken through near Büllingen, but now no one knew where it was. When the Bastin family came out from Sunday Mass just down the street, they saw Gen. Timberlake and Peter Rupp standing at the front door of the Hôtel du Moulin talking things over. Regardless of the uncertain situation, Rupp told the general he had a nice lunch for them. As 1 p.m. drew close, even Timberlake could hear the rumble of guns and then a louder racket of machine gun fire. *What was that?* Longson wondered to himself.[20] Timberlake ordered his intelligence officer, Sgt Kelakos to investigate. Headquarters had advised Timberlake to move his headquarters to Stavelot. The move was made in the morning, leaving behind a skeleton crew of three officers and three enlisted men under Lt Col John C. Tredennick. The men were to stay at Hôtel du Moulin with the general to maintain communications.

At daybreak that morning, on 17 December, another U.S. force of about fifty vehicles had arrived unexpectantly at Timberlake's HQ. Capt. Seymour L. Green found himself in Ligneuville with the service company of the 27th Armored Infantry Battalion and the kitchen, maintenance, and supply trains of the 9th Armored Division's 14th Tank Battalion. Coming from several miles north, he had orders to assemble in the town before proceeding to St Vith. Meanwhile, the rest of the 14th Tank Battalion and the 27th Armored Infantry had been ordered from Ligneuville and Schoppen to Nieder Emmels near St Vith an hour and a half after midnight.[21] The U.S. 106th Division was in trouble. After a wrong turn in Waimes, Green had shown up at daybreak with about fifty vehicles.

There was also a single M4A3 tank dozer (a Sherman mounting a bulldozer blade) and a 105mm assault gun there from the 14th Tank Battalion, both in need of maintenance. He also had a hundred men jumpy about rumours of German paratroopers. Rather than pushing past Ligneuville, Green decided to wait for some of his straggling trucks. Simultaneously, Lt Dornan, his maintenance officer, ventured to Battalion headquarters 10 miles to the east near Breitfeld. There, he learned of 'enemy attacks all over the place … look out for yourself'.

After breakfast Green approached Gen. Timberlake in the street in front of the Hôtel du Moulin. People from the village were walking to church as if all were normal, but tanks of the 7th Armored Division had been moving through the town all morning. The armor had evidently raced down to the Ardennes from Holland to stem trouble to the south. Timberlake's G-2 – an intelligence officer had little more: 'No one knows exactly what is going on,' Green told Lt Dornan. 'Things are SNAFU.'[22]

Weirdly, Timberlake seemed more concerned with losing his posh digs to Green or anyone else than he was about the Germans. 'This is a tempest in a teapot!' he complained to Green. 'If we have to leave, we'll be back by Christmas!'[23] Green thought it very strange that Timberlake – a general –

wanted a promise from him that he would give up the Hotel Rupp after he returned. And according to the battalion after-action report, Green was warned by a messenger on foot at 2.30 p.m. that an enemy armored column was approaching from the north.[24] He saw to it that his less battle-worthy trucks were sent off north toward Stavelot, where they would be out of harm's way. He had the truck column of the service company and the single tank placed on the small road leading into the main road, left facing north up the N23. Any German advance would surely run across the tank.

Green's intuition was on target. Just up the road, the Waffen SS armored column was advancing as fast as 25 ton German tanks could drive toward Ligneuville. Werner Sternebeck and his two tanks and two half-tracks were in the lead, but not far behind was tank driver Manfred Thorn and Panzer #734. 'Drive at once to Engelsdorf and make contact with the Spitze of Sternebeck!' The order of Werner Poetschke was still ringing in Thorn's ears from their hasty meeting back at the crossroads. 'We rode along toward Engelsdorf,' Thorn recalled. 'Some of the American vehicles still had their engines running. SPWs passed by me. Vehicles were everywhere – there were a lot of our vehicles on the road. SPW people jumped up on the trucks and looked inside them. They were looking for booty.'[25] He passed them by. As Thorn worked the brakes of his Mk IV tank while clanking down the steep hill and negotiating the sharp turns to the right, it became clear that something was wrong. One slip here and … the road dropped off steeply on the left.

Thorn pulled off to the shoulder of the road 400 to 500m south of Baugnez. Just after Thorn stopped, a Mk V Panther with two SPWs behind it came zooming around the curve and passed him without stopping. It was Arndt Fischer's Panther #152 moving ahead with Peiper and Diefenthal in his wake. At least one additional panzer, that of Klingelhöfer, passed by and joined in pursuit behind Peiper.[26] A minute or two passed. However, arriving next behind Thorn was the Mk IV #731 of Hans Siptrott. He stopped to offer assistance to Thorn.

Did he need help? 'No,' Thorn replied, but the brakes were shot; they would have to be repaired somehow. Beyond that, Thorn could see that Siptrott was seething with anger. Although Jochen Peiper admired Siptrott as a tank commander, he had one clear flaw. Unlike blowhards like Werner Wolff, Siptrott had a quiet, most unmilitary voice, speaking almost in a loud whisper. During practice drills, those under him complained of trouble hearing him. But when Thorn saw Siptrott jump from his tank, he bellowed loudly.

'He was absolutely fuming and angry.' Thorn looked up from inspecting the brakes. 'Oh, what's up?' Siptrott walked up, 'I could kill Fleps, I could throttle him!' he said, 'I've already given him a kick in the rear.' Siptrott explained that Fleps had fired twice back at the crossroads – without his approval.[27] 'Why had he fired?' Thorn asked. Siptrott shook his head.[28] 'The prisoners up there …' Siptrott motioned with his hand to his rear, '*Jetzt haben sie gerade da oben alle erschossen!*' – Well, now, they have shot them all – '*Scheiße!*'[29] 'All of them?' So that was the raft of machine gun fire Thorn had heard after driving from the crossroads.

'What are you going to do now?' Thorn asked. Siptrott looked nervous. A *Großer Scheißdreck* – a total shit storm. That's what Fleps had brought on.

'I'm going to put him on report!'[30] Siptrott went on. Soon he returned to his tank and Fleps, who remained inside. They drove off. Not long afterward, with makeshift adjustments, Thorn was satisfied that he could continue driving in his tank down into Ligneuville.

Meanwhile, back at the Hôtel du Moulin, Gen. Timberlake and his skeleton staff were still oblivious to their danger. Presently, Herr Rupp served up a beautiful lunch. Everyone sat down to eat over the white linen tablecloths. For Longson, it seemed bittersweet; the place was warm, the delectable aromas of Herr Rupp's foods perfumed the air, and there was even a Christmas tree in the corner. *No one wanted to leave this place*, he thought.

But Longson's nostalgic reverie was interrupted when an AA-gun tractor came roaring down the road like a bat out of hell, zipping by the mullioned hotel windows. 'There are tanks coming down the road!' the driver yelled. He didn't stop. Timberlake and Tredennick huddled briefly. There had already been a false alarm like that the preceding day. He ordered Sgt Kelakos to take a jeep up the road and report back. In the meantime, they would eat lunch and prepare to depart. Shortly, Kelakos was off, and Rupp and his staff resumed serving the meal. Minutes passed. Then, just as the steaming soup was being ladled, Kelakos burst through the door. 'Tanks are coming down the road,' he said breathlessly, 'they are less than five minutes from us!' Timberlake noisily scooted his chair away from the table. 'We've got to get out of here!' he shouted. Everyone dropped their soup spoons.

In U.S. Army military parlance, they evacuated – if that was the proper word. It was more like a panic. The command left in such a hurry that several members of his staff in other locations near the hotel were not even aware of the bug out. Jim Longson:

> They gave me all the secret stuff – notes and papers – and I took it in the back and burned it on the ground. It was windy and cold and I burned the papers in a hurry. 'Get it done, Jim, you're driving the truck.' There was a truck ahead of me and there were four in my group, but it was the first time I had driven a 2½-ton truck. The general was in his 1940 Ford sedan – the last vehicle out. It was maybe five minutes before we got out of there. There was me and one other man. We drove out of there in a big hurry – I didn't grab any of my things – I only had the clothes on my back.[31]

Jimmy Longson gunned the accelerator, worried about the American flag that the Bastin family now kept displayed at their home. Would he ever see them again? There was little time to think, now he had to just steer the roaring truck up and down the narrow Ardennes roads, shouldered by snow and ice, hoping the enemy did not catch up to them. Timberlake and the little column of four vehicles raced out of town.[32]

Alphonse Piront, a young boy of 13, was also in Ligneuville that day, then living at the top of the hill toward Pont, 2km south-west of Ligneuville. A typical boy, he often used a treasured pair of binoculars to gawk in fascination at the Allied and German aircraft and buzz bombs that flew overhead that autumn. But now, hearing strange sounds from down in the town, he and his parents ran out of the house to investigate. Alphonse peered through his binoculars down the road. In the distance he could see German tanks coming down the hill from Baugnez toward the town. Like most boys of 13, Alphonse was excited by the war and had collected plenty of American patches, insignia, and trinkets that proudly adorned his clothes. The Americans in the town seemed to like it when he wore them. But seeing the advancing Germans, Alphonse ran inside and tore off the insignia and threw it all away. 'We heard a lot of loud shooting, and even though it ended quickly we all ran to the basement and hid.'[33] Little Thèrése Bastin was still in shock over the sudden departure of Jimmy Longson and the Americans. Now, just after Sunday Mass, Hitler's Third Reich was back in town.

> When the Germans came into town that Sunday I was at the window of our home at my father's side. We saw the first tank that came into the village and I'll never forget the appearance of the German standing in the turret. He was so stern looking. We heard shooting and my father yelled out 'Let's get out of here!'[34]

At 1 p.m. the *Panzerspitze* under Werner Sternebeck raced through the streets of Ligneuville. Expecting to find a U.S. Army general and his staff, they cornered only a few frightened American soldiers. They sped on further to the bridge over the Amblève just south of the Hôtel du Moulin. Peiper had ordered them to seize the bridge and hold it. The tanks of Sternebeck and Tonk took up defensive positions just short of the bridge while an SPW – likely of the 11th Company – deposited infantry to crawl forward to check the stone span for explosives. Manned by mess Sergeant Lincoln Abraham, a 50-calibre machine gun barked to life from the rear deck of an immobilised assault gun, but it was soon raked with fire. Abraham was killed by return fire, but his defense kept German heads down long enough for most of the 14th Battalion service vehicles under Capt. Francis E. Voegeli to dash north-west out of the town towards Stavelot.[35] Another of Peiper's SPWs had attempted to ford the river just east of the stone bridge, but was hit midstream by a gun round that decapitated its driver.[36] Still, the bridge was under Sternebeck's control by 2 p.m.

In the meantime, Arndt Fischer was racing hell-bent for Ligneuville directly in front of the SPW of Diefenthal and Peiper. Just after capturing Büllingen and sloshing fuel into his tank, 'I got a message on the radio from Peiper that said, "Engelsdorf is occupied." That was Ligneuville of course. On the way, I interviewed an American officer and there is a major headquarters in Engelsdorf,' he said. Peiper gave his adjutant, Arndt Fischer, a direct order:

> 'Proceed immediately to Engelsdorf and take the bridge and wait on the other side of the town. Units behind should proceed immediately to Engelsdorf.' I got out of my tank and told Sternebeck personally. I don't think his radio was

> working. 'We have to proceed immediately to Engelsdorf and the main column has to come up quick.' I got back on the radio and addressed all the companies. Now the situation was that Sternebeck was ahead with his single tank and 3–4 SPWs. But that was clearly not enough. Peiper came up to me at the crossroads, 'Fischer proceed.' He got back in the SPW right behind me and we took off. I was the umbrella for his thin-skinned SPW. As I drove down into Engelsdorf, vehicles were burning and exploding and most of the Americans had their hands up. We drove ahead. Sternebeck got there with full surprise. I got there about ten minutes later.[37]

The Americans left in such a hurry that the SS men found their lunch at the Hôtel du Moulin still on the table, the cigarettes still smoking, and the glasses half-empty. The soup was just cold. Within ten minutes, the bulk of Peiper's forces would be there. But Sternebeck's *Spitze* had been sighted by the M4-A3 American tank dozer under Captain Seymour Green. The tank prepared to challenge the next vehicles of the enemy roaring into Ligneuville.

Green, in charge of the little detail of the 9th Armored Division in the town, had been standing 100 yards north of the hotel just after being brushed off by Gen. Timberlake. He was working with his supply trains up on the hill road just above town. When the bulldozer raced past him, he drove off to catch it. Green looked up just in time to see Timberlake and his four vehicles dash out of town. The captain and his driver, Pfc. Stanley, jumped in their jeep and high-tailed it back beyond the hotel. 'Get the outfit ready to move,' he yelled to 1st Sgt Page Schenk.[38]

Green sprang from the jeep and walked along the left side of the road just beyond the hotel, where the road to Baugnez curved off to the right and headed uphill. As he reached the curve, he was confronted by a German half-track with several tanks and other armored vehicles only 25 yards away. 'They saw me,' Green recalled. 'I had a carbine!'[39] Instinctively, he dropped his weapon, as the Germans motioned him to the right side of the road where they met him. Some of the enemy laughed, shouldering rifles and pretending to prepare to shoot. He nervously held his arms high. He watched as the first few tanks and armored cars went by him. Then an American jeep with a German in it and driven by an American from the 3rd Armored Division stopped beside him. The German ordered him to get in; he had no choice but to do so.

Green was relieved of his wristwatch.[40] The German officer who captured Green was likely SS Ustuf. Kurt Kramm, who had originally been in the amphibious vehicle of Gerhard Walla only to mount a captured jeep at the crossroads. With his impressed American driver, he set off for Ligneuville. When Kramm had arrived at Baugnez, he had already seen the executed Americans lying dead in the field. Now, he came across the Mk V Panther of Werner Poetschke just before Ligneuville:

> I met Stubaf. Poetschke at the street curve before Engelsdorf. He was about to walk on foot into Engelsdorf because fighting was still going on there. He gave me the order to wait there in front of Engelsdorf to assemble the motorised

> reconnaissance platoon and then follow the column with some additional American vehicles. 'There are also some prisoners of war among them, you know what to do with them,' he added. He meant without a doubt that I should have them shot. It was the first time during my career that I received an order of that kind and I hesitated. Then, I decided not to pass Poetschke's order on to my men, and had the prisoners of war searched for weapons. It was an American captain, two or three NCOs, and four or five privates. The captain I searched myself and took a wristwatch from him and detached his shoulder patch. Shortly before standing with my pistol in front of the prisoners of war, the American officer said to me, 'We are prisoners of war,' and I answered him in the exact German translation because at that time I spoke English improperly. 'Yes, Captain, I make prisoners of war.'[41]

First a half-track and then a German tank had suddenly rumbled down the street in front of the hotel. Sternebeck stopped his tank in front of the Hôtel du Moulin. The German tanker bellowed loudly from his turret. Peter Rupp peered out cautiously after seeing the flags at the hotel had been changed. Sternebeck stood in the tank and brusquely asked the hotel manager about the whereabouts of the American headquarters there. Rupp looked at his watch; it was 2.20 p.m.[42] 'Those gentlemen left fifteen minutes ago,' Rupp said in clear German, 'but they will be back before Christmas!'[43] Sternebeck didn't laugh; he gunned his tank engine and clanked on toward the Amblève bridge, the Panzer IV of August Tonk following behind him.

Rupp was cool – he was an innkeeper in the border nation of Belgium who had learned the art of flexible allegiances. He himself had been born German and his diminutive Swiss wife, Balbina, was even less worried. Their daughter, Mary, had been married to a German since 1930, as she was quick to tell any of the new visitors. Just then two SS non-commissioned officers from one of the half-tracks strode up to the door.

'Where did the Americans go?' they demanded from the doorway. 'I don't know,' Rupp replied. 'Nonsense! You know. We're going to look in the hotel and if we find one American, we'll kill you in the same room.' They had missed capturing the American headquarters. 'Go ahead,' Rupp said moving ahead. 'I haven't any Americans here.'[44] One of the SS men produced a revolver and forced Rupp to enter his hotel at gunpoint. They went through every room in the hotel, but no Americans were found. Convinced that Rupp was on the level, the SS man allowed him to go about his business.

Although Capt. Green was now captive on the captured American jeep, his scattered forces in Ligneuville recovered from the surprise of Sternebeck's bold stroke. The massive Panther #152 of Arndt Fischer came roaring down the road, with Peiper just behind in Diefenthal's SPW. As the steel behemoth rattled noisily down the hill, Fischer was observed by the Sherman tank dozer in a defilade ambush position just north of the Hôtel du Moulin on a side road off the highway. The tank dozer was positioned on a slight hill by a barn, pointing toward the Ligneuville approach route. When Fischer turned the curve toward the hotel right by the post office, he swelled in the sights of the

Sherman. Its gunner hit the Panther in the rear with its 76mm gun from just 100 yards away. Sliced through by the anti-tank round, it burst into flames. A second vehicle, an SPW just behind it, was also struck. Peiper and Diefenthal were just behind that vehicle. Zwigart, being an experienced driver, realised the danger and swerved for cover with Diefenthal's SPW, pulling in just behind the church.

Inside the blasted tank, Arndt Fischer's black leather panzer jacket was still soiled with fuel from the hasty refueling in Büllingen – a matter of dangerous consequence:

> By then the Americans had figured out that someone had come through Engelsdorf. A Sherman was there in the village. I drove down toward the bridge real fast and could not see it. From 50 metres or so I got a full hit. My tank driver was killed. The radio man was also hit. My leather uniform, soaked with gasoline, burst into flames. 'Come out!' I yelled. I jumped out the top and jumped into a deep snow-covered ditch that was by the road and rolled in the snow. Peiper's SPW behind us had to back off. Somebody was firing at me from the building above. Peiper's SPW stopped that with machine gun fire. After a time, more of our tanks showed up and knocked out the enemy tank. Peiper came to me in the ditch and bandaged me up. I was terribly burned. Peiper, who gave me first aid, was so irritated that he put on the bandage backward.[45]

How did Peiper describe the chaotic arrival in the village? 'We entered Ligneuville at top speed, received machine gun fire, and got to approximately the center of the village.'[46] Stopping 500m beyond the Baugnez crossroads where the road entered the woods, Peiper and his crew looted an American jeep while waiting for Fischer's Panther and several half-tracks to pass by them. After the Mk V passed by, Peiper and Diefenthal pulled in right behind him and roared off. Peiper recalled, 'Ligneuville was reached by the point shortly after 1 p.m.'[47]

> In the center of the village, that tank which was in front of me was knocked out by a Sherman coming from the right. I saw the Sherman standing 50 metres to the right of me; he was standing in a blind corner, so I could not reach him with my weapon. I then jumped out of my car – my recon – with my crew and ran with close-combat weapons into a house to knock out this tank from the rear of the house though a window with a Panzerfaust. In this moment, as I ran to the house, my recon car was also knocked out. Thereupon we destroyed the Sherman[48] and went out of the house the same way we came in … and it was almost impossible to stay there because the ammunition from my recon car was exploding at this time. With the aid of two others of my crew I then put the fire out on the three or four of my men who were rolling themselves around on the ground. I also bandaged the adjutant of the 1st Battalion [Fischer] who had been wounded as the first tank was knocked out. It was very unpleasant there because we couldn't move from the spot where we were because burning ammunition was exploding all around us. In the meantime … So, I bandaged the adjutant of the 1st Battalion, Lt Fischer, who had suffered severe burns on his face and hands.[49]

SS messenger Karl Paul Fröhlich, in Diefenthal's vehicle, described the scene:

> Before the bridge in Engelsdorf, Fischer's tank explodes. There is another shot and our SPW is hit. I see our assistant driver's head flying through the air. All the doors of the SPW open and everyone runs out. Peiper hides behind a wall. I run across the street and head up a hill. As I run up, I see an American with a gun. '*Scheiße!*' This is the end. Suddenly, the American drops his gun and puts his hands up.[50]

Diefenthal added his own recollection:

> We later on followed the road down to the south, practically up to Ligneuville (Engelsdorf) to a house on the right side of the road which was a bakery. Just when we were at the bakery, a Mk V, which was the last one [sic, in front of us] was shot up. I saw Ustuf. Fischer when he left his burning vehicle. Peiper left my SPW immediately and took cover from the shooting of the American tank. Before we went into the bakery, Peiper and I and the radio operator stood in the street beside each other and then suddenly, this radio man had his head shot off by a shell from the tank and thereupon we jumped into the bakery. I did not spend much time in the bakery with Peiper, perhaps ten minutes. I received the order from Peiper to see that this area from which were receiving fire was cleaned out. Neither Peiper nor myself were firing any weapons at the tank. I had Panzerfausts in the car, but in the car there remained only the driver and he was driving very fast to bring the car across the street under fire, to the cover of the bakery.[51]

Meanwhile, Diefenthal crept back along the road to direct one of the SPWs of his 12th Company just to the rear with a 7.5cm cannon. He directed them to engage the menacing Sherman off the side road just ahead. After a sharp exchange of gunfire, the tank dozer was hit. The Sherman was now in flames, Diefenthal grinned when he reported this back to Peiper. 'That's just fine …' Soon Diefenthal's grenadiers were fanning out through the town to mop up any remaining resistance. Peiper continued:

> After about forty-five minutes had elapsed, Poetschke arrived at that place on foot. He didn't tell me where he had been. He merely reprimanded his adjutant because he was wounded, because he had no business being out front. At the same time, Diefenthal, who had come up to me, reported that the town was completely under control. I was also informed that a high-echelon American CP had been located in the hotel there, which according to the restaurant innkeeper's testimony, had been disturbed at their dinner [sic, lunch].[52]

Peiper arrived in the hotel lobby. 'Just before we arrived, the entire [American] staff had got away,' Peiper recalled with disappointment. 'A giant banquet was there in a large room with large California grapes garnishing exotic foods we had not seen or known.'[53]Kurt Kramm later told of the scene:

> Several minutes later I saw Stufbaf. Poetschke coming back with Ustuf. Fischer who was wounded. I walked toward them and received the order to ride in the radio SPW [Bucheim] as the acting adjutant. Poetschke went toward the front again and I went back to my vehicle and gave the order in the presence of Rottf. Walla and Oscha. Ochmann to wait there for the motorised reconnaissance platoon, to follow them, and to send the prisoners back in the first empty service vehicles.[54]

Ochmann was displeased with the orders to guard the American trucks and the prisoners. Just as the single Sherman was knocked out north of the hotel, the assault gun near the bridge was forced to surrender as well. Behind Peiper was Panzer #702 of Schaefer and with the tank of the company commander after that. 'Arriving in Engelsdorf,' Rolf Erhardt recalled, 'we first saw Panzer #702 unharmed and ahead of that the burning Panther of Arndt Fischer. There too, was Peiper and likely Diefenthal and several SPWs.'[55] The SPWs belonged to Georg Preuß' 10th Company that showed up and commenced a short combat with the smattering of Americans left in the town. An SPW from 11th Company was also hit. Peiper attempted to destroy the Sherman A3 with a Panzerfaust, but a soldier from the panzer grenadiers beat him to it.[56]

Karl Paul Fröhlich was in Ligneuville when Peiper's troops first entered the town. Even though events were deadly for some captured Americans, others surrendered without mishap. But for Fröhlich, who had fought with the Leibstandarte since 1941 in campaigns stretching across Europe, the action in Ligneuville was almost his last.[57]

> I was in the right side of the road and there was a road fork which was going up there and there were two Shermans [sic, armored vehicles] standing at the fork with trucks. I had received orders to cover up the dead and locate trucks by Maj. Poetschke. I went out to the trucks in order to take a blanket or a shelter from one of them in order to cover up the dead. And as I went up the hill there, there were two American soldiers there who had their rifles pointing toward me. And I said to them, 'Hands up!' and they dropped their rifles and about four or five more men came from behind the house and also held up their hands … I then took them down the road and Colonel Peiper told me to leave them there, that the walking wounded could pick them up and take them back.[58]

Meanwhile, Panzer #632 appeared with SS tank driver Heinz Noack at the helm. At 4 p.m., his Mk IV panzer had passed by the Baugnez crossroads without stopping. He saw, with his own eyes, the dead Americans lying in the field there, but had no idea what had happened. When he reached Ligneuville he was surprised at first to see American soldiers milling about in the village – which he had understood was in German hands. Soon it became clear that these were the fake GI commandos of Skorzeny's Panzer Brigade 150.[59]

The U.S. 27th Armored Infantry Battalion service company had been in the process of moving to a new bivouac area east of St Vith. 'We ran into a concentration of Germans who immediately opened fire on us. We immediately stopped the vehicles and jumped into the ditch on the side of the road ... There were ten men in my group. We exchanged fire with the Germans, who were about 25–30 yards away ... they were beginning to get closer and were using flamethrowers on our trucks. The first sergeant of our group decided to surrender. He threw up a white flag and surrendered for the entire group. We dropped our guns and walked with our hands up and the Germans ceased firing.'[60]

Now, Green could hear a lot of firing from his perch in the captured jeep. Some of his service company was able to escape the melee, but others were hit or cornered and forced to surrender. Some fled on foot cross-country. Sporadic fighting went on for an hour.[61] Green was still riding in the captured American jeep driven by a man from 3rd Armored Division when a young German in an SS uniform flagged him down. He ordered Green to get out of the jeep and join a group of other prisoners at the roadside. The SS man grabbed Green's arm and spun him around so his back faced him, all the while waving a pistol.

Green stood motionless, hoping for the best. He could hear the SS trooper mumbling something about air raids on Hamburg. But nothing happened; the youthful SS man 'cooled off and wandered away'. They were marched off toward the Hôtel du Moulin and once inside were placed in a room upstairs. But soon after they were settling down there, one of the German guards entered their room shaking his head. 'They just shot some of your comrades,' he said, pulling out family snapshots taken from the dead men.[62] Green didn't recognise any of them.

For both Seymour Green and Arndt Fischer the Ardennes Offensive was over. Both spent the evening of 17 December in the Hôtel du Moulin. Fischer was badly burned and spent the night in the hotel, attended to in Gen. Timberlake's bedroom. 'I'll never forget that I went to sleep looking at the American flag over my bed.' The next morning Skorzeny's people were at the hotel, but they had no additional medical help. Fischer's burns were bad and Peiper twice sent divisional orderlies to replace his bandages.[63]

Peiper made sure that his friend Fischer was taken care of, but he wanted to see what he could learn from Captain Green. He had missed General Timberlake, but what could he learn from Captain Seymour Green that might help him to reach the Meuse in the next day?

Chapter 13

HÔTEL DU MOULIN

No one ever stopped when they were winning.
—Hemingway, A Farewell to Arms

In Ligneuville, Belgium, the innkeeper of the Hôtel du Moulin, Peter Rupp, saw the American soldiers being rounded up as he peered from his kitchen window.[1] Presently, an SS sergeant with a pistol separated a group of eight soldiers from the other Americans and marched them off to the side of the road across from the hotel. One of the unarmed Americans was Joseph P. Mass of the Service Company of the 27th Armored Infantry Battalion, 9th Armored Division. This was part of Combat Command B that was ordered down from Faymonville to St Vith.

> Everything was normal on the morning of the 17th. Being told to move out was normal ... Well, at about ten o'clock there was light. There was me and Penny in the C&R. There were two jeeps and there were eight of us. There was a six-by-six supply truck with a canvas top, two jeeps, and that was it. We were part of the service company; there were about thirty in the entire thing, but they were scattered all over. The column had eight of us. We followed the leader, our 1st Sergeant Schenk. He was in one of the jeeps and he led the group and we all followed. We headed to our destination. We didn't even know where we were going. We travelled about two hours. There was hardly any traffic, only an army jeep or two. We were out for about an hour and we saw a convoy of American cars coming by. It was a continuous convoy and it was going toward St Vith ... We waved at them and tried to be friendly and they just looked at us and didn't wave or anything. They kept on going. Looking at the bumpers we could see that they were from all kinds of different outfits. These convoys must have continued for an hour or so. There were so many of them that they were jammed on the road and were stopped in some places. We saw officers outside their stopped vehicles talking to each other. Traffic was stopped in places. So, I remember a sign that said Ligneuville was about 5 kilometers ahead. We didn't see any more American cars. We came around a bend in the road as we

approached Ligneuville and we heard a couple of shots. And there just in front of us was a German tank! It was about a hundred yards away. I had never seen a German tank, but we knew it was immediately. There was nothing we could do. We pulled over on the side and road. We were dazed.

… It looked like the whole German army was approaching. I had never seen so many tanks and vehicles and soldiers in my life. We went from one column of tanks and vehicles that were American and then just down the road ran into this. We could hear firing going on. I don't know who they were shooting at. There was a lot of shouting and hollering. Schenk says, 'There's nothing we can do. We have to surrender. What chance would we have? It's the whole German army.' We were about 50 yards away around a horseshoe bend in the road. We are all too scared to say anything back. We dropped our guns and raised our hands and then about ten German soldiers came up to us and marched us back to where the congregation of German soldiers had made a bonfire.

They seemed mean. They had long coats and shouted loudly. I couldn't understand them, but they shouted loudly at us. To this day I remember that. I was so frightened. No one in our group said anything. We were all scared stiff. We had our hands held high and they kept guns at our backs. I didn't turn my head right or left or look any direction except straight ahead. I was afraid to make a move. They marched us back to where a large number of German vehicles were located. They moved us to a place that was an opening in front of the vehicles on the side of the road. They lined us up so we were facing some fields. There were a lot of vehicles in the town and they had us facing the fields off the road. We could still hear shooting going on. All eight of us were there. They marched us down the road and had us turn to face the fields.

They pushed us with their guns and they twisted me after I stopped in the road and had me face away from the road. They were hollering at us. They twisted us around and pushed us that way and I was looking straight ahead. There was still a lot of shooting going on. And I heard a shot and it seemed to be next to me. And Carter was standing next to me on my left side. I guess they pushed him, because he fell forward into the slight recess in the field off to the road and I heard a shot. And then I realised what was going on. And I realised that my turn was next because I was next to him. So, I braced myself. I heard hollering behind me and I prepared myself for the shot and I gave a quick jerk and the gun went off. The shot went through the back of my neck and the bullet came out of my windpipe. I went down. They thought I was dead. I was not unconscious. To this day, I remember the impact of the shot. It was like being hit in the head with something big. It was a stunning blow. Then I passed out. Evidently, they got the rest of the guys, but I didn't hear anything. Later, I found that the others had been killed. I must have laid there for two or three hours, because when I woke up it was dark. I had sense enough to decide to get out of there. I knew they might come by with a wagon and take the bodies and bury me alive.

So, I saw a clump of bushes about 25 yards away. My neck was swollen and frozen blood was congealed on the wound and I couldn't turn my neck. I managed to roll under the bushes and then passed out there again. I slept there all night and awoke the next morning. I was about 25 yards away from the road. During the night I heard a couple of vehicles come close to where I was hiding, but the major convoy of Germans seemed to have passed. The next morning, I couldn't move my neck. I couldn't see over to where I had been shot. My neck

> was twice its normal size and I couldn't move my head and I was sitting there in a daze. Then I realised there was an old farmhouse about 50 yards away. A villager in the house came creeping toward me when he saw me. He brought me something warm to drink and he told me where to go.[2] He motioned for me go down the road to a big building. I started going to where he told me to go. And just outside the building he told me to go, there were German soldiers standing outside of the house. He had told me to go to the Hôtel du Moulin. And the German soldiers were in front guarding it so they stopped me. One of the guards spoke English and asked me, 'How have you been wounded?' I guess my response saved my life. I told them, 'I didn't know. I just woke up on the ground and I have been wounded. I got up and came here.' Then they dragged me in and said, 'Are you an American?' I said, 'Yes, sure.' They took me into the hotel. There were lots of Germans inside in black dress uniforms. They looked to be using the place as a headquarters. Then they took me back into one of the rooms and there was Captain Seymour Green and Lt Dornan from my company. And there were four of our enlisted men. Green asked me, 'What happened?' I told him … And when he heard, he got real mad and started hollering for a German doctor to tend to my wounds.[3]

Having previously been with the SS Totenkopf Division, SS Hauptscharführer Paul Ochmann later admitted shooting the prisoners.[4]

> On 17 December 1944, it was just starting to get dark. I saw near the village entrance to Engelsdorf about eight American prisoners of war standing on the right side of the road in front of a house. Their hands were either clasped about the neck or raised above the head … When I saw these prisoners, I went to an SPW, standing in the immediate vicinity of the house in which sat Untersturmführer Hering, platoon leader of the 9th Panzer Pioneer Company. … I was in a bad mood because I received from Untersturmführer Kramm, one hour before, the order to remain in Engelsdorf and guard thirty American vehicles captured as well as eight American prisoners of war … For these reasons, I went to SS-Ustuf. Hering and said to him, 'Here are eight prisoners, they should be shot, I need another man!' … Hering told me that I should go to the next vehicle, and that Sturmmann Suess would go with me …
>
> Together with Suess, I led the prisoners past the SPW of Ustuf. Hering (to the north) over to the other side of the road … I formed them at the right edge of the road … because there the bodies could drop right down the steep terrain without lying in our way. I then indicated to the prisoners with my hand that they should place themselves with their backs toward me and then face toward the slope as I intended to kill them with a shot to the neck and I know that by a shot in the neck (*Genickschusse*), the victim falls forward. Thereupon I shot the first American prisoner of war in the neck from a distance of about 20 centimetres. The American was doubtlessly dead from the motion he made – I saw that he fell forward. Then again with my pistol I shot the second American in the same manner. I know from my service with the *Totenkopf einheit* that this is the customary way to shoot people.[5]

Ochmann said he shot four or five, while Suess killed the rest. Afterward, Suess and Ochmann came upon another group of eight prisoners in the town who, instead of executing, they escorted into the Hôtel du Moulin. 'I was of the opinion that enough prisoners had been bumped off,' he said in his statement. Ochmann then remained around the hotel until the following day, then he left in a captured American vehicle.[6]

Two local women, 33-year-old Marie Lochem of Ligneuville and her 25-year-old sister, Josephine, had seen the atrocity take place.[7] When the Germans arrived that afternoon, there was noise from shooting all over. 'The *Schwartzer klapen* are back,' Josephine worried to her sister, Maria.[8] One of the German tanks pulled up right in front of their house as they moved to the back of the room and watched the big, metal beast through the windows. Just then, there was the loud crack of gunfire as an American Sherman blasted Fischer's tank from high ground above their house. Marie and Josephine, petrified with fear, watched the gunfight from the back of the house. Across the street, Anna Willems hid in the basement.

Just then, the German tank exploded into flames directly in front of their front door. The soldiers in the tank were badly burned and aid men brought them into the house. Eventually, Dr Franz Neumayer treated Arndt Fischer for burns. Josephine remembered seeing how badly they were burned as the groaning German soldiers were pulled inside. Meanwhile, guns crackled. Frightened, both women ran out of the house to safety in the barn when the firing started. There was a lot of shooting just in front of their house, but eventually it calmed down. Still, they huddled in their safe place until night.

Marie and Josephine watched cautiously from the barn as two German soldiers in black uniforms separated eight American prisoners from a larger group of two dozen U.S. Army soldiers, who were then led away. The remaining eight American soldiers were then lined up on the south side of the road between 25 and 50 yards from where the girls watched. 'The German soldier who shot the eight American soldiers with the pistol was standing approximately 5 feet from each of the American soldiers he shot.' Marie Lochem was amazed that none of first group of men seemed to run. 'The American soldiers just stood there with their arms down at their sides while the shooting took place.'

Hiding in the barn, the two girls peeked out of the cracks in its wooden slats to see the Germans line up the Americans along the road. 'Look through the boards, they are killing them.' They shot the American soldiers in the neck at the side of the road. To Josephine it was horrifying. The American soldiers 'fell like bowling pins into the ditch'.[9]

After the shooting was done, Marie heard the two German soldiers discussing whether the eight Americans should be buried. 'If they left the bodies, the Americans might retaliate against them.' Regardless, the Germans left the corpses where they were shot. The following day it began to snow, their frozen forms disappearing under a spreading blanket of white. The eight dead men from the 9th Armored Division were lying in death by the road entering Ligneuville: T/5 John Borcina, S/Sgt Joseph F. Collins, T/4 Casper S. Johnson, Pvt. Clifford H. Pitts, Pfc. Michael B. Penny, S/Sgt Lincoln Abraham, Pvt. Gerald R. Carter, and Pvt. Nick G. Sullivan.[10] All had been shot in the back of the head or in the face. Today a simple monument just before the Hôtel du Moulin denotes the shooting, which occurred about 50m north of the monument, on the east side of the road.

Rupp had seen the whole thing from the kitchen window of the Hôtel du Moulin. He had seen a large group of American prisoners being gathered near his hotel. Then a smaller party of nine men were marched off north from the hotel along the road. To Rupp's shock he then saw the SS trooper point his pistol at the first man in the line. There was a loud report and Rupp turned inside his hotel where another SS man was standing. 'The American prisoners are being murdered!' he shouted, but the trooper paid him no attention. Meanwhile, Rupp heard one shot after another at brief intervals. He returned to the door just in time to see the SS sergeant pointing his Luger at the head of the last American still standing from the group. The GI – who looked very young to Rupp – spun away and tried to run, but the SS man grabbed the young man, pushed his pistol barrel into the open mouth of the youth, and pulled the trigger. A hideous blast and the soldier fell limply with the other bodies sprawled by the road. The SS man walked briskly away, but Rupp was too shocked to do anything more.

Later the other fourteen soldiers were being herded into the lobby of his hotel. Behind them was a stocky SS sergeant – one of the men who had done the shooting he had just witnessed. Rupp could tell that the sergeant intended to execute these Americans, too. 'They are wounded and haven't got weapons. They can't defend themselves.' Rupp ran up to the SS man, losing his cool, and addressing him firmly in his native tongue. Didn't the soldier know he had been born German? The SS non-commissioned officer shouted at Rupp, 'You're all spies!'

'Murderer!' Rupp shouted back, 'You killed eight of them. I saw you put the pistol in their mouths!' The German sergeant swung at Rupp catching the 69-year-old squarely in the jaw. He was sent reeling to the floor, bleeding and missing two teeth.[11] The man was likely SS Sergeant Paul Ochmann.[12] In spite of that sudden blow, Rupp still protested to the face of the SS man. 'That's not right,' he complained holding his mouth, 'they're prisoners.'

'Shoot them,' the SS man railed to a younger one with him, 'the Belgian swine first.' Rupp thought he was a goner. But at that point, a German officer in a black SS tanker's uniform suddenly showed up from the front of the hotel. 'Leave them alone Hauptscharführer!' he said, pushing the snarling German out of the way. He clearly outranked the SS sergeant and looked to be the man in charge.[13] He helped Rupp to his feet. 'You're right, Mein Herr,' he began, 'It's a shame how some people treat prisoners.' He looked with scorn to the stocky SS sergeant standing just off to the side. 'Sergeant, put these men in that room and treat them as you would want the *Amis* to treat you.' The man who had saved their lives was Jochen Peiper.[14]

The snarling SS man backed down. Soon the fourteen Americans were crowded into a room on the main floor of the hotel. The frenzied atmosphere seemed to soften, but only a little – Rupp's daughter Mary asked to tend the seven wounded Americans. 'Go to the devil!' one of the guards complained, but then allowed her in anyway. In spite of the actions of 'the good German', tempers remained on edge. From the kitchen Rupp knew he needed to keep the Germans happy, thinking at once of the wine and cognac he had hidden in the cellar to protect it even from the earlier American occupiers. From their hiding place, Rupp cradled bottles of cognac and champagne inside his overcoat and ascended the stairs. Once inside the hotel, he passed the bottles to his daughter, Mary who was still bandaging the wounded.

'Give the guard a good cognac so I can talk with the prisoners.' She agreed with Rupp, using the chance to go see the prisoners. Captain Green was there and had noticed that Rupp spoke German to the SS men. 'Are you Belgian or German?' Green asked. 'Belgian,' he replied, asking about him and his men. Green wouldn't tell him more than his name rank and serial number. Rupp was friendly as he proffered cognac; Green said the liquor was welcome, but his men were really hungry.

Rupp went downstairs to the kitchen, where his staff was still busy preparing food for the German officers downstairs. During the evening of 17 December, SS General Wilhelm Mohnke had arrived at Ligneuville after just having navigated the road, jammed with German traffic from Born. At the Hôtel du Moulin, he had set Up command headquarters for the 1st SS Panzer Division complete with communications trucks at the rear of the hotel.[15] Blue rings of cigar smoke filled the air as SS men had turned the hotel dining room into the forward command post.

Rupp entered the kitchen. 'Prepare fourteen good plates with vegetables, meat, and good sauces – all hot.' Rupp and his staff were so busy serving the German officers downstairs that no one challenged the eight trays of food that were sent upstairs at 8 p.m. But when Rupp went into the kitchen to get the other six, a German SS officer caught him coming out. Where was the food going? 'To the prisoners,' Rupp answered. 'That's a crime to do that for such swine!' said the SS officer. Rupp protested, 'Well, you don't give them anything, so I have to!' His feisty wife Balbina suddenly appeared and injected herself between the two men. 'Look here,' she said, 'I am with the Swiss Red Cross and I have orders to look after all prisoners.' She was a neutral citizen of Switzerland to boot, squawking indignantly at the German officer while Rupp headed up the stairs with the last food. When he came back down, he crept once more into the secret cellar and returned with his arms full of bottles. That worked, Rupp making one trip after another to the hideaway to retrieve more booze. Soon the Germans now slapped him on the back as warm cognac and fine wine oiled edgy nerves.

Peter Rupp went upstairs to speak to the American prisoners in his hotel. With food in their bellies and kindness from his daughter, they felt growing trust. Some men gave Rupp their jewellery to keep lest it be lost in captivity. The prisoners could not know that the brave man may have just saved their lives.

Downstairs a council of war convened. Peiper was there in the SS officer huddle in the dining room with Wilhelm Mohnke. Had any of the traffic mess been sorted out? Peiper's spirit was flagging:

> My own situation was obscure. Not only did things not develop according to plan, but we were low on gas, had but little sleep since the 14th … I sensed that my flanks were completely open and had the uneasy feeling that nobody followed either. No radio contact could be established since my departure … Toward midnight, a naval lieutenant reported to me. He belonged to the Skorzeny outfit and had worked his way up the point by hitch-hiking. From his report, it appeared that all the rear was a traffic chaos and all infantry and artillery trucks had bogged down in the mud between Honsfeld and Ligneuville … I now felt for the second time, that the big strike was over.[16]

Peiper looked to sort out his confused order of battle. Reports from his messengers indicated that hundreds of vehicles including tanks were left standing along the roads to the rear, the victims of mechanical trouble, air attack, and inept driving.[17] The directional confusion at Büllingen and beyond had left both the 6th and 7th Panzer Company in rag-tag march order, shot up, and in need of fuel. As a result, Peiper ordered that the 1st SS Panzer Company under SS Ostuf. Karl Kremser would now lead the advance with Junker and Klingelhöfer's company pulling up the rear. After reorganising for an hour, Peiper pointed Kremser's Panthers west and sent them off. Their mission was to negotiate the sharp-bending narrow roads that led to Pont, Beaumont, and Lodomez towards Stavelot.

To be sure, Kampfgruppe Peiper had narrowly missed a major battle. Only by minutes that afternoon did it avoid colliding with Combat Command R of the 7th Armored Division. The near miss was made clear at the CCR command post at Recht that same night. Just before 9 p.m., a wild-eyed driver for the chief of staff rushed in blathering about how he and Col Church M. Matthews had been ambushed about 4.45 p.m. that afternoon, running into an enemy armored column just outside Ligneuville near Pont, Belgium.[18] Matthews and his driver had suddenly come across the enemy armored column after taking a wrong turn looking for the command post. Their jeep was fired upon, and both men leapt into the ditch. In the wild scramble to escape, they became separated in the dark. The driver escaped on foot, but he could not locate the missing colonel.[19] German tanks were running amok behind American lines.

The force that had ambushed Col Matthews had indeed passed through Pont that afternoon. By three o'clock in the afternoon Peiper's column was again on the move out of Ligneuville, snaking up the tortured road toward Stavelot. 'At that time, a change in the order of march took place,' Peiper later recalled, 'and the 1st Panzer Company, which had been further toward the rear, took over the spearhead and continued in the direction of Stavelot.'[20] By dusk they had reached the tiny hamlet of La Vaulx Richard, only a mile from Stavelot. For the moment, SS Sturmbannführer Werner Poetschke was in command, while Peiper stayed behind at the hotel to interrogate the American prisoners. There, with SS Obf. Wilhelm Mohnke, Peiper sought alternate routes ahead.

One of the guards went looking for Seymour Green. As captain, he was the senior officer among the prisoners. Around 9 p.m. the guard motioned Green to a room downstairs. When he entered the dining room near the hotel lobby, Green was somewhat relieved to find the SS officer who came to their aid the previous afternoon. A Knight's Cross dangled from his neck – the SS leader was none other than Jochen Peiper.[21] At first he seemed busy talking to others of high rank in the corner of the dining room with its magnificent wooden beams and ornate furniture. Sitting at tables with linen tablecloths, the SS officers were waving hands and issuing orders as they pored over a map. Meanwhile, an SS radioman worked nearby, but Green could not understand their animated conversation.[22] For his part, Peiper was upset that being deep in the hilly, forested valleys of the Ardennes neutralised the powerful radio in the communications SPW of 1st Panzer Battalion outside the hotel, and he could not get in contact with division and then corps headquarters back at Manderfeld. Rupp, the hotel owner, showed up occasionally with more food or drink. As Green waited, the Germans smoked cigarettes and cigars. Presently, Peiper excused himself from his headquarters.

Jochen Peiper had hoped to interrogate a captured American general that night, but the bird in hand was only a captain. For his part, Green was surprised at Peiper's good English and his easy-going manner. They moved off to comfortable seats away from the headquarters' bustle at the end of the Rupp dining room. In any case, he invited the American soldier to take up a seat at a small table. 'Good evening, Captain,' he announced in clear English. He leaned forward politely offering Green a cigarette. Peiper lit up and took a puff.

'How do you like our tanks?' he began in good English. Green shrugged his shoulders. 'Who are you, Captain?' Green mouthed his name, rank, and serial number.

'Are you Jewish?' Peiper asked. Seymour Green had brown hair and brown eyes. More than that, Grün was a very common Jewish name in Germany. The American was surprised.

'No, I am early American stock,' Green said. Actually, he was from Ardmore, Pennsylvania, but didn't offer that detail.

'Oh,' Peiper responded, bounding one hand on his mouth, as if he were an American Indian right out of a Karl May novel. He grinned, but Green looked bored. 'You'll go to a good POW camp,' Peiper added. Was he saying there were *bad* POW camps? But the SS officer hardly paused, asking the captain where the divisional command post was located and then laughing at his question. Green just stared ahead. 'We never find anything from officers,' Peiper sighed, 'but we'll find out from one of your privates.'

There was an uneasy silence. 'You Americans aren't going to like the Russians,' Peiper finally announced. It was Peiper's standard line. 'We're fighting for an honorable peace, you know.' Green remained deadpan. Peiper seemed frustrated not to get a rise out of Green. Then Peiper rose from the table and held up a book. '*An American Tragedy*,' he repeated, reading the title from its cover. 'A perfect title, don't you think?' It was Theodore Dreiser's 1925 classic novel about the dark side of the American dream. It was likely left behind at the hotel by Timberlake and his crew, but the gift fit Peiper's quirky habit of planting his nose in classic literature during any breaks at the fighting. 'Now, I'm going to read this book,' Peiper said patting the cover – a chance to understand the enemy. 'I think I'll enjoy it!'

Peiper saluted curtly and said goodbye, letting Green return to his men. The Pennsylvania man found his men huddled in their room, sleeping. Several were wounded and being attended by Rupp's daughter. It was after 10 p.m. Green's interrogation ended. Peiper was dead tired. He walked across the street to where Diefenthal and others were catnapping on cots across from the bakery. He joined them. Just a short close of the eyes …

By midnight, the Germans were drinking one toast after another in the lobby of the Hôtel du Moulin – this one for the Führer, this one for dead comrades, another to their women, and some even sang songs of the Homeland. The fourteen American prisoners were forgotten. By 5 a.m. even Peter Rupp himself was nodding off, the only sound was the snores of German SS men and the low crackle of a radio set droning in the background.

The next day, thoughts of executing the Americans were gone along with the threatening SS sergeant. That morning German guards brought in a badly wounded American, who Rupp spoke with briefly. The prisoner had been shot through the neck and could hardly talk above a croak. Rupp could understand that his name was Joseph – and Rupp thought he was dying. It was Joseph Mass. He was taken to the room at the Hôtel du Moulin where Seymour Green and the other Americans remained as prisoners. On 20 December they would be transported from Ligneuville back east as prisoners into Germany.

What happened to the spearhead that Peiper dispatched toward Stavelot? An early witness was Nicolas Schugens, a Belgian customs agent in Wanne. Schugens had recently been transferred from Wanne to Steinbruck for a border assignment and was due there for work on Monday, 18 December. As his sister lived in Ligneuville he planned to bicycle by for a visit. Preparing to leave Wanne, he learned there was a football match scheduled that Sunday afternoon between the local team and British RAF radar crews based in Stavelot. Nicolas left in the afternoon, reaching Stavelot to see American soldiers strolling with well-dressed Belgian girls by a stone bridge. There, he turned to the south to pedal up the steep rise that led to Ligneuville. Another kilometer ahead in Logbierme, Schugens met a rural policeman. 'The Germans are in Manderfeld!' he said excitedly to the 26-year-old young man. The *garde champêtre* had left the border town the day before – everything was confusion. 'It's not possible!' Schugens shouted back, 'You're crazy!' Schugens wagged his finger. 'In Stavelot there are girls on the soldiers' arms and a football match going on so it's impossible the Germans are close by!'

But then, a little further down the road, Schugens ran into the old trout fisherman, Gabrille, who everyone knew in the region. 'Nicolas, where are you going?' he yelled, waving him down. Schugens braked to a stop. 'I'm going to my sister's in Ligneuville,' Schugens said from the bike. 'No!' the old man shouted, 'the Germans are in Ligneuville!' Schugens shook his head and mounted the bike once more. 'Wait! Wait!' the old man cried. 'You're mad,'

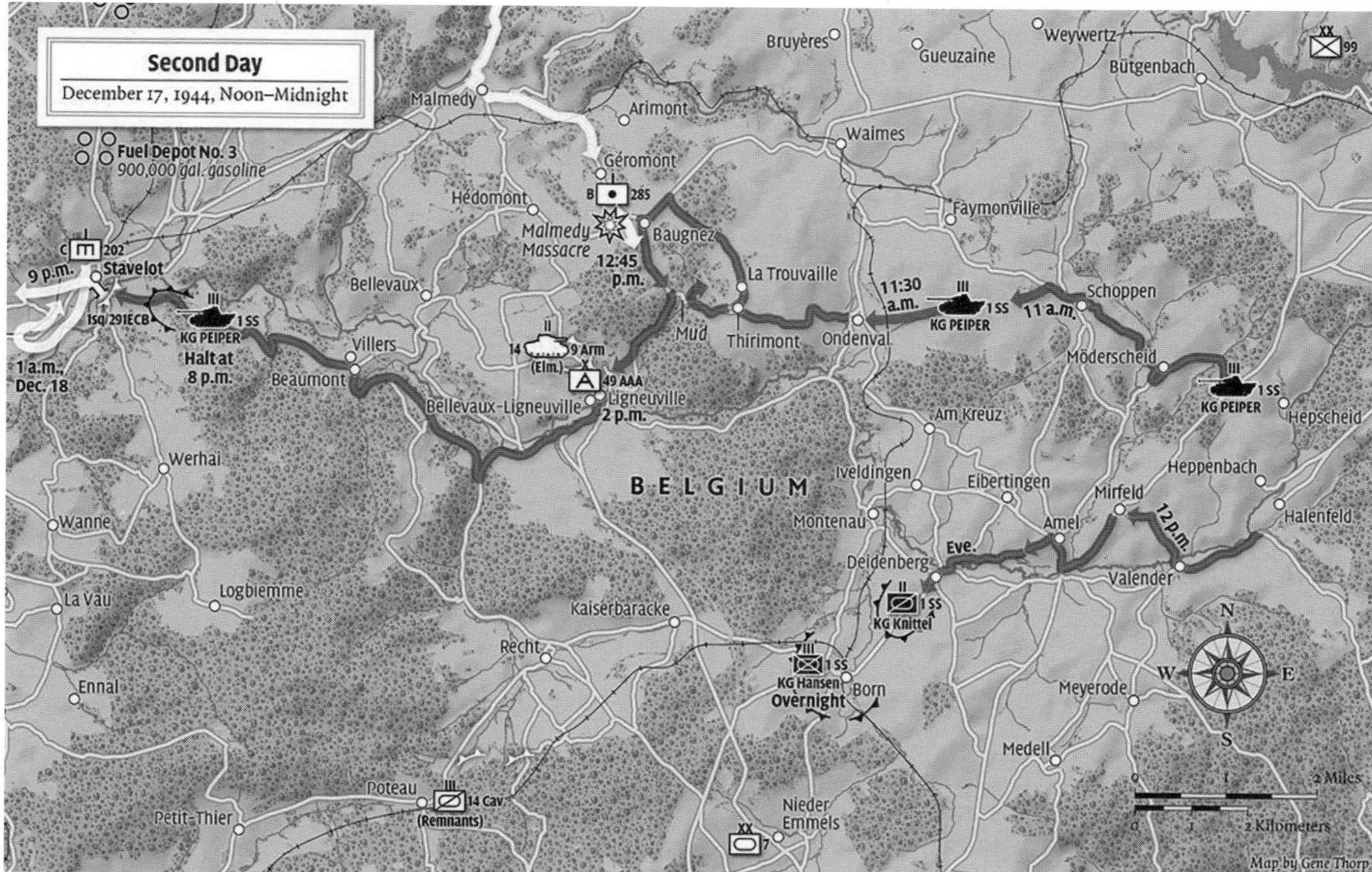

Second Day
December 17, 1944, Noon–Midnight
Fuel Depot No. 3
900,000 gal. gasoline
202
Stavelot
9 p.m.
1 a.m., Dec. 18
1Sq/291ECB
III
1 SS
KG PEIPER
Halt at 8 p.m.
Malmedy
Hédomont
Malmedy Massacre
Géromont
B
285
Arimont
Bruyères
Gueuzaine
Weywertz
Bütgenbach
99
Waimes
Faymonville
Baugnez
12:45 p.m.
La Trouvaille
Thirimont
Mud
Ondenval
11:30 a.m.
KG PEIPER
Schoppen
11 a.m.
Möderscheid
Hepscheid
Bellevaux
Villers
Beaumont
Bellevaux-Ligneuville
Ligneuville
2 p.m.
14
9 Arm
(Elm.)
49 AAA
Am Kreuz
Heppenbach
Halenfeld
Werhai
BELGIUM
Iveldingen
Eibertingen
Mirfeld
12 p.m.
Amel
Montenau
Eve.
Deidenberg
Valender
II
KG Knittel
Wanne
La Vau
Logbiemme
Kaiserbaracke
Recht
KG Hansen
Overnight
Born
Meyerode
Ennal
Medell
Poteau
14 Cav
(Remnants)
Petit-Thier
Nieder Emmels
7
N
W
E
S
2 Miles
2 Kilometers
Map by Gene Thorp

Schugens said pedalling off, 'I don't believe it!' But Gabrille was an old-timer Ardennais; if prone to exaggeration like every fisherman, two warnings in a row were worrisome. Soon Schugens was coasting downhill, glad there was no one on the road. Still, he listened intently as his bike clicked downhill.

It was only when Schugens got to Refat – a clump of houses at a hairpin turn in the road hugging the Amblève river – that the young customs agent heard strange sounds. Puzzlement gave way to panic as almost immediately afterward a loud rip of machine gun fire almost caused Schugens to fall off his bicycle. 'There were trees between me and the Germans, but they were only about a hundred yards away from me. They were across a curve in the road from where I was, but I could see them. The bullets were zipping over my head. I turned around and pedalled as fast as I could back to Refat.' From there, he ducked on to a narrow forest trail to get away.

Schugens drove his bicycle forward as fast as he could go. When he got to Wanne, the football match was over, but he grabbed a few possessions and then looked up the local mayor, Monsieur Georis.[23] 'The Germans are in Ligneuville!' he flatly told him. 'You're crazy!' Georis retorted. Schugens knew the reaction; it had been his own scarcely an hour before. 'Do what you like,' he said straddling his bicycle, 'I'm leaving.' He pedalled for Trois-Ponts.[24]

Meanwhile, in the village of Stavelot further north up the road, Edmond Klein and his fiancée, Lèona Fourgon, ignored the military traffic in town that afternoon. Intent on their date, they went to the movies at the Cinema Casino. Yet the attempt at wartime romance failed when the darkened theatre in the late afternoon was interrupted by a call out for Edmond Klein. It was Lèona's sister who came with word from their father for the young girl to return to Francheville at once – the Germans were somewhere nearby. That sounded impossible to Klein, but dutifully, he, his fiancée, and Albert Gustin mounted the Gillet 350 motorcycle and buzzed up the steep Rue du Vieux Château up to the heights above Stavelot. Soon they were puttering through the tiny farming hamlets of La Vaulx Richard, Lodomez, and Beaumont.

It was around 5 p.m. when the motorcycle trio rounded the narrow, curving road between Refat and Francheville to suddenly see a large shape in the road. '*Tiens … Un char Américain*' – Look, it's an American tank – Klein called out to his friends.[25] *Thank goodness*, he thought. As they drew closer to the vehicle, they could see a figure standing in the turret of the armored vehicle. He seemed to be studying a map. 'They are Germans!' someone else called. Even though they were now only 5m from the tank, Klein twisted on the throttle hard and wheeled his Tour du Monde right past the tank. He leaned forward as if that would help them around the curve to Francheville. They zipped on past and had nearly reached the hairpin turn some 100m further on when a barrage of machine gun fire enveloped them. The bullets seemed to be everywhere, thuds and a fiendish zipping sound. Then one pierced the front tyre, and the trio were certain they would die if they continued on. Klein zoomed off the road and lost control of the bike. The three passengers were thrown free of the vehicle, unharmed and in a recessed shoulder that shielded them from additional bullets. Taking stock, they quickly abandoned the motorbike and headed into the dense woods.

Nearly half an hour later, Leona's sister, Louise, arrived on the same road coming from Stavelot, delayed by the fact that her transportation was a pedal-powered bicycle. As she neared Beaumont, she heard the loud hammer of automatic weapons and nervously discussed the situation with a woman standing on her doorstep in the village. The sound of shooting ended as soon as it started. Yet, determined to reach her home in Francheville, she pedalled on. As she crossed the tiny bridge straddling the tiny Noir Ru creek, she heard loud motors ahead but continued resolutely. Next, about 50m beyond the bridge, even in the darkness on the road, she could see she was facing a tank. Aghast, she watched as the hatch on its steel turret swung open. 'Hello … Hello,' she heard. Even in the near darkness she could make out a white star on the side of the tank. They must be Americans. *Amazing,* she thought to herself, *these GIs really forget the war when they meet a young girl.* Just then she pedalled beyond the tank to find an American jeep posted by the intersection on the Refat road to Francheville. From the jeep, a soldier hailed her in perfect French, '*Mademoiselle, où allez-vous?*' – Miss, where are you going?[26] The soldier got out of the jeep and walked over.

Louise straddled the bike and stopped, amazed in the gloomy light to see that the occupants behind the man appeared to be wearing German helmets. 'I am going home,' she said to him, 'to my house in Francheville.' She forced composure.

'From where are you coming?' he asked.

'From Stavelot.'

The French-speaking soldier then seemed to address the other in the jeep in German. 'Are there Americans in Stavelot?' he continued.

'Yes,' she said, 'they are coming constantly since this morning.'

'And are there tanks?'

She nodded again. 'Yes, they fill the streets.' And she had told him exactly what she had seen, for earlier that day, the tanks of the 7th Armored Division had filled the streets of Stavelot, unaware those tanks were headed for St Vith. With that, the French-speaking soldier bid her goodbye and Louise Fourgon resumed pedaling ahead. But she had not gone more than 200m when she grew so nervous that she fell off the bicycle and then fled on foot toward her home.

Was an American tank leading Peiper's battle group? And now did the leaders of Kampfgruppe Peiper believe American tanks filled the streets of Stavelot? Whoever the misled SS officer was, it was not Jochen Peiper, for the impetuous SS commander would not be there until much later. Meanwhile, his battle group point crept forward to reach the big, serpentine hillside turn above Stavelot around 10 p.m. The main column closed up at midnight. When Peiper arrived he was not pleased. 'Our column was terribly stretched out like an accordion.'[27]

> In my estimate we reached Stavelot at about 2000 or 2100 hours. I had at once attempted to take the town in one rapid attack. That, however, proved impossible

> because all our infantry troops who were not available were not strong enough and because the tanks had no chance to go into action along the road ...[28]
>
> It was impossible to take the town. The whole town was full of American vehicles and a large number of columns were passing the town from north to north-west. With the weapons at our disposal, we fired into the town and attempted at least to disturb the traffic of these columns. Then an American column attacked on the road, but I can't say with certainty whether this was in the evening or the early morning hours. This attack was conducted by American infantry on our left flank ... The terrain was much higher on our left. We were in a closed formation on the road at the time of this attack and we defended by directing the fire from the weapons on our vehicles to the left ... It was after dark or in the early morning hours.[29]

But the truth was that Jochen Peiper was not near Stavelot that Sunday night. After his unsatisfying talk with Captain Green and the inability to contact headquarters, he was exhausted. Had the Pervitin worn off? As during all big offensives, many of the officers in his command were likely popping the methamphetamines.[30] Peiper had now been up for seventy-two hours. That night, one woman in Ligneuville, Anna Willems, claimed Peiper had slept briefly that night across from her house:

> In December '44, I lived in Ligneuville with my brother, in the bakery, right across from the post office. I saw Peiper several times. He himself was very friendly, something I can't say of all his soldiers. He said that we should best stay in the cellar, because of the danger and the situation. He and some of his officers slept several hours during the night of 17–18 December, in a barn behind the bakery on field mattresses.[31]

Peiper's excuse for not attacking Stavelot that night? 'That night, we attempted to capture Stavelot,' he would later write, 'but the terrain presented great difficulties. The only approach was the main road and the ground to the left of the road fell off very sharply and to the right of the road rose up very sharply.' But it was clear that Peiper and his underlings had been fooled by a squad-strength counterattack by engineers led by a Lt Col Pergrin. 'As darkness fell, we observed heavy American traffic, all moving westward without blackout restrictions ... There was a short curve just at the entrance to Stavelot where several Sherman tanks and anti-tank guns were zeroed in ... At 1800 hours a counterattack circled around a high hill 800m east of Stavelot and hit my column.'[32]

> My own infantry strength was too weak and I decided not to attack until it got light the next day. Also I tried to reconnoitre a new road bypassing Stavelot ... During the night I committed an armored group – that is to say a weakened Panzer Company, which had the mission of reaching Trois-Ponts by way of Wanneranval and Aisomont. During the night I only received one message from this company, which notified me that they were running into severe terrain difficulties. On the 18th at 0600 hours, I started the attack on Stavelot. At this time,

> much demolition could be seen in Stavelot, especially three large fuel dumps. The infantry advanced to the outskirts of the city [*sic*], but they were stopped because a heavy barrier had been erected behind which Sherman tanks and anti-tank weapons were standing.[33]

That same Sunday evening, the leadership of the 6th Panzer Army pondered an offensive going off rail. Hermann Priess and the 1st SS Panzer Corps held a council of war at the Igelmonderhof in Manderfeld, the eight-room farmhouse of Joseph Henzius.[34] Otto Skorzeny was present with Sepp Dietrich and a bevy of adjutants. Thwarted from Hitler's proposed mission of infiltrating across American lines, Skorzeny was looking for a new mission for his Panzer Brigade 150. The major concern of the leadership group now was supporting Jochen Peiper's battle group, which was now strung out for miles along roads jammed with traffic. An order had to be given that moved every truck with fuel – escorted by a junior officer – to the front. Sepp Dietrich emoted his confidence in Peiper, who was closing on the village of Stavelot with the SS tank regiment. It was night, and he envisioned that Peiper right now was pushing through American lines and driving straight for the Meuse.

In the meantime, liaison officers entered the farmhouse throughout the night with little news of what was going on at the front. Most reports said roads were still jammed. Skorzeny had decided that his disguised troops would not be committed to battle until the two SS tank divisions had crossed the difficult Hohes Venn plateau. And then he preferred to move his fake tanks at night. The von der Heydte parachute operation was supposed to spring this loose, but *Operation Stösser* hadn't panned out either. Strong winds and inexperienced pilots had scattered the paratroopers all over. And other than Peiper's surgical strike, the American front was holding. Skorzeny approached Dietrich's capable chief of staff, Fritz Krämer. 'I am so badly equipped,' he began, 'that only with a big breakthrough can I carry out my mission to the Meuse river … I gave it twenty-four hours more, so now I cancel. Do you have a job for me?'[35] Could his tank brigade be instead committed as a regular combat unit? Perhaps they could unhinge the American resistance on the right flank of Kampfgruppe Peiper.[36]

While Jochen Peiper himself was questioning Seymour Green and catching a catnap, Werner Poetschke, and a coterie of Skorzeny men in American jeeps and uniforms, scouted the winding road of approach to Stavelot on the afternoon of 17 December. In the tiny hamlet of La Vaulx Richard just south of Stavelot, the Americans in the village left in a hurry at 4 p.m. and many of the townspeople joined them. By then, nearly all the young men in the village had fled.

The German approach up from Ligneuville was creeping along in the dark at a pace slower than a man could walk. The advance consisted of infantry from 11th SS Panzer Grenadier Regiment 2 and a few Panthers from Kremser's 1st Company. Even if Poetschke had wished it, the heavy tanks were not leading – and the reason had nothing to do with temerity. This narrow serpentine road is treacherous, and indeed dangerous to negotiate at night even in a car.

Driving a tank in that darkness was a nightmare; the driver could hardly see anything through the narrow slits. And hearing was impossible inside the tanks, too; the din of the tanks' engines and tracks drowned out almost everything else. Any defender would hear the tanks approaching in the still night from more than half a mile away. To assist the tanks, the two captured jeeps with Skorzeny commandos aboard led the advance, stopping from time to time, turning off the engine to listen for any sounds ahead. Then they would drive forward another 100m. All during this time, the tanks fully expected to encounter an ambush.

Without Peiper, the advance slowed to a groping crawl.

Chapter 14

BEFORE THE AMBLÈVE

They came back
To widows,
To fatherless children,
To screams, to sobbing.
—Aeschylus

On the afternoon of 17 December, Monsieur Albert Petit, a farmer in La Vaulx Richard was on his way back home after attending the Sunday gathering of the farmers' union in Stavelot. He arrived at 4 p.m. just in time to find many locals fleeing the village. All said the Germans were coming.[1] Some people, such as Charlotte Petit and Georges Blaise, intended to go, but could not bring themselves to leave their elderly uncle, Joseph Willem, at their home midway between Lodomez and La Vaulx Richard. Similarly, Albert Petit had no choice but to stay as he and his wife, Fina, had a 2-month-old baby at home. After he arrived breathless at the door, his wife pleaded to go too, but he argued against it. They had a simple dinner, listening briefly to the BBC as they always did at 7.15 p.m. The London announcer told them there was a big German offensive in Belgium. Albert carefully dimmed all the lamps and went to bed.

The Belgian couple were awakened by shooting in the night. Soon afterwards, machine gun fire shattered the windows and both ran to the basement with the baby. At 5 a.m. there was knocking at the door and soon Germans in long overcoats came inside. They spoke French and asked for a *fricassee* – fried bacon and eggs. Fina cooked for them what little she had. The Germans in their home appeared to settle down, although Albert was relieved when they left.

For Albert Petit, the sounds of shooting and gunfire went on for days.[2] It would not be until 11 January, when the Americans took the village back, that Albert would learn that his uncle, Joseph Willem, and two cousins, Georges Blaise, Charlotte Petit, had been brutally murdered at the other side of the village. They had been killed with a group of American soldiers.[3]

Who had done it? Sometime in the evening of 17 or morning of 18 December, twelve men of the 27th Armored Infantry Battalion of the 9th Armored Division were captured on the road that passed through La Vaulx Richard south of Stavelot. Sometime that day – no American or Belgian witnesses survived – the GIs and three civilians were marched outside the house across the road into a wooded copse of trees on the hillside overlooking the village and shot down in cold blood.[4] Today, a simple stone monument memorialises the deaths of these individuals, but until now little has been known of how they met their fate. Significantly, major German units were in the area that afternoon, including elements of the Kampfgruppe Peiper, but particularly Gustav Knittel's reconnaissance battalion.

A clue as to those responsible comes from the testimony of SS Schuezte Ernst Mahl, who was with the headquarters company of SS Ostuf. Heinz Goltz's section of SS Panzer Reconnaissance Battalion 1. Elements of the battalion had arrived in La Vaulx Richard at around 1 p.m. on 18 December – just in time for two Mustang fighter planes from the 67th TAC Recon Group to spy sixty vehicles led by tanks (Heavy SS Panzer Battalion 501) and armored cars on the march towards Stavelot. Mahl's headquarters company was strafed by American fighter-bombers of the 387th Fighter Squadron at 3 p.m. for an hour and a half. After that the SS men climbed out of the cellars and ditches, evidently eager to get rid of the prisoners they were holding.

Mahl claimed to have seen Coblenz and Dröge discussing the fate of the captives, but a careful evaluation shows that Coblenz and much of the 2nd Company had already passed through Stavelot when the fighter-bombers struck. The officer in question may have been Heinz Goltz, whom Mahl claimed to have seen in the vicinity.[5] Another possibility is Martin Leidreiter, who was collecting his scattered 3rd Company and were already responsible for other killings in Wereth the previous day.[6] In any case, Goltz's group would be implicated in several brutal executions of Belgian civilians around Stavelot. Ernst Mahl:

> Eight American prisoners of war together with three Belgian civilians were shot … It was an elderly man, a younger one and a young woman. I have seen personally how these people were led up a hill to the forest and that was done by Uscha. Wolf of my company and two SS men … I know they were shot because immediately after they were led into the forest, I heard about four to five bursts of 9–10 rounds each.[7]

Jules Fabritius and his pregnant daughter-in-law Julia had also elected to stay behind in their home on the northern outskirts of La Vaulx Richard. Julia's sister-in-law, Simone, also remained behind in the village. Both of their husbands were in greater danger, having left in mid-afternoon on bicycles along with most of the male youth of the village.[8] Julia had two other young children that would have had difficulty keeping up with the other refugees who streamed north towards Huy that afternoon.[9] When the Germans arrived just after 4 p.m., the tanks and vehicles motoring through the town let loose machine guns on any of the homes with windows lining the streets. The window glass was shot out and Julia fled with her children to the basement.

At 7 p.m. two U.S. jeeps stopped outside their home. Julia glanced out of the upstairs windows. 'Here are some more Americans!' she announced to Simone. She had no sooner spoken, than soldiers burst through the doorway. Seeing their khaki uniforms, Julia at first thought they were GIs. The rude guests knocked over chairs and pilfered the cupboard, demanding water and food. Their French seemed odd too. It became apparent the 'Americans' were, in fact, German. Various weapons and German accoutrements poked out from behind motley khaki uniforms. 'We are returning to Paris!' one crowed. Thankfully they later left.[10]

There was more trouble for the local villagers in La Vaulx Richard. Looking to help Peiper seize Stavelot by subterfuge, the Skorzeny men took two locals by force: Emile Claude and Jules Califice.[11] Emile was a veteran of the First World War and Califice knew the local terrain like the back of his hand. The Germans forced both at gunpoint into American jeeps in the column. Emile Claude was to help the fake GIs get past the Americans that were likely ahead.

Yet, an attack would need more than Judas goat commandos to move forward. Werner Poetsche thrust Kremser's 1st Panzer Company beyond the village of La Vaulx Richard. Here, the narrowness of the hill-bound roads were such that a Panther would barely fit on the paved section. The 3rd platoon was leading the advance, with the Panther of Erich Strelow at the point and the 2nd and 1st platoon coming up from behind.[12] 'We drove the entire night through various villages without meeting any of the enemy,' remembered Hans Hennecke in Panther Nr. 111. 'But in front of Stavelot, we stopped. Breisemeister [Panther Nr. 114] appeared and reported to me.' Breisemeister said his tank was losing steering fluid, which had to be constantly refilled. He told Hennecke how he stopped at the [Baugnez] crossroads to refill fluid and found weapons in a civilian house, which he then burned to the ground.[13] Later, he said, some of the American soldiers in the field across by the house had suddenly stood up and run for the woods. But Breisemeister's alibi about torching the Bodwarwe Café and the escaping American prisoners was not on the mind of Peiper's tank leaders the night of 17 December.

The problem was the approach to Stavelot. Beyond La Vaulx Richard, the spindly road wound up and then around a gnarly granite cliff-side with a 90 turn that allowed only a single-vehicle approach. The darkness was complete, infantry support was lacking and the Americans would almost surely defend that place. Poetschke ordered the tanks to test the waters and see if the Americans might have missed defending the precipice on the edge of Stavelot.

They hadn't. Lt Col Pergrin had ordered a squad of his Company C of the 291st Engineer Combat Battalion to protect the bridge at Stavelot. The assignment fell to Sgt Charles Hensel, who on the afternoon of 17 December expected to be going again between the sawmill at Trois-Ponts and their cush billets at the Château Froidcour in La Gleize. 'You aren't going to be going to the mill tonight,' the 2nd Platoon leader, Lt Warren Rombaugh told him by phone a little after 4 p.m. 'Good,' Hensel replied, 'You mean we are going to have the night off?'[14] 'Not exactly,' Rombaugh corrected, 'You're going to Stavelot and set up a roadblock.' He provided details; there was a big enemy armored column rampaging about around Malmedy.

Sawdust was sounding better all the time. Yet, Hensel had his orders. All thirteen men of his 3rd squad were soon turned out and told that this night was looking to be a really different adventure. Rather than cutting timber for winterised huts, they might have to actually fight the enemy. The Sergeant told each man to bring every weapon they could lay their hands on. In the squad truck they loaded a .30 calibre machine gun, a bazooka, an assortment of mines, TNT charges, rifles and extra ammunition. Still, it wasn't much.

Driving off from La Gleize at around 5 p.m., they should have been in Stavelot in twenty minutes, but moving east they found themselves upstream against 7th Armored traffic flowing west of Trois-Ponts. It took them over an hour to go the distance. Arriving in Stavelot, Hensel found the town a hubbub of activity; there was no attempt at a blackout. Many trucks roamed about with headlights blazing. 'There was an air of confusion,' an impression made indelible by the growl of an unusual number of buzz bombs streaming overhead towards Liège.[15] According to orders, Hensel proceeded immediately to the stone bridge across the Amblève river at the south end of town. It was unguarded and there was no one there.[16]

Hensel drove on across the bridge, planning to set up a roadblock and then later come back to wire the bridge for destruction. Their truck then slowly geared up the narrow road the locals call Vieux Château, rising above Stavelot to the hairpin turn at the top of the hill. They turned around and came back just below the sharp curve in the road at La Corniche and parked facing downhill. In the darkness the squad began to lay out an alternating pattern of mines just below the road bend and covered it with the bazooka and machine gun.

Meanwhile, on the quiet streets of Stavelot, old resistance fighter Albert George was visiting his sister at her home by the bridge to discuss the disquieting BBC broadcast they had both heard.[17] Could the Germans really be in Malmedy? Albert left to take a look about. Then right around 8 p.m., he saw and heard Hensel and the engineer platoon go by, an American stopping them briefly to check his identification. Ten minutes later, all was quiet save the gurgling Amblève. As he walked along the road to Wanne, he saw another group of soldiers approaching. Thinking them more GIs, he quickened his step. Yet, as he drew near, the five men drew weapons so he hoisted his hands to play it safe. Then a surprising raspy voice in the darkness. '*Wo ist die Brücke?*' George was staggered; they were Germans, looking for the bridge. He could see their characteristic helmets. Without thinking, he pointed the way to them and the five men disappeared into the night. Albert George fled in the opposite direction.

Meanwhile, Sgt Chuck Hensel knew nothing of enemy infiltrators bluffing their way into Stavelot. Instead, he made his way up to the heights above the town to set up the ordered roadblock. The position was chosen as only a combat engineer could see fit – just below a point where the road from Ligneuville turned sharply down before a glacial granite wall on one side and a sheer drop on the other. A line of unlinked mines were placed across the road at that point. Hensel covered the position with a well-sighted .30 calibre machine gun and a bazooka team.

On the other side of the road, Corp. Eugene Morris and Pvt. Gadziola shouldered their rocket-in-a-stovepipe, immediately before some Belgian farm buildings – the Ferme Resonnet.[18] The idea was to hold fire until any Germans stumbled on the mines and then let them have it with every weapon Hensel's squad possessed. Meanwhile, Hensel realised he would need a lookout to alert his ambush teams when the enemy was about to come around the curve. Just 30–40 yards up the road to the south on the other side of the precipitous curve was a dilapidated stone guardhouse that had been built during the First World War to help protect from German invaders in a different age. Hensel's assistant squad leader, Corp. Morris, sent Pvt. Bernard Goldstein with his rifle to the abandoned blockhouse to keep a look out for any approaching Germans. Goldstein remembered the uncertainty, his fear – 'pitch dark'.[19]

It was 7.30 p.m. Hensel was about done and having second thoughts about leaving Goldstein on watch by himself. The deep night created an eerie blindness and nothing could be seen on the uneven ground, raising the prospect of nosing unwittingly into the enemy. Worried for Goldstein, Hensel escorted Pfc. Charles Bauer to the Jewish boy's outpost to give him company. The two men had just rounded the sharp curve and were within 300ft of Goldstein when they heard the motors of armored vehicles, growling low as if they were idling.

The events from the other side of the fence are quickly told. SS tank battalion commander Werner Poetschke's order to seize the bridge during the darkness went to Heinz Tomhardt's 11th Company reinforced by engineers of 9th Panzer Pioneer Company, which had also arrived in front of Stavelot.[20] They were to be prepared to deal with mines and, if lucky, capture the bridge in one bold move. Indeed, a jeep full of Skorzeny men had already passed through the American defense earlier that evening and reported little American presence. Now, the German engineers and panzer grenadiers edged cautiously forward. Goldstein had only been in the abandoned guardhouse for about twenty minutes when he heard German voices and the sound of vehicles 'creeping along'. Goldstein, who spoke German, could hear enemy on the road just above him discussing how to proceed.

'Halt!' he bellowed in English. 'Who goes there?'[21] No sooner than the word come out of his mouth, than Goldstein wondered what had possessed him. Shooting broke out instantly. Hensel could see Germans jumping off the armored vehicles in the sudden illumination of muzzle flashes.

Goldstein returned a shot with his rifle, but one of the big German guns on the vehicle before him belched a big shell and 'the noise and flame was like an earthquake'. Hensel and Bauers pulled back around the craggy bend in the road away from the tracers and near the Resonnet Farm.[22] Each were worried about Goldstein. What had happened to him? In fact, he had escaped. Terribly frightened by the gunfire in the darkness, he had scampered up the hill that went over the big rock by the bend in the road. What they thought was a tank appeared to nose ahead when a bazooka team of Corp. Morris and Pvt. Gadziola loosed a poorly aimed rocket that hit the vehicle. Nevertheless, it stopped, after which Pfc. John Leary and Pfc. Francis Lynch on a .30 calibre machine gun showered the hulk with lead.[23] The beast pulled back.

Still concerned about Goldstein, Hensel led several of his men in an attempt to reach him, not knowing that Goldstein was already running like hell from the scene. Each time Hensel and his men advanced, single shots from their carbines were met by a brace of automatic weapons fire.[24] Yet, the Germans seemed more than impressed with the enemy's riposte. Thinking they had run into serious resistance, the SS men ordered a halt until reinforcements could be brought up.

Hensel, too, gave up trying to rescue Goldstein. Instead, they needed to backtrack and try to reach and defend the bridge over the Amblève river. Leaving the mines in place, Hensel and his men hastily boarded their truck and without starting the engine coasted down to the bridge so as to not alert the enemy. Oswald Siegmund, with 11th Panzer Grenadier Company was driving a captured jeep:

> The battle group was stopped, it was dark, and Peiper told me to drive with my jeep in the direction of the Americans. A machine gun troop of two men boarded the jeep and we started to roll down the hill without starting the engine. Having passed a first cliff I had to start the engine of the jeep in order to keep on rolling down the hill. When we passed the second cliff there was a bang and I could see a muzzle flash. Although I tried to stay as close as possible next to the cliff, I immediately drove the jeep into the ditch. Trying to find the machine gunners, I realised that I was alone. Under fire from the Americans, I returned uphill till I reached Peiper, who was smiling. I was then dismissed by Peiper.[25]

Approaching the Stavelot bridge, Hensel had found a platoon-sized group of engineers already wiring it for demolition. He didn't know the officer, but recognised Pvt. Lorenzo Lipularo, who was driving Lt Cliff Wilson's jeep, the 291st motor transport officer. Wilson asked if all of Hensel's squad were accounted for as demolition was imminent.[26] Hensel said they had left one man up there, but Wilson told him he and his squad were relieved, and were to proceed to the bridge in Trois-Ponts to help guard it. Even though several of his men were upset to leave Goldstein behind, Hensel obeyed and at 11 p.m. their truck crossed the Stavelot bridge bound for Trois-Ponts. About that same time, Col Wallis Anderson's headquarters at the Hôtel Crismer in Trois-Ponts learned that Hensel's roadblock had been attacked by German tanks and forced to pull back to the bridge at Stavelot.

Anderson could not know that the enemy too, had lost their nerve. Only two platoons of the 11th Company panzer grenadiers were available, with the rest stuck in traffic: 'We halted on the road near Stavelot in the evening,' remembered SS-Oscha. Rudi Rayer, 'After we had been there for some time, the 11th Company was ordered to attack and capture a bridge in the town and to hold it.' Then there was the sharp encounter with Hensel's squad at La Corniche – conjured to be all the bigger by the unconcealed U.S. traffic streaming through Stavelot down below the north-facing cliffs. 'The company took up a position of all-around defense. Enemy tanks rolled continuously on the other side of the bridge and we waited for a counterattack. We were fired at from every side without being able to do much in the dark.'[27]

Anderson was now very worried as Hensel and C Company of the 51st Combat Engineer Battalion had not yet arrived to help him defend Trois-Ponts and Pergrin was still holding Malmedy with 180 men and not a single anti-tank gun. Lt Joe 'Blinky' Chinlund's C Company of the 202nd Engineer Combat Battalion in Stavelot was stuck there without orders – things were so confused that Anderson had forgotten about this unit.[28] Yet, it was obvious that the enemy was drawing near; all day Chinlund watched the 7th Armored Division choke the streets heading east to stop the Germans somewhere on up ahead. On his own initiative, Chinlund sent two of his men to check on the big fuel dump near Franchorchamps – a failed reconnaissance because its guards would not let his men ahead without the password.[29]

The last straw was the mass exodus of anxious refugees walking and pushing carts, across the rabble of the withdrawal of the 629th Engineer Light Equipment Company and the 962nd Engineer Maintenance Company at 10 p.m. At midnight, Chinlund pulled out of Stavelot and joined the general mass exodus of support units from that town on the Amblève. Meantime, Wilson's few men attempted to wire up the span for demolition – unknowing that two engineer volunteers helping with that preparation were Skorzeny men. Their help amounted to sabotage.

Then, at midnight Pvt. Goldstein, shaken but unwounded, appeared at the Amblève bridge before Stavelot.[30] There he found a good friend, Pvt. Lorenzo Liparulo, who was manning the span with several engineers. The officer at the bridge, Lt Cliff Wilson, sent the two men on a reconnaissance up the hill toward the hairpin turn. Yet, Goldstein knew there was trouble up that way, and they parked their jeep just a short distance up the Route du Vieux Château across from the Tannerie Dumont. They listened for any sign of the enemy, with Goldstein still edgy and smoking nervously. Suddenly, out of nowhere, German infantry appeared on both sides of their jeep and opened fire with automatic weapons. Liparulo was mortally wounded in the head and Goldstein was struck three times in the right hip and leg. Thinking both Americans were dead, the German infantry moved back up the hill. Meantime, Goldstein flung himself out of the jeep and, unable to walk, began crawling back towards the bridge.

Fifteen minutes after midnight, the withdrawing little column of C Company 202nd Engineers ran into Col Anderson on the road near Trois-Ponts. Professing difficulty in contacting Chindlund's battalion commander, Anderson quickly directed them to return to defend the bridge at Stavelot. For those in Chindlund's Company, all seemed total SNAFU – driving sixteen trucks back and forth in the darkness. Bucking traffic in the night, by 1 a.m., Chinlund organized his men in a house 100 yards from the bridge over the

Amblève, with a machine gun covering the span. S/Sgt Felix Skuta ordered John Stevenson to begin deploying a bracket of mines to deny crossing to the north side. Yet, this was interrupted when part of the 526th Armored Infantry Battalion arrived, with orders to defend the bridge on the *south* side.

> My orders from my Company Commander were to mine the bridge; we were to hold it until relieved. I went over to mine the bridge with six men. Each man carried two mines and we mined them, laying them on the track on the bridge so that no vehicle could go between them. We did this with two rows staggered. We pulled their pins out, then went back on the side we came from. Just then, though an armored infantry unit came up and went right up to the bridge. An officer came up from the first half-track and said, 'Get your mines off the bridge, we're going over.' My superior, S/Sgt Felix Skuda, told me, 'Okay, get the mines back off, those guys are going to cross.' We did that while the line of half-tracks waited, loaded with infantry. It took us about five minutes.[31]

In the meantime, A Company of the 526th Armored Infantry Battalion and a section of guns from the 825th Tank Destroyer Battalion had been redirected by First Army. They were to deviate their march from Spa to Malmedy and proceed directly to Stavelot. Under command of Maj. Paul J. Solis, the Executive Officer of the 526th, the task force defending the U.S. First Army had orders to cross over the Amblève and block all the roads leading north and west.[32] Sgt Lou Celentano was with the 825th TDs moving to the Ardennes, unhappy that they had been rousted from a nice château in the countryside near La Reid, Belgium. There, he and the boys had been living high for a week with real beds, warm comfort, and even a nicely decorated Christmas tree. 'We all thought the war was almost over and it was Christmas ...'[33] Now, they were sent south into heaven knows what – 'stuck in a half-track towing a 3in gun and confusion like I had never seen before'.

The story of the 526th Armored Infantry Battalion was unusual. Stateside, they had trained for months of top secret training with obsolete M-3 Grant tanks designed to blind the enemy with brilliant arc lamps (*gizmos*). They shipped to Wales for further training with the unlikely weapons and then on to France. Company A landed at Utah Beach on 25 August, disturbed to see crosses all over a beach still covered by the wreckage of the first days of the invasion. Their action in France had been nothing, really – just excessive encounters with Calvados. Their secret Gizmo tanks were never employed and their substitute covert mission to nab top Nazis in France came to naught when the Germans fled after St-Lô.[34]

Now in the autumn of 1944 they were living the good life at the Château de Grimonster, south of Liège in Belgium. Their billet was a magnificent twenty-room château on a lake – a spendy resort serving the upper crust. 'It was a vacation really,' one of the anti-tank gunners remembered. Some of the GIs even travelled to Liège to eat ice cream and take in a movie. A hunt earlier that month for wild boar with Baron Pierre Descamps was the most they'd used their weapons since D-Day.

On 16 December, Pvt. Lee W. Galloway took a hot bath and relished an evening at the cinema in Liège with pin-up beauties Gail Russell and Diana Lynn. But there were ominous developments that Saturday. Everyone nervously noted a bevy of V-1s roaring over the estate.[35] Galloway, who fancied himself a budding writer, kept a journal: 'Rumours all day that we might pull out,' he wrote. Some laughed, but 2nd Lt Charles L. Beardslee sternly warned them to be ready to "fight for their lives". No one believed him.'[36] Where were they going anyway?

The answer was Stavelot, Belgium. They lost their way more than once in the darkness, but after training at night for months most of the 526th men thought the sunless hours a friend. Groping their way into Stavelot, Maj. Solis soon fed two squads of 526th infantry, a 57mm anti-tank gun and several half-tracks and towed guns of the 825th into positions along the Vieux Château leading to the bridge. Several guns of the 825th, such as that of Celentano, would have their weapons sighted to over-watch the river. The unconventional order seemed curious to Celentano and the other three men, Jack Armstrong, Martin Hauser and Jonas Whaley, as they watched enemy tracer rounds in the night: hold their position for six hours.[37]

Jack Armstrong seemed to have a premonition, for he suddenly asked Burnette and Celentano to make sure to help his wife Margaret if he didn't come back. Armstrong, Burnette and Whaley were chosen to go across the river, while Celentano and Hauser were to cover them. They set up their guns in a park north of the Amblève river – some 900 yards away from the road where he was told the Germans might appear.

Meanwhile, ill-fated Pvt. Bernard Goldstein, his hip shattered by German bullets, somehow managed to crawl back to the bridge at around 2 a.m. There, he found it controlled by members of the 526th Armored Infantry Battalion. Goldstein was soon evacuated.

On the German side, after a quick nap in Ligneuville, Peiper and Diefenthal were back in their SPW and motoring north towards Stavelot. By 1 a.m. they were in the western part of La Vaulx Richard, staying at a gabled house:

> I spent the night before Stavelot in Diefenthal's [SPW] vehicle and I went up to a house next to the river in the morning, where I had a conference with my commanding officers and it was there that I ordered the attack for the next morning. I also ordered the 7th [Panzer] Company was to move towards the south and try to get behind the enemy and take Trois-Ponts.[38]

The house was just under a kilometer south-east of Stavelot. There, Peiper saw his company commanders. Karl Kremser with the 1st Panzer Company was up first. 'The situation was presented to me,' Peiper recalled. 'The town is like a fortress,' he was told,' and we have not been able to get off the road without infantry.' Gustav Knittel with SS Panzer Reconnaissance Battalion 1 had also arrived with other unwelcome news. 'He told me that there were a lot of [American] men at the crossroads who had been bumped off.'[39] While Knittel's report would seem to have been second hand (his reconnaissance troop took a different route), Peiper would later maintain that this was the first time he heard of the shootings at Baugnez that became known as the Malmedy massacre.

Besides the weariness and hunger of many of his men, Peiper saw the gnarly winding roads from Ligneuville burning precious petrol at an alarming pace. Now, Peiper's intuition failed him. Was it the forty-eight hours of non-stop advance amid frustrating delays, the desire to quiz an American officer, or the rich food and drink from Peter Rupp? Peiper was not before Stavelot at dusk when his first elements rose to the craggy height above Stavelot. An opportunity was lost.[40]

The point Mk. V tank of Peiper's assembling column was that of SS Oscha. Erich Strelow. SS Rttf. Eugen Zimmermann was the gunner for the lead Panther of Kremser's 3rd Platoon. 'During the night, we arrived high above Stavelot,' Zimmermann, recalled. 'At times we could see vehicle headlights in the town and even hear them.' From the vantage of his Panther, the time looked ripe to strike. 'I had the impression that the Americans were leaving.'[41] Yet, late in the night, German engineers moved past his tank, supposedly to help secure the bridge. In the meantime, Peiper personally designated his Panthers to lead the attack. 'Only a few shots were heard, otherwise it was quiet.' In the dark, the dense tank columns closed up behind Kremser's halt on the Stavelot road. Christ's 2nd Panzer Company pulled up right behind them:

> We were then standing the whole night before Stavelot. And then because the road in front of me had been cleared once again I was able to overtake the rest of the battalion outside of Stavelot. There the battalion was standing in readiness and was preparing itself for the attack on Stavelot.[42]

Without Peiper's plucky presence, SS nerves failed to plunge into the murk of the sharply curving road descending to Stavelot. Certainly Poetschke had orders. But darkness had thickened the fog of war: first there had been the madcap bazooka and machine gun fire of Hensel and Goldstein, giving the impression that a thicket of anti-tank defense lay ahead. Peiper had dissolved Sternebeck's diminished *Panzerspitze* and combined it with the rest of the 6th and 7th Panzer Company and the 3rd Panzer Pioneer Company. Their assignment was to feel out a less obvious approach from Wanne to Trois-Ponts and seize the bridges there. Poetschke awaited Peiper's decision, but the regimental commander was not in place until after midnight. Now, gazing down towards Stavelot from the mount of Diefenthal's SPW, Peiper himself was fooled.

Meanwhile, on the other side of the hill, the mood at Gen. Courtney Hodges' U.S. First Army headquarters in Spa fell off the scale. Hodges and his headquarters had been enjoying the good life in Spa. Since 25 October there had been billets in hotels rather than tents, with the famous mineral baths and even a band to pump out tunes on Sundays.[43] Even the infantry replacement obsession faded. Now, on Sunday night, nerves were on edge. The dark shape of a German night fighter appeared in the pre-dawn hours, and a falling bomb cratered the road not far from the Hotel Britannique.

Now the foreign press in town of in Spa, well aware of the artillery, the stray bombs, and the rumours from the front, were demanding to know what was going on. They had got along so well all through the autumn with Hodges and his staff. The official press haunt was at the Hotel Laaken, but most of them hung out at the more comfortable Hotel Portugal. The First Army representative from the Hotel Britannique seemed uncharacteristically tongue-tied. 'There is nothing much to say,' he began, 'except that the German has broken through at several points.' The answer to most of the fevered questions was 'No,' and the officer departed with an unsettling remand: 'The situation is extremely fluid.'[44]

The correspondents filed their gap-ridden stories, made worse by the censors with their blue pens. That night there was a curfew bell and the reporters watched the Belgians of Spa, so warm and gracious the last weeks, now shuttering up their shops and pulling in American flags. Back at the Hotel Portugal, the proprietor gave the journalists more unhappy news: there would be no dinner; the cook had fled 'so the Germans can't get him'.[45]

The clutch of reporters settled into Room 6 to drink away their troubles. The sign over the big double doors: 'Here we grow the biggest and most beautiful hangovers in the world.' 'Come on everybody!' bellowed Pete Carroll, an Associated Press photographer, 'bottoms up for the First Army Press Song!' Soon everyone was singing the unprintable ditty. But when moods waned, Hal Denny with the *New York Times* became serious. He had already endured retreat and capture in Tunisia a year before. 'You mean I have to clear out all the junk in my room?' the titian-haired international correspondent Lee Carson, complained, 'Goddamn the Germans!'

Not far south of Spa, on the other side of the Amblève river, and peering through binoculars into the inky darkness, stood one of those Germans: Jochen Peiper. The SS battlegroup leader saw a seemingly endless procession of headlights running along the road to Stavelot that paralleled the Warche River to Malmedy. From atop the towering hills just south of the river, 'we could observe heavy traffic moving from Malmedy towards Stavelot,' Peiper reported, 'and Stavelot itself seemed clogged up by several hundred trucks.'[46] He could not know that he was watching the evacuation of a million gallons of fuel from a nearly undefended fuel depot on the other side of the river. The deed was carried out in great haste by the 897th and 3562 Ordnance Companies. Before the offensive, Peiper had been given a map marked with known American headquarters and supply depots. He knew there was one fuel depot near Spa and another smaller one from which he had snatched of 5,000 gallons in Büllingen.

Peiper's spotty intelligence was oblivious to the colossal mass of fuel near Francorchamps.[47] Nestled under the pines just north of the road were stacks of 200,000 5-gallon jerricans – enough to take the entire 6th Panzer Army to Antwerp and beyond. The fuel was being hoarded by Eisenhower for the advance from the Roer River into the heart of Germany. That logistical prize was only guarded by sixty ill-armed Belgian soldiers. The unlikely defenders were from the 3rd Company of the Belgian 5th Fusilier Battalion under command of Capt. Jean Burniat with a tiny headquarters at the foot of the Francorchamps road. Peiper did not even know about the Belgians or the fuel.

In the meantime, the U.S. First Army quartermaster, Col Andrew T. McNamara, was just short of a heart attack. He was ordered to rapidly evacuate the 3 million gallons of fuel. When the *London Daily Herald* reporter Iris Carpenter and other correspondents attempted to get back to Spa from Eupen by jeep, they came upon 'a fantastic sight' on reaching the road that led through Pepinster through Theux. 'Bumper to bumper, the First Army headquarters trucks were jammed, loaded with supplies and pulling out as fast as they could.'[48]

Peiper, on the other side of the river and seeing the massive truck columns, judged the town of Stavelot as 'heavily defended', and waited for Preuss's infantry to close up. In fact, other than the trucks evacuating the fuel, there was little in the way of combat presence in the town: Company C of the 202nd Engineer Combat Battalion remained without orders. But all day on the 17th, its members noticed tanks of the 7th Armored Division going through Stavelot heading for the rear. It was troubling 'I wonder what this is all about?' everyone in the little engineer company was saying.[49] Peiper remembered:

> I arrived with my leading elements – Mark IV tanks, infantry on half-tracks and engineers – at Stavelot at dusk. Of course we did not stop, but tried to enter the little town out of the movement. However, Stavelot is a natural little fortress and a huge rock blocks the entrance. As soon as the first vehicle rounded this commanding position on the descending road, it was knocked out when leaving the narrow S-band curve. Unfavorable terrain did not allow my armored vehicles to leave the road and to deploy. Thereupon, my armored infantry dismounted and attacked abreast along the road. All in all [we had] perhaps 60 men. This unprepared attack was repelled by anti-tank guns and snipers. I decided to await the arrival of more infantry, as my tanks were completely unfit for this occasion, and the element of surprise was no longer on our side.
>
> While my column waited on the road – everybody asleep, on both flanks secured by small infantry forces, there was heavy traffic in Stavelot and the biggest surprise – a counterattack on the left flank. A U.S unit, perhaps a platoon descending the slope to our left, yelling and firing. Though my hat was off to them, we had to drive them off. My own situation was obscure. It was clear that things were not developing according to plan. We were low on fuel and had but little sleep since the 14th, and food was not worth mentioning. I sensed that my flanks were completely open and I had the uneasy feeling that nobody followed either. My radio contact could not be established since my departure … Towards midnight, a naval lieutenant reported to me. He belonged to the Skorzeny outfit and had worked his way up to my point by hitch-hiking. From his report, it appeared that all the rear was a traffic chaos and all infantry and artillery trucks had bogged down in the mud between Honsfeld and Ligneuville. They had stubbornly followed my route of advance, disregarding the shortcuts my tanks

> made through several forests in order to appear from unexpected routes. I now felt for the second time that the big strike was over.[50]

In any case, Peiper expected a fight and wished for infantry support for the punishing assault he had in mind. 'Despite that, one could have taken the town during a night attack. I decided against that, because none of our own troops were following and I did not want to wage war on my own with just a few men!'[51] Further, he had enlisted a couple of 'special guides' from Skorzeny's Panzer Brigade 150 to see if American attempts to blow the stone bridge across the river could be thwarted. Peiper put little stock in the fake Americans, but without the bridge he would not risk a night assault.

Skorzeny's Trojan Horse jeep teams did produce results. Cap. von Behr had passed through Malmedy earlier that day in an American jeep with three other commandos – unknowing that such rider-ship would soon become a tip-off. So plentiful was transport that American jeeps seldom had more than a driver and two passengers. Nevertheless, von Behr had ended up in Malmedy through a wrong turn. 'We had more luck than sense!' he later told Skorzeny when reporting to him in Ligneuville. He announced that Malmedy was practically undefended. In any case, around midnight, Col Pergrin sent an urgent message to his Company A commander in Werbomont to send all available bazookas and rocket ammunition to him in Malmedy. Two GIs, T/4 Jeff Elliot and Pfc. Red Anderson, volunteered to drive the bazookas to Pergrin, motoring off from Werbomont at 12.30 a.m.

'Don't be heroes,' their commander had warned. 'If you run into trouble, abandon the jeep and get the hell out.'[52] It was a dangerous mission – they were likely to run into the enemy. An hour later they passed through Trois-Ponts running against the grain of traffic pouring to the west. They were on the western outskirts of Stavelot when they saw headlights coming their way.

At first they pensively drew their weapons, relieved to see a single American officer getting out of the jeep facing their own. None of the other U.S. uniformed soldiers in the other jeep said anything or even left the vehicle. Was the road clear to Trois-Ponts, he wanted to know? Elliot told him it was and the officer was seemingly satisfied to return to his jeep, which sputtered off to the west. Elliot and Anderson, on the other hand, heard what sounded like tank tracks in the night. They scooted on towards Malmedy – unaware that they had just met Capt. von Behr's jeep team that would soon report to Peiper that the road to Trois-Ponts was clear – at least for now.[53] Why had Peiper not wrested Stavelot in a pre-dawn night assault?

> The terrain [before Stavelot] was extraordinarily unfavorable, sloped down very much towards the left and a hairpin turn was right outside the town so that everybody passing by this curve was knocked out by several American tanks and tank destroyers which were located behind road blocks at the edge of town. My own attacking infantry remained at the edge of town and suffered heavy casualties and had to dig in.[54]

Meanwhile, back at the Baugnez crossroads after the terrible events that Sunday afternoon, 20-year-old Madeleine Lejoly-Jacob, living just west of the road junction, had stayed in the cellar for hours with her mother and father. That evening she ventured upstairs to see great walls of flame consuming Madame Bodarwe's café just to the east. The waves of fire and heat were terrifying enough, but above the loud crackle of the flames consuming the building just 60m away, she heard pitiful moans. In a near panic the young woman hurried back to the cellar. Yet at dawn the next morning, Madeleine still heard the baleful moan. She urgently told father, Henri Lejoly-Jacob. Soon, he ventured outside to find the source. There he was shocked to find three dozen American bodies in one tangled mass. Then he followed the sound of the moans:

> I found two wounded American soldiers in a shed by my house. There were also two dead American soldiers on the ground in the vicinity west of my house. My cousin Henri Lejoly [Quirin] came to my house and we found the two wounded soldiers in the shed and he and my wife and daughter gave them first aid treatment, food and drinks. We left them in the shed because we were afraid of the Germans. Two Germans soldiers came and found these wounded Americans in the shed on Monday [the 18th], and one of the German soldiers wanted to kill them, but the other one kept him from doing it. After one or two days, one of the American soldiers died and we took him out of the shed and placed him on the ground. German soldiers continued to come to the house for several days.[55]

Indeed SS-Schütze Angelo Accetti, who had been part of a punishment platoon of the Leibstandarte engineers, was being brought up to the front on 19 December. As he passed by Baugnez he stopped at the Lejoly house by Baugnez to see if the Americans were in the vicinity:

> I saw American vehicles … and at the crossing before I got to Malmedy, I saw 60–70 American dead lying in a field. There was a lone house on this corner and there was an American wounded man in the barn of the house.[56]

Accetti talked to the man and woman of the house. 'I never saw so many [dead] in one spot.' But while admitting they had heard a lot of shooting a couple of days before, the couple claimed to not know much. They told him that there was a wounded man in the barn 'and I went back to give him some cigarettes'. Accetti then drove on to the north and ran into an American roadblock, where he was wounded and taken prisoner.

On 20 December the area came under artillery fire and Lejoly and his family were moved to another house, where they stayed in the basement until 1 January 1945. 'While we were at this house, some German soldiers said that the wounded American soldier in the shed at my house had been picked up and carried away by soldiers of the German army.' The episode's end remains a mystery.[57]

Chapter 15

HERBSTNEBEL

In human affairs, there is no room for certainty.

—Virgil

On the night of 17–18 December, the deep-winter fog descended thickly over the Ardennes battlefield, largely leaving both American and German combatants in the dark. In particular, the Allied side of the hill saw deepening gloom. 'The situation developed badly during the day,' wrote the U.S. First Army diary keeper, Maj. William Sylvan. At the nearby V Corps headquarters in Eupen, artillery shells fell sporadically as the intelligence officer nervously reported many twin-engined German planes flying overhead. At 3.30 a.m. he noted that German aircraft disgorged multi-colored flares and Luftwaffe parachutists, who floated down in the night over a wide area from north of Aachen to the outposts of the U.S. 78th Infantry Division near Simmerath.[1] Another German Crete-like airborne operation – this time with saboteurs? At the same time, front-line troops reported powerful assaults from the enemy all along the Ardennes front. Where was Col Dickson, the intelligence officer who had warned of all this?

The tall and handsome West Pointer Monk Dickson had been footloose in Paris on 17 December 1944 on a four-day leave. 'I was a lone heretic now,' he remembered.[2] On that Saturday, in the City of Lights, Dickson tried to forget the war, more worried about whether GI thieves in Paris might steal his sedan than about the Germans. Just after breakfast, his intelligence superior, Brig. Gen. Edwin Sibert, from Luxembourg City rang on the phone. Words were short. Come to Luxembourg at once. There was big trouble on the First Army front; the phone line might not be secure.

So much for Paris. Dickson threw his bags together and was soon motoring east. The day was foggy, damp and cold when he arrived in Luxembourg City. There he found Edwin Sibert in a state. Sibert did not like Dickson or 'his backroom boys'.[3] The sentiment was mutual. Dickson 'hated Sibert and the latter reciprocated'.[4] Dickson had his reasons. He had run intelligence for Bradley through the incredible mess of Kasserine Pass nearly two years before, and had earned a reputation as an devout pessimist. Now, with Bradley promoted to head of the 12th Army Group, Dickson had been left behind in First Army while Bradley had plucked Brig. Gen. Edwin Sibert out of the artillery to head his intelligence. Dickson saw his superior as overconfident and cocky. He didn't know what it was like to be chased around by German tanks. To add insult, Sibert had been among the vocal critics who considered Dickson a pain. Maj. Gen. Kenneth Strong from the SHAEF office had asked Sibert to call Dickson on 15 December and set him straight about these 'alarmist views'. Attempting to reach Dickson, Sibert found the First Army G-2 had already left for Paris. They could enjoy Christmas without Dickson's constant nagging.

Now, the two men met in Luxembourg City's Hotel Alpha. Before the two men in the G-2 chambers of Bradley's 12th Army Group was a big, outstretched map. On the Ardennes cartography, where there had been few signs of the enemy previously, were now a dozen enemy divisions and more than a few question marks. 'The situation is obscure,' Sibert ventured as Dickson studied the map. Sibert, who had predicted the enemy was nearly ready to fold tents, had been caught in the 4th Division sector visiting Radio Luxembourg when the offensive opened, shocked by the profusion of artillery shells falling. Back at the regimental CP, Sibert listened as reports filtered in that Company E of the 12th Infantry Regiment, an experienced outfit, was under withering assault and totally surrounded in Echternach. Parachutists were landing up north and there was word that an SS tank column had blown through the line in the Losheim Gap.

Dickson shook his head, motioning to the many red enemy flags, 'It's all in Estimate Number 37,' he carped.[5] One by one, the enemy reserves he had called out were now pinned on Sibert's maps with angry red arrows. Sibert didn't say a word. 'He was shaken.'

From Luxembourg City, Dickson sidled once more into his sedan, trying to coax warmth out of its heaters as he drove to Bastogne. There, he conferred briefly with the VIII Corps commander, Maj. Gen. Troy H. Middleton and his G-2. Soon it became obvious that the front before them was buckling under heavy enemy pressure. At least three panzer divisions were identified and smashing ahead. The 110th Regiment of the 28th Division was overwhelmed.[6]

Worst of all, two regiments of the 106th Infantry Division were totally surrounded on the Schnee Eifel just south-east of St Vith across the German border. Dickson conveyed the message from Bradley that he should pull out from Bastogne and move 17 miles further west to Neufchâteau.[7] Middleton agreed that he would be of little use if captured, but he resolved to stay in Bastogne until he could brief the 101st Airborne Division that he expected shortly. Their provisional commander, Gen. Anthony McAuliffe, had just arrived. Maj. Gen. Matthew B. Ridgeway, in charge of the airborne corps, arrived at dark. 'The gloom inside that headquarters,' Ridgway recalled, 'was thicker than the fog outside.'[8]

As darkness closed, Dickson hurriedly left to return to Spa and Gen. Hodges, driving up the main highway toward Liège. The paved road seemed lonely – even spooky. When Dickson reached the town of Aywaille further north, he ran into Col Francis P. Tompkins, commander of T-Force, a special headquarters reconnaissance team of the 12th Army Group.[9] In the darkness, Tompkins told his old friend that they were moving up before Spa, as word had it that the enemy was threatening. Spa was his destination, too, Dickson said. This time they were expecting combat, said Tomkins and not their usual cush guard assignment. One suggestion: if Dickson was going to Spa, he had better take the roundabout route as the Germans were running amok.

Once burned, twice cautious. Dickson had already been captured at Kasserine. He circled wide to the north before driving into Spa from Theux. Dickson knew the T-Force with their secret counter-intelligence mission; if Hodges was using his palace guard as a combat force, that was 'really scraping the bottom of the barrel'.[10] It was late during the pre-dawn hours of the 18th when Dickson arrived and met Hodges. The enemy was attacking like wild hornets. The situation in Spa was chaotic at best. Cooks and clerks were issued weapons and told to man mortar pits dug around town. In the meantime, a group of U.S. Army historians in Spa were issued thermite grenades to help burn sensitive papers. 'Remarkable, how little we know of the situation,' wrote one.[11] Fearing reprisals if the Germans arrived, local gendarmes freed twenty-one Belgian collaborators, only to have disgruntled American MPs round them up again.[12] American flags hanging from many shop windows in Spa now swiftly disappeared.

At noon, Gen. Hodges closed himself into his office in the Hotel Britannique, took no calls, and – head in hands – appeared profoundly depressed. Visited during the day by Ernest Harmon, the commander of the U.S. 2nd Armored Division pronounced him 'the most shaken man I have seen anywhere'. Hodges 'almost went to pieces'; Gen. Bradley in Luxembourg City considered relieving him of command.[13] His chief of staff, Maj. Gen. Bill Kean, took unofficial temporary command.

That night, Monk Dickson arrived to find a haggard Hodges conferring with his staff. Dickson recommended that First Army HQ move at once back to Chaudfontaine near the Meuse, but Hodges seemed determined to stay in Spa. Even that morning he had refused to call off the attack of the 2nd Infantry Division.[14] Hodges was encouraged in his denial by his dyspeptic chief of operations, Col Truman C. 'Tubby' Thorson. 'We'll seal them off here,' Thorson swept across the map as if diagramming football options, 'and stop them there.' *Really?* Dickson shook his head. The reported German spearhead was already beyond the pass where Thorson had called for them to be headed off. 'You'll stop them at the Meuse!' Dickson blurted.[15]

At 10.15 p.m. Col Dickson was interrupted in his deliberations with Hodges' staff to take a call from Maj. Adolph G. Rosengarten, Jr. He was the super secret guy – the U.S. First Army ULTRA representative. Beyond the ULTRA stuff, which was looking more suspect each hour, at Dickson's behest Rosengarten conveyed conventional battlefield intelligence. He told Dickson of his conversation with a wounded American soldier:

> At 1830 hours, 17 December 1944, I interviewed Pvt. Homer Ford, Co. C, 518th MP Battalion. He was on traffic control today at the intersection of #32 and #23 at approximately L-8199 in the afternoon. German tanks fired on some American trucks. The drivers scattered and about two hundred men were rounded up by the Germans, including the informant. SS troops dismounted from their vehicles and searched the Americans. When they were finished, the Germans lined up the Americans and shot them with MGs, machine pistols, etc. The informant was wounded, fell on his face, and later escaped.[16]

Ford was sent on to U.S. First Army in Spa, where he was debriefed by Col Alvin B. Welsch. The place Ford described was just south of Malmedy – and uncomfortably close to the HQ at Spa. Dickson went straight to Hodges, demanding they move their headquarters back while there was time. To provide intelligence to other commands, he promptly issued G-2 Periodic Report #191. It led off ominously: '1st SS Panzer Division identified in V Corps Sector ... The enemy launched a full-scale counteroffensive on the V Corps' southern front before 0600 hours ... this attack made considerable overall progress with advances of 12–20 kilometers.' Dickson included a full page on the 'Massacre of American PWs'.[17]

At twenty minutes after midnight, Col Throckmorton, on the Operations staff, told Dickson of a report received through engineer channels: 'as of 2300 hours, two or three enemy vehicles fired on engineer troops commanding a roadblock just east of Stavelot.'[18] Dickson was getting word of Sgt Chuck Hensel's improvised defense, but Stavelot was just 8 miles away from Hodges' headquarters. Could this be Peiper and the 1st SS Panzer Regiment?

'The *Boche* is staking his life on this drive,' Sylvan wrote in the First Army war diary. There were tank-led counterattacks everywhere, parachutists landing and enemy spies operating behind friendly lines. 'As ample witness to the extent to which the *Boche* are carrying out this bid for victory came a story tonight which measures up to and matches anything thus far published of *Boche* brutality and atrocity.' Sylvan was referring to the Malmedy massacre. 'They were herded together into a side field and an SS officer fired two shots from his pistol and immediately came the crackle of machine gun fire and the whole group was mowed down in cold blood ... There is absolutely no question as to its proof – immediate publicity is being given to the story.'[19]

Against all advice, Hodges elected to stay in Spa, but it was an uneasy night. German planes growled across the dark sky, made more ominous by a fitful procession of buzz bombs. The next morning, Gen. Elwood Quesada, in charge of the supporting XIX Tactical Air Force, took a cue from the enemy. If they could fly in this murk, then so could his boys. He made sure each pilot heard about the enemy shooting prisoners.[20] Quesada implored them to find the enemy column beneath the clouds and 'give the Nazis hell'.

Meanwhile, Jochen Peiper sat in the late night with Jupp Diefenthal in his SPW high up in the forested hills just a couple of kilometers short of Stavelot. From Peiper's perch, he could look down into the town, and the Ambleve below. All evening, his armor and infantry crawled up on the Ligneuville road, assembling to launch a full-blooded blow across the Amblève. At daybreak on the 18th he would strike, thrash the enemy, and push for the Meuse river.

Chapter 16

STAVELOT

And down by the trenches
in front of me a cemetery
has been sown
with forty-six-thousand soldiers
after such sowings we must
wait with serenity for harvest …[1]

To its 5,000 inhabitants, the old Belgian village of Stavelot was famous for three icons: its legendary founder, Saint Remacle, its famous poet son, Guillaume Apollinaire, and its weirdly eccentric annual festival, the *Carnaval du Laetare*. The mundane? Many of the people in the town worked in its tanneries, renowned throughout the region for high-quality leathers.

For officers of the Waffen SS, Stavelot was not famous, but infamous. The village along the Amblève and the surrounding region stirred contemptuous recall of the dogged Belgian opposition centerd there during the German occupation. The town was right on the borderline between the French- and German-speaking parts of Wallonian Belgium, and the ancient tensions were only accentuated by time itself. As much as Malmedy-Eupen served as a nexus for German ideas during the occupation, Stavelot was the focus of the Belgian Resistance.[2]

In 1940, a company of cyclists of the Chasseurs Ardennais, quartered in Stavelot, rose to fight the Germans the first day of the invasion. After the German occupation, Stavelot became a focal point for the Belgian resistance. Indeed, when the Germans first came through in 1940, most of the men of military age took off, even though there was no fighting in town, leaving behind only the old men, younger boys, women, and children.[3] Yet the men who fled did not really leave.

Made up of intrepid Belgian youths who hid in the forested hills of the area, the secret *Armée Blanche* near Stavelot was a locus of anti-German activity

SS officer Jochen Peiper is received by Adolf Hitler at his Wolfsschanze headquarters in East Prussia on 27 January 1944. In the meeting, Hitler awarded to Peiper the Oak Leaves to the Knight's Cross. (Hoffmann)

Peiper pictured outside Hitler's Wolfsschanze headquarters after receiving the Oak Leaves. (Hoffmann)

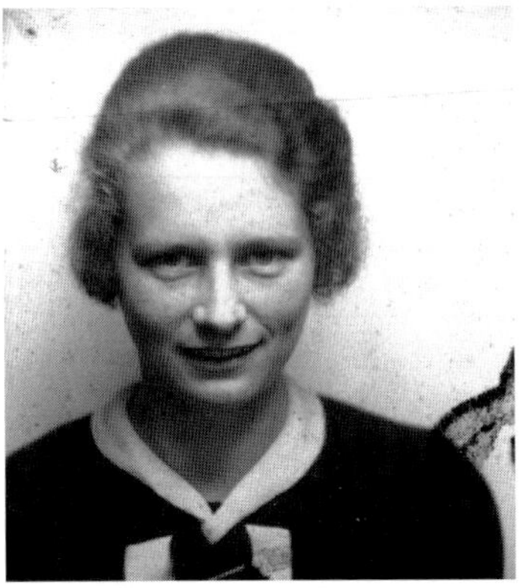

In 1936, Hedwig Potthast joined Heinrich Himmler's secretarial staff. Eventually the young woman became Himmler's secret mistress. Potthast was also very close to Jochen Peiper and his wife Sigurd, before the war (Sigurd was also a Himmler secretary) and they maintained a close correspondence during the conflict. (BA-K)

Peiper addresses his assembled 1st SS tank regiment on 9 November 1944. The regiment was being reconstituted for future operations near the Westphalian town of Rahden. (Lippl)

The Mk V tank crew of SS-Uscha. Valentin Bersin at Rahden during Peiper address. Bersin's crew (Pz #122) consisted of SS-Strm. Rau, Figura, SS-Uscha. Woch and SS Strm. Georg Kotzur—the radio operator. (Lippl)

Peiper confers awards to members of his tank regiment at Rahden, Germany. With new operations coming, Peiper sought to inspire his command on 9 November 1944—the annual celebratory National Socialist occasion when Hitler had staged his *Bierkellerputsch* twenty-one years earlier. (Lippl)

SS-Stubaf. Werner Poetschke, the leader of Peiper's I. Panzer Battalion pictured with his adjutant SS-Ustf. Arndt Fischer during the autumn of 1944. (Fischer)

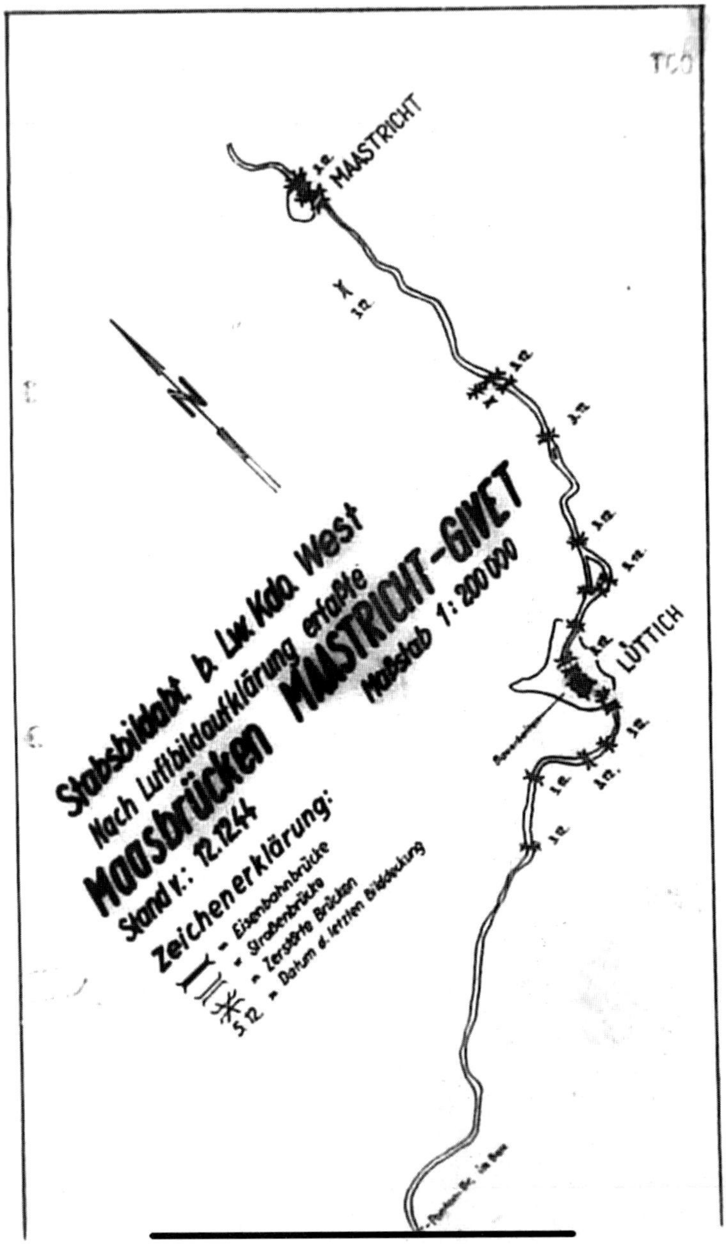

On 12 December 1944, the reconnaissance office of *Luftwaffen Kommando West* compiled a dated aerial evaluation of the Meuse River bridges over the recent weeks. These bridges would be a key objective for *Kampfgruppe Peiper* and the panzer spearheads. Some photos were obtained by the Arado-234 jets of *Kommando Sperling*, but coverage was spotty. Other than Huy, most bridges between Namur and Liège were still down. (NARA, T-311 Roll18).

SS Kreigsberichter Ferdinand Rottensteiner took photos of Mk V "Panther" tanks serviced under cover of Eifel forests prior to the Ardennes Offensive. (Suddeutscher Verlag)

The Allied Commanders: (Left to right): Lt. Gen. Sir Miles Dempsey, British Second Army; Lt Gen. Courtney H. Hodges, U.S. First Army; Field-Marshal Bernard L. Montgomery; Lt. Gen. William H. Simpson, U.S. Ninth Army; Gen. Harry Crerar, Canadian First Army, 1945. (NARA)

SS-Ostf. Werner Sternebeck was one of Peiper's most aggressive tank leaders and the head of the battlegroup *Panzerspitze* in the Ardennes. (Hans Behrend).

A German 88 mm flak gun is pressed into service in the initial barrage on the Allied lines, 16 December 1944. Nearly two thousand guns took part in the barrage along the Ardennes front, but much it was ineffective as it was unobserved and fired by map. (Gregoire)

Hôtel du Moulin in Ligneuville was the headquarters of the 1st SS Panzer Division beginning on 18 December 1944. Paul Rupp is no longer proprietor, but the hotel, still open and famous for its *haute cuisine*. It was the scene of dramatic events from 17-20 December 1944. (Shepperd)

U.S. prisoners of war of the 99th Infantry Division, guarded by a nonchalant member of the German 3rd Fallschirmjäger Division, march through Merlscheid towards Lanzerath and captivity. (BA-K)

A wrecked Mk IV Panzer of the Panzerspite under Sternebeck, which was destroyed when it took a wrong turn and proceeded north towards Wirtzfeld. There, it was struck down by anti-tank rounds from an M10 TD of the 644th Tank Destroyer Battalion. (NARA).

A German SPW (halftrack: Sd.Kfz. 251/1) of *Kampfgruppe Peiper* passes through the village of Honsfeld on 17 December 1944. At the far end of the road is a Möbelwagen FlaK Panzer (Sd.Kfz 161/3). To the right is an abandoned U.S. M3 personnel carrier which has been taken over by new owners. (NARA).

SS Troops in the Belgian town of Honsfeld scrounge for fuel. The Germans were desperately short on gasoline at the start of the Ardennes Offensive (NARA).

German Fallschirmjäger (parachute) troops traveling behind Peiper try on boots from Americans killed in the confusing battle in Honsfeld. (NARA)

On the morning of 17 December, the SS Kriegsberichter snapped a photo of an the air attack against *Kampfgruppe Peiper* near Büllingen. The strafing, by P-47s of the U.S. 366th Fighter Group ended at 10:20 AM. More than a dozen Luftwaffe fighters intervened and two U.S. fighter bombers were shot down, although seven German fighters also fell.

The knocked out Mk V Panther of SS Ustf. Arndt Fischer shown in Ligneuville in 1945. U.S. troops stand with the tank in front of the *Hôtel des Ardennes*—which is still in operation, but renamed the Hotel Saint Hubert. (NASM)

A tank-worthy J-bridge installed by German engineers over the blown rail overpass near Losheimergraben. Note the FlaK 38 2-cm anti-aircraft gun posted by the bridge. (NARA)

The Malmédy massacre field showing bodies of some of the 84 Americans killed in the Baugnez field and environs. Photo taken on 14 January 1945 after heavy snows. (NARA)

SS-Strm. Georg Fleps who admitted firing the first shots into the surrendered Americans at the field in Baugnez. (NARA)

SS-Oscha. Hans Siptrott who commanded the Mk IV tank #731 at the Malmédy crossroads. Siptrott claimed he was ordered to fire upon the Americans in the field at Baugnez. (NARA).

German SS grenadier of *Kampfgruppe Hansen* signals the way forward at the Poteau crossroads after the defeat of Task Force Mayes/ U.S. 14th Cavalry Group, 18 December 1944. (NARA)

Moving along Rollbahn E on 18 December, *Kampfgruppe Hansen* passes the Kaiserbarcke crossroads northwest of St. Vith. The shortage of transport in the German army is reflected in high ridership. (Gregoire).

Famous photo of a Königstiger #222 of Heavy SS Panzer Battalion 501 at the Kaiserbaracke crossroads on 18 December 1944. The Fallschimjäger are likely members of the secret troop,12/FJ Rgt. z.b.V.,associated with the Skorzeny operation. This specialist troop accompanied Peiper all the way to Stoumont. Tiger #222 was lost in Stavelot. (NARA)

Elements of *Kampfgruppe Knittel* at the Kaiserbaracke crossroads on 18 December 1944. This series of photos shows unknown SS officers of the 1st SS Reconnaissance Battalion posing atop an amphibious *Schwimmwagen.* In the past, it has been claimed to show Peiper – completely untrue. (NARA)

Standing in his command car amid a total traffic jam on Rollbahn E, SS Brigadeführer Wilhelm Mohnke, the commander of the *1st SS Panzer Division* is on the road from Büllingen. Reaching Ligneuville, he would make his headquarters there: 18 December 1944. (Gregoire).

Just north of Ligneuville, several Americans were killed by the road, executed by SS-Oscha. Paul Ochmann with *Kampfgruppe Peiper*. (NARA).

Ernest Natalis of Stoumont who met Peiper or Poetschke during the battle and helped cool tempers. (Natalis)

The heavily contested bridge across the Warche River at Stavelot. The ancient stone span was the scene of extensive fighting in the battle by the U.S. to deny a supply path to *Kampfgruppe Peiper.* (CRIBA)

Heavy Königstiger of s. SS Panzer Battalion 501 passes a line of prisoners of the U.S. 99th Infantry Division near Lanzerath on the morning of 18 December 1944. Too slow and ponderous for Peiper's tastes, the heavy tank battalion brought up the rear of his battlegroup. (NARA)

throughout the occupation. Although poorly armed, the bands boldly carried on a covert guerrilla war against the invaders from the east, derisively referred to by locals as the *verts de-gris*, the 'green-greys'. One of these young men, Emile Wolwertz, became a leader of the resistance in the area and fought against the Germans for years. Just before being captured in 1943, he killed himself in the woods and became a martyr for the local boys, including Marcel Ozer.[4]

Ozer was a typical member of the resistance; he had one brother in forced labor in Germany and both he and his other brother had been arrested and imprisoned in 1943 on the logical suspicion of being part of the resistance. Modelled after the Free French and supported by the women of the town and its elders, these bands made life treacherous for SS men who were active in the area during the summer 1944 flight to the German border. When the Gestapo released Marcel in 1944, he re-joined the resistance. 'There were about two hundred of us around Wanne,' he remembered.[5] But all were so deficiently armed that their actions were more like the nuisance of juvenile delinquents than the deadly partisan bands in Russia. Still, they hated the SS men. For the Waffen SS, Stavelot was a 'nest of bandits'.[6]

Even if the U.S. First Army conceded that the Belgian resistance had been effective in thwarting Hitler's occupation of the Ardennes, the situation there remained byzantine.[7] Hodge's intelligence officers worried about a toxic mix of pro and anti-German groups in the Belgian Ardennes. In early December the U.S. First Army disarmed the last Belgian resistance groups. First and foremost were the Rexists, led in absentia by local fascist hero Leon Degrelle.

Degrelle was a recent recipient of the prestigious Knight's Cross with the Oak Leaves, earned while fighting in the east with the SS as an Obergruppenführer. He had always vowed to return to 'liberate' Belgium. The Rexists, now driven underground by the American liberation, were nevertheless still active in Ardennes with both pro-Nazi espionage and mayhem, as evidenced by the brazen political murder of Count Louis d'Oultremont during the liberation in August 1944.[8] That Malmedy was only 10km away only trebled tension in Stavelot.[9] Everyone in Malmedy spoke German or Walloon – and there were a number of Nazi sympathisers. However, any SS men operating west of Malmedy were likely to find the French-speaking Stavelot locals less than hospitable. That part of the Belgian Ardennes was culturally schizophrenic.

An early case in point came on 6 September 1944, when, after fleeing France, the legendary Kurt 'Panzer' Meyer was captured by members of the *Armée Blanche* in Durnal, east of the Meuse river. And two days later, the same organization ambushed SS Knight's Cross-holder Stubaf. Hans Waldmüller.[10] On Friday, 8 September, Waldmüller was in a motorcycle with a sidecar, hauling back east through the Ardennes toward the German border with his adjutant, SS Ustuf. Maquardt. As the officers of the 12th SS Panzer Division sped through the thick pine forests from Werbomont toward Stavelot, members of the Belgian resistance just west of Basse Bodeux pulled a cable across the road. Waldmüller, his adjutant, and the driver were sent sprawling from their motorcycle. The adjutant was shot in the head and Waldmüller himself was hacked to death with a knife.[11]

Four days later, on 12 September 1944, Stavelot was liberated by American troops, but not before the local Gestapo apprehended seven Ardennes youths supposedly involved in the ambush. The group was sent to Verviers, where four were shot and the rest jailed.[12] The SS did not forget; both Meyer and Waldmüller were long veterans with the Leibstandarte. Indeed, Waldmüller had graduated from SS officers' school at Braunschweig, as had Peiper.

When 23-year-old Marcel Ozer had returned home to Stavelot after the American liberation that September he surprised his happy mother. He and his other resistance buddies were bitterly disappointed to be disarmed. Some of these resistance comrades had even considered volunteering for service with the 5th Belgian Fusiliers that were being filled out as an adjunct force with the First Army, but that seemed a let down. Their duties were mostly standing guard over motor pools or other black market targets: long, cold hours at Herve, Aywaille, or the fuel dumps near Spa. The uniforms were poorly fitting British throwbacks with the bowl-shaped British helmets and the weapons nearly an afterthought. There seemed to be little chance to fight the Germans, and Marcel, like many others, returned to the agrarian life. He resumed work at the local dairy and a budding romance with girlfriend Juliette. 'We thought the war was over.'

Twenty-five-year-old Beathe Wetz, living with her parents at 15 Grand Place, was also relieved when the Americans had arrived in September 1944.[13] Her father was the patron of the Hôtel du Perron in Stavelot and the war had begun for her when the neighbour next door woke everyone up on 10 May 1940. 'Wake up! Wake up!' she shouted. 'The war is here!'[14] When the occupation began that Friday, many elected to flee, but Beathe's father, Edward, thought this was folly. 'We will stay here,' he insisted. 'Besides, where would you go? If you go to France, the Germans have taken that, too!' Still, the young men left. Beathe's brothers stayed away – one hid in south Belgium trying to avoid German conscription and the other remained in the Belgian Congo. There was a double standard for the sexes. Being a pretty, young, blonde girl with dark blue eyes meant that Beathe was treated well by the Germans, but no one wanted them around. 'We were scared a lot,' she recalled. 'It was a terribly sad time.' Food was short; the family always kept suitcases ready to flee. Beathe Wetz almost gave up music.

'I could not live without the piano,' said Beathe. Having taken lessons since she was 9, she treasured the Zimmermann upright her father had gifted her. Before the war, Beathe had daily practised her favorite pieces: Bach, Debussy, Schümann, and Rachmaninoff. Warm tones filled their comfortable living room. Their home was in an imposing, multi-storey, twenty-nine-room structure constructed in 1868 from Pierre de Taille – the greyish-blue masonry stone indigenous to the region. The stout structure seemed to always be billeted with soldiers. During the German occupation, she seldom played, the Zimmermann was a barometer for her Belgian mood.

When the Americans came that autumn, her mood lifted. As before, there were now more than a dozen young soldiers staying at their home. Yet unlike the taciturn German soldiers during the occupation (who seemed proper enough), the U.S. Army GIs were different: casual, relaxed, and friendly. C Company of the 202nd Engineer Combat Battalion was stationed in Stavelot in early December, just after her birthday, and the commander and many of the men were billeted at her home; the American boys predictably sought female companionship, and provided chocolate as they practised their French. Beathe had learned some English at school and after the American boys got the word from Lt Joe Chinlund – no fooling around – a little friendship developed.

When some of the Americans found Beathe had a piano, they urged her to play. She played Mozart and Beethoven's *Pathétique* for a happy few, but one soon brought her sheet music for more contemporary tunes. Beathe could sight read music, and soon she was playing the songs for which they yearned: 'Let Me Call You Sweetheart', 'Always', and 'Deep Purple'. It wasn't unusual for more than a dozen appreciative Americans to crowd into their living room. That was the scene at the Wetz household during the late afternoon of Sunday, 17 December. All day heavy American traffic had rumbled through town, but the soldiers gathered at her home just the same. The first sign of trouble came at about 6 p.m. – an American soldier rushed into the living room and interrupted mid-recital.

The messenger addressed the lieutenant in excited speech so rapid that Beathe could not catch it. 'All of a sudden the whole house of soldiers started running around madly, grabbing guns in a great hurry.'[15] Guns in hand, they all ran out of the house, jumped into vehicles, and sped off.[16] The family was mystified. After midnight a number of the GIs came back. Chinlund had reached as far as Trois-Ponts when he was ordered to return to Stavelot to guard its bridge. When the lieutenant returned he seemed pre-occupied. Beathe asked about the earlier alarm. 'Nothing,' he told her, 'nothing at all.'[17]

Neither Beathe's mother nor father seemed convinced; most of the other soldiers were gone and the traffic in town continued at an uneasy pace. When Chinlund got back to Stavelot to the home, Pfc. Stanley Aldinger, his radio operator, said the lieutenant lay in a bed 'shaking like a leaf'. That night Chinlund questioned Aldinger, 'What's the signal for retreat?' Sounds of shooting outside interrupted their conversation. 'Well, it is impossible to stay here,' Chinlund said.[18] He ordered Aldinger to go down to the bridge and report back. The private took his rifle and was off to find Pfc. Howard Meyer of the 202nd.

That night, Beathe tossed and turned in the small room behind the kitchen, where she and her parents slept. As with other farming towns along the Amblève in Belgium, Stavelot was deeply religious – in fact, there were five separate services at St Sebastien's Church each Sunday. As always, the main mass at 10 a.m. was most heavily attended. There, farmers could receive the Eucharist after sleeping a little late, friendly conversation with friends after the service, and perhaps quaff a *petite gouette* – a small drop – in one of Stavelot's nineteen cafés.[19]

As the faithful approached the church from the Avenue Ferdinand Nicolay at 10 a.m., they saw two U.S. Army jeeps racing through town from Malmedy. Strange, here in the Ardennes, the American GIs seemed to almost take Sundays off. And when the church crowd emerged an hour later, they were confronted by the sight of tanks and vehicles of every size and type moving bumper to bumper along the Rue Henri Massange. So dense was the traffic that it was difficult to cross the street. What was this?[20]

Questions from curious local boys revealed that the Americans were all from the 7th Armored Division. Even Pfc. Paul Kohli of the 202nd Engineer Battalion, a farm boy from Ohio who had been in town for days, was stumped by the sudden traffic. Each vehicle's occupants had a different explanation. They all wanted to know if anyone had any liquor. Where were they going? 'Search me?,' said one GI, 'I just follow the vehicle in front of me.'[21] As the parishioners returned home, the farmers and shopkeepers debated the events over wine. Reaching his doorstep on the Rue Vieux Château south of the Amblève river, Albert Sougné, confronted another improbable sight.

Immediately before his gaze was Noël Hubert of Refat hustling down the road, followed by his family. Hubert was pushing a cart covered with blankets and other random items – even a canary cage. At first, Sougné flashed back to May 1940 when the Germans had come. 'Where are you going, Noël?' the Stavelot native chided. 'Are you moving?' 'Don't laugh, Albert!' he retorted, plodding toward the bridge. 'The Germans are in Ligneuville and everything is burning there!' No sooner had Hubert disappeared down the road than a wheeled flood of refugees on bicycles spilled into town from the same direction.[22]

Meanwhile, in the darkened cave of the Casino Cinema during the Sunday matinee, someone yelled shrilly in the middle of the film. 'The Germans are coming!' Stolen kisses forgotten, the lights came up. Everyone spilled outside into the winter gloom to witness a stream of refugees. 'The *verts de-gris* were back!' Then an announcement from the mayor of Stavelot – a curfew was in effect immediately.

Marcel Ozer worried with everyone else. 'It's not possible!' Ozer's mother cried out. Yet seeing many other locals streaming through Stavelot, many townspeople grabbed a few possessions and joined them. Ozer's mother wanted to stay, however, so he and his family joined many others hiding in the cellars of the big Abbey and the dairy. During the night no one slept, but Ozer and his other friend from the resistance, Raymond Blaise, wanted to retrieve their weapons 'and see if we could do something'. Just before dawn he and Blaise left the dairy and headed for the south side of the bridge across the Amblève river. As they approached the bridge in the pre-dawn, they could see four or five American soldiers on the other side of the street. 'Let's go over and see what's going on.' After a few steps, Ozer was petrified to see the closest soldier's upper sleeve. It was adorned by a silver eagle-Waffen SS. The man raised a machine pistol. '*Raus!*' he cried. 'Get lost!' Both walked briskly back to the dairy, hearts pounding.

Now, the Leibstandarte Adolf Hitler was poised above the town, with SS Obersturmbannführer Jochen Peiper in charge. For time-obsessed German planners, *Wacht am Rhein* had fallen badly behind schedule. All but the most jaded called for the panzer spearheads to reach the Meuse river by the evening of the second day – or at worst – the third. Things had certainly gone differently in May 1940, when the German 28th Infanterie Division had reached Stavelot nine hours after the beginning of Hitler's offensive in the west – albeit in good weather and against scant resistance.[23] Now, four and a half years later, Hitler's most trusted SS tank leader had arrived before Stavelot in the middle of a cold December night.

Kampfgruppe Peiper had made no real advance progress since 9 p.m. the previous evening – forty hours since the start of the offensive. With Peiper absent for several hours, his battle group languished for hours in the road between Beaumont and La Vaulx Richard, worried about Pvt. Goldstein's challenge at La Corniche. Was there a way to circumvent the perceived enemy strength along the main road? Peiper could not know that the fabled enemy in the dark was no more than a squad firing rifles, a lone machine gun, and an American soldier who had not fired a bazooka since basic training.[24]

To German eyes, the threat below seemed magnified by the non-stop U.S. traffic visible in the darkened streets of Stavelot. Even though duped by phantom headlights and shots in the night, Peiper was back in control and ready to add a spark beyond La Vaulx Richard. At 2 a.m. he ordered the half-tracked 11th Company under SS-Ostuf. Heinz Tomhardt to dismount and assault a densely forested hilltop known as Stokeu on the southern outskirts of Stavelot. He was to use whatever troops were available. 'After the counterattack was repulsed, I committed more armored infantry to attack Stavelot again.'

Meanwhile, Jupp Diefenthal arrived surprised to find Skorzeny's jeep teams waiting. 'On a hill overlooking Stavelot, a group of Skorzeny people with three jeeps each with four men under the leadership of Oberleutnant reported to us. The 1st lieutenant wanted to go with our group following our advance to be able to drive fast (*abzurauschen*) after a breakthrough into behind-enemy lines.' The commandos did not offer to help reconnoitre the American defenses, but Diefenthal and Peiper agreed the *Einheit Stielau* troops could tag along with him.[25]

Peiper's idea was to coup the bridge without alerting the enemy at the roadblock he thought was stoutly defended at La Corniche.[26] Otherwise the crossing would surely be demolished by the American engineers already encountered. His infantry would take a small track, a farmer's trail called La Bergerie, rising on the wooded hills from the Ferme Petit to the Ferme Rensonnet. The trail was unsuitable for anything beyond cows or walking foot soldiers. Emerging from the high forested hill south of Stavelot, they would dash on to the Route de Stokeu to take the bridge in a short infantry rush in the dark. As Peiper always said, 'night is our friend'. At the end of the ambling 2.5km approach, they were to seize the old medieval stone bridge that he needed to pass his 46-ton Panthers across the Amblève river. If possible, one platoon was to cross the river upstream to take the bridge by surprise from the north side. But would that even be possible with the swift river current?

The infantry mission fell to the 1st platoon under SS-Ustuf. Willi Horn and the 4th under SS-Oscha. Rudi Rayer. The approach proceeded more like a hesitant game of infantry hide-and-seek than a full-out assault. The luckless Bernard Goldstein and his ill-fated buddy, Pvt. Liparulo, had run afoul of Tomhardt's grenadiers sometime after midnight, but the advance of the grenadiers progressed only in a dilatory fashion. It was after 5 a.m. when the SS panzer grenadiers struck Task Force Solis – a small unit built around Company A of the 526th Armored Infantry Battalion. Still, before dawn the SS troopers reached the heights south of Stokeu, while others filtered into the houses along *Chem du Château* just south of the Amblève river bridge. Meanwhile, the lead tank of Erich Strelow was on the road waiting, noticing that a platoon of infantry and engineers moved ahead of their parked Panthers. Their orders were to secure the bridge and remove mines. They heard some firing, but then all went silent. What?

Had Peiper's attack come at midnight, they would have found the bridge covered by no more than a squad of American infantry – perhaps not even that. Company C of the 202nd Engineer Combat Battalion had left the previous night, only to be ordered by Col Anderson to return to protect the bridge. However, there was an hour where the span was totally undefended. Skulking back to Stavelot, it wasn't until 1 a.m. that 'Blinky' Chinlund had his few bazookas and heavy machine guns in place to cover a daisy chain of mines on the bridge. [27] Even then, the men were so sleepy that a local youth, René Bourgonjon, coming back from a visit to his girlfriend in Hénoumont, was able to approach from the Stockeu road and cross the bridge in the darkness, avoiding the mines with his bicycle. Reaching the other side, his clanging bicycle chain woke Pfc. Jim Jackson and Nick Marinucci, who had fallen asleep behind the tripod of their 30-calibre machine gun.[28] The Americans thought the Belgian was a German spy and held him.

At 3.45 a.m., Task Force Solis began to arrive in Stavelot. Named for its commander, Maj. Paul Solis, its vanguard was Company A of the 526th Armored Infantry under Capt. Charles A. Mitchell. There was also a company of tank destroyers from the 825th TD Battalion. Maj. Solis had received orders from his battalion commander, Lt Col Irwin, to move combat elements across the bridge to defend its southern approach. Capt. Mitchell recalled:

> I set up our CP in the Engineer Building near the bridge. At 0430 hours I sent the 2nd platoon and one section of TDs along the route to the left to occupy the 202nd Engineers' roadblock. I sent the 3rd platoon off to the right to establish a roadblock and kept the 1st platoon around the CP for internal security.[29]

Obediently, at 5.30 a.m., portions of Mitchell's company and Lt Doherty's platoon moved to the north side of the span in several half-tracks. Lt Harry A. Willyard, commander of Mitchell's 2nd squad, insisted to S/Sgt Felix Skuta of the 202nd that he remove the mines so they could pass to defend the approach on the other side of the bridge. Outranked, the sergeant directed John J. Stevenson to do so. Soon, two half-tracks driven by Pfc. John Stredwick and T/5 John Osborne moved across the river and began to climb the Route du Vieux Château.[30]

All the while Capt. Charles A. Mitchell was unaware that he was sending the combat team into the lion's jaws. Diefenthal's panzer grenadiers were now collecting in the darkened streets and houses on the other side of the Amblève river. There was another critical oversight: in directing Mitchell to take over, Solis did not check to see if the span had been prepared for demolition, assuming that both the 291st and 202nd Engineers in Stavelot must have done so. In fact, Mitchell knew nothing about orders to destroy the bridge; neither did Paul Kohli with the 202nd. They had been ordered to guard the bridge, but not to destroy it.[31]

More half-tracks soon crossed over, ferrying machine gunners of the 2nd squad – S/Sgt William Heuer and Jack Ellery and their crews – to set up a defense of the bridge. At the same time, tank destroyers of Company A of the 825th TD moved across the river as well. The half-tracked combat team under Lt Willyard was to drive up to the roadblock previously occupied by Charles Hensel and the engineer squad at La Corniche. His two half-tracks had ascended the Vieux Château road about halfway up when Willyard ordered the engines cut so they could listen. By radio, Willyard called Capt. Mitchell on the other side of the river. He reported all was calm.

Some of Willyard's men seem to have made it to La Corniche, if only to run into the assembling column of the Kampfgruppe Peiper near the Ferme Rensonnet. There, Americans knocked on the door of the farmhouse, only to be warned by Ernest Rensonnet that the Germans had been there around midnight.[32] Two of the captive Belgian guides, Jules Califice and Emile Claude, were guiding the head of Kampfgruppe Peiper down toward the bend in the road past La Corniche. They moved in two captured American jeeps: Skorzney men with panzer grenadiers coming behind.

The farmer's frantic protestations finally understood, they ran back quickly to turn a heavy machine gun against the German column approaching La Corniche in the darkness. Claude and Califice used the confusion to escape, amazed to find themselves unharmed. But the Germans were not so lucky, with several seriously wounded from 50-calibre machine gun fire.[33] Willyard first reported to Mitchell of running into a small enemy patrol. It got bigger. The shooting swelled into an automatic weapons firefight. With a fireworks-like shower of gun flashes all around, Willyard ordered the half-tracks to pull back. They were taking fire from all directions. At 6 a.m. Mitchell moved his CP into the church in the town square, taking advantage of its height to give him a better view of the bridge across the Amblève.

Meanwhile, on the other side of the Amblève, Lt Jack Doherty, commanding the towed anti-tank guns of the 825th Tank Destroyer Battalion, set up an observation post of the road coming down from La Corniche 1,000m away. Before dawn, his crews had made their way up to the Allée Vert along the road to Malmedy .[34] This road paralleled the river on the north side, and would allow the GIs to ambush the enemy when they tried to enter town on the one good road. Doherty had been leaning against one of the stout elm trees lining the road, steadying his binoculars to gaze across the river toward the road at the top of the hill. Peering through the haze just before daybreak, he saw a shadow on the road above. Small-arms fire crackled and there was a faint metallic squealing sound. He had never heard German tanks, but when he saw orange flames suddenly spew from one of the shadows, he knew it was his quarry. There was a very short delay until he heard an exploding round and not far away. Doherty ordered Sgt Martin Hauser's gun unlimbered and the crew moved into well-rehearsed action, turning the 76mm towed piece toward the distant hill across the river.

The Americans, too, had been spotted. Just then another shell exploded among the trees lining the road, quite near the crew hurrying to prepare their riposte. But as the minutes passed, Doherty's crew worried that a head-on shot against a German tank at that distance would only glance off. They only had a few armored-piercing rounds and wanted to wait for their target to move across their field of view and expose their less-protected sides. The Germans would have to traverse a 300m distance naked of cover and perpendicular to their waiting guns. Broadside shot. But as they waited, a swirling mist took the targets in and out of view. When the German tank appeared again, they were shocked to see it bolt quickly down the road with more tank shapes zooming right behind. Doherty was exasperated. 'Shoot when you get the chance!' he urged Hauser. 'We didn't come here to watch a Kraut parade!'[35] Quickly, his crewmen fired, but the accompanying tracer of the first round showed it zooming above the target. Now, with the ambush betrayed, the gun crew fired as fast as they could load, sight, and shoot. Sgt Hauser's men punched off four additional rounds, but with the fog, jitters, and difficulty of firing uphill, all seemed to miss.

Doherty ordered Hauser's gun to be hastily moved to a new position closer to town. When Hauser resumed fire, he was joined by a second 76mm under Sgt Louis Celentano about 100m west. Meanwhile, S/Sgt Vester Lowe brought up more ammunition. Even with both guns blasting away and more shells fired, they could not seem to hit the German tanks in the foggy morning. Also, other 57mm gun crews of the anti-tank platoon of 526th Armored Infantry Battalion under Lance Corp. William Ewen and S/Sgt William Jensen had set up not far away. They, too, joined the fire, but with their puny AT weapons, piercing the thick steel hide of distant German tanks was unlikely. They banged away all the same. Unfortunately, as the towed gun crews fired, the return attention of the Germans on the hill sent a blizzard of shells and long-range machine gun fire cascading into the Alleé Verte. As the ammunition dwindled for each of the guns and shells began to burst all around them, the crews sought cover. Their efforts were brave, but the gunnery failed to still the German armor. Peiper's tanks now raced down the hill across the river, barrelling as fast as a Panther could go.[36]

A hell rapidly developed around the American gun positions. Curate André Raskin had just celebrated early Monday morning Mass at St Sebastian

Church, and arriving at daybreak at the little Chapelle Saint Louis, located about half a kilometer away on the east edge of Stavelot.[37] Even with a sparse audience, at 7.45 a.m. he began the Eucharist … '*Pater Noster*'. A stunning explosion shook the ancient chapel, the walls struck by the first shell aimed at the nearby American gunners. Plaster fell. After rising from the floor, Raskin prayed.

The household of young Yvonne Gruselin was on edge since the previous evening after hearing the shooting across the river up on the hill at La Corniche. As the shells began to shake their home, young Yvonne stole outside to watch the American gunners firing away at the enemy on the other side of the river. Now, a battery of American quad-mounted 40mm Bofors anti-aircraft guns (203rd AAA AW Battalion) stumbled into the fight not far from the Gruselin home, moving along the Malmedy road in their attempt to re-join the 7th Armored Division. Tracers ripped across the river going both directions. High up on the hill Yvonne saw shells flying like big orange sparks and striking the Rensonnet Farm. Even at a distance, she could see the barn's roof burst into flame. Scared crazy, Yvonne dashed back inside.[38]

High up the hill, Joseph Rensonnet had watched as the gunfire and flames enveloped his cowshed. Looking out as his son Ernest raced back to the main house, he was seized with one thought: 'the *bêtes*!' With gunfire crashing down, he and his son ran back to the cowshed to evacuate the fifty cattle in the barn. They entered from the back and threw the doors open. 'Gee up!' he yelled as the cows mooed woefully inside the blazing barn. The frightened animals thundered out in a near stampede, Rensonnet and his son herding them away amid bullets and shells. The father and son emerged choking from smoke to find themselves in the barn courtyard confronted with a weird scene. Two Waffen SS infantrymen were readying to shoot one of their pigs, which had just been turned loose. Pulsing with adrenalin, Resonnet stopped them by standing between them and the pig. There were shouts – Ernest fully terrified by his father's bold move.[39]

Pfc. Howard Meyer and Corp. Donald Necina of C Company, 202nd Combat Engineers, were still hiding in the bushes by the north-side bridge. In spite of the odds, they had survived both placing the mines on the bridge that evening and then removing them at the insistence of a cocky TD officer. But after the American half-tracks and guns crossed, red and green flares burst like stars in the sky. Soon the night was filled with ear-splitting bangs and explosions. 'We could see gun flashes,' Meyer remembered. Those guys 'had run into those krauts'.

Just then, the engineer squad was joined by Pfc. Stan Aldinger, who had come down to see what was happening; Chinlund was not willing to leave headquarters. Then, the sounds of grinding machinery: on the bridge – a tank. Nervously, Necina shouldered the bazooka and loosed the rocket at the looming shape. After a shower of sparks burst against its front, the iron beast stopped and began firing madly at everything.[40] Machine gun fire was all over. Meyer blasted off a belt of 30-calibre MG rounds, but for what? 'We have nothing to fight tanks like that!' Aldinger said. 'We ran,' Meyer remembered, 'we ran as fast as we could go.'

Meanwhile, Sgt Martin Hauser's 76mm remained concealed among the trees before Jean Jacob's house along the Avenue Ferdinand Nicolay. Although replenished with ammunition and firing across the river once more, the smoke from the burning farms now prevented effective observation on the approach route for the German tanks. Later, the mostly residential buildings themselves along the Rue du Vieux Château obscured the line of sight. But after the first flock of German tanks had passed by, Hauser spied a panzer halted near the postman's house. After a few tense moments, he managed to get off a shot. The 3in round hit Panther #115 broadside, penetrating the hull and igniting the engine, which soon oozed thick, oily smoke. The Americans cheered their first victory, but the entire German crew under SS Uscha. Hans Richartz escaped to take refuge in the home of Marcel Loxhet just across the road. Cowering inside, Loxhet was shocked when a bleeding black-uniformed German panzer man burst into his home. He and Marcel Breuer, his brother-in-law, treated the bleeding SS tanker and offered he and other Germans water before they left.[41]

At about the same time that Hauser hit his mark, the nearby gun of Sgt Celentano managed to hit another tank and damage its transmission – likely Hans Hennecke's Panzer #111. Celentano, too, was frustrated as he watched the crew of the stricken tank jump out and run for cover – his machine gunner had hesitated.[42]

> In the midst of all this fighting when the tanks stopped, my machine gunner froze. We watched as one of the tank's turret opened up and men started to jump out. I looked up and Ben had his fingers on the trigger of the 50-calibre, but he wasn't firing. I was yelling, 'Fire! Fire!' but nothing happened. I jumped up on to the half-track and got behind him and with my fist hit his hand hard. His hand released the trigger and I swear only one bullet came out of that gun. But I looked up to see one man coming out of that tank get hit with that one bullet.

By now the first half dozen German tanks had gone by and Doherty's ammunition was dwindling once more. He could hear the wail of steel tracks and musketry down near the bridge. There was no sound from the guns of Armstrong or Whaley, Doherty unaware of their earlier fate. Would the Germans cross and swallow up his little platoon, and run them down from behind? With few other options, Doherty sent off a frenzied message to Maj. Solis and the 526th. The German tanks were already across the river and they were pulling out of town. Swearing under his breath, Doherty ordered one of his guns to be wheeled into position to fire down the road to protect their rear.

What had happened to those assigned to hold the bridge? Out in front of the ancient stone span, sleepy machine gunners had set up on the south side. Cpl James Landgren of the 526th was more impressed with the darkness of the night than Capt. Mitchell's warning:

> When we reached the other side of the river we heard what seemed to be tanks or half-tracks. The person closest to me was Bill Kenny. He helped me haul a 30-calibre air-cooled machine gun. I carried the machine gun, and he carried the ammo boxes. We also had M1 carbines strapped on our backs. We talked to each other in whispers: 'What is going on?' We walked about ten minutes up the road. We took a road that went directly east across the river. It was wooded on the right-hand side alternating with pasture; there were some houses on the left. When we heard the sound of the tank treads, we put the gun on the south side of the road. Bill Kenny was handling the ammunition; I held the machine gun. I said, 'Let's find out what's going on and send somebody back to see what we should do.' Staff Sgt Jack Ellery was back there on the east side of the bridge.[43]

Assigned to reinforce Willyard's two half-tracks were two towed 3in guns of Lt Jack Doherty's 1st platoon, Company A of the 825th TD Battalion. In the darkness, the second half-track of Sgt Jonas Whaley first took a wrong turn down the Rue des Iles. Driving their half-track towing a 3in gun all night, William Gilman longed to reach their destination so he could sleep. But rather than climbing the hill to reach Armstrong, Whaley found his half-track rattling along on a street that paralleled the Amblève. Bob Hammons was with Whaley and crew:

> There was an unusual quietness as we prepared to set up our 3in guns in town when we heard what seemed to be tanks revving up. Lt Jack Doherty sent two squads across the Amblève river while another two squads were set up on the street [to fire across the river]. Sgt Armstrong was in the first half-track and Sgt Whaley, myself, and crew were in the second. As we crossed the bridge over the Amblève, we went to the left and down a dead-end street. With that wrong move, we turned around and started back. As we travelled this short distance back to the right road, residents were opening up their doors to see what we were doing. We told them to turn off the lights.[44]

Eventually, realising the error, they awkwardly doubled back to the bridge and from there clanked up the hill as ordered. Meanwhile, Sgt John Armstrong in the other half-track had already ascended the Route du Vieux Château to the turn-off on the Route de Somagne. They halted just across from some brick houses on the left side of the road.[45] As Whaley proceeded up the street to join him, a military policeman stopped them and warned that the enemy was just up ahead. That soon became obvious. Creeping ahead in their half-track, they came across a jeep on the right side of the road just beyond the bridge with a dead American slumped over the wheel. It was Pfc. Lorenzo Liparulo, who had died earlier that night in an encounter with the Germans lurking on the south bank of the river. Whaley was intent on joining Sgt Jack Armstrong. He had just sighted the other half-track when a brilliant star-flare illuminated the road, buildings, and pastures.

Tracers zipped through the night under the illumination of the flare. Whaley yelled for his crew to detach the 76mm gun, and everyone jumped off to pirouette the gun as if on a state-side drill. But that action soon seemed unwise, for the gun crew came under an ugly fusillade with bullets bouncing off the baseplate. Whaley and Armstrong conferred urgently under the din. In seconds, they decided to pull back to the bridge. It soon became obvious that the enemy had infiltrated the houses and hedges that lined the road. Sgt Armstrong began to slowly pull back, as Whaley followed, choosing to abandon the gun. Hammon recalled:

> As we approached the road and turned left up the hill, I noticed a jeep moved up against a building. The driver had been shot and I thought he was dead … As we moved up the hill [along the Rue du Vieux Château] all I could hear was the sound of our tracks on the street echoing against the houses on the left side of the road. As we reached the top of the hill, a cold drizzle had begun and all of a sudden, flares went up and lit up the whole area. The 1st squad had hit a trip flare and then there was a lot of firing from the Germans and also fire from GIs on the other side of the river. We were caught in the crossfire and tried to get out. In the scramble to get back down the hill, Sgt Armstrong's half-track slid into a ditch. We backed up and threw a towline and pulled them out. They passed us as we were trying to get the towline back on our track as we dodged the tracers. Suddenly, there was a ball of fire and an explosion in the half-track of the 1st squad in front of us. Immediately, we all tried to get out of both tracks. We disconnected a 30-calibre machine gun from the pedestal mount and someone handed it to me as I was already on the ground. I think it was Leonard Walsh and we scurried into a tin shed nearby. I was standing by the door with the MG as three others stood behind me (Walsh, Eichorn, and Willi Banes). We realised we were outnumbered and decided to go into a nearby house to set up the machine gun. We found a door open in the basement and hurried up to a bedroom. At the window, we could see the Germans coming over a bank and watched as two of them with burp guns shot Sgt Armstrong and Richardson as they were trying to get out of their burning half-track. Eichhorn, standing next to me, was angry at what he saw and raised his carbine to shoot them, but I noticed he had mud in the barrel and I stopped him. I decided we had better get out of there as tanks were already coming down the road.[46]

Meanwhile, the two infantry-loaded half-tracks of the 526th, including Lt Willyard and S/Sgt Dewey Lowe, had been similarly assailed in their position further up the road near La Corniche. They began a panicked action to pull their vehicles back down to the river. Yet as they approached the position of the tank destroyers, the enemy pulled a cable across the road that nearly turned over Lowe's half-track, driven by Daniel Osborne. Several men bailed from the vehicle as enemy fire enveloped everything. Lt Willyard managed to evade the trap, collecting several men from the crippled sister armored personnel carrier and backing down to the river.

At about the same time that Willyard ran into an ambush, the TD-towing half-track of Sgt John Armstrong drew near the line of brick houses on the right side of the Chemin de Château road 200m from the bridge. As they motored toward the bridge the men crouching in the half-track were suddenly stunned by a bright flash and a loud explosion. The back of the vehicle was shattered by a German Panzerfaust rocket. Hand grenades exploded. Sgt Armstrong stood up and yelled, 'Get out!' A chorus of voices barked 'Heil Hitler!' from the ditch.

The driver, Conley Leach, was killed immediately by bullets, which struck him in the back. His body collapsed over the wheel and on the horn, which howled in an unworldly dissonance. Machine gunner Frank Richesin was hit, too, crying out in anguish, while Leo Brunette scrambled over the hood of the half-track. Three men attempted futilely to scramble out of the back of the stricken vehicle. Tony Calvanese fell wounded from a hand grenade, but his crewmates, Gallagher and Williams, fell dead on top of him after being cut down by machine gun bullets. Even wounded, Richesin the gunner, Armstrong, and Brunette attempted to run. Only Brunette survived the lethal rain of automatic fire as they tried to dash to the house of Edmond Becker. The other two were cut down by the door. As the half-track caught fire, Tony Calvanese pushed out from under the other bodies to escape the burning vehicle and crawl. He had no confidence he would get even a few yards away, but at least he would not burn to death.

In the meantime, the half-track of Sgt Jonas Whaley following behind Armstrong's escaped the deadly trap. Seeing what happened to Armstrong's vehicle, the driver hastily pulled off to the right. Flames leapt from Armstrong's half-track before them, the enemy continuing to pour bullets into the conflagration. It seemed clear that the SS grenadiers were on both sides of the road – even behind them. The entire crew fled the vehicle and made for the houses that lined the road or followed Sgt Whaley, who ran for the bridge down the road.

Meanwhile, on the other side of the Amblève the 1st platoon of Company A of the 526th, with fifty-six men and several machine guns and bazookas, remained just north of the bridge on the right side of the Rue Gustave Dewalque, the main street through town. At 6.30 a.m. platoon leader Lt Charles F. Beardslee ordered S/Sgt Edward V. 'Vic' Brennan to unload his machine gun from his half-track and move his squad down by the bridge. To clarify a confusing tactical situation, Beardslee took Pvt. Dante M. Casa with him to the bridge for a personal reconnaissance. The choice of Pvt. Casa was understandable; the Mexican American had an unauthorised Browning Automatic Rifle (BAR) and loved to fire it:

> Lt Beardslee and I went down to the bridge that crossed the river. From behind a stone wall we observed two knocked-out American half-tracks on the opposite side of the river, one of which was burning and illuminating the area. We also observed three SS troopers looting the trucks and four more a little further away. I knew I could fire on the three SS troopers on the truck, but Beardslee said don't fire and to stay there until he could bring down the machine gun squad. The Germans were firing from the opposite side of the river. Being there alone, it seemed like a lifetime. Tracers and bullets were flying over my head and hit the stone wall and the houses behind me. I also heard their tanks moving in down the narrow roads, backing into houses. I was scared and cold. The machine gun squad finally arrived. I whispered to them to be silent. They moved down to a brick wall to the left of the bridge and took position.[47]

By the time Sgt Vic Brennan arrived, Germans sprayed wildly with a steady, if off target, gunfire. Sighting his big machine gun, the California native opined that the Germans had not located their position and ordered his men to hold their fire.[48] At that time a Belgian man holding the hand of two children suddenly bolted across the bridge. Dante Casa was still hugging the wall on the north side of the bridge, lying prone and pointing his BAR across the span. As they approached, Casa called on them to move on. They ran even faster, but no sooner had they reached safety than two German SS men with submachine guns ran charging behind them.

> I yelled in German for them to halt and throw their hands up. They were close together and bumped into each other at the sound of my voice. Then they fired. I fired, too, emptying my clip. It happened so fast and as the smoke cleared, I saw them dead. I felt dazed and my nose was bleeding.[49]

His face slammed by the recoil of the BAR, Casa was convinced he had been shot and ran, only stopping when he reached the square. Now, Beardslee's men found themselves pinned by enemy machine gun bursts, throwing themselves on the ground or hugging recessed doorways for cover. As Casa ran, he could hear the racket of machine gun fire banging away behind him.

Momentarily, marksman Lt Alfred Duesdieker, was able to rally Beardslee's platoon to overcome spreading command paralysis and set up a defense on the north side of the river. Seeking a stout place to make a stand, he remembered the First U.S. Army map depot in a building the locals called Beurrerie des Ardennes, just 30m from the bridge. Soon Duesdieker and Beardslee's platoon found themselves defending a kitchen truck left behind by the 202nd Engineers and the U.S. Army map storehouse. The building was replete with mountains of topographic maps, but not one of Stavelot. 'We do not even have one to know where we are,' he noted, 'but at least we will eat!'[50] That sortie ended when Pvt. John Mills moved to the building's window, only to have the glass shattered by bullets that tore into the stacks of maps.[51] 'Let's get the hell out of here!' Duesdieker yelled.

Meanwhile, also on the north side of the river, Mitchell placed two of his guns and a platoon of men before the vulnerable bridge along with another 57mm anti-tank gun located at the north edge of Stavelot. Mitchell intended for these placements to repel any German move toward the Franchorchamps road to the north and its million-gallon fuel dump. The rest of the troops (Mitchell's 3rd Platoon of the Company under Lt James J. Evans) were held in reserve at the marketplace in Stavelot, to serve as a backstop.

Then a strange incident: at the command post in the town square of the T-Force commander, Maj. Paul Solis, a soldier appeared in a faded American uniform and missing a helmet, but warning that hell was breaking loose. The Germans were right on top of them. The man spoke in a tortured English, but no one suspected at the time that the would-be Chicken Little might be a Skorzeny commando. A number of the interpreters in T-Force spoke with thick accents.[52] Yet Solis himself now became suspicious of the man – even though he had more pressing problems with his entire company currently under attack. Solis told the soldier to get back to his unit.

Some would later say that Solis had been spooked.[53]Alarmed by the nearing squeal of tank tracks and a crescendo of gunfire, Solis worried about the large cache of fuel stored on the Franchorchamps road, and sent his adjutant, Lt John Pehovic, to check on its security. Pehovic soon arrived at that place and nearly panicked to find no one minding the mountain of petroleum cans. He roared back toward Stavelot in his jeep to warn Major Solis. He had just left the stacks of fuel when he came across two half-tracks of the 526th heading to the west. Pehovic waved them down. 'I made them turn around,' he recalled. The air was filled with metallic howls of German tanks. Pehovic told the crews to get back to the fuel dump along the Franchorchamps road nearby – and quick.[54] Meanwhile, Solis was nowhere to be found. He had moved to the north side of Stavelot away from the endangered bridge, leaving its defense in the hands of Capt. Mitchell. It was the last time Mitchell saw him all morning.

Yet Solis may really have encountered a clandestine enemy commando. Not far away, the firing in the north end of the town slowed – at least enough for young Beathe Wetz to head back home from the house where she had taken refuge when shells were exploding. As she reached the Grand Place, she saw some soldiers in the customary green uniforms of the U.S. Army. *Ah,* she thought to herself, *the Americans have come back.*[55] She walked toward the nearest one in a friendly gesture. 'Halt!' he called out in German. 'Don't move.' Then one of the Germans in an American uniform came around and poked a rifle in her back. 'Don't be afraid,' the other one told her, 'I need something to drink.' 'Well, I live at that house there,' she said, motioning to the big building at #15, 'I will go there and get you some water.'

One German dressed as an American followed behind Beathe with his gun drawn. She quickly walked up to the steps and knocked on the door – she didn't dare go inside. The door opened. 'Mother, could you bring this soldier some water?'

Her mother seemed pleased but puzzled. 'I can do better,' and she soon returned with a cup of hot coffee. 'Oh, you have chased the *Boche*,' her mother gushed. 'Good!

Beathe stomped forcefully on her mother's foot. '*Please*, Mother,' she whispered in Walloon. 'He is one of *them* – he is not an American!'

Beathe's mother shook in a spasm, hurriedly excusing herself to the kitchen. Meanwhile, the young woman tried to keep her cool. 'Hey, you look pretty young,' Beathe said to the German gulping his coffee.

'I am 17,' he said proudly below the doorstep, 'and I am SS.'

'Thank you,' she nodded, deftly stepping back. Once inside, Beathe carefully closed the big wooden door and turned the lock. She collapsed, nearly fainting in relief.

Chapter 17

HESITATION

The worst calamities that befall an army arise from hesitation.

— Sun Tzu

The view from the German side? At 6 a.m. on 18 December 1944, Peiper was now fully in control of his battle group with tanks and half-tracks, bunched up on the road near the Rensonnet Farm on the cliffs above Stavelot. But still the question: why had he waited all night? Fuel deliveries to his tanks were tardy and he was not inclined to second guess his decision the previous evening. 'I could have taken Stavelot during the evening of the 18th [17th–18th], at the cost of my little infantry cover force, but only to run out of gas on the other side. I would not have been able to hold the place. During the night, my outfits closed up and at daybreak I attacked Stavelot properly prepared,' Peiper would later claim. 'Though I had given away a precious night, the opponent had not made much use of it, at least concerning the defense of "Fort Stavelot".'[1]

The morning was cold – 38 degrees and overcast, but nothing like Russia. On the other hand, the morning drizzle and ground fog would help cloak his baldly obvious approach.[2] His orders: immediate preparation for a full-scale assault. He had a brief huddle with Karl Kremser of the 1st Panzer Company, who would smash any resistance before them, and Jupp Diefenthal's grenadiers would root out anti-tank weapons. As stealthy trickery to seize the bridge before dawn had failed, he would fall back on the usual *modus operandi* – full speed, all guns blazing.

Meanwhile, Sgt Herb Barnes decided it was time to pull back to the bridge, ordering Cpl James F. Landgren to cover their retreat with his big Browning machine gun. Norman Pihaly, Philip Archambault, Harvey Schirrmacher, and Kelly Cornet were among those who ran back toward the bridge as he continued to fire blindly to the south. Landgren and his machine gun crew kept up the fire, but were desperate to get away:

> There were twelve of us in the squad; others set up with their M1s as soon as we heard the sounds. We waited there for no more than ten or fifteen minutes. We got word that we were to get out of there and get back across the river as best as we could. While we waited for the word, the tank tracks seemed to change directions (from the south rather than the east). We had no bazooka or anything that would stop a tank. No one said anything; we knew the enemy was right there. We could hear other sounds, motors, and engines. As soon as we heard that [orders to get back across the river] and I thought the others were now far enough back toward the bridge, we jumped up and ran down the road as fast as we could. It was very dark. I threw the firing bolt to the machine gun away and we abandoned the gun. I turned to the south to cross the river; Kenny went the other direction. I was going across the field when the firing started. Something hit me in the leg below the knee. There was large haystack close by and I rolled under that until I figured I could move again. Kenny ran the other way.[3] I loosened my boot; there was blood in the bottom of it. I put the boot back on loose. I must have dozed off that night. When I came to, it was 6 a.m. or 7 a.m. and very foggy. But I could see under it. Up the road, facing to the west toward the river, I could see a big German column on the road right in front of me. I could have hit them with a stone. There were bushes in between us and I was just on the other side of a haystack. I was slightly elevated so I could see down on it very well. Then there was a break in the column and I saw my chance. I ran across the road hobbling on my leg, but I went pretty fast.

Landgren ran to the closest house, which was occupied by Marie Louise Rochelinval, her sleeping grandfather and her daughter Paulette. 'Very early in the morning, we heard a noise at the front door. My mother went to see who it was and all of a sudden a soldier, his uniform in tatters, no shoes on his feet, fell inside the entranceway. He was wounded …'[4]

> I went straight to the closest house near me and knocked on the door. I spoke just a little French, but I didn't say a word. The door opened, and this little lady took my arm and helped me inside. While inside, Marie Louise took my boot off and put me on a bed. She took my sulphur pack from my kit and wrapped the wound with bandages.[5]

Lt Evan's 3rd platoon, under Sgt Barnes, had been hit as they moved up the Route de Wanne. Machine gunner Pfc. Norman Pihaly deployed there with Pfc. Harvey Schirrmacher, Philip Archambault, and Pfc. Kelly Cornet. Before he left to cross the bridge to the north side to get help, Evans told them to set up their 30-calibre weapon near the tannery overlooking the Stokeu road to the south-east. In the darkness, fear rose sharply; the men had never been in action. Soon after Evans left, Cornet became nervous. The men could see dark shapes coming out from the treeline at Stockeu hill facing the Wanne road 'wearing long coats and looking like ghosts'. One of the men with Archambault wanted to fire at the shapes, but Cornet cursed him. With the enemy all over, they'd be good as dead if he revealed their position. Cornet wanted to run and the frustrated machine gunner told him to go. 'The lieutenant ain't coming back,' Cornet said as he took off, 'you're staying for nothing!'[6] Down below towards the bridge, machine guns barked. The blasts eddied back and forth. Schirrmacher took off, too, and disappeared into the night.

Now alone, Pihaly and the other soldier fired the machine gun wildly into the night, not knowing from whence the enemy gunfire emanated. Soon ammunition ran low and the gun was so hot he thought the barrel would melt. 'We were sitting ducks,' Pihaly recalled. As the Germans rushed the bridge with tanks, 'The Germans opened up on us with machine pistols.'[7] Huddling behind the machine gun's backplate, they dived to the ground as bullets ricocheted. Both scattered, but Archambault ran west, away from the main action to cross the Amblève at Crespin's footbridge west of the stone bridge. Reaching that place, he was amazed to find both Cornet and Schirrmacher – weaponless and clueless – hiding in the woods. Norm Pihaly crossed the footbridge, then dashed behind the tannery, swimming for his life across the pond to its rear.

Under powerful blows, the two platoons peeled back in disorder with German infantry in hot pursuit. To cover the chaotic withdrawal, Sgt Jack Ellery had set up a rearguard machine gun position on the south edge of the bridge. But as the remnants of the two platoons and a single, surviving half-track pulled back across, Ellery himself was shot, hit in the back as he tried to reach a half-track on the bridge to get more ammunition. Meanwhile, on the north side of the bridge, Capt. Mitchell was barely in control, listening by radio as Lt Willyard's half-tracks sent back word of ominous sounds of tanks. 'This place is really unhealthy,' he confided, 'we've got to do something different if we want to get back to the other side of the river.' Soon it was every man for himself. Two squads found the tiny footbridge at Crespin's tannery to cross the river just west of the embattled main stone span.[8]

The Americans ran a gauntlet of fire, with several wounded as a platoon of the enemy attempted to rush the crossing. One American sergeant held off the charging panzer grenadiers with a Thompson submachine gun. One running was Anthony Calvanese – a private of the 825th Tank Destroyer Battalion from Massachusetts:

> It was dark, just before dawn, and our two half-tracks headed across the bridge across the Amblève river. On the other side we saw enemy tracers firing at us from the hillside above. We tried to pull back and set up, but ran into a ditch while trying to turn around. We tried to get back across the bridge. Sgt Armstrong was with us. Sgt Whaley was behind us. I was manning the 50-calibre machine gun. Just before reaching the bridge, we saw tracers coming across and we were hit by 25-calibre machine gun fire. We had our armor plate up, but our windshield was down so we could see something through the darkness. The bullets crashed through the windshield. The driver was killed instantly and the six others died just like that. There were bullets everywhere. I was hit in the thigh and fell down with bodies falling on top of me. One of my buddies, Ben Murphy, somehow got away. I knew I wouldn't last long in that half-track and had to pull the body of Bernard Gallagher off me. I jumped out of the half-track and made my way into a nearby building.[9]

Although hit by a bullet in the right thigh, Calvanese managed to hobble across the way into an abandoned brick home, to open its door, and to collapse improbably in an easy chair. He sat by the window, the room's interior eerily illuminated in orange tones by the blazing vehicle outside. The pain in his leg rose sharply and Calvanese attempted to crudely treat his wound with a sulphur bandage. 'I could see the half-track was now on fire and the SS men were walking around it in the firelight.' Calvanese had not been in the house long when one of the troopers saw him inside and took a shot. Shattering the window, the bullet missed, but Calvanese threw himself on the floor. Terrified that the SS man would soon enter to finish him off, Calvanese crawled quickly on the floor to the rear of the house. He squeezed out of a window.

At the exit, fear trumped prudence, for after pushing himself through the window, he clawed clumsily at the ledge before falling awkwardly over 20ft to the back street. He landed hard, but then rose from the ground, stooped in pain. He still managed to hobble off. Somehow he made his way towards a dairy on that side of the river, helped by an unknown Belgian. Reaching the entrance, the American found the interior filled with terrified locals. Two were Marcel Ozer and Raymond Blaise, who had just returned from their risky brush at dawn with SS men by the bridge. Although the townspeople took in the wounded American, Ozer worried to the elders. If the Germans found a GI in here, they would surely shoot everyone.[10]

Calvanese's decision to move out of the house was fortunate. Minutes after he was gone, there was vigorous banging at the wooden door of Jules Crismer on the same street, just a few steps from the bridge.[11] Pulling the door open, Crismer was surprised to see a German soldier walk inside as if he owned the place. '*Salut Moncheu Crismer*,' the youth strode forward to glare in his face, scowling in a Wallon dialect, *'N'a ti des Americans volà?'* – Are there any Americans here? The man in the German uniform addressed Crismer in Walloon – the indigenous Belgian language. The Stavelot native shook his head. The youth ignored him, motioning two other SS uniforms into the home. Inside, they burst into the various rooms, weapons drawn. Crismer did not recognise the youth, but was shocked just the same. 'Who are you?' he demanded, 'and how do you know my name?' 'I cannot say,' the youth told him, 'because of my mama.'

In his business, Crismer dealt daily with the farmers in the area – he was well known for miles around. Obviously, this boy was one of the Wallonian youths from Malmedy who were now fighting with the SS and looking to not draw attention to his family. After ransacking the house, and not finding Calvanese or other Americans, the Walloon SS man left. Crismer never saw him again, not knowing that he was hardly finished with the Germans that day.

Meanwhile, as the Americans fled to the north side of the river, the Germans attempted to use their momentum to capture the span. Reaching the south side of the bridge, SS Ustuf. Willie Horn rallied his men into a headlong charge, leading himself. The bold effort was met by a hail of fire. The SS officer fell wounded midway across the bridge, tumbling to the cobblestones. Their leader chopped down mid-stride, the remaining panzer grenadiers fled back over to the houses south of the bridge. Rudi Rayer, in charge of the SPW-mounted 11th Kompanie, had steel for his men:

> We stopped toward evening on the road just outside of Stavelot – 2 or 3 kilometers outside of town. After we had been standing there for some time, the 11th Company received the order to take on foot a bridge in town and hold it. The company consisted at that time of the remains of the 1st and 2nd platoon. Owning to technical damage, part of the company was left back on the road. Of my platoon, only the Wilfer group was with the company. The bridge was reached, but we could not hold it. The company, which was at that time in a difficult position, dug itself in front of the bridge. On the other side of the bridge, enemy tanks rolled by continuously and we expected a counterattack. We were fired on from all sides without being able to do much about it in the darkness. We had heavy casualties, among them 1st Lt Tomhardt, 2nd Lt Horn, and many others. By the order of the commander, Diefenthal, I took over command of the company.[12]

Horn was still alive and crawling on the bridge when an anti-tank round hit nearby and 'tore him to pieces'.[13] At the top of the hill, Peiper did not hear about Ustuf. Horn's fate, but decided the tanks should be employed at first light. During the momentary possession of the bridge, engineers along from 9th Panzer Pioneer Company checked for explosives, but determined that it was clear. Oswald Siegmund took part in the attack:

> Our company commander received his first combat order on the 18th: Attack Stavelot dismounted and capture the bridge in the center of the town. The order was issued at 3 a.m. and at 4 a.m. the company jumped off. They first met six, and later three American reconnaissance vehicles. They reached the bridge at 6 a.m. and Ustuf. Horn was killed in action. The company was unable to capture the bridge. More enemy reconnaissance vehicles attacked from behind, two were knocked out in close combat. Thank God, at 8 a.m. the tank point arrived. Tomhardt was wounded, our company heavily depleted.[14]

Peiper was displeased. 'We approached the outskirts of the village, but got bogged down because of stubborn American resistance at the edge of Stavelot. We suffered fairly heavy losses, twenty-five to thirty casualties. Since I did not have sufficient infantry, I decided to await the arrival of more.'[15]

Meanwhile, with the Germans threatening to capture the bridge, Mitchell had deployed his two remaining guns – one was towed some distance on the Malmedy road so that it could blast at the Germans approaching the bridge across the river. The other gun was located in the marketplace and sighted down *le Châtelet* – the road emerging from the bridge.

Up at the top of the sharply bending road at La Corniche above Stavelot stood the farm of Joseph Rensonnet. In spite of the excitement the preceding night with the momentary contact between the Germans and Charles Hensel's engineers, the situation had calmed down by midnight. Rensonnet and his family slept fitfully until they rose as usual before dawn. Being simple farmers,

Joseph Rensonnet and his son, Ernest, had to attend to their daily routine caring for livestock. He and his son moved to the attached cowshed at 7.45 a.m. to fodder the fifty head of cattle, spreading hay into the various pens such that each beast received its morning meal.[16] The work took twenty minutes as usual, at which point Joseph walked to the stairs that led to the main part of his home. As he climbed, he nearly fell in shock, thrown off balance by a deafening roar that shook the high walls of his farm. Instinctively, he yelled for his son. 'Ernest, where are you? Come fast!' 'Yes,' Ernest said, 'I am coming!'

Yet the boy hesitated. Ernest raised the corner of a tarp covering a window in the cowshed. He could not believe his eyes, for only a few metres away from the window was the muzzle brake of a German cannon. He bent down further and could make out a huge tank at the end of the cannon, blue smoke wafting away from the gun muzzle. Up the road as he looked back was one tank after another stretching back to the rocky wall at La Corniche. Then another deafening blast as the tank fired again, Ernest Rensonnet dropped the tarp and scampered back to his father and safety, terrified as a machine gun stammered to life. Now at 8 a.m., when it became light enough to see, the Amblève river valley thundered with German shells and rockets joined by clattering squeals as German tanks positioned themselves on the Vieux Château road just above the cowshed of Ernest Rensonnet.

Meanwhile, Lt Maynard L. Rogers had ordered Sgt Carl A. 'Smitty' Smith to bring his thirteen-man 57mm gun crew down to the bridge to stop the enemy. On risk of insubordination, Smith protested, 'I'm not going to do it.' Dead bodies lay on both sides of the street, and bullets seemed to be streaming from the other side of the river. Several half-tracks had not come back from the other side of the river, and one burned brightly in the street. 'I wasn't about to get my men killed. I was not going to do that.'[17] Smith confronted Rogers. It was suicide, he told him.

Smith struck a compromise: 'I'll take part of my squad down there if you can get smoke down there.' Rogers ordered smoke mortar shells and soon their approach was cloaked. Smith broke the squad in two and took only a few down to the gun: Pfc. Roscoe L. Taylor, Pvt. Lloyd J. Fisher, Pvt. Samuel Bohn, and Pvt. Frank Kristancic. In the gloomy early morning, Sgt Carl 'Smitty' Smith hauled his 57mm gun crew just across from the north-end bridge, in front of Brennan's machine gun positions positioned right by the bridge before the Dizier house .[18] There, Sgt Smith's crew quickly detached the 57mm from the half-track and limbered the gun on to the little back street of the Quai des Vieux Moulins.

Sgt Paul Brumfield of platoon headquarters was down by the bridge, peering out from the window of the third storey of a building there. 'A big tank is coming!' he yelled down to the group manhandling the gun. 'It's coming!'

Smith replied in an urgent but hushed tone: 'Shut up, you idiot! We don't want to let them know we're here!'

When the gun was in place, Brumfield asked Sgt Smith to stay with him to load. He sent the others with their weapons into the building to his left, on the immediate left side of the bridge. When a German tank came across the bridge, they would cross broadside to his gun just 30ft away. It would be a perfect ambush, but would the 57mm gun be able to penetrate the German armor? In the meantime, terrified Belgians abandoned the homes near the north side of the bridge – most of the dwellings now riddled with bullet holes and shattered glass. Brennan now relocated his two machine guns so fields of fire would not endanger Smith's gun crew.

Two privates of Lt Beardslee's 1st squad were still in place on the north side of the bridge in the hardware shed of Adolphe Foguenne's home. Poking his M1 rifle out a window, Pvt. Samuel J. Bohn shot down one of a group of SS panzer grenadiers approaching the bridge. They all scattered, but as he reloaded, his buddy Lee Galloway yelled that German tanks were approaching. Frantic, they located a bazooka and ammunition. Galloway would load as the two readied to blast the first tank when it came around the bend. Bohn passed his M1 to Lt Beardslee. Alas, when the steel beast clattered towards them, the low stone wall near the bridge made it impossible to get a clean shot. He shouldered the weapon just the same.

Shaking with fear, Bohn shoved his stovepipe-like weapon out of the window and quickly drew a bead on the distant tank. Galloway loaded and then patted his shoulder – the bazooka was loaded. Bohn pulled the trigger. The first rocket roared off but missed the tank some 80m away. Galloway helped him reload and in seconds he fired another round. It missed, too, both flying high. 'Damn! Give it to me!' Now, Pfc. Earl Moody took the bazooka from Bohn and tried again – another miss. The giant metallic reptile growled across the bridge spitting fire.

With only one rocket remaining, Lee Galloway wielded the weapon to quickly set loose the spark-tailed round. It flashed ahead against the big Panther now waddling down the middle of the bridge. Alas, his rocket, too, glanced off – without exploding.[19] Carl Smith saw the failed attempt too. In their haste they had failed to remove the arming pins.

The Germans had seen them, for bullets now ricocheted off the sides of the Foguenne house. 'Damn!' Capt. Mitchell cursed as he watched the bazookas bounce off from his vantage in the church steeple.[20] At 9 a.m. he radioed battalion for reinforcements. No reply.

On the German side of the river, perched on Diefenthal's SPW at the top of the road just below La Corniche, Peiper held binoculars to his eyes, peering down into the valley toward Stavelot. Having watched as his grenadiers swept the Americans back over the bridge, the time for committing his armor looked ripe. In order to make his armor difficult targets, Peiper ordered his tanks to approach the bridge at maximum speed. With that, the Mk V Panther tanks – Oscha. Erich Strelow in the lead – rattled down the steep Rue du Vieux Château at 25mph, as fast as a 50-ton steel beast could go.

Strelow's panzer was concealed by smoke from the blazing Itche farm, struck earlier by the American fire. Strelow's tank driver, Rttf. Heinz Biwald, paused briefly before the home of carpenter Camille Nicolay. Strelow disgorged a few engineers off the hull of the tank, who removed several mines laid out in the road. That done, he ground on toward the river. But only a little further ahead, he now found his way blocked by the abandoned half-tracks of Sgt Whaley and Armstrong. Biwald gunned the Panther's powerful Maybach engine and bullishly pushed the half-tracks off the road. The bridge loomed ahead.

After racing down La Rue du Vieux Château and turning for the bridge at breakneck speed, the Panthers were fired on by two well-camouflaged anti-tank guns. On the other side of the bridge, Sgt Vic Brennan waited nervously, having set up his two MG crews to provide flank protection for the AT guns.[21] The Germans sensed the tempo as mortars and artillery now pelted the town, a flare allowing Brennan to identify two enemy soldiers stealing across the bridge. In the dim light they came under Brennan's machine gun. One was killed and the other wounded.

With great difficulty, Sgt John Stevenson of the 202nd Engineers had placed mines on the bridge in the darkness by 2 a.m. covered by machine gun guards at either end. His comrade, Pfc. Howard Meyer, recalled that he was never so frightened in his life, worried that the Germans would hear his teeth chattering as he hauled the mines on to the bridge.[22]

Meanwhile, buttoned up inside the iron beast, SS Oscha. Erich Strelow was nervously oblivious to the quiver of failed rockets that had harmlessly missed or bounced off his tank. He was looking ahead to the Amblève crossing, having been warned by radio to watch out for Obstuf. Horn, who had been wounded midway across the span. But as his lumbering Panther approached the bridge, Strelow's gunner, Eugen Zimmermann, saw no sign of the SS officer; instead, he only saw the lifeless body of an American sprawled out across the entrance to the span. It was S/Sgt Jack Ellery, who had been shot down in the infantry firefight for the bridge.

Ordered to charge, Strelow did not hesitate. He throttled the Panther tank engine and charged across the bridge, crushing the American soldier's form as he clanked across the narrow cobblestone reach. Yet as he proceeded, he saw the limp body of a German soldier on the right walkway across the bridge. Was he alive? With the drumbeat of gunfire and bouncing lead, Strelow could not pause, doing well to avoid driving over the fallen comrade.

Now, emerging from the north end of the bridge, the gun crew under Sgt Carl Smith prepared to hit the juggernaut broadside from a tiny alley at point-blank range – just 30ft.[23] The problem was that their gun was only 57mm. The tank crossed the bridge and then a flash and ejection of smoke hit directly into the side of the brute. With the blast came a weird, screeching echo, the sonic signature of an armor-piercing shot glancing noisily off the Panther. Sgt Smith remembered vividly:

> We were in a blind alley and the German tank came up in front of us. He didn't know where we were. We hit him at a distance of 30 feet. We hit him squarely, but it glanced off. The second shot took his sights out, but they didn't knock them out. He shot twice, but both shots went over us – but nearly blowing down the building behind us. The tanks kept shooting into the buildings – over our heads, but we had to get out of there. We didn't have anything heavier than the 6-pound bullet in our 57mm gun and you might as well throw a rock at those

> heavy German tanks. But the tank we hit didn't move for a while after we hit it. Everything happened so quickly there was hardly any time to think – *just get the hell out of there!*[24]

The anaemic 57mm anti-tank round couldn't pierce the thick armor of its mantle as the steel battle wagon turned angrily toward them. A return blast from the German gun somehow missed the crew, but went on to explode inside Pauline Livet's café, spilling dust, smoke, and a spray of shattered spirits into the street. Another blast from the 57mm gun ricocheted off before the deafened gun crew took to their feet.[25] Even so, the concussion caused the German gun to careen wildly skyward.[26] Strelow's gunner was horrified to see the American anti-tank gun:

> Peiper himself ordered my tank to lead the attack on Stavelot. The attack was planned to jump off at dawn. The entire crew received detailed instructions. An enemy anti-tank gun should have been in position directly behind a sharp curve to the left. The best thing to do: shift into high gear and go flat out. Further information that came in during the night was that the bridge was secured but that an Ustuf. was lying directly on the bridge, no specifics as to whether he was wounded or already dead. I thought, for heaven's sake, don't pass over him. At daybreak we all were wide awake and we received the order to start the engine and began moving. We met no resistance. The anti-tank gun was there but we rammed it aside and continued toward the bridge. For heaven's sake, the Ustuf. wasn't lying on the bridge. We had hardly crossed the bridge when we received the first hit. My driver was screaming, 'Gas pedal blocked – we are hit!' I saw an anti-tank gun directly behind the corner of a house to the right. 'Radio operator – Fire!' The 7.5-centimetre gun missed the target and was now pointing toward the sky. The driver accelerated and drove over the gun. The tail of the gun broke off and landed on the hatch of the radio operator. Fierce fire from all directions continued.[27]

Peiper's own account of the capture of Stavelot:

> At dawn, I committed another armored infantry company against Stavelot. I withdrew two Panther tanks 200 metres from the edge of town and instructed them to charge Stavelot at maximum speed. They drove around the curve firing rapidly. The first Panther tank was hit, and it burned, but it had so much initial speed that it penetrated the anti-tank obstacle at the curve and damaged two tanks. The second Panther used this opportunity to drive through and seize the bridge at Stavelot. We followed up with other vehicles and the Americans evacuated town.[28]

Even having destroyed the American anti-tank gun and having thwarted an ambush, Erich Strelow's Panther was nonetheless momentarily incapacitated, blind, and unable to properly aim its gun after the two hits. Even so, he proceeded cautiously down the street aware that Panther #111, under SS Ostuf. Hans Hennecke, was right behind him – or so he thought. 'In the middle of the bridge, my tank was hit by anti-tank fire,' remembered SS officer, Hans Hennecke. 'I changed my tank and took over the tank of Ostuf. Kremser.'[29]

> The tank of Richartz was hit and burned out [further up the road]. Ostuf. Kremser was seriously wounded. I ran forward to his tank, helped to dress his wounds, and got orders to take over the company and to carry the attack toward Trois-Ponts. I boarded the company commander's tank and passed through Stavelot.[30]

Outside of Stavelot, Hennecke convinced Roland Knörringer, a tank mechanic, to leave his captured American jeep to ride into town atop his Panther. From his position behind the turret as they drove down toward the bridge, Knörringer suddenly saw Ostuf. Kremser hobbling into a house next to the road. Knörringer jumped from Hennecke's Panther in order to find out what had happened to his company commander. Reaching him by the house just before the bridge, Knörringer discovered that Kremser was painfully wounded in his leg. Medics descended and before came the morphine haze, Kremser gave him an order. Hennecke was to take over the company. When he returned to Hennecke's tank, he found that it, too, had been hit by American anti-tank fire. Both he and Hennecke then boarded Kremser's tank, which was less damaged and had the preferred radio equipment to control the company.[31]

What happened to the planned American ambush? The German armor had descended the hill so fast that half a dozen tanks had roared past by the time the 76mm gun crew of the 825th Tank Destroyer Battalion on the other side of the river had drawn a bead. Yet the gun under Sgt Louis Celentano now found targets as the enemy armor rumbled down the hill.[32] A round from his gun struck Panther #115 under Richartz and another seemed to have taken out the tank of Hans Hennecke (#111).[33] However, following Strelow's Panther was another Mark V, likely that of the company commander (Panther #101 of Karl Kremser).[34] Attempting to drive across the bridge behind Strelow, the Panther was hit by a bazooka about midway across the span.[35]

Seeing German tanks approach from the gloom that Monday morning, S/Sgt Boyce L. Williams, Pvt. William H. Darden and one or two others of his headquarters rifle squad took off with a bazooka to find a way to hit the German tanks barrelling for the bridge. The men ran into Camille Sougné's three-storey brick house on the left side of the bridge. Clambering up the stairs, they posted themselves by the second-floor window overlooking the bridge, but were too late to hit the first tank. They set up just the same. Another tank waddled warily onvto the bridge. They pointed the bazooka and the rocket hissed from their window perch, flashing against the front of the tank 30m away. 'Hit!'[36]

> We got into a house right by the bridge and went upstairs. I think William Darden was with me, but I can't be sure. We knocked out one of the German tanks. We fired on it with a bazooka from the open window. The tank had nearly gotten across the bridge when we hit it. The Germans stayed in the tank and we shot at anybody who came close to it. The Germans would come up within 5–10 feet of the tank and they would try to attach a cable to the tank. We were shooting

> infantry as they showed themselves. We stayed right at that window and fired the bazooka. We were each firing M1 carbines and picking off Germans as they tried to get to the tank. They kept trying to get a cable attached to the tank.[37]

Stunned by the explosion, the German tank crew locked the transmission and stalled the engine in the middle of the bridge. Each attempt to restart on the engaged clutch stalled. Now the walls of the Sougné house were pelted with gunfire. Williams and the others dropped to the floor as the window glass exploded from a hail of bullets. Someone looking through one of the rear windows of the house called out to tell Williams the Company A half-tracks were pulling out. They dashed from the house as machine gun slugs cut ugly pits into its brick walls.

Meanwhile, the situation was critical for Kremser because once the tank was immobilised. the Americans on the other side pelted the tank with bullet fire. Anti-tank fire could not be far behind. In a brief lull, Kremser jumped from the tank, sprinting through a gauntlet of gunfire until he arrived breathless at the Crismer house on the south side of the bridge. There he convinced less-than-enthusiastic members of the 9th Panzer Pioneer Company to help him rescue the tank. He arranged for fire to smash all the buildings on the other side so that a chain could be moved to the marooned tank in the middle of the bridge. Another Panther managed to pull it back to the entrance of the span, but Kremser was badly wounded outside the Crismer house while making the arrangements. His loader, Roland Knörringer:

> Obstuf. Kremer had called me over to his tank, where I had to fix the range finder of the gun as his gunner was not able to see. While I was working on it, Obstuf. Kremser got off the tank. I learned then that he had been wounded at this very moment. I got off the vehicle, too, and went to him. Then I witnessed that Ustuf. Hennecke was ordered to lead the first company. Obstuf. Kremser was bandaged and we took leave of him. Ustuf. Hennecke took over the command of the company and got into the tank of the chief.[38]

Peiper was meanwhile with the spearhead tanks just before the bridge with the flak panzer of SS man Karl Wortmann just behind him. 'There was heavy fire in Stavelot,'

> While waiting, our infantry dismounted and moved along either side of the tank column for security. Two soldiers came up with a young American PW. Peiper was personally with the foremost tanks at the bridge at Stavelot. When Peiper saw the young 'milky faced' prisoner, he told Wortmann to take him back and let him go. 'I am not going to capture children.'[39]

After clearing the bridge, Briesemeister's tank, another Panther, and Peiper in Diefenthal's half-track along with another SPW of Tomhardt's 11th Company moved on across the span. Kremser, meanwhile, was carried into the Crismer house on the south side of the bridge for medical care – he would eventually be evacuated. At the same time, Hennecke arrived and on orders from Werner Poetschke took over Kremser's tank, which seemed only to be slightly damaged. Hennecke hardly knew the tank crew, but the important thing was that command Panther #101 had an experienced radio operator, already working with the other twenty-odd tanks of the company. One radio put him in direct contact with the other tanks of the company, and another radio was tuned into the frequency of Peiper's SPW.[40] Be on the lookout for the anti-tank guns, Peiper warned over the radio.

Now in charge of the 1st Company, Hennecke in Panzer #101 crunched ahead north into the village of Stavelot. Meanwhile, the Americans on the other side, including Lt James Evans and the 3rd squad, had misread the effectiveness of Sgt Smith's 57mm blast against the lone German tank on their side of the bridge. No other tanks had followed, and the steel beast had not moved since being smacked by the round from Sgt Smith's AT gun. *It had been maimed or knocked out*, Evans hoped. With the Germans stopped, they would move from the Place Wibald.

Yet as Evans moved forward, Strelow's Panther suddenly creaked to life. Its long cannon swerved right and belched an explosive round. The shell detonated against the cobblestones, emitting a spray of deadly shrapnel. Lt Evans fell dead in front of the Café Henriette Carls. The bold American attempt to recapture the bridge failed. Sgt Chris Breuninger:

> Lt James Evans, Jim Lego, myself, and several other members of the 1st platoon withdrew behind a building about 70–100 yards up the street … We could see a tank successfully cross the bridge and stop momentarily as it entered Stavelot. The tank – I believed it to be a German Panther – was broadside to Sgt Smith's gun. As it started to move slowly, Sgt Smith fired two shots at the tank, causing it to stop. There was complete silence. Not hearing any firing, Lt Evans and the rest of us thought Sgt Smith had knocked out the tank. In order to observe more fully what had happened, Lt Evans and Jim Lego stepped out into the roadway. At that precise instant the Germans observed the movement and fired their 88mm gun. The shell hit directly in front of Lt Evans, causing shrapnel fragments to smash into his body. It was apparent he had not survived. Lego was hit in the shoulder … The rest of us had not exposed ourselves to the direct firing of the shell, but the explosion caused a portion of the building to fall, and power and telephone lines fell on us. I helped Jim Lego, who was seriously wounded, to his feet. About then the German tank started to move forward. We heard a call from up the street to withdraw.[41]

Sgt Smith and his gun crew were also trying to get away from the debacle at the bridge, but lost one man in their dash to freedom:

> We saw a second tank get disabled on the bridge. We didn't know who did that or how it happened. I thought maybe it was a mine. I saw them push the one we were shooting out of the way and the second one come up and push it out of the way. Six rounds and we shot them all off. And when they were shot off, we had nothing left to do, but to get out of there. So, we went down the alley. There was

> lots of shooting now. They had snipers up in the buildings on the other side of us. We went through a blown-up building to get out of there. The buildings were reduced to rubble. I went first out of the building [and ran] to the right. I was pushing the guys out. I instructed them how to get out of there. We zig-zagged out one at a time, each running like hell. The sniper had a burp gun. [Pvt. Lloyd] Fisher got shot when he came out. Cpl Robert Hyde and I pulled Fisher into a building, but when we looked him over, he was already dead. We took off his dog tags. We also tended to Roscoe [Taylor], who got shot in the butt. The slug went right through the stock of his rifle and didn't go in far, but his butt was bleeding. Most of the other guys were up three or four stories. Sam Bohn was firing a rifle and he shot the sniper who killed Fisher. There was a lot of machine gun fire. But Bohn got us out of there by shooting that sniper.[42]

Most of the men made it back in desperate rushes to the Place du Marché in the center of town, where the 526th and elements of the 202nd Combat Engineer Battalion were assembled. Should they make a stand? As the shooting picked up, Pvt. Paul Kohli convinced S/Sgt Felix Skuta that they should drive their jeep out of town while they still could.[43] With his other buddies from the 202nd, John Stevenson made a similar decision. Meanwhile, the armored infantry company attempted to evacuate the aid station at the Athénée – the school in town. Wounded Bernard Goldstein and others were being treated there. Now they would be evacuated.

At the same time, SS panzer commander Erich Strelow cautiously nosed his tank up the main road through town, eventually ascending the Haut Rivage. The Americans in the town seemed stunned, pulling back and close to panic.

Even with the losses and brave fighting by the Americans, with more of his strongest tanks ready to punch across the river, Peiper seemed on the verge of firm control of Stavelot. With a secure logistical lifeline across the Amblève river he could burst beyond American lines and head for the Meuse. Or could he?

Chapter 18

THE BRIDGE

Whoever said the pen is mightier than the sword obviously never encountered automatic weapons.

— Douglas McArthur

Young Beathe Wetz was still worried about the Americans soldiers that previously had hurriedly left her house. Had they returned to the Grand Place where previously they had their headquarters: Company C of the 202nd Engineer Combat Battalion. So much shooting and everyone had just left.

Seized once more with foolhardy curiosity, Beathe ran down the street by herself to take a look. Turning on the Rue Neuve she gasped, nearly bumping into German tanks that were turning left at the Rue du Haut Rivage. There was no shooting, but young Beathe was only 6m from one of the tanks. When SS soldiers appeared alongside the giant steel monsters, one glanced at her with disdain. The young woman skulked away in fear. She raced back home just as a shell smashed into the roof of St Sebastian Church.[1] She fell to the cobblestones, bruised but unwounded.

A Belgian woman at the home where Beathe sought cover motioned her inside as the shells exploded anew. 'Come in! Come in!' Beathe took refuge, waiting for the shooting to end.[2] Back at the multi-storey Wetz home, two U.S. soldiers, Stan Aldinger and Howard Meyer, showed up breathless, disgusted to find that everyone else in the company had deserted their headquarters, leaving abandoned vehicles and ammunition strewn about. It was a bug out.

Meanwhile, down at the bridge, the sight of 50-ton tanks rushing towards them was too much for the already shocked infantry of Company A, 526th Armored Infantry. Most of the men fled to stout brick buildings for cover. With his driver, Sgt Jack Mocnik, Capt. Mitchell sprinted from one street to another to encourage the squads under his command, his characteristic pipe clenched in his teeth.[3] 'By this time the Germans controlled Stavelot completely, and it was very easy for our parents to earn $10,000,' Howard Meyer recalled sarcastically. That was the death benefit for American parents whose son was killed in battle. Following Mitchell, he was petrified. Gunfire ripped up and down the cobblestone streets.

With German tanks now prowling the narrow roads, Mocnik found many of the men beyond being rallied. Mocnik cursed some GIs cowering by the schoolhouse and told them to get their rifles. Meanwhile, Mitchell radioed First Army from Stavelot: 'Have met a strong enemy force and am in desperate need of physical aid.'[4] A little later, at 9.43 a.m., an ominous message came: 'Company A withdrew from Stavelot. Enemy across in force … Many U.S. casualties. Request ammunition support at once.' Simultaneously, as the fight for the bridge raged, Lt James Evans waved his reserve 3rd platoon forward until he was felled by an artillery burst. That message was relayed to First Army at 10.30 a.m. with an ominous rejoinder: 'Tanks approaching roadblock #3 …' The radio went dead. Capt. Mitchell ordered his command post to move to the high ground on the north end of town.

After escaping from the debacle at the bridge, 22-year-old machine gunner Pfc. Philip Archambault was with his Kentucky GI buddy, Pvt. Kelly Cornet. They took cover in the doorway of a building as the Germans blazed across the bridge. What should they do? 'Beats the shit out of me,' Cornet mumbled.[5] Archambault shook his head; it was the Kentucky youth's response to everything. But the Maine native spoke fluent French and asked the housekeeper for refuge. She agreed, but after stepping inside, both men became nervous as they gazed through the lace-lined windows. Tanks and half-tracks loaded with Germans were cruising down the road not more than 200 yards away.

'*Merci, Madame!*' Archambault thanked the woman. She became visibly agitated when they refused to stay for coffee. '*Les Allemands!*' he called out as they bolted out the door. The two men scattered, moving from one house to the next to get away from the Germans. Archambault wanted to cross the Amblève, but his hayseed sidekick couldn't swim. Concealed in a copse of woods, they watched the glow of German cigarettes in the gloom, waiting until they vanished so they could dash out of town to disappear into the wooded trails to the north.[6]

Another from the same hard-luck group, Pfc. Norman Pihaly, ran up the hill behind the bridge until confronted by a young woman emerging from a home's cellar. '*Americain ou Boche*?' It was Anna Schutz, a 31-year-old woman from Lorraine, who spoke broken English after working at the U.S. Army map depot in Stavelot. 'American!' Pihaly called back. He spoke French and was pleased to hear her question, but looked nervously over his shoulder. The loud racket of gunfire crackled. Anna signaled Pihaly to follow her to the basement of a home where she and her children had taken refuge. Inside the cellar were four other women and some children. He was to hide in the apple bin, they insisted. There he hid, covered with apples and a family blanket.[7]

With news that the Germans were back, many other Stavelot civilians made themselves scarce. Eight-year-old Marcel Massotte followed his father to the basement of a big, stout building near their home, the Château Lambert. There they joined thirty other townspeople at Les Quartiers – many women and children. At 2.30 p.m. that Monday someone rang the doorbell. Answering the door, 53-year-old Tony Lambert was confronted in the entrance by two SS men carrying pistols. Hearing gunfire, Marcel's father, Lèon, rushed upstairs.[8] He gasped. There was Monsieur Lambert lying in a pool of blood with SS men standing over his body. 'Are there Americans here?' one SS man shouted. With guns pointed his way, Massotte threw up his arms. Luckily, he spoke German. 'No, just civilians – old men, women, and children,' he replied, 'come in and see for yourselves.' Soon the troopers followed him into basement. 'You didn't think we would come back, did you?' one snickered as they passed down the stairs, 'now we will soon be in Brussels and then Paris!'

The German men reached the basement, where all of the Belgians cowered in fright. Strangely, two of the Germans were in American uniforms. Shouting to the group below, the SS men ordered the women upstairs to cook for them. Lambert's daughter Claudine offered them beer and wine, but when that ran low, one waved a pistol and demanded more. Claudine brought cognac from the cupboard. Marcel's father Lèon could see they were SS men. Downing the cognac, they prepared to leave. 'We're going to come back and kill you all,' they laughed drunkenly. Lambert's heart pounded.[9]

Back on the south side of the bridge, Peiper marvelled that the Americans had not destroyed the span. As more tanks managed to cross the old stone structure, with the heavy firepower reaching the north side, the Germans had the upper hand. John Stevenson was with the 202nd Engineer Combat Battalion in the middle of Stavelot that morning:

> In the schoolhouse we were just sitting down to pancakes as I remember. It was still dark and just breaking daylight. Suddenly, the German sent up flares and I knew they weren't ours. Then the Germans let loose and shooting began. We all ran out from the breakfast table. No one knew where everyone else was. Most of the action was right at the bridge about three blocks from the school. Other people were coming and going. I remember it was just breaking light, but everyone was running around. I remember thinking to myself that those half-tracks must have run right into the Germans on the other side. There was a lot of machine gun fire after the other people got to the other side. We started down toward where the noise was coming from. Then one of the civilians, a woman, came out of her house and ran up to me saying, '*Boche, Boche!*' and started pulling on my coat and pointing to it while repeating that. I think she was trying to tell me that they had American uniforms.
>
> We decided we couldn't help much and we began to look for a position at the railroad track. We got up to the [northern] edge of town by some woods. Mortars started coming in and I jumped into a crater. An empty stone house was nearby. Then, I said to my buddy, Pfc. Robert Lehnert, 'Hey, Bob, let's get in this basement.' The words weren't even out of my mouth and a shell went through it. Next, Bob looked over the valley and said, 'Hey there a lot of them over there!' We had left some fellows [from the 202nd] with machine guns down there [to cover the bridge]. We could hear a lot of firing and wondered if they would make it out ... We didn't stick around and instead started going on up the hill away

> from town. We could hear tanks down in the valley and I was concerned that we were going to be surrounded so we headed up the hill.[10]

Some civilians had not left town. Céline Ozer and her family were still at their food store at the corner of the Haut Rivage and Henri Massange Street. When the first German tank came down the road, she and her family sensibly fled to the basement. But there, the cellar was frigid and expecting they might be there a long while, Céline decided to climb the stairs to fetch a sweater. As she reached for a woollen garment in the closet, she heard a loud shout out in the street. She turned to a nearby window and looked out onto Rue du Henri Massage, shocked to see a long cannon emerging behind the lace. The gun barrel looked like a snout on a big, iron beast that stopped right in front of their grocery. As she watched, a metal hatch atop the vehicle flipped open and a figure in a dark uniform emerged. His head was topped with a cap and covered by headphones. Looking away, the man shouted loudly, but even understanding German, Céline could not hear what he was saying over the loud din of the tank's motor. Just then the turret revolved left so the big cannon faced down the street. '*Los!*' the German shouted. He dropped down under a clanking hatch an instant before a thunderclap rocked the house, the glass shattering from the concussion. Céline ran, convinced the house would soon collapse.

The German tank had sighted the Americans and their TD guns under Lt Jack Doherty at the other end of the street. A tank round ripped apart Doherty's unoccupied jeep. The trap was sprung. As the leading tank reached the intersection of route Le Châtelet, they came under machine gun fire and the menacing muzzle of one of Lt Doherty's 76mm AT guns pointed down the Ferdinand Nicolay Avenue. After shooting across the river, Doherty's guns were still in position across from the Degbomont house.

The first round of Sgt Hauser's gun slammed into Strelow's panzer, hit still again, but failed to pierce its thick armor plate. The round glanced off and exploding into the glazed storefront of the Pharmacie Gillet. So struck, Eugen Zimmermann in Strelow's panzer quickly fired a wild shot at the ambush team before turning his Mk V up a side street and climbing the steep Haut Rivage to Neuve Street to avoid the gun. It was a circuitous path down the narrow, stone streets, but soon he reached the road that led west out of town to Trois-Ponts. Meanwhile, the gun crew kept shooting at the German armor roaring across the bridge until they could see they had been bypassed and were in danger from panzer grenadiers jumping off the tanks. One of Tomhardt's SPWs arrived and put the American anti-tank men under machine gun fire. The Americans spiked the gun muzzle with a phosphorous grenade and fled. Doherty and others with him were wounded, lucky to escape, abandoning their guns and jumping aboard the few operating jeeps to scoot away east toward Malmedy.

But the upper hand momentarily came back to the American defenders when Battery D of the half-track-mounted anti-aircraft guns of the 203rd AAA

Battalion, looking for the way to St Vith, wandered into the fight. Their entry into the battle forced the German infantry to take cover until Captain Eaton ordered them on to St Vith, Belgium after five men were wounded:

> We were riding along peacefully in convoy when we came to an abrupt halt in Stavelot. At first we did not know why, but when we saw the tracers streaking across the valley, it became clear. My M15 half-track with two 50-calibre machine guns and a 37mm cannon stopped in the center of the road. We heard machine gun fire crackling over our heads. Soon the whole battery was firing back at the houses … The enemy fire quickly subsided, but the mortars continued. Next thing I saw was a big Tiger tank [sic] headed for our column and there was no way we could compete with him. The captain must have given the order for withdraw and the others began to move off.[11]

The AA half-tracks departed and the German infantry were soon fanning out through the town. By 10 a.m. the German armor now had the bridge firmly in hand and were pushing back the remnants of the engineers and armored infantry, away from their advance route to the west.

Jochen Peiper was now hardly focused on Stavelot, his attention turned to the next objective – the three bridges across the Amblève and Salm rivers at Trois-Ponts, just up the road. While fighting still raged in Stavelot, his tanks slipped down the streets to emerge on the hard-surfaced road that took them that direction, more than a little surprised to have seized Stavelot and its bridge.[12] He would leave consolidation of the town to the infantry coming up behind him.

In Panzer #101, Hans Hennecke now clanked up the Rue du Gustave Dewalque behind the half-dozen other tanks and vehicles ahead of him. He listened over the radio as Peiper warned of anti-tank guns lurking off to the right. Hennecke had likely heard from Strelow that he had been struck by a gun off to the right, for when he came to the entrance to the Place Wibald, he ordered the tank to pause in front of the Café Henriette Carls where Lt Evans lay dead.

Hennecke rose in the turret, wary of gunshot. At the same time, two terrified Belgian families emerged from the bicycle repair shop of Louis Gillain seeking refuge from the gunfire smashing into their homes by the river. The two families boldly made their way down the street in the same direction the tanks were moving, walking right along next to Hennecke's panzer before walking off to the right at the Rue du Châtelet. Why would two Belgian families move so boldly down the street with all the shooting? Léon Colinet said it was because neither the Colinet nor Tombeux homes had basements. They were seeking refuge in the cellars at the town hall.

At around 10 a.m., Léon Colinet, his father, his wife Pauline Livet, and their young daughter Gaby took refuge in a nearby building with a cellar, where they were joined by the Tombeux family – Marcel and Maria and their two children.[13] Yet that building with its café seemed terribly exposed as the SS troops came across the river. First, there was the shooting on both sides, but then the Colinet-Livet house was right next to where the Americans under Sgt Smith had fired their anti-tank gun at Erich Strelow's Panther. When the German tank fired back, it shattered the front of the café and a hail of bullets and gunfire made it unhealthy to remain there. Yet in searching for a new safe haven, Léon Colinet was under a dangerous misunderstanding. From the cellar, he reckoned that the engines they heard in the streets were the American Sherman tanks.

During a pause in the shooting after the engine noise faded, Colinet convinced both families that they should follow the Americans away to the north and take refuge in the City Hall's big, deep cellars. *'C'est le moment! On y va!'* – It's time! Let's go for it! The two terrified families spilled out into the street from the bicycle shop, finding themselves between tanks. Shots rang out and not far away. Joseph Colinet hurried to catch up with what he thought was an American tank just ahead, seeking its protection. Behind him was his son Léon cradling a blanket with their daughter Gaby in his arms. A few paces after Léon was his wife, Pauline, wrapped in a fur coat, and Marcel and Maria Tombeux, carrying their infant, Michel.

As Léon Colinet ran toward the Place Wibald, he shuddered and stopped mid-step. The tank just ahead … it was too big … its cannon too long to be an American one. On the back of the tank he saw a black cross outlined in white. 'Watch out!' he said in a low voice to the others approaching him, 'They're Germans!' But those behind him could not hear over the loud, rattling tank engines. At least the tanks seemed closed up. Maybe they could get by unnoticed. They walked by one panzer near the home of Camille Dupont. Yet, as they approached the Café Henriette Carls, a man in a black uniform emerged from the turret of the big tank lurking by the Place Wibald.

Léon Colinet did not know that the man he saw standing in the tank was SS Untersturmführer Hans Hennecke, the SS officer just having recently taken command of the 1st Panzer Company. Hennecke wore headphones over his ears, but instinctively turned to see the little group of civilians approaching his tank from the right side of the street. Although petrified, Léon Colinet stood tall as if assured with composure. *'Bon jour,'* he nodded as he passed. The German grinned back and motioned with his hand. But any reassurance from that event was countered by a horrifying sight. Beside the tank was the body of Lt James Evans – sprawled out in front of the Café Henriette Carls. He had been killed there just ten minutes before. Both Joseph and Léon had to step over the body, accompanied by shrieks of fear from Pauline Livet and Maria Tombeux. The entire group abruptly turned right down the Rue du Châtelet and hurried along the road, walking a little faster with each step they took away from the tank.

About 20m away from the Panzer, Léon Colinet saw something disturbing out of the corner of his eye – movement atop the tank he had just passed. Stepping faster, he canted his head just enough to see a man on the tank behind him pull out a machine pistol. 'It's not possible,' he mumbled to himself. Then a ripping sound – the staccato burst of a machine gun. Everyone ran as fast as they could. Joseph Colinet was hit in the shoulder but continued to sprint.

But Pauline Livet and Maria Tombeux collapsed from a volley of bullets in the front of the home of Berthe Courtjoie. Marcel Tombeux was hit, too, in the chest, howling to his wife attempting to come to his aid. 'Move yourself and the baby to the house!' – his final words. Unharmed, his daughter, Marcelle was pulled from the arms of her dying father to duck away with her mother. Still clinging to her other young child, Michel, Maria Tombeux managed to crawl to the house with both children.

Léon Colinet was unharmed, turning toward his wife, Pauline, who lay badly wounded and bleeding in the street near Marcel. He started to go back to retrieve her, but now the German tank leader had emptied his machine gun and now fired a pistol at him. At the time, Colinet was still holding his little daughter Gaby and felt the concussion as the pistol round struck. Amazingly, the bullet struck the multi-folded blanket and was stopped without hurting Gaby.

'Save yourself and the baby!' Pauline called out. Léon Colinet ran down the street and turned into an alley. There, he helped his wounded father, Joseph, move away from the terrible scene. Meanwhile, a neighbour, Émile Crasson, on the street witnessed the entire event while hiding behind a stone wall near his home.[14] After the German tank passed, Marcel Tombeux attempt to get up, but then collapsed to the pavement while Pauline Livet crawled pathetically, moaning until she stopped moving. With the first German tank gone, Crasson rushed out into the street, only to have another SS panzer approach. This tank, too, began shooting at him as he tried to pull her limp body off the cobblestones to the Parmentier house at the corner. Machine gun bursts swept the length of the Rue du Châtelet, and Crasson had to dive for cover once, but he eventually was able to drag Pauline's riddled corpse to the house. Léon Colinet was waiting. The survivors made their way to the town hall.

What would Hans Hennecke recall of those events? After the war, he produced a detailed sketch of the incident, but claimed the fatal shots came from his radio man, Willi Gelfert.[15]

> On 18 December 1944, I drove with my tank through the village of Stavelot between approximately nine and ten o'clock in the morning. My tank had the number 0101 – the tank of the company commander, Obstuf. Kremser. Kremser had been wounded immediately before the events described herein and I had taken over the company at the same time I had taken over his tank. When I reached the spot marked #1 on the sketch, my tank was travelling very slowly at a walking pace because the road was rather narrow. At this time I was standing in the turret of the tank. The turret was open and I was looking out at the road. On each side of the road stood approximately four to five women [*sic*] and they were looking at the tanks as we drove by. Suddenly, and without having received an order, radio man Strm. Willi Gelfert started firing with his machine gun at the women who were standing on the right of the street, approximately 20 metres away. He fired to the right approximately three short bursts. Two women on the right side ran into the doorway of a house, and two or three of them were hit and collapsed … Due to the policy which I knew had to be followed in the campaign, I could not announce an order forbidding this, although it would have been

> technically possible ... I saw how two or three women collapsed after being hit. All of the two or three had been hit in the chest because they collapsed in the way which is typical of shots in the chest, namely, forward. Approximately two women succeeded in escaping into a house. I can remember the scenes distinctly, but I cannot remember seeing a child.

Hennecke claimed that he soon moved on with his tank and never spoke to Willi Gelfert about the shooting. Not knowing his newly taken over tank crew, Hennecke blamed the wounded Kremser, saying he had likely given orders to '*Feuer frei*' with their weapons – an edict that had included the civilian population.[16] Gelfert did later speak to SS Strm. Fritz Eckmann. Eckmann was following behind Hennecke in Pz. #102, commanded by SS Hscha. Leo Skotz:

> We drove through Stavelot ... At this time we were the second tank behind the company commander tank. We drove slowly. At this time Obstuf. Hennecke was Company Commander because Obstuf. Kremser was wounded in Stavelot. Just as we had reached about the middle of the village, a group of fifteen to twenty women and children [*sic*, there were eight] hurried out of a house on the right-hand side of the road and attempted to cross the road. Several of the women carried babies in their arms. As the group came out of the house, I saw the radio operator's machine gun of the company commander's tank firing at them and three to four women were hit. The rest of the group succeeded in reaching the left side of the road where additional machine gun bursts brought another three or four women to the ground. One of the women hit carried an infant, and they both fell to the ground. Another woman came running to her, picked up the baby, and ran with the rest of the survivors into a house. The radio operator in the company commander's tank was Strm. Willi Gelfert. Several days later when I was in La Gleize, he boasted how tough he was at shooting those civilians and he described in detail the motions of the women as he was strafing them with machine gun fire.[17]

The citizens of Stavelot were hiding. However, learning the Germans were taking possession of the town, those hiding in the dairy were deeply worried. If the SS came and discovered the American Tony Calvanese in the building, they would surely kill everyone. The first idea was to get him back to the Americans. Marcel Ozer volunteered to wade across the river to get help from the Americans on the other bank, but setting foot in the icy water convinced him the current was too strong. He ended up swimming back to the south shore and traipsed back to the dairy, cold and sopping wet. There, he and the others came up with a plan. A local Red Cross girl, Mme Berthe Beaupain, managed to get a stretcher from the Red Cross building. They would evacuate Calvanese, disguising him as a wounded Belgian. As crazy as it sounded, Marcel Ozer and Louis van Lancker would carry Calvanese on the stretcher covered with a sheet. Mme Beaupain came along in her Red Cross uniform with her brother and Father Antoine Bernard.

The brave Belgian group walked boldly down the street cradling Calvanese on the stretcher with Father Bernard walking in the lead. They reached the south side of the bridge, having to wait for one of the Panther tanks to cross the span so they could head to the north. On impulse, Ozer and Lancker dashed in behind the tank creeping across the bridge. Following in its dangerous wake, the group was horrified to sidestep the body of Sgt Jack Ellery hideously smashed into the cobblestones. Gunfire crackled and Mme Beaupain and Father Bernard, escorting the stretcher, crouched instinctively. A few steps further on, Ozer saw a dead German officer propped up sitting with his chin limply down and his legs folded off to the side so the tanks would not harm him. Just beyond was the north side of the bridge. Ozer and Lancker and the others dashed off to the right to a nearby brick building, gunfire seemingly popping off everywhere. The others of the group left, but Ozer and Calvanese made their way into the far recesses of its cellar with Calvanese, where they would hide once more.[18]

As the Germans consolidated their hold on the town, some American soldiers in the upper stories of buildings sniped at the tanks as they passed down the streets below, leading many of the Germans to believe that the townspeople of Stavelot were firing at them.[19] Peiper took no time to clarify soldier or civilian:

> While driving through the town, we were fired at by infantry from various directions. From where that came from, it was impossible to determine in such a situation. To silence it, we fired – driving at full speed – into houses, roofs, and so forth. If the direct effect may not be great on a hidden enemy, the effect on morale is quite extensive. It certainly did not happen that we consciously fired at civilians, but their activity cannot be excluded. Later on the inhabitants of Stavelot expressed a lot of good things about their combat activity.[20]

As Peiper's tanks emerged from Stavelot on to the road to Trois-Ponts, Mme Jeanne Gengoux was at the window of her kitchen, surprised to see German tanks roaring down the road. She was just recovering from her astonishment when she saw the machine gun of a passing half-track swivel toward their house. She screamed to her children to get down, but a blast of machine gun bullets shattered the window, enveloping the room. Fourteen-year-old José Gengoux was hit in the stomach and died shortly thereafter. His sister, Germaine, was shot in the right hand; her right ring finger had to be amputated that night. Just a few houses down, Joseph Albert and his daughter Denise were hiding in the basement as the tanks rumbled down the road. Hearing a noise in the house above, Monsieur Albert went up the stairs to find himself confronted by SS men. Were there Americans there? Albert insisted no, but his daughter heard the loud shots as her father was murdered.[21] Peiper claimed the townspeople were terrorists:

> We took Stavelot on the morning of the 18th. When we penetrated [the town], many civilians shot at us from the windows and openings in the roofs. My only goal was for the bridge near Trois-Ponts. I thereupon had no time to spend on those civilians and continued driving on, although I knew that the resistance

> in the town had not been decisively broken … 1st Lt Kremser, CO of the 1st Company, and 1st Lt Tomhardt, the commander of the 11th Panzer Company, were left behind, wounded … Shortly after we left town, some Belgian civilians came and severely mistreated our wounded, pouring hot water over men in many cases and shooting constantly into us with pistols over the heads of the wounded. First Lt Kremser was wounded a second time because of this. First Lt Tomhardt and several others were able to escape from town secretly and gain liberation. In the meantime, violent resistance had been reopened in town consisting of newly arrived American soldiers and civilians. With help of a few tanks of mine, which followed behind some infantry, we succeeded in the counterattack to get our wounded out.[22]

Capt. Mitchell ordered his company to pull back once the enemy tanks surged from the bridgehead and the grenadiers swarmed through town. Although Maj. Solis had intended to pull up into the hills north of town, in the chaos, most of his troops pulled back helter-skelter along the road to the east bank toward Malmedy.[23] 'It was a damned mess,' Sgt Mocnik remembered.[24] He and Capt. Mitchell drove away from the embattled square, heading up the road to the fuel dump near the Haute Levée. There, they found two lone Belgian soldiers in British uniforms guarding the endless stacks of jerricans.[25]

Meanwhile, Maj. Solis had come upon two truckloads of engineers from 3rd platoon of Company C of the 291st Engineer Combat Battalion under Sgt Ed Keoghan. Keoghan and his engineers had been trying to make their way back to La Gleize from Sourbrodt when they arrived at daylight just west of Stavelot to find the village under attack just below them. Concluding they could no longer get to La Gleize, the little group was accosted by Maj. Solis in a jeep with a truck of infantry just behind. 'Have you got anything to fight tanks with?' Keoghan shook his head, replying, 'I've got one anti-tank rifle grenade for a carbine.' No matter. 'Okay,' Solis ordered, 'Position your men in these farm buildings. Guard this road. German tanks are coming!'

With that, Solis took off. Although Keoghan thought the orders were ridiculous, he obeyed, posting men with carbines. Expecting the worst, he and his men prepared an ambush from the farm buildings and haystack of Henri Wansart just west of town. They waited apprehensively in the cold mist. The first hour was the most anxious, as the sounds of fighting and tank tracks filled the air. Yet nothing came. Then, a second lonely hour … and after that, a third. Nothing appeared on the road until Solis himself arrived to give the engineers a new assignment – help the Belgians guard the fuel dump.[26]

Moving further down the road, Sgt Mocnik found 'GIs loading gasoline into their vehicles as fast as they could at the far end of the dump and hauling it off.'[27]

Company C of the 202nd got out of Stavelot, too, covered by the 50-calibre machine gun fire of Pvt. Wesley Hillary who kept enemy heads down. 'We started going on up the hill away from town, as we could hear tanks down there,' one member recalled. 'I was concerned that we were going to be surrounded. There was a big gasoline dump there. We walked until we found a truck. One guy was loading the truck with jerricans and we all pitched in and got it loaded in a hurry and jumped on top. We got him to drive off. Behind us, we saw a terrific fire as we left.'[28]

It was true. Capt. Jean Burniat of the Belgian Army's 3rd Company, 5th Fusiliers Battalion had been briefed the previous night by Capt. Harry Sturgis, Commander of the 3814th Quarter Master Supply Company. Capt. Burniat was told that the Germans were on the move and the three big fuel dumps in the area (Spa, Franchorchamps, and Stavelot) could be in danger. Arriving at the huge Géronstère Depot #2 near Spa early that morning with his English interpreter, Roger Hardy, Burniat was informed that telephone lines were out.[29] Capt. Burniat drove straight ahead to warn Lt Albert Detroz at the Château Malacord headquarters in Stavelot. They arrived before daylight, just in time to see flares lighting the sky and sounds of gunfire. Burniat and his interpreter roared off in their Bedford truck to see if the Franchorchamps dump was secure. Just as Lt Pehovic before him had discovered, Burniat found it open for enemy capture. On the spot, he told a flustered Lt Detroz to act as he saw fit, and then hastened back to Spa to warn everyone with the U.S. First Army. The Germans were in Stavelot.

Setting aside panic, Lt Detroz sought to secure the Depot #3 with sixty lightly armed men. He ordered his Belgian infantry to prepare a roadblock using jerricans that could be set on fire. The jerricans were stacked along the right side of the Vielle Route near La Bicoque – the farm of the Rey family. The picturesque farm was now dominated by the stacks and stacks of fuel cans. Suddenly, a GMC truck driven by Pvt. Calvin Hales, who worked with the Belgians, was hit by a German artillery round and a loud racket of gunfire ominously echoed in the valley. Pfc. Theo Lauter of the 3814th QM Gas Supply Company was billeted in a house between Stavelot and Franchorchamps. He was awakened the morning of 18 December by loud explosions drawing steadily closer. 'Our platoon sergeant arrived on the scene with orders for us to pack up and get out of there as the Germans were in Stavelot and on the other side of the Amblève river.'[30]

At about the same time, an American half-track approached the fuel dump towing a gun. It was Lt Jack Doherty again with the last remaining towed gun from the disastrous gun duel before the bridge. Close behind him was Maj. Solis. Solis directed two rifle squads of his remaining 3rd platoon and its single 57mm anti-tank gun under S/Sgt Malcom Irwin to block the road to Franchorchamps. He personally ran to the fuel dump to warn the Belgians of the enemy's imminent approach.

Moving forward in a half-track, Solis came across Lt Albert Detroz, who flagged him down excitedly.[31] Detroz made it known to Solis that he understood that the Germans could hardly miss an attempt to capture the fuel. Detroz turned to Pvt. Robert Tille to fire his Bren gun into a collection of jerricans piled in the middle of the road. Even though the bullets ripped open the cans, the fuel was not set alight. But using bayonets like can openers and a burning rag worked, and the flames soon spurted skyward in a fire that erupted so quickly that those setting it had to pull back abruptly. A hellish orange petrol blaze boiled upward. 'It was a Dantesque sight,' one present remembered, 'a wall of flame and smoke spreading high into the sky.' The Rey farm was just outside the reach of the massive fire.

Having gone to Spa to warn of the German approach, Capt. Burniat and Roger Hardy attempted to return to Lt Detroz and the fuel dump from the north. Yet coming from Franchorchamps, their driver Théo Peeters suddenly found their path blocked by dozens of fuel jerricans thrown in the road near the Ferme Bonaparte. Obviously, someone had hauled the cans on to the tarmac, whereas the cans had been previously stacked neatly on the left shoulder of the road. Flaming explosions ahead of them eerily illuminated the jumble of fuel cans in the road. To clear the obstacle, Hardy got off their GMC truck and laboriously hauled off the fuel cans. He worried the scene looked to be a perfect enemy ambush. Anticipating the worst, Burniat covered Hardy's swift removal with a Sten gun, both expecting the enemy to rise up out of the ditches and turn their position into a flaming pyre. Fortunately, the two finally moved beyond the roadblock, thankful to find other Americans and Belgians guarding the mass of the fuel dump further to the south.[32]

With V Corps all too aware of the debacle developing near Stavelot and Malmedy, the 30th Infantry Division was rushing towards Peiper. Gen. Hobbs had sent the 117th Infantry Regiment under Col Walter M. Johnson from Eupen the night of 17 December towards that zone. Infantry-laden trucks bucked heavy traffic made up of desperate Belgian refugees and all manner of U.S. Army traffic heading in the opposite direction. Col Richard W. Stephens, the chief of staff, conveyed the word on Stavelot: 'They want Col Johnson's outfit to take that place quick ... They want to stop this thing and cut it off before it gets any deeper.'[33] Progress was slow, with nighttime raids by the Luftwaffe, seemingly determined to delay the U.S. convoys with poorly aimed bombs and illuminating flares. In the town of Berverce, Johnson met his superiors, learning that he was to send his 1st Battalion to Stavelot, the 3rd to Malmedy, and hold the 2nd in reserve. Yet reaching Malmedy, traffic came nearly to a standstill. With such a traffic jam, it took two hours to clear the town.[34]

All morning of the 18th, the 1st Battalion, U.S. 117th Infantry Regiment of the 30th Infantry Division had been in the snarl. Motoring south of Eupen, Capt. John E. Kent and others huddled around a radio in the back of their slowly moving GMC truck. Axis Sallie was on the air claiming that the Germans had split open the Western Front. 'The Fanatical 30th Division, Roosevelt's SS troops, are en route to rescue,' she cooed, 'but this time they will be annihilated.' 'We thought it was funny,' Kent remembered.[35] But finding that they were now ordered to defend bridges approaching Malmedy gave them an uneasy feeling.

By dawn on 18 December the mission of the 1st Battalion was changed to circle north toward Stavelot in an attempt to relieve Company A of the 526th Armored Infantry Battalion. Word had it that the road from Malmedy to Stavelot had already been cut. 'We de-trucked two miles from the town,' Kent remembered. 'We found armored infantry personnel eating K-rations and the men said simply: "Germans chased us out of town."'[36] Company A advanced on the right side of the road and Company B took the left, the men soon coming across the aftermath of the burning roadblock and Belgian guard units that warned them of the enemy up ahead. On the orders of Lt Col Frankland, the burning had been stopped – but not before 145,000 gallons of fuel had gone up in flames. The remaining 800,000 gallons were then evacuated by truck by the 3814th Quartermaster Gas Supply Company to Spa, where they were hastily loaded on to trains to take them out of enemy reach.[37]

Contrary to the cinematic Colonel Hessler in the Hollywood *Battle of the Bulge*, Jochen Peiper did not approach the fuel dump with its vast stores of fuel. While the pall of boiling flames and towering smoke would have seemed to have attracted the attention of the fuel-strapped SS tank column, Peiper remained totally unaware of the massive fire.[38] Indeed, when the pyre erupted, Jochen Peiper was already further west, heading with the spearhead to Trois-Ponts. 'I had no idea of a U.S. gas dump being at Stavelot,' Peiper later wrote, 'but if a huge amount of petrol had been ablaze, I would have known.'[39] In reality Peiper's eyes were fixed to the west with orders to drive fast. What happened 2km behind him might as well have been in Berlin.

The German armor continued to wind through town – first the Panthers of the 1st and 2nd Panzer Company and then half a dozen of the super-heavy Königstigers of the attached SS 501st Panzer Battalion. However, that the German grip on the town was less than complete soon became obvious, as two Tigers were lost in the streets to American fire. Pvt. Lee Galloway of the 526th hit a German Tiger with a bazooka that afternoon.[40] Meanwhile, the panzer regiment laid down a smokescreen across the Amblève to veil its movements through town. Up on the hill above town, Capt. Mitchell relayed a message to First Army at 11.07 a.m. that his 'company is taking up defensive positions on the north side of Stavelot' and was requesting artillery missions on targets of opportunity as soon as they could see them.[41]

Peiper was unaware that the arriving U.S. 30th Infantry Division had orders to seize and hold the town.[42] With no infantry to spare, Peiper only controlled the narrow network of twisting streets he used to emerge west of town. He made no effort to consolidate his grip on Stavelot. That task fell to the *Landsers* of the 3rd Fallschirmjäger Division to the rear.[43] In fact, the Luftwaffe troops were many kilometers to the east, most having gone no further than Faymonville.

Having seized the bridge across the Amblève, Peiper's real concern was getting quickly to Trois-Ponts some 6km away on the hard-surfaced N23 and seizing its bridges across the confluence of the Amblève and Salm rivers. The Salm River was not a very imposing body of water, yet it cut a deep swath into the surrounding treed landscape. Approaches were difficult and predictable. Immediately in the wake of Peiper's rushing spearhead was SS Uscha. Karl Wortmann in his flak panzer:

> Finally, the advance could continue after the bridge over the Amblève and the area around it had been cleared by our engineers. But when our advance began, very strong small-arms fire was opened from all the windows around us. Also

> anti-tank fire hit our column. The Americans tried to prevent the column from crossing the bridge. The roads in the town were very narrow and bumpy. The column formed up again very slowly. Trois-Ponts was 5–6 kilometers away and there were several stops. During these occasions we were spotted by an American reconnaissance plane, but failed to realise it.[44]

It was an event soon to have dramatic consequences.

Chapter 19

DASH

In the midst of chaos, there is also opportunity.[1]

'The Führer is excellent,' the radio crackled expectantly. Like many in the heart of Germany, Sigurd Peiper likely followed the progress of the war on the radio each morning. As always, the broadcast from the *Deutsches Nachrichtenbüro* and *Radio Berlin* covered events almost two days before, but Hptm. Ludwig Sertorius, Hitler's favorite news commentator, was ebullient. 'Strong German forces after a short but tremendous artillery barrage, launched a mighty offensive from the Westwall,' he began. He had information for his listeners, who had been wondering why there had been no news from Hitler for weeks.

> In all tranquillity, we let the enemy guess, lie, and provoke, because we didn't want to tell the world the reason the Führer surrounded himself with a veil of secrecy – because he planned and prepared the German offensive during these last days and weeks to the last detail.[2]

'At 5.30 a.m. on 16 December, our forces overran the first American forward positions between the Hohes Venn in Belgium and the northern part of Luxembourg … The enemy was completely taken by surprise. The U.S. First Army,' Sertorius blustered, had been 'cut in two.' Then a note of feigned caution. 'We have no illusions that we can be in Paris tomorrow,' he continued wryly, 'but the offensive has succeeded brilliantly.'[3]

That cold, foggy Monday, 18 December 1944, found Peiper scudding away from Stavelot in Jupp Diefenthal's armored half-track along a seam that cut the length of grain of the U.S. First Army lines in Belgium. From Peiper's anxious perch – a cold metal seat – he watched the narrow road unwind just beyond the gun muzzle of the lead Panther tank ahead of him. Inside the jolting SPW with Paul Zwigart at the wheel, Peiper stared at a topographic map in its clear Lexan case. The village of Trois-Ponts, 'Three Bridges', was just ahead. Ever since his days of leading armored half-tracks in Russia, Peiper appreciated the gravity of bridges: seize them or suffer. Indeed, Trois-Ponts was an obvious communications center in the Ardennes. Studded with roads, rails, and bridges, the N23 entered the town after first passing under two big railway overpasses before it joined with the North and South N33.

Moreover, in that town, both Panzer Rollbahn D and E established by *Heersgruppe B* planners converged. Peiper had decided to advance along the more direct Rollbahn E that went through Werbomont and Hamoir to the Meuse river. 'We proceeded at top speed toward Trois-Ponts,'[4] Peiper recalled, seemingly unaware of the bloody mayhem left in his wake. His attention was firmly fixed on reaching the Meuse at Huy. It was there where he had crossed the Meuse during what he saw as the triumphant conquest of France in 1940.[5]

Still, Peiper would first have to get across the rushing Amblève river. Riding behind the advance, he could see that the terrain before the bridge town of Trois-Ponts was distinctly unfavorable for tanks. There, the confluence of the Amblève and Salm rivers cut deep gorges with tree-lined cliffs and sharply turning roads hugging the scant, flat ground along the riverbed. Additionally, deploying off the sparse road network would be even more difficult than at Stavelot. Indeed, from Stavelot, the road hugged the Amblève on the north bank with steep hills rising to the north. At the entrance to Trois-Ponts, the road is straddled by two giant viaducts carrying the railways, one going toward Stavelot and the other to Comblain-au-Pont. Once through the second tunnel, the road from Stavelot then joins the N33, which connects Trois-Ponts to Liège via the route from La Gleize to Stoumont.

Following just behind the two lead tanks, Peiper was acutely aware of his vulnerability. 'Driving one after another along a narrow road,' he would later remember of his advance to Trois-Ponts, 'one could not get off the path.' His tanks moved single file on roads that would barely accommodate one. The sweeping formations of Russia – the tank companies neatly echeloned in depth and seeking *Keil und Kessel* on a wide front – meant nothing in the torturous Amblève river valley.[6] Nor did the 2km range of the Panther or Tiger tank guns. All targets appeared only 100m or so ahead on the winding Ardennes roads. 'We were never stronger than our lead tank,' Peiper worried.[7]

Those who lived in the valley were troubled, too. That Monday afternoon, on the road to Trois-Ponts, newlywed Juliette Antoine was in her two-storey brick home on the Ferme Antoine on the south side of the Route de Trois-Ponts.[8] Hers was one of the last houses reached before Trois-Ponts. Born in La Gleize, young Juliette Legros had been courted by her teenage sweetheart, Maurice Antoine, since before the war. Yet after Belgium was occupied in May 1940, Maurice had been conscripted into the German army – a move he resisted with many others by going into hiding and even joining the Belgian Resistance. With other *refractieurs*, he hid in the hills between Vielsalm and Trois-Ponts. Finally, in September the Americans had liberated Belgium and their romance flourished anew. Things seemed to return to normal, so they married in a gala celebration on 16 November 1944.

Yet exactly a month after their wedding on Saturday, 16 December, Maurice Antoine was surprised to hear from a friend that Malmedy had been shelled by big guns. And when both Juliette and Maurice went to Mass the following Sunday in Stavelot, they emerged to find the roads choked with refugees streaming from the east. Both saw Americans, but they didn't seem casual or fun-loving as usual. Instead, they saw a GI gun crew working to point their machine gun down the road to the east. The next morning, the stream of refugees reached a flood, and both decided it would be best for Maurice to go to Liège. If the Germans found him … Neither wanted to ponder that possibility. Maurice buried some American cartridges he had from his resistance days in the garden, and said a tearful goodbye. It had been a wonderful honeymoon, both agreed, but there was no time. 'Three kisses and he was gone.' To fight the tears, Juliette decided to make bread.

Just after 10 a.m. there was gunfire outside and everyone took cover. The lead German tank was shooting at everything that moved.[9] They could not know that just 300m down the road at the charming French-style farm of Léon Mignon, the tank's machine gun had fired at a group of civilians standing by the road who thought the approaching tank was American. Horror descended on the homes aligned along the road to Trois-Ponts. Soon after, an SS man came into the house and fired at the entire family with a submachine gun. Mignon's wife, Maria, and two of his daughters, Marie and Monique, were killed in the blast. Léon himself fell to the kitchen floor and feigned death. After the SS man left, Léon escaped to the loft with his surviving 2-year-old daughter, who had gone unnoticed.[10] Nearby, Alphonse and Catherine Depas suffered a similar fate. Even though the two families attempted to flee into their homes, Julien Hourand was killed in the doorway of his farmhouse and Marcel Hourand was wounded in the leg even as he dashed into the kitchen.[11]

At the Antoine farm, the shooting rattled the building and most took to the basement. One exception was hired hand Léonard Nailis, who poked his head up to look out the window facing the road to see what all the racket was about. Glancing at the big machine approaching, he saw bright flashes and dropped instinctively. His reflex likely saved his life, for as he dropped to the floor, a hail of gunfire shattered the window, one bullet crashing into his parents' photo that hung on the opposite wall of his room. As machine guns crackled with rounds slamming into the walls and windows, Nailis crawled through the house looking to hide with the others.

Then, there was someone at the door – they didn't knock; they just came in. They were SS troops, but Juliette was shocked to see that some getting off the vehicles were in American uniforms. They came in as if they owned the place. Two strode into the kitchen where they were kneading loaves. They drank the milk that Juliette was using to make the bread. The SS men seemed famished; they ate everything in sight.

In the village of Trois-Ponts, André Nicolay, a boy of 16, awoke with his father and 12-year-old brother, Michel, from a fitful sleep.[12] They had always lived in their modest brick home located on the Rue de Coo before the bridge over the Amblève river. It was another foggy day – typical for that time of year – and everyone was jumpy and afraid since the previous day. Since Sunday, refugees had been fleeing through town and there were rumbles of gunfire in the distance. That morning an American soldier had showed up at their home pounding on the door and shouting. The soldier was beside himself, but the language barrier made it impossible to know exactly why. It was clear that he was cold, however, and their father invited him in for hot coffee. Fortified with warmth, he left in a big hurry.

As he departed, the family heard closer sounds of shooting from the direction of Stavelot. André and his father stood in the doorway on the street as both watched an American gun crew hurriedly drive through town with a half-track towing the gun into position. Minutes later there were reports of cannon fire. The American anti-tank gun at Vieux Moulin had been destroyed. André's father was worried. He had already received his call-up papers from the German army and had not gone. With the occupation, Hitler moved the German border from its present location east of Krinkelt to Franchorchamps and considered all the people of Malmedy to be ethnic Germans *Volksdeutsche* and part of the Greater German Reich.[13] André had ignored the edict. His father urged his eldest to take off. His younger brother, Michel, wanted to go along but his father said he would stay in the safety of their home. As the sound of the shooting to the east increased, André mounted his bicycle and sped away toward La Gleize.

Before the action began, the hilltop town of Trois-Ponts was headquarters for the 1111th Engineer Combat Group and Col Wallis Anderson at the Hotel Crismer just to the left before the bridge crossing the Salm river.[14] The small town of 1,400 was defended by the 140 men of Company C of the 51st Engineer Combat Battalion, recalled from sawmills near Marche and led by the battalion executive officer, Maj. Robert B. Yates.[15] At 1.40 a.m. Col William H. Ragland, the chief engineer at Hodges' headquarters, called Anderson to make sure he understood that the bridges at Trois-Ponts must not to fall into enemy hands.

Unlike at Stavelot, and with more time, they had seen to it that more than a ton of C-4 explosive was wired to destroy each span. The key thing, however, would be to give the engineers with the detonator key adequate warning of the enemy armor's approach. The approach of the N23 to Trois-Ponts passed under two towering railway viaducts – one of the roads emerging from them going on into Trois-Ponts proper and the other turning west to La Gleize. At 7.50 a.m. Capt. Schueber of the 51st announced to Anderson by radio that his roadblocks before Trois-Ponts were in place while other engineers wired the bridges. Meanwhile, a gun crew of the 526th Armored Infantry Battalion had become lost in its move to Stavelot. On the morning of 18 December, the crew paused in Trois-Ponts after its towing half-track broke down between Aywaille and Remouchamps.

In light of the deteriorating situation, Anderson commandeered the crew of the half-track, and ordered his S-4, Capt. Robert N. Jewett, to have them set up their 57mm anti-tank gun 200 yards east of the twin railway viaduct, not far from the Hotel Liffange, and about 100m from the bridge. Another dozen men under Lt Richard Green including some of the 3rd Platoon, C Company, 51st Engineers, and other wayward members of the 526th Armored Infantry and Company A of the 291st Engineers were set up in ditches across from the 50mm MG in front of the hotel. Further, on the west side of the viaducts,

Capt. Sam Scheuber of the 51st had set up a 2½-ton truck mounting a crewed machine gun to serve as a backstop.[16]

As all this went on, 60-year-old Marie Adèle Job, the manager of the Hotel Liffrange, stood at the window of the dining room, seized with worry as she watched the American gun crew set up not far from her establishment.[17] Soon her two brothers joined her at the window. 'This looks to turn out bad,' One suggested they run off down to the road to Coo. But the other said no. Just then Capt. Robert Jewett, Anderson's S-4, roared up in a jeep and began directing the Americans to sight their weapons, lay out mines, and prepare for the enemy. Shortly, he placed Lt Green in charge of the mine-laying operation up ahead while he directed preparations for the gun crew. Mme Job was now really frightened.

Meanwhile, back in Trois-Ponts, Col Wallis Anderson plainly heard the cacophonic din of battle from the direction of Stavelot. At 11.05 a.m. he hastily readied to depart Trois-Ponts with his 1111th Engineer Group headquarters intending to head back to Basse Bodeux just a short distance away. Anderson told those under him he was not bugging out, but was under orders from First U.S. Army to co-ordinate the engineers outside of harm's way. Anderson encouraged his men. 'We have come several thousand miles to fight the Nazis,' he reminded, 'not to withdraw from them.' Each of the three bridges of Trois-Ponts were wired for demolition without fail. His engineers were to blow each sky high the moment the enemy approached.

The road from Stavelot to Trois-Ponts followed a tortured path, winding through two railway underpasses with a 90-degree turn before it reached the river. At the exit of the second underpass was a T-intersection with the Amblève river to the south. At the intersection, the road either turned left to go through Trois-Ponts and reach the three bridges that gave the village its name, or to the right ran along the bending curves of the river without crossing. Peiper wished to proceed left and cross the river directly to Werbomont, then the Meuse river.

About 50 yards beyond the position of the 57mm gun, a jeep was posted with two more U.S. soldiers another 50 yards further up with a daisy chain of mines that they would pull across the road to halt any enemy advance. There was not long to wait.

Less than an hour after leaving the maelstrom in Stavelot, at 11.30 a.m. a dozen tanks of Kampfgruppe Peiper were heard before they were seen, coming out of the ground fog before the east side of Trois-Ponts. With the tanks roaring toward Hotel Liffrange, Cpl Bruce W. Frazier and Pfc. Ralph J. Beiker first took two rifle shots at the men standing in the turrets of the German armor, but missed. While the Germans dropped inside their tanks and buttoned up, Frazier and Beiker hurriedly yanked two dozen mines across the road and then rolled away from the ditch to run as fast as they could to get back to the jeep. Frazier fired it up and threw the vehicle in gear. As the lead tank fired its machine gun, Frazier and Beiker wove down the road at full speed. 'They're coming!' one called out to those in the Hotel as they raced by.

Nevertheless, as his lead Panther reached the unconcealed mines, Strelow climbed out of his tank and pushed them aside while his bow machine gunner blasted the ditches to make sure no one else was lurking by. Twice struck, Strelow's gun-shy gunner, Rttf. Eugen Zimmermann, urged Uscha. Ernst to radio for support. The *Amis* had to be ahead of this minefield and he had no gunsight! Where were the panzer grenadiers? 'Irmgard, this is Carbide, over!'[18] Yet the Fu 5 UHF transmitter had pitiful range in the Ardennes hills. No reply. Soon Werner Poetschke and Peiper himself approached on foot to see the reason for the halt. The result was predictable: get moving. In less than a minute, Zimmermann and the rest of the crew were rolling forward, not stopping for any bullet fire from the MG at the Hotel Liffrange, whose outgunned crew had elected to run off south for survival.

Two hundred yards east of the viaduct the four-man crew of S/Sgt Albert Smith's 57mm anti-tank gun found themselves facing the lead Panther. 'Now, let's be damned sure they are Jerries,' one of the team called out. Perhaps they waited too long because the third tank in the column fired off several rounds before they could even fire one. One round slammed behind them; another zipped only inches above their heads, and still another hit a tree behind them. Deadly fragments of steel and wood whirled through the air although wounding no one. The enemy identity settled, Corp. Donald Hollenbeck put the German tank in his sights – it was at nearly point-blank range – and ordered Pvt. Dallas Buchanan to pull the trigger. The shot streaked ahead, slamming into the Panzer Mk V in a shower of sparks.

What the gun crew couldn't see was that the 57mm round had bounced off its sharply angled steel glacis plates – up to a 100mm thick. Against hope, the American crew reloaded as they saw the German beast stop. In fact, driver Rttf. Heinz Biwald had hit the brakes in shock. Now seeing all was okay, he idled in the road to help Rttf. Eugen Zimmermann fire back. The precision Zielfernrohr F-12, a telescopic sight, had been blasted away in the earlier encounter with Carl Smith in Stavelot. Zimmermann now squinted one eye to look down the open breech of the swivelling KwK 42-gun barrel. Peering down the length of the tube, he sighted the American gun ahead. Tank traffic backed up behind him, but he paid no attention. Strm. Heinz Hoffmeister slammed an explosive anti-personnel shell into the breech as they approached the ground before the rail overpasses:

> The order 'sharp left' came over the radio. At that moment we were hit, but thank God, it was only a graze. Apparently, we were moving too fast. I was able to exactly recognise the anti-tank gun and aimed the cannon, not with the optics, but directly along the barrel, at a stone wall immediately behind the anti-tank gun. One explosive shell and there was no more resistance.[19]

Zimmermann's HE shell struck the base of the 57mm gun, killing four Americans tending the weapon instantly, and stunning Pfc. Andrew Salazar.[20] In near panic, Capt. Jewett gathered up the fleeing survivors on the west side of the tunnel at the T-intersection into his nearby half-track. They raced off to safety along the N33 toward La Gleize.

Even with the 57mm gun destroyed, the German tanks had to slow, evidenced by the sound of squealing steel on asphalt. It was a challenge for the big panzer forms to clear the underpasses and negotiate the gnarled curves. Even more, the cannon and anti-tank gun shots immediately alerted the demolition crew of the combat engineers guarding the bridges ahead. As if on signal, the American Troops on the other side of the river commenced to fire. 'We kept sniping at them from across the river,' remembered Major Yates, 'but every shot of ours seemed to draw about a thousand in return.' Still observing from the other side of the river with binoculars, Col Anderson counted nineteen armored vehicles in the German advance. Peiper:

> We were standing below the railway bridge and received rather severe infantry fire from the bridge across the river further down. At that time seven to twelve prisoners of war were brought over to me. One of them told me that he belonged to an American engineer battalion and that they were ordered to stop our advance by demolition. I, myself, sent them on back without guards.[21]

Boom! As Peiper took cover in his command SPW under the railway overpass, he saw streaks of bright light up further up just before a thundering explosion. Wood splinters and debris rained from the smoking rubble.[22] He and Diefenthal got out of the SPW and walked past the stalled tanks up ahead.[23] He didn't need word back from those ahead to know that the bridge before him across the Amblève had been blown to smithereens. Then, the other span to the right exploded. It was just after noon:

> Driving one after another along a narrow road from which one could not get off, we were never stronger than our lead tank. This tank was hit by an anti-tank shell in the mantlet from a gun that was in position in the left ditch. The tank finished off the anti-tank gun with an explosive grenade at good, full speed. We did not encounter any other resistance. The bridges were blown up before we could get to them. There was no trace of Maj. Yates, merely some mines that were lying openly on the road.[24]

When the smoke drifted away, Peiper could see the characteristic three-storey brick houses in the narrow streets of Trois-Ponts appearing just beyond through the dust, but the wooden bridge had gone. 'We destroyed the anti-tank gun,' Peiper recalled with feigned regret, 'but then the enemy blew up the bridge in our faces.' He was angry; the pesky engineers were no match for his tank troops. 'If we had captured the bridge at Trois-Ponts intact and had enough fuel, it would have been a simple matter to drive through to the Meuse River early that day.'[25]

The mood of the SS men in Peiper's column seemed to over-match their leader's dismay. Had the civilians been helping the Americans in the town? Col

Wallis Anderson, the commander of the 1111th Engineer Combat Group, was in Trois-Ponts looking down from the road to Brume. Through the stereoscopic lens of his field glasses he saw the trestle bridge explode. 'After the bridge was blown in Trois-Ponts, practically in their faces, I saw the Germans pause briefly to look the situation over, kill a civilian man and woman with apparently no provocation whatsoever, and then turn north-west.'[26] Other Americans saw the same sight. According to witnesses, a German tank approached the blown bridge and two black-uniformed SS men emerged to examine its damage. Seeing an elderly man and wife in front of the adjacent house, two SS tank men shouted for the couple to come forward. One SS man then shot the woman with a pistol, who collapsed into her husband's arms just moments before he, too, was shot. The two SS tankers then remounted their vehicle and headed off toward the village of Coo.

With that, Louis Nicolay had seen enough and dashed with his son into a neighbour's basement. For the night they were safe and Nicolay was pleased that his oldest son had left town. Yet the following afternoon, the SS searched the houses along the river in a wicked mood. Soon they pulled André Nicolay's brother and his father from the basement, lined them up against the wall of their house, and shot them. Louis fell mortally wounded, but young Michel had only been shot through the hand and ran away screaming. An SS rifleman ran after the boy while other SS men laughed. One man, Edmond Georgin, ran to the river and swam across, only to have his right arm almost severed from machine gun fire from the other bank. Other Belgians were executed in their homes.[27]

Meanwhile, the Americans watched the entire episode from just the other side of the surging river. Enraged, Maj. Yates of the 51st Engineer Combat Battalion personally fired at the cruel SS spectators, dropping one before they disappeared.[28] Sadly, young Michel Nicolay had stumbled on his way to the river and his pursuer had caught up with him and stabbed him to death with a bayonet.[29] In all, eleven civilians were murdered that afternoon. While the orgy of killing went on, a Belgian woman, Madame Lifrange, who spoke German, boldly approached the Germans who were executing those in the village. 'You men are crazy!' she yelled. 'What are you doing?' 'We have just killed two *Maquisards*' – partisans – they announced. Madame Lifrange would later learn that the partisans they referred to included her two older brothers.[30]

Meanwhile, the feint of the 6th and 7th Panzer Companies approached along the tortured road from Hinoumont to Wanne and Aisomont, having set off from Vaulx Richard at 8 a.m. To negotiate the forest trails, they had impressed a Belgian guide from that village, Fernand Hopa, whose bullet-riddled body was found on 19 December near Bûtay just a few kilometers south of his home.[31] The objective of the armored approach was still another bridge that crossed the Salm river south of Trois-Ponts near the railway station. If that could be taken, Trois-Ponts could be taken from the rear. Yet their progress along the road was slower than a man could walk as the track to Wanne was treacherous. Many tanks mired during the slow advance.

One platoon of C Company of the 51st Engineers under Lt Fred Nabors had checked this approach, too, by setting up a roadblock on the approach road near Noupré. The position wasn't much, but it bristled with an explosive lace of mines laid across the road covered by two bazookas and a few men with small arms.

At 11.30 a.m. three Mk IV German tanks approached the position, attempting to detonate the mines with a stream of machine gun fire. A short exchange of fire with an ineffective bazooka shot sent the defenders scurrying for safety back through the woods. The tanks then dumped off German infantry, who busied themselves removing mines so the tanks could proceed. The panzer group pressed on, but when they reached the railway overpass near the rail station high on the hill above Wanne, they found the partly repaired structure insufficient to bear the weight of anything more than a motorcycle.[32] At 12.30 p.m. the Americans had blown up the big stone span in town that carried the N23 across the Salm near the Hotel Crismer. There was one last possible German approach – a bridge across the lower Salm river near Grand Halleux a couple of kilometers south of Trois-Ponts.

The infantry with the Mk IVs stuck up on the hill near Aisomont now descended down the forested reverse slope to try to seize the southernmost span from the north. At first the German grenadiers thought they had found it undefended. In fact, a squad of five men from Company A of the ubiquitous 291st Engineer Combat Battalion hid in the bushes on the west side of the bridge with orders to blast it on sight of the enemy. While Sgt Jean B. Miller clutched the detonation key, SS troopers started to warily cross the bridge. When the first two were mid-span, Miller twisted the key.[33] That crossing, too, crashed into the river with an ear-splitting roar.

With that final reverse, the 6th and 7th Panzer Companies received orders to double back and join the main advance through Stavelot to Trois-Ponts and La Gleize – a countermarch that would consume the entire day.[34] And for them, there was a further complication: in spite of topping off with fuel in Büllingen, both of the Mk IV companies were now running short on fuel. Some of the Mk IVs would stay behind in Aisomont and Wanne waiting for petrol. SS Uscha. Rolf Ehrhardt, the tank driver for the 7th Panzer Company commander, recalled:

> The night in Lodomez ended with the order: 'Flanking attack via Wanne to Trois-Ponts. 7th Company and 6th Company (with Mark IV tanks) as well as the 3rd Engineer Company (Sievers).' We lined up where Roman Clotten rode at the point, because his radioman was from Alsace and spoke French well. As I remember, the Americans had withdrawn, but secured the entrance to Wanne with several mine barriers. I, myself, did not get to Wanne, as I was stuck in Hénumont because of difficulties with the carburettor for a short while. [In Wanne] Roman Clotten as well as a platoon leader radioed about rifle fire from basement and dormer windows and about recognising civilians. In the meantime, it had become noon. Then came the order: 'Back to the initial position in Lodomez and follow the spearhead!' Trois-Ponts had been taken by the main

> element. The road to Lodomez was very difficult. Because of the difficult terrain, many Mark IVs had burned up so much fuel that they stopped. They had to be refuelled with reserve cans, which were in short supply because of the danger of fire. Naturally, that took time. Then, suddenly, the American attack planes arrived, which caught us with the bulk of the vehicles on the hillside without any cover. The gunfire and bombs had no serious consequences, but again, they cost us important time and precious fuel.[35]

Peiper fumed in Trois-Ponts. While he waited for word of seizure of either of the other two bridges, the commander of his heavy Tiger battalion arrived. Here was Heinz von Westernhagen, the commander of Peiper's lumbering 2nd Panzer Battalion – the 501st SS Heavy Panzer Battalion. Peiper asked him about the situation in his battalion. Eyeing the blown bridge, 'Bad luck,' they agreed. Yet Westernhagen, who had toiled up the roads past Baugnez the preceding afternoon, had something else to tell his superior. 'Among other things, he told me in this conference that a mix-up had happened at Ligneuville and that a rather large number of prisoners had been shot there. He did not know any details, nor who had given the order to do that.'[36] Peiper claimed he was too busy with the problem of exploding bridges to ask for clarification about Westernhagen's '*Durcheinander*'.

To his trained ear, the muffled explosions verified the negative news Peiper now got over the radio. The bridges were gone, and he had pissed away another hour. No more waiting, Peiper ordered the entire column to turn right and west on the N33. Soon they passed through the little ridge-line village of Coo, then toward the tiny hamlet of La Gleize just eight curving kilometers away. In the gorge of Roanne-Coo, the loud racket of machine guns announced the arrival of Peiper's armor.

Arsène Gabriel was driving from Stoumont in his farm truck when he was enveloped by machine gun fire as he made a turn toward Coo. His radiator was holed, but Gabriel quickly turned around and sped off. Moments later, the armor approached Moulin Marechal, causing two locals walking on the road to dive into the underbrush by the road as bullets flew. They dared not move as fifty tanks and half-tracks zoomed down the road. The point of the Kampfgruppe Peiper was firing at anything in their path. At nearby Borgoumont, Ruy, and La Venne, all the young Belgian men took to the roads.[37]

There was one bridge in La Gleize, and otherwise a road that led to Stoumont, Remouchamps, and eventually to the Meuse at Liège. As before, Peiper ordered his tanks to race at top speed for the village. The route was vexing to Peiper's audacious sensibilities, winding through the canyon-like Amblève river valley from one serpentine curve to the next. Boulders, curves, and trees seemed to invite ambush. Yet while his radio crackled, Peiper listened as his tanks reported clear driving. Maybe he had finally shaken free.

Meanwhile, having escape Trois-Ponts, André Nicolay was still pedalling furiously to reach La Gleize. As he slowed to ascend the steep path toward La Gleize, he could see American aeroplanes flying over his left shoulder, evidently to attack the German column approaching. Were they catching up? He pedalled faster. On the way, he passed Lucien Hurlet from Parfondruy with a horse and cart and a herd of sheep, moving along the road at Coo to the east from where he had just come. He was fortunate to just get into La Gleize to hide as he saw the first German tank approaching in the distance.[38]

In La Gleize was 17-year-old Gerard Gregoire. As early as 16 December, Gerard's father, Etienne, had warned him that things were amiss. Coming back from Stavelot by bicycle the previous afternoon, he and his friend Arthur Beauvois had watched the night sky shimmer a splotchy red to the east.[39] The next day Gregoire had trouble getting back home from school because long columns of the GMC trucks of the U.S. 7th Armored Division now jammed the road between Stavelot and Trois-Ponts. By nightfall, he could see artillery flashes on the eastern horizon. Everyone in La Gleize had the jitters. Huddling around a radio, London's BBC had little to say about the drama upon them. That evening there was a dance at the local café, the Echo des Campagnes. It was cold outside. Even though the band Ramonfosse from Theux emoted sweet sounds with saxophone, trumpet, and violin, Gerard was too anxious to dance. Several American GIs were at the party. Suddenly, regular partygoers from Ligneuville burst into the café. 'The Germans are coming back!' Everyone scattered.[40]

On the morning of 18 December Gregoire awoke to the sounds of townspeople evacuating. The streets were filled with trucks, bicycles, and carts. The Americans were leaving in haste. At 9 a.m. his father, Etienne, watched as a column of American jeeps loaded up with some fifty GIs left town and headed off west toward Remouchamps. Even though Etienne decided to stay, not all agreed. 'I don't want to see the Germans again!' his neighbour Joseph Cara crowed from the street. 'You're crazy,' his father told them. 'They are not coming back.' But as the sounds of fighting grew closer later that morning, even his father changed him mind. Soon they all set off by bicycle for the town of Huy on the Meuse.[41]

In La Gleize was 12-year-old Jeannine Kalbusch, who had become friendly with the Americans of the 291st Engineer Combat Battalion that autumn.[42] The previous evening, the casual mood of the GIs seemed to change, and a line of GMC trucks moved out of town. The next morning the town police officer was yelling in the street, '*Les Allemands sont au Vieux Château à Stavelot!*' – the Germans are at the route leading into Stavelot! When he arrived at the turreted Château Froidcour, the upscale headquarters of Company C of the 291st, he learned they were pulling out of La Gleize. Most of their combat platoons had been sent to Malmedy already. Now, the last of their vehicles drove away from the trimmed courtyard before noon. Victor Kalbusch returned at 11.30 a.m., saying that the Americans had been ordered to pull back to Werbomont. At her father's urging, Jeannine began readying three bicycles to leave. Meanwhile, 18-year-old Serge Fontaine on the outskirts of town tried to also ready bicycles for himself and his sisters. For the Kalbusch and Fontaine families it was too late – they could hear barking gunfire. The Germans were already in the streets.

Andre Nicolay had seen the tanks coming as he raced on his bicycle into La Gleize. Just after noon, Peiper's reconnaissance elements reported after ascending through the village of Coo they had reached the hilltop village of La Gleize. Anticipating American resistance in the hamlet, the 1st Panzer Company, personally led by the Panther of Hans Hennecke, raced through the narrow streets spraying doors and windows of houses with machine gun bullets.[43]

Jeannine Kalbusch was coming back with her father from Targnon when she reached La Gleize in time to see the first German tank enter the town. 'It was shooting, raking the whole place with machine gun fire.' She noticed the village clock at 12.10 p.m.[44] The parish priest was nearly blinded by shards of glass from a bullet-shattered window before he dived into the cellar at the Georges' farm. Madame Alice Collard and Monsieur Joseph Mathias, the local postman, were shot between Madame's house and the school, both collapsing atop each other in death.[45] 'The Germans were shooting at anything as they passed,' remembered Serge Fontaine. His 25-year-old cousin, Madeleine Dumont, thought the Americans were returning and ran out of the house clutching binoculars. Even before she could look, she was blasted in the chest in the doorway of her farm home in Werimont, and collapsed in the arms of her sister.[46]

Presently, Hennecke's Mk V tank yawed left on a minor road at the south end of the hamlet to push for a bridge across the Amblève to the west that led to the village of Cheneux. Passing by the stately Château Froidcour, the column of tanks descended to the south to look down upon the Cheneux bridge. 'We saw some persons rushing around the bridge,' Peiper later recalled, 'and since we had to expect that this bridge, too, would be blown right in front of our noses, the point stopped and opened fire.'[47] The 'persons rushing around the bridge' were actually a local man and four Belgian women who stood watching the approach of the tank column. The man, Joseph Gilson, announced he thought he could see a star on the tank. But he was wrong; it was a German cross. The Panther barrelled toward the bridge shooting as it came.[48]

The Belgians were struck by the fusillade. One of the victims was the mother of 10-year-old Paul Servais, who was living in Cheneux near the village of Monceau.[49] Paul's mother, Rene, his 8-year-old sister Betsy, and Lèa Goffinet had been talking together near the bridge. Madame Goffinet was hit in the knee by the gunfire and 57-year-old Madame Maria Hulot, hiding behind a nearby hedge, was killed instantly. Gilson, too, was wounded in the thighs, but managed to stumble away. Meanwhile, Rene and Betsy hobbled off to hide in a nearby culvert. They crawled inside the tunnel as tanks and half-tracks ground overhead.

The SS took no time to consider the dead woman or others who had scattered. Instead, a quick check of the big multi-arched stone bridge revealed no explosives and, better yet, it appeared stout enough to support heavy tanks. Peiper arrived shortly. Pulling out a map in Diefenthal's SPW, Peiper could see that by crossing the Amblève there, he could proceed to the Meuse via Werbomont where there was just a small tributary to be crossed – the Lienne Creek. Just after 1 p.m. his tanks started to sally forth from the bridge toward

Cheneux, still intent on pushing west as quickly as possible on the N23 to resume the advance on Rollbahn D. Even after the bad luck at Trois-Ponts, Peiper thought it might still be possible to reach the Meuse by nightfall. Meanwhile, the three escort Skorzeny jeep commandos reappeared. 'The Skorzeny team informed us they were leaving us to head off for the Meuse,' Diefenthal recalled. 'We wished them good luck. '*Hals und Beinbruch!*' – Break a leg![50]

In the tiny village of Cheneux, 24-year-old Suzanne Boutet was milking the cows when came sounds of shooting outside. The previous night, her brother had showed up at 3 a.m. saying the Germans were in Stavelot. Her brother, her husband Emil, and many other young men took to the roads to escape, but now on Monday afternoon, she was still surprised to see Germans passing through the village – lots of tanks and vehicles. She and her family ran to the cellar to hide.[51] Father Durrier soon offered sanctuary for all women and children at the church.

Other Belgians in Peiper's line of advance agonised in waiting. Walthère Jamar, the village notary in the tiny village of Chevron, was living as he always had in a two-storey stone house not far from Werbomont. Seized with doubt that Monday morning, Monsieur Jamar visited his neighbors the Firmins to ponder the rumours. He scribbled nervously into his diary:

> In the morning, when listening to the news on the radio at the Firmins' house, I learn the Germans between the towns of Aachen and Trier have launched a violent counteroffensive with many troops and impressive amounts of rolling stock … Ida [Lebouote], our maid, upon return from Neucy tells us that she ran into refugees coming from Stavelot and Trois-Ponts, who told her that Malmedy has been taken by the Germans and that they are now approaching Stavelot. Again, we are very worried … From my window, I look eastward at the route de Stavelot and I see streams of refugees as far as I can see. Again there is panic! Many people from Les Forges and from Chevron talk about leaving.[52]

Peiper didn't know it, but he was now fated to run afoul of the 82nd Airborne Division. When SHAEF had released the 82nd and 101st Airborne Divisions from strategic reserve, the developing crisis before Bastogne to the south immediately demanded that one of the two be sent to that place, so the 101st was re-routed in route to that direction. Yet Peiper's shocking penetration drew Maj. Gen. James Gavin's 82nd Airborne Division like a magnet.

'On the 17th, I went to Spa in the rain that night,' Gavin remembered, 'The next morning at 10 a.m. we had a meeting with [Pete] Quesada and Kean (William B. Kean, the First Army Chief of Staff). The problem was where to put the airborne division. Bill Kean looked over the situation map and a messenger gave him a yellow message. 'A German armored column just arrived and we blew the bridge.' Kean pointed to Werbomont on the map. That seemed to be a good indication of where Gavin might send his command. 'Bill, that's good news. It looks like a good place. We'll go and hold there.' 'Till then we were scared. Everyone was scrambling from town.'[53]

Gavin arrived at noon in Werbomont. Making a personal reconnaissance east toward Trois-Ponts, he found the Salm a 'roaring mountain stream'. There, at the bridge was a lieutenant engineer. 'What is the situation?' Gavin asked.

'These people say the Krauts are coming over the hill,' the engineer gestured to the span.

'What are you going to do?' Gavin asked.

'I'm going to blow this bridge sky high.'

Satisfied, Gavin went on to Bastogne and talked to corps commander Troy Middleton, who didn't seem to know where the 28th Division still existed to his front. Gavin was unimpressed with the possibility of being surrounded. In the airborne, being 'cut off is standard operating procedure'.[54]

Meanwhile, a displaced captain of Task Force T of the 12th Army Group witnessed an animated discussion pondering the need for the 82nd Airborne to displace from the Salm river and pull back. The Germans had a lot of tanks. During the discussion, a grizzled airborne NCO walked over and slid his boot heel along the ground. 'That's as far as they go,' he grinned.[55]

While Peiper pushed his tank drivers, now roaring from the bridge at Cheneux, the bad news reached the U.S. First Army headquarters. The foreign press in town at the Hotel Laaken in Spa were demanding to know once more what was going on even with the headquarters packing. A terse briefing by 'Casey' Dempsey, the press representative, of the First Army told them precious little, other than the disquieting news that enemy 'parachutists were thick in the woods for miles around'. After he left, other reporters volunteered rumours that German tank columns were 'shearing ahead so fast, nobody knew where they could be expected'.[56] Dempsey wouldn't say. They'd have to go to V Corps in Eupen to find out more.

Soon, British-born reporter Iris Carpenter and companions were careening around hairpin turns to Eupen, warned by Dempsey to be back by night. On the road, they followed behind an armored car that stopped twice to fire at something they could not see. 'This road is lousy with parachutists,' its driver complained. Reaching Eupen, Gen. Gerow expressed astonishment that the reporters had left Spa. If they wanted to save anything there, they should hightail it back there as quickly as they could. 'The whole headquarters is pulling out!'

Meanwhile, a prisoner from the Heavy Weapons Company of Kampfgruppe von der Heydte – 420 men in all – told interrogators of their mission to hold the road intersection at Belle Croix until 1730 hours, when they would be relieved by both the 1st and 12th SS Panzer Divisions.[57] To add credence to that threat, both of the SS divisions had been identified by now in the Krinkelt to Honsfeld areas. One armored battlegroup – Peiper's – had boldly overrun Büllingen the day before and was now perilously close to Hodges's headquarters. Moreover, a captured prisoner from the 6th Panzer Company told interrogators just after midnight on 17 December that the mission of the tank battle group of the 1st SS Panzer Division was to get a bridgehead across the Meuse river. 'Enemy is east of Malmedy and has patrols north and south of the town,' American intelligence brooded, 'Situation critical … Ten enemy tanks in Stavelot and ten more approaching.'

The night before, Hodges had 'Big' Bill Simpson, in charge of the Ninth Army, at his headquarters. Both West Pointers, Simpson had fought with Hodges since 1916. To Simpson, Hodges looked shaken. 'The situation was clouded and confused – we were trying desperately to find out what the hell was going on,' Hodges later recalled. 'The fog was down and our air units could not see anything.' Simpson offered both the U.S. 1st and 30th Infantry Divisions. 'I think you are going to need them.' Capt. William Cox with the G-1 section of the First Army had just come from Bastogne by jeep. 'I arrived to find everyone in a dither,' he said. What was going on? 'The Germans are coming!'[58]

That same night Gen. Leland Hobbs with the 30th Infantry Division also came to Spa. 'I didn't know what the big deal was,' he later recalled. 'I saw Hodges. He was being pressed by his staff to pull out. I came to get info. They were vague and advised us they were moving out. They didn't appear to know much about what was going on and were mainly interested in leaving. The weather was terrible.'[59] By that time Hobbs had funnelled the 120th Infantry Regiment toward Malmedy and the 117th Regiment toward Stavelot, both of which seemed under immediate threat. Hobbs had held the 119th Infantry in a state of 'high alert' in the V Corps center of Eupen in case the 1st Battalion of the 117th was unable to contain the Germans at Stavelot. But with the bastion at Stavelot having mostly pushed the Germans out of town, and SS tankers obviously pressing toward Spa and the 1st Army HQ, Hobbs now moved his 119th Infantry chess piece to Theux, departing just after noon on 18 December.[60] That assignment, too, was not fated to last, for word that German armor was north of Trois-Ponts meant that two avenues of approach to Liège were open to Peiper. One route lead south of La Gleize to Cheneux, then Werbomont, and Aywaille. The other route wound along the north bank of the Amblève river to Remouchamps.

With either approach, Peiper would be within striking distance of the massive U.S. Army Ad Sec (Advanced Section, Communications Zone) fuel and ammunition depots spread between Verviers and Liège.[61] Lt Gen. John H.C. – 'Jesus Christ Himself' – Lee, in charge of the supply services, knew that the entire U.S. plans to assault the Roer inside Germany would be damaged irrevocably if the enemy tank column got there. Capture or destruction of the millions of gallons of carefully accumulated fuel and munitions at the railyards at Kinkempois near Liège might set the Allied war effort back by months.[62] At Theux, Hobbs met Col Edwin M. Sutherland and bade him to proceed immediately to Remouchamps and to divide his command into two columns: one to protect the southern approach and the other to screen any enemy advance toward Stoumont.

The following morning, the already bleak atmosphere at the U.S. First Army headquarters in Spa strayed into new territory. The aroma of military undoing became unmistakable under the gilded hotel chandeliers and posh carpets. 'The situation deteriorated rapidly today,' Maj. William C. Sylvan recorded in the First U.S. Army diary. Some officers were fretting over the possibility that they'd need to evacuate the hotel's carefully stocked liquor supply.[63] Col Benjamin 'Monk' Dickson, was there and edgy too.[64]

Closer than the massive depots at Liège, there was a huge 4 million gallon fuel dump nearby – the greatest ever assembled in Europe – that seemed ripe for Peiper's plucking. Lt Col Lowell S. Love with the Armored Section of the U.S. First Army was asked to do something – anything. Love's reserves were scant – only five half-tracks, three M10 TDs, and a few dozen hands who were mostly cooks, clerks, and military police. There were plenty of chiefs in Spa, but precious few Indians. With these sparse resources, Love 'volunteered' several officers to set up roadblocks.[65]

At 10 a.m. four roadblock teams moved out with a single half-track and gun for each man. Deep in the lonely fir-lined roads, they waited with weapons at the ready – desk-bound officers who had not held an M1 in months. Love told each officer that their radio was as important as their gun. First Army would need a quick warning if the Germans came up this far. All morning they waited anxiously, peering into the mist down the roads leading to the south-east, worried by sounds of distant firing.[66]

Back in Spa, Hodges finally met Maj. Gen. Lawton 'Lightning Joe' Collins, the commander of the VII Corps. 'Nice to see you Joe,' Hodges said, noting that 'Big Bill' Simpson in charge of the Ninth Army was loaning Collins's Corps to him 'until we can straighten out this mess down here'. In the meantime, 1st Lt E.W. Kann at the U.S. First Army prisoner of war enclosure near Henri Chapelle telephoned the G-2 of the U.S. First Army with the latest about the SS tank column now seen in Stavelot. The SS prisoners were more security minded than the lot he was used to seeing, but he pried things loose:

> Prisoner from 1st SS Panzer Regiment, 1st SS Panzer Division states that there are two battalions in the regiment. First Battalion has four companies consisting of fifteen to seventeen Panther and Mk IV tanks each … One corps Tiger Battalion is attached to the regiment with four companies of fifteen to seventeen Tiger tanks. The regimental commander is PEIPER.[67]

It was five minutes till noon when Dickson got the phone call. The prisoner had been captured at Büllingen, mentioning that the whole SS tank regiment – 120 tanks – was attacking west. These were the SOBs rampaging west of Stavelot now, and just 8 miles from their headquarters. They were also the ones who had been in the vicinity of Malmedy when the whole lot of a battery of a Field Artillery Observation Battalion had been murdered after surrendering. Dickson quickly turned to his dog-eared copy of the War Department's Order of Battle of the German Army.[68] Flipping through the Roster of Senior Military Officers, there was his name:

> *PEIPER, Joachim, 30 years, Waffen SS, Obersturmbannführer, last promotion 30 January 1944. SS officer since 1935. Leibstandarte Adolf Hitler.*

Dickson let that sink in. Meanwhile, in his big chamber on the second floor of the Hotel Britannique, Gen. Hodges watched as aides chalked new German positions on the map's transparent overlay with red grease pencils. Maj. Gen. Kean took telephone calls while Dickson frequently popped in and out the door with the latest information.[69] By 1330 hours both Maj. Harry Webb and Capt. Andrew Lundberg from the 1111th Engineer Combat Group had arrived about an hour apart from each other with news from Trois-Ponts, where the engineers had dynamited three bridges there to prevent being overrun by German tanks. According to a wide-eyed Lundberg, these Germans didn't seem the defeated *Volkssturm* types. They were SS men with big tanks. After the spans had been blown in their faces, the Germans had shot civilians unlucky enough to be seen on the eastern side of the Salm river.

Simultaneously, Maj. Bristol, piloting a Cub spotter plane, burst into the Hotel Britannique: there were German tanks just a few miles away! And Dickson knew it was not just any enemy tank column: it was the Leibstandarte Adolf Hitler under an intrepid SS colonel named Joachim Peiper. His tank group had bypassed Malmedy, Dickson told everyone, and were headed their way in several columns. 'They are from the 1st SS Panzer Division.' Sylvan reminded everyone that was the same group that had shot down dozens of surrendered Americans the preceding day. Even a lumbering German tank could be here in an hour.

Monk Dickson entered the room. 'General, if you don't want to get captured, you'd better get out of town. The Germans are only a mile away.' Hodges listened without response. 'General, there's no time to lose!'[70] Dickson was alarmed.

There were ugly rumours that Hodges had 'gone to pieces'. One staffer saw him at his desk, head in his hands, and he had spent most of the previous day locked in his office.[71] In fact, his chief of staff, Maj. Gen. William B. Kean – whom Dickson had derisively nicknamed 'Captain Bligh' – was calling the shots. The immediate order: the headquarters would soon be moved at once to Chaudfontaine 19km distant and near the Meuse river. By afternoon most of the section personnel had been sent back to Chaudfontaine, save Hodges, his immediate staff, some military policemen, and C.I.C. people.[72]

An exception was *New York Times* reporter Harold Denny. Denny continued to hang around – mostly because he smelled a good story.

> Our move was decided upon and carried out suddenly yesterday afternoon. Those of us who had been living in that little city and going over to Germany daily to cover the battle knew, of course, of the German penetrations, but I hardly expected that they had made it advisable for us to move. Yesterday, we journeyed to the front and found it extremely 'fluid' as military men put it. Roads that we had previously travelled in perfect security were no longer safe ... We found out what we could, and the group of us who lived in this particular town thought it well to return to it before roving Germans might close in behind us.[73]

Denny had been in Spa all autumn with Hodges, and this was the most exciting day he had ever seen. Yet as he penned quick notes, he was certain that his shadow-like killjoy, Maj. Eugene Nute, U.S. First Army chief censor, would prevent him from reporting this blockbuster. Later that afternoon, Denny watched with amazement as Nute headed off with others to a ridge south of Spa to challenge the enemy with an M-1 rifle. Lt Col Joseph Stancook, the U.S. First Army pay cheque officer, was put in charge – a finance officer was setting up a makeshift blockade of clerks, cooks, and bakers![74] Denny couldn't believe it. Coming back inside the hotel, he found Dickson cracking jokes. Hodges wouldn't leave so he laconically pondered his fate; would he and his staff make good prisoners?[75] Denny was not excited about becoming a captive of the German army. That had already happened to him once in Africa.

> We got [back] there and the decision was made to move further back into Belgium. We began to hurriedly pack … The Luftwaffe in its new numbers and boldness had again made the night noisy with flares and bombs trying to hamper our transport and communications, and buzz bombs grumbled along overhead in increasing numbers.
>
> As we packed, the air was full of German and American planes. It was cold and large patches of the sky were clear. Fleets of aircraft at high altitude moved in crisscross patterns of white vapor trails, like the tracks of figure skaters on ice. There was a tremendous boom as a bomb or long-range German shell fell at the edge of town. Two of us were packing our jeep and trailer in front of the hotel where we lived. A gently bred old lady asked in English if we were leaving. 'Oh, no,' my companion replied. 'Oh, good,' she replied politely. 'It would be horrible if the Germans came again.' Then we looked up. On the balcony across the street a woman with a worried, resentful face was hauling in an American flag which she had displayed in our honor. A little later when we left town, there was hardly an American flag to be seen of the scores that residents had put up. We went down to pay our hotel bill. Some of us had not enough ready Belgian cash. 'That's all right,' the landlady assured one of my friends. 'You will be back in a couple of days and you can pay me back.' But there were tears in her eyes when we departed … We ourselves were to have given a Christmas party for the children of the town who had been so hospitable and frank in their joy at our coming and the Germans' flight. Now we knew they wondered what would happen to them … We were side-tracked for a long time in front of a school and the children were gathered along the roadside, shouting endlessly in unison, '*Vive l'Amèrique: a bas les Boches!*' Their teachers were amassed on the front steps. They waved to our GIs in the brave V sign and then began singing, 'The Star Spangled Banner' in French.[76]

Gradually, the town's entire population seemed to have gathered in the streets, their expressions etched in worry. Denny and the other reporters waved and smiled, trying to put on brave faces. Soon, all were in tears as they motored off for Liège.

First Army diary keeper William Sylvan approached Hodges, worried of a report that there were tanks just 2 miles down the road. Reinforcements? 'Bill, those aren't ours,' Hodges sighed, 'they are German tanks.'[77] Hodges seemed dazed. A stream of new communiqués showed the enemy armor was on the move just to the east. Dickson motioned to a waiting Piper Cub aeroplane at the headquarters airstrip. 'General,' he said calmly, 'I suggest you leave now.' Hodges wanted assurance the backstop airborne divisions were in place. Sylvan:

> About three o'clock this afternoon there were reports that tanks were coming up from Stavelot headed toward Spa. They were definitely identified at La Gleize. Only a small roadblock and half-tracks stood between them and our headquarters. Shortly before four o'clock the whole headquarters, with the exception of one officer in each section, was sent out to man the road [block] leading into town. Colonel Dickson came to General Hodges to say that he thought he ought to be prepared to leave at once and that a Cub plane was waiting at Maroon strip to take him away. By one of the fortunes of war that can never be explained, tanks turned south-west from La Gleize … This was the greatest of good fortune.

Sylvan knew they had no heavy weapons and would have been quickly routed and, 'between us and them was our largest gas dump consisting of two million gallons, enough to keep a panzer division rolling for thirty days'.

Hodges wanted to meet with Gen. Gavin, who was bringing down the 82nd Airborne Division to halt the enemy. But Gavin did not appear at the appointed hour – a strong incentive to leave. It was completely dark when they departed for Chaudfontaine 15 miles to the rear, led by an armored car bristling with weapons. As their car made its way to the north-west, German nightfighter aircraft fitfully dropped bombs and flares on the dark road.

Near Pepininster, a V-1 buzz bomb screamed down on to the column, hitting a truck containing the G-4 traffic-control section, killing all fourteen of its occupants – their mangled bodies spread across the road. At midnight, Hodges and his exhausted staff pulled into Chaudfontaine, moving into quarters in the Palace Hotel and the Hôtel des Baines. 'Buzz bombs, passing at frequent intervals overhead, made the night not particularly restful.'

Chapter 20

'THE DAMNED ENGINEERS ...'

May God have mercy on my enemies, because I don't.

Gen. George S. Patton

Maj. Gen. Elwood 'Pete' Quesada was a prima donna in the U.S. Ninth Air Force, an organization already filled with dashing figures.[1] On the morning of 18 December 1944, Quesada, the IX Tactical Air Commander, received an urgent request from the U.S. First Army. A 15-mile-long column of German tanks and half-tracks had been sighted less than 10 miles from the headquarters of the U.S. First Army at Spa and not much further from Pete Quesada's headquarters in Verviers. Peiper had been counting on fog to veil his movements. Unbeknownst to German leadership, had his panzer column turned north, much of the defending U.S. V Corps might have been trapped by the enemy armor. How was the endangered U.S. unit to find such a rampaging enemy cloaked by foul weather? With a cloud ceiling of barely 200ft, the murk was impossible for low-level reconnaissance.

Challenged to somehow hit the Germans, but needing to find them first, Quesada phoned Col George W. Peck, the commander of the 67th Tactical Reconnaissance Group. Might any of his hot-rod P-51 fliers be willing to brave the 10/10 fog to find an enemy panzer column. Two of 'Peck's Bad Boys' volunteered: Capt. H. Richard Cassady from Arkansas, and 2nd Lt Abraham Jaffe, from New York. Gen. Quesada spoke to both men personally. Abe Jaffe was unsure of what good this would do; looking outside at the dirt strip at Mons, Belgium, all he could see was mist. 'Nobody can fly in this,' he said to Cassady. Still, he loved his souped-up F-6 Mustang and he and Cassady would try to do what Quesada asked for.[2] The rumours were that the Germans were on the move. Nervous Belgian locals even asked Cassady's liaison officer to return the swastika-emblazoned flag given to him in case the Germans came back.[3]

> There was little change in the weather. I sat near the phone connected to our group headquarters back at Gosselies – waiting. The remaining pilots waited

> in our makeshift ready room, some sleeping, some reading, some playing cards or writing letters. Then after a long wait, the phone rang. It was Capt. Scott of Group Operations with word that we were tasked with a *must* mission. Who would volunteer?

'Al, we got a hot one,' Cassady ventured. Looking outside, Jaffe was dubious, but if 'Sak' was going, he would, too. The two pilots were given three points to reconnoitre, all south-east of Liège. The two buzzed off from the Belgian airfield just after noon, the air being so obfuscated that the two flew in close formation just to see each other. Luckily, both were guided by SC-584 radar. The flight there was uneventful, as their two Mustangs flew high over a vast expanse of grey cotton below. Both pilots kept radio silence, with Cassady typically humming gospel hymns into his oxygen mask and jotting down anything he saw on his knee pad.

Quesada's 27-year-old combat operations chief, Col Gilbert L. Meyers, considered a fighter-bomber mission to hit the enemy should Cassady and Jaffe find anything. In his mind, there was only one man to call – Col Ray J. Stecker and the 'Hell Hawks' of his 365th Fighter Group. Meyers knew Stecker from the early days with the Ninth Air Force when he flew Curtiss P-40s in North Africa. There, Stecker had boldly flown his plane above the enemy at tree-top level – eyeballing Rommel's tanks hiding under Tunisian olive groves without getting cut up by enemy flak. He had flown so low the Germans had difficulty training their guns. Within the U.S. Ninth Air Force he had a reputation for bravado. The Hell Hawks, flying P-47 'Jugs', had been up on a mission earlier on 18 December, only to be called back – impossible weather. When the phone rang in the operations tent, Stecker thought it was to confirm the obvious: the day's flying was over.

'That Jerry column you hit the other day,' Meyers began, 'has been reinforced and has broken through our lines near Stavelot.' Stecker shook his head. 'Well, there is now nothing between it and the English Channel but service troops, cooks, and bakers!'[4]

'But the weather –' Stecker interrupted.

'I know,' Myers nodded, 'the weather is down to the deck and it will probably be suicide ...' He paused. 'But Goddamn it, Ray, we've got to get something in there or the bastards will be in Liège! If you can just send in a four-plane flight, it might work.'

'I'll see what we can do,' Stecker said, hanging up. He was soon on the phone to Maj. George R. Brooking, whose 386th Squadron had been on standby since sunrise. Brooking joined his other men in the frigid operations tent at Chièvres, Belgium. Stecker addressed them right off. No mincing words. 'Men,' he began, 'this is going to be rough, but the Krauts have given us a hell of a kick in the pants at the front.' There was a rampaging SS armored column. They must find them in this terrible weather and give them a pasting.

Cassaday and Jaffe spent a half an hour-long immersion in the fluff on the first checkpoint. 'Deadbeat,' one of them radioed back – airman lingo for nothing. Both men had the same idea, a dangerous one. Could they fly down low enough? The Mustangs had to descend to treetop level – dangerously close to the undulating 450ft hills. 'It was so foggy,' Jaffe said later, 'we had to fly in the valleys, sometimes at less than a hundred feet, in order to miss the hills and still be able to see the ground.'

On one descent, they narrowly missed running into a hillside when they came out of the clouds. Nothing. When they both pulled back up to 6,000ft, Jaffe was shaking. 'Let's cool it and get out of here.' But Cassady wanted one more try – 90 degrees left from the last terrifying descent. Down they went again, and the view ahead glowed a little lighter. Then, suddenly they were through the clouds just above the trees near Stavelot zipping along at 250 mph. Before them, just below, was a serpentine column with scores of enemy tanks and armored vehicles. 'More war hardware than I had ever seen,' remembered Cassady. 'Holy hell!' he yelled, 'Where are you?'

'Right on your ass!' Jaffe called out.

'Do you see that?' They banked sharply and made another pass. 'I think we found them,' Cassady called out laconically. It was 1.35 p.m.

'We made three runs over that column, and the Germans were so surprised to see us they didn't fire until the last run,' remembered Capt. Cassady, 'We could see the Germans' faces as they fired rifles at us. There were machine guns, 20mm flaks, and pistols, too – everything they had.'[5] Cassady could see the flashing, small-arms fire – but worried most about Jaffe who was behind him in the narrow valley as their nose cameras recorded the length of the German column. Both men were soon on the radio giving the precise coordinates of Kampfgruppe Peiper.[6] Immediately, word flashed to the 365th Fighter Group already in the air; they were near the target. By that same time Maj. Brooking had become frustrated with the opaque cloud cover below him and the unproductive circles about the target. 'I am going down there to poke around by myself,' he called out.

'You're crazy,' said his wingman, Lt Thoman, but he obediently followed Brooking into the murk.

Like Cassady before him, Maj. Brooking found himself not more than 20ft above a concentration of German tanks and armored vehicles, all rolling along serenely. Both hunter and hunted were surprised. Brooking was shortly at the other end of the valley and calling the rest of his flight down. The other P-47s joined the two already there, but this time they were greeted by a popping flak. Undaunted, they buzzed right across the column dropping their bombs and firing machine guns. Capt. Wells dropped his two bombs in the middle of half a dozen tanks on a road near the top of a hill. Wells thought he clobbered them. The other Thunderbolts also dropped their bombs, after which each plane made three strafing runs. The German flak now sent glowing sparks roaring up from the ground. 'I've been hit badly, Brook!' Lt Price suddenly called over the radio. 'I'll try to belly land somewhere.' Others saw his P-47 streaming smoke and fire and disappearing into a fog bank to the north. Last heard, he declared himself descending at treetop level and looking for anything without hills and trees – a bad bet.[7]

On the ground, from his hiding place along a stone garden wall, André Nicolay had watched the lead German tank coming toward La Gleize behind him where the curve in the road overlooks the road coming up to it. As he peered from his hiding spot, he saw the German tanks thread their way through town to the south. With La Gleize sitting atop a ridgeline, he had a clear view of the village of Cheneux below. More American aeroplanes materialised through the cloudy overcast overhead and soon they were roaring down on the Germans. A typical Belgian boy of 16, André fancied himself an expert on wartime aircraft identification from posters. The American machines seemed to be guppy-shaped Thunderbolts, but he was very excited to see a few fork-tailed P-38 Lightnings.[8] It was after 2 p.m.

At once, Meyers sent all of Stecker's 365th and also a squadron each from the 366th and 404th Fighter Groups. Meanwhile, Cassady and Jaffe remained over the target to guide the P-47s to the quarry. Eventually, he would shuttle seven waves of four fighters to strike Peiper's column. Each of Stecker's newly arriving 'Jugs' twisted and threaded through the fog-laden Amblève Valley to smite the SS battle group with bomb and bullet. Soon, Lt Wells called out that he, too, had been hit, but unlike Price, thought his crate was still airworthy – just punched full of holes. On Brooking's orders, Wells was soon sputtering away, escorted back to an emergency airfield by Lt Thoman. Meanwhile, the squadron commander remained over the target. At 1535 hours Brooking taxied in at Chièvres Air Base after 'landing on fumes' in a 10/10 fog.[9]

Peiper himself witnessed the German side of the air attack.[10] Motoring along in Diefenthal's SPW, Peiper had eagerly crossed the Amblève river bridge. From there the road curved sharply up along a steep hill ascending toward Cheneux. Yet at that moment – 2.40 p.m. – the thick overcast parted momentarily and the American *Jabos* struck like hornets. The head of the tank column was just beyond the bridge at Cheneux when a flock of P-47s swooped down. Bombs rained down while bullets ripped across the road. Sixteen P-47s in the first wave struck the SS column. Peiper's serpentine road-bound battlegroup was strung out over 30km, all the way from Cheneux, back to Lodomez, before Stavelot.

Two SPWs were hit near the bridge while a 500lb bomb detonated in front of a nearby brick farmhouse, and explosions and cannon fire disabled Panther #131 of SS Oscha. Adolf Thomas and a nearby command car. Peiper was not hit, but the bomb strikes were close to Diefenthal's SPW. Just up ahead, Werner Poetschke scurried under a tank to take cover while Peiper jumped off Diefenthal's SPW to scramble to an old Belgian bunker across from the Dumont farm. The dank interior was filled with water and mud. Bombs exploded. Kurt Kramm, Poetschke's adjutant, was among those wounded. Peiper found himself joined in hiding by the leader of his reconnaissance battalion, Gustav Knittel:

> At the railway just north of Trois-Ponts, I caught up with the tail of the column of the Combat Group Peiper, driving with Col Peiper himself, who was riding a half-track together with Maj. Diefenthal. I got into the vehicle of both commanders

> and drove along with them to just outside Cheneux – approximately 800 metres before the bridge. During the air raid from 1300–1500 hours, I took shelter with Peiper in a pillbox, 200 metres south-west of the Amblève bridge at the entrance to Cheneux.[11]

As Peiper later recounted after the war, just as Heinz von Westernhagen told him of the shooting at Baugnez only an hour earlier, now Knittel, too, told him of the same incident. '*Die haben 'n ganze Menge auf der Kreuzung umgelegt*' – They've bumped off quite a few at the crossroads.[12] Peiper must have reflected bitterly on the irony: hiding in a fetid, old Belgian bunker under a withering air attack while his reconnaissance battalion commander informed him that his men had shot scores of prisoners the preceding day.

Although the tanks tried to hide under the conifers lining the right side of the road between the bridge and Cheneux, the planes found them, making one strafing pass after another. Eventually, the first wave departed and Peiper's convoy re-formed itself on the road. One of his Panthers became stuck in the ditch with a broken track on the road to Grand Pont.

However, in less than half an hour, as Peiper's tanks and half-tracks re-emerged from hiding to dash to Rahier, they were hit once again by P-47s of the 390th Squadron, 366th Fighter Group, and the 396th Squadron of the 368th Fighter Group. Beginning at 3 p.m., the planes swarmed over the valley, the German convoy scudding for cover under tree branches or in the shadows of houses. Over the course of the afternoon, three dozen Thunderbolts menaced Kampfgruppe Peiper from one end to the other.

Watching raptly from a woodpile in Roanne, Serge Fontaine could see the planes roaring along the length of the tank convoy spitting bullets and bombs, only to pull up and circle back to mete out more in 'an infernal merry-go-round'.[13] Meanwhile, at the eastern terminus of the SS column, two rocket-firing British Typhoons from 247 Squadron at Eindhoven attacked the tail of the battle group near Stavelot.

Peiper and his men were not the only ones endangered by the Allied strafing. Madame Servais and her daughter, Betsey, were still hiding in their refuge near the Cheneux bridge when American fighter-bombers descended on the German column. As the bombs dropped, they were joined in their refuge by an SS man running for cover. Bellowing, he forced Madame Maria Goffinet out of hiding so he could take the spot. Just then, a bomb from one of the planes exploded near one of the German tanks, spraying her with shrapnel. Another bomb levelled the Dumont farmhouse, killing Goffinet and Jules Dumont. Maria's friend, Joseph Gilson, was also wounded. Badly hurt, Mother Servais fell in the ditch. Unwounded, her daughter Betsy ran through the woods to their home in Monceau south-east of Cheneux. 'Come and help! Mother has been hurt at the bridge!' she screamed to her brother Paul.

They found a wooden farm cart and set off with their oldest sister, Jeanne, toward Cheneux. But on reaching the road, they found they had to leave the horse and cart; the road was covered with burning tanks and vehicles.

Meanwhile, she and Maria's friend, Gilson, were taken to the Château de la Vaulx Renard to be tended by German medics.

As the Allied aircraft zoomed, bombed, and strafed, the Wirbelwind flak tanks of Peiper's 10th Flak Company banged away at the P-47s with their quad-mount, 20mm cannon. They claimed to hit several. At least one Thunderbolt was seen careening out of control to disappear in an ugly smudge of smoke beyond the tree-lined hills to the north.

Lt Walter Butts, at one of the U.S. First Army's emergency roadblocks south of Spa, saw three P-47s buzz by his single half-track roadblock in the deep woods. At the intersection of the forest-lined road from Spa that led south to Andrimont and Cour, his squad-sized force waited at the south end of the largest petrol depot on the continent: over 2 million gallons.[14] It was a logistical prize beyond the enemy's wildest dreams.[15] Yet other than the pandemonium at First U.S. headquarters in Spa, Butts didn't sense the enemy was anywhere nearby. It was exceedingly quiet where he waited with a squad in the thick Bois de Géronstère.

Still, it was impossible not to worry as non-stop crews on quartermaster trucks lifted up full loads of jerricans and hauled them away as fast as they could. Looking on, Butts scratched his head; it would take days for the trucks to move this pile of fuel even with the crews working round the clock. Waiting, he and his men saw glowing tracer rounds arcing up toward the planes to the south. That SS German tank column must be close by. Butts saw two planes hit near Moulin du Ruy, one of them leaving a smoking trail before crashing just to the south-east. The half dozen men in his half-track now gripped their weapons and strained to see down the road. Were the Germans coming?[16]

Karl Wortmann was one of those who Butts saw firing at the planes. During the afternoon between Stavelot and Trois-Ponts, he recalled that his column stopped briefly. He observed a light enemy reconnaissance plane dipping out of the clouds and running the length of the column. 'Within an hour we were attacked by an overwhelming force of fighter bombers.'[17]

> The cloudy and overcast winter weather had somewhat broken and the sun shone for a moment. The march formation was located on a narrow mountain road and stretched out for two kilometers. A long, rocky wall stretched along the right side of the road, falling off steeply into a valley. When sixteen Thunderbolts attacked them from one side of the valley, the vehicles stood without cover on the long stretch. There wasn't the slightest chance for them to withdraw. The panzer crews and grenadiers crawled under their steel mounts, a defenseless and powerless offering on a silver platter.
>
> The two flak panzers immediately opened fire with their four-barrel weapons and let go with everything they had. However, the 'violinists of the air' attacked piteously, firing their on-board weapons and dropping bombs. It was hopeless for the men of the flak panzers against sixteen attacking aircraft because too many were attacking at once. They blazed away in a manner at one and all and made the pilots unsure and prevented the enemy from accurately engaging their targets. The eight barrels spit out an enormous amount of rounds, which was

> indicated by the flak clouds … Their panzer turrets turned lightning fast to the right and to the left as required to drive off the enemy aircraft.
>
> One Thunderbolt was set ablaze by our panzer flak guns, falling out of the sky several seconds later. After a half hour, the enemy aircraft veered off, Obstuf. Peiper thanked the men in the flak panzers.[18]

Later, the American wild hornets returned. The aerial attacks went on for nearly two hours. In all, Meyers sent out seven four-plane flights up until it became too dark to fly. When the planes departed at 4.10 p.m., two Panthers (one near Stavelot) and one Panzer IV and five SPWs had been destroyed along with perhaps a dozen other vehicles.[19] Some forty men were wounded – pulled into farmhouses and mills by civilians. However, the biggest casualty for the Germans may have been time.[20] Two hours were spent cowering under trees while the planes strafed the column from Cheneux to Rahier. And the single, knocked-out Panther hit on the road to Cheneux effectively blocked the way until a very narrow, steep shortcut could be used to reach the village.

Even as far back as Stavelot, the roads were under air attack. In Königstiger #133, SS Oscha. Werner Wendt lumbered along in Peiper's wake, reaching the bottom of the steep descent approaching Stavelot around 1 p.m. He and Jürgen Wessel in #105 and Jürgen Brandt in #131 pulled their hulks off the path to let the faster portions of Knittel's reconnaissance battalion pass by. 'The road is under strafing,' he wrote in his diary, 'At 1500 hours, Obstuf. Wessel and a second Tiger crossed the bridge across the Amblève without a hitch. Oscha. Brandt and Wendt with additional tank leverage moved on toward the bridge. As they crossed, both tanks were attacked by a fighter-bomber. Brandt was hit in the tank tracks and had to stop 30m beyond the bridge to repair the damage. Now, Stavelot was hit by light artillery and bazooka fire and Wessel decided to back up and in so doing rammed into a two-storey house. Debris from the house buried Panzer #105. The crew could only dig out with much effort.'[21]

Up on the hill in La Gleize, young Serge Fontaine could see the American aeroplanes converge on the German tank column moving in the valley below leading to Werbomont. 'Great!' he called out to his father. Both could see the SS tanks scatter off the roads. 'I think the Germans are done!' the youth called out at twilight. The night had become quiet until there was a knock at their door. It was two Americans. His father hushed his son and quickly conducted the men to the stable, where he hid them in a haystack.[22] During the night, the growl of German vehicles increased. In the morning the Americans were gone and the Germans were back.[23]

Back on the road, Peiper remained firmly focused on resuming the advance on Rollbahn E along the N23 to the Meuse. However, before that goal was possible, there remained one more bridge, this one a sturdy span across the Lienne Creek. He knew he must have it. At around 4.30 p.m. the lead tanks reached the N23 a little south of Froidville and turned up the road to hove in on the bridge. As usual, they rushed full throttle ahead and sprayed their path with machine guns. Peiper would later claim that he mounted Ustuf. Walter Krause's SPW after emerging from the bunker.[24] However, it seems likely from two eyewitnesses that he instead resumed his seat in Diefenthal's SPW and proceeded west with the tanks.[25]

If the fighter-bombers had exacted only moderate physical damage on Kampfgruppe Peiper, the delay was catastrophic. Back at Haute Bodeux, Col Wallis Anderson with the 1111th Engineer Combat Group followed the repulse of Peiper at Trois-Ponts with one blown bridge. As Anderson consulted a map, it was clear to him the German tanks were attempting to thread to the west. He reasoned that they would be striking for La Gleize and then Cheneux, where they could reach the road going to Werbomont. It was too late to send a detail to La Gleize; word arrived that the Germans were already crossing the bridge at Cheneux. Looking ahead, he saw there was another bridge across the Lienne Creek at Neufmoulin near Habiemont.

He quickly called Captain James H. Gamble in charge of Company A of the 291st Engineer Combat Battalion demanding a demolition team be sent at once to that crossing. Although the creek was even less substantial than the Amblève river, its approach cut deeply into the hilly terrain, making it impossible for a Panther tank to otherwise cross. Gamble agreed to try to blow the 180ft trestled span, but told Anderson there were only about fifteen of his men left in Werbomont. Gamble warned the men to hurry to the span. As luck would have it, when the men were given the assignment, they found that the truck they had to use to reach the crossing had a badly burned valve and with its stuttering engine it could go no more than 10mph. Consequently, it was 3 p.m. when the little truck reached the bridge, packing wire, carbines, and lots of TNT. Given Gamble's warning, they were surprised to reach the place before the Germans.

A momentary scare came at 4 p.m. when they heard vehicles approaching from the east – and they were still not done setting the charges. Yet listening closer, they heard the familiar thunking of American trucks. It was a small convoy including Gen. Anderson himself. He and Sgt John L. Scanlan had left the forward CP Trois-Ponts at 4 p.m. and under orders from U.S. First Army were pulling back to Modave.[26] On the way, they had come upon a long line of Belgian civilians trudging to the west. During a pause along the road, Scanlan heard someone knocking on the door of the command car. It was an old Belgian couple. 'Please Monsieur,' the old man began in broken English. 'Take us with you – we are Jewish. We couldn't stand another five years under the Nazis.' Scanlan and Anderson made room for the couple.[27]

Had it not been for Quesada's slashing fighter-bomber attack on the Germans between Cheneux and Rahier, no one in the little convoy would have escaped, for Anderson and the others passed by the Habiemont bridge only thirty minutes ahead of the Germans. Nor without the air attack would the detail from 2nd platoon, Company A of the 291st Engineer Combat Battalion under Lt Alvin Edelstein have been able to finish wiring up the trestled bridge with 2,500lb of TNT.[28] Approving their handiwork, Anderson and Scanlan left at 4.15 p.m.

Just thirty minutes later, on the road between the Habiemont bridge and Cheneux, another drama unfolded. It would later be called 'the jeep incident'. During the headlong advance when Kampfgruppe Peiper had been stung by the attack by fighter-bombers, the armored spearhead had come to a standstill on the Cheneux road and tank traffic jammed up for half an hour. Just then an American jeep came racing towards them. SS radio man Hans Rineck had been in Diefenthal's SPW with Peiper during the advance – a post he had held since being assigned to Leibstandarte in October 1944.[29] At 3.30 p.m. on 18 December 1944, as the column resumed its dash to the west, Peiper was in the van of the spearhead. According to at least two witnesses, Peiper was in Jupp Diefenthal's SPW, driven by SS Rttf. Paul Zwigart.[30]

In the late morning at 11 p.m. Col Wallis Anderson at Trois-Ponts had sent a message to Maj. Harry Webb to warn the U.S. First Army about a report of Tiger tanks 'swarming' in Stavelot. Yet events developed rapidly; the SS column was turned back at Trois-Ponts by a string of blown bridges, with the Germans skirted rapidly off to the north-west. Anderson knew that in the event of any advance toward Spa or Stoumont would almost certainly catch the U.S. First Army by surprise. With some anxiety, at 12.30 p.m. Col Anderson also dispatched his motor liaison officer Capt. Andrew F. Lundberg to the U.S. First Army in Spa. He was to warn them that the Germans had crossed the bridge to the north of Trois-Ponts and were likely headed their way.[31] Webb first, and then Lundberg reached Hodges's headquarters to personally warn the chief engineer that afternoon. They were in danger, both insisted.

With their mission accomplished, Lundberg and Webb raced back to reach Anderson, who both assumed was still in Trois-Ponts. Knowing the need for tank-busting ordnance to help stop the enemy armor, Lundberg had piled the jeep high with mines requisitioned from First Army. With Pfc. James M. Snow Jr at the wheel, the two crossed the Habiemont bridge near Werbomont at about 4.30 p.m. that afternoon. Maj. Webb was right behind them in another jeep. In the fading daylight, it was hard for Snow to see the road ahead. Just then, he suddenly emerged from the ground fog to see a big shape right ahead. There was a loud rip of gunfire; their jeep had smacked right into Peiper's column.[32] In fact, the American jeep ran into a rock wall, narrowly avoiding a direct collision with the SPW in which Jochen Peiper was riding. Meanwhile, the jeep behind Lundberg carrying Maj. Harry Webb and his driver also screeched to a halt, but the men were able to jump from their vehicle and escape into the woods.[33] There was one civilian witness, 50-year-old Ghislain de Thier, whose country home, Les Roches, was immediately across from the incident:

> The morning of the 18th we saw some refugees coming down the main road who announced to us that the German tanks were very near. I hesitated to believe those with bad news as I had seen the comings and goings of American jeeps in the road that afternoon without the least sense of panic. But at three o'clock, we had to face the facts. Soon thereafter, I witnessed an attack by Typhoons firing rockets against German tanks that had suddenly appeared on the secondary road a hundred metres above our house. The Germans, having taken possession of a place called 'Poteau de Rahier', had cut the Americans of Bodeux off from a path to Werbomont. It was at this moment at approximately 4.30 p.m. that I saw

> a jeep going up rapidly from the Lienne valley to the main road … I had a heart-breaking sensation for I knew the Germans were only about a hundred metres higher and I could do nothing to prevent their encounter. The meeting was short and tragic. The first tank came out from behind the bend that concealed it from their eyes. For a second there was an infernal crackle of gunfire … then an icy silence. Private James Snow lay inert in the jeep. Soon they had given their lives … The German tanks continued to come down the road and pass in front of our property.[34]

Assistant radio operator Hans Rineck described the moment from inside Diefenthal's SPW with Peiper:

> There were two American soldiers sitting in it. A tank opened fire on the jeep with its machine gun and the jeep collided with our SPW. The assistant driver in the jeep had been hit severely by the machine gun burst and was dead, while the driver was only pretending to be dead.

Captain Lundberg had been shot by the first burst of tank machine gun fire and slumped over lifeless in the jeep. However, the driver, Pfc. Snow, of Stokes County, North Carolina, was petrified with fear, but still alive and feigning death.[35] Hans Rineck was the radio operator in Diefenthal's adjutant's SPW (Rttf. Gottfried Neckerauer) immediately behind the SPW with Diefenthal and Peiper and driven by Zwigart:

> I received an order to carry the dead man out of the jeep. I noticed the other one was not dead but was only pretending, and I said, 'He is still alive.' From the right side of the road the man who at that time was a Rottenführer by the name of Paul Zwigart came running. Zwigart grabbed the American who was feigning death out by the collar and dragged him from the jeep and pushed him in front of himself and the American raised his hands above his head as a sign of surrender … As I put down the body of the dead American on the left side of the road, near the edge of the wood, I heard shots fired on the right side of the road. I looked toward the right and I saw Zwigart firing shots from his pistol which he aimed at the American. The American collapsed under the fire … I asked Paul Zwigart, 'Why did you shoot him?' He answered, 'You do not understand, in an armored spearhead you cannot bother with a single prisoner of war.'

Rineck claimed to be too far away to hear if Zwigart received any orders from anyone else in the command vehicle before shooting the prisoner. Rineck said he was preoccupied with hauling the body of the dead American driver to the other side of the road and did not hear any orders. But he did add that there was no resistance from the American or any attempt to escape when he was shot. And when Zwigart shot the prisoner, Rineck claimed to approach him to question his judgement.

For his part, Peiper carefully avoided saying anything about Zwigart and the jeep incident. 'The bombardment of our spearhead was uncomfortable,' he later recalled, 'but not dramatic, the damage was minor, because the fighter-bombers operating at an altitude of only 20 metres attacked across the direction we were driving, but not along our column.'[36]

> On the other side of the bridge, my column was attacked by a heavy American air raid. The road on the other side takes a sharp curve and goes up to Cheneux and the tank at the point was blown to pieces by a bomb right there. It was therefore not possible to pass by this tank for a while. We made desperate attempts to pull it back toward the rear, but nevertheless lost at least two and a half hours. I then ordered Diefenthal to proceed at once in the same direction at great speed to reach the main road and to prevent [the enemy from seizing] the next bridge near Neucy.[37]

When questioned, Peiper said he had re-joined his command SPW: 'At the bridge at Cheneux, I was reached for the first time by my command group and I mounted a radio vehicle of this group and I received a report of all radio messages that had come in from my communications officer, which, of course, had not reached me before then.' Yet it is significant that Peiper, even though incriminated by Zwigart's testimony, could not produce witnesses who were in his hypothetical 'command vehicle' other than SS Rttf. Walter Landfried at the Malmedy trial.

However, if Peiper was not clear on his whereabouts, others in Diefenthal's SPW were explicit. Hans Assenmacher, the SPW radio operator, had also been with Zwigart, Diefenthal, and Peiper in an SPW just behind the tank spearhead when a fighter-bomber attack halted their advance.[38] The traffic jammed and they waited impatiently:

> We had been standing on the road for several minutes when somebody from the tank out front started suddenly to shout, 'Americans, shoot!' I tried to get my machine gun, but by the time I had got into position, another machine gun was already firing. I got back into my seat … I saw an American jeep drive past the two Panthers which were standing on the right side of the road in front of us and I saw them drive up to the SPW of the adjutant on the left side of the road. Shortly thereafter, the men from the Panther and SPW approached the jeep. I saw Rottenführer Zwigart, who was down there, walk over to the jeep and pull the American, who was driving the jeep, out from behind there. The assistant driver appeared to be dead and was carried out by another man. Rottenführer Zwigart then took the American in front of our vehicle and went to the back of the SPW and there said to Sgt Fackelmeyer, 'Paul give me a machine pistol.' Sgt Fackelmeyer gave him a machine pistol. Zwigart then went back to the American who was standing at our vehicle. He pushed him along in front of him, the American turned around briefly, and Zwigart motioned for him to go ahead. After the American had walked forward two or three steps, Zwigart shot him down with a burst from his machine pistol. Then he returned to the SPW and handed the machine pistol back up.[39]

The Panther of Kurt Plohmann, a member of the 1st Company of the Panzer Regiment,[40] had been put out of action near Stavelot on 18 December and on orders he had mounted the Panther of SS Oberscharführer Erich Strelow. Plohmann was still riding on the tank after the fighter-bombers struck on 18 December when the panzers headed west from Cheneux and were turned back by the blown bridge:

> We stopped for a short while and then an American jeep approached us coming from the opposite direction. The point of the tank column opened fire on the Jeep. One American soldier driving the jeep was killed instantly. The second soldier in the jeep played dead and had to be taken to this position. Thereupon, a man from the SPW came down to the Jeep and pulled the soldier out of the jeep by his collar. The German soldier then shot the American soldier with a machine pistol on a small side path next to the highway.

To be sure, Zwigart's SS career did not inspire the view of a compassionate soldier. Upon entering the SS, he had been a member of the SS Totenkopfverbände, 2nd Death's Head Regiment. Of all the Waffen SS units, those with the Totenkopverbände were most likely to be assigned to concentration camps. Some 43% of the officers assigned to the concentration camp system had pulled stints in the Waffen SS.[41] Zwigart then later moved to the Leibstandarte in 1940 in Russia and there was steeped in a pitiless campaign.[42] Not surprisingly, in Zwigart's description of his actions on 18 December 1944, there was no denial:

> As far as I remember, it was close to four o'clock in the afternoon [of 18 December] about 1 kilometer from the village in which we had the heavy air attack, and I saw a Panther standing on the left side of the road ... on the right-hand side of the road stood some SPWs of our battalion. I drove past the SPWs and stopped about astride the Panther on the right side of the road ... Diefenthal, who was sitting behind me, shouted to the commander of the Panther asking what happened and told him to proceed ... Afterward, Hauptsturmführer Diefenthal took the map into his hands and [he] as well as Obersturmbannführer Peiper looked at this map. While we were doing so, the adjutant's SPW approached from the rear and came to a halt in between us ... At approximately the same time, an American jeep whose driver apparently did not know we were there, came driving toward us at great speed. One of the vehicles beside us opened fire. The driver of the jeep was apparently hit and drove into the front of the adjutant's tank [sic SPW] ... Someone, I believe it was Unterscharführer Rineck from the adjutant's tank, dismounted and stood around the jeep without anything happening. Thereupon Hauptsturmführer Diefenthal gave me the order, 'Zwigart remove the jeep – we don't have any time.' While still in the SPW, I noticed the two Americans in the Jeep appeared to be either dead or wounded. I went to the Jeep where Unterscharführer Rineck called my attention to the fact that one of the Americans still lived and just pretended to be dead. I shouted at the living one that he should get up, getting hold of him at the same time ... The American dismounted the Jeep and I could see he was not wounded. I was very mad at the Americans for obvious reasons, because just before that, we sustained a heavy air attack.[43]

Then a confession implying that Peiper and Diefenthal saw his shooting of a prisoner as a pedestrian event – hardly noteworthy.

> For that reason, I knew that my superior, Haupsturmführer Diefenthal, and my commander, Obersturmbannführer Peiper who was also present, wouldn't mind if I shot the prisoner, so I decided to shoot him. I was asked at the interrogation how I knew that Diefenthal and Peiper would agree, and I said that I 'knew' them. I have been long enough in the Waffen SS to know that even if no specific order is issued to shoot a prisoner of war, the officers at least don't mind it. Also, I knew the Obersturmbannführer as a radical SS man. It was known in the regiment that he, before he came to us, was Himmler's adjutant and right-hand man.

Zwigart borrowed a machine pistol from Paul Fackelmeyer directly under the eyes of Diefenthal and Peiper. 'At that time, comrades in some of the vehicles and some standing at the sides shouted loudly and encouragingly, "Go ahead – bump him off …"'

> It was just like the 'Leipzig Fair'. … From all sides I was watched with curiosity; the noise of the encouraging shouting, and between Obersturmbannführer Peiper hollering to Haupsturmführer Diefenthal repeatedly, 'Quick! Let's go! We don't have any time …' When I asked for the machine pistol, I saw Peiper on the opposite bench, sitting on the blankets which I had spread out for him. He glanced at me quickly and impatiently and then looked at this map. There is no doubt that Diefenthal and Peiper knew what I was going to do, but they were disinterested … Before the edge of the woods, when the prisoner had walked about three steps in front of me, I drew my gun and aimed at his head and fired a burst of ten to fifteen shots into his head, whereupon the American immediately fell dead. I took a short look at the body. He was already dead; he had a huge hole in his head and blood flowed in streams … Rineck then removed the watch from the body and immediately after the shooting, he shouted joyously, 'Now, at least I have a watch!' As I returned, Diefenthal asked me what was inside the Jeep. I replied, 'Mines,' and thereupon he hollered at me that I should once and for all get the jeep out of the way. He did not say anything about the shooting.

'Quick! Let's go!' Peiper had emphasised. The jeep was blocking the road over which his sorely delayed tanks were to advance. 'We don't have any time …'[44] Zwigart's shooting hardly delayed the Kampfgruppe Peiper at all.[45] By 4.40 p.m. they were advancing forward once again.[46]

Back at the bridge, between 4 and 4.30 p.m., Corp. Fred Chapin worked his way under the trestle, wrapping its thick wooden piers with bulging packs of TNT laced with prima cord. It was growing dark at 4.45 p.m. when he rolled out his wire along a ditch and placed his detonator in an abandoned German sentry box some 30m behind the crossing. At that moment, in the gloomy twilight up ahead, Chapin thought he saw ghostly forms over the brow of the hill. There were sounds, too.

Enemy tanks? Just then, one of them opened fire. A shell exploded off to Chapin's left. 'Blow! Blow!' Edelstein yelled, wildly waving his arms. Chapin wrenched the key, instinctively ducking and instantly saw a brilliant flash followed by a thundering roar. Chunks of wooden debris rained down where the bridge had been. It was 5 p.m. Peiper was only a few vehicles back from the lead tank and saw the detonation. It was the second time in six hours that he had a bridge blown up in his face. 'The damned engineers!' he shouted in frustration. 'The damned engineers!'[47]

Pfc. Shorty Nickell, one of Chapin's engineer buddies, watched the detonation with satisfaction. 'Thar she blows!' he heard someone shout from the creek bank. Momentarily cloaked by the massive cloud of smoke and debris, Chapin and Pfc. Shorty Nickell took off up the road leading west away from the German armor. They had nothing with which to contest those monsters, although some other engineers had left belts of mines across the road in case the Germans got through. But they didn't. Frustrated with the loss of the bridge, the SS vehicles poured a fountain of fire across the narrow banks of the creek into the treeline and up the road. Chapin and Nickell ran headlong to get to a waiting truck. Chapin thought he was hit, but discovered instead that a bullet had sliced his canteen in two on his cartridge belt.[48]

So anxious was the driver of their truck to get away from the ordnance flying about that Chapin and Nickell had to run to get on board. Luckily for them, the truck was still challenged to move much at all. As the two stretched toward the back of the receding truck bed, helpful hands reached out to hoist them past the tailgate. They fell inside, happy to be rolling slowly away to Werbomont. 'Gun this thing!' they told the driver. His foot pushed the pedal to the floorboard.

Other GIs could not run fast enough to reach the truck and so trudged up the road. Presently, they were approached by an American jeep and found themselves confronted by a two-star general. It was Gen. James Gavin of the 82nd Airborne Division. After a sharp salute, they quickly assured Gavin the bridge was blown. He wanted to know how many tanks there were. 'Between three and five,' one man ventured – at least when they took off. They didn't stick around to see more arrive. Gavin smiled knowingly and thanked them.

Chapter 21

INTO THE NIGHT

Speed is the essence of war. Take advantage of an enemy's unpreparedness.[1]

Worried for the sad procession of Belgian refugees he had watched all afternoon, Wathère Jamar gazed from his picture window in his two-storey home in Chevron, Belgium. Out east across the valley across the Ardennes at sunset were the cold waters of Lienne Creek just 2km away. The road angled from the hills in the distance to pass obliquely by his house:

> Around 5.30 p.m., while darkness settles over the country, I am … looking at the route de Stavelot, when I see a big tank on the very same road, heading for Neufmoulin. At the same time, a young boy running in the front of the house yells, 'Look there!' Right after that I see a huge explosion, in the direction of Neufmoulin. At the same time I see the flashes of cannon shots and the long lightning streams of machine guns. I also see a great ball of fire of a greenish color slowly descending to the earth … The bridge at Neufmoulin has been blown up … One thing is certain: the Germans are close by. We go to bed fully dressed, and of course are worried …[2]

After the smoke cleared from the Habiemont/Neufmoulin bridge detonation, Peiper got out to take a look, but there were no crossing options. The Lienne Creek was not much of a body of water, but the problem was the creek bed's clay-like soil. Obersturmführer Hans Hennecke was there:

> In Cheneux, we were surprised by fighter-bombers which attacked us. We had major losses. Oscha. Thomas's tank was burned out and Rock and Knörringer were wounded. I moved on with another tank as I was ordered to reach the Maas River at all costs. I reached the point with [Erich] Strelow near Neucy. His tank had run out of fuel. It started to get dark and it took some time till the entire armored group arrived. The Neufmoulin-Habiemont bridge near Neucy was

> destroyed. Peiper issued the order to turn around and drive to La Gleize in order to continue the attack via Stoumont with the 2nd Company as point.[3]

Jamar watched as the Germans pulled back to try to cross a ford in the river just to the right of the bridge ruins. Yet the vehicular footing there was found treacherous for SPWs much less lighter tanks. Peiper had to change direction again. He ordered both the 10th Company and 11th Company to scout for bridges across the Lienne that could carry his tanks. Soon it was dark. Clattering about, the 11th Company now under Oscha. Rudi Rayer (Heinz Tomhardt had been wounded in Stavelot) located a small bridge near Les Forges and moved across, blasting their path with bullets, and killing Monsieur J. Minguet as he stood in the doorway of his home.[4]

Soon Rayer's half-tracks drove south to the destroyed span at Neufmoulin. After reaching the blown-up bridge, they missed finding the N23 in the darkness and drove on to Trou de Bras to the south by mistake. Ordered by radio to return to Peiper's main column, Rayer's lost reconnaissance team seized a local Belgian man, Monsieur Gilsonnet, and planted him on the hood of their lead half-track with orders to steer them back to Neufmoulin. Reaching that place, they released the greatly relieved Belgian man.[5]

Meanwhile, at 10 p.m. the 10th Company (Obersturmführer Preuß) found a bridge 4km north-east of Neufmoulin at Moulin Rahier. Both SPW companies had orders to find different bridges and then continue to move to Werbomont once reaching the other side. However, they discovered the bridges too rickety to support tanks. Undeterred, his lighter SPWs and two flak vehicles drove on toward Chevron and Habiemont but they were nearly destroyed when drawn into a trap. Karl Wortmann went with Preuss in his Wirbelwind. His driver, Erich Miechen, worried as to whether the unsteady wooden structure could support their 22-ton weight. They clambered across and the second flak vehicle followed:

> We drove south till we reached the blown-up bridge and followed Georg Preuss a short distance toward Werbomont. During our advance, we reached a house on the right side of the road. All the windows were wide open. In front of us, we saw shadows moving and we stopped immediately. Headlights turned on and in the same moment there was a loud crash. We were trapped. It became a difficult task to get out of there.[6]

In the meantime, Col Sutherland with the U.S. 119th Infantry Regiment had reports of German tanks as far west as Chevron. Consequently, he sent Lt Col Hal McCown's 2nd Battalion with the support of four M-10 tank destroyers from Company A, 823rd TD to cover the threatened approach. In the end, orders and map symbols translated to individual soldiers. McCown arrived in the area of the Habiemont bridge just after dark, creating a bit of a stir with the division because he moved out of radio range. Other elements of the regiment reported a build-up of German armor west of La Gleize north of the Amblève.[7]

McCown promptly sent ahead a combat team under a man he saw as one of his more effective combat leaders: 1st Lt effectively Edward C. Arn. Arn had landed in Normandy on 12 June 1944 and served with the 30th Division, earning battlefield commissions that eventually led to his leadership of F Company. Even so, Arn was a stoic. 'I had written too damned many letters home,' he remembered. All told, F Company lost 128 men killed and another 600 wounded in the war. He himself, was wounded twice. While his soldiers needed to get the job done, Arn advised his platoon commanders to be careful with their men. 'There's nothing between us and the enemy, but our field jacket,' he reminded them.[8] Arn recalled moving to Werbomont:

> The whole move to our detrucking point couldn't have been more than a hundred miles. Nevertheless, it took all night … The roads were clogged with fleeing civilians, military vehicles, and turn-tail GIs of all ranks and types heading away from Belgium. It was a real mess and those truck drivers on that particular night deserved awards of some type. 'Axis Sally' from Berlin announced on my truck's radio 'the fanatical 30th Division – Roosevelt's SS troops – is going to try to rescue the First Army.' How she knew that our division was involved was quite beyond me … Eventually, as dawn was breaking, stiff-cold Fox Company stalwarts climbed out of the trucks. We headed south. During that morning McCown's jeep roared to a screeching stop. Signalling the company to halt, I double-timed to the colonel, who already had spread his map on the hood of his jeep.[9]

'Arn, here is where you are,' McCown said pointing to a topo map, 'I want F Company in Vielsalm with the place secured by nightfall.' He moved his finger across the contour lines.

'Sir,' Arn protested, 'that's a good distance from there.' He asked what intelligence knew about the enemy disposition to the east.

'Not much,' McCown answered, handing him a dog-eared map, 'There's an enemy counteroffensive under way in considerable strength and we must contain it.' McCown stood up straight and saluted. Arn did the same. 'Fast! Now, move!'

McCown's jeep scurried off. F-Company resumed their march. Arn could see that reaching Vielsalm was out of the question, but there was a village named Chevron about 8 miles ahead. With any luck, they could reach it by nightfall. 'The road we were on followed a very small river or creek called Grandmont Rivulet. A wooded hillside sloped down to the edge of the road on our left and to the tiny stream's banks on the other side. It was a damned scary situation.' Arn placed a small squad of Ken Austin's 3rd platoon in the lead and communicated with them from the middle of the column via walkie-talkie. It was about dark when Arn's 3rd platoon reached Chevron, where the tiny stream met the Lienne Creek. 'It was very, very dark,' Arn remembered. 'One could scarcely see beyond his nose.' On a hunch Arn ordered a tank destroyer from battalion headquarters and was quickly assured that one was on its way.[10]

> There were two or three sharp curves in the road between me and Neufmoulin. I had no way of viewing the place in the gloom of the night. By runner, I ordered Austin to set up a roadblock for the night. I also ordered the machine gun section of the weapons platoon to move forward. Austin's bazooka man was there, too.

When they were dispatched to guard the approach to Werbomont, to set up an improvised ambush, Arn worried he might soon run into the enemy as reports filtered in of German armor nearby. Lt Ken Austin was on the walkie-talkie. 'Jesus Christ, Lieutenant!' he whispered into the microphone, 'there are tanks or something, I think headed toward us from the east! They are firing wildly and point-blank!'

Arn could hear the bang-bang over the transmitter. 'Do you think they have any idea where you are?'

'No sir, I think they're just coming on in the dark and firing away.'

'Good! Don't expose your position and hold your fire!' Arn quickly ordered 2nd Lt Ray Beaudoin's 2nd platoon up on the high ground above Austin just as one of the TDs clanked up the road. Arn flagged down the TD and gave the commander the situation. There were two or three curves in the highway ahead. 'Take a position on this side of the first curve!' Arn yelled above the engine noise. 'Shut your motor off and when the lead vehicle – whatever it may be – rounds that curve, let them have it.

> A Kraut vehicle lumbered around the curve. The TD's muzzle-blast was terrific and nearly blinded me as I tumbled partway down the slope on my side of the road … It proved to be a German half-track and the TD's shell had destroyed it completely, thus blocking the road perfectly … I could have kissed that TD commander … Within seconds, I heard a blast from one of the company's bazookas. I discovered later that one of Beaudoin's bazooka men, Pfc. Mason Armstrong, had worked his way from the high ground north of town into the second storey of a residence and had fired down on two Kraut half-tracks, knocking out both.[11]

Pfc. Mason Armstrong had taken his squad of twelve men into a small, two-storey house at the edge of the town of Chevron. After sunset, it became very dark. 'You couldn't see your hand in front of your face,' Armstrong remembered. 'We could hear the Germans coming up the road from the east … We had a tank destroyer up the road and we decided to let them go by. There was a squad or more of German infantry. We could hear them talking and worried that they would see the tracks in the dirt road from our vehicles. A half-track went by and in the dim light we could see it was loaded with Germans. Just then a real ruckus broke loose and we began firing at the noise.'[12] Armstrong had trained with the bazooka at Ft McClelland and now pointed the weapon at the Germans from an upstairs window in the house, but it was so dark he couldn't see a thing. 'We were lucky and hit one of the half-tracks.' A torrent of machine gun fire came back – a terrible racket – and the half-tracks were firing with their cannon. In the momentary flashes of the gunfire he could see one of the half-tracks turning around and backing up toward their house. He fired again and disabled the last half-track, although both the Germans and the Americans in the house were firing at anything and everything. 'It was lucky we didn't kill each other,' Armstrong said. 'No one knew who was who.' The man next to him at the window was killed when he was hit by cannon fire that tore off his entire shoulder.

In a short minute Preuss's reconnaissance team was shattered by intense small-arms fire. Then, German infantry tried to storm the building firing upon them, but the other members of Armstrong's squad fought them back with carbines. In the end, the enemy finally left, abandoning the third half-track. 'What remained of the enemy effort could now be heard withdrawing to the east on the other side of the Lienne.' Even with the night again quiet, Armstrong and his men spent restless hours at the house. At dawn Arn pushed a roadblock out beyond the bridge across Lienne creek.[13]

That morning as Arn was preparing to move the remainder of F Company into blocking positions near Neufmoulin and its important bridge, he heard a jeep roaring down the road behind him. Looking back, he saw it screech to a halt. Out popped a tall, lean, paratroop officer with two stars on his helmet. 'Who's in command here?'

'I am sir, Lt Arn, F Company, 119th Regiment, 30th Division,' Arn leapt up saluting, 'At your service!'

'I'm Jim Gavin of the 82nd Airborne Division.'

There was Gen. Gavin again. He waved away Arn's salute and wanted a tour of the place where the scene occurred where the SS column had been turned back. Surveying the macabre scene of broken machines and dead SS troopers, Gavin seemed pleased. 'Looks to me, Lieutenant, as if you've had quite a night of it!'

'Yes, sir,' Arn agreed, 'but my men have set up a roadblock.'

'Good!' Gavin gestured, 'You'll be pleased to know my people will be relieving you here.'

'Yes, sir!' Arn snapped. Gavin wrote about the day in his own field diary:

> I visited the locality at daylight on 19 December and found about five armored vehicles, armored cars, and self-propelled guns knocked out with several German dead lying about in the road ... It appeared quite clear that this was a reconnaissance party of the German armored column that had been endeavouring to move from Trois-Ponts to Werbomont and had succeeded in crossing the bridge at Les Forges.[14]

Meanwhile, the U.S. 3250th Signal Service Company intercepted the radio transmissions from the Kampfgruppe Peiper detailing the mission gone wrong. At 1932 hours Peiper flashed to Preuss, 'Take Werbomont and await further orders.'[15] At 2040 hours the recon group signaled: 'Our position is 6 kilometers SW of Werbomont.' In the meantime, Peiper encouraged them, 'All speed to Werbomont with two groups.' Peiper was obviously referring to Tomhardt, who was lost with the 11th Company to the south. But by 2134 hours the

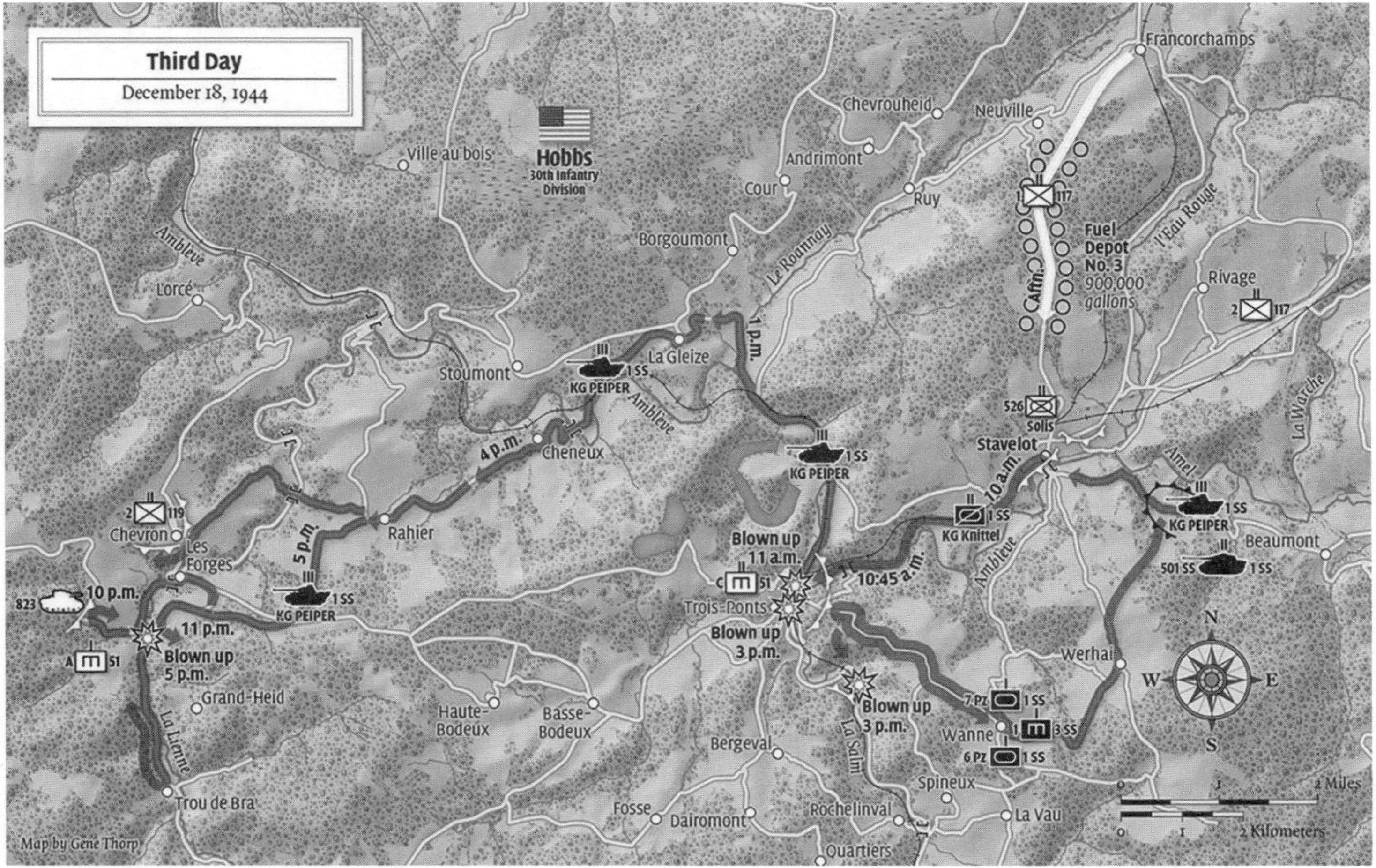
Third Day
December 18, 1944
Hobbs
30th Infantry Division
Ville au bois
Chevrouheid
Neuville
Francorchamps
Andrimont
Cour
Ruy
Borgoumont
Le Roannay
l'Eau Rouge
Fuel Depot No. 3
900,000 gallons
Aftn.
Rivage
La Warche
Amblève
Lorcé
Stoumont
La Gleize
1 p.m.
KG PEIPER
1 SS
Solis
Stavelot
Amel
Cheneux
4 p.m.
Rahier
Chevron
Les Forges
5 p.m.
10 p.m.
823
11 p.m.
Blown up
5 p.m.
Grand-Heid
La Lienne
Trou de Bra
Haute-Bodeux
Basse-Bodeux
Blown up
11 a.m.
Trois-Ponts
Blown up
3 p.m.
10 a.m.
KG Knittel
10:45 a.m.
Beaumont
501 SS
Werhai
Wanne
7 Pz
6 Pz
3 SS
La Salm
Bergeval
Spineux
Fosse
Dairomont
Rochelinval
La Vau
Quartiers
N
W
E
S
2 Miles
2 Kilometers
Map by Gene Thorp

unidentified point leader of the 10th Company tersely told of trouble. 'I have been thrust back.' And just before 10 p.m., 'My position on the road at Oufny. There are four shot-up, tank-destroyer half-tracks in front of me … I await orders.' But now, a clarification. 'A scout car with Preuss is coming with a new mission,' came the order at 2202 hours: 'Stay where you are.' Yet by the time Preuss arrived, it was clear that the mission had failed – no bridge. Thus, it was almost an hour later, at 2301 hours, when Peiper signaled the troops to 'all go back to the take-off point'. For his part, Preuss recalled losing three SPWs and over a dozen panzer grenadiers killed or wounded.[16]

> The 10th Company was committed to quickly advance against Werbomont. The advance moved through Rahier-Froidville-Chauveheid-Forges-Habiemont. Apparently, because of an incorrect location report and believing that we were still within our own security belt, we fell into an American-armored ambush near Oufny and suffered heavy casualties.[17]

After that debacle in which Peiper personally re-called Preuss over the radio. U.S. intelligence people eagerly interrogated some of Preuss's men captured on the other side of Lienne Creek.

> PW from 10th Company, 1st SS Panzer Division captured … PW stated that seven armored personnel carriers came across the bridge after dark last night. His was knocked out by 2nd Battalion, 119th Regiment. PW was in high spirits about progress of the war. They have plenty of tanks and have captured enough American gasoline to run for a while.[18]

If only it were true; in spite of capturing fuel at Büllingen, Peiper was already short. He looked to turn his tank column around on the road in the night – a military feat even in daylight and out of contact with the enemy. There was no choice – he had to drive back to La Gleize since he did not have engineering capability to put in a heavy tank bridge. Had he taken the Trois-Ponts bridge on the 18th, or even the span over Lienne Creek, he maintained that he could have reached the Meuse that night.[19] Now, repulsed, he would instead try an attack toward the west through the torturous Amblève river valley in the direction of Stoumont. At the same time, the attached 84th Flak Sturm Battalion took up positions just west of Cheneux to guard that crossing of the river. By 11 p.m. Kampfgruppe Peiper rested between La Gleize and Stoumont, exhausted both in spirit and of fuel. Many sleep-deprived SS men took over houses in Cheneux just south-west of La Gleize. Only five Panzer IVs of Junker's 6th Panzer Company managed to reach Peiper's group at around midnight; the rest didn't have enough gasoline.

The fuel situation faced by Kampfgruppe Peiper on 18 December became dire. Karl Wortmann's flak tank broke down on the road back to Cheneux.[20] Soon they were passed by all the other tanks and then left alone on the road. 'As time passed, it became quite uncomfortable,' Wortmann recalled. They were all alone in the cold. And as light began to form in the eastern sky, he and his crew heard tank noises off to the west.

Anticipating the worst, the vehicle's driver, Günther Sträter, set up a machine gun as the sounds grew louder, but Wortmann found that the noise was coming from four German vehicles: King Tigers, moving at barely a walking pace, and a pair of the beasts with massive chains were towing the other two. 'I ran up and stopped them,' Wortmann recalled. He recognised one as Hstuf. Mobius in charge of the 2nd Company of the 501st SS Panzer Battalion. Mobius explained that they had nearly run out of fuel by the blown bridge and had to drain two of the tanks and use the petrol in the other two vehicles to tow all of them back.[21]

Feldwebel Karl Laun with the 84th Flak Sturm Battalion was at the rear of Kampfgruppe Peiper approaching Stavelot on the 18th and seeing similar signs of fuel depravity. 'Marking our route of advance off both sides of the road are immobile Tigers and Panthers,' he jotted into a diary. 'Everywhere, a frantic search for gasoline. They even approached our flak piece with solicitations for a few liters of gas.'[22]

Hermann Staritz, the commander of an infantry gun, a 'Bison' or *Grille*, of the heavy 13th Company, was moving with a buddy in a captured American jeep. 'In the morning, we proceeded to Stavelot and hid ourselves because people were shooting from the windows. We were lucky to have an American jeep we were still driving so they didn't shoot at us.' But like everyone else, Staritz and the infantry guns continued west and left Stavelot to those coming up from behind. 'We closed formation, but then the Jabos came as we advanced toward Cheneux. The bridges were blown in front of us.'[23]

When Arndt Fischer had been badly wounded leading Peiper into Ligneuville on 17 December, a replacement for the adjutant of the 1st SS Panzer Battalion was already heading for that town. SS Ustuf. Rolf Roland Reiser had ridden by motorcycle to Peiper's adjutant, Hstuf. Han Gruhle, at his headquarters by the blown-out railway trestle in Losheim. Reiser had been told to report there as he was now transferred from the 2nd Battalion in Rahden. Gruhle told the Transylvanian SS officer that he should report immediately to Stubaf. Poetschke. Where was he, Reiser wanted to know? Gruhle had no idea, suggesting he hitch a ride on a supply vehicle and ask his way forward. Poetschke would be near the point – follow the tank tracks.

Reiser walked down the road until he stopped a *Schwimmwagen* driven by SS Uscha. Dieter Kreye of the headquarters company of the 1st Panzer Battalion. Reiser and Kreye then moved through Honsfeld, where there was still some shooting and Allied air activity. At about 1600 hours Reiser and company reached Büllingen, following a dozen Tiger tanks moving through the village, still being pounded by artillery. Yet moving west of that village in the darkness, Kreye and Reiser followed the muddy tank tracks until their vehicle sank into the mud. The two men spent a fitful night sleeping in their *Schwimmwagen*, not extricating their vehicle until the following morning when a Panzer IV *Beobachtungswagen* [observation tank] appeared and offered to haul them out with a steel cable.[24] Once extricated, the two men continued to follow tank track imprints on muddy trails. Soon they churned ahead on a road, turning west at Thirimont, and then came across other stuck half-tracks as they slogged forward.[25] In spite of everything, at around 12.30 p.m. on 18 December, they arrived in Ligneuville to find the division headquarters.

Reiser spoke with SS Hstuf. Paul Ochmann in the town, also with the headquarters company who alerted him that the 1st Panzer Battalion was still further on ahead. There were prisoners in the hotel across the street, but Reiser claimed Ochmann told him nothing of the shooting further up the road at Baugnez or those in Ligneuville.[26] Noting Arndt Fischer's burned-out tank, Ochmann pointed out that Fischer had already been evacuated. Reiser lunched at the Hôtel du Moulin in Ligneuville and at 1330 hours left with Ochmann in a captured U.S. Army vehicle. 'We could only ride a short while because American planes attacked steadily.'

Only at 5 p.m., when the *Jabos* left the skies, were Reiser and Ochmann able to continue on toward Stavelot. About a kilometer before Stavelot at a road fork, Ochmann and Reiser came upon several SPWs and other vehicles. Reiser dismounted and struck up a conversation with Ostuf. Rudi Mäule, then assigned to headquarters 1st SS Panzer Regiment. Mäule informed Reiser that Poetschke and Peiper were further up ahead as the tanks had pushed through Stavelot by noon. The road through town was yet under enemy observation. Ochmann elected to wait for some other vehicles of his platoon, so Reiser continued on with Mäule.

However, aware of the gauntlet from Americans still holding out in Stavelot, the two SS men waited until total darkness at 2100 hours to follow behind elements of Knittel's 1st SS Panzer Reconnaissance Battalion. Under cover of darkness, Reiser and Mäule passed through Stavelot without trouble and later reached the village of Cheneux, where they came across a shot-down Panther and a column of vehicles grinding west. At 2 a.m. on the morning of 19 December Reiser asked where Poetschke might be? Still further ahead at the point. Yet even in the darkness, Reiser could see the traffic was now stopped and then slowly rolling back east. Soon news came by word of mouth; all the snarled traffic was turning around. Baffled, Reiser waited patiently by the road. Next, word came that Poetschke was in the panzer of Ostuf. Friederich Christ, in charge of the 2nd Company. Reiser would wait.

With Kampfgruppe Hansen and the 1st SS Panzer Grenadier Regiment still stuck trying to dislodge the Americans in Poteau, it was clear to the divisional commander, SS Obf. Wilhelm Mohnke, that Rollbahn E was jammed. Hansen had at first brushed aside the remnants of the 32nd Squadron, 14th Armored Cavalry, just before Poteau. Yet attempting to move beyond on the road, Hansen slammed squarely into Combat Command A of the 7th Armored Division that had just inserted itself into a perimeter defense of St Vith anchored in Poteau. Repeated infantry assaults were unable to dislodge the stubborn American defense.

The Ardennes roads remained atrocious. Kampfgruppe Sandig – 2nd SS Panzer Grenadier Regiment – supposedly following right on Peiper's heels on Rollbahn D, was, in fact stuck in traffic while leaving Büllingen at nightfall on

17 December and did not reach Ligneuville for another twenty hours. A young company commander in Sandig's regiment recorded the frustration on 17 December:

> It turned out that things did not go as the staff officers had planned on their green tables. The long Army worm, jammed up on the narrow roads, along with defective vehicles and ill-considered operations caused many unit commanders to lose time that would later have a deadly effect. Instead of the planned departure at 0800 hours, the battle group was still at the same place in the afternoon. It was already growing dark when a gap appeared and Gruppe Sandig could begin its march to the front. Only late at night was Stadtkyll passed, where the stop of several hours occurred on the serpentine road because a panzer with track damage blocked the road. Only after Feldmarschall Model appeared and the panzer was summarily pushed aside by the following vehicle, was the advance able to continue … The roads were slick as we moved through the Eifel highlands. There was another traffic jam … We stopped again … Shells from American artillery![27]

With Kampfgruppe Sandig snarled in traffic jams west of Büllingen, there was a vacuum in Peiper's wake. Thus, Mohnke ordered Gustav Knittel to detour his reconnaissance battalion, waiting as a second echelon for Hansen, along Rollbahn D to Peiper's rear. On the afternoon of 18 December, while Peiper was bearing down on Neufmoulin, Kampfgruppe Knittel raced north to the village of Pont, a small hamlet north of Ligneuville, and then toward Stavelot.

In Stavelot the U.S. 30th Infantry Division used its infantry of the 117th Infantry Regiment and the attached 843rd Tank Destroyer Battalion to slowly recapture the town in escalating street fighting. At 4.30 p.m. the SS again briefly got the upper hand when Coblenz's 2nd Company of Kampfgruppe Knittel emerged from hiding and resumed their move though Stavelot. Yet rather than leave his forces to shoot it out in wild street fighting in the town, Knittel rode on, leaving his companies behind to meet with Peiper, who was pulling back at the Cheneux bridge. Moving along with Coblenz to the rear were six Mk IVs, two platoons of engineers in SPWs, and three King Tigers that smashed their way through Stavelot. A fourth King Tiger was damaged by enemy fire, however, and effectively blocked the bridge access to any further German traffic. Even worse for Peiper, by 8 p.m. the American infantry and tank destroyers overcame the few SS vehicles and infantry squads still in Stavelot marketplace and by daybreak were back in control of the stone bridge across the Amblève river. Peiper was cut off.

Having survived an ill-advised encounter with German tanks on the Rue Neuve in Stavelot the preceding day, Beathe Wetz and her mother now took refuge in their big cellar at the square honoring St Remacle. Her father had escorted the whole family to the basement while racing through the house to clear signs everywhere of the recent American billets. 'Oh no, the Germans are back!' her mother wailed, watching the heavy boots stomp by. The Americans had left so suddenly, there were several Army trucks on the street, and Germans showed up to gleefully pilfer each. Soon there were signs that the

Americans were arriving. Beathe heard tanks grinding down the streets as gunfire near and far caused her and her mother to hold each other:

> The air smelled of powder – filled with smoke and fog. You could not see across the street. At night on the street, the houses next to us were burning. The sky was red with fire. In the light of the fire, I could see a German tank at one end of the street and an abandoned American tank at the other end. Then, I saw an American soldier on the sidewalk just in front of my house, fighting a German soldier with a bayonet. They struggled with each other, shouting and grunting. Suddenly, the American stabbed the German and he fell in agony, screaming. It was horrible – a horrible vision. And all through the night, in the basement we could hear him calling for God and his mother. When you hear something like that, you can never forget it.[28]

Even if bitter house-to-house battle in Stavelot now found the Americans inexorably gaining a costly upper hand, by midnight Kampfgruppe Knittel had linked up with Peiper – who paid little attention to his rear. Even so, half of Peiper's tank regiment strength had not crossed north of the Amblève because of fuel shortages, choking traffic, or mechanical troubles. In particular, part of the Tiger battalion had not moved on from Stavelot as tardy fuel deliveries made further advance impossible.[29] Also, although Peiper reckoned the 3rd Fallschirmjäger Division would be marching in his wake, the 9th Fallschirmjäger Regiment was only reaching the village of Schöppen – far to Peiper's rear – by 19 December.[30] Meanwhile, his opposite in the 12th SS Panzer Division, Kampfgruppe Kuhlmann, was still stuck fast in tough fighting in the twin villages of Rocherath-Krinkelt, barely off the start line. Peiper knew his right flank was exposed and open.

By midnight Jochen Peiper was back in the village of La Gleize and collecting his troops on the outskirts of the village for an advance along the road to Stoumont the following morning. Some claimed that a group of fifteen Americans were shot along the wall of the church in La Gleize that afternoon, but although there were multiple post-war confessions by young, impressionable SS grenadiers (likely seeking to curry favor with their U.S. captors), there was little physical evidence for that atrocity.[31] If any such shooting did happen, it was nothing like the magnitude of the executions at Baugnez or even Honsfeld.[32]

Back at the massive fuel dump south of Spa, Lt Walter Butts sat patiently with his men in foxholes just south of the enormous stacks of fuel-laden jerricans. As the gloom in the forest gave way to darkness, every sound and movement seemed threatening. At about 8.30 p.m. on the 18th the men around the single half-track began hearing tank engines in the valley to the south and Butts thought the enemy might be headed his way. He pleaded urgently with the men currently loading fuel for the quartermaster company and convinced sixteen to join his little squad. The men had rifles and a truck and that was about it. Increasingly worried, he radioed Spa for immediate reinforcements. At midnight Col Love came to the roadblock and went back to

Spa to commandeer a couple of 90mm guns from the 110th AAA Gun Battalion that had just come down from bivouac in a château in Creppe, south of Spa.[33] If the German tanks came up that road that led south to Cour and La Gleize, perhaps the guns could stop them.

Late that afternoon, and 16km north-west of Stavelot, Joseph Leroy was returning from Lorcé to the sanatorium in Stoumont on his motorbike. As Leroy puttered along, he came upon slower-moving American tanks headed toward Remouchamps. The Germans were up ahead, the Americans warned; turn back. Leroy ignored them – he drove on ahead to Targnon and then to the sanatorium where he worked. There, Leroy learned from Dr André Bastin that it was more than rumour. 'Nobody wanted to believe it,' the Abbé C. Hanlet recalled.[34] But facts intruded on aversion; the Germans were already in La Gleize and looting everything there. Another person whispered that he had seen German tanks just down the road in the darkness hiding under the trees.[35] 'We all agreed to keep the silence and not worry the sick people there.'

Still, Dr Bastin was worried. His wife had just given birth ten days before. He set off himself for his home in the woods just north of La Gleize. As he left, Bastin could only shake his head as he observed entire families moving on bicycles and carts, all awkwardly laden with bedding, clothes, and all kinds of possessions. Ten weaponless American soldiers walking on foot showed up amid the refugees, saying they were headed to Liège. Then came, a young Belgian man frantically pedalling west of Stoumont. The Germans were already in Coo.[36]

That night, at Hitler's headquarters at the Eagle's Nest, reports filtered the progress of *Wacht am Rhein*. Peiper's advance was still the deepest of any of the panzer spearheads, advancing so fast that his command always seemed to be out of radio contact. At 10.20 a.m. word had arrived at Hitler's briefing that the 1st SS Panzer Division was in Stavelot. Then, another dispatch forty minutes later described their approach to Trois-Ponts. 'The tanks are south-west of there,' the evening report commented, but noted that the mass of the division dawdled to the rear. 'Recht was taken at 14.30,' it went on, but 'pulling up the mortars and artillery on the roads, which are sometimes completely covered with mud, is very difficult.'[37]

Back at his command train deep in the Black Forest, SS head Heinrich Himmler, was receiving a healing treatment from his Finnish masseur, Felix Kersten.[38] Unlike his patient's mental doldrums in autumn, Kersten found Himmler almost giddy. The big, winter counterattack was going well, he told a doubting Kersten. 'Our offensive has been worked out in detail by the Führer in person,' the Reichsführer SS explained. And then there was the Blitzkrieg-like dash of Peiper and the Leibstandarte Adolf Hitler. Peiper was, after all, Himmler's previous adjutant. The *Lötlampen Abteilung* – it was just like Russia. 'We have only to maintain this rate of advance,' he confidently assured, 'and by the 26th of January we'll have reached the Channel coast.'

'What then?' Kersten wanted to know. 'Then our troops will be free to drive the Russians out of Europe,' Himmler assured.[39] Kersten said not a word.

In fact, Jochen Peiper in Belgium at the spearhead point of the offensive was thinking nothing of the Russians, or even the Channel coast. He had experienced serious repulse that Monday. Well after midnight, Peiper lay exhausted in La Gleize after one repulse after another. Following a short nap in Diefenthal's cramped SPW, Peiper moved to the point of the column. He encouraged his weary panzer men to prepare for a big advance at dawn.

In the meantime, the U.S. 30th Division's 119th Regiment left Aachen in heavy traffic. Lt David F. Knox, in charge of L Company, was sitting in the back of a 2.5-ton truck worried about Luftwaffe night-fighters circling overhead in the inky sky. 'It wasn't good to be moving,' he wrote in his diary. Soon their truck column was lost in the fog, finding themselves on a dirt road and heading in the wrong direction. Some of the German planes were buzzing noisily overhead, some dropping flares. 'One of the colored drivers said, "If I don't die tonight, I ain't never going to die!"' Somehow they got turned around as rumours swept the column that the Germans had counterattacked and the 78th Division had lost an entire battalion. At 2 a.m., as the column advanced haltingly, Lt Col Roy Fitzgerald, in charge of the 3rd Battalion, spoke to Knox. 'The best information was that about thirty tanks were headed our way.'[40] Great.

Bucking traffic and expecting the worst, by 9 p.m. on 18 December, Fitzgerald's 3rd Battalion arrived in Stoumont along with two platoons of Company A, 823rd TD Battalion. The riflemen jumped from their trucks and began setting up blocking positions. Fitzgerald was also pleased to have help from two 90mm AT guns assigned from the 143rd AAA Gun Battalion under Lt Donald McGuire. Two companies were to set up in the town itself. Meanwhile, Knox and Company L and three 57mm guns from headquarters occupied a small knoll north of Stoumont. The place was a cluster of stone houses known as Rouat:

> I went back and moved the company up to our area. It was dark by then and it must have been at least 2200 hours. We set up without much trouble. The anti-tank weapons set up in our area also. I went down to battalion to tell them of our situation and see if they had any more information … Maj. Rogerson was sitting in the corner. He had the story that the tanks we could hear moving were stuck down near the river. No one seemed to be concerned about the situation. Capt. [Francis J.] Del Bene, the S-3, said, 'If they try to come after us in the morning, we'll sure give them hell!' I shared my situation and went back … There was no question about the tank activity; there seemed to be plenty of it. I could hear the Germans hollering to each other. I spent the rest of the night getting anti-tank mines put out.[41]

Although the rifles and guns of the 823rd TD Battalion now barred immediate passage toward Stoumont, Peiper's men didn't seem to notice. Instead, the SS lead tanks bivouacked on the road, openly celebrating their crushing advance in the forests west of La Gleize. Having detrucked on the other side of Stoumont, Lt George Rehkopf, leading 1st Company of the 119th Infantry, ordered a night-time patrol to enter the town and make sure it was clear. That mission fell to S/Sgt Walter C. Kos of Company I, 119th Infantry, and four other men.

Stoumont was quiet enough, but upon reaching the eastern outskirts of town, Kos and his combat patrol came upon a flickering light in the St Anne woods. Kos and the others crept stealthily forward: a blazing campfire in the wood. The bright flames exposed thirty big tanks and half-tracks by the campsite, the SS troopers smoking and joking. 'A lot of shouting and hollering,' one reported, 'sounds like a bunch of drunks.'[42]

Having seen enough, Walter Kos and his little patrol pulled back just enough to get on the radio. They had come upon a bivouac of enemy tanks, he told his company commander. They needed artillery to strike the enemy partying just east of Stoumont.[43] When Rehkopf phoned the battalion, he was ridiculed – they didn't believe him. The lieutenant ordered him to set up his 3rd platoon in a defensive position just west of the SS tankers.[44]

Even if Peiper saw the net closing in on his deep incision into the American lines, his hardened SS tank men remained boldly confident. Peiper ordered Diefenthal's panzer grenadiers to circle around to the north of Stoumont to help with the envelopment he planned at daybreak.

While Peiper's men celebrated in the woods east of Stoumont, young Belgian Paul Servais was trying to get back to find his mother, Lèa Goffinet. She had been shot by the Kampfgruppe Peiper as it had approached the bridge at Cheneux.[45] When Paul and his sisters reached the Château de la Vaulx Renard, they were ushered inside to find only German wounded. Awkwardly, an SS medic told them their mother had been moved to the mill at the Moulin Gillet. Reaching that place by foot, Paul and his sisters found their mother inside, in terrible pain. The German medics told them that there was nothing they could do; her body was riddled with shrapnel. Both the German and wounded civilians were crowded in one room – a gruesome scene of blood and screaming people.[46] His young sister was hysterical.

Outside the mill, Paul's felt, eyes stared blankly ahead as German vehicles burned in the road. Even there, he could hear screams inside. His father, Rene, soon appeared. In the middle of the night, Paul's mother asked to see her son. He went inside with his father to find his mother fading. 'Please take care of your little sister.' Paul's father, Rene, was devastated. 'It is the end of everything,' he confided to his son. Monsieur Gillet offered to help Rene with the boy.

Monsieur Gillet took the youth back with him to Monceau to gather some wood from the local carpenter. Returning from Monceau and carrying planks, two SS troopers challenged Paul and Mr Gillet at the top of the hill. '*Nein!*' he called out. They could not pass. Gillet lost his temper. 'You son of a bitch,' he screamed, 'you killed my wife and she was a fine woman and I am going through.'[47] Gillet held Paul's hand tightly, and the SS men let them pass.

That morning, Tuesday, 19 December, arriving back at the mill near Cheneux, Paul wrenched himself free of Monsieur Gillet's hand to rush inside. In the cellar, he was confronted by his mother, dead and still. Around her were others, dead and dying. When Monsieur Gillet came inside to bring him away, the boy was inconsolable. Paul Servais could not speak. He followed Monsieur Gillet back to his workshop. There, he watched in dazed silence as Gillet made a simple wooden coffin.

Chapter 22

CHENEUX

Cannon to the right of them, cannon to the left of them, cannon in front of them …[1]

Ulysses, Tennyson

On the morning of Thursday, 19 December 1944 Jochen Peiper's long tank column had recoiled from the attempt to reach the Neufmoulin bridge south of the Amblève. He had aimed to punch through the thick woods of the Bois de Xhoris to the Meuse river beyond. No more; there was no bridge. Just to the rear of Peiper's push, apprehensive Belgian villagers huddled in the cellars of their homes in Cheneux. Venturing tentatively above ground, they still heard the muted rumble of tanks and the thunder of distant guns. The tiny hamlet of eighty-seven French-speaking souls was just south of La Gleize, but after being repulsed, Peiper's column pulled back to collect there. Now, the Germans crossed to the other side of the Amblève and drove off towards Stoumont and the Meuse.[2]

Yet even having pulled back from the thrust toward Werbomont, Peiper sought to retain the bridgehead across the Amblève as a hedge for future operations. That was possible; the teletype at Sepp Dietrich headquarters of the governing 6th Panzer Army hourly anticipated the arrival of Kampfgruppe Telkamp in the zone near Vielsalm. This was the panzer regiment of the 9th SS Panzer Division under the leadership of SS Stubaf. Eberhard Telkamp, the Hohenstaufen Knight's Cross tank leader. Elements of Telkamp's panzer regiment motored into place near Recht, if laggard due to flagging fuel deliveries and tortuous traffic jams from stubborn American resistance.[3] Over the last two days, the U.S. 7th Armored Division had steadfastly defended the road nexus radiating from St Vith, making Poteau nearly impossible to bypass.[4] 'Other than the hard-surfaced roads, the tracks are muddy,' Heeresgruppe B complained, 'greatly hindering motor traffic.'[5] Obf. Sylvester Stadler's

Hohenstaufen was to smash through the deeply incised forested valleys near Salmchâteau, and turn to the north-west to reach Peiper.

The other prospect for relief was from the Leibstandarte itself. Seeing Peiper's plight, SS Obf. Wilhelm Mohnke now sought to move his 1st SS Panzer Grenadier Regiment and his artillery to Wanne to reinforce the division's remaining tanks and tank destroyers there. If that could be accomplished speedily, Mohnke intended to push aside the Americans in Trois-Ponts – build a bridge if necessary – and crash beyond its cobblestoned streets to Brume, Monceau, and then Cheneux. That would link up with Peiper. The last reports to Mohnke told of only some weak U.S. engineer platoons in Trois-Ponts. The news from the rest of 6th Panzer Army was hardly good; Kampfgruppe Kuhlmann, the sister battlegroup of the 12th SS Panzer Division, was still embroiled in a village battle for Rocherath-Krinkelt near the start line.[6] Still, it was news of Mohnke's plan on the evening of 19 December that led Peiper to hurry the 7th Company under Hstuf. Leopold from La Gleize to a position west of Cheneux to hold possession of that town.[7]

In fact, Mohnke's intelligence was lacking, for the 82nd Airborne Division now barred the real estate over which the 1st SS and the newly committed 9th SS division proposed to advance. To preserve that option, Peiper himself ordered the 84th Flak Sturm Battalion into a defensive position to defend the bridge and Cheneux. Knowing these troops were regular army, he added SS infantry for stiffening resolve. Feldwebel Karl Laun:

> In the afternoon, we advance in forced march tempo to a bridge in the direction of Cheneux. In the beginning our mission is defined as bridge protection. But hardly have we reached our destination when Peiper requisitions one of our platoons for infantry commitment. To an ever-increasing degree does the SS rely on the prowess of the flak units to refill their badly decimated ranks … Prior to taking cover, they displayed their courage by ordering the herding-together of all civilians in Stoumont.[8]

In the meantime, Peiper's casualties from the failed advance on Werbomont – many from the bombing of the column on 18 December – continued to file back in a sorry cavalcade to the east. They came in ambulances or mud-splattered trucks – even walking wounded – all drifting back. Passing through Cheneux, they converged on a makeshift German hospital that had been established in the Château Froidcour west of La Gleize. Given Peiper's new directive, the battlegroup stance in Cheneux changed to a beehive of defense. Rearguard elements of Kampfgruppe Peiper sited flak wagons behind houses, while infantry dug in machine guns and sited a few available artillery pieces. To deal with American infantry who might try to turn the flanks through the woods, they dug foliage-covered holes for camouflaged snipers.

For the residents of Cheneux, the chief worry on 19 December consisted of straggling SS men, some who were dead tired, others who seemed less than enthusiastic to re-join Peiper's charging advance. Dupont Émile was given the job of serving notice to all the local that everyone must go immediately to the school. As the SS men grew short tempered, many civilians wilted with fear. Directed to the church, obediently, they came out into the street. The village inhabitants were aghast. Were the Germans planning to kill them all in one place like in Oradour and Tulle in France? Fearing the worst, some of the men hid instead. Monsieur Jean Prince cowered in a corner of his loft and Joseph Boreux and Jules Forêt sought hiding places at their farm. Houses further down the way toward Rahier did not get the warning and the Boutet, Gaspard, and Delvenne families remained at home. Fleeing toward the church, the Grosjean and Louis families were terrified.[9]

Peiper had been right. American infantry companies, assembling just to the west, were intent on throwing him out of Cheneux. And they were not just any American infantry – they were the All-Americans. The 504th Parachute Infantry Regiment was an immensely proud unit within the realm of the big egos that populated the U.S. Army airborne forces in the Second World War. The airborne troops bragged of exceeding toughness – even rivalling the Marines. Certainly they were brave, but also known for their willingness to fight under foolhardy conditions. Indeed, they were more like Peiper's grenadiers than anyone in the American army would want to admit. While they were not fanatic (at least in the sense of killing innocents who got in the way), there was no denying that the *esprit de corps* of the airborne came down to a willingness to sacrifice.

'All of us were volunteers,' remembered S/Sgt Frank Leslie Dietrich with Company C. 'We were challenged and proud. If you survived paratroop school there was a great feeling of being special.'[10] The training had been arduous; many washed out training that stretched from Ft Benning to Ft Bragg. The big allegiance was to the 504th itself. When Dietrich had begun training in 1942, there had been no 82nd Airborne Division, but there was a 504th, one of the original parachute infantry regiments. The division itself had been in action since 10 July 1943.

Eventually, the 504th moved to England in April 1943, coming under the command of Col Reuben Henry Tucker III. They jumped at Sicily, where their aircraft had been badly shot up by the U.S. Navy who mistook their aerial armada for the enemy. Tucker's plane was one of the few to reach the drop zone, riddled with 2,000 holes. At Salerno beachhead in September 1943, there had been many wounded in the first days and Dietrich watched as replacements arrived to almost immediately become casualties. 'We tried as hard as we could to take care of the new guys,' he remembered, 'but the old-timers looked out for each other.'

Later the 504th was used in the Arnhem operation, where the Grave bridge was seized in a crossing made in flimsy canvass boats under fire. Dietrich was convinced that without the leadership of Tucker, personally directing tanks and artillery to pin the enemy on the other side, most would have died. There were still terrible losses and when the 504th had been sent back to Reims, Sgt Dietrich felt plenty lucky to be alive.

And what about the *crazies*? Born in 1922, Morris 'Mike' Holmstock saw himself as an average kid who got out of a Philadelphia bakery business to volunteer just like everyone else. As a result, he became a raw paratrooper recruit in Toccoa, Georgia, simply because the paratrooper guys looked good on the recruiting poster.[11] Starting out, Holmstock was with the 3rd Battalion of the 506th Parachute Infantry Regiment at Toccoa. There, he took in all the preliminaries: jumping out of 250ft mock towers, training with live ammunition, and the like. Unfortunately, their regimental commander, Col Robert F. Sink, had read somewhere that the Japanese were hoofing it 100 miles in forced marches over three days. 'We can do better, boys!'

Carrying full equipment, Holmstock and the rest of his battalion walked about 135 miles on back roads, all the way from Atlanta to Ft Benning, in only three days – paying the price in agonising foot pain, blisters, and exhaustion. 'It was pure hell.' At Ft Benning, it just got worse, with midnight marches, endless drills, and pointless guard duty. Hated even more than Sink was Capt. Herbert M. Sobel, in charge of E Company. But the real kicker was that Sink and Sobel under him seemed to enjoy all the physical and mental abuse. Regardless of effort and attention to detail, each soldier was cursed – sentenced to demeaning punishment, constant physical abuse, and endlessly condemned a 'worthless shithead soldier'. Soon Holmstock learned to hate Col Sink – and hate the colonel from North Carolina in a way a Pennsylvania boy didn't know was possible. He asked for a transfer – anywhere but with Sink and Sobel.[12]

Even released, Holmstock was labelled a malcontent and ended up with the 541st – a holding outfit for airborne replacements – and was soon shipped overseas. 'I joined the 504th in February of 1944 in Italy. 'It took me about two hours on the beach at Anzio to know what combat was all about,' he remembered. Yet the actions in Italy earned the 504th a reputation with their German enemy that stuck with the regiment. 'Devils in Baggy Pants', the diary on a dead German soldier called them. Regardless of enemy respect, the men of the 504th found the experience of war a clear vision of hell. Pvt. Glynn Arrington estimated he had been on the front line of the 82nd Airborne for more than a hundred days by December 1944.[13]

At Camp Sissone in Reims, France, the 82nd Airborne men were able to rest up for a few weeks. Everyone was out for a pass to Paris. Those who were left behind could still go into town and see movies, and the old French barracks were 'a real luxury compared to being on the line'. There were wood stoves, hot chow and there always seemed to be poker or a game of craps under way. Dietrich avoided the dice, but he did very well at cards. Corp. George D. Graves, Jr. remembered Sissone with near revelry:

> In 1944, 17 December was a more than usually pleasant winter day. The sun was shining. People were humming around the CP in good spirits as Paris passes were providing something to look forward to for those who had not gone on first quota. It was Sunday. Plans had been prepared for some ground company parties on Christmas. Our mess hall had been well decorated and a big

> 'Merry Xmas' painted on the wall. Christmas trees had been gathered from the surrounding countryside. There was nothing startling in the morning news on the radio. Bucky Neumeyer was still finding it hard to spend the large amount of cash he had won on payday. We decided it would be nice to have a supply of champagne for Christmas … I felt myself in a position to ask for a pass to Reims … After detrucking in Reims, I ran into old Mike Kogut, the 1st Sgt of Company H and 'Suzie' Souza. We debouched to a hotel and sampled a bottle of champagne. Leaving the hotel, we went to see the famous cathedral which was certainly an impressive sight … We soon found another café which sold Anisette. The proprietor was a Corsican and we were soon spieling Italiano with him. Before we left we managed to trade him on two bottles of cognac and four bottles of wine for some cigarettes, which was quite an accomplishment … It was dark when we got to the best nightclub in town. The atmosphere was quite luxurious and the orchestra better than average.[14]

The cosy merriment did not extend to others such as Pvt. Glynn Arrington, who had been on guard duty. 'It had been a cold, miserable day,' he recalled, 'by midnight it was sleeting and getting colder by the hour … After I got back from guard duty, my gun-section sergeant told me to go to the supply room and get my gun and all the ammo I could carry. There's some action up in the Ardennes, someone told us; we're needed up there.' Another paratrooper woke Frank Dietrich. 'The Germans are coming!' 'That's bullshit,' he grumbled, 'today is my day off.'[15]

Meanwhile, fortified by champagne, cognac, and beer, Graves stumbled back into Camp Sissone at 1 a.m. He was, in his own words, 'in a highly exhilarated frame of mind.' Even assigned at the S-1 at HQ, young Graves was still reeling from the alcohol.

> I had to be assured by about twenty different people before it finally sank in that it was anything but a joke. We were told the Germans had broken through the First Army front on about a fifty-mile line … By eight o'clock, groups of long, trailer-troop carriers began to arrive. We had heard the news on the radio early in the morning … Parachutists had been dropped and the Luftwaffe had been most active. This made the prospect of travelling in long, cumbersome vans in a large, slow convoy most undesirable. We would be a delicious target for the Luftwaffe if they came out … Our serial, the first, pulled out of the gate at Camp Sissone at 1017 hours for destination unknown. We were packed into the truck like sardines in a can. It was cold and damp. I had a bad headache and felt generally miserable … We all agreed that the situation must be pretty bad to throw us in helter-skelter. No one gave much of a damn about looking at the countryside.[16]

The soldiers motored into the spruce and fir forests of the Ardennes in the back of uncovered, rail-sided cattle flatbed trucks. 'We rode all day,' Glynn Arrington remembered. 'We rode toward Bastogne, but then went by that town and detrucked at Werbomont, Belgium. 'It was dark by that time and we could see buzz bombs going overhead on their way to Liège.'[17] 'It was misty and rainy,' recalled Frank Dietrich:

> At 3 a.m. [19 December] after our truck had become lost amid the confusion on the roads and in the pitch-black of night, we arrived at our destination, which turned out to be the little Belgian village of Werbomont ... We took over a Belgian farmhouse for a CP. The former GI occupants, we learned from the Belgian owner, had taken off in great haste for the rear at 5 p.m. the previous afternoon. Such was their hurry that they left behind a large pot of coffee, a full case of 10-in-1 rations, bread, and even uneaten pork chops ... I sat around the kitchen listening to the staff talking about the situation ... It was known that there was only one battalion of the 30th Division between us and the onrushing Germans ... We had no anti-tank support except our 57mm pea shooters ... I had three cups of delicious coffee while waiting for morning. The Belgian who owned the house groaned inwardly as we began to use up the bread, sugar, milk, coffee, and jam that our GI predecessors had left behind in our rush to the rear. He said that forty-six flying bombs had landed in Liège the day before. His family had fled westward on foot earlier in the day ... We got some news on the radio in the CP at 9.30 a.m. The BBC said the First Army was in retreat ...[18]

On Tuesday, 19 December the scattered truck columns of the 82nd Airborne collected in the area around Werbomont, preparing to move out to cover the roads east of that point. The 505th Regiment would move east to cover Trois-Ponts, while the 504th would move to the north-east to cover the area south of La Gleize where the enemy had pushed through the previous day. Meanwhile, the Belgian householder at the 504th headquarters hastily packed a suitcase and departed, imploring the airborne soldiers not to steal from his house. Corp. Graves had not slept in thirty-three hours:

> I was exhausted so about 3 p.m., I unrolled my pack and lay down on the floor to get some sleep. At 1730 hours Capt. Hauptfleisch shook me and told me to get up and be ready to move out immediately. I asked him whether it was forward or backward. He laughed and said, 'Forward.' That was how it always was, moving on a moment's notice. The colonel held a meeting of the Battalion commanders, after which Capt. Hauptfleisch gave us a briefing. The regiment was going to try to seize the town of Rahier about eight miles north-east of Werbomont. It was not clear if the enemy held the town. The 1st and 2nd Battalions were to move out at 1800 hours with headquarters company following the 2nd Battalion ... The night was pitch-black and we formed silently on the road outside the CP. A heavy fog had descended and the air was damp and chilly ... It was 1930 hours when the last of the 2nd Battalion passed us and we fell behind their column ... We set off at a pretty fast pace and despite the dampness of the night, I was soon sweating. The country was hilly and heavily wooded ... After marching about two miles, we began to hear the rumble of artillery, the first I had heard since coming to Werbomont ... I said a little prayer asking God to guide us through the night ... We arrived at the little village of Rahier at about midnight. There was a great deal of firing of all types to the north and east of us. A moon had come out so it was possible to see the houses in the village. Not a living thing outside ourselves stirred. The death-like calmness was eerie. After looking around the village without much success and banging on locked doors, I got the village schoolmaster out of bed ... He let us into his house. The staff took over

> the kitchen as a coal stove there was suitable for coffee … The battalions had all reached the area and were engaged in digging around the town for an expected attack.[19]

That night, Col Ruben Tucker received orders from Gen. 'Slim Jim' Gavin. Under his leadership the 504th would start to turn the vice on Peiper's forces from the south. Part of the mission would involve wresting Cheneux from the enemy, but one cautionary objective, too, would be to fend off Peiper should his tankers come crashing back down the road from La Gleize.

> At 7 a.m. I went down to the CP to do some interpreting as the colonel wanted to get the town completely evacuated of civilians to get them out of harm's way. I found the house attached to the dance hall crowded with children, old men, and women. It was hard to tell them that they must leave, quickly. One old lady about age 80 started to cry. I helped them carry some trunks full of clothes and china down into the cellar … I tried to impress upon them without scaring them too much that it was for their own good that they must leave. They grabbed a few scraps of food and some blankets and left on foot, going right down the road to Werbomont. It was a heart-rending sight to see an old couple hobbling along, leaning on each other. I didn't feel half sorry for the children as they were too young to know what it was all about.[20]

At daybreak on 20 December, the 504th prepared to seize Brume and Cheneux:

> All morning long, terrific firefights were going on in the surrounding area. The 2nd Battalion was dug in across the road from the house on a large sloping field … At about 1300 hours the 1st Battalion passed by the house on the road going toward Cheneux, which we heard was the battalion objective. The boys were in very high spirits and I heard one man shout out, 'Four more shopping days before Christmas. Pass it back.' That seemed like a hell of a good joke and the men roared with laughter. Lt [Robert] Madruga, who had just come back from the hospital in England the day before we pulled out for Belgium after being wounded in Holland, stopped off at the CP to joke with us and said he was still full of good old IPA [a British ale], which was a hell of a way to go into battle.[21]

Gen. Gavin wanted Tucker's 504th Parachute Infantry Regiment to clean out Cheneux and link up with the 505th Regiment at Trois-Ponts.[22] That would create an unbroken line along the Salm river to bar the enemy from thrusting west. The 1st Battalion commander issued orders for the assault in their assembly area in Rouge Thier.[23] Company A, under Maj. John T. Berry, was to seize the village of Brume, while the other two were to capture the village of Cheneux. Company A's assignment was easy; Brume was captured quickly on the afternoon of 20 December against only very light resistance.[24] Cheneux was another matter.

Unknown to Col Tucker, Peiper had situated strong forces in the town: Maj. Wolfgang von Sacken's 84th Flaksturm Abteilung with its five hundred men and fourteen flak wagons.[25] These featured four 20mm guns mounted on a half-track chassis – dangerous to strafing Allied aircraft, but lethal to any infantry caught in the fury of their guns.[26] The flak battalion also included sixteen light machine guns, and more than a score of Panzerfaust teams.

Beyond that force, the shot-up remainder of Ostuf. Heinz Tomhardt's 11th SS Panzer Grenadier Company arrived after big losses the previous day in Stoumont. Also, on the morning of 20 December, Cheneux was reinforced by the 6th and 7th Panzer Grenadier Companies of Hstuf. Schnelle's 2nd Battalion of the 2nd SS Panzer Grenadier Regiment.[27] These SS troopers from Kampfgruppe Sandig had just crossed at the Petit Spai bridge backed up by five 105mm guns of the 1st and 2nd Artillery Batteries.[28] All in all, the forces in Cheneux amounted to a reinforced battalion, albeit bristling with automatic weapons.

It was 1 p.m. on 20 December when the men of 1st Battalion marched off from Rahier in two staggered columns to seize Cheneux. In the lead, Company B under Capt. Thomas C. Helgeson walked cautiously up either side of the road, peering into a thick ground haze with only 200-yard visibility. Company C followed right behind. The C Company commander was a replacement officer with much less experience than many of the old-timers in the regiment. As S/Sgt Dietrich saw it, there were just too few of the 'Willi and Joe' types left. He wasn't pleased; their platoon leader, Lt Vern G. Freisinger, had never been in combat.

Led by Col Willard 'Willi' E. Harrison, the paratroopers came under fire from SS sharpshooters 500 yards east of Rahier. Sgt Dietrich could hear a loud racket ahead as soon they began to move. Having run into them many times in the past, he instantly identified the violent chatter of an MG 42. Dietrich hated them.

Back towards Rahier, Preuss's SS panzer grenadiers had abandoned a 7.5cm gun mounted on a half-track the day before, which was now brought up to lend support to the lightly armed airborne men.[29] Just before 3 p.m. the captured vehicle was ordered to go into position on the road between the attacking platoons. Driven by Pfc. Russell P. Snow – a clerk from regimental headquarters – the stubby, close-support gun was operated by Pfc. Harold Kelly and Pfc. Harry Koprowski of the regiment's 57mm anti-tank squad.[30] The men had never even seen such an enemy vehicle, must less fired its weapon, but after some lurching back and forth and blasting off two test rounds the half-track was ready to go. Seeing at the last minute that there would be no one to cover the driver and two impressed gunners, they knew help would be needed. Those driving and firing were certain to be a target for the enemy.

'Get on that damned half-track!' Capt. Helgeson yelled to two nearby BAR (Browning Automatic Rifle) men. Obediently, Pvt. Thomas A. Holiday and Buland Hoover mounted the German SPW pointing their automatic rifles off ahead. Soon they were clanking down the frozen road moving just ahead of the gaggle of airborne infantry trotting down the road.[31] Threatened with envelopment, the previously bold enemy squad fled down the road, one of the enemy being captured and another killed. The PW turned out to be a prisoner from the 6th Company, 2nd SS Panzer Grenadier Regiment, who reported the fighting had seen the company drop to ninety men from the 120 who had left Germany four days before.[32] While he said no tanks were in Cheneux, there were 'some flak wagons'.

B Company's third platoon on the right flank drew enemy fire. The second platoon leapfrogged above the third and swept the hillside, as skirmishers pushed forward. After moving about 300 yards further, they discovered and silenced another machine gun nest. Yet resuming the advance down the road into thick mists with only a 50-yard visibility, the airborne troops were soon confronted by a sudden fury of enemy fire as they pressed closer to Cheneux. 'We went down this road ahead of the company,' Holiday remembered, 'When we got down there, they were set up all across this hill. The Krauts had a hell of a lot of stuff down there.' Their armored half-track no longer felt so safe, 'There were 20mms zinging off all over this thing.'

Deploying with two platoons astride the road, Company B charged forward 400 yards out from the treeline across open pastures devoid of cover and criss-crossed by fences that ran perpendicular to the line of advance. Even though the left platoon set up a base of fire to cover the right platoon's advance, the enemy defenders opened a devastating hail of automatic bullet fire on the left platoon. Simultaneously, the move of the right platoon ended when it was pinned to the ground by devastating crossfire from two 20mm flak guns and two MG 42s.

Kelly and the BAR men in the captured half-track shot down an enemy effort to flank their position but were frustrated with the limited transverse of the 7.5cm gun. Shortly, German mortar fire began to drop on to the two pinned platoons, killing six men right away and destroying the company radio.[33] The support platoon, which remained on the edge of a copse of trees, attempted to turn the enemy right flank with the two forward platoons still paralysed under a rain of bullets.

Peiper's defensive rearguard had automatic weapons arrayed in depth as well as another flak wagon on the American right. These guns and a squad of SS infantry pinned the airborne flanking movement, and the German half-track fighting under American hands could only fire blindly into the tracer-laced fog. As dusk gathered, the American thrust was hit by enemy fire, with Pfc. Kelly wounded and ammunition exhausted. The driver instinctively pulled back. In the meantime, the Company B commander attempted to make contact with his battalion commander as well as the head of Company C. Under heavy fire and without radio, confusion spread. In the gathering ground haze before nightfall on 20 December, Company B pulled back 200 yards, where contact was finally re-established with Company C. A perimeter defense was set up at the edge of a densely wooded stand west of Cheneux and the assault platoons were sorted out and casualties evacuated. Mike Holmstock of Company B:

> At 6 p.m. it was getting dark and there was a fog settling in and we moved in a single-file line along the dimly lit road. We came out of the woods and into a clearing. Suddenly, there was machine gun fire and we circled back into the woods. We stayed in the woods for a little bit. We had a useless 2nd lieutenant with no combat experience. At one point there was a tree burst with phosphorous and he panicked thinking it was a gas attack. 'Piss in your handkerchiefs!' he yelled. 'And climb a tree!' We ignored him. We had all seen combat; he hadn't. The NCOs ran the show – take my word for it. The good officers got killed.[34]

Meanwhile, Cpl Fred Nix ordered a reconnaissance with the 3rd platoon and took a small patrol that reached the railway track, from where he was able to peer into the village. The long shadows of the blue-forested hills grew. Nix was an old-timer, too, and what he saw gave him pause – antennas rising from behind stone houses in the town. German armor lurked back there. At 1845 hours the B Company commander, Helgeson, was called for a meeting with his superiors. Nix and Dietrich had just got back from a patrol with news for the 1st Battalion: there were tanks in the town. As they left the meeting, they could hear SCR 300 radio at Harrison's CP with the voice of Col Rueben Tucker, the commander of the 504th, barking on it. 'Have I got to come down there and take you by the hand?'[35]

The airborne soldiers had few heavy weapons: a couple of anti-tank pieces and two M36 tank destroyers of Company B, 703rd Tank Destroyer Battalion. However, unlike the less-than-enthusiastic members of the army flak battalion fighting under the SS, the airborne troops who would fight for Cheneux that day were hardened veterans.

At dusk, Col Tucker ordered the leader of the 1st Battalion, Lt Col Harrison, to get going. 'We will take that town!' Tucker insisted. The new assault was to feature both B Company moving right of the road and C Company on the left with the two self-propelled M36 tank destroyers in support. In the early darkness, B and C airborne companies regrouped at the edge of the village. They would attack under the cover of darkness at 7.30 p.m. on both sides of the road with the two tank destroyers pushing with them down the road.

The B and C companies reached their assembly point in the woods west of Cheneux at about 7 p.m., only to be immediately pummelled by German mortar rounds. At 7.30 p.m. the new American assault moved off with B Company on the right and C company on the left. In particular, C Company had no cover at all, moving across naked pastures just south of Le Chêne Bois. B Company had trees to their right, but moved along the right shoulder of the road. After a gulp of whisky, the infantry advanced in four waves running at 50m intervals. They disappeared into the fog as they crossed the open fields east of Rahier.

The plan immediately went sour. 'For some reason, the 90mm guns revved engines, which only served to alert the enemy,' Dietrich remembered, 'and being shit-scared, the bastards did not move.' At the same time, the infantry flooding across the darkened pastures and fields on either side of the road found their way blocked. They became tangled in numerous barbed-wire fences that lay perpendicular to the assault. Streaming tracers illuminated the night. With only a single pair of wire cutters, Dietrich and the others of C Company attempted to thread through the closely spaced fences. Illuminating star shells burst overhead. 'Two or three fences before we reached the town, a Kraut mortar, and hand grenade came in.' 'Let's get them!' Dietrich yelled. Some ran forward and tried to bound over the fences. Many became ensnarled.

Company B on the right side of the road had pushed forward in four assault waves. The last wave was ordered to remain in the woods until instructed to move forward. That time came during the evening, with the assault moving across gently sloping ground – also devoid of cover – and negotiating four barbed-wire fences. As soon as they emerged from the woods to cover the 400-yard distance, the enemy caught Company B in the clearing by the right side of the road. The first two waves of airborne infantry were swept by devastating enemy fire, with many squads almost eliminated down to a single man. All but twenty-eight men of Company B were shot down and most of them sought cover in the woods that lined the south side of the road.

T/Sgt Dock O'Neal led the 1st platoon from the woods south of the main road. In spite of terrible enemy gunnery and coiled wire, O'Neal and a few survivors who were still standing now moved toward Cheneux. They tried to use any cover given by the trees on their right. As they approached a fork in the road, they spied a house in the gloom on the south side of the road.

Like a giant machine gun, a flak wagon in the home's shadow was firing into the trees, trying to chop down the advancing troopers. Flashes from its obscenely loud, multiple-gun barrels provided an eerie, strobe illumination of the crossroads as the big 20mm rounds cut down tree limbs and men alike. The sergeant directed ordered them to hit the flak wagon with a bazooka, but before the rocket could be launched, O'Neal was badly wounded in the leg by shrapnel. He rolled down the slope from the road, but soon managed to climb back up, seeing it had been hit by the bazooka round and was burning. A German soldier was trying to climb out of the burning vehicle and was on fire himself. O'Neal shot him down with his .45-calibre pistol.[36] Mike Holmstock:

> As it was getting dark, we formed a skirmish line. Tucker was informed we had pulled back to the treeline and he said: 'We never give up territory … the 504th motto is "Strike and hold."' Tucker was pompous – he had a strong ego. His orders: 'Take that town.' We came back out of the woods and entered the two-acre meadow on the slope of a hill at 6 p.m. There was a single strand of barbed wire to keep the cows at bay. The fellow next to me said he was a .30-calibre machine gunner. 'Would you take this box of MG ammunition for me?' 'Yeah, I'll take it.' I came to a first line of barbed wire and went over it. Next, I came to a second strand of barbed wire and I said, 'I'll go under this one.' Just as I tried to shimmy under the wire, all hell broke loose. Really, all hell. It was like a hundred machine guns opened up. I was *really* scared. I could see German tracers going over my head only inches away. I was scared as hell and lay as

> flat as I could and prayed. We were caught in the open field and I was right in the middle of it.

The assault resembled rushes across no-man's-land in the Great War. Like Company B, Company C on the left found itself still tangled in barbed-wire fences with many men cut down.[37] Few reached the western-most houses in Cheneux. 'We kept going forward,' Dietrich remembered, 'and kept losing people ... They just decimated us.' The advance stalled. The automatic weapons fire was the heaviest ever experienced by the 504th. Mme Boutet, hiding in her henhouse in Cheneux, was deafened by a German machine gun in front of her door. The Americans fired back. Her house was enveloped by machine gun bullets that blew out every window and smashed ugly holes in the walls. 'It was the most terrible fire anyone in our outfit had ever seen,' remembered Pfc. Glynn Arrington of Company B:

> They had enfilade fire (fire from two directions) on us and it was devastating ... The green men in the outfit wanted to look up at the tracers and I had to force their heads back down ... We continued on toward the town a few feet at a time ... there was barbed wire everywhere and it was slow ... I had never encountered fire like that ... It was inconceivable that anyone could live through that much fire ... There is no way to describe the terror ... Anyone who said they were not scared was not there or was a liar. We crawled about a half mile during the hours it took us to take the first building and get behind it. We got at that first building at about 8 p.m. ... The noise was deafening – you couldn't hear! And the stench of burned powder was overpowering. Men were dying all over the place; the wounded were moaning terribly. It is not like in the movies ... Here, in real life, when a man was hit he merely fell and if he were conscious, he would call a medic. We lost an awful lot of men there ... When a man got hit, if he smoked, the first thing he wanted was a cigarette, even before the medic would give him a shot of morphine. I heard many call out: 'Medic! Medic!' and then 'Will somebody please light me a cigarette?' ... After the men saw [Pvt.] Donald Simpson on the wire fence, dead from a 20mm shell, we did not have any more trouble getting them to keep their heads down ... Really there are no words in any language to describe the chaos.[38]

Company C was north of the road across from Company B, facing at least four light machine guns. Flares arced overhead. Trying to make his way forward across the barbed wire, Frank Dietrich saw men falling all around him. One was Pfc. Raymond D. Levy, the smallest man in the regiment, but one of the toughest. The Jewish boy was moving beside Dietrich when he was hit while scaling a fence. 'I can still see an awful vision in the battle. Levy carried an incendiary grenade and one of the tracers set it off. Hanging on the barbed wire, his body burned in a grotesque scene, illuminating the night.'

Leaving that hellish vision, Dietrich followed the glowing tracers. He darted forward, hugging the road. Mortars exploded; at one point, he was hit in the back by shrapnel, but it didn't seem too bad. Jumping up and sprinting ahead in the darkness, he suddenly found himself facing three Germans firing a machine gun close by the road. 'I spotted them the same time they saw me.' With his Thompson, he blazed away at the dugout as the Germans twisted the machine gun barrel toward him. Slugs from his Thompson killed the two men assisting the gunner, but the enemy weapon now flashed at him ominously. Rounds struck Dietrich's submachine gun and shattered his left hand.

Even yanking on the trigger with his arm strength, the gun refused to fire, but the man shooting at him was only a few yards away, Dietrich rushed toward him from the side. As the German turned to face him, Dietrich threw the 11lb submachine gun at him, squarely slamming into his chest. The man fell back in the foxhole just as Pfc. Orin Guidry came up beside Dietrich and killed the soldier before he could get up with a blast from his Browning Automatic Rifle. Although saved from death, Dietrich was wounded and without a weapon, having given his pistol to another soldier before the battle. 'I turned and started back and was determined to get to those 90mm SP guns that had failed to move forward and cost us so many men. If I had the goddamned pistol, I would have killed those bastards.'

> As I returned, I could see dead men everywhere. There were many wounded medics so those who were able were very busy. I came across Pfc. Danny Serilla, who had been shot in the head. It was the third time he was wounded, but he was still conscious. I supported him with my right arm and helped him back and took him to the aid station. It was a terrible scene; only darkness hid the gruesome scene there, but nothing protected you from the sound.[39]

Only twelve men were left in Dietrich's platoon of thirty-four. Five of the old-timers with his unit died before Cheneux: Ferrell, Fox, Bloomberg, Levy, and Duquette. The inertia of a third human wave of airborne soldiers carried the assault to the defending line, and the first house in the town was seized from the Germans. Survivors hugging the ground in Cheneux were soon witness to a cannon duel between the two American tank destroyers and the SS howitzers firing from the Delvenne farm.

In the meantime, the operations officer of the 504th sent an optimistic picture back to division mentioning only enemy losses from the interrogation of a prisoner from the 6th Company of the 1st SS Panzer Grenadier Regiment. '[Enemy] has no tanks – has flak wagons. Probably two more, but not certain. … Fight for Cheneux going well.'[40]

What 'well' meant seemed ridiculous even for a paper summary. Savage fighting raged through the fire-swept streets of Cheneux that night as the American airborne infantry stalked the killers on the flak wagons. A private of Company C slipped on to the shadowed deck of a 20mm flak gun and armed only with a knife climbed up and killed the gunner from behind. A desperate battle continued, too, for Company B. After the first two waves had been shot down by enemy machine guns, the third and then fourth waves rushed from the woods on the right side of the road with a war cry. These men pushed forward across the broken bodies in the fields and managed to reach the village by 10 p.m., where survivors of Company C were in a desperate fight. By this time there were no officers left in B Company, with more than sixty casualties suffered.

Mike Holmstock was nearly one of them. For what seemed like an eternity, he was stuck out in the field under fire. Petrified, he and others hugged the ground as tracers flashed overhead. As things trended even worse, S/Sgt William P. 'Knobby' Walsh rallied Holmstock and an additional dozen survivors to B Company to charge another 20mm flak gun. Halted by a 'wall of fire', Walsh crept within 20ft of the gun but was severely wounded when his left arm was pierced by shrapnel from a tree burst. Undeterred, Walsh got help from another trooper to pull its pin, crawling back to hurl the grenade into the flak wagon's cockpit, silencing its crew.

> That was the longest minute of my life. I prayed: 'I'll do anything to get out of here ... Three flak wagons were firing 20mm rounds on the road and had an MG gunner near the front wheels firing low. They were really spraying that field. One of my friends, [Melvin D.] Isbel, was wounded in the back. Total chaos – much yelling and screaming amid sheets of gunfire. Above the din, I heard Sgt 'Knobby' Walsh yell: 'Let's get the son of a bitches, they're killing us!' Later he came back from in front of me and shouted, 'Somebody get me a goddamned hand grenade!' He ran off and used one grenade to knock out one of the flak wagons ... Moving forward, I saw the first wagon and it was out of commission; Knobby had wiped it out. I came to the second one and standing right beside it, emptied the entire magazine of eight rounds into the cab and never stopped to look. It was an eerie scene; the darkness and fog was momentarily brightened by gun flashes.[41]

One hundred and twenty Germans were killed, and twenty-six were taken prisoner. 'Our boys practically beat them back with our bare knuckles,' claimed Lt Col Warren Williams, the commander of the 1st Battalion, 504th Parachute Infantry Regiment. In mid-afternoon, the battle raged fiercely; the most bitter fighting ever experienced in the war by the paratroopers. Dead Germans sprawled grotesquely beside their shattered vehicles. The knocked-out vehicles included three 20mm flak guns, several half-tracks, a reconnaissance car with an 81mm mortar, two towed 105mm guns, and two self-propelled guns. 'We cracked into them at night at the edge of this village,' Williams said after the battle, 'we had to fight them with anything we had.'

Sgt Al Vraback of Kansas City led the bazooka team that silenced many of the guns. 'These three flak wagons were giving us the most trouble,' he said. 'They set them up right in the middle of the street and turned them on us. I had six bazookas when this thing started. Now, I only got two, but we knocked out those guns.' 'After the bazooka men shot holes in the vehicles, we ran up and tossed grenades into them and killed the German crews,' said Sgt Samuel D. Crenzo. Sgt Michael Jalowey of Rhode Island, 'I never missed a day in Africa, Sicily, Italy, or Normandy, but this was the roughest I ever saw ... I didn't see how we could make it.'[42] Even so, by 5 p.m. Cheneux was partly in American hands.

Apparitions of SS men and American paratroopers stalked each other in the fog, some of the GIs taking momentary refuge in Cornélie Boutet's cellar. There was fighting inside the home while Mme Boutet hid in the henhouse. At the Delvenne house nearby, the Americans took possession of the house in a maniacal charge, only to be forced out by thrown hand grenades.

Corporal Graves was still in Rahier at headquarters with Col Reuben Tucker. Yet even there, remote from the Cheneux carnage, the scene was grim. Artillery shells crashed about, tracers blazed up the road, and V-1 buzz bombs chugged overhead. Meanwhile, the radio static was punctuated with shouted messages. Capt. Hauptfleisch brought in the first SS prisoner, who bragged that Tucker's headquarters would shortly be wiped out. The commander of his tank battle group, he said referring to Peiper, 'was already sure to be on the way to Antwerp!' Graves remembered:

> I was lying open-eyed, listening to the bursting crack of 20mm shells around the house with a great deal of apprehension, when Lt Madruga, whom I had just talked to earlier in the day, burst into the house bleeding badly from two wounds. He said they had to have more ambulances up in the 1st Battalion area in a hurry. A few moments later, Capt. [Charles W.] Duncan (Battalion S-3), an old soldier who had seen a lot of fighting as a company commander and was not one to be easily excited in the heat of battle, came in saying the 1st Battalion was being cut to ribbons.[43]

At nearby Monceau, the airborne attempted to support the assault of Cheneux by showering the village with bullets and missiles. However, their advance towards the main part of the village was met with deadly machine gun fire from the ridge. All the bazooka carriers and infantry squads were shot down or forced to the ground. Company C now penetrated the enemy main line of resistance and killed twenty in hand-to-hand fighting, but lost an equal number of their own. As the battle reached a climax, two enemy platoons fled from the town, which had become a hellish netherworld. The commanding officer of C Company was wounded, with the executive officer taking over and forlornly attempting to rally his men inside enemy positions. Meanwhile, another wave of infantry from C Company emerged from the woods in the darkness.

They, too, rushed toward the town as the Germans dropped mortars on them and swept their ranks with machine guns. By the time they reached the advanced positions in town 400 yards further on, another fifty casualties were suffered. At 10 p.m. the remaining three officers of the eight in the company sought to reorganize the shattered platoons.

Attempts to rally the survivors of Company B and C under S/Sgt Clyde A. Ferrier to forward movement in Cheneux were met by heavy fire from yet another 20mm flak wagon 200 yards further on. In the tracer-lined darkness the M-36 TD could not see the enemy and would not move forward. At that point the battalion commander took things into his own hands and ordered the reserve light-machine gun platoon forward under his personal leadership. However, reaching the enemy lines and throwing down tripods, they were plastered by 20mm gunfire from a flak wagon that methodically killed the crews of five of the eight machine guns.

> From every side, from what seemed like every square yard of ground, the wounded screamed and moaned for morphine … Jeeps and ambulances raced up to where the wounded lay.[44]

In desperation, the battalion commander ordered the tank destroyer forward with parachute infantry clinging to their deck. Even though the infantry had to dive for the ditches when the TD came under fire, the 90mm gun fired two rounds, one of which hit and blew a flak wagon apart. That night the battalion commander established a temporary CP in a knocked-out half-track in town, attempting to organize his depleted infantry platoons in a defensive perimeter to ward off any attempted enemy counterattack.

By 11 p.m. when the regimental commander, Col Tucker, arrived at the CP, the 1st Battalion had tenuous control of Cheneux and the decision was made to attempt to push on to the river. 'Ninety men dug in with Panzerfausts and flak weapons contacted,' Tucker optimistically radioed to division just after 11 p.m. 'Opposition at Cheneux *fini* except one flak wagon.' Yet forty-five minutes after announcing *fini,* Tucker was calling for the elimination of five flak wagons hitting them with punishing fire from the village.[45] Feldwebel Karl Laun described the scene from the other side:

> The din in the village of Cheneux is maddening, a fact to which I can personally testify as I am selected to stay at the bridge. In vain I do try to point out to Herr Major Sacken that an employment of our pieces near the bridge is suicide plain and simple. For an incessant artillery and mortar fire seems to be zeroed in on this point. I inspect the first piece and already find one man of the crew wounded. He is evacuated. I return and hear that another man has disappeared without a trace – probably by a hit. And then I find Lt Porep severely wounded. When I place the unfortunate guy at the major's feet, Sacken becomes concerned over his own safety. In the meantime, I have already taken it upon myself to order the survivors of my platoon to retreat. Simultaneously, the SS was cajoled into new positions behind Cheneux by threats, kicks, and curses of their officers. At night, American infantry counterattacks twice. We suffer heavy casualties …[46]

So heavy were American losses that night that at 1.50 a.m. on 21 December there was a lull in the fighting where stretchers were brought forward to evacuate the wounded. Just over half an hour later, Col Tucker flashed word to the division: 'HAVE TOWN (CHENEUX).' Meanwhile, during the momentary suspension in the fighting, the Germans continued to force the civilians out of their cellars to evacuate them to the school. '*Zur Kirche!*' They were escorted down the road by a white flag. The church was hardly a refuge.

As the battle picked up once more in the night, a Mk VI Königstiger ground forward by the chapel and with each gun blast the walls of the entire structure trembled. Through the church windows, the surroundings turned blood red – four farms were blazing.[47] Those inside expected each hour to be their last.[48] Mike Holmstock:

> From the other side of the house came a Kraut half-track backing out toward the road I was on and I fired back and they immediately pulled in behind a house. We never did go in the house and got no fire from inside.
>
> I crossed the road and standing next to the house I noticed there was a doorway at the ground floor. I went on back down to the back of the house. The half-track went to the other end of the field and resumed firing … I ducked down and realised I had been hit between the eyes with a piece of shrapnel and started to bleed. Soon I could taste blood in my mouth. I thought, *You can get killed in this goddamned place …* Not sure what had happened that night. It was all a blur. I do remember fighting by the church … there was firefight in the cemetery there. Behind that was a barn used for cows and there was some light there from burning buildings and I could see silhouettes of soldiers in combat. It was like cowboys and Indians. We slowly picked off the German defenders and then hid until the next victim was found. Everyone had their own private war.'[49]

When dawn arrived the following morning, the battle resumed with undiminished violence. 'Receiving quite a lot of 20mm and SP fire,' the 504th reported to division at 5.05 a.m., 'but town is still under our control.' Yet less than three hours later, at 7.45 a.m., the Germans began a half hour artillery preparation on the American positions, followed by a rush forward by enemy infantry back into the town. Part of the SS infantry of 7th Company had arrived back from Stoumont with orders to help stabilise the situation in Cheneux.

Even with renewed street fighting, the German counterattack failed and another flak wagon was destroyed in the early morning by a direct hit by an American 81mm mortar. The SS assault wave was shredded. The panzer grenadier company commander, SS Hstuf. Leopold, was killed and Hstuf. Herbert Schnelle, in charge of II Battalion, was badly wounded.[50] Most of the 84th Flak Sturm Battalion now pulled back, but Tucker's plan of pushing on to the bridge was abandoned. 'Ran into stiff opposition; fighting is on right now.' Still, the 1st Battalion was so damaged that nothing more could be expected than clinging to their tenuous hold in Cheneux. Company B was finished. When daylight revealed the scene in Cheneux, Glynn Arrington confronted disturbing scenes. 'Everywhere you ran, you were dodging body parts … It was a really gruesome place.'[51] On the German side, Karl Laun was getting out:

> A German counterattack at dawn is stifled by enemy fire. Nobody shows any inclination to fight – not even the SS. As a matter of fact, they are the first ones to withdraw. Suddenly, one of our tanks makes an appearance near the bridge.

> Again, a frantic solicitation for gasoline. Draining all vehicles, including the Volkswagen, and the wrecked prime movers, we scrape 30 gallons together. The Tiger continues toward Cheneux.[52] I am damned glad I don't have to be in the inferno prevailing in that village.

Mike Holmstock with the airborne:

> There were many casualties. Only eighteen of our company were left standing after daybreak. I looked at the field the next morning and the field was red with blood and broken, smouldering equipment and tires. Helmets, packs, rifles strewn about. Dead men lay everywhere and many bandaged wounded were walking about. The next morning I was at the back of the house we held. The walls were only two cinder blocks high and Pfc. Johnny Barton sat next to me … Why are you shaking?' I asked. 'Same reason you're shaking.' I couldn't hold a glass of water.[53]

Meanwhile, the 3rd Battalion attacking from the fields south of Cheneux remained pinned down by German fire. Amid growing awareness of near tactical disaster, Col Tucker altered his plan of action, swinging two companies of the 3rd Battalion under Lt Col Julian A. Cook to the south side of Cheneux to attack up from the Monceau road. Luckily for Tucker, fog obscured the view of his men, surging forward in bull rushes – above the Cheneux position. If the that manoeuvre had not been hidden from the enemy, it too, would likely have been shot to pieces.

By dint of great effort, by 4 p.m. on 21 December several of Cook's infantry companies assembled in a copse of trees. They suddenly fell upon the German positions from the north – a direction that thwarted the carefully sited flak guns and MG 42s that had murderously denied the approaches from the south and west. Now, the renewed assault – knots of men sprinting through the streets, farms, woodsheds, and the ancient mill armed with carbines, submachine guns, and even knives – grappled with the German troops who emerged to meet them in single combat. Soldiers shot each other with automatic weapons at point-blank range and grenades exploded just beyond arm's reach.

In the middle of the little hamlet in the gathering gloom at the end of the day, several fires illuminated the cruel arena – 200m of Belgian dairy farmland strewn with dead bodies, burning houses, and animal corpses. By 9 p.m. of 21 December the Germans had mostly been forced from Cheneux, killed, or captured.[54] The German survivors fled across the railway bridge over the Amblève river to join Kampfgruppe Peiper in La Gleize. Elements of the 504th's 3rd Battalion liberated the La Vaux Renard farm on the east edge of Cheneux, which housed many wounded. The next morning, the American paratroopers gingerly approached the church in Cheneux and released its shaken civilian inhabitants.

Maurice Prince crawled carefully from hiding in his attic loft, ecstatic to be alive after all the shooting, bombs, and burning. He emerged into the foggy light to an epiphany. He felt, he himself had become a Belgian Lazarus. He persuaded one of the U.S. airborne soldiers to let him milk his bellowing cows. Then, feeling beyond harm, Prince nearly danced his way back past the smoking ruins. Afterward, the Belgian farmer chewed on a stale sugar beet. After a two-day fast of fear, the vegetable tasted like manna from heaven. It was a tiny spark of hope amid devastation, but for Maurice Prince, it was a new life.

Chapter 23

PROFESSOR NATALIS

No clever fighter disdains his foe.[1]

Professor Ernest Natalis was an improbable man to find in the diminutive Belgian town of Stoumont.[2] Before the Second World War, the professor was a schoolteacher there and a sizeable fish in a small pond. Stoumont was in the heart of Wallonia, 45km south of Liège, but was not particularly noteworthy. Yet as the Stoumont schoolmaster, Natalis believed it was his duty to imbue his pupils with all of the historical significance that their 130-dwelling settlement deserved. The village was picturesque and bucolic – a cluster of dwellings on a jutting hillside plateau that ranged above a forested rise and fall of beech, spruce, and birch.

The region drew its origins from an old Roman road that crossed the property. It had been inhabited by the Eburon tribe as far back as 57 BC. In time, Stavelot–Malmedy became a principality of the Holy Roman Empire under St Remacle. In AD 651 the King of the Franks, Siebert the 3rd, deeded Stoumont. Like most of the surrounding fiefdom, Stoumont had not escaped the wars that were periodically sweeping through the region. In 881 the Normans ravaged the area and the English–French Hundred Years' War eventually lead the Lord of Froidcour to build a fortified castle with towering turrets of grey slate that strategically overlooked the entire valley from one mile east of the village. That military accomplishment seemed not to have helped its owner, for, on 24 October 1415 the lord was felled by arrows on the field of battle at Agincourt. In 1794, in the French Revolutionary War, the left flank of the defeated Austrian armies had streamed through Stoumont when French General Jean-Baptiste Jourdan prevailed.[3] Yet, there was no fighting.

The real event that became the catalyst for modern Belgium was Napoleon's singular defeat at Waterloo on 18 June 1815, which led to the Treaty of Versailles. Stoumont's only real claim to a piece of that history was that one of its citizens, Monsieur Leroy, was killed fighting for Napoleon that day. For centuries Stoumont and its deep, hilly forests had been known for its clean air. To take advantage, in 1912 a large rest home and rehabilitation center was built there to house the elderly. St Edouard's Sanatorium was a quarter of a mile outside the north-western outskirts of town. Modern times did little to change the place. Agriculture was king, and the railway coursing through the valley along the gurgling Amblève river helped commerce. The First World War had seen little happen in the town, but everyone there was aware of the terrible stories of German civilian massacres along the Meuse river not far away in August 1914.[4] When the Germans came through in May 1940, there was no fighting in Stoumont, only billets. The peaceful town knew little of the war's earlier turmoil.

Other than the unsavory character of the local NSDAP Gestapo office, the German occupation of Stoumont in 1940 was nothing unusual, for unlike Stavelot, there was little organized activity by the Belgian *Armée Blanche*. There was keen awareness of the violence of their Teutonic neighbors to Belgians to the east thirty years before. 'We are happy they did not renew the horrors of Dinant and Aerschot,' Natalis recalled. 'We recognised it as good grace.'[5]

The 500 inhabitants living in the village looked up to Natalis for good reason. The professor was a Renaissance man – an accomplished, well-read scholar who spoke fourteen languages. Natalis was a fine-looking Belgian of average height, presenting a professorial air in the way he carried his thin frame. At 47, he was losing his hair and had a small moustache, adding to his studious appearance. The professor was devotedly Catholic. In January 1944, a German aeroplane crashed in the hills just north of Stoumont and Natalis insisted that the townspeople should go up to the crash site to help the wounded. 'Somebody has got to help them,' the professor explained. 'They are human beings.' There were survivors – some burned – and Natalis saw to it that the injured were brought to the attention of the village physician, Dr Rene Robinson.

Personally, Natalis was devoted to his wife, Alice, who bore him six children. One of these, 14-year-old Therese was with her father in Stoumont at their home near the school on 17 December 1944. She was there when rumours of the German offensive swept the village. The proceeding night they watched with dread and fascination at the sparks of gunfire in the eastern night sky was accompanied by distant booming. Natalis said nothing to the children. But that night, the Americans drove into town in a manner Natalis had never before seen. They always seemed so casual that autumn. This was different.

Lt Col Roy G. Fitzgerald knew nothing of the history of Stoumont, nor Ernest Natalis, when he rushed the companies of his 3rd Battalion, 119th Infantry Regiment into the village that evening. Fitzgerald's men moved into Stoumont with little opportunity for sleep or looking about. They had little idea of the lay of the land, much less enemy dispositions.[6] With a central location, he impulsively chose the Natalis home across from the school as their command post. Many 'Old Hickory' riflemen were unaware they were now in Belgium rather than Germany, from where they had trucked the night before.

On paper, Fitzgerald's battalion was slightly understrength, but had two platoons with eight towed 76mm guns from the 823rd Tank Destroyer Battalion. Sensing a critical assignment, Gen. Hobbs allotted ten M4 Shermans from Company C of the 743rd Tank Battalion to Col Edwin M. Sutherland, the commander of the 119th Infantry Regiment. Sutherland, in turn, provided the reinforcements to Fitzgerald. However, these were not yet in place; they would only arrive at the 119th CP at 6.15 a.m. on the 18th. Theoretically, the 3rd Battalion also had the dedicated fire of eighteen self-propelled M7 'Priest' 105mm howitzers of the 400th Field Artillery Battalion. Yet, at daybreak these were just reaching firing positions south of the Amblève and some 6km west of Stoumont at Chession. With all the confusion, they were blind; there were no forward observers in place.

As soon as Fitzgerald set up his CP in the Natalis' kitchen, the house bustled with runners – some coming in to ask directions as they were lost in the darkness. Other elements were located in the school across the way. Static-laced messages crackled over the radios as the U.S. Army set up guard points. Natalis was fascinated by the scene, but knew enough to move the rest of his family into his home's basement.

As the night wore on, the professor – clearly understanding the English GI lingo – gathered that the Germans were getting close. At 1.45 a.m. word came from excited riflemen that an enemy tank hit a hasty minefield laid by I Company. The incident took place on an unpaved farm track 200m north of the main N33 road. In fact, the vehicle that exploded was an SPW mistaken for a tank by American soldiers watching in the dense fog.[7] By 5 a.m. two 3in guns – part of Company A, 823rd Tank Destroyer Battalion – radioed Fitzgerald that they had to pull back under fire.

Details came later; the gun crews were surprised by more enemy half-tracks that materialised out of the mist. Just before dawn the battle noise picked up. Natalis could see the American commander looked increasingly worried. Having only taken over command of the 3rd Battalion after the Roer river offensive, it was Fitzgerald's first combat action. 'Gentlemen,' Fitzgerald worried to his orderlies, 'it looks like we may all be prisoners tomorrow.'[8]Natalis had never heard such words from American soldiers. He hurried to the cellar.

Inside the basement's damp recesses, Henri-Joseph Natalis, the professor's elderly father, and Alice with their six children sat quietly. Natalis announced he was about to set off for Dr Robinson's house on the east edge of town. There, maybe he could see what was happening. He left parting words: under no conditions were they to leave the cellar nor even go upstairs. Knowing he might run into the Germans, Natalis grabbed a few items that might come in handy. With that, the village professor swung the door open, ascended the steps, and disappeared into the fog.

Another puzzled citizen of Stoumont that morning was 21-year-old Raymond Beco. A typical young Belgian, he still could not believe on 16 December that the Germans might be coming back. Raymond had been 16 in 1940, and even though short in stature, was called up for the Belgian reserves just before the German onslaught. Beco experienced military defeat in the disastrous days of May 1940, where even the Chasseurs Ardennais could not protect their own. Eventually, he returned home to the occupation that stretched on for four years. Yet, after the U.S. Army liberation in September 1944, Beco felt safe because of the laid-back comportment of the Americans. The Germans were gone.

That autumn in Stoumont, there were 'cowboy' engineers – C Company of the 291st Engineer Combat Battalion – living in their 'castle,' the Château Froidcour.[9] For these Americans, life seemed humdrum as Christmas approached. Beco, like many other Belgians, sought to find the way back to a normal life. On Saturday, 16 December, he and friends travelled to Verviers to see the movie *The Mark of Zorro*. Yet when the youths came out of the theatre, the heroism of Tyrone Power and libidinous visions of the lovely Linda Darnell faded like vapour. In front of the marquee, they were greeted by the booming of distant gunfire. A lot of traffic seemed to be moving towards the Baraque Michel.[10]

More than puzzled, Beco stayed in Verviers overnight, but returned to Stoumont the following day. The road was clogged with refugees relating fantastic rumours, all the time hustled along by military traffic going the other way. All the same, Raymond arrived in time for church service on Sunday evening. Nothing felt out of the ordinary, but at the end of Mass someone ran excitedly down the spiral staircase. 'The Germans are coming back!' Raymond shook his head; he couldn't believe it.

Each Sunday evening, a group of Raymond's friends would get together to make music – happy jazz. Beco played the piano, another squeezed the accordion, while still another added sweet tones from a saxophone. The party was in La Gleize that night, where there were twenty-one young people gathered. By now, the word of the German threat was on everyone's lips. The famous Sunday party fizzled. Sullen youths departed.

The next morning, 18 December, Beco and other locals could hear the Germans moving down the road from La Gleize to Cheneux. Soon, American Piper L-4 observation planes swooped down over the panzer column, followed by angry AA guns firing. Then, the vectored American fighter-bombers came in and strafed. Raymond was in his house in Stoumont and even from there he could see the fighters looking like metallic birds flitting past his window. That seemed enough for his father, Emile, who gathered up his entire family – Raymond had four sisters – and headed for St Edouard Preventorium that afternoon. It was stout. Maybe they would be safe there.

In time, Beco and his family took refuge in the sanatorium cellar along with more than two hundred others. Not much happened that night, so he came out of St Edouard's and found American soldiers casually smoking cigarettes in half-tracks posted on the street. The GIs asked Beco if he knew where the Germans were. 'I don't know,' Beco told one who spoke French, 'but I saw them earlier today on the road to Cheneux and they might come up the road.' He motioned toward the Château Froidcour. Beco thought the Americans were clueless. They didn't even seem to know about the road that came into town from the chapel. Even his brief stint with the Belgian army told him they were badly positioned. All the same, he ducked back inside.

At the Château Froidcour, the center of local blue-blood nobility, the head housekeeper, Céleste Masson, was awakened by the rumble of vehicles on the road in front of the castle. Trucks? The day before, Company C of the 291st Engineer Combat Battalion had hurriedly left the Froidcour at noon to head for Malmedy. As the last of the American vehicles departed, the caretaker had painstakingly removed all signs of the U.S. Army star from the courtyard. The event dismayed Capt. Lawrence Moyer and the Americans who had been there all autumn.[11]

Now, Masson could be pleased with his foresight. That Tuesday, the housekeeper warily looked out from the ground floor while 20-year-old Chantal de Harenne peered from the three-storey-high castle turret. In the distance, the young Belgian woman saw vehicles approaching from the east. They were not the familiar drab-green color. She ran down to warn others. Although young Chantal saw the German column approach from her high vantage, Masson on the ground floor did not.[12] The housekeeper prepared to go out and feed the cattle as he always did. When he arrived at the farm courtyard in the gloomy dawn, German soldiers approached. '*Amerikaner?*' they asked. Masson waved his hands, feigning surprise. '*Non!*' he said, '*Seulement les vaches!*' – only the cows. He went about feeding the animals although chilled by the sight of silver threaded runes on their collars: SS men. When he was done, Masson decided it was time to make himself scarce.[13] One of those Germans arriving was Jochen Peiper himself.

In the misty night, the SS leader reached La Gleize. From there, he motored a little further east to make his headquarters at the building on the east side of the Château Froidcour – the caretaker's house. The impressive medieval castle was a perfect headquarters for Peiper – a dominating, stout structure with stone ramparts, 360-degree fields of fire, and two high turrets with a dominating vantage. On the unusual clear day in the High Ardennes, one could see the entire valley all the way to Stoumont. To the south, there was an expansive view of Cheneux and the rolling terrain below. And from the east side of the castle heights, if fog did not obscure, an observer could see as far back as Trois-Ponts.

Just before dawn on 19 December, Peiper's divisional liaison, Hstuf. Gerhard Nüske, arrived at the Froidcour to give his commander an unwelcome message from Wilhelm Mohnke: Stavelot had been recaptured by the Americans. His supply line was cut. Where was the Fallschimjäger that were supposed to have secured that place? Were the Luftwaffe ground formations worthless? The unemployed Hermann Göring conscripts knew more about Paris than fighting. At least Peiper had a clutch of the old-guard German paratroopers – borrowed Skorzeny men. These were from 12th Company, Fallschirmjäger Regiment z.b.V. (*zum bersondern Verwendung*: for special duty) that had ridden his tanks all the way from Losheim – changing from the fuel-challenged Tigers to Panthers at Stavelot. Rather than from the 3rd Fallschirmjäger Division, they were part of Skorzeny's assigned troops for Panzer Brigade 150. They would still be fighting from Peiper's tanks in Stoumont.[14] He desperately needed infantry support to fight with his tanks.

Beyond distraction with tottering logistics, Peiper still fixed his attention on the westbound N33. He ordered immediate preparation of all operational tanks of the panzer regiment to be thrown down that road, supported by Diefenthal's 3rd Battalion/2nd SS Panzer Grenadier Regiment. Bolstered by elements of the 9th SS Panzer Pioneer Company, the tough paratroopers would march south, parallel to the road, using thick woods to mask their approach. The self-propelled infantry guns of the 13th SS Panzer Grenadier 2nd Regiment would bombard from La Gleize as needed. Peiper planned to hit Stoumont with everything he had – which, in spite of post-war tallies, was not all that much. Nevertheless, he would throw everything into the fray.

Peiper had some thirty-five tanks in La Gleize: one Königstiger, twenty-one Panthers, five Mk IVs, and one Flakpanzer IV.[15] Eventually, four more Tiger IIs would arrive from Cheneux along with the Flakpanzer IV of Karl Wortmann from the misadventure toward Werbomont. One token Panzer IV of the 7th Company under Oskar Klingelhöfer also showed up, albeit without the rest of the company.[16] The driver, Rolf Ehrhardt, had nursed the tank to La Gleize by scrounging fuel wherever he could find it, but now in Wanne he and Klingelhöfer left their ailing #701 and exchanged Panzer IVs with Rttf. Walter Eichhorst. Peiper worried that for the first time in the offensive, his Kampfgruppe was split up; about half of the strength of the tank regiment remained on the other side of the river with no bridge now to reach him.[17]

Beyond that, all offensive plans were dominated by the supply situation. While a small truck convoy from Kaiserbaracke–Logbierme–Wanne had reached him by crossing the light bridge at Petit Spai just before dawn, that drop in the bucket was insufficient for his fuel-thirsty panzer group. They were able to bring some fuel and evacuate a few wounded.[18] Still, there was not nearly enough petrol to move most of his armor west and have any chance to advance. 'My Panthers and Tigers can't eat hay,' Peiper had complained.[19] A standard consumption unit, a *Verbrauchssatz*, of 100km for the heavily motorised Kampfgruppe Peiper required at least 10 metric tons of petrol in the mountainous Ardennes terrain to even get close to the Meuse.[20]

During 18 December, just before midnight, half a dozen Mk IV tanks of the 6th Panzer Company arrived from Wanne-Stavelot; the rest of Junker's company remained too short on fuel to reach Peiper. The added armored strength was to supplement the bulk of SS Ostuf. Friedrich Christ's 2nd SS Panzer Company that was to take over the job as the spearhead panzer unit for the first time.

As the entire tank column turned arduously around after being rebuffed at the blown Habiemont bridge, the 1st Panzer Company that had led the advance from Cheneux was now at the rear of the inverted procession and also lowest on fuel. With their tank crews exhausted from the failed dash to Neufmoulin the preceding day and fuel tanks nearly empty, Peiper would leave the eight tanks of Hennecke's 1st Panzer Company in reserve in La Gleize.[21] They would wait for resupply and function as a reserve. Indeed, Hans Hennecke's own

Panther #111, which had broken down after the Stavelot battle with engine trouble near the Petit Spai Bridge, would be repaired by driver Bahnes in time to make the trip and become the very last tank to reach Peiper in La Gleize.

The tank strength for the attack on Stoumont on the morning of the 19th totalled thirteen Mk Vs, with three to five Mk IVs from the 6th Panzer Company that would follow the assault as a second echelon.[22] To add to that were more than a dozen SPWs laden with infantry of the 11th Company and an SPW assault gun platoon (7.5cm guns) of the 12th Panzer Grenadier Company. With elements of Rumpf's 9th Panzer Pioneer Company, Peiper would send infantry filtering through the woods south and north of La Gleize to trap the Americans.

Alongside the new company leadership, the commander of Peiper's 1st Panzer Battalion, Werner Poetschke, transferred to the mount of Panther #201, the command tank of SS Ostuf. Freiderich Christ and the 2nd Panzer Company. Although Christ had been with the tank regiment for some time – having been wounded in Normandy and five times before that in the war – he had only commanded his company for a month.[23] That situation was an example of the officer-costly system of leading from the front that was so pervasive in the Waffen SS. Along in the attack would be both Werner Poetschke and Hans Gruhle (Peiper's adjutant), and himself.[24] Peiper would co-ordinate the show from just to the rear.

Experience was not the only problem in the leadership of the panzer regiment. According to Erich Rumpf, while Christ was a favorite with Werner Poetschke, he was not well liked. 'He was arrogant against all the other company leaders and was always bragging,' the commander of the 9th Panzer Pioneer Company would later write. 'Christ was always talking big during the war games, but in real combat he was weak. He was a word hero.'[25] At first, Hans Gruhle had been at the rear of the column with the supply trains. Some said it was because Peiper was already concerned at the beginning of the attack about the importance of maintaining an unbroken fuel supply. Yet some in the know in the 1st Panzer Battalion said it was because Gruhle himself was not aggressive enough for Peiper. Arndt Fischer was more favored in the front-line adjutant role by both Peiper and Poetschke.[26]

Meanwhile, Erich Rumpf's ears were likely burning, too. Bernhardt Dietz, training for the Leibstandarte, had gone AWOL in Westphalia, finding himself shipped off to the penal platoon of Rumpf's 9th Panzer Pioneer Company. Arriving near Ligneuville on 19 December, Dietz found that members of the punishment platoon kept to themselves and were considered such misfits and untouchables that they were not allowed to mingle with the other units. Still, while he was camped there, he spoke with an SS trooper named Jansen, who told him about how dozens of American prisoners had been shot down two days before on the road south of Malmedy. This was the kind of organization he had fallen into. Soon Dietz learned that Rumpf, himself, was exceedingly unpopular with the luckless men of his *Strafzug* (the punishment platoon). 'Rumpf had given orders that anyone who talked about this murder would be shot.'[27]

Condemned for cowardice earlier on 19 December by Werner Poetschke, Christ would get a chance to show his mettle. The attack plan beyond Stoumont that afternoon seemed certain to lead his steel steeds straight into the enemy. In any case, from La Gleize, Peiper planned to knife past Stoumont, recrossing the Amblève west of Targnon near Lorcé, and then race to Aywaille before continuing on for the Meuse. Still, Christ's tanks seemed certain to run into the enemy.

In the meantime, SS Ustuf. Rolf Reiser was waiting on the road from Cheneux for Poetschke to pass back toward La Gleize. He was to report to him for duty. Learning that his future superior was with Christ's Panzer #201, Reiser flagged it down. Sure enough, Werner Poetschke popped out. He had been transferred to his command, Reiser told him. Poetschke ordered him to board the tank, intending to bring him up to speed on the situation.

Inside the tank, Poetschke spoke impatiently. Since his adjutant, Arndt Fischer, had been wounded as well as his ordnance officer, Kurt Kramm, Rolf Reiser would immediately become his new adjutant. Reiser agreed. Somebody might tell him why the entire tank column was going backward. 'Tanks could not advance on the road,' Poetschke told Reiser, 'because the bridge was out.' They would recoil a few kilometers and take a different path to the Maas. Had he seen a supply column to the rear? 'The fuel in the tanks would soon be exhausted,' Presently, they arrived in a village, which Reiser learned was La Gleize as they dismounted. Reiser's first task: order all the tanks to line up bumper to bumper along the road that led west from La Gleize. He then ushered the company and platoon commanders to Poetschke's headquarters in the village.

It was completely dark when Poetschke told him he was headed off to find Peiper. An hour later, Reiser came to a stone farmhouse in La Gleize to find a meeting there just breaking up. 'After that, Poetschke gave the order of attack on Stoumont to the company commanders and went to sleep for one or two hours.'[28] Stoked by cigarettes and coffee, Peiper stayed up to manage the preparation for the move he hoped would at least spring his tanks free. Leaving La Gleize proper, he moved his forward CP to the Château Froidcour. At 2 a.m. the fourth platoon of the 11th Panzer Grenadier Company arrived by the castle in their SPWs. Peiper ordered them to park their vehicles and steal though the woods to check for the enemy on the N33 up ahead.

The small force of grenadiers was gone all night stumbling in the darkness, but sent word that the N33 was clear. Other sections of the company moved forward in their SPWs and stole into the edges of Stoumont, removing mines in the night and bringing the U.S. tank-destroyer guns under fire. 'In the darkness and the fog, visibility was zero' and three of the four American TDs in town were soon abandoned or destroyed. They succumbed to confused encounters with the enemy on foot and half-tracks that appeared as if apparitions almost on top of the gun positions.[29] Waffen SS disdain for the enemy manifested once more. Members of the fourth platoon claimed to have shot seven American prisoners being sent to the rear 700m west of the Château Froidcour.[30] Whether this was true or not, for Peiper back at the caretaker's house by the Froidcour, it mattered little. He would attack immediately.

Peiper's tactical method remained uninventive – a sudden charge of armor and men before the sun rose. It always worked on the Eastern Front. Yet here in the west, shell-happy American artillery and their buzzing air force could ruin such hammer-blow tactics by raining explosives before Peiper's combat teams pushed forward to engage the enemy. That was what had happened to Herbert Kuhlmann at Avranches in Normandy.[31] It was the reason to hit when observers were blind or sleeping. 'The night is a friend of the weak,' Peiper's said over and over.

However, on 19 December the SS panzer leader looked approvingly on the dense mist hugging the Amblève Valley. Nature's own smoke would hide his weakness – too little infantry, too few cannon, not even enough tanks. Still, under the fog, he would attack with everything he had to give the impression of a much larger force At least with the dense fog, both the hated U.S. Army Air Force and their artillery would be blind. In a battle without lots of artillery, the Americans would have to stop him with rifles and manoeuvres. The curving narrow roads and steep hills were another consideration:

> I immediately proceeded to reconnoitre Stoumont. The results of the reconnaissance were that heavy enemy concentrations were in Stoumont. Upon that I planned and prepared an attack on the town on Stoumont for the early hours of the 19th. Contrary to my first plan, I was not able to attack Stoumont at dawn because there was a heavy fog. The attack began at 9 a.m. [sic].[32] The terrain was very unfavorable. I was hardly able to make use of my tanks. The enemy had dominating positions, a large number of anti-tank guns, and tanks also.[33]

At 3 a.m. an SS reconnaissance vehicle exploded on top of a mine laid by Company I. At 6.45 a.m. American mortars commenced to fall. True to Peiper form, at 6.15 a.m. a phalanx of eleven Panthers surged toward Stoumont, striking down the road and pushing into town from the south. Five Panzer IVs of the 6th Panzer Company would follow up as the second echelon. 'The attack was favored by fog,' Peiper would recall years later. His tanks were supported by the fire of three 'crickets' – self-propelled, 150mm infantry guns. Peiper ordered the tanks deployed off road, to the extent possible, because staying on that path 'would mean being shot down with certainty. The center of gravity was to the right of the road, carried out by our own weak infantry, with the tanks providing fire protection.'[34]

At 7 a.m., with the 9th Panzer Pioneer Company in support, another lead vehicle hit a mine, which seemed to be the signal for a shooting duel.[35] 'Because of the terrain, tanks were unable to leave the road,' Peiper recalled. 'Strong fire from Stoumont and heavy flanking fire from the north from your (U.S.) 30th Infantry Division checked our attempts to enter Stoumont.'[36] So dense was the fog that by the time the American saw the enemy, the SS tanks were already among them and overrunning elements of Company A, 823rd TD Battalion.

'We used the technique of sending in two to three tanks at maximum speed and eventually broke into and cleared out the village.'

What had it been like on the receiving end? Having sighted the enemy's campfire bivouac the night before, S/Sgt Walter Kos was now waiting anxiously. He and the rest of the 3rd platoon of Company I, 3rd Battalion remained in a defensive position facing the road. Frustrated that battalion did not call down artillery on the enemy concentration, Lt Rehkopf had ordered Kos to 'hold them as long as you can'. But after seeing the big German tanks the night before, Kos worried that wouldn't be long. He set up a bazooka team supported by machine guns. 'At 6 a.m. we could hear their tanks starting up,' he recalled, 'We knocked the first tank out and it blocked the road. They pushed the tank off the road and then we were helpless.'[37]

'You are on your own,' came a frantic message to Sgt Kos. His I Company was to 'Get the hell out of there any way you can.'[38] That warning was too late as German tanks now flooded through K Company and swept behind Kos and his men. Kos gallantly led his 3rd platoon and directed anti-tank gunfire that struck another two German vehicles, which just seemed to increase the ferocity of flashing gunfire. Soon, it was every man for himself.[39]

'We were cut off. We fought house to house, but their tanks came right in. We were captured by SS troops. They lined us up against a wall and were ready to shoot us.' Kos thought their captors seemed young, drunk, and wild. Luckily, an officer came by and seemed to change the course of events.[40] 'Then a [German] camera man came by and took our pictures instead and ... On the way back, they searched us and took cigarettes and candy and booted us in the ass ... we were taken back to La Gleize and put in a cellar.' There, also captive in the cellar, were many other men from the 119th Regiment. Kos was surprised to find the leader of the 2nd Battalion, Maj. Hal McCown. 'This did not look good.'

At 7.30 a.m. Christ's column of fifteen tanks approached Stoumont in the fog. Werner Poetschke was right behind Christ at mid-column. The lead German tank was Panther #225 of Rttf. Franz Prahm. As their steel mount rounded the turn, it took small-arms fire from the first house on the left, which was promptly showered with lead. A squad of SS grenadiers rushed into the house and flushed out an American infantry squad there.[41]

When the tank curved further into the village and came toward the church, it came into the sights of a 3in gun of the 823rd that had been placed there. The American gun crew fired quickly, hitting the Panther four times However, but on its thick frontal armor; all the hits bounced off harmlessly although, no doubt, jolting the panzer crew inside. Yet a bigger gun was just metres down the road, west of the church. At 7.30 a.m. the 90mm gun posted just west of the Robinson house fired several rounds at Panther #225 only 40m away. A lucky shot sheared off the 75mm gun barrel and although other shots bounced off the tank.

Prahm's panzer crew attempted to escape while they could, the 90mm gun still firing at them – a final round actually piercing the tank's armor. The tank smoked and caught fire with little opportunity for survival. 'The escape hatch flew open,' Cpl Humphrey of Sarnowski's gun crew recalled, 'and the crew just boiled out of that tank. The first man out, a little guy in a black uniform and beret, got away from us and ducked into the brush. The outpost men around the gun killed the rest as they spilled out. While they were jumping and being killed, we fired one more round into the center of the tank.[42]

Horst Vollprecht was in Panther #231 motoring up behind Prahm. 'We were closed up pretty well,' he said of the tank column, 'about ten metres [apart] …'

> [Prahm] drove until he got to the first right turn inside Stoumont. He was knocked out there … We were standing there. The whole company was supposed to drive through town one after another, but since Prahm's tank was knocked out, the company deployed in the field. Prahm got almost to the church. He must have received several hits, because I saw the whole crew get out. And shortly thereafter he must have received another hit, because the tank started burning … The first fire must have come from the direction of the church … [the later fire] came from the left, because after he received the hit, the tank started burning – bursting into flames immediately … fire came from the town in Stoumont, from anti-tank guns, machine guns, and then from Sherman tanks on the right.[43]

Panther #225 had been hit by a 90mm round that penetrated the hull and started a fire. From there, the situation embodied the dread of every panzer man: escaping from a crippled, flaming tank under enemy gunfire. There could be few greater nightmares. Even if the *Panzerlied* gloried it as an 'honorable grave', who would want to die that way?[44] Twenty-year-old Werner Zander, Hübler's gun loader, described the end of their luck:

> By daybreak of this foggy day, our tank received an order to drive at the point. We drove up to the first house without being bothered. Slowly we proceeded along. After a few metres, already we were hit several times from an anti-tank gun in our front armor plate and cylindrical mount. Our motor stopped. As a result of these hits, our cannon failed and our turret had a jam. We were unable to defend ourselves anymore. The commander, SS Cpl Prahm, gave orders to dismount. I left the tank [first] through my loader's hatch and took cover in the ditch. Now, I could observe the following: the radio operator dismounts, runs to the left around the tank, and falls from machine gun fire. The driver [Strm. Heinz Bieler] also got out, ran alongside the tank on the left to the rear, and when he reached the idler wheel, the tank was hit again. One of the driver's legs was torn off. The tank started burning from that last hit. Gunner [Hans-Georg] Hübler appeared in the loader's hatch. I shouted at him to dismount immediately. Hübler left the tank and leapt over to me in the ditch. Without waiting any longer, we worked ourselves to the rear in the ditch. In front of a tank of the 2nd Company, we crossed the road.[45]

There was no celebration from Sgt Sarnowski's gun crew as the enemy tank burned. Immediately to the rear, the platoon leader, Hscha. Heinz Knappich, saw Prahm's tank gush ugly flames and frantic men jump the burning hulk dodging and being hit by a hail of bullets. Seeking to give cover for the men attempting to escape or hide, Knappich in Panther #221 started to drive around the broken machine, but several AT rounds struck nearby – near misses. One round clanged into the armor but did not penetrate. Knappich pulled back and got on the radio to Ostuf. Christ.

Natalis and the others hunkered down in the Robinson cellar, shrinking further into a corner as the din of destruction above grew louder. After the war, three young crew members of Sepp Knappich's Panther #221 confessed to having fired on a group of twelve to fifteen American prisoners emerging from a house after Prahm's tank was destroyed – an event made large in the eventual prosecution of Leibstandarte war crimes in the Ardennes.[46] At the trial, Vollprecht, who described the scene in Stoumont in detail, denied, however, seeing bodies of American soldiers shot outside the Robinson house. It was a battlefield incident.[47] In any case, American resistance at the entrance to Stoumont collapsed after Prahm's tank was destroyed.

During those minutes of tense fighting, the SS and parachute infantry sought out the offending American anti-tank guns. They quickly blew up the American ammunition half-track and sent the gun crew diving for the ground. Sgt Sarnowski destroyed Gun 2 with a rifle grenade. Showered with exploding shells and cordite, Sarnowski ordered the gun crew to leave the fire pit and fight on as infantry. Pvt. Albert A. Darago and Pfc. Ronald E. Seamon were among those recruited.

Seeing Panzer #225 blasted and its crew shot down, the tank advance paused. For fifteen minutes the tanks behind Prahm held off, standing still or pulling back. Then, Werner Poetschke appeared and snarled a direct order, 'Christ, get your tanks moving forward!'[48] Ostuf. Christ ordered the advance to resume, but Hscha. Sepp Knappich in Panther #221 was having nothing to do with that. He radioed Christ that he had been hit, too. There was an American anti-tank gun out there ready to blast anyone else who dared move up.

At 9 a.m., commanding from a roadside ditch just to the rear, Peiper hastily launched the 9th Panzer Pioneer Company and part of Diefenthal's panzer grenadiers to help with the street fighting ahead. Soon, the infantry took out the remaining positions of Company I on the main road and brought Company K under flanking fire. Confronted by both tanks and intense small-arms fire, Capt. Bruce Crissinger's four towed 3in guns proved useless as their crews were forced to take cover from deadly bullet fire. By 9.10 a.m. Company I fell back to the church under heavy pressure. Only the presence of Macht's tanks from the 743rd Tank Battalion avoided complete collapse. The 743rd reported destroying two cannon-mounting German half-tracks.[49] After being knocked out, SS Uscha. Anton Motzheim abandoned his skewered vehicle and pulled back on foot east along the N33. He and his crew continued until they were personally stopped by Peiper, near the Château Froidcour:

> On the morning of 19 December, 1944, a few hundred metres before Stoumont, after my vehicle had been knocked out, I was stopped by Ostubaf. Peiper, who was standing with Hstuf. Diefenthal near an SPW. Hscha. [Jochen] Thiele was

> also with this SPW in the immediate vicinity. Peiper questioned me about the outcome of the attack. During this time a group of fifty to eighty American prisoners of war passed by and the German guard asked Peiper what should be done with the prisoners. Peiper answered, 'First of all, take them to La Gleize then we'll see further.' When I told Peiper that I had been knocked out, he gave me the order to fight with my crew as infantry. However, a little later on the same morning, I received the order to drive to La Gleize with three K.W.K.s [SPWs mounting a 7.5cm cannon] which needed repair. I arrived in La Gleize between ten and eleven o'clock the same morning, when I met Peiper, who was standing with Stubaf. Knittel, commander of the reconnaissance battalion, and Stubaf. Poetschke, the commander of the 1st Panzer Abteilung. Peiper called me over and asked what I was doing in La Gleize, since I had received an order from him to fight as infantry. Just as I was standing there, Poetschke said to Peiper, 'Ostubaf. Peiper, here are two more prisoners of war.' Peiper answered in an indifferent and disdainful manner, 'As usual.' From Peiper's answer, I concluded that both prisoners of war would be bumped off.[50]

Amid the confusion of Peiper's blunted advance, a knot of Fallschirmjäger infantry rushed to the scene of Prahm's burning tank just before the Robinson house. Under fire, they provided first aid to Strm. Heinz Bieler, who was severely bleeding. The paratroopers quickly set up machine guns and hauled out grenades in the shadow of the Robinson house while a Panzer IV of the 6th Panzer Company curved wide behind the garden to outflank the American defenders. In moments, Werner Poetschke showed up on foot, having left his own command Panther, #151, just up the road. The entire panzer column now idled without moving. Indifferent to bullets zinging about, Poetschke grabbed an abandoned Panzerfaust lying in the Robinson yard and ran forward. Ironically, rather than using the weapon to hunt down American anti-tank crews, Poetschke shouted that if his tanks on the road did not move forward, he would shoot them down himself.

'The attack itself was studded with severe crises,' Peiper recalled, 'and in one of these crises the tanks of the Battalion Poetschke attacking on the right flank proceeded to pull back so I gave Poetschke the order to take a hand there at once.'

> Poetschke himself left his tank, took hold of a rocket launcher, went over to every tank and threatened every commander to shoot him down at once if he would go back even one metre. In that manner, the backward movement on this flank was stopped, while at the same time, I myself organized everything that was lying in the ditch, including the Company Rumpf, for an attack on the town, which made the decision.[51]

Four of Christ's Panthers left the N33 and waddled forward cross-country north toward Rouat to eliminate the deadly, anti-tank gun positions from the flank.[52] Spying Sherman tanks lurking behind a house, the Panthers stood off in the fields and engaged the M4s of the 2nd platoon, C Company 743rd Tank Battalion in a duel in the fog, a contest that eventually sent the American armor into retreat. Yet at about the same time, more of Lt Macht's tanks showed up to prop up the teetering positions of Company I and L, on the center and right of the village, respectively. The SS advance stalled once more.

Leaving his position, by the road, Peiper mounted a *Schwimmwagen* driven by Paul Fröhlich. He ordered Fröhlich to speed west. They splashed along the muddy road to appear at the Robinson house on the eastern edge of the village, conferring over sporadic gunfire with Poetschke, Diefenthal, and von Westernhagen. Prahm's destroyed Panther continued to belch flame and smoke while Peiper surveyed the dismal scene. Although the SS leader only remained about ten minutes, two other vehicles drove up. One was the Mk IV panzer of Hstuf. Oskar Klingelhöfer, the sole representative of the missing 7th Panzer Company, driven by Rolf Ehrhardt. They had driven all the way from Wanne to La Gleize and now to Stoumont. Peiper ordered Klingelhöfer to go back to locate his own company and the rest of 6th Company in Wanne. He was commanded to use them right away to help Gustav Knittel seize Stavelot by launching a blow from the south. Klingelhöfer must have looked thoroughly whipped for Peiper uncharacteristically ordered him and his crew to take a short nap before leaving.[53]

The second vehicle that appeared was an SPW ambulance under Hstuf. Dr Rudi Neumeier on the medical staff of the 1st Panzer Battalion. After pulling up, Neumeier and his crew brought the wounded into the sturdy basement of the Robinson house, where some thirty American prisoners were held. Fritz Willecke described the scene: 'We went into the house, leaving our tank parked outside and there was an American medic lying there. He was dead.' The American medic was sprawled out on the floor, his body covered with shrapnel wounds. Going past the dead American, they placed their own wounded on the floor. 'We went upstairs to look for food for the wounded and suddenly, we heard shouting outside. We looked down and saw a sergeant from our regiment taking about thirty armed Americans out of the cellar.'[54] As they emerged, Peiper ordered the American prisoners to be taken back to the Château Froidcour. The Waffen SS leaders came upon a large-calibre U.S. anti-aircraft gun in which Peiper immediately took an interest in using against its former owners. SS officer Gerhard Nueske:

> Peiper beckoned a U.S. medic who was standing by the door of the house to come closer and asked him in my presence if there were still U.S. soldiers in and around the house. At the same time, several civilians came out of the house and approached us. Peiper sent them back, telling them that there was still fighting going on and they should stay inside. He told Gruhle to have the civilians sent into the church as soon as the firing ceased. Peiper also issued an order that the U.S. medic was to be brought to the medical aid station immediately, as he would surely be needed. On our way back to the house, we were surprised by heavy artillery fire. Thereupon, he ordered Gruhle, his adjutant, to establish the command post in the Stoumont castle [Château Froidcour]. Then Peiper left and drove to Stoumont railway station together with Poetschke in Poetschke's jeep. Peiper ordered Fröhlich to bring the regimental radio station there.[55]

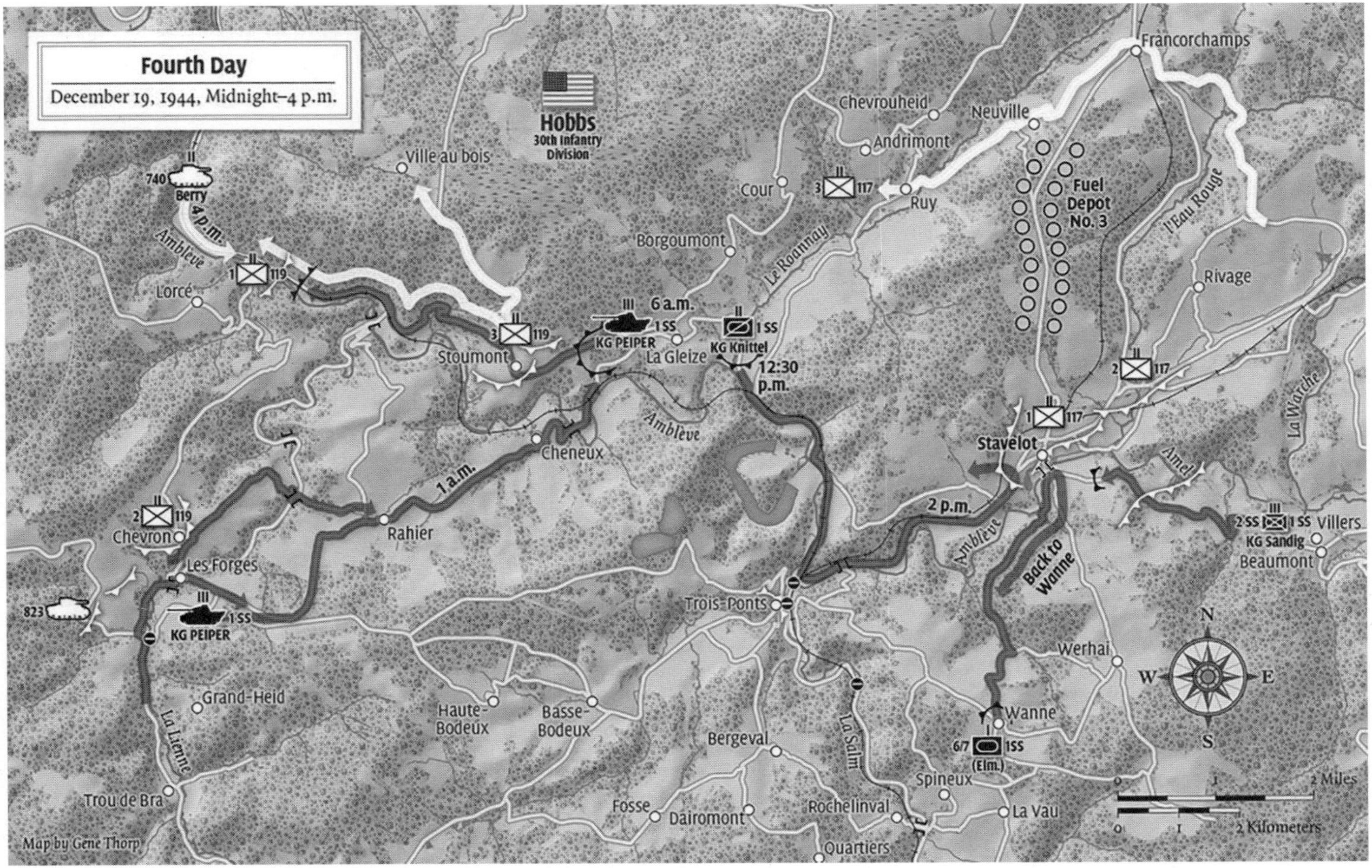

Fourth Day
December 19, 1944, Midnight–4 p.m.
Hobbs
30th Infantry Division
Ville au bois
740
Berry
4 p.m.
Amblève
Lorcé
1 119
3 119
Stoumont
6 a.m.
1 SS
KG PEIPER
La Gleize
1 SS
KG Knittel
12:30 p.m.
Borgoumont
Le Roannay
Cour
3 117
Ruy
Chevrouheid
Andrimont
Neuville
Francorchamps
Fuel Depot No. 3
l'Eau Rouge
Rivage
2 117
1 117
La Warche
Stavelot
Amel
2 SS
1 SS
KG Sandig
Villers
Beaumont
Amblève
2 p.m.
Back to Wanne
Cheneux
1 a.m.
Rahier
2 119
Chevron
Les Forges
823
1 SS
KG PEIPER
Grand-Heid
La Lienne
Haute-Bodeux
Basse-Bodeux
Trois-Ponts
Bergeval
La Salm
Werhai
Wanne
6/7
1SS
(Elm.)
Spineux
La Vau
Rochelinval
Quartiers
Fosse
Dairomont
Trou de Bra
N
S
E
W
2 Miles
2 Kilometers
Map by Gene Thorp

As morning wore on at the Natalis home near the school in the west of town, there was no further news from the professor who had set off to Dr Robinson's house. In the darkened basement, the noise of battle rose sharply. Was Ernest okay? In fact, Professor Natalis was still at the Robinson home while a knot of German paratroopers fought with the Americans in the north end of town. It was far too dangerous to try to leave. Natalis and Dr Robinson took refuge in the home's big, partially buried, stone cellar. Already since the previous evening American soldiers had hidden there with Alice Robinson, her children, and a dozen neighbors. In the morning the sounds of heavy fighting and gunfire only ended when SS tanks pulled up. Suddenly, the cellar door swung open. '*Heraus!*' an SS man yelled.

The Belgians and the Americans emerged from the basement.[56] Nearly a hundred spilled out into the streets, hands held high. Fallschirmjäger and SS men seethed in anger to find twenty American soldiers among the score of civilians in the Maison Robinson. One of the German paratroopers had been seriously wounded just outside the house. Now the professor's fluency with languages paid off. He spoke clearly in *Hochdeutsch* (proper high German) to the surly armed mob milling about. Professor Ernest Natalis addressed one SS man in the group. 'We need Dr Robinson here to be allowed to come and help an American soldier near the house who is dying.' Even though his German was good, that seemed to be the wrong thing to ask. Several in the group mocked him: *Partisan!* An SS man put the muzzle of his gun to his neck. Suddenly, the man retracted the pistol. 'Here comes the commander,' he gestured. Natalis understood him perfectly.

In a moment of bad timing, as the SS officer approached, the entire Natalis family – including his elderly father and children – came walking down the road from the west. Natalis's wife had got worried with Ernest's long absence and after the fighting stopped, they received permission from the Germans on the other end of town to walk back to take refuge in the Robinson cellar. It was 11.30 a.m.

The man who approached was an impeccably dressed SS officer with a Knight's Cross dangling from his neck. He was likely Jochen Peiper, or possibly Werner Poetschke.[57] Regardless of which, the meeting almost immediately got off to a bad start. With the cold December weather, Natalis was characteristically wearing a beret. 'You don't wear a hat when speaking to a German officer!' The SS leader snatched his cap and threw it down. Natalis reached down to pick up his hat. As Natalis rose from the ground, he thought quickly, asking for a doctor to come and treat the children in the basement. 'No!' the SS officer scowled, 'All you people are terrorists!'[58] 'You may know the order of march and things military, sir,' Natalis protested. 'But you do not know the mentality of the population here.' The SS men motioned the Natalis kids, father, and mother to get off the street. Obediently, they did. Meanwhile, the conversation between their father and the SS officer continued.[59] 'You are protecting the *Amis* and you were in the cellar together with them.'

'No, my Oberst,' Natalis complained in proper German. 'You are making the war. You have a mission and some orders, but the civilians who are on your road do not make war on these villagers.' Out of his pocket, Natalis took out a calendar for 1944 and pointed to Friday, 21 January. 'What is the connection?' the SS officer complained impatiently. 'There was a crash of a Luftwaffe plane flying from Bremen to Chièves on that date carrying thirty-five German men,' Natalis explained. 'They crashed just up there at the Fagnes de Monthouet.' Natalis motioned to the north. 'All the people from here helped and saved many of them.' They had been transported to the hospital in Spa. Natalis even had a snapshot of the smashed aeroplane. 'As you can see from this diary, we are humanitarians,' he said, passing over the diary and photo. 'We rescued the Germans from this plane earlier this year and we expect you to treat us the same.'

The SS officer nodded knowingly and announced he would spare the population of Stoumont. 'You must protect the people in this house, my own and also the abbey,' Natalis insisted. The SS officer spoke briefly to the SS men present and sharply suggested the professor get back to the cellar. The Germans now rounded up the people from the village and put them in St Edouard's, the church, and the Robinson house cellar.[60]

Rttf. Georg Ebeling was present at the Robinson house that day in the command tank of Peiper's adjutant, Hans Gruhle. He remembered Peiper encountering a Belgian civilian in Stoumont. 'It was generally said among us,' he recalled, 'that the commander is in a bad mood.'

> I noticed how Stubaf. [sic] Peiper beat a Belgian civilian on his hat ... I was standing on the street in front of the house behind which later on an American was shot. On the road in front of this house, Stubaf. Peiper was standing with Ustuf. Krause. I stood right next to Stubaf. Peiper – not more than 2 metres away. A civilian – medium sized, and slim with grey hair as far as I could see below his hat – came to Peiper and wanted to ask something. Stubaf. Peiper, however, did not let him finish, but hit him with his open hand on his head and shouted, 'Get out of here' or something similar. The civilian was frightened, turned, and went away. When he went away, Peiper said, 'One should lock up all the people in the church and blow it into the air!'[61]

During that fearful morning one Stoumont family suffered the fate of others at Stavelot, Trois-Ponts, and elsewhere. Unlike the younger men of the village who had left before the Germans arrived, 74-year-old Emil Servais stayed to move his grandchildren. During the surge of German tanks and grenadiers into Stoumont that morning, Servais ushered other elderly and children into his cellar for protection. However, hearing someone enter his home, he ascended the stairs to the door. There, he was confronted by two men of an SS tank crew, who shot Servais without explanation.[62]

Meanwhile, Professor Natalis, having survived a confrontation with Peiper, returned to his family in the basement of the Robinson house. Madame Natalis was relieved to see her husband, even though terrified by the events. Another twenty-one were in the cellar. Young Alphonse Prince was among them, stifling hunger, fear, and thirst. That night he watched Dr Robinson tend to a wounded German soldier. In spite of Robinson's skills, the young paratrooper died before morning, the Belgian boy anguished to witness 'horrible and cruel suffering'.[63]

In the deteriorating conditions of the dark cellar, Robinson, his twins, and the Natalis family huddled for four days – living on old apples and a few American jerricans filled with fetid water.[64] In time there were nearly forty people in the cellar. A neighbour woman from Stoumont went crazy in the darkness. Mme Natalis's 6-year-old daughter, Gabrielle, had Down's syndrome and laughed continuously. Therese Natalis was only 14. 'It was all we could do to keep our heads.'[65]

Chapter 24

STRIKE FOR THE MEUSE

If the enemy leaves a door open, you must rush in.

Sun Tzu

By early morning on 19 December, Peiper's forces in Stoumont had the upper hand. German tanks hit the American roadblocks on the east at the same time that Diefenthal's grenadiers swarmed from the north. The SS troopers charged down the pastured hills into Rouat, defended by Company L of the 3rd Battalion. Company K, originally assigned to defend the southern exposure of Stoumont, was drawn into the fight. The assailed Americans wavered, only recovering their balance with the last-minute arrival of ten urgently requested tanks of C Company, 743rd Tank Battalion, under Lt Walter D. Macht.[1] Pushed forward, four tanks charged ahead in support of Company I, and Company L at Rouat with the American infantry and tanks counter-assaulting a determined enemy. This new effort faltered when both American armor ran into a single much bigger German tank. The massive iron beast boldly ruled the street, its steel armor repelling all the American TD gunnery that bounced harmlessly off its glacis plates. The crews of the American towed guns were wounded by German sharpshooters spotting them in the fog.

So ended the American bid to seize the initiative, as Company I recoiled back into Stoumont, only able to extricate themselves because Macht's tanks and McGuire's TD kept hitting German armor shooting at them. Still, a new problem emerged as Macht's tanks ran low on ammunition. Radio messages at 7.25 a.m: 'Our 3rd Battalion is being attacked by a strong force consisting of infantry and tanks,' it began, 'One of our TDs has been overrun by the enemy and force seems to be quite strong.'[2]

An hour later, orders came to the 119th Infantry Regiment at the pivotal location of Halte (today called Naze) that the combat team was to protect the strategic bridge crossing the Amblève river. McCown's 2nd Battalion had been held at Werbomont to protect the Habiemont bridge. Now on the afternoon of 19 December, 2 Battalion was ordered to move from the Werbomont area to Remouchamps and act as divisional reserve. Yet, it was Sutherland's 3rd Battalion that was now put to flight. German armor poured into the streets of Stoumont, outflanking Company K on the south-west edge of town.

By 10 a.m. Companies I and K fell back from Stoumont. Maj. Vodra Philips, the battalion S-3, ordered Lt Macht to get his tanks out of town. To prevent encirclement, Lt David Knox, commanding Company L, commenced to pull his infantry back as well. The American defense in Stoumont wavered. In the fog, cannon thundered and machine guns crackled as the big German tanks sought out the hold-out American foxholes.

The German attack split into two wings, one smacking Company I and its four 76mm anti-tank guns to the south-east and the other hitting Company L to the north. One German tank was temporarily immobilised after it ran down another TD gun, but the SS infantry flooded behind it into town, reaching all the way to the sanatorium. Twenty Americans were captured. A wild battle took place at town cemetery where a lone machine gun held up the Germans until it was blasted away. Threatened with envelopment, the American infantry pulled away from the church at 9.15 a.m. Lt David F. Knox was in charge of L Company in Rouat:

> Just before daylight I checked the men in position and changed some of them. Then four tanks arrived in our defense area, which made us feel much better. All the men were alerted before daylight because we realised anything might happen. At about 0830 hours tanks or half-tracks began to come over the rise to our front. The tankers wasted no time with them. Two were knocked out and no more appeared to be trying to come over. We realised, however, that there were plenty behind. We knew this because they kept throwing direct-fire rounds into our buildings. At the same time there was a hell of a fight going on to our right, in the area defended by Companies I and K. At about this time, Lt Parramore called me on the sound-powered phone and told me these two companies were getting pushed back. That wasn't good because our flank would soon be very vulnerable. I immediately checked with battalion. They told me that there had been some trouble, but everything would be okay. I could hear the other company commanders on the radio occasionally … It was now about 0900 hours. Lt Parramore called me again and told me that Companies I and K were getting pushed back again, and that I had better find out what was expected of us. That was a mighty good idea … I called on the radio, 'Hello, Thorn 3, Hello Thorn 3, we are concerned about the situation on the right, can you tell me what is going on?' Here is Col Fitzgerald's answer that I will always remember. 'I, too, am concerned – the situation is *grave*. You will continue to hold.' So I told Lt [James F.] Parramore we would have to hold … He had a little more realistic picture of the whole thing because he could see the men practically running to the rear.[3]

By now, the American infantry positions were under vigorous attack from two sides – grenadiers filtering into the town from the north, while big Panthers ground up the road. At the same time, a trio of tanks split off in a flanking move to cut off the U.S. retreat north towards Monthouet.[4] Soon American soldiers attempting to flee from the tanks overrunning their foxholes found their way barred by interlocking fields of fire. Company L of the 3rd Battalion now blocked a move for the Peiper to turn north. The larger problem was the effort to cover the retreat of the 3rd Battalion near Rouat while the American armor pulled out:

> I kept close to the radio. The Germans had, by this time, set up a machine gun or a tank just behind the rise to our front 250 yards and were firing machine gun fire down the street just outside our CP. At about that time, I heard Lt [Robert J.] Kane, the company commander of Co. K, call up very excitedly. I knew he was being overrun by plenty of tanks from his flank and the rear. Our orders were to hold. It wasn't good. At about this time, the tanks with us started to pull out. I wasted no time in getting hold of the radio. I said, 'What do you mean to hold and you take the tanks away? What do you mean?' The answer: 'Continue to hold and cover withdrawal of the battalion.' Lots of things went through my mind in a hurry. It sounded like an order to sacrifice Company L to save what they could of other units. I asked, 'Give me clarification. It is useless without tanks. How long do you expect us to hold?' Then I got the answer I wanted. 'I will leave that to your judgement,' Col Fitzgerald said. My mind was made up. We had better get out and in a hurry. Lt Parramore had told me too much about the situation on the right to make the answer anything else. Everyone was to start working back in small units. The machine gun crew would cover us and then get back also. [Sgt Joe] Kirby left with most of the CP group to let the rest of the men know about the plan.[5]

Running back 150 yards, Lt David Knox found most of his company holed up in a house. The German machine gun fire had everyone pinned and an attempt by a jeep driver to race out ended in his death in a hail of bullets. 'We can't stay here,' Knox pleaded. 'Let's go up this hill and into the woods.' Lt Kennedy agreed and started off with Knox, but only a few men came with them as bullets flew. Then McWilliams, Knox's driver, had a brainwave – the smoke grenades in that jeep! Soon nearly thirty fled to the east, as the wooded scene disappeared under blue-grey clouds.

The Germans must have feared a counterattack, but screened from enemy eyes, Knox and his men climbed uphill into the forest to avoid capture. At one point, they heard their Sherman tanks pulling out and decided to come back down to the road to hitch a ride. Yet as they approached the edge of the woods, they saw a big tank emblazoned with a black cross. Back up the hill they ran. 'They had seen us and put some fire at our feet.' Still, Knox moved cross-country in the gloom by compass to the north-west, and he and his party eventually re-joined the rest of his company. Despite having thirty men missing, he learned his company was by far the strongest remaining of the ravaged 3rd Battalion.

When the German tanks and infantry moved forward once again, the American resistance melted. Strings of deposed infantry and armor streamed back through Stoumont. Peiper's men claimed ten Sherman tanks had been destroyed – another exaggeration. 'The attack outcome was uncertain for some time,' Peiper recalled. 'It was decided by the 3rd Panzer Pioneer Company (Sievers), which went around the town in a wide swing and suddenly fired on the western exit from Stoumont. That action did the enemy in.'[6]

> After my reconnaissance had given me a clear picture of the enemy situation in Stoumont, I assembled for the attack at approximately 0600 hours on the morning of the 19th. The troops I had with me were a grand conglomeration and a mixture of all units I had with me at that time. I had tanks from my own tank regiment, panzer grenadiers from the 2nd Regiment, an AA unit of the Luftwaffe, an artillery unit of our own division artillery, and at least one reinforced company of paratroopers, which were mounted on my tanks during the whole advance. I had at most six more tanks from the 2nd Battalion – the Königstiger battalion – and because the speed at which we were advancing was too great for this unit after Stavelot, they were unable to keep up with us. The attack on Stoumont was a difficult one because I couldn't attack with an extended armored front and the point vehicles could only fight from the road. Enemy resistance was great and was constantly fed by troops coming in from the north and the west. This was the first time I was able to realise that a strengthened American opposition was in the making. After about two hours of combat, Stoumont was taken by my tanks. We captured approximately 200 American soldiers.[7]

In Stoumont, Hstuf. Oskar Klingelhöfer's driver, Rolf Ehrhardt, reached Peiper:

> Held up by unforeseen circumstances, we reached the commander on the morning of 19 December during the heavy fighting for Stoumont. A shot-down Panther, several burning vehicles, a heavy 92mm [sic, 90] American anti-tank gun, battle noise and smoke, and the bodies of dead comrades formed the backdrop for our conversation at the entrance to Stoumont. As I remember, Peiper ordered us to 'Get some hours of sleep and tomorrow morning bring up the 7th Company.'[8]

Meanwhile, the 3rd Battalion of the 119th Regiment looked to reorganize shattered elements. The 3rd Battalion was nearly destroyed with many taken captive, and now First Army was demanding that Gen. Hobbs block any enemy excursion up the road from Stoumont to La Reid – at all costs. Unfortunately, Hobbs had no uncommitted troops. For the moment, Capt. Carlton E. Stewart took over command after Lt Col Fitzgerald was relieved at the regimental command post at Halte. The new commander informed Lt Knox leading Company L, that despite the few weapons they had remaining, they were to block the road to Spa in case the SS tankers came that way. 'Half the gasoline in Europe is down that road.' Most of the men in the roadblock had never been in combat. 'What are you going to stop them with?' Soon Knox was instructing the company chaplain on how to fire a bazooka from a freshly dug foxhole. 'I felt happier when he told me an armored combat team would be up shortly.' It was 10.30 p.m. on 19 December; in just an hour and a half, he would be 25 years old. With no enemy in sight, an exhausted Lt Knox soon fell into a deep sleep.

While Knox slumbered in the woods, 200 captive members of his battalion were marching east in long lines along the road toward Germany with their hands on their heads. More than half of the rifle strength of the battalion and nearly all of its equipment had vanished.[9] At the west end of town, Peiper's protégé, Jupp Diefenthal, glared at the frightened American youths plodding eastward.[10] After seizing Stoumont, jubilant SS men gathered in front of the Café Gregoire to celebrate with captured cigarettes and local beer.

Eventually, the many American prisoners would reach the Château de Froidcour. There, the Germans placed them in rooms in the big cellar, where the south-east corner had been converted into a field hospital.[11] An entrance on the west end of the basement was used to bring in the wounded or to carry out the dead. For young Mademoiselle de Harenne it was a horrible sight. Many SS men were severely burned from the bombing the preceding day near Cheneux.

At about 10 a.m. Oscha. Walter Ropeter in Panther #222 reached the center of Stoumont to find American resistance evaporating. The infantry of Knox's Company L had fled to the north under cover of smoke as the Sherman tanks of the 2nd platoon, Company C of the 743rd Tank Battalion, pulled out from Rouat. In the center of Stoumont, Ropeter conferred briefly with a second Panther commander – likely Heinz Knappich in #221. Orders were to drive immediately west. After a short conversation, both tanks sped off toward Targnon.[12]

At mid-morning, the 119th Regiment sent a shrill message to division. 'Current [3rd Battalion] forced back from its position in town. All TD s destroyed. Tank ammunition critical. Request more tanks, it's urgent.'[13] While Company L pulled back deep into the woods, Company I (who would only emerge from battle with twenty-four men) and Company K were forced to pull back along the N-33 while German tanks nipped at their heels.

Luckily, the endangered infantry were covered by Lt Macht's ten Sherman tanks. At 10.40 a.m. Hobbs, the 30th Infantry Division commander came to the 119th Regimental CP at Halte (Naze) to see things for himself. The Germans were still barrelling down the road on a collision course with the 119th Regimental headquarters. Hobbs promised the 740th Tank Battalion from V Corps and his own reserve battalion of the 117th Regiment to strike at La Gleize from the rear. Maybe that would call off Peiper's smashing attack.

Henry F. Klein of D Battery, 110th AAA Gun Battalion, had been ordered to deploy his #2 gun with an M51 tractor in an anti-tank stance west of Targnon. 'I stopped at Stoumont Station,' Klein later remembered, 'but rejected it as a suitable position because of a limited field of fire. The road was snake-like.' Klein pulled back on the N33 about half a mile north-west of the railway building. As noise of fighting picked up, gun commander Sgt Bill Nelson helped sight his 90mm piece while stragglers from other units set up small arms to defend the weapon in case the Germans showed up.[14] Nelson and his improvised gun crew waited pensively as several Sherman tanks rattled back. Then, the last American tank halted on the road ahead of their position and stood there defiantly facing east. More infantry stragglers arrived. Had the

Germans been stopped? Klein knew things were better when some men pulled out cigarettes.

Meanwhile, Capt. Leon Kent of C Battery, 143rd fumed that he had not been able to get his two AA guns out of Stoumont before the SS battle group had overrun the town. When it became clear the third available 90mm gun could not reach the village before it fell to the enemy, Kent ordered Lt McGuire's gun to be turned around and pulled back to the railway station west of Stoumont. Even then, there was no time to properly emplace the massive piece. It was simply splayed out on the wet cobblestones between the curving road and the railway station building, its exposed 90mm barrel facing east. Then a discouraging sign: while Kent endeavoured to turn the gun around, infantry streamed past. The last vehicle out of Stoumont was a jeep with an officer in the backseat yelling at Kent – likely Lt Thomas Springfield.[15] His men had pulled a daisy chain across the road just to the rear, he said, but this was the last of them. 'Next thing up this road will be Germans,' he called out.[16]

Stoumont having been captured, two of Peiper's infantry companies – Rumpf's 9th and Sievers's 3rd Panzer Pioneer – mopped up the remaining resistance in the town. At 10.30 a.m. approximately five Panthers of Christ's 2nd Company lined up on the N33 and charged forward with the 10th Panzer Grenadier and 11th Panzer Grenadier Companies in their wake as infantry support.[17] Eventually, other tanks would follow, but Friedrich Christ was intent on displaying personal bravery after being reprimanded by Poetschke. There was no room for cowards in Peiper's nihilistic domain.

As the U.S. 119th Regiment's 3rd Battalion pulled back in disarray, there was the developing American impression that unless a stand was made, there was nothing to stop the Germans. Liège was only 25 miles away. The big problem was that Macht's tanks didn't have enough ammunition to hold for more than a single salvo of anti-tank shot. Macht was able to entice a few infantrymen to help bolster his position, but not enough to keep SS scouts from drawing within Panzerfaust range. In the meantime, the 1st Battalion, having been sent to help the 3rd in Stoumont, arrived too late to assist.[18] Instead, the battalion had to pull off to either side of the N33 in haste at noon to prevent being overrun, its retrograde move having left the village of Targnon undefended when the German tanks arrived just minutes later.

Peiper's chief worry now was fuel. The Panzer IVs of 6th Company along with Rumpf's SS Pioneer Company were sent back to La Gleize as there was not enough petrol for a full-blooded attack using all the tanks. Moving west, Peiper left some of Sievers's tough, armored engineers – the 3rd Panzer Pioneer Company – to consolidate his grip on Stoumont. At his point, Peiper's spearhead now only possessed seven Panthers, two Wirbelwinds with Rayer's 11th Company on SPWs, and one platoon from Sievers's company. Still, Peiper would press forward with these units, hoping for a quick victory and resupply by morning.

Moving ahead, Friedrich Christ's road-bound tank column clanked down the fir-lined slopes and hairpin turns that descended and rose on the chain of hills of the deeply incised Amblève river valley. Kent and McGuire's gun crew hurriedly prepared their 90mm gun as there were few anti-tank resources to defend the 119th Regiment's headquarters. Realistically, the SS tankers knew that both American infantry with bazookas and anti-tank guns likely lay in wait in the wooded curves. The rational course was to make the advance with an infantry-heavy combat team to protect the tanks, but not under Peiper. No time, full speed. Even so, Christ's tank driver, Otto Lessau, recalled that Christ was petrified. 'We all were,' he insisted.[19]

Peiper seemed indifferent to losses. He almost seemed proud of them. 'You will go ahead at high speed on the assigned road,' Peiper had ordered just before the Ardennes attack. 'Your task will be fulfilled after you have been blown up. The one who will take over after you is the tank right behind you. If shooting has to be done, it will be done while moving. There will be no stopping for anything.'[20] Was that clear?

Any way one cut it, Peiper's devil may -care style of warfare had smashed the 119th Regiment's 3rd Battalion in Stoumont. The American unit lost all its tank destroyers with many of its men in captivity. Col Sutherland, who would relieve Lt Col Fitzgerald of command at noon that day, reported heavy casualties: eight killed, thirty wounded, and 203 missing.[21] Company A of the 823rd TD battalion reported one killed, four wounded, and sixteen MIA.[22] Peiper, however, experienced few losses in the fighting in the cloaking fog, largely due to the lack of U.S. artillery support. He lost a single Panther, #225, and two SPWs.

As always, higher headquarters on both sides were behind events. By 9 a.m. U.S. First Army, currently relocated near Liège, received word that the tank group of the 1st SS Panzer Division that had sent them packing the day before now threatened to burst into the clear. 'What is the situation down there this morning?' Gen. Thorensen, the G-3 with First Army wanted to know. 'This morning, first thing, our Blue Battalion of Crisis [119th Infantry] ... was hit hard and some elements were overrun. Our Red Battalion was used in there to assist it ... Then at 1-S [Stoumont] they were attacked and the Germans really seemed to want that place badly. We are holding our own.'[23] Hobbs ordered the remainder of Sutherland's shattered battalion gathered as an emergency backstop.

Gen. Gerow with V Corps sensed things getting out of hand and suggested that Gen. Gavin with 82nd Airborne take over responsibility for the sector. Yet the situation facing Leland Hobbs was not like a college American football game where coaching was the problem. Here it was the other team that was the problem – the Kampfgruppe Peiper – with their weapons and willingness to sacrifice. An hour later, at 10.35 a.m., a report from the 119th deflated all remaining optimism. 'What is the status of McCown?' Hobbs asked. His battalion was being brought up after being relieved by the airborne. 'He is on his way up here,' came the response, but 'Currant [3rd Battalion] is being pushed back fast.'

Then, just minutes later, the regimental commander of the 119th Regiment revealed the bad cards. 'The situation here is critical,' he began, 'and our tanks are about out of ammo. We have lost all our TDs and ATs. They have been forced out of the town. Herlong is filling the breach. I have sent for tanks, but we only have four ... There is a force of thirty or forty tanks pushing them back now.' Hobbs reminded him that Lt Col Samuel T. McDowell's 3rd Battalion of the 117th Regiment was being sent down to stabilise the situation by putting pressure on the enemy at La Gleize. 'I want you to hold that together,' Hobbs insisted. 'We will have to have some tanks to do that,' Sutherland said, specifically requesting available armor to be thrown behind their threatened center. HQ 30th Division: 'I will see what I can do.'[24] Stoumont was toast; by 10.30 a.m. Peiper had cleared all remaining American resistance.

SS man Josef Pichler, a motorcycle messenger with the 3rd Panzer Pioneer Company, had just reached the village of Stoumont. At 10 a.m., after taking six prisoners of war, he hooked up with his company commander, Franz Sievers:

> The company was ordered to make a search of the location looking for PWs. By order of Sievers, Schäfer commanded the group leaders to march all PWs back to the first aid station at the Sanitorium St Edouard of Stoumont. During the search, the village of Stoumont was under constant heavy fire by the enemy.

Nearby, the Catholic sisters at St Edouard's Sanatorium moved the mattresses and bedding down to the cellar, anticipating the worst on the morning of 19 December. Everyone moved below ground just as the first shells started to fall. At 9 a.m. the sounds of fighting grew near the sanatorium and minutes later the Germans came through with a flock of tanks and infantry, sweeping up twenty Americans as prisoners. The rest of the Americans pulled back hastily on the road to Targnon, the German tanks in hot pursuit. In minutes, German SS men were everywhere, taking food in the kitchen, setting up machine guns in the first-floor windows, and siting guns in front of the building. The peaceful, religious sanctuary for mentally disabled children and young girls quickly morphed into a fortress. For the SS it was *Festung St Edouard*.

Pichler took shelter from the artillery fire at a small grocery shop in Stoumont, when two additional American prisoners showed up with a wounded German. The wounded SS man got a bandage from Ustuf. Karl-Heinz Rose, the medical orderly with the 3rd Panzer Pioneer Company, and then was packed up into a departing ambulance. Presently, another three American prisoners showed up, after which Oscha. Willi Schaefer asked the commander of the 2nd platoon, SS Uscha. Max Beutner, to move them back to the Château Froidcour.[25] With that, Sievers and Schaefer set up a command post near Stoumont at the sanatorium. There, Pichler witnessed a half an hour meeting between Sievers, Peiper, and Poetschke.[26] Breaking from their huddle, Peiper headed back off to the east while Sievers remained at the sanatorium.[27]

In an early post-war account, Pichler didn't mention that his commander, Franz Sievers, had been involved in a war crime during the advance through Stoumont. Indeed, in his eventual testimony at the Malmedy trial, he indicated that on 19 December SS Oscha. Willi Schaefer brought in a wounded American to Stoumont and Schaefer then asked the SS officer what to do with him. Contrary to the testimony of the enlisted man, Sievers said he ordered him to be sent to the aid station. Later Sievers claimed to have learned that this man and another had been shot by Schaefer, but indicated it was Max Beutner (conveniently deceased) who had ordered the dirty deed.[28] Still, the balance of evidence would suggest that a war crime had really occurred and that Sievers and the 3rd Panzer Pioneer Company were at its root. Not surprisingly, many of the same men supposedly involved were also accused of the killings at Baugnez.[29]

Had the Kampfgruppe Peiper murdered American soldiers in Stoumont? In the eventual trial, a specious accusation would come from Uscha. Hans Pletz, the driver of Christ's Panther #201, that his commander had ordered him to fire on a group of more than twenty American prisoners collecting by a grocery store at the center of Stoumont. However, the author's critical examination of this episode reveals that it almost certainly did not occur.[30] What very may well have transpired, however, was the shooting of several American soldiers by Joachim Hoffmann and Gustav Sprenger near a Stoumont home on the orders of Franz Sievers:

> After parking my SPW, Uscha. Rose, our company medic, who was riding in my SPW, and the crew of our SPW and went into a house … From there we went to a store in front where I parked my SPW. From there, Rose and I walked to the tavern. It was about nine o'clock in the morning. We stayed in the tavern for about half an hour and then returned to our SPW, taking some lemonade with us. From the SPW, we went into house #24, which was still occupied by civilians, and we cooked some food. We were there about an hour and a half. Then Rose and I returned to our SPW … then Rose left. At this time, standing in the intersection were Sievers, Schaefer, and Pichler … While I was standing by my SPW, I saw two American soldiers come around the corner … They had a wounded German soldier with them who was wearing a black German panzer uniform and was said to be the crew member of a knocked-out tank. As the Americans approached, they were unarmed and carrying the wounded German soldier, one with his arms under the wounded man's legs. From where I was standing near my SPW, I observed that Oscha. Schaefer, who speaks a few words of English, spoke to the two Americans … Then Oscha. Schaefer called me. … 'Take the two prisoners away.' … I asked, 'Where shall I take them?' Then Schaefer turned to Ostuf. Sievers and they talked, but in a such a low voice that I could not understand or hear what they said. I was about 5 metres from them. I could only see that Sievers looked at me and made a nod of his head to Schaefer … Schaefer approached me as soon as Ostuf. Sievers nodded and said, 'Knock them off' and pointed down the street. I answered that I had never done such a thing before. He replied, 'You are a coward. I give you the order. Go ahead.' I could not say anything more because Schaefer was the company troop leader … Sievers was no more than a ½ of a metre to 2 metres from Schaefer and was bound to have heard the order.
>
> I took the machine pistol off my shoulder and marched the two Americans down the street … They were walking ahead of me, 1 or 2 metres from me. They were unarmed and had their arms clasped behind their heads. When we reached a point, as one of the two American prisoners turned to me, I shot him in the chest with a burst of three to four shots from the machine pistol. Thereupon, the other prisoner turned toward me and I shot him in the chest with a similar burst

> from the machine pistol … They fell to the ground and did not move anymore or show any signs of life … As I was walking back and had gone about 10 metres, I met Rttf. [Josef] Pichler, who asked me where the two Americans were lying and why I was white in the face … I did not answer but went back to Oscha. Schaefer and reported I had carried out his order … Ostuf. Sievers and Schaefer both stood at the same spot where I had left them previously … After making my report, I returned to my SPW …[31]

In a statement of his own, Joachim Hoffmann, an SPW driver in 3rd Panzer Pioneer Company, largely corroborated Sprenger's version.[32] Twenty minutes after Sprenger shot the two Americans in Stoumont, both Sprenger and Hoffmann saw Rttf. Willi Biloschetzky and Strm. Greber – also of their company – escorting two other American soldiers carrying a wounded GI on a stretcher. The two SS men, joined by Sprenger, escorted the pair carrying their wounded buddy to the same spot.[33] This time – likely seeing the other two dead men – the Americans attempted to run, but were chopped down by machine pistol fire before they could reach the corner of the house. With that grisly action over, Sprenger perpetrated yet another. Sprenger approached the wounded American on the stretcher, now lying in the road where he was dropped, and dispatched him with a point-blank burst of machine gun fire into his heart.[34]

SS Rttf. Josef 'Sepp' Pichler, the messenger with the 3rd Panzer Pioneer Company, talked of the incident after the war with comrades even before being moved to Schwäbisch Hall – although not mentioning his own participation.[35] Willi Schaefer, who had given the orders, confirmed how Gustav Sprenger had shot two American soldiers who had been carrying a wounded German tank man.[36] 'At my question to Sievers of what should be done with the American prisoners of war,' he answered, "I shall have them shot."'

And there were other statements from other members of the same company – Gustav Neve and Siegfried Jaekel – also attesting to the incident.[37] Jaekel recalled the exact expression that the battle-hardened Sievers had used in ordering the first two Americans shot: '*Jede Menge Barcelona* – which meant that everything was to be mowed down.' And unlike some of the other fabled killings in Stoumont and La Gleize, this time bodies were found. A Belgian tailor from Stoumont, Albert Jourdain, would later confirm he had found five dead Americans in Stoumont by his house at the location indicated by Sprenger, who marked on pictures where he had executed the men.[38] 'I saw some dead American soldiers who were on the path that runs by my house,' he declared.[39] After the end of the war, but well before the trial or even Schwäbisch Hall, the incident made the rumour mills at the internment camps housing Waffen SS men.[40] That the Sievers incident happened became more likely given a corroborating galaxy of statements as well as the physical evidence cited by Monsieur Jourdain.[41] Even so, it seems a safe assumption that Jochen Peiper knew little of these incidents.

The head of Kampfgruppe Peiper still focused on his prime mission of reaching the Meuse. Although he did not know it, Allied intelligence was on to him. They had just captured a map that identified his tank regiment as leading the prime push as well as his objective.[42] Nevertheless, for Peiper, the time for a final strike to shake his column loose seemed at hand: the Americans were fleeing down the N33, discarding equipment as they went.

There was one big problem. Before any regimental-scale advance, Peiper would need supply trucks to reach them from Rollbahn D. Unfortunately for Peiper, the tank-rolling road had been interdicted by the Americans capturing Stavelot the day before. He urgently dispatched Gustav Knittel to auger his way into that town from the west. The battle swirled around Peiper in chaos:

> After the first prisoners were brought back from the enemy line of resistance and my attacking infantry disappeared into the town, I drove into town promptly with a jeep. Since violent fighting was still happening on that front, I stopped at the first house on the left-hand side [Robinson house]. An American anti-tank gun was standing next to that house, as was a knocked-out and a burning Panther, so I assumed the clearing of the town would take a while yet. I planned to establish a message center in this house first. Some of the officers of my staff as well as Poetschke, Westernhagen, and Nueske arrived at my place, as did my communications officer. At that time I saw an American medic standing at the house, leaning against the door. Since there were some American wounded and dead still lying around in the area, and since the vicinity did not look to be very secure, I notified the medic to come over and asked him a few questions, the subject of which was whether there were any more Americans in the houses in the vicinity. That was not an interrogation, but a measure of security.
>
> A large number of civilians flooded out of the houses at the same time. They were gesturing wildly and approaching me. I gathered from the confusion of voices that they wanted to go back into the town in order to milk their cows. I chased them back and made myself understood to them that this was somewhat too early now. And I ordered my adjutant to see to it that after the combat mission had ebbed down somewhat that all of the civilians would be taken to the church. At the same time, I ordered that the medic would be taken to the aid station, since we could use him, and then went to an American anti-aircraft position which was quite near the house in order to determine whether these weapons were still of use. A severe artillery barrage started, when I returned, which forced me to take cover. That meant that I jumped into the house from the rear, but since the hits were very close, I got out again and lay by the window on the other side. I met my adjutant and some other men who were taking cover there, and I ordered my adjutant to establish a C.P. at a distance from that point, since the artillery was zeroed in too well at that point. Then, together with Maj. Poetschke, I got into his jeep and drove through Stoumont, met Capt. Diefenthal on the western edge of town, and ordered him to follow the escaping enemy at once and see to it that all the vehicles would not stop under any conditions, but would instead increase their speed.[43]

Peiper claimed Werner Poetschke's bravery carried the day in Stoumont:

> A quickly organized attack came to a standstill because at the edge of the village there were four anti-aircraft guns and six heavy anti-tank guns as well as several

> enemy tanks at the forest edge north of Stoumont that closed the crucial road with their fire. Clearly realising that a ruthless, headlong assault would have success there, Poetschke put his tank at the point and led by example at the front. Nevertheless, the attack failed to break through and several tanks began to slowly pull back to again reach the reverse slope. At this moment of crisis, SS Stubaf. Poetschke was filled with bright fury. He bailed out of his tank, grabbed a Panzerfaust, and threatened to shoot down his own tank crews if they rolled back one more step. This brutal measure was the deciding factor. Oblivious to the murderous fire and his own losses, the tanks pushed ahead, firing wildly into the village and causing a great panic that broke the stiff opposition. One hundred and fifty prisoners, four AA guns, five heavy anti-tank guns, four Shermans, and an abundance of equipment and enemy dead fell into our hands.[44]

Not long after Stoumont was firmly in German hands, the SS colonel had a short conference in La Gleize with Gustav Knittel, who had arrived with his battalion:

> The conference with Knittel happened at La Gleize at about 12.30 a.m. Knittel reported at this time that only about two-thirds of his battalion had arrived in La Gleize and that the rest of it was lost somewhere to the rear because the enemy had completely taken Stavelot again and that his vehicle situation would [not allow him to] continue in a westerly direction any longer. I then ordered him to turn around at once, to clean up Stavelot, and ascertain whether our main route of supply which went through Stavelot would be secure. Knittel asked me to make some tanks available for this undertaking, but I could not do that and I had to send him away looking rather annoyed at the time because this was not a very nice mission for him.[45]

Peiper's command now spread out awkwardly 16 km from Stavelot to Stoumont, requiring that he divide command responsibilities. 'I put Maj. Poetschke in charge of Stoumont, Lt Col von Westernhagen in charge of La Gleize and temporarily, Maj. Wolf in charge of the flak battalion in Cheneux.' While Peiper said he knew that things were grave in Stavelot, 'I was of the opinion that the troops who were following us would not have any trouble breaking that resistance.' Indeed, a Panther of the 1st Battalion arrived in the course of the afternoon, driven only by its driver (who had repaired the beast), telling Peiper of being fired on repeatedly in Stavelot, but still able to drive through the town to reach him. Soon Knittel would clear up the situation, Peiper opined, and supplies would flow once more.

On the other side of the fence, Gen. Hobbs had clearly focused on the predicament of the 119th Infantry Regiment, with a report from Col Sutherland. 'The battalion we have in Stoumont is getting pushed around; the enemy has forty tanks there.'

Gerow: 'I thought the situation was more favorable there.'

Col Stephens with 30th Division was in on the call at 10:55 am: 'It was earlier, but I just got word that they lost their TDs and got pushed out of Stoumont.'

'How did they lose their TDs?' Gerow asked with a clueless touch.

'Tanks knocked them out,' Stephens responded.

'Did you get the tanks?'

'Yes,' Stephens said, claiming something that wasn't true. 'But we can't trade even with them.' The Germans had big tanks.[46]

At the American command post of the 119th Infantry in Halte, the air was electric. At 11.25 a.m. the 119th Regiment reported that the 3rd Battalion was 'disorganized and withdrawing past our C.P.'[47] Half an hour later, the same source claimed the remnants of the battalion were sorting things out before being sent to block the road leading north out of Stoumont. When it became clear the defense of the 3rd Battalion was collapsing, Sutherland ordered his reserve 1st Battalion to reinforce his wavering forces.

At 10 a.m. Company C zoomed off in trucks, but by the time the soldier-laden vehicles reached Targnon, the column began to buck foot traffic of nearly panic-seized members of Companies I and K falling back. Capt. Donald R. Fell had the trucks continue another 500 yards, where the men dismounted. They then marched toward Stoumont, under orders to contact Lt Col Fitzgerald. In fact, when they reached the outskirts of the town, they found the situation impossible – bullets and shells zinging everywhere and no sign of Fitzgerald. Consequently, Capt. Fell and Lt Macht began a slow retreat back in the direction they had come. In the meantime, Sutherland and Maj. Philips conferred urgently at the regimental CP. 'We were greatly outnumbered,' remembered Cpl Harland Whitcomb of C Company, 743rd. 'We had to retreat.'

> Our tank was sitting at the end of the street. Our tank commander got out to look around. While he was gone, I saw a German tank starting to pull out in the street about a block away. As the tank turned and faced down the street, I fired an armor-piercing round into him … By the time the tank commander returned, we retreated down the street past an anti-aircraft 90mm gun and crew. Just as we passed them they fired at something we could not see. We set up a roadblock just beyond the gun.[48]

Sutherland elected to establish a defensive line east of their position at Halte – well aware that beyond their last-ditch position, the only thing between the SS and Liège were ten replacement tanks manned by untrained personnel of the 90th Ordnance Battalion. These men were not tankers; that option seemed plenty desperate.

Presently, the German armor rumbled down the road, passing through the little hamlet of Targnon at about 10.40 a.m. That Skorzeny commandos moved with Peiper's advance was clear. That morning, Monsieur Gilbert Collard of Targnon was returning home from Esneux on his bicycle after placing his daughter in a shelter there. Collard was increasingly worried by the sound of big gunfire the closer he drew toward home. On the way, he met Ernest Jacot of Stoumont and in the interest of saving their hides, the two men took the less-obvious approach to Targnon by coming down the country road that led from Chession south of the Amblève.[49]

The two men had just crossed the Lienne Creek at Neûr Pont when two soldiers in American olive-drab jumped out from bushes by the road in front of them. 'Identity papers!' they shouted in bad English. The sound of their voices was at once Germanic to Collard's ear. A glance down showed feldgrau pants and tired-looking German boots. A gun muzzle pointed at each man. Collard's identity card revealed him as a member of the Red Cross. '*Doktor*?' the sentry now asked, lapsing into his mother tongue. Collard struggled with his German. He was more of a doctor's aide. '*Gut!*' the sentry said lowering his weapon. Collard and his companion must go to the Bonmariage farm, he said, where wounded comrades needed care.

In moments both men were pedalling madly for the bridge across the Amblève that led into Targnon just a short distance away. However, upon reaching that span, the bicyclists found Waffen SS men in panzer grenadier uniforms, who signaled them to stop. There was a request for papers again, this time in accented French. Collard listened carefully; the tone was not German. The SS guards of Diefenthal's battalion seizing the Targnon bridge during the morning assault were Walloon.[50]

Collard explained that he was a medic and he was supposed to help some wounded Germans at the Bonmariage farm. Biking further, the two men arrived at the farm only to discover that the three German victims were only lightly wounded and had been treated. Yet Targnon now seemed an unhealthy place – Peiper's tank column had just passed through and bullets whistled outside. Both Belgians excused themselves from the grenadiers, who were setting up a 75mm gun by the farm. They ran from the cover of one house to the next. When Gilbert reached his home, his wife opened the door. He was visibly shaking. 'Your nerves!' She brought a bottle of brandy. For Gilbert Collard, even slugging down a quarter liter of *eaú-de-vie* did not still him – he groped his way down into the cellar.

While the worry of the two Belgian men was real enough, there was little fighting in Targnon as Peiper's tanks and panzer grenadiers threaded down the winding valley road. Moreover, the 'special guides' holding the bridges could not fight the battle. Beyond Targnon was another matter. As the German panzer column emerged from a copse of trees hugging the valley floor, they clanked double-time for the Stoumont rail station, but came under American eyes from the surrounding hills. A volley fire from the 197th and 400th Field Artillery Battalions plunged about the tank column, causing the panzer men to button up. The company commander, Ostuf. Friedrich Christ, fell from second position to third.[51]

What American armor would be available to stop Peiper's pulsing panzer thrust? The uncommitted U.S. First Army unit that Hobbs had promised was the 740th Tank Battalion. Arriving from Neufchâteau, they hurriedly scrounged any vehicles available at the ordnance depot 4 miles north at Aywaille. Col Rubel, in charge of the battalion, had been trying to get tanks for a month; now First Army told him he would crew anything armored at the Sprimont tank park.[52] However, tank crewman T/5 Clarence O. Webster drew the line at an available armored car; they hadn't trained for that so they kept poking around the tank park.[53] Even considering the emergency circumstance, the available vehicles seemed 'a hopeless mess': fourteen Shermans, five DD – Duplex Drive – amphibious tanks, and one M36 tank destroyer in for repair. The rag-tag group could only equip Company C under the command of Capt. Raymond Berry. The tanks were hardly combat ready. All the radios were British, and the GIs knew nothing about operating them. Hand signals in battle?

Still, when Rubel arrived at Aywaille, he found jittery MPs preparing its defense and nervously advising that an enemy armored column was less than 12 miles away. At about noon, Capt. Smithers, the S-3 of the 119th Infantry, met Capt. Berry on the road to Remouchamps and asked how soon he could get his jury-rigged tank unit rolling. Capt. Berry was eager for the fight. 'They're bastard tanks, but we're shooting fools,' he whooped.

Berry moved his fourteen tanks to Halte around 2 p.m., ready for fighting. Gen. Hobbs, who was in Halte, was unimpressed. 'They aren't ready for anything,' he told his G-3.[54] In spite of that, he told headquarters that Herlong's battalion would attack to capture Stoumont by nightfall.

Well before Berry arrived, Christ's panzer company roared ahead. By now, SS Oscha. Walter Ropeter's #222 was the lead Panther, with Knappich just behind. Although the German tanks were largely unharmed by the momentary U.S. artillery cannonade, it had the potentially critical effect of alerting American forces ahead.

Swinging around the curve, Ropeter's tank came into the sights of Gun #1 of C Battery, 143rd AAA Gun Battalion, which Capt. Leon Kent had hurriedly located at the rail station. Pfc. Harry M. Lane advised Sgt Alexander M. Sarnowski at the 90mm gun to check and make sure no Germans were trying to sneak down the rail line while everyone's eyes were fixed on the road. 'I ran out and took a position behind some box cars,' Lane remembered, 'The Germans were close and saw me and started shooting. I started to run to the corner of the station and tripped on the tracks and fell flat on my face. A spray of bullets whistled over me.'[55]

'They got Lane!' someone on the gun crew called out, but Harry Lane surprised everyone, jumping to his feet and sprinted to the station. As he hugged the brick building, at least seven deafening shots blasted from the big 90mm gun nearby. Several rounds struck the first two German tanks coming down the N33.[56] It was approximately 10.45 a.m.[57]

On the receiving end, SS Oscha. Ropeter's tank was sliced open by an anti-tank round 200m east of the station and caught fire. The driver and radio operator were killed and Ropeter and two others were badly burned. Almost immediately, Panther #221 of Hscha. Heinz Knappich just to the rear, attempted to pull ahead past the flaming hulk, but it, too, was hit by several 90mm rounds. The tank was stopped but, contrary to Kent's vantage, it was not destroyed.[58] A single German SPW attempting to follow up was blasted. In any case, the first Panther effectively blocked the road, and the second tank would go no further. After regrouping in the woods, the Germans attempted to resume the advance. Grenadiers of the 11th Panzer Grenadier Company encircled the two-storey brick railway station but grew more timid as the Panthers could no longer protect them.[59]

With traffic backed up, Horst Vollprecht in Panzer #231 emerged from his tank long enough to examine Knappich's damaged Panther just ahead of his own. A Panzer man was always interested in how well their steel battle wagons could resist being pummelled. Panther #221 had sustained several deflected hits on its frontal armor without being knocked out. Eventually, it pulled out and was sent back east after taking on wounded men from Ropeter's destroyed vehicle. The advance was delayed for about forty-five minutes – galling to Peiper. As Vollprecht prepared to re-mount his tank, he saw Peiper and Jupp Diefenthal in animated conversation discussing the next move over a map.[60]

Shortly after the U.S. anti-aircraft gun, employed as a powerful anti-tank piece, had been knocked out at Stoumont station, Peiper arrived to supervise Ropeter's destroyed Panther being pushed off the road. That done, the advance was to resume. As they moved out at noon, the radioman in Koch's tank, SS Oscha. Erwin Aumer, overheard Friedrich Christ polling each of his panzer commanders to report on their fuel stores.[61] Looking at the clock-shaped fuel gauge, he could see his own was nearly empty.

Horst Vollprecht, the driver of Panther #231, under Ustuf. Helmut Koch, was immediately behind the panzer of Christ, having passed Knappich's vehicle while leaving town. Ahead of them was Brauschke's vehicle, which he believed to be the lead tank in the assault. 'We came to a stop about 300 metres before the railway station because the tank of Sgt Ropeter was knocked out by anti-tank fire coming from the station. After the panzer of Sgt Ropeter had been knocked out, Lt Koch told me that infantry would try to knock out this gun.' SS Hscha. Rudi Rayer with the 11th Panzer Grenadier Company described the infantry assault:

> After the 9th Company and part of the tank unit had taken the town of Stoumont, the battalion and the 11th Company drove within the battalion through Stoumont and reached the town's railroad station. After the first tank had been shot down by an American anti-tank gun positioned at the railway station, I was ordered to take the railroad station with the 11th Company in an on-foot attack. After a short resistance, we took the railway station.[62]

By noon the anti-tank position was wiped out, but Rayer's company was punished by heavy artillery from the newly arrived 197th FA Battalion, soon firing from Nonceveux.

> A short time later our tanks came up front and were ordered to continue the attack. A short distance beyond the railway station, the other tank that was driving up front was shot down at once. Again, the 11th Company got the mission to attack in close combat the invisible enemy tanks in the woods and to eliminate them. After heavy losses, the attack on foot had to be called off and we had to withdraw again. Then we got the order to cover the right of the march

> column. After we had been lying there under the heaviest artillery fire for several hours, the commander ordered me to drive after dark with the 11th Company to Cheneux.[63]

The end came when an SPW with blazing machine guns showered the two-storey brick structure with lead while grenadiers ran forward. 'Let's get the hell out of here!' McGuire yelled. He and the others spiked the gun and pulled back 400 yards west, where Herlong's 1st Battalion set up a blocking position.[64] American resistance at Stoumont station was smashed.

Chapter 25

THE FINAL THROW

And if faithless luck abandoned us one day,
and we don't return to the homeland
The deadly bullet hit us, we meet the fate, then
the Panzer is our honorable grave ...[1]

The latest repulse to Kampfgruppe Peiper beyond Stoumont did not assuage American fears on the ground. On the phone with Col Sutherland was the 30th Division chief of operations, Col Stephens. He wondered if 119th Infantry Regiment could cover the tear in the American defenses. 'This situation here is a lot worse than you realise,' he said, 'I have one battalion – Herlong's battalion – on the road. The 3rd is practically out of the fight. It was badly disorganized, and Fitzgerald was wounded and evacuated.' Stephens attempted to bolster Sutherland's flagging spirits with word that the 740th Tank Battalion was on the way. 'You at least have enough [troops],' Stephens insisted, 'to keep them from getting loose.' But Sutherland had other news. 'They are shooting at my CP right now.'[2] Talk was cheap.

Fortunately, the earlier German bombardment on the U.S. regimental HQ at Halte (Naze) at 11 a.m. was limited to a few sporadic rounds – Peiper's shell-firing Crickets having insufficient ammunition for more.[3] Surprised not to have been overrun by noon, Col Sutherland regained his confidence. His 1st Battalion established an in-depth defense in front of the CP at a point where the paved N33 (today the N633) wound through a highly sloped cut with the Amblève river on the left and railway tracks on the right. At 1210 hours, Company C, 743rd Tank Battalion reported they had 'fallen back to the 1st Battalion position', with the worrisome rejoinder that they were followed the entire way by enemy tanks.

Luckily, by the time Lt Macht's C Company, 743rd Tank Battalion, knew they were short on ammunition, word came that other tanks were on the way to reinforce. As B and C Companies of the 119th Regiment were deploying on either side of the road, Lt Macht then suggested to Lt Col Robert Herlong that all three companies make a stand with his tanks and any others they could convince to stop. The place chosen by Macht for the defense was midway between Stoumont station and just before the regimental CP at Halte. This location had a sharp turn in the road between Stoumont and its rail station. The military operation would be most feared by any attacker: a crossfire ambush. The swept curve in the road meant that enemy tanks approaching would not see the danger until they wallowed in the kill zone.

Between the river and the road was a railway track on a narrow cut. On the north side of the river the terrain rose sharply into thick woods. Moreover, the section of road had an extremely steep ridge on its right side that was lined with trees. It would be impossible to deploy off the road there – it was the most channelised terrain in the length of the entire advance of Kampfgruppe Peiper. Realistically, infantry could only approach along the railway cut or attempt to filter awkwardly through the sharply forested slopes (there was an open, treeless area north of the train station). However, the most vital point was that any tanks would be confined tightly to the road in single-file formation. If Macht and the other defenders could put away the enemy lead vehicles, Peiper's entire column would be jammed. As the tankers, both American and German knew, a 50-ton iron battle wagon disabled on a one-way road amounted to a defensive barrier. Even if pushed aside, anti-tank gunners would be zeroed in and waiting.

Unless breaching the blocking position, it was virtually impossible to outflank Herlong's barrier. The incised waters of the Amblève river was just to the south of the curving road and the steep, sloped woods of the Vielle Venne rose quickly on the north. The 90mm guns would further backstop the position just behind the ambush. Meanwhile, Herlong sought to augment the position with the tanks of the 740th Tank Battalion being hastily moved into position. Amid the disaster with the 3rd Battalion, Sutherland had also anxiously deployed the twelve arriving howitzers of the 197th FA Battalion to the village of Nonceveux.

Meanwhile, the three American rifle companies of 1st Battalion deployed on either side of the road in hasty defenses were expecting German tanks to descend upon them at any moment. However, all that worry merely translated into a few sporadic rounds from a hidden German gun and some infantry feeling out the American defenses. Indeed, the available SS strength likely amounted to only a single infantry platoon and a single tank. In any case, Herlong had nearly an hour to improve his bushwhack. Soon Capt. Berry's tanks of the 740th arrived (although dismayed to learn Macht's Shermans had 'retired' to the rear to fetch ammunition).[4] 'We probably would not have had the heart [either] if we had known what was there,' Capt. Berry recalled, 'We almost had no information as to what was in front of us. … We were nervous as hell.'

German leaders of the final push assembled in Stoumont, with Peiper himself directing a blow that was to at last send the Americans reeling to the west in full flight. Josef Diefenthal:

> About five to ten minutes after the conveyance of the prisoners of war, Col Peiper and Maj. Poetschke arrived in a jeep. I was at the crossroads at Stoumont on the

> main road toward Stoumont Station. Col Peiper gave me the following order, which I remember precisely still today: 'The Americans are running! Keep to their heels and raise their V.O. (beginning speed).' I was hurriedly grouping [assembling] the point and started it when I mounted my SPW and continued driving with the point myself. As enemy tanks and anti-tank guns blocked the narrow road west of Stoumont Station, at the sharp curve about 250 metres west of the station, the pursuit came to a halt. I stopped abreast of the station, and sat down in a road ditch, taking messages and studying my map. A few seconds later, Peiper and Poetschke were already in their jeeps with me so they must have ridden directly behind me from the crossroads at Stoumont. After the situation was explained, Col Peiper ordered the line held and to await further orders after supply arrived. After approximately one and one-half to two hours, Col Peiper and Maj. Poetschke parted from us, Col Peiper with the indication that perhaps in the afternoon hours [the next day], a conference of the commanding officers would take place and they would now go back to La Gleize to give Knittel the commission [assignment] to establish communication with the division.[5]

The sparse road network leading west now influenced German prospects. Horst Vollprecht described the delay at the rail station:

> The company remained there for quite a while. The platoon leaders went to the company commander [Christ] and I then got out and then went to the tank of SS Hscha. Knappich – who was behind us – and I looked at the hits which the tank of Knappich had sustained. I also saw Col Peiper, together with Diefenthal there. They were standing at the road with a map. After that, the company proceeded along the right turn behind the station.[6]

Just after noon, after the hulk of Ropeter's tank was bulldozed off the road by another Panther, Peiper's tank assault resumed, but now with only five tanks remaining: Uscha. Horst Krüger leading in #215, Christ in #201, Koch in #231 and Kaufmann in #211. Brauscke in #232 brought up the rear. Seeking a modicum of infantry support, some panzer grenadiers rode atop the tanks as they pushed beyond Stoumont station. Two hundred yards further up was the sharp bend in the road where the Americans were aligned in their 'last-stand position'. On the map today it is about 400 yards to the curve, with the 'farthest penetration' monument for Kampfgruppe Peiper another 130 yards west. Just to the west, tanks and anti-tank guns bolstered a foxhole line with 1st Battalion protecting regimental headquarters at Halte.

Hobbs also worried the enemy might charge down the road to their rear from Targnon across the Amblève, ordering the 400th Armored Field Artillery Battalion to leave seven of its M7 Priest self-propelled howitzers on the hill near Chession (the rest were to move to Nonceveux with the 197th FA Battalion), where they were to act as tank destroyers if German armor approached.

At noon, Gen. Truman C. Thorson, the G-3 of First Army, was on the phone to the 30th Division commander about Stoumont. 'We are having real battle over here,' Hobbs told him, 'but it is a little obscure.'[7] Thorson got to the point. 'We just received a report that down at Stoumont, there is an unimproved road going north and there are some tanks going north on that trail.' Hobbs: 'We have directed that they block that place.' Thorson made sure he knew the gravity. 'We have a large gas dump we must protect. That is why I want you to be watchful of those roads to the north. It is not very far from where you are fighting.'

So urgent was the request that Hobbs was present at the 119th Regimental headquarters to make sure the mission had priority. The secondary road curved north of Stoumont to eventually reach the hamlet of Montoûyet, where a provisional company raised from the detritus of the 3rd Battalion now moved.[8] North of this place, any German armor would eventually run into the huge fuel dump, the town of Spa, and the evacuating U.S. First Army headquarters.

While this went on, Dr André Bastin of the sanatorium in Stoumont reached his home near Borgoumont north of La Gleize, although he had bicycled that morning against the grain of German tank traffic. He knew his trip was dangerous – even foolhardy – but worried for his family. Reaching his house by the little villa known as Tchéoux – Tscheous now – he was relieved to find his wife and their 10-day-old baby safe. But almost immediately, Bastin was shocked to see three American soldiers outside his door in a jeep. He pointed out a German tank just down the road attempting to camouflage itself on the heights near Chemin Renontige near the entrance to La Gleize to the north.

From the balcony of his home, Bastin counted six German vehicles – SPWs and amphibious jeeps heading for them. Amazingly, one of the Americans still in Borgoumont fired a single rifle grenade against the patrol. It exploded and although the Germans fired back with a fury, the altercation seemed to be enough to compel the unusually timid SS men to pull back south. Watching the road down in La Gleize, Bastin's wife counted fifty-two trucks and three motorcycles in the column, but not a single tank.[9] But at about 11 a.m. three half-tracks loaded with panzer grenadiers passed though Bourgoumont and headed north through the village of Cour.

That same morning, east of Stoumont and north of La Gleize in Cour, young Belgian Jean Dumez was headed north to the speak to American soldier friends in Andrimont just a few kilometers further on. For the last two days, U.S. Army truck convoys had feverishly evacuated the two million gallons of fuel stored by the road just to the north. Then, at 11 a.m., Dumez scurried to one side of the road, suddenly confronted by two half-tracks loaded with SS men coming up from the south. '*Benzin*?' one German man called out. They had guns. 'Up there,' he nervously motioned north.[10] That seemed to be enough and the half-tracks roared on. Even where he stood, he could soon hear shooting up ahead. What happened? Soon after leaving his location, the small German column ran into the hastily assembled defense before the Géronstére fuel depot.

The place of confrontation was a crossroads called 'Vète Creû'. The roadblock there was the Hollywood-like improvisation of Lt Col William Fiske – a man who otherwise managed the palace guards at the First Army headquarters. Fiske's irregulars awkwardly spread out a hasty minefield that covered an assortment of weaponry from the bottom of the First Army barrel: two 90mm guns of the 110th AA Battalion with four M51 trailers, mounting electrically driven quad .50-calibre machine guns. Also available were two M8 armored cars from the 125th Cavalry Reconnaissance Squadron; and a lone half-track. In addition to the gun crews, the position was bolstered by a 'band' of infantry – a hundred nervous cooks and guard troops from headquarters. Men from Capt. Reiver's Company D of the 110th AAA Gun Battalion were the backbone:

> They picked the road junction that each battery was to defend. Ours was the gas dump. We started to set up our defense about 11 p.m. It was drizzling, we travelled under blackout conditions on a narrow dirt road, half of which was taken up by 5-gallon cans of gasoline. We drove right by the spot we were to defend, which turned out to be a good thing. It was not a road junction, but a fire break in the forest. There was no way to turn around … We were attempting to set up our two 90mm guns to cover the road to La Gleize when one of them slipped off the dirt road into the soft, forest mud. Our M4 prime movers were really Sherman tank chassis with built-up superstructures which held the gun crew and sixty-three rounds of ammunition and powerful winches … After much digging, the gun came loose from the mud and we got into position. While this was going on, the other men set up the three M51 machine gun mounts, several bazookas, and our seventy-five men in strategic positions … We placed some land mines, large enough to blow up a tank on the road before the enemy could reach the gasoline.
>
> Our plan was to let the Germans hit the land mines which would blow them up or shoot them if they stopped to shoot the mines … I wondered how accurate the reports on the enemy could be, so I asked for a volunteer to work his way through the underbrush and let us know exactly what to expect. Sgt Monaghan, in charge of the machine guns, volunteered. He came back to tell us the entire area was full of German tanks, the likes of which he had never seen.[11]

When the lead German armored car stopped short of the minefield, two SS men got out to investigate. Fiske gave the word, and everyone at the roadblock opened up. 'Jerry must have thought he hit a regiment,' Lt Walter Butts, the commander of the fuel dump defense recalled later. 'I don't know how much damage we did, but we made a hell of a lot of noise. After ten minutes the column pulled out. We just let it go.'[12] They really had no choice.

> Finally, we heard some noise and here came the Germans. We could only see them through an opening in the forest; they were not huge tanks, but light armored vehicles. We could have fired on them, but I said to wait until they got closer. Suddenly, the Germans started to shoot … The Germans were shooting at the land mines … Suddenly, one of our quad machine guns opened up. I had not given the command to fire and all hell broke loose. The Germans fired everything they could and we did the same. We did not fire our 90mm guns because the Germans were downhill from us and the 90mm gun will not depress below horizontal. The Germans fired at the machine gun which had started shooting, destroying it and killing the operator and wounding another man. There was so much shooting, it sounded like the invasion all over again. Then just as suddenly, the shooting stopped and the Germans ran. We couldn't believe it.[13]

Not long afterward Dumez saw the half-tracks that had accosted him; they streamed back the other direction through Cour carrying wounded grenadiers. However, Lt Fiske did not have the resources to counter anything more than an enemy scouting party. Well aware of the importance of protecting the Géronstére fuel dump, the 30th Division ordered that the 3rd Battalion of the 117th Regiment be relieved of its defensive position at Malmedy on 19 December and be sent there to stabilise the teetering position.

Upon arrival, Lt Col Samuel T. McDowell assigned his Company K the mission of blocking the road from La Gleize–Cour to the vital ridge south of Spa. By nightfall Cour was filled by K Company of the 3rd Battalion, 117th Infantry Regiment, that had hastily moved there. The following morning, a further twenty tanks of Task Force McGeorge of the 3rd Armored Division arrived in the village and moved on Cour. At the same time, Company L and some of the tanks were ordered to take the high ground south of Roanne in order to take under fire any enemy movement out of La Gleize to the east. They had almost been too late.

On the other side, Gen. Hobbs was also under pressure. Maj. Gen. Gerow, in charge of the U.S. V Corps, grew impatient after the 82nd Airborne took over the defense in the Werbomont–Cheneux area. That was supposed to allow the 2nd Battalion of the 119th to strike Peiper, but instead the 3rd Battalion was whipped before anything could be done. At 6 p.m. the 505th Parachute Infantry Regiment under Col William E. Eckman moved toward Basse-Bodeux, Brume, and Trois-Ponts, while the 504th Regiment under Col Ruben H. Tucker was charged with covering the south side of La Gleize. As usual, Gavin seemed fully confident.[14] Hobbs, on the other hand, was more concerned with the very survival of his 119th Regiment:

> Gerow: 'Tell your fellow [Sutherland] that he has got to get hold of those people [Peiper] and wipe them out.'
> Hobbs: 'He has a tough job.'
> Gerow: 'Those people haven't gotten any artillery and he has. He can break it up.'
> Hobbs: 'We have just gotten a report that there are a lot of tanks rolling his way.'
> Gerow: 'He has a lot of TDs and AT stuff and can get them set up and knock the hell out of them.'[15]

In fact, Gerow was suffering from command denial. What the 30th Division was facing was fully as bad as the mayhem Gerow had seen leading the 29th Division on D-Day at Omaha Beach. Two guns of the 110th AAA Gun Battalion had pulled back to the line; one was located at the regimental headquarters at Halte and the other, Gun #3 commanded by Sgt Lloyd Noteboom, appears to have been in the line with the 1st Battalion.[16]

Just before 1 p.m., retreating U.S. infantry and the ten remaining tanks of C Company, 743rd Tank Battalion, streamed down the road – the last being mistaken for a German tank and fired upon, but not hit. There was a short pause. Soon after, the din of tanks and German motors grew closer.

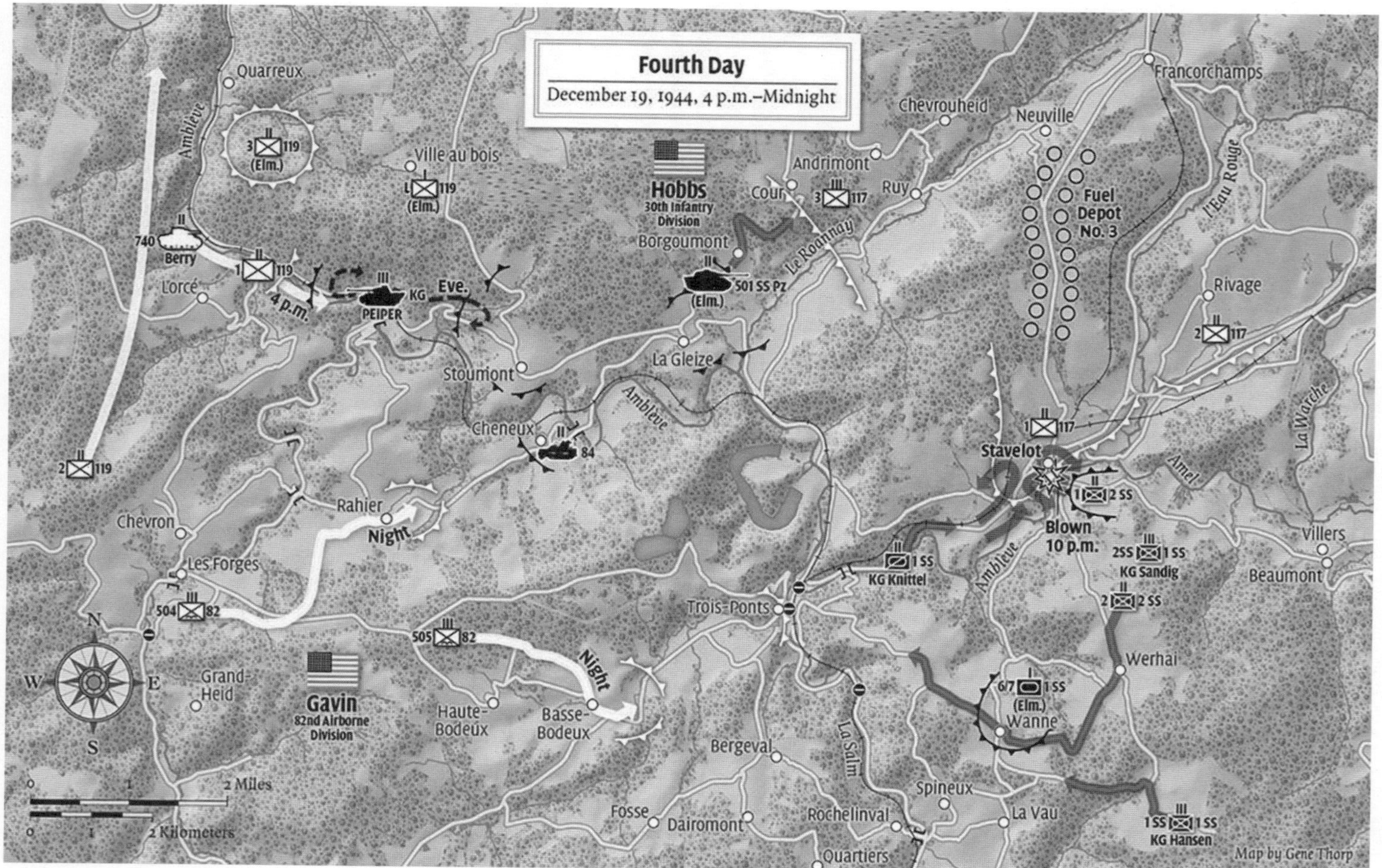

Fourth Day
December 19, 1944, 4 p.m.–Midnight
Hobbs
30th Infantry Division
Gavin
82nd Airborne Division
Quarreux
Amblève
Ville au bois
Berry
740
Lorcé
4 p.m.
KG
PEIPER
Eve.
Stoumont
Cheneux
84
Rahier
Night
Chevron
Les Forges
504
82
505
Grand-Heid
Haute-Bodeux
Basse-Bodeux
Night
Borgoumont
501 SS Pz
(Elm.)
La Gleize
Cour
Andrimont
Ruy
Chevrouheid
Neuville
Francorchamps
Le Roannay
Fuel Depot No. 3
l'Eau Rouge
Rivage
117
119
La Warche
Amel
Stavelot
Blown 10 p.m.
1 SS
2 SS
KG Knittel
KG Sandig
Villers
Beaumont
Trois-Ponts
Werhai
6/7
Wanne
La Salm
Bergeval
Spineux
La Vau
Fosse
Dairomont
Rochelinval
Quartiers
KG Hansen
2 Miles
2 Kilometers
N
S
E
W
Map by Gene Thorp

Approaching vehicles down the road spitting machine gun fire made it certain that German tanks would soon slam into their ambush. The first – Panther #215 of Uscha. Krüger – came into sight driving down the road toward the 1st Battalion ambush position just 300m before Halte. The driver, Strm. Oskar Guttmann, reckoned all hell broke loose 400m past Stoumont station. They were fired on 'from the front, the left, and the right'; tank and anti-tank rounds zinged off their thick armor while machine gun bullets sounded like hail pelting the armor.[17] A U.S. gun scored a direct hit on the Panther, badly wounding Krüger, and backed up the entire column with the crew bailing out. Somehow, Guttmann got out of the tank, as did Strm. Karl Daub and the two gunners. Both Krüger and Guttmann were wounded and later taken back to the Château Froidcour.[18]

The Americans on the other side were mostly unaware of the extent of the German effort. They couldn't see. Headquarters merely recorded their positions being hit by a single, hidden tank and some infantry who had attempted to infiltrate their position.[19] Meanwhile, learning of the impending arrival of the 740th Tank Battalion, Lt Macht in charge of Company C, 743rd Tank Battalion, decided to fire at will at the grinding sounds of German tank engines just up ahead. Firing blind, the soon-to-be-departing M4s blasted anti-tank rounds straight up the road. An M10 tank destroyer of the 823rd Tank Destroyer Battalion was also enlisted to help the nervous American infantry and it, too, fired at ghostly forms just ahead. Which gun destroyed Panzer #215 is uncertain – the 743rd Tank Battalion claimed it a 'probable' since Krüger's Panther did not burn.[20] For good measure, the 1st Battalion bracketed the road and the woods on their left with 60mm mortar fire where German infantry had been collecting. Although they could not know it, their unsighted riposte halted the final Sunday punch of Jochen Peiper in the Ardennes.[21]

On the German side, the 4th platoon of the 11th Panzer Grenadier Company under Rudi Rayer was ordered to filter through the woods on the right side of the road. The plan was to roll up the American positions ahead and bring the threatening anti-tank guns under fire. A few SPWs would push up the road while Brauschke's Panther #232 advanced in concert. 'A short distance beyond the railway station, the other tank driving up to the front was again shot down at once,' Rayer said, recalling the end of Krüger's tank, 'Again, the 11th Company got the mission to attack in close combat the invisible enemy tanks in the woods and to eliminate them. After heavy losses, this attack on foot had to be called off and we had to withdraw again.'[22] They were only able to pull back with great difficulty to a point just west of the train station. There, they set up defensive positions. Herbert Stock participated in the failed action, attacking with the 11th Company in a *Schützenpanzerwagen* with SS Hscha. Hans Hendel.

> In this vicinity, I participated in an attack through the woods with the 11th Panzer Grenadier Company, but was unable to get through as we were opposed by three American tanks and a numerically superior infantry force. Then Rttf. [Kurt] Wittwer reported to Ostuf. Preuss, who was then commanding not only his 10th

> Company but also our company … We held our position in the woods near the railway station until about 2100 hours on 19 December. Then we withdrew and returned to Cheneux.[23]

Although Rudi Rayer was leading on the ground, the infantry attack fell under the overall leadership of Ostuf. Georg Preuss since Heinz Tomhardt had been wounded in Stavelot. When Wittwer returned to Stoumont station to report to Georg Preuss, he found him in a command post in a house across from the station. (The 'house' is probably the hotel, about 200ft east of the actual station on the same side of the highway.) His reaction to the terrible losses? 'Now it is time for the 11th Company to be burned up [*verheizt*],' he shrugged.[24] Preuss had a reputation for utter ruthlessness – and even contempt – for the welfare of his men. After the battle, this was the man who Peiper would recommend for the Knight's Cross.[25] As Erich Rumpf would later dryly comment, 'Who was in good favor of Peiper, also gets a lot of decorations.'[26]

About an hour after Rayer and Stock descended into the deadly woods west of Stoumont station, the remaining Panthers of Christ's shrinking company assembled with their commander back at Stoumont station. They looked to renew the advance after Ropeter's tank had been destroyed. The gathering fog was now so thick they were unaware of the fate of Krüger's vehicle just ahead. Still, Christ had orders to advance from Poetschke, who now briefly returned to the Château Froidcour with Peiper. Sensible or not, the order was non-negotiable.

While neither the Americans nor the SS tankers could see each other in the ground mist – visibility was only a few metres – the panzer commanders could not see the jaws of the trap they now entered. The fog of war was never more real. Uscha. Brauschke in Panther #232 now resumed the lead, moving on the right side of the curving, tree-lined road and followed by Panther #211 under Ustuf. Heinz Kaufmann. There was no way to deploy off the narrow road with the firs on the left and railway tracks beyond that. Further back was Ustuf. Koch in #231 and Uscha. Freidrich bringing up the rear in #202. Meantime, Christ in Panzer #201 stayed back near the rear of the column, ostensibly to direct the action, but more likely to simply attempt to find out what was going on.

Rumbling forward at 3 p.m., trouble began as soon as Brauschke rounded the sharp bend in the road before reaching the hamlet of Naze. Artillery shells commenced to fall about in a sharp barrage.[27] In several mad seconds, Brauschke saw a bright flash strike Kaufmann's Panther just before the sharp bend in the road that left the railway tracks. So thick was the wafting clouds of ground fog that the loader, Stm. Helmut Nestler, could see nothing ahead. Panicked by the flash-bang of enemy guns in the murk, they fired at least one round ahead, but could not see who fired at them.[28]

Panther #232 was now clanking ahead into certain near destruction. Several more rounds were fired unobserved into the fog, with more explosions around them. In heart-pounding panic, driver Rttf. Erwin Szyperski tried to turn the house-sized Panther around.[29] In so doing, he ran the 50-ton tank off the right side of the road. *Reverse!* The tank would not come out of the ditch. Panther #232 was now an immobile, steel box, its vulnerable side armor facing the enemy and its guns turned the wrong way.[30] In total pandemonium, the crew boiled out of the turret and fell back through the fog on foot. Soon they passed by Koch's #231 still moving forward. Further back, they came across the angry leader of the 1st Panzer Battalion, Werner Poetschke:

> When Untersturmführer Kaufmann's tank was knocked out, I attempted to turn my tank to get out of there in a hurry, and in doing so, I got stuck in the ditch. Our crew abandoned the tank and started to walk back on foot in the direction of Stoumont in order to report ... As Unterscharführer Brauschke revealed to Hauptsturmführer Poetschke the situation – that we had left our tank – he got very angry, pulled out his pistol, and yelled to Brauschke that '... if you don't get that tank out of the ditch, I'll shoot you.' Brauschke and I turned around in order to get back to the tank.[31]

In fact, Brauschke, Rolf Ritzer, and Szyperski did reach the abandoned panzer, but by then the 740th Tank Battalion was moving up with the American infantry counterattack:

> We rushed back to the tank and I was just about to let the motor run, when our tank was hit in the side and was in full blaze of fire in a split second. With comparatively serious burns on both my hands and face, I succeeded at the last moment to get out of that tank and my comrade Rolf Ritzer accompanied me in the direction of La Gleize to the main field dispensary which was established there.[32]

In far-fetched statements likely to suit interrogators, Rolf Ritzer and Ewin Szyperski claimed to have shot American prisoners nearby their abandoned tank. Georg Bunda, the assistant gunner in Panther #231, vehemently denied any such happening. Their tank was able to move close enough to the curve in the road to see the danger. 'Kaufmann and Brauschke's tanks were out of action. Kaufmann's [*sic*: Brauschke's] tank was stuck in the ditch alongside the road. Our own infantry was not in front of us; neither were there any U.S. prisoners.'[33]

The story from the American side? Sensing a turning high tide, at 1.35 p.m. Gen. Hobbs, now at Halte to give Sutherland some backbone, ordered Herlong's 1st Battalion to counterattack towards Targnon. An early move ran afoul of the 11th Panzer Grenadier Company moving cautiously through the woods. As the American infantry groped their way forward through the fog, they came upon Kaufmann's abandoned Panther #211 and a destroyed SPW with a German ambulance, likely blasted while trying to rescue SS wounded from the tank.

At 2.10 p.m. Hobbs met the 740th Tank Battalion on the road from Remouchamps and ordered them to join the 1st Battalion assault, but they had no ammunition. It would be over an hour before they were ready to move forward. At 3.30 p.m. Rubel's column of tanks appeared, collecting ammunition while Herlong pondered his prospects. In the fog and battle confusion, he was not aware that a gun of the 143rd AAA Gun Battalion had first halted Poetschke's spearhead just outside of Stoumont station. Nor was he aware of the blind shooting through the fog by the departing 743rd Tank Battalion and a tank destroyer. All that took place two hours before and had halted the pinnacle of Jochen Peiper's final effort. Herlong thought more German tanks would soon come charging down the road. He waited for the 740th to advance.

Yet rather than wait for the inevitable enemy slam, Herlong seized on the idea of a tank-led attack with each of Berry's fourteen armored vehicles accompanied by a squad of infantry. It was a reckless decision, but Herlong was strangely buoyed by Berry's oddball tank outfit. Smart or not, at 4 p.m. the American counterattack got under way, the tanks moving single file down the road with the infantry striding cautiously alongside in the foggy near-darkness. Lt Charles D. Power's platoon lead the way, with Powers himself straddling a tank.[34]

And what of the German account of the same action? In one of those odd military chemistries of timing, the advance of the U.S. 740th Tank Battalion coincided with a renewed effort by Christ's company to move ahead with the rest of his few tanks. In the German lead was #232 (Brauschke) with #211 (Kaufmann) right behind, who had only recently arrived at Stoumont station.[35] Even more than before, a thick ground haze reduced visibility to zero. Powers moved cautiously as if he were a high-noon gunman, thinking the first shot would likely carry the day. He and his tank driver hugged the inside of the road as they rounded the curve just west of Stoumont station. As they came out of the turn, a dark shadow hove into view. It was a Mk V Panther approximately 200 yards off in the haze. With excited instructions to the gunner, Powers got off a round, which hit the mantle of the Panther and ricocheted into the thinner armor below. By any accounting, it was an incredibly lucky shot. The tank was burning, but in fact, it was the tank of Horst Krüger, which had already been abandoned after being struck two hours earlier.

Powers then clanked on another 50 yards ahead of Krüger's hulk and spotted still another enemy apparition and again got off a round. Another lucky shot – this one penetrated the lower front plate. The gun round struck the mount of Kaufmann's Panther #211. Amazingly, Powers moved on further until the hazy outline of still another Mk V appeared. However, here his 76mm gun jammed as Powers considered evasive action: the enemy tank was sending armor-piercing shells his way. All missed, which seems likely as the rounds probably came from Brauschke's #232, which fired blind at the Americans.

Meanwhile, S/Sgt Charlie W. Loopey, commanding the lone M36 TD behind Powers, managed to squeeze off a 90mm round that pierced the Panther's cupola. Pumped on adrenalin, Loopey's gunner planted two further rounds into the German tank – almost certainly Brauschke's #232 that had just been abandoned in the ditch.

'After a very violent mutual fire duel, we were finally knocked out,' Horst Vollprecht recalled.[36] Vollprecht was in Panther #231, commanded by Ustuf.

Helmut Koch – the fifth tank in the column starting out from the little signal house next to the rail station. As he recalled, Brauschke's panzer was 80m ahead of theirs; the fog hung just above the tank turret, but everyone was buttoned up as anti-tank rounds and machine gun fire zipped about. It was about 4 p.m. when they pushed ahead hesitantly.

> There were four tanks in front of us. To our left front was the tank of Sgt Krüger and on the right side of the road was Brauschke's tank. Behind Brauschke's tank, one of the tanks was standing in the ditch – the panzer of Ustuf. Kaufmann. By Kaufmann's tank, the tank of Sgt Herzog was standing also by the right side of the road. After we had received the anti-tank fire, we pulled back some. It was quiet for a while until the artillery firing started again. That kept up for about an hour … The four tanks were still ahead of us … After the artillery firing was over, the Americans fired some smoke shells. When the smoke cleared there was some slight fog on the road and I could observe about 200 metres ahead of our first tank, some American infantry or anti-tank troops attacking from the railway tracks toward the road. These shapes, however, were only seen for a very brief time … then they'd be taking cover again. We fired one of two rounds of fragmentation at these infantry … After that it remained quiet … Our tanks kept receiving artillery fire and then the artillery fire stopped for a while and then another American infantry attack started through the bushes on the right side of the road. The American infantry got quite close to us. We fired our tank grenades and fragmentation rounds into them … After Herzog's tank took over the point and had been hit by a tank destroyer, 2nd Lt Koch told me through the intercom that a [German] infantry outfit had tried to knock out these anti-tank weapons.

Worried of the danger of close assault, the few remaining Panthers of Christ's company pulled back. 'Our tanks kept receiving artillery fire … then another American infantry attack started through the bushes on the right side of the road. The American infantry got quite close to us. We fired tank grenades …'[37]

Vollprecht said the assailed German tank spearhead remained at that position for a half an hour until Christ, his company commander, ordered all his tanks to peel back to toward Stoumont. It was 4.30 p.m. Oskar Mauer, the first gunner in the same tank, told a similar story describing strong artillery fire that descended on them after the aborted push.[38] At 4.45 p.m. the 1st Infantry Battalion reported that they had 'knocked out three Mk V tanks with our tanks'.[39]

'We pushed westward to seize a bridge west of Stoumont,' Peiper recalled of the span over the troublesome Amblève at Halte to Lorcé. 'This was about as much as we could do with the gasoline we had.'[40] In fact, they never captured the desired bridge. The furthest lunge westward of Kampfgruppe Peiper withered. Did Peiper think his advance had been beaten? 'Certainly, Captain Berry did not stop our further advance. We did not want to go any further. We had hardly any infantry and only tanks without gasoline!'[41] Yet it seemed clear that there was a failing of courage, too. Uscha. Otto Lessau, the driver of Christ's Panther #201, remembered a terrified company commander during their advance past Stoumont.

In any case, for the purposes of the advance of the 740th Tank Battalion, the three destroyed Panthers effectively created a barrier on the path to Targnon. Satisfied with the counterblow to German aims, Herlong's infantry moved cautiously just beyond the abandoned tanks and established a defensive line west of Stoumont station. Peiper pulled back and made no further attempt to break this line – seeming to cede victory to the 119th Regiment. In darkness, at 5 p.m., Herlong's 1st Battalion began a groping attempt to push further past the rail station toward Stoumont, but was held up by German gunfire.

The furthest penetration westward of the Kampfgruppe Peiper had been stopped a kilometer from their intended river crossing at Lorcé and 45km from the Meuse River. Aware of mounting tank losses, Ostuf. Christ got on the radio and ordered his remaining Panthers to hold where they were. He was running out of fuel and now the American artillery fire commenced to fall to their rear. Back at Stoumont station, the four remaining Panthers of 2nd Company collected in the early night. Friedrich Christ himself was wounded by a shell burst in the evening as his company headed back to Stoumont.[42] By 10 p.m. Herlong's steady advance reached Targnon, moving into the vacuum vacated by the SS withdrawal.

Peiper insisted the end of his advance was more a result of his dwindling fuel supply than any ability to overcome Herlong's infantry.[43] 'We did not know we were out of gasoline until the town had been seized,' Peiper later said:[44]

> I then followed the attacking point with Poetschke, and met them again at the railway station of Stoumont – several kilometers west of the town proper. There, I got out of the vehicle and walked to the first tank. The tank was standing right behind a sharp, right-hand turn which was under severe American anti-tank fire. On the right, on the north end of the woods, more enemy infantry was located and a lot of firing [was going on]. There, I met Diefenthal and 1st Lt Christ, the commander of the 2nd Panzer Company, in the ditch and we had a short conference about the situation with a map. By that time, it was quite definite that due to our fuel situation, we could no longer continue to attack. Therefore, I had to abandon my intention of capturing the next bridge, and ordered my men to hold the position we had achieved until further notice … I returned with Poetschke and stayed in my C.P. for a very short time. That was about twelve o'clock. The C.P. had, in the meantime, been established in the big castle located between Stoumont and La Gleize. I ordered the C.P. to be taken out of the castle and to be moved to a small house located directly on the road Stoumont–La Gleize since wounded were already lying in the castle and I had no intention of installing my C.P. under the flag of the Red Cross. Then, I continued to drive to La Gleize with Maj. Poetschke.[45]

The final throw was over. Peiper pulled back.

Chapter 26

THE SANATORIUM

By this hour tomorrow, we shall have defeated the enemy, or we shall not see another again. [1]

To U.S. First Army intelligence mavens peering into their crystal balls in the early morning hours of 20 December, the deep advance of Jochen Peiper still looked to endanger the entire Allied front. If the German columns reached the Meuse near Liège, logistical concerns could portend disaster.

Although the 30th Division had blunted its Sunday punch the preceding day, parts of its 119th Regiment were badly mauled. Another attack like that the next morning might splinter the entire fragile American line. The 82nd Airborne Division had arrived on the Salm river line to deny Peiper's push to Werbomont. While that action had seemed to immediately stabilise the situation, the collapsing defense of St Vith by the U.S. 7th Armored Division was another nearby calamity. Would the entire U.S. VIII Corps line fall apart?

Strong German reinforcements were appearing in the G-2 maps in the vacuum of Gavin's dangling right flank: Otto Remer's armored Führer Begleit Brigade, SS Obf. Sylvester Stadler's 9th SS Panzer Division, and the German Army's 116th Panzer Division. A withdrawal – indeed a retreat – appeared necessary, something entirely foreign to Gen. Matthew Ridgway's operational thinking. The overtaxed 30th Infantry Division would have to stop Peiper alone.

Although successful at turning back Peiper's latest headlong lunge toward the Meuse, Herlong's 1st Battalion of the 119th Infantry had suffered losses in the previous day's fighting. To backstop the situation, Hobbs had ordered McCown's 2nd Battalion to hurry from Werbomont to the village of Targnon just down the road from where the German tanks had been stopped the previous day. They made the move, picking up fifteen anti-tank Teller mines in the road east of Targnon after they moved past the knocked-out Mk V tanks.

Gen. Hobbs wanted help. He was on the phone to Gen. Gerow with V Corps in Eupen. 'We have some very lucrative air targets,' Hobbs complained. 'The last report I got was that the fields are clouded in,' said Gerow. 'It is clear as a bell here,' Hobbs continued on, exaggerating. 'The trouble is all the fields are clouded in,' Gerow retorted.[2]

If Peiper's tankers had been thrown back in their lunge westward from Stoumont, they had hardly given up on controlling the town. Tough infantry forces, including the 3rd Panzer Pioneer Company, focused on wresting St Edouard's Sanatorium in the western sector of the town back from the Americans as the first stage toward complete eviction. 'The order was given to seize and hold Stoumont at all costs,' recalled a member of the 3rd Panzer Pioneer Company.[3] Peiper himself stopped by the sanatorium that night to give Sievers added ginger:

> In the afternoon of the 20th, I was in the C.P. of Sievers in Stoumont, one more time with Poetschke. His C.P. was in that building [the sanatorium] and in the cellar of that house I visited a large number of civilians – there were several nuns and over a hundred children there – and I calmed them down. I gave Sievers some particular instructions concerning the defense.[4]

To those who knew him, Franz Sievers with the 3rd Panzer Pioneer Company was an old '*Rabauke*' – a rowdy – tough and merciless. Sievers would later proudly tell others about fighting in the sanatorium. 'I shot a lot of people in close combat,' he said. After acquiring a half dozen Panzerfaust rockets, Sievers told how he had advanced along the upstairs hall of the sanatorium by firing a Panzerfaust into one room after another to drive the enemy off. The whole building shook with each blast. On 20 December, I was thrown out of the castle by an American counterattack. Stubf. Poetschke gave me the order on the same day to start another counterattack in order to get back the lost positions.'[5]

For a short time, only the kitchen remained in German hands and Sievers kept it that way. He repelled the Americans in the upper corridor by blasting through the hall before firing into different rooms to clear them out. Then, he also fired a Panzerfaust into the second-floor rooms, remembering the 'Americans cried terribly'. One witness later related how 'this will show them what it is like if you want to throw the old Sievers out of the house'.[6] The fighting was ferocious – no quarter.

Sievers had orders to retake the place. At 10.45 p.m. he launched a short, but brutal firefight, battling for individual rooms. Then at 11 p.m. in the deep darkness of 20 December, the Germans of his company launched a desperate counterattack against the place. Between fifty and a hundred SS men supported by several tanks firing from the north end of the sanatorium descended on the position fighting 'like crazed men'.

'Heil Hitler!' That was the collective shout as a platoon of Sievers's SS grenadiers charged into the building from the woods to the north. The bloody fighting – with gun, grenade, and even knives – eddied back and forth with some rooms changing possession twice during fighting. Within fifteen minutes the Americans were forced to pull back completely from the main building.[7]

One group of eleven soldiers, led by Sgt William J. Widner, held out in an adjoining structure (the Annex) while the remainder of Companies B and C built up a line along the hedge not 30m from the sanatorium. Several other limited German counterattacks came against the American line outside the sanatorium during the evening hours.

At some point on that day, 20 December, Max Hammerer of Sievers' 3rd Panzer Pioneer Company admitted a 'mercy killing' of a badly wounded American soldier.[8] Hammerer had found the American soldier partially buried in debris at the sanatorium and groaning in pain in a hallway in the building. He dispatched the man with two pistol shots – one in the head and another in the heart. He later blamed his company commander, Franz Sievers, who he claimed had told him prisoners would not be taken.[9]

Maj. Hal McCown and the 2nd Battalion of the 119th Infantry Regiment were still being held in reserve by the 82nd Airborne, but itching to be committed.[10] 'I am being held in mobile reserve,' he radioed to division, 'I would like to know if La Gleize is taken?' 'No,' Hobbs told him. 'We don't have that.' Hobbs explained to McCown that an armored unit was trying to help take the place, but that seemed unlikely given the road-bound nature of the terrain. As the 119th was now attached to the 82nd Airborne, it was unclear if support of the airborne troops was his new assignment. 'No,' McCown told him. 'Our mission is to take Stoumont, but I am prepared to go around over that road to the north or drive through Herlong.'[11] Soon McCown would have the mission he was asking for – an audacious sweep to cut between Stoumont and La Gleize. Maybe the troublesome but trapped SS tank column could be sliced into two pockets.

Meanwhile, Maj. Singleton, with the 117th Regiment, watched helplessly as a panzer column left La Gleize to the west. 'There is a big enemy tank column moving west from La Gleize to Stoumont … it is a hell of a bunch.' Col Frankland radioed that their artillery in Stavelot was too busy to do anything about it. 'Can we get any air? … it has cleared up over Curlew area (1st Battalion, 117th Infantry) and they say they need air bad. There is a lot of stuff there.' But then the negative word from above. 'They just can't go now,' Col Ralph Hill of V Corps relayed.[12]

At dusk at the Stoumont train station, Gen. Harrison regrouped his forces, which had been committed the previous day. Along with Herlong's battalion, he would again have Company C of the M4 tanks under Lt Col Rubel reinforced by some self-propelled tank destroyers of the 823rd TD Battalion. Civilians hid in the strongest cellars as German shells commenced to fall.

For the 119th Infantry, attempts to reach Stoumont from the west in a cloudy haze made for a hesitant, creeping attack – hardly what headquarters had in mind. At 8.30 a.m. the 1st Battalion's A–C companies moved forward with the assigned 740th Tank Battalion, but encountered enemy minefields, losing one vehicle. The combat team reached Targnon, the tiny knot of houses midway between Stoumont and its rail station, at mid-morning.

As Herlong's 1st Battalion with the 740th Tank Battalion started off that morning, they ran into a Mk V on the road, but the lead 2nd tank platoon commanded by Lt John E. Callaway knocked the Panther out with a single round that blew off its gun muzzle. Then, as Harrison's combat team moved into Targnon, the SS panzer grenadiers let loose with machine gun fire, sending civilians scurrying into cellars. By noon, however, they had pulled back from Targnon to the wooded slopes just north-east of town before Stoumont. One Sherman tank hit a mine as it moved beyond the village. Intense machine gun fire broke out when American engineers attempted to clear the minefield. Attempting to push up the N633 into the thick forest belt between Targnon and Stoumont, the initial U.S. attack was repulsed, as was a reactionary German counterattack. A bit further on, Callaway's tankers shot down two half-tracks, one of these burning before the wooded slopes east of Targnon, not far from the Sherman crippled by the minefield. The 1st Battalion then spent much of the remaining daylight removing five successive minefields covered by enemy fire.[13]

Then about 500m short of Stoumont, the leading tank commanded by Lt David Oglensky was hit by a well-camouflaged German gun firing from the north, but he found the crippled beast could still move. As it was growing dark and Herlong feared a German night-time counterstrike, he ordered Oglensky to turn his tank broadside to the road to create a temporary barrier. Nevertheless, the attacking force had advanced 2 miles by nightfall, which left the tank-infantry team within 400m of Stoumont.[14] At 5.25 p.m. the 119th Infantry Regiment reported losing a tank to enemy fire and halting before Stoumont so American artillery could work over the town.[15] That was the American way.

Meanwhile, Herlong's infantry edged closer. Just north of the road over which Herlong had advanced sat the sanatorium, now occupied by the SS men. At dusk, several platoons of B and C companies were ordered to seize the place, which overlooked Stoumont. In the sanatorium itself, the morning of 20 December began with an ominous quiet. It drizzled through the cold night. Prisoners taken that morning reported Preuss's 10th Panzer Grenadier Company had a hundred infantry in the town with a handful in the sanatorium, while artillery spotters located three German tanks. That prompted 155mm artillery fire on Stoumont from 9.15 to 10.15 a.m.[16] In the meantime, some forty unlucky locals who had evacuated from the Elsenborn area now sought refuge in the stout cellars of St Edouard's. By midday there were 250 Belgians in its cave-like underground.

The sanatorium was weakly occupied by Peiper's forces. Even so, the American infantry only reached it after a violent German response. By dark, the 119th Infantry Regiment with its attached 823rd TD Battalion and 740th Tank Battalion attacked toward Stoumont once more at 4 p.m., reaching within 500m of the west entrance of the village. There, at a sharp bend in the road, they were halted by heavy resistance from infantry, tanks, and direct-fire weapons.[17]

Still, the American infantry of the 1st Battalion, supported by tank fire and artillery, soon cleared the place by nightfall on 20 December. 'We inched forward all day long,' remembered Lt Bud Strand with Company D of the

1st Battalion describing the action on the 20th. 'At dusk part of our unit had control of the Sanatorium on the high ground. The high ground to the east of Stoumont was vital to our attack and we dug in.'[18] The GIs of Old Hickory warily occupied foxholes around the estate.[19]

In the late night, at the command post at Targnon, the 2nd Battalion of the 119th contemplated a move to recapture the bastion at St Edouard's. During the night the Americans drove a few tanks to a dominant position near the sanatorium, but the SS men possessing the place anticipated that move – a panzer blasted away the lead tank in the early dawn just as it was brought into position. The Germans then rushed the heights of Rouat, forcing the Americans to quickly pull back. At the same time, the advance along the Amblève road, the N33, failed entirely, with the lead Sherman taking several direct hits. Soon three American tanks were burning, blocking the road and any further effort.

Meanwhile, three of Capt. Berry's tanks of the 740th attempted to approach along the road from the south-west, but were handicapped by the terrain, which sloped sharply right into German gun sites. During the night the SS tankers floated bright flares over the American positions, which lit up the positions of Berry's Shermans such that the Panthers in Stoumont rapidly destroyed two of the American tanks and forced the others to pull back west of a house about 150m west of the sanatorium.[20] 'We retook Stoumont in a night attack with Sievers's 3rd Panzer Pioneer Company, reinforced by another few tanks,' Peiper would sardonically recall, 'because we were too weak to do it in daytime.'[21]

> On the night of the 20th to the 21st, I made a counterattack in Stoumont when I regained the positions we had lost. In the course of this, two officers and, I believe, thirty-five men were captured in a castle-like building in the western part of Stoumont. Combat in this house was particularly severe. Fights took place for every individual room and the tanks on the outside had to shoot down the individual rooms which were pointed out to them by the infantry inside.[22]

At 2 p.m. another German counterattack hit Company C in the U.S. center, which was only fought off with difficulty. Even so, by mid-afternoon on 21 December, a spirited firefight threw the Germans out of the building once more. Following the action, Companies B and C deployed on the north end of the road while Company A set up on the south side and observed nervously as the new occupants of the sanatorium took to the basement. Herlong regrouped his battalion before Stoumont. He left C Company in the sanatorium itself, B Company in foxholes to the north, and Company A watching the road by the exploded tank in front of the southern entrance to the smashed building.

Meanwhile, on the afternoon of 20 December, the 119th Infantry set up positions to block any German forces pushing to the north where they might threaten the American fuel depot. In the process there was a short firefight at 5 p.m., during which the Americans captured two NCOs of the SS 9th Panzer Pioneer Company that were dug in by the roads and backed up by three Panther tanks.[23]

To cover the area north of Stoumont, the eighty survivors of the 3rd Battalion lay in reserve near Monthouet, now reinforced by two batteries of the 110th Battalion AA and a few self-propelled tank destroyers under Capt. Carleton E. Steward. Meanwhile, having previously run afoul of that defense, the SS had organized their own strongpoint on the heights of Belleville and the crest at Rochette in a hedgehog position with tank guns facing three directions. Around 11 a.m. a group of Sherman tanks of 3rd Armored Division's CCB, F Company, under Task Force Jordan crossed the lines at Monthouet and pushed towards Compère's farm. There, they came upon SS sappers laying mines. '*Amerikaner!*' members of the lead tank heard as the German troopers scattered into the trees.

Anticipating trouble, the M4s opened machine gun fire, spraying the sides of the road ahead. Even so, 30m ahead, the lead Sherman hit a mine. That seemed a signal for the Germans lying in wait. In moments, the second M4 exploded from an anti-tank round as the American column was pelted by machine gun fire. Karl-Heinz Hagestedt, a member of Erich Rumpf's SPW, knocked out one of Task Force Jordan's Shermans with a Panzerfaust.[24]

With that setback, the task force pulled back to the edge of the woods, with both sides resigned to an afternoon shootout near Prévot's farm. Even darkness did not bring an end to the musketry – a standoff in the mists north of Stoumont. Attempts were made to find other routes to the east of the enemy-infested road, but there were no alternatives.[25] Meanwhile, the group of enemy tanks and infantry that had stopped Task Force Jordan's column pulled back to the village of Rouat.

Some twenty-two Americans had been made captive during the earlier German sweep of the sanatorium. Before morning, they would be transferred as captives to the Château Froidcour, leaving behind two GIs and two SS men too badly hurt to be moved. SS Uscha. Rudi Rayer had been seriously wounded by an artillery concussion while moving his SPW-mounted platoon of the 11th Panzer Grenadier Company to Cheneux. He now lay with the other SS casualties in the Froidcour:

> From 20–23 December, I was lying in the cellar in great pain, partly unconscious. I remember that one day when all the wounded were still able to walk, we were ordered to return with the battalion. The others were told we would be handed over to the Americans, and we would be exchanged as soon as possible. Two Belgian women and a German medic took care of us in the castle. There were about thirty to forty wounded Americans with us in the castle.[26]

The 30th Division commander, Gen. Leland Hobbs, made his headquarters at the three-storey brick Hôtel des Bruyères in Franchorchamps to the east. Against his better judgement, he divided his attention between the two big battles he faced. One was the critical defense at Stavelot to keep the door shut on supply for Peiper. The other action was ferocious fighting in Stoumont and La Gleize. On 20 December there was little good news. Corps was insisting that 30th Division close the gap between Stavelot and St Vith – most improbable.

Thus, the urgent request for the 120th Regiment to close the gap with the 7th Armored Division disappeared when corps revealed its desire to take away the 291st Engineer Combat Battalion – a move the 30th quickly protested. Also, there was the dangling flank with the U.S. 1st Infantry Division near Waimes. Hobbs instead endeavoured to form an artillery center of gravity around Franchorchamps. Soon the hamlets of Baronheid and Neuville bristled with gun tubes.

At 10.42 a.m. came more questions about the status of the 119th Infantry. Had they retaken Stoumont? 'Col. McDowell is operating from the right,' came the response, 'but he is fog-bound. He is working his way through the woods [to that place], but he ran into some stuff. He is getting a lot of direct fire personally.' Enemy shooting was so intense it was clipping limbs off trees. Col Frankland was there, too, but 'getting pecked at'.[27]

At 2.12 p.m. the 119th Infantry was still a kilometer west of Stoumont dealing with belts of minefields and well-ranged fire; one of the accompanying tanks was knocked out. Col Hill, with V Corps G-3, pleaded for air support, but word came that airfields were still socked in and 'there isn't much hope they can get up'.

By 9.02 a.m. on 20 December, Company K of the 3rd Battalion of the 117th Infantry, moving from Spa, had organized a company-sized raiding party to proceed south of the village of Cour toward La Gleize. GIs on the ground reported 'it is so foggy that they can't see a thing down there'.[28] The infantry, escorted by twenty Sherman tanks of 3rd Armored's Task Force McGeorge, managed to pass through Cour to reach Borgoumont by 11 a.m. Bob Kaufmann was in the advance with 36th Armored Infantry as they pushed for La Gleize by crossing Nabonruy Creek:

> After some time, our squad was called together and we were ordered to move out … We crossed the bridge and a short distance later, we moved off the right side of the road and began ascending the hill. There were barbed-wire cattle fences to deal with and the only sound that could be heard was the squad leader's wire cutter snipping wire fencing … The several of us who crossed the brook had not gone too far when we heard the frightening sound of the bolt of a machine gun being moved back into the load position. No sooner had we hit the ground, when the machine gun opened fire. Fortunately for us, the gun had been pre-sighted on the bridge we had just crossed. But no sooner had the machine gun opened up, when we were suddenly overwhelmed with rifle fire, not only from our front, but along the full length of our flank. Then there was the pop of a fire gun and the eerie, shimmering light that gave the landscape a ghostly and unreal complexion. The German defenders began yelling at us to surrender. In the midst of all that, explosions resulting from hand grenades began erupting among our men, splattering us with dirt. Our squad leader whispered for us to withdraw. There were at least three new men in our squad and this baptism of fire was something no one had expected. We tried to squirm around to get out of there. After slithering on our bellies for a considerable distance, we decided we were beneath the trajectory of fire and stood up and made our way down the rest of the hill, heading toward the stream. Crossing the bridge was out of the

> question because of the machine gun. We were forced to make our way through the chilly water. We finally made our way back to buildings where the rest of our platoon had remained.[29]

At 3 p.m. Bastin and his wife spied an American tank column approaching from Roanne. This was Company L of the 117th Infantry Regiment supported by a few tanks from Company A of the 743rd Tank Battalion. Those manning the SS roadblock anticipated this move, and after numerous anti-tank rounds, the lead American tank burst into flames. In the fire, smoke, and confusion, the other four tanks pulled back. Shortly afterward, German tanks took their place and ruled the terrain. However, Lt Robert A. Peters, the 3rd Battalion's AT officer, was satisfied, having disabled one of the panzers. Company L consolidated its position in Roanne and held that position all the following day, but efforts to put pressure on La Gleize were stymied.

'The Americans arrived just in front of Borgoumont,' remembered Dr Bastin at his home in the same village. 'The men kept asking questions: the number of German tanks, the calibre of the guns, SS or Wehrmacht.' The official word from the Americans was as follows: at 12.12 p.m. the Company K of the battalion supported by Task Force McGeorge pushed forward. A few patrols reported reaching the edge of La Gleize at dusk, but there they ran into a hornet's nest of tank gun and automatic fire.[30] The repulse eventually devolved into a resurgent SS counterattack with two platoons of Company K temporarily surrounded. Only through determined action by the rest of the company were they able to pull out to defensive positions in the darkness.[31]The remaining troops of the battalion stayed in defensive positions in Roanne and Moulin-du-Ruy, with both sides trading automatic weapons fire.[32] Dr Bastin:

> The Americans decided to penetrate into La Gleize. They invited me to join the column to show the soldiers the little footpaths, the creeks, and machine gun nests. There were 25 tanks, 200 infantry, and 12 of the F.I. from Spa whose commander was Mickey Decerf. They had bad equipment, but these courageous, young boys were marching before the tanks. After one hour, we approached the village. The Villa Closset was hidden in the thick fog. We lay on the ground and the lead tank fired a shell in front of the house … We went further … A new stop because a machine gun was firing in the fog. A soldier had been hit in the leg. Two feet from my left shoulder, the earth was suddenly raised by bullets. I knew enough from that; I won't go any further. But everyone was thinking the same and the word passed around – 'We go back.' Something exploded in front of the tank where I was lying … it was a mine. As we pulled back … the head tank driving back also hit a mine and was soon burning. The rubber of the track burned … The soldiers were not happy they were on recon.[33]

As confusing as were the mines and fog, the armored action of Task Force McGeorge ended that day when the mist lifted briefly in the afternoon. A panzer watching Borgoumont from the south fired once and blew up the M4 of Lt Carl E. Wanamaker, who died with his entire crew. Company K attempted an infantry counterattack on the nearby village of Hasoumont to blunt SS control, but this move to the south at 6 p.m. was soon checked. Two squads were again temporarily surrounded by German defenders. When Company K pulled back toward Cour, it counted many casualties. And at a place called Chenaî, north of La Gleize, the American infantry got a taste of the pitiless nature of their adversary. In this old Belgian farmhouse, an American night patrol discovered the bleeding and lifeless bodies of Françoise Istasse and Arthur Delvenne sitting in armchairs, their legs covered by blankets, shot in their sleep.[34]

Later, Herbert Stock with the 11th Panzer Grenadier Company would describe a scene chillingly similar. Stock maintained that Uscha. Heinz Klipp with the 1st platoon of the company had shot ten Americans captured in the woods near his foxhole.

> After seeing these dead soldiers, I entered the same house behind which they were lying and in the house I saw two dead civilians, each of whom were still sitting in a chair. Both of these civilians were about 60 years of age. Later, Uscha. Klipp boasted that he had let someone shoot them.[35]

That night, in spite of German mortars that landed sporadically in their village, Dr Bastin and his wife fell asleep reassured by the Americans who remained in the village. The next day, 21 December, was worse. The American tanks had pulled back to Roanne 4–5km north-east of La Gleize. 'We don't learn anything about the operations; we won't understand the movements of the troops …'

At 3.14 p.m. on 20 December the 117th Infantry Regiment was asking if their 3rd Battalion strike had reached La Gleize. Answer? No. 'The Jerries have a strong roadblock north-west of La Gleize, supported by tanks and infantry. Our task force is having quite a fight there.'[36] The battalion of the 117th Infantry attacking reported being stopped when a patrol came across two enemy tanks in the zone in which L Company was to assemble at Roanne. [37]At dark the U.S. divisional commander awaited word that the 117th with Task Force McGeorge had penetrated into La Gleize. It never came. 'They are getting 20mm, mortar, and tank fire.' Instead, the U.S combat teams pulled back.

There was still danger to the north. If the SS tankers turned that way, they might catch up with the massive fuel dumps still being evacuated. To hem them in, Col John Welborn, the acting commander of Combat Command B, 3rd Armored Division had split his unit into three battalion-sized task forces to contain Peiper.[38] The forces of CCB moved out of La Reid, just south of Spa, at 8 a.m. Task Force Jordan under Maj. John W. Jordan was to attack from north of Stoumont with the remainder of the 3rd Battalion, 119th Infantry, to slam the door shut on that German approach.[39] Meanwhile, Task Force McGeorge, under Maj. Kenneth McGeorge with Company K of the 117th Infantry was to close the net on Peiper from the north-east – although they had to change their planned route as the path south of Spa proved too narrow and muddy to support tanks.[40] At the same time, the largest tank force, Task Force Lovelady, of Col William B. Lovelady was to be attached to the 117th Infantry. The combined team was to

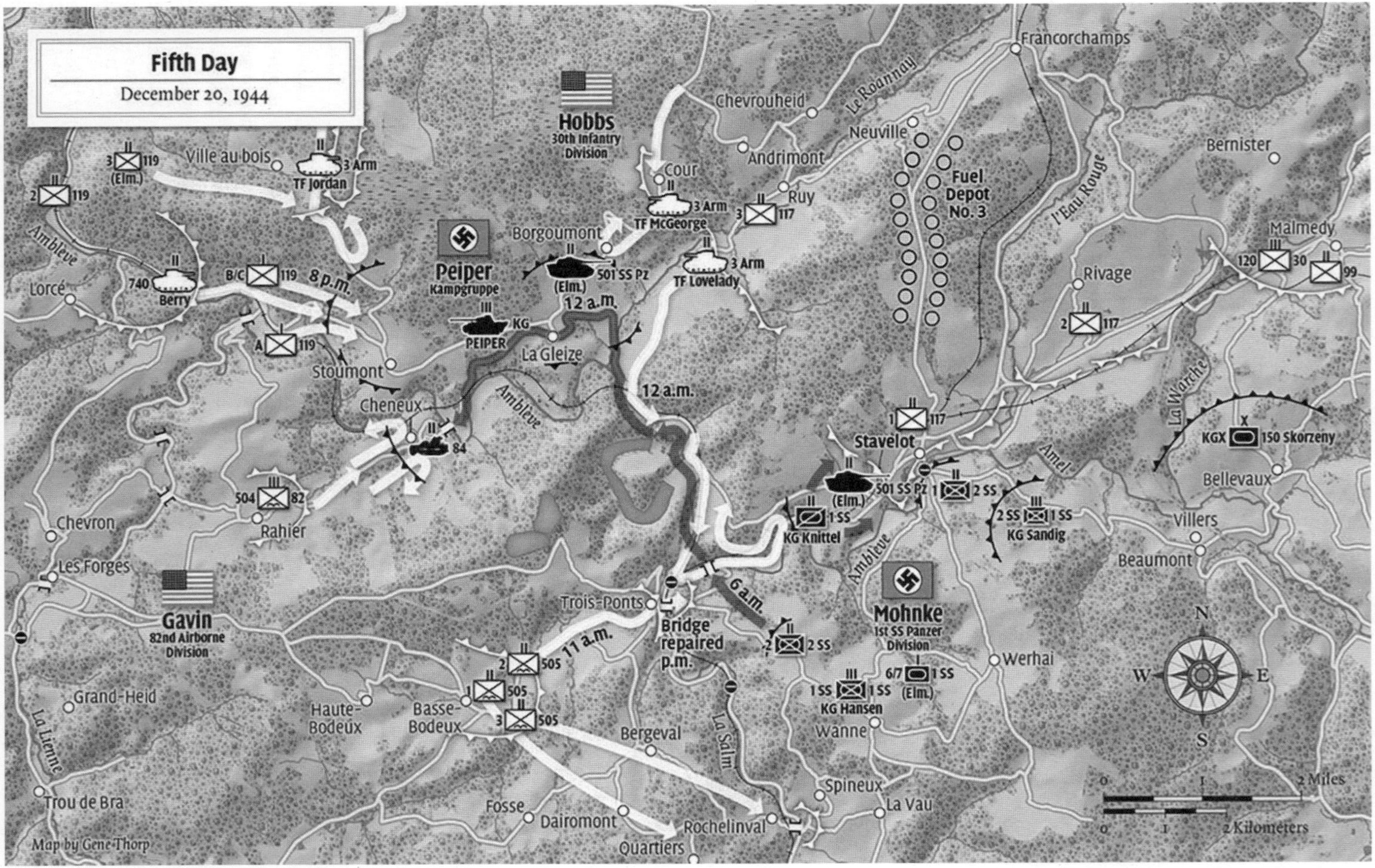

Fifth Day
December 20, 1944
Hobbs
30th Infantry Division
Peiper
Kampgruppe
Gavin
82nd Airborne Division
Mohnke
1st SS Panzer Division
Ville au bois
TF Jordan
3 Arm
Lorcé
Ambleve
740
Berry
8 p.m.
Stoumont
Cheneux
84
504
82
Rahier
Chevron
Les Forges
Grand-Heid
La Lienne
Trou de Bra
Borgoumont
501 SS Pz
(Elm.)
12 a.m.
KG
PEIPER
La Gleize
Cour
TF McGeorge
TF Lovelady
Chevrouheid
Andrimont
Ruy
Neuville
Le Roannay
Fuel Depot No. 3
Francorchamps
l'Eau Rouge
Bernister
Malmedy
Rivage
La Warche
KGX
150 Skorzeny
Bellevaux
Villers
Beaumont
Stavelot
Amel
KG Sandig
KG Knittel
6 a.m.
Trois-Ponts
Bridge repaired p.m.
11 a.m.
505
Haute-Bodeux
Basse-Bodeux
Bergeval
La Salm
Fosse
Dairomont
Quartiers
Rochelinval
Spineux
La Vau
Wanne
KG Hansen
Werhai
N
E
S
W
2 Miles
2 Kilometers
Map by Gene Thorp

clear the highway between La Gleize and Stavelot, where increasing German attacks were threatening to reopen supply lines to Peiper.[41]

Nothing went smoothly. Both TF Jordan and TF McGeorge ran head-on into the enemy and were stopped about a quarter of a mile from their objectives of Stoumont and La Gleize, respectively. In the meantime, the forty odd tanks and half-tracked infantry of Task Force Lovelady were supposed to approach La Gleize from the east.

Lovelady's advance party proceeded from Roanne at 2.20 p.m. on 20 December. At that time, Lt Albert E. Hope's E Company ran across two small groups of the enemy not far from the Coo railway station: a few trucks and a couple of towed 105mm howitzer guns of the 1st Battalion of the divisional artillery attempting to reach Peiper. The second column was led by a *Schwimmwagen*, escorting a self-propelled, 150mm howitzer (the only Hummel in the 1st SS Panzer Division), two SPWs, ammunition trucks, and some infantry.[42] Both columns were shot up and dispersed.

Hope radioed back to Lovelady of his satisfactory encounter and received orders to proceed on toward Stavelot driving via Trois-Ponts. Yet the SS commanders were now warned. Near Trois-Ponts, Hope's tanks ran into infantry of the 2nd Battalion of Rudolf Sandig's 2nd SS Panzer Grenadier Regiment that had crossed at the wooden Petit Spai Bridge earlier in the morning.[43] In the heavily wooded road, Panzerfaust-wielding grenadiers with sited anti-tank cannon picked off the first light tank, then the fourth and then those in between. As the tanks blew up, the SS men sprayed the crippled vehicles with machine gun fire. Lt Hope was killed, and Maj. George Stallings took over the tiny combat team in Petit Coo, now cut off from the rest of Task Force Lovelady in the triangle at the confluence of the Amblève and Salm rivers.[44]

Meanwhile, back at La Gleize, Rolf Ehrhardt and Oskar Klingelhöfer had slept the night of 19 December in a La Gleize basement. Upon arising in the morning, they looked to fulfil Peiper's orders to them the day before by going to Wanne to fetch the missing 7th Panzer Company:

> By daybreak we started, but before the viaduct on the road to Coo, an SPW with an orderly officer from the division staff came toward us. He stopped and told us that the broad was blocked a bit further down by American tanks. We put down at the mill [Moulin Marechal] and took over protecting the road to Coo. The duty shortly became official; there was a Königstiger, commanded by Ustuf. Georg Handtusch, as well as a small detachment from the reconnaissance battalion with an armored Puma, and a *Panzerschreck* platoon. With us, this became blocking position Mill. My Mark IV stood behind the bower, the Königstiger in the yard, and the Puma between some trees along the road. All barrels were aiming at the road curve … No doubt we would have prepared a hot reception for the Americans. The expected attack did not happen and the 20th passed quietly, but without boredom. I made several reconnaissance walks, especially up the slope toward Werimont. From time to time there was heavy fog, and we depended more on ears than eyes. Motor sounds from the road Coo–Franchorchamps constantly kept us alert. Once when we heard idling engines, I set off on foot and

> I recognised six American tanks, but the distance was too far for the Panzerfaust, and not too great for the machine gunner. Suddenly, bullets flew past my ears and I could only save myself by an Olympic-style hurdle over a fence – to a stone wall. After an anxious quarter of an hour the tanks departed to Coo.[45]

When Ehrhardt got back to the Moulin Maréchal, he worried the Americans might be almost upon them. He went up into the farmhouse there and sat on the top floor with binoculars looking out at the road running above them and the other side of the little Rognany Brook that meandered close by. Nothing. Satisfied, as the day ended, he came down to the kitchen in the half-basement, where he found an operating stove and some food. A little pilfering the pantry and Ehrhardt was soon frying potatoes, the aroma soon attracting other hungry men. The kitchen at the Moulin Maréchel buzzed 'like an ant hill'.

> This swarm was suddenly hit by an unannounced volley of machine gun fire. An American raiding patrol had worked itself unnoticed along the brook within a close distance – about 30 metres of the house. The panic that broke out in the kitchen was indescribable. Some men tried to go up the stairs, but the door to the staircase was blocked by other men seeking cover. I myself, and six to eight comrades threw ourselves below the window. I can't say how long the fire lasted … We expected hand grenades through the windows and a Uscha. and I tried to break out. But the fire stopped as suddenly as it had begun. A Puma fended off the spook … The *Amis* were able to disengage without losses. With the firepower of the Puma, that was really a miracle … In the afternoon, I again posted myself at the attic window. In the meantime, the fog had lifted and I had a good view of the road. I discovered an American armored column coming from the direction of Franchorchamps – two-thirds were tanks – driving slowly in march formation.[46]

The American tanks spied by SS driver Ehrhardt were part of Task Force Lovelady approaching from Roanne toward the junction of N33. To Klingelhöfer, Ehrhardt advocated an improvised ambush. Their Mk IV would stay on the left of the mill and Königstiger #211 on the right would allow a good portion of the vehicles to pass by through the forest on the road above them. The Tiger would then shoot down the point tank. 'We will hit the last tank we can reach, and then we will clean up both sides toward the middle.' The Americans would have no possibility to escape; the road was too narrow. However, when Klingelhöfer and Ehrhardt presented this plan to Hantusch, he refused. 'Firing uphill!' he scowled. 'I am young and not weary of life. And I have only 3 centimetres of steel over my head!'[47] A powerful American tank force had cut the road between La Gleize and Trois-Ponts, just what Peiper had directed them not to let happen.

Later out of frustration, Ehrhardt and another group of reconnaissance men went on another patrol in the dark, coming across a group of Americans attempting to repair a vehicle. Confronted by submachine guns, most escaped, but Ehrhardt managed to take an American prisoner. 'The very young soldier was in shock. He wept and his whole body shook.' Several SS troopers escorted the prisoner back to the mill for a personal interrogation by Peiper.

'The information learned was important, but hardly cheerful.' Peiper discovered the young soldier's tank unit had come from the Düren area.[48] The 3rd Armored Division was on the way to encircle his thrust behind American lines. Hardly welcome news given the heavy fighting in Stoumont and Stavelot further east.

Meanwhile, at Hitler's headquarters at Adlerhorst, Wednesday, 20 December went by with little new word on Sepp Dietrich and his favored 6th Panzer Army. Word did come that the 1st SS Panzer Division was busy throwing back attacks on Stavelot, which was now effectively in American hands. 'No new reports from the Kampfgruppe Peiper 25 kilometers west of Stavelot,' the summary mentioned.[49] However, by morning on 22 December, the same report told of offensive failure: 'The Kampfgruppe Peiper is concentrating around La Gleize since repelling all enemy attacks after air supply did not come through.'[50]

Shortly before supper, Brig. Gen. William K. Harrison with the 30th Infantry Division returned to Gen. Hobbs's headquarters from visiting the V Corps headquarters in Eupen. There, he found Hobbs 'somewhat depressed and dissatisfied with the 119th Infantry which he had visited during the day'. The necessity of co-ordinating both the 30th Division and CCB, 3rd Armored, made it important the armor be attached to the 30th at 5 p.m. on 20 December. The next step was to place all the forces involved in the Stoumont–La Gleize pocket under a central commander.

Radio signals in the broken Ardennes terrain were notoriously unreliable and Lt Col Courtney Brown, the executive officer of the 119th in Halte, was only in sporadic communication with the forces fighting in the sector. Peiper had the same problem, complaining that the only reliable communication with division from his radio set came from Morse code.[51] Indeed, the FuG.5 radios in Hans Gruhle's command Panther in La Gleize by his headquarters could not even raise the division. Instead, the larger Fu G.12 80-Watt radio set in Oscha. Sepp Diener's SPW was set up right outside of Peiper's CP. With this radio SPW, Peiper was at last able to raise Mohnke in Wanne 10km away.[52]

At 1750 hours on the night of 20 December, an exasperated Maj. Gen. Hobbs was on the phone to Col Sutherland. 'We've got to have that town the first thing in the morning,' he complained, 'there has been too much stalling north and south … Get those troops moving and into the town the first thing in the morning … As for the battalion commander of that battalion (the 3rd), I want him relieved.' Sutherland: 'I have already done so.' Hobbs was nearly beside himself. 'I don't want any excuses about getting in there. Get going! … and when you do that, immediately move east and make contact with La Gleize.' 'I already have McCown ready to do that.' Hobbs: 'Get started early.' 'We'll do the best we can.'[53] That wasn't what Leland Hobbs wanted to hear.

The 3rd Battalion in Stoumont had taken quite a beating and lost nearly two hundred men, now captive. Lt Col Roy Fitzgerald was relieved of command. The nearly disastrous action the previous day had shown the lack of cohesive leadership in repelling Kampfgruppe Peiper. Harrison was a natural choice for the job, particularly as he had skilfully managed the division during the Operation Cobra action in Normandy. Moreover, the brigadier general was now familiar with both the ground and troops. By way of contrast, Col Edwin Sutherland had been nearly paralysed with worry the previous day; his idea of tactical finesse was 'simply to go barging ahead'. At 7.40 p.m. Hobbs told Harrison to take over the whole regiment.[54]

> I and an aide left the CP immediately after talking to Hobbs and went a roundabout way to the 119th CP at the west of Stoumont on the road to Liège. The direct route was blocked by the Germans. Because of reports of German parachutists in the area, we carried our weapons ready to shoot, but to our relief nothing happened. Arriving at the CP at about 10 p.m., I found that an order for an attack at daylight had already gone out to the troops. I looked at the situation map and decided to let the attack go off as planned since not knowing the situation, I figured I might obtain some urgently needed success and at least it would give a better picture of the situation. The attack started as planned, but made no headway … When I got to the front, I saw the Sanatorium … It was a short distance off to my left and in the advance there was a knocked-out Sherman tank. It had been captured and used by the Germans. The U.S. white star markings were on it – I suppose this was to deceive us. The Germans had taken the Sanatorium during [the earlier] night, but at the moment I did not see indications that they were still occupying it … If they had been in it, they would probably have fired on us. A sergeant told me he had been in the fight for the Sanatorium and admitted the SS soldiers were 'right fanatical'. … The sergeant told me that on the outside of the Sanatorium the men were dug in – not a strong force. The Germans worked their way in close in the dark and then fired a number of their bazooka rounds and immediately charged. We lost some men and the Sanatorium. If you've seen the one-shot German bazooka, you know it can make a real big bang when its shell explodes.[55]
>
> After looking over the ground I decided that the only way to recapture Stoumont was to make a holding attack with the seriously depleted 1st and 3rd Battalions and an envelopment with the 2nd, holding one company in reserve. The attack was launched, the 2nd Battalion moving around through the woods to the north to come in from behind. They actually started to set up a roadblock on the Stoumont–La Gleize road I believe. They were discovered and the battalion commander was captured. He and his small group ran into a strong German patrol in the woods. After that, neither wing of the attack made any progress, so we pulled back the companies of the 2nd Battalion to secure positions for the night. Although the attack itself was not successful, it scared the Germans into pulling out of Stoumont and to re-join the remainder of their forces in La Gleize. We followed up and set up my CP in the château of Stoumont [Chateau de Froidcour]. The Germans had ransacked the place, including the wine cellar.[56]

On the other side, Jochen Peiper himself could find little encouraging that Wednesday:

> On the 20th, the conditions became much more strained; I was out of communications with the division and the supply line had not been cleared either.

> Reconnaissance patrols were sent out in the direction of Stavelot and returned without performing their task [of re-establishing contact with the German forces south of the bridge.] Furthermore, reconnaissance patrols of mine could notice enemy concentrations north of La Gleize. In the afternoon heavy attacks from the west were made in Stoumont. Cheneux was attacked from the south-west and about forty-five tanks passed us by going east toward Stavelot.[57]

Chaos prevailed in the gloomy Ardennes. No one knew exactly what was going on. For the U.S. First Army, 20 December developed as another bad day. Otto Skorzeny still had a fifth column commando operation motoring around U.S. rear lines as well and the von der Heydte parachutists seemed to be showing up all over. In fact, Baron von der Heydte himself had been wounded and would later surrender to U. S. forces in Monschau on 24 December.

Seemingly, the von der Heydte operation had miscarried, but one interrogation of a Fallschirmjäger officer had struck a new intelligence nerve. There were still 300 planes at the airfield at Sennelager, one excited paratrooper told his interrogator, with a capacity of 4,000 men. 'It is quite possible that these paratroopers could land in our uniforms,' the worried G-2 continued. 'In the event of such a paratroop landing in our sector, panic must be avoided. *Just don't be surprised!*'[58]

Chapter 27

IN THE CAULDRON

I don't know what effect these men will have upon the enemy, but by God, they frighten me.

Duke of Wellington

Surrounded. That was the military situation Jochen Peiper faced on 21 December 1944. While the American defense on the 18th and 19th had been haphazard and inconsistent, by that Thursday Peiper's forces were fully outnumbered. Reinforcements – from the 3rd Armored Division – swarmed around his battle group. His single tank battalion – along with the equivalent of two infantry battalions and a flak detachment – had little in the way of heavy artillery and a rapidly diminishing ammunition supply.

There was now almost no fuel. By that date, the Americans had encircled him with the equivalent of four tank battalions, twelve infantry battalions, two tank destroyer companies, and twelve well-supplied artillery battalions.[1] Knittel's reconnaissance battalion and a few Tigers near Trois-Ponts were able to add gumption, but not enough to counter the crushing enemy advantage.

Both Jochen Peiper, stuck in the pocket between La Gleize and Stoumont, and Gen. Hobbs, attempting to contain him, could see they were mutually overextended. Each leader stood in buildings, planning on maps, telephones, and radios as to how to annihilate the other. On that same day, Hobbs ordered the 30th Division to tighten down its stranglehold on Kampfgruppe Peiper, while denying enemy attempts at rescue. The noose on Peiper tightened near Stavelot with the recapture of Ster, Renardmont, and Parfondruy, revealing horrific civilian atrocities committed by Knittel's men.[2] Nevertheless, all attempts to cross the Amblève river to relieve Peiper were turned back.

On the west side of Peiper's advance, Gen. Harrison's plan of attack for 21 December involved a squeeze play on Stoumont and a thrust from the east on La Gleize. The sequence was as follows: the 2nd Battalion of the 119th under

Maj. Hal McCown would conduct a wide envelopment to the north, then turn south and strike Stoumont from the east, seizing the road midway between Stoumont and La Gleize and thus setting up a strong all-around defense.

Meanwhile, Herlong's 1st Battalion along with Berry's tanks would cast the SS men out of the Stoumont Sanatorium and then move into the town from the north-west. Simultaneously, Task Force Jordan and the 3rd Battalion would outflank the enemy from the north. Task Force Harrison had orders to attack at 7.30 a.m., seize Stoumont, and reduce all resistance north of the Amblève river. Once that mission was complete, they were to make their way to La Gleize to join up with a battalion of the 117th Infantry Regiment assigned to evict the Germans from that place in conjunction with Task Force McGeorge of CCB, 3rd Armored Division.[3] However, before the American attack could get started, at 7:20 a.m., a piecemeal German counterattack towards Harrison stopped everything. That effort was blasted by American artillery, however, forcing Peiper to pull back. At the end of the engagement, Gen. Harrison called off the advance until later on the 21st.

The news was not good from Lt Col Robert Herlong, who stood in the way of Peiper's thrust: Companies B and C were decimated. In the twenty-four hours since commitment, the 1st Battalion of the 119th Infantry Regiment had lost more than two hundred men and five platoon commanders. B and C Companies were badly weakened and down to about sixty men each. Still, under a new plan, the attack would resume at 12.45 p.m. simultaneously both from north and west with co-ordinated artillery fire. By then the 2nd Battalion under Maj. Hal McCown would have sliced into the thick woods of the Bois de Bassenge north and east of the road. That would cut the enemy pocket in half. Or so went the plan.

Gen. Leland Hobbs, in charge of 30th Division, was on the phone with Col Russell F. 'Red' Akers with the U.S. First Army. 'How is the thing going?' Akers asked stoically. 'Sticky,' Hobbs admitted. 'How about the west?' Rather than describe the body blows he was taking, Hobbs preferred to tell how he was dishing it out to Peiper's battle group. 'At Stoumont, they have had two attacks this morning; they are being hit at La Gleize, too. There is sort of a pocket in there …' Akers remarked that Hobbs must have half of the 1st SS surrounded. That was one reason for their trouble, Hobbs agreed. 'They are trying to get out,' he reckoned, 'forward or backward or something.'[4]

The Germans still held the sanatorium in Stoumont. Raymond Beco remembered the Germans coming down the long steps at 10 a.m. on 20 December. Bursting into the cellar, the SS men boasted loudly to the frightened civilians that they would 'soon be in Liège!' Beco thought they seemed 'all hopped up' and their attitude 'fierce'.[5] Several Americans in the sanatorium were totally surprised and dropped their weapons. The SS men did not shoot, but one did swing in anger at a GI with his rifle. 'You'll have no trouble from us if you leave us alone,' one German told the priest, 'but if you shoot at us as they did in Stavelot, then we will treat you as we did them.'[6] Within minutes, the Germans took over the entire building, but mostly left those in the cellar alone. The big worry now was gunfire. Large-calibre artillery began to fall and the entire building shook. Each hour it seemed to grow closer. By 21 December the Americans had rained hundreds of shells on Stoumont.

Even the first night, the fighting swirled outside the sanatorium. Amid loud firing and shell bursts, the terrified people in the sanatorium cellar were placing mattresses up against the walls hoping to stop shrapnel. A large, German panzer posted itself outside the main hall while U.S. artillery shells from the 197th FA Battalion whistled down from Nonceveux. As the shooting picked up, everyone in the cellar recited the last rosary. Eventually, the battle noise faded, only to crackle occasionally through the night – an evening of fitful sleep for the 200 there.

The 740th Tank Battalion had lost five Shermans in front of the sanatorium on the outskirts of Stoumont, blocking access to the road. At noon, under a smokescreen, tank recovery vehicles of the 740th Tank Battalion cleared the hulks. The remaining tanks, with Company A, ground toward the village.[7] Charging ahead in haste, one of the Shermans surprised the panzer at the crossroads and put it out of commission. The tanks continued their push that took them all the way into the village, confronting a foxhole line of SS grenadiers on the main street. Expecting the worst, the Shermans fired point blank at the German infantry by Dr Robinson's house. The only survivor – wounded in the eye – was pulled into the cellar with the other civilians to be treated by the Belgian physician. But the headstrong American tank had ventured too far ahead and was soon hit by an anti-tank round.

At 4.02 p.m., Gen. Hobbs rang up his chief executive officer, Gen. Harrison. 'What is the real picture is down there?' 'The second battalion is alright,' Harrison replied, but we are out of contact with McCown … I think we can stop them.' Yet, Hobbs was uninterested in just stopping Peiper; he wanted the Germans thrown back entirely. Had the tanks he had sent along to Harrison helped? 'They didn't get anywhere,' Harrison complained. 'The trouble is that the only places where tanks of any type can operate are on two sunken roads. The Germans have big tanks, so tanks have been of no help to us.'

'You are not going to make more attacks?' Hobbs asked.

'I wouldn't risk it with these people,' said Harrison. 'As a matter of fact, I have pulled Herlong back a couple of hundred yards so he wouldn't invite attack. Stewart has pulled back to the edge of the woods with CCB and they are holding the north road.'

'Are you planning to attack again tomorrow?'

'No, I wouldn't advise it,' Harrison warned, 'That place is very strong. I don't think with those troops we have now, without some improvement, that we can take the thing. That is my honest opinion. They [we] are way down in strength. Trouble is that you can only get light artillery fire on the town and the Germans can shoot at us with tank guns and we can't get tanks to shoot back at them unless they come out and get hit. We had three tanks knocked out.'[8]

In the meantime, the infantry of the 1st Battalion, moving with armor, advanced 200m from Targnon and entered the sanatorium. There, scenes of desperate hand-to-hand combat commenced. Some American captives were freed, but a violent German response ensued with guns of all calibres smashing into the sanatorium. The GIs were able to hold on to the building until 3 p.m., but heavy losses continued. With the heavy enemy fire, the battalion-sized American group and their supporting tanks pulled back by 4 p.m. to avoid being enveloped in darkness.

Twenty-five-year-old Karl Wortmann was in one of the SS flak tanks and witnessed the fighting around the sanatorium. His vehicle was out of ammunition, but from the high ground near La Gleize he could see American troops swarming over the massive building. Although he thought his remaining flak tanks could have helped with the battle, he had been forced to send most of them to Cheneux to reinforce the threat there. In the end, he could only afford to send a second flak tank to help Peiper's forward redoubt:

> With its massive construction, the Sanatorium looked like a fortress. However, shells from enemy tanks, anti-tank guns, and artillery were wearing away the walls. In the end, it looked like a ruin, the roof threatening to collapse. The few panzer soldiers who were not yet wounded, didn't want to give up and continued to fight bitterly. It then became clear to each: the Sanatorium had become a defensive bastion. If it was lost, the Americans could march on to La Gleize. So, the Americans assaulted the Sanatorium's ground floor and the panzer men withdrew to the upper floors. Bitter fighting took place, man against man. Our comrades threw hand grenades downstairs to the lower floors and fired their rifles and pistols to open a way to escape the fortress. Of my second flak panzer, only three returned; the rest had been killed or wounded.[9]

During the terrible fighting in the Stoumont Sanatorium on the evening of 21 to 22 December, children and l'Abbe C. Hanlet, a Catholic priest, cowered in the basement of the building with women and children. Raymond Beco, the young Belgian boy from Stoumont, was still there with the others. Just before noon on Wednesday, one of the priests heard the Germans among them call out, 'The Americans are only 150 metres from the building!' Minutes later, they could hear machine gun fire with 'bullets sounding like hailstones smashing into the building'. Everyone was terribly frightened. Beco could hear fighting going on upstairs. Only later did it become calm. Had the Americans captured the place?

Beco hastily pulled back into the catacombs. Presently, some others appeared at the door of the basement. This time, they were SS men. The building was now half occupied by Germans and half by American hands, with loud shooting overhead. Two Germans were bellowing in anger from the door. Beco turned to his father and said, 'We're in deep trouble again.'

Brig. Gen. Harrison was on the phone to Hobbs explaining his failure to seize Stoumont: 'The attack jumped off on time,' he said. 'They got about 200 yards and got small arms fire and were stopped. McCown is going to try to work down on the other side.'

Could the 119th kick the SS men out of Stoumont? 'I don't think the other battalions can be counted on to do much. They both had night attacks. I doubt very much if they can accomplish it. I am considering pulling them back and putting down artillery and smoke so they can hold what they have got.'[10]

Later, when asked if he was moving further on to La Gleize, Harrison revealed he had lost communication with McCown, but had left a platoon to watch the mines being dug into the road between Stoumont and La Gleize.

During the early morning of 21 December, McCown's F Company was attached to the 1st Battalion to bolster the splintering line of 1st Battalion by the sanatorium. Still, only Companies E and G were available for the wide sweep through the woods north to Stoumont.

Maj. Hal McCown had ordered his 2nd Infantry Battalion to proceed across country toward La Gleize. The battalion had lined up just west of Targnon on the other side of the 90mm gun that had knocked out Peiper's furthest penetration on 19 December. On the early morning of 21 December, McCown's infantry companies marched off on a wide-arching sweep east with the mission of finally swinging south to block the Stoumont–La Gleize road. A cross-country move through heavy underbrush made for tough going. McCown:

> I had only recently taken over the battalion and was naturally trying to do everything myself. Before my attack to put the finishing bit on surrounding Peiper's troops in the Stoumont area, my regimental commander pulled my largest company (F Company) from me to attach to the 1st Battalion who was holding Peiper frontally to the west of Stoumont. To the south, the Amblève river blocked Peiper's armored task force.
>
> To the north was our 3rd Battalion, which had been badly mauled from its initial encounter with Peiper on the first day of contact and had nearly two hundred casualties. The 3rd Battalion was in a holding position and not even in contact with the Germans, but it was to push forward at H-hour and move in on Stoumont with my unit to administer the coup de grace. My unit, two companies strong, planned to push deep to the east on a northerly axis above the Stoumont–La Gleize road, cut south, chop the road, mine and block it. Then at H-hour, we would attack Stoumont with the 3rd and 1st Battalions moving at the same time in order to hit the Germans from all sides.

It was an imaginative plan and the first stages went well. Captain Ed Arn's F Company reached positions north-east of Stoumont, where they dug in to create a roadblock. Presently, McCown showed up at the F Company position with two men. 'What's out ahead here, Arn?' The enemy was not far away, Arn ventured but McCown was unmoved. He suggested that Arn might want to bring his men along to help bag the enemy. Arn politely refused. He had an order directly from division to assume a defensive posture as they were a reserve. McCown complained. Arn said nothing, but watched McCown and two enlisted men disappear down into a forested hillside.[11]

In McCown's plan, Capt. John L. Faris in charge of G Company and Capt. Warne Parker with E Company were to move east and then south to a point between La Gleize and Stoumont.[12]

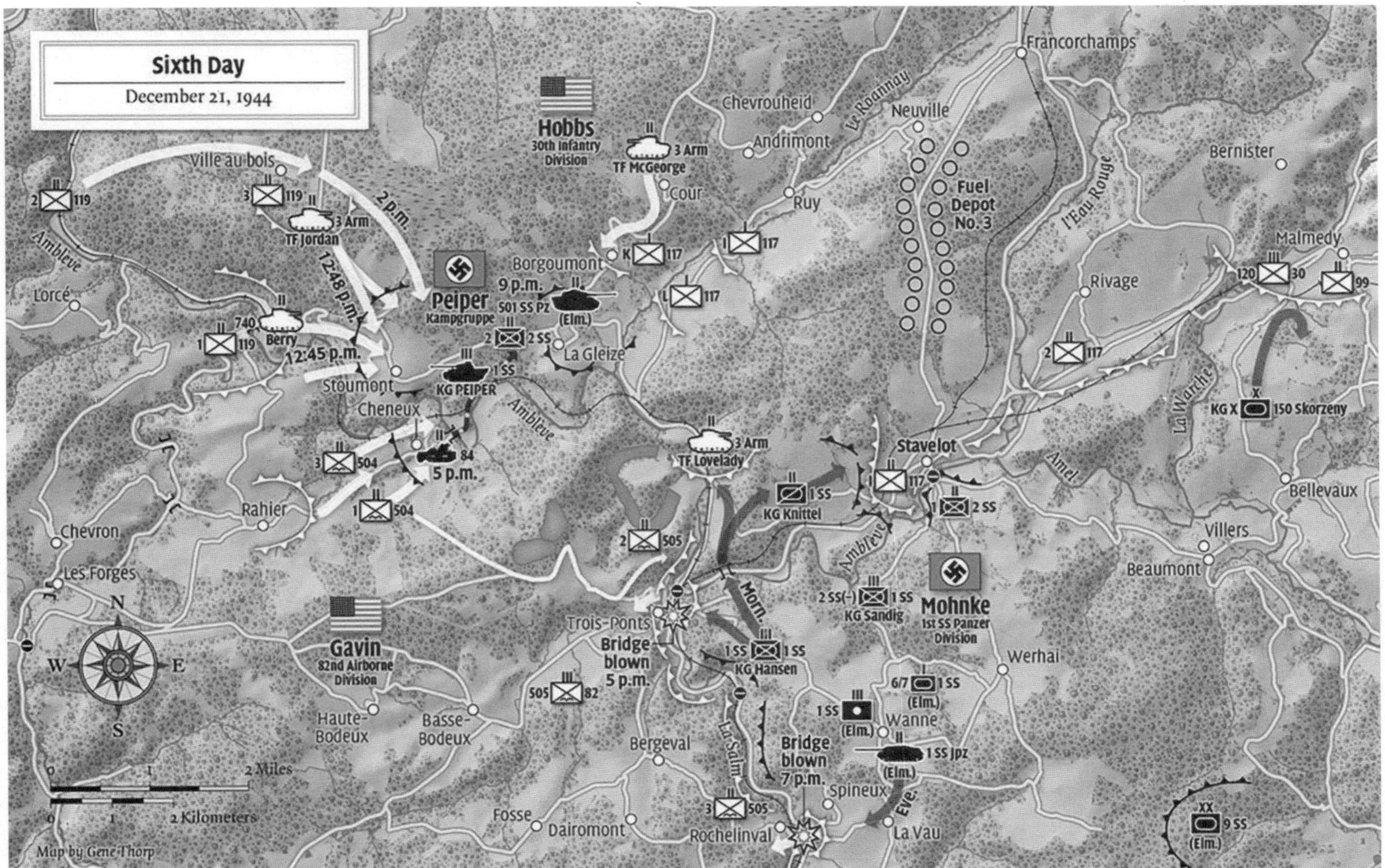
Sixth Day
December 21, 1944
Hobbs
30th Infantry Division
Peiper
Kampfgruppe
Gavin
82nd Airborne Division
Mohnke
1st SS Panzer Division
TF McGeorge
TF Jordan
TF Lovelady
KG PEIPER
KG Knittel
KG Sandig
KG Hansen
KG X
150 Skorzeny
Fuel Depot No. 3
2 p.m.
12:48 p.m.
12:45 p.m.
9 p.m.
5 p.m.
Bridge blown 5 p.m.
Bridge blown 7 p.m.
Morn.
Eve.
Francorchamps
Chevrouheid
Neuville
Andrimont
Bernister
Malmedy
Ville au bois
Cour
Ruy
Borgoumont
La Gleize
Stoumont
Cheneux
Rahier
Lorcé
Chevron
Les Forges
Rivage
Stavelot
Bellevaux
Villers
Beaumont
Trois-Ponts
Werhai
Wanne
Spineux
La Vau
Rochelinval
Bergeval
Haute-Bodeux
Basse-Bodeux
Fosse
Dairomont
Amblève
Le Roannay
l'Eau Rouge
La Warche
Amel
La Salm
2 Miles
2 Kilometers
Map by Gene Thorp

Here, they were to use an attached squad of engineers to block a road between the two towns with trunks of blown-down fir trees to contain any enemy advance. As usual, E Company was in the van on the 1km march, but when Sgt MacKay and Capt. Faris reached the road, McCown was keen on tromping ahead. 'Major,' MacKay warned, 'I'm the last guy on the right of the battalion.'[13]

The two men Arn saw with McCown were enlisted soldiers of E Company. Faris had been with McCown since daybreak as they plodded forward. 'I've been bothering you all morning,' McCown said to Faris and MacKay. 'I am going down here,' he said, motioning to the west, 'to see what a German smells like.'[14]

The two men with McCown, Pvt. Earl Barefoot and Pfc. James Winters, were dubious of McCown's intentions. Barefoot had seen enough of McCown to know the score. 'He didn't get down for nothing,' Barefoot recalled of McCown under fire. 'He was totally brave – too brave for his own good.'

During the foot march, led personally by Maj. McCown, only sporadic mortar fire fell. The surprise seemed to have worked, for the two companies reached the Stoumont–La Gleize road in the early afternoon. Indeed, Company G laid down a hasty minefield on the road before the Germans suddenly appeared both from La Gleize and Stoumont. These were grenadiers of Preuss's 10th Company. A sharp exchange of gunfire took place at 4 p.m., where increased firepower from SS half-tracks and armor forced the Americans to pull back.

Drawing back from the melee, several noted that the battalion commander was missing. McCown had been on a personal reconnaissance of the German positions. Two other men with him reported back telling of a narrowly avoided capture. At the same time, the other two prongs of Harrison's co-ordinated attack ran into heavy resistance. The word back to the division was as bad as it was terse. 'Major McCown captured,' it began, 'with map boards and all regimental installations on it.'[15] McCown continues:

> On the afternoon of 21 December at about 1600 hours, I, my radio operator, and orderly were captured by a German patrol which had us covered from all sides in a trap; a machine gun fired over our heads and individuals from another patrol closed in on us from three directions. At that time, I was moving away from the front line where I had inspected the front-line positions of my battalion which was flanking Stoumont from the Germans' rear. I was taken back to the German CP at Stoumont and as I passed through the town, observed preparations everywhere for departure among the Germans. The German commander later told me it was the appearance of my troops on his rear in Stoumont that caused him to evacuate the town that night. The German patrol took me back to the main headquarters at La Gleize, passing through several areas where firefights were going on between my men and the surrounded Germans. Knowing my own plans for the capture of Stoumont were put into effect at that time, I was halfway expecting to be recaptured before I reached La Gleize.[16]

Command reverted to Maj. Nathaniel J. Laney, the executive officer of the 2nd Battalion. No sooner had he taken over for McCown than he was ordered to pull the men back to the west of Stoumont, lest they too be encircled. In the interim, Faris blew down the trees across the road between Stoumont and La Gleize just in time to find the smoking logs under submachine gun fire coming from a German motorcycle and a staff car. Land mines and bazookas took care of the incursion, but Faris knew that McCown, having gone further along, would be running directly into the Germans who were coming up from behind.[17]

Pvt. Earl B. Barefoot was the runner for Capt. Warne R. Parker, McCown's Company E commander. No one liked Parker, including Barefoot.[18] 'He was a coward, but more than that he was mentally ill. He would hide in basements, and he would shake whenever there was any shooting outside.' Yet, Company E fought well largely due to the bravery of S/Sgt Harold L. Holycross. He was the leader of the 2nd Platoon of Company E – a man Barefoot thought 'was the greatest soldier I ever met. He ran that whole company, even though Parker was supposedly in charge. Parker kept him around to run the whole show – he just followed after Holycross like a dog, going from one basement to the next and giving the craziest orders.'[19] In the autumn, Holycross and Company E had turned in a much talked-about combat performance in turning back a German counterattack on 16 October near Wurselen.

Since taking over the battalion in November, McCown had decided that E Company was his best bet to lead an attack. Now, in Ardennes as the 2nd Battalion moved between Stoumont and La Gleize, the two privates from Company E were along. Barefoot would serve as McCown's runner and help him locate Capt. Parker, who was supposedly up ahead, looking to cut the road to La Gleize.

> I went down the road with Colonel McCown and Pfc. [James C.] Winters. He was trying to get ahead; he wanted to find Capt Parker. 'He is supposed to be up here,' he said. I tried to tell him he was not around. Though he was nowhere close, he was behind us. I kept saying, 'He is going to get us killed.' He thought the captain was ahead of us. McCown would have really been unhappy if he knew the truth. I told him, 'The captain is not up ahead!' But he wouldn't listen to an enlisted man. I had already dropped back. I knew the captain was in a basement to the rear and we were going the wrong way. I said, 'Winters, drop back.' Then, I heard the guns go off – *bang, bang, bang*. I said to Winters, 'They've probably killed him – let's get out of here …' I didn't have to say much more to him. We were both running back … If the Germans had captured us instead of McCown, I doubt they would have taken us prisoner. I was happy to get out of there.[20]

McCown:

> My capture was as sheer a piece of stupidity on my part as any personal act I have ever committed … I left my command post and soft-skinned elements to the rear of the 3rd Battalion to the north, swung down into the valley and

> successfully mined the road, felling trees across it to prevent armored vehicles from reinforcing La Gleize. At H-hour my two companies jumped off, moving west toward Stoumont. We could hear shooting and artillery which we assumed was the 1st and 3rd Battalions starting their attack from positions closer to the town. My work with the two companies was now in good shape, so I moved with my operations sergeant and radio operator back to the slope to the north, well to the rear of my attacking companies. My aim was to contact the flank of the 3rd Battalion to prevent any unfortunate brush of our own troops firing into each other. The slopes were thickly wooded with occasional small clearings. Suddenly, a German soldier appeared to our front. I thumbed the catch on my weapon, an Italian Beretta submachine gun and dropped him with three shots on semi-automatic. Realising the 3rd Battalion must have been slow in making its move, I moved with my companions still further to the north to dodge any loose Germans in the area. We had not moved more than a hundred yards when we spotted three more Germans moving toward us from the front in deployed formation. We hit the ground. Shortly after, small arms from the rear were fired directly over our heads and a voice shouted. *'Kommen sie hier!'* I looked around and spotted what looked like a platoon deployed across the trail along which we had come. They had apparently been trailing us since I dropped the first German. We stood up with our hands in the air and that was that.[21]

Circling around and attacking from the north-east, the infantry of McCown's 2nd Battalion rapidly cleared the wooded heights and crossed the road known as 'de Harenne' at 2 p.m. They breached the Stoumont–La Gleize road near St Ann Chapel. An hour of infantry bull rushes brought the Americans close to the Froidcour, but they were unable to reach that place, finding any approach blocked by machine guns. Still, during the short time the GIs held the road, they were able to blast down three large trees across the roadway. Back and forth traffic between Stoumont and La Gleize would be impossible until the wooden trunks were removed. However, the results were not what was hoped for as the incursion came under heavy German fire with threat of envelopment in the woods. Sensing a trap, at 3.15 p.m., Brig. Gen. Harrison ordered 2nd Battalion to pull back fast.

While this mayhem played out, in Stoumont, Task Force Jordan of the 3rd Armored with his infantry and tanks resumed the assault from Monhouet toward Rouat north of the village. Moving 300m further on, the Sherman tanks were stopped once again by anti-tank fire from the crest of Rochette and Belleville. Attempts by the shaken infantry of the 3rd Infantry Battalion to challenge the enemy ended under a cascade of automatic weapons fire from the crest. Soon there was direct fire from five German tanks. The Americans halted and then directed artillery on the German defenders and the sunken road that led toward Stoumont. A spasmodic firefight took place at 1 p.m. One of the German tanks was temporarily halted by a hit from a Company K bazooka, but not for long.

With the continued pea soup fog, all the requests for air support fell flat. Even artillery observers for Peiper's limited gunnery resources were nearly blinded. Nevertheless, a big 155mm howitzer in Nonceveux nearly 8km away ranged in on Stoumont via direct fire and commenced to blast the Germans who were still stubbornly holding out. For the civilians in the sanatorium's big cellar, and those taking refuge in Dr Robinson's home, the gunnery was terrifying. Some were crazed from the bouts of pounding and gunfire.

The situation was as dire for Jochen Peiper. His column was out of gas and he would have to circle the tanks. Peiper now pulled back his command post to the castle of the towering Château Froidcour between Stoumont and La Gleize – a point of strategic observation of the entire Amblève river valley. For a short time, he stayed at the caretaker's house. On that Wednesday, Peiper took the two frightened women at the villa and ordered them to work for him in the kitchen to feed his staff. Peiper ordered the other twenty-eight members of the household staff of Baron de Harenne – gardeners, butlers, and housekeepers – to help fetch whatever was needed for his temporary command post and medical facility.

An immediate sewing session produced big bed sheets adorned with large red crosses. By noon, the Red Cross insignia would be draped over the towers of the castle where the wounded – both German and American – were housed in its dark basement. Yet, the fog made it impossible for the American artillerymen to see the red cross and at least a dozen shells fell near the castle. One blew in a section of the roof. 'The Americans are really bandits!' Peiper raged at one of the Baron's workers. 'Now, they are shooting at the wounded!'[22]

Yet, Chantal de Harenne at the house recalled Peiper as an frenzied SS man who brought no harm to anyone there. 'He was always running from one place to another.'[23] The tactical prospects from the German side at the château grew depressing. 'On 21 December, the American attacks again increased in intensity,' remembered Rolf Reiser.

> Our defense was severely affected by the shortage of fuel and ammunition. We could not permit any panzer movement and had to be sparing with the tank ammunition. Every panzer shell had to hit its target … During the withdrawal, our command panzerstopped near Schloss Froidcour. In the lower rooms of the castle lay more than a hundred German wounded, most of whom had to be left behind … It was difficult to bid them farewell, especially when given an imploring look and a squeeze of the hand, yet we had to make known our own inability to help.[24]

Peiper's adjutant, SS Hstuf. Gerhard Nueske, was with his commander when they pulled out from the castle, and shuttled a short distance east to the town of La Gleize. He would remain with Peiper at his C.P. on the east end of town for the rest of the fighting.[25]

The properties in Stoumont, including the sanatorium, had been seized the day before by Herlong's 1st Battalion when it first passed through town. However, that evening the institution there had become the focus of Peiper's frustrated spearhead group. Franz Siever's panzer engineers slammed into the 1st Battalion positions in combat chaos in the darkness. So desperate became the fight that Hal McCown offered his F Company to Herlong. Yet, the company commander, Edward C. Arn, was not interested in joining disaster:

> On a hunch, I took only a runner with me. I'll never forget the distraught condition of Herlong and his staff officers. His command post was in a large barn, as I recalled, behind St Edouard's. The point-blank tank fire had converted the entire hill into a blazing and exploding conflagration. Parts of the Sanatorium caught fire, shells detonated all over the place, and the command post was wallowing in complete confusion. The orange flames of the tanks' guns and the screams of terrified people huddled in St Edouard's basement completed the chaotic picture. Herlong's infantry were taking a terrible beating. Herlong managed to scream at me to commit my kids … He and I argued over most of the night and I took one hell of a verbal going over.
>
> Nevertheless, I never ordered one Fox Company rifleman into that bloody mess. It would have been stupid to have done so … At daybreak, we snuck back to my command post near Targnon.[26]

The American intentions were this: the 119th Infantry and the 1st Battalion with some support of the surviving elements of the 3rd Battalion would attack at 8 a.m. and seize Stoumont while the 504th of the 82nd Airborne Division would attack from the west. Lt David Knox was still in charge of Company L, recovering with the shattered 3rd Battalion at nightfall 20 December:

> We were alerted to go back into Stoumont. It would be done that night, the regimental commander said. We got ready and went to the assembly point. A sadder bunch of men I have never seen. Morale was low. They knew what had pushed them out of town – Hitler's 1st SS Panzer Division. They knew how much armor was there. Capt. Stewart wasn't in favor of the move … He finally convinced Col Sutherland to throw artillery through the town all night and try to go in the following day.[27]

In the misty night, Knox made his way to battalion headquarters. There, he was dismayed to learn that the plan for attacking Stoumont had changed four times during the night:

> By about 0800 hours we were in position above the town. It was so foggy that we couldn't see over 25 feet,' reported Knox. The town was 500 yards ahead, so given the fog, the attack was postponed until 12.45 p.m. 'The artillery barrage started and we took off with it … It was so foggy that one of our men found himself within 10 yards of a German MG before he knew it. Collins was the hero there. He knocked one position out with his BAR. Collins then turned the gun on the other German crew and knocked it out as well, but the entire action left everyone confused and blind. I told Col Stewart that contact was lost on our right and there was nothing to do, but pull back … Finally, we got word to hold up for the night. We organized with the light tanks and dug in.'

On the other side, almost out of fuel, Karl Wortmann and his flak panzer crew pulled back from Stoumont to La Gleize. They were surrounded, under a cold drizzle, with no food, fuel, ammunition, and nothing to drink. Seeking even a slight distraction, Wortmann led the men in an old student song that he now had set to new words:

> *Keine Granate Im Panzer mehr.* No more shells in the Panzer.
> *Und der Tank war auch sehen leer.* And the gas tank is empty too.
> *Bauch, Knurrrt Magen.* In our bellies, our guts growl.
> *Aber des woll'n wir dem Ami nicht sagen.* But we won't tell the *Amis* about that.

In La Gleize itself, matters were tense. Fifty Belgian civilians remained in the village, although for the most part huddling into densely packed home cellars for protection. Peiper's conduct of the battle for the village would have to be orchestrated with little remaining fuel. Accordingly, the tanks were carefully sited, camouflaged, and dug in as reinforcements from Schnelle's panzer grenadier battalion arrived to bolster Peiper's defense.

No petrol also meant that Diefenthal's and Sievers' SPWs, mounting otherwise helpful automatic weapons, remained parked in silence. More than two dozen tanks stood silent and unmoving in Monsieur Hakin's orchard – a place known as Pré de Froidcour, which was located south of the main square in town. Also, all but abandoned were the six self-propelled infantry guns (13th Infantry Heavy Gun Company under Ostuf. Koch) with no more 150mm shells. (They had started with only eighteen rounds for each vehicle.) The lack of artillery was infuriating for Peiper. By the time he reached La Gleize, the village was already under a withering bombardment by more than a hundred American tubes with a seemingly endless supply of ammunition.

While the others had run the escapade to pierce beyond Stoumont, SS Ustuf. Hans Hennecke had manned his lone Panther sentinel in the town, aware that the Americans had seized Stavelot and were drawing nearer. Then, in the fog they heard the sound of tanks moving from the road to Trois-Ponts. 'We drove our Panther into position,' Hennecke recalled, 'in order to give the Americans a reception.'[28] But as the grinding sounds drew close, Hennecke cocked his head to listen. Out of the fog emerged a Panther. Hennecke held his fire, when the hatch of the tank swung open. It was Hennecke's own first vehicle that had been shot down at the entrance to Stavelot on 18 December. Popping out of its hatch, was Rttf. Bahnes – his driver.

Soon Bahnes was explaining how he and his men had cannibalised another German tank for transmission parts to get the Panther operating – all the repairs taking place under American noses on 19 December. Eventually, a mechanic had patched together its drivetrain such that it could operate awkwardly in third and fourth gear. With those improvised repairs, he had raced across the bridge with the Panther's turret swinging wildly. The Americans had been so surprised by the sudden apparition that Bahnes had driven though Stavelot and made his way on to La Gleize. Now, on 21 December, Bahnes's Panther was the last German vehicle to make its way to Kampfgruppe Peiper in the cauldron.

Back at the sanatorium, the Americans were using TD fire to get the upper hand on Peiper's troopers still holding out. Sgt Widener, who was still holding out in the annex next to the sanatorium, directed 90mm fire from an M36 tank destroyer that blasted big 90mm holes in the crumbling walls. Later, several of the M10s joined in the fusillade and fired dozens of rounds into the multi-storey structure from close range – an eerie scene of noise and gun flashes. By early afternoon, the front of the building teetered near collapse, its facade gashed by ugly shell holes.

The American infantry were now able to use hand grenades to force their way into two shell-ravaged rooms. However, the SS troopers countered this move by calling up a Panther to the rear of the building, which fired round after round into the ground floor. German tanks forced the TDs to pull back. The American effort to recapture the building failed again with twenty-two men pinned inside the building. A bazooka team climbed to the top of the sanatorium attempting to destroy the tank from above, but observant SS men knocked out the bazooka team with a spurt of bullets from machine guns. Shortly after, the Germans brought up at least two 20mm flak wagons, which made further American infantry advance into Stoumont all but suicidal.

After a personal reconnaissance on his belly, Capt. Berry's tanks made an effort to climb the boggy track to the sanatorium courtesy of a hastily fashioned corduroy road. Three Shermans and a TD gun moved right up to the sanatorium and the ubiquitous Lt Powers managed to sneak around to the right of the château and destroy the Panther that had checked every American move. Next, the American armor covered the withdrawal of nearly two dozen Americans, but then had to pull back when SS gunners on the high ground to the north-east of the sanatorium ranged in anti-tank rounds and threatened to shoot down Berry's tanks.[29]

A brace of Peiper's remaining panzers also checked the attack from the north on Stoumont by Task Force Jordan and the battered 3rd Battalion of the 119th Infantry. Although the infantry with tank support managed to reach a line on the east side of the road almost to the edge of Rouat, the Shermans ran into the same accurate anti-tank fire as suffered the day before and had to pull back once more.

Without armor, the infantry withdrew to the cover of the woods for the night after reporting observing tanks astride the road from La Gleize to Stoumont.[30] Not much more could be expected; the 3rd Battalion was still recovering from having been overrun two days before.

Most of the civilians had left Stoumont proper, but those who stayed risked the unending rain of shells.[31] At the church in Stoumont, more than a hundred people took refuge even as the structure was slowly pounded. During the night of 20–21 December, the sanatorium became a horror realm of close combat and death. Those in the cellar could hear machine guns still rattling away. As the bullets struck the walls like hail, the priests led everyone in prayer. Next, they heard more footsteps along the floor above and barking guns on either side of the building. Raymond Beco and his father thought it was the end – a fight to the finish.

Suddenly, a door swung open to the cellar. *'Civils!'* someone yelled. It was an American soldier. The cellar-bound refugees were overcome with joy. That evening some people from the cellar went up with the Americans and made food in the kitchen and returned to share the limited victuals with those in the cellar. The Americans settled into the rooms on the ground floor and kitchen, seemingly pleased with hot water for making coffee. 'The day has been tough,' the GIs told them, 'but the losses to the enemy are terrible … Tomorrow we head for Germany!'

Any relief was all too short. At midnight the area around the sanatorium was engulfed in renewed automatic weapons fire. A shell fell in the pantry, exploding and filling the hall with smoke and powder. Down in the 30m-long cellar, the Mother Superior passed out wet handkerchiefs. 'We were praying to St Rita a lot,' Mia Hurlet remembered as a young girl. Another shell hit near the basement window, which exploded with a crash, and all the children hastily moved to the middle of the cellar. Amazingly, no one was hurt, but the cellar ceiling trembled with each blow. Several wounded Americans were brought down the stairs.

Now, the door to the cellar suddenly opened again, this time to reveal a squad of angry SS soldiers with submachine guns slung over their shoulders. The Americans in the cellar threw down their arms. The enemy approached and cursed loudly. One of the SS troopers raged upon finding that one of the Americans had a radio. He smashed it to pieces on the floor. 'We should burn you all here!' he screamed.

'What have we done wrong?' the priest begged.

'You are hiding prisoners!'

'No,' he protested, 'they hide for themselves. There are only children here and some women here praying … What business do you have to make this a battlefield?'

The young SS man calmed down, particularly after seeing the badly wounded soldier – an American who had lost a lot of blood and couldn't be moved.

Young Jenny Lejuene, who was among the Belgians in the cellar, worried that the Germans might kill everyone. She sat next to the American soldier who was badly hurt and could not be evacuated. The SS trooper stood guard, took two cigarettes out of a pack in his hand and calmly lit both, handing one cigarette to the American. The wounded man took a big drag. Soon, in turn the American was offering the German chocolate from his shirt pocket. The SS man nodded in appreciation. 'Thank you,' he said, 'but I can't eat it. It's covered in blood.'[32]

As the hours passed, the injured American soldier's condition worsened, and the priest in the cellar administered last rites. 'I understand you,' the American said weakly. His wife was Catholic and he thanked the priest before fading.[33]

On the morning of 22 December, the walking wounded were marched off for the Château Froidcour just before the American artillery got to work once again. Outside, in the streets above, U.S. Army soldiers and SS troopers stalked each other outside like high-noon gunfighters. From the afternoon to the evening, the battle went on. Grenades exploded in the grand hall above, causing even the stone to shudder. A section of the cellar ceiling collapsed. Those seeking refuge in the space had grown to 250 as others fled there from the bombarded village. Everyone now huddled away from the walls as bullets bounced off the exterior masonry like hammering hails and blew out the window glass in the barred basement.

The streets outside were lethal. Two civilians died from the shelling while running for cover: Florent Laborer and his sister Marie. Then came a sudden explosion at the sanatorium; a shell collapsed the cellar's arch and filled the dark underground once more with smoke and dust. Under near panic, one of the priests rushed up the stairs to request a momentary truce. Even as he moved up the stairs, he could hear shooting. Yet, as he approached the kitchen from the cellar, an SS man there could only see an unknown figure coming from the darkness and fired two pistol shots. Amazingly, the shots missed, but the priest ducked back down to the cellar.

Returning to the blackness, the priest pleaded for the crowd to calm down; there was no sanctuary above. In the early evening, the Germans came down to the cellar themselves.

Previously enthusiastic, now 'they seemed tired and discouraged'. The priest asked to have everyone evacuated to safety. 'Impossible,' the SS men said. 'The house and the village are surrounded by enemies. The first one of you who ventures out on the road will be killed.'[34] But for all their bluster, the SS men now seemed to wilt. On Friday morning, 22 December, the priest and the Mother Superior were determined to leave. The two priests conducted the communion while the faithful in the cellar knelt on mattresses. When the sacrament was complete, the interior of the cave was oddly silent. The sounds of shooting had finally stopped. Going above, to the wrecked kitchen, the priest found that the SS men had left. Sister Louise and Sister Catherine volunteered to seek out Dr Robinson. The forlorn group left the sanatorium, led by two sisters carrying a white flag.

But then, at 9 a.m., as they walked, the shooting rose again; this time it was the American guns once more. The sisters raced quickly down the road to Stoumont as the guns thundered overhead, somehow reaching the Robinson cellar unscathed. Back at the sanatorium, as the first artillery fire struck, one of the wounded Americans took a bed sheet to an upper-floor terrace. He waved it vigorously to implore the American guns to stop.

United with Dr Robinson in the cellar, the doctor directed the nuns to U.S. Army lines. The nuns implored them to help, but the GIs were suspicious. Skorzeny commandos dressed as nuns? The Americans demanded to know more, but first provided some soup. 'There are many children in the cellar!' one nun pleaded before taking a bite. 'Are there any Germans?' 'Yes, but they are wounded,' said Sister Agnes, now stammering. 'There are Americans there in the cellar, too. Many are wounded.' Ambulances were soon assembled. 'Please go as soon as possible.'[35]

* * *

On the following morning, 22 December, Harrison was explaining his inaction to Hobbs. 'I understand there won't be any air today.'

'That's right,' said Hobbs. 'Now we have got to take aggressive action there and find out what the enemy in there is trying to do.'

La Gleize and Stoumont remained important, Hobbs insisted, 'We've got to get that area cleaned up.'

'We're going to try to knock them out today,' said Harrison. But that did not seem to suit Hobbs.

'Well go to it then,' he insisted, 'and put all the artillery there you need.'[36]

German plans were also afoot. Not far away on the Baron's Froidcour estate, Peiper consulted his commanders. One, Benoni Junker, was right there, wounded in the cellar. Later that afternoon, Peiper left the castle to order his forces to pull back from Stoumont before first light on Friday morning, 22 December. The SS commander left about eighty of his wounded men in the care of Dr Dittmann at the Froidcour.

Later that day, the 119th Infantry Regiment recaptured Stoumont from the small SS rearguard that Peiper had left behind. At about 10 a.m., Gen. Harrison decided to make a personal reconnaissance of the terrain just west of the sanatorium 'to figure out how to attack the place'. The streets were like a shell-ruined ghost town – quiet. As he approached the building, two civilians emerged, yelling that the Germans were gone. Harrison ordered a patrol to investigate, which soon found the blasted-out sanatorium deserted. The 1st Battalion occupied the ruins without firing a round. Two or three seriously wounded Americans whom the Germans had left behind with several of their own told how the enemy had abruptly departed at 4 a.m.

Some German elements pulled out later. After the fog lifted on 22 December, Task Force Jordan watched as six Panther and Mk IV tanks moved east across the open pastures before Rouat. There was no exchange of fire, but the German show of force gave Maj. Jordan pause.

He delayed his attack from the north until 1.05 p.m. so that the 391st Field Artillery Battalion could plaster Rouat with a time on target (TOT) shelling. Then, at 1.20 p.m., Task Force Jordan and the 3rd Battalion of the 119th moved forward, entering Rouat just after 2 p.m., claiming the 'fighting in the town was a house-to-house business'.[37] Task Force Jordan consolidated its grip on Rouat the night of 22 December while sending a platoon of light tanks to reconnoitre a route to La Gleize. This move ended upon discovering an enemy roadblock backed by heavy tanks.[38]

Lt Bud Strand with Company D of the 1st Battalion 119th Infantry Regiment was still facing Stoumont on 21 December but relieved the enemy was gone. 'Orders came to continue our attack even with our depleted forces and pressure was then put on from the west where we were and also from the north … We brought 155mm howitzers to the high ground and fired 95lb shells directly into Stoumont. With the pressure on 22 December, Stoumont fell to us.'[39]

Meanwhile, the SS surgical team under Dr Willibald Dittmann in the Château Froidcour's dank cellar continued their grim medical effort until they were captured by the Americans. Dr Dittmann's makeshift field aid station was flooded with casualties, the wounded, the dead, and the dying – all mixed together in terrible misery. Medical supplies ran thin as the few medics tended to the suffering by the light of weak candles. In the cellar, a wounded American man laid next to other moaning German troopers, their comrades attempting to soothe them with old songs of the Fatherland. Dittmann and two American doctors performed surgery without anaesthesia, operating with a horrifying assortment of saws and scissors otherwise 'used by the gamekeeper for cutting up deer and wild boar'.[40] Orderlies moved out the dead on stretchers to pile them upon the castle lawns – a horrifying scene.[41]

In combat exhaustion, not all of Peiper's men got the word. 'Today's brace of vaunted supermen were captured by our 1st Battalion in Stoumont,' the 119th Regiment G-2 reported, 'their company pulled out of that town during the night while they slept peacefully in a cellar.'[42]

At 4 p.m., on 21 December, Jochen Peiper first arrived in La Gleize at the house of Mme Boulanger. His forces in Stoumont commenced to pull back, taking a secondary road to the south since the Americans still had the N33 under fire near St Anne's Chapel.

In Stoumont, the 1st Battalion and the 740th Tank Battalion advanced just after 2 p.m., reaching the ruined church at 2.45 p.m. 'We have Stoumont complete,' Harrison phoned back to Hobbs at 3.14 p.m., 'they pulled out ahead of us.' Hobbs wanted to know about La Gleize. 'Your mission is to take both.' At 3 p.m., the fierce bombardment ceased abruptly, and Sherman tanks clanked forward into Stoumont, followed by a wave of cautious American infantry. Peeping from the cellar windows of the wrecked sanatorium, Mia Hurlet saw a man displaying a white flag with red crosses, floating from a truck. It was 3 p.m. on 22 December. 'We came out of the cellar, stepping over dead soldiers lying on the stairs.'

Corpses and rubble were everywhere – horrible scenes of death. The rooms above were scarcely recognisable – ugly holes in the walls and ripped ceilings. Blood over walls and floors. Even amid the gruesome scene, Raymond Beco and his father were overjoyed to see the American helmets marked by red crosses. 'Everybody out!' one called out.[43] Leaving the sanatorium, he was haunted by another vision. There in the muddy road, surrounded by smouldering vehicles and a smashed ammunition box was the body of an SS trooper, his young face staring blankly up to the sky while an American GI rifled his corpse for papers. *He only looks 16*, Beco thought. Beco suffered nightmares from that scene for the rest of his life.

Soon, Americans were standing outside the sanatorium cellar, forming a line to help the children out. The children, shocked with sullen faces blackened by powder and dust, were quietly loaded into the trucks. One young child cried uncontrollably, wailing that she had lost her shoes. One of the GIs took the girl in his arms and then produced a pair of dull-green socks and pulled them on to her feet. They were too big, but the child stopped sobbing. Jenny Lejuene burst into tears.[44] Soon the 250 evacuees began a trek to safety near Lorcé. If St Edouard had been devastated, not a single Belgian child who took refuge there was killed or even hurt.[45]

Under orders from Gen. Hobbs, the Americans aimed to move beyond the wrecked village. At 5 p.m. on Friday, 22 December, the 2nd Battalion, 119th Infantry had recaptured the Château Froidcour. Arriving at the castle, they not only found fifty German wounded, but freed a dozen Americans. Baron Harenne's family and his housekeepers were soon evacuated with the others to Lorcé. The hulks of war lay scattered and broken on the road. Strewn from the Stoumont rail station to the St Anne Chapel was wrecked German equipment: one Königstiger Panzer Mk VI, eight other tanks, three half-tracks, one anti-tank gun, and ten other vehicles.[46]

Jochen Peiper's headquarters company had left only an hour before the Americans arrived. The SS commander of Kampfgruppe Peiper had slipped away again.

Chapter 28

MCCOWN

A prisoner of war is a man who tries to kill you and fails, and then asks you not to kill him.

Winston Churchill

As Jochen Peiper made his defensive headquarters in the little Belgian village of La Gleize, American artillery gunners trained their tubes on the place. So repulsed, it would be the place where he would circle his panzer wagons and make a last stand – unless support could reach him. Waffen SS messenger Paul Fröhlich was in a cellar with Peiper and the panzer staff. Once, while outside of the basement, they heard an incoming artillery round and Peiper fell to the dirt, but by the distant noise of the explosion they realised that it was not a close hit. Fröhlich was still standing, but looked to the other side of the road as if he saw nothing. Still, he couldn't help smiling. Peiper smiled back.[1]

> I had my C.P. about halfway between Stoumont and La Gleize, and since the position had become much more serious on the 21st, I considered giving up Stoumont. In the early afternoon of the 21st, an American major was brought to my C.P. Simultaneously, the road about one hundred yards away had been cut by American troops. Trees had been demolished there – there were mines hidden in between them – and the danger of Stoumont being cut off became obvious … He [McCown] was captured by members of Diefenthal's battalion. I put one or two questions to him, since I was in pretty much of a hurry because there was severe firing about 100 metres away from me at that roadblock, and I had to count on Americans looking into my quarters at any minute. I therefore ordered McCown to be taken to La Gleize at once and then participated in the counterattack on the roadblock. I saw clearly that the enemy now perceived my undefended northern flank, which had been represented by the big forest between La Gleize and Stoumont, and I had to expect that stronger American forces would follow these troops which had cut the road. This place, where

> the road was cut, was eliminated again with all available messengers, liaison officers, and the latter part of Preuss's company. At the same time, I made plans for evacuation of my main aid station, which was located in the castle [Froidcour]. All slightly wounded persons were taken to La Gleize. About fifty more severely wounded, who were now no longer able to be transported, as well as some fifteen Americans and some medics were left behind [at the castle]. Since I was faced with the possibility of being surrounded simultaneously in Stoumont, La Gleize, and Cheneux, I decided to withdraw to La Gleize with all my troops, while still attempting to keep control of the bridge south-west of La Gleize, since I had not yet given up hope of troops following us behind. At dusk on 21 December 1944, the units withdrew from Stoumont to La Gleize. A severe crisis which had developed in Cheneux was cleared up by the personal action of Capt. Diefenthal. At that occasion a Belgian civilian had beaten in the head of one of my men, thereby yelling '*Vive la France!*'[2]

Now an American officer prisoner in the Battle of the Bulge, Maj. Hal McCown was first taken to the gardener's house at the Château Froidcour to meet Peiper at his CP. 'Our short conversation was interrupted by someone shooting through the window,' the SS commander would recall.[3] Peiper interrogated McCown briefly but could get nothing out of him.[4] Name, rank, and serial number. McCown, on the other hand, made mental notes. 'I did my best to determine the objectives of this unit.'

From still enthusiastic SS men with Peiper, McCown learned that this 'division would be the first element in Liège'. Col Peiper questioned me fruitlessly several times about road and bridge conditions in the Maastricht area.'[5] McCown listened as Peiper boasted that they had only got this far by capturing fuel, that ammunition had to be preserved, and how resupply could not be expected. The important thing was finding a bridge strong enough to get the rest of his column from Trois-Ponts to La Gleize. He'd then resume the advance. Peiper had McCown removed to La Gleize under escort. McCown glanced at his watch. It was 4 p.m. on 21 December 1944:

> I was taken to the cellar containing the commander of the German troops, whose name I later found out was Lt Col Peiper, 1st Regiment, 1st Panzer SS Adolf Hitler Division. An interpreter (Josef Becker) who had spent sixteen years in Chicago, USA, served as interpreter. I later found out that the majority of the German officers spoke English fairly well. The colonel spent a few minutes trying to get technical information from me, but seeing the attempt was worthless, sent me away again. I was taken to a cellar containing a 2nd lieutenant and several high-ranking NCOs; they were dressed very faultlessly in their black Panther [*sic*, Panzer] uniforms, each with several decorations. I mentally noted, at the time, that this would probably turn out to be one of their 'bluff' attempts to get information. The light of a small electric bulb in the cellar fell mainly upon my face, leaving the other occupants and the rest of the room in semi-darkness. One of the NCOs drew his Luger, examined his clip, reloaded the weapon, and laid it on a table in front of him. It was with difficulty that I managed to suppress a smile at these obviously studied and rehearsed preparations in a place so identical with what intelligence officers back in the states teach our troops to expect when

> in the hands of the enemy. The only distracting feature, of an otherwise perfect setting as far as they were concerned, was the frequent crashing of American artillery concentrations – sometimes uncomfortably close.
>
> The next thirty minutes were spent in an attempt to extract from me information I had refused to give the commander earlier that afternoon. I was surprised to see that as my failure to respond to their threatenings [*sic*] continued, they grew no angrier, but instead seemed to lose interest in the procedure. Finally, I was taken to another cellar where a warrant officer searched me thoroughly, taking my flashlight and knife, but leaving me my wristwatch, ring, the little food I was carrying, and my personal papers. I was conducted to a very small cellar which contained four other American officers, all lieutenants of my own regiment. We exchanged information about our present situation.[6]

Rolf Ehrhardt, coming with a message from Hstuf. Klingelhöfer, entered the cellar in La Gleize just at the time Peiper was reintroduced to the American officer:

> I happened to be present as the American Lt Col McCown – Staff Officer of the 30th U.S. Infantry Division – was led to Peiper as a prisoner by Oscha. Max Bergmann. The tall officer had to stand bowed in the low door as he introduced himself with a casually correct salute. Peiper got up from the table and offered McCown his hand. I did not understand anything of the following conversation, but had the instinctive feeling to [my] experience [of] two personalities, who had much in common in bearing, correctness, education, and attitude.[7]

McCown seemed impressed by his captors:

> An amazing fact to me was the youth of the members of this organization – the bulk of the enlisted men – were eighteen or nineteen years of age, recently recruited, but from my observations thoroughly trained. There was a good sprinkling of both privates and NCOs from the years of Russian fighting. The officers for the most part were veterans, but were also very young. Col Peiper was 29 years old, his tank commander was 30; his captains and lieutenants were between 19 and 27 years of age. Their morale was high throughout the period I was with them, despite the extremely trying conditions. The discipline was very good. The noise discipline on night movement … was so perfect I could hardly believe they could accomplish it. The physical condition of all the personnel was good, except for a lack of proper food which was apparent more strongly just before the escape of the unit. The equipment was good and complete with the exception of some reconditioned half-tracks among the motorized equipment. All men wore practically new boots and had adequate clothing. Some of them wore parts of American uniforms, mainly the knit cap, gloves, sweaters, overshoes, and one or two overcoats. I saw no one, however, in American uniforms or in civilian clothes. The relationship between the officers and men, particularly the commanding officer, Col Peiper, was closer and friendlier than I would have expected.[8]

The immediate issue for Peiper was what to do with McCown. With an American infantry battalion on the road between Stoumont and La Gleize, his

Tough Paratroopers of the 82nd Airborne Division move up from Werbomont, Belgium to block the *Kampfgruppe Peiper's* path westward. (NARA)

Ears cupped from the cold, tank leaders on a Mk V Panther advance through the snowy forests of the Ardennes (Bildarchiv Preussicher Kulturbesitz).

SS-Uscha. Paul Zwigart pictured prior to the Malmédy Landsberg trial where each defendant received a number. In the trial (and afterwards), Zwigart confessed to killing an American soldier who had surrendered from a jeep on the road to Cheneux. This incident took place on the afternoon of 18th of December 1944 while Peiper and Josef Diefenthal looked on from their SPW. (NARA)

Knocked out Panther Nr. 131 on the road to Cheneux. The bridge at Cheneux can be seen in the background. The medium tank was disabled by an U.S. air attack by the 366th and 404th Fighter Groups. (NASM)

North of Stavelot was the massive U.S. First Army Fuel Depot #3– almost a million gallons of gasoline largely stored in jerricans stacked at intervals over the 8 km of road leading back to Franchorchamps. (NARA)

Cleaning up the aftermath of the fiery roadblock on the Franchorchamps road. Maj. Paul Solis of the U.S. of the 526th Armored Infantry Battalion, burned 124,000 gallons of gasoline to block the road north to the larger cache of nearby fuel—over 800,000 gallons. Faced with a wall of flame, the lead panzer turned back, Peiper did not attempt to capture the fuel as he did not know of its existence. Filmakers of Warner Brother's Battle of the Bulge would suggest otherwise. (NARA).

On December 18th in the village of La Vaulx Richard, SS officers, SS-Stubaf. Gustav Knittel and Ostf. Heinrich Goltz of the 1st SS Panzer Reconnaissance Battalion look skyward at U.S. aircraft swirling about the Ardennes while studying a map to plot their advance. (NARA).

Kampfgruppe SS Knittel's control of the streets of Stavelot had been tenuous and brief. A coordinated counterattack by the 117th Infantry Regiment of the U.S. 30th Division with tank destroyer support of the 843rd TD Battalion on December 18th expelled the few troops left behind. Only the dead remained. (NARA)

Alarmed at the German advance, in the town of Malmedy, the 120th Regiment of the U.S. 30th Infantry Division set up defensive positions covering the bridges with machine guns on both sides. (NARA)

The battle in Stoumont at the Robinson house is seen in this image. SS-Stubaf. Werner Poetschke is turning to retrieve an unfired Panzerfaust in the swirling battle. Poetschke would then use the anti-tank rocket to threaten friendly tanks that did not advance. (Transit Film).

Just beyond Werner Poeschke in the fighting at the Robinson house in Stoumont, a group of Fallshirmjäger sets up a machine gun alongside the hedge while shielding a comrade wounded from U.S. small arms fire. On the right Panther Nr. 225 burns after receiving a direct hit with SS-Strm. Hans-George Hübler and Werner Zander taking refuge under fire in a nearby ditch. (Transit Film).

During the morning assault towards Rouat, just east of Stoumont, a Panther of the Poetschke's 2. Kompanie passes an abandoned 76mm gun of the overrun 823rd TD Battalion. Fog and smoke drifts across the La Gleize-Stoumont road. (Transit Film)

Under cover of smoke from the fighting, SS panzergrenadiers mop up U.S. resistance down the Rue du Village in Stoumont. (Transit Film).

In Stoumont, the lead Panther Nr. 225 (SS-Rttf. Franz Pram) advancing just beyond the Robinson house is hit, killing most of the crew. The two survivors are rescued from the burning wreckage while Werner Poetschke orders the advance to continue. (Transit Film)

One of Peiper's tank leaders in action in a Mk V Panther in Stoumont on 19 December. (Transit Film).

The battle of Stoumont won by *Kampfgruppe Peiper*, SS-Hstf. Jupp Diefenthal, commander of Peiper's III Battalion motions captured American soldiers of the 119th Regiment up the 'Rue du Village' to the rear. Diefenthal wears his characteristic tan sheepskin jacket. (Transit Film).

Camouflaged by pine boughs, the crew of a Wirberwind FlaK tank of *Kampfgruppe Peiper* fires at remaining resistance in Stoumont. (Transit Film)

The battle over in Stoumont, surrendered U.S. soldiers from the 119th Infantry Regiment are escorted east along the N33 roadway. (Transit Film)

U.S. prisoners are gathered in Stoumont in front of the Café Grégoire, 19 December 1944. (Transit Film).

Heavily armed SS panzer grenadiers celebrate the rapid conquest of Stoumont, with cigarettes from captured American soldiers and appropriated beer from the Café Grégoire. (Transit Film)

Near Stoumont rail station, just west of Targnon, three wrecked Panther tanks mark the end of the road for the spearhead of *Kampfgruppe Peiper*. The tank furthest west was Pz Nr. 215. of SS-Uscha. Kruger (NARA).

Grim-faced airborne soldiers of the 504th Parachute Infantry Regiment pass through the village of Rahier before entering Cheneux—the scene of some of the bloodiest fighting of the Ardennes Campaign. (NARA).

On 21 December 1944, Jagdpanzer IV Nr. 101 of SS-Hstf. Otto Holst collapsed the flimsy wooden bridge at Petit Spai. The tank destroyer and span fell into the Amblève when the 25-ton TD attempted to cross. (CRIBA)

After the bridge at Petit Spai collapsed, German engineers with SS Pz Pio. Battalion 1 attempted over a period of two days to construct a new bridge nearby. Deadly U.S. artillery fire on the construction site ended the effort, destroying the trestle and killing many SS engineers. (Pallud)

On December 20th and 21st, a desperate back and forth battle took place for possession of the sanatorium in Stoumont, dubbed *Festung Sankt-Edouard* by the SS troops fighting there. (Cavanagh)

Maj. Hal D. McCown, commander of the 2 Battalion/119th Infantry Regiment who was captured as Peiper's prisoner and held from 21-24 December in La Gleize. After long midnight conversations with Peiper, McCown escaped from Peiper's band as they fled on foot through the deep woods between La Gleize towards Wanne, Belgium. (U.S. Army)

A U.S. bazooka team of 325th Glider Infantry Regiment sets up on the road to Werbomont, ready to challenge any German advance: 23 December. (NARA).

U.S. infantry approaches abandoned Tiger Nr. 223 of *schwere SS Panzer Battalion 501* on the outskirts of La Gleize after *Kampfgruppe Peiper* had left on Christmas Eve. (Author's Collection)

Regimental command Panther Nr 002, likely originally belonging to Peiper and then his adjutant, Hans Gruhle, was abandoned on Christmas Eve near La Gleize. (CRIBA).

SS-Uscha. Manfred Thorn during 1944. Thorn was the tank driver of Panzer Nr. 734 and would spend Christmas in the village of Wanne where Peiper's escaping battlegroup arrived on foot, wet and exhausted. (Thorn)

Mk IV Ausf J of the 1st SS, likely from the 7th Kompanie in transfer to the Lutrebois area south of Bastogne at the end of 1944. Kriegsberichter Fritz Jäckisch. (Suddeutscher Verlag)

On 14 January 1945, U.S. forces retook the snowed bound Malmédy crossroads at Baugnez. There, they uncovered the dozens of executed American soldiers just south of the burned out Café Bodarwe. Standing is Lt. Col. Alvin B. Welsch in charge of the U.S. First Army Malmédy massacre investigation. The grim events at the Malmédy crossroads would dog Jochen Peiper for the remainder of his days.(Corbis)

After the Ardennes Offensive, Obersturmbannführer Jochen Peiper cradles well-used binoculars during the final fighting in the East in 1945 (Westemeier)

combat team in the westernmost village was in danger of encirclement. He sent out word that Stoumont must be evacuated. Then too, it seemed inevitable that Cheneux would soon be lost.

The 1st Battalion of the 119th Infantry had suffered the brunt of the second battle to recapture Stoumont. Casualties totalled 106, with sixteen killed, sixty wounded, and twenty-eight missing (twenty-four of the missing were later liberated at La Gleize). Company A of the 823rd TD Battalion reported only four serviceable M-10s and four 3in guns after the battle.[9] On the German side, left behind in Stoumont were sixty to eighty SS men too badly wounded to withdraw with the others to La Gleize.[10]

At the other end of the fighting against Peiper's perimeter, on 21 December, Maj. Stallings' combat team still held its encircled positions east of La Gleize while the rest of Task Force Lovelady consolidated the Ster–Parfondruy area finding dozens of murdered Belgian civilians. Patrols from Stallings' group found the enemy stubbornly holding the high ground to the north-east. When Lovelady was ordered on 22 December to take this hill, Stallings found that he could not use the road on which he entered Parfondruy since it had been cut by the enemy.

A radio message arrived from Leibstandarte division commander Wilhelm Mohnke that some of Max Hansen's men were now across the Amblève river with orders to advance via Coo to rendezvous with his forces at La Gleize. Peiper's Waffen SS infantry, as well as Peiper himself, pulled back towards La Gleize, avoiding the obvious N33 by taking the parallel road to the south that passed the Masson farm.

Eventually, a battalion of Kampfgruppe Hansen infiltrated through the woods near Petit Coo. The following day, the 22nd, they overran the battalion aid station by 5 p.m, cutting the road leading south to Stallings' marooned troops.

Hansen's 3rd Battalion then thrust northward from its assembly point near Trois-Ponts, using the hastily repaired footbridge at Petit Spai. Moreover, the SS panzer grenadiers had pushed toward Parfondruy and repelled further efforts to expand the American toehold in Ster by a sweeping movement that had pushed down into the tiny hamlet of Biester – just south-east of Coo. On signal, the heavily armed grenadiers rushed out of the forested Bois des Moines, charging downhill at a full gait. By the opening to the waterfall, the Americans had bolstered their assets with an infantry company from the 120th Regiment. As the SS troopers crossed the fields before the railway, the American machine guns mercilessly cut them down before they could reach Biester. This butchery spelled the end to their advance to seize the railway bridge over the Coo waterfall. More than 160 corpses were counted in the fields. Still, Task Force Lovelady was now effectively cut in half, reporting at 3.50 p.m. that it was now under accurate heavy weapons fire.[11]

On 22 December, SS-Ostubaf. Max Hansen ordered his command to prepare for still another attack to at last break through to Peiper in La Gleize. His 1st Battalion moved from the line between Renardmont and Ster that had been seized the previous day. However, the new plan was set back when SS

Stubaf. Emil Karst, in charge of the battalion, was killed while on personal reconnaissance. Hstuf. Herbert Rink took over but found his troops stopped cold by elements of Task Force Lovelady standing their ground in the Bois de Ancre.

Meanwhile, in the village of Petit Coo, a scrambling fight developed in which the Americans had armor and the Germans – without the bridge at Petit Spai – did not. Amid heavy losses, the grenadiers were eventually forced to pull back. At nightfall on 22 December, Hansen made the decision to call the thing off. He relayed the message to Mohnke in nearby Wanne some 9km away. The division commander then flashed it to Peiper's basement CP at the Maison Georges in La Gleize. 'During the night, a division message informed us that the attack by Gruppe Hansen was suspended, and therefore there was no longer any hope of relief.'[12]

Just to be certain Mohnke could not get relief to Peiper, on the morning of Saturday, 23 December, Company A of the 105th Engineer Battalion blew up the bridge straddling the waterfall. In the meantime, not far away, part of Task Force Lovelady was still trapped. Maj. Stallings tried to punch his way out of the encirclement once more, only to lose two more tanks. His situation neared desperation, save for the ability of Stallings to call down artillery on the SS grenadiers encircling them. The men of his group, such as S/Sgt James K. Cullen, began to consider a distasteful possibility. 'The situation in E Company area was becoming critical. With ammo almost depleted, Stallings at one point had contemplated surrender.' Surrounded for two days, Cullen and his men were frustrated with the difficulty of confronting those surrounding them. The SS infantry hid in the woods, but dropped mortars on their position – one of which had already killed Lt Verna L. McCord:

> As a squad leader, my world was centerd on a very small area: the men of my squad who were fighting, eating, and sleeping. We knew we were up against SS troops and that we were cut off with a river behind us … We talked about being taken prisoner. The general agreement was that we were not going to be prisoners very long because we had seen what the Germans had done to civilians in Trois-Ponts. One of our medics had a small Beretta pistol, but said he would swim the river before he would become a prisoner.[13]

From 22 to 24 December the fighting eddied through Petit Coo and Biester and the surrounding area, with Hansen's men seemingly bent on victory or death. Only on 24 December at noon did Stallings' Shermans succeed in breaking out of the vice. They suffered very significant losses, but. Max Hansen estimated he lost at least five hundred men in the fighting between 20 and 24 December attempting to fight a way across the Salm to Peiper in La Gleize.

All the while, Allied intelligence experts puzzled over a decrypt on 20 December from the 1st SS Panzer Division telling of momentarily re-establishing contact with Kampfgruppe Peiper. The communiqué complained of the spearhead being short on both fuel and ammunition and requesting resupply.[14] Was there a secret conduit to the trapped battle group?

There were other worries, too, in Allied intelligence circles. Word came on 21 December that the corps could expect another enemy airborne operation the following night. One of the captured Skorzeny men – a ranking officer – told his interrogators that among the sixty English-speaking commandos were specialists in kidnapping and assassination of leaders in high places.[15] Then, just a day later, a member of the Kampfgruppe Peiper arrived in the U.S. First Army POW cage to corroborate a disturbing story:

> Two German soldiers who do not know each other … told of a plan to kidnap Eisenhower. This mission is to be carried out by a group of men under command of Lt Col Skorzeny … The group has reported to have left on the mission in six light trucks to be dressed in British uniforms.[16]

Dwight D. Eisenhower, the Allied leader of all forces in Europe promptly became a prisoner in his own headquarters. A game of spy-vs-spy ensued as an Eisenhower lookalike double was driven around the streets of Paris to lure out Skorzeny and his assassins. Round the clock surveillance was posted on the *Café de la Pais*. Even with jittery Parisians and MPs, the whole thing came to nothing. Skorzeny later claimed the kidnapping operation was a rumour that, once started, he never made any attempt to stop.[17] Meanwhile, Paris was gripped by rumours. One tale claimed that parachutist commandos were moving into town disguised as Americans or British. Traffic snarls and short tempers dampened any holiday enthusiasm. Two German agents were captured by nervous *Gendarmes* in the city, who learned they had been there all along, having never left Paris in August.[18] While Skorzeny's mission to infiltrate American lines and capture Meuse bridges had come to an ignominious end and he was ordered to disband his Trojan Horse brigade, Peiper was still trapped in La Gleize.

***

For Belgian civilians hiding in the basements of La Gleize, life was hellish: lying on straw mattresses in the dark, deprived of food and any sanitary means. And with increasing bomb blasts and sleep now impossible, many in the subterranean holes became paralysed by fright. Some hallucinated.

In the cellar of Arthur Georges' brick house in La Gleize, Peiper made his headquarters. The location was strategic. From its perch, the front windows looked out over all the roads north toward Hassoumont and the church just to the west, and the back windows overlooked the steeply curving Grand Route rising from Coo to the east.

When Peiper took over command there, he made adjustments to ensure any enemy effort to seize the place would be snared in a web of tank crossfire. The terrain made the directions of the American advance against La Gleize obvious. Based on long experience in Russia, Peiper and Poetschke knew how to sight tank guns. They further knew from Normandy that without artillery and tanks, the American infantry were reluctant to confront German armor.

Poetschke established two main defensive positions: Werimont Farm, which dominated the N33 road passing below going east to Moulin du Ruy and a terrain feature called the Dinheid, and the Les Montis area just west of La Gleize, which provided direct observation of roads approaching Stoumont as well as the path from Cheneux.

Peiper sensed the road from Borgoumont on the north as his defensive weak point because there was no dominating high-terrain position that prevented an infantry assault through the woods lining the road crossing Nabonruy Creek. Fortunately for him, the Americans were loath to attempt any infantry assault without tanks, much less heavy artillery support.

Unfortunately for Arthur Georges, his family had not fled La Gleize before the Germans came, and were now trapped in their old farmhouse. Worse, their home would become the nerve center of Kampfgruppe Peiper. While Peiper, Poetschke, and the leadership of the tank regiment took refuge in the basement, Georges and his family tended a wounded SS soldier in the cellar. Above them roared continuous explosions from American artillery bombardment. With the shelling, the roof of the cellar shook in a thunderous drumming with falling bricks. Another shell burst blew in part of the basement wall and sent fragments through the cellar window, wounding Monsieur Georges in the head. Georges fled outside. There, he manhandled part of the trunk of a splintered tree in front of the hole in the basement and then returned to move the wounded SS man to a less-exposed corner of the cellar.

Peiper's armored bastion to the south was also under bombardment. At Werimont Farm, Peiper sited two King Tigers and a long-gunned Puma reconnaissance car. Yet the huddle of heavy German armor at the position was a tantalising target for American artillery observers. By day's end, the old farm had been struck by shelling from American guns, mortally wounding Madeleine Dumont. Amid the chaos, Rolf Ehrhardt moved the Mk IV tank of the 7th Company commander to the farm, where they made headquarters in the basement of an adjacent building. Ehrhardt's crew comrades – radioman Helmut Rentsch, first gunner Engelbert Bock, and loader Peter Mühlbach – spent time in the tank while he stayed with Klingelhöfer and Maj. von Sacken from the 84th Flak Sturm Battalion in the basement. There, they were joined by the Tiger commanders Ustuf. Handtusch as well as Ostuf. Helmut Dollinger, who led #213.[19]

The other hilltop position, south of La Gleize – called the *Dinheid* by locals – was a dominating perch, so much so that the American infantry could not possibly hope to close with the position without first being punished by enemy fire. On that same day, east of La Gleize the Americans again struck out from Roanne-Coo and finally forced the stubborn SS grenadiers from the Moulin Maréchal and established a foxhole line stretching from the mouth of Roanne down to Werimont. But that success was only possible because that action came in a wooded draw, not under the nose of the triad of tanks firing from the Dinheid.

On the opposite side of La Gleize to the north, at 10.40 a.m. on the 21st, some fifteen tanks of Task Force McGeorge reinforced by a few additional Shermans from the 743rd Tank Battalion and the attached Company K of the 117th Infantry pushed south to seize La Gleize. The tanks and infantry advanced 1,000 yards against strong resistance – unable to close the final distance to the village.[20] McGeorge was confronted by several German tanks, surprised to find that one was an M-4 Sherman with U.S. markings otherwise operating cozily with the enemy. It was knocked out, but further progress proved impossible. A roadblock consisting of Rumpf's panzer engineers backed by four Mk IVs, a Panther, and a King Tiger checked every further move. The American infantry grimly dug in north of Nabonruy Creek, between La Gleize and Borgoumont.[21]

Meanwhile, Peiper worried about the repeated armored attacks of Task Force McGeorge from the north. At 10 a.m. the following day, the 22nd, he directed a tank-led counter-assault along the road moving from Borgoumont. Forces from the evacuation of Stoumont were available. At around 8 a.m. elements of Sievers' 3rd SS Panzer Pioneer Company went into position in front of a group of buildings on the road leading to Borgoumont. The command post was established in the northernmost building, but Sievers' company was out of effective communication with Peiper in La Gleize proper.[22] Tiger II #334 from Heavy SS Panzer Battalion 501 and three or four Panzer IVs of the 6th Company were sent with them on the mission. With infantry support from Sievers, Tiger #334 and several Panzer IVs charged up the road beyond Les Tcheus.

The American view of the action was quickly told. Before La Gleize, at 1 p.m. on the 22nd came a report from 30th Division observers on the other side that 300 enemy infantry and four tanks (a Tiger and several Mk IVs of the 6th Company) were moving towards the American roadblock on the way to Borgoumont.[23] This news came as the assault of Task Force McGeorge moved forward to seize La Gleize from the north. However, the armored column had only proceeded about 800 yards when they smacked into strong resistance.

In fact, McGeorge had been drawn into a trap. Just before reaching La Gleize the column was suddenly enveloped by fire from both sides of the road. The Americans' assault was thrown into confusion, and they pulled back. Eventually, the task force managed to fight its way out of the snare back to Borgoumont. German losses were heavy, too. Franz Sievers' 3rd Panzer Pioneer Company was heavily engaged in the fighting around Borgoumont and the Sanatorium. Max Beutner was killed and later buried in La Gleize.[24] Max Hammerer was also wounded by shrapnel and could only be evacuated to the improvised aid station in La Gleize after the American mortar fire ceased.[25]

True to form: the counterattack stopped any initiative Company K may have had left. Tiger #334 destroyed one Sherman before it was knocked out by a 90mm gun of 143rd AAA Bn firing from the Roanne area. However, both Panzer IVs, #625 and also Junker's #601, were destroyed after being pounded by U.S. artillery. At 3 p.m., during a break in the gunnery, the surviving German tank crews bailed out and ran back to La Gleize.[26]

Meanwhile, having been turned back at Borgoumont yet again, Maj. McGeorge moved his Company I of Sherman tanks across the secondary road to the N33 and attempted to push directly up the road into La Gleize from the east – an action Peiper had been anticipating. By this time, Werner

Poetschke had posted his Panther #151 by the Werimont tank group, which effectively overlooked the American advance. Even though rushing forward after a sharp artillery barrage on the enemy positions, the American tanks were channelled on to a road that ascended at a steep angle directly into the German tank sights. At 3 p.m. Tigers posted on the road and from Werimont shot down the lead Sherman as it crossed the ridge. Its hulk blocking the road, efforts to move it signaled the Germans to shell the length of the column. As others attempted to deploy off road near the 'Minières', the American armor drove into a minefield and lost two more vehicles as the infantry attempting to draw alongside were pelted by machine gun fire.[27] The entire armored convoy pulled back 300 yards.

Still, another attempt at 1.30 p.m. on the 22nd met a similar fate to the debacle of Company K the day before. The SS counterattacked so enthusiastically with armor and panzer grenadiers that Maj. McGeorge had to fall back lest his column be enveloped. 'Our squad was caught in a sudden burst of machine gun fire,' Bob Kaufmann recalled:

> The men on the right side of the road flung themselves into the ditch … the slightest movement brought a response from both the machine gun and the 75mm. Two of our men called out that they were wounded … The order came to pull back … We were once again forced to reverse direction and crawl back to the shelter of the woods 100 yards behind us … Our concern was the two wounded men.[28]

Having failed twice, Task Force McGeorge pulled back. Like everyone else, Bob Kaufmann dug in once more. Maj. Kenneth McGeorge himself had enough of this approach, too, deciding that an attempt on the Amblève road to his left might yield better results for the next day. Consequently, he moved Company I of Shermans over to that road (La Rosier–Andrimont to Ruy) for an advance on the morning of 22 December. Luckily for McGeorge, the two tanks and a Puma of 'Blocking Group Mill' had been called back to La Gleize by Peiper, who looked to consolidate his hold on the hilltop village.[29]

In the hamlet of Hasoumont, which Task Force McGeorge had attempted to wrest from German control the preceding day, Belgian local Albert Delvenne was trying to tend to his neglected farm animals. During the day, he had been coming with his wife to Hasoumont to tend the cattle. Yet on 21 December he knew he needed to take some water to his chickens in a small coop in the place Renontige. Delvenne brought water to the hens and added some feed, but on his way back home, he found his way blocked by an SS man in front of the house of Monsieur Dumont.

The SS trooper screamed that he was a spy and pointed a pistol at his head. Delvenne protested quietly. It wasn't true, he told the German and then calmly took out tobacco, paper and rolled a cigarette and then lit it up. 'So, you are not afraid to die!' said the SS youth. '*Non!*' Delvenne replied, raising his voice. 'Then go!' the SS man said. He and his wife were hustling off for Borgoumont. By dark they had reached that place, the sentry quickly sending them to the U.S. headquarters at the home of Jules Legros for a debriefing.

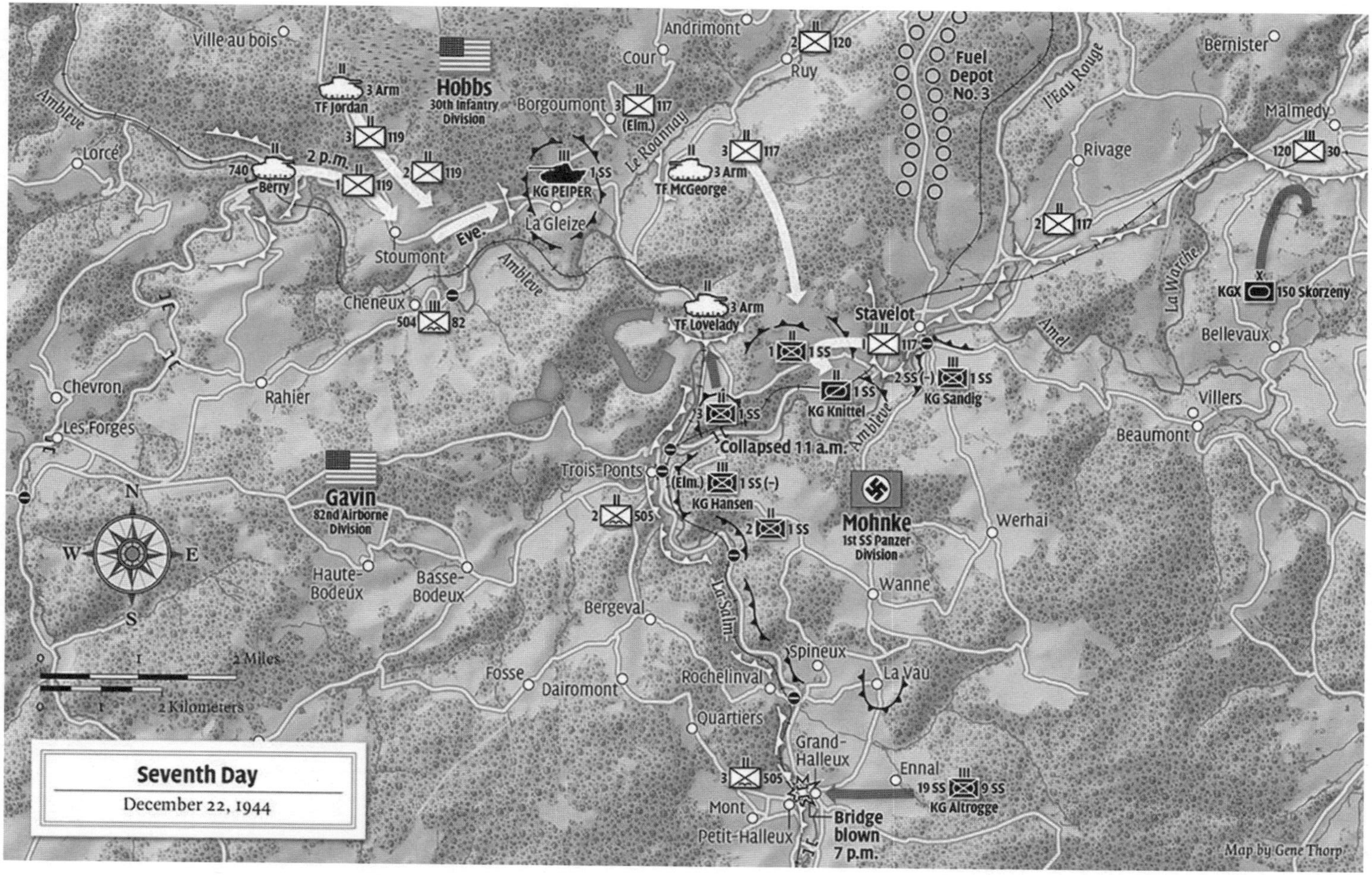
Seventh Day
December 22, 1944
Hobbs
30th Infantry Division
Gavin
82nd Airborne Division
Mohnke
1st SS Panzer Division
TF Jordan
3 Arm
TF McGeorge
TF Lovelady
Berry
740
2 p.m.
Eve.
KG PEIPER
KG Knittel
KG Sandig
KG Hansen
KG Altrogge
KGX
150 Skorzeny
Collapsed 11 a.m.
Bridge blown 7 p.m.
Fuel Depot No. 3
Ville au bois
Lorcé
Ambleve
Stoumont
Cheneux
La Gleize
Borgoumont
Cour
Andrimont
Ruy
Le Roannay
l'Eau Rouge
Rivage
Bernister
Malmedy
La Warche
Bellevaux
Villers
Beaumont
Amel
Stavelot
Trois-Ponts
La Salm
Chevron
Les Forges
Rahier
Haute-Bodeux
Basse-Bodeux
Bergeval
Fosse
Dairomont
Rochelinval
Quartiers
Spineux
La Vau
Wanne
Werhai
Grand-Halleux
Petit-Halleux
Mont
Ennal
2 Miles
2 Kilometers
Map by Gene Thorp

The western part of La Gleize remained quiet on Friday morning, 22 December, as Task Force Harrison, the reinforced 119th Infantry Regiment still had its hands full securing the battered streets of Stoumont and evacuating panicked civilians. American soldiers cleared out the Château Froidcour and the St Anne's woods west of La Gleize.

Early that morning, Peiper appeared at the home of Joseph Dewez on the northern outskirts of La Gleize. They would have to leave. Dewez called him '*Grand seigneur*' – the great lord – who was attended hand and foot by his soldiers as civilians left their homes in Hassoumont. 'But where are we going to go?' Dewez protested. The German said they needed room for their wounded in the cellar.[30]

For two days, artillery drumfire had been falling on little La Gleize. Down in the crowded cellar was a discouraging scene. Four soldiers were breaking apart chairs to feed a small fire for warmth. Soon ten badly wounded German soldiers were brought in and placed on hay strewn across the floor. Amid the moans, over to one side, Jesus on the cross appeared to look down over the macabre scene. All through the day, the Germans grew in number; by morning of 23 December there were nearly thirty there – artillery rounds exploding close by and seeming to defy its protected status.

With that fifteen Belgians in his cellar – the families of Boulanger, Creutz, Gregoire, and others – gathered coats and a few possessions to file outside of the cellar. They emerged in the northern part of La Gleize to find the fog had been replaced by swirling snowflakes. There was no artillery, and Émile Boulanger, his wife, and two children gathered their things, intending to hurry elsewhere. However, coming out of the cellar, SS men challenged them anew. Who had given them permission to depart on their own? There were language problems.

Soon Peiper appeared and said to let them all go. For a time, it was quiet. 'Let's go quickly,' Boulanger urged.[31] The Gregoire Lambert family, the Creutz boy, and several others joined. The artillery could start at any time. Nervously clutching bedding and a few possessions, the frightened Belgians hustled along the road toward La Venne. However, the anxious party had only reached the farm by Werimont when the guns started again. They tried to run faster, but SS troopers emerged from Werimont Farm and waved for them to stop.

The SS men turned them around, back to the La Gleize church. Bombs fell. Reaching its entrance, they ran inside. The commander of the lead Panther of 1st Company, Panzer Rgt. 1, Rttf. Eugen Zimmermann, was among the wounded:

> On 21 December 1944, I was severely wounded by a mortar fragment in the right arm and hip in La Gleize while I was dismounting from my Panther. During a pause in the firing, I was carried by my comrades into the La Gleize church. I still clearly see the Red Cross flag hanging from the church. At that time, the church was full of wounded and civilians so that I had to be placed close to the church doors. The proximity to the exit was evidently my salvation. No sooner had I laid down when tanks and artillery fired at the church. A large stone fragment struck a severely wounded comrade next to me. I did not know him … 'I'm thirsty!'

> he groaned. I was too, but there was nothing to drink. The firing on the church caused great panic, especially among the civilians. For me, there was only one thing to do: Get out! I crawled to the exit. I was overrun by those capable of running. I got out and was able to find some cover behind gravestones.[32]

All through 22 December the shells exploded. That night, a deafening blast sent masonry tumbling, ripping open the wall behind the choir. The church tower took a hit, teetering precariously as the interior filled with dust and smoke. Sleepless terror was interrupted by shell blasts and more SS stretcher bearers bringing in wounded. Then, another a volley of shells struck, blasting away an entire wall, which now looked as though it would collapse and kill everyone.

The Germans were nowhere to be seen, so through the gaping breach, the little group of Belgians led by Émile Boulanger ran outside, helping each other to move down the shell-pocked streets of La Gleize. Reaching the house of Yvan Hakin south-west of the town, they were again turned away from its cellar by Peiper's men inside. So repelled, the little group took shelter in the cow stable of Lambert's home until the worst of the shelling stopped. By morning, they took off again in the direction of Cheneux, until finally challenged by Americans.

Mme Jules Delvenne had a similar experience, being ordered by impatient SS men on the morning of 22 December to leave La Gleize. Mme Delvenne quickly left with her baby wrapped in blankets. She found her way to La Venne south of town near the Amblève, where she joined others in the cellar there. They were relieved that she and her baby were okay.[33]

That night, the officers of Kampfgruppe Peiper huddled in the cellar of the Dewez farmhouse opposite the church. Even though he was surrounded, Peiper held out hope. 'At the time, I was of the conviction that a regiment sent by my division would come in to relieve me. Further, in the course of the day on 21 December, I heard some very loud combat noises north-east of me, and was of the opinion that this was due to the Hitler Youth Division. In the course of the 22nd, it became clear to me that I was completely surrounded and that relief was improbable.'[34] There, Rolf Reiser, Werner Poetschke's adjutant, helped co-ordinate the shrinking defense perimeter. Reiser was with Peiper on the night of 21–22 December:

> After a half-quiet night the enemy had not attacked and we had long ago become used to the constant artillery fire – a steadily increasing drumfire greeted the morning. Contact with the leaders who were in defense positions was only possible by messenger. The messengers made indescribable efforts on that day, moving through murderous artillery fire within direct view of the enemy. The Americans suspended their drumfire at 1400 hours and attacked along all the roads leading into the town with tanks and infantry.
>
> Obstuf. Peiper ordered: 'Everyone to the defense!' We left the command post. Panzer men, messengers, radioman – armed with machine pistols, carbines, and Panzerfausten – took up positions in the ruins and waited for the enemy. Beside me, in the niche of a broken wall in a building, stooped a sharpshooter

> who was firing at the American infantrymen advancing along the road ditch. With their numerical superiority in tanks, the Americans were able to advance across the road from Stoumont and Borgoumont up to the first houses. All the attacks were repulsed with counterattacks and bitter fighting lasting for hours. At twilight, the enemy suspended the attack and withdrew. Prisoners and wounded from both sides were taken to the few overfilled basements and treated.[35]

'Here we made temporary radio contact with the division,' Reiser would later recall. 'During the night before 22 December, a garbled radio message was received announcing an air supply mission for the next night.'[36] That potentially good news was overshadowed by bad: the division radioed that the relief attack by Gruppe Hansen to reach them had failed.

The American captives huddled in the La Gleize cellars with the Germans. Bob Hall, taken prisoner on 19 December and taken to La Gleize, remembered Peiper – speaking English and questioning the group of American POWs. Like McCown, Hall told Peiper nothing. 'I recall one of our soldiers had cigarettes and on the pack was written – BUY U.S. WAR BONDS – and the English-speaking German officer really got a chuckle out of that.'[37]

> I was four days in that cellar. It was all Americans in that cellar. One of our guys, Max Levine, was with us, although I guess there was another couple of guys, too. When we got out, there was 152 of us. The Germans came in and wanted to know if anyone spoke German. And Max being Jewish, he could speak their language and they used him as an interpreter. It was a huge cellar and I was clear on the other side of the cellar. Max would call for three or four guys to come and I asked him what these guys were doing. 'They are making us load ammunition for them. This one time, Max was hollering. They want six of us and they will take all of us if no one comes. Six of us went up and there were two dead Germans laying out in the street – one I remember had a shot through his head – and the guards were pushing us with their rifles. That was when I expected to get shot. I could tell they were angry. They were digging and digging and I got a bad blister. It occurred to me that they might shoot us and put us in the holes we were digging, but they put the two dead Germans in the holes. And then the shelling started and we dug so fast. I had terrible blisters from the digging in the cold. Finally, the shelling got so bad, that they sent us back in. We got back in the cellar and I was there for four days. I guess it was on the 23rd when this Col McCown told us that 'You are probably going to get out soon. They are encircled.' They moved a good part of us out of there. We had nothing much to eat – some raw potatoes, a rotten apple … But we were really treated pretty well by the Germans in La Gleize. They were encircled and didn't have much themselves. I didn't see anyone mistreated.[38]

Later that night of 21 December at 11 p.m., Peiper summoned Hal McCown to his headquarters:

> I was again taken to the cellar headquarters of Col Peiper. I found him in a very much different mood than the cold, impersonal attitude which he used formerly.

He and I talked together from 2300 until 0500 hours the next morning – our subject being mainly his defense of Nazism and why Germany was fighting. I have met few men who impressed me in as short a space of time as did this officer. He was approximately 5 feet, 8 inches in height and 140 lbs in weight, long dark hair combed straight back, straight, well-shaped features with remarkable facial resemblance to the actor, Ray Milland. He is the holder of the Iron [sic, Knight's] Cross with Oak Leaves and had fought in Russia for a long period of time and briefly at Mortain and Caen.

To his surprise, McCown found Peiper fully convinced that Hitler would win the war.

He was completely confident of Germany's ability to whip the Allies. He spoke of Himmler's new reserve army quite at length saying that it contained so many new divisions, both armored and otherwise, that our G-2s would all wonder where they all came from. He did his best to find out from me the success that the V-1 and V-2 were having and told me that more secret weapons like those would be unloosed. He said a new submarine campaign was also opening up and that they had been told there was considerable tonnage sunk in the English Channel just recently from the recent underwater attack. The German air force, he said, would now come forth with many new types and which – although inferior in number to the Allies – would be superior in quality and would suffice their needs to cover their breakthrough in Belgium and Holland and later to the French coast.[39]

Peiper lectured him earnestly on European history and remained a stalwart advocate of National Socialism:

Peiper strongly defended Hitler and his programme. He admitted many wrongs had been committed, but also mentioned the great good he believed Hitler was doing, specifically the elimination of the Communist menace and his Napoleonic concept of a unified and more productive Europe [with the] master race running things and elimination of undesirable persons and peoples. Peiper was a devout Nazi and was at one time the adjutant of Himmler. Peiper had a well-developed sense of humour and said he would like to take me with him to the Russian Front and let me see why they had to violate all the rules of land warfare in dealing with the Russians – both soldiers and guerillas – since the Russians observed no rules themselves. He was most careful to point out that German behavior was circumspect on the Western Front.[40]

McCown learned that early American attempts to reach La Gleize had fallen apart. On every approach where American tanks came out, they were picked off by the German tanks with their bigger guns and thicker armor.[41] Still, the Americans still had Peiper firmly surrounded. As if to make certain, on 21 December the 82nd Airborne had seized Cheneux to the south-west. In the meantime, early on 22 December, McCown's parent infantry division, the U.S. 30th, endeavoured to close its trap on Peiper. At 1 p.m. Task Force Harrison attacked south-east with the 3rd Battalion of the 119th Infantry and Task Force Jordan.[42] Under a noisy curtain of artillery fire from the 391st FA Battalion, they advanced against heavy resistance from infantry and tanks. They reached the center of Rouat by 2.30 p.m.[43] At that same time, the 1st Battalion, 119th Infantry, moved through Stoumont headed east but was halted by tank fire from the outskirts of La Gleize. Lt David Knox and the other companies of the 3rd Battalion got orders to help in its capture with a move from the north:

> On 22 December we got the order just after noon to jump off again at 1415 hours. This time we would have tanks with us for sure. The usual artillery preparation would be given. Faces looked mighty scared. I wondered if the men would go. Woody was the bright spot. He told the men 'Come on, these tankers are really doing a job.' ... The men started forward with the tanks. Company K was on our right. What do you know, they were moving across an open area and not drawing a single round of fire and neither were we! The Germans had pulled out! We were soon in our old town and our jeep was still there ... We found two of our men. They had been hidden in a cellar all the time.[44]

The tanks of the 3rd Armored joined the push. 'Stoumont taken by TF Jordan,' the tank team radioed at 3.10 p.m. 'Mission accomplished.'[45] Forty minutes later the 30th Division S-2 added that twelve to fifteen German tanks had pulled back to the east to La Gleize and that the Germans had more or less abandoned Stoumont.

That night, on the German side, the Luftwaffe seemed not to have been clued in to Peiper's new retrograde coordinates. At 8.20 p.m. Task Force Jordan reported that German planes dropped flares and several paratroopers from a single plane in over Stoumont. At 9.10 p.m. the combat team announced they had rounded up five paratroopers who had landed near town. But that was night-time confusion; soon it became clear that at least some of these were supply canisters floating down between La Gleize and Stoumont.[46] Although Jordan made a pensive move toward La Gleize, the lone road for an approach made this altogether unpromising.

The 2nd Battalion of the 119th Regiment was still attempting to cut the road between Stoumont and La Gleize, but was stalled in the woods by mortars and roadblocks. The barrier was one Company G had originally established the day before, now taken over by the Germans and reinforced by infantry and tanks. In Sgt Elmer MacKay's platoon was an older 35-year-old soldier, Paul 'Pop' Hibner. After everyone went to the ground with the shelling, MacKay looked about to see if his men were okay. As the explosions went on, MacKay was shocked to see 'Pop' Hibner walking about and studying the ground. 'What the hell are you doing?' MacKay shouted.

Hibner said he was looking for his false teeth. Shrapnel whizzed through the air.

'Get down you idiot!' MacKay yelled.

'Don't worry,' Hibner gushed. 'I am dodging the bigger pieces!'[47]

Soon E Company was pulling back once more. By 3.15 p.m. on 22 December the battalion had reached its objective. From Borgoumont, civilians such as Dr Bastin watched La Gleize being shelled.[48]

> I spent the night in the Dumez house in Borgumont. For the first time since the beginning of the week, it was raining. I came back to my home in the early morning to have a look around and learn the news. The front line was along the Nobonruy [creek] 300 metres from my house. The sentry [thought I was a Belgian fighter] and I were allowed to pass the checkpoint. The Germans were waiting for me at my home. They asked a lot of questions and sent me to the cellar … The Germans concentrated in La Gleize were searching for a way to withdraw. To my knowledge they hoped to breach Borgoumont and find a way through the woods to Roanne and Stavelot. At 10 a.m., they brought a certain number of tanks to the fields around my house that I heard passing along my cellar. The American tanks were only 300 metres from there. Both sides began to fire at each other. This time a German tank was hit and exploded when the artillery began to fire on the houses … The German tanks withdrew at about 3 p.m. At 5 p.m. the guns were firing more and La Gleize was taking all the shells. It was during that night that all the houses were burning. In the morning [of 23 December], the civilians had been chased from their houses [by the Germans] and had taken refuge in the church [in La Gleize] or in La Gleize where eighty people had hidden …[49]

The next morning Dr Bastin looked out to see that La Gleize was now a smoking ruin. 'At first I saw the church had disappeared, but I could see pieces of burnt walls and smoke around them … I looked back to my poor, wounded house.' During the constant shelling Dr Bastin thought the church would be completely levelled. But looking ahead, it was still there. He was so surprised that he broke out laughing.

North of La Gleize, the members of Company K of the 117th Infantry worried they would soon be asked to attack again. Maj. Singleton, the 117th S-3 operations officer, asked if there were any 90mm guns? 'North of La Gleize,' just between those two churches,' he radioed to division, 'is a tank as big as two houses … Our tanks have fired at that tank, but he continues to just sit out there in the open.'[50] Artillery, air strike – anything. Later, came a frustrated communiqué from Col William D. Duncan with the 743rd Tank Battalion. His own Shermans could not contest the German behemoths. They needed some 90mm tank destroyer guns. 'I know where you can get some German tanks,' he swore, saying the enemy armor was blithely motoring about 'as if they are having driving instructions'. The only good news seemed to be that the 119th had finally wrested Rouat.

South of La Gleize, at Peiper's key blocking position at Werimont Farm, physical deprivation wore on German nerves. Rolf Ehrhardt was there:

> We had no warm meals since 13 December; we only had marching rations for three days. None of us had a full stomach; many of us had not eaten anything for days. A few sugar cubes and a few frozen apples from the upper rooms of

> the farm were our only food for several days. My crew did have some pieces of bread. But the C.O. and I did not ask for any. It was not enough for dividing it up. The same thing with sleeping. One could not think about it. I believe, from the beginning of the attack until the breakout I slept more than one uninterrupted hour only once or twice.[51]

East of La Gleize, Task Force Lovelady with its attached Company E of the 120th Infantry Regiment continued to hold roadblocks and clear the enemy from around Stavelot, but were held up by unfavorable terrain and tough German resistance. Company E, which had taken Parfondruy the previous morning, had been ordered by Task Force Lovelady to return to Arrêt de Coo, halfway between Coo and the Moulin Marechal, but by mistake had marched to Roanne. So, on the morning of 22 December, the company was ordered to counter-march south to re-join Task Force Lovelady, which was now under siege.

The company ran into the enemy north of Arrêt de Coo, unable to reach Lovelady and taken under fire themselves. There were now no more than one hundred effectives in the company, and the 2nd Battalion, 117th Infantry Commander Lt Col James W. Cantey pushed Company F into the gap between Company E and L.[52] Inconclusive fighting continued, but eventually Cantey added Company G, which had been the sole division reserve. The German move was intent on isolating both Task Force Lovelady and the 30th Division infantry companies.

Meanwhile, on the night of 22–23 December, all the American artillery zeroed in on Peiper's bastion in La Gleize. At Neuville, the 113th Field Artillery Battalion funnelled hundreds of artillery shells into the town, including the deadly new proximity-fuze rounds. On the morning of 23 December some 220mm cannon in La Reid joined in the gunnery. La Gleize began to collapse and burn. More than a dozen times, Rolf Ehrhardt went to Peiper's headquarters in La Gleize with messages from Oskar Klingelhöfer holding at Werimont Farm. Peiper directed the defense of the eastern perimeter. 'The place was like a pigeon coop,' Ehrhardt remembered, as messengers constantly went back and forth.

> Not far from the church, in a house on the right side of the road, where one could see from the rear windows north toward the villages Roanne and Borgoumont, was the command post 'Peiper'. The cellar was vaulted and built from natural stone. It was not roomy. A peculiarity of the space was a very large table made from a fist-thick stone plate. In this room was Ostbaf. Peiper, when he was not elsewhere with his men. During the last few days of the action in La Gleize I escorted Hstuf. Klingelhöfer several times to the cellar and was a bystander during conversations and a recipient of orders. The radio station was in the cellar of a house on the way to the farm … At the beginning of occupation of this cellar, I had set up a small cast iron stove at the request of Peiper. Despite the improvised chimney set-up with several stovepipes through the tiny cellar window, the stove actually worked. Peiper thanked me and asked me what my future professional plans would be. I answered: 'Perhaps 'TFO' [Technical Officer Oven] – a joke.

> Among the troops the engineering officers for motor vehicles were called 'TFK'. My version 'TFO(fen)' caused Peiper to laugh heartily.[53]

With the fighting growing more hopeless, the willingness of young SS troopers to sacrifice themselves began to lag. 'I was present when Peiper received the report that one of the engineers was trying to desert,' Rolf Ehrhardt recalled. 'To this, Peiper answered that this man deserved to be killed.'[54] Rolf Reiser claimed that Peiper and Poetschke in La Gleize had enjoined the shooting of American prisoners on 22 December, while Hal McCown was coddled:

> On this day, I heard Obersturmbannführer Peiper saying at the command post of the battalion to Sturmbannführer Poetschke that he would have part of the prisoners of war shot. Peiper's words were 'I am going to have part of the prisoners of war shot …' That prisoners of war were shot, I know from a remark of Sturmbannführer Poetschke. I was present a few hours after the above orders to shoot prisoners of war were given. Sturmbannführer Poetschke conversed with an American major who we were keeping in confinement. The name of this Major was MacGown [sic] or similar. I have to admit that the manner in which this Major was treated stayed in my memory, especially because it touched me comically. Obersturmbannführer Peiper and Sturmbannführer Poetschke took care of him … and talked to him as friends, while orders existed to have other American prisoners shot. Among other things, I remember that this American Major inquired of Poetschke where the other prisoners of war were. I myself don't speak English. However, I can remember that this question of the American Major was translated by the interpreter into German and that Poetschke said in German, 'These prisoners were shot, but you don't tell him anything …' On 23 December 1944, after the issuance of the above orders, I saw in La Gleize about 60–70 metres left and behind the schoolhouse in a gully, the corpses of ten to fifteen American prisoners who had been shot. I am not sure about the exact number.[55]

While there was some evidence of isolated shootings of individual prisoners around La Gleize by SS troops, there was no evidence for a mass killing as there was at Baugnez – particularly the large execution the prosecution would later claim took place by the church wall. There were multiple witnesses, however, who said that six to eight Americans were shot 'as target practice' just outside La Gleize on 22 December.[56] There were also the claims that over a dozen Americans were shot in town by tank crews of Hscha. Knappich and Drechsler.[57] If this were so, however, where were the bodies when American graves registration crews arrived?

That no massacre occurred in La Gleize, as would later be claimed by Malmedy trial prosecutor Burton Ellis, is clearly indicated by two key pieces of evidence. Firstly, the Stoumont–La Gleize battle zone was liberated by the 30th Infantry Division much earlier than the crossroads at Baugnez. Even so, as Old Hickory took over the devastated scene of the La Gleize fighting, no reports emerged of large numbers of bodies of executed American soldiers being discovered. Nor was there any mention of war crimes evidence from the soldiers themselves who liberated this zone from 22 to 24 December.

Finally, there were no indications from local villagers – including the town priest, Louis Blockian – of malevolent wrongdoing.[58] And those Belgian civilians included the village priest who had passed by the church wall repeatedly. Why then would these German SS youths be admitting something that never happened? 'These [alleged] shootings are probably the result of the "hope for release",' said Grainger Sutton – a defense attorney at the later Malmedy trial. 'An accused would admit anything to be released from their present intolerable surroundings in Schwäbisch Hall.' Blokian, who had been in La Gleize from 18 to 24 December, had only seen the body of one dead U.S. soldier – the charred corpse of an American hanging from the turret of a burned-out Sherman tank. Other Belgian witnesses, Alfred Kreutz, Armand Baltus, and Maria Gregoire, had seen little else suspicious in town either.[59]

However, that isolated shootings of American prisoners occurred seems likely as these were often indistinguishable from combat-related casualties even to trained graves registration crews. Indeed, members of the 12th Panzer Grenadier Company would later admit firing on three American prisoners outside the 2nd platoon command post in La Gleize on 22 December – corroboration of Peiper's admission. Two of the Americans were supposedly killed, with one escaping.[60] Peiper himself told Maj. McCown about that specific incident on the night of 22–23 December. Although he regretted having to shoot the Americans, he said, he recommended McCown tell his men not to attempt escape. In fact, that specific conversation was recalled by McCown in his trial testimony as well as from Peiper himself.[61] Still, McCown would claim he neither heard of nor saw any abuses of his men at the hands of the SS troops.[62]

Peiper would later testify 'that he had decided to fight to the last man in La Gleize, until he received a garbled radio message from higher headquarters advising him to evacuate La Gleize and return'.[63] What is certain, however, is that Peiper had ordered one of his own SS men to be shot – for threatening desertion. Gerhard Walla, from the headquarters company of Poetschke's 1st Panzer Battalion, had been in the cellar of the schoolhouse in La Gleize. That was Werner Poetschke's command post on the morning of 22 December as the Americans blasted the place with artillery.[64] In the small cellar was Poetschke, Peiper himself, as well as SS. Ustuf. Rolf Ritzer, Ustuf. Steininger, and SS Ostuf. Erich Rumpf. They talked over the situation. Things weren't looking good and some of their men were looking to bug out.

Rumpf told Poetschke and Peiper that one of his company had left his position and removed his SS insignia. 'Peiper said this man had to be shot,' Rumpf recalled. The SS panzer engineer officer was soon out of the CP on other business when SS Ustuf. Hans Hennecke came through the door. 'After Hennecke entered, Lt Col Peiper told him to order Rumpf to form an execution detail for this man.' The shooting party was to report to Hennecke, who promptly left. According to Walla, five minutes later, Hennecke showed back up at Poetschke's CP 'and reported the execution of the order'. Hennecke addressed Peiper and Poetschke at the command post. Poetschke waved him away. 'Over there with you,' Poetschke answered, 'my den is already crowded enough.' In the room with Peiper and Poetschke was his adjutant '*Väterchen*' – the nickname for Rolf Reiser. Reinhard Maier was with the Panzer Signals Battalion.[65]

> The command post of the 1st Panzer-Abteilung was transferred on the afternoon of 21 December under the command of Stubaf. Poetschke to the schoolyard in La Gleize. It was not possible to take up radio communications from La Gleize due to the heaviest artillery fire of the Americans … For this reason, from 2 p.m. on 21 December up to the 24th, I was in the basement of the command post because it was nearly impossible to move outside … During this time, I always saw Ustuf. Rolf Reiser at the command post of the battalion, where he had also been on the 22nd. In the forenoon of this day I was present as a witness when some officers were present at this place, among them Obstuf. Peiper, Stubaf. Poetschke, Ustuf. Steininger, Ustuf. Buchheim, Ustuf. Reiser, and others. On this occasion I heard that Obstuf. Rumpf reported to Obstuf. Peiper that one man of his company had left his post without permission. I heard that this event had been discussed by the three mentioned officers and Poetschke said that this [man] ought to be executed by a court martial for cowardice. After Ostuf. Rumpf left the command post, I heard Poetschke order that Rumpf must form an execution detail out of his own men and sent Ustuf. Hennecke with that order … I remember that the AWOL man of the 9th Pioneer Company had been executed by the execution detail of Rumpf on the evening of 22 December 1945 [*sic*] in front of the command post of 1st Panzer-Abteilung.[66]

When did Peiper himself first sense the total failure of *Wacht am Rhein*? 'The first indication we had was a message on 23 December 1944 at 1700 hours ordering us to break out toward the east with our vehicles and men,' Peiper would later lament.

'When I received that message I realised that our only chance was to break out without any vehicles and wounded.'[67] Peiper had done that repeatedly in Russia – many times – but never like this, and never against the *Amis*, encircled, under attack, and behind enemy lines.

Peiper's old comrade in charge of the Tiger tanks, Heinz von Westernhagen agreed. Now located with his few huge tanks in La Gleize, von Westernhagen viewed Peiper's unrelenting advance as brave if foolhardy. 'As always, again we were in the deepest mess,' he wrote home from the front. 'We were the spearhead of the attack. Already on the first day we broke through the American positions and penetrated deep into the rear. It was a wild chase with frantic shooting. In the end we were cut off and encircled. For five days we sat like a mouse in a trap without food and little ammunition and got hammered by American artillery.'[68]

Even at Hitler's headquarters, it was clear that Peiper's prime attack spearhead assigned to lead the way to Antwerp was now in danger of total destruction. The Heeresgruppe B report was grim: 'Concentric attacks against Kampfgruppe Peiper and from the south-west against Stavelot continued under the heaviest employment of artillery.'[69] His Führer's final great gamble lost, now it was up to Jochen Peiper to somehow escape to fight another day. The view of one of the regular army men in Peiper's attached flak battalion:

> 22 December
> This morning, we get new orders: to throw a circular defense around La Gleize. With this order the *Landsers* begin to realise that we are cut off and encircled. I had a premonition of this. Like a flash, I realise the deadly seriousness of the situation. Should the Yanks catch us here together with the SS – caught together and hung together. And these SS madmen want to fight to the last man – including us. The boys of my platoon have become taciturn; passively, they have accepted their fate. Like robots, they go through the motions of carrying out the order which I pass down from the Battery commanding officer. I know damned well that only utmost alertness and interest could see the men through in this critical moment, but these qualities are lacking as much as the motor fuel in our gas tanks.[70]

On the night of 22–23 December Peiper called Hal McCown back to his headquarters once more, looking to engage him in 'intellectual' conversation. By now, McCown and Peiper were almost at ease. 'The substance of the conversation was the same as the night before, on general subjects centring mainly on politics,' McCown recalled. Their conversation was frequently interrupted by gusts of heavy American artillery fire that 'never let up for any period'.[71] Had they discussed prisoners of war?

> Early in the conversation, Col Peiper brought to my attention an incident which had occurred that day … He stated that during an American armored infantry attack coming from the east, supported by smoke and artillery, that the American troops had approached among the first buildings on the eastern side of La Gleize – actually at the south-eastern road since the road was the axis of the attack. He said that at this time, several American PWs who had been employed in work details in La Gleize had attempted to escape by running. He said that in the confusion, to which he himself was a spectator, and could testify to the same, that approximately nine PWs were killed … Col Peiper stated also that he was sorry it had occurred and for me to announce to the remaining PWs in the town not to attempt to run in the future or they would be shot and he did not want any future [incidents] … Col Peiper had decided to consolidate all of his wounded, who had been spread out in the cellars around the town, with the few American wounded … Col Peiper said he was planning to move them into the large church … at the southern end of town. He was very much interested in my opinion as to whether the American artillerymen would fire on the church. I was able to give him no satisfaction that they would not and told him that any concentration placed on the town would probably strike the church as well.[72]

Before daybreak, McCown again returned to the large cellar in La Gleize. The 135 American prisoners were still there and in reasonable spirits.[73] 'I had been with them long enough and had made considerable pep talks to them to get their feelings rather high. They knew they would be released shortly since the German situation was bad.'

After the war Peiper recalled his continuing probing discourse with Maj. McCown that night. 'I tried to avoid letting McCown know the tight spot I was in. It was my first opportunity to speak in a friendly manner and on a human basis with an opponent. It was a big contrast to the cruel and inhumane fighting style of the Eastern Front and I was therefore very glad to see that real front-line soldiers speak the same language.' According to Peiper, McCown told him, 'the Americans' task in the war was to pull British chestnuts out of the fire.'

> I recall he said, 'Well, I guess the war is over on this front for me, so I'll help you fight the Russians …' We had a long conversation about the Jews … He wanted to know why we persecuted the Jews and so I tried to explain to him the Jewish situation in Germany, how it came about. I told him we see America only through the eyes of propaganda and you do the same about Germany. … I asked him if all influential positions in the States were held by Jewish people. He told me something about the strong financial interest they had and I believe I said, 'OK, when this war is over, I'll pay back your support against the Russians and help you hang the Jews.'[74]

'These remarks were made in a joking manner,' Peiper later said, as if to defend McCown from negative connotations. 'We exchanged addresses and hoped we would meet again after this bloody war was over.' But '*Help hang the Jews?*' Even perversely viewed as a joke, the content reflected the unvarnished view of Jochen Peiper: SS warrior anti-Semite.

Chapter 29

LA GLEIZE

There is nothing as bad as war … When people realise how bad it is they cannot do anything to stop it because they go crazy.

Hemingway, *A Farewell to Arms*

It was two days before Christmas 1944 in Hitler's *Adlerhorst* headquarters. That Saturday in briefing room in Haus #2, a staff officer scribed concentric, heavy, blue pencil lines on a situation map south-east of Liège. Blue strokes affixed Jochen Peiper's tank group far east of the Meuse River where the Führer's planners had forecast him to have crossed. On the map, he and his spearhead battlegroup, labelled '1.SS', were now corralled, encircled, and confined to defensive positions on the hills and ravines arrayed around La Gleize. That hilltop village and the otherwise pastoral farms south of it around the hamlets of Werimont and La Venne comprised the only Belgian real estate still held by Hitler's lead SS tank group. A week before they threatened a new Dunkirk in the west; now they were hemmed in and hunted.

New pencil marks on Hitler's map displayed angry, red arrows directed at the blue island that was the Kampfgruppe Peiper.[1] Like steel versions of Wild West covered wagons, Jochen Peiper's tanks were now totally surrounded 50 miles from their start line. Under siege: that was the best description of Peiper's predicament, for he and his men were now cut off, unsupplied, and under concentric assault.[2] Each hour the moat thinned.

Even though the U.S. First Army finally had Peiper trapped, the weather prohibited use of their most potent weapon: air power. With a full, armored combat command and two tank battalions, the Americans theoretically had a numerical advantage. *Theoretically* was the key word. Tank manoeuvrability would be good, for Ardennes soil with its mud-like tendencies was now 'frozen hard as stone'. However, the broken terrain and the impossibility of off-road deployment made most tank approaches obvious on La Gleize. Then too, the Germans fielded superior armored fighting vehicles, both in guns and armor, and made any potential American tank advantage a mirage. Surprise would also be impossible as the village yielded a commanding vantage over the surrounding area. No matter what approach the Americans used, they would surely run into every weapon Peiper and his 1,600 surviving men could bring to bear. For advancing U.S. riflemen, cold ground made it nearly impossible to dig foxholes for cover when they came under fire. Artillery was the sole remaining advantage and the American commanders aimed to exploit that to the fullest.

From his station just west of La Gleize, SS Uscha. Karl Wortmann surveyed Peiper's encirclement from the mount of his camouflaged flak panzer. On 22 December he was not more than 300m from an American anti-tank gun, which was thankfully oblivious to his presence. It would be easy to wipe out the crew of the American gun, Wortmann opined, but with no more ammunition, perhaps it would be best to save his rounds: 'By now, we have already spent several days and nights in the open air outside the village … Each night after dark, I have gone to our command post in the village. There is hardly any news. Every man in this inferno knows that we are in a lousy situation and a worsening one at that. Supplies of fuel, food, and ammunition broke off the day we were encircled …[3]

Frustrated by the inability to breach the boundaries of Peiper's *Kessel* kill zone, orders from U.S. First Army were to lay down a massive artillery bombardment on Kampfgruppe Peiper. Things got started in La Gleize the morning of the 22nd, as witnessed by Karl Laun and anti-aircraft gunners of the 84th Flaksturm Battalion:

> For breakfast, we get a double helping of artillery and mortar fire. We helplessly stand by as an anti-tank gun is jockeyed into position. Just a few minutes later it broadcasts overtures for our benefit. And already the fourth round dissects one of our cannon. Then we become cognisant of the fact that only two of our tanks are still manoeuvrable, while just about eighteen Shermans race around, firing relentlessly from one and then from another direction … I have given up all hope of getting out of this hell alive. Herr Major Sacken stages an appearance among us in the afternoon. The boys wink at each other knowingly; the good Major is really scared stiff. Verbose though he likes to be, he keeps his trap shut and silently cowers in his hole … approximately 700 dejected souls remain.[4]

Messenger Rolf Ehrhardt raced down the streets from Peiper's headquarters:

> The village of La Gleize was under constant harassing fire from the American artillery. For some reason, I had to go along the road to the road fork. I proceeded ducking low along the houses on the right side of the road. Suddenly, an explosion came 20 metres in front of me. Roofing tiles crashed down on me while I was down in the gutter along the house wall. When I started to get up, the same thing happened again. Five or six times I was down in the dirt. Aside from fear, a grudging admiration rose for the precision of the enemy artillery. Apparently, every time they hit the same spot within one metre. I wanted to leave this devilish hole with an energetic jump, but surprise left me breathless. In a narrow yard

> between two houses a Panther fired round after round toward the north. Because of the proximity and the muzzle blast, roofing tiles flew around and I, old rabbit, let myself be fooled and mistook the tank-gun shots for incoming detonations.[5]

Monsieur Etienne Gregoire Lambert was huddled in the church with the German wounded and other Belgians, hoping to survive from one hour to the next. From 8 a.m. onward, a rain of shells fell on the village.[6] The Red Cross flag now seemed to mean nothing; the streets were choked with dust and cordite. Everyone's ears rang from the deafening explosions. Then, at 11 a.m., the first shell struck the church, causing St Joseph's altar to fall on to two German soldiers who were otherwise unscathed.

Starting at 1 p.m., an even heavier wave of shells descended on the town. The gunnery went on for more than fifteen hours. In the afternoon, two more shells blew holes in the ceiling and at 3 p.m. the church tower exploded and then collapsed, temporarily burying the church refugees in stones and plasterboard. Lambert and his little group ran out into the street. Some wanted to run behind the school, but SS men in foxholes shooed them away. Now the group made their way back to Lambert's own home. In its garden was a horrifying sight – two dead Germans, one with no head. He carefully shielded his daughter's eyes and conducted his family to the cellar door. In a last glance at the top of the stairs , Lambert looked out over a blazing perdition. 'How can we live in this hell?'[7]

By midnight, the American gunners were cascading white, phosphorus shells into the narrow streets. Karl Wortmann remained in his flak tank:

> I am surprised when suddenly there is a roar of big shells over our heads. Our eyes go the village. Shell after shell follows at short intervals, and after the fourth shot, the spire of the church subsides and crashes to the ground. Shivers go down my spine. The school and the cellars are full up with our own as well as American wounded … Right in the center of the village, close by the command post of Obstuf. Peiper, 164 American prisoners are accommodated in two cellars … Uninterruptedly, the Americans keep on firing the deadly incendiary shells into the village. On this afternoon of 22 December, we witness La Gleize being completely razed to the ground within just an hour. The village perishes and with it many of my comrades. When it gets dark, I try once again to reach the command post, but smoke and rubble make any advance impossible. It is a dreadful sight – comrades to whom I try speaking are hardly able to utter a word. On the way back to my tank, I remember my crew's request: 'Bring us back something good to eat.' Thank God, they have not lost their black humour.[8]

Maj. Hal McCown was still in Peiper's custody:

> I was taken back the morning of 22 December and again placed in the small cellar with the four other American officers. All that day, American artillery pounded the town incessantly, even the guard detachment – consisting of five Germans – came down into our cellar with us, which was heavily overcrowding the tiny room. In the afternoon a 105mm shell made a direct hit on the wall of

our cellar, throwing the German sitting beside me halfway across the room. A hole approximately 2½ feet in diameter was knocked in the wall. Lt Henley and Lt Youmans of my regiment helped pull the German out from under the rubble and got him on the floor of the undamaged part of the cellar. Within another few minutes another shell landed a few feet from the hole in the cellar wall and shrapnel and stone flew through the room. Lt Henley was killed instantly and three Germans were wounded. One of the Germans died within about thirty minutes. We administered first aid as well as we could. For several hours the shelling continued without appreciable let up and the dead and wounded together with those unhurt were cramped close together in the unharmed half of the cellar. Late in the afternoon, parties of American enlisted men came into the cellar and removed the dead and wounded; the litter bearers told me that German casualties had been heavy throughout town.[9]

Eventually, the Americans were moved to a new cellar. Bob Hall recalled Peiper himself, coming to their new place of imprisonment, to fetch McCown. That same day, Wilhelm Mohnke's headquarters of the 1st SS Panzer Division moved to the château in Wanne, Belgium.

Wanne was on a steep, wooded hill just 8 straight-line kilometers to the south-east of Peiper's men but separated by the confluence of the Amblève and Salm rivers. There in the communications vehicle set up at the divisional headquarters, the *Feldfernschreiber* clicked off a priority message signed by Hitler himself. Who had committed the atrocity being reported by the Americans? 'When I heard of the shooting of 120 American prisoners near Malmedy,' reported Genobst Alfred Jodl, 'I immediately, on my own initiative, had an investigation started through OB West so as to report the result to the Führer.'[10]

A man in the communications car from the 1st Company of the Panzer Signal Battalion received the message on 25 December 1944. He overheard a short conversation between his commanding officer, SS Ostuf. Helmut Liebrich, and an SS Master Sergeant of the 2nd Company. Liebrich said they had discussed the matter of the incident at Malmedy with the Operations Officer, SS Stubf. Ralf Tiemann. An investigation had been made, related radio operator SS Rttf. Gerhard Ellhof, with negative results.[11]

Meanwhile, at U.S. First Army headquarters, wounded prisoners of Kampfgruppe Peiper, such as Benoni Junker, had been taken captive at the Château Froidcour on 22 December.[12] By 27 December U.S. interrogators had pieced together information on the culprits of Baugnez. Evidence 'indicates that the mass murder of U.S. PW s at K8101 was probably committed by the CT (Combat Team) of Einheit Peiper … The CT was at the head of the German column in the Malmedy area at the time the atrocity was committed.' Who was responsible? Lt E.W. Kann, in charge of the POW cage with U.S. First Army, ventured a guess to his superiors, 'It is pointed out that OST (SS Lt Col) PEIPER was regimental CO of the 1st SS Pz Regt,' he wrote. What had Peiper told them about the fight? 'Germany lifts itself for the last time. If it doesn't succeed this time, we have lost.' And then Kann connected the dots. 'OST. PEIPER always travels at the point of his column,' the captured men said.[13]

Jochen Peiper was hardly focused on what had happened days before at Baugnez, but rather the real possibility that La Gleize would be his last battle. 'Until that time,' he would later say, 'I had the intention of defending the town until the last man, even if no aid would come.'

> Our position at La Gleize had become very difficult. The town itself consists of a few houses only. It is surrounded by mountains and offers very excellent artillery observation points to the enemy. Further to the north and west, the forest is very close to the town and offers good lines of approach to infantry. In view of the great enemy artillery superiority, it was only a matter of days that the whole town was shot to rubble. It was hardly possible to move in the streets. All squares of the streets of the town were under direct machine gun and tank-destroyer fire. Connected with that was a very great increase in our own casualty rate. The town hardly had any cellars. The few cellars which were available were used for the prisoners and wounded. The prisoners represented a terrific burden to me at that time, but it happened constantly that the guards who were standing outside the cellars in which the prisoners were kept ran away during the artillery fire.
>
> On the evening of the 21st while inspecting the lines of combat, I saw a number of Americans – I think about eight – lying at the edge of the town, shot. I wasn't able to make any investigation since it was dark and very lively firing was going on. I continued on my way to the CP of Major Poetschke and I asked him whether he knew anything about those American soldiers I had seen out there. And he said, 'Yes.' They had been shot in the course of an enemy attempt to escape during the afternoon – on the afternoon of the 22nd. In the afternoon, the enemy had attacked with very strong infantry – very strong tank concentrations from the west and very strong infantry concentrations from the east. They had penetrated the outermost houses. The whole town was filled with fog and the impression one had was that the infantrymen were in front of our doors. I myself jumped out of my cellar with a machine pistol while my adjutant began burning secret matter. At that time, I saw the whole town full of brown figures, but could not decide whether they were attackers or escaping prisoners. In connection with that attack, Poetschke related the incident just mentioned.[14]

Radio communication between Peiper and divisional headquarters had been non-existent since leaving Ligneuville on 17 December. Periodically, Peiper had sent out word of 'our tactical situation and our supply, but received no receipt'. There had been rumours in the encirclement that fuel drums would be floated down the Amblève river to them, but even the most optimistic had a hard time believing such a scheme. On 21 December fleeting radio contact was established, but the exchange was discouraging. Peiper told of being desperately short on fuel and under escalating assault, while the division offered help – air support. 'Rudel will come with his battle planes,' the message began, 'Direct him toward targets with suitable signal means.'

Peiper knew Hans Ulrich Rudel well; he was the famous Luftwaffe pilot from Silesia – a Stuka tank-busting specialist on the Eastern Front who had blasted Soviet T-34s in Peiper's path more than once.[15] Yet as Peiper looked out from the stone house that was his headquarters, he could hardly see across the street. La Gleize was totally socked in – bathed in an impenetrable mist. Kampfgruppe Peiper was living in a cloud and Peiper thought the Luftwaffe must be, too. 'Rudel should first let us know he is in the area by signalling us with a fog horn!' Peiper replied.[16] Visibility was zero. Not surprisingly, no tank-busting Stukas were seen over La Gleize that day or otherwise. Rudel wasn't even flying.

That Thursday, 21 December, Peiper sent messages informing the division of his desperate plight and looking for a briefing on the odds that the sister battle groups would cut through to him. SS Stubaf. Ralf Tiemann was nestled in his radio truck near the castle in Wanne, listening to Peiper, who could evidently not hear his own transmissions. Tiemann responded, but Peiper did not acknowledge reception. 'Where is our support from the air?' Peiper called out. 'We have fired our last mortars and have no more ammunition.'[17] Another man from the newly arrived Panzerwerke Company under SS Ostuf. Werner Stöckel was in the signals room asking corps about the whereabouts of some replacement axles. He overheard even worse from Peiper: '*Gebt mir Treibstoff und Munition sonst gehen wir vor die Hunde!*' – 'Send me more fuel and ammunition or we go to the dogs!'[18]

Everyone seemed to be listening in on Peiper. As Allied intelligence observers eavesdropped on the 1st SS Panzer Company on 21 December, they learned that the Luftwaffe was considering an attempt to drop Peiper fuel along with a hastily requested Luftwaffe ground attack specialty unit *Sonderstaffel Einhorn* from Italy.[19] The resupply mission didn't happen, and a text of frustrated explanation from German planners flashed from Fldm. Model directly to Hitler's headquarters. 'After air resupply did not come through, the elements of Kampfgruppe Peiper are concentrated around La Gleize after repelling all enemy attacks.'[20] In a conciliatory tone, the same report to Hitler called for stepped-up attacks by the rest of the Leibstandarte. At 5 p.m. there was another radio message, brief and disheartening. The attempt by Kampfgruppe Hansen to break through to him had failed. The resupply mission would be rescheduled the next day.

At Peiper's CP in La Gleize, Karl Wortmann overheard that fuel supplies would be dropped by parachute on the night of 22 December and that *Auntie Ju* transports would circle La Gleize before dropping them. Wortmann, a 25-year-old flak panzer gunner, warned his otherwise eager men of the 1st platoon not to fire on the German aircraft – a prudent warning given that just about everything in the air now seemed to be American or British.

At 8 p.m. on 22 December a small doddering flock of Junker transports of *Transportgeschwader 3* droned over the village. SS men on the ground fired off flare pistols to guide them. Soon the transports were spitting out a small trail of supply canisters by parachute.[21] The deadly 3.7cm flak guns of Wortmann's platoon remained silent. In spite of ground signals, the SS men watched most of the packages under silk canopies waft in the moonlight into American lines to the west. Had the Luftwaffe not received word that Peiper no longer controlled Stoumont? Wortmann observed small groups of German patrols try to worm their way to the canisters. '*Kein Gedanke daran!*' – 'Don't even think about it!' All were pushed back by alert American fire.[22] 'The whole night through, we could not get those canisters out of our thoughts. On the following day, we saw through the binoculars that quite a number of canisters were lying in no-man's-land, which was only 200 metres wide. A light snow was falling . . . Our cursing did not help us any!'[23]

The packages surprised the locals. One Stoumont farmer awoke to find a wooden Luftwaffe *Abwurfbehälter* filled with cigarettes and schnapps in his cow pasture; another parachute-draped box was chock-full of 9mm Luger pistols.[24] Karl Laun was unsurprised by the supply drop's failure:

> We occupy the south-east side of La Gleize, facing the railway bridge. Everybody digs and claws to gain the slight cover of mother earth. With a wood saw, we fell a few trees and roll them over our foxholes as protection against shrapnel. We add a few shovelfuls of dirt and place a prime mover right over a four-man, slit trench ...
>
> On the other side of the river, we spot American infantry. Our propaganda machine at once starts to work. 'You see, boys, the Americans are retreating ...' In the evening, the American artillery cuts loose. We crawl like moles into our trenches. Hunger overpowers me, but in spite of this, I don't dare to get one of my booty U.S. rations only about 30 metres away. The artillery shells fall as thick as hail into our positions.
>
> During the night, a plump Ju 52 hums above us and throws down barrels with gasoline. Many of them land on the American side, where there is an overabundance of this juice without our involuntary contribution.
>
> In the distance, behind our lines, we hear the grumbling Werfers; again, a gala occasion for the *Herrenmenschen* to feed us a good line. 'Hooray, they are coming!' But nothing came. Another morale booster is not long in coming. The SS Division Hitler-Jugend and Hohenstaufen will 'box' their way through to us. But nothing comes. Only the monotonous whine of the enemy artillery assumes an even more intense tone.
>
> In the small hours of the morning, I find my blanket which I had stuffed into my foxhole. It is frozen, board-stiff, but our American comrades sympathise and obligingly send over a few phosphorous grenades to warm things up.[25]

Peiper accepted his disappointment stoically. 'Co-operation with our planes was good,' he would later write with an ample dose of sarcasm. They had fired tracers into the air as the Ju 52s had approached to let them know where they were. 'The air drops failed because we were encircled in too narrow an area and most of the stuff was bound to fall among the Americans.'[26] Peiper only received a single fuel drum – a few liters to power generators for radio transmitters and a few sloshes into empty fuel tanks to move a Panther or Mk IV into better firing positions.[27] Even worse, the 6th Panzer Army informed them that no further air support of the Peiper battle group could be expected.[28] 'A little Stalingrad?' thought Karl Wortmann.

While Peiper railed at Luftwaffe incompetence, frustrated American ground commanders, in particular Maj. Gen. Matthew Ridgway in charge of XVIII Airborne Corps, wanted a hell-like aerial bombardment of enemy-held

La Gleize. His preference, he said, was 'to wipe it off the map'. Lt Col Robert Herlong pleaded against that approach to Gen. Hobbs, 'I've got a lot of men in that town, and we'd kill all of them,' he offered. 'Give us one more day.'[29] Besides, Hobbs had already had enough experience with American bombers hitting his division by mistake – and that happened in Normandy with good weather. Besides, earlier saturation bombing efforts seemed to have little effect on the tenacity of strong battle forces.

Hobbs' caution made little difference, for on 23 December the Ninth Air Force again bombed his men in error. The tragedy came about when twenty-eight B-26 Marauders from the 322nd Bomb Group of the Ninth Air Force were scrambled to hit the German railhead at Zülpich, some 32km east of the border. Most of the planes of the mistaken mission realised they were off course and aborted the mission. However, six planes, thinking they could hit an alternate target, released eighty-six 250lb bombs over Malmedy, Belgium, thinking it was Lammersum, Germany.

Malmedy normally had a population of 5,000, but many locals had been evacuated after 16 December. Yet given events in the days that followed, Malmedy became a magnet for 1,300 refugees from the surrounding towns of Büllingen, Butgenbach, and Rocherath as they were captured by the Germans. So quickly did the population swell that the Mayor Joseph Kluckers, had just returned to help restore civil order. And so when the bombs fell at 3.26 p.m., the town teemed with more than 4,000 Belgians and American army troops.

One moment, one mistake and terrific destruction and loss of life followed. The 3rd Battalion of the 120th Regiment suffered most for its companies were located all through the town. The kitchens of Companies K and L were wiped out, with most of their staffs killed, and many of Company M were injured. All over there were scenes of horror. Sgt Frank Palco, an aid man with Company M, found himself following a panicked Belgian girl to an air raid shelter. In the smoking center of town, he saw the structure collapsed by a direct bomb hit. Inside, Palco found three women still alive, but in terrible pain and pinned underneath fallen roofing beams that had crushed their legs. Though without surgical tools, the sergeant pulled out scissors from his aid kit and performed field amputations – a horrific process without anaesthetic, but one that saved the lives of two of the women.[30]

For Gen. Hobbs, the errant bombing was the last straw. At 6.02 p.m. he was on the phone giving Gen. Matthew Ridgway an earful. He understood that corps wanted an air strike and sure enough 'we got a medium [bomber] strike this afternoon and it hit Malmedy and created quite a big fire – the houses are burning and a lot of civilians were killed and wounded and some of our troops were casualties.'[31] Ridgway protested that he had nothing to do with the bomb attack. He couldn't even get a mission assigned. That did nothing for Hobbs, who was now on the phone to V Corps and Chief of Staff Col John G. Hill. 'Did you know that our own bombers bombed the hell out of Malmedy yesterday?'[32] T/4 Wilson E. Rice, of the 30th Infantry Division Medical Department, recorded:

> A lot of the 120th Infantry Regiment troops were there … It's not so bad until they begin bringing in women and children. One little girl, about nine years of age, and her brother, about five came in on the same litter. The little girl was not hurt so badly, but the little brother is in pretty bad shape. That little girl really took my heart. There she is without her parents and looking after her little brother.[33]

Malmedy's agony was not over. The following day Col David Pergrin of the 291st Engineer Combat Battalion, having survived the discovery of the atrocity at Baugnez and the direct attack on Malmedy by Skorzeny's people the week before, was now digging survivors out of the rubble in town from the mistaken bombing the previous day. He was nearing a Belgian trapped in a cellar when another wave of B-24 Liberators struck. Pergrin, too, was temporarily buried in the exploding rubble. Scores of civilians died, and frantic calls came from the 120th Regiment. 'They just bombed us again. They just dropped a half a dozen bombs on us. We want that stopped. They have hurt our troops badly.'[34] Hobbs was on the phone to First Army. 'Our own air wants to beat us at this game,' he said. 'I ask that … whatever they do tomorrow, that they be kept off us.'[35]

Still the bombs came. On Christmas day four Marauders of the 387th Bomb Group mistook the smoking ruins at the center of town for German-held St Vith, which was being bombed to smithereens. At 2.30 p.m. another brace of bombs struck the scarred center of town. With the town packed with refugees, at least 125 further Belgian civilians and thirty-seven American soldiers were killed, and many more were wounded.[36]

Experienced hands of the U.S. 30th Infantry Division called the U.S. Air Force 'the American Luftwaffe'.[37] On this, both sides agree. Peiper: 'The Luftwaffe, through long hibernation and a high standard of living, had become a gentlemen's weapon, which lent no ear to the needs of the petty infantry soldier, but spoke uneasily of poor flying weather.'[38]

Despite the disadvantageous terrain, spotty radio communication resumed between divisional commander General Wilhelm Mohnke in Wanne and Peiper. 'We have 320 wounded and 120 wounded Americans and 300 American prisoners in cellars …' Peiper reported. Two radio reports arrived from division that night. 'If Kampfgruppe Peiper does not punctually report its supply situation,' went the first, 'it cannot reckon on a running supply of fuel and ammunition.' And then another: 'Six Königstigers ready for action east of Stavelot. Where do you want us to send them to you?' Peiper couldn't believe it. The promised fuel cans had just floated down the river into the puzzled hands of the Americans surrounding him. 'Via air lift to La Gleize!' Peiper scowled.

SS Stubaf Ralf Tiemann was listening to the radio transmissions in Wanne. 'Let me out, you assholes!'[39] Peiper cursed over the static before switching off the radio. Soon Peiper and his officers hunkered down in the darkened La Gleize cellar as the artillery shelling picked up again. On the morning of 23 December another transmission arrived from Mohnke. 'Can you break out with all vehicles and wounded?'[40] The American artillery shelling had reached a hellish din. 'Last chance to break out tonight,' Peiper sent back. 'Without wounded and vehicles. Please give permission!'[41]

> Convinced that in the course of the day, I would get permission to break out of La Gleize, I immediately started the necessary preparations and worked out a schedule … My radio operator kept asking: 'Where is the main line of resistance – where is a covering position? May we break out?' In the course of the afternoon our breakout preparations had progressed to such a point that there was no more return … Toward 1700 hours the following message was received: 'State when and where you will cross our lines with all wounded and vehicles.' Thereupon I blew my top and had the radio car blown up. We never received permission to break out, but did so on our own account.[42]

The American prisoners did not know the gravity of Peiper's decision. 'Up until the 23rd at noon, I decided to keep La Gleize until the last man,' he admitted after the war. 'And I told my commanders, if all of us should perish here, our prisoners are not going to survive us [either], since I thought it impossible that all of us would die here and the next day a hundred and fifty Americans would get new weapons and fight against the German Army.'[43]

In any case, Gen. Hobbs was under increasing pressure on 23 December to erase Peiper's stand at La Gleize. He and CCB of the 3rd Armored Division arranged four separate concentric attacks from each point on the compass rose all timed to get under way at 8.30 a.m. To aid the assault waves he organized formidable artillery support. The 197th Field Artillery Battalion, supported by the 119th Cannon Company and a rogue 155mm gun under the personal direction of Col George K. Rubel, would pour direct fire on the SS from nearby the Château Froidcour.[44] In the castle there, Brig. Gen. William K. Harrison had set up his headquarters, although he was momentarily disappointed to find that Peiper's men had thoroughly ransacked its extensive wine cellar:

> From the top of the château, I could get a good view of the village of La Gleize, at least the side that faced us. It was on a bend in the river and could be strongly defended against attack from the side where I was. The river prevented attack from the south and south-west. The only direction from which I could hope to attack successfully was from the woods to the north of the village. I was assured by a liaison officer from the 82nd Airborne that they held the south bank of the river, sealing the Germans in. CCB, 3rd Armored Division, Brig. Gen. Boudinet was operating east and north-east of La Gleize and was put under my command. But there was no way I could give anything more than very general instructions to Gen. Boudinet to co-operate in the attack the next morning against the east of town. Gen. Ridgway visited me in the afternoon [of the 23rd]. I showed him the situation and told him I planned to take La Gleize the next morning.[45]

The lead element of the multi-pronged assault would come from Col Robert Herlong's reinforced 1st Battalion, 119th Infantry, Task Force Jordan of the 3rd Armored and some towed guns of the 823rd Tank Destroyer Battalion. At 8.30 a.m. the combined force attacked toward the south end of La Gleize along the road that approached the town from Cheneux. 'On 23 December we moved toward La Gleize and we had by this time received heavy artillery support from our rear.'[46]

Jordan's armor led, but in the vicinity of the road junction north of La Venne along the Werimont road they came under enemy eyes.[47] His armor had scarcely advanced forward when they ran into a minefield covered by anti-tank fire. At 10.30 a.m. Harrison was on the phone to Hobbs. 'They are pretty much through the woods down there,' he said of Boudinet's CCB. '[They] are temporarily slowed down at defending minefields on his left. They are defended by light tanks and a company of infantry.'[48] Attempting to remove the mines, they were ambushed by a Panther and a Mk IV situated on a reverse slope from the Dinhè terrain between La Gleize and La Venne. Two Shermans were hit right off, one burning, and Maj. John Jordan himself sought refuge from the enemy guns stalking anything that moved. Eventually, the minefield and felled trees were removed, and the combat team proceeded 300 yards further. There, however, they were raked by heavy automatic weapons and tank fire near the Mouton crossroads. Another tank was lost. Still, CCB's tanks reached the edge of the woods about 1,000 yards from the church in La Gleize. Going any further, Jordan reckoned, would be suicide.

Herlong sent the ranking officer of Company A of the 823rd Tank Destroyer Battalion, Capt. Bruce Crissinger, for a recon. 'See what you can do about it,' he said to Crissinger.[49] He was supposed to uncover Peiper's tank positions for M10 tank destroyers in waiting. Yet as Crissinger and Lt Art Cunningham stole some 500 yards east of Stoumont, they, too, were both pinned by machine gun fire, 'the bullets so close to our heads that they cracked like Chinese firecrackers'. Cunningham was wounded and crawled to the rear and safety, but at 3 p.m. Bruce Crissinger was rousted from a ditch by two German paratroopers fighting with Peiper.[50]

> We then climbed a steep, high bank on the north side of the railway track into a grove of evergreen trees and into a rather large, covered bunker. There, I was jammed in with several Germans, some of them officers while the good old American artillery continuously pounded the grove. One of my captors asked me my name. I told him my name was Crissinger. '*Ja*,' – Yes, he said, 'a German name.' He said his name was Schultz. It was not a happy group.
>
> I was then turned over to a rather small, thin soldier with a hairlip who was carrying what appeared to be a British Sten gun. He took me through various manned positions, machine gun nests, and so forth. As we came up a lane toward La Gleize, a Mk IV tank swivelled its periscope to get a good look at me. I was turned over to an interrogation officer in a building. He was originally from Chicago and spoke perfect English. He had a shrapnel hole in his helmet and he was not very happy either. From there I was taken across the little village to a house and into the cellar. There were already thirty or forty GIs in the cellar including four A Company men. A big SS soldier with a submachine gun sat at the top of the cellar stairs. Sometime during the afternoon, a kettle of peeled and boiled potatoes was passed around. Each man took one. They were properly salted and delicious.[51]

A second arm of the concentric attack emerged from the west near the Château Froidcour with the 3rd Battalion of the 119th Infantry Regiment crashing forward with support from Captain Berry's Company C, 740th Tank Battalion. Col. Rubel's straight-ahead tank advance from Stoumont toward La Gleize 'fizzled out and no gain was made'.

> The enemy was covering our advance with all kinds of fire. Most of it came from La Gleize, but the thing that stopped us was the flanking fire from the high ground north-west of the town. This fired caused us a lot of casualties.[52]

Given the sparse road network, the assault pushed along the obvious approach on the N33. Moving cautiously forward, at 8.30 a.m. they ran into a roadblock where the lead tank was knocked out by anti-tank fire. By 1.10 p.m. the roadblock was clear, and the battalion pushed 150 yards further until it was checked once more by a hail of 20mm flak fire from La Gleize. The infantrymen were able to link up minutes later with the tanks of CCB, 3rd Armored, but they could go no further.

'Can we get any air?' Gen. Harrison radioed back to division, 'we have twenty Panther tanks in this town.' 'There isn't much chance of it,' Hobbs admitted.[53] At least one company became lost and took most of the day to reassemble. Lt David Knox commanded Company L, 3rd Battalion of the 119th Infantry:

> It had been a very cold night. Frost was on the ground. The three rifle companies were supposed to approach the town over three different routes or roads. According to the map it looked good – phase lines to check in on and all sorts of big plans ... By noon, we realised that we were on about the only road there was and also that the road we were on didn't seem to be on the map. It was very confusing. There was no route into town. Over on the other side of the draw we could see a red parachute that had been used to drop supplies to the German troops ... Night came and we ground-hogged for the night. The whole night was spent in trying to get artillery lifted that was falling very near our 3rd platoon. Everything was being dropped in La Gleize that night. *Everything.* As I shivered, I thought, *Tomorrow is Christmas Eve.*[54]

Meanwhile, other elements of the 3rd Armored tightened the noose on Peiper by launching assaults from the other cardinal directions. That Saturday afternoon, infantry of the 117th Infantry Regiment along with elements of D Company, 36th Armored Infantry Regiment, advanced down the road from Borgoumont toward La Gleize. Dashing forward after a rain of mortar fire, the American infantry managed to push past the Nabonruy stream and worm in close to the north edge of the village. There, enemy resistance stiffened and the advance stalled. The 117th's G Company also moved on La Gleize from the north to assist, but with the fog of war they were given a jump-off line that did not bring them into contact with the enemy.

To the east, Task Force McGeorge along with a platoon of road-bound Shermans from the 743rd Tank Battalion did manage a bull rush from near Roanne toward La Gleize before being badly cut up by German tank and machine gun fire.[55] They stopped once more at the Minières. Eventually, the two predatory Königstigers that had punished the advance from south of La Gleize near Werimont Farm were taken under fire by those brave Shermans surviving the challenge. Rolf Ehrhardt was still with his Mk IV at Werimont Farm:

> On the opposing slope a number of American Shermans drove up. The cannon of the Mark IV was of little importance because of the long distance. But the extra-long, 88mm guns of the two King Tigers and the 75mm cannon of the Panther would have easy play with the Shermans, which at these distances were certainly inferior. Was it a feeling of revenge? The American formation was recognised early enough for coming into a favorable firing position for us. Now it was time. After the first miss of one of the Tigers, unexpectedly the Shermans turned to face us and opened up firing rapidly. That drove me from my observation post on the second floor, fleeing into the basement. From there we followed the fighting acoustically. The shells and mortars from the Americans blew through the house. The basement was soon overcrowded with people, who waited for a pause in the fire to count the number of Shermans that had been shot down. Limestone mortar fell from the vaulted ceiling. The discharge from the super-cannon of our Tigers was easily distinguishable from the incoming hits. In our minds, every round fired by 88mm cannon was a hit. Suddenly, the Tiger commander Hantusch burst into the cellar, both hands pressed to his head, and yelled: 'That was Hantusch's last yell!' His Tiger received several hits that shook up the sensitive weapons system so much that the electric firing mechanism had broken down. By another hit on to the turret, Hantusch was slightly wounded in his head and had left the smoking tank, which could burst into flames any moment. Minutes later the second Tiger commander, Ostuf. Dollinger, came into the cellar, bleeding heavily from his head and without a word. After he had been bandaged, he reported that the discharge smoke made it impossible to zero in. The rapid, incoming fire spoiled the last chances of hitting. Numerical superiority of the eight to ten Shermans nullified the superior weapons of our tanks. Dollinger's Tiger got a hit that 'amputated' the front third of the cannon. Another illusion dashed, we were now depressed.[56]

Unknown to McGeorge, both of the German steel monsters were put out of action by damage to their sensitive electrical firing mechanism.[57] However, the American assault from the east faltered just the same. 'The Task Force tried to attack around the bend and to come up the hill into La Gleize,' commanders later described, 'However, the enemy fire remained too strong.' By 3.30 p.m. they were defending rather than advancing and were even forced to fall back. That night, they removed mines and trees that had been felled across the road, preparing for the big assault on Christmas Eve.

Dismayed with the lack of progress, Gen. Leland Hobbs contacted Brig. Gen. William K. Harrison with the 119th Infantry Regiment, asking him to plan on capturing La Gleize the next day without fail. Harrison was not confident. 'There are at least fifteen of those big tanks left there, plus a sizeable infantry force. I am not planning on making an all-out attack on it today.'

Hobbs: 'If I get you the air, will you go? … Can you wind it up?'

'I am not sure,' Harrison replied. 'We have not cleared up the roadblocks. I know you want to do that, but all that is left of the 1st SS is in there, and they are not giving up. We have lost three tanks already today.'[58]

Meanwhile, at 3.10 p.m., Maj. Trearse, the air support officer, announced that an air strike would be coming within minutes to hit Peiper's forces in front of the 3rd Armored, Combat Command B. Then, just twenty minutes later came a frantic call from Trearse, 'Planes are bombing Malmedy. We haven't a line left to anybody in town,' he said. 'Call them off!' Another air support mission gone terribly wrong.

At 8.43 p.m. that night Gen. Ridgway, in charge of XVIII Corps, called up Gen. Leland Hobbs to impress on him that La Gleize had to be taken, otherwise a surrounded group of Task Force Lovelady was in jeopardy. When could Hobbs eliminate the SS stronghold? 'I can't promise you, but I hope by noon.' Ridgway then delivered bad news: the U.S. First Army wanted the elements of CCB 3rd Armored pulled out pronto.[59] The 2nd SS Panzer Division was now ruthlessly smashing the shaky American defensive line near the Baraque de Fraiture crossroads just to the south, and armor was desperately needed.

How would the 30th Division capture La Gleize without armor? 'It is an almost impossible task unless we have something to replace them,' Hobbs pleaded. 'Do everything you can not to pull them away. I can't guarantee the situation without them.' Ridgway agreed to attempt to delay pulling out the armor, but pressed Hobbs again to get on to eliminate the enemy in La Gleize. 'I am just trying to meet the pressure from the army [First U.S. Army], which is very insistent,' he said, hanging up the phone.[60] That much was true. The following morning at 10.30 a.m. Field Marshal Bernard Law Montgomery appeared at Ridgway's headquarters in Werbomont to peer over his shoulder.[61] It was mortifying. Entrusted by Eisenhower with the entire northern front, the British commander had ordered the 82nd Airborne to pull back – an unwelcome mission for Ridgway or Gavin. In any case, the 30th Division would be on their own, and no proper British advice would change the fact that it would suffer declining resources against Tiger tanks. Christmas Eve would see a headlong attack against a fanatical SS opponent, an operation sure to be a bloodbath.

At 8.46 p.m. Hobbs was in contact with Brig. Gen. Boudinet about the mess of his Task Force Lovelady – still trapped yet ordered to pull out to go to First Army. 'Pretty stiff fighting,' came the report … Enemy holds the road on the west of the woods along the river.'[62] It was like double queen's *Zwischenzug*; if Hobbs had Peiper surrounded on the Ardennes chessboard, Mohnke had Lovelady in the same jaws.

'I just presented the facts to the corps commander,' Hobbs said of his tense communication with Ridgway, 'and he directed me to hold everything where it is for the time being.' That was good, Boudinet said. 'We will have to keep them here.' Indeed, Task Force Lovelady was still trapped. Otherwise 'you gave me an almost impossible job.' No sooner had he hung up than Hobbs was back on the phone with Col Ralph D. Eaton, the chief of staff with XVIII Corps. There was now a request to pull the 291st Engineer Combat Battalion in use all across the front, but particularly at Malmedy. 'We will move them as soon as we can … but we can't afford to be weakened … We cannot pull these people away. I impress that on you as well as your boss.' He fumed. Without CCB 3rd Armored, 'we haven't the armor we need.' And the enemy troops they were dealing with weren't just typical German forces. Without tanks to support his foot troops, 'those people' – the 1st SS Adolf Hitler – 'would run wild down there and I couldn't stop them.'[63]

Frustrated by the stubborn German resistance that turned back his 740th Tank Battalion that afternoon, Col Rubel on the western side of La Gleize took matters into his own hands, commandeering a 155mm artillery gun, which he had brought up to the Château Froidcour. He set the gun up just south of the château and called up another platoon of Shermans mounting 105mm guns to join in the gunnery. 'Crunch Junior' – that was the name made up by the 30th Division artillery observer for Rubel's direct-fire battery improvisation. T/5 Clarence O. Webster was a bow gunner in one of Rubel's irregulars, operating in a tank without an operable radio:

> Our 1st platoon of A Company with five tanks with 105mm guns set up just south-east of the 155mm gun. These guns were out in the open and visible from La Gleize. Expecting gunfire from La Gleize at any time, we began to fire on the town where equipment and soldiers were moving around. It was devastating firing the guns point-blank into the town. The destruction was really horrible. We shelled the village all afternoon on the 23rd until darkness set in.[64]

Rubel chose the targets himself for the 155mm gun, blasting 192 rounds into La Gleize over open sights. The 105mm tanks joined in. Never having been in combat before, Clarence Webster was unnerved by the experience – dead bodies were lining the lane of the château and the devastation in western La Gleize before him looked horrible, as he watched men running from buildings while he blew them apart. Moreover, the fighting the preceding two days had shaken his confidence. He and his buddies had witnessed Germans using a captured Sherman tank. The enemy had fanatically rushed toward their tanks with Panzerfausts. They were not driven away by warning shots; only mercilessly shooting them down stopped the SS infantry from wielding anti-tank rockets.

Across the way, Jochen Peiper was stoic. Although each American attempt to reach La Gleize was turned back, the noose had tightened, dramatically. And Rubel's guns and the other tubes of the 30th Infantry Division were blasting his command post apart. Expectantly, he followed the progress of Kampfgruppe Hansen's grenadiers just to the east. If they could break through, they could get out of this hellish netherworld.

The SS infantry east of Peiper now stretched a skirmish line through the woods north of Trois-Ponts to expand their bridgehead along the N33.[65] The infantry battle raged all day, but at no point did Hansen break free of the 2nd Battalion, 505th Airborne Infantry Regiment and Task Force Lovelady in the continuing battle for Petit Coo. The airborne strengthened their positions before the 10th SS Panzer Grenadier Company in Noupre. Indeed, further American attacks beginning at 9.30 a.m. were now strongly supported by artillery and a few tanks between Stavelot and Coo.[66] This counterpunch pushed back the SS grenadiers and left one company surrounded and embattled. A wounded SS evacuee grimly reported the comrades he had left behind aimed to fight to the last man.[67]

The Americans suffered, too. Maj. George Stallings' group from Task Force Lovelady had been isolated for more than a day by the advance of Kampfgruppe Hansen across the Petit Spai bridge and into their rear at Biester.[68] The German infiltration through the woods had overrun the battalion medical aid station at the Boulangerie Thonon (near Coo) and cut the road leading south to Stallings. Four M4 tanks of the little combat team fell prey to anti-tank weapons launched from the timber-lined roads. Lt George Gray's recon platoon, surprised by the suddenness of the German infantry assault on Petit Coo, took refuge in cellars, only to later be taken captive.[69]

'We're just fine, thank you!' Stallings had reported over a static, bedevilled radio link on 22 December.[70] However, at one point on 23 December, the ammunition supply grew critical and Stallings contemplated surrender – a last resort given growing awareness of the fighting methods of the Waffen SS.[71] Such had been underscored when the 3rd Armored and six rifle companies of the 120th Regiment recaptured the hamlets of Ster, Renardmont, and Parfondruy from the Germans. They found scores of Belgian civilians brutally murdered by Kampfgruppe Knittel.

By dent of a big effort, Col Lovelady got his forces back to Grand Coo in a position to sweep the enemy from the high ground and pry open the road to Stallings. At daybreak on 23 December the attack began through the Bois de Lancre, but the light M5 tanks with E Company of the 2nd Battalion, 120th Infantry Regiment, did not recapture the aid station at Petit Coo until 11.15 a.m. Two tanks were lost. The fighting that morning was ferocious.[72]

To reorganize, Task Force Lovelady's infantry pulled off to the high ground just east of Petit Coo. While this went on, the Stuart tanks standing in a column on the N33 came under heavy anti-tank fire from the SS infantry in the woods. Three additional companies – F and G – of the 2nd Battalion, 120th Regiment and Company L of 3rd Battalion / 117 Regiment came to Lovelady to protect his armor. The battalion-sized infantry contingent from 30th Division would fight as Task Force Hickory. By 4 p.m. Biester was finally cleared of the enemy.[73]

Although elements of the 1st SS Panzer Grenadier Regiment continued to hold out in the Bois de Moines, German losses in the 1st and 3rd Battalions trying to link up with Peiper were terrific. The 12th SS Panzer Grenadier Company had now lost its second commander. Knight's Cross Holder SS

Ostuf. Frank Hasse, commanding the 11th Grenadier Company, was also killed. SS Oscha. Heinrich Nebel was in Petit Coo:

> During the night, the Americans pulled out of town and placed it under fire the next morning. Ostuf. Hasse's command post was located along with the Panzerschreck platoon in a building on the edge of Petit Coo. An enemy tank was set up at the entrance to a tunnel. Our Panzerschreck platoon was ordered to put it out of action and [in the process] lost all its weapons … Ostuf. Hasse was killed during the further course of the fighting. Our battalion commander Hstuf. Böttcher was also seriously wounded in the fighting. Ostuf. Haft from 10th Company took over command of the battalion.[74]

Meanwhile, the tattered troops of the 1st SS Panzer Reconnaissance Battalion pulled back to Madame Antoine's farm along the river just west of Stavelot, under the steel umbrella of the four-remaining operational Königstigers watching over the vicinity.[75]

With the end of prospects for a conclusive American assault into La Gleize on 23 December, U.S. artillery observers unleashed a blistering cannonade. At 2.30 p.m. the central part of La Gleize became an artillery hell. American heavy gun batteries firing from Targnon, La Reid, Franchorchamps, and Neuville began an unremitting fire. So fast was the shelling at times that firing cannoneers were forced to pour water over steaming barrels. Adding to the lethality, the guns of the 113th FA Battalion in Neuville rained down proximity-fuzed POZIT artillery rounds that burst in the air over the target and sprayed the ground with deadly shrapnel.[76] Surviving troopers were soon driven to the cellars by the incessant gunnery. That night, divisional artillery reported more than 1,200 rounds fired into La Gleize. Observers saw a village in flames.

Planning between shell bursts in La Gleize, Peiper and his men prepared to slip away. On the afternoon of 23 December, his officers held an urgent conference of war in his headquarters at the home of the George Family around a bulky stone table. Diefenthal, Poetschke, and others were there.[77] With news that they would try to leave, 'some glow came into the eyes of the hard, worn-out faces'.[78]

At first, Peiper had contemplated several escape routes – one back toward Stavelot with Knittel, another to move south-east toward the crossing at Petit Spai, or to head further south into a heavily forested region where U.S. airborne troops had set up along the Salm river. However, as he planned, word came back from a reconnaissance carried out by one of the Skorzeny men the preceding day.[79] The only path open was the nearly impassable wooded terrain to the south. Peiper would cross the Amblève river and push towards Basse Bodeux to the Trois-Ponts road. Even if unpromising before, perhaps 'the old man' – 36-year-old Max Hansen – and his 1st SS Panzer Grenadier Regiment would snatch the bridgehead at Coo. Then they could meet up there. Orders went out; they would leave that night. Vehicles would be blown up. Karl Wortmann:

> The night is closing in and going to be colder and some snow is falling. Freezing and starving, we lie there in our foxholes … Every now and then I doze off. Each night we have to spend here seems longer and more unbearable than the one before … I hear something … I raise up, hearing voices in the dark night and run toward them. 'Merry Christmas! Merry Christmas!' I hear them repeating. 'What's going on? Christmas is only tomorrow,' I reply. 'No, it's right now,' he shouts back. He is a messenger from the command post. What is this password? I want to know. 'Immediate escape – blow up tanks and follow!' he says and then runs off. I wake my crew and they quickly realise what's up.'[80]

What to do with the wounded and the prisoners? Leibstandarte men too badly wounded to walk like Benoni Junker were left in the company of SS Ostuf. Dr Willibald Dittmann, the medical officer of Diefenthal's 3rd Battalion. What would become of the American prisoners? That was still unsettled. Peiper gave the final instructions: 'Breakout 0200 hours. Password: *Frohe Weihnachten*' – Merry Christmas![81]

Chapter 30

'PASSWORD MERRY CHRISTMAS'

O Tannenbaum, o Tannenbaum,
du kannst mir sehr gefallen.
Wie oft hat nicht zur Weihnachtszeit
Ein Baum von dir mich hoch erfreut.
O Tannenbaum, o Tannenbaum,
du kannst mir sehr gefallen.[1]

They would break out. At first, Peiper only allowed his officers to know of the La Gleize escape plan. The others were informed at the last minute to keep the notion secret; someone from Kampfgruppe Peiper could easily become a prisoner.

That afternoon of 23 December, Peiper had his star prisoner, Maj. Hal McCown, brought past the steel gate of the timbered farmhouse where Peiper had established his headquarters. When the American major arrived at the cellar, Peiper complained, 'the Americans were using a heavy-calibre, direct-fire weapon to fire on houses in La Gleize and to knock out my tanks'.[2]

McCown shrugged, but Peiper complained anyway: this fire – or the observers of it – came from the château where he had left both German and American wounded. He would not fire on the place, but McCown told him it was American policy to evacuate prisoners from anyplace from which fire would emanate. That seemed to suffice for Peiper, who returned him to the larger group of American prisoners. Just after dark, McCown was called back still again – this time to find Capt. Bruce Crissinger of the 823rd Tank Destroyer Battalion in Peiper's company.

Peiper had to break the news to Maj. Hal McCown that they would shortly abandon La Gleize. 'I led McCown to believe we were still in control of the situation and that we were just called back. He then smiled and said, "Well,

Colonel, I've been always looking forward to riding in a King Tiger." He did not know that he was going to walk!'[3] McCown continues:

> Late in the afternoon of 23 December I was called once more to Col Peiper's headquarters. He told me he had received orders from the commanding general to give up his position and withdraw to the east to the nearest German troops. He said he knew it to be impossible to save any of his vehicles – that it would have to be a foot withdrawal. His immediate concern was what to do with the American prisoners, of which he had nearly 150, as well as his own wounded. He dictated to me a plan of exchange whereby he would leave all American prisoners under the command of the senior PW, a captain, to be turned over to the American commander as the Americans entered the town the next day. He said his wounded would also be left in the cellars in La Gleize and that he would leave a German medical officer in charge of them. He had previously left a considerable number of wounded in the château in Stoumont which had already been captured by the Americans. In exchange for the American prisoners, all German wounded would be turned over to the 1st SS Panzer Division wherever they might be when the wounded were assembled. I would then be released back to the American lines as I would be the only prisoner retained during the foot movement of the Germans east from La Gleize. I told Col Peiper that I could not give him any assurance that the exchange would be carried out as it was a matter for higher headquarters. He said that he fully understood.[4]

'This proposal is a farce!' McCown flatly told Peiper.[5] Peiper could not have cared less. McCown was his golden hostage.[6] Who knew what value he might have in the hours to come? In Peiper's plan, another ranking American prisoner would be entrusted with the German wounded. That man would be Capt. Crissinger, who had been captured at 3 p.m. After dark, Crissinger was captive in a La Gleize cellar. He recalled:

> At 7 p.m. that night we heard fire crackling overhead in the house above courtesy of the American artillery – maybe white phosphorous. We were ordered up the stairs and outside by the guard. Everything was orderly, but the scene in the street beside the house was chaotic. The town was on fire and slowly being smashed to pieces by artillery. While our thirty to forty GIs were huddled together, we were wondering what would come next. Our wild-looking guard was now swinging around his submachine gun and yelling 'Officer! Officer!' in accented English. I finally realised he meant me and I identified myself as an officer. I was taken to the command post of SS Lt Col Joachim Peiper … The CP was in a cellar. There was a blanket for a floor. I went down and realised who was in command. I snapped my absolute best salute. He returned it. He was a very good-looking man who spoke slow, good, but not perfect English. There were three or four other officers with him.

'Did your guns knock out any German tanks?' Peiper asked the tank destroyer captain. 'Yes, we did,' Crissinger said. Peiper told Crissinger about a German gunner in a Tiger tank – Michael Wittmann – who had destroyed thirty

American Shermans in one day. Did he know of it? The Ohio native shook his head. Never mind, Peiper continued.

> Shortly after that, Maj. Hal McCown was brought in. He gave me a quick surprised handshake. After a little conversation, the purpose of the meeting was made clear. Peiper's force was surrounded and out of fuel. They were going to abandon all their equipment and escape through American lines that night, taking McCown along as a hostage.

'I was to lead an ambulance convoy under a flag of truce loaded with German wounded who were in the cellars of La Gleize through the German lines,' he would later recall. 'When this was accomplished, McCown would be released. Peiper wrote a note explaining the plan, which I later gave to Col Sutherland. He rightfully ignored it.' Crissinger continued:

> What I took to be a German sergeant then came in and reported to Peiper, giving him the Nazi salute. I thought Peiper returned it half-heartedly. He was given several orders by Peiper, to each of which he replied '*Jawohl!*' He then saluted again and beckoned me to follow him. As we were leaving, McCown again shook my hand and said to me, 'If I am ever to see my family again it's up to you.' I was then taken by the German sergeant through the wrecked and burning town with artillery shells falling constantly.[7]

Everything now happened quickly. On the dining room table of the home of the George Family in La Gleize, Peiper left his map board where he had followed the enemy moves with colored pencils. And he left a book he had been reading: *Deutsche Geschichte – German History* – by Richard Suchen (1940). Someone left an MP40 submachine gun on the table – all signs that the move was made in haste.[8] Orders, maps, and codes were hurriedly burned and hand weapons gathered. Marcel Boulanger's house was vacated at 10 p.m., the SS putting the torch to their previous domain. The entire farm went up in flames. The *Lötlampen Abteilung* – Blowtorch Battalion – was a label for which Peiper had become known over the war. Marcel Boulanger was thankful that at least his animals were released.

Even leaving, Feldwebel Karl Laun with the 84th Flaksturm Battalion saw little that was promising in Peiper's situation:

> A starlit night sky hangs over La Gleize.[9] It has grown bitter cold. The flames, still bursting from the ruins, flicker spookishly. In between – as if demonstrating that the end is at hand – the American artillery punctuates the death sentence of this town. Since last night the impacts lie exclusively in this small place. The field hospital has to be moved to the comparative safety of the cellars.

At 2 a.m. Peiper assembled his battle group – carrying side arms and packs – and marched off with them accompanied by Maj. McCown.[10] The men had left Germany with only three days' rations and many were famished, so those with any food at all carried it like a treasure. SS Uscha. Rolf Ehrhardt lugged along two bottles of brandy in his pack. They set off south from the main square down a secondary, sunken dirt road – *'Le Coulée'* – towards Werimont Farm. Peiper asked McCown to give his word that he would not try to escape.[11] McCown bluntly informed Peiper that as a professional soldier, it was his job to try to escape. Peiper said nothing, but immediately assigned two guards to watch over the American officer.

> At 0300 hours on 24 December, the foot column began to move. Col Peiper and I moved immediately behind the point, the remainder of his depleted regiment moving in single file. Col Peiper told me he had 800 men to evacuate. I later watched the column pass three separate times and this number was correct according to my own estimate. We crossed the Amblève river near La Gleize on a small highway bridge and moved generally south, climbing higher and higher on the ridge line. At 0500 hours, we heard the first tank blow up and inside of thirty minutes the entire area [of La Gleize] occupied by Col Peiper's command was a sea of fiercely burning vehicles, the work of the small detachment he had left behind to complete the destruction of all his equipment.[12]

McCown had grudging admiration for military discipline in Peiper's battle force: 'The noise discipline on night movement was so perfect,' he would later relate, 'that I could hardly believe that they could accomplish it.' Was Peiper discouraged during the walk out from La Gleize? Hardly. 'I saw him give a slap of encouragement on the backs of heavily loaded men as we were climbing the steep hills,' he said and a 'couple of times he spoke cheering words.'[13]

So quiet was the evacuation at the dark hour, not everyone got the word or saw the single red flare fired off at 3 a.m., including a group of fifty men north of La Gleize who were mostly wiped out during the final assault.[14] Strm. Helmut Naumann had been wounded in the left shoulder during the bombardment the day before:

> Inwardly, I had prepared myself to stay behind as a wounded who would become an American prisoner of war. But then our company troop leader came and said to me: 'We will take my Naumann with us.' Although my left arm was bandaged, my feet were still alright so I was able to walk. I wasn't aware of any exhaustion due to my wound and I also didn't feel any pain. When the password 'Merry Christmas' was issued I joined the column at the rear as I wasn't combat-ready due to my injury. Thanks to my injury I was freed to wear a weapon. As my left arm was unusable I couldn't climb our SPW and therefore I had to leave behind my baggage, amongst which was a picture of my girl, my watch, and my steel helmet. I wasn't aware that I would miss the helmet later. Soon after we had gathered on the road we started to march in a single file into the woods. Our company troop leader, an Uscha. whose name I have forgotten, helped me during the first hours in particular when we had to climb uphill. I owe him so much.[15]

Others were literally in the dark. That night Karl Wortmann was standing guard in La Gleize when he heard a baleful sound – someone crying. Wortmann wanted to know what was being said. '*Frohe Weihnachten*' – Merry Christmas – the soldier said, explaining that it was the password for evacuating La Gleize. He had been left behind.[16] Wortmann ran to his flak panzer and woke the crew. 'We're all in trouble!' he yelled. Wortmann and his flak men grabbed machine pistols and filled their pockets with egg-shaped grenades. The crew trotted off on foot in the darkness toward the south.

At first, they nearly panicked to come across the abandoned foxholes of the 9th Panzer Pioneer Company – not a good sign. 'Suddenly, one of my crew detects a lot of footprints in the thin, newly fallen snow and we follow at a brisk pace.'[17] After tense minutes, they caught up with the rear of the column, marching down a rocky, descending trail that locals called La Coulée. The march was vigorous; there was little chance to catch their breath.

Even the few Skorzeny guides with the column were no help in guiding Peiper's posse through the maze of darkened trails. As they first entered La Venne after descending the steep hill from La Gleize, the German march column passed by Albert Legros' farm, where a mass of refugees was sleeping uneasily. The farm was snuggled up against the Amblève river just south of La Gleize. Earlier in the week, members of the 2nd SS Panzer Grenadier Regiment had already occupied the other homes of the little village, eating everything in sight before they departed. But on 22 December as the U.S. artillery commenced to flatten La Gleize, more Belgians arrived to escape the deadly bombardment. By Friday night eighty-two lost souls had taken refuge in Legro's straw-floored cellars.[18] It was so crowded that he even moved his livestock from the stables to make more room. That evening eight German *Fallschirmjäger* arrived at the farm, frightening Legros with their talk of SS harshness. They claimed to have survived a parachute drop that evening to accompany the containers dropped to Kampfgruppe Peiper.[19]

The following evening, there was another knock at the entrance to the farmhouse. Opening the door, Legros was confronted in the dim candlelight by a man completely dressed in an American uniform, but with a German SS man holding a gun right behind him. Legros was speechless. 'Which is the way to Brume?' the man wearing American garb demanded in French. 'It is this way,' Legros motioned beyond the door to the south, 'you certainly speak good French.' 'I learned it in New York!' the 'American' replied with intended irony. 'What do you want?' Legros asked. Again, the man demanded information about the way to Brume, but Legros said the village was accessible only by forest trails. He was unsure of the best route and soon the French-speaking 'American' soldier and his SS tough were inside demanding Legros direct them. 'We need guides!' the German commando said, confronting the huddle of civilians in the cellar. Waving a gun, he pointed to Yvan Hakin and young Ernest Gason in the basement. 'You and you!' Without a word, Laurent Gason stepped forward to take his son's place.[20] He would not let his 17-year-old boy be used as a hostage – a pawn in war.[21]

With no choice but to co-operate, Hakin and Gason emerged from the basement under gun muzzles. They found themselves in the cold night confronted by a number of other Germans disguised as GIs, leading a long parade-like column of SS men. Peiper and a captured American were somewhere behind the point and the rear of the column was said to include thirty or so lightly wounded men. A box of cartridges and a Panzerfaust were thrust on the Belgians to lug along as they embarked with the heavily armed SS group. The Germans demanded help to find passage across the Amblève and then directions to Aisomont.[22] Even worse, the SS officer closest to them informed them that should their advice cause the German column to run into American soldiers, the first shots would be for them.

The two Belgians conducted the SS column cautiously to a little footbridge across the river at La Venne at 4.30 a.m.[23] The Americans were sleeping in some of the nearby houses by the river and some of the Germans removed their clicking, hob-nailed boots to slip through. Even so, there were close calls. 'At one point, we came upon an American guard smoking,' remembered SS Infantry gunner Hermann Staritz, 'and we had to pull back and go around him.'[24] In less than an hour they had passed under the railway viaduct through La Venne and crossed the Amblève river over the rushing current. They marched up a steep, craggy forest slope into the deep clefts of the forests of the Bois de Stalons.

The uphill trek along switchbacks on a logging trail was exhausting. Many men – some carrying mortars – were staggered.[25] In the darkness, SS Ustuf. Oskar Klingelhöfer slipped and sprained his ankle. But for Peiper it was another forced march, reminiscent of days with the Hitler Jugend where he and his brother had excelled. *Full pack; all day.* Up they went.

As they ascended towards the top of Mont St Victor, Peiper paused at one point. He could see all the way back to La Gleize. Artillery was now slamming into the largely vacated village. Eventually, the shelling ended, and tiny figures could be seen running into the village in rushes, as Wortmann remembered the scene:

> The steep and narrowing forest path demands of everyone the very last ounce of strength. We heard panting and groaning – small wonder that we are all weakened after more than a week without food. Our knees dodder; each of us is near collapse and ready to drop. But there is only one thing on our minds – hold out! It is still dark. After a long time, we have reached a height which allows us to pause for breath. We are standing in a clearing and the eyes of our 800 men turn back to La Gleize. There, we see a burning graveyard. Not only are the houses ablaze, but our tanks and vehicles are, too.[26]

Soon the Americans would know they had pulled out of La Gleize. In fact, that realisation came at 10.28 a.m. on 24 December, when the operations officer with the 119th Infantry used a field telephone to advise General Hobbs:

> Notify the Task Force on the other side of town [La Gleize] that we have taken it and to be on the lookout for the enemy infiltrating through. We have recovered all of our men who were taken prisoner with the exception of Major McCown.

> He was seen at 11.30 last night with the German Task Force commander, a lieutenant colonel, and apparently they were trying to get out.[27]

At sunrise, the tired remnants of Kampfgruppe Peiper were atop Mont St Victor, the 520m-high forested hill between La Venne and Brume. The sun rose in a rosy-red orange to the east. The cloudy, grey veil had finally departed and to Hal McCown, Peiper almost seemed giddy with delight. As they walked, Peiper stopped and turned to McCown while pointing to a small fir tree covered with hoarfrost and radar-decoy tinsel from American aircraft. 'I promised I would get you a Christmas tree,' Peiper beamed. 'There it is.'[28] McCown said nothing, but silently vowed that he would find a way to escape – a real Christmas present.

'At daybreak, there was a clear blue sky,' Rttf. Staritz recalled. 'The *Jabos* were out and I worried they were looking for us. Then we saw some American infantry moving forward slowly as if they were looking. We went the other way, walking around in a big semicircle.'[29]

The column then ventured hesitantly south toward Brume, but after spotting Americans in the village, they looped back up the hill into a heavily wooded section. At 8 a.m. Peiper signaled his men to take a break in the thick woods of a deep ravine called Trou des Mouchettes just west of where two mountain-top reservoirs are today. Through that day the 800–900 men concealed themselves in the forest ravine as American aeroplanes roamed the blue skies overhead. For Staritz, a particularly worrisome sight was a low-flying American Piper Cub that buzzed the area.[30] The cold, bright sun seemed to reveal everything on the Mont St-Victor. To evade aerial detection, the SS men carefully hid under frosty fir boughs.

While his men hid for hours in the frozen recesses of the Trou des Mouchettes, Peiper and several officers doubled back and ventured to the eastern edge of the tree-covered hilltop. Although temporarily disoriented while traversing the dense woods, upon reaching the summit he consulted his guides. By using a map and compass he could finally make out signs of a battle just a kilometer below his vantage point. On the edge of the Bois du Layinster, on a bald spot near its crest, Peiper could peer through the trees down the steep slope toward Coo.

Peiper had hoped to be back to friendly lines by now, originally planning to escape over the narrow bridge at Coo. He could then join the German salient west of Biester effected by the strong assault of 1st SS Panzer Regiment of Kampfgruppe Hansen. Until noon the beleaguered command group waited up on the hill, looking for evidence that Hansen's grenadiers filtering through the Bois des Moines might reach the village of Coo. Hansen was only a kilometer away. Yet that didn't happen. The noise of the battle was clearly audible up on the mountain. Even without a radio Peiper knew that the panzer grenadiers of 3rd Battalion were in desperate combat. If only SS Ostubaf. Max Hansen could capture Coo's waterfall bridge, Peiper could steal over to the friendly side in the night.

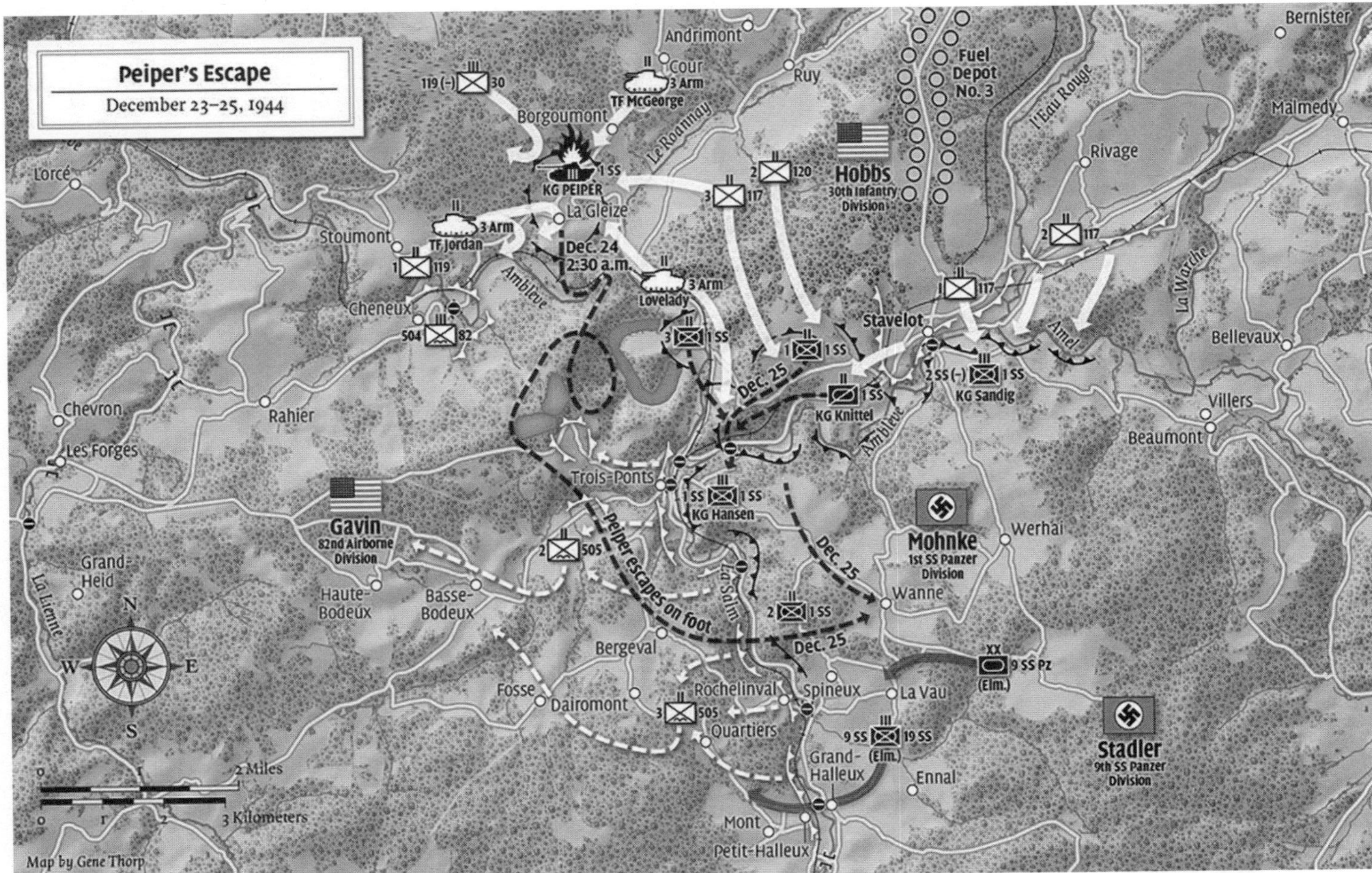

Peiper's Escape
December 23–25, 1944
Map by Gene Thorp
Andrimont
Cour
TF McGeorge
3 Arm
Ruy
Fuel Depot No. 3
l'Eau Rouge
Bernister
Malmedy
Rivage
Borgoumont
Le Roannay
KG PEIPER
La Gleize
Hobbs
30th Infantry Division
Lorcé
Stoumont
TF Jordan
Dec. 24
2:30 a.m.
Lovelady
Ambleve
Cheneux
Stavelot
La Warche
Amel
Bellevaux
KG Sandig
KG Knittel
Dec. 25
Villers
Beaumont
Chevron
Rahier
Les Forges
Trois-Ponts
KG Hansen
Gavin
82nd Airborne Division
Peiper escapes on foot
Mohnke
1st SS Panzer Division
Werhai
Wanne
Grand-Heid
Haute-Bodeux
Basse-Bodeux
La Salm
La Lienne
Bergeval
Fosse
Dairomont
Rochelinval
Spineux
La Vau
Quartiers
Grand-Halleux
Ennal
Stadler
9th SS Panzer Division
Mont
Petit-Halleux
2 Miles
3 Kilometers

What Peiper didn't know was that after their headlong charge to Petit Coo on the morning of 24 December, the SS infantry attempting his relief was now under a crushing assault by tanks of Task Force Lovelady. Intense house-to-house and tree-to-tree fighting flared. In noting the direction of the enemy push, the U.S. First Army decreed that the bridge by the Coo waterfall be dynamited. Courtesy of Company A, 105th Combat Engineer Battalion, the span went up with a roar at noon.[31] Even if he could not see it, Peiper knew the consequences of the thundering explosion having already experienced plenty of reverses compliments of the U.S. engineers. Plan B vaporised. Back in the ravine, Werner Poetschke tracked down Rolf Ehrhardt, who still had bottles of brandy:

> Nearly all the comrades have laid themselves down under the big conifers and have stretched out their tired limbs. The wide branches, heavy with snow, are sagging almost down to the ground and make good cover. There is a long silence; everyone is too worn out to talk. Then from somewhere, a low tune can be heard: 'Silent Night, Holy Night'. Someone of the 800 men have subconsciously begun to hum. Others have joined in. In little time, the melody has sparked from man to man, becoming unified and distinct as if a conductor is leading. It is like a large choir singing in the open woods. No one cares about their skill – it is the emotion in their hearts. Now, even brave men have a subtle feeling. My thoughts wander back home to relatives. At this moment, each one of us knows. It really is Christmas![32]
>
> We are still dreaming when there is a loud booming in the sky. This was not little angels descending from heaven. The noise grows louder and louder and we realise it is three formations of heavy American bombers which are headed east. More than forty are painting long condensation trails in the sky. Long after they are gone from view, the noise of the planes is still ringing in our ears. Our hearts bleed, watching them fly past us in perfect parade order and heading to Germany.[33]

The Allied bomber formations were so numerous, Rolf Ehrhardt recalled that 'their vapour trails were like lines on music'.

> It was almost a familiar picture. But one thing was new for me. Now and then a Flying Fortress left the formation and pitched down smoking. The cause of that was small dots at the tip of the vapour trails, usually moving steeply upward. We saw one of the few attacks of German jet interceptor fighters against incoming bomber formations. It was a small shadow of the promised wonder weapons.[34]

Also, hiding in the deep forest on the mountain top, Karl Wortmann and his men were surprised to find themselves inexplicably seized by the Christmas spirit. It was an improbable feast of charming winter scenery, but joy bubbled up just the same. 'The twigs of the tall and straight fir trees were covered with thick layers of ice,' he recalled, but hunger gnawed nonetheless 'even with slopes and valley meadows looking picturesque under a gloss of snow … Who among us is enough of a romantic to absorb the charm of nature at the moment?'

Just after dark, Peiper suddenly appeared and told everyone it was time to go:[35]

> We had to be careful. I was really afraid as we were in a bad way. Quietly, in a long single file, we went down the hill shouldering our weapons. I was carrying a heavy machine gun. Peiper was going up and down the line to encourage everyone. Peiper told me to give the gun to someone else if it got too heavy. I told him I thought I could manage it ... The walk was most strenuous and many of us were sweating in spite of the cold.[36]

McCown was still with Peiper, but under constant guard. McCown had come to know several personalities among the SS men: SS Lt Col Heinz von Westernhagen and SS Captain Rudi Neumayer. There were two other officers whose names he heard often: Diefenthal and Poetschke.[37] SS Rttf Karl-Paul Fröhlich, who seemed to be a runner for Peiper, guarded McCown most of the time. Fröhlich seemed friendly enough, but kept a pistol trained on him during the long march. 'Can you ask him to take this gun off me?' McCown asked Peiper at one point. McCown now had a white cloth attached to his helmet – to identify himself as a prisoner. Peiper, the proper soldier, thought that looked ridiculous – 'like an umpire in a tactical exercise'. The SS colonel spoke to Fröhlich. 'He will put down his gun,' Peiper said grinning, 'if you promise not to escape.'[38] McCown said he couldn't agree. 'Okay, then,' Peiper nodded, signalling them to resume the march. McCown pushed on:

> The foot column was closed into a thickly wooded slope on a very high hill. Col Peiper, his staff, and myself with my two guards spent all day of the 24th reconnoitering for a route to re-join other German forces. No food was available at any time after we left La Gleize; the only subsistence I received was four small pieces of dried biscuit and two swallows of cognac, which one of the junior officers gave me. The German regimental surgeon [Dr Rudi Neumayer, of the 1st SS Panzer Battalion] later gave me a piece of Charms candy, the sugar of which did me a lot of good during the later long march.'[39]

Meanwhile, posing as Americans, the 'special guides' venturing west of his column got a warm welcome from civilians in Beauloup earlier in the day. This caused Peiper's group to stay with the plan to veer east and south to avoid any Belgian settlements. At sun set, Hakin and Gason helped guide the SS men to the 'Fontaine Marquet' to avoid Brume, moving south to arrive at the precipitous wooded ridge line overlooking Henri-Moulin on the N66 highway. The column curved south as they approached a small, religious shrine nearby at the Cavalry de Croisette. With that, the German SS officer closest to Hakin took it upon himself to ridicule the Americans they were trying to elude. 'What kind of '*Kultur*' do these American monkeys have?' he laughed, making ape-like sounds. 'But how would you know?' Belgians such as Hakin were terrified.[40]

The column was long and strung out as they started down through dark forests to cross the N23 (now the N66) west between Trois-Ponts and Basse Bodeux. Peiper's men silently trudged down narrow forest trails in the cold twilight. They took a short break as darkness closed by 5 p.m. It was cold under a clear, cold sky. The night was studded by stars – Christmas Eve. 'The *Jabos* were gone,' Hermann Staritz remembered. 'I remember it well because I was thinking about home and the *Weinachtsbaum* and we were sitting in the woods. I was sitting with Major McCown and Peiper's driver, Paul Fröhlich.'

Threading down a line of steep switchbacks, the SS battle group headed south intending to sneak across the main road N66 west of Henri-Moulin. Even though it was dark when Peiper's men debouched into the little valley, they were momentarily devoid of cover crossing the road. Given the risk, the long file of men split up into squad-sized groups to sprint across the highway. When the column with its slower tail of stragglers and the wounded finished the descent, though, gunshots rang out and everyone scattered. Some ran back up the hill. The fire came from U.S. vehicles motoring down the N66 or perhaps a lone American outpost at the Henri-Moulin mill. With the shooting, Yvan Hakin and Laurent Gason, having feigned illness to straggle, used the distraction to dash from their guards. They ran headlong into the dark, dense forest.[41] Other Germans, wounded or exhausted, were separated from the main column.[42]

Befuddled by the confusion, Karl Laun and a section of the 84th Flak Battalion headed off west, passing east of Basse Bodeux. Helmut Naumann was wounded:

> We suddenly received fire from machine guns and mortars. We were well trained for these moments and we all hit the ground in order to avoid being hit by ricochets. We stood up again when the firing stopped after a while and continued the march. A small group of five men then realised that we had lost contact with the men in front of us. As we had been in contact with the enemy only minutes before we were not allowed to shout, therefore, we discussed what to do next. We were unable to see anything in the dark night and we also didn't know the direction. We had no choice; we had to stay where we were and wait for the morning to come before we could walk on. We spent the rest of the night in our thick coats, lying close to each other in the snow. At dawn we stood up and continued to march without a real target. With my injury I walked at the end of the column. We stumped through coniferous forest, sometimes also through thickets. This was very hard for me as I didn't have a steel helmet. As I couldn't use my left arm, I only had the right arm to keep the branches away which would have otherwise hit my face. I can't remember additional details. Suddenly, I had lost the men in front of me and found myself alone in a thicket. Even in that moment I didn't dare to shout because I knew that I was still between the lines. So I had to help myself.[43]

Hal McCown was disappointed not to get away, but amused that Peiper seemed lost:

> At 1700 hours, just before dark, the column started moving again on the selected route; we pushed down into a valley in single column with a heavily armed point out ahead. The noise made by the entire 800-man group was so little that I believe we could have passed within 200 yards of an outpost without detection. As the point neared the base of the hill, I could hear quite clearly an American voice shout 'Halt! Who is there?' The challenge was repeated three times, then the American sentry fired three shots. A moment later, the entire column was halfway back up the hillside in only a few minutes. A German passed by me limping who was undoubtedly leading the point as he had just received a bullet through the leg. The Col spoke briefly with him, but would not permit the medicos to put on a dressing; he fell in the column and continued moving on without first aid. The point moved along the side of the hill a distance of half a mile, then again turned down into the valley, this time passing undetected through the valley and [across] the paved road which ran along the base. Several vehicles 'chopped' the column, but at no time was its presence detected. The entire 800 men were closed into the trees on the other side of the valley in an amazingly short period of time. I could tell then that Col Peiper was basing his direction of movement on the explosion of American artillery fire as the probable location of his friendly forces. His information as to the present front lines of both sides was as meagre as my own as he had no radio and no other outside contact. He continuously consulted his map, thus proving that he was quite thoroughly lost.[44]

Now Peiper commenced an effort to feel his way to the south-east through extremely rough terrain to somehow cross the Salm river.[45] He avoided roads and villages, walking parallel to a small streambed. Time was running out and an outpost of the 456th Parachute Artillery Battalion had already reportedly sighted, '400 troops moving from Brume, well-armed and headed east'.[46] McCown:

> We continued moving … continuously up and down the rugged hills, crossing small streams, pushing through thick undergrowth, and staying off and away from roads and villages. At around 2200 hours, Col Peiper, his executive, and his S-3 disappeared from the forward command group. I and my two guards were placed in charge of the regimental surgeon, whose familiar Red Cross bundle on his back made it easy for me to walk behind. I tried in vain to find out where Col Peiper went; one friendly enlisted man of Col Peiper's headquarters told me that Col Peiper was very much tired out and I believe that he and a few selected members of his staff must have holed up in some isolated house for food and rest – to be sent for from the main group when they had located friendly forces.[47] The change of command of the unit also wrought a change in the method of handling the men. A young captain in charge of the leading company operated very close to me. My knowledge of Latin as well as the German I had picked up allowed me to understand to some degree practically every order he issued. I heard him tell my guards to shoot me if I showed the slightest intention of escaping, particularly when we neared the Americans.[48] Whereas Col Peiper had given a rest break every hour or so, there were no breaks given under the new command from that time until I escaped. The country we were now passing through was the most rugged we had yet encountered. All of the officers were continuously exhorting the men to greater

> effort and to laugh at weakness. I was not carrying anything except my canteen, which was empty, but know from my own physical reaction how tired the men with heavy weapons must have been. I heard repeated again and again the warning that if any man fell behind the tail of the column, he would be shot. I saw some men crawling on hands and knees. I saw others who were wounded, but who were being supported by comrades on either side up the steep slopes; there were fully two dozen wounded in the column, the majority of whom were going along quite well by themselves.[49]

In the late night, the troop skirted Bergeval and ended up in the forest facing a meadow north-west of the village. Once St Jacques was found to be held by the Americans, the exhausted column assembled to hide in the dense treeline west of the Parc St Jacques highway and worked their way to the east. It was at this point that Peiper and several other officers disappeared for a number of hours. Where were they? Rolf Ehrhardt recalled how near panic seized the column when he, Dr Neumayer, and Oskar Klingelhöfer realised that Peiper was nowhere to be found, nor was Poetschke or Diefenthal.[50]

Dead on their feet, many of the men were now snoring at the wooded edge of the meadow near Bergeval. None had had anything to eat for over twenty-four hours. Eventually, another SS officer stepped forward to reorganize the leaderless group, rousting many who were sleeping.

With the unfriendly attitude of the young SS officer now in command, the prospects for McCown's escape dwindled and only the friendliness of Paul Fröhlich – who offered a cigarette after one gruelling segment – reassured him he would not be shot on the spot. Even when the American major had stumbled, the officer thrust a pistol into his back.[51]

Sometime in the late-night hours, Peiper and the others made it back to the column, ostensibly after having reconnoitred the approach up ahead. At this point McCown recalled some discussion about resting for the night in Bergeval. He also remembered drama as the Germans had struggled up the 9% grade to Mont de Fosse, preparing to move to St Jacques:

> We approached very close to where artillery fire was landing and the point pushed into American lines three times and turned back. I believe the Germans had several killed in these attempts. Finally, the commander decided to swing over the ridge and come down into the next valley and try to reach their lines. I was firmly convinced by this time that they did not know where they were on the map as there were considerable arguments from among the junior officers as they held their conferences. At around midnight the condition of the men was such that a halt would have to be given as well as warmth and food provided. I heard the captain say that he would attempt to locate a small village where the unit could hole up for the rest of the night. At approximately 0100 hours, I believe I heard word come back that a small town was to our front that would suffice. At this time, I was not forward near the point – my guards held me back near the position which was occupied by the covering force between the village and the west – towards the American rear.

All the SS men were awakened in the treeline. The plan was to skirt north of Bergeval, cross the Parc de Saint Jacques road and then descend into yet another valley. Next would come yet another climb up a steep stream bed to reach the cliffs overlooking the Salm river.

In Bergeval itself, recon SS men burst into the farmhouse of Arthur Deroanne demanding that he help locate a crossing over the Salm river. The Belgian man would guide Peiper's march column to a ford south of Trois-Ponts and mostly north of Rochelinval by way of the high crests near Fosseuheid. Had Peiper's luck finally ran out?

Groping forward through the thick woods, they ran into the skirmish line of Capt. Archibald A. McPheeter's Company I of the 505th Airborne Infantry Regiment somewhere between the top of the bluff and just before the railway tracks. At one point, they were challenged by an American sentry 'Who goes there?' 'We are American soldiers,' Jupp Diefenthal called out in an unconvincing German yell. There was a brief exchange of gunfire against the sound of rushing water.[52] It was 1 a.m. – an hour after midnight on Christmas Day. In Bergeval the Gaspar family heard the shooting to the east.[53]

Contact was momentary, but confusion spread as the airborne troops worried their lines had been pierced in the darkness and the German enemy had somehow got behind them. The sound of automatic weapons crackled in the woods. Some of Peiper's men dived for the ground while others ran hither and yond. 'We came into a deep forest,' SS gunner Hermann Staritz recalled, 'and as we moved ahead, the enemy suddenly fired at us with mortars. Everyone was running in my direction. Peiper yelled at them. "Everybody run toward me!" he shouted. "Hurrah!" Sometime later the mortars stopped firing.'[54] Karl Wortmann was still up ahead at the head of the column.

> Our way leads downhill and with vigorous strides … but we meet with an unexpected and awkward surprise: Americans suddenly emerge from the forest … Comrades immediately behind us see what is happening and the Americans become frightened and go to the ground. The sudden, increasing gunfire gives everyone fright. Some of the guys panic and part of the column runs toward the slope and scatters. There are wounded men and shouts for medics.[55]

When Staritz and Paul Fröhlich looked up, the American major was gone. As he had warned Peiper, he had used the opportunity to slip away.[56] In just a few mad minutes, the firing was over, and the escape column formed up again. 'Where is McCown?' Peiper called out to Fröhlich. Staritz and Fröhlich were chagrined to tell Peiper they had lost their quarry. He told Peiper the American disappeared during the firing just moments before. 'It doesn't matter,' Peiper said, 'if he is killed, it is from American bullets.'[57] The German column had run into gunfire from the 82nd Airborne Division. Hal McCown:[58]

> The outpost had already moved into position before firing broke out not very far from where I was standing. My guards and I hit the ground, tracer bullets flashed all around us, and we could hear machine gun bullets hitting the trees very close

> over us. The American unit, which I found out later was a company [I Company, 505th Parachute Infantry Regiment], drove forward to clear what it obviously thought was a stray patrol, this time using mortar fire as well. The mortar fire fell all around on the German position. I do not know if my guards were injured or not. Shrapnel cut the trees all around us … I could hear commands being shouted in both German and English with the latter dominating. There was considerable movement around me in the darkness. I lay still for some time waiting for one of my guards to give me a command. After a while, I rose cautiously and began to move at right angles from the direction of the American attack, watching carefully to my rear to see if anyone was covering me or following me. After moving approximately 100 yards, I turned and moved toward the direction the American attack had come from.[59]

'I whistled "Yankee Doodle" as loudly as I could,' McCown recalled, worried that his odd dress might earn him a bullet from nervous GIs. After all, he was wearing American fatigues covered by a German tanker's jacket and a knit cap loaned by Peiper for warmth.[60] *At least it was dark*, McCown thought as he turned at right angles to the German column he sought to leave behind.

Sgt William T. Dunfee of I Company, 3rd Battalion, 505th Parachute Infantry Regiment, had been on patrol in the area near Bergeval that night. Due to the loss of St Vith to German forces and the encirclement of Bastogne to the south, General Eisenhower had consented to the wishes of Field Marshal Bernard Montgomery to pull the American positions back from the Salm river and shorten American lines in the U.S. First Army. That meant that the 82nd Airborne Division would *withdraw* – a dirty word closely related to *retreat*. They had never done that in the entire divisional history. 'No ground gained was ever relinquished,' General James Gavin had boasted. Now, they had been ordered to pull back. Dunfee recalled:

> About 2100 hours on Christmas Eve, we were all packed up awaiting orders to move out. Fortunately, our machine guns were still dug in, covering the shallows of the Salm to our immediate front. We were lying back dozing, when all hell broke loose. The Germans came from our rear, shooting and yelling like a bunch of Indians. I didn't have to see them to know who it was; the German machine guns' rapid rate of fire and their pink tracers told me so. The Germans wanted to go home for Christmas, too. We immediately hit our foxholes and started firing. I would estimate a company-strength group started through our area. Some made it to the river and some didn't … When the smoke cleared, we realised we were attempting to withdraw through an enemy force who was withdrawing through us. That may not be unique in military history, but it was a new experience for us. When we finally pulled out around 2230 hours, we were attacking to our rear.[61]

After the chaotic encounter with the enemy, the woods fell silent, weirdly illuminated by the bright, waxing, gibbous moon overhead. It was spooky. After a few tense minutes, Sgt Raymond 'Mike' Maikowski of his squad heard movement off by the road. Maikowski slipped the safety off his M1 rifle as he heard someone whistling in the dark. Maikowski was a veteran paratrooper who had been fighting with the 82nd Airborne since North Africa in May 1943. Having survived four parachute jumps all the way from Sicily in 1943 to Market Garden just weeks before, he was not about to let a whistling German commando do him in on Christmas Eve 1944. Maikowski motioned his weapon at the form in the undergrowth just before him. 'Put your hands behind your head,' he swaggered, 'and get your ass out here where I can see you!'[62]

On the other end of the gun muzzle, McCown heard the M1 safety click off. 'I'm Maj. Hal McCown, 30th Infantry Division!' he blurted out as he emerged from the shadows. He thrust his hands upward. 'I've been captive for days by five to eight hundred Germans!' The man Maikowski saw before him sounded GI – a twangy Arkansas accent, but the panzer jacket looked plenty suspicious. 'Sure, you are!' Maikowski took no chances. Still, under close inspection, Hal McCown soon headed back up the line of command.

While McCown sought to surrender to paratroopers, Peiper's column moved on, a number of wounded men supported by comrades. 'We were so frightened, we had almost forgotten the cold and our hunger,' Wortmann recalled, 'but there is no doubt that we must soon somehow cross the Salm river and find our front line.' Again, patrols were sent out, but several returned after running into an increasingly wary enemy or an otherwise impossibly steep descent. The bridges, particularly the attractive one by Rochelinval, were all guarded by the enemy. The Salm crossing that Peiper chose comprised an unlikely stretch interrupted by a steep rock face that paralleled the railway tracks. Getting there involved a bush-whacking, cross-country scramble from the end of switchbacks – an 18% grade steep enough to make for a difficult descent, but an unlikely enough approach to not be guarded by the Americans.[63] Fatigued men slid, climbed, or scrambled down the steep hill toward the Salm – the silence being interrupted occasionally by a barking dog or rifle fire. At one point, Peiper appeared to encourage his men down the precipitous slope – so inclined that many had to scoot down the ice-crusted slope on their behinds. The sound of the rushing water grew ever louder, but the men had to jump the last 10ft down to the railway tracks:

> In front of us, the River Salm runs along the valley – the rushing water of a mountain river. What shall we do now? There is no bridge. Several brave ones swim across the icy water ... Most of the comrades are now squatting on the railway embankment, which is a little higher up on big stone. Three metres below, we see before us the foaming and gushing water of the River Salm.

As Wortmann watched, those who had swum across helped the taller men with extended arms. Soon a score had formed a human chain across the surging waves. They slowly wove and stumbled across the icy current. Wortmann joined:

> Now, it is our group's turn. The water is cold as ice and with all our remaining strength, we lean against the strong current. Though I stand 1.93 metres high, the

> water reaches my chest. We balance over the big rocks that lie on the riverbed. The 30-metre width of the river seems an endless distance … Some comrades are carried off and drowned. Comrades who reach the other side go for shelter. Adjoining the strip of forest and parallel to the highway is the road from Trois-Ponts to Grand Halleux. By the time, the last comrades cross the river, it has become day … An American tank comes by. We hide and then wait. We line up roughly on the road and in a march formation go a short jog down the road toward Grand Halleux. A narrow path leads off the left side of the road in the opposite direction steeply up the rocks. By the time the tank comes back, we are already high up above the road. The path leads up over an open plain. We are totally frozen in our wet rags.[64]

Karl Wortmann remembered that once they were 100m above the road, they couldn't resist waving their caps and shouting 'Merry Christmas' to the next U.S. patrol who drove down the road. Karl Laun recalled a nightmare trek all the way from La Gleize, now crossing the icy Salm:

> We reach a railway overpass, after that the Salm, a small river, but with the temperature of 10 degrees below zero [sic], a crossing of even this creek does not constitute one of the niceties of life. Two men stumble and disappear in the whirlpool of the swollen river. I am icy wet as I reach the opposite shore. The reception committee already awaits us – one of our SS friends. One can't recognise his rank in the darkness, but he shows his superiority by dealing out curses and kicks to the stragglers. On the other side of the river, these courageous gentlemen are very quiet and subdued, but now knowing the last American sentries are safely behind them, they at once assume the typical SS arrogance.[65]

Hermann Staritz told his story from the Bergeval area. 'As we proceeded, we heard a couple of vehicles on the road below. We went across the road and took cover on orders.' The Germans then found American trucks that had been abandoned and loaded with K-rations.

> We got something to eat and then we went on to the Salm river. Reaching it, we went up and down the river, looking for a place to cross. I helped look for a shallow spot and found one. We held on to each other and made a human bridge across the river. I was holding the man in front of me by his coat sleeve. The water was ice cold and up to your chest and moving fast. It was even harder for me as I was still carrying an MG 42 on my shoulder. We were all freezing after getting out – our clothes became frozen stiff. Reaching the other side, it was about 3 kilometers up the hill to Wanne. It was an hour walking in the dark and the town was under fire when we got there. Our comrades thought we were the enemy. 'Become prisoners, we won't fire …' We called out that we were German, too. When we reached the village, we were lost souls. It was 6 a.m. on Christmas morning. We had to wait for vehicles to haul us away. We had lost about fifty men from La Gleize – some in the river. In the evening, we were driven back. We were moved to Petit-Thier and we got medical attention. For me it was over – I had a frozen foot.[66]

Peiper, too, would remember 'Holy Night 1944' well – wounded as he was while trying to find a way through American lines and then across the frozen Salm. 'I swam through the icy floods of a rapid stream with my brave comrades,' he would later write to his father, 'following a desperate breakout of [an] encirclement ... my situation not alleviated by a hand shot through and a drowning man attached to my pants!'[67]

All those in his column were numb when they reached the steep, tree-covered bank on the other side. Shaking with cold, the 800 men were soon traipsing up an almost impossibly steep, gravel road threading through thick forests towards Wanne. The 15% grade made standing upright difficult and frequent rests would be needed, even for the Waffen SS toughs. Then a surprise. As the nearly frozen men straggled across the road in small groups, an American jeep approached, but so shocked were they to see the long SS column that 'they couldn't turn around fast enough'.[68] As soon as they appeared, they were gone, Peiper's men breathing a sigh of relief. They had only hand arms.

Before reaching Wanne, Karl Wortmann recalled the rag-tag group being shelled by American artillery as they emerged from the Bois des Echevin. 'It was very steep on the other side,' Paul Fröhlich recalled.[69] The SS men gathered in the woods, but waiting long was not an option. Their soaked uniforms commenced to freeze in the cold air and the shivering men stomped and clapped arms and hands to keep from freezing in place. On the edge of hypothermia, they plodded off to another very steep climb towards Aisomont. Nervous villagers told them other Germans were just to the north.

Twenty-four hours after crossing the Amblève river, Peiper and the remnants of his exhausted battle group reached the little hilltop village of Wanne. Peiper estimated he had only lost thirty men during the escape from La Gleize. When Peiper's men finally reached the village, they were greeted as a band from a lost civilisation. Reaching Wanne, everyone collapsed.

'Looking into mirrors,' Peiper recalled, we do not recognise ourselves. We are unshaven, unkempt, and filthy from head to foot. Our uniforms are frozen stiff and it is hard to get them off. But the room is nice and warm. Freed, we let ourselves fall down on layers of straw. When we wake after a deep and endless sleep, Christmas is over.'[70]

Manfred Thorn, Hans Siptrott, Georg Fleps, and the others of the 7th Panzer Company had been holed up in Wanne for several days, their tanks stationary, low on fuel and unable to cross and come to reach Peiper. Both men spent Christmas eve in a basement by their Panzer IV, hungry and cowering under gusts of American artillery fire that swept the town. At one point, Siptrott noticed that there was a bit of flour, sugar, and eggs in the pantry of the home they occupied. The men had been gnawing on apples and raw potatoes for two days. 'I knew how to cook well,' Siptrott recalled, having learned from his sisters. Risking that an artillery observer might see his lit oven, Siptrott spent an hour above ground to produce an apple cake.[71]

What Siptrott did not relate was their holiday conversation in the basement in Wanne. Particularly telling was the recollection of tank gunner Werner Löhmann, the gunner in Pilarzek's Panzer #734. Löhmann recalled that when he was in Wanne, Georg Fleps from Siptrott's tank told him about his actions near Malmedy during idle conversation. As Fleps related it, two SPWs with MG 42s had fired on the prisoners on orders. 'Upon that I pulled my pistol and fired several shots into them, too.'[72]

While Jochen Peiper swam the cold Salm on Christmas Eve to escape and Hans Siptrott baked a cake in Wanne, the 30th Division commander, Gen. Leland Hobbs, was planning a hard battle to capture the village Peiper had just abandoned.[73] Brig. Gen. William K. Harrison and Col Walter Johnson, with the 119th and 117th Regiments, would lead the assault. At 7.22 a.m. Hobbs telephoned Harrison to see 'if they were all set'.[74] Nothing over the preceding days had shown Harrison that the morale of the 1st SS Panzer Division had diminished. Indeed, the fighting against his attack from the east the preceding day suggested nihilistic determination to fight to the death.

The hill north of La Gleize was very heavily wooded, and patrols had found it free of the enemy – potentially a weak point. Harrison planned to employ his rested 2nd Battalion of the 119th Infantry, first concealed by the dense woods to swing into battle from that direction, in concert with Task Force Jordan of the 3rd Armored Division. Hobbs told both commanders that 'this thing must be pushed hard to clean out that pocket as soon as we possibly can'. He hung up, telling both regimental leaders to 'go to it'.[75]

The next day his troops would gingerly enter the rubble of La Gleize unopposed. They would find the village bastion altogether abandoned. Other than the wounded left behind, all the SS troopers and Peiper, their leader, were gone.

Chapter 31

VANQUISHED

Glory is fleeting, but obscurity is forever.

Napoleon

Although having escaped encirclement in La Gleize, Jochen Peiper was missing. In the following days, word would trickle out that 'parts of the missing battle group had fought its way back'.[1] There was little other news at higher headquarters of what had become of Peiper.

Hitler's commanders wondered, too. On 24 December German high command had reported an attack in progress to open a way to Peiper in La Gleize. Perhaps looking to not call Hitler's attention to the gloomy fate of his favored spearhead, the relief mission failure was not detailed on Christmas Day. Instead, a communiqué described how an intrepid officer from the panzer reconnaissance battalion had been specifically dispatched to cross the Amblève, reach Peiper, and tell him to fight his way back to the division. Von Rundstedt's headquarters worried on Christmas morning because 'since yesterday there has been no radio contact between 1st SS Panzer Division and Kampfgruppe Peiper.'[2]

After walking for thirty hours behind American lines and swimming the Salm, on Monday, 25 December Jochen Peiper and his exhausted members stumbled into the castle in Wanne looking 'like walking icicles'.[3] It was 10 a.m. Ralf Tiemann, the divisional logistics adjutant, was there. With Peiper was Jupp Diefenthal, Heinz von Westernhagen, and Rolf Möbius – Tiger commanders. To Tiemann they looked terrible – dirty, unshaven, totally whipped:

> On that day, I was on the outskirts of the village [Wanne] as the news was announced that Peiper had appeared. I then saw some of the first of the men emerge from the woods. They made a sorry sight. Some were on their own, some in small groups of twos and threes, and some were supporting others who were at the end of their strength. All were shivering from the cold and using their last

> reserves of energy to reach their billet – [longing for] the warmth of a bed, for they had waded through the river and were soaked through to the skin. What is burned into my memory was the sight of Paul Fröhlich. Some of the men had climbed out of their winter coats when crossing the river because of being weighted down; others had lost their coats in the swiftly flowing water … Paul Fröhlich still had half of his … it was ripped neatly from the button holes. His only comment was, 'So many hours for so few miles.' And then he disappeared.[4]

Peiper scowled when he spoke at last to the divisional operations officer. 'We left with 3,000 men from Germany and now we have 717,' he said hoarsely. He motioned back with his hand. 'You can find the others the whole way along our path.'[5] Peiper claimed to have suffered a near heart attack, passing out, and being taken to the aid station of his regiment, where he was seen by Dr Kurt Sickel. His right hand – wounded during the escape across the Salm – was bandaged. Peiper threw back a cognac, complaining he had not slept in nine days, and fell into a deep slumber.[6]

'Prosit Neujahr!' At the Führer's *Adlerhorst* in the Taunus Hills near Ziegenberg, the bunker complex was covered with snow and ice. At midnight on 1 January Hitler had ended a long silence, at last addressing the German people. Even if his voice warbled flat and tired over the *Grossdeutscher Rundfunk*, he mocked the Western Allies for having failed to make anything out of their victories of August 1944 – now it would be the Third Reich who would be the victor a year later. In August 1945, 'Germany will rise like a phoenix from the ashes … from its ruined cities and go down in history as the miracle of the twentieth century!'[7]

It was cold and clear when General Heinz Guderian, the acting chief of staff of the Army High Command, arrived in *Adlerhorst* from Poland. The white landscape glittered in the weak, low-angle sun. Upon arriving, Guderian and his aides were disarmed by menacing SS guards, who inspected their briefcases and looked for bulges in their uniforms. Everyone was careful to use only the Hitler salute. At the usual war council, Genmaj. Reinhard Gehlen, the resident chief on matters of Soviet intelligence, gave a sobering appreciation of the situation in the east. He warned of imminent calamity from a new, Russian winter offensive. There were charts and tables alluding to a fantastic Russian numerical advantage. The defense on the Eastern Front, Guderian told Hitler, 'was a house of cards'.

The German leader would have none of it, calling the estimates 'idiotic'. Guderian hastened to Gehlen's defense, saying if that was crazy, then he should be shackled, too.[8] Yet Hitler was still focused on the Ardennes – the last, faint twinkle of German offensive panache. He had just launched still another offensive, Nordwind, in the Alsace. While shaking the Allied defenses around Strasbourg, it soon faltered just like *Wacht am Rhein*, although the German leader was still trusting those dedicated to him. 'In the last analysis, they show themselves in the capacity to hold on, in perseverance and fanatical determination,' Hitler said. 'That's the decisive factor in any victory.'[9]

At 5.06 p.m. that day, Genlt Bodo Zimmermann reviewed the situation in the west. 'The pressure point is again the area around Bastogne,' he began. Hitler, meanwhile, took special interest in his SS troops: Zimmermann read aloud the order that had gone out: 'The Führer has ordered the 1st and 2nd SS Panzer Corps with the 1st, 2nd, 9th, and 12th SS Panzer Divisions to begin immediately to assemble for rapid refitting behind Army Group B.' Any attempt by local commanders to appropriate the SS forces for local use would lead to their relief.[10] Peiper's two SS adjutant friends, Johannes Göhler and Otto Günsche, listened alongside Hitler. 'The Leibstandarte is outside [the Bulge] now?' Hitler looked up for confirmation.

'Yes sir, the Leibstandarte is outside,' nodded Zimmermann. 'Only Kampfgruppe Peiper is missing, as it lost its way at Malmedy at the time and is now being pulled back by Field Marshal Model.' On 27 December, after two days' rest, Peiper's men and the two dozen available tanks of the division were assembled around Emmels, north-west of St Vith.[11] They would shortly be shuttled south.

Zimmerman didn't have the facts right – *Hitler's Own* certainly had not become lost. Yet Hitler knew that Waffen SS scion Jochen Peiper and his charge were the lightning rod of that command. 'We have to make sure we activate these units again as quickly as possible,' he emphasized. 'Field Marshal Model is not that stupid …' Model was holding on to Kampfgruppe Peiper as an insurance policy. Any rupture of his lines and Peiper's blow torch could be brought forward to cauterise the wound.

Meanwhile, the holiday mood was subdued at Hitler's headquarters. Compared with the bunkerised existence in East Prussia, his secretary, Christa Schroeder, liked the rustic digs at *Adlerhorst* – small log cabins nestled deep in the wooded slopes near Bad Nauheim. On 24 December, while Peiper and his men hid in the deep conifer forests west of Trois-Ponts, Schroeder and Gerda 'Dara' Christian went with Hitler out on his afternoon walk. From the doorway of his quarters, the trio emerged into the woods, bathed in bright sunlight beaming through a cold, crystal-blue sky. From one edge of the horizon to the other stretched contrails of American bombers streaming toward the Reich. The snow crunched under their winter boots as sunlight shone weakly through the trees.

High above the pines, sunlight glinted off the distant, metallic wave of B-17 bombers as if they were a vast school of silver minnows in a blue sea. Usually quiet, Schroeder suddenly faced Hitler almost in tears. 'Do you think, *mein Führer*,' she pleaded, 'that we can still win the war after all?' Hitler paused. 'We must,' he said.[12] There was nothing more. Dara looked away as if wishing to disappear. In awkward silence, they continued walking. Reaching the doorway to the headquarters, the cold quiet and the sunlight was gone. Inside, all was still abuzz – adjutants running with papers, noisy teletypes, and jangling phones – the relief of distraction.

Mental exhaustion seemed to be the tonic for worry at *Adlerhorst*. SS Captain Johannes Göhler was the new adjutant liaison of the Waffen SS to the Führer himself. Peiper knew Göhler well – he had been among the SS horsemen under Gustav Lombard during the early days and in April 1941, Goehler had been on the staff of the SS Kommando of the Reichsführer SS after graduating from the SS Junkerschule in Braunschweig.[13] Like Peiper, he went into battle in Russia after graduating, but Göhler fought in the favored manner for a budding Waffen SS hero – on horseback. There, he rode with the 3rd Squadron of the 1st SS Reiter Regiment under Lombard, who would be later implicated in the killing of Jews in Ukraine's Pripet Marshes in July 1941 by the SS Cavalry Brigade.[14]

Such knowledge was hardly public; Hannes earned the Ritterkreuz for knocking out two dozen Russian tanks while under SS Brigf. Hermann Fegelein in November 1943. Yet now in late 1944, the 26-year-old native of Bischofswerda saw himself at the apex of his career, assigned to operate as the senior SS officer under Fegelein and reporting directly to Hitler.

On Thursday, 21 December 1944, Hannes Göhler was writing to his wife, Ursula, from the adjutant's quarters. 'I need rest badly,' he wrote in catharsis, 'I have not slept in forty hours and work has to be continued in a few hours … However, I wanted to let you know that I have been promoted to Sturmbannführer. The Führer signed my promotion in my presence.' Four days later, as an exhausted Jochen Peiper trudged through ice-crusted forests from encirclement in La Gleize after losing every tank and gun, Göhler seemed giddy at *Adlerhorst*:

> I have a small Christmas tree. It is not large and it stands in a tin can wrapped with colored paper. It is decorated with tin foil and pine cones. Even a few presents are under it. The adjutant of the replacement army gave me a book, General Oberst Guderian a few bottles of wine, Gruppenführer F. [Fegelein] some smoking material and a folder with photographs of horses … But we did not have much of a Christmas. Yesterday was a day like any other, that is, full of work and stress. We also worked during the night except for a brief break. For dinner, we had a really good meal. Feldmarschall Keitel made a brief, beautiful speech. Then we sat around the lit Christmas tree for a short while, and then we went back to work again. Today is not much different. This morning I met my supreme chief. Again, he offered me his hand and talked to me, and also asked about all of you and about my family … He still remembered we have two small children, that our daughter was born on the day I arrived here. I would do anything and sacrifice everything for this man. He is so wonderful, I cannot describe it in words. How grateful I am that I can be a witness to this time![15]

Others were less euphoric. Before falling on to his cot in exhaustion, Karl Thöt, a stenographer at *Adlerhorst*, jotted a few notes in his pocket diary: 'Taking endless notes on 24, 25, and 26 December. For the first time, this year a Christmas celebration did not take place. Instead, we had roast goose on Christmas Eve, pheasant on Christmas Day, and roast pork on the second Christmas holiday. Above all, much work – thirty-four hours of taking notes.' Thöt dutifully recorded the words of Hitler's late-night, tea-laced conversation as if they were notes of gold for historical posterity.[16] 'On

Christmas Eve I did not get to bed until 0230 hours,' Thöt wrote. 'The next day was up till 3 a.m. and then 4.30 a.m. the following evening.'[17] That was Hitler's schedule, too.

Peiper, having collapsed in the Leibstandarte headquarters in Wanne, Belgium, on Christmas Eve, now awoke from his stupor on the 25th. He made his way to the headquarters of Wilhelm Mohnke to file a report of his Ardennes actions. That report remains curious, as rather than bragging of Peiper's audacious advance, it instead spoke glowingly of what had transpired at the Baugnez crossroads. For those actions, his divisional commander, Wilhelm Mohnke, enthusiastically recommended the Obersturmbannführer for the Swords to the Knight's Cross. Such endorsements would be made on the unit commander's own after-action report. Mohnke's composition at division headquarters the day after Christmas spoke in admiring tones of Peiper's actions on 17 December:

> Without regard for threats from the flanks, and only inspired by the thought of a deep breakthrough, the Kampfgruppe proceeded via Möderscheid–Schoppen–Faymonville to Ligneuville and destroyed at Baugnez an enemy supply column. Then, after annihilation of the units blocking their advance, they also succeeded in causing the staff of the 49th Anti-Aircraft Brigade to flee.[18]

As Baugnez was specifically named, there could be little doubt that the incident referred to in the three-page commendation is what would become known as the Malmedy massacre. And by his own admission, Peiper had learned of the incident a day after it occurred and a week before Mohnke formulated his description. Why would such an incident – a smudge – be singled out for a decoration? Translation of the ambiguous German term used for annihilation – *Vernichtung* – is one issue. Conventional interpretation would see it as simply describing the battlefield destruction of the enemy. However, within the National Socialist lexicon, *Vernichtung* could also enjoin the killing of an enemy. After all, the concentration camps at which Jews were being liquidated were referred to as *Vernichtungslager* – elimination camps.

The likelihood remains that after years of savage ideological war on the Eastern Front, men of the Waffen SS had come to admire such harshness. Certainly, that is the way Himmler would have seen it. The correct interpretation will probably never be known, but it cannot be discounted that Peiper and Mohnke understood *Vernichtung* to embrace the killing of prisoners of war. Rather than a blemish on one's record, such an event was an accolade. As a convalescing Peiper witnessed the final winter battles around Bastogne, the recommendation for his promotion was forwarded speedily on to Hitler's headquarters.

That same afternoon of 26 December, the situation at Hitler's *Adlerhorst* headquarters reflected morose tension. The day had witnessed a series of crushing reverses. The German 7th Army had been nearly forced back to the German border, the haggard men of the prime spearhead of the Kampfgruppe Peiper had not only been stopped, but had barely escaped total destruction in

La Gleize. Even worse, U.S. Gen. George Patton's 4th Armored Division that day had broken through the siege around Bastogne and his attack from the south was steadily increasing the threat of trapping the entire German salient. Finally, although the 2nd Panzer Division had nearly reached the Meuse river, it was now out of fuel and under terrific attack by Allied fighter bombers and the U.S. 2nd Armored Division.

Genobst Alfred Jodl confronted Hitler. 'Mein Führer,' he implored, 'we must face the facts squarely. We cannot force the Meuse!' Hitler searched for an explanation. 'We have had unexpected setbacks,' he admitted, 'because my plan was not followed to the letter, but all is not lost.'[19] He described how, if Bastogne was eliminated, that Field Marshal Model's advance on the Meuse could continue. That edict seemed less than convincing. At the close of the day Reichsmarschall Göring quietly approached Hitler. The two men began to argue. Finally, Göring lost his patience. 'The war is lost!' he blurted. The Reichsmarschall meekly suggested that Hitler seek a truce. Hitler could contact Count Folke Bernadotte, whose father was the brother of Swedish King Gustavus V. Surely, he would help with armistice negotiations. Hitler flew into a rage. 'I forbid you to take any step in this matter!' he shouted. 'If you go against my orders I will have you shot!' Göring departed.

What about Peiper? At one point during his convalescing days in the Ardennes he had the occasion to speak to Genflm. Model, who stopped by at headquarters. Things looked gloomy as the Bulge collapsed under American counter-blows as the head of Heeresgruppe B strode into the Leibstandarte headquarters east of Bastogne near Bras.[20] Model stared at Peiper with his monocle, before congratulating him instead on his 'big success'. Peiper shook his head. 'I and the rest of the bunch got out with only a walking stick, hat, and a songbook.'[21]

'With all respect, Genflm. Model, Sir,' Peiper added, 'I don't know what you mean about success. I lost my entire regiment.'[22]

'Don't talk nonsense,' Model protested. 'That was a great success.'

'How could it be? We did not even make it across the Maas.'[23]

'We didn't really even expect to,' said Model. He recited the old Prussian motto: aim too high, if you want to hit low. 'The Americans are assembled on one side,' he gestured. 'The Russians are on the other.' He drew pointed forefingers together. 'The pincers were supposed to close and the Reich would be cracked like a nut. We have won two months.'

'We could only hit one side,' Model continued. 'The American assembly was totally confused and now we could turn against the Russians.' Peiper surmised that the German political leadership believed the war could no longer be won militarily. He recalled his conversation with Josef Goebbels the previous spring where he said their big hope was to split the Allies.

Kampfgruppe Peiper was formally disbanded. 'This was a year of outstanding events and we were able to carry the load of its responsibility so capably that the world looks upon us with admiration.' It was Goebbels on the radio enthusiastically addressing the German people – an ironic address clearly heard all over Europe:

Our belief in victory is steadfast. We have to prove to our dead heroes that they did not die in vain and their belief in Germany and the future will be a symbol to us …

The enemy tries to split the nation and the Führer by claiming he is ill and by spreading vicious rumours. But in fact, I never saw the Führer happier and healthier and more full of plans than he is today. He spends many sleepless nights planning to ensure the future of Germany. The whole world looks in astonishment and amazement at our fortitude and strength. We are the greatest nation in the world and our destiny is victory.[24]

The Führer was happier than ever?

Peiper's partner with the heavy tanks, Heinz von Westernhagen, was between pride and exhaustion when he wrote home on 29 December:

Dear Mother!
Christmas is over and we have some difficult days behind us. Right now we're resting for a few days, sleeping off the Christmas stress, while we care for our frostbitten limbs and prepare for our next action.

This time we were always in the thickest mess. We were at the point of the attack, and on the first day were already able to break through the American positions and push far behind their lines. It was a wild hunt with a great amount of shooting – but finally we were cut off and surrounded. For five days we sat without rations and with little ammunition while, like a mouse in a trap, we were smashed by American artillery.

Early on 24 December we agreed to break out – it succeeded. For thirty hours we marched behind the American lines, breaking out on Christmas Eve around midnight from behind their positions. Then we swam a raging stream with a ripping current under MG fire, making it across only by summoning up all our strength. Still, some brave soldiers died, either because their strength was no longer sufficient or their hearts failed. I dragged a wounded man along with me. And in the morning hours of the first day of Christmas we arrived back again in our lines, looking like walking icicles.

We thumbed our nose at the Americans and got the German Army's 850 soldiers back. That is our pride. Now we prepare for new action … I don't have any more time, and must go take care of my wild soldiers. To you, I send heartfelt greetings and health in the New Year. I am convinced that this will be the last year of the war. I greet you.
Your son, Heinz[25]

Like Peiper, Knittel's reconnaissance battalion commenced to find a way back across the Amblève river, albeit without Tiger tanks, vehicles, or heavy weapons.

In the night of 24 to 25 December, order was given that the company was to leave the bridgehead and withdraw to Wanne. The withdrawal started at 0500 hours; I marched back with the commander, Ustuf. Gerlach and Uscha. Eckschlager, and several men along the Amblève river until we reached the destroyed [Petit Spai] bridge 3 kilometers west of Stavelot. There we crossed the river on an emergency

> bridge. From there, we had a brief assembly in the basement of an isolated house 300 metres south-east of the bridge, in order to be protected from the enemy artillery fire. Next, after a brief stop, we continued our retrograde march on the road to Aisomont and Wanne.[26]

Madame Antoine and her neighbors had now been hiding in their cellar for days while Knittel had made his headquarters at her house along the Amblève:

> Time became very confused. We were in a dark cellar and we didn't know what day it was. Sometimes the Germans came in and we were always afraid, but most of them just came in to sleep. Our days and nights meant nothing. There were sounds of vehicles coming back and forth and sometimes we could hear gunfire – usually distant. Then on Christmas, the Noel, things became quiet. 'They've gone, they've gone!' we whispered to each other in the cellar. We got out of the cellar and looked about. They had taken all of my husband's shirts, the livestock was all dead, and the house was smashed and reeked from an overflowing toilet. There were German bodies lying about. One German was sprawled out dead in the living room. Shells were still falling and we went back to the cellar. On 27 December, another neighbour, Leonard Nalis, came while we were still in the cellar. On that day, shells began falling on the farm at the backdoor cellar entrance. The Americans were here and the Germans were shelling us from Wanne. One shell fell through the barn wall and exploded inside, killing four cows. We let the rest of the cows go. When we came outside we were struck by how dead everything seemed. There was not a sparrow to be seen. Everything was smashed.'[27]

Along with Knittel, the two battalions of the 1st SS Panzer Grenadier Regiment who had stubbornly defended the forested hills west of Trois-Ponts would also filter back across the river over the following day to take up position on the wooded heights just across the Amblève along the Grand Faye. To their right, the remainder of the 2nd SS Panzer Grenadier Regiment concentrated in the Bois de l'Abbaye south of Stavelot. The ranks of the SS infantry had been thrashed over the preceding days; 500 men had been lost from the merciless mission to gain Peiper's relief.[28] On the roads leading up to Stavelot, the U.S. Army Air Force caught the German columns in the open. 'The sky was full of our fighter planes,' remembered one American GI. 'They had a field day … The roads were littered with Hitler's junk.'[29] After the debacle SS Oscha. Heinrich Nebel with the 12th Company huddled dejectedly in Wanne:

> I was sitting with my commander, Hstuf. George, in a basement that served as our command post. A small *Weichnachtsbaum* with a pair of tallow candle lights illuminated the dusky room and reminded us it was Christmas evening. The raw truth did not allow us to get too sentimental. Too many of our comrades were gone … On that same night, comrades from the Panzergruppe Peiper reported to us so they could warm up. They had swam the Salm and were thoroughly soaked.[30]

In Roanne, Belgian civilian Serge Fontaine was worried about his grandmother:

> I went to Werimont to see if she was okay. I saw shell holes, dead cows, and destroyed trees. There were bodies of American soldiers laying about. When I came to the farm it was terrible. There were seven or eight armored vehicles there. The place was completely destroyed; the farm had burnt. My grandmother had just come back from La Venne with my cousins. They had nothing left. Everything had burned except some jars of jam in the cellar. That was all they had. In the evening, they came back to Roanne with me.[31]

Peiper drove to Blanche Fontaine, where he established his own command post in Petit-Thier.[32] Peiper dutifully did his paperwork, quickly composing a recommendation for his old pals from the SPW battalion. He first wrote a commendation for Jupp Diefenthal for the Ritterkreuz on 26 December and Georg Preuss two days later.[33] In flowery prose, Diefenthal was cited for his bold advance on Stoumont on 18 to 19 December and Georg Preuss for his actions at Büllingen – an accolade that strained credibility, unless getting lost and hiding in the woods qualified for special merit.

Meanwhile, the remaining detritus of the panzer regiment moved to the area around Petit-Thier–Burtonville. Perhaps Peiper had 'suffered two concussions due to tank fire', as his medical report said.[34] Along with him was Dr Kurt Sickel, the 37-year-old regimental surgeon and former concentration camp doctor, who set up something of a relaxation center for the divisional commanders.[35] As a Belgian village, snow-cloaked Petit-Thier was not much to look at – a middling, large, forester's house, with a priest's quarters and surrounding buildings, one of which was a pigsty. Sickel cleverly packed a fuel drum with heavy stones in a small outbuilding and converted it into a sauna. At last, a means to get rid of head lice. Sickel specifically mentioned Peiper as among the visitors.

One critical event took place at Petit-Thier – and one that would dog Peiper for the rest of his days. This was the late December incident, where Peiper had supposedly presided over the execution of a frostbitten American soldier.[36] The GI had been taken captive while wandering lost north-west of St Vith amid the frosted conifers of the *Forêt Domaniale du Grand*:

> Peiper was a highly educated man, recited Shakespeare in large quotations by heart, and spoke English fluently … He tried to interrogate the man in English. The American was incapable of speaking in spite of all his endeavours. As Peiper described it, his talking was more of a bark. There was silence for a few seconds when Peiper and Sickel established that the man was too weak to talk. The sergeant [Wichmannn] asked Peiper, 'What shall I do with him? Should I bring him upstairs?' The small dispensary was upstairs. Sickel looked at his superior; Peiper gave Sickel a meaningful look and Sickel replied to the sergeant: 'Get the swine out and bump him off.' The body was found at exactly the same location which the sergeant described. At the future trial, Sickel confessed to the crime, and was among those whose death sentences were commuted. His statement and the confessions of Peiper and Wichmann checked out in all details.

Corroborative evidence by the witnesses stated Wichmann had boasted right after the crime was committed.[37]

Peiper's adjutant, Hans Gruhle, did not deny that the American had been shot:

I was present when the American soldier, caught in the Petit-Thier forest, was brought to the commanding officer of the 1st Panzer Regiment, Colonel Peiper, for the purpose of interrogation … The prisoner's hands and feet were wrapped with rags and according to the regimental surgeon, he had third-degree frostbite. His physical condition was so weak that he could not even hold the cup of coffee, offered by Col. Peiper, and had troubles keeping the cigarette. I had the impression that everyone present had pity on him. At the question from Col. Peiper to the regimental surgeon as to whether his weakness could be overcome, the surgeon denied negatively with his eyes and head. I was not in the room when the prisoner was led out.[38]

Peiper's detailed recollection, which, while professing compassion, seemed strangely detached from the suffering of the prisoner and saw his execution as a matter of mercy:

In the first days of January 1945, according to my estimate, it was about the 10th of the month, I was at my command post in a small castle in the neighbourhood of Blanche Fontaine. As I recall, this castle had the name Petit-Thier. One of my men, I would not recognise him again, shoved an American prisoner of war into the room for me. This prisoner of war was in a completely exhausted condition, apparently half-starved and frozen. He looked like a mummy. He had rags wrapped around his feet. According to his looks, I estimated this American to be at least fifty years of age. I questioned this man as to which division he belonged, but he was so exhausted that he could not talk; he could only utter inarticulate sounds. I still know, however, that he was 27 years of age, which especially struck me by his looks. His skull looked like a death's head. He was not able to name his division to me, and I think I found out his age from his papers.

At this time, Stbf. Dr Sickel, the regimental surgeon of the 1st Panzer Regiment, LSSAH and at that time also the command of the Regimental HQ Co. 1st Panzer Regiment, was present. I further have the certain belief that also O. Stubaf. von Westernhagen was in the room, perhaps along with H. Stbf. Gruhle. We were just going to have coffee, when the prisoner was brought into the room. After I had seen that the prisoner was too exhausted to be able to talk, I offered him a chair and a cup of coffee and a cigarette, as I felt pity for him. He chattered his teeth, however, so much that he could neither drink nor smoke. I endeavoured to learn from the prisoner to which division he belonged and to find out other military details. All he was able to utter with a voice more similar to barking than talking signified that he had kept himself hidden in the woods for fourteen days.

When Dr Sickel, the regimental surgeon, saw that an interrogation was futile, he said, 'This is of no use anymore! Help arrives too late here.' Thereupon I asked Dr Sickel: 'What shall we do with the man? Shall he go to the aid station?' Dr Sickel replied, 'The best is we give him a mercy shot! Anyway, he won't make it anymore. Take the poor devil away.' I have been asked if I remember if Dr Sickel

> said to the soldier who brought him in 'Outside with the swine! Bump him off!' Such a statement was not uttered in my presence. Dr Sickel and I acted obviously out of pity for the prisoner … I admit to having given Dr Sickel, on the basis of his medical opinion, the authorisation to shoot the prisoner … He left the room immediately with the prisoner and his guard.[39]

The civilian commentary on the events at Petit-Thier cast conclusive doubt on Peiper's innocence. Beginning on Christmas Day, soldiers of the exhausted Peiper troop had begun filtering from the village of Wanne to Petit-Thier, occupying the sturdiest and most comfortable homes. The local priest of the village, the Curé Calhay, remembered seeing the Germans come into the village, surprised by their rag-tag demeanour – particularly for an elite SS unit with Hitler's name. 'It was not the Army of 1940,' remembered the priest. In his quarters at the forested château near Tinseux, Jochen Peiper arrived, but the mood was darkly suspicious. The Curé had heard of the terrible civilian killings in Stavelot, Trois-Ponts, and Wanne. He knew, too, that Peiper's men were suspected.

The SS members immediately began questioning the priest, the mayor, and the schoolteacher who had stayed behind. *L'Armée blanche?* – the White Army? Everyone had to watch what they said or did. Indeed, one civilian, Frans Carpentier, was taken out and shot on Christmas Day when the SS accused him of misleading them. Carpentier had claimed to the SS men that the road to Vielsalm was clear, while a tank motoring that way hit a mine, wounding six. The SS were there until 16 January.[40] There had been a series of murders where the panzer regiment had lagered: Wanne and then Petit-Thier.

Camille Gerardy, of the village, said he discovered the murdered American soldier in question. On 27 January 1945, the forestry worker had claimed to have come across the dead GI on the edge of the thick woods off to the side of the roads some 300m from his house. The black-haired young man lay face down in the snow with one arm outstretched as if to reach for a photo of a woman who lay on the icy ground just beyond his reach.[41]

In any case, on the morning of 28 December, the 'unemployed' Peiper accompanied Ralf Tiemann as the divisional command post moved south.[42] Peiper, Tiemann, and Mohnke called on the commander of the 5th Fallschirmjäger Division in its command post in a railway tunnel south of Schimpach.[43] The parachutists had been cut to ribbons in the fighting over the preceding two weeks and could give little information on the circumstances at the front. The strongest tank unit in the division was now the SS 7th Panzer Company, which had but ten Mk IVs – but ironically included the tanks of Hans Siptrott, who was present at the scene of the shooting at the Malmedy crossroads.[44] On the night of 28 December the dregs of the divisional strength threaded their way from St Vith to Trois Vierges to Oberwampach east of Bastogne. Now the Leibstandarte would be used to achieve what Hitler himself had ordered: the capture of Bastogne.[45]

Whatever happened, Peiper elected to temporarily leave his command post. The regimental surgeon, Dr Kurt Sickel, signed a document on 30 January

1945 indicating that Peiper had suffered *commotio cerebri* in 1945.[46] Normally, this would be interpreted as a 'concussion', but some postulated the term indicated a physical and/or 'nervous breakdown'.[47] Certainly, the cause was there. 'During the whole offensive, my men and I ate very little, and slept still less,' Peiper recalled.'[48]

Meanwhile, at Hitler's headquarters, the edict to erase Bastogne coincided with a visit from Heinrich Himmler that afternoon. The SS leader was in the process of readying his a new attack in Alsace–Lorraine on New Year's Eve. Preparations for that were plodding along, even amid unfavorable news from the Ardennes. Still, on Thursday, 28 December, Hitler sternly lectured Himmler's assembled generals with an exhausting post-mortem of what had gone wrong in the Ardennes. 'First of all, there were the terribly bad roads ... To a panzer division, ten lost hours can mean under certain circumstances, the loss of an entire operation.' Hitler was clearly thinking of Peiper. 'That happened in Heeresgruppe B with the Leibstandarte ... In the last analysis only the spearheads did the fighting.'[49]

On the following day, Hitler arranged a short meeting with Genflm. von Rundstedt about the need to seize Bastogne. 'At the moment, victory seems a long way off,' Martin Bormann wrote from Hitler's headquarters. 'The day before yesterday the enemy flew over three thousand sorties on the Western Front. Their aircraft fly when, how, and where they like ... German planes are nowhere to be seen.'[50] Von Rundstedt said they would put in an attack to wrest Bastogne.

On the ground, the planners of the XXXIX Panzer Corps organized the assault. It would consist of two opposing thrusts south-east of the market town. On paper, the Leibstandarte would join up with the other tank-led pincer thrust from the Führer Begleit Brigade. Both would attack the Bastogne corridor from the opposite direction with the intent of again cutting off the crossroads town. In Peiper's place would be Werner Poetschke leading whatever tanks could be found. His objective was Assenois, just south-west of Bastogne. The southern group, organized around the infantry strength of the 1st SS and 2nd SS Panzer Grenadier Regiments and led by old infantry hand Max Hansen, was to punch forward through Villers-la-Bonne-Eau, cut Patton's arterial road from Martelange to Bastogne, and contact the western claw of the German advance around Hompre. Although Hansen's grenadier companies were 40 per cent below strength, they would be supported by the few Tigers of Kampfgruppe Möbius – at least those that could forage enough fuel and had not accompanied Peiper to the La Gleize debacle.

On the late evening of 29 December, Poetschke and his tanks crunched across the snow-crusted Tarchamps–Lutremange road under bright moonlight. By morning, 30 December, all was in place. Pushing forward in the single remaining Panther, Poetschke led the remnants of the 1st SS Panzer Regiment (mainly the 7th Panzer Company) through the heavily wooded terrain. Peiper was not leading the action, but showed up at Poetschke's command post as an interested spectator.

Poetschke's improvised tank assault was doomed from the start. Before dawn on 30 December the tanks felt their way forward out of dense ground fog in the early morning, grinding through the Bois de Jean Collin as they rumbled forward to the north-west. So thick and blurring was the murk and mist that the two tank groups turned in different directions to completely different fates. The six tanks of the 6th Panzer Company turned west – reaching all the way to Remoifosse, north of Hill #535. American observers heard more than they could see, but soon determined the noises weren't friendly. The German tank commander in the lead panzer could see the main Martelange road when an avalanche of American artillery fire fell before him. This repulse was quickly followed by shattering tank rounds from the U.S. 4th Armored division. They halted warily – one panzer after another going up in flames.

Peering through the fog, American P-47 fighter-bombers marked the German tank positions of the northern attack group with smoke and buzzed down, dropping napalm and flinging rockets. Even tormented by the *Jabos,* Poetschke refused to stop. 'Drive fast!' he yelled at his driver. As the panzers dashed from one woods to another, across the snowy landscape between Lutrebois and Lutremange, the eager fighter-bombers shot up several German tanks not disabled by the blizzard of American shells. They claimed to have left three tanks burning.[51] Crews of crippled panzers attempting to escape from their metal chariots were chased and machine gunned as they fled across the snow-crusted fields. Not more than half a kilometer away, a different story unfolded.

At about 9.30 a.m. SS-Uscha. Manfred Thorn and the rest of the 7th Panzer Company arrived at the hill before Lutrebois. The lead panzer, Panzer #701, stopped just before the forest, with the seven tanks lined up one after another on the road. American fighter-bombers struck at them awkwardly in the mists and German infantry emerged from the trees as if to join the SS panzer column but were then chopped down by an unseen enemy. Manfred Thorn wanted to follow the other tanks, but just then his radio buzzed with an order to advance north. He drove on ahead. Soon the entire 7th Panzer Company drove in wedge formation across the frozen, open fields of white toward Sainlez – unaware that the U.S. 4th Armored Division had taken possession of Lutrebois behind them. Manfred Thorn in Panzer #734 rolled just behind his platoon leader, the indefatigable Hans Siptrott, in Panzer #731. At first, there was no resistance, but they could see and hear the violent reaction elicited by the other tank group just ahead. Ominously, they lost all radio contact. In the same panzer column with Thorn was Rolf Ehrhardt.

At one point on that strange day, Ehrhardt heard a tapping sound on the driver's hatch. He opened the metal plate amazed to see battalion commander Werner Poetschke and his adjutant Rolf Reiser standing just outside. Their Panther had been knocked out in the air attack and they had hoofed it through snow, dodging shellfire as they sprinted from tree to tree to check the status of the other tanks. What a crazy *Kampfschwein.* Never mind the situation, Ehrhardt implored, where was the front? In this fog, he and his crew were completely

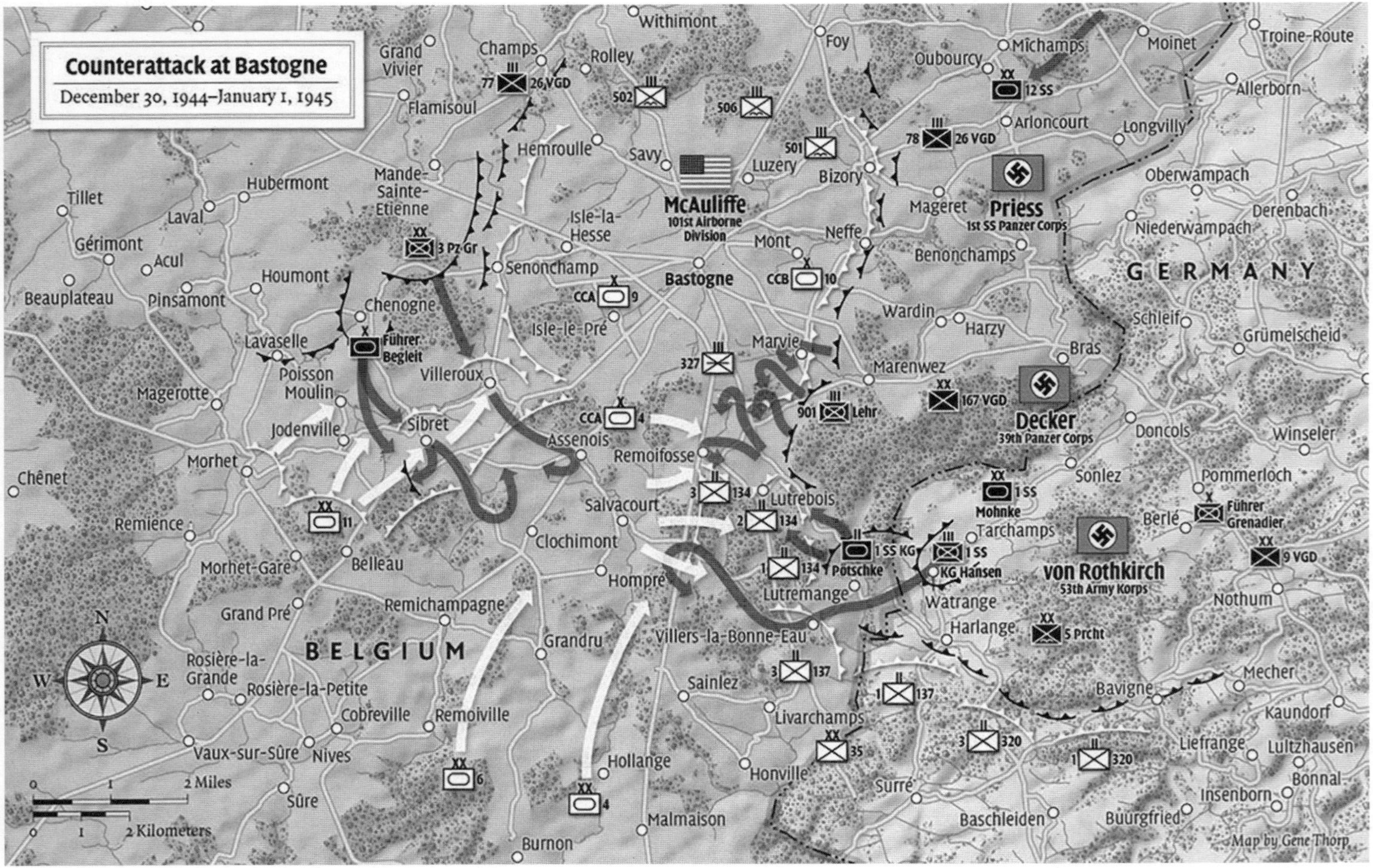
Counterattack at Bastogne
December 30, 1944–January 1, 1945
McAuliffe
101st Airborne Division
Priess
1st SS Panzer Corps
Decker
39th Panzer Corps
von Rothkirch
53th Army Korps
GERMANY
BELGIUM
Bastogne
Withimont
Foy
Champs
Rolley
Grand Vivier
Flamisoul
Hemroulle
Savy
Luzery
Bizory
Oubourcy
Michamps
Moinet
Troine-Route
Allerborn
Arloncourt
Longvilly
Mageret
Oberwampach
Derenbach
Niederwampach
Benonchamps
Mande-Sainte-Etienne
Hubermont
Tillet
Laval
Gérimont
Acul
Isle-la-Hesse
Mont
Neffe
Senonchamp
Houmont
Beauplateau
Pinsamont
Chenogne
Isle-le-Pré
Wardin
Harzy
Schleif
Grümelscheid
Lavaselle
Poisson Moulin
Villeroux
Marvie
Marenwez
Bras
Magerotte
Jodenville
Sibret
Assenois
Remoifosse
Doncols
Winseler
Morhet
Chênet
Sonlez
Pommerloch
Lutrebois
Salvacourt
Remience
Clochimont
Tarchamps
Berlé
Morhet-Gare
Belleau
Hompré
Watrange
Nothum
Grand Pré
Remichampagne
Lutremange
Harlange
Grandru
Villers-la-Bonne-Eau
Rosière-la-Grande
Rosière-la-Petite
Sainlez
Bavigne
Mecher
Cobreville
Remoiville
Livarchamps
Kaundorf
Vaux-sur-Sûre
Nives
Hollange
Honville
Liefrange
Lultzhausen
Sûre
Surré
Bonnal
Insenborn
Malmaison
Baschleiden
Buurgfried
Burnon
77 26 VGD
502
506
501
12 SS
78 26 VGD
3 Pz Gr
CCB 10
CCA 9
Führer Begleit
327
901 Lehr
167 VGD
CCA 4
1 SS
Mohnke
3 134
2 134
1 134
1 SS KG Potschke
1 SS KG Hansen
Führer Grenadier
9 VGD
5 Prcht
11
3 137
1 137
3 320
1 320
35
6
4
N
S
W
E
2 Miles
2 Kilometers
Map by Gene Thorp

disoriented. Even if they didn't know where they were, their enemy was intent on finding out. For just then, an American Piper Cub observation plane zoomed noisily out of the low clouds, passing so low and lazily overhead that Ehrhardt thought he could have thrown a rock and hit it.[52]

That sight proved a bad omen; within minutes, artillery fire shadowed their every move. Just before 3 p.m. the 7th Company thrust was neatly ambushed by hull-down tanks and tank destroyers from 4th Armored Division that fired from the rear.[53] Eight tanks fell in ten minutes.

Manfred Thorn's tank narrowly avoided the same fate. His tank commander, SS-Uscha Horst Pilzarek, thought he saw American infantry on the left side of the road, but curiously, none fired – a trap. 'Turn around!' Pilzarek shouted suddenly, 'The company is burning!'[54] 'I turned around in a hurry,' recalled Thorn, 'and drove on past the burning tanks as quickly as possible.' As anti-tank gun rounds smashed around him, Thorn gunned his engine, pulling in behind a haystack at a farm on the outskirts of Lutrebois – waiting two hours until dark to dare pull out. He watched warily as the knocked-out panzers on his right blazed in the twilight.

At 5.30 p.m. Thorn at last dared to pull out, immediately attracting artillery fire from opportunistic American observers. Somehow, however, he found another surviving tank of their company in a mad dash to the woods to the east and together they motored blindly through the thick forest, reaching friendly lines near Bras. Surprisingly, there they found most of the surviving tank crews of the panzers destroyed in the mad minutes that afternoon. Siptrott was there, as was Ehrhardt. Both had their panzers shot out from under them. That night, when Poetschke hitched a ride with Roman Clotten back to his command post on one of the few remaining Mk IVs, it was to inform Jochen Peiper that six of the 7th Company panzers stood burned out in a line on the road north-west of Lutrebois. The single Panther had also been lost.

While Poetschke impaled his tanks on American gunnery and air power, the morning of 30 December began as grenadiers and heavy tanks of the southern attack group surged through the snow-packed farming village of Villes-la-Bonne-Eau to the south. Fighting raged for each farmhouse, pasture, and barn until the infantry attack soon stalled due to a lack of sufficient artillery. All the while the Americans dumped one salvo of shells after another on the village.[55] Yet even that did not stop the seven Tiger tanks, which lumbered up to point their 88mm snouts directly into the stone houses in an attempt to blast the Americans out. Losses were high. In the confused battle for Villers-la-Bonne-Eau the 35th Infantry Division lost nearly all of Companies K and L of the 137th Regiment – 168 men. Only Sgt Webster Philips made it back to American lines.[56] But the SS troops paid a high price. The fifteen houses of the hamlet became a magnet for some six thousand shells fired by American guns over succeeding days. Yet, try as he might, Poetschke's two panzer thrusts were unable to get closer than 200 yards to the Bastogne–Martelange Road. It was over.

Peiper went to the front to look for his remaining tanks. There wasn't much left; the 7th Panzer Company was in a bad way, having lost six of its eight remaining tanks.[57] Peiper was enraged by what he saw as needless sacrifice – Poetschke was punishing crews by launching them into a suicide mission. According to several sources, he and Poetschke exchanged heated words about the action. Even if the penalty platoon had become an institution in the SS divisions, Poetschke had a brutal reputation for taking things a step further.[58] The previous May, Teddi Wisch had presided over a divisional inquiry against Poetschke for 'misuse of disciplinary action' – a euphemism for punishment by nearly killing subordinates.[59] Peiper took up an audience with Sepp Dietrich. 'It takes twice as long to train a tank man as an infantry man,' Peiper complained. 'Think it over.'[60]

Hans Siptrott narrowly managed to escape the melee unscathed, but decried Poetschke's attack. 'Rudi Ribbentrop always had taken care, but he wasn't there anymore,' Siptrott complained. 'I was an old hare and you became one by finding a way not to do orders that were stupid.' This time it wasn't possible, even for an experienced NCO who had seen his share of losses from reckless action. 'I liked Peiper as he led by example, but I can't say the same for Poetschke. I didn't care for him.'[61]

On the other side of the fence, the master of American bravado, Gen. George S. Patton, saw the repulse of the 1st SS Panzer Division as decisive. 'Unquestionably, this was the critical day of the operation,' he wrote on 30 December. 'There was a concerted effort on the part of the Germans, using at least five divisions, to again isolate Bastogne.'[62] Hitler's blustered effort 'to erase Bastogne' using his namesake command had failed as Patton moved up additional forces. Meanwhile, the Third Army commander motored into Bastogne, zipping along in a jeep up the shell-pocked route from Martelange. The Leibstandarte had just been repulsed and smoking tank carcasses littered the roadside. Once inside the wrecked Belgian market town, Patton personally decorated Brig. Gen. Anthony McAuliffe – the man who burnished 'Nuts!' into the annals of American military folklore.

If the Leibstandarte had been rebuffed in its bid to recapture Bastogne, they still possessed plenty of fight, as the U.S. 6th Armored Division attested when they attempted to repel the division near Michamps on 3 January. U.S. tankers bravely stood down the dozen German tanks that sallied from Wardin only to find that their 75mm shot bounced off the King Tigers 'like marbles off a brick'.[63] 'My boys pulled back for the first time,' a sullen Maj. Gen. Robert H. Grow worried, 'and the 1st SS Panzer Division attacked into the middle of our retreat.' The 6th Armored Division left smouldering armored hulks as it pulled back; a lethal curtain of artillery was the only thing that stopped their enemy.

George Patton, who had been ebullient just days before, was sobered by the enemy resolve. He had been at Grow's command post when the Germans took it under fire 'We can still lose this war,' Patton penned into his diary on 4 January, 'The Germans are colder, hungrier, and weaker than we are for sure. But they're still doing a great piece of fighting.'[64]

It was true. Kampfgruppe Hansen now gave assault rifles to everyone who could walk and planned counterattacks on the Americans when companies were down to thirty-five men. Still, prisoners coming into the POW cages of the U.S. Third Army – recent replacements for the division – professed to be 'very eager to see combat and still believing victory'.[65]

East of Bastogne at Schimpach, the 5th Fallschirmjäger Division was unhappy to be sharing its headquarters with the SS troopers whose fighting Patton admired. Maj. Gen Ludwig Heilmann, commander of the 5th Fallschirmjäger Division, didn't mince words:

> The staff of the 1st SS Panzer Division located next to my command post now became a very dangerous neighbour … the command of the division was taken from me and subordinated to the SS. The Oberführer Mohnke, commander of the SS Division and General [Hans-Kurt] Hoecker, took possession of my command post in an imprudent way … The SS spread the rumour that paratroopers peacefully sat together with the Americans in the cellar of a house in Villers-la-Bonne-Eau and had drunk the pledge of brotherhood. The 1st SS Panzer Division said to one of my military policemen that one ought to set a *Nationalsozialistischen Führungsoffizier* on the throat of the Parachute Division. My Ic [chief of staff intelligence] officer listened in on a telephone call made within the SS staff which read as follows: 'Now it is high time that this paratroop division is cleared out.'[66]

On Thursday, 11 January 1945, a teletype message flashed from Berlin to the headquarters of the 6th Panzer Army. It was addressed to Joachim Peiper: 'In consideration of your continuous display of heroism, I award you the Swords to the Oak Leaves of the Knight's Cross.' It was signed by Adolf Hitler himself.[67] Within days there was a glowing press release, dutifully reproduced in the *Tegernsee Tal*, for the local war hero.

Peiper was only the 119th German soldier to receive this military honor, but given the chaotic conditions as he physically recovered from the debacle of the previous month, he did not personally receive the swords from 'the hand of the Führer'. That perfunctory honor seems to have come from Sepp Dietrich. Indeed, up until that point, no one participating in *Wacht am Rhein* had received an award approaching it in stature.[68]

The panzer regiment pulled out of the Bastogne battle on 9 January near Doncols and, by 10 January, were back in the region near St Vith. Peiper and the staff of the tank regiment camped there until the rest of the division loaded up on trains in the Eifel, before heading off for Cologne.

Peiper, ailing once more, seems to have gone in another direction. After leaving, he made his way south, to visit the family home in Rottach Egern. That January the mood in the skiing resort was subdued. The order to send war-wounded to the Tegernsee hotels had been rescinded, but that was only because they were brimming with maimed soldiers.[69] In the meantime, Gen. Walter Warlimont, living in nearby Gmund, was asking Himmler for the use of his concentration camp labor, who had just finished a new air-raid bunker in town. He wished to construct a personal one for his quarters.[70]

As the war careened out of control on Peiper's 29th birthday, 30 January, the ordinary festivities of the *Machtergreifung* seemed maudlin. But as always, Hitler made the ceremonious address to mark the movement's seizure of power:

> The fight against this Jewish Asiatic bolshevism had been raging long before National Socialism came to power … However grave the crisis may be at the moment, it will despite everything, finally be mastered by our unalterable will.[71]

Chapter 32

FINIS

Only the dead have seen the end of war.

Plato

The streets of Rottach Egern were buried deep in snow and cold on Tuesday, 30 January 1945 as Peiper likely listened to Hitler's speech. The local mood was grim – too many 'died for the Führer' notices in the paper – the ugly, Maltese crosses checkering the back pages of the newspaper. It was Peiper's birthday. In Berlin, Hitler's ministry of war production, Albert Speer, handed his superior a terse report concluding the 'Thousand Year Reich' was over.[1] Hitler knew it too, so confiding to his Luftwaffe adjutant, Nicolaus von Below:

> I know the war is lost. The enemy superiority is too great. I've been betrayed … I ought to put a bullet through my head. I lacked hard fighters. Model and Dietrich are such, and Rudel … But we will not capitulate, ever. We may go down, but we will take the world down with us.[2]

It was Hitler's own vision of a perfect defeat for his failed German Reich – a Wagnerian apocalypse. That evening on 30 January, eager Soviet infantry of the 89th Guard's Rifle Division reached the Oder River and skated across the ice to form a strategically important bridgehead just north of Küstrin. Overmatched German defenders were thunderstruck. The Red Army was not 50 miles from Hitler's Berlin bunker.

Peiper himself, too, would soon come under scrutiny. That the Malmedy incident was of grave concern to the Allies became apparent to the German foreign minister at the end of December when Roosevelt's State Department cabled 'the strongest possible protest':

> U.S. Urgent–Allegation
> Please request the Swiss to inform the German government that a group of fifteen survivors have reported that on December 17 in the fighting south of Malmedy

> about 130 members of an American Field Artillery Observation Battalion were taken prisoner by German forces. The prisoners were stripped of their valuables and equipment, herded into a field, and submitted to machine gun fire from tanks at a range of approximately one hundred feet. The American government protests most vigorously against this gross violation of the Geneva Prisoners of War Convention ...[3]

Caught in a severe winter storm over the holidays in Washington D.C., U.S President Franklin D. Roosevelt himself warned the Germans who were still fighting, 'None who participated in such acts of savagery will go unpunished.'[4] Just a month later at the conference at Tehran, Stalin rose to his feet during the banquet finale. 'I propose a salute to the swiftest possible justice for all of Germany's war criminals – justice before a firing squad,' he began. 'I drink to our unity in dispatching them as fast as we capture them, all of them.' Meanwhile, Roosevelt's Treasury Secretary, Henry Morgenthau, Jr, was so appalled by the emerging magnitude of German war crimes that he supported the early British position advocating summary execution.

On 27 January 1945, the Office of the Inspector General of the U.S. First Army forwarded word of the need for a full investigation of the Malmedy incident to General Omar Bradley with the 12th Army Group.[5] General Hodges reminded Bradley that there were at least two Belgian witnesses to the atrocities. Henri Lejoly of Bavjnez had fearfully watched through the window of his home as the Germans jostled the Americans in the field and brought up half-tracks with machine guns. As it looked like the Germans were preparing to shoot the American soldiers, Lejoly moved away from the window and hid, moments later hearing loud machine gun fire. Soon after, he heard his neighbour, Frau Adele Bodarwe, run into her house. 'Oh my God!' Lejoly had heard his neighbour scream. He never saw her again.[6]

Also, on Tuesday, 30 January 1945 Eisenhower and SHAEF itself opened their own inquiry. At Harrogate in Yorkshire, U.S. Army Lt Col. John S. Voorhees and Lt Col J.H. Boraston of the British army convened the investigation to consider the Malmedy allegations. Of the witnesses who spoke to SHAEF that day, 26-year-old Sgt Henry R. Zach of the U.S. 3rd Armored Division had a disturbing testimony of being shot in the field, feigning death and then desperately crawling wounded to find help the next day.[7]

There was no German response, but the world press revealed the Malmedy incident in widespread coverage. On 10 February 1945, the Associated Press in London reported a German broadcast in English to American troops on the Western Front declaring that brutal acts like those at the outset of the Ardennes breakthrough were justified by national preservation. There was little doubt that 'Hans of Arnhem' referred to Malmedy: 'If you have a numerically superior opponent fighting a smaller one and the smaller one knows that his very existence is at stake, he will – because of his inferiority – have to resort to means that appear hard and brutal.'[8]

With an eye towards total mobilisation for battle, Josef Goebbels, Hitler's propaganda minister, began to incorporate the Allied warnings of how they would eviscerate Germany at the end. Certainly, the victors would be looking for the commander of the 1st SS Panzer Regiment.

While Peiper convalesced, the U.S. 30th Infantry Division looked to attack and recapture the crossroads at Baugnez where the Malmedy atrocity had taken place. Deep snows now starkly outlined the Ardennes terrain. Private Francis Edwards thought the snow-encrusted trees 'made for a beautiful Christmas-like sight', but toiled with everyone else to fashion camouflage outfits out of bed sheets, drapes, and anything else to help blend in with the icy white. Otherwise, the olive-drab uniforms stood out invitingly for the enemy gunners.[9] Even then, they would approach enemy lines under cover of darkness.

Although a tiny patrol on the night of 30 December from the 120th Regiment had found the crossroads free of the enemy, they ran into an enemy outpost.[10] The following night, three hours into the new year, two platoons of B Company set out across the snow to test the enemy defenses near Baugnez, now in possession of the 3rd Fallschirmjäger Division. Trudging through deep snow, when the main body of the ten-man raiding party reached the crossroads, they came under fire from an enemy strongpoint to the south. In minutes, Capt. Murray Pulver, in charge of Company B, found the entire night operation in danger of destruction.

A sparkle of lights blinked in darkness – a fan of German automatic weapons fire from the woods and a nearby house caught the patrol in an exposed enfilade. Rifle grenades dropped out of the black sky and exploded willy-nilly, killing the patrol leader and another GI, and wounding several others. During the chaos, a platoon sent to flank the enemy on the right stumbled on uneven humps in the snow. In the bright moonlight, a few of the 'uneven humps' were uncovered to reveal bodies in the massacre field, twisted and frozen, lying on top of each other. But there was little time to look further. Still under fire, the patrol retreated and captured a scrawny paratrooper in the woods near the house. Captain Pulver could only report that the Germans were still plenty strong around Baugnez–Thirimont.[11]

So costly was that attempt, along with frigid windblown snow, that a renewed attempt at the crossroads was postponed for more than a week. Another push came on 12 January 1945, when the 30th Division battled once more for the crossroads – now covered with 2 to 4ft of drifted snow and pockmarked by craters from artillery fire. That night, infantrymen of the 119th Regiment of the 30th Division dug foxholes around the foggy crossroads only to find in the daylight that they shared the snowy field with victims of a mass killing. Pvt. Herschel Nolen of Durant Oklahoma awoke to find a dead man in a grotesque, rigid posture with its outstretched arms nearly reaching his foxhole. 'There are others around here still lying under the snow,' he said waving his hand. 'If that's the way they want to fight – then that's alright with us,' Nolen said. 'But let us fight that way, too.' Private Glenn L. Hubbard in a nearby foxhole agreed, 'If the people back home could see this, maybe they would stop their bickering.'[12] By the morning of 13 January the 120th Infantry Regiment had largely retaken the area.[13]

The folks back home could not see the scarred and blackened crossroads with the gutted and burned-out café. Along the road leading by the café off to the north were a dozen or so wrecked American trucks and jeeps, abandoned and now partly covered in white. Bare birch trees stood out starkly against the white snowfield, the ground pitted by dark splotches of shellfire. The grey bark of the trees that bordered the field was split and gleaming yellow from exploding shrapnel. Only two dozen yards from the charred ruins of the café were the exposed bodies of the young Americans killed in the field.

Even though most of the bodies were hidden in the snow, here and there, the frozen death forms were exposed by icy winds. The contorted corpses, edging out of the snow, gave a macabre appearance. Several lay face-up with their hands held over their heads and their mouths half open as if totally surprised by death.[14] One snow-dusted face looked straight ahead as if lost in eternity, staring up at the dark-blue sky criss-crossed by bomber contrails. Several fell huddled together, looking as if they sought warmth from the cold. One soldier clutched his stomach in a death spasm while a medic with a bullet hole through his Red Cross armlet stared straight ahead in a fixed gaze. Birds or small animals had eaten the eyes out of some victims.

Later, the German barrage lifted and fifteen prisoners from the German 3rd Fallschirmjäger Division were escorted through the lines from the embattled village of Thirimont to the south.[15] Helmets off with their hands over their heads, they looked weary and expressionless. 'I feel pretty low on these Jerries,' ventured Sgt James Warnock of Belton, South Carolina. He knew the German soldiers they had captured would soon be off to the rear – a place warmer and safer than his foxhole in the death field at Baugnez. 'After seeing what we have seen here, it makes you wonder why we take prisoners,' he said.[16]

Was Kampfgruppe Peiper's reputation from Malmedy behind them at the close of the year? Evidently not. In late December 1944, a prisoner of the 26th Volksgrenadier Division was wounded and hospitalised for two weeks at Bad Bertrich in the Eifel in the former hotel, Haus Schneider. There, he shared a room with an SS Gefr. Heinz Weber, who had fought with Peiper in the Ardennes. During their two weeks together convalescing, Weber boasted that his unit had captured several *Amis* near Bastogne, but since 'we have no time for prisoners', the GIs were led aside to the edge of a wood and executed with pistol shots to the head.[17]

On Peiper's arrival in the snow-encrusted village of Rottach Egern, a special gift from SS leader Heinrich Himmler was waiting with the mail: a *Weihnachtsgabe* containing scarce foodstuffs, two pounds of coffee, special tea, red and white wine, cognac, and a hundred real tobacco cigarettes. The gift was reserved for generals, but for his long-favored adjutant, Jochen Peiper, Himmler made an exception. Upon arrival, the SS officer looked distinctly unwell. Sigurd Peiper had lit the twelve candles of the ceramic SS *Julleuchter* to celebrate the dark winter holidays – even darker in 1945. Now she found her husband's mental countenance frayed – even worse than in December – and his gaunt yellow features suggested jaundice. All attacks in the West had failed and the German defense on the eastern border of the Third Reich trembled near collapse.[18] Peiper only stayed a few days with the family to celebrate his birthday.

Departing home, Peiper headed off to consult Himmler, before going on to Berlin. Himmler was his old boss from 1939–41 and his wife, Sigurd, had worked for K.H. (König Heinrich: the inner circle code name) before that. Later, Peiper would re-join his division.[19] Peiper was met at the Birkenwald rail station by fellow SS adjutant Werner Grothmann. Grothmann quickly took him to Himmler's inner sanctum in his special command train, the *Sonderzug Steiermark*. The train idled in the snowy birch grove 50 miles north of Berlin.[20] Also present from their days together with Himmler, was Peiper's old office superior, SS Obgruf. Karl Wolff. Wolff was recently back from Italy, where he had been supreme commander of SS forces there. Now, under Himmler's direction, Wolff was covertly seeking to establish some diplomatic solution out of a lost war. 'Up until the end of January, I still believed in victory ...'

On 4 February, Peiper was in deep conversation with Himmler and Heinz Lammerding, the former commander of the 2nd SS Panzer Division, with Wolff also present. Peiper's reportage of the Ardennes operation to Wolff was cynical. Peiper '... told me that 3,000 aircraft had been promised to take part in the offensive,' recalled Wolff, 'whereas not a single one of them was seen and that the enemy had been able to put up an umbrella over the Rhine.'[21]

Peiper said he had lost every tank that he had taken with him to cross the Meuse – with most abandoned for lack of gasoline. Faced with chronic fuel shortages, Himmler told his audience of crazy schemes, reporting that Nazi engineers were working on the chemistry to distil petrol from fir tree roots. Without a hint of irony, Himmler then advocated soldier-powered rickshaws to transport ammunition. The failure in the Ardennes and the Alsace had done nothing to still Himmler's talk of coming secret weapons. He praised SS engineer Hans Kammler, who had just arrived at Birkenwald to hint at a new 'diabolical' weapon; one that would reputedly would make all motors cease to function.[22] For Peiper, listening to such fare after coming from the gritty fighting front, must have been difficult to stomach. Peiper still had the war to fight. Having been cast out of the Ardennes, he would be heading off to lead a final panzer attack in the East.

On 7 February, Himmler and his entourage left in their armored train for Berlin to meet Hitler. Upon arriving in Berlin, Himmler, Grothmann and Peiper toured the smashed and smoking ruins of the capital. Peiper's old family home in Wilmersdorf had been blasted away and the SS and Gestapo headquarters on Prinz Albrechtstrasse was thoroughly wrecked. Nearby streets were impassable from rubble. The SS Reichführer put on a brave face.[23] That night, Himmler's group, including Peiper, dined with Hitler at the Reich Chancellery. Also there was SS adjutant Hermann Fegelein, Reichsleiter Martin Bormann and Hitler's mistress, Eva Braun. Grothmann and Peiper sat at an adjoining table.[24]

The destruction of Berlin dominated the conversation; nearly 3,000 had died in the smoking ruins. With the wave of a hand, Hitler ordered that his mistress depart the following day for safety at Berchtesgaden in the south. She didn't obey. Then Peiper departed too; he had to be back to the Leibstandarte for a new attack operation. Hitler demanded the Hungarian oil fields be recaptured.

If a nutty scheme, Peiper had tied his star to Hitler; there was no choice but to obey.

How to end a war gone wrong? SS Lt Col Jochen Peiper would simply keep fighting. If National Socialism and Hitler could not be saved, Peiper would at least give unflagging battle to their enemies. From his perspective – loyal to the end – it was a cruel fate. He would end the Second World War still fighting with his SS panzer division in Austria's storied forests near Vienna. Hitler's name remained embroidered on his cuff sleeve. 'When the Führer was needing his Leibstandarte most,' Peiper later said with agonised regret, 'fate separated us from him.'[25]

EQUIVALENT RANKS OF WAFFEN SS, GERMAN ARMY AND U.S. ARMY IN 1944

SS	Abbrev.	German Army	Abbrev.	US.Army
Reichsführer-SS	RFSS			
		Generalfeldmarschall	Genflm	General of the Army
SS-Oberst-Gruppenführer	Obstgruf.	Generaloberst	Gen.O.	General
SS-Obergruppenführer	Ogruf.	General	Gen.	Lieutenant General
SS-Gruppenführer	Gruf.	Generalleutnant	Gen.Lt.	Major General
SS-Brigadeführer	Brigf.	Generalmajor	Gen. Mj.	Brigadier General
SS-Oberführer		Obf.	–	–
SS-Standartenführer	Staf.	Oberst	O	Colonel
SS-Obersturmbannführer	Ostubaf.	Oberstleutnant	OTL	Lieutenant-Colonel
SS-Sturmbannführer	Stubaf.	Major	M	Major

SS	Abbrev.	German Army	Abbrev.	US.Army
SS-Hauptsturmführer	Hstuf.	Hauptmann	Hptm.	Captain
SS-Obersturmführer	Ostuf.	Oberleutnant	Olt.	1st Lieutenant
SS-Untersturmführer	Ustuf.	Leutnant	Lt.	2nd Lieutenant
SS-Standartenjunker	Stjk.	Fähnrich	Fhr.	Cadet
SS-Sturmscharführer	Stuscha.	Hauptfeldwebel	HFw.	Sergeant-Major
SS-Hauptscharführer	Hscha.	Oberfeldwebel	Ofw.	Master Sergeant
SS-Oberscharführer	Oscha.	Feldwebel	Fw.	Staff Sergeant (T/5)
SS-Unterscharführer	Uscha.	Unteroffizier	Uffz.	Sergeant (T/4)
SS-Rottenführer	Rttf.	Obergefreiter	OG	Corporal
SS-Sturmmann	Strm.	Gefreiter	G	Private 1st Class
SS-Mann	Man.	Schütze	Schtz.	Private

ENDNOTES

Prologue – A New Dunkirk

1 At the turn of the century, hotel was still in business, now incarnated as the *Hotel Bayern* and ever popular with as a party destination for the well-to-do crowd on New Year's Eve. Information on the history of the hotel courtesy my journalist friend, Dr Michael Heim.

2 See '*Betr.: Bestätigung der Verwundungen und Erkrankungen des SS-O-Stubaf. Joachim Peiper, Kdr.Pz-Rgt.1 zwecks Einlage in das Soldbuch,*' signed by Dr Sickel and Hans Gruhle on 30 January 1945 at the regimental command post. The copy in the Ernst Klink archive shows a handwritten note at the bottom of the copy: '8.44: (Herzschlag)?'

3 Interview with Ralf Tiemann, 21 October 1995. Also interview with Rolf Reiser, 15 May 1997.

4 For Sigurd Peiper's discussion with her husband's doctor, see letter Sigurd Peiper to Hedwig Potthast, 11 November 1944, *NSDAP Hauptarchiv*, Himmler Collection, Microfilm Roll #99, Hoover Institution, Stanford University.

5 Interview with Gerhard Walla, 10 May 1999. Seeing Peiper in December 1944 as Werner Poetschke's adjutant: 'He was a nervous wreck …'

6 Toland Interview with Jochen Peiper, 10 October 1963, John Toland Papers: The Last Hundred Days, Library of Congress, Box 15.

7 Helmut Heiber, ed., *Hitlers Lagebesprechungen*, Deutsche Verlags Anstalt, 1962, p. 620.

8 Originally dubious of the assault rifle in that it would require still another non-standard issue of ammunition (7.62mm), Hitler personally test fired the side-arm and became an enthusiastic proponent. Of course, the weapon was too little too late, but made from stamped metal parts and almost half the weight of the U.S. Browning Automatic Rifle (B.A.R.), it was issued in large numbers to hastily assembled German conscripts in the autumn of 1944. At the front, even a single untrained soldier firing off bursts from its 30-round clip (500–600 rpm) could keep heads down of an entire enemy platoon in contact. Indeed, the MP 44 design was enthusiastically copied by the Russians at war's end into the immensely popular modern Kalashnikov AK-47 assault weapon.

9 In a production miracle to meet Hitler's demand, his armaments minister, Albert Speer, managed to manufacture nearly 2,900 single-engine German fighters in the single month of September 1944—virtually tripling production compared to the year before. All this was accomplished while Germany was pounded by a rain of bombs. Most of the new production were not jets, but mostly the increasingly outdated Me-109 piston-powered aircraft.

10 Albert Speer, *Inside the Third Reich*, Macmillian, NY, 1970, p. 470.

11 This story became a sensational book, *Hitlers Bombe*, by Berlin historian, Rainer Karlsch (Deutsche Verlags Anstalt, 2005) which claims that not only were the Germans much closer to crude nuclear weapons than previously supposed, but that three tests were conducted in early 1945, one killing hundreds of inmates near the military training center in Thuringia near Ohrduf. However, Karlsch's proof of these brazen claims are sketchy at best. See Klaus Wiegrefe, 'How Close was Hitler to the A-Bomb?' *Der Speigel*, 14 March 2005.

12 Indeed, there had been a German program to develop an atomic bomb. On 15 September 1941, two great physicists, Germany's Werner Heisenberg (the uncertainty principle in physics) met with Denmark's Niels Bohr in Copenhagen. First, he informed Bohr as to his conviction that Germany would win the war, saying 'it was therefore quite foolish for us to maintain the hope of a different outcome of the war.' Heisenberg shocked his old mentor with one claim: he now led a project in Germany to develop atomic bombs and if the war went on long enough, he was certain it would be settled by these terrible new weapons. Bohr said little. ('I listened to this without speaking since a great matter for mankind was at issue, in which, despite our personal friendship, we had to be regarded as representatives of two sides engaged in mortal

combat.') Although the discussion proved the end of the longtime friendship of the two colleagues, Bohr sowed the seeds of doubt in Heisenberg's psyche. When he returned to the Kaiser Wilhelm institute after his argument with Bohr, the convinced German officials in charge that the atom bomb project was too expensive and unrealistic for the short war under way. Thus, the German military abandoned the project in 1942 just as the American Manhattan Project was just getting under way. Heisenberg's motives have been the inspiration for much post war speculation as even telling Bohr was a major breach in security. See Thomas Powers, *Heisenberg's War*, Knopf, NY, 1993 and *www.nbi.dk/NBA/papers* and *www.werner-heisenberg.unh.edu*. For the secret weapons rumor in the 2nd Panzer Division in the autumn of 1944, RG 407, Entry 427, Records of the U.S. First Army, 101—2.13, Box 1495, U.S. First Army PWI Report No. 12, '304 Panzer Grenadier Regiment,' 26-27 October 1944.

13 'Spot Interrogation of Ernst Schaefer: German Information on the Atomic Bomb,' Headquarters, Third Army Interrogation Center, 19 September 1945, NA, RG-498, UD-247A, Box 1289.

14 Kreipe's jotted record of Hitler on 19 August: *'Darauf einstellen, dass im November offensiv wird—wenn der Feind nicht fliegen kann.'* Jodl Diaries, 1937-1945, Records and Documents Related to the Third Reich, David Irving Collection, Microform Ltd., Microfilm Roll 16, MS Nr. P-215, p. 316.

15 'Interview with Genobst. Alfred Jodl: Planning the Ardennes Offensive,' ETHINT-50, 26 July 1945, NA, RG-238, Foreign Military Studies.

16 'He was glad instead because the explosion and the shock received had relieved him of the neurotic trembling of his right hand. He took that as one more good omen and felt himself inspired to prepare to the last detail, the Ardennes Offensive … This offensive was, as far as a military layman can judge from all I have seen or heard, was in planning and scheming, entirely Hitler's work.' Recollections of Dr Ewald Reynitz, Microform Ltd. David Irving Collection, *Hitler's War*, Film 97125, Reel 4.

17 'Forest of Arden' Location of Shakespeare's, *As You Like It*, Act V, Scene 1.

18 Jodl's war diary for 11 September 1944, Kom. Nr. 96, *op. cit.*, p. 323.

19 'Hitler couldn't understand why the west didn't take the chance to fight against the East. He knew the East was the most dangerous military enemy … He could have won against the Russians if the West held off attacking into Germany … Hitler couldn't understand why the West helped Jewish communism. Guderian saw the realism of the front, but Hitler saw beyond.' Interview of John Toland with Otto Günsche, 16 October 1963, John Toland Papers, The Last Hundred Days, Library of Congress, Box 16.

20 In the autumn of 1757, Frederick the Great was beset by enemies on all sides and defeat appeared certain. The French had invaded the territory of his Anglo-Hanoverian allies, a Franco-Imperial army was threatening Saxony, an Austrian army 110,000-strong had marched into Silesia and even the lumbering Russians had moved against him. Boldly striking out, within a month Frederick transformed his fortunes. At Rossbach on 5 November he smashed the Franco-Imperial army in half a day. With a forced march to Silesia, he won perhaps his greatest victory exactly a month later, crushing the Austrian Army at Leuthen.

21 'War experiences of General Sepp Dietrich and Colonel Joachim Peiper.' 1 May 1953, written in April 1946 while awaiting trial at Dachau, USAMHI, D811, D5 C.3, Carlisle, PA. Handwritten original in author's possession.

22 *'Persönliches Kriegstagebuch des General der Flieger Kreipe,'* NA, RG-238, Foreign Military Studies, MS P-069.

23 *Inside the Third Reich,* Speer, p. 528, For comparisons of the planning for the offensives in the Ardennes in both 1940 and 1944, see Magna E. Bauer, *Comparison Between Planning for the German Ardennes Offensive in 1944 and Operation 'Gelb' in 1939/1940,'* MS R-44, OCMH, April 1950

24 The staff exercise was co-ordinated by Gen. Jodl and the *Wehrmachtführungsstab* and provided five possible courses of offensive action when submitted to Hitler on 9 October. For details, see Schramm, MS A-862, *op. cit.* Hitler rejected the alternative options believing they failed to promise decisive success.

25 The planning for the German offensive and the jousting match between his generals to scale down the 'Big Solution' (Ardennes to Antwerp) to the 'Small Solution' (Aachen-Ardennes pincers converging on Liège to trap the U.S. First Army) is a large and complex story. For a comprehensive overview using German sources, see Charles von Lüttichau, 'The Ardennes Offensive: Planning and Preparation,' three chapters of roughly 150 pages with maps, MS R-14, prepared for the Office of the Chief of Military History, Washington D.C., 1953.

26 Although Wilhelm Keitel was roundly criticized as Hitler's yes man and sycophant, Jochen Peiper liked him. 'He was a gentleman with a somewhat awkward complexion, but you always had the feeling that he could be relied on. Keitel was closest to Hitler, not because he was a slave, but because he believed … Hitler has such a strong influence and magnetism that all people under his influence couldn't resist him.' Jochen Peiper, John Toland Interview, 10 October 1963, *op. cit.*

27 'Hitler: Detailed IPW Report #12,' Headquarters U.S. Third Army, Office of the Assistant Chief of Staff, G-2, 25 April 1945, NA, RG-407, 103-2.13 to 2.18. 'He [Hitler] was very technically minded and he was outstanding in recognizing the importance of mechanized equipment on modern warfare … Through his ability to view highly complex problems without reserve and caution, he was capable of seeing things and saying things that startled his professional military leaders.'

Chapter 1 – 'Hold the Reins Loose'

1 Keitel's promise of 17.5 cubic meters (4.6 million gallons) of petrol and 50 trains of ammunition, Schramm, *op. cit.*, pp. 261-262. By mid-December the required accumulation for the offensive had been built up, albeit with only 7,500 cubic meters of fuel immediately on hand in the camouflaged Eifel depots. Jodl Diaries, *op. cit.*, p. 391. The original gasoline allocation to the *Fifth Panzer Armee,* for example, was reduced from 3 to 2.5 consumption units (theoretically sufficient to go about 250 km on level roads, but in the hilly Ardennes for only perhaps 125 km). ('Consolidated Report from PW s from 1SS Panzer Division,' U.S. First Army PWI Report, 27 December 1944, NA, RG-407, 101.1- 3.2, M.L.-2125, Box 1497). Resupply without an active truck convoy behind the moving panzers would be almost impossible. The rest was on the other side of Rhine River and would require trucks or trains to bring it up—an egregious error on the part of the German logistical planners, for in transit it would be vulnerable to Allied air attack and gummy roads. The other problem was the available stores since the Germans reckoned on a 2,000 cubic meters per day consumption for the operation. Ideas of bolstering the nine-day supply with captured fuel bordered on fantasy.

2 Hitler: 'I cannot wait until the weather gets better.' Walter Warlimont, *Inside Hitler's Headquarters 1939-45,* Praeger, NY, 1964, p. 492.

3 *'Richtlinien für das Angriffverfahren der Operation Wacht am Rhein,'* OB West KTB, Anlage 50, 18 November 1944, NA, RG-242, Records of German Field Commands, Microfilm Roll T-311, Roll 18.

4 Schwerdtfeger, W. 1986, 'The Last Two Years of Z-W-G,' *Weather*, 41, p. 129-191. Also, Harold A. Winters, *Battling the Elements: Weather and Terrain in the Conduct of War,* Johns Hopkins University Press, 1998, pp. 50-56. Hitler would later promote both Schuster and Schwerdtfeger, his 'weather prophet,' based upon the favorable forecast. Ironically, after the war, Prof. Schwerdtfeger would hold a prestigious position at University of Wisconsin in the Department of Atmospheric and Oceanic Sciences. Hitler on 28 December: 'The best omen [for the offensive] was the weather development which had been forecast by a young weather forecaster who actually proved to be right. The weather situation allowed us to camouflage the final build up so the enemy failed to recognize it.' Parker, 1991, *op. cit.*, p. 214.

5 'Interrogation Report No. 34: Cover and Deception Prior to the Ardennes Offensive, Genmaj. Otto Remer,' 30 August 1945, Third Army Interrogation Center, NA, RG-498, UD-249, Box 1293.

6 The Allies believed that Genflm. von Rundstedt was in charge of the German forces in the West. This is quite clear from Benjamin Dickson's Estimate #37 where he indicated that 'German generals are obviously now conducting their operations without intuition ... an obvious smack against Hitler's often invoked *Führerprinzip*. They expected the experience field marshal to pursue a cautious military course based on husbanding his reserves and making a limited counterattack once the Allies penetrated across the Roer River. Although many took to calling it the *Rundstedt Offensive* after the war, the old field marshal vehemently protested that appellation as he had little to do with its inception or execution. Indeed, he was insulted by the designation: 'The Rundstedt Offensive.' The only troops he controlled during the offensive, he maintained, were the 'guards outside my headquarters.' 'Special Interrogation Report Field Marshal Karl Rudolf Gerd von Rundstedt,' 1 February 1946, *op. cit.* Von Rundstedt referred to Sepp Dietrich as 'a fool' and a 'former *Wachtmeiser*' in complaining about his assignment to lead the strongest army in the Ardennes. 'Conversation between Genlt. Schimpf and Gnlt. Von Rundstedt, 1 May 1945,' C.S.D.I.C.(U.K.) S.R.G.G. 1334C, U.S. First Army PWI Interrogations for 1945, NA, RG-407, 101.1- 3.2, M.L.-2125.

7 'Why Does Hitler Stay Silent? Illness, Even Death is Rumored,' *Milwaukee Journal,* 12 November 1944, p. 2.

8 'German Troops Want Assurance on Hitler,' *Washington Post,* 14 December 1944, p. 2. An unconfirmed report said three commanders on the Eastern Front demanded 'something must be done in order to convince troops that Hitler was neither dead, insane or being held captive.'

9 For details: Anthony Cave Brown, *Bodyguard of Lies*, Harper & Row, NY, 1975.

10 Declassified documents show that 'Communications intelligence gave clear warning of the German counteroffensive in the west ... The timing of the attack was revealed only on very short notice ... There were no clear indications of where on the front the attack was likely to take place, nor how big an effort it was to be.' 'Post Mortem Writings on Indications of the Ardennes Offensive, December 1944, Lt Col. Harry L. Dull, Jr., Classified Annex to USAWC Military Research Programme Paper: The ULTRA Study, 23 May 1977, Communications Intelligence (COMINT) in the Prelude to the Battle of the Bulge,' SRH-112, NA, RG-457, Records of the National Security Agency.

11 Bradley related the success of the German subterfuge in his memoirs: 'so conspicuous were these telltale signs of von Rundstedt's apparent intent to nab us astride the Roer, that we probably should have sifted them for evidence of deception. But if anyone on the Western front sniffed in those preparations an intent to mislead us on a German offensive elsewhere, he certainly did not share his suspicions with me.' Omar N. Bradley, *A Soldier's Story*, Henry Holt, NY, 1951, p. 439

12 On 22 August 1914, a series of pitched battles took place in the southern reaches of the Ardennes around Rossignol, Neaufchâteau and Bertrix. Indeed, Erwin Rommel first smelled gunpowder in the battles in wooded hills around Ethe near Virton. 'In The Ardennes Country: A Military Survey of the Battle Ground,' Incl. 2 to VII Corps G-2 Periodic Report 8, Bitter Woods Papers, *op. cit.*, Box 17.

13 Both field marshals tried futilely to get Hitler to settle for a more modest strike. Von Rundstedt crafted—*Plan Martin*—a double envelopment with a strong attack on a narrow front through the Ardennes with a second pincer to emerge from Roermond, the jaws ultimately converging on Liège to ensnare the U.S. First Army. Model's Unternehmen *Herbstnebel* "Autumn Mist" plan was even more straightforward—a sabre-like assault by 20 divisions on a 40-mile front through the Ardennes but designed to turn north just before the Meuse. Again, the quarry was the U.S. First Army, but with less ground to be covered to reach the objective. See Percy E. Schramm, 'Preparations for the German Ardennes Offensive,'NA, RG-338, Foreign Military Studies, MS # A-862.

14 Hans Kettgen communicated with Peiper in early 1976 in a detailed interview about many aspects of the war: 'I spoke to Peiper and he was cool and dry: "We must face the facts, Sepp Dietrich was a party general and even if he had some leadership qualities, they were not comparable to his rank for the time: Bernadotte and Budyonni were daredevils; Dietrich was not." To my thinking, Peiper was right.' Hans Kettgen to Richard Schulze Kossens, 20 February 1976, BA-MA, RS7/ v. 498.

15 'Special Propaganda Questionnaire: Gen. d. Inf. Günther Blumentritt,' 14 January 1951, MS B-344, NA, RG-238, Foreign Military Studies, p. 8.

16 'Ardennes Offensive, December 1944, Plans, Scope and Inquest,' SHAEF, Intelligence Party (OKL) Report No. 22, 23 July 1945, USAF HRC, Maxwell AFB, Montgomery, AL.

17 David Irving, *The Secret Diaries of Hitler's Doctor*, New York: Macmillian, 1983, pp. 200-201.

18 Speer, *op. cit.*, p. 528

19 'Three infantry divisions were to make the initial breakthrough, after which the panzer divisions were to race for the Meuse … Reconnaissance units could have gotten through a hole in the line. Once behind the three American divisions there would be nothing to stop them. By moving night and day, 80 km was the maximum expectation. I expected them to reach the Meuse by the second day if everything went fairly well.' 'An Interview with Genobst. Alfred Jodl: Ardennes Offensive,' ETHINT-51, 31 July 1945, NA, RG-238, Foreign Military Studies. The non-combat march rate of a panzer formation was approximately 150 km/day, whereas an infantry formation could march 25-30 km/day. The hilly Ardennes in winter could modify these expectations, however. Against Hitler and Jodl's opinion that the Meuse could be reached in a single day, von Mantueffel, leading *5.Panzer Armee*, reckoned it would take four days to reach the crossing. Von Manteuffel Interview, *op. cit.* One German shortcoming: their reconnaissance had not established that many of the bridges across the Meuse River, retreated across in September, had been dynamited and were no longer serviceable. This included the span at Ombret-Rawsa.

20 Mohnke had taken command of the forming panzer battalion at the end of 1941, but was replaced by Georg Schönberger at the end of 1942 and given command of the Leibstandarte's expansive Feldersatz Battalion. Later in 1944, he was given command of the *SS Panzer Grenadier Regiment 26* with the *Hitler Jugend Division*. In the press release accompanying his Knight's Cross promotion, he was credited with stopping and destroying 34 Allied tanks in the fighting around Caen. See Mohnke's BDC file. Mohnke was not well liked in the Waffen SS and had a serious problem with opium addiction. Author's interview with Ralf Tiemann 21 October 1995.

21 For Mohnke's opiate addiction: '*Dolantin-Sucht des SS Sturmbannführers Mohnke*,' 12 February 1942, NA RG 242, T-175, R108, F2631614. For Peiper's preference to have Albert Frey become the new commander of the Leibstandarte in the autumn of 1944, Letter Albert Frey to Jens Westemeier, 18 February 1994.

22 Peiper's medical file, *Achiv Deutsche Dienstestelle (WASt), Nr. II/1- 112.827*. The document shows Peiper evacuated from France on 2 August 1944, admitted to *Res. Laz Tegernsee* on 6 August 1944 and being released on 7 October 1944. For Himmler's visit to the Obersalzberg to visit Hedwig Potthast on 3 October: *The Bormann Letters*, H.R. Trevor Roper, ed., Weidenfeld & Nicolson, London, 1954. For Himmler's drive from Obersalzberg to Hitler's headquarters at *Wolfschanze* in East Prussia, see Bormann's note to his wife on 7 October 1944.

23 Toland Interview with Richard Schulze-Kossens, 6 July 1972, FDR Library, Box. 58.

24 Speidel described Dietrich as an uneducated country yokel but possessing common sense. I saw on a piece of paper where Dietrich had written to Speidel in the fall of 1944, 'With cordial greetings, Yours, Sepp Dietrich (and *not* Heiler Hitler).' 'The 20 July Putsch: Genmaj. Alexander von Pfuhlstein,' 7th Army Interrogation Center, 10 April 1945, SAIC/2, 290/56/2/4-5, Box 72. '*Mit kameradschaftlichen gruss, Ihr Sepp Dietrich (und nicht Heil Hitler).*'

25 The Allied assessment of Dietrich came from a detailed appraisal in August 1945: 'Probably no officer in the German Wehrmacht has had more abuse heaped upon him than Oberstgruppenführer Josef 'Sepp' Dietrich, former commander of the 1 SS Panzer Corps and 6 SS Panzer Army. His position as the senior military officer of the Waffen SS has made him the favorite whipping post of both the Allied press and the German General Staff … A few minutes conversation with the man explains to some extent his reputation. Physically 'Sepp' Dietrich is the antithesis of what Hitler would like to have us believe was the Aryan superman. Short, about 5' 7' tall, squat, broad, dark face dominated by a wide nose, rapidly dwindling hair, he resembled more the butcher that he started to be back in 1909 and 1910 than the general he became in 1933. Born in Memmingen, Swabia, he possesses a rich Bavarian accent that no amount of Berlin society has

been able to refine of its rough, natural tones. His vocabulary, for which he constantly apologized, is replete with down to earth words of the foxhole and the beer cellar … He is garrulous and conceited, and was eager to impress his interrogators as a soldier free from the political intrigues of National Socialism … In May 1928, he joined the National Socialist Party after an unsuccessful series of odd jobs. 'I was not a Nazi until hunger forced me to become one,' he explained.' 'Special Interrogation Report Oberstgruppenfuehrer Josef 'Sepp' Dietrich,' Canadian Military HQ, Historical Section, London, 29 August 1945, NA RG 407, E427, Box 19540, WWII OPNS Reports 1940-1948, 1st Army, 101.2.13 1945, The Adjutant General's Office.

26 Although Peiper later claimed to have driven the Panther, (e.g. ETHINT-10), this was not the case. Instead, the tank had been driven by Hans Hennecke, who affirmatively reported back to Peiper the following day. Interview with Arndt Fischer and Rolf Reiser, 15 May 1997.

27 John Toland, *Battle: The Story of the Bulge*, Random House, NY, 1959, p. 102.

28 For awareness of genocide in the wake of Hitler's armies within the Roosevelt and Churchill administration since mid-1941. See Richard Breitman, *Official Secrets*, Hill & Wang, NY, 1998.

29 W.H. Lawrence, 'Nazi Mass Killing Laid Bare in Camp,' *New York Times*, 30 August 1944. Although Lawrence described how he had doubted the veracity of some Soviet evidence of German war crimes in the past he claimed himself so shocked as 'to believe any story of German atrocities, no matter how savage, cruel and depraved.'

30 Jochen Peiper to Charles Whiting in 1969; related to author in interview in York, U.K.: August 2001.

31 'Memorandum for the President, Donovan to Roosevelt,' 20 March 1944, Office of Strategic Services, Roosevelt Safe Files, FDR Library, Hyde Park.

32 'Rumpf testimony,' *op. cit.*

33 'Handwritten testimony of Erich Rumpf,' Case 6-24, RG 549, Box 7.

34 Robin Lumsden, *Himmler's Black Order*, Sutton Ltd. Gloucestershire, 1997, p. 221.

35 Himmler to the assembled Volkssturm in Bartenstein, East Prussia on 18 October 1944, NA, RG-242, T-175, Roll 93, F 2614201—4393.

36 *The Bormann Letters*, edited by Hugh T. Roper, Weidenfeld & Nicolson, London, 1954, pp. 119-120.

37 'Report on Gebhard Himmler,' 12 June 1945, 21 AGp DIC/D/CI/18, NA: RG-407, Records of the 12th Army Group Mobile Field Interrogation Unit #4, Box 81. (290/56/2/5).

38 'What's Himmler got that Hitler hasn't?' Willi Frischauer, *Daily Herald*, 15 November 1944, London.

39 *'Heil Himmler!' Nachrichten für die Trupp*, 19 November 1944. The piece did not escape notice from Himmler's office records, NA, T-175, Roll 118, F2643381-85

40 'Heinrich H. drove to the Westwall yesterday; we are in daily communication by telephone. He is tackling his task as commander in chief of the Replacement Army with magnificent energy … Martin Bormann on 2 September 1944: H.R. Trevor Roper (ed.), *The Bormann Letters*, Weidenfeld & Nichols, London, 1954, p. 96.

41 'Certain unreliable elements seem to believe that the war will be over for those as soon as they surrender to the enemy. Against this belief, it must be pointed out that every deserter will be prosecuted and will find his just punishment. Furthermore, his ignominious behavior will entail the most severe consequences for the family. Upon examination of the circumstances, they will be summarily shot.' 'Confidential,' Reichsführer SS, 10 September 1944, captured German document, Annex No. 3 to G-2 Periodic Report No. 176, VIII Corps, NA, RG-407, U.S. First Army G-2 Records.

42 That Peiper was back at the panzer regiment HQ by 13 October is verified by his recommendation for the *posthumous* recommendation for the Knight's Cross for Josef Armberger, who had been killed in the fighting in Normandy on 20 August 1944. BDC file for Josef Armberger, NA, RG-242, SS-Officers, A3343-SSO-017. That Poetschke had been in nominal charge of the tank regiment is clear from the BDC file for Herbert Kuhlmann (NA, RG-242, SS-Officers, A3343-SSO-070) for whom Poetschke signed for his recommendation for the German Cross in Gold on 30 September 1944. Kuhlmann's recommendation came after the attack of the Panther battalion under Peiper on 18 July 1944 in which 134 British tanks were destroyed and by his later action in the desperate fighting near Chambois on 20 August 1944 in which Kuhlmann led the last of the Leibstandarte tanks to temporarily halt the American advance. Kuhlmann was handed over the command of the *SS Panzer Regiment 12* with the *Hitler Jugend Panzer Division* at the end of October 1944 when the previous commander, Obersturmbannführer Willi Hardieck was transferred to Otto Skorzeny and *Panzer Brigade 150*.

43 Even after arriving during October, Peiper left the training of the tank crews to Poetschke in Weitzendorf. The adjutant to the *I. Panzer Abt.*, Rolf Reiser, claimed to see Peiper only once there for the final live firing exercise before transferring to the west (interview on 8 January 2006). Further interviews with Timm Haasler of Günter Borchers *9. Panzer Pionier Kompanie* and Karl Wortmann with the flak panzer company reveal that they were personally welcomed by Peiper near Rahden on 27 October and early November 1944, respectively. Thanks to Timm Haasler for this information. Clearly, Peiper was at the Panzer Regiment headquarters on 1 November 1944 given his formulaic conciliatory letter to Josef 'Sepp' Armberger's father on that date as provided to author by Heinz Stutterecker. 'Please forgive me as I have been in the hospital for a long time and am just getting the opportunity to write to you …' In the Normandy fighting,

Armberger knocked out four Sherman tanks with a Panzerfaust afterwards he was killed in the heavy fighting in the area north-east of Mossey/Evreux On the 31 October 1944 he received the Knight's Cross posthumously

44 'Police Battlegroup Zimmermann: First Army PWI Report No. 5, 15/16 October 1944,' NA, 101-2.13, Box 1496. While Himmler declared that 'All eyes are on Aachen,' by 9 October, the evacuation of the city was considered complete.

45 *SS Battalion Rink* (SS Ostuf. Herbert Rink) consisted of three under-strength companies of 80-90 men each which assembled in Tornholt, Germany around 1 September and were made up of about 60% ex-Luftwaffe personnel with the remainder coming from the SS training and replacement battalion for *SS Panzer Grenadier Regiment 1. Kampfgruppe Diefenthal* (SS Hstuf. Josef Diefenthal) consisted of Rink's small battlegroup and two other companies (Schmidt, Woelky) who had joined *Kampfgruppe Diefenthal* in the fighting in September. On October 12th *Kampfgruppe Diefenthal*—bolstered by twelve 20mm flak guns and a dozen tanks from the *108 Panzer Brigade*—counterattacked the penetration of the U.S. 30th Infantry Division across the Siegfried Line near Bardenberg, only to be shunted to Aachen when the fighting there grew grim. '30th Infantry Division G-2 Periodic Report No. 117,' NA, 330-2.1, October, 1944, Box 7569. Their interrogators characterized the prisoners as 'shabby and decrepit deserters' who protested that 'Captain Diefenthal and other officers conveniently disappeared on the way and 1st Lt Rink took command in Aachen.' First Army PWI Report No. 9, 14/15 October 1944,' also, 'KG Diefenthal: First Army PWI Report,' 20/21 October 1944, NA, 101-2.13, Box 1496. 'Far from having the expected arrogant Nazi attitude, PWs were bitter against their own leaders for using them as cannon fodder … Lt Rink who never left his bunker in Aachen told his men to hold to the last and as a last resort to save a bullet for themselves.'

46 The higher chain of command: The OKW, or Oberkommando der Wehrmacht was Hitler's highest headquarters. OB West (Oberkommando West) was FM von Runstedt's headquarters in charge of all forces on the Western Front. Heeresgruppe B was FM Walter Model's Army Group B which included all forces in the Ardennes Offensive. The Sixth Panzer Army, led by Josef Dietrich, was under all these headquarters.

47 Jodl, ETHINT-50, *op. cit.*, p. 16.

48 'The city of Aachen had no particular operational importance. But it was the first German city to be assaulted and its defense to the last ought to have been a shining example for the troops, the German people and the enemy, of the ruggedness with which we would fight for our Fatherland.' Alfred Jodl, 'The Operations after the Breakthrough to Avranches, NARA, RG-338, FMS, A-927.

49 'Interview with Gen. d. Pztruppen, Hasso von Manteuffel,' 12 October 1966, Bitter Woods Collection, Box 3, John S.D. Eisenhower Papers, Eisenhower Library, Abilene, KS. When inviting von Rundstedt to meet Hitler with him on 2 December 1944 in Berlin, the aging iconoclast waved him off— 'You go,' saying arguing with Hitler was pointless. He said he would be sending his chief of staff to save them both. Of Genflm. Model, von Mantueffel said, 'He was personally brave, driving and a good General Staff officer, but during the Ardennes he drove everyone frantic "bending the bow until it broke."'

50 Von Rundstedt quotes: Günther von Blumentritt, *Von Rundstedt*, Odhams Press, London, 1952, pp. 268-269. 'It was a nonsensical operation, and the most stupid part of it was the setting of Antwerp as its target. If we reached the Meuse we should have got down on our knees and thanked God—let alone try to reach Antwerp.' 'Special Interrogation Report Field Marshal Karl Rudolf Gerd von Rundstedt,' 1 February 1946, NA, RG-407, 7th Army Interrogation Center, Box 1954P. Also, B.H. Liddell Hart, *The German Generals Talk*, Quill, NY, 1948, pp. 276-277.

51 Charles von Lüttichau, *Interview with Thuisko von Metzsch on Operations of Army Group B and its Role in the German Ardennes Offensive, 1944*, MS R-10, OCMH, Washington D.C. May 1952.

52 Jodl, ETHINT-50, *op. cit.*, p. 7.

53 For Skorzeny's oft-described meeting with Hitler, I used several sources to triangulate the dialogue: Most important was John Toland's revealing interview with Skorzeny on 28 September 1957, Toland Papers *Battle: The Story of the Bulge*, LOC, Box 8. I also consulted secondary sources: Otto Skorzeny, *Skorzeny's Secret Missions*, E.P. Dutton, NY, 1950, p. 219-235; Charles Foley, *Commando Extraordinary*, G.P. Putnam & Sons, NY, 1955, p. 114-116. Otto Skorzeny, *My Commando Operations*, Schiffer Press, Atglen, PA, 1995, pp. 326-328.

54 See 'An Interview with Otto Skorzeny,' 12 August 1945, ETHINT-12, NA, RG-238, Foreign Military Studies. When Skorzeny was dismissed, he was further briefed by Genobst. Alfred Jodl and told that he should attempt to locate uniforms and truck himself. Skorzeny announced amazement at the thousands of tanks, guns and jet planes that would be available. But Jodl lowered the expectation when he told Skorzeny that 2,000 planes might be available, but no more than 140 of these would be jets.

55 In fact, the notice did reach Allied intelligence, but was so preposterous that it was initially discounted as a propaganda ploy. Yet, continuing reports kept the intelligence on the Allied radar screen. In its daily periodic intelligence reports, the U.S. First Army on 2 December mentioned the captured of an order dated 30 October 1944 calling for 'English speaking units in the German Army' and another dated 7 October which noted that Otto Skorzeny had set up a school at Friedenthal near Oranienburg looking for English speakers 'with an American dialect.' G-2 Records, U.S. First Army, NA, RG-407, 101-2.2.

56 John Toland's interview with Otto Skorzeny, *op. cit.*

57 'IPW Report 105,' IPW Team 46, 23 December 1944, G-2 Records: 30th Infantry Division,' NA, RG-407, 330-2.2, Box 7594.

58 'German Preparation for the Bulge: Observed from the Other Side,' *The Bulge Bugle*, August, 2010, p.12. 'We knew it wasn't a social call or trying to be nice, but they seemed to make it just that.'

59 NA, RG-338, Records of the MIS 6824 Detailed Interrogation Center, Consolidated Interrogation Report, 6824 DIC (MIS) M. 1033, 12 Feb. 1945, Box 90.

60 Skorzeny used an English teacher, Obtl. Lothar Stielau, to help evaluate the 400-500 English speaking volunteers. In particular, they were looking for 'Category One' types with a good command of English, an American accent and a working knowledge of slang. 'After a fortnight … we found ourselves faced with a frightful result.' The first category—mostly sailors—numbered only ten men. The second category was made up of men who spoke more or less fluently, numbered 30-40, but many displayed heavy English accents. The third category who could 'make themselves understood' had about 150 odd men. The category 4 volunteers 'lads who had not completely forgotten what they learned at school' totalled 200 and the vast remainder could simply say 'yes and no.' Skorzeny, *Skorzeny's Secret Missions, op. cit.*, pp. 228-229. Equipment and uniforms remained a problem too; only 34 jeeps and two Sherman tanks had been obtained by 21 November and one of the Shermans developed transmission problems and had to be left behind.

61 'Division strength on 3 December 1944 was 18,430 which wasn't what it should be (22,000) Worse, the tank drivers only had about 4 hours driving experience on average and the crews had spent three weeks cleaning up bombed out cities rather than training.' Rudi Lehmann to Hubert Meyer, 10 May 1979, BA-MA, RS7, v. 509.

62 Rudolf Lehmann, 'I SS Panzer Corps: 15 October—16 December 1944,' NA, RG-338, Foreign Military Studies, MS B-577.

63 Interview with Werner Ackermann, 22 December 2010. Also, similar input from Manfred Thorn who was with Panzer 734 in the *7. Kompanie*.

64 'Unlike, the movie,' Ackermann told the author, 'there was no foot stomping!'

65 '*Komm zurück zu mir, Ich warte auf Dich.*' Schumann had played piano from childhood and frequently serenaded anyone who would listen in Russia. Interview with Horst Schumann, 8 March 2006. Later Schumann and Helmut Jahn, being radio experts from Peiper's command tank were reluctantly reassigned by their leader. 'I am recruiting a special radio company for the Reichsführer SS that will be in the Black Forest,' Peiper told Jahn, 'so I will send you there.' He then turned to Schumann, 'I recommend that you try to disappear in Nuremberg.' He told Schumann he had a small parting gift. From the regimental commander's small personal field library, Peiper handed Schumann a book, *Herr Heinrich,* a popular history of King Heinrich the First by Fritz Vater (Ehler Verlag, Berlin, 1941). 'This book will be good for you,' Peiper told him without further explanation. It was on Himmler's old recommended list—a book on the king who his former boss saw as his previous incarnation. (See 'Interrogation of Gottlob Berger,'30 October 1947, NA, RG-238, M1019/R6/666.) Schumann went to leadership school in Nuremberg, while Jahn was assigned to the radio unit for special tasks for Heinrich Himmler in the Black Forest.

66 *Tagebuch von Benoni Junker*, 1—11 September 1944, Courtesy Timm Haasler. Junker had started out the war as an SS officer in 1940 as a member of *Totenkopf Regiment 3*. Later he fought in Russian with *SS Division Nord* and then later transferred to *SS Panzer Regiment 1* in 1943. BDC file for Benoni Junker.

67 Interview with Werner Ackermann, 13 March 2010. 'There were really bad ones like 'Machen' Preuss and Poetschke; they were really bad. They had a really bad reputation. Junker could not be compared to them. He was really very human whereas they were awful. Preuss especially was always proud of his losses. 'Look, we have lost twenty more!' There were really some bad ones in the Leibstandarte, but we were new [recruits] and surprised.'

68 *Tagebuch von Benoni Junker*, 21 March—27 November 1944, Also, interview with Karl Paul Fröhlich, 20 March 1996.

69 Himmler: 'We really need to waste no words on the subject of alcohol … With the hundreds of thousands of men we're losing in the war, we can't afford to lose still more men though addiction to alcohol and self-destruction … Leaders who allow their subordinates to hold drinking parties in their companies will be punished.' Himmler's infamous speech to SS men at Posen, Poland on 4 October 1943, IMT, *op. cit.*, PS-1919. The speech is also reproduced in Bradley F. Smith, Agnes F. Petersen (eds.), *Heinrich Himmler. Geheimreden 1933—1945,* Propyläen Verlag, Frankfurt am Main, 1974

70 Author's interview with Reinhold Kyriss, 20 May 1997. The *Himmelfahrtskommando* was considered a 'journey to heaven mission'—high risk at best. Peiper used them as punishment for the actions of his officers whom he considered in need of discipline.

71 There were varied reasons for those finding themselves on the punishment platoon. While Sternebeck and Asmussen were clearly there for excessive drinking and fist fights, August Wien was punished due to disappearing from his command (*5. Panzerkompanie*) during the Normandy Campaign on 12 August 1944 and then arriving without explanation to the *6. Panzerkompanie* in the fall of 1944. Gerhard Stiller via Walter Schüle to Mike Smeets, 23 September 2002.

72 Interrogation of SS Rttf. Guenther Boese, 1st Panzer Battalion, 1st SS Panzer Regiment,' First U.S. Army PW Combat Team, 23 January 1945, NA, RG-153, Case 6-24, Box 73. Peiper: 'Not the best *Menschenmaterial*.' Staatsanwaltschaft Flensburg 2 Js 437/56 AR 491/66. Now on file at Bundesarchiv Ludwigsburg 124 AR 491/1966.

73 One captured prisoners of war from the *II.Battalion, 2.SS Panzergrenadier Regiment* of the Leibstandarte commented that in the fall of 1944 'The LAH is no longer an elite unit that it was before its commitment in Russia. The men are no longer specially selected; since January 1943 not only volunteers are to be found in their ranks, but draftees as well. There is also a considerable number of former Luftwaffe men in the division. Nevertheless, the morale is very high and relations between officers and enlisted men is excellent. The officers always accompany their men, regardless of the danger involved in a mission and the casualty rate among them is very high.' U.S. III Corps, G-2 Periodic Reports, 'Daily IPW Report No. 16,' Annex No. 2 to G-2 Periodic Report No. 24, 1 January, 1945, NA, RG-407, 203-2.1.

Chapter 2 – A Forest Dark

1 'Interrogation of SS Mann Quack of *10 Kp, 2.SS Pz Gr Regt*,' U.S. First Army PWI Report No. 6, 21 December 1944, NA, RG-407, 101.1- 3.2, M.L.-2125, Box 1497. According to Quack the tactic was first successfully attempted in training on 10 December 1944.

2 'The Attack Orders of the Three Armies Taking Part in the Ardennes Offensive,' Percy E. Schramm, Appendix 2. 'Preparations for the German Ardennes Offensive,' NA, RG-338, FMS, MS # A-862. Schramm took the attack orders from surviving parts of the OKW War Diary for the period. The German original is Percy Ernst Schramm, *Kriegstagebuch des Oberkommandos der Wehrmacht*, Bernard & Graefe Verlag, Frankfurt am Main, 1961, Band IV.

3 Charles von Luttichau, *The Ardennes Offensive: Progressive Build up and Operations*, OCMH, Research Section, November 1952.

4 Tabulation taken from the original records: NA, RG-242, T-311, Roll 18, Frames 210020-25, Field tank strengths taken from 'Schw. Waffen Pz. Division, 10.12.1944' as supplemented by *OB West* maps for the period: eg. Bundesarchiv.RH 2 W/608 for 17 December 1944. Artillery strength for *1.SS Panzer Division* was 30 Field Howitzer 18/40, 18, s. field howitzer 18 and 4 10-cm cannon, although a few self-propelled artillery pieces showed up later.

5 'Häschen, I want to send to you with the letter my little Christmas presents for your children. Helge may have fun with the little shopping bag. My little kids happily carry rolls or butter home in one. For Nanette, the doll actually is not yet a toy. But I wanted to see, if I could make such a doll. You will recognize in the *dirndl* the leftover material from shortening my own *dirndl* and recall some of the nice time we had together in Tegernsee. Maybe Helge will like the doll and will dress and undress it with just as much eagerness and enthusiasm as Hini. It is just too bad, that we cannot telephone at least on the 24th. We both, again, shall light up the Christmas tree for the children without Papi. My thoughts shall be with you and yours heartily' Letter Sigurd Peiper to Hedwig Potthast, 11 December 1944, *NSDAP Hauptarchiv*, Himmler Collection, Microfilm Roll #99, Hoover Institution, Stanford University.

6 Franz W. Seidler and Dieter Zeigert, *Hitler's Secret Headquarters*, Greenhill Books, London, 2004, pp. 188-197. Also R. Raiber, 'Guide to Hitler's Headquarters,' *After the Battle*, No. 19, 1977.

7 Martin Bormann to Gerda Bormann, 11.12 1944, H.R. Trevor Roper (ed.), *The Bormann Letters*, Weidenfeld & Nicholsen, 1954, p. 148. 'I have asked for Bühler to come here, otherwise the vegetable supplies for the Chief are sure to be in the same mess as my communications apparatus.'

8 The conversion work for Ziegenberg castle was fantastically expensive in labor, expense and concrete—38,000 cubic meters. For camouflage, Dr Todt had planted 2,000 trees, 33,000 shrubs and seeded hundreds of acres of lawns with the farmhouses prominently displayed for aerial eyes while the blockhouses and bunkers were hidden with sod or netting. When first built in 1939, Hitler was displeased, saying he wouldn't stay in a place that suggested he was a '*pferdeliebenden Adeligen*'—a horse-loving nobleman. Yet, in December 1944, it appeared the logical place. Joining Hitler soon after the offensive opened, Himmler would make his accommodations in *Schloss Kransberg* some five kilometres to the north. Seidler and Zeigert, *op. cit.*, pp. 46-57.

9 RG 338, Records of the MIS 6824 Detailed Interrogation Center, Boxes 88-92, MIS/Y X/156: 20 March 1945 Viebig was not inspired by the infantry he had been assigned. Jokes were making the officers' rounds that the Volksgrenadier might as well be called the '*Metalsturm*: lead bones, gold teeth and silver hair.'

10 'An Interview with Obstgrf. Sepp Dietrich: Sixth Pz Army in the Ardennes Offensive,' 8-9 August 1945, ETHINT-15, NA, RG-238, Foreign Military Studies, p. 6. In the interview Dietrich claimed not to have known where the attack would be or of the particulars of the plan. This was clearly in error as Dietrich had held a closely supervised map exercise the week before.

11 Shulman's interview with Dietrich in September 1945: Milton Shulman, *Defeat in the West*, E.P. Dutton, NY, 1948, p. 229.

12 Author's interview with Hinrich Springer, 19 May 1997.

13 *'Auch ein schlechter Ruf hat seine Verpflichtungen'*. Also, a bad reputation has its commitments.' Rumpf, NA RG 549, Box 7 and Box 32. That Peiper indeed used this as his unit's motto is verified by his own letter to Häschen Potthast in March 1943: 'We have become known beyond the borders of our division because of our successes and because of our persistence and enduring matter-of-factness. But even a bad reputation has its obligations— (I freely quote Zarah Leander) Our reputation precedes us as a wave of terror and is one of our best weapons. Even old Genghis Khan would gladly have hired us as assistants'. Letter from Jochen Peiper to Hedwig Potthast, 24 March 1943, *NSDAP Hauptarchiv*, Himmler Collection, Microfilm Roll #99, Hoover Institution, Stanford University. *'Aber auch ein schlechter Ruf verpflichtet*—But a bad reputation has its obligations'—Peiper reveals that his favorite wartime motto was taken from Nazi wartime cinematic diva Zarah Leander. The lyric comes from the song 'Yes Sir!' from the film *'zu neuen Ufern.'* According to Zwigart, Peiper would shoot his prisoners with a clear conscience.

14 Rumpf, *op. cit.*, NA RG 549, Case 6-24, Box 32.

15 'Interrogation of Preuss,' no date, NA, RG-549, Case 6-24, Box 31, p. 14.

16 'LSSAH,' BA-MA, RS/4/1270. The concentration of the various elements of Kampfgruppe Peiper is detailed on Maps ?

17 Wortmann memories, *op. cit.*

18 Peiper testimony, 21 June 1946, *U.S. vs. Valentin Bersin,* Case 6-24, RG 153, R3, p. 1903.

19 Other key *Kampfgruppen* panzer leaders in the Waffen SS divisions: *12.SS (Hitler Jugend)*: Stubaf. Herbert Kuhlmann, *9.SS (Hohenstaufen)*: Stubaf. Eberhard Telkamp and *2.SS (Das Reich)* Stubaf. Ernst-August Krag. Each commanded a *Kampfgruppe* with their given name.

20 Toland interview with Otto Skorzeny, 28 September 1957, John Toland Papers Battle: *The Story of the Bulge,* LOC, Box 8. Skorzeny complained personally to Hitler about this deficiency with the result that a few of the available Arado 234 jet reconnaissance aircraft of *Kommando Sperling* were earmarked to snap photos of the bridges for Skorzeny on 3 December 1944. Danny Parker, *To Win the Winter Sky,* Combined Books, Conshohocken, PA, 1994, p. 123.

21 Statement of Joachim Peiper to Ralph Shumacker, 21 March 1946. NARA, Case 6-24, RG-549, Box 6.

22 U.S. vs. Bersin, *op. cit.*, pp. 1903-1904. 'After that, the 1A talked to me about the attack by means of a map and then gave me the entire orders.' Question from the Court: 'Did he explain to you what he meant by fighting fanatically?' Peiper: 'He did not especially explain that, but what the expression meant was no concern for one's person and material and unconditional preparedness.'

23 'When I was received on 14 December by Division Commander, Oberführer Mohnke, he told me he was present at the meeting with the Führer and that on his orders, it had to be fought with special brutality … It has to be fought without humane inhibitions and one should remember the victims of the bombing terror.' Statement of Joachim Peiper, 21 March 1946, RG-549, Case 6-24, Box 6.

24 Affidavit of Oskar Klingelhöfer, 18 March 1946, NA, Case 6-24, RG-549, Box 6.

25 Statement of Friedrich Christ, 17 December 1945, NA, Case 6-24, RG-549, Box 6.

26 Regarding the differences with 1940: 'And there was the third dimension—the enemy air force.' Interview with Peiper from 1971 provided by Hans Kettgen to Harvey T. Rowe and then to author, p. 6 of transcript.

27 *Rollbahn D,* which was assigned to Peiper by Fritz Krämer, was unpaved for a stretch west of Honsfeld to Schoppen and also between Pont (2 km south-west of Ligneuville) and Logbierme (3 km south-east of Wanne). The road was exceedingly narrow for a number of stretches and any sections which had been used by the Americans for supply that fall would be only useful for one-way traffic as the snow cover would be packed and narrow.

28 Peiper, ETHINT-10, *op. cit.*, p. 7.

29 Peiper statement at the Malmedy trial, Case 6-24, p. 1905.

30 *U.S. v. Bersin, op. cit.*, pp. 1906–1908.

31 A captured German document revealed the magnitude of the gasoline problem for the tank regiment. On good roads, a panzer grenadier battalion like the SPW-equipped *III. Battalion/SS Pz-Gr. Rgt 2,* under Jupp Diefenthal would require 8,500 liters of fuel to move 100 kilometers. In rough terrain, like that in the Ardennes, that number rose to14,000 liters. However, the panzer's fuel requirement was quite another matter. A full-sized battalion of 76 Mk IV tanks and its supply column would require 27,000 liters of gasoline to move 100 km on good roads and 53,000 liters in rough terrain. However, the heavier Panthers and Tigers were a more severe logistic burden. A Mk V battalion with 76 tanks would require 48,000 liters on good roads and 76,000 liters in rough terrain. And, for only 45 Tigers in a Mk VI b battalion, the numbers were 39,000 liters on good roads and 71,000 liters on roads in rough terrain. Peiper's Mk IV and Mk V elements made up only about a single equivalent battalion of about 70 vehicles in a mixed battalion, but he also had a full-strength Tiger battalion and several other elements that needed fuel to move: an artillery battalion, a self-propelled flak company of flak tanks, two engineer companies on SPWs and an Army flak battalion. Thus fuel requirements for *Kampfgruppe Peiper* remained a daunting issue—likely at least 200,000 liters to move the battlegroup 100 km forward. NA, RG-407, G-2 Periodic Report No. 196, VIII Corps, 30 December 1944, 208-2.1, Box 3965.

32 Statement of Sepp Dietrich to Ralph Shumacker, 22 March 1946, NARA, Case 6-24, RG-549, Box 33.

33 Charles Whiting interview with Otto Skorzeny, as cited in *Jochen Peiper*, Leo Cooper, South Yorkshire, 1999, p. 48.

34 Statement of Hermann Priess to Morris Ellowitz, 16 April 1946, NARA, Case 6-24, RG-549, Box 6. 'The part of the speech of the Führer in which he occupied himself with terror methods, was.' Terror is to be met with terror. Any resistance is to be broken ruthlessly. The Führer did not explain what he meant by terror. I interpreted the phase referring to terror as meaning that the enemy air attacks on the civilian population would be avenged.'

35 Statement of Rudolf Sauer, 15 May 1946, NARA, Case 6-24, RG-549, Box 25. Original German statement in Box 9; Sauer's claim was never rescinded.

36 U.S. v. Bersin, *op. cit.*, p. 1909.

37 Skorzeny, ETHINT-12, *op. cit.*, p. 10.

38 Statements of SS Einheit Grabowski, NA, RG-338, Records of the MIS 6824 Detailed Interrogation Center, Consolidated Interrogation Report, 6824 DIC (MIS) M. 1033, 12 Feb. 1945, Box 90.

39 U.S. v. Bersin, *op. cit.*, p. 1912.

40 U.S. v. Bersin, *op. cit.*, p. 1910.

41 'Löhman Statement re: main Malmedy Incident,' POW enclosure D-104, RG 338, Records of U.S. Army Commands, Records of HQ U.S. Army Europe (USAREUR), Index to Defendants in the Malmedy Case (6-24), Reference Witness Statements, 290/59/18/5. Another separate statement taken in an entirely different POW cage (E-67) came from one SS Rottenführer Karl Nohr, a crew member in the tank of Roman Clotten. 'On the evening of 15 December 1944, the platoons of the *7.Kompanie* were lined up in a wooded area for orientation. Siptrott addressed the entire platoon, telling them, among other things, that they should fight in the old SS tradition, keeping in mind the thousands of civilians who had died back home during the bomber attacks, and for that reason, to fight ruthlessly taking no prisoners of war.' To be fair, Siptrott vehemently denied these allegations in an interview with the author. On that occasion, Nohr's statement was read. Siptrott's response: 'I deny that completely.' Did he speak to his men the night before the attack?' 'Yes I did, but speaking quite normally.' Interview with Hans Siptrott, 17 May 1997.

42 Interview with Reinhold Kyriss, 20 May 1997.

43 In the Schwabisch Hall statement of Arndt Fischer on 31 March 1946, he wrote that during the briefing of company commanders at Blankenheim on the 15th of December 'Stubaf. Poetschke spoke about that we should not take any prisoners where the military situation absolutely required it. Poetschke also declared that this was a secret order.' At his trial, Peiper denied that any such discussion ever took place, nor that there was a separate regimental order: U.S. v. Bersin, *op. cit.*, pp. 1913-1915. Fischer would later denounce his Schwabisch Hall statement, both at Landsberg and personally to the author in an interview on 15 May 1997. However, Fischer's liaison officer, SS Ustuf. Kurt Kramm, was at the same meeting and contradicted Fischer's later denials in several statements. After the war, Kramm was considered a turncoat by the other old SS veterans who rebuffed his attempts at contact. Rolf Reiser, who worked diligently for decades to exonerate the Leibstandarte, made early denials as to the existence of such orders. 'That a verbal or written order concerning the shooting of American POWs during the offensive in December 1944, through officers of the Panzer Regiment or 1st Panzer Division has been ordered, it is not known to me at all. I never received such an order nor heard anything about it.' Statement of Rolf Roland Reiser, 3 January 1946, NA, RG-549, Case 6-24, Box 37.

44 Fischer's original 9-page handwritten statement (including a detailed sketch of the layout of the Forester's house in Blankenheim) (are you sure? Mike Smeets gave me a copy of that sketch, and it is signed by Hans Gruhle (Peiper's original adjudant) with its transcription and translation is in NA, RG-549, Case 6-24, Box 9. For statements agreeing with Fischer's original mention of the 'secret' order that prisoners be shot when conditions warranted, see statements of Kurt Kramm, Friedrich Christ, Oskar Klingelhöfer – you need to pick a spelling – either -hoefer (umlaut), or -höfer. It appears both ways throughout the manuscript, Benoni Junker and 2nd Lt Hans Buchheim. In particular, Kramm's courtroom statements to that effect at the trial were never repudiated. 'We will fight in the same manner as we did in Russian in the action that will follow,' he recalled Peiper saying, 'The certain rules that have applied in the West until now will be omitted.' Kramm's testimony is U.S. v. Bersin, pp. 186-222.

45 Peiper: *'De kommende Einsatz wäre die letze Chance den Krieg zu gewinnen. Win ein Sturmwind müssten wir angriefen. Der Feind muesse eine wahnsinnige Angst vor der SS bekommen. Dies sie unsere Verpflichtung.'* 'Handwritten statement of Hans Hennecke, 13 March 1946, NA, RG-549, Case 6-24, Box 36.

46 Testimony of Hans Hennecke on 11 December 1945 to Dwight Fanton, NA, RG-549, Case 6-24, Box 23.

47 *'Auf Kriegsgefangene legen wir keinen Wert!'*—Georg Bunda was the gunner with Panther 231 in Christ's company. 'Interrogation Notes #1,' Interrogations of defendants or other SS men held at Dachau by the defense team in April and May 1946, Willis Everett Archives, courtesy James Weingartner. In screening results done prior to Schwäbisch Hall, Stm. Hans Hübler and Karl Daub, in Pz. 225, claimed that 'Christ told his men to fight a ruthless fight and conduct themselves in such a way as to spread terror among the American troops and made it clear that prisoners of war would not be taken.' Screening Results 10–19 December 1945, IC#78, Ellis Papers.

48 Statement of Gerhard Nueske, 31 January 1948, NA, RG-549, Case 6-24, Box 51.

49 'The word *impossible*', speech of Himmler to *SS Oberabschnitt* commanders on 17 July 1942. Krausnick and Bucheim, *op. cit.*, p. 329. For 'hopeless operation' Jochen Peiper to Charles Whiting in 1969 interview.

50 We had no hope, but were determined to perform our duty to the bitter end. '*Wir hatten keine Hoffnung, waren aber dennoch entschlossen bis zum bitteren Ende unsere Pflicht zu tun.*' Peiper, '*Kommentar zum Buch 'Massacre at Malmedy,*' *op. cit.*, p. 2.

51 Not all these heavy tanks were operational, however. According to panzer man, Werner Wendt, no more than 30-35 of the Tigers were combat ready on December 16th: Author's interview with Werner Wendt, 21 May 1996. This agrees well with the period Heeresgruppe B situation maps which show 30 operational Tigers on 19 December with 8 in short-term repair. There was also a remarkable rate of mechanical breakdown of the heavy tanks on the hilly and mired Ardennes roads so that the number seen at the front was lower still. Horst Stumpf, 'Tank Maintenance: Ardennes,' 11 August 1945, NA, RG-238, Foreign Military Studies, ETHINT-61.

52 'A German Report on the Engagement in the Ardennes Offensive Involving SS Tank Detachment 501,' by Werner Wendt, prepared for *The Pekan*, publication of the 526th Armored Infantry Battalion WWII, Vol. 12, No. 1, March 1992. Born in 1921, Wendt had been on the Russian front since July 1941, serving as a gunner in the fighting on 6 March 1943 in which as gunner of a Tiger I, he personally destroyed 17 Russian tanks in fierce battalion before his own tank was destroyed.

53 Interrogation of Gefr. Alfred Franz, 2100 21 December 1944, NA, RG-407, 30th Infantry Division G-2 Records, 330-2.2, Box 7593. Franz had been with the Panzer Division Gross Deutschland on the Eastern Front, only to be pulled out on 9 November and sent to Grafenwöhr to join *Panzer Brigade 150* under Otto Skorzeny due to his knowledge of English. In November during their special training, he and his other paratroopers were addressed by Gen. [sic] Skorzeny 'emphasizing the coming operation as deciding the war.' Just before the Ardennes assault, Franz reported that he and the other 130 men of his company were addressed by his commander, 1st. Lt Brewko who told him and the others 'not to take any prisoners.' Separated from the rest of Skorzeny troup, they would ride the tanks of an attacking *Panzergruppe*. In addition to standard firearms, each squad had one light machine gun, and approximately five Panzerfauste. The infantry element of *Panzer Brigade 150* would include *II Battalion, 12 FJ Regt. zBV* as organized into *Kampfgruppe Schaefer* (1st–6th Kompanien) and *Kampfgruppe Schluckebier* (7-12 Kompanien). *KG Schluckebier* was to make the breakthrough in German uniforms after which *KG Schaefer* was to follow and exploit the breakthrough in American uniforms to fan out and seize bridgeheads over the Meuse River. As envisioned *Operation Greif* would advance over the following roads: a) Trois-Ponts-Basse Bodeux–Villettes–Bra–La Fourche–Haaren–Deux Reys–Roche–a Freus; b) Petit Thier–Ville de Bois–Vielsalm–Salmchateau–Hebronval–Regne–Manhay–Mormont–Roche a Frene; c) Aisne–Juzaine–Domal–Tchigne–Oneux–Amas–Ocquier– Vervoz. 'Annex No, 3 to G-2 Periodic Report 182, VIII Corps,' 21 December 1944, NA, RG-407, VIII Corps, G-2 Records, 208–2.1

54 Although the *1.SS Panzer Division* showed only a single self-propelled Wespe artillery on its organization chart on 3 December 1944, just before the attack (BA-MA, RH 10/312) it received some additional panzer artillery that were committed in support of *Kampfgruppe Peiper*. See Jean Paul Pallud, *Ardennes 1944: Peiper and Skorzeny*, Osprey, London, 1987, p. 61-62. According to Tiemann, the self-propelled elements were assigned at the 1st battalion which had a '*gepanzert*' designation. Tiemann, *op. cit.*, Vol. IV/2, p. 22 and p. 76. The self-propelled guns were in the 1st and 3rd batteries: '1 SS Pz Artillery Regiment: Third U.S. Army: G-2 Periodic Report No. 218,' 15 January 1945, NA, RG-405, 103.2.1.

55 Eberhard Kosch *Betr. Ardennen Offensive: Aufstellungs und Vorbereitungszeit*, prepared by Kosch for Toland, Schriesheim, Baden, Library of Congress, John Toland Papers, Battle of the Bulge, Box 37.

56 'Interview with Trautgott Schmidt, 1st SS Panzer Division,' 18 October 1982, Charles B. MacDonald Papers, Folder: 1st SS Panzer Division, USAMHI, Carlisle, PA.

57 Interview of Charles MacDonald with Karl Wortmann, 16 October 1982, Charles B. MacDonald Papers, U.S. Army Military History Institute, Carlilse, PA.

58 Statement of Anton Motzheim, 28 February 1946, NA, RG-549, Case 6-24, Box 8.

59 Statement of Herbert Stock, 9 April 1946, NA, RG-549, Case 6-24, Box 7. Original handwritten statement in same box. 'I know that the term '*Rabatz*' is used in the fight by SS soldiers and means that everybody is free to have as much fun as he wants in shooting at everything—at property, civilians and prisoners of war.' However, this term could have various interpretations depending on context. In an interview with Werner Ackermann on 22 December 2010, the former Leibstandarte veteran indicated the term could mean big trouble and chaos. However, it could also mean to 'clean the enemy out.'

Chapter 3 – The Secret

1 For ULTRA decrypts on German plans on troop strength and equipment levels: PRO: DEFE 3, (Defense Ministry) HP 3935, 3971 and 4086, Kew, London.

2 'It was my memory that the appearance of men and equipment of these panzer divisions in the Ardennes opposite the VIII Corps was lightly dismissed by the weekly SHAEF G-2 summaries … I had noted for

some time an attitude of disparaging the German forces, referred to as ulcer battalions, etc. Some American G-2s at lower levels seemed to have become infected with this comic opera type of description in an effort to be witty.' Gen. William K. Harrison to John Toland, 30 April 1958, John Toland Papers: *Battle: The Story of the Bulge*, Box 35.

3 On the receiving end were Obtl. Horst Götz (*Kommando Sperling*) and Lt Erich Sommer (*Kommando Hecht*). The later made the first jet reconnaissance mission of the war on 2 August 1944 snapping a panoramic display of the American and British landings at Normandy from 35,000 feet, without the Allies even being aware of their existence. In late November 1944 the job of photographing the Meuse crossing became an unavoidable priority: 'Constant bad weather in the target area as well as over our airfields prevent the execution of the job for over a week,' remembered Sommer, 'Finally, in the early morning hours of 3 December, a radio message arrived directly from *Luftwaffen Kommando West* ordering the reconnoitering of the Maas river crossings between Dinant and Liège at whatever the cost.' [Smith and Creek, p. 158] Later in the afternoon, Oblt. Werner Muffey from *Kommando Sperling* was able to take some suitable photographs in spite of a 3,300 ft cloud base.

4 'Sunset Daily Intelligence Reports: December 1944—January 1945, Sunset 779, Part I, Signaled on 17 December 1944,' NA, RG-457, SRS-1869, Records of the National Security Agency.

5 'Records of the Combined Services Interrogations Center,' U.S. 12th Army Group, NA, RG-165, Entry 179, Box 749.

6 'G-2 Periodic Report No. 175: U.S. VIII Corps,' 9 December 1944, NA, RG-407, VIII Corps, G-2 Records, 208—2.1. In fairness to the G-2s, in the same summary reported the bulk of the Leibstandarte was in the area east of Düren (Weiler).

7 U.S. First Army PWI Report No. 4, 13 December 1944, NA, RG-407, 101.1—3.2, M.L.-2125, Box 1497.

8 'V Corps Artillery G-2 Unit Journal,' 16 December 1944, NA, RG-407, Entry 427, 205-ART-2.2, Box 3047.

9 'G-3 War Room Journal: December 15, 1944,' 21st Army Group briefing at 2315, SHAEF War Diary for December, NA, RG-331, Entry 58, Box 23.

10 Maj. Gen. Sir Kenneth Strong, *Intelligence at the Top*, Cassel, London, 1968, p. 211. Said Eisenhower's G-3, Maj. Gen. Harold R. Bull: 'In the back of our minds was the thought: No Goddamned fool would do it. It would certainly be their dying gasp. Strong became steadily more worried over the radio silence … We did not think they would come out in the open,' Charles MacDonald Papers, USMHI, Box 6.

11 Dickson: 'Military intelligence is largely a gambling game. Fashioned of cold logic based on knowledge of military commanders and their habits, plus bits and pieces of information from good and bad sources … Some seem to regard G-2 as a crystal ball department, although it is no more so than well-paid and respected scouting systems in baseball and football. Neither, I might point out, can predict absolutely what the opposition is up to.' 'We wouldn't be Warned in the Bulge,' By Col. B.A. Dickson and Ivan H. Peterman, John Toland Papers, Box 36.

12 John Eisenhower interview with Col. Benjamin A. Dickson, 1 November 1966, Bitter Woods Papers, Box 1; Also letter Ivan H. 'Cy' Peterman to John Eisenhower, 7 November 1966, Box 3.

13 'The Nazi party in Belgium … with the members of the SS Wallonia, now believed still active with the German armed forces, are the major threat as regards to sabotage and espionage.' 'G-2 Estimate No. 25: Counterintelligence in Belgium,' Col. B.A. Dickson, U.S. First Army, 11 September 1944, NA, RG-407, 301-2.2, G-2 Records of the 1st Infantry Division, Box 5058.

14 Interview regarding wartime Spa with historian Guy Lebeau, Stavelot, 19 October 1995.

15 'My intended function was to receive and evaluate the Ultra produced by the specialists at Bletchley Park, who then radioed the material deemed pertinent to First Army's present and future operations to the special liaison unit or SLU, attached to its headquarters. This unit, composed of English personnel, used the 'one time pad' and wrote out Ultra on slips of paper which had to be destroyed within 24 hours. Supposedly, I would discuss the material with the G-2, Col. Benjamin A. Dickson, in the light of our other intelligence and with him brief First Army's highest echelon on its import at least once a day. Ultra because of its high classification was not disseminated below the level of field army. Ordinarily, each morning, Colonel Dickson would personally brief the top echelon on the total of our intelligence product.' Adolf G. Rosengarten, Jr. 'With Ultra From Omaha Beach to Weimar, Germany—A Personal View,' *Military Affairs*, Vol. 42, No. 3, October, 1978, pp. 127-133. Rosengarten had been with the ULTRA section with U.S. First Army since March 1944.

16 Bradley's G-2, Brig. Gen.Edwin Sibert, described these shortcomings well: 'Many of the things we learned in training in the dark days of '42 and '43 were discarded too readily in the flush of victory in the summer and fall of '44 … In December '44 it was the old story of overconfidence all up and down the line.' Letter to John Toland, 1 Feb. 1958, Toland Papers, LOC, Battle, Box 36.

17 Author's interview with John S.D. Eisenhower, 3 January 1997. 'Col. Dickson was something of an opportunist and would rush to signal the Commanding General without proper evaluation … I suggest that if one has little confidence in the messenger, one is not likely to give full credence to the message.' Rosengarten letter 4 June 1982 to Charles MacDonald, Charles B. MacDonald Papers, USMHI, Box 6.

18 'Summary of Enemy Movements: Headquarters U.S. First Army, Report No. 10,' 11 December 1944, NA, U.S. First Army, 1.01-3.3, Box 1529. 'The prisoners identified the men as belonging to the Division LAH by their armbands. PW s stated that they did not talk to them because of the unfriendly relationship between the Army and the SS.'

19 'G-2 Estimate No. 37, 10 December 1944,' Headquarters First U.S. Army, Eisenhower Papers, Bitter Woods, Box 3. This was Monk Dickson's famous Estimate No. 37.

20 The full interrogation of Elise Delé is in U.S. First Army, G-2 Records, NA, 101-2.2, Box 1874. The story is covered in dramatic detail in MacDonald, *op. cit.*, p. 11-14.

21 'Interview with Col. Benjamin A. Dickson,' 1 November 1966, John S.D. Eisenhower, Bitter Woods, Box 1. Also in the First U.S. Army (FUSA) briefing room were Lt Gen. Charles E. Hart (artillery officer), Maj. Gen. Robert W. Wilson (G-4 in charge of logistics) and Brig. Gen. William B. Kean (his chief of staff). Dickson pointed out that although the First Army G-3, Brig. Gen. Truman C. 'Tubby' Thorson down-played his warning, others of the special staff took special note of Estimate 37. For instance, Col. Andrew T. McNamara, the FUSA quartermaster halted the movement east of more gasoline from the depots west of the Meuse and Col. John B. Medaris and Col. William R. Amspacher likewise suspended further forward movement of ammunition and medical facilities, respectively. This story is essentially repeated in another account by Dickson, 'We wouldn't be Warned in the Bulge,' By Col. B.A. Dickson and Ivan H. Peterman, 1949, John Toland Papers, Box 36.

22 Toland Interview with Peter C. Haines III, no date, Toland Papers, LOC, Battle, Box 36. 'A few days before the Bulge I chatted with Col. Monk Dickson—several of us were there just after supper. He pointed out that his analysis of the German dispositions gave him a pessimistic view. He and G3 were in reverse positions. I kept the situation map with respect to armor. [Capt. William] Cox and I, a few days before the Bulge, were at the map arguing where the Germans would make an attack. We argued. Cox said it was the Ardennes.'

23 Dickson's exclamatory 'It's the Ardennes!' at Hodges headquarters was verified by First Army correspondent, Cy Peterman in a letter to John Eisenhower, 7 November 1966, Bitter Woods Papers, Box 3. Peterman was with the *Philadelphia Inquirer*. See also, 'The G-2 Battle of the Bulge,'Benjamin Dickson, John Toland Papers, *Battle: The Story of the Bulge*, Box 36. However, in his interview with John Toland on 15 July 1957, Hodges claimed Dickson never made his concern clear: 'Anyone who said they anticipated a big blow never told us.' Toland Papers, LOC, Battle, Box 36.

24 Charles B. MacDonald, *A Time for Trumpets*, Morrow, NY, 1985, p. 56.

25 Forrest C. Pogue, *The Supreme Command*, OCMH, U.S. GPO, Washington D.C., 1954, pp. 369-371.

26 For background on the District of Columbia when the Ardennes fighting broke: *The Washington Post*, December 13–18th 1944.

27 'Replacements Dearth Plagues Eisenhower,' *Washington Post*, 16 December 1944, p. 1.

28 It was important to understand 'what education has done to the German youth.' Eleanor Roosevelt, 'My Day: Columns from 1944,' 16 December 1944. Eleanor Roosevelt Papers Project.

29 'Actually, the only inaccurate element in the Russian's story was the date of the attack. It took place on the 16th and not the 17th.' Gen. William K. Harrison to John Toland, 30 April 1958, John Toland Papers: *Battle: The Story of the Bulge*, Box 35. Harrison claimed that the interrogation of the prisoner had also been witnessed by another young officer in the 106th Division who was serving in the medical battalion.

30 'Consolidated Interrogation Report, Annex 1 to G-2 Periodic Report No. 182, HQ VIII Corps, 16 December 1944, NA, RG-407, U.S. First Army G-2 Records, deserted to Roth, Belgium on 15 December 1944, 5 Co., 295th VGR, 18 VG Division. The prisoner revealed that the coming big attack would be supported by a new secret weapon which consisted of a shell that would 'freeze' the vicinity which it detonated.

31 'It is now certain that attrition is steadily sapping the strength of German forces on the Western Front and that the crust of the defense is thinner, more brittle and more vulnerable than it appears on our G-2 maps.': 'Weekly Intelligence Summary No. 18 for Week Ending 9 December 1944,' 12 December 1944, Headquarters 12th Army Group, SHAEF War Diaries, NA, RG-331, Entry 176, Box 40.

32 Edwin Sibert to John Toland, 1 February 1958, John Toland Papers, *Battle: The Story of the Bulge*, LOC, Box 36.

33 '612th Tank Destroyer Battalion, Action Against Enemy, Reports After Action,' 4 January 1945, NA, RG-407, TDBN-612-0.3.

34 The 612th had trained on self-propelled M-10 tank destroyers stateside. But after transferring to Europe they learned in early 1944 that they would soon convert to being a towed TD gun outfit. 'We didn't like it,' remembered, William Littlejohn with Company B of the battalion. Nor did any of the nine others of his crew. 'I was a driver on the M-10 crew and a halftrack driver with the towed guns.' The M-10 crew was five men, whereas ten were needed on the towed version. Interview with William Littlejohn, 11 March 1996.

35 Interview with Francis C. Hayes, Company B, 612 TD Battalion, 18 February 1996.

36 Interview Will C.C. Cavanagh with Wilhelm Osterhold, *Checkerboard*, publication of the 99th Infantry Division, March-April 1991.

37 Account of Oberschutze Schwarzmüller, *Der Soldat*, December 2004.

38 Gerhard Engel, *Heeresadjutant bei Hitler 1938-1943: Die Aufzeichnungen des Major Engel*, Hildegard Kotze (ed.), Stuttgart, 1974, p. 97. Engel would be severely wounded in the Ardennes fighting on 29 December 1944. In his memoirs, Engel said nothing about Peiper, but had plenty negative to relate about his days with Hitler. Having read Albert Speer's *Inside the Third Reich* in 1975, Peiper saw Engel as another 'historical opportunist.' A more appropriate title for the army adjutant's book, Peiper related to friend Fritz Kosmehl, might be 'A Spy in Hitler's Court.' Peiper to Kosmehl, 17 December 1975.

39 'An Interview with Obst. Joachim Peiper,' 7 September 1945, NA, RG-338, Foreign Military Studies, ETHINT-10, p. 10.

40 Stephen M. Rusiecki, *The Key to the Bulge: The Battle for Losheimergraben*, Praeger Pub., Westport, CT, 1996, pp. 18-19.

41 Warlimont, *op. cit.*, p. 485.

42 'Ob.Kdo. H. Gru. B, Ia Nr 0270/44 g.Kdos.Chefs. vom 15.12.44,' BA RH 19 4 /84.

43 'Life at the moment is beastly. Even the miserable little walk I took today has left me stiff and sore, because it's the first exercise I've had in years ... If only peace would come! If this war continues much longer all my hair and teeth will fall out and I shall become a real poor old gaffer!' H.R. Trevor Roper, *The Bormann Letters*, Weidenfeld & Nichols, London, 1954, pp. 148-149.

44 For Hitler's schedule on 15 December 1944: the chronology kept by his man-servant, Heinz Linge. NA, RG 242, T-84, Roll 22. Linge Diaries. For 'great emotional crisis.' David Irving, *The Secret Diaries of Hitler's Doctor*, Macmillian, NY, 1983, p. 204-205. For Himmler's schedule, '*Termine des Reichsführer SS am 14-16.12.1944*,' NA RG 242, T-175, Roll 112, 2637613-16. Himmler returned to Sonderzug Steiermark at Eppstein on the evening of 15 December. He spoke to Hitler at 4.30 PM on 14 December and at 5 PM on 15 December before the attack.

45 '*sondern such den Beginn eines neuen Abschnitts den ganzen Westfeldzuges*.' 'OKW/WFSt/Op.(H) West, Tagesmeldung vom vom 15.12.1944,' BA-MA, RH 19/IV/ 76.

46 'Heinz Windenhayn. 4 Co, SS Pz Gren Regt, 1. SS Pz Div LAH,' First Army PWI Report, No. 8, 17/18 December 1944, NA, U.S. First Army, G-2 PW Interrogations, 101-2.13, Box 1497.

47 The order was signed by Dietrich. Tiemann, *op. cit.*, Vol. IV/2, p. 27.

48 'First Army PWI Report: From the Bulge to the Rhine, Diary of Feldwebel Karl Laun,' 11/12 March 1945, NA, RG-338, U.S. First Army Interrogation Reports, ETO-MIS-Y, Box 64. (290/56/2/3).

49 According to SS enlisted man Ackermann, the crew members of Panzer IV Nr. 635 were SS Uscha. Heinz Phillip (commander), Sturmmann Albert Braun (gunner), Reinert (loader), Georg Köhler (Radioman) and Werner Ackermann (driver).

50 Author's interview with Werner Ackermann, 13 March 2010. Follow up interviews on 8 August and 22 December conducted by Ann Shields.

51 'Wien was a real fanatical type too ... He lost his life quickly after the start of the attack in the Ardennes when a shell tore off his head. Wien and Sternebeck were like each other.'

52 Ackermann's interview with author on 13 March 2010 as verified in followup interview on 8 August 2010.

53 'Statement of Werner Ackermann, Panzer Number 635,' 4 January 1946, NA, RG-549, Case 6-24, Box 36. 'During that time, the men had lit a fire where I stood.'

54 'Tonk was a really nice person and he was not one of the rowdies' that Ackermann kept running across in the Leibstandarte.

55 Interview with Hans Siptrott, 15 July 2012.

56 Clemency plea of Hans Siptrott, 12 July 1946, U.S. v. Bersin, *op. cit.*, p.3238-39. Peiper's recommendation for Siptrott's German Cross in Gold is found in Siptrott's BDC file and is dated 30 December 1944, but signed by Peiper the preceding October 20th.

57 Interview with Hans Siptrott, 17 May 1997. Klingelhöfer was not well liked. 'He was one of the most conceited officers. During the time he belonged to the division staff, he did not consider it necessary to shake hands with younger officers.' Handwritten statement of Erich Rumpf, NA, RG-549, 'Rumpf's Description of Personalities,' Case 6-24, Box 32.

58 Interview with Hans Siptrott, 23 November 2007. Courtesy Mike Smeets. Fleps participation with the *7. Kompanie* in Normandy is described in his own testimony where he indicated he had witnessed a Canadian prisoner executed by SS Uscha. Rolf Erhardt and Rttf. Wesenberg. Statement of Georg Fleps to A. Salomons, 6 March 1946, PRO WO/309/256, Kew. Fleps also recounted his military career in the post-trial pleas for leniency although his claim of only 75 days of combat was exaggerated. U.S. v. Bersin, *op. cit.* pp. 3215-3216. For Fleps as a rough character and not being well liked: interviews of Timm Haasler with Werner Ackermann of *6. Panzer Kompanie*, 22 February and 9 March 2005. In those interviews, Ackermann mentioned that Fleps was involved in nearly killing a comrade in a POW camp in the summer of 1945 before he was brought to Schwäbisch Hall.

59 For Peiper's poor health on the eve of the offensive: interview with Gerhard Walla with the staff company of I.*Panzer Battalion*, May 2005. Interview courtesy of Mike Smeets. 'Peiper was a wreck' said Walla, who

indicated that command of the forward spearhead unit was handled primarily at the beginning by Werner Poetschke.

60 'An Interview with Obst. Joachim Peiper: 1 SS Pz Regt,' 7 September 1945, NA, RG-338, Foreign Military Studies, ETHINT-10, p. 9. 'If our own infantry had broken through by 0700 as originally planned, my answer is yes, I think we might have reached the Meuse in one day.'

61 *'Auf Wiedersehen in Amerika und gute Überfahrt!'* Story of Eberhard Kosch from 16-page MS (*Betr. Ardennen Offensive: Aufstellungs und Vorbereitungszeit,* prepared by Kosch for Toland, Schriesheim, Baden, no date, Library of Congress, John Toland Papers, Battle of the Bulge, Box 37.

Chapter 4 – Wacht am Rhein

1 Max Schneckenburger, *The Watch on the Rhine, Stanza* 4.

2 'An Interview with Obst. Joachim Peiper,' 7 September 1945, NA, RG-338, Foreign Military Studies, ETHINT-10 What would he do differently? 'Have no artillery preparation and keep the horse-drawn artillery from clogging the roads … Attack with combat teams and tanks at the same time as infantry. An unsupported infantry attack wastes too much time.'

3 'Report by Rolf Ehrhardt, 7. Panzer Kompanie, 1. Panzer Regiment, LSSAH, Ardennes Offensive,' Copy provided to author by Wolf Mauder, translation by Helmut Thiess.

4 PW Max Denisch of *SS Panzer Regiment 12,* captured near Krinkelt, Belgium on 18 December 1944 who reported to his interrogators that 'hopeful and certain we went into battle.' He also quoted Hugo Kraas, the *Hitler Jugend* panzer division commander: 'We'll throw the Allies out of France and victory will soon be ours.' NA, RG 407, First U.S. Army, G-2 Journal, 101-2.13 POW Interrogations,' Box 1952. He also said that Kraas had told them that 'I ask and expect you not to take any prisoners with the possible exception of officers, who might be kept alive for the purposes of questioning.'

5 Testimony of SS Sturmmann Oskar Mauer, Malmédy Massacre Trial, pp. 2160-2175. Mauer was gunner in SS Ustuf. Helmut Koch's Panther #231. For other rumors of thousands of planes and secret weapons, testimony of SS man Heinz Conrad, *ibid, p. 341.*

6 Interview with Werner Wendt, 21 May 1996. 'Our training and experience was still pretty good. Our replacements were not bad and there were still a lot of veterans. And for the replacements, we always had the pick of the crop, even for the lower level people.'

7 Arndt Fischer's personnel data: NA, RG-242, BDC Files, Waffen SS Officer, A3343-SSO-208. Also statement of Fischer 31 March 1946, NA, RG-549, Case 6-24, Box 6. One can only imagine what Fischer saw at the concentration camps from 1939.

8 'This must be understood in understanding his behavior.' Interview with Arndt Fischer, 15 May 1997.

9 For Peiper's displeasure with Gruhle: interview with Arndt Fischer, *ibid.*

10 Interview with Fischer, *op. cit.: 'We* had known about the operation for a time. Two weeks before we went to Blankenheim in the Euskirchen front and every day we had a sand-box exercise. We knew the area and all the company commanders were present. The sand box replicated the area up to the Meuse River. The first part of the model was rendered in great detail. During the division headquarters discussion, we were told who was marching in what direction and Peiper learned which units would go on various march routes. Skorzeny troops were supposed to pass our tanks and then take the bridges ahead. We tried no alternatives, but repeated the exercise several times.'

11 In Normandy, the Allies had learned to plaster any German tanks with turret command designations with plenty of gun fire to paralyze enemy command. To confound such efforts, after escaping the hell of Falaise, Werner Poetschke decided that lettering like '001 or 002' would not be used. His personal *I. Battalion* command Panther would be designated '151' and his adjutant's (SS Ustuf. Arndt Fischer) would be '152.' This worked fine as Kremser's *1. Panzer Kompanie* had no 5th platoon. Thanks to Timm Haasler for this information.

12 Interview with Rolf Reiser, 15 May 1997.

13 Statement of Anton Motzheim, 28 February 1946, NA, RG-549, Case 6-24, Box 9 (both handwritten and transcribed and translated statement).

14 'The [commando] unit was provided with 80 soldiers with good language proficiency, and out of that they made up two groups. Group 1: A pure sabotage group consisting of 8 jeeps of which 3 jeeps were directly under his [Skorzeny's] control during the offensive. Group 2 consisted of six Jeeps and was a commando/reconnaissance group with radio equipment. They divided themselves into two groups—a 'short distance team' with 4 jeeps, and a "long distance team" with 2 jeeps. The short range team came back intact after almost two days. And what happened to the long range team? In front of me lays an issue of *Life* [magazine]. A brutal photo essay shows the shooting of three German spies. One of these was a personal friend of mine.' Anonymous member of Skorzeny commando team from Wilhelmshaven, *Der Spiegel, 'Brie*fe, Panzerbrigade 150' 10 January 1951. Depending on source, the number of jeep teams varied from 14 to 29.

15 'The 150 linguists were formed into a unit named 'Einheit Stielau' taken from 1st Lt Stielau, the company commander,' 'Order of Battle Notes period ending 222200 December 1944,' G-2 Records, 30th Infantry Division, NA, RG-407, 3330-2.2, Box 7594. Oblt. Lothar Stielau was an English high school teacher at the *Oberschule zum Dom* from Lübeck, an early Hitler Youth leader and in autumn 1944 was in charge of the 'English speaker's group'or *Einheit Stielau* for Otto Skorzeny at Grafenwöhr. In 1945, Stielau received the Army Honor Roll clasp for his service as a linguistics trainer with SS *Jagdverbände/Sondertruppen der RFSS* as part of *Kampfgruppe Solar* in the Ardennes (Solar was the codename for Skorzeny). Born in 1908, Stielau had joined the NSDAP and the SA in 1932 and ten years after the war joined the *Deutsche Reichspartei* as its chairman in Lübeck. In a weird post war episode, it would be Lothar Stielau, in 1958 who questioned the authenticity of the Anne Frank diaries and was then sued by Otto Frank the following year. Stielau lost his job, but remained active in right-wing circles in the 1960s with the likes of Hans Ulrich Rudel, Hans Venatier and Otto Remer, See 'Was schrieb das Kind?' *Der Spiegel, 14/1959,* 1 April 1959 and also: 'Rechts ab zum Vaterland,' *Der Spiegel, 18/1967,* 24 April 1967.

16 In spite of many attempts to discredit such a theory, the possibility that Skorzeny intended to assassinate Eisenhower cannot be completely dismissed. An interrogated *Einheit Stielau* commando told of having been sent to an SS interpreter's school at Berlin-Oranienburg with thirty others in October where he learned that a special Fifth Column was to precede a new offensive in the west with various missions, but also 'kidnapper gangs were to capture high ranking officers.' 'IPW Report 105,' IPW Team 46, 23 December 1944, G-2 Records: 30th Infantry Division,' NA, RG-407, 330-2.2, Box 7594. Still another interrogation by First U.S. Army of a different commando revealed claims for a specific plan to capture or kill Eisenhower, 'IPW Report No. 193,'20 December 1944, FUSA G-2 Reports, NA, RG-407, 101-2.2. Research compendium completed for the author, 'Panzer Brigade 150,' by Timm Haasler.

17 Account of Heinz Rohde; Jean Paul Pallud, *The Battle of the Bulge: Then and Now, After* the Battle, London, 1984, p. 112. Also, *Der Spiegel, 'Mit* Shakespeare -Englisch,' 10 January 1951.

18 Composition of Werner Sternebeck's Spitze consisted of two Panthers, five Panzer Mk IVs and two SPWs and supporting engineers of *9.Pi.Kp.* under SS-Oscha. Rudolf Dörr.
—SS-Obstuf. Werner Sternebeck (Spitze commander), Mk IV (#614)
—SS-Uscha. Hans-Jürgen Bahrend (*1.Pz.Kp.*),(#113), Panther
—SS-Uscha. Valentin Bersin (*1. Pz Kp*: #122), Panther
—SS-Oscha. August Wien (*6.Pz.Kp:* #631), Mk.IV (KIA in Büllingen)
—SS-Ustuf. Karl-Heinz Asmussen (*6.Pz.Kp.*: #612), Mk.IV
—SS Hscha. August Tonk (*6.Pz.Kp.*: #623), Mk.IV
—SS-Schaf. Horst Rempel (*7.Pz.Kp.*: #725), Mk.IV (KIA in Büllingen)
—2 SPW from *9.Pi.Kp./SS-Pz.Reg. 1*: one under SS-Uscha. Erich Held and the other under SS-Rttf. Wemmel.

Immediately behind the Sternebeck's Spitze came the vanguard *10.SS Panzergrenadier Kompanie* under SS Hstuf. Georg Preuss. Next were Oskar Klingelhöfer's *7.Pz.Kp.,* in Mk. IVs as part of the main body of *Kampfgruppe Peiper.* This included *1st SS Pz. Kp, 11th Pz Gr Kp, 6 Pz Kp, 9 Pz Pi Co., 7th Pz Kp., AA Kp of Rgt, 3 Pz Pi Kp, 2 Pz Kp, 13th PzGr Kp, the SS s. Pz Bn 501,* then *84. AA Bn* of the Luftwaffe.

19 *Rollbahn E* to the south of Peiper would be used by the advance of by *Kampfgruppe Hansen* and the reinforced *SS Panzer Grenadier Regiment 1,* with the reconnaissance battalion—*Kampfgruppe Knittel*—advancing freely on the available roadway net from his rear. So limiting was the road network that *Kampfgruppe Sandig* and *SS Panzer Grenadier Regiment 2* would advance in echelon behind Peiper's lead on *Rollbahn D,* and well to the rear.

20 With the good fields of fire on the Roer River plan on 17-18 November 1944, the Königstigers of *Heavy Panzer Battalion 506* destroyed more than three dozen Sherman tanks of the U.S. 2nd Armored Division near the village of Puffendorf. See Charles B. MacDonald, *The Siegfried Line Campaign, OCMH,* Washington D.C., 1963, pp. 530-533.

21 In the Hollywood cinematic epic on the *Battle of the Bulge,* Colonel Martin Hessler, a highly fictionalized Peiper (portrayed by Robert Shaw), is delighted to command a brigade of Tiger tanks. The real Jochen Peiper was less enamored with ownership of a battalion, knowing that the ponderous steel behemoths excelled in the long range tank gunnery contests on the open plains of Russia, but not in the closed terrain of the Ardennes. They also burned twice as much fuel a kilometer as did the Mk IVs. 'The Tigers were far to the rear in my column,' Peiper made clear. '*Kommentar zum Buch 'Massacre at Malmédy von Charles Whiting,'* p. 5, September 1971. Copy from Ernst Klink and provided by James Weingartner.

22 ETHINT-10, *op. cit., p. 9.*

23 Handwritten statement of Erich Rumpf, NA, RG-549, 'Description of Personalities,' Case 6-24, Box 32.

24 Interview with Reinhold Kyriss, 20 May 1997.

25 Interview with Werner Ackermann, 13 March 2010. 'Sternebeck liked to lead the attack. I can't imagine he didn't want to. He was a fanatic like Wien and was totally crazy to get the Knight's Cross.'

26 'I received company punishment for six weeks from the regimental commander (Peiper). The *Spitzen* platoon was in a sad situation. For punishment, I was assigned to the point as a messenger so I could

risk my life.' Interview with Gerhard Walla, *Stabskompanie, I. Panzer Abteilung, 1.Panzer Regiment,* 10 May 1999, Anspach, Bad Württemberg. Walla would not tell the author the 'minor infraction' that had led to his assignment.

27 'Statement of SS Rottenführer Guenther Boese, 1st SS Panzer Battalion,' 23 January 1945, NA, RG-153, Case 6-24, Box 73. Rumor had it that Bersin was guilty of numerous transgressions which got him in trouble with Peiper. 'The SS always had its strict code of honor, and murder and especially rape (which was also *Rassenschende*) would be severely punished.'

28 Interview with Reinhold Kyriss, 7. Panzerkompanie, 20 May 1997. 'Peiper punished trivialities sternly.'

29 The crew of Sternebeck's Nr. 614 included the star-crossed first gunner, SS Rttf. Roland F. Messner who described the first day of the offensive in the trial of Otto Skorzeny: 'Testimony of Roland F. Messner,' 22 August 1947, U.S. v. Otto Skorzeny et al., NA, RG-549, Case 6-100, Box 77. The driver was SS Rttf. Heine with Hscha. Georg Spaeter, the former commander moving to the position of loader. During the eventual trial of the Malmédy men, Messner would serve as a 'spy' for the prosecution. Sternebeck had just been married the month before.

30 ETHINT-10, pp. 10-11.

31 Testimony of Joachim Peiper, 25 August 1947, U.S. v. Otto Skorzeny, NA, RG-549, Case 6-100, Box 79.

32 'Commitment of the I SS Panzer Corps During the Ardennes Offensive,' Hermann Priess, NA, RG-338, Foreign Military Studies, MS # A-877, p. 6.

33 As briefed by SS Ostuf. Hardieck, Peiper was told that the tanks of Skorzeny's Panzer Brigade 150 were to point their guns to the nine o'clock position and leave them there throughout the initial advance. All commando soldiers were to take off their steel helmets and all the vehicles were marked with small yellow triangles on the rear. For a much more complete description, see Michael Shadewitz, *The Meuse First and then Antwerp, J.J.* Fedorowicz Pub., Winnipeg, 1999.

34 Testimony of Joachim Peiper, 25 August 1947, U.S. v. Otto Skorzeny, NA, RG-549, Case 6-100, Box 79. 'The *Kampfgruppe Hardieck,* as long as it was attached to my combat group … was to wear German uniforms to avoid any misunderstanding. Later on, if they succeeded in getting ahead of me in the direction of the enemy, they were to wear American uniforms.'

35 For the need to preserve the panzer divisions for the advance to the Meuse and beyond: Priess, MS A-877, *op. cit., p. 7.* When asked what he would have done differently in designing opening assault of the Ardennes offensive, Peiper was clear: Besides instituting a speedier method of supplying gasoline, he would insist on no artillery preparation and an attack with infantry on tanks at the beginning of the assault. 'An unsupported infantry attack wastes too much time.' ETHINT-10, *op. cit., p.* 24.

36 ETHINT-10, *op. cit., p. 13.* Peiper to U.S. Army Interviewer Ken Hechler: 'Your 99th Infantry Division put up very light resistance. In fact, the resistance was so light that it was a pity to have wasted so much artillery on them.'

37 See Charles B. MacDonald, 'The Neglected Ardennes,' *Military Review,* April 1963. Also, 'In the Ardennes Country: A Military Survey of the Battleground,' Incl. 2 to VII Corps G-2 Periodic Report 8, *Bitter Woods Papers, Abile*ne, KS, Box 17.

38 Said one prisoner: 'As much as I formerly believed in Almighty God, so do I now believe in German victory within three months.' 'In memoriam of 3 Para Division,' 12/13 Dec 44, First Army Special Report, NA, RG-407, 101.1- 3.2, M.L.-2125, Box 1497.

39 *Ibid,* 'The typical PW from this division [now] is not the cocky kind described above [from Normandy]. Rather he is a slight, self-conscious, disillusioned sort of fellow with little self-confidence and barely any security mindedness.'

40 Strength: Tagesstarke, 1.12.44, 3 FJ Division, Combat losses and experience in battle leading up to the Ardennes taken from *LXXXI Armeekorps,* T-314, Roll 1589. 'Personnel and Equipment of 3rd Parachute Div,' NARA. It should be noted that the division was in serious fighting north of the Ardennes at Merode-Lucherberg (4-6 December) and near Obergeich as late as 10 December such that it 5th Regiment would need emergency replacement before commitment to the Ardennes. McDonald, *Siegfried Line Campaign, op. cit.,* 509-510 and 583-586.

41 The German 3rd Parachute (3rd Fs.Jg.) Division had the following units available on 16 December (III./5 Rgt and III./8 Rgt. did not join the division until after 19 December). Roppelt, *op. cit.* and Nikolaus Thomas, *Von der Front,* Grenz-Echo-Verlage, Eupen, 1995.

—Krewinkel-Afst area: I./ and II./Fs.Jg.Rgt. 5 supported by elements of II./Fs.Jg.Rgt.8 which only had the three companies (5, 7 and 8) in platoon strength.

—Hergersberg area: I./Fs. Jg.Rgt. 8

—Losheim- Hüllscheid-Merlscheid: I./Fs. Jg. Rgt. 9 in the lead (11 officers and 513 NCO and enlisted men (EM), followed by II.Fs.Jg.Rgt. 9 (13 officers and 457 NCO & EM and III/Fs.Jg. Rgt. in reserve (9 officers, 389 NCO & EM.

42 Fritz Roppelt, *Der Vergangenheit auf der Spur: 3. Fallsch. Jg. Division,'* Hössbach b. Aschaffenburg, 1993. According to Roppelt, the 3. Pioneer Battalion and 3. Panzerjäger Battalion were both poorly trained

and without sufficient heavy weapons. According the commander of the 9. FJ Rgt, 'only the 1st Battalion, trained by Obstlt Schenk zu Schweinsberg was fit for combat.'

43 'We heard of the beginning of the Rundstedt Offensive and so we were all in a good mood. Forward again after many backstrokes and the depressing withdrawal from France.' Leonardt Maniura, 'Impression Report on the Campaign in the Ardennes in 1944/45,' Charles B. MacDonald Papers, U.S. Army Military History Institute, Carlisle Barracks, PA, Box: German Army and Paratroops, *3rd Fallschirmjäger Division*, translation by Dieter Kopac, 1983.

44 Walter Wittlinger to Richard Byers, 2 December 1985. Letter provided to author by Byers.

45 Timm Haasler interview with Vincent Kuhlbach, 29-30 September 2002. Also Rudi Frühbeißer, *Opfergang deutscher Fallschirmjäger Normandie—Ardennen, Nuremberg*, 1966. While Frühbeißer's chronicle of the regiment was an accurate well-researched document, the same cannot be said for a later book, '*im Rücken der Amerikaner,*' which German paratrooper and American veterans alike characterized as 'pure fiction.'

46 '*Kriegstagebuch Ob.West, Anlagen Befehle und Meldungen vom 11.12-20.12.1944,*' BA-MA, RH 19 IV/84 D, Ia Nr. 10697/44 geheim. Von Rundstedt's message closed with: 'May you feel inside yourselves the sacred obligation to give your all and to perform superhuman feats for our Fatherland and the Führer!'

47 Hans Zeplien, *Beginning of the Battle of the Bulge*, former commander of the 14th AT Kompanie of Grenadier Regiment 89, Charles B. MacDonald Papers, 12th Volksgrenadier Division, Carlisle Barracks, PA.

48 Fischer interview, *op. cit., Also* interview with Fischer, 1 December 2006, courtesy Timm Haasler.

49 'No doubt, the artillery fire at other places on the front was heavy, but never reached the intensity announced.' 'Report by Rolf Ehrhardt, 7. Panzer Kompanie, 1. Panzer Regiment, LSSAH, Ardennes Offensive, 16 Dec. to 18 Dec. 1944,' Copy from Ralf Tiemann, translation by Helmut Thiess.

50 Interview with Reinhold Kyriss, 20 May 1997.

51 Interview of Mathias Heinzius by Nikolaus Thomas, Igelmonderhof/Manderfeld, 5 January 1997.

52 Interview of Matthias Goenen by Jean Philippe Speder, 15 February 2003. 'We stopped and talked. Everybody was wondering what was going on and what we should do. Coming from Lanzerath, several American vehicles appeared, passed by and stopped some 200 meters past the crossroad. Soldiers removed a machine gun from one of the trucks and entered a small patch of forest. There was also a small tank in the column which stopped further down the road to Lanzerath. Some of the soldiers came to us and told us to leave. All of a sudden a lone shell exploded on the road. The Americans flew towards the forest and no more trucks were to be seen. We civilians, dashed to a nearby house and sought cover. From where we were I could see the road leading to our village and coming towards us there was a group of German paratroopers. Just as they were reaching the crossroads, shells began to rain and big explosions shook the house. The Germans opened fire. I could hear the noise of their machine guns. They were firing at the Americans we had seen. We were definitely at the wrong place and I was scared to death. Bullets were now ripping holes in the walls and big chunks of the ceiling were fall. Girls and children were crying and several people were wounded. The fight finally died down. … As we emerged from the dust and smoke, the German column was already on the move toward Lanzerath. We found ourselves on the German side … The sensible thing was to go back to Merlscheid and that's what we did.'

53 Maj. Günther Holz, 'Panzerjäger 12 in the Battle of the Bulge,'*Alte Kameraden*, 1972, Charles B. MacDonald Papers, U.S. Army Military History Institute, Carlisle, PA. 'At first everything seemed to go ahead without major difficulties. There was hardly any enemy resistance. The devastation caused by the drumfire inhibited our advance, but represented no real obstacle … Where we had assumed a defeated enemy, we found neither dead nor wounded soldiers, only empty and shattered positions … Only after the forest had been reached at dawn … they found strongly fortified and occupied American positions. Each pillbox meant severe fighting and the advanced slowed down.'

54 'The artillery's preparatory fire lasting half an hour reached the foremost enemy strongpoints and positions as well as that of the … presumed gun positions in the rear and road crossings, approach routes, villages, woods and other points where it was presumed that troops had gathered … I myself did not think very much of this artillery preparation and I already told OB West and the chief of staff of the 6. Panzer Army. The proposal I made … in the evening of 15 December … was to the effect to postpone the beginning of the offensive until the break of dawn to be able to effect a short preliminary adjustment of fire with a few roving guns to effect observed firing … This proposal was rejected.' Walter Staudinger, 'Artillery Leadership and Artillery Assignment during the Course of the Ardennes Offensive,' MS B-759; also 'The Artillery Command of the 6 Panzer Army During the Ardennes Offensive, 1944-45,' MS B-347; and 'Sixth Panzer Army Artillery in the Ardennes Offensive,' ETHINT-62: All NA, RG-338, Foreign Military Studies.

55 For perspectives on Gen. Gerow, interview with John Eisenhower, 3 January 1997.

56 'The German Breakthrough,' Combat Interview by F.C. Pogue and J.M. Topete, 3rd Battalion, 394th Infantry, CL-184, USAMHI, Carlisle Barracks, PA.

57 'Der Deutsche Fallschirmjäger.' 1964, p. 8-9. 'The 9th Paratroop Regiment in their Offensive against the Americans,' Charles B. MacDonald Papers, U.S. Army Military History Institute, Carlisle, PA.

58 Between 24 November and 16 December 1944, some 1,091 V-1 'Buzz Bombs' were launched towards Liège, Brussels and Antwerp over the U.S. V Corps in the Ardennes from locations in Germany within the zone of operations of the German *6. Panzer Armee*—Hollerath, Berk, Basem, Hallschlag, Stadtkyll and Birget. The closest locations were only one to three miles from the front lines of the U.S. 99th Division in the Ardennes: 'Buzz Bomb Alley,' Dick Byers, *The Checkerboard, Febru*ary 1992.

59 'The I SS Panzer Corps During the Ardennes Offensive,' Rudolf Lehmann, NA, RG-338, Foreign Military Studies, MS # B-779, 1954, p. 20.

60 The point platoon *Spitze* was commanded by Werner Sternebeck as punishment for indiscretions in the autumn of 1944. Some said he had also exhibited cowardly behavior in Russia. See 'Affidavit of Kurt Dethlefs,'21 March 1946, NA, RG-549, Case 6-24, Box 39. Note that other the members of Sternebeck's Spitze were also being punished. Asmussen, Tonk, Wien and Rempel were dedicated drinking buddies with Benoni Junker (see Junker's diary entries for summer 1944) and Sternebeck and Asmussen had smashed up a tavern in the earlier fall. Further, Wien had disappeared from command when things got hot in Normandy and Bersin was known to everyone in the tank regiment, even the regimental commander, as an incorrigible rowdy. 'Bersin was a soldier who always got himself into trouble and got locked up during the times between battles,' Peiper commented to U.S. Army interrogators, 'However, he was known as a very brave soldier.' RG-549, Records of U.S. Army Commands, Records of USAREUR, 'Index to Defendants in the Malmédy Case (No. 6-24) Reference Witness Statements,' Card for Valentin Bersin, 290/59/18/5.

61 Michael Shadewitz, *The Meuse First and then Antwerp, J.J.* Fedorowicz Pub., Winnipeg, 1999, p. 85.

62 Zeplien MS, *op. cit.*

63 Otto Skorzeny, *Wir kämpften—wir verloren*, Helmut Cramer Verlag, Königswinter, 1975, p. 293.

64 John Toland Interview with Otto Skorzeny, November 1963, John Toland Papers, LOC, The Last Hundred Days, Box 8.

65 *Ibid*, Skorzeny to Hitler 'I must put this condition on our commitment, because we are so badly equipped and trained.'

66 Otto Skorzeny, *Meine Kommandounternehmen: Krieg ohne Fronten,* Wiesbaden: Limes, 1976, 272. Also: An Interview with Lt Col. Otto Skorzeny, Commanding Officer for Operation 'Grief', 'Battle of the Ardennes,' U.S. Army, Robert E. Merriam, Oberursel, 12 August 1945, Eisenhower Presidential Library.

Chapter 5 – Rollbahn D

1 'An Interview with Obst. Joachim Peiper,' ETHINT-10, NA, RG 338, 7 September 1945, 7.

2 The story of Nick Matchnick, from Cavanagh, *op. cit.*, p. 94.

3 Rusiecki interview with Osterhold, Rusiecki, *op. cit.*, p. 28.

4 Cavanagh, *op. cit.*, p. 81.

5 Cavanagh, *op. cit.*, p. 94.

6 Peiper specifically clarified this question with his American interrogators in September 1945: 'Obst. Peiper has stated that his regiment's route lay from Scheid to Losheim to Losheimergraben to Hünningen and Honsfeld ... The map also shows the northern route of 1 SS Pz Div as springing from Lanzerath, but Obst. Peiper states that this route was taken only after the Losheim—Losheimergraben route proved to be unusable because of resistance and the blown bridge.' 'An Interview with Obst. Joachim Peiper: 1 SS Pz Regt.,' 18 September 1945, ETHINT-11, NA, RG-338, Foreign Military Studies, p. 1.

7 'March routes did not have to be rigidly adhered to. Each division had express permission to deviate from prescribed routes whenever the situation demanded—such as weak spots in the enemy positions etc.' 'Commitment of the I SS Panzer Corps During the Ardennes Offensive,' Hermann Priess, NA, RG-338, Foreign Military Studies, MS # A-877, p. 12.

8 ETHINT-11, p. 2.

9 Peiper's War, *op. cit.*, p. 333-337.

10 In a letter to Mike Smeets (8 February 2006), Waffen SS veteran Ulrich Felden remarked that he was not too keen on the leadership of Herbert Kuhlmann in 1944, saying the commander of *SS Panzer Regiment 12* 'lacked the necessary elan' and was *'Kriegsmüde*—war weary.'

11 At the very worst, if *Kampfgruppe Kuhlmann* was close by and using the road, Peiper could have advanced to Losheimergraben and then turned off to the left to Eichelsberg to pick up *Rollbahn D* just north of Lanzerath.

12 Other accounts place the seizure of Losheim at 10.10 AM, Priess, *op. cit.*, p. 24.

13 Charles Whiting, *Jochen Peiper,* Leo Cooper, 1986, p. 49. Based on Whiting's 1969 interview with Peiper.

14 ETHINT-10, *op. cit.*, p. 12.

15 Interview with 1st Lt Neil Brown: William C.C. Cavanagh, *Dauntless: The History of the 99th Infantry Division,'* Taylor Publishing Company, 1994, p. 101-102.

16 Story related to author by Will Cavanagh, 13 October 1995.

17 Remarks of Wilhelm Osterhold in touring the Ardennes battlefield in September 1988; provided to author by Richard Byers.
18 Story told to Will Cavanagh by Siegfried Moldenhauer during battlefield tour in September 1988. In a strange twist of fate, after the war, looking for a job, Moldenhauer was offered a job that saw him become a profitable distributor for Coca-Cola in Germany.
19 Interview of Timm Haasler with Hans Böttger on 1 April and 9 June 2003.
20 Letter Wilhelm Osterhold to Arthur Mings, 24 November 1988; provided by Richard Byers to author. 'With one unlucky strike, the battalion had lost two thirds of its strength and the remaining rest had all hands busy bandaging the wounded buddies and then carrying them back to the road where they might be picked up by ambulance. At the moment, the first battalion was knocked out and it took almost a full week until the battalion had some fighting strength again.'
21 Obstlt Wilhelm Osterhold in charge of the *48th Grenadier Regiment* would earn the Oak Leaves to the Knight's Cross for seizing the Losheimergraben crossroads—albeit 36 hours later than Peiper had anticipated. Genlt. Gerhard Engel, '12th Volksgrenadier Division,' MS# B-733 and MS # B-027, NA, RG-338, Foreign Military Records, 27 December 1947. Also: Stephen M. Rusiecki, *The Key to the Bulge: The Battle for Losheimergraben,* Praeger Pub., Westport, CT, 1996. Ruseicki conducted extensive interviews with Osterhold.
22 ETHINT-10, p. 9.
23 ETHINT-10, *op. cit.*, p. 8.
24 Testimony of Roland Messner, *op. cit.*
25 Interview with Reinhold Kyriss, *op. cit.*
26 Interview with SS Uscha. Werner Wendt, 26 May 1996.
27 'It's a long night, but the difficulties of convoy driving are keeping me awake. Dead silence in Kronenburg—not a soul in sight.' 'First Army PWI Report: From the Bulge to the Rhine, Diary of Feldwebel Karl Laun,' 11/12 March 1945, NA, RG-338, U.S. First Army Interrogation Reports, ETO-MIS-Y, Box 64.
28 Interview with Werner Ackermann, 13 March 2010. The engine in the stricken Panzer IV would be pulled and eventually replaced, but the tank was not ready to move forward for nearly two weeks after which the operation in the Ardennes was largely over.
29 ETHINT-10, p. 13. The Germans blew the bridge across the railway line at Losheimergraben on 3 September 1944—a development that was a hardship for the civilians in the region that autumn: Alois Krings and Hubert Jenniges, *Losheim: 1486—1986 Zwilchen Geltern und Heute,* PRO D&P, Grafische Betriebe, St Vith, 1987.
30 Statement attributed to Peiper by Paul Zwigart: Richard Gallagher, *Malmedy Massacre,* Paperback Library, 1964, p. 35. 'We drove on the highway from Blankenheim to Dahlem and reached a point between those two at the Forsthaus Schmidtheim at about 8 AM on 16 December. Here we stopped. At noon, we resumed to Stadtkyll over Kronenburg over Hallschlag to Losheim.'
31 Peiper's testimony on 21 June 1946: U.S. vs. Valentine Bersin, Case 6-24, NA, op. cit., pp. 1917-1918.
32 Peiper's testimony on 21 June 1946: U.S. vs. Valentine Bersin, Case 6-24, NA, op. cit., p. 1918. For more evidence against the army plan to lead with an artillery barrage: 'Corps headquarters had repeatedly requested that there be no preparatory artillery barrage, but that the artillery open fire with the beginning of the attack … Corps held the view that by an artillery preparation of one hour on this completely quiet front, the advantage of secrecy would be surrendered one hour too soon. The attack troops would thereby be deprived of a great advantage, the surprise factor, without gaining any essential support. Corps headquarters' request in this connection was refused.' 'The I SS Panzer Corps During the Ardennes Offensive,' Rudolf Lehmann, NA, RG-338, Foreign Military Studies, MS # B-779, 1954, p. 2.
33 ETHINT-10, p. 25.
34 After spending a frustrating day with Peiper at his headquarters, on the night of December 16th. Genmaj. Gerhard Engel met in the woods east of Losheimergraben with Obstlt Osterhold with the *48th Grenadier Regiment* and Maj. Gunther Holz with his tardy assault gun detachment to devise a plan to seize the crossroads. He was under great pressure form SS Gruf. Hermann Priess, the division commander explained. The panzer columns were backed up for miles—*Kampfgruppe Peiper* included. 'We must seize the crossroads at dawn. The timetable for the panzer attack is 24 hours behind schedule. Priess insists that the offensive will fail if the crossroads is not seized.' Rusiecki interview with Osterhold; Rusiecki, *op. cit.*, p.123.
35 'In the last days, now we have to fight with Luftwaffe bastards from Paris.' Interview with Jochen Peiper, 10 October 1963, John Toland Papers: The Last Hundred Days, Library of Congress, Box 15.
36 Ludwig Havighorst to author, 20 September 1995. As commander of the engineer company of *9. Fallschirmjäger Regiment,* the commitment in the Ardennes was the first ground combat in his ten years of soldiering. Beginning in August 1940, he had flow more than 400 missions in He-111s as a navigator or bombardier in the Luftwaffe, mostly with the Boelcke Bomber Wing.
37 Capt. Stanton H. Nash, commander 820th TD Battalion, to author, 26 November 1996.
38 Interview with Carl Johnson, 3rd Platoon, Company A, 820th TD Battalion, 29 December 1996. 'We kept dropping back every day on orders until we ended up at Esneux, Belgium.' The TD men pulled out at 10:30

AM, spraying their German pursuers with machine gun fire. Company A, 820th Tank Destroyer Battalion, After Action Report, December 1944,' NA, RG-407, TDBN-820-C.

39 'The I SS Panzer Corps During the Ardennes Offensive,' Rudolf Lehmann, NA, RG-338, Foreign Military Studies, MS # B-779, 1954, p. 21.

40 Havighorst letter, 20 September 1995, *op. cit.*

41 820th TD Battalion: After Battle Report, December 1944: https://tankdestroyer.net/images/stories/ArticlePDFs2/820th_A_Co._AA_Report_Dec._1944_-_Retyped.pdf

42 Hugh M. Cole, *The Ardennes: Battle of the Bulge,* OCMH, Washington D.C., 1965, p. 147.

43 32nd Cavalry had been at Vielsalm the night before the attack enjoying a U.S.O. show. At 7 AM, they got word that they were to proceed immediately to Manderfeld to relieve the 18th Cavalry which 'was in big trouble and under assault by five German tanks.' Toland Interview with Bob Reppa, John Toland Papers, LOC, Battle, Box 36.

44 14th Armored Cavalry Group (Mecz) and its work in the Counteroffensive, Combat Interviews, 32nd Armored Cav. Sqd., Lt Jack Shea, NARA, RG-407, Combat Interviews, 23 January 1945, Phase I, p. 14. Many of the German troops fighting in the Ardennes had likely been provided with doses of the methamphetamine, *Pervitin,* which saw side use in the war, particularly during large-scale offensives. Norman, Ohler, 2015. *Blitzed: Drugs in the Third Reich.* Penguin Books, New York, NY.

45 Interview with Robert Reppa, 30 November 1996. Describing Holzheim on 16 December, 1944: 'I was outside with our guns facing Andler or Schonberg. I noticed the local people cleaning up the town and taking back in the American flags. A young officer, Captain Martin with Troop C of the 18th, stopped by to see me. It was late in the afternoon and was getting dark and he said, 'I'm leaving and I'm going back, if you're smart you'll do the same.' After a bit, I looked at a map and I could see he was right. I would be soon cut off.'

46 Interview with Adolf Schür, 14 October 1996. 'For the past 50 years, people have been criticizing Adolf Hitler, but during the war, no one here criticized him. We thought of ourselves as Germans. In 1920 the Versailles Treaty said you are Belgians. It did not make any difference to the way people here saw themselves. We speak German; we are German. In 1940, most people did not know much about National Socialism, but the Germans were here and they were German, and we welcomed them. We were *Volksdeutsche.* And when the government says, come and help us shoot planes down, you really don't have much choice.'

47 Adolf Schür interview, *op. cit.*, 'The shelling lasted over an hour. The snow was black with holes where the shells had landed.'

48 Author's interview with Sanny Schugens (nee Schür), 13 October 1995.

49 See folder marked '*Hauptwachmeister Büllingen/Aachen: Gendarmeriekreis Malmedy: gez. Kempenich,*' and '*Geheimde Staatspolizei:Aachen,*' and similar documents, 1941-1944, NA, T-175, Roll 15, F2517893-8048.

50 Author's interview with Sanny Schugens *op. cit* ... Although she never saw them again, Schugens recalled the names of two of the TD men: (White and Parker)'Before I saw the first German, I ran about the house pulling all the American trousers and jackets and maps that were hanging up and rolled them up and stuffed them into the basement under the bin of potatoes because I didn't want the Germans to see them.'

51 For account of the participation of C Battery, 371st FA with the I&R platoon; letter and attachments of Peter Gacki to author, 28 January 1995.

52 'Action at Lanzerath,' By Warren Springer, *The Checkerboard,* March 1990.

53 To Bouck and Springer, the sudden departure of the TD men from the Schür household looked like 'a bug out,' but Bouck couldn't blame them for it was common knowledge in the U.S. Army that for towed TD guns, the first shot was usually the last (MacDonald, *op. cit.*, p. 108). Although the TD crews of Lt Arculeer's 2nd Platoon, 820 TD Battalion did pull after communications were cut by the shelling at 5:30 AM, the parent 18th Cavalry Squadron made that arrangement legal by ordering the guns attached to Col. Mark A. Devine's headquarters to Manderfeld at 9.40 AM. Company A, 820th Tank Destroyer Battalion, After Action Report, December 1944,' NA, RG-407, TDBN-820-C. In a letter to the author (26 November 1996) the head of the battalion, Capt. Stanton Nash wrote that: 'Arculeer pulled back on orders of Col. Damon of the 18th Cavalry which I relayed to Lt Arculeer ... I guided the M-8 with the radio to the second platoon where Arculeer was in Lanzerath. They had received artillery fire, but there was no ground attack at the time ... In the meantime, Lt Brown of one of the HQ recon units reported tanks to the west of us probably headed for Andler.' There had never been any formal attachment at all of the guns to Lyle Bouck's defense, until armored assault brought all available elements back to Manderfeld.

54 Interview with Bouck, 9 February 1996.

55 The young girl in Lanzerath, Tina Scholzen, who had supposedly pointed out the I&R positions up on the hill in some accounts, had instead indicated to the Germans the direction that the three guns from the 820th TD Battalion had exited the village. For these facts: *Lanzerath Revisited,* 1 August 1997, by Richard Byers, provided to author.

56 Author's interview of Adolf Schür, 18 October 1995. Also MacDonald interview with Schür, 10 August 1981, Charles B. MacDonald Papers, USMHI, Carlisle, PA.

57 Author's interview with Lyle Bouck, 9 February 1996 and several follow-up letters. Also, extensive interview notes of John S.D. Eisenhower with Bouck in 'Bitter Woods' papers at the Eisenhower library in Abilene, KS.

58 Rudi Frühbeißer, *op. cit.* loss figures for 16 December 1944. Although Frühbeißer was later involved in a fabricated history of paratroopers functioning as Skorzeny commandoes, his *3 Parachute Division* history is generally reliable. In the *3. Fallschirmjäger Division* history, Fritz Roppelt detailed the losses by company in Lt Col. Schenk zu Schweinsberg's *I. Battalion/9 FJR*: they totaled 137 killed, wounded and taken captive in the first two days of fighting. Roppelt, *op. cit.*, p. 426. Most of these were lost at Lanzerath.

59 Wittlinger to Byers, *op. cit.* Vincent Kuhlbach agreed claiming, 'very high losses when we tried to attack Americans in well camouflaged and fortified positions.' Kuhlbach interview, *op. cit.*

60 Adolf Schür told the author in an interview in Lanzerath on 18 October 1995 that he had seen 27 dead of the German paratroopers buried in the temporary grave across from the Café Palm. Other villagers put the number at 30-40, Roppelt, *op. cit.*, p. 427.

61 Adolf Schür interview, *op. cit.*

62 Peiper trial testimony, U.S. v. Bersin, *op. cit.*, p. 1920.

63 Interview with Arndt Fischer, 15 May 1997.

64 'This way I may have lost 5-7 halftracks, which of course be repaired.' Peiper to Lyle Bouck, 9 December 1966.

65 American writer, Richard Gallagher interviewed Benoni Junker in the early sixties, sprinkling Junker's Ardennes recollections in his little-known book, *Malmedy Massacre* (Paperback Library, New York, 1964). He also spoke with SS Rttf. Gerhard Schaeffer who was in Siptrott's #731.

66 Peiper's synopsis of the day's frustrations: 'We fell in line much too late, because a blown up road bridge could not get repaired in time … Second, because an enormously clogged up road was there because a Volksgrenadier Division, which was supposed to clear in front of us our own mine fields, which they had not cleared … We decided ourselves, shortly before darkness fell, it does not matter, we get going. We then cleared the mines ourselves by driving onto them, which was justified for lack of time.' Interview with Joachim Peiper from 1974, transcript from Hans Kettgen and courtesy of Harvey T. Rowe.

67 Diary of Karl Laun, *op. cit.* The doodle-bug Laun refers to is the German V-1 or 'buzz bomb.'

68 In a letter to Michael Reynolds on 1 October 1985, Werner Sternebeck wrote that he had not been ordered to sacrifice vehicles by rolling over mines. He said the vehicles had been lost because the engineers had difficulty in finding all the mines. See Michael Reynolds, *The Devil's Adjutant*, Sarpedon, 1995, p. 72. Regardless, in several accounts, Peiper claimed that in interest of a rapid advance, he had purposely sent tanks ahead without prudent mine removal. Peiper to Toland, 22 February 1959; Peiper to Bouck, 9 December 1966. Also, Peiper's testimony at his trial. Also in another document written by Werner Sternebeck in 1983 and provided by Wolf Mauder to the author (*'Bericht über den Vormarsch der Panzerspitze der 'Panzer Gruppe Peiper von Losheim bis Engelsdorf am 16. und 17.12.1944,'*), he did not dispute Peiper's claim, saying instead that the mine removal operation had not been sufficient. It seems likely that Sternebeck did not receive an order to sacrifice his tanks to the minefield, but rather that Peiper had ordered him to proceed knowing full well that the darkness and the need for speed made adequate precaution impossible.

69 Sternebeck to Mauder, May 1983, *op. cit.*

70 The story of the defense of Bouck and the I & R platoon against overwhelming odds was largely overlooked by Dr Hugh Cole in his official U.S. Army account of the Bulge published in 1965 (*The Ardennes Campaign*, US G.P.O., Washington D.C., p. 85). Angering its veterans, however, the episode was brought to the attention of John S.D. Eisenhower who was preparing his own account of the Bulge in 1966: *The Bitter Woods*, GP Putnam, NY, 1969. Often retold after that publication, the story was covered by Jack Anderson with the *Washington Post*. 'Why Private Tsakanikas Should Get the Medal of Honor,' *Parade*, 25 March 1979. Bouck also spoke with Charles B. MacDonald (*A Time for Trumpets*, William Morrow, NY, 1985) and Gerald Astor (*A Blood Dimmed Tide*, Donald Fine, NY, 1992). In addition to numerous letters and a detailed interview, Bouck prepared a 10-page essay elaborating on his memories for the author: ('Intelligence & Reconnaissance Platoon 394th Infantry Regiment, 99th Infantry Division: 16 December 1944, Lanzerath, Belgium,' February 1996). Recently, the story has been made into a full-length book: Alex Kershaw *The Longest Winter*, DaCapo Press, Cambridge, 2004. Other than the numbers of Germans killed at Lanzerath, there have been some controversies about the action at Lanzerath: contrary to what is written in Rusecki's account (*op. cit.*, p. 102), Billy Queen was not killed while trying to run from his position. Joseph McConnell, who was in the foxhole with Queen wrote to Lyle Bouck in 1990 that the artilleryman had been hit in the chest soon after the fighting began.

71 ETHINT-10, p. 14.

72 Today the Café Scholzen can be found just before the old schoolhouse in Lanzerath. In the 1990s, the café was found just before the old schoolhouse, then the Calypso nightclub.

73 Author's interview with Bouck, 9 February 1996.

74 Jochen Peiper to Lyle Bouck, 9 December 1966. Letter courtesy Bouck.

75 Baron von Hoffmann was an Luftwaffe Oberst or Colonel while Peiper was an SS-Obersturmbannführer or Lieutenant Colonel.

76 Although Alex Kershaw's account of Lyle Bouck and the I &R platoon in the battle for Lanzerath (*The Longest Winter)* is admirable for its drama and scope, some of the dialogue on pages 118-119 is invented, taken from a version created with artistic license by Stephen Rusiecki (*The Key to the Bulge,* Praeger, Westport, CT, 1996) which is, in turn, loosely based on a letter written by Peiper to Lyle Bouck dated 9 December 1966. Bouck, was witness to the verbal feud between Peiper and Hoffmann, but was unable to understand the exchange in German. Author's interview with Bouck, 9 February 1996.

77 This was an erroneous conclusion Peiper would repeat over the years. Commenting on Charles Whiting's book, *Massacre at Malmédy,* Peiper said of the Lanzerath fighting: 'This 'Western' has been copied from the [John S. D] Eisenhower book [*The Bitter Woods]* and is based on the fantasies of Lt Bouck. The losses of the paratroopers in Lanzerath were negligible.' Jochen Peiper, 'Kommentar zum Buch 'Massacre at Malmédy von Charles Whiting,' p. 1; Courtesy James Weingartner. While, the losses were nothing like estimates of 400 killed and wounded from the *I. Battalion* of *9 FJR* (Bouck letter to Peiper, 26 November 1966)—they were still considerable—perhaps a third of that figure according to records of the parachute regiment. The combat strength of the *I. Battalion* on the eve of the attack was 11 officers and 485 NCOs and enlisted men; with recorded losses to the battalion in the first two days of fighting as 137 killed and wounded. Fritz Roppelt, *Der Vergangenheit auf der Spur: 3. Fallsch. Jg. Division,'* Hössbach b. Aschaffenburg, 1993, p. 426. Indeed a temporary mass grave of some thirty paratroopers was dug across from the Café Palm in Lanzerath after the battle.

78 ETHINT-10, p. 15. In defense of von Hoffmann, it is true that SS Oscha. Kugel's Tank #632 of the *6. Panzer Kompanie* was sidelined after hitting a mine between Lanzerath and Buchholz Station after leaving that evening. Interview of Heinz Noak with Timm Haasler, 2005.

79 U.S. v. Bersin, *op. cit.*, p. 1920.

80 In fact, they were 3rd Platoon from the 1-4./FJ Regt. 9, under the command of Fw. Vincent Kuhlbach, Fw. Schneider and Fw. Josef Schega, all under the command of Lt Günther Wabnik. Some of these paratroopers can be seen ridings the Königstigers pictured at Kaiserbaracke, Deidenberg and Ligneuville. Nominally, they were returned the next day to their parent division but a company of Fallschirmjäger travelled further west to Stavelot with Peiper. Maj. Taubert was the son of SS Ogruf. Siegfried Taubert who Peiper knew from his days as Himmler's adjutant. Taubert's eldest daughter married SS Chief medical officer, Dr Ernst-Robert Grawitz who reported directly to Himmler.

81 'Bericht des Oberst a.D. Helmut von Hoffmann, Kommandeur FS Rgt 9 über seinen Einsatz in der Ardennen Offensive,' as recorded by Dieter Bechtold, 5 November 1984.

82 Interview with Arndt Fischer, 15 May 1997.

83 Author's interview with Lyle Bouck, 9 February 1996.

84 Ludwig Havighorst to author 10 February 1996.

85 Peiper, 'Kommentar zum Buch 'Massacre at Malmédy,' *op. cit.*, p. 4.

86 Peiper's account of the engagement at Lanzerath from his interview in 1974 (Hans Kettgen courtesy Harvey Rowe): 'Around midnight, we arrived at a village in which a paratrooper regiment was located. This regiment of paratroopers was subordinated to me by radio from corps headquarters. I had a brief speaking connection with the corps and they told me: There is a paratrooper regiment in Lanzerath; it is assigned to you immediately. They are stuck. We arrived there around midnight. Things were totally quiet. No rounds fired all around, while one would assume a few hours after the start of such an offensive quite some nonsense would be going on. After some difficulties, I had found the command post in which a colonel with his staff and a bunch of soldiers sat in a large room, giving the impression of total apathy, as if they were waiting for being taken prisoners. And I was then an Obersturmbannführer – a lieutenant colonel, while he was a colonel. The balance was on my side, with my decorations and the fact that he merely had the War Service Cross 1st Class, but with swords. And I said you are assigned to me; do you know that? He said yes, I know that. Then I asked him how the situation is here. To which he replied something like we sit here in the middle of the forest and the forest is totally mined, with snipers in the trees and barriers. We just cannot get through. We twice attacked with a battalion and both times we were pushed back. Then I asked where is the battalion commander? It was said that he is not here, but we could look for him. Then came a lasting impression of the war for me. Suddenly an army captain, whom I had not seen or noticed just two or three seats away, suddenly said to me, colonel, sir, I am asking you that you intervene energetically. I have, sort of, been assigned as army liaison but they actually never attacked. I took that as a sign for having to be rather ruthless. And I asked what actually had been done. And he said, nothing is happening here. To which I replied, pay attention, in order not to lose any time, we shall get ready for immediate attack. From you, I would like to have a battalion that combs through the forest to left and right of and in line with us, so that our tanks will not be annoyed by enemy infantry. I shall report to you the readiness at such a time and your battalion commander shall report to me at such and such a time. And then I left him to himself and left. No, rather I said do not let us be by ourselves. Then we got

ready. Everything in complete darkness and no paratroopers anywhere. Then came some figures. They all had slept in houses. I remember I called for an officer. And a senior sergeant showed up, with the German Cross in Gold, and he told me, Sir, it is a crying shame what you are doing with us. Our new commander comes from the Reich Air Ministry. We once used to be quite an outfit, but what is being played with us is quite a mess. That, on the subject of paratroopers. They certainly had been great guys, but in the end, they were sitting in a boat like ours. They no longer are what they used to be in Crete. We could not find any officers, so we grabbed a few energetic sergeants and I said: Boys, do you have anything? They answered, yes, we have a company here, or so. We let them mount our vehicles and we took off. And we took off as the spearhead, without encountering any resistance in this forest.'

Chapter 6 – The Ardennes

1 Marshal Phillipe Pétain before 1940. 'So long as we make certain dispositions,' Alistair Horne, *To Lose A Battle*, NY: Macmillan, 1969, p. 102.

2 'If anyone anticipated such a big blow, they never told me. My lasting impression of the Bulge: I was so tired.' Toland interview with Courtney Hodges, 15 July 1957, Toland Papers, Battle, LOC, Box 36.

3 John S.D. Eisenhower, The Bitter Woods, Robert Hale, 1969, p. 199. Porsché likely called one of the assault guns with the *244th Sturmgeschutz Brigade*, 'a Tiger tank.'

4 106th Infantry Division, Report of Actions Against Enemy, December 1944, 8 January 1945, NARA, RG 407, Entry 427, 106-1.1.

5 For Hodges' character, author's interview with John S. D. Eisenhower, 3 January 1997. Also, Charles B. MacDonald, *The Mighty Endeavor, NY,* Oxford University Press, p. 406-407. Although Hodges was a stickler for spic-and-span, he frowned on adorning uniforms with service and decorations, calling them 'brag rags.' 'Precise Puncher,' *Time Magazine, 16 Oc*tober 1944.

6 Interview with Clarence Hubner, Toland Papers, *Battle: The Story of the Bulge*, Library of Congress, Box 36.

7 'Hodges—a Self-Made Mystery Man,' by G.K. Holdenfield, *The Stars and Stripes, 5 Oct*ober 1944.

8 Hodges favorite dish: Tomato and onion salad. 'Lt. Gen. Courtney H. Hodges,' by Don Whitehead, *Cosmopolitan Magazine, Octob*er 1944, Courtney Hodges Papers, Eisenhower Library, Abilene, KS, Box 23. 'We join with all our hearts in this celebration by a great people whose children have crossed the ocean to bring us deliverance.'

9 Hodges was an expert skeet shooter and marksman and had been instrumental in having the American infantryman armed with the light weight rapid-firing carbine rather than bolt action rifles for the war. He had also been a champion of the bazooka, saying that American infantryman need a chance—even if desperate—to stop enemy tanks. Still, examining enemy weapons, he would later declare that he envied the submachine guns and anti-tank rockets (*Panzerfaust*) being supplied to German men in 1944. Hodenfield, *op. cit.*

10 First U.S. Army, G-2 File, 16 December 1944: 'First Light Report: 16/6045,' Also, Artillery Intelligence Report No. 185. NA, RG 407, FUSA. 'A heavy to intense artillery programme commenced along the entire Army front at 0530 hours and continued at this rate until about 0800 hours.' Eleven large-calibre shells landed in Malmédy, three in the middle of town doing significant damage there.

11 'Master A.A,' 170200, U.S. First Army G-3 Files, NA, RG-407, 101.3.3, Box 1529.

12 Charles R. Codman, *Drive, Atlan*tic Monthly Press, 1957, pp. 200-201.

13 Charles B. MacDonald, *A Time for Trumpets, Morrow*, NY, 1985, p.96-97, 199. Just before being sent up north to Honsfeld to the 99th Division rest center, the Berlin born actress was detoured back to Paris after shellfire enveloped the front on 16 December. The decision was hurriedly made by the regimental executive officer of the 394th Regiment, Lt Col. Frederick Maxwell. Letter of E.B. Smart to Dick Byers, 10 January 1991. Alex Kershaw, *The Longest Winter, DaCapo* Press, Cambridge, MA, 2004, pp. 66-67.

14 John Toland, *Battle: The Story of the Bulge, Rando*m House, NY, 1959, p. 27-28.

15 For the segment on Eisenhower: John S.D. Eisenhower, *The Bitter Woods, DaCapo* Press, 1969, pp. 213-214.

16 In the incident, five thieves dressed as American GIs commandeered a six-by-six truck carrying fifty-three cases of liquor. As consolation, the held-up drivers were each given a personal bottle of Old Grand Dad before the brigands disappeared—truck, booze, and all: 'Have a cool Yule, fools!' one said in parting.

17 Present were Generals Bradley, Bedell Smith and Maj. Gen. Harold R. Bull, Air Marschal Sir Arthur Tedder, Eisenhower's deputy commander at SHAEF, and General Carl 'Tooey' Spaatz, the senior American airman in Europe.

18 On 16 December, Montgomery had signed an intelligence appraisal by his 21st Army Group which would later prove embarrassing: NA, RG-331, Entry 176, SHAEF, Box 45 (Also *Bitter Woods Papers, Box 31*), 21st Army Group: Annex 2 to Periodic Report #180, 'SHAEF's View of the Enemy Situation,' 'The enemy is at present fighting a defensive campaign on all fronts; his situation is such that he cannot stage major offensive operations. Furthermore, at all costs he has to prevent the war from entering a mobile phase; he has not the transport or petrol that would be necessary for mobile operations … The enemy is in a bad way.'

19 Maj. Gen. Kenneth Strong, *Intelligence at the Top: The Recollections of a British Intelligence Officer, Doubleday*, NY, 1968, p. 213.

20 Interview with Field Marshal Montgomery, 1 October 1966, John S.D. Eisenhower, *Bitter Woods Papers, Abilene*, KS, Box 2. Later during the offensive, one of Montgomery's messenger liaisons was arrested and temporarily detained by Gen. Joseph Collins who thought the officer was one of Skorzeny's spies.

21 12th A Gp G-2 Periodic Rpt, `162300, Dec 1944, in Royce L. Thompson, 'American Intelligence on the German Counteroffensive: 1 November – 15 December 1944,' prepared for U.S. Army Historical Division, November, 1949, NARA, 2-3.7 AE.P-1, p. 253-259.

22 *'Ich habe dem Führer am ersten Tage des Angriffs berichtet, dass die Uberrashung völlig gelungen ist.'* 'An Interview with Genobst. Alfred Jodl: Ardennes Offensive' ETHINT-51, 31 July 1945, NA, RG-238, Foreign Military Studies. Worried about secrecy a month before on 18 November, Jodl had called for expulsion of all less security-minded Alsatians from front line divisions in the Ardennes. 'Jodl Diaries,' NA, RG-242, Entry 166, MS #P-215.

23 David Irving, *The Secret Diaries of Hitler's Doctors, op. cit.*, p. 204.

24 Obstlt Schuster had been the *Regeirungsdirecktor im Wetterdienst der Luftwaffe*. Jodl had been apprehensive that the weather might clear as 14 and 15 December had been foggy as the meteorologist had forecast. An Interview with Genobst. Alfred Jodl: Planning the Ardennes Offensive,' ETHINT-50, 31 July 1945, NA, RG-238, Foreign Military Studies.

25 *'Nun sage noch einer was gegen die deutsche Luftwaffe!'* 'Typed transcript of shorthand diary kept by Ministerial a.T. Karl Thöt. 16 December 1944,' Microform Ltd. David Irving Collection, *Hitler's War, Film* 97125, Reel 4. December 16th: 'Unfortunately, I missed the heavy fire this morning at 0535 hours which commenced our attack in the West. Exactly one half year after the first attacks by our retaliation weapon against England. I still slept at that time!' Ewald Reynitz was another of Hitler's conference recorders.

26 'Lage-Unterrichtung Ia/Heeresgruppe B: 10:30 Uhr, 17.12.44,' BA-MA, RH 19/IV-84. However, this report would seem premature as a day later, Army Group B was reporting no word from von der Heydte. The 3rd Panzer Grenadier Division was now moving towards Hellenthal with the objective to move through the Elsenborn area and link up with the missing paratroop operation. The other contingency was that a battlegroup of 12th SS Panzer Division would link up with the paratroopers. John Paul Pallud, *The Battle of the Bulge, Then and Now*, After the Battle, London, 1984, p. 68.

27 This and the following quotes: 'OB West: Tagesmeldung vom 16. 12.1944 and 'Morgenmeldung vom 17.12.1944,' BA-MA, RH 19/IV-84.

28 Crew members of Panzer Nr. 001, SS Ostuf. Joachim Peiper (commander), SS Oscha. Otto Becker (driver), Wilhelm Nusshag (code radio), SS Rttf. Paul Schiereg (long wave radio).

29 Peiper to John Toland, 22 February 1959, LOC, John Toland Papers, Battle of the Bulge, General Correspondence, Box 108.

30 Interview with Sanny Schugens, 13 October 1996. 'The next morning I remember seeing tanks coming down the road. The new German soldiers were SS, but we did not know the difference at the time. There were a lot of them and they seemed to pass through town for a long time. It was very cold. At Christmas, there were still SS here. Some of them stayed here in our house and they all stayed in the kitchen since that was the one room that was heated where there was a stove. There were four chairs in the kitchen and an old armchair. The Germans sat on the chairs; we were forced to sit on the floor. We resented it; my mother was 60 years old. 'What was it like when the Yanks were here? Were they correct and polite?' the SS soldiers wanted to know. I said without thinking, 'We didn't have to sit on the floor when they were here!'

31 Interview with Sanny Schugens, *op. cit.*

32 Author's interview with Adolf Schür, 14 October 1996.Mueller told Schürr that the SS men never said anything to his and his nephew. They had just taken them away from the group of the Americans behind the barn and shot them. Interestingly, the author interviewed another soldier of the 612th TD Battalion taken prisoner in Honsfeld on the morning of 17 December, who saw the shooting as they were being marched through Lanzerath later that day. 'We finally were marched along side the road towards the east and I saw the Germans take an elderly man and boy out from our group. We could see they took them behind a barn. The boy was 14 and the old man seemed to be in his 50s or 60s. Then we heard some shooting and I knew they were dead.' Interview with Ralph J. LeBlanc, 612 TD Battalion, 13 March 1996.

33 Author's interview with Adolf Schür, 14 October 1996. The long line of prisoners that Schür observed marching through town included T/4 Luther C. Symons. The 394th Infantry Regiment lost 596 officers and enlisted men captured in the Bulge—most of the strength of an entire battalion. See Cavanagh, *Dauntless, op. cit., p. 119*.

34 As Peiper organized them, Sternebeck's *Panzerspitze* would lead from Lanzerath in concert with Preuss's 10 Pz Gr Kp, 12 PzGr Kp,then commanding officer of *III Abt* and Peiper in a command vehicle. *6 Pz Kp* with Untersturmfuhrer Steininger because Junker was ill (according to the post-war alibi of Junker), *11 PzGr Kp, 7 Pz Kp, 9 Pz Pi Kp, 13 Inf How Kps, AA Kp of Rgt, 1 Pz Kp, 2nd Pz Kp, 12 Pz Gr Kp* (other part), *SS Hvy Pz Abt 501*, then the *84th AA Bn* of the Luftwaffe.

35 'When I arrived, my tanks were lined up in columns and I ordered them to form on both sides in closed, tight formation with these paratroopers. I got very angry and called the commander of the parachute unit, but nobody came. Then I got on my recon and went on ahead. We went on a road that is not shown on the map—it runs from Lanzerath on a direct north-west route because I knew the railway station at 990985 [Buchholz Station] was still held by the enemy. I had no contact with the enemy in these woods. In the vicinity of the railway station, we received additional artillery rounds. At approximately six o'clock in the morning, we entered Honsfeld at top speed and surprised a reconnaissance battalion there.' U.S. v. Bersin, *op. cit., p. 1995*. Statement is an excerpt from Peiper's interrogation by Dwight Fanton on 25 August 1945.

Chapter 7 – Honsfeld

1 Interview with Reinhold Kyriss, *7. Panzer Kompanie*, 20 May 1997. 'On all the roads that ran through the forests in the Ardennes. Every second of every minute, we worried that an anti-tank gun could finish us.'

2 Sternebeck, *op. cit.*, 1983.

3 Peiper testimony from Malmedy trial., U.S. v. Bersin, *op. cit.*

4 ETHINT-11, p. 6.

5 It should be noted here that the author had taken small liberties with Peiper's testimony given the roughness of the translation. However, in all issues where the exact context of the language is important, any interpretation or alteration will be mentioned. Here the translator originally said, 'at that time considered themselves to be ambushed secretly,' which the author altered to its English equivalent 'considered themselves subjected to a surprise ambush.'

6 'An Interview with Obst. Joachim Peiper,' 7 September 1945, NA, RG-338, Foreign Military Studies, ETHINT-10, p. 6.

7 Interview with Andre Schroeder, Honsfeld, assisted by Will Cavanagh, 23 October 1996.

8 Schroeder interview, *op. cit.*

9 Havighorst letter, *op. cit.*

10 Sternebeck *op. cit., 1983.*

11 The tail of Peiper's column was all the way back in Losheim moving in fits and starts due to the heavy traffic. Feldwebel Karl Laun with the *84th Flak Sturm Battalion* wrote in his diary: 'We approach Losheim at dawn. Just before we get into the town, a battle group turns off to the left and it becomes ominously quiet … Everyone deceives himself into believing that we are still secure in the second echelon. The typical fate of a Landser [soldier] to stumble around in a blackout of ignorance. We get a cold thin pea soup … Another halt is called before Losheim. Suddenly intense artillery fire breaks loose and everybody crouches in the ditch … That sort of thing would have been frowned upon earlier in the war, but "*tempora mutantur et nos in illis*"—times change and we change with them. The artillery on both sides of the street fires a total of two rounds. We advance 500 meters and stop again.' 'First Army PWI Report: From the Bulge to the Rhine, Diary of Feldwebel Karl Laun,' 11/12 March 1945, NA, RG-338, U.S. First Army Interrogation Reports, ETO-MIS-Y, Box 64.

12 '801st Tank Destroyer Battalion: Action Against Enemy, Reports After Action Report,' 1 January 1945, NA, RG-407, TDBN-801-0.3. Also, letter and enclosures from Donald F. Dembowski, 801 TD Battalion, 25 May 1995. The 801st was attached to the U.S. 99th Division. Sgt. Gallagher was later able to escape in the confusion of 17 December 1944.

13 Given that Creel saw a German cross on the side of the tank, this almost certainly would have been a Mk IV as the Panthers of the LAH had the German cross painted on the forward hull, whereas the Panzer IV had the cross on the sides. Thanks to Timm Haasler for this insight.

14 'One of my men, Theobauld, later told me, 'We woke up the next morning, and we were completely surrounded. We could already see a long column of German tanks up and down the road.' Most them became captive. Author's interview with Bob Reppa, 32nd Cavalry Squadron, 30 November 1996. Also original notes of Toland's interview with Reppa, John Toland Papers, *Battle: The Story of the Bulge*, LOC, Box 36. Also, Lt Jack Shea, 'Fourteenth Cavalry Group and its Work in the Counteroffensive 16-31 December 1944,' Combat Interview, 23 January 1945, NA, RG-407, p. 28-29. Reppa spent the rest of the war as a prisoner in Stalag 13B in Hammelburg, Germany.

15 '801st Tank Destroyer Battalion: Action Against Enemy, Reports After Action Report,' 1 January 1945, NA, RG-407, TDBN-801-0.3. The rest of the battalion in the vicinity was roughly handled. Company A and the 2nd recon platoon deployed south of Honsfeld was hit by the German advance from Lanzerath losing most of its equipment (seventeen 3-inch guns and eighteen halftracks) and eventually filtering back to friendly lines at locations from Krinkelt to Robertville.

16 'Report of Rolf Ehrhardt,' *op. cit.*

17 Pvt. Jim Foley to Rex Whitehead, 29 August 1945.

18 Andre Schroeder interview, *op. cit.*

19 Given the accusations of war crimes in Honsfeld, the author conducted extensive interviews with surviving members of the 612th TD Battalion. Thanks to Jack Flanagan and Don Smart with the battalion association for his assistance in investigating this episode.

20 Letter W.T. Hawkins to author, 14 November 1995. 'We could not understand why we were moving up as everyone else was moving in the opposite direction.' Hawkins helped the author with the organization and locations of the defenders in Honsfeld, particularly in clarifying discussions on 17 February 2007 a decade after our original contact.

21 In interviews with several members of Company B, they told of resenting Captain Kennedy's departure that night—particularly as a number would be shot and all the rest made prisoner in Germany for the remaining months of the war.

22 Interview with Francis C. Hayes, 612 TD Battalion, 18 February 1996. 'Company B moved in, found quarters, and went to bed. I was in the third story of a house with Stegall, Hawkins, and Lt [William J.] Gribbin. Lt William Baysek was downstairs.' Remembering those days said Hayes: 'Those poor boys didn't have dog's chance.'

23 Both Peter Mueller and Brodel would later be shot by Germans in Lanzerath. See previous chapter and interview with Adolf Schür.

24 Don Smart, 'Terror at Honsfeld,' *World War II, Battle of the Bulge Commemorative Edition*, December 2004.

25 Although emotions were running high, Townsend surrendered the men in his house at approximately 10 AM. He did not see any of his men shot. Townsend to author, 4 March 1996.

26 Not getting out in time to surrender with the others, Charlie Sisco hid in the basement of the house for two days until discovered by the enemy and made a POW.

27 Sgt. Fayne Haynes and Lt Grandy and the others of the 1st platoon made their quarters in *Haus Spelzen* in Honsfeld.

28 Interview with George Block, B Company, 612 TD Battalion, 4 March 1996.

29 This section from author's interview with Elmer F. Haynes, 24 February 1996.

30 Interview with George Block, B Company, 612 TD Battalion, 4 March 1996.

31 Testimony of S/Sgt. Billy F. Wilson, 612 TD Battalion, 9 August 1945, NA, RG-549, Case 6-24, Box 8.

32 'Some of my comrades and me went back and got rifle grenades which we then used to set the farm building on fire. But by the time we did that, they were gone.' Account of Rainer Bender, *5.Fs.Jg. Rgt. 9*, information provided by Arnold Wesenberg with the *3rd Fallschirmjäger Division* Veterans Association, September 2002. Thanks to Timm Haasler for this source.

33 Interview with Elmer F. Haynes, 24 February 1996. After he was taken captive: 'We went on down the street about a block and there was Hayes and guards saw he had a knife on him. They roughed him up. There they grouped us up together. They roughed us up and fired over our heads. They seemed wild and kept shooting their guns over our heads. There were two German speaking civilians. Papendick talked to them. They stayed with us. Germans thought they were collaborators. As we got to the edge of the town that afternoon, they took these two out (old man and boy) and lined them up along the wall of a house which looked like a chicken house on the left side as we were marching out. And they shot them. We heard the shots and saw them dead by the building. They then just marched us on off. These German troopers were along the side of the road as we marched and one hit me in the jaw. As were going out of this town, there were many German tanks lined up and the American air force started dropping bombs, but they missed off to the right of us. My leg was hurting like the dickens … Just as we marched up the hill, this tank swerved over to the left and came right through us. Everyone got up out of the way. I had my hand on the tank and pushed myself off and rolled down the embankment. I got back to the road as they hollered at us. We marched about twelve miles until dark along the snowy road.'

34 One of these men was probably Pvt. William Bradley with Sgt. Devers group. Testimony of Wilson, *op. cit.*

35 As for the German vehicle doing the shooting, it seems most likely that it was Panther 101 of the leader of the *1. Panzer Kompanie* Karl Kremser. Prior to their refueling in Büllingen on 17 December, an enlisted man in his company, SS Rttf. Ernst Köhler of Panzer #111 described in trial testimony that he had witnessed eight or so American soldiers come out of a shelled building under a white flag. 'When they were about 10 meters away from his vehicle, Kremser's vehicle opened fire with machine guns on them … there were about 50 rounds. They fell forwards and continued lying there.' U.S. v. Valentin Bersin, Case 6-24, NA, RG-549, Testimony of Ernst Koehler, 29 May 1946, pp. 949-954.

36 Block Interview, *ibid*, 'When I came home, I wrote to his sister and told her of his death … Then they took us all up and lined us up again and they took our overcoats or galoshes; we thought we would be killed. They didn't kill anymore though. But as we walked back they swung at us with guns and the tanks swerved towards us while we walked. We walked for the bulk of the day. We came to a little town and we went into a big basement-like dungeon under this house with big heavy stone walls. We were there for two nights; then they marched us back and put us on railroad cars. We eventually ended up in Hammelburg at Stalag 13C.'

37 Interview with Woodall, *ibid. Also* 'Testimony of Morris Woodall,' 10 September 1945, NA, RG-153, War Crimes Case Not Tried, Case 6-188.

38 Interview with Morris Woodall, 14 November 1995. 'After landing in France, I was scared just about all the time.'

39 'Testimony of Charles O. Huttoe,' to Jack Solomon, Miami, FL, 13 August 1945, NA, RG-549, War Crimes Cases Tried, Case 6-24, Box 8. 'We had decided to surrender, and the officer in charge gave the order to cease firing. He then held out a white flag and stuck it out of the window, and after he had done this for a few minutes some of the Americans in the house began to walk out, holding the white flag. There were 12 of us in the first group. They had all walked out of the house and were already clear when the Germans shot them all down in cold blood … There was S/Sgt Billy F. Wilson and Pfc. James Crowell from Tennessee, also a member of the 612th … There was about 200 of us as we began to march to the rear … This unwarranted shooting occurred all the way along the road as we marched to the rear. As the tanks passed by, the German soldiers would shoot at us and we had to jump into ditches or behind any cover we could find.'

40 Testimony of Billy F. Wilson, 6 July 1946, Sweetwater, Texas, NA, RG-549, Case 6-24, Box 41. Also, testimony of Capt. George W. Scott and Pfc. Herbert E. Williams (16 &17 February 1946) who picked up Wilson between Elsenborn and Butgenbach at 4 PM, NA, RG-549, Case 6-24, Box 33.

41 Testimony of Anton Motzheim, 28 February 1946, NA, RG-549, Case 6-24, Box 8. Motzheim's detailed map could not be located in Box 8, but a duplicate can be located in the same series in Box 40. Motzheim said he did not investigate whether the American was dead because an American air attack suddenly caused him to dive for cover. 'I shot this American because Hscha. [Jochen] Thiele had given me the order that morning not to take any prisoners of war.' In the eventual trial, Motzheim took the stand to deny these charges and complained that he composed the statement only after being beaten. Yet, in a statement made on 12 February 1948 and designed to aid Motzheim who was still imprisoned, Paul Pfalzer, who had been in Motzheim's SPW verified that just before arriving in Honsfeld that two flak panzers ahead of them had been knocked out and that he charged Motzheim with destroying the enemy anti-tank weapons with their machine guns. 'That order was fulfilled and the *Panzerabwehrkanone* was destroyed. There were no prisoners made.' He agreed that they were attacked by American aircraft, but said they did not stop. 'Declaration of Pfalzer,' Case 6-24, RG-549, Box 58.

42 Affidavit of Siegfried Jaekel with detailed maps, 1 March 1946, NA, RG-549, Case 6-24, Box 7. Similar affidavit for Joachim Hoffmann from 6 March 1946 is in Box 6. Finally the earliest of these is from Gustav Sprenger from 15 February 1946 (Box 38) although Sprenger said the prisoners had not been shot when he passed by.

43 Interrogation of Siegfried Jaekel on 15 February 1946 by Ralph Shumacher, NA, RG-549, Box 38. In the same statement, Jaekel said he and his crew had shot eight American prisoners marching back along the road just south of the airfield near Büllingen. 'During the whole offensive, whenever we saw prisoners of war coming back along the road with their hands raised, we shot them … There were at least four other occasions.' The interrogation of Jaekel was done in the presence of SS enlisted man Gustav Sprenger, manning another SPW in the same unit, who corroborated many of the described events.

44 William T. Hawkins to author, 18 November 1995. 'All of our towed guns were still coupled to the halftracks that morning, however, some of the men uncoupled one gun from the 1st Platoon which I was a part of. Then one gun from the 2nd platoon was unhitched and got into action. I distinctly know two of the lead [German] tanks were destroyed by these two guns of ours.'

45 Interview with Francis C. Hayes, 612 TD Battalion, 18 February 1996.

46 Hawkins to author, 14 November 1995.

47 Interview with Francis Hayes, *op. cit.*

48 'Interrogation of Pvt. Amos H. Atkins,' 31 August 1945, NA, RG-153, War Crimes Cases Not Tried, Case 6-188. 'I was captured at about 1000 hours on 17 December 1944 in the town of Honsfeld, Belgium. T/5 'Johnnie' Stegall of Company B, 612th TD Battalion, was with me when we were captured. We were soon joined by approximately 250 other prisoners of war and began a march to the east into Germany.' During one of the attempts to surrender, Pvt. E.R. Davis had been shot, but only sustained a minor head wound when the bullet creased his skull after piercing his helmet. Davis had clearly seen Stegall shot by a German soldier from one of the tanks.

49 'Testimony of Sgt. John M. Dluski,' 18 September 1945, Indiantown Gap, PA, NA, RG-549, Case 6-24, Box 8. Also, interview with Devers Bryant, B Company, 612 TD Battalion, 10 March 1996.

50 'A boy across the road in front of me [Elmer Haynes] fired on the tanks and knocked out some. I fired three rounds into a barn where there was German machine gun nest. There was a barn about 100 yards away. We shot in the door and the window of the barn where they had pulled up hay in front the machine gun. The German infantry was surprised to find us there, but they noticed after we started firing. Their infantry came back on up the road and tried to come on back up the road after they passed us by. They came back and hemmed us in, and they saw our gun. They thought we had left the gun and did not

know we were there. They came back up the road from the north. They were bringing everything they had—even pushing wheelbarrows. Haynes was firing about the same time we were. There was a lot of small arms fire; the German infantry were shooting back. I saw the tanks coming up towards us. I can still see a German standing in his tank, firing a burp gun at me. I was hit in the hand and the shoulder. We were out behind the gun. The gunners thought they were going to kill us all. Sgt [Robert A.] Beaty, Pvt. [William E.] Bradley who was loader, T/5 [Edward C.] Sapp who was halftrack driver, were good friends in the unit. They were all among those on his gun crew, and all were killed. Of the ten men on my gun, five were killed, and the rest of us were taken prisoner. The bullets came from a tank that was about 20 feet away. They had overrun us. So much going on. 'We better give up or they're going to kill us all if we don't.' Five of our gun crew was killed in the bullets that hit us. So much was going on that you couldn't tell what going on … It was just getting light.' Bryant was later witness to the shooting of several comrades. 'I saw Stegall killed and [Pvt James M.] Milliner killed as well. There were so many more of them than us. They ran over Milliner with a tank. The rest of us put our hands up and they marched us away.'

51 'Sworn Statement of T/5 Charles L. Morris' and 'Sworn Statement of Ronayne G. White,' Company B, 612 TD Battalion, 7 February 1945, NA, RG-549, War Crimes Cases Tried, Case 6-24, Box 8. Both men agreed that they had seen Pvt. William E. Bradley, who was killed in Honsfeld that day.

52 For the identity of the crushed gunners in Honsfeld: Story of Andrew Donaldson: 'Report of the 39th Annual Reunion of the 612th TD Battalion Association,' *op. cit.*

53 Story of Sgt. Clinton Patrick: 'Report of the 39th Annual Reunion of the 612th TD Battalion Association,' Indianapolis, IN, 5-9 August 1992 as provided by Jack Flanagan. Story of Patrick strangling the German soldier from account related by Hayes, 'Terror at Honsfeld,' *op. cit.*

54 'Terror at Honsfeld,' by Don Smart, *World War II Magazine, November* 2001.

55 'Running over wounded PW with Tiger Tank in Honsfeld, Belgium: Perpetuation of Testimony of Andrew S. Pratz, Pvt, testimony to Don. B. Berston, Judge Advocate General's Office,' 28 March 1947, NA, RG 153, 'War Crimes Cases Not Tried,' Case 6-156. I saw five American soldiers killed by approximately 15 German soldiers while our soldiers were attempting to surrender on 17 December 1944 … Our soldiers were shot down while holding up a white flag in an attempt to surrender. The flag was about 12 x 12 inches and mounted on a short stick so the Germans could not help but see the flag waving in the air. Four of the Americans were killed outright, and the fifth American soldier was wounded and went down pleading for aid. About that time a German Tiger [*sic*] tank came down the street of this village and maliciously ran over the one surviving American who was throwing his arms about in a terrified manner. The tank operator could not help but see the man lying there in a helpless and wounded condition.'

56 'Terror at Honsfeld,' *op. cit.*

57 Interview with William Littlejohn, 11 March 1996. 'They woke us up and told us "The krauts are all over!" And they were. We got up and looked out the window and they were there in big numbers. There was already a lot of shooting … We had been overrun. There was officer in the house, Lt Chandler, my platoon leader, and he told the whole group there was no use continuing. Somebody went out with a white flag and there was firing as they came out.'

58 'He told me of tanks running over a road full of bodies and how horrible it was … I was afraid he wouldn't sleep last night.' Letter Rugh Agnes Riley to author, 22 February 1996, writing of the experiences of her husband Talmadge C. Riley, 612 TD Battalion. Riley was Sgt. Townsend's gunner in the 2nd platoon.

59 Interview with Walter Fickers, assisted by Will Cavanagh, Honsfeld, Belgium, 19 October 1995.

60 The place where Schroeder saw the seven shot American soldiers was the three-story home of Josef Collas (*Haus Krütz*), where Lt Gribbin and his group had been posted. It is right across from the *Haus Spelzen* forming a courtyard where the bodies were found. For the trial later in Dachau, Schroeder drew a detailed map of Honsfeld where he described what he had seen that day. 'Honsfeld: Map of Andre Schroeder,' 27 March 1946, Prosecution Exhibit 73, NA, RG-549, Case 6-24, Box 7.

61 Interview with Andre Schroeder, *op. cit.* After the battle, the town was wrecked. There were dead Germans everywhere. They left and stayed with Mrs. Schroeder's family near Reuland until August of 1945 and came back to repair their damaged home. When the Americans came in February, he told them, 'There are a lot of Americans dead here; seven or eight of them were murdered at the yard at this house. That young kid over there knows all about it.' Then an American officer spoke to him in German. Later he was requested to go to Dachau. He went on the bus to Dachau—25 or 30 people. He testified there about these events. He was only on the stand for five minutes. He looked at the German defendants. During the offensive, they were dirty and had beards. But there they were clean and well kept. I didn't recognize any of them. But for him, the trial was an adventure; he was chauffeur driven and stayed there for eight weeks.' Even today, Honsfeld is a serious farming community. Schroeder farms each day; when we found him, he was busy cutting wood for winter.

62 Henrich Signon, 'Honsfeld,' in *Kriegssschicksale 1944-45: Beiträge zur Chronk der Ardennenoffensive zwischen Venn und Schneeifel, St. V*ith, 1969, p. 92-95.

63 'He described that they had lined them up in one row before firing.' U.S. v. Bersin, NA, RG-549, Case 6-24, Trial Testimony, Testimony of Andre Schroeder, 28 May 1946, pp. 911-918.

64 'Erna's father had fought with the German army and returned after the war to learn of his daughter's fate. An autopsy was performed; she had been killed by 16 bullets in the chest—most likely a machine gun.' Schroeder interview, *op. cit.*

65 'Testimony of Pvt. Max Drechsner, 11th Company, 3rd Battalion, 999th Brigade,' taken by Capt. Alfred T. Bogen, First U.S. Army, 29 January 1945, NA, RG-549, Case 6-24, Box 8. Drechsner drew a detailed sketch showing that there were a number of bodies across from the stone house where abandoned anti-tank guns were found. Weinfurtner: 'I saw six bodies in the open and also indications that more were under the snow. The bodies laid with their hands over their heads and gave the impression that they were murdered. All six men that were in the burying detail were convinced that they were murdered.'

66 Cole, *op. cit.*, p. 261.

67 Twenty-two members of the 612 TD Battalion who were killed in Honsfeld with three other medics taken prisoner and pressed into service of the Germans. '612 TD Battalion: Lest We Forget,' no date, courtesy Jack Flanagan. In addition to the 19 on this list, Pvt. Cecil Mann, Sgt. Darwin R. Wortman and T/5 William J. Laukkonen were also killed in Honsfeld as evidenced by the exhumation of the mass grave at the local cemetery. 'Sworn Statement of Maj. Jack B. Day, HQ V Corps,' 22 February 1945, NA, RG-549, Case 6-24, Box 33.

68 Interview with Morris Woodall, Judge Advocate General's Office, 22 August 1945, War Crimes Cases, No Tried, Case 6-188.

69 In 2006, the remains of T/5 Michael Kardos were discovered having died in Stadkyll in Germany on 29 December 1944 while in German captivity. No further details are yet available and no word on the fate of the other two captured medics has surfaced since the war.

70 Members of the 612 TD Battalion shot while attempting to surrender on 17 December: Pvt. William Bradley, Pvt. James Milliner, T/5 Edward Stegall, Pvt. John Crowell, T/5 Robert Thomas and Pvt. Cecil Mann. The three missing medics: T/5 Michael Kardos, Pfc. Robert Farley and Pfc. James J. McGinity.

71 Others exhumed from the mass grave in Honsfeld on 5 February 1945 that could have been those shot by the *Haus Krütz* are: Pvt. Homer K. Reedy, Sgt. Darwin R. Wortman, Pvt. Everett Locke, T/5 William J. Laukkonen and Pvt. Leo J. Kroll. The documenting report indicated that the 'listed bodies were in such a condition that it was impossible to determine the nature of the wound that caused death. From the conditions of these bodies, it appeared that they had been run over by vehicles or tanks.' Sworn Statement of Maj. Jack B. Day, HQ V Corps, U.S. Army, 22 February 1945, NA, RG-549, Case 6-24, Box 33.

72 'Not all the Germans were bad guys … Only a few bad apples caused the shootings.' Interview with Jack Flanagan, 612 TD Battalion Historian, 2 March 1996.

73 Account of Rainer Bender, *op. cit.*

74 Roppelt, *op. cit., p. 433.* The losses in Honsfeld included Lt Manfred Rottenberg who had taken over as a company leader in the *II. Battalion* at the last moment and had been one of the paratroop leaders mounted on Peiper's tanks.

75 Interview with Vincent Kuhlbach, 29-30 September 2002, courtesy Timm Haasler.

76 'Action Against Enemy, Reports After/Action, HQ 612th Tank Destroyer Battalion,' 4 January 1945, NA, RG-407, TDBN-612-0.3. Also: Maj. James B. Kemp, 'Operations of the 612th Tank Destroyer Battalion, 2nd Infantry Division, in the Battle of the Bulge,' Advanced Infantry Officer's Course, 1949-1950, Ft. Benning, GA.

77 Although Fayne Haynes had claimed his gun crew (himself, Pvt. Hawkins, Pfc. Woodrow Burpo and Pfc. Robert Taylor) had destroyed both flak wagons, others believed that George Block's gun had struck down one. Letter W.T. Hawkins to author, 25 February 2007.

78 Recollections of Karl Wortmann, Cuppens archive, courtesy Timm Haasler. After the war, Vögler would frequently correspond with Georg Preuss as evidenced by the many letters in the later's Landsberg mail file. Vögler had been with the LAH since 30 January 1942 and had been a party member in the NSDAP since 1 March 1938. After the war, Voegler came to Peiper's defense: 'I never got a written or oral order of Col. Peiper according to which prisoners or civilians were to be shot. Being of the firmest character and known as one of the best and soldierly most unobjectionable leaders of his troop, Col. Peiper never acted or spoke in any situation as long as I know him personally—and that is since 1941—contrary to his upright and gallant attitude.' 'Affidavit Karl Heinz Voegler,' 11 August 1949, Oldenburg, NA, RG-549, Case 6-24, Box 53.

79 Interview with Jochen Peiper, 1974, from Hans Kettgen as provided to Harvey Rowe and then to author. Peiper also repeated this same scene in testimony at the Malmedy trial in 1946: 'Major [Siegfried] Taubert was the commanding officer of the airborne battalion which joined us in the attack on Honsfeld … this whole regiment was under my command at the time. Evidently due to some mistake, no time limit was set on this and I did not know that the regiment proper has a different mission after Honsfeld was taken. Maj. Taubert then told me that they had first to wait for an order from his regiment and I was annoyed and told him for them just to stay back in Honsfeld and hide. I ordered him to immediately mount all his paratroops

on my vehicles, to advance with me at top speed to Büllingen. He created all kinds of difficulties by saying he had no orders to advance that far and that he had to wait for orders from his division, and I screamed at him and told him he could go to the devil, to dig himself in at Honsfeld and I would advance myself. He stayed in Honsfeld … [But] all of them did not stay there. I found out that I had a company of parachutists with me for the first time in La Gleize while attacking Stoumont.' U.S. v. Bersin, *op. cit.*, pp. 1921-22, 1996.

80 Prisoner count from Roppelt, *ibid. Peiper*'s assessment of captured war material in Honsfeld is from ETHINT-10, *op. cit.*, p. 15.

81 AAR (after action report) 612thd TD Bn: Some 19 men of the company and its reconnaissance platoon were killed in Honsfeld. These losses established by a roll call of Company B conducted on December 18th in Sourbrodt. According to the village priest, Henri Signon, three medics of the 612th TD Battalion were captured and made to travel at gun point with the *Kampfgruppe Peiper* on 17th December and were never heard from afterwards. For the story of the capture of the medics: account from the Honsfeld village Mayor, Gerard Palm. In 1950, T/5 Michael Kardos was found to have died in Stadtkyll on 1 January 1945—just before the exodus of the Leibstandarte from the Ardennes. Strangely this happened with the hospital in town, which was caring for German casualties bombed by the U.S. 322nd Bomb Group in a raid on New Year's day. The other two Americans are still listed as missing in action: Pfc. Robert Farley and Pfc. James J. McGinty. It is possible that one or both of these men died in the same bombing raid—182 in the hospital died that day with many being unidentified. Thanks to Don Smart, the 612 TD Battalion historian and to U.S. Historian Bill Warnock for this information. 'Narrative of the Investigation: Case #5936,' HQ American Graves Registration Command, European Area, U.S. Army, 1 January 1950.

82 Laun diary, *op. cit.* 'After having been given that shot in the arm [Peiper's order of the day], we await nightfall. Two of my pieces alternately have to draw each other out of the mud while moving into the bivouac area. Other gun crews were smarter and just stayed behind, marooned in the mud. I start to settle down when a Tiger wakes me up, dangerously close. We might have had mincemeat there.'

Chapter 8 – Into the Storm Wind

1 *Panzerlied*: '*Ob's stürmt oder schneit, ob die Sonne uns lacht, der Tag gluehendheiss oder eiskalt die Nacht, Bestaubt sind die Gesichter, doch froh ist unser Sinn es braust unser Panzer im Sturmwind dahin.*' The famous tanker's song was composed in 1933 by Kurt Wiehle. In interview with Rolf Reiser by the author on 15 May 1997, he described how the *Panzerlied* was often sung in the training schools, although in late 1944 near the front, 'we were often not in a mood for singing.'

2 Interview with Paul Zwigart, 20 May 1997, Anspach. 'Preuss frequently went out on patrol without protection or proper reconnaissance and sometimes got in trouble.' Also extended handwritten statement of Erich Rumpf, NA, RG-549, 'D. Rumpf's Description of Personalities,' Case 6-24, Box 32. 'Who was in good favor of Peiper, also gets a lot of medals: Diefenthal, Preuss, Sievers and Sickel.' Dr. Sickel was particularly disliked and was called by the officers of the regiment *'Sie-Ekel'*— ('You Bastard').

3 Interrogation of SS Ustuf. Julius Steinert, 21 December 1944, U.S. First Army PWI Report No. 6, NA, RG-407, 101.1—3.2, M.L.-2125, Box 1497. 'The LAH died in France and will never be the same. The replacements—youngsters—have not received sufficient training.' Steinert was taken prisoner after Preuss's failed attack towards Werbomont on 19 December and interrogated at the 77th Evacuation Hospital.

4 According to a detailed deposition in the Malmedy trial by Poetschke's orderly, SS Ustuf. Kurt Kramm, (U.S. v. Bersin, *op. cit.*, p. 209) the organization of the units of *Kampfgruppe Peiper* was as follows at they advanced from Lanzerath: Spitze platoon (Sternebeck), 10. SS PzGr. Kp (Preuss), tanks of Poetschke and Fischer, Peiper and Diefenthal in the later's III Abt. SPW, 6. Pz Kp (Junker), 11. Pz Gr. Kp (Tomhardt) 7.Pz. Kp, (Klingelhöfer), 9 Pz Pi. Kp (Rumpf), 10. (Flak) Kp (Vögler), 3. Kp./ SS Pz Pi Kp 1 (Sievers), 1. Pz Kp (Kremser), 2.Pz Kp (Christ), 12. Pz Gr. Kp. (Thiele), 13. (IG) Kp. (Koch), s SS 501 Abt (von Westernhagen), 1/ SS/Pz Art. Rgt. 1 (Kalischko), Luftwaffe Flak Abt. 84 (von Sacken).

5 Wittlinger letter, *op. cit.*

6 U.S. v. Bersin, *op. cit.*, pp. 1923-1924.

7 Peiper's crew in command tank 001 on 16 December 1944 included veteran driver, SS Oscha. Otto Becker, Morse code radio operator, Wilhelm Nusshag and voice radioman SS Rttf. Paul Schierig. The gunner is unknown. Interview with Wilhelm Nusshag, SS Rottenführer Rgt. Stab Kp. 10 May 1999. Also letter from Nusshag to author, 28 March 1999.

8 Evidence that Peiper switched to Diefenthal's SPW at this point comes an important facet in the sequence of events before later reaching the Baugnez crossroads. 'Testimony of Josef Diefenthal to Dwight Fanton,' Wiesbaden, 14 November 1945. (NA, RG-549, Case 6-24, Box 33). Note that this testimony was before any of the alleged abuse at Schwäbisch Hall. Q: 'Was Peiper riding in your vehicle when you left Büllingen?' A: 'Yes' Q: 'How long had he been riding in your vehicle at that time?' A: 'Standartenführer Peiper mounted my vehicle before the airfield at Büllingen.' Diefenthal said of Zwigart— 'a good natured fellow and an excellent driver.'

9 Interview with Wilhelm Nusshag, SS Rottenführer Rgt. Stab Kp. 10 May 1999. 'On 16 -17th December [1944] it was still dark when everything started moving. Then it happened that our tank was disabled near Büllingen. There was an engine failure. The driver and I stayed with the tank. We tried to get it fixed and somebody came from ordnance and got the tank moving. We drove ahead, but we couldn't catch up with the battle group. They had gone to La Gleize. We only got as far as Recht and then drove to Wanne and that was as far as we could go.'

10 Peiper testimony described how he personally clarified the route to Poetschke on the outskirts of Honsfeld on the morning of 17 December, U.S. v. Bersin, *op. cit., p. 1923.*

11 Testimony of Joachim Peiper, U.S. v. Bersin, *op. cit., p.* 1921.

12 Sternebeck's account, *op. cit.,* 1983.

13 American intelligence officers worried at the time that the observation planes captured by the Germans might be used against them: NA, RG-407, 301-2.2, U.S. First Infantry Div., G-2 Journal for 18 December, Box 5072: 'Enemy captured *89 W* and *89 C* liaison planes from 99th Division intact. Artillery of the 2nd Infantry Division lost ten planes and CCB, 9th Armored lost two more at Büllingen.'

14 'Personal History: A Journal of Experiences and Photos Across Europe During WWII,' Roger D. Phillips, 254 Engineer Combat Battalion, copy in author's possession. For the description of the fighting from Georg Preuss, Tiemann, *op. cit.,* p. 39.

15 '254th Engineer Combat Battalion: After Action Report: December 1944,' dated 1 January 1945. NA, RG-407, EN BN-254-0.3. Casualties amounted to two officers and 67 enlisted men.

16 Yager's 'German officer in a cream colored jacket' was most likely, Josef Diefenthal in charge of *SS Panzer Grenadier Battalion III* as few others had a jacket of this color. For details of this episode, author's interview with Grant Yager, Pittsburgh, 1 July 1995. Also, 'Deposition of Sgt. Grant Yager' (28 September 1945) and 'Testimony of T/4 Preston H. Davis,' (25 October 1945). NA, RG-153, 'War Crimes Cases: Not Tried,' Case 6-107. For Romaker's exclamation: Letter Grant Yager to Ralph G. Hill, 2 July 1982. Charles B. MacDonald Papers. For the description from the German side, Sternebeck, *op. cit.,* 1983. Needless to say, Diefenthal's testimony, either at Schwabisch Hall or before, did not say anything about shooting an American soldier at the entrance to Büllingen.

17 Recollections of T/Sgt Edward C. Vickstrom, 254th Engineer (C) Battalion on 17 December 1944, 5 August 1996. 'I made it across okay and joined up with six to eight other GIs, none being 254 [Engineer Combat Battalion] men, and we took up positions along a wooded fence line several hundred yards NW of Büllingen. We could see lots of traffic in the Butgenbach direction but couldn't determine if it was German or U.S. Probably some of both amidst all the confusion. We had one or two TDs from 612th TD Battalion in support who fired several rounds at tanks making feints in our direction.'

18 Phillips, *op. cit.*

19 Sternebeck, *op. cit.,* 1983.

20 'Heros of the Elsenborn Ridge,' Parker, *Battle of the Bulge, op. cit.,* p. 147.

21 Tiemann, *op. cit.,* p. 39.

22 U.S. v. Bersin, *op. cit.,* pp. 1924-1925.

23 Letter Arnold Betcher to author, 2nd Quartermaster Company, 2nd Infantry Division, 6 January 1997. Those captured and forced to do the fueling were from the Service Platoon.

24 'G-4 Journal and After Action Report, 2nd Infantry Division,' December 1944, NA, RG-407, 2nd Infantry Division, 302-4.3.

25 U.S. v. Bersin, *op. cit.,* pp. 1925-1926.

26 Letter Roger Foehringer to author, September 1995. By Christmas 1944, Foehringer ended up in Stalag 13C in Hammelburg.

27 'Report of Rolf Ehrhardt, *op. cit.*

28 Approximately 5,000 gallons of MT-80 gasoline and 25,000 rations were captured. Given that many of the German tanks were likely halfway down through their 700 liter capacity, the fuel was enough to fully top of fifty German tanks. Royce L. Thompson, 'Overrunning of Installations, the Ardennes Campaign,' Washington D.C.: OCMH, 12 Feb 1953, 2-3.7 AE.P-24.

29 Gen. Michael Reynolds, *The Devil's Adjutant: Jochen Peiper, Panzer Leader,* Sarpedon, New York, 1995, p. 83.

30 U.S. v. Bersin, *op. cit.,* pp. 2355-2356.

31 Letter Ralph G. Hill, Jr. to author describing his experiences, 19 January 1995.

32 Interviews with Karl Paul Fröhlich 20 May 1996 and 19 May 1997.

33 Sternebeck, *op. cit.,* 1983.

34 Rttf. Albert Braun was the gunner in #631. After Wien was decapitated when their tank was struck; the crippled tank was driven back to Büllingen where Wien's body was removed and the tank prepared for further service. Interrogation of Rttf. Albert Braun, IC #1, 'Screening Results 15 to 24 November 1945,' Malmedy Investigation, Ellis Papers.

35 For description of the mistaken foray by *Kampfgruppe Peiper* north towards Wirtzfeld: Interrogation of SS Strm. Franz Mohr, IC #1, 'Screening Results 15 to 24 November 1945,' Malmedy Investigation, Ellis Papers.

Mohr was the cannoneer of Panzer #615. He, the commander, SS Rttf. Peter Kasparek and SS Strm. Theo Becker (driver) were all taken captive after their tank was shot and destroyed. SS Strm. Scharnert (loader) and Ross (the radio operator) were killed. Although Junker would later claim to be incapacitated because of his foot injury, in his early interrogation, Franz Mohr clearly placed him in Büllingen at about 7:30 AM during the heavy artillery fire on the town. There, Junker ordered the tank of Rttf. Kasparek to take the lead followed by an SPW, then Panzer #613 (Fremdling) and then Panzer #631 of Wien.

36 For the story from the American side, see Danny S. Parker, 'Heroes of the Elsenborn Ridge: 644 TD Battalion,' in *Battle of the Bulge,* DaCapo Press, Cambridge, MA, 1991. The M-10s shooting the German tanks and halftracks were Sgt. Tom Myers in C-12 and C-9 under Sgt. George Holladay.

37 U.S. v. Bersin, *op. cit.,* p. 1926.

38 These included aircraft of the 389th and 391st Squadrons, 366th Fighter Group.

39 'From G-2 Air, IX TAC: Troop Movement,' 0945 Hours, G-2 Records V Corps, NA, RG-407, V Corps, G-2 Records, 205-2.2, 17 December 1944. The map co-ordinates refer to the area between Honsfeld and west of Büllingen.

40 Danny S. Parker, *To Win the Winter Sky,* Combined Books, Conshohocken, PA 1994, p. 152 & pp. 172-173. The P-47s claimed seven enemy aircraft shot down to the loss of two of their own destroyed by flak, whose gunners noted the German ME-109s being 'evidently very reluctant to enter into dogfights.'

41 Laun Diary, *op. cit.*

42 Main source for this section: AAR for 47th Field Hospital, 'Resume of Activities for Month Ending 31 December 1944: 47th Field Hospital' and 'Report of Events by Maj. John W. Henderson, 3rd Platoon, 47th FH,' 9 January 1945, NA, RG-407, No Box list.

43 The account of Capt. Warren and associated quotes are taken from Dr Clifford L. Graves, *Front Line Surgeons,* Fry and Smith, San Diego, 1950, pp. 243-245.

44 Interview with Ruth Nance Elbrader, 18 November 1995. 'The television show MASH is fiction. Although women heavily outnumbered men—40 enlisted men for every six nurses, doctors were all business. They were all tired and usually exhausted. No way that anyone wandered into an operating tent. It was very professional. Enlisted men were always respectful: no snide remarks, no swearing or anything like that. We did not have time for friendly discourse. Off time, everyone was exhausted and went straight to sleep. But if nurses did want a date, they were not too hard to come by.'

45 The 3rd platoon was eventually evacuated back to Spa, only to be ordered back from there on the 18th of December as the Germans threatened to overrun the U.S. First Army headquarters. They left once again, heading back to Liège where 'buzz bombs were falling like crazy.' Two weeks later, Ruth would learn that her husband, another soldier had died fighting in the Lorient in the South of France.

46 On the morning of 17 December, the 1st platoon of Company A of the 801 TD Battalion deployed west of Hünningen reported firing on a column of tanks and halftracks advancing from Honsfeld to Büllingen. They claimed to knock out four tanks and a halftracks—doubtless an exaggeration—but likely was the gun section that cost *Kampfgruppe Peiper* two tanks just outside of the town. Counter fire from the German column destroyed one 3-inch towed gun and wounded the platoon leader. '801st Tank Destroyer Battalion: Action Against Enemy, Reports After Action Report,' 1 January 1945, NA, RG-407, TDBN-801-0.3.

47 Statement of Walter Köbler, 28 August 1953, NA, RG-549, Case 6-24, Box 48. Köbler had been with the 2. *Panzer Kompanie* since November 1943.

48 Schommer to Giles, 19 March 1964, Janice Holt Giles Papers. At first Schommer didn't believe Smith had really seen a tank. 'That was impossible, as we were winning the war.'

49 Janice Holt Giles, *The Damned Engineers,* Houghton Mifflin, NY, 1970, p. 74-75. The village of Amblève is normally known to the German speaking locals as Amel.

50 'At daybreak the next morning, all was quiet and I made my way back to Thirimont. I went back to my daily work on the farm until we were evacuated sometime around Christmas.' Interview with Alphonse Grosjean, Thirimont, 1 October 1996, Thanks to Jean Philippe Speder for assisting the author.

51 Statement of Georg Preuss, 2 April 1946, Handwritten confession and typed transcript are both in NA, RG-549, Case 6-24, Box 8. Also clarifying points by statement of Karl Hey, 4 February 1948, RG-153, Case 6-24, Box 81. For further testimony of the guilt of Preuss relative to the shooting of the flyer, see U.S. v. Bersin, *op. cit.,* testimony of Herbert Kohles and Rudi Knobloch, 29 May 1946, pp. 928-937.

52 In a 19-page undated interrogation of Preuss in the fall of 1945 or early part of 1946, Preuss was asked why he hid in the woods for so long: 'Q: Did you think it was important to re-establish contact with the regimental column? A: It was only possible for me to contact any fighting groups where I heard noise. I couldn't know that Peiper was already advancing out of Büllingen. I was trying to get in contact with any fighting groups to find out what was going on. Q: You knew Peiper was in a hurry? A: Yes Q: You knew he would be right behind you, didn't you? A: I didn't know that—I only saw Americans behind me.' With Preuss missing, command of the four platoons of *10. Kompanie* fell to SS Uscha. Aschendorff. 'Interrogation of Preuss,' no date, NA, RG-549, Case 6-24, Box 31. In spite of getting lost and hiding in the woods for most of a day, Peiper would later recommend Preuss for the Knight's Cross.

53 The eleven executed black men were discovered by the U.S. 99th Infantry Division on 13 February 1945 after they recaptured the region: Pvt. Curtis Adams, Cpl Mager Bradley, Pvt. George Davis, S/Sgt. Thomas Forte, T/5 Rob L. Green, Pvt. Jim L. Leatherwood, Pvt. Nathaniel Moss, Pvt. George W. Motten, Pvt. William E. Prichett, T/4 James A. Stewart and Pvt. Due W. Turner. Each man was subsequently examined and autopsied.

54 Thanks for NARA archivist Richard Boylan for originally pointing associated records. 1st Lt Herbert Peterfreud of the 395th Infantry Regiment found the bodies by the main road in February 1945: 'They showed signs of brutal treatment … some men's heads had been bashed in by rifle butts, others showed signs of being bayoneted, others showed bullet holes in one or more parts of their bodies.' Also, 'The Wereth Eleven: Remembering the Invisible Soldiers in the Battle of the Bulge,' Norman S. Lichtenfeld, Mobile, AL, copy provided to author. Also, www.wereth.org.

55 Testimony of Mathias and Maria Langer and Maria Martes of Wereth, Belgium, 19 February 1945 as related to 1st Lts. Herbert Peterfreud and John Polachek; NARA, RG-549, War Crimes Cases Not Tried, Case 6-102, Wereth incident.

56 '*Schnelle Gruppe Knittel and Wereth*,' manuscript prepared for author by Timo Worst, February 2007. The *3. Panzer Reconnaissance Kompanie* composed of amphibious VW *Schwimmwagens* was surveying roads in this zone since Knittel did not know if he had to follow *Kampfgruppe Peiper* or *Kampfgruppe Hansen* the following morning. The head of the company, Martin Leidreiter was scouting the northerly routes in case Knittel would be ordered to follow Peiper. The group in the Wereth area were scouting the roads towards Poteau in case Knittel would be ordered to follow the southerly route with *Kampfgruppe Hansen*. There was also still another reason: Knittel reported problems moving the truck supply columns from Kronenburg through the heavily forested zone near Wereth. Although Ostuf. Martin Leidreiter was clearly not a member of the jeep team that perpetrated the atrocity, he was the leader of the unit and was later photographed in La Vaulx Vaux Richard on 18 December 1944—the same day that another atrocity was committed in that same locale. See Jean Paul Pallud, *The Battle of the Bulge: Then and Now, After the Battle*, London, 1984. Note that the photo on p. 155 is *not* Leidreiter whereas the photo on page 152 is not of Goltz, but is, in fact, Leidreiter. *Schnelle Gruppe Knittel* advanced in the wake of *Kampfgruppe Hansen* moving via Holzheim on 17 December to pause at the Belgian village of Born just north of St. Vith to reorganize at nightfall.

57 U.S. v. Bersin, pp. 1927-1928.

58 In Cpl Cummings, jeep was 2nd Lt Lloyd Iames and Sgt. Vernon Anderson. Others of the recon company included 1st Lt Thomas McDermott, T/3 James McGee and Cpls. Edward Bojarski and Walter Wendt, Sgts. Henry Zach and Marvin Lewis and Pvts. John Klukavy and William Barron.

59 Author's interview with James Cummings, Bakersfield, CA, 25 September 1996.

60 Cummings interview, *op. cit.* In a separate statement on 19 December 1944 to U.S. First Army Headquarters, Cpl Edward Bojarski of the same recon company estimated that they were a mile and a half south of Waimes on the highway N-27 when they were captured. NA, RG-153, Case 6-24, Box 76. However, from Bojarski's description of the 'embankment on the right side of the road,' Belgian historian Henri Rogister (*op. cit.*) concluded that the location may have been between Ondenval and the exit of Möderscheid on the way to St. Vith.

61 Letter Walter Wendt to author, 21 December 1998. In an earlier letter, the author sent Wendt photos of Werner Poetschke and Jochen Peiper, but Wendt was unable to identify the officer who spoke and laughed at him near Waimes on 17 December 1944.

62 Cummings interview, *op. cit.*

63 U.S. v. Bersin, pp. 1927-1928.

64 Ray received his commission from President Roosevelt in 1939; his brother Roger was also an Academy graduate. Ray ended as a prisoner in the city of Limburg: 'The POW collecting point was a huge barn; there were hundreds of Americans in there. It was getting close to Christmas now … We sang Christmas carols in this crowded place. After that I was transferred to the 2nd floor of a chateau in the same compound and was placed in solitary confinement. I could hear German soldiers drilling outside and singing 'Lili Marlene' as they marched. I did get some food, but I had no human contact for days. On New Year's Eve came word that the commanding officer wanted to see me. I went down the flights of stairs to his office that night. He spent 3-4 hours questioning me over New Year's but mostly it was just talk. He drank a good deal more of Johnny Walker than I did. He said he didn't think it was right I had to spend New Year's up there … The next day, we marched on foot and we eventually we ended up in Hammelburg. I was there for the next two and half months until the camp was liberated.'

65 Interview with Col. Ray, *op. cit.*

66 The history of the 100th Ammunition Battalion records that Col. Ray departed 'shortly before noon.' Thanks to Bill Warnock for assisting with tracking down the details of Col. John Ray's capture.

67 This was likely Cpl Bradley Reeves of the FUSA HQ Company who was reported missing on 17 December, 1944 and was never heard from again.

68 It seems certain that Col. Ray was sent to ASP 126 which was on the road near Waimes, operated by the 57th Ordnance Ammunition Company. Travel from Verviers to Spa to Waimes would likely have taken him through Malmedy by the Baugnez (massacre) crossroads east towards Waimes. See Lida Mayo, 1968. *The Ordnance Department, On Beachhead and Battlefront,* OCMH, Washington D.C., p. 304. Just before noon this road was occupied by the *Kampfgruppe Peiper.* Although Ray never got to the artillery supply point, the immobile supply depot was prepared for demolition using a daisy chain of mines and prima cord. In the early afternoon, the entire depot was detonated with a deafening roar that could be heard for miles.

69 Interview with Col. John Ray, Natick, MA, 15 and 18 May 1998.

70 Peiper to Toland, 22 February 1959. LOC, John Toland Papers, Correspondence, *Battle: The Story of the Bulge,* Box 108.

Chapter 9 – 'Everything Has Changed ...'

1 Adolf Hitler, *Mein Kampf,* (Franz Ehrer Nachfolger GmbH, 1925; 1939, English edition, Chapter 11, 'Nation and Race.'

2 'Typed transcript of shorthand diary kept by stenographer Karl Thöt. 17 December 1944,' Microform Ltd. David Irving Collection, *Hitler's War,* Film 97125, Reel 4.

3 OKW/WFSt/Op.(H) West 'Tagesmeldung vom 16.12.1944,' BA-MA, RH 19/ 4/ 84.

4 John Toland, *Battle: The Story of the Bulge,* Random House, NY, 1959, p. 39. The source for this oft quoted conversation was clarified in Toland's interviews with Balck in 1963, found in the *Last Hundred Days* archives at the Library of Congress.

5 'V Corps Artillery G-2: Unit Journal,' 17 December 1944, NA, RG-407, 205-ART-2.2, Box 3047.

6 Hansen Diary, Charles B. MacDonald Papers, USAMHI, Box 7. Lt Col. Hansen was Gen. Bradley's aide.

7 Hansen Diary; also Omar Bradley, *A Soldier's Story,* Holt Rinehart and Winston, NY, 1951, pp. 454-456. With word that Skorzeny's American uniformed commandos were operating behind American lines (some said there was a goon squad aiming to capture Eisenhower.), Bradley experienced some difficulty confirming his identification. Over the following days as he travelled back and forth to the U.S. First Army, he was challenged three times by edgy sentries to prove his identify. Once he was held up briefly because he could not remember the identity of actress Betty Grable's current husband.

8 'Without material—weapons, ammunition, artillery and tanks—there is no fun in war.' Recollections of his father, interview with Franz Josef von der Heydte, Landshut, 18 March 2010.

9 John Toland's interview notes with von der Heydte in 1957, John Toland Papers, LOC, Manuscript Division, *Battle: The Story of the Bulge,* Box 38.

10 One plane-load of parachutists had been dropped far to the north, in the sector of the U.S. 104th Infantry Division near Weisweiler, west of Düren and above the Hürtgen forest. The bewildered jumpers possessed a map on the Monschau area, but were totally in the dark relative to their mission, expecting to be briefed upon landing. '3rd Armored G-2 Journal,' 181200, NA, RG-407, 603-2.2, Box 12203.

11 'Voluntary Statement of Prisoner of War LD 882 Oberstlt. Friedrich von der Heydte,' 2 November 1945, P.W.I.S LDC/835 (a)-Te/JR, U.S. First Army, INT/9, NA, RG-407, 101.1—3.2, M.L.-2125, Box 1514.

12 Peiper interview from Kettgen, *op. cit.*

13 *To Win the Winter Sky, op. cit.,* p. 162. The P-47s strafed Peiper's column repeatedly dropping their bombs on the mostly densely packed roads. The German fire found its mark, however, and hit the mount (or plane?) of 2nd Lt John D. McCarthy. McCarthy was so low that he never had a chance to get out, slamming into the Ardennes countryside. Soon the 388th Squadron under Capt. Robert M. Fry showed up to relieve Capt. Slinde's pilots. Fry's P-47s continued to bomb and strafe the German traffic; they claimed 15 destroyed vehicles before they departed.

14 For 'vapor trails,' Carpenter, *op. cit.,* p. 207, Reports of Me-262: U.S. First Army, G-2 Journal, Box 1875, 101-2.2. 'Nine positions strafed at 2150 A by one jet-propelled plane. No casualties.' (K-677196—K684138).

15 'Fernschreiben! 16.12.44, OKW/WFSt/O.(H)/West,' Ia Report, *OB West Tagemeldungen,* BA-MA, RH 19 IV/84 D, p. 138.

16 *'Mit Shakespeare-Englisch,' Der Spiegel, Nr.2,* 10 January 1951, pp. 10-15 and letter to editor, *Der Spiegel,* 10 January 1951, p. 11. Also, Gerald Astor's interview with Rohde, *A Blood Dimmed Tide,* Donald Fine, NY, pp. 101-104. In the first 24 hours of the attack Otto Skorzeny's English-speaking jeep teams roamed the Ardennes, nearly at will. One of the semi—fluent commandos, Feldwebel Rohde, had learned passable English while visiting his father in Woodstock, New York. Yet, now he narrowly avoided detection when he realized that no American vehicles were using blackout headlights and hastily removed theirs. Nor were most American jeeps riding with four men packed into each. Watching the Meuse bridge at Huy, Rohde worried that with searchlights were trained on the bridge and perhaps the Americans were wise to their mission. Later, the much relieved Ahrensböck native, successfully returned to German lines.

Chapter 10 – The Blowtorch Battalion

1 Recollection of admonition from Leibstandarte division commander, Wilhelm Mohnke to Jochen Peiper; Statement of Peiper, 21 March 1946, NA, RG-549, Case 6-24, Box 6.

2 Interview with Reinhold Kyriss of the *II Panzer Battalion*, 20 May 1997. 'He was totally unpredictable.'

3 Comrade Rolf Reiser remembered that Peiper had been ill when he left the tank regiment in the summer of 1944—a fact recalled by most who knew him. Gerhard Walla, with the tank regiment, thought in December 1944 that Peiper was a nervous wreck. Pervitin? To him, Peiper was more of a figurehead leader while Poetschke was the true leader of the tank regiment. Did Peiper have a nervous breakdown after Normandy? Sigurd Peiper's letters to Hedwig Potthast in the fall of 1944 reinforce that judgement.

4 Kyriss interview, *op. cit.*

5 'Beförderung des SS Ustuf. Poetschke, 1./SS-A.A.' 16 May 1940 and 'Beurteilung des SS Obersturmführer Poetschke,' 19 September 1940, BDC File for Werner Poetscheke, NA, BDC A3343-SSO-386A.

6 Kyriss interview, *op. cit.*

7 'Vorschlaglichte Nr. 3173 für die Verleihung des Ritterkreuzes des Eiserner Kreuzes,' signed by Peiper on 24 April 1944. For the disciplinary action: 'Feldgericht der Leibstandarte SS Adolf Hitler: Mißrauch der Disziplinarstrafbefugnis: SS Haupsturmführer Werner Poetschke,' 18 May 1944, BDC File for Poetschke, *op. cit.* The action was over harsh treatment of a motorcycle platoon during the actions at Kharkov in January 1943.

8 There is corroboration for Peiper's uneasy relationship with Poetschke. In a 1985 interview with Gerd Cuppens, Hans Hennecke in Lübecke told the Belgian researcher: 'Poetschke and Peiper were not at all friends,' he confided, 'and sometimes they would argue.' Gerd Cuppens, *Massacre a Malmedy*, Editions Heimdal, Bayeux, 1989, p. 60.

9 'Statement of SS Rottenführer Guenther Boese, 1st SS Panzer Battalion,' 23 January 1945, NA, RG-153, Case 6-24, Box 73. Boese joined the SS in 1942, being assigned to the LSSAH as a motorcycle messenger. From there he served continually with the division and was wounded twice in Russia. 'During training Poetschke had employed a punitive method already used by him in Russia. This was known as 'Strahlen' and consisted of having to run or march carrying two tank suspension parts of great weight in their arms. No man had ever lasted a full hour with this. But the punishment was frequently given for three or four hours which meant repetition on subsequent days until the spirit and body of the man was completely broken ... His comrades hated their commanding officer for this.' In the Ardennes, when his jeep had fallen out due to bad gas, Poetschke accused him of cowardice and made him ride exposed on the outside of tank from Derenbach (east of Bastogne) to Neuville. 'There was great bitterness in the battalion that men were uselessly and cruelly sacrificed—especially because neither Poetschke nor Peiper were ever present when a really hot attack came off.' '*Die Kampfmoral war sehr dadurch gesunken—With that the fighting morale dropped.*' He was captured near Neuville on 17 January 1945 after being sent on a mission to bring back a pig for the panzer regiment kitchen near Petit Thier, Belgium.

10 'Interrogation Report: Rottenführer Gunther Boese,' 23 February 1945, NA, RG-549, Case 6-24, Box 22. Hennecke derision: '*Da habe ich in die Franzosen anständig hineingepfeffert!*'

11 Author's interview with Otto Dinse, 21 May 1996. 'Every night we were on wild rides deep inside Russian lines. We didn't even know where the front line was ... Peiper always took advantage of things. He always had a tank platoon with his battalion. They were an armored tank group. He attacked at night broke through 60 km north that took the Russians completely by surprise. One cannot imagine; the enemy was standing on the dark street and we just marched right through. I had the tank of the adjutant and we didn't even have communications with the division headquarters ... It goes like this in Russia: at 4 or 5 in the morning the sun rises and then the Russian artillery begins, and then at 8 AM in the morning the tank battle starts along with other fighting. But we took off at 12:01 AM and drove around. We did this with tank attacks also. We did it time after time. We nicknamed the halftracks "open coffins," so we always had a company of tanks along. The *Schützenpanzerwagen* were only strong enough to stop rifle rounds; if an anti-tank gun fired on it, it was gone. Accordingly, Peiper always got tanks to go along and he attacked with tanks intermingled with SPWs. He would lead with an SPW out front with a tank behind a few and then there would be a few more SPWs with another tank. This is the way Peiper organized his attacks. We lost some tanks and some SPWs, but the enemy would always try to take out the tanks first. But that's how we rode all our attacks.'

12 Peiper testimony, U.S. v. Valentin Bersin, *op. cit.*, pp. 2031-2032.

13 Asked when he first saw the American trucks south of Malmedy being fired upon, Peiper ventured that it was sometime between '1300 and 1330 hours.', *ibid.*, p. 1929.

14 Peiper's testimony at the trial on pages 1927-1928 of the stenographer's transcript is at odds with numerous other accounts of those in Diefenthal's halftrack who do not recall Peiper having left the vehicles as he described in the trial. In a Schwäbisch Hall statement, Hans Assenmacher, Diefenthal's radio operator, clearly places Peiper in the SPW beside Diefenthal as they approached the crossroads. Moreover, even in

his later statements from Landsberg intending to exonerate his colleagues such as that of 5 November 1947, (RG 153, Box 81), Assenmacher maintained that Peiper was with them when the first sounds of gunfire were heard, even mentioning that Peiper himself ordered the firing stopped from their SPW.

15 Sternebeck as related to Rolf Reiser at Ebensee. Statement of Rolf Roland Reiser, 3 January 1946, NA, RG-549, Case 6-24, Box 37. 'I remember how Sternebeck once told me that he had met a troop of American POWs, led by a Captain. They were passing by his panzer. He waved his hand for them to go back further. He also spoke about a shooting behind him and that American soldiers were running away, or trying to run away and that he had shot with his pistol a few times.'

16 Werner Sternebeck, *'Bericht über den Vormarsch der Panzerspitze der 'Panzer Gruppe Peiper von Losheim bis Engelsdorf am 16. und 17.12.1944,'* His recollections from 1983 were kindly provided to author by Wolf Mauder.

17 SS Oscha. Rudolf Dörr claimed that his SPW in the *Panzerspitze* first had the assignment to pick up mines for the attack group, but 'became stuck in the woods after Büllingen and we had to be left behind. We were later pulled out by a tank and re-joined our outfit at Stavelot.' Dörr had been captured at La Gleize and was interrogated on 16 January 1945 by Maj. Oliver Seth at the 168th Gen. Hospital, 'Testimony of S/Sgt. Rudolf Dörr,' NA, RG-153, Case 6-24, Box 70.

18 SS Rttf. Ohlrogge's crew included Strm. Büttner (driver), Strm. Till (MG), Strm. Süsse and Strm. Lüsse (medic). Thanks to Timm Haasler for preparing the summary research document, 'Summary 9. (Pi.)/SS-Pz. Rgt.1' for the author.

19 'Statement of Rolf Reiser,' 3 January 1946, NA, RG-549, Case 6-24, Box 37, p. 6. At Ebensee POW Enclosure Nr. 2 in Barracks Nr. 20, Ustuf. Helmut Pönisch was located in the same room with Reiser (he 1943, he had attended the *1. SS Panzer Junker Lehrgang* tank leader instruction course in Putlos with Reiser). While rooming with Reiser, Sternebeck had brought in an issue of *Yank* magazine that showed shot Americans at Malmedy. Sternebeck then remarked to those present saying, 'that he will probably be held responsible for that because he led the point of the offensive, despite the fact that he did not have anything to do with all that.' Ralph Schumaker said of Reiser: 'He proved very meticulous in formulating the sentences of the statement. Was always in a co-operative cell in D Block.' SS Ustuf Helmut Pönisch had been in the summer of 1941 on the staff of the *Kommandostab RFSS*. Later, he met Rolf Reiser at the *ISS* tank training school in Putlos in 1943. He fought with the staff of *I. SS* panzer Regt 1 in Normandy.

20 This could have been Gerhard Walla who claimed to be left alone with the prisoners for some time.

21 For Tonk handing the prisoners over to a tank driven by Manfred Thorn: 'Screening results from SS Rttf. Alfred Krafft,' IC #78, Screening results from 15-24 November 1945, Ellis Papers, in author's possession. While Thorn told the author in several interviews that he encountered Werner Poetschke guarding the prisoners, he does not recall seeing Tonk at the crossroads, so this point remains in doubt. Retired Bundeswehr panzer officer, Wolf Mauder, has studied the movements of *Kampfgruppe Peiper* in detail and while disputing that the U.S. convoy could have been moving when Thorn sighted it at the front of the vanguard, he estimates that the distance from Sternebeck's point tank to the vanguard following up as approximately 2 km with a time interval of 10-15 minutes. The author believes this could have been as short as five minutes, but certainly not more than 15 minutes. Interview with Wolf Mauder, 19 May 1997, Heppenheim.

22 Interview with Gerhard Walla, 10 May 1999.

23 Peiper's testimony: *ibid*, U.S. v. Bersin, pp. 1927-1932.

24 Also in the SPW of Dörr (Platoon commander) with Maute was Uscha. Held (SPW commander), Rttf. Hoeppner (driver), Strm. Hoppe (MG#1), Strm. Franke (MG#2), Strm. Heinz Kappermann (radio operator) and Strm. Gramlich. Statement Heinz Kappermann, 23 December 1944, NA, RG-549, Case 6-24, Box 41 and Statement of Erich Maute, 22 January 1946, Box 32.

25 Peiper's testimony: *ibid*, U.S. v. Bersin, pp. 1929-1930.

26 Interview of Arndt Fischer by Timm Haasler, 12 January 2006, courtesy Timm Haasler.

27 Interview with Manfred Thorn, 23 March 1996, Butgenbach, Belgium.

28 It was standard procedure in the German army that the platoon leader or company commander tried to be as near to the point as possible, but never leading the attack because the loss of the unit leader could cause the entire assault to break down.

29 Interview with Manfred Thorn, 23 March 1996, *op. cit*.

30 Follow-up interview with Manfred Thorn, 11 May 1999.

31 Interview with Hans Siptrott, 17 May 1997, Esslingen.

32 This was likely the SPWs of Dörr, Wemmel and those with Rumpf and the rest of *9. Panzer Pionier Kompanie*.

33 Thorn interview, 23 March 1996, *op. cit*.

34 In the author's interview with Thorn on 11 May 1999, he vividly recalled the words from Poetschke before the café: *'Fahren sie auf nach Engelsdorf und nehmen die Verbindung auf zur Spitze Sternbeck.'*

35 'Testimony of Rolf Ehrhardt, 30 October 1946, NA, RG-549, 'English Summaries and Translations of German Documents Related to War Crimes,' 290/59/18/2-5, Box 13. After leaving the crossroads,

Ehrhardt related that: 'About 600 meters further on we overtook car [Panzer] 734 of Pilaypik [sic, Pilarzek] which had stopped because of some defect. I cannot give the exact order of the motor vehicles of my company. Schraeder, Unterscharführer and 734 were ahead of me (out of sight). As I overtook 734, I arrived in Engelsdorf before him … I cannot give the exact time when I arrived in Engelsdorf. It must have been a short time after 2nd Lt Fischer's Panther had been hit as I still saw Fischer (wounded).' In Ehrhardt's detailed recollections of the Ardennes events from 1981, he told of having trouble descending down to Ligneuville. 'The road required some attention because the technology of the Mk IV was not designed for going down curves downhill. Arriving in Engelsdorf, we first saw [Panzer] No. 702 unharmed [Schraeder's tank] and also the burning Panther of Fischer, Peiper—and likely Diefenthal too—as well as a number of SPWs.' Report from Rolf Ehrhardt, *7 Kompanie, 1. Panzer Regiment*, LSSAH, no date, but 1981, 18-page report provided to author by Hans Behrend, Aspach.

36 'As commandant of the spearhead tank of the 7th Company, I was not an eye witness to the events at the crossroads.' Statement of Heinz Schraeder, 22 September 1947, NA, RG-549, Case 6-24, Box 15. Note that after Thirimont, Panzer #734, driven by Manfred Thorn was actually ahead of Schraeder.

37 Testimony of Edward Bojarski to Lamar Tooze, U.S. First Army HQ, 19 December 1944, NA, RG-153, Case 6-24, Box 76.

38 The very important testimony of Arvid Freimuth was taken at Dachau on 30 October 1945, at Dachau well before the investigation at Schwäbisch Hall. NA, RG-549, Case 6-24, Box 31. However, within the Schwäbisch Hall investigation, Freimuth later committed suicide claiming that he had perjured himself—possible since his only confession at Schwäbisch Hall had nothing to do with the crossroads incident and concerned alleged shootings at La Gleize. The author used the 30 October 1945 statement as its contents contained nothing controversial but did shed light on Peiper's actions at the crossroads on 17 December 1944. The crew of Freimuth's SPW included SS Ustf. Heinz Hendel, SS Rttf. Kurt Wittwer, Strm. Olaf Jassen, Strm. Herbert Stock and Rttf. Günther Heinrichs.

39 Testimony of Josef Diefenthal to Dwight Fanton, 14 November 1945 in Wiesbaden. NA, Case 6-24, RG-549, Box 33. This 32-page interview with Diefenthal remains one of the center pieces of the early investigation.

40 While it will be shown that Poetschke almost certainly ordered his subordinates to shoot the American prisoners, the possibility that Peiper told Poetschke to do away with the captives cannot be excluded. Indeed, Paul Zwigart, who was driving Diefenthal's SPW at the crossroads told SS NCO medic Josef Frank precisely that while both were held in captivity in the fall of 1945. 'Zwigart driver of the vehicle in which Peiper and Diefenthal were driving at the time of the shooting at the crossroad, told Frank, Schlachter, Moosbrugge and others that Peiper gave the order at the crossroads.' Dwight Fanton's Personality Card Index File, NA, RG-549, Case 6-24, Index to Defendents in the Malmedy Case, Reference Witness Statements, 290/59/18/5. Card for SS Uschaf. Josef Frank, *7 Panzer Kompanie*. While most rumors prior to Schwäbisch Hall charged Poetschke with the origination of the orders to shoot the prisoners, some hearsay continued to attribute the original source to Peiper. For instance, SS Uscha. Emmerich Bukor, in the headquarters battery of the artillery regiment recounted to American interrogators in the fall of 1945 that 'he had heard about the murder in Hungary in February 1945 from Richard Huber of the *II. Battalion*, that he had heard from others that Peiper had given the order to other officers to shoot the Americans and that the order had been carried out.' Interrogation of Emmerich Bukor, IC #73, 'Screening Results 15—24 November 1945,' Ellis Papers.

41 Testimony of Josef Diefenthal, 12 December 1945, NA, RG-549, Case 6-24, Box 33.

42 Kuhlmann was in charge of *SS Panzer Regiment 12* of the Hitler Jugend Panzer Division, at that hour involved in a ferocious battle with the U.S. 2nd Infantry Division in the twin villages of Rocherath-Krinkelt, not far from their starting point. They would never advance closer to Malmedy than Butgenbach.

43 This conversation and all the particulars in this section from the statement of Hans Assenmacher, 6 and 11 February 1946 at Schwäbisch Hall as witnessed by Ralph Schumaker, NA, Case 6-24, RG 549, Box 36.

44 Freimuth Statement, *ibid*, page 9. Paul Fröhlich had also been in Peiper's SPW since Büllingen: 'Peiper was very concerned with time. Peiper reached the crossroads and yelled out some orders to get moving.' Author's interview with Frölich 19 May 1997.

45 Although Hans Assenmacher produced statements in 1948 alleging mistreatment at Schwäbisch Hall and errors in his account of the 'Jeep incident' incriminating Paul Zwigart, he never re-canted his version of the events with Peiper at the crossroads on 17 December 1944. See Affidavits, 17 June and 19 November 1948, NA, Case 6-24, RG-549, Box 70.

46 Interview with Paul Zwigart, 20 May 1997, Anspach. 'I liked Maj. Peiper, but I cannot talk about Diefenthal. We cannot speak about him.' The author's interview with Zwigart was exceedingly tense, with comrade, Dr Franz Neundorff standing by him. The jeep incident at Cheneux was placed off limits before the meeting.

47 Author's interviews with William Merriken, 4 July and 22 September 1995. In both interviews, Merriken recalled after they had surrendered and were walking back to the crossroads a tall panzer officer who called out 'Chauffeur! Chauffeur!' asking them to drive the trucks, now abandoned by the 285th FAOB.

48 Interview with Gerhard Walla on 10 May 1999, Aspach.

49 'Testimony of Rolf Erhardt at Oberursel,' 30 October 1946. RG 549 'English Summaries and Translations of German Documents Related to War Crimes,' 290/59/18/2-5, Box 13. 'While I was in captivity, I heard about the events in [near] Engelsdorf from Rottenführer Reinhard Meier that he had been present when Poetschke had answered the question of a messenger of what to do with the prisoners, with "Kill them!"' Note that this testimony came *after* the trial.

50 Testimony of Josef Diefenthal, Wiesbaden, 12 December 1945, NA, RG-549, Case 6-24, Box 33, p. 7. This early investigative interview with Dwight Fanton is the most important document dealing with Diefenthal in the Ardennes operations. After this 32-page interview, Diefenthal later pointedly avoided any discussion of his and Peiper's movements at the crossroads.

51 BDC file for Erich Rumpf, NA, RG-242, A3343-SS0-055B, Frame 589.

52 'Who, at that time, was not proud of the man, who without hesitation staked their life for the fatherland.' Letter Elly Rumpf to Parole Board, 16 September 1946. NA, RG-153, Case 6-24, Box 84. 'In case he has done wrong and has done what he is accused of, [then] he acted under the pressure and terrible confusion of war and it really was a desperate situation at the time.'

53 'The main care [sic, job] of the company leader was from the battalion Poetschke that all those soldiers were against his will, transferred to the 9th company who had been punished in their former companies and were considered particularly undisciplined, for which reason they had to serve a special term of probation in the 9th company. Almost all of them were soldiers of long service … Rumpf referred to this order as an attempt of the battalion commanders to clear themselves of all soldiers that were inconvenient to them and difficult to deal with … I know that shortly before the removal to the area west of Cologne, Rumpf rang up the regiment several times for the purpose of being relieved from the post of a company leader and to be removed to another unit. Rumpf, was however, ordered to stay in his position.' Affidavit of Gunther Borchers, 5 August 1947, NA, RG-153, Case 6-24, Box 80.

54 Statement of Walter Fransee, 21 March 1946, NA, RG-549, Case 6-24, Box 33.

55 'All inhabitants of the village were shot, man, woman, or child. Rttf. Schmidt, who was then the radioman for the company commander, Hstuf. Nüske told us, when we caught up with the baggage train that Rttf. Vorst allegedly beat the children to death with an iron bar.' 'Kriegsverbrechen im Osten,' Statement of Walter Fransee, 1st Platoon, 9 Pz Pi. Bn, 1 SS Pz Rgt., handwritten statement and transcription and translation by Helmut Thiess, George Washington University, Gelman Library, William Perl Papers, Box 6, Folder 51.

56 However, in writing to American historian John Toland in 1959, Peiper would challenge these notions. 'I regret that you do not write history,' he said criticizing Toland's account, 'but prefer to still cling to the old and primitive pattern of the Nazi brutes slaughtering civilians and violating the laws of war and peace … For a man with intelligence and reason, such a one-sided and biased story should be under his dignity. And above all: what is the good of it?' Peiper to Toland, 22 February 1959. Library of Congress, John Toland Papers, *Battle: The Story of the Bulge*, Box 108, Folder 'P.'

Chapter 11 – At the Crossroads

1 Prince Fontinbras to Horatio: *Hamlet*, Act V, Scene II.

2 'Also, tell your men and impress on them so you don't experience failure, that no one must stay behind because every man and every vehicle are needed.' Statement of Erich Rumpf, 22 March 1946. Handwritten and translated typescript are in NA, RG-549, Case 6-24, Box 7.

3 Letter Jochen Peiper to Hedwig Potthast, 24 March 1943, *NSDAP Hauptarchiv*, Himmler Collection, Microfilm Roll #99, Hoover Institution, Stanford University. Originals at the Bundesarchiv Koblenz, '*Nachlass Heinrich Himmler: Korrespondenz Hedwig Potthast*, Bestand N 1126/37. This letter is very significant to an understanding of Peiper view of fighting. '*Aber auch ein schlechter Ruf verpflichtet*—But a bad reputation (*schlechter Ruf*) has its obligations'—Peiper revealed that his favorite wartime motto was taken from Nazi wartime cinematic diva Zarah Leander. The lyric is from the catchy tune, 'Yes Sir!' from the film '*Zu neuen Ufern*.'

4 Interview with Al Valenzi, 26 September 1995. Also, testimony of T/Sgt. William Merriken to Ralph Shumacker, 9 October 1945, Wiesbaden, Germany, RG- 549, Case 6-24, Box 30. Both men heard Peiper's utterance at the head of the surrendering American column.

5 This chapter of the book is largely distilled from the author's more detailed account in *Fatal Crossroads* (2012). Additional accounts and details, particularly from the American side, can be gleaned there.

6 'Screening Results 24–29 November 1945,' witnesses interrogated by Capt. Hoelzl, pp. 1-2, Ellis Papers. 'Maier then asked Poetschke if he thought the messenger had received the correct order. Poetschke asked the messenger who was at the crossroads. He replied: "*Ostuf. Rumpf*". Poetschke then recalled the messenger and asked him to repeat the orders and the messenger said: "Shoot the prisoners" Poetschke then said, "Correct," and dismissed the messenger.'

7 According to Erich Rumpf's own testimony, his personal orderly and messenger was SS Rottenführer Richard Weck. No statements or testimony of Weck survives, and his driver SS Karl Viel refused to talk. The number of U.S. POWs being led back from just beyond Baugnez was considerably less than fifty. They were essentially being rounded up and walked back to the collection point. See *Fatal Crossroads, op. cit.*, pp. 61-73.

8 Reinhard Maier was in Room #24 of Barracks 'D' at IC#78 and talked to SS Rttf. Hubert Brückner with the *7.Kompanie* who was prisoner there. 'Peiper had nothing to do with it,' Brückner remembered Maier saying, 'He knows the whole story, that Poetschke gave the order and that when interrogated, he will tell all about it.' 'Screening Results 15–24 November 1945,' witnesses interrogated by Capt. Shumacker, Ellis Papers.

9 The SPW of Hering was driven by Schuetze Paul Buth with Strm. Fritz Pupkulies as one of its machine gunners, Strm. Spaeh its messenger and Sturmann Walter Fransee its radio operator. Rest of the 8-10 man crew is unknown. Statement of SS Schütze Paul Buth, 26 March 1945.

10 Statement of Willi von Chamier, 21 March 1946, witnessed by Ralph Shumaker, both 3-page handwritten statement with detailed map are in NA, RG-549, Case 6-24, Box 8. In the map, von Chamier shows the exact locations of Rumpf and his own SPW. Lined up across the prisoners just before the shooting, on his map, were three SPWs from another unit and four tanks.

11 Von Chamier, *op. cit.*, The crew of the SPW consisted of Oscha. Wedeleit (leader), Uscha. Helmuth Haas (leader of 1st squad), Rttf. Katcher (MG Gunner 1), Uscha. Willi von Chamier (MG Gunner 2), Uscha. Biotta (Rifle 1), Schuetze. Max Rieder (Rifle 2) and Schuetze Corzieni (Rifle 3). Von Chamier had been a steel worker in Dortmund prior to the war. In April 1943, von Chamier was moved from his duty as a Luftwaffe flak gunner to the Waffen SS with the tank regiment of *SS Panzer Regiment 1*. He was captured on 20 December 1944 and transferred from a POW camp in the U.S. to Dachau for the trial, arriving on 20 March 1946. He confessed before William Perl, Ralph Shumaker and Burton Ellis the following day with his statement written that afternoon. Like nearly all of the Malmedy men, von Chamier would repudiate his confession on 11 April 1948, NA, RG-549, Case 6-24, Box 47.

12 Statement of Walter Fransee, 21 March 1946, NA, RG-549, Case 6-24, Box 33. Two detailed sketches showed the locations of the men shot by Hering as their SPW passed the crossroads.

13 Those claiming to have seen Rumpf at the crossroads at the time of the massacre were so numerous: both Rieder and von Chamier in statements claimed to have seen Rumpf himself fire into the prisoners with a pistol after calling for them to fire as well. Dörr claimed to crew-mate Kappermann that Rumpf had told him to order the tanks present to fire into the prisoners, but he was having none of that. The medic in the same SPW, Erich Maute, corroborated this account. Also machine gunner Strm. Fritz Pupkulies in screening in the fall of 1945 before Schwäbisch Hall said that his commander, Rumpf, should know about the massacre as he was already there waiting when they arrived and saw the bodies lying in the field. ('Screening Results 24-29 November 1945,' interrogations by Capt. Hoelzl at IC#1, Ellis Papers.) SS man Bernhardt Dietz went AWOL from training in Westphalia and was sent to the penal platoon of the *9. Pz. Pi. Kompanie* in the Ardennes. 'When they were camped near Engelsdorf on the 19th or 20th of December, a man by the name of Jansen told him about the murder at the crossroads and said that Rumpf had given orders that anyone who talked about this murder would be shot … Rumpf was very unpopular with the *Straf* platoon.' 'Screening Results 15-24 November 1945,' interrogations by Morris Ellowitz at IC#1, Ellis Papers. Note that these interrogations were done prior to Schwäbisch Hall. Finally, the following members of Franz Siever's *3. Panzer Pi. Kompanie*, who were implicated in the massacre, all told of seeing SS Ostuf. Rumpf at the scene when it took place: Joachim Hoffmann, Gustav Neve, Siegfried Jaeckel and Gustav Sprenger.

14 Since both Rehagel and Rumpf were present—and both were in need of alibis excusing them culpability at Baugnez—the possibility emerges that the SS officer the members of Panzer Nr 711 saw speaking to Rehagel near the crossroads was Rumpf himself.

15 Slightly different to Rumpf's earlier claim, the weight of evidence suggests that Hennecke's tank showed up immediately after the massacre had taken place. See statement of Hans Hennecke, 17 January 1946, NA, Case 6-24, RG-549, Box 8. Indeed, Hennecke's tank had side-swiped the SPW of Erich Rumpf on the right side of the road at the intersection which had elicited numerous curses from Rumpf. 'I drove very slowly further, Uscha. Richarts followed me … As I was passing the house which lies on the right side of the street, I stood in the turret of my tank looking in the direction I was going. Ernst Rock, my loader, stood behind me … Strm. Rock called to me, 'Untersturmführer, there lie some men and they are all dead.' I turned around and saw 15 or 20 dead Americans were lying to my right on the field. I saw them lying in a heap, and from the manner in which they were lying, I could see that they had not fallen in combat. No weapons were with them.' Hennecke remained with that version of the story, both in his first interrogation by Dwight Fanton on 11 December 1945 in Schwäbisch Hall (Box 23) and even in his later legal effort at exoneration from Landsberg. See statement of 11 April 1948, NA, Case 6-24, RG-549, Box 55.

16 Statement of Erich Rumpf, 22 March 1946. Handwritten and translated typescript are in NA, RG-549, Case 6-24, Box 7. Rumpf includes five sketches with legends which are in the same series, Box 25.

17 Statement of Joachim Hoffmann, 6 March 1946, U.S. v. Bersin, *op. cit.*, pp. 645-567. Original is in RG-549, Case 6-24, Box 6 with Hoffmann's detailed map of the crossroad incident. Even though Hoffmann would later repudiate his statement as did many others, it is significant that a typed transcript of an interrogation of Hoffmann regarding the crossroads incident survives from 15 February 1946 (Case 6-24, RG-549, Box 38).

Q: You passed Beutner's vehicle on the right?

A: Yes. When the SPWs of the 2nd platoon passed Beutner's SPW, he was still sitting on his SPW and shouted to every vehicle. 'Go and bump them off—all of them.' We stopped near the south end of the field. We stood parallel to the ditch.

Q: Before the first shot was fired, how long were you there?

A: One to two minutes. During this time, the entire crowd on all the vehicles started shouting, 'Bump them off! Bump them off!' I remember that Bode, Beutner and some more people from other SPWs were among them. There was quite some excitement. The men took out their weapons. We only had one machine gun—the front gun mounted permanently and after we arrived Toedter alone mounted and fixed the rear machine gun. I took the machine pistol and left my driver's seat and posted myself in front of the right corner of my SPW. Shortly after I posted myself there … Witkowski said, 'Well boys, let's go on and let them have it.'

18 Interrogation of Gustav Neve by Ralph Shumacker, 6 March 1946, NA, RG-549, Case 6-24, Box 26. Within the interrogation transcript, Neve changed his story completely after being confronted with Gustav Sprenger—from saying the Americans had already been shot when he arrived, to confessing to active participation in the shooting with detailed hand-drawn sketches. This exchange makes it clear, however, that an agreed upon tactic of the guilty in the crossroads shooting was to claim that the Americans were already shot when their vehicle arrived—or conversely that all the Americans were still standing there and unharmed.

19 Machine gunner, Heinz Stickel in the same SPW 'I received the order from Witkowski to shoot the prisoners who were standing in the pasture.' He claimed to have obeyed since SS Ustuf. Seitz had told them before the offensive that 'You will not take any prisoners of war in this offensive.' Statement of Heinz Stickel, 18 April 1946, NA, RG-549, Case 6-24, Box 7.

20 Statement of Joachim Hoffmann from 20 March 1946, Case 6-24, RG-549, Box 6. Regarding the actions of Beutner: 'He told Witkowski that they were going to shoot the prisoners and to move on down the road out of the way so that they would not be in the field of fire.' Regarding Diefenthal: 'In my affidavit dated 6 March 1946, in which I told all I know about the shooting of American prisoners of war in the Eifel offensive, I mentioned having seen an officer wearing a yellow jacket at the crossroads north of Ligneuville … On this date I saw a man in Cell E-53 at the prison in Schwäbisch Hall. The man I saw in this cell is definitely the same man I saw in the yellow jacket. When I recognized him this morning, a guard opened the door of his cell and told him to state his name. He gave his name as Josef Diefenthal.'

21 Affidavit of Gustav Neve, 6 March 1946, U.S. v. Bersin, pp. 667-672. The original and detailed map drawn by Neve is in Case 6-24, RG-549, Box 6. 'After we had come to a halt, I heard Beutner tell Witkowski that the weapons should be loaded and made ready so we could 'bump off' the American prisoners … Finally Beutner gave the order to fire and everybody opened up with their weapons.'

22 Jaekel statement: U.S. v. Bersin, pp. 681-692. The original statement and large detailed map is in Case 6-24, RG-549, Box 7. Jaekel named Hans Toedter and Harry Ende as helping him load, man and fire the machine guns in his SPW, although these men were never located or brought to trial.

23 Statement of Heinz Stickel, 18 April 1946, U.S. v. Bersin, pp. 705-706. That of Marcel Boltz: pp. 711-715.

24 Not surprisingly, two other NCOs who were in Beutner's SPW—Rttf. Ernst Goldschmidt and Max Hammerer, were evasive in their statements regarding the events at the crossroads although the members of Hoffmann's and Sprenger's crews clearly placed them on the scene. However, Hammerer did tersely admit that 'at the crossing which leads to Engelsdorf … our SPW came to a halt and I was present as American prisoners of war were shot.' Statement of Max Hammerer, 11 April 1946, U.S. v. Bersin, pp. 1411-1412. However, Goldschmidt insisted awkwardly at the Malmedy trial that the 60 Americans had already been shot when the 2nd Platoon SPW reached the crossroads—a fact disputed by five other witness statements which placed him on the scene when the shooting took place. Trial testimony of Ernst Goldschmidt, U.S. v. Bersin, *op. cit.*, pp. 2398-2434. Indeed, so perilous was Goldschmidt's nervous performance at the trial, that defense counsel Everett sought to cut short his testimony. Interestingly, Hans Oettinger, who was working as a carpenter in Hedelfingen would later come out of the woodwork to testify in Max Hammerer's behalf (who was sentenced to die by hanging)—a risk since Oettinger himself and the others in the SPW he drove at Baugnez participated in the shooting. 'Sworn Statement of Hans Oettinger,' Munich, 19 December 1947, NA, RG-153, Case 6-24, Box 80.

25 Statement of Heinz Friedrichs, 21 March 1946, NA, RG-549, Box 9. Friedrichs was an 18 year old SS grenadier in the SPW of Uscha. Gerhard Schumacher. When they were preparing to fire on the prisoners—a mission that was aborted at the last moment, Friedrichs looked away. 'I told him I could not stand it, whereupon he called me a coward.' Unable to depress his cannon on the prisoners, an Obersturmführer in

a pionier uniform who appeared to be in charge, [likely Erich Rumpf of the 9. Panzer Pionier Kompanie] ordered Schumacher to proceed to Engelsdorf as a tank was coming up that 'would do the job.'

26 Statement of Siegfried Jaekel, 1 March 1946, witnessed by Ralph Shumacher, NA, RG-549, Box 7. Original handwritten statements and detailed maps are in Box 7.

27 Trial testimony of Marcel Boltz, U.S. v. Bersin, pp. 2464-2528.

28 Interrogation of Siegfried Jaekel on 15 February 1946 by Ralph Shumacher, NA, RG-549, Box

29 As apparent from the accounts here, there were at least three versions of what happened from German sources: one where the instigator of the shootings was Erich Rumpf and another where it was Max Beutner—convenient because he was killed in the later fighting. A final version has both Rumpf and Beutner involved, but Fleps the source of the first shots. For further detail, Fatal Crossroads, pp. 239-241.

30 The SPW was likely that of Max Beutner of the *3. SS-Pz.Pi. Kompanie* which had bridging equipment rack-mounted on their *Sdkfz 251/7 Pionierpanzerwagen*. Thanks to Timm Haasler.

31 Siptrott's statement, U.S. v. Bersin, pp. 561-562. 'Several hundred meters further south we stopped because of a traffic jam. At that spot, Fleps left the tank. We stopped approximately five minutes and Fleps was absent.' Author possesses a copy of Siptrott's original handwritten statement as well as the drawing that went with it. The diagram showed his tank #731, Clotten's tank behind him as well as two other tanks of Dubbert and Koch behind those. However, in his recollection, Siptrott was hazy on the exact march order and did not realize that Pilzarek's tank with Manfred Thorn as driver was actually up ahead of his own as well as two other tanks: 702 with Heinz Schraeder and 701 with company commander, Oskar Klingelhöfer. Author's interview with Thorn (23 March 1996 and 11 May 1999) and Siptrott (17 May 1997).

32 Given the author's reconstruction of the events at the crossroads, the 'SPW commander' giving Siptrott and Fleps the order would have been SS Uscha. Max Beutner in charge of the 2nd platoon of the *3 Panzer Pionier Kompanie* which several accounts place on the scene with Beutner relaying orders from Werner Poetschke in a Panther present immediately before the events took place.

33 In Fleps' original handwritten statement, he says that Siptrott scornfully referred to the men in the SPW as: '*dise Elende Hunde*—these miserable dogs' After he first fired, an MG on one of the SPWs opened up and he then shot again, felling a lone man who remained standing. He claimed that Siptrott began to drive away as soon as he fired the second shot.' Statement of Georg Fleps, 5 January 1946, NA, RG-549, Case 6-24, Box 7.

34 Fleps' statement, *op. cit.* Fleps said that after leaving the scene at the crossroads that 'We stopped again by the first house on the left side of the road, i.e. the house indicated as No. 9 on my sketch (which is just 30 meters or so behind the massacre field), because the column had stopped and besides our track was slightly damaged. I left the tank to take booty. I took some cans of condensed milk and corned beef from an American truck. There I saw to the right of the street behind a fence, three Americans lying who were either dead or wounded … I saw there three men from another vehicle of another company—I believe they belonged to the Mk V tank. Two were obviously dead … the third one gave the impression that he was still living. The people ahead of me, who I assume belonged to the Mk V, fired about two shots at the American and I shot once into his head. We were standing at his feet.' Fleps also recounted his story that earlier in the war, he had seen SS Uscha. Rolf Ehrhardt and Rttf. Wesenberg shoot a wounded Canadian POW at Tilly in July 1944.

35 Interrogation of Roman Clotten at Ebensee, 1 October 1945, NA, RG-549, Case 6-24, Box 31. Who had ordered the prisoners shot at the crossroads? Clotten ventured in this early statement that it had been Poetschke who had given the original orders.

36 Statement of Roman Clotten, 22 January 1946, NA, RG-549, Case 6-24, Box 7. Clotten's statement included a detailed sketch which was very similar to others given by other members of his company as well as others made by members of Rumpf's *9. Kompanie* and Siever's *3. Kompanie.*

37 Whether Dubbert's tank was on the scene when the shooting transpired is one of the unresolved questions in the author's laborious research to recreate the chronology of the event. Although Clotten's testimony and the sketch of Siptrott placed SS Uscha. Dubbert on the scene and firing into the prisoners, neither he nor any of his tank crew (Strm. Anton Stephan, Hans Muling, Strm. Menzel and Rttf. Alfons Ziesemann) were ever called to testify at the trial. This may be because SS Rttf. Alfons Ziesemann claimed that when their tank approached the crossroads, the Americans had already been shot minutes before. Prior to arriving at the crossroads he heard a lot of shooting which 'he recognized as fire from machine guns … As he passed the corner where the crime took place he saw many Americans dead and he knew from the way they were lying that they had been shot down.' He claimed that the tank ahead of him was commanded by SS Uscha. Heinrich Burk. Interrogation of Alfons Ziesemann, IC #1, Screening results from 24-29 November 1945, Ellis Papers. Also, Georg Fleps in a statement dated 4 March 1946 (NA, RG-549, Case 6-24, Box 22) claimed to have spoken with SS Oscha. Erich Dubbert on the night after the shooting in a farmhouse on the outskirts of Stavelot where Dubbert said 'he had shot and killed four American prisoners of war who were still alive at the road crossing before Engelsdorf.' The grim implication was that the main shooting had already happened and Dubbert finished some off. Thus, it is possible that Clotten mistook Koch for

Dubbert just behind him although Clotten claimed that Dubbert fired with a machine pistol whereas Koch clearly shot with a swivel-mount MG-34 according to the testimony of Reicke.

38 At Bliesheim on 13 December, Clotten claimed to have been told by Klingelhöfer, that no quarter would be given in the upcoming operation. 'We should revenge our women and children who have been killed by airplanes and said "No prisoners will be taken."' And on the eve of the offensive his platoon leader addressed them saying that they would 'fight in the old SS spirit and should not show any mercy to the enemy.' 'I would have hindered Bock in this shooting,' Clotten later said, 'had I myself not been incited by the speeches of our Company commander, Ustuf. Klingelhöfer and our platoon leader, Ustuf. Muenkemer.' Statement of Roman Clotten, 2 April 1946, NA, RG-549, Case 6-24, Box 7. It is noteworthy that while other repudiated their statements in totality, Clotten never denied that Bock had shot at the crossroads, but said that he had only joined in after others had already started the shooting. 'I have always expressed my free opinion disapproving of the shooting … At that time I had a gunner, who was a very young man and a soldier with no combat experience at all and at the time of the incident at the crossroads had the first direct touch with the enemy.' 'Appeal for Review: Roman Clotten,' Landsberg/Lech, 7 November 1947, NA, RG-549, Case 6-24, Box 49. Clotten had been a driver at Hitler's headquarters since 1940, but was transferred to fight with the Leibstandarte only in May 1944.

39 The originals of these very significant sketches of the events at the crossroads can be seen in Case 6-24, RG-549, Box 7, 'Statement of Roman Clotten.' In the author's assessment, Clotten, Siptrott's and Joachim Hoffman's Schwäbisch Hall sketches, when taken together provide a cohesive picture of the events at the crossroads on 17 December 1944. Clotten reckons that Heinrich Burk's panzer #714 was ahead of Siptrott's although uncertain in his recollection. In fact the Panzer ahead of Siptrott was #734 of Pilzarek containing driver Manfred Thorn who had managed to take the lead of the entire *7. Kompanie* given the trouble with mud and tracks which Siptrott and the others had encountered. Perhaps most significantly at all, unlike many of the other statements made a Schwäbisch Hall, that of Roman Clotten was never retracted. In Landsberg in an appeal for review of his sentence of 10 year imprisonment on 7 November 1947, Clotten charged that he had been abused by William Perl, but 'I admitted to him [the investigation officer] that the gunner of my tank had fired once as a reaction after the general turmoil had started … I had a gunner who was a very young man and a soldier with no combat experience at all, and at the time of the incident at the crossroads he had his first direct touch with the enemy … I had nothing to do with the shooting. The fact that my gunner fired once as a nervous reaction, when the general firing had started, can certainly not be interpreted as a violation of any written law.' Also, Kurt Mai, who had also been with the *7. Kompanie* said, in a statement on 21 October 1947, that he had a conversation with Clotten later in the war: 'I remembered that he spoke once in the presence of myself and some comrades … He said at this time, that this was a very dirty mess (*grosse Schweinerei*) to which he would never give his consent.' Case 6-24, RG-549, Box 49.

40 Interrogation of Roman Clotten by Dwight Fanton at Ebensee on 1 October 1945. Case 6-24, RG-549, Box 31.

41 Trial testimony of Hans Joachim Piper: U.S. v. Bersin, pp. 578-586.

42 Author's interview with Hans Siptrott, 17 May 1997. In the interview, Siptrott agreed that Fleps had fired at the crossroads and that he had later kicked him in anger on the way down into Ligneuville. See *Fatal Crossroads* for more details.

43 Affidavit of Otto Arnold, 7 January 1948, NA, RG-153, Case 6-24, Box 81.

44 Author's interview with Hans Siptrott, *op. cit.* It is noteworthy that in Gerd Cuppen's 'reconstruction' of the Baugnez proceedings he cited an anonymous German officer he interviewed on 1 August 1988, who had been at Baugnez. Although Siptrott was an NCO, the quotes Cuppens used (and the fact that he was in frequent communication with Siptrott that year) makes it likely that the description of the deadly moment came from the man Peiper nicknamed 'Spitze:' 'in such a [tense] situation, a small event is enough to set off a disaster. It is enough that the nerves of single idiot cracked up so that he presses on the trigger of a machine gun.' Cuppens, *op. cit.*, p. 113.

45 John Bauserman, *The Malmedy Massacre*, White Mane Publishing Co., Shippensburg, PA, 1995, p. 23.

46 This psychological phenomenon has much in common with the varied perceptions victims have in car crashes. Some details, on which attention is focused, will be recalled in great detail, but with many other circumstances and images hardly register in memory at all or are distorted and filled in by the brain. Similarly, witnesses to a crime scene will have notoriously different perceptions of the same event—a reason why multiple witnesses are so important to a thorough investigation.

47 Testimony of Werner Löhmann at the Malmedy trial, U.S. v. Bersin, *op. cit.*, p. 548-550. Löhmann was the gunner with Horst Pilarzek's Panzer #734 of the 3rd platoon of the *7. Panzer Kompanie.* He made a virtually identical statement at Schwäbisch Hall on 7 March 1946, NA, RG-549, Case 6-24, Box 32. However, in that statement he recalls the briefing given to the platoon by Hans Siptrott just before the attack. 'The enemy must learn to fear us again. Therefore, we will fight in the old SS spirit. There is a new order that no prisoners of war will be taken.'

48 Hoffmann's statement of 6 March 1946 (*op. cit.*): 'As far as I can remember, the first shots were from Beutner's SPW.' Jaekel's statement of 1 March 1946 (*op. cit.*): 'My recollection is that the first fire I heard was pistol

fire from Beutner's SPW.' Neve's statement (6 March 1946, op. cit.): 'I heard Beutner tell Witkowski that the weapons should be loaded and made ready so we could bump off the American prisoners ... Finally Beutner gave the order to fire and everybody opened up with their weapons.'

49 'I am quite sure that I saw him fire.' Statement of Max Rieder, 26 March 1946, *op. cit.*

50 Statement of Siegfried Jaekel, *op. cit.* Jaekel named many of those he saw shooting at the crossroads, both in his SPW and those of Beutner, Bode, Sprenger. The SPW of Oettinger shooting also showed up just as the shooting started, and participated in the 'mercy shootings' that followed. Years later, co-operative members of the *9. Panzer Pionier Kompanie* would attempt to provide some cover for Erich Rumpf. An example is the affidavit of Joachim Braunroth of Michelstadt on 19 April 1948 (NA, RG-153, Case 6-24, Box 81) claiming that 'Rumpf did not give any order for the shooting,' but then later wrote that 'After a short stop in front of the crossroads, which lasted about 5-10 minutes, the column proceeded and we drove past the crossing in the direction of Engelsdorf. At the crossroads, we saw about 40-50 dead Americans which we passed. At the crossing at that time was standing one officer in tank uniform and some German soldiers in grey uniforms. Vehicles standing there were a German tank, an SPW and 10-15 American lorries.'

51 Statement of Gustav Sprenger, 27 February 1946, Case 6-24, RG-549, Box 7. Sprenger was one of the few witnesses who claimed to have seen SS Obstuf. Sievers at the crossroads—something denied by his other comrades. All agreed, however, that SS Ostuf. Erich Rumpf was on the scene.

52 Sprenger's plea for mitigation of his death sentence in the trial: 'I was continuously taught that every order had to be carried out and that refusal to obey an order would be punished extremely, even with death.' From November 1943 up until I was wounded, I participated in the Russian Campaign with the LSSAH. Fighting in Russia was very hard and ruthless. The nameless cruelties the German prisoners of war who were taken by the Russians had to suffer, shocked me deeply.'

53 Testimony of Walter Fransee and Paul Buth, U.S. v. Bersin, 27 May 1946, pp. 762-779.

54 Those implicating Hubert Huber in administering mercy shots to those in the field were numerous: Testimony of Kurt Plohmann, Horst Kiefer, Walter Landfried, Rudolf Zimmermann, Adolf Weiss and Kurt Dethlefs, 27—28 May 1946, U.S. v. Bersin, *op. cit.*, pp.792 -835. The likely soldier who was forced to get up by Huber and then shot in the head was 2nd Lt Lloyd Iames as witnessed by S/Sgt. Henry Zach. Indeed, Huber himself admitted the shooting, describing its particulars in gruesome detail: 'I fired the final shot directly into the center of his forehead. During my years in the German Army, I have seen many dead soldiers, both enemy and our own, and there is absolutely no question that this soldier was dead after I fired these shots at him.' Huber drew a detailed diagram showing his movements in the field on a map showing where the American bodies had been found. He estimated that the man he had shot a point blank range was the body tagged as #38—1st Lt Thomas McDermott. (Indeed, the autopsy, McDermott was found to have been shot in the left forehead at such a close range that there were powder burn marks.) Also, Huber described how members of his own crew, Panzer Nr. 625, participated in shooting at the prisoners in the field with the tank machine gun. He named SS Strm. Martin Grischatz as the gunner, SS Stm. Schroeder (loader) and SS Schutze Schreier (the radio operator) who eventually also came into the field with pistols along with SS Uscha. Rudi Storm and another man of Briesemeiseter's Panzer Nr. 114. Affidavit of Hubert Huber, 16 February 1946, NA, RG-549, Case 6-24, Box 27 (the handwritten original is in Box 9).

55 Huber's tank gun loader—a young, enlisted Waffen SS man named Karl Heinz-Schroeder had left the Hitler Youth to join the Waffen SS at 18 because of their better food and equipment. Schroeder had been assigned to Huber's tank as a loader for the Ardennes Offensive where they were 'given orders to keep pushing forward no matter what.' However, Schroeder was wounded during the offensive and taken prisoner near La Gleize. After capture, Schroeder was first sent to the U.S. to Ft. Eustis where he met *Afrika Korps* veterans who still thought Germany might win the war. He then spent a brief time at Ft. Pickett in Virginia and was repatriated to Germany through Belgium where he was held for six months by the government for war crimes investigations.

56 While Huber of the *6. Panzer Kompanie* and members of the *3. Panzer Pionier Kompanie* were apprehended, it remains curious that more than half of the named individuals implicated in shooting the Americans lying in the field were curiously missing and unavailable at the Malmedy trial.

57 'Look at these bodies,' SS Sturmmann Hans Knospe, recalled of his remark to his squad leader with the *9th Kompanie III Panzer Grenadier Battalion*, 'There was some dirty work here.' 'Screening Results 15 -24 November 1945,' Ellis Papers. Witnesses interrogated by Lt Schweitzer.

58 Interview with SS veteran tanker at the *Hotel Sonnenhof*, Aspach, May 1997. Name withheld on request.

59 Several American survivors would put the time interval between the departure Peiper and the main shooting as a matter of minutes at most. Many of the forty-odd American survivors saw Diefenthal in his easily to recognize tan leather jacket along with Peiper in their vehicle and were able to relate the timing of the events after the departure of their command SPW.

60 Peiper's revealing letter to John Toland, 22 February 1959. Library of Congress, John Toland Papers, *Battle: The Story of the Bulge*, Box 108, Folder 'P.' The letter was written after an extensive discussion between Otto Skorzeny and Peiper as to whether it was worthwhile to communicate with Toland. The New England

author was writing an account of the events at Malmedy in his bestseller for Random House that was published that same year.

Chapter 12 – Ligneuville

1 Napoleon Bonaparte quoted by one of his aides: R.M. Johnston, *The Corsican*.

2 Despite the technical dazzle of the German V-weapons, personal experience with the weapons tended to diminish their luster. A useful example comes from the autumn of 1944, when the U.S. 1st Infantry Division captured a few German infantry with the *9th Fallschirmjäger Regiment*. When captured 17-year-old Walter Blehm was cocky as a V-1 buzz bomb screamed overhead. 'Germany will win this war,' he crowed, 'our secret weapons …' His voice trailed off as a thunderous noise erupted. The V-1 had detonated only 150 yards away. Everyone fell to the mud. When they were rousted up, the lack of damage from the resulting blast looked to be altogether unremarkable. 'Well if that is to decide the war, we lost already,' one prisoner ventured while wiping off mud. Blehm was even less impressed: '*Was fuer eine Scheisswaffe!*' 'Selected Intelligence Reports June—November 1944,' Office of the A.C. of S., G-2, 1st U.S. Infantry Division, Germany, 1 January 1945. 1st Infantry Division: NA, RG 407, 301-2.0: Box 5030.

3 Letter Joseph P. Barrett, 15 August 1995. Barrett was with the 474th AAA Battalion under Timberlake.

4 On 17 December 1944, a V-1 hit the quartermaster depot in Liège, blowing up 400,000 gallons of gasoline. Even worse, on the day after Christmas, a V-1 hit the 28th General Hospital, ironically killing a German POW being treated there. Benjamin King and Timothy Kutta, *Impact: History of Germany's V-Weapons in World War II*, DaCapo Press, Cambridge, 2003, p. 284. Several of the Malmédy survivors were treated at the hospital as Al Valenzi recounted to the author: 'Ken [Ahrens] and I were taken to Liège later that night [the 17th]. We wanted to stay together. They took us to the same hospital, but they put him in a different ward. I was in shock. They fixed us up and put us in beds. The next morning, there was an officer who came in from the Inspector General's office who spoke to us. I told them what I could. Then we were getting buzzed bombed in Liège and we had to evacuate that whole hospital. Then they put us in a train. Ken and I were separated and we didn't see each other anymore. I was nearly in a panic in the evacuation. The train headed for Paris. Everybody was worried that the Germans were going to get to Paris. They gave me a shot and put me out.' Interview with Al Valenzi, 26 September 1995.

5 Interview with George Dalferes, 49th AAA Brigade, 10 March 1996.

6 'The Forty Niners: Unit History of the Headquarters and Headquarters Battery 49th AAA Bridgade, December 1,1942 to May 9, 1945,' Maj. Michael G. Kelakos, US. Army Military History Institute.

7 All quotes from Jim Longson, interview with author, 27 April 1996 and several clarifying letters.

8 'Operations of the 49th AAA Brigade in Europe, 1944 to May 9, 1945,' June 6, 1955.

9 Joseph Barrett to author, September 1995. 'I realize that rank had its privileges,' he wrote, but 'to fight through eleven months of combat from homes that are in a class of the Vanderbilt Mansion is ridiculous.'

10 Interview with Thèrése Bastin, Ligneuville, 20 March 1996.

11 Longson interview, *op. cit.*

12 The engineers were members of the 508 Engineer Light Pontoon Company, NARA, RG-407, AAR December 1944 for 1121 Engineer Combat Group, 5 January 1945.

13 'The Ardennes Breakthrough,' unpublished account of operations of the 49th AAA Brigade provided by Theresa Kelakos, p. 39.

14 The frequency of sighted Buzz Bombs can be seen in the reports of the 27th AIB records for 16 December 1944 which recorded fifteen V-1's seen and heard during the daylight hours: 'Unit Journal 27th Armored Infantry Battalion,' RG 407, 609-INF(27)-1.2, Box 15885.

15 A V-2 rocket hit the Rex Cinema on the *Avenue de Keyser* in Antwerp at 3.20 PM on December 16th killing 567 people including 296 service men. They were part of a capacity crowd watching the film *Buffalo Bill*. With the opening of the Ardennes Offensive, the Germans had begun bombarding their objective Antwerp, rather than London.

16 Cecil E. Roberts, *A Soldier From Texas*, Ft. Worth, TX, 1978, p. 49.

17 'Unit Journal 27th Armored Infantry Battalion,' for 16 December, *op. cit.*

18 HQ Combat Command B, 9th Armored Division, After Action Report, 1-31 December 1944, NA, RG-407, 609-CCB-0.1 to 3.2, Also, letter of Arthur Gjertson to author on 19 December 1996. Gjertson was former Master Sergeant of HQ 14th Tank Battalion.

19 Interview with Peter Rupp, August 1957, John Toland Papers, LOC, Manuscript Division, *Battle: The Story of the Bulge*, Box 37.

20 Years later Jim Longson would realize that the small arms fire they heard to the north was the shooting of American prisoners up the road at Baugnez. Interview with Longson, *op. cit.*

21 After Action Report, Headquarters 14th Tank Battalion, 1- 31 December 1944, NA, RG-407, 609-TNK(14) Bn. Also After Action Report for 27th Armored Infantry Battalion for the same period: NA, RG-407, 609-INF(27)-0.1 to 0.7. These two elements comprised the majority of Combat Command B of the U.S. 9th

Armored Division. The 14th Tank Battalion had been in the vicinity of Ligneuville since 13 December, being held in readiness to assist the U.S. 2nd Infantry Division in their assault on the Westwall. However, after the German attacks around St. Vith on 16 December, the tank battalion departed Ligneuville before dawn on December17th. The 14th and 27th AIB closed to Breitfeld and Steinbruck, Belgium at 10 AM on the same day.

22 Account prepared for John Eisenhower by Seymour Green, Valley Forge, PA, May 1969, John S.D. Eisenhower Papers, The Bitter Woods, Box 2.

23 Toland interview with Seymour Green, 1957: John Toland Papers, LOC, Manuscript Division, *Battle: The Story of the Bulge*, Box 37.

24 After Action Report for 14th Tank Battalion, *op. cit.* The report indicated that the Service Company was assailed by both small arms and tank fire within ten minutes of the warning. Most of the Service Company was able to escape from the firefight and withdrawal to Bellevaux- Stavelot and then to Werbomont by nightfall. The battalion Service Company lost four fuel or cargo trailers and a kitchen truck, an assault gun and a tank dozer in the firefight in Ligneuville.

25 Quotes from Thorn: Interviews with Manfred Thorn, 23 March 1996, 11 May 1999 and 21 December 2007.

26 The march order of the tanks is made clear by the statements of Rolf Erhardt. 'Testimony of Rolf Ehrhardt, 30 October 1946, NA, RG-549, 'English Summaries and Translations of German Documents Related to War Crimes,' 290/59/18/2-5, Box 13. After leaving the crossroads, Ehrhardt related that: 'About 600 meters further on we overtook car [Panzer] 734 of Pilaypik [sic, Pilarzek] which had stopped because of some defect. I cannot give the exact order of the motor vehicles of my company. Schraeder, Unterscharführer and 734 were ahead of me (out of sight). As I overtook 734, I arrived in Engelsdorf before him … I cannot give the exact time when I arrived in Engelsdorf. It must have been a short time after 2nd Lt Fischer's Panther had been hit as I still saw Fischer (wounded).' Thus, it seems possible that 702 stopped with Thorn after his tank became disabled and waited until Siptrott arrived to continue on.

27 It is noteworthy that in his own statement, Georg Fleps indicated that Siptrott had given him the order to fire after complaining to the SPW commander at the crossroads that he did not have sufficient ammunition. 'The commander said something to Siptrott whereupon Siptrott , who saw that I already had my pistol in my hand, gave me the order: "Shoot".' This statement and the original handwritten version by Fleps given on 5 January 1946, is in NA, RG-549, Case 6-24, Box 7. Adding to this is Siptrott's own statement of 7 January 1946 where he said he had ordered Fleps to shoot since 'I thought it was within the scope of SS Hstuf's Klingelhoefer's order … telling us that we should not take any prisoners.' Thus, the contemporary statements of Thorn and Siptrott contradict earlier statements. However, in an affidavit made on 7 January 1948, the radio operator of Siptrott's tank, Otto Arnold, testified that 'I do recollect that Hans Siptrott most severely rebuked the loader Fleps at that time, as this gunner had fired upon some prisoners on his own accord without having received any order. Furthermore, the commander made it known to the soldier, that he had in mind to report this incident to his superiors.' NA, RG-549, Case 6-24, Box 67.

28 In the author's interview with Hans Siptrott on 17 May 1997, he recalled his reaction to Fleps's shots at the crossroads. 'I was sitting on top of the tank looking out and Fleps was the loader and popped out of the loader's hatch. He was out of the hatch to his waist [he showed the author how Fleps stood and how he reached from the commander's hatch with his leg to kick him]. I kicked him into the backbone and hit my shin bone and hurt myself. I told him, "Why are you firing?" I kicked him, because I didn't know why he shot. I was surprised. And we continued driving on.' When Siptrott reached Ligneuville , he recalled seeing Fischer's tank burning. He and his tank crew paused in the town and did not resume the march to Stavelot until later on the night of the 17th. In a pause near Ligneuville, Strm. Werner Reicke, the loader in Panzer Nr. 712 was approached by Georg Fleps who proudly announced. 'On the road crossing which we just passed, American prisoners were shot and I had fun shooting among these American soldiers.' Reicke indicated that Fleps had boasted of the incident several times to others in the *7.Kompanie* in Ligneuville and Wanne. Statement of Werner Reicke, 12 February 1946, NA, RG-549, Case 6-24, Box 33. Manfred Thorn in Panzer Nr. 734 remembered Flep's cavalier attitude: 'Fleps boasted to fellow soldiers prior to reaching Engelsdorf that he had acted independently.' NA, RG-153, Case 6-24, Box 81: 'Sworn statement of Manfred Thorn,' 20 October 1947.

29 Interviews with Manfred Thorn, 23 March 1996, 11 May 1999 and 21 December 2007. After his tank was fixed, Thorn continued on in his tank to Ligneuville, some 500 meters ahead. When he got then, there was already a Panther burning ahead—that of Arndt Fischer.

30 'Had Fleps not fired,' Thorn posed to the author, 'perhaps it [the massacre] would never have happened.' Interview with Manfred Thorn, 23 March 1996. However, Thorn did not seem to be aware of the preparations for the shooting by the 3. *Panzer Pionier Kompanie* when they were described to Thorn in a follow-up interview on 21 December 2007.

31 Interview with Jim Longson, *op. cit.*

32 Timberlake and his little party passed through Stavelot later that afternoon, not stopping until they reached Bomal, Belgium 20 miles further west along the Ourthe River, later that night. On the 18th of December,

the units of the 49th AAA Brigade passed through Liège to the little town of Lambermont where contact was made with the U.S. First Army at 1400 hrs. 'Ardennes Breakthrough' *op. cit.* Jim Longson would try to get back to Ligneuville and the Bastin family later in December, but the Germans still held that place and Longson had to return to General Timberlake without finding out the status of the family. It would only be after the war in June 1945 that Longson would return to find that although Ligneuville was devastated and there was a hole in the roof of Julie's house, the Bastin family were still fine. Longson and the Bastin family maintained a friendship which lasted more than 50 years after the war.

33 Interview with Alphonse Piront, 20 March 1996.

34 Bastin interview, *op. cit.* When German SS tank men returned to Ligneuville in the 1980s on a personal tour, Thèrése met Werner Sternebeck whom she had seen in the first tank that day.

35 Narrative: Combat Command B, 9th Armored Division, 16-25 December 1944, prepared for author by Cecil E. Roberts, 1996. In the contemporary plaque to the American dead killed in in Ligneuville, the name of deceased Lincoln Abraham is inverted to Abraham Lincoln.

36 Paul Fröhlich described this incident in the author's interview *op. cit.* Also, Timm Haasler kindly provide a photo of the immobilized SPW in the middle of the Amblève.

37 Author's interview with Arndt Fischer, 17 May 1997.

38 Green interview, *op. cit.*

39 Green account for Eisenhower, *op. cit.* 'They could easily see me. I stopped and they stopped. I felt helpless and sort of silly.'

40 The German in the jeep was likely Ustuf. Kurt Kramm as corroborated by both Kramm and Roman Clotten. In a statement by Clotten, he said that he saw Ustuf. Kramm riding in a captured jeep in Ligneuville where he captured several Americans he tried to interrogate although unable because of the language barrier. Statement of Roman Clotten, 1 October 1945, NA, RG-549, Case 6-24, Box 31.

41 Statement of Kurt Kramm, 16 March 1946, NA, RG-549, Case 6-24, Box 32. Important sketches by Kramm are separated in the source material and are in Box 41 of the same series.

42 During this time, the Belgian clocks were set to GMT +2 whereas German clocks were set to GMT+1 which explains the discrepancy in timing between German and Belgian sources for the timing of events in Ligneuville. Thanks to CRIBA historian, Henri Rogister for this information.

43 In author's interview with Arndt Fischer (15 May 1997) he related this story that had been told to him by Werner Sternebeck when both returned to Ligneuville on a personal and anonymous tour in the 1980s.

44 Toland interview notes with Peter Rupp, *op. cit.*

45 Interview with Arndt Fischer, *op. cit.* In the hit that disabled Panther Nr. 152, Arndt Fischer was badly burned and Strm. Wolfgang Simon, the driver, was killed. All the others were wounded: SS Rttf. Josef Duda (gunner), Strm. Günter Weseman (loader) and Strm Günter Ikrat (radioman). Thanks to Timm Haasler for this information.

46 U.S. v. Bersin, *op. cit.*, p. 2000.

47 Peiper's testimony from U.S. v. Bersin, p. 1936. Peiper described the Ligneuville encounter twice in his trial testimony. The earlier account: 'Right upon entering the town I suddenly saw in front of me the vehicle of Lt Fischer. That vehicle had been set on fire. I thereupon stopped about 50 yards from the vehicle and recognised a Sherman about 80 meters to my right. He was just about to aim his cannon at my vehicle. I thereupon ordered the driver of Diefenthal's vehicle to pull the vehicle back at once, which he did, whereupon we remained at a protected corner of a house. Another halftrack that followed passed by us and was knocked out at that moment.' According to the author's interviews with Karl Paul Fröhlich (20 May 1996 and 19 May 1997), this was likely the SPW Fröhlich saw destroyed coming right after he entered Ligneuville in Diefenthal's SPW. Peiper continued: 'I took a Panzerfaust and ran into the house in order to attempt to knock out the Sherman from the rear window, but it was knocked out at the very moment by another tank … I then ordered Diefenthal to clean out the town with his grenadiers'.

48 Before Peiper could reach the tank with his Panzerfaust, it was destroyed by a 251/9 SPW of the *11.SS Panzer Grenadier Kompanie.*

49 Peiper's testimony at the trial, *ibid*, pp. 2001-2002. The recon vehicle that Peiper describes as having been knocked out could not have been Diefenthal's halftrack, but most likely the halftrack coming right behind them which Zwigart and Fröhlich agreed was destroyed.

50 Interviews with Karl Paul Fröhlich 20 May 1996 and 19 May 1997.

51 Testimony of Josef Diefenthal, 12.12.1945, NA, RG-549, Case 6-24, Box 33. Also, detailed annotated map drawn by Diefenthal to illustrate the action: '*Marschband beim Kampf der Spitze in Ligneuville.*'

52 U.S. v. Bersin, p. 1936.

53 Hans Kettgen interview with Jochen Peiper, 1971 provided by Hans Kettgen to Harvey T. Rowe and then to author, p. 11 of transcript.

54 Statement of Kurt Kramm, 16 March 1946, NA, RG-549, Case 6-24, Box 32.

55 In Ehrhardt's detailed recollections of the Ardennes events from 1981, he told of having trouble descending the downgrade to Ligneuville. 'The road required some attention because the technology of the Mk IV

was not designed for going down curves downhill. Arriving in Engelsdorf, we first saw [Panzer] No. 702 unharmed [Schraeder's tank] and also the burning Panther of Fischer, Peiper—and likely Diefenthal too—as well as a number of SPWs.' Report from Rolf Ehrhardt, *7 Kompanie, 1. Panzer Regiment*, LSSAH, no date, but 1981, 18 page report provided to author by Hans Behrend, Aspach. What is the 'Aspach'?

56 For years, accounts have described how the Americans lost two Shermans and an M-10 destroyer in Ligneuville. The source of the inaccuracy is Peiper's post war account in ETHINT-10, *op. cit.* In actuality, the Americans only lost the single Sherman tank-dozer, the immobilized 105mm assault gun, a kitchen truck and a one ton trailer of the 27th Service Company in Ligneuville. Roberts, *op. cit.*, pp. 50-51.

57 Interview with Paul Fröhlich, 20 May 1996. Born on 9 September 1920 in Frankenheim, Fröhlich had joined the SS in 1940 as a non-commissioned officer and went straight away into the Leibstandarte. He first fought in the Balkans and then in Russia serving as a driver for the tank regiment commander Schönberg. In the Ardennes in December 1944, Fröhlich had been with the motorcycle reconnaissance platoon with the tank regiment, but had been given a ride in Diefenthal and Peiper's SPW on 17 December as they entered Ligneuville.

58 Testimony of Paul Fröhlich, U.S. v. Bersin, Case 6-24, *op. cit.*, pp. 2782. From Ligneuville, Frölich would ride to Stavelot in a captured American jeep.

59 Interview of Heinz Noack with Timm Haasler, March 2005. The tank had been delayed by a track repair which took place south of Honsfeld earlier that morning.

60 Testimony of Joseph P. Mass, 27 July 1945, Parma, OH, NA, RG-153, War Crimes, Cases not Tried, Ligneuville, Boxes 67-69.

61 Ehrhardt claimed, that while in Engelsdorf, his first gunner, Stm. Helmut Langhammer was seriously wounded by a bullet shot to his stomach. 'The round was fired from a house at the slope on the right entrance to the village. As I understand, an infantry soldier smoked out the marksman—a civilian.' Ehrhardt's *op. cit.*

62 Green account for Eisenhower, *op. cit.*

63 Fischer interview, *op. cit.*, The next morning: 'They asked me if I wanted to go back to divisional headquarters ... I said yes. I was wrapped in an '*Ami*' blanket and the others with me had American uniforms. We were quiet and careful. They had a special-colored cloth to allow them to be identified by our people. I reported later that day to the divisional first aid station. Recovering from burns took time: 'The divisional staff assigned me to a home hospital near Gorlitz. In February, 1945 I was sent to the training staff as a reserve.'

Chapter 13 – Hôtel du Moulin

1 Rupp's story is taken from John Toland's original handwritten notes from his 1957 interview with Peter Rupp (John Toland Papers, LOC, Manuscript Division, *Battle: The Story of the Bulge*, Box 37) and then supplemented by the published account: 'The Brave Innkeeper of 'The Bulge,'' *Coronet Magazine*, December 1959, pp. 168-152.

2 The man who helped Joseph Mass was M. Matthieu Lamby, of Ligneuville, who had seen Mass get up from the group of shot soldiers and later offered him aid. Although Lamby is no longer living, his story was related to Madame Therese Lochem who was interviewed at the author's request on 23 May 1997 by Jean Philippe Speder.

3 Author's interview with Joseph P. Mass, 13 September 1995. Also, letter to author 10 April 1997.

4 Born 28 January 1914 in Lower Saxony, SS Hscha. Paul H. Ochmann had joined the Waffen SS in November 1941 with SS Totenkopf 'Thuringen.' In the Ardennes, he was with the motorcycle platoon of Poetschke's *I.SS Panzer Battalion*. Ironically, even though crossing Peiper at Ligneuville, Ochmann was promoted for his performance in the Ardennes being designated SS Hauptscharführer on 1 January 1945. NA, BDC File A3343-SM-N044.

5 Statement of Paul Ochmann, 29 March 1946, pp. 958-961.

6 Jochen Peiper ignored Ochmann's statement made in Schwäbisch Hall, detailing both his career with Totenkopf, as well as his observed deed in Ligneuville. 'This 'story' was brewed together by the prosecution and paid Belgian witnesses,' the SS colonel would complain, 'If it would have been true, Ochmann would have been hanged and not released in a few years.' Peiper was commenting on the description of the episode by Charles Whiting on page 45 of *Massacre at Malmédy*. '*Kommentar zum Buch 'Massacre at Malmédy von Charles Whiting*,' September 1971. Although Peter Rupp would later tell how he saw Ochmann shoot the American prisoners, he did not testify for the prosecution. Although under a sentence of death for years, Paul Hermann Ochmann was released from Landsberg on 9 June 1955. He lived quietly, as did many of released Malmedy men, frequently attending reunions of 7th Panzer Kompanie after the war.

7 Statement of Marie Lochem to Capt. George W. McBurney, Ligneuville, 24 January 1945, NA, RG-153, War Crimes, Cases not Tried, Ligneuville, Boxes 67-69.

8 Author's interview with Josephine Lochem, 25 March 1996, Ligneuville. *Schwartzer klapen* appears to have been a local Belgian term for the German army.

9 *Ibid.*

10 NA, RG-153, War Crimes, Cases not Tried, Ligneuville, Boxes 67-69. Those executed were from the following units of the 9th Armored Division: 27th Armored Infantry Battalion, Service Company (Borcina, Collins and Carter); the 14th Tank Battalion, Company B (Johnson, Pitts, Abraham and Sullivan) and the 27th Armored Infantry Battalion, Company B (Penney). On 24 January 1945, Maj. William E. Kamus, the Regimental Surgeon with the 120th Infantry Regiment examined the bodies. Sullivan, Pitts, Abraham and Carter were killed by bullets striking them in the back of their lower skull. Johnson and Penny were shot in the mouth and Collins and Borcina were executed by shots fired into the left eye and nose, respectively. Today, Borcina, Collins, Johnson, Pitts and Penney are buried at Henri Chapelle; the others were returned to the U.S. There are discrepancies between the civilian accounts on the number of victims, but the number of eight is, in fact, correct.

11 In Toland's interview with Rupp, he identified the man who had knocked out his two lower teeth as an SS sergeant. He claimed to have heard other SS troopers call to him as 'Ochmann.'

12 That Ochmann was at the Hotel the afternoon and evening of the 17th with Gerhard Walla was made clear in the statement of Kurt Kramm, 16 March 1946, NA, RG-549, Case 6-24, Box 32. 'Early on the 18th before Stavelot, I learned from Rttf. Walla that Oscha. Ochmann had stayed at the Hotel Rupp on the evening of the 17th and had brought into the hotel in Engelsdorf an additional 10 POWs after searching the houses to the eight prisoners of war [already there]'

13 The officer was Jochen Peiper himself as later realized by Seymour Green in a letter to Maj. Glen Strange.

14 'The good German' who had protected Green and the other prisoners from being shot was identified in Toland's interview with Rupp as the same officer who later interrogated Green that night. As this is firmly established to have been Peiper, it was then the SS colonel, likewise, who stopped Ochmann from executing the other American prisoners held at the hotel. The younger soldier with Ochmann was likely Suess.

15 Interview with Ralf Tiemann, 21 October 1995. Tiemann replaced Dietrich Ziemssen as the Ia (Division, General Staff Officer)) for Mohnke at the Hôtel du Moulin in Ligneuville after Ziemssen was wounded. Tiemann gave the author a complete description of the scene there with Mohnke's and Skorzeny's headquarters. Tiemann was not pleased with Mohnke as the divisional leader. Mohnke was a morphine addict and unpredictable. As Tiemann recalled, the divisional headquarters remained at Ligneuville until December 23rd when it moved to Wanne over a muddy forested road via Logbierme.

16 Peiper to John Eisenhower, 4 April 1967, Eisenhower Library, John S.D. Eisenhower Papers, Bitter Woods, Box 17.

17 Motor [mechanical] troubles had reached 'an unprecedented scale'within the Leibstandarte. 'Consolidated Report from PW s from 1SS Panzer Division,' U.S. First Army PWI Report, 27 December 1944, NA, RG-407, 101.1- 3.2, M.L.-2125, Box 1497.

18 Letter Carl K. Mattocks to Robert Moranda, February 1955, 7th Armored Division, in author's possession.

19 See Combat Interview with Maj. Fred Sweat, S-3, at CCR CP on 28 December 1944, GL-247, ML Series, NA, RG-407 . Also, 'S-3 Journal, CCR, 7th Armored Division,' NA, RG-407, 607-CCR-3.2, Box 15678. 'Driver of Col. Matthews, Chief of Staff, reported to CCR CP with info of having escaped from column of German vehicles of approximately 30 tanks and 30-35 other vehicles. Present whereabouts of Col. Matthews is not known. Approximate position of German column- 792978, moving west.' The map co-ordinates of 792978 correspond to Pont, Belgium Half an hour later, Maj. Gillis was reporting to the 7th Armored Division CP that he believed Col. Matthews had been captured. Matthews' body would later be found near Pont in January 1945.

20 *Ibid*, p. 1937.

21 Green did not originally identify the officer as Jochen Peiper in the interview with Toland, but the good English spoken, plus the various themes described—and even the language—strongly suggest that this was the SS colonel.

22 This scene described by interview notes of Maj. Glen Strange with Capt. Seymour Green prepared for author, 25 October 1995. Strange indicated that Green later realized that it was Peiper who both 'had admonished some of the SS soldiers and they were treated better after that.' and also had interrogated him on the night of the 17th.

23 Another witness to Nicholas Schugens frantic warning in Wanne was M. Paul Engelebert, Interview with Engelbert, 19 October 1995. 'The day the Germans arrived here there was a football match taking place between some of the young men of this area and some of the English had a soccer match and the soccer match had finished and the ladies of the town had prepared a feast with lots of food for after the game at the chateau and there were American and Belgian flags flying. Suddenly Nicolas Schugens showed up during the match and said, 'The Germans are coming!' And the men there told him, 'It's not true and it's not true!' 'Yes, yes,' he told them, 'it is true, they are coming.' So they had to hide all these flags quickly and

the English took off in a hurry. The English were ground liaison men. The Germans showed up the next morning (the 18th). M. Tobas, was the school teacher in Lierneux, and took care of the football in the village and these Brits were based in Lierneux and were radar people and were based there. He had gotten the Brits to come to the village to play that Sunday. The Brits took back off to Lierneux after Schugens warning. The Germans arrived here on the 19th. They could hear all the shooting in Stavelot the day before and they knew Schugens was not lying.'

24 Author's interview with Nicolas Schugens, 13 October 1995. In Trois-Ponts: 'It took me hour to get across the road, there was so much American traffic on the road. I was still on my bicycle. I was trying to get to Huy and the Americans were heading to St. Vith ... I went to Basse Bodeaux and I stayed there and thought, 'With all these American tanks and stuff, the Germans will never come here.' Then we saw American soldiers on foot in Basse Bodeux on either side of the road and I said, 'It's not normal that they should be on foot. Let's get the hell out of here.' We left.'

25 For the account of Edmond Klein and the Fourgon sisters: Hubert Laby, *18 Décembre 1944: Stavelot, Dépot* Légal, Faimes, 1994, p. 49.

26 *Ibid*, pp. 50-51. The possibility remains that the honest statement of Louise Fourgon regarding Stavelot ('American tanks fill the streets') to the Germans on the road to Refat may have critically altered the intelligence perception within the *Kampfgruppe Peiper* on the night of December 18th. While not definitive, no fewer than three Belgian account claim to have seen an American tank with a white star in the vanguard of the battle group on 18 December.

27 Peiper interview with Kettgen, *op. cit.*

28 *U.S.* vs. Valentin Bersin, NARA, Case 6-24, testimony of Joachim Peiper, p. 1937.

29 *Ibid*, p. 2003.

30 During World War II, German soldiers made use of the methamphetamine drug Pervitin (methamphetamine hydrochloride), commonly known as 'speed,' to enhance alertness and endurance. Norman Ohler. (2015). *Blitzed: Drugs in the Third Reich*. Penguin Books, NY, NY. The use of Pervitin was not limited to the Ardennes Offensive but extended to various military operations throughout the war. This was particularly prevalent during periods of intense combat. Dr Otto Ranke, a German military doctor, conducted research on the effects of Pervitin during the war. His work, which includes studies on the drug's impact on soldiers' performance and endurance, is documented in medical literature of that time. Soldiers reported increased alertness and reduced fatigue after taking the drug in spite of serious health consequences for soldiers, including addiction, psychological issues, and physical deterioration. O. Ranke, 1941, The significance of the benzedrine in the therapy of war psychoses, *Zeitschrift für die gesamte Neurologie und Psychiatrie*, 172(3-4), 267-27.

While specific citations related to the Ardennes Offensive might be limited due to the wartime secrecy surrounding drug use, it is clear that it was used in the Ardennes in 1940 and almost certainly again in 1944. 'When Hitler heard about the plan to invade through Ardennes, he loved it. But the high command said: it's not possible, at night we have to rest, and they [the allies] will retreat and we will be stuck in the mountains.' But then the stimulant decree was released where soldiers were to take 1-4 Pervitin tablets daily, and that enabled them to stay awake for three days and three nights. Interview with Norman Ohler, Rachel Cook, High Hitler: How Nazi Drug Abuse Steered the Course of History, *The Guardian*, London, 16 Sept 2016. That Pervitin was used the Leibstandarte soldiers in the Ardennes Offensive seems highly likely. The army ordered 35 million methamphetamine tablets for the troops prior to the Ardennes operation in 1940 and a similar distribution in 1944 seems likely. Peiper's unusual behavior during the offensive—awake for days and then collapsing, which witnesses described as a nervous condition. While circumstantial, such behavior is consistent with Pervitin use. Author communication with Norman Ohler, 18 Jan. 2024.

31 Cuppens interview: Anna Willems, *Massacre a Malmédy? op. cit.*,19 February 1988, p. 52.

32 Interview with Joachim Peiper: 1SS Panzer Regiment:11-24 December 1944,' RG-338, Foreign Military Studies, ETHINT-10. Although Peiper described his regiment's actions in some detail, his information is undoubtedly second hand as he did not arrive at his tanks' spearhead until around midnight given the time spent in Ligneuville interrogating Captain Seymour Green.

33 'Because we had to take the bridge at Stavelot at all costs before it was destroyed, I now had to advance at all costs. I gave the order to three Panthers to take a running start and at top speed crash down to the tank barrier.' U.S. v. Bersin, p. 2005-2006.

34 Interview with Mathias Henzius, 5 January 1997. Also, Nikolaus Thomas, *Von der Front: Die Kriegsjahre 1944-45 im Raum von Eifel und Ardennen, Grenz* Echo Verlag, Eupen, 1995, pp. 75-76. The farmhouse in Manderfeld had been the HQ during the fall for part of the U.S. 14th Cavalry Group all through the fall of 1944—the troopers leaving so hurriedly on the night of the December 16th that Christmas packages from the States were abandoned.

35 Toland interview with Otto Skorzeny, 28 September 1957, John Toland Papers Battle: *The Story of the Bulge*, LOC, Box 8.

36 Description of the scene at the Manderfeld headquarters on the night of 17 December: Letter Otto Skorzeny to John S.D. Eisenhower, 16 April 1966. John S.D. Eisenhower Papers, Bitter Woods Research Papers, Box 16, Eisenhower Library, Abilene, KS.

Chapter 14 – Before the Amblève

1 Interview with Albert Petit, 21 March 1996.

2 Petit *op. cit.*: 'On the Monday, the 18th, the Germans installed a workshop a repair shop to repair vehicles in La Vaulx Richard and on that same day the village was bombed and strafed. The bombs all fell in the trees and the house was not damaged … On the Tuesday [19th December], some other SS men showed up and they were Austrians with German shepherd dogs came then, and they were really nasty. They shoved a pistol into my neck and told me "You are a terrorist." "*Nicht Terrorist*," I told them. I had a pile of *Signal* magazines in the living room and I showed them that. I fooled them with that. They said, "Okay, you are pro-German, you're alright." Up until Christmas, the Germans who stayed here, they were alright to us and they brought him [me?] meat. They helped us milk the cows—some had been farmers before their service—and my wife cooked food for all of us. On Christmas day, the group that was here went down into the village to get meat and one was killed. It was a sad day. Everyone was crying. The Germans slept in the basement with us." We got along. At Christmas the Germans staying at our house were very sad and did not celebrate Christmas. They were sick of the war and sick over the loss of their friends.'

3 Neighbors had seen a German tank stop in front of the house of Joseph Willem on the evening of 17 December before he and his daughter and son in law had disappeared.

4 The victims at La Vaux Richard are S/Sgt. Walter W. Arter, Pfc. Harry A. Czaplinski, T/5 William G. Edmonds, Pvt. Myrl M. Gion, Pvt. Dave H. Glotzer, Pvt. Donald A. Hoffer, S/Sgt. Edward W. Kadluboski, Pfc. Carl N. Millard, Pfc. Belen Reys, Pfc. Rolf O. Runge, T/5 Donald A. Spencer and T/5 Klass Visser. All were from the kitchen and supply crew of the 27th Armored Infantry Battalion which had been in Ligneuville on 17 December. The civilian victims were Mme. Charlotte Petit (31 yrs) and her husband M. Georges Blaise (30 yrs) and M. Joseph Willem (72). The bodies were discovered on the hill above the village on 18 January 1945. For the fact that the soldiers had been earlier in Ligneuville: Robert J. Peterson, 'Very Dark Day for the 27th Airborne Infantry Battalion,' *Gravel Agitator: Newsletter of the 27th Airborne Infantry Battalion,* Winter 2007-2008.

5 Goltz's headquarters company was in La Vaulx Richard until after the fighter bombers departed as corroborated by SS reconnaissance officer Bernhard Bartels, Affidavit, 15 March 1948, NA, RG-549, Case 6-24, Box 21.

6 I am thankful for the careful assembly of a march time-line and supporting documents for this analysis done by Timo Worst and Hans Weber. In post war accounts, Leidreiter endeavored to place himself elsewhere on the 18th of December, but the photographic evidence (he was photographed in the hamlet with Knittel before the later left) as well as other testimony by Coblenz and corroborating testimony indicates otherwise. Based on available evidence, Leidreiter was one of the first to arrive at La Vaulx Richard during the late evening of 17 December or the early morning hours of 18 December. When passing through the La Vaulx Richard, Coblenz recalled seeing an officer but refused to name him given the sensitive circumstances; it is possible it was Leidreiter The re-constructed sequence of events:
Night of 17-18 Dec: Leidreiter arrives in La Vaulx Richard
12:00 Noon: Knittel reaches Leidreiter and converses with him in the village where he is photographed.
12:30: Knittel leaves village and crosses bridge into Stavelot behind Peiper's tanks
14:00: Coblenz leaves La Vaulx Richard with 2 Kompanie and crosses bridge with Tiger tanks of 1.SS Pz Abt. 501.
14:45 Leidreiter leaves La Vaulx Richard with Gieseke and half of 3. *Kompanie*. Leaves Hstuf. Haschenberger behind to collect his company. Leidreiter manages to cross the bridge under fire, but Gieske's thin-skinned *Schwimmwagens* wait behind buildings just south of the bridge.
15:00 American fighter bombers of the 365th FG strike Stavelot and La Vaulx Richard. Coblenz's men hide in western portion of Stavelot. Leidreiter hides near bridge on the north side. Goltz's headquarters company is held up in La Vaulx Richard
16:30-17:00 Fighter bombers depart . At La Vaulx Richard, the American soldiers and Belgians are marched up a wooded hill and shot, likely ordered by Ustuf. Heinrich Dröge and possibly witnessed by Ustuf. Hachenberger and Obstuf. Wagner.
17:00 Gieseke attempts to move across the bridge after the air attacks end, but finds their way blocked by fire.
17:30 Leidreiter approaches Coblenz for loan of his heavy platoon to help seize the bridge so his company can cross. He realizes this mission is impossible.

7 'On 18 December 1944, we approached Stavelot. At that time, there was an American prisoner of war on our vehicle. The American was one of the 6-8 prisoners of war who had been turned over to the

reconnaissance battalion early that day. A short distance before Stavelot, it was necessary to make a stop because of an air attack … After the air attack I returned to the SPW where I had been riding. I observed a number of officer of the battalion talking [and gesturing]. Sitting on the ground nearest the house before Stavelot, I saw 6 to 8 men. They were wearing American uniforms. Immediately before this shooting, a discussion took place between Ostuf. Coblenz, the leader of the 2nd Company and Ustuf. Dröge of my company, Ostuf. Goltz, my company commander and a Hstuf. who was the doctor of my company whose name I don't know anymore … ' Statement of Ernst Mahl, 7 May 1946, NA, RG-549, Case 6-24, Box 32. Several statements from other sources indicated the SS Ustuf. Dröge was implicated in several of the terrible shooting of civilians around Stavelot. Mahl's statement perfectly described the composition of the group of American soldiers and civilians who were shot near Vaulx Richard, but ascribed their shooting to a Ustuf. Wolf of the Heinrich Goltz's headquarters group. Mahl indicated that Coblenz, Goltz and Dröge were present prior to the shooting, but Coblenz could not have been present as Mahl clearly indicated it took place when the strafing from American fighter bombers was over and this would have been after 4 PM when Coblenz and his men were hiding from the air attack in the western part of Stavelot. Also see testimony of Mahl at the Malmedy trial: Testimony of Ernst Mahl, U.S. v. Bersin, *op. cit*, pp. 1037-1051. 'As your company approached Stavelot, did your company make any stops?' the prosecution asked. 'Yes, outside of Stavelot.'

Q: 'Why did they stop?'
A: 'We had an air raid.'
Q:'During the air attack did you see any Americans?'
A: 'Yes, we had some prisoners of war … six to eight … They were with us during the time of the air raid.'
Q: 'What was done with these Americans?'
A: 'They were shot after the air raid.'
Q: 'What were the Americans doing?'
A: 'They were standing next to a house.'
Q: 'Were there any German soldiers around them?'
A: 'Yes, there were officers … They were holding a conversation.'
Q: 'Who was in this group of officers?'
A: 'Obersturmführer Wegner [sic, Wagner], 1st. Lt Coblenz, 2nd Lt Droege, one 2nd Lt from the second company and one Captain who was our doctor.'
Q: 'What did you see happen after that?'
A: 'I saw Sgt. Wolf and other men take these prisoners from the house to the woods and after they disappear I heard shooting'.

8 Interview with Julia Fabritius née Terf, 20 March 1996.

9 Julia Terf's family was not nearly so lucky: The SS shot her father, François Terf, in the passageway to his house in Parfondruy. In the same village, a similar fate befell her 34-year old sister, Jeanne and her 10-year old son, Paul, who were shot while sitting at the table in their home. The Germans went into houses and began killing people indiscriminately.

10 Julia's oldest child was four and the other two years old. She put them to sleep far away from any windows as those seemed to attract German machine guns when vehicles passed though the town. There was the sound of shooting after midnight and at 5 AM the SS woke up the Fabritius family and started bringing wounded Germans inside their house. These were wounded being brought back from the firefight as Goldstein's road-block. The Germans forced Jules to make coffee for them before banishing the entire family to the cold stable outside. Both knew better than argue with the Germans; they left the house without complaint.

11 Interview with Jules Fabritius, 20 March 1996. At the first opening of fire by the American roadblock, both Belgians escaped their captors by jumping from their jeeps into the darkness. Califice was further back in the column and jumped off too. The fire was coming from Americans on a nearby farm in Amelvot. After seeking shelter in the ditch, Emile Claude got up and ran away.

12 'In the evening towards 20.00 hours our panzers were stopping at the entrance of the town Stavelot.' Affidavit of Kurt Briesemeister, 05.04.1948. The march order of the half dozen Panthers of *1. Panzer Kompanie* approaching Stavelot on the night of 17 December was Strelow's 3rd platoon, the 2nd platoon, Kremser's 101 and Skotz's 102 of the company troop and then Hennecke's 111 and behind them Richartz in 115 and Briesemeister's 114 bringing up the rear in delayed by the need to constantly refill the steering oil. Since the *1. Kompanie* had halted before Stavelot, the *2. Kompanie* also closed up to them that same night. Timm Haasler assisted me with the puzzle pieces to discern Peiper's attack order before Stavelot.

13 Breisemeister told Hennecke that he had burned down the cafe, not only after finding weapons in the home, but after being fired upon by the civilians at Baugnez. See 13 page undated handwritten statement of Hans Hennecke from 1945 or 1946, NA, RG-549, Case 6-24, Box 36. This statement also contains detailed tactical information about the operations of the *1. Panzer Kompanie*. Thanks to Timm Haasler for transcription and translation.

14 Interview notes with Charles Hensel by Janice Holt Giles, 6 February 1969, Damned Engineers Papers, Western Kentucky University.
15 Interview with Corp. Eugene Morris, 8 December 1968, Janice Holt Giles Papers.
16 Corp. Morris thought the bridge had been inspected when they crossed and was found to be wired for domolition. However, Hensel did not recall that event and the issue is uncertain.
17 Story of Albert George: Laby, *op. cit.*, p. 58.
18 Morris interview, *op. cit.*
19 Interview notes with Bernard Goldstein by Janice Holt Giles, 9 May 1969, Damned Engineers Papers, Western Kentucky University.
20 'We reached the outskirts of Stavelot about 2000 hours on the evening of 17 December 1944. Here the company had to dismount and advance as infantry. The SPW's of the company were left on the road before Stavelot.' Affidavit Heinz Friedrichs, 11.Kompanie, 21 March1946.
21 In his interview, Morris also heard Goldstein shout 'Halt!' to the German vehicles. 'Imagine a solitary soldier with an M1 rifle challenging a tank … He deserved a Bronze Star.'
22 For a very detailed assessment of the positions of Goldstein, Morris, Hensel and others as well as the mines: Letter and maps Andre Banneux to Janice Holt Giles, 29 January 1969, Giles Papers, WKU, Banneux folder.
23 Even though Goldstein claimed the vehicle was a tank, it seems likely that the apparition he saw in the darkness was an SPW of *11.Kompanie* that was leading the assault with the *1.Panzer Kompanie.* This speculation is given further credence by the fact that Hensel saw infantry jumping off the 'tank'—much more likely to be panzer grenadiers unloading. Moreover, gunner Rttf. Eugen Zimmermann in Strelow's Panther in the lead mentioned nothing about being fired on by a bazooka prior to arriving at *La Corniche.*
24 Shaken, but unwounded, Pvt. Goldstein had scampered up the giant rock to the west of the curve in the road and eventually made his way from the scene all the way back to the bridge at Stavelot around 11 PM.
25 Oswald Siegmund, *Meine Ehre heißt Treue, Essen* 1992, p. 62.
26 It is possible that the platoon was from the 202nd Engineer Combat Battalion, although the AAR for that unit nor the author's interview with one of its members provided further evidence.
27 Statement of Rudolf Rayer, Dachau 26 April 1947, NA, Case 6-24, RG-153, Box 80.
28 Chinlund's company had been recently transferred from operating sawmills in Luxembourg with 3rd Army to 1st Army, and then temporarily attached to Anderson's 1111 Engineer Combat Group. 'After Action Report 202 Engineer Combat Battalion, December 1944,' NA, RG-407, ENBN-202-0.3. The company had been in Stavelot for five days, enjoying comfortable billets in Belgian homes and busying themselves improving roads and removing old German roadblocks. Yet, most of the men of Chinlund's company viewed Stavelot as a holiday, strolling the streets, trying to meet Belgian girls and photographing the *Place Saint Remacle* in the town.
29 Those in the party were S/Sgt. Felix Skuta and his driver, Pfc. Paul Kohli. Both men aroused the suspicion of the guards of the 3814 Quartermaster Company. Of Swiss derivation, Kohli had a clear German accent and Skuta's Polish tinged English hardly helped further. See Interview with Paul E. Kohli, Ohio Historical Society, Columbus, OH.
30 Interview notes with Bernard Goldstein by Janice Holt Giles, 9 May 1969, Damned Engineers Papers, Western Kentucky University.
31 Interview with John J. Stevenson, Company C, 202 Engineer Combat Battalion, 2 February 1996.
32 The battalion was under the command of Lt Col. Carlisle B. Irwin—a spit and polish WWI veteran—but its company would not fight together in the Ardennes. At 1630 on the 17th of December, the battalion was ordered to proceed to Remouchamps to join the 99th Infantry Battalion with both to proceed to Malmédy via Spa. 'After Action Report 526th Armored Infantry Battalion, December 1944,' NA, RG-407, INBN-526-0.3.
33 Louis Celentano to author, 825th Tank Destroyer Battalion, 19 May 1995.
34 Letter William Selden, 526th Armored Infantry Battalion, 17 February 1991. In desert training at Camp Bouse in Arizona, their biggest worries were snakes and scorpions.
35 Author's interviews with Sgts. Boyce L. Williams and Carl A. Smith, 526th Armored Infantry Battalion, 23 and 25 September 2008. Also, '*A History of Company A: 526th Armored Infantry Battalion,*' Norman Pihaly, ed., Wiesbaden, Germany, October 1945.
36 'Lee M. Galloway: Army Experiences 1943 -1946,' undated hand-written journal, courtesy Tom Hanchett. Also, 'Company A Goes to Battle,' Lee Galloway, *The Pekan, Vol.* 12, September 1992.
37 Celentano to author, June 1995. 'The fateful night as we stood talking and watching the beautiful tracers in the sky Leo Burnette, who was a member of Jack's [Armstrong's] crew joined us as we talked in whispers in the dark. We were scared because of what we saw in the dark. But we were mostly scared because no one knew what was going on.'
38 Peiper testimony, U.S. v. Bersin, p. 1937-1939.
39 Peiper interview with Hans Kettgen, *op. cit.*, p. 11. Peiper's exact description of his conversation with Knittel: '*Ich habe dann am Abend, am Abend dieses Tages habe ich den Kommandeur der Aufklärungsabteilung, die*

mir seitweilig unterstellt war, Knittel, gesprochen, und der sagte mir übringens, da in der Straßenkreuzung, der war sehr viel freige-kommen, da lägen deine ganze Menge, die sind umgelegt worde.'

40 Historians have long pondered how isolated rifle fire and a single bazooka shot from Hensel's dozen men would cause Peiper's spearhead to halt before the big bend in the road, and then wait for eight hours while the Americans reinforced the bridge. If *Kampfgruppe Peiper* had continued down the road that night, they would have reached Trois Ponts and crossed the river there before daybreak. By morning they would have crossed Lienne Creek and confronted Company A of the 291st in Werbomont which was ill prepared for any real defense. By nightfall of 18 December, they would have reached Ouffet and then Ombret Rausa on the Meuse River and likely run out of gas there—and probably attracted the attention of the entire 82nd Airborne Division. The speed of Peiper's advance if he had broken through Stavelot on the night of 17/18 December can be gauged by his progress on the following morning. Breaching the Amblève bridge defenses and shaking loose from the defenders by 1000, Peiper drove to Trois Ponts (6 km away) by 1100 and even with reverses and going through La Gleize reached the Habiemont bridge before Werbomont by 1600. Even assuming progress at night against scattered opposition would be half that rate (3 km/hr), departing from Stavelot at 2200 on the 17th, he would have reached Trois Ponts at midnight and Werbomont 16 km further on the 18th at 0530 assuming he proceeded down *Rollbahn E*. Ombret Rawsa on the Meuse River, some 42 km from Werbomont would be reached by the afternoon at 1300 assuming that a daytime advance rate of 6 km/hr resumed, or just after nightfall if a rate of only half that could be maintained. Relative to the fuel supply, Peiper essentially ran dry near Targnon, albeit after a failed advance and backtrack from La Gleize to the blown Habiemont bridge. This was a back and forth trip totaled 29 km with likely some further fuel wasted from the awkward turnabout. The advance from Stavelot to Targnon was 18 km. This shows that KG Peiper had enough fuel to travel about 50–60 km from Stavelot. The distance from Stavelot to Ombret Rawsa on Rollbahn E was 65 km. Likely, some of Peiper's light elements would have reached the Meuse to almost completely run out of gas there while others would be strung out without fuel all the way back to Ouffet.

41 Eugen Zimmermann as quoted in Tiemann, *op. cit., p. 59.*

42 Interrogation report of Friedrich Christ, no date given, but October 1945 at Wiesbaden, NA, RG-549, Case 6-24, Box 28.

43 Hodges was an avid rifleman and a veteran of World War I. The previous week he had been working with local hunters in the Ardennes to procure a new custom made Belgian-made shotgun. Courtney Hodges Papers, Eisenhower Library, Abilene, KS, Box 25.

44 Iris Carpenter, *No Woman's War,* Houghton Mifflin, NY, 1946, p. 208.

45 Carpenter, *op. cit.*, pp. 208-209 for all of the quotes from First U.S. Army headquarters.

46 'An Interview with Joachim Peiper,' 7 September 1945, Kenneth Hechler, ETHINT-10, NA, RG-338, Foreign Military Studies, p. 18.

47 'An Interview with Joachim Peiper,' *op. cit., p. 8*. Question: 'Did you realize that you came within 300 yards of a three million gallon dump at Spa?' Answer: 'With a typical gesture, Obst. Peiper shrugged his shoulders, smiled rather arrogantly, and said in English, 'I am sorry.' He didn't know the existence of the gasoline dump.'

48 Iris Carpenter, *No Woman's War, Hough*ton Mifflin, NY, 1946, p. 211.

49 Interview with Stevenson, *op. cit.* 'You have to realize how confusing things were that evening. Contrary to what people have said, we did not run out of there. Things were totally confusing; nobody ever expected the Germans to be close by.'

50 Jochen Peiper to John Eisenhower, 4 April 1967, Bitter Woods Papers, Abilene, KS, Box 17.

51 'I arrived at Stavelot with meager resources. The town was hard to get at. The first tank was hit, as it barely stuck its nose around the corner. The attack had be made by infantry, but at this time we certainly did not have more than 30—50 men. Their immediate attack got stuck in defensive fire.' *'Kommentar zum Buch 'Massacre at Malmédy von Charles Whiting,'* by Jochen Peiper, September 1971, p. 8.

52 Interview with David Pergrin, 15 December 1982. Charles B. MacDonald Papers, U.S. Army Military History Institute, Box 6, 291st Engineer Combat Battalion Folder.

53 Giles, *op. cit.*, p. 203-204.

54 Peiper testimony, U.S. v. Bersin, p. 1937-1939.

55 Statement of Henri Lejoly-Jacob (age 50) to Lt Col. Alvin B. Welsch, 6 January 1945, Also statements of Johanna and Madeleine Lejoly to Welsch on 4 January 1945, NA, RG-549, Case 6-24, Box 23. The dead American who died in the shed and then was moved outside was almost certainly S/Sgt. John D. Osborne who was found in mid-January 1945 just outside of that place. Moreover, the autopsy of Osborne found the bullet hole through his left knee and the improvised dressing which Lejoly had helped administer. Osborne, however had received a severe blow to the head, which was listed as the cause of death. The other two dead Americans who Lejoly saw outside his house when he went outside on 18 December 1945 were Privates Stanley I. Piasecke and Keston E. Mullen who were found just west of his home, both found in autopsy to have been killed by shots to the head.

56 Testimony of Pvt. Angelo Accetti to Maj. Oliver Seth, 189th Station Hospital, 17 January 1945, NA, RG-153, Case 6-24, Box 70. Accetti was captured on the 19th of December,'When I was captured about 800 yards further on I told the American Captain [that] there was a wounded man back in the house.'

57 It seems almost certain that the man who survived in Henri Lejoly-Jacob's shed was either Pvt. Louis A. Vario whose body was found 18 kilometers east in Neuhof, Germany or Pvt. Elwood Thomas whose body has never been located. Vario's body was not discovered and buried until 8 February 1945. When his body was disinterred on 12 September 1947, a post mortem evaluation determined that he had been shot in the back. ('Information from Burial File,' Data produced for the author from John Bauserman, 2007). The weight of evidence, however, is that the man who was in wood shed at the Henri-Lejoly Jacob house was Pvt. Thomas. This becomes much more likely since Michael Skoda, who had taken refuge in the Joseph Mathonet house just down the Hedomont road, was later conducted by the Germans to see a wounded American in a house near the crossroads. When Skoda saw the man, he recognized him as Thomas from the 285th FAOB, who was badly wounded.

Chapter 15 – Herbstnebel

1 'V Corps Artillery G-2: Unit Journal,' 17 December 1944, NA, RG-407, 205-ART-2.2, Box 3047. Allied intelligence worried that the Germans knew the position of the V Corps headquarters, as a number of space flares landed close by the headquarters.

2 'Algiers to the Elbe,' Benjamin A. Dickson Journal, Charles B. MacDonald Papers, USAMHI, Box 6, Intelligence Folder.

3 Edwin Sibert to Toland, 1 February 1958. Toland Papers, Battle, LOC, Box 36.

4 'Interview with Adolf G. Rosengarten, Jr.,' 22 February 1947, USAMHI, Papers of Dr Forrest C. Pogue. Rosengarten was the ULTRA officer in the U.S. First Army Headquarters.

5 'Interview with Col. Benjamin A. Dickson,' 1 November 1966, John S.D. Eisenhower, Bitter Woods, Box 1.

6 'Report of the VIII Corps After Action Against Energy Forces in France, Belgium, Luxembourg and Germany,' entries for 17 December, NA, RG-407, VIII Corps AAR, December, 1944.

7 Frank James Price, *Troy H. Middleton: A Biography,* Louisiana University Press, Baton Rouge, 1974, pp. 226-227. 'Before Middleton left on the morning of 19 December for Neufchateau, he counseled Brig. Gen. Anthony McAuliffe, who would become famous for his 'Nuts!' response to a German request for surrender. 'Now Tony, you're going to be surrounded before long. But don't worry; help is on the way from Patton. You've got fine me … I'd prefer not to leave this place but Hodges has told me I have to go.'

8 Ridgway, Gen. Matthew B. *Soldier: The Memoirs of Matthew W. Ridgway,* Harper Brothers, NY, 1956, p. 114. As Ridgway got up the following morning in the headquarters, he overhead a conversation between two soldiers in a hallway at Middleton's headquarters illustrating the great uncertainty: 'We'd better get the hell out of here.' The reply: 'We can't. They've got us surrounded.'

9 Eisenhower interview with Dickson, *ibid.*

10 T-Force included the 526th Armored Infantry Battalion and the Norwegian 99th Infantry Battalion (Separate). Letter Capt. S.M. Harris of T-Force to author on 3 October 1992. The 526th had been located in Remouchamps when the German counterattack took place. Harris drove to the U.S. First Army HQ on the morning of the 16th to see a friend and found the place 'a disturbed ant's net.' 'My friend had little to say to me other than that things were a mess.' Before being shipped overseas, the 526th had trained in the desolate Arizona desert with special tanks with CDLs or Canal Defense Lights—powerful arc strobe lamps (13 million candlepower) mounted on an M3 tank chassis that were designed to blind the enemy in night attacks—so secret that even Harris did not know about them. 'I roomed with the Battalion operations officer in Remouchamps. They had been told it was secret and they damn well kept it so.' As the 526th did not bring its top-secret CDL tanks (nicknamed *Gizmos*) to Europe, they were given a counterintelligence mission to gather information on enemy secret weapons as they liberated major cities and otherwise to serve as a sort of palace guard for the 12th Army Group. See Stuart L. Daniels, 'The Mystery of Our Most Secret Weapon,' *The American Weekly,* 11 August 1957. Also R.W. Koch, 'The Secret of Camp Bouse,' *The CHP,* February 1991.

11 Pogue's entry for 19 December 1944: 'Germans have the good ground now for armor, as we did from Paris. Much complaint about our failure to go to the Rhine in September.' Forrest C. Pogue, *Pogue's War,* University of Kentucky Press, Lexington, 2001, p. 295.

12 'The Defense of Spa,' 518 M.P. Battalion, History of the Ardennes Campaign, NA, RG-498, Records of the ETOUSA Historical Division, Ardennes Campaign, Box 2.

13 For various sources on the atmosphere at Hodges headquarters during the chaos on 17 December: Rick Atkinson, *The Guns at Last Light,* Henry Holt, NY, 2013, pp. 440-443.

14 Iris Carpenter, *No Woman's World,* Houghton Mifflin, NY, *1946,* pp. 208-213.

15 Dickson may have been mindful of information just made available from POW interrogations: '1st SS Task Force—P/Ws insist that mission is to get a bridgehead across MEUSE River. Task Force has 12 Mk IVs and

17 Mk Vs, Co. of PGR and Co paratroops riding tanks. Platoon of armored flak.' NA, RG-407, V Corps G-2 Journal and File, 17 December, 2037 hrs, 205-2.2.

16 'Maj. Rosengarten to G-2, Record of Telephone Conversation: G-2 Journal No. 111,' 2215 17 December 1944, NA, RG-407, G-2 Journal, 101- 2.2 U.S. First Army, Box 1875.

17 'U.S. First Army, G-2 Periodic Report No. 191,' 18 December 1944, NA, RG-407, U.S. 1st Infantry Division, G-2 Journal and File, 301-2.2, Box 5072. 'Suddenly for no apparent reason, one or two shots were fired into this group of defenseless prisoners by the Germans engaged in guarding them, and almost immediately two of the German tanks began spraying the prisoners with machine gun fire.'

18 'G-3 Master (Col. Throckmorton),' 0020A 18 December 1944, NA, RG-407, G-2 Journal, 101- 3.3 U.S. First Army, Box 1529.

19 'War Diary of Maj. William Sylvan,' Courtney Hodges Papers, Eisenhower Library, Abilene, KS, Box 25.

20 U.S. Army official historian, Forrest C. Pogue, were less inclined to see the shooting at Malmedy as solely an SS aberration. Pogue had followed the U.S. First Army in the autumn of 1944 and recalled hearing of the shooting after evacuating Spa, Belgium: 'The whole matter of killing prisoners had been on my mind since the Huertgen Forest fight. I recalled ugly stories about some unit's record in regard to the killing of prisoners. During the period of the Ardennes, I visited a headquarters on the Malmedy road and was told that a sniper had just shot one of their men on an outpost. The men were looking for the German and said that if they captured him they would shoot him. An armored infantry lieutenant, noting my surprise, said his outfit had captured enemy soldiers on a recent occasion and, after saving two for questioning, disposed of the rest. His excuse, was that being tankers, they couldn't handle the others. Others spoke of opening fire on enemy soldiers who seemed to be on the point of surrendering, so that there would be no need to shoot them later ... Placed against this sort of testimony and this sort of reasoning, a massacre like the one at Malmedy is brutal only because it is larger or calculated to provoke terror.' Forrest C. Pogue, *Pogue's War*, University of Kentucky Press, Lexington, 2001, pp. 297.

Chapter 16 – Stavelot

1 Excerpt from *Cote 146*- 'Hill 146:' Guillaume Apollinaire joined the French army in December 1914 and was posted to the front in April 1915. On 17 March 1916 he received a shrapnel wound to his temple for which he was invalided out of the army.

2 Prior to the French revolution, the district of Eupen-Malmedy was divided into three parts: Eupen belonged to the Duchy of Limburg, St. Vith to Luxembourg and Malmedy to the Imperial Abbey of Stavelot-Malmedy. Annexed by the French empire during the Napoleonic era, the district became of Prussia in 1814 after Napoleon's fall some 16 years before the foundation of Belgium came into being. The district remained Prussian, later German, until 1920 when it became part of Belgium as decreed by the Treaty of Versailles. However, even on the first day of Belgian rule, an anti-Belgian movement came into existence, aiming at the return of the region to Germany. In May 1940, Hitler claimed the area with its population of about 60,000—mostly German speaking citizens—to be returned to the Reich. A large portion of these people, German through cultural background– probably consider themselves as much German as Belgian. Even today, evidence of this schism is still observed where road signs with French spelling such as *Bullange*, are crudely whitewashed with the alternate German spelling—*Büllingen*.

3 That the Belgian resistance was very active in the region and just being disbanded was made clear in a directive from the U.S. First Army on 3 December 1944 which called for all 'Belgian resistance groups' to cease their activities and turn in their arms to U.S. military authorities. Col. R.S. Nourse, to all Corps, Divisions and Separate Commanders, 'Belgian Resistance Groups,' U.S. First Army: G-1, General Correspondence, NA, RG-407, 101-1.1 The orders did not apply to the officially sanctioned Belgian Fusilier Battalions, however.

4 Interview with Marcel Ozer, 25 May 1997.

5 Interview with Marcel Ozer, 14 October 1995.

6 The German perception was verified on this point even viewed by local Belgians. In an interview in April 2003, Joseph Dejardin, a local Belgian historian recalled that 'Stavelot was called a 'Partisanen-nest', that's correct. The AS (*Armee Secret*) and the *Armee Blanche* were the two parties here in Stavelot.' Transcript of taped interview provided courtesy Mike Smeets.

7 For Col. Benjamin Dickson's view of the complex situation in Belgium, see 'Counterintelligence in Belgium: G-2 Estimate No. 25,' 11 September 1944, U.S. First Army, NA, RG-407, U.S. First Army G-2, 301-2.2, Records of U.S. First Infantry Division, Box 5058.

8 Born in January 1887, Comte Louis d'Oultremont, the head of a noble family known for participation with the Belgian resistance, was murdered on the grounds of his five-turreted castle at Ham-sur-Heure 10 km south of Charleroi on 12 August 1944 by two car-loads of Rexist thugs. The killers of d'Oultremont and his 40-year old governess, Mme. Schmidt, were apprehended after the war and executed. At the time, Louis's son, Lt Edouard Comte d' Oultremont was a commando leader on the

3-man 'Team Andrew' that parachuted behind German lines near Charleville in August 1944. Their objective—right out of a Hollywood thriller—was to sow mayhem and link up with the French Maquis as the Americans approached: Roger J. Spiller, *'Jedburgh Team Operations in Support of the 12th Army Group,'* Combat Studies Institute, U.S. Dept. of Defense, October, 1991. Thanks to Henri Rogister for helping to uncover details.

9 In 1933, a Dr Dohnen from Germany went to Eupen and began to gather around him a group of young fanatics which organized along SS lines. They were thoroughly indoctrinated with Hitler's ideology and trained under strict quasi-military discipline performing night marches, terrain exercises and the like. By 1934, he and Joseph Kerres had organized 150 youths, then given them an innocent sounding cover-up name, the '*Verein fuer Natur und Heimatkunde*'—the Nature and Homeland Club. Another even more fanatical group—the '*Segelflugverein*'—the Glider Club in Eupen and the *Bogenschuetzen Verein* in St. Vith organized in the same fashion. In 1939, hand-picked members of the organizations were secretly taken into Germany for further training. In May 1940, these operatives were used during the invasion of Belgium within '*Battalion z.b.v. 800.*' This clandestine military formation operated in civilian clothes ahead of the panzer divisions securing bridges, guiding German columns and carrying out Fifth Column activities. Further this seems a likely inspiration for Hitler's brain-wave for the Skorzeny commando operation in 1944. So dedicated were the Belgian youths of the *Segelflugverein* and their splinter groups that many of the youth later were absorbed into the Waffen SS and fought with Germany throughout the war. 'The Pro-German Movement in the Eupen-Malmedy Region of Belgium 1920-1940,' U.S. First Army, Annex No. 2, 11 December 1944, NA, RG-407, 1st Infantry Division, 301-2.2, G-2 Records, Box.5071.

10 'BDC File for Johann Waldmüller,' NA, RG-242, A3343-SSO-2188. Waldmüller had entered the SS in 1937, became a platoon leader in the Leibstandarte in July 1940, eventually rising to the rank of SS Obersturmbannführer in 1944. Killed in Belgium on 8 September, Waldmüller just received the Ritterkreuz for his actions with *12. SS Panzer Division* on the invasion front just two weeks earlier.

11 Even today, the locals around Stavelot, Belgium describe this incident with pride. Author's anonymous interview with Stavelot resistance fighters 1996-1997.

12 Smeets interview with Joseph Dejardin, April 2003: 'The Belgians who believed were responsible, were arrested and brought to the *Feldgendarm*-post here in Stavelot (located at the square *L'Histoire*). From there to Verviers. 4 out of 7 were shot. Two of them were men who had married girls from Stavelot—one from Brussels and one from Mons.'

13 The square is now known as Place Saint Remacle in Stavelot towards the north end of town.

14 Interview with Beathe O'Neill (nee Wetz), 3-4 February 1996. When interviewed, Ms. O'Neill still owned the large building at 15 Grand Place, purchased by her father before the war.

15 In a letter to Gen. Michael Reynolds on 16 January 1990, Capt. William Doyle insisted that Chindlun was 'a bad apple' and left the company pretty much on its own. 'It was like living in a dream world … you had no idea what was happening. He had no leadership ability.'

16 In interviews with the author 17 July 1997 and 20 June 2010, Howard Meyer insisted they had heard 'machine gun fire up on the hill south of town' and that Chinlun and Sgt. Dale Renfroe had later told him that with binoculars, they spotted what they thought were German tanks up on the hill across the river. This is what led to the rapid exodus from Stavelot.

17 Headquarters of C Company 202 Engineer Combat Battalion located themselves at Beathe's home. Author's interview with Stevenson, 2 February 1996 and letter to Michael Reynolds, 8 February 1990. Stevenson was the squad leader of 1st Platoon under Sgt. Felix Skuta. 'My squad was staying in a large mansion-type house. We had no specific assignment. The attitude of the men was very relaxed. We all thought the war was far away and almost over … We began to notice friendly military units moving through Stavelot, apparently to the rear. As the day went on, it appeared to me that our Company Commander, Lt Chinlund had not been informed about what was happening. Late in the day, sometime after the sun had gone down, our company formed a convoy and set out in the direction the other units had been travelling … We arrived at some type of headquarters … As I understood it, C Company received orders to return to Stavelot to defend the bridge until relieved.' In fact, C Company had reached Col. Anderson with 1111th Engineer Combat Group in Trois-Ponts who ordered them to return to Stavelot.

18 Interview with Stan Aldinger, 22 June 2010. At 6 AM, Chinlund decided to pull C Company out of the battle and head towards Verviers—without warning Meyer and 15 others down near the bridge that he was pulling out. After returning to Stavelot that night, Chinlund had ordered Meyer and five others down to the bridge where they set up mines to be covered by machine guns.

19 This episode from Hubert Laby, *18 Décembre 1944: Stavelot,* Dépot Légal, Faimes, 1994, pp. 34-35. I am appreciative of Mr. Laby's help with the author's research in 1997 and his gracious permission to use stories in his important account. Other sources for this chapter are two studies by Serge Fontaine, *'Les Cartes de la Bataille de Stavelot,'* and also, 'The Fights of 18 December 1944 in Stavelot,' CRIBA, Liège, January 1991. Thanks to Henri Rogister for a translation by Raymond Goémé.

20 Letter Guy Lebeau to Hubert Laby, 20 February 1995. Courtesy Hubert Laby.

21 'Paul E. Kohli Account of Stavelot Belgium, 16 -18 December 1944, 202 Engineer Combat Battalion,' MSS 1018, The Columbus World War II Roundtable Collection, Courtesy of Ohio Historical Society, Columbus, OH.

22 Laby, *op. cit.*, Albert Sougné stayed in Stavelot, unable to convince his aging parents to take to the roads.

23 See *Der Feldzug im Frankreich*, Lage 10.5.1940, ABDS, NA, Record Group unknown, map copies in author's possession provided by George Wagner in the 1970s.

24 Peiper's adjutant, Hans Gruhle, seemed to have been equally impressed with the squad-level counterattack by Sgt. Charles Hensel. 'Toward midnight on 17 December, the panzer assault halted at a point close to the outskirts of Stavelot. An infantry attack, lacking sufficient force, was stopped by defensive fire in front of the American positions.' 'Kampfgruppe Peiper: 15-26 December 1944,' MS C-004, Foreign Military Studies, USAMHI.

25 Diefenthal to Tiemann, 5 March 1986. Ralf Tiemann, *Die Leibstandarte, Band IV/2*, Munin Verlag, Osnabrück, footnote, p. 84.

26 In fact, the infantry of *11. Kompanie* had been in place on the road before Stavelot since 8 PM. For the planned surprise assault on the bridge, the panzer grenadiers left their SPWs on the road and moved on foot, carrying only the firepower that could be shouldered in the darkness. Affidavit of Heinz Friedrichs, 21 March 1946.

27 'After Action Report, 202 Engineer Combat Battalion, December 1944,' NA, RG-407, ENBN-202-0.3. Until 11 December Company C of battalion had been with the VIII Corps operating two sawmills near Bettembourg, Luxembourg until ordered to V Corps to help outpost the village of Stavelot. On the evening of 12 December, they reported to Col. Anderson at Trois Ponts who located Company C in Stavelot.

28 Story of René Bourgonjon: Laby, *op. cit.*, pp. 68-69. Convinced he was a German spy, the suspicious youth was taken back to the company CP near the café of Pauline Livet in Stavelot for questioning before being released.

29 'Personal Narrative of the CO of Company A, 526th Armored Infantry Battalion,' interviewed by Capt. Franklin Ferris, 7 January 1945, in 'The German Offensive of 16 December 1944: The Defeat of the 1st SS Panzer Division Adolf Hitler,' NA, RG-407, 218.2-1, XVIII Corps G-2, January, 1945, Combat Interview 94, Box 24037. 'Arrived at Stavelot at 0400 18 December 1944. Picked up Maj. Solis and Lt Pehovic from Battalion headquarters. Company of one platoon of TDs parked on the road on the outskirts of Stavelot while Maj. Solis, Lt Pehovic and myself went into town to get the situation from the Engineer Company that was in town at the time. They had a roadblock across the river up on the hill and it had been fired on and the men retreated back into town.'

30 Today the *Route du Vieux Château* is rendered on maps as the *Chem du Château*.

31 'I was not informed, nor was I aware that the bridge was supposed to have been prepared for demolition.' 'Recollections of Dr Charles Mitchell,' 526th Armored Infantry Battalion, prepared for author, February 1995. Also, interview with Paul Kohli, *op. cit.* where he specifically recalled that Company C of the 202nd did not prepare the bridge for demolition. The problem seems to have arisen from the haste with which Col. Anderson gave Chinlund orders at midnight on 17 December in Trois Ponts. Chinlund heard that he was to defend the bridge, rather than prepare it for demolition. And even if he had received orders to dynamite the span, so stalwart were its old stone piers that hours of preparation with many bundles of TNT would have been required to prepare to bring it down.

32 Laby, *op. cit.*, pp. 88-89.

33 Several of the SS wounded were treated at the home of Julia Fabritius back in La Vaulx Richard. One of them was Karl Kremser.

34 Today on contemporary maps, this is Rue Marlennes.

35 Bob Hammons to author, June 1995, Also, Laby, *op. cit.*, p. 106.

36 Maximum speed of the Panther was still not fast by Peiper's standards compared to armored personnel carriers. The maximum speed for the *Panther Mk V Ausf G* is listed as 38 km/hr or 24 mph. Both the Mk IV and *Königstiger VIB* had similar top speeds. The *Sd Kfz 251* SPW could go up to 53 km/hr or 33 mph. Chris Ellis, *Tanks of World War II*, Octopus Books, London, 1981.

37 Laby, *op. cit.*, p. 109.

38 Laby, *op. cit.*, p. 169.

39 Father and son survived the confrontation at their burning farm, only to witness still another surreal scene later that morning. A flock of their geese wandered into the road in the path of a German truck loaded with infantry, and they saw the truck stop and patiently wait for the geese to squawk across the road. Laby, *op. cit.*, p. 175.

40 Interview with Donald Necina, 21 June 2010 and Stan Aldinger, 22 June 2010.

41 Laby, *op. cit.*, p. 118.

42 Letter of Louis Celentano to author, 19 May 1995.

43 Interview with James Landgren, 1 February 1997.

44 Account of Bob Hammons, 825th TD Battalion, composed for author, June 1995.

45 Sources for operations in Stavelot on December 18th: Laby, *op. cit.* Also, Will C.C. Cavanagh, *A Tour of the Bulge Battlefield,* Leo Cooper, London, 2001, pp. 90-91. In Sgt. John Armstrong's halftrack: Leo Brunette, Conley Leach (driver), Frank Richesin (machine gunner), Bernard Gallagher, Anthony Calvanese, Fowler Williams and Douglas Newman. The halftrack of Sgt. Jonas Whaley included Cpl Bob Hammons, driver William Gilman, Willie Banes, Gaylord Eichorn, Joseph Bowen and Leonard Walsh. During the attempt to find the *Route du Vieux Château,* the two halftracks became split up in nighttime driving.

46 Hammons account, *op. cit.,* 'We took refuge in a potato bin in the basement. We hid our MG under a mattress ... Not long after we got there, a German soldier came in and took up a position at arm's length from the potato bin where we were. He stood there and watched, as we did, at the battle raging outside. There was a half window on the street side of the basement and we could hear the clanging of steel against steel while tank motors revved up. We realized they were pushing the halftracks and guns off the road so they could pass. Back in the potato bin, Willie Banes who had driven all night to get there, had gone to sleep and was snoring pretty loud. I expected the German to open up with his burp gun at any time. But somehow they didn't notice us.' The next day the Americans hid the entire day in the house, escaping at dusk by leaving through a rear door of the house while the Germans were occupied. All three men managed to move under cover of darkness down to the Amblève, crossing over a small dam by the reservoir at the east edge of town.

47 'Stavelot- Another Perspective,' Dante M. Casa, *The Pekan,* March 1991. 'When Company A landed in France, our halftracks stopped at a stack of Browning Automatic Rifles (BARs). I confiscated two BARs and 300 rounds of clips. At the time, I never realized it would save my life.'

48 'I had both machine guns covering the bridge when two soldiers approached in the half light walking towards us. I held our fire until we could see the outline of their German helmets. We fired on them with rifles as we did not want to give away our gun positions.' Brennan to author, 26 April 1995.

49 Casa, *op. cit.,* 'I searched for a medic and to my relief, my nose was still there.'

50 I used the interview transcript of Alfred Duesdiecker, May 1998, courtesy of Tom Hanchett, 526th Armored Infantry Battalion Association. Also, Laby, *op. cit.,* p. 99.

51 Oft repeated story of John Mills as related by his widow to author, 17 September 2008. Also Mills letter to the editor, *The Pekan,* January 2005 and email transcript of John Mills to Hanchett, 7 July 2000.

52 The story of the 'spy' in Solis's command post comes from Lt John V. Pehovic, the S-1 with the 526th, '12 Hours in Stavelot' *Bulge Bugle,* November 1999.

53 Two anonymous members of Company A of the 526th Armored Infantry Battalion told the author that Solis was 'a garrison commander,' similar to Lt Col. Carlisle B. Irwin, who would not be found anywhere near the front line. Clearly from the author's research, Capt. Charles Mitchell led the forces of the 526th that engaged the enemy in Stavelot that morning.

54 Pehovic, *ibid.*

55 Interview with Beathe O'Neill, *op. cit.* Eventually Beathe would marry a Lt from the 117th Infantry Regiment of the 30th Infantry Division, who introduced himself to her after the battle.

Chapter 17 – Hesitation

1 Jochen Peiper to John Eisenhower, 4 April 1967, *Bitter Woods Papers,* Eisenhower Papers, Abilene, KS, Box 17.

2 Weather in nearby Herve, Belgium on the morning of the 18th: NA, RG-407, 301-2.2, U.S. First Infantry Div., G-2 Journal for 18 December, Box 5072.

3 William Kenny and Steve Howell ran further to the right and ended up swimming the Amblève in an attempt to escape.

4 'We laid the solider on a bed, my mother tended to his wounds as best as she could, gave him something to eat and then, in the warmth of the house, he fell asleep.' Letter Paulette Comté to Julia Ozer, 23 April 1996. This and preceding quote, courtesy Jim Landgren.

5 Landgren interview, *op. cit.* 'Then there was knock at the door and this time it was German soldier. I was in the bedroom towards the rear of the house. I heard them talking in there in German. "Any other Germans in the house." "No" "Okay, we're coming back and we're going to take over the house." Marie Louise hustled me down into the basement. Down there was her 9 year old daughter. It was dark, but they had oil lamps. There was a small chicken coop that adjoined the basement. You could get in there from the basement. The daughter took me out to it and there was a little ladder going up to a little loft—it was more like a shelf. There was straw enough to cover up. It was cold, but I had a tanker's uniform on. They were heavy coveralls. I had a jacket with heavy material and I had paratroop jump boots. The bandaged leg was still not hurting; maybe it was the cold. I had not been in the loft more than ten minutes when a whole squad of Germans came in the basement to use it as a command post. There was a lot of firing now. They were assaulting the bridge. The Germans were attacking the town from the south. Lots of heavy fire right across the river. I had a knife; that was all. The Germans used that little chicken coop as a latrine so

there was a lot of traffic. I have never been sure how long I was there. I had two D-bars (hard chocolate) and a canteen of water. I stayed there awhile. I don't remember them; they say they brought me water. I was there at least four days. I was so worried about how the hell I could get out of there that I didn't think much of the leg … But one morning, apparently the Germans were looking for eggs and when I woke up I staring at a German. He was so startled he pitched over backwards. Then three or four raced in from the basement with their rifles and I came down from the shelf. I was very startled to see the SS emblem on their uniforms. There was a lieutenant who spoke English. They searched me and I was pretty wobbly. I had class ring on my hand (Notre Dame) and they were trying to pull it off. They were pretty rough. The lieutenant stopped them. I was sitting facing the wall. He offered me some cold bacon. I tried to chew it but I couldn't get it down. I had the dry heaves. I was in bad shape. "I didn't care at that point." The German lieutenant then took my ring off. He looked over the ring and then offered it back. But I gave it back to him, "You might as well keep it because I won't have it very long." The lieutenant then seemed to search for something to give me in return. He gave me a very small picture of himself. I threw away the picture as fast as I could. I didn't want to get caught with a picture of an SS officer. I don't know how much time went by. I may have been there 4-6 hours. It was dark. The Lieutenant and I crawled down the road. It was under fire. We went to the home of Josef Demoulin about four houses down. They took me into the basement. There were three German officers sitting at a table in the basement with a candle. One of them, seemed elderly and higher ranking. They asked me questions in German. I didn't say a word. I heard the elderly ask the Lieutenant if I was "*Kranke*?"—hurt. He spoke with him for a minute, but I could understand a little. "He had been hiding in house down the road, where the Grandfather and the little girl are." They shrugged their shoulders at me. Then they took me out of the house and I was put under two guards. When he turned me over to the two guards, we crawled back to the east. We were there for a short time. When the two soldiers came up. He said, "Good luck" to me in German—I understood that—and left. We were standing up then. The two guards took me back and we got into a German jeep and went back to a very large house or a hotel. It was evidently a CP for higher ranking officers. This was five or ten miles from Stavelot. There was a concentration of vehicles and many people coming and going into it. I was taken into a large room and there were many officers and people at large table with radios. [This was likely Ligneuville] They were sitting around smoking cigarettes. There was a *Life* magazine lying on the table. They asked me questions. By this time I was a little more composed. All I did was to give my name rank and serial number. "We know who you are and you were with the 106th Infantry Division." There were pictures of an American tank on the cover of the *Life Magazine*; they tossed it towards me. The house seemed more like an estate than a hotel. "You were in New York a month ago." They didn't look at my dog tags. I kept quiet and I didn't say a word. They led me down the hall and they opened the door and there were 20-25 young Germans in there. They sat me down. They were singing Christmas carols. "Silent Night." No one made any aggressive moves to me. On the contrary, soon, we were all drinking and smoking. After maybe half an hour they took me out of the room and put me in the basement. It was a dark basement with water on the floor. I sat on the furniture down there and was allowed to keep this half a bottle of schnapps. It kept me warm. They were very young soldiers. The next morning we walked away and we came to another town. There were two American air force personnel who were there and we walked east. It was cold and the road was snow covered. We walked a while and then these Hitler Youth stopped us and forced the fliers to take off their fur lined slipper. They poked them with bayonets. They wanted my boots and I started to complain. Just then, a German command car came racing up. A German officer got out and back handed the young German soldier carrying the air force boots. He cursed them and made them give back the boots and screamed at them so more. We would have lost our feet if that had not happened. He left and we walked. We walked a long time. Later we ended up on a train in boxcars. I was with a group of American soldiers, but I had no idea what day it was. I ended up in Stalag IVB in Muehlberg and was liberated by the Russians in early May.'

6 Interview of Mike Smeets with anonymous member of 526th Armored Infantry Battalion, provided to the author on 20 October 2008.

7 Norman Pihaly to author, 8 February 1996.

8 Mitchell account, *op. cit.*

9 Interview with Anthony Calvanese, 14 June 1997. Calvanese had entered service in 1942 and had been with the 825th Tank Destroyer Battalion since before the landing at Normandy. Still, the 825th had mainly security duties for the 12th Army Group and their deployment in the Ardennes was their first combat action.

10 Interview with Julia and Marcel Ozer, 14 October 1995, Stavelot.

11 Story of Jules Crismer from Laby, *op. cit., p.* 95.

12 Declaration of SS Oscha. Rudi Rayer, Dachau, 26 April 1947, NA, RG-549, Case 6-24, Box 28. In another statement dated 27 October 1947 (Box 38), Rayer clarified that 'After heavy losses on our side we succeeded in reaching the bridge and we established ourselves there till we were picked up by our own tanks … Besides many other dead comrades, the company commander, SS 1st Lt Tomhardt was wounded

at Stavelot.' By way of contrast in Tomhardt's many statements after the war, he never said anything about his fighting near Stavelot.

13 Screening of Günther Heinrich at Ebensee, 1945. SS-Ustuf. Willi Horn was born at Walsleben (30.04.1920-18.12.1944), and joined the 12./LSSAH by January 1, 1941. Horn died at Stavelot as the platoon leader of 11.(gep.)/SS.PzGrenRgt.2 LSSAH (Tomhardt). Willi Horn is buried at the cemetery at Lommel (Belgium) under unknown soldiers (Volksbund Deutsche Kriegsgräberfürsorge e.V.). He was killed during the capture of a bridge in Stavelot , while his Kompanieführer Ostuf. Heinz Tomhardt was wounded.

14 Oswald Siegmund, *Meine Ehre heißt Treue, Essen*, 1992, p. 64.

15 'An Interview with Obst. Joachim Peiper: 1 SS Panzer Regiment' ETHINT-10, Freising, 7 September 1945., NA, RG-238, Foreign Military Studies.

16 For the story of Ernest Rensonnet, Laby, *op. cit.*, pp. 105-106.

17 Interview with Sgt. Carl Smith, 25 September 2008. 'The officers were all back in the village square in Stavelot with Lt Rogers and Mitchell and a 1st Sgt. and Lt Beardslee and they were watching from a tall building. The officers didn't come down where the fighting was. Did you know that the sergeants did most of the fighting? I did and it was my responsibility to take care of those men.'

18 Later that morning, the SS troopers would set the Dizier and Adolphe Foguenne houses ablaze—likely to deny the structures just to the north-east of the bridge to the Americans who had fired from there against the Germans crossing the span all morning.

19 'Lee M. Galloway: Army Experiences 1943-1946,' undated hand-written journal, courtesy Tom Hanchett, entry for 18 December 1944. 'We went out of the shack as a shell had hit it while we were in there and dropped a lot of dust on our head.'

20 In 1995, Capt. Mitchell told the author he had personally observed the German tank assault across the bridge, seeing bazooka rockets glance off the Panther.

21 Because the American 2nd and 3rd squads on the south side of the bridge were fleeing under attack, Brennan's men in the buildings flanking the bridge had to hold their fire to make certain that vehicles crossing the bridge were not American. In this way, the halftrack of Lt. Harry Willyard was able to cross the bridge without being mistakenly fired upon. Still, Brennan's men had to wait until they had clearly identified if vehicles crossing the bridge were unfriendly.

22 Author's interview with Howard Meyer, 20 June 2010. 'We were not ordered to blow the bridge, but to protect the bridge.'

23 Capt. Mitchell, in Ferris interview, *op. cit.*: 'The tank continued on across the bridge where it came under direct fire of an AT gun manned by Sgt. Smith and Pfc. Taylor. They fired point blank at the tank. The tank fired its 88mm gun at them, but was unable to depress its muzzle far enough to hit them. In the face of the approaching tank, Sgt. Smith and Pvt. Taylor continued to fire at the tank until it threatened to overrun the gun.'

24 Interview with Carl Smith, *op. cit.*

25 Running down the little street: *Quai des Vieux Moulin*, the two men, Sgt. Carl Smith and Pvt. Roscoe Taylor ran past the house of Adolphe Foguenne where they met up with Pvt. Lee Galloway and other men with Lt Beardslee attempting to flee north from the German tanks and infantry now flooding across the bridge. Several men were killed or wounded at the end of the street when the Germans took their retreat under a withering fire from a cross street. Some of the others of the AT and machine gun crews hid themselves in the attics of some of the buildings on the *Rue du Gustav Dewalque*.

26 Brennan to author, 26 April 1995. 'About that time Sgt. Carl Smith and his 57mm anti-tank crew came down to the bridge. I gave him my positions covering the bridge with flank protection, worried that the Germans might try to wade the river on foot. About this time, it was just daylight and we observed a Tiger tank [sic] approaching us on the bridge. The tank stopped only about 15 yards in front of Sgt. Smit. He fired three rounds at the tank—it was a direct shot. The tank's armor was too thick for the rounds to penetrate, but his crew fed one round after another into the gun. The tank made no attempt to return fire, but the tank kept coming on. We were given orders to pull back to the town square. We then ran to our halftracks and moved back.'

27 Zimmermann in Tiemann, *op. cit.*, p.81. Afterwards: 'We drove uphill, the fire faded away and we had made [it?] through Stavelot. Via radio we called the weapons mechanic because our gun was totally screwed up.'

28 Peiper, ETHINT-10, *op. cit.*; Peiper got facts wrong in his retelling. Although the first tank (Strelow) was hit, it was not destroyed, but reached the bridge. The 'two Sherman tanks' were actually two halftrack towed guns of the 825th TD Battalion. Also, Strelow's tank, after being hit, had run over one anti-tank gun and caused another to be abandoned.

29 Statement of Hans Hennecke, 14 January 2006. Courtesy Timm Haasler.

30 'In front of Stavelot, Knörringer had also boarded the tank as a gunner. A short time later, Stubaf. Poetschke appeared and pushed me to move on.' See 13 page undated handwritten statement of Hans Hennecke from 1945 or 1946, NA, RG-549, Case 6-24, Box 36.

31 Interview with Roland Knörringer, 1 October 2008, courtesy Timm Haasler. Knörringer had joined the LAH at the same time as Rolf Reiser, moving to the *1. Panzer Kompanie* in November of 1944. 'The company had

an *I-Staffel* (Maintenance section), equipped with a one ton halftrack. In general he should have driven with this vehicle but Hennecke asked him to stay close with the tanks and therefore he took his toolbox and mounted Hennecke's tank. As there was no free space inside the tank he stayed outside on top of the engine compartment. On the way to Stavelot, he remembered a wooded area where they discovered a deserted American tent camp. They dismounted from the tanks and started to search for American K-rations. As they didn't have had much time everybody took whatever carton they could find. Later during another break he opened his carton, expecting to find some good food but the content of his carton were several boxes filled with 10 rosaries each. Although he was very disappointed about it he didn't throw the boxes away, instead he handed over the rosaries to civilians in the next town they passed through. The other thing he remembers is that they captured an American jeep which he took over as his vehicle. He drove with this jeep till Stavelot.'

32 Letters Louis Celentano to author: March 17th, May 19th and June 5th 1995.

33 In their After Action Report for 18 December, the 526th TD Battalion claimed to have knocked out four German tanks in Stavelot—likely a typical exaggeration. However, it does seem likely that together the 825th TD and 526th did temporarily knock out three tanks—those of Richartz (Nr. 115), Kremser (101) and Hennecke (111), although the latter two were soon back in action.

34 In his important book, Hubert Laby (pp. 129-132) indicated that the German tank hit midway across the bridge was that of Hans Hennecke, and Kremser's tank (0101) was hit by one of Sgt. Celentano's rounds that shot down the tank of Richartz on the *Vieux Chateau*. Kremser then arrived at the Crismer house and tried to prod some engineers into action to retrieve Hennecke's tank and was shot outside near the bridge. While this scenario remains possible, another seems more likely: that it was Kremser's tank, in fact, that was hit by Pvt. Mill's bazooka on the bridge. Reasons: When examined after being left in La Gleize, Kremser's tank showed frontal damage to the tank similar to what would be expected from a bazooka hit, whereas Hennecke's original Nr. 111 look pristine on the gun turret, but showed damage as if hit from the side. In statements after the war, Hennecke claimed to have been hit in 111 while he was descending to the bridge, but before he actually reached the span. After his tank was damaged, he and his crew made their way on foot towards the bridge to find Kremser had been wounded and was located in the Crismer house. He then boarded Kremser's tank now just south of the bridge entrance on Poetschke's orders and proceeded on into Stavelot. Further, Hennecke penciled two detailed sketches outlining precisely this sequence and location of vehicles in his statements at Schwabisch Hall and one from the trial itself: See 'Sketch of Stavelot Incident drawn from Recollection: Hans Hennecke, Nr. 57,' Case 6-24, RG-549, Box 54. Also, 'Statement of Hans Hennecke,' and labeled sketch, 13 March 1946, Case 6-24, RG-549, Box 6 and Box 8. However, Laby and witnesses are indeed correct that the damaged Panther was towed off the bridge. In the John V. Pehovic's account '12 Hours in Stavelot' *Bulge Bugle, Novemb*er 1999, the member of the 526th wrote, 'The Germans brought up a tank that attempted to cross the bridge, but it was quickly immobilized. The Germans then brought up a monstrously huge Tiger Royal tank [sic] which pulled the wrecked tank from the bridge.'

35 Expert Timm Haasler has helped the author attempt to reconstruct the confusing fight for the Stavelot bridge. Since Strelow's tank was likely from the 2nd platoon of the *1. Panzer Kompanie*, it is very possible, or even likely, that other tanks of that platoon followed Strelow across before Kremser was hit by Sgt. Boyce William's squad in the middle of the bridge. In his handwritten statement cited above, Hennecke indicated that before he continued across the bridge in Kremser's 101, that 6-7 German Panthers had proceeded before he crossed. In Hennecke's post war sketch of the action, he showed that Panther Nr. 124 of Uscha. Daniel Mayer was ahead of his Nr. 0101 when he proceeded across the bridge.

36 Contrary to Hubert Laby's helpful book (pp. 129-130), it was not Pvt. John Mills who fired the rocket from the Sougné house that morning. Nor was he ever at Ft. Knox, having trained at Camp Fanin, Texas. See John G. Mills to editor, *The Pekan*, January 2005, p. 23. Also email of John Mills to Tom Hanchett, 7 July 2000. Although part of Williams' headquarter squad, Mills was separated from the others at the map depot and left the scene with Sgt. Al Duesdieker to return to the Stavelot town square. It seems very likely that the man who shot the second tank from the Sougné windows was Williams' second bazooka man, Pvt. Bill Darden.

37 For the story of the bazooka attack against the second German tank, Interview with Boyce Williams, 526th Armored Infantry Battalion, 23 September 2008. It is also noteworthy that in the author's interview with Sgt. Carl Smith, that while he and his gun crew blasted the first tank into Stavelot, he also saw the second tank temporarily halted on the bridge, but never had an idea why it stopped. Interview with Sgt. Carl Smith, 25 September 2008. Williams was unhappy that he and his squad were forgotten: 'The first thing I knew, the whole outfit had pulled out, but there was no word to us. Mitchell had never gotten word to us. We decided we had better get out. And we worked our way to the other side of the street and we got to the hospital. The Germans were now firing down from the church.'

38 Roland Knörringer 3 January 1948, NA, Case 6-24, RG-153, Box 82. After passing through Stavelot, Hennecke 'ordered me to turn the turret. While I did so, the gun tube knocked hard against a wall, so that

the range finder got damaged. We stopped, and I tried to fix this again, but did not succeed … A few hours later, I was wounded myself by an airplane.'

39 MacDonald interview with Karl Wortmann, 16 October 1982. Charles B. MacDonald Papers, USAMHI, Folder, '1st SS Panzer Division: Leibstandarte Adolf Hitler.'

40 After Hennecke replaced Kremser as the commander of Nr. 101 his new crew was: Rttf. Albert Mussmecher (driver), Rttf. Roland Knörringer (gunner), Rttf. Georg Erhard (loader) and Strm. Willy Gelfert (radio operator). Hennecke left his previous crew to repair the damage to Pz. Nr. 111, parked in front of the home of Lucien Servais. Willy Bahnes, its driver, supervised the replacement of its gear box by salvaging essential parts from Richartz's Nr. 115 that had been hit on the *Rue du Vieux Château*.

41 'Killed in Action—Lt. James Evans,' Account by Chris Breninger, A Company, undated, courtesy Tom Hanchett.

42 Interview with Carl Smith, *op. cit.*

43 'Paul E. Kohli Account of Stavelot Belgium, 16 -18 December 1944,' *op. cit.*

Chapter 18 – The Bridge

1 Howard Meyer, C Company, 202nd, was in the square in a halftrack when he saw a shell blast the church roof, just as later recalled by Beathe Wetz. (Interview 20 June 2010).

2 Interview with Beathe O'Neill, *op. cit.*

3 M/Sgt. Jack Mocnik, '30 Hours of Hell: 17th and 18th December 1944,' Pittsburgh, KS, provided to author. 'Old Mitchell and me—scared as hell—were wandering like tourists on a Sunday stroll … I knew what bullets sounded like when they pass near your ears and I thought that maybe crawling on our bellies was a better mode of transportation.'

4 AAR 526th Armored Infantry Battalion, December, 1944, NA, RG-407, INBN-526-0.3. Radio log for 18 December 1944.

5 Interview with Philip N. Archambault, 26 February 1996.

6 Not all of the veterans of Company A, 526th Armored Infantry Battalion had a glorified picture of the action in Stavelot, disturbed that some members did not own up to having run scared under assault: 'As I think of it now, it makes me wince that Captain Mitchell tried to stop the Germans with a platoon of infantry and a ridiculous 57mm so-called anti-tank gun.' Anonymous member of the 526th Armored Infantry Battalion to Mike Smeets, provided to author, October 2008.

7 Letter Norman Pihaly to author 8 February 1996. 'Then as dusk, Anna came and said that a neighbor who leaned towards the Germans knew I was there and she guided me across the street (36 de la rue Neuve) and up steps to a stone dog house. Removing the dog, she put me in and blocked the entrance with the dog. I was still wet and very cold. It was a large shaggy mixed breed who loved company and kept me warm all night … The next morning, Anna and the children brought me an apple and a piece of dark bread that I shared with the dog. Later that day, after artillery and mortar barrages, Anna ran to me saying, "The Americans are here. Come quickly!" I was so happy to see the tall 30th Division rifleman that I held out my hand. "Put your fucking hands on top of your head, right now, or you are dead." He asked my outfit, but walked me to his captain's outpost, where I could tell my story.' Pihaly then moved to Malmédy where the town was bombed on 19 December. Anna Schutz received a personal commendation for Gen. Dwight Eisenhower for her courage. Also, letter of Anna's daughter, Marie Fernand Cottin to author, 9 January 1996.

8 Interview with Marcel Massotte, 19 October 1995. Assisted by Will Cavanagh and Guy Lebeau. For other background on the murder of Tony Lambert: Georges Thone, ed. *Les Crimes de Guerre commis pendant la contre-offensive de von Rundstedt dan les Ardennes: Stavelot*, Royaume de Belgique, Ministère de la Justice, Commission des crimes de Guerre, Liège, 1945, pp.14-15.

9 A few days later, the surviving civilians at the *Château Lambert* were discovered and evacuated to safety at the center of town by GIs of the 2nd platoon, Company D of the 1st Battalion of the 117th Infantry Regiment under 1st Lt Frank Warnock including Sgt. Michael Cirullo, Pvt. Fred H. Vendt and S/Sgt. C.L. Griffin. 'Echos of the Past: Letters from the Ardennes,' by Frank Warnock, provided to author 1994.

10 Interview with John J. Stevenson, Company C, 202 Engineer Combat Battalion, 2 February 1996. 'But we weren't heroes in Stavelot. We didn't stick around and started going on up the hill away from town. We could hear tanks down in the valley and I was concerned that we were going to be surrounded so we headed up the hill … The four of us spent the night up the woods laying on the ground. In the morning we started walking. We didn't know which way to go, so we waited until buzz bombs passed overhead and we knew where they were coming from and headed the direction they were going. We walked until we found an American truck on the road. And there was one guy loading the truck with jerricans and we ran up to him and pitched to help in exchange for a quick ride. We got it loaded in a hurry and jumped on top. Just as we drove off there was a terrific explosion and fire behind us. We were trying to find our outfit. We went into Spa, Belgium and there was company truck there that took us to our headquarters.'

11 'I think the Germans were more surprised than us.' Walter J. Davis to author, 203 AAA AW Battalion, 20 April 1996. On their way out of town Company D of the 203 AAA AW came across the fuel dump on the Franchorchamps road where 'men were running around like mad ... I asked what was going on and they said they were going to set fire to the gasoline, so I told them to hold up until we fill our tanks.' Albert J. Bepersti to author, 7 May 1996. The engagement at Stavelot occurred at 8:10 AM until almost 9 AM: NA, RG-407, 203 AAA AW Battalion, S-2 and S-3 Journal for December 1944.

12 'If our not attacking during the night [of 17 December] was a mistake,' Peiper later recalled, 'the Americans made up for it by not putting Stavelot into a defensible position ... There was no heroic defense of the bridge.' *Kommentar zum Buch 'Massacre at Malmédy von Charles Whiting,'* September 1971.

13 Story of the Colinet and Tombeux tragedy: *U.S. v. Valentin Bersin*, Testimony of Maria Tombeux, 29 May 1946, pp. 921-927. Testimony of Antoine Colinet, 31 May 1946, pp. 992-1000. Other details from Laby's account, *op. cit.*, pp. 142-146.

14 Story of Émile Crasson from Laby, *op. cit.*, pp. 145-146.

15 Statement of Hans Hennecke, 13 March 1946, RG -549, Case 6-24, Boxes 6 and 8 including original handwritten account in German, English transcript and sketch.

16 *Ibid*, Hennecke's commentary Gelfert's firing on the civilians in Stavelot: 'Of course, I could have shouted to him "Cease fire" as soon as he started firing to the right. However, this would have meant to act against an order which had been issued by Obstuf. Kremser in front of the assembled company. This order essentially stated that no prisoners of war should be made, and that in the spirit of the old fighting Waffen SS, panic and terror should be spread amongst the enemy as well as amongst the civilian population.' During the Malmédy trial, Hans Hennecke attempted to repudiate his previous confession from Schwäbisch Hall, claiming that the statement about shooting the civilians had been made under pressure from Lt William Perl in a mock trial staged by him and Harry Thon. U.S. v. Bersin, *op. cit., Testi*mony of Hans Hennecke, 25 June 1946, pp. 2179-2210. However, the statement made by Hennecke on 13 March 1946, was witnessed by Ralph Shumacker and not Perl as seen in the original handwritten documents. After the Malmédy trial while imprisoned at Landsberg, Han Hennecke would enlist an affidavit of the gunner of Pz. #101, in which former SS Rottenführer Roland Knörringer claimed not to recall Willi Gelfert shooting the civilians as Hennecke had earlier admitted. 'Affidavit: Roland Knörringer,' 27 January 1948, Both in NA, RG-153, Case 6-24, Box 82. However, Hennecke unknowingly contradicted his comrade's statement by denying that Gelfert was in the tank with them as a radio operator in 101 when the incident took place. 'Concerning the Malmédy Case: Hans Hennecke to the Judge Advocate,' 15 January 1948 (Also Box 82).

17 Statement of Fritz Eckmann, 25 February 1946, (includes handwritten original) NA, RG -549, Case 6-24, Boxes 7. 'When Gelfert was boasting of this occasion, present were tank crews of Obstuf. Kremser, Obstuf. Hennecke, Hscha. Skotz and Hscha. Pidun.'

18 Ozer interviews, *op. cit.* Ozer would stay with Calvanese in the brick building until he could turn the American soldier over to the 117th Infantry Regiment when they recaptured Stavelot.

19 Marcel Ozer told the author that one civilian man in Stavelot, Alfred Buche, bragged that he had shot at two German soldiers in the early morning hours of 18 December before the SS battlegroup had crossed the bridge. Interview on 14 October 1995. However, this does not match with German claims that civilians in Stavelot had fired on the Germans from windows as their column passed through town. The likelihood is that these shots were fired from American soldiers of the units still in Stavelot (526th Armored Infantry Battalion, 202 Combat Engineers or the arriving 117th Infantry Regiment). Alfred Buche was an employee at the electrical generation plant in town and had been a devoted member of the Resistance. When the Germans came he quickly destroyed many secret papers at his home. However, he stayed behind to help the Americans, but was later suspected by suspicious GI s of being a German spy. After convincing them otherwise, Buche would open the locks at the electrical generation plant to drop the level of the Amblève at great personal risk. By doing so, Buche made it possible for the Belgians still holed up in the dairy on the south side of the Amblève to come over to the north side to safety. '*Les évéments dramatiques de l'hiver 1944,*' unknown periodical provided to author by Armand Reutsch, 11 December 1954.

20 Peiper, *Kommentar*, *op. cit.*

21 Henri Rogister, *Sur les Traces Sanglantes des Troupes de Joachim Peiper: 16—24 Décembre 1944*, CRIBA, Liège, May 1994 p. 133.

22 Peiper testimony, U.S. v. Bersin, pp. 1937-1939. Peiper's adjutant, Hans Gruhle, echoed Peiper's charge about the people of Stavelot: 'The battle for Stavelot was rendered particularly difficult by the fact that the U.S. forces were actively supported in combat by civilians of the Belgian resistance movement, a condition that had been encountered previously in Büllingen.' 'Kampfgruppe Peiper,' MS-C004, *op. cit.*

23 Losses for Task Force Solis were two men and one officer killed, 15 wounded and twenty men missing. The attached platoon of the 825th TD Battalion lost six men killed and two wounded in the fighting. Source: AARs for both battalions for December 1944.

24 Mocnik, *op. cit.* 'As we went up the hill where the gas dump was, we came upon two halftracks. The men were firing 50 cal and 30 cal shells into the cans of gas, but the gas never caught fire. The GIs jumped out of

the tracks and started going up the hill opening 5 gallon gas cans and spilling them on the ground. Finally, they got a gas can on fire. Mitchell told me to go on. As we got to the far end of the gas dump, we met Maj. Solis for the first time that day. We burned about a quarter mile of gas. Damndest fire you ever saw. The cans would explode and fly though the air like a rocket trailing fire and smoke. When we got together the men set up a road block with one 57mm anti-tank gun and a bazooka.'

25 Lt Pehovic had been so alarmed to find the gasoline undefended that after his hasty reconnaissance that morning, he hurried back to the company CP at the *Place du Marché* in Stavelot to warn Maj. Solis, but he was nowhere to be found. Instead Pehovic found Capt. Mitchell and a few evacuating engineers, who quickly convinced him they needed to get out the of the center of town while they still could. Pehovic, *op. cit.*

26 Janice Holt Giles, *Damned Engineers, op. cit.*, pp. 232-234. Eventually, around noon, Solis returned and ordered Keoghan and his men to go north-east to help defend the large fuel depot there. However, the traffic on the road was so jammed that when he got the depot, the fires were being extinguished and there were lots of American defenders already there from the 30th Division. Frustrated, he took matters into his own hands, moving his two trucks on through Franchorchamps to head for Malmédy. The best bars were in Malmédy, he joked with the driver of his truck. After all this cold waiting around, 'If we can't find something to eat, at least we can get a good drink!'

27 *Ibid.*

28 'We spent the night up the woods. There was four of us and spent the night laying on the ground and in the morning we started walking. We didn't know which way to go, so we waited until buzz bombs passed overhead and we knew where they were coming from and headed the direction they were going.' Interview with John Stevenson, 5 February 1996. Company C of the Battalion ended up returning fire at the enemy tank force passing through Stavelot until 10 AM when 'when superiority of the enemy force necessitated a withdrawal to Spa.' AAR 202 Eng Combat Battalion, *op. cit.* Even if lauded in the predictably self-serving battalion accounts, Company C suffered no casualties in the fighting at Stavelot.

29 Depot #2 near Spa was the First Army's largest cache of gasoline: 2.11 million gallons. Its evacuation to storage yards west of Liège began on the night of 18 December with a continuous stream of trucks and 400 rail cars used. With great effort, the mass of the gasoline was removed by 22 December. Royce Thompson, *op. cit.*

30 December 18th 1944 between Spa and Stavelot, Pfc. Theo Lauer, 24 June 2002, 3814 QM Gas Supply Company, 1st Army, CRIBA, courtesy Henri Rogister and CRIBA.

31 '*Un Certain Bataillon en Decembere 1944 ou Les Feux de L'Hiver*,' Roger Hardy, May 1983, Charles B. MacDonald Papers, USAMHI, Carlisle, PA, Box 7.

32 Hardy, *op. cit.* Hubert Laby hypothesizes that German paratroopers who had landed near the village of Ruy may have created the undefended roadblock before fleeing from the area, Laby, *op. cit., p.* 71.

33 Telephone conversation between Col. Stephens, Custom 5 and Col. Harold E. Hassenfelt, 181300A December 1944, NA, RG-407, 30th Infantry Division G-3 Records, Box 7633.

34 Capt. Franklin Ferris, 'The German Offensive of 16 December 1944: The Defeat of the 1st SS Panzer Division Adolf Hitler,' NA, RG-407, 218.2-1, XVIII Corps G-2, January, 1945, Combat Interview 94, Box 24037. pp. 3-5.

35 'Stavelot, Belgium, 17 to 22 December 1944,' Captain John E. Kent, *The Bulge Bugle*, February 1998, pp. 22-23.

36 Later Gen. Leland Hobbs, the commander of the 30th Infantry Division would complain to First Army that a number of U.S. Army units had fled Malmedy before their arrival. 'I have a list of people that were in Malmedy that pulled out and left a lot of top secret documents,' Hobbs told Col. Aikens. 'G-3 Journal, 30th Infantry Division,' entries for 200944, 20 December 1944, NARA, RG-407, 30th Infantry Division, 330-3.2, Box 8815. Who were those taking off and leaving sensitive documents behind? Hobbs listed them: 304th Ordnance Company, 100 Quartermaster Battalion, 69th Replacement Battalion, 72nd Replacement Battalion, 203rd Ordnance Depot, 134th Medical Group and the 44th Evacuation Hospital. The later unit had been the field hospital which had initially received the wounded survivors of the Malmedy massacre. Not surprisingly, when examining the records at the National Archives, the author found that none of the AARs survive for the December 1944 period.

37 Depot #3 was the second largest U.S. First Army fuel dump. Moving the million gallons of gasoline out of harm's way was no small feat. Even with non-stop truck loads, it was Christmas Day before the fuel was relocated. The dump contained 798,000 gallons of MT-80 gasoline and 305,000 gallons of diesel and oil. A total of 123-167,000 gallons were burned in the flaming roadblock—without authorization of the U.S. First Army Quartermaster. Royce L. Thompson, 'Overrunning of Installations in the Ardennes Campaign,' OCMH, R-24, Washington D.C., 12 February 1953.

38 'Obst Peiper denied that any of his men moved towards these dumps … Before the start of the offensive Obst. Peiper was given a map with known American headquarters and supply installations. He knew of the gas in one dump near Spa and also of the gas in Büllingen. He did not know of the presence of the other dump south of Franchorchamps.' ETHINT-11, *op. cit.* However, in his account prepared for the author, Capt. Mitchell did claim that two German armored vehicles—likely halftracks—followed them up towards

the fuel depot, but turned back after finding the southernmost stretch of the road to Franchorchamps blocked by a massive fire.

39 Peiper to John S.D. Eisenhower, 4 April 1967, Bitter Woods Papers, Box 17. Peiper was quite insistent on this episode. 'Nothing against Maj. Solis,' he wrote to John Toland, 'but don't you think that something like that should be known to us? We knew neither of the gas dump nor the road block. Moreover, from a tactical standpoint, a gasoline barrier would have attracted our interest and instead of moving westward, we might have turned toward this most interesting direction. To sum it up: none of us ever heard of this incident.' Peiper to Toland, 5 April 1959, John Toland Papers, Battle, LOC, Box 108.

40 Mitchell account, *op. cit.*

41 AAR 526th Armored Infantry Battalion, radio log, *op. cit.*

42 Peiper: 'Without waiting to mop up Stavelot, the German forces continued their westward advance. For the time being, no forces were available to secure the advance road leading through the western edge of Stavelot.' MS-C-004, *op. cit.*

43 In fact the German parachute division had advanced no further than Ondenval and Thirimont and would make no effort to follow Peiper's advance beyond those places. Meanwhile, *Kampfgruppe Sandig* with two panzer grenadier battalions of *SS Panzer Grenadier Regiment 2*, and nominally assigned to *Rollbahn D* right behind Peiper was still tangled up in massive traffic jams and by the morning of December 18th was still virtually parked on the roads between Amblève (German: Amel) and Ligneuville.

44 Letter Karl Wortmann to Haasler, 6 September 1999. Courtesy Timm Haasler.

Chapter 19 – Dash

1 Sun Tzu, 'The Art of War.'

2 'communiqués on Fighting on Various Fronts: Germany,' and 'Nazis Say Thrust has Cut 1st Army,' *New York Times*, 19 and 20 December 1944. 'Details will be announced later,' the Sertorius called out over the air, 'as to not give information to the enemy, but the great offensive, with support of strong formations of our fighter bombers is taking a favorable course.' The DNB news agency further reported 'Eisenhower, the man who has been regarded as the prototype of methodical warfare has been coerced to make improvised methods of defense.'

3 'Nazis Report Sweeping Gains,' *New York Times*, 19 December 1944. How were such news broadcasts viewed by the German people? Former Bundeswehr officer, Hans Dieter Bechtold, was only ten years old in December 1944. 'Like everyone, we listened to the radio at home about the great Ardennes Offensive was taking place. We all had a hope that somehow victory would be realized even at this late hour.' Interview with Bechtold, 21 May 1996.

4 Peiper, ETHINT-10, *op. cit.*

5 During the German invasion of France in 1940, Peiper had been at Huy with the Leibstandarte to cross the Meuse after Heinrich Himmler, the Reichsfüher SS, dropped him off there to meet the division the day before. See Hitler's Warrior, *op. cit.*, 57-58. Peiper was assigned to reach the Meuse River and cross at Huy or Ombret Rawsa (Amay) (Hermann Priess, 'Commitment of the I SS Panzer Corps during the Ardennes Offensive (16 December -25 January 1945,' 'Fürdas ISS Panzer Korps vorgesehene, Strassen,' Anlage 2, MS A 8-77, (NARA), Also see Pallud *op. cit.*, 20-21 and 69-71). Except for Huy, all of the other bridges across the Meuse River were down, having being destroyed during the German autumn retreat. The exact status of these bridges is documented in an important SHAEF report on file at the National Archives in the UK: WO 219/2139, 'Battle of the Ardennes: Deployment and use of reserves, threatened areas etc. and report on the battle with maps, SHAEF December 1944- February 1945' (Kew, UK: National Archives). Many thanks for Andrew Dlugolecki for pointing out this important document. Note that on ETHINT-10, page 7, Peiper himself indicated that his planned route was Werbomont to Tinlot then Huy.

6 The favored formation in open Russian terrain was the *Panzerkeil* or blunt wedge with tank companies sweeping ahead on a 1—3 km front and seeking to breakthrough and surround the enemy by sudden concentration on a vulnerable point (*Keil und Kessel*—Wedge and Cauldron).

7 Jochen Peiper, '*Kommentar zum Buch 'Massacre at Malmedy von Charles Whiting*,' September 1971. Copy courtesy of James Weingartner.

8 Interview with Juliette Antoine, 19 October 1995. Assisted by Will Cavanagh and Josef Dejardin. Today, the shell marks are still plainly visible on the upper east side of the walls of Madame Antoine's home on the *Route de Trois Ponts*.

9 Everywhere along the route of the *Kampfgruppe Peiper*, one can even today see evidence that the walls and facing windows in each home and building were shot to pieces as the tank column approached. This was standard assault procedure within the battlegroup—known today as fire suppression. However, Peiper's battlegroup never concerned itself with whether the targets might be civilians—quite different than methods advocated by modern combat forces.

10 Henri Rogister, *Sur les Traces Sanglantes des Troupes de Joachim Peiper: 16—24 Décembre 1944*, CRIBA, Liège, May 1994, pp. 134-135. Léon Mignon and his surviving daughter would be discovered hiding in their home a week later by three American soldiers of the 117th Infantry Regiment including Lt Edward H. Cope.

11 Laby, *op. cit.*, pp. 163-164.

12 Interview with André Nicolay, Trois Ponts, 26 March 1996. Assisted by Will Cavanagh.

13 Until 1815 Malmedy had been autonomous, although German speaking. However, after Napoleon's loss at Waterloo, it was Prussian and then after the German defeat in World War I it was at least nominally French. Again in 1940, Malmedy was again made part of Hitler's Reich.

14 Anderson had located his headquarters at the hotel on the Avenue Joseph Lejune since 8 November 1944. The engineer combat battalions he controlled included the 291st in the zone of Stavelot-Malmedy, the 51st in the region of Marche, the 296th in the vicinity of Sourbrodt and the 300th at Pont-de-Bonne. The various engineer companies were far flung, but at least provisionally linked by SCR-284 radio communication to the various battalions which could convey coded messages up to 45 km or voice by 15 km, depending on terrain.

15 On 17 December, the C Company of the 51st Engineer Combat Battalion had been operating sawmills in Marche. Weapons included 8 bazookas, and ten .30 or .50 calibre machine guns. 'All of a sudden, on 17 December, somebody said, "All hell's broken loose. The Germans have broken through!" We got in a truck with all our stuff and went quickly to Trois Ponts ... We heard on the radio that the Germans were executing prisoners so we were determine to defend to the last.' C Company arrived at Trois Ponts just before midnight on 17 December. Interview with Jose E. Marquez, 51st Engineer Combat Battalion, 29 December 1996.

16 Other than After Action Reports, a primary source for the actions at Trois Ponts: Ken Hechler, *Holding the Line: The 51st Engineer Combat Battalion and the Battle of the Bulge, December 1944—January 1945*, Studies in Military Engineering No. 4, U.S. Army Corps of Engineers, Washington D.C., April 1988. Also, Serge Fontaine, *Trois Ponts: Decembre 1944, Quand les Ponts Volaient en Eclats*, November 1992.

17 Laby, *op. cit.*, p. 158.

18 Zimmermann's account in Tiemann, *op. cit.*, p. 61.

19 Zimmermann: 'We cautiously negotiated the underpass. I thought for sure there would be another anti-tank gun. It was quiet! But the bridge on the left was blown.'

20 The gallant, but ill-fated anti-tank team were from 3rd Squad, of the anti-tank platoon of Company B of the 526th Armored Infantry Battalion: Lillard B. McCollum, Donald D. Hollenbeck, Dallas N. Buchanan and James L. Higgins. Today, the graves of Higgins and Hollenbeck are found at the U.S. military cemetery in Henri Chapelle. Pvt. Andrew Salazar was wounded in the leg. Fontaine, *op. cit.*

21 Testimony of Joachim Peiper, U.S. v. Bersin, p. 1941.

22 The destroyed span over the Amblève was a wooden trestle bridge that had been constructed by the 291st Engineer Combat Battalion the previous October. Originally the bridge had been an ancient stone work, but on the German invasion on 11 May 1940, it had been blown up by Belgian engineers to be rebuilt in wood by the Germans during the occupation only to be destroyed again when they fled in September 1944.

23 Zimmermann, *op. cit.*, 'The bridge to the left was blown. Stubaf. Poetschke and Obstuf. Peiper approached on foot to see what the problem was.' Meanwhile, when Strelow attempt to move off to the right, he found his path blocked once again by a pile of mines in the road. 'I decided to aim the cannon at the middle of the explosives. Close the hatches! Fire! The pile of mines blew into the air with an extraordinary explosion.' That much was true as the resulting detonation severely damaged the nearby homes of Octave Formatin and Frédéric Ernst.

24 Peiper, *Kommentar*, *op. cit.* In the encounter at Trois Ponts, Yates had been mentioned in the account of author, Charles Whiting*: Massacre at Malmedy, (NY: Stein and Day, 1971)*, 75.

25 Peiper, ETHINT-10, *op. cit.*

26 Wallis Anderson to Janice Giles, 31 January 1969, Damned Engineer Papers, W. Kentucky University. In the author's interview with André Nicolay on 26 March 1996 in Trois Ponts he identified the couple shot by the bridge as 59 year old George Warnier and Mme. Alexandrine Murtzen, his common-law wife. *Chez les Warnier* was just ten meters from the bridge. The fate of the Monsieur Warner was also witnessed by neighbor Edmond Georgin who saw an SS man shoot the couple with a holstered pistol. See Matthieu Longue, *Massacres en Ardenne,* Racine, Brussels, 2006, p. 164. According to a timeline established by Matthieu Longue (who had access to the original Belgian investigation in the 1948 Liège trial), the Warnier couple were shot down just minutes after Peiper left the blasted bridge site at 12 noon.

27 On 25 December, local Trois-Ponts resident, Joseph Polis, not only found the body of Michel Nicolay, but also Celestine and Louis Nicolay and Jean and Marie Burnnotte-Debosines, all lying on the ground and each executed by a bullet through the head. Madame Georgine Corbisier-Evard had been shot in her bed. Later, American Army officers found other Belgian dead (Jules Pregardien, Pauline Counet, Irma Boutet, Oscar Job and Gustave Job) murdered in the SS killing orgy near the site of the destroyed Trois Ponts

bridge on 19 December 1944. Commission des Crimes de Guerre, *Les Crimes De Guerre: Stavelot, Décembre 1944—Janvier 1945,'* Georges Thone, Liège, 1945, pp. 16-18.

28 Hechler, *op. cit.*, pp. 25-26.

29 Interview with André Nicolay, 26 March 1996, *op. cit.* 'André's uncle would later find young Michel sprawled on the ground near the Amblève with his throat slit where he died. Returning from La Gleize after the battle, André found his dead father on the side of the house. All told, he had lost his father, his brother, his grandmother and a cousin in the killings.

30 Still later, when the SS were forced out of La Gleize and from the villages around Parfondruy and Ster some of them returned to Trois Ponts. In a show of anger they rousted 26 of the village from their homes and herded them into a basement. Just before locking the door they told them, 'We're going to kill you all, but we have to get a machine gun. That will be the quickest way.' Horrified, those inside protested, 'At least you spare the children.' 'No,' the Germans pronounced, 'You've all got to die—this whole race has to die.' But those in the basement decided they would not go down without a fight. One, Frederich Ernst, told them, 'We'll take them on them with axes.' But the Germans never came back. Nicolay interview, *op. cit.*

31 Hubert Laby, *op. cit.*, p. 168.

32 Fontaine, *op. cit.* The railway bridge near the Trois Ponts station had been demolished by the Germans in September and had only been partly repaired.

33 Giles, *op. cit.*, p. 248.

34 '18 December/44: 7th Tank Company [and 6th Pz Company and the 3rd Pioneer Company were directed to the left on by-ways via Wanne to take important bridges and secure them. Approximately 2-3 km on the hill before Stavelot [Lodomez],[they were to prepare to] attack. Moreover, some tanks stuck in soft ground With the delay, only reaching the starting point before Stavelot at dusk. [Then came the] decision of the leader of 7th Company (Klingelhoefer) to continue to drive at night. Radio staff tank had an engine defect and was unable to move. We participating alone [to proceed] in the 7th Company commander's tank in the trip to La Gleize. In La Gleize, reporting to the regimental commander. [He] orders new formation of [the] column for the attack to Stoumont.' Statement of Rolf Buchheim, Dachau, 5 November 1947, NA, RG-549, Case 6-24, Box 28.

35 'Report by Rolf Ehrhardt, 7th Panzer Kp., 1 Panzer Regiment, LSSAH Ardennes Offensive, 16 Dec. to 25 Dec. 1944,' composed in 1981, provided to author by Wolf Mauder translation by Helmut Thiess.

36 Peiper's testimony at the Dachau trial, U.S. v. Bersin, *op. cit.*, pp. 1939-1940. 'Our conversation about this matter was not comprehensive at all because the importance of the technical problems would not permit that … My road of advance from Trois Ponts on west could not be maintained and I had to find another crossing somewhere.'

37 Serge Fontaine, *Stoumont-Cheneux—La Gleize,* Decembre 1944, CRIBA, Liège, 1970, p. 7.

38 Nicolay interview, *op. cit.*

39 Interview with Gerard Gregoire, 28 March 1996. Local historian Monsieur Gregoire was long-time the proprietor of the *December '44* museum in La Gleize. Gregoire died in 2021. With its Königstiger tank, the museum arguably possesses the most famous battlefield relic in the Ardennes. The tank, Nr. 213, was the mount of SS Ostuf. Helmut Dollinger and saved on a lark by Jenny Geenen, the former innkeeper of the destroyed *La Fermette* in La Gleize. When Geenen observed an American tank recovery team hauling the armored beast from Werimont farm to be turned into scrap metal she offered the GIs a bottle of cognac. They accepted, leaving the town of ruined town of La Gleize with the Tiger as a lasting memento.

40 Both Serge Fontaine and Gerard Gregoire corroborated the story of the aborted dance in La Gleize in separate interviews. As late as 2000, the *Echo des Campagnes* is still in business in La Gleize right across from the museum and advocating Jupiler beer for the thirsty.

41 *Ibid,* When Gerard Gregoire and his father returned to La Gleize on 9 January 1945, they found their village completely smashed. Their home was gone; only the chimney remained.

42 'The Americans were pleasant enough, but leaving, everyone worried about their possessions … We really didn't like the Germans, but we had our share of hassles with the Americans.' Interview with Jeannine Kalbusch-Goffinet, La Gleize, 29 March 1996.

43 Those killed in La Gleize as the *Kampfgruppe Peiper* first entered were Madeleine Dumont (age 25), Alice Collard (36) and Joseph Mathias (58).

44 Kalbusch-Goffinet inteview, *op. cit.* Mme. Goffinet insisted to the author that she clearly saw the first German tank to enter the town and that it was crudely camouflaged to resemble an American Sherman. 'It had a muzzle brake on the barrel, but was painted khaki and I knew it was not an American tank. I remember this tank very clearly.' If one of Skorzeny's camouflaged tanks had come with Peiper's advance, it seems likely that it would have been discovered with the armored vehicles left behind by the *Kampfgruppe Peiper* in La Gleize.

45 Interview with Maria Georges of La Gleize by Marie France Gregoire, no date, but 1990s.

46 Interview with Serge Fontaine, Roanne, 20 October 1995. Also, interview with Julie Marechal of Werimont by Marie France Gregoire, no date, but 1990s.

47 Testimony of Joachim Peiper, U.S. v. Bersin, p. 1941.

48 In a 1991 interview with Gen. Michael Reynolds, Hans Hennecke, returning to the Ardennes, insisted that there were American soldiers near the Cheneux bridge when he opened fire. Also, two years later, the local historian, Gérard Gregoire, revealed that Gilson had been unwisely wearing a GI top coat. Reynolds, *op. cit.* p. 130. However, Reynolds correctly pointed out that at a range of only 300 meters in good visibility it would be difficult to comprehend how the SS troopers would mistake four women and a Belgian man for a group of American combatants.

49 This story from author's interview with Paul Servais, in Rahier, 28 March 1996, assisted by Marie France Gregoire. Another woman in the group, Mme. Delvenne was wounded in the arm.

50 Diefenthal account in Ralf Tiemann, *Die Leibstandarte, Band IV/2,* Munin Verlag, Osnabrück, footnote on p. 84. 'Days later the Oberleutnant with two of his men showed up again. They were the last survivors from his team. When he reported in exhausted to our front line before Cheneux he asked to hang out with us for the rest of our raid.' Diefenthal to Tiemann, 5 March 1986.

51 Interview with Emile and Suzanne Boutet, Cheneux, 27 March 1996, assisted by Will Cavanagh. 'When the Germans first came through, they just passed through. But when they came back, they eventually came down to the cellars and said, "*Raus! Raus!*" Get out. They wanted us to cook food for them. We cooked what we had left from the Sunday dinner—the meat and potatoes. We spent the Monday and the Tuesday in the basement in the village and then on the Wednesday moved to the church.'

52 Walthère Jamar, 'Another Bridge too Far … Another Longest Day: Chevron: A Belgian Village,' Annotated diary of Mr. Jamar, CRIBA, Liège, Jamar Sneiderman Historical Fund. Thanks to friends at CRIBA for permission to use this text.

53 Toland interview with James Gavin, 20 August 1957. Toland Papers, Battle, Box 34.

54 Gavin certainly did not reckon on being attacked in Werbomont while his men were still off-loading from trucks on the afternoon of 18 December—which is precisely what would have transpired had the American aircraft not delayed *Kampfgruppe Peiper* from 2–4 PM.

55 Letter Capt. S.M. Harris to author, 3 October 1992.

56 Carpenter, *op. cit.*, p. 210. Also, David W. Hogan, *A Command Post at War: First Army Headquarters in Europe, 1943-1945,* (Washington D.C.: Center for Military History Pub 70-60, 2000), 171-216.

57 'V Corps Artillery G-2 Unit Journal,' 17 December 1944, NA, RG-407, Entry 427, 205-ART-2.2, Box 3047. Entry for December 17th at 2030 hours.

58 Interview with Cox and Hodges in Box 36 of Toland Papers, *Battle,* LOC.

59 Toland interview with Leland Hobbs, no date, but 1957, Toland Papers, Battle, LOC, Box 35.

60 Capt. Franklin Ferris, 'The German Offensive of 16 December 1944: The Defeat of the 1st SS Panzer Division Adolf Hitler,' NA, RG-407, 218.2-1, XVIII Corps G-2, January, 1945, Combat Interview 94, Box 24037. p. 23.

61 ADSEC was Advanced Section of the Communications Zone. Had the German armored columns reached the area around Liège or just north of Namur, the entire supply chain for the U.S. First and Ninth Armies would have been seriously disrupted, with equally serious implications for army-wide combat effectiveness. Col. William Whipple, Logistical Problems During the Ardennes Offensive, *Military Review,* Vol. 28, May 1948, pp. 18-26.

62 *Ibid.*

63 Forrest C. Pogue, *Pogue's War,* University of Kentucky Press, Lexington, 2001, p. 291.

64 'U.S. First Army Diary, William Sylvan,' Eisenhower Library, Abilene, KS, Courtney Hodges Papers, Box 25. Also, John S.D. Eisenhower interview with Monk Dickson, Bitter Woods, Box 1. 'There was no panic,' Dickson remembered.

65 These were: Capt. Olaf W. Christopherson, 1st Lt Walter R. Butts and 2nd Lt Donald Miles and Capt. John. L. Fellows and Capt. James W. Gooley.

66 'Defense of the Spa Gas Dump,' by 1st Lt Walter R. Butts, Jr., in Ferris, *op. cit.* The defensive positions were: north of Franchorchamps at road junction 735087 (Lt. Miles), 2) near Baronheid at road junction 745104 (Capt. Fellows), road junction at 679071 (Lt. Butts) and 4) on a hill above Stoumont just to the south of Moutoûyet (Capt. Gooley). The positions were occupied at about 10 AM that morning.

67 'Record of Telephone Conversation: G-2 Journal No. 48,' Lt Kann (PWE) to G-2 First U.S. Army, 18 December 1155A, NA, RG-407, G-2 Journal, 101- 2.2 U.S. First Army, Box 1875.

68 U.S. War Department, *Order of Battle of the German Army,* Military Intelligence Division, Washington D.C., June 1944.

69 'Hodges Nearly Captured by Enemy in Bulge Dec. 18th,' by Harold Denny, *New York Times,* 4 June 1945.

70 Toland, *Battle, op. cit.,* pp. 96-97; the conversation is taken from Toland's interview with Dickson, The original notes are in Toland Papers, *Battle,* LOC, Box 36.

71 Carlo D'Este, *Eisenhower: A Soldier's Life,* Macmillan, NY, 2003, p. 646.

72 At the end of the December, the War Department cabled U.S. First Army headquarters and asked them to send home the officer responsible for the enemy mounting a surprise attack on U.S. Forces in the Ardennes. By that time, the First Army was in Tongres, Belgium still in their 'retreat headquarters.' When Gen. Kean

asked Dickson about the request. It certainly wasn't his slip, he told Kean, handing him a copy of Estimate No. 37 and suggesting he re-read it. 'It's all in there, Monk,' Kean said motioning to the copy, 'I remember you beat the map before you left us warning, "It's the Ardennes!" What a pity you didn't make it more emphatic.' Nobody was sent back to Washington. 'We wouldn't be Warned in the Bulge,' By Col. B.A. Dickson and Ivan H. Peterman, John Toland Papers, Box 36.

73 'Joy Becomes Gloom in a Belgian Town,' by Harold Denny, *New York Times*, 20 December 1944, p. 1. 'You wonder what is going to happen to your recently freed friends when the Germans come back.'

74 Paul Scott to author, 16 July 1996.

75 In Denny's article, he claimed that the improvised sections sent off from Spa had fought with the enemy on the 18th and prevented Spa's capture. Denny was likely relating second hand, the defense of the 526th Armored Infantry Battalion before Trois Ponts although his version is highly fictionalized. To the author's knowledge there was never an advance on Spa that afternoon, the closest being Peiper's push beyond Stavelot to La Gleize.

76 'Joy Becomes Gloom in a Belgian Town,' *op. cit.*

77 Stephen T. Wishnevsky, *Courtney Hicks Hodges*, McFarland, 2006, p. 158. This account is verified by the account in the Sylvan Diary, *op. cit.* for 18 December. Other quotes from Sylvan diary.

Chapter 20 – 'The Damned Engineers ...'

1 *To Win the Winter Sky*, *op. cit.*, pp. 179-180.

2 Author's interview with Abraham Jaffe, 30 May 1996.

3 Letter Richard Cassady to his parents, no date, but February 1945. Copy provided courtesy Abraham Jaffe. In the letter, Cassady expands on the brief story about their exploits that appeared in *Time Magazine* ('World Battlefronts') on 15 January 1945. 'Sak' Cassady was nicknamed for his penchant for sleep.

4 Charles R. Johnson, *The History of the Hell Hawks*, Southcoast Typesetting, Anaheim, CA, 1975, pp. 347-348. In actuality, on the 17th, the 386th Squadron of the 365th Fighter Group had been vectored to attack truck and horse drawn convoys of the *326th* and *277th Volksgrenadier Divisions* the preceding day. See *Winter Sky*, *op. cit.*, pp. 161-162.

5 'The Story of the IX Tactical Air Command,' IX TAC History, USAF Historical Office, Maxwell AFB, p. 30.

6 Richard Cassady letter, *op. cit.* When Cassady and Jaffe landed, Gen. Quesada was on the phone immediately. 'Okay son, do you think we can get the fighter bombers in there?' Cassady said yes.

7 In fact, Price managed to make a perfect belly landing behind German lines in a clearing near Francorchamps. Although shaken up as his Thunderbolt barrelled over the ground, he got out of his stricken plan and began running to the west, avoiding roads and staying in the woods. On 20 December, he found troops of the 120th Regiment of the 30th Infantry Division. They took Price prisoner as there was some doubt about his allegiance due to suspicion about German paratroopers and the fact that Price carried a German Luger rather the traditional Colt .45. Johnson, *op. cit.*, p. 348.

8 Nicolay interview, *op. cit.* The P-38s that he saw were the 506th squadron from the 404th Fighter Group which claimed to attack 40 vehicles just south east of Stavelot that afternoon. The first wave of planes struck Peiper's column at just after 2 PM as observed by 25-year old Serge Fontaine, hiding behind a woodpile in the village of Roanne. Fontaine, *op. cit.*, p.8.

9 Other flights of the 365th against Peiper that afternoon: 1st Lt Howard R. Dentz: four planes at 1450 over Stavelot and Maj. Arlo C. Henry led four planes of the 387th Squadron at 1500 to attack the enemy near that same time. Other flights hitting the column: Capt. Neal Worly at 1530, Capt. Robert E. Robinson at 1540 and Capt. Samuel E. Saunders at 1555. Col. Stecker himself led the last flight against the SS battlegroup, hitting supply lines of the 1. SS Panzer Division near Blankenheim. Even if the Hell Hawks claim of 56 vehicles and 15 tank and halftracks destroyed was a blatant exaggeration, the fact that the P-47s had delayed *Kampfgruppe Knittel* in following up behind Peiper had much to do with the capture of the river crossing in Stavelot by American forces the following morning.

10 'I had an air attack outside of Cheneux ... This air attack lasted for about two to 2 ½ hours ... We arrived at Cheneux at about 1530 to 1600 hours.' Peiper's testimony at the Malmedy trial, U.S. v. Bersin et al., *op. cit.*, p. 2005.

11 Affidavit of Gustav Knittel, 8 May 1949, NA, RG-549, Case 6-24, Box 59. The statement by Knittel, taken at Landsberg while Peiper was still under a death sentence, was clearly meant to establish that Peiper stayed at the Cheneux bridge rather than going with Diefenthal—a fact disputed by several in Diefenthal's SPW. The implication was to remove Peiper from being witness to the shooting of the American by Paul Zwigart. 'After the air raid, I was eyewitness to how Col. Peiper gave a combat commission to Maj. Diefenthal for continuing the drive in the direction of Rahier. Diefenthal left by himself. I parted from Col. Peiper at Cheneux in order to look for my battalion in the area of Stavelot.' Another clear sign that Peiper remained with Diefenthal comes from his continued insistence that he was nearby when the Habiemont bridge was blown. Had he stayed behind at Cheneux, this would not have been possible.

12 Remark verified by Peiper's corrections to Whiting's book as submitted to Ernst Klink. Jochen Peiper, '*Kommentar zum Buch Massacre at Malmedy* von Charles Whiting,' September 1971.

13 Fontaine, *op. cit.*, p. 9. The Belgian man wrote of seeing the second wave of attacking fighter-bombers creating much more damage than the first creating great confusion along the rear of the column. Fontaine personally witnessed bombs hit or nearly hit five additional tanks (one on the road in front of the Dumont farm), with damage to more than a dozen halftracks and trucks.

14 This was Fuel Depot #2 with 2,110,920 gallons of gasoline and 115,000 gallons of oil and other petroleum products. Evacuation of the massive depot (K-683110) began on the night 18 December with round the clock effort loading of the jerricans into 400 waiting railcars made available by the 25th Regulating Station. The Franchorchamps Depot #3 (K-742060) contained approximately 1 million gallons of gasoline and POL although 123,000 gallons—the 20 southernmost stacks of jerrican were burned in the flaming roadblock on the road leading from Stavelot. Not only were the Belgians involved in setting the fire, but also a captain with the 272nd Field Artillery Battalion. The remainder of the depot was evacuated from the evening of December 17th – 19th. Royce L. Thompson, 'Overrunning of Installations, the Ardennes Campaign,' Washington D.C.: OCMH, 12 Feb 1953, 2-3.7 AE.P-24.

15 The 3,000,000 million gallons of gasoline at the Géronstère and Franchorchamps fuel depots was 50% greater than the total amount of fuel Hitler had accumulated for the entire *Wacht Am Rhein* offensive, According to Genobst. Jodl, Hitler's chief military planner, by mid-December the required accumulation for the offensive totaled 7,500 cubic meters of fuel on hand in the camouflaged Eifel depots. Jodl Diaries, *op. cit.*, p. 391. (7500 cubic meters = 2,000,000 gallons).

16 Butts report, *op. cit.*

17 Wortmann to Haasler, *op. cit.*, 6 September 1999.

18 Karl Wortmann, Tiemann, *op. cit.* Vol. IV/2, p. 62. The account was essentially repeated in the letter of Wortmann to Haasler in a letter dated 23 November 1999.

19 'By the end of the afternoon, this column had been bombed and strafed from one end to the other with over 100 vehicles left damaged or burning on the road.' As always, the Allied air claims against ground targets were greatly exaggerated relative to the actual results: the three fighter groups claimed 32 tanks and 73 other vehicles destroyed. 'Unit History IX Fighter Command and IX Tactical Air Command,' 1 December to 31 December 1944, File 536.02, USAF Historical Office, Maxwell Air Force Base.

20 Reynolds, *op. cit*, (p. 131) describes Belgian reports of SS casualties being moved to the Gillet mill and the Château de la Vaulx Renard near Cheneux.

21 'A German Report on the Engagement in the Ardennes Offensive Involving SS Tank Battalion 501,' By Werner Wendt, *The Pekan*, Vol. 12, Nr. 1, March 1992. 'Obscha. Wessel climbs in the next tank to come by and goes through the rue Hottonruy on as far as Trois Ponts. Brandt's repair of his tank takes a lot of time. Because of the narrowness of the street, no other tank could pass by. As Brandt was again ready to start his tank, it was getting dark. Since Brandt and I had lost all contact with anything ahead, we decided to wait … so Brandt and I stood the entire night in Stavelot. About 30m away from the bridge, towards the market place, some paratroopers had dug in. A few cyclists pass us in the night since these are quite a bit more narrow than tanks. Apart from a few rifle shots, the night transition to 19 December was practically peaceful.'

22 Interview with Serge Fontaine, *op. cit.*, The Americans given refuge were from the 526th Armored Infantry Battalion that had escaped the debacle at Stavelot. One was Philip N. Archambault of Tucson, Arizona and the other was Norman Pilhaly.

23 Interview with Philip Archambault, 26 February 1996. Pfc. Philip Archambault, who spoke fluent French, was still with his clueless buddy, Pvt. Kelly Cornet. 'We ended up behind enemy lines all that day, trying to find a place to hide. A civilian man had been with us all day long as a guide. We came to a farmer working who motioned to us: "Oh, come, I'll take you to our house." People there were apprehensive about having American soldiers in their houses; Germans would kill them if they hid the enemy. "No, it would put you in danger." I said. "Do you have another place you could put us?" "Yes, in a hay loft." It was a foggy day, and we went up in the hay loft. Soon it was dark. There was no food. It was just Kelly Cornet and myself. Time lost all meaning and we wondered what had happened to our keeper. He said he would bring some food. But after a while I could hear voices, and they were German, and pretty soon the hay loft shook. I worried, "How do they know we are here?" Many things raced through my head. Pretty soon there was gunfire over our heads. I guess we are in no-man's-land. I said, "Kelly, we're getting out of here." I jumped from the hay loft. Kelly yelled, "Your flashlight is on!" There was some bullet fire, but I couldn't turn it off. We crept and crawled out of there—I don't know where we went. We went from there and to a house, and some people let us in and gave us fried eggs and a piece of black bread. They told us the Americans are in Coo. In the morning we headed off for there. I remember climbing through a rather swampy area and going up a hill covered with evergreens. I thought, *God, this is going to be a different kind of Christmas!* On the way to Coo, I was very thirsty and drank from a stream. Kelly hollered, "Don't drink." There was a dead German upstream. We saw animals that had been blown up from mines or shell. Kelly wanted to go back.

"No," I said, "If we go back, we could hit a land mine." We finally came to a place where the Americans had bivouacked and found some D-rations. A whole pile of them. We went through it but all were empty: no food. We finally came across an American guard, but he was fast asleep. I was angry at his nonchalance. We wandered down a road he told us to go down. Soon we were in the village of Coo There were doctors there who treated us. But they still didn't have food, but at least they gave us some coffee. It tasted wonderful. In the village, they wanted us to help find bodies. And while we did this ghastly work, I remember a terrible scene that has always haunted me: a man and his two children, a boy and girl and they were ambling along looking for his wife. And they found her and his two children were following with his dead wife's stiff corpse in the wheel barrow. The little boy was crying and the little girl was dazed. The girl had blue eyes and blonde hair and was about 4 years old. The boy was about 7. I have had nightmares about that time ever since, but less frequently since I talk about it now. Christmas time is most difficult. It was just a sad kind of thing. I don't remember Christmas Day, but the man and his children with his dead wife in the wheel barrow haunts me.'

24 At the Malmedy trial, Peiper's personal attorney, Dr Eugen Leer looked to help out Peiper with the sticky jeep incident involving Paul Zwigart on the road to Cheneux on 18 December. As planned, Landfried said he had been there in his halftrack when the air attacks began—taking shelter in one of the first house in the village. The U.S. fighter bombers strafed and dove at them for what seemed like an hour, after which they started up the road to the west again. 'Did you see Col. Peiper after you left?' Leer asked. 'Yes … We had been driving on a side road and as we hit the main road, Col. Peiper was standing by a pillbox outside of Cheneux.' 'Do you know who Col. Peiper rode with from then on?' 'Yes,' Landfried said. 'Lt. Col. Peiper, together with SS Ustfuf. Krause, mounted my SPW and we then went into Cheneux on the main road into a forest. On that main road, we made a right turn and continued on. Since the bridge was out, we had to turn around and at that time, when we turned around, Lt Col. Peiper got out of my vehicle and mounted the vehicle of Major Diefenthal, I think. We turned around and moved back about two vehicles behind Major Diefenthal.' But the significant thing was that Landfried testified that Peiper changed to Diefenthal's vehicle when it was already dark—a claim that was at odds with testimony from both Paul Zwigart and Hans Assenmacher. U.S. v. Bersin, *op. cit.*, Testimony of Walter Landfried, pp. 2905-2910.

25 It is significant that Hans Assenmacher, who was in Diefenthal's SPW later told the court as a prosecution witness that Peiper had been in Diefenthal's vehicle when they encountered an American jeep at just after 4 PM on the road to Rahier. Testimony of Hans Assenmacher, 4 June 1946, pp. 1272-1279. Even more importantly, writing his parents from Landsberg prison on 24 and 28 March 1947, Zwigart charged: 'Peiper won [over] a tank driver, Landfried of his regimental staff, who told the following lies in his favor before the court: *Peiper mounted his armored vehicle at Cheneux, after dark and rode with it to the blown up bridge where he changed back to my carrier* [italic for emphasis]. The truth, however, is as even my prosecution witness Assenmacher confirmed before the court, that Peiper mounted my vehicle in daylight at about 16:00 hours—half an hour before dusk—shortly before the mentioned incident when the jeep arrived … Peiper was negotiating in daylight at the blown up bridge in my vehicle with a jeep crew of Skorzeny troops … Thus, you can see that Peiper is pretending to be innocent by faking his absence during the occurrence with the jeep. Diefenthal is also pretending to be innocent.' Letter Paul Zwigart to Family, 24 March 1947 and forwarded to Col. Willis Mr. Everett, Jr. on 20 April 1947, NA, Case 6-24, Box 70. In the statements Zwigart never denied that he shot the American prisoner, but claimed that he was ordered 'to take care of the situation' by Jupp Diefenthal. That this issue remained a difficult one for Peiper, however, is revealed from a letter requested and obtained from Paul Fackelmeyer who had been the assistant radioman in the SPW. 'On 18 December 1944, after the fight for Stavelot was over, the regimental commander, Peiper, rode a stretch in the SPW of my then battalion commander, Diefenthal. It was at the fighter bomber attack at the latest, however, that Peiper left our SPW.' Affidavit of Paul Fackelmeyer prepared for Jochen Peiper, 26 August 1949. After the Malmedy trial saw his death sentence over the shooting, Zwigart again affirmed that he had shot the American soldier in the jeep that day. 'In the presence of my superiors, and on instigation of my comrades standing around me, I interpreted it as an order, which was my highest military duty … In the heat of battle, I lost my head … Soon thereafter I considered the wrong that I committed.' Then Zwigart choked with emotion. 'I beg this high court to place themselves in my position,' he implored, 'and bring out a merciful sentence.' *U.S. v. Bersin*, pp. 3218-3250. Moreover, Zwigart never recanted his responsibility for the shooting, but complained that an enlisted man was being used to cover for officers giving the orders who were at least as guilty.

26 'After Action Report 1111 Engineer Combat Group, December 1944,' NA, RG-407, ENGP-1111–0.3 -3.17.

27 'There were smiles mingled with their tears when we finally left them off safely in Modave.' John Scanlan to Janice Holt Giles, 13 October 1969, Giles Papers, personal correspondence.

28 Story of Edelstein and Chapin, Giles, *op. cit.*, pp. 260-261.

29 Testimony of Hans Rineck, 4 June 1946, pp. 1263-1270.

30 When the author interviewed Paul Zwigart on 20 May 1997, it was done on the condition that there would be no discussion at all about the jeep incident at Cheneux. 'It is difficult for me to talk about this time,'

he explained, 'I was buried by rubble in Normandy in 1944. My nerves were very bad.' In the interview Zwigart was accompanied by other Leibstandarte veterans—at least nominally for moral support, but likely to keep stories straight. However, in the course of the hour, Zwigart made it very clear to the author that he did not care for Josef Diefenthal.

31 'Unit Journal, 1111 Engineer Combat Group,' entries for December 1944, NA, RG-407, ENGP-1111–0.3. On 19 December, in the Unit Journal, Capt. Lundberg and Pfc. Snow were reported as missing since 1600 18 December. They had run into the *Kampfgruppe Peiper* shortly after crossing the Habiemont bridge. One jeep behind him, carrying Maj. Harry Webb and his driver also screeched to a halt, but were able to jump from their vehicle and flee into the woods.

32 Janice Holt Giles to Wallis Anderson 10 February 1969, Damned Engineer Papers, Western Kentucky University.

33 Trudging through the woods, and hitching rides Maj. Webb and his driver would not show up back at the Modave headquarters until late on the 19th of December: Unit Journal, 1111 Engineer Combat Group, *op. cit.*

34 Letter Ghislain de Thier to Mrs. Lundberg, 23 April 1945. Copy courtesy Henri Rogister. In the fall of 1944, after the V-1 robot bomb campaign had made staying in Liège dangerous, the Belgian man and his wife fled to their country home near Rahier in the Ardennes. After seeing Andrew Lundberg shot on the 18th of December 1944, he wrote the Captain's mother in the spring of 1945: 'We owe so much to all those young men who came from far away to die here at our home so that our children will have the same life of freedom that their parents have enjoyed.' From the Ghislain de Thier's description, it is clear that he did not closely witness the events during the encounter—likely hiding with his wife. He heard two bursts of gunfire, surmising that Snow and Lundberg had first fired on the SS column—a fact none of the German accounts mention. More likely, he instead heard the jeep initially fired upon and then the gunshots which killed Lundberg.

35 Special thanks to Bill Warnock for helping to identify Capt. Andrew F. Lundberg and Pfc. James M. Snow, Jr. who were killed west of Trois Ponts on 18 December 1944. Capt. Lundberg, a native of Kalamazoo, Michigan is buried today at the U.S. Army cemetery at Henri Chapelle (A-2-35). The body of Pfc. James Snow was returned to North Carolina for burial after the war.

36 'This was because of our defensive fire.' Jochen Peiper, '*Kommentar zum Buch 'Massacre at Malmedy von Charles Whiting*,' September 1971.

37 Testimony of Joachim Peiper, 21 June 1946, U.S. v. Bersin, *op. cit.* pp. 1941-1942. In a letter to John Toland, 22 February 1959, Peiper said he saw the bridge blown at Neufmoulin. 'After passing La Gleize, we were happy enough to find the next Amblève bridge undamaged and proceeding towards Cheneux. Just short of the steep and winding curve of this hamlet we were caught by low-attacking U.S. fighter-bombers and lost perhaps 5-7 vehicles. At dusk we reached Rahier just in time to see the bridge go skywards. A probing attack launched by the half-track Company (Preuss's 10th Company) over a bridge a little father north that was not fit for tanks go into an ambush and was almost annihilated.' Toland Papers, 'Battle,' LOC, Box 108.

38 Testimony of Hans Assenmacher, 4 June 1946, pp. 1272-1279.

39 At the eventual trial of the Malmedy dependants, Hans Assenmacher was closely questioned to see how Peiper and Diefenthal had reacted to Zwigart's execution of the American prisoner:

Q: How far were you sitting from the place where Zwigart shot the American?

A: About four meters.

Q: Were you in a position to observe whether your passengers, Peiper and Diefenthal were in the back of the vehicle at that time?'

A: Yes.

Q: When Zwigart came to the vehicle and asked for the machine pistol, did either Peiper or Diefenthal make any statement to Zwigart?

A: No, they said nothing.

Q: When Zwigart marched the American over towards the vehicle, did you hear any shouting?

A: I heard people yell, 'Paul, bump him off.' Obersturmbannführer Peiper was sitting on the right side facing the direct they were driving, on the bench, on top of several blankets which were folded up … At the last instant, I saw Diefenthal's head bending over a map.'

40 Testimony of Kurt Plohmann, 4 June 1946, pp. 1280-1283.

41 See Charles W. Sydnor, Jr., *Soldiers of Destruction: The SS Death's Head Division*, Princeton University Press, 1977 and French L. MacLean, *The Camp Men: The SS Officers who Ran the Nazi Concentration Camp System*, Schiffer Military History, 1999, Atglen, PA. In the later reference, some 16 officers within the concentration camp system had previously been with the Leibstandarte Adolf Hitler—not including either Arndt Fischer or Dr Kurt Sickel. Zwigart described his early career this way: 'I entered the SS in November 1939 and received my SS schooling in the concentration camp Dachau. From Dachau, I was ordered to the concentration camp Buchenwald. From Buchenwald, I again returned to the concentration camp at Dachau … I have not killed or mistreated prisoners either in Buchenwald or Dachau. From the concentration camp Dachau, I was transferred in the middle of March 1940 to the LSSAH to which I belong

to up to this time. Since June 1941, I belonged without interruption to the same battalion—which is now called the 3rd … This battalion, now commanded by Haupsturmführer Diefenthal was part of the 2nd Panzer Grenadier Regiment LSSAH.'

42 Zwigart: 'In Russia, generally we did not take any prisoners at all. When the fighting became heavier and the German advance slowed down, prisoners of war were only taken in special instances. On various occasions we burned down whole villages with our blow torches. I remember two cases; one in the spring of 1943 when we expressly received the order near Kharkov to set a village afire and 'bump off' all inhabitants 'including women and children. When I say we, I mean the third battalion which at that time was led by Hauptsturmführer Peiper. As far as I know he originated the order personally. Our battalion was, at that time cut off from the main unit, and operated on its own … I myself did not see Haupsturmführer Peiper, who was with us at the time, shooting at civilians. However, it was generally known that he actively participated in this action … After wiping out of the village, our battalion was 'rewarded' with the name Blowtorch Battalion and from thereon, our tactical symbol was the Blowtorch and remains so up to today.'

43 Statement of Paul Zwigart, 11 February 1946, pp. 1288-1293.

44 After the war, while both Diefenthal and Peiper were prisoner at Landsberg, Diefenthal enlisted the help of other veterans in a transparent campaign to deny that Peiper was in Diefenthal's SPW when the jeep incident occurred. According to the convoluted testimony, the shooting was the product of Zwigart's motivation alone. Karl Heinz Flacke charged that 'if it proved to be true' that Zwigart shot the prisoner, 'it was a single action resulting from the inexcusable motives for which no other person can be made responsible.' Affidavit of Karl Heinz Flacke, 14 April 1948, NA, Case 6-24, RG-153, Box 80. Even more improbable was Diefenthal's claim that he too was not in his own SPW! Totally contradicting his earlier statements, he claimed to have remained behind at the Cheneux bridge with he on foot and Peiper on a bicycle (!) while Zwigart drove his SPW forward to commit the war crime by himself! Affidavit, Josef Diefenthal, Landsberg/Lech, 15 January 1948, NA, Case 6-24, RG-549, Box 50. It is significant, however, that at the trial that Hans Assenmacher testified directly before the court that both Diefenthal and Peiperwere present in the SPW and seemed totally unconcerned with Zwigart's actions shooting the American other than to order him to hurry up so that the road could be cleared.

45 Josef Diefenthal's confession, predictably attempted to move culpability for the incident from himself and Peiper to Zwigart and further claimed not to remember what happened to the prisoners in the jeep: 'On the 18th December 1944, about 1400 hours we were strongly attacked by Jabos in and before Cheneux. On the same day I drove in my SPW from Cheneux in the direction to Werbomont. Other than myself in my SPW were; the driver—SS Unterscharführer Paul Zwigart—then Rottenführer; the radio-operator—Rottenführer Assenmacher, and the radio-operator Rottenführer Fackelmeyer. Around 1500 hours when I was about to study the map, I suddenly heard machine gun fire from one of the vehicles in our column. I put away my map and ordered the driver Paul Zwigart, Headquarters, *III Battalion, 2nd Panzer Grenadier Regiment, L.S.S.A.H* to stop. I saw a Jeep come towards us at great speed. While it came towards us, another vehicle of ours shot at the Jeep. The Jeep then drove against a rock which bordered the road on the left side, as seen from my direction of travel, with a crash. In the Jeep were two American soldiers or officers who pretended to be dead, but in reality lived. However, I can no longer remember, how I knew that they pretended to be dead, yet in reality still lived. At this place I gave my driver Paul Zwigart the order to get the Jeep out of the way, because the Jeep blocked the road. I gave him no order to effect what he should do with the prisoners. I did not attach any importance to the question of what he should do with the Americans but was only interested that the road should be cleared and for this reason, I cannot remember any longer today what happened to the prisoners. I know that I was impatient and wanted to proceed as quickly as possible. It is possible that I called to Zwigart 'Quicker, Quicker.' However, I cannot remember it any longer. From this place it was still about 2 kilometers to the bridge which, however was blown up as we soon found out. As we could not get further, we therefore again had to return on the same road.' Sworn statement of Josef Diefenthal, (both handwritten original and translated transcript), NA, 27 March 1946, Case 6-24, RG-549, Box 9.

46 By the morning of the 19th of December, the Germans had left the vicinity of the home of Ghislain de Their when they pulled back to La Gleize. During the afternoon, he found his home 'Les Roches' in the middle of 'no-man's-land' between the German and American line. At 3 PM, the Belgian ventured down to where he had seen the jeep run into the German column:

> 'I was coming down through the woods until I reached the edge of the road. All was calm, not one soldier and no friend or enemy … On the edge of the road just at the opening to the woods, I came across the body of Captain Lundberg. He was outstretched on his back with his eyes half-open. His face was calm and quiet. He must have been hit in the heart by one burst, the glove covered left hand was clenched in a fist folded back towards his head … He did not look to have suffered … Across on the other side of the road, the jeep is stopped by the front door of an abandoned farm.'

Ghislain de Thier found the body of James Snow fallen out of the jeep by the abandoned farm, his body covered by shattered glass from the jeep's bullet riddled windshield. Overcome by emotion, he said a prayer for the two dead men. 'I have a heart breaking pang as I learn first hand of the meaning of this horrible war.' Letter Ghislain de Thier, 23 April 1945.

47 'The book's title has finally been decided, and is taken from what the German commander said about the outfit when the final bridge was blown in his face: "The damned engineers! The damned engineers!"' Letter Janice Holt Giles to John Scanlan, 10 August 1969, Giles Papers, personal correspondence. The quote very likely came from an unpublished interview of André Banneux had with Jochen Peiper in 1963 in Stuttgart as Giles consulted Banneux extensively for her book before the two researchers had a falling out in the last months prior to the book's publication. Banneux alludes to Peiper's comment about his trouble with engineers and bridges engineers in his letter to Giles on 20 March 1969. For Banneux's interview with Peiper, see Banneux letter on 11 March1969 and Giles' response on 18 March 1969: 'What Peiper told you concerning the attitude of his men and his inability to control them is almost precisely what he told Lt Col. Charles Perry of the Adjutant General's Office … This is an excuse and it will not serve. German discipline was rigid and excellent. His men understood perfectly well that they had been turned loose to kill at will.' Janice Holt Giles Papers, *op. cit.*, Banneux Folder.

48 Letter Fred Chapin to Janice Holt Giles, 8 July 1969, Giles Papers.

Chapter 21 – Into the Night

1 Sun Tzu, 'The Art of War.'

2 Jamar Diary, *op. cit.*, the destruction of the bridge likely happened 30 minutes earlier than noted in Jamar's diary as noted by CRIBA researchers.

3 'I received the order to try to reach La Gleize with the *1.* Company, organize the defense of the village and wait for supply. I marched back by stages, towing some of the tanks and reached La Gleize before noon on 19 December … I was in charge of the defense of the western part of La Gleize. My command post was in the cellar of the school.' Previously untranslated 13 page handwritten statement of Hans Hennecke, no date NA, RG-549, Case 6-24, Box 36. Transcribed and translated by Timm Haasler.

4 Fontaine, *op. cit.*, p. 10.

5 'Statement of Rudolf Rayer,' 27 October 1947, NA, RG-549, Case 6-24, Box 38. 'After a short delay, we drove on in the direction of a place—I believe the name of the place was Werbomont. After the bridge spanning this place had been blown before our eyes, I got the order to find another passage over the river with the 11th Company. In a distance of about 2 kilometres from the first bridge, I found another crossing point, but this one was only passable for light tanks. I received the order to attack Werbomont with the 11th Company alone … The 10th Company [Preuss] was to follow me at an interval of ten minutes. After two of the tanks [SPWs] at my disposal had been disabled by mine and the 10th Company had almost been destroyed by American tanks [this was the blocking position of Lt Arn], I got the order over the radio to stop the attack on Werbomont and turn back.'

6 'A good portion of the road was running in a ravine like valley. Years later, Georg Preuss told me that had we taken the bridge intact, we would have run into an ambush. Preuss sent out reconnaissance parties led by experienced NCOs, who found the first village was free whereas two other villages were occupied by the enemy. Preuss told me several times that the Americans were fully aware of our whereabouts; they were really waiting for us. They even mentioned his name in their radio messages.' Wortmann to Timm Haasler, 22 September 1999, *op. cit.*

7 Telephone conversation from Col. Brown, Executive Officer of the 119th Infantry, 182200 December 1944, NA, RG-407, 30th Infantry Division G-3 Records, Box 7633.

8 Arn to author, 17 July 1995. 'I have cried out with all my heart against war. There is nothing romantic or glorious about it.'

9 Arn to author, 3 August 1995 and 'The Battle of Neufmoulin,' by Edward C. Arn, composed at the author's request. Regarding Maj. Hal. McCown: 'I respected him. He was all-soldier.'

10 According to the regimental AAR, available were four M10 Tank Destroyers and three 57mm anti-tank guns from the attached 823st Tank Destroyer battalion.

11 'Battle of Neufmoulin,' *op. cit.*

12 Interview with Pfc. Mason Armstrong, 27 January 1996. Arriving in France as an infantry replacement in the summer of 1944, Armstrong received the Distinguished Service Cross for his actions on 18 December 1944.

13 An earlier account of the same action was summarized in Capt. Franklin Ferris, 'The Defeat of the 1st SS Panzer Division Adolf Hitler,' January 1945. This account was based on Ferris's interview with Lt Edward C. Arn on 4 January 1945. NA, RG-407, 218.2-1, XVIII Corps G-2, January, 1945, Box 24037. 'Reconnaissance cleared his advance as far as Werbomont, so he moved his battalion as far as that town on trucks. From Werbomont, the men proceeded east on foot. By the time that F Company, leading the march reached the

little settlement of Habiemont on the Lienne River, three kilometers east of Werbomont, it was dark. The bridge over the river at this point had been blown by First U.S. Army engineers, but Maj. McCown's map showed another crossing one kilometer to the north … When scouts in front of F Company were fired on from a house on the west bank on the river, Maj. McCown decided to dig in on the high ground above the river for the night. Edward C. Arn dispersed his men and the two M-10s made available to him. He had just finished placing the forward TD gun into position, and the infantrymen along the side of the road were still digging their foxholes, when at about 2200 five enemy halftracks passed the house occupied by Lt Austin's platoon. The leading halftrack mounted a 75mm assault gun which fired two rounds into this house and so stunned Lt Austin's men that they retired to the cellar. The column of halftracks proceeded up the road. Not a shot was fired at it until the lead halftrack approached within about 40 yards of the first TD gun. The driver of the lead halftrack at this point, flicked on his headlights, apparently in order to make out the bend in the road. Instantly, the TD gun put three rounds into this halftrack which went up in flames and lit up the entire area. The American soldiers on the sides of the road and in the first house passed by the enemy, now opened up with all weapons. One of the halftracks was knocked out while it was attempting to make a U turn. Another one was abandoned. The remaining two managed to turn around, but were stopped by bazooka fire as they passed the house occupied by Lt Austin's platoon … The enemy made no further effort to break through F Company's road block.'

14 Personal account of Gen. James Gavin, 'Story of the 82nd Airborne Division in the Battle of the Belgian Bulge,' NA, RG-407, G-2 Records, XVIII Corps. McCown's battalion was relieved by the 82nd Airborne Division the following day at 3:30 PM. According to the assessment of Capt. Ferris: 'It is of interest to note how close they came to breaking through to Aywaille. If they had arrived at F Company's roadblock an hour or so sooner, they might have broken through before Company F was in position to stop them.' In fact, Preuss's disastrous advance across the Lienne Creek represented the furthest penetration west of the *Kampfgruppe Peiper*.

15 'G-2 Message Log from 3250 Signal Service Company,' 18 December 1944, G-2 Records, U.S. V Corps, NA, RG-407, 205-2.1-2.2.

16 In March 1996, the author interviewed a farmer at Les Forges who said that the Germans had abducted a civilian to help guide them to the Neufmoulin bridge. Today, the bridge at Les Forges remains small, but not wooden as it was in 1944. After the war, local farmers in the area impressed Preuss's abandoned halftracks into farm service until they broke down in the 1950s.

17 Account of SS Hstuf. Preuss: Tiemann, *op. cit.* Vol. IV/2, p. 64-65.

18 Account of the captured German grenadier: 'Story of the 82nd Airborne Division in the Battle of the Belgian Bulge,' NA, RG-407, G-2 Records, XVIII Corps.

19 Experienced Bundeswehr tank man, Wolf Mauder, estimated that had Peiper captured the 'big highway at Werbomont, they could have advanced further, but they would have stopped 20-30 km ahead under any circumstances. Before moving on Peiper would have had to be resupplied and that wasn't going to happen with Stavelot in American hands.' Interview with Mauder, 19 May 1997, Heppenheim.

20 Story of Karl Wortmann on night of 18 December from Tiemann, *op. cit.*, Vol. IV/2, p. 67.

21 Others did run out of gasoline in Cheneux. Maurice Prince of that village, told the story to Marie France Gregoire that the evening of December 18th, an older SS soldier showed up at their farm pushing a motorcycle. He seemed friendly enough, and chose to spend the night while other Germans pushed on by going from west to east. '*Keine Benzin*' he said pointing to his motorcycle. 'For you!' he said getting off the machine. The following morning, the magnanimous SS man left, asking the way back to Malmedy. '*Deutschland kaput!*'

22 'First Army PWI Report: From the Bulge to the Rhine, Diary of Feldwebel Karl Laun,' 11/12 March 1945, NA, RG-338, U.S. First Army Interrogation Reports, ETO-MIS-Y, Box 64. (290/56/2/3). 'Before Stavelot, the masses of SS concentrate. Obviously, there is trouble brewing in town. And yet, indeed, our AA outfit receives the honor of being allowed to advance through this purgatory. My vehicles are the last one to be given this dubious honor. There is small-arms fire and mortar barrages aimed directly at us. I miraculously escape being hit by shrapnel. A few splinters get into my eyes and I can't see a thing as we advance into town. A few knocked-out Panthers stand by the roadside. It is said that Belgian patriots took care of them with Panzerfausts. There is a giant crater in the road. All men go on a pick-shovel detail. A few arrive in time to witness another example of SS heroism. Three civilians, among them a woman and a girl, are vanquished by a burst from a machine pistol. The reason for their shooting is smilingly proffered by the SS: 'They did not know the password.'' An Austrian regular army sergeant, Laun was from Vienna and with the 2nd Battery of the 84 Flak Sturm Battalion.

23 Interview with Hermann Staritz, 12 May 1999.

24 Reiser indicated the tank recovery panzer was commanded by Ostuf. Neugebauer, *1st Battery, 1 Battalion of SS Panzer Artillery Regiment 1.*

25 Statement of Rolf Roland Reiser, 3 January 1946, NA, RG-549, Case 6-24, Box 37, Reiser appears to have followed the path of Preuss that led into the marshy woods west of Thirimont and east of Ligneuville

where several vehicles were marooned in mud. Thus, he avoided the path that would have led him past the dead Americans in the field at Baugnez.

26 *Ibid*. 'In Engelsdorf, I did not hear anything about the shooting of American POWs. I only saw American POWs who were quartered in the hotel on the right side of the road.' Yet, Reiser's insertion of this statement regarding his conversation with Paul Ochmann is telling. By several witnesses, (including Ochmann's own admission) the SS Sergeant had participated in the shooting of more than half a dozen American in Ligneuville the previous afternoon.

27 K.H. Schulz, *'Die Freiwillige,'* Vol. 1, 1965. For progress of Kampfgruppe Sandig, see Tiemann, Vol. IV/2, *op. cit.*, Karte 19.

28 Interview with Beathe O'Neill, 3-4 February 1996.

29 One of the paratroopers of *12 Kp., Fallschirmjäger Regiment z.b.V.* that rode on Peiper's King Tigers in the Ardennes reported that the Mk VIB used 8 liters of fuel to go only 0.3 miles. This is possible as the flat road consumption rate for the Königstiger was 4.8 L/km or 7.7 L/mile. Hilly terrain might double that value. 'As a consequence, the tanks which started out east of Malmedy suffered a shortage of gasoline when they reached the vicinity of Stavelot.' The paratrooper then changed from the seven King Tigers they rode to several Panthers that then moved on to Stoumont, 'First Army, PWI Report No. 9, Para Regt. z.b.V.,' 25 December 1944, NA, RG-407, 101.1- 3.2, M.L.-2125, Box 1497. Peiper preferred the Mk IV in battle. The Mk Vs (4.1 L/km) also used a lot of fuel relative to the Mk IV (2.3 L/km), so that not only was it easier to find bridges for the Mk IV battalion, but the petrol requirements differed quite a lot as well – 80% more fuel to move a Mk V Panther than a Mk IV. Tigers used double fuel: Mk VIB: 4.8 L/km.

30 In fact, the *3. FJ Division* had been assigned to advance through the Losheim Gap, but then to turn to the north-west to assume a blocking position near Malmedy. For the assault plan, see *'LXVII Armykorps,'* NA, RG-238, T-314, Roll 1597. Being the southernmost attack force in the *6.Panzer*Army, and given the failure of *12.SS Panzer Division* to advance, Peiper had no recourse but to rely on other elements of the Leibstandarte for his flank protection.

31 Affidavits: Armin Hecht, 6 April1946, Fritz Rau, 12 March 1946, Fritz Gebauer, 16 April 1946, Heinz Gödicke, dated 13 March 1946, Wolfgang Richter, 16 April1946, NA, RG-549, Case 6-24, Boxes 8 and 9. The crew of the first of two SPWs involved included Uscha. Heinz Klipp (1st Platoon Leader), Rottf. Armin Hecht (Driver), Rottf. Karl Stellner, Strm. Hans Dirnberger, Gren. Ernst Pliester, Gren. Günther Bösel, Gren. Wolfgang Richter and Gren. Heinz Gödicke. The affidavit of Wolfgang Richter was typical of these: 'As we drove through La Gleize I saw a church which was surrounded by a wall to the left of the route of advance for tanks. On the right-hand side of the road was a house. We passed this church about 20m and stopped in the middle of the road. About directly in front of the church, at the wall to the left of the road, if you drive in the direction of Stoumont, there stood about 10 to 15 American prisoners of war. I know now that they were American prisoners of war because they wore American uniforms which I know. I was able to see that they were prisoners of war because they carried no weapons and stood there with raised arms, their hands clasped behind their heads. A few minutes after we had stopped our platoon leader Uscha. Heinz Klipp gave the order to bump off these prisoners. With this I want to say that he gave the order to the whole crew. Immediately after he had given the order "Commence firing", these prisoners were shot. The weapons used by the individual persons I am not able to say today any longer. I personally used my carbine .98 and shot about 4 to 5 rounds, which I fired at the height of the chest of one prisoner. I saw him as well as the other prisoners slump to the ground. I am positive that the prisoners were dead because I could not see any of the prisoners moving around or make any noise. Immediately after this shooting was finished Uscha. Klipp gave the order to drive on.' In another statement, Herbert Stock claimed an initial shooting of about ten Americans happened by the La Gleize church at about 2 PM on 18 December as Peiper's column passed through, implicating an Rttf. Wittwer and Arvid Friemuth. Then, later after retreating from Cheneux to La Gleize, he stated that another group of 15 were shot by the church wall on 22 December on the orders (*Masche! Masche!*) of Ostuf. Georg Preuss. 'Affidavit of Herbert Stock,' 15 March 1946, NA, RG-549, Case 6-24, Box 9. Significantly, however, no physical evidence for a mass of shot American soldiers was ever found in the eventual trial of the Malmedy defendants in La Gleize or seen by called Belgian witnesses. U.S. v. Bersin, *op. cit.*, pp. 3081-3099. Stock repudiated his Schwäbisch Hall statements on 3 April 1948 (Box 54).

32 The post war confessions of young SS men of SS Uscha. Rudi Rayer's *11.Company* admitting the shooting of 15 Americans on 18 December along the church wall in La Gleize were likely invented. Unlike the other killings in Honsfeld, Baugnez, Ligneuville, Stoumont, Trois Ponts and Cheneux, no physical evidence (i.e. bodies) were ever linked to the confessions. Those claiming to have been witnesses included: Fritz Gebauer (17 yrs), Armin Hecht (20), Rudi Rayer (23), Heinz Gödicke (17), Fritz Rau (17), Theo Rau (26) and Wolfgang Richter (18). Perhaps most importantly, four Belgian residents of La Gleize (Father Louis Blokian, Alfred Kreutz, Armand Baltus and Maria Gregoire.) testified at the trial or via deposition, that although present at several times on the afternoon of 18 December, they saw no bodies of American soldiers killed by the cemetery wall. Interview of Wilbert Wahler with Alfred Kreutz, 11 June 1946 and interview of Father Louis Blokian, Miles Rulien with Maria Gregoire and Armand Baltus 15 June 1946, U.S. v. Bersin, *op. cit.*, pp.

2818-2827. All the SS men were all young and eager to satisfy their captors to earn early release or a lighter sentence. Later, the statements of each youths were repudiated while they were held at Landsberg.

33 Butts, *op. cit.*, The guns of the 110th AAA Gun Battalion (two 90mm and four multiple 50mm guns) arrived at the fuel dump at 4 AM on the morning of 19 December.

34 Abbé C. Hanlet, *La Tragédie de la Maison St-Edouard à Stoumont et Histoire du Préventorium*, 19-22 December 1944, H. Dessain, Liége, 1945.

35 'Bourgoumont and the Battle of the Bulge,' as told by Dr André Bastin in 1951. Translation by Benno Dedecker of La Gleize in 2005. Dr Bastin's home was at a place called *Les Tscheous*.which is just north-east of La Gleize and south of the village of Borgoumont.

36 Abbé C. Hanlet, *La Tragédie de la Maison St-Edouard à Stoumont et Histoire du Préventorium*, 19-22 December 1944, H. Dessain, Liége, 1945.

37 'Tagesmeldung vom 18.12.1944,', OKW/WFSt/O.(H)/West,' Ia Report, *OB West Tagemeldungen*, BA-MA, RH 19 IV/84 D, pp. 229-233.

38 That Himmler was located, as Kersten claimed, is verified by a secret French intelligence communiqué on that same date from French Secret Agent X/2 which found 'Himmler, two generals and 20 other personnel in a railway tunnel near Triberg on way to Donaueschingen in the Black Forest.' The informant learned little more than Himmler's presence as civilians in Triberg were kept away from the railway restaurant by glaring SS guards. G/ d. c./6 S. R .O. S.D.A. 7, Nr. 828, 18 December 1944, ML Records of Adj. Gen Office 'French Intelligence Summaries,' NA, RG 407, Location 250/ 65/ 9/1, Box 24218.

39 Himmler on 18 December 1944: Felix Kersten, *The Kersten Memoirs 1940-1945*, London, Hutchinson & Co, p. 229.

40 Letter David F. Knox, 2 October 1984, including account of the Ardennes fighting written by Knox in May 1945; courtesy Gen. Michael Reynolds.

41 *Ibid.*

42 'G-2 Message File and Journal,' 2130, 18 December, 30th Division Reports, NA, RG-407, 330-2.2, Box 7593.

43 'At 182200 the 3rd Bn, 119 Rgt was blocking an estimated 30-40 tanks in the vicinity of Stoumont. The enemy tanks were in a bivouac area and were very noisy, talking loud and smoking cigarettes apparently unaware of our presence ... During the night an enemy tracked vehicle was knocked out by a mine field near Stoumont. At 6 AM a build-up of approximately 15 tanks and a small force of infantry was observed on the road east of Stoumont.' NA, RG 407, XVIII Corps, G-2 Records, 218-2.2, Box 4972.

44 Walter Kos to author, 7 August 1995.

45 Interview with Paul Servais, *op. cit.* Also, interview with Marie Gillet by Marie France Gregoire, no date, but 1990s. Paul's pregnant sister, Betsy, had been wounded in the arm in the same encounter with the Germans by the bridge at Cheneux. At first, they had hauled their wounded mother back to their home in Cheneux, only to find the building smashed by an American bomb intended for the *Kampfgruppe Peiper*.

46 'My mother suffered a lot. I saw a lot of dying people. You can't imagine ...' Paul Servais told the author weeping, 'It is important to understand the terrible way of war.' Paul stayed with the Gregoire family, living in a stable until Christmas Day. When Paul and his father and sisters returned to Monceau in January he remembered the horror of having to remove dead bodies from the road to get their cart down the road to Cheneux.

47 Monsieur Gillet's wife was Maria Hulot who had been killed at the bridge that morning. His daughter was wounded.

Chapter 22 – Cheneux

1 Alfred Lord Tennyson, *Charge of the Light Brigade*.

2 Thanks to Mathilde Schmetz and Gérard Grégoire and his daughter Marie-France for canvassing the locals and assisting in obtaining interviews.

3 Elements of the *9. SS Panzer Division* had reached Manderfeld as early as 18 December, but terrible road conditions and thick traffic kept them from reaching the area around Poteau until 48 hours later. 'Excerpts from Journal of the 20th SS Pz Gren Regt,' Translation of Captured Documents, Incl. No. 1 to G-2 Per. Report No. 199, 13 January 1945, NA, RG 332 Records ETO Historical Division: Records of the Ardennes Campaign, 1944-1945, Box 2.

4 Wilhelm Tieke, *Im Feuersturm letzter Kriegsjahre*, Munin Verlag, Osnabrück, 1975, p. 424. In an effort to push aside the 7th Armored Division blocking their way west, the *9.SS Panzer Regiment* lost five Panthers in a charge forward near Poteau on 21 December, including the personal mount of Stubaf. Eberhard Telkamp.

5 'OB West: Tagsmedlung vom 19.12.1944,' BA-MA, RH 19/IV-84.

6 To the south the Fifth Panzer Army, was drawing further west than Peiper. Genflm. Hasso von Manteuffel's spearheads were now nearing the key road junction of Bastogne and sweeping north-west of it through Houffalize, aiming to cross the Meuse River between Namur and Dinant.

7 Willi Detering, 'Ardennen: Operation 'Wacht Am Rhein',' *Chronik 7./ 8. Kompanie*, Stetten, 1992, p. 201.

8 'First Army PWI Report: From the Bulge to the Rhine, Diary of Feldwebel Karl Laun,' 11/12 March 1945, NA, RG-338, U.S. First Army Interrogation Reports, ETO-MIS-Y, Box 64. (290/56/2/3).

9 Over the day, a total of 145 shells exploded in and around Cheneux being fired by batteries of the 376th Airborne Artillery Battalion attached to the 82nd Airborne.

10 Interview with Frank L. Dietrich, 19 November 1995.

11 Interview with Morris Holmstock, 26 November 1995.

12 The character of Capt. Herbert Sobel was popularized in *Band of Brothers* by Stephen Ambrose and HBO mini-series which followed it. Due to a near mutiny of the NCOs in Company E, Col. Sink had to transfer Sobel at the beginning of 1944.

13 There were 12,604 wounded in action of which 4,850 returned to duty, and there were 1,535 missing in action. Glynn Arrington to author, 19 June 1995.

14 'Blood and Snow—The Ardennes,' Corp. George D. Graves, Jr. S-1 Section, 504th Parachute Infantry Regiment,' provided to author by Louis Hauptfleisch.

15 Dietrich interview, *op. cit.*

16 'I was most surprised to find all the lights burning brightly in the CP. Stopping in to investigate, I was further amazed to see all our equipment packed, people running around in great excitement, and the whole CP in a general uproar. I asked what in the hell was going on. Sgt. Griffin told me to get my personal equipment ready to move out at 9 a.m.' Graves, *op. cit.*

17 'Memories,' by Glynn Arrington, composed for author, June 1995.

18 Graves, *op. cit.*

19 *Ibid.*

20 *Ibid.*

21 *Ibid.*

22 For a complete account of the 504th Parachute Infantry Regiment before and after Cheneux, Phil Nordyke's excellent history: *More than Courage: The Combat History of the 504th Parachute Infantry Regiment in World War II,* Zenith Press, Minneapolis, 2008.

23 'Narrative of Action of the First Battalion, 504th Parachute Infantry at Cheneux, Belgium on December 20-21, 1944' provided to author by Louis Hauptfleisch, the chief executive officer of the 504th PIR.

24 Combat Interview with T/Sgt. George W. Corporan, 2nd I & H, 1st Battalion, 504th Parachute Infantry Regiment, NA, RG-407, 82nd Airborne Division, GL-458, Box 24058. This combat interview provides a framework for the actions on Company B on 20 December 1944.

25 'Flaksturm Abteilung 84,' research compendium assembled by Timm Haasler for author, November 2009.

26 Composition of the heavy weapons of the *84th Flak Sturm Battalion* that the Americans would face: *1. Batterie*: nine 3.7 cm flak (Flak-vierling Sd.Kfz. 7/2. *2. Batterie*: nine 2 cm Sd. Kfz. 7/1Flak-vierling 38 (half tracked), *3.Batterie*: nine 2 cm Flak-vierling 38. Only the *1.* and *2. Batterie* were involved in the action at Cheneux.

27 Part of the *7. Panzer Grenadier Kompanie* of *II. SS- Panzer Grenadier Regiment 2* was recalled from Cheneux to Stoumont on 20 December 1944 and did not return until the following morning. Detering, *op. cit.* Thanks to Timm Haasler for his compendium composed for the author: 'Cheneux: 20—21.12.1944,' 7 April 2010.

28 Several other 10.5 cm guns of Butschek's *5. Batterie* remained at the Petit Spai bridge, although its leader moved on to La Gleize without his guns.

29 While this was reported by the Americans as a 'Jerry halftrack mounting a .77 calibre,' it was, in fact, a *Schützenpanzerwagen Sd. Kfz. 251/9-D* with a 7.5 cm gun mounted on a limited transverse mount. This was likely one of the vehicles from Georg Preuss's *10.Kompanie* which had been abandoned near Rahier in the ill-fated run towards Neufmoulin bridge 36 hours before.

30 Ray Fary to author, 22 April 1996. Fary was with the 80th Airborne AA Battalion from which Kelly and Koprowski volunteered to man the German halftrack.

31 Phil Nordyke, *All American, All the Way: The Combat History of the 82nd Airborne Division,* Zenith Press, Osceola, WI, 2005, pp. 596–597.

32 'G-2 Journal, 1725, 20 December 44,' G-2 Records of 82nd Airborne Division, NA, RG-407, 382-2.2, Box 10413.

33 Corporan interview, *op. cit.*

34 Interview with Morris Holmstock, Company B, 1st Battalion, 504th PIR, 26 November 1995.

35 Dietrich interview, *op. cit.*

36 Story of T/Sgt. Dock O'Neal as recounted by his son, on 30 August 2006 on an Internet forum for the 504th Parachute Infantry Regiment: http://forums.strikehold504th.com.

37 C Company lost 14 killed and many wounded; there were only about 130 men in an airborne company.

38 'Memories,' Arrington, *op. cit.*

39 Dietrich, *op. cit.* Dietrich was evacuated to Malmedy on 21 December and then to Paris and Wales for rehabilitation. 'To be honest, I was usually afraid of making too many close friends, because it hurts like hell to lose them.'

40 'S-2, 504 to G-2,' G-2 Message File, 1725 and 1910, 20 December 44,' G-2 Records of 82nd Airborne Division, NA, RG-407, 382-2.2, Box 10413.
41 Holmstock interview, *op. cit.*
42 'U.S. Men Seal Foe in Belgian Pocket,' *New York Times,* 23 December 1944.
43 Graves, *op. cit.*
44 'The Battle of Cheneux,' NA, RG-407, 382-Inf(504)-0.3.
45 'G-2 Journal, 2215, 20 December 44,' G-2 Records of 82nd Airborne Division, NA, RG-407, 382-2.2, Box 10413. At 2300 hours Lt Miles provided further commentary from G-2 forward that sounded less confident as faced with a tough enemy: 'Five flak wagons, lots of bazookas, some mortars and dominating automatic weapons … Destroyed four flak wagons. [Enemy] well dug in west of town with approximately 90 men—good fighters.'
46 Laun, *op. cit.*, entry for 20 December.
47 The farmhouses of Servais, Forêt and two of Joseph Prince burned to the ground that night.
48 Two in the village died that night that had not come to the church. Joseph Boreux was cut down by shrapnel while he fled when flames started to consume his home. Not far away, Jules Forêt freed his cattle from the burning stables to the fields, but when he emerged from his blazing home he was shot in the forehead.
49 Holmstock interview, *op. cit.*
50 Detering, *op. cit.* description of action on 21 December 1944. SS Hstuf. Schnelle would later be évacuated with the rest of *Kampfgruppe Peiper* from La Gleize across the Salm River to Wanne on a stretcher.
51 'Thank God there was only one Cheneux … Later that morning I was trying to help clean out a house of the enemy. I stuck my head in a door and saw a dirty looking bird raising his weapon at me. He was fast with his gun—just as fast as me. I swung up my Thompson and blasted him. The mirror in the room shattered … I was really shook up.' Memories, Arrington, *op. cit.*
52 Laun, *op. cit.*, entry for morning of 21 December: 'the enemy artillery bursts have somewhat subsided. In the morning hours two of my best comrades and I are selected to form a *Panzervernichtungstruppe* (tank elimination crew). Six Panzerfauste, one machine pistol and we constitute a formidable force which will be able to stop all enemy tanks. Our battle plans concentrate around the selection of the most favorable retreat route.'
53 Holmstock interview, *op. cit.* 'That very morning, we only had eighteen men left in the town, and I thought, *at least we don't have to fight anymore* and here come twenty replacements. *Shit,* he thought, *they'll make us go back.* We were all tattered and ragged, and a mess. When Capt. Helgesson, our Company Commander, saw what had happened to us he went berserk and Sgt. Amadando Castgno had to hold him down that night. After that Helgesson disappeared for three months' The eighteen survivors of B Company must be understood in context; full authorized strength of a parachute infantry company was 152 men, but typical line strength in fall 1944 was around 130.
54 'Have town (Cheneux).' Col. Tucker sent prematurely to division at 2225 on the night of December 20th. However, all through the night of the 20th and the following morning the records recorded continued fighting in the town. G-2 Journal Files, *op. cit.* More realistically, on 21 December at 2030 the S-2 of the 504th announced that 'enemy cleared from Cheneux to south bank of the river from 638019 on west to bridge at 644016.'

Chapter 23 – Professor Natalis

1 Frederick the Great to his soldiers before the Battle of Leuthen, 4 December 1757.
2 Author's interview with Madame Therese Natalis, Stavelot, 27 March 1996 and interview notes of John S.D. Eisenhower with Ernest Natalis, 10 October 1966, Bitter Woods Papers, Box 2. Also, letter Paul Natalis to author 5 February 1997 and enclosed article by Prof. Ernest Natalis: '*La Bataille de Stoumont,*' no date.
3 'A Short Sketch of the History of Stoumont,' Ernest Natalis, copy provided to author by the professor's son, Paul Natalis. In the 8th and 9th Centuries, the region was brought into the Catholic faith by the Benedictines in Stavelot. The Benedictines ruled the tiny region from 651 until 1794 during the French Revolution.
4 In August 1914, the German army coming through the Ardennes had executed hundreds of innocent Belgian civilians in villages stretching from Herve to near the Meuse River at Andennes, Seilles, Aerschot and Dinant. See John N. Horne and Alan Kramer, *German Atrocities, 1914: A History of Denial,* Yale University Press, 2002. As would happen in WWII, the Germans in 1914 were obsessed with the idea that the Belgians in the area were partisans.
5 'Dans La Tourmente: Secteur de Cheneux- La Gleize et Trois Ponts- Wanne,' *Journal des Ardennes,* no date, courtesy Paul Natalis.
6 Line strength in the three companies Fitzgerald's 3rd Battalion: 145 officers and men (Company I), (Company K) and 165 (Company L). Authorized strength in 1944 was 193 officers and men. Capt. Franklin Ferris, 'The German Offensive of 16 December 1944: The Defeat of the 1st SS Panzer Division Adolf Hitler,' NA, RG-407, 218.2-1, XVIII Corps G-2, January, 1945, Combat Interview 94, Box 24037.

7 119th Infantry Regiment Unit Journal, NARA, RG-407, 330-INF (119) 3.2, 19 December 1944. The burning SPW almost certainly came from the *11. Panzergrenadier Kompanie* which ran a reconnaissance towards Stoumont at 2 AM. (see *Duel in the Mist, op. cit.*, p. 33).

8 Natalis, *op. cit.*

9 Janice Holt Giles, *The Damned Engineers*, Houghton Mifflin, NY, 1970, pp. 12-13.

10 Interview with Raymond Beco, 23 March 1996.

11 Giles, *op. cit.*, pp. 242-243.

12 Interview with Mme. Georges de Harenne at the *Château Froidcour* by Ann Hamilton Shields, 9 August 2010.

13 Serge Fontaine, *Stoumont-Cheneux—La Gleize, Decembre* 1944, CRIBA, Liège, 1970, p. 11.

14 'First Army, PWI Report No. 9, Para Regt. z.b.V.,' 25 December 1944, NA, RG-407, 101.1- 3.2, M.L.-2125, Box 1497. On the origins of the German paratroopers of 12/ Fallschirmjäger-Regiment z.b.V. riding with Peiper, Email Timm Haasler and research summary: 16 July 2021.

15 Left behind due to mechanical troubles, or a laggard pace from roads, traffic or fuel shortages were 25 Mk IVs (mostly of the *7. Panzer Kompanie* in Wanne), 13 Mk Vs and 28-35 Mk VIb. This count from a document ('Tanks North of the Amblève) prepared for the author by Timm Haasler on 5 January 2009. This count does not include two additional Mk IVs (622 and 702) which were taken back to Rahden for long-term repair. Also, the following eight tanks had been lost in combat action to the *Kampfgruppe Peiper* by the morning of 19 December: Panther 233 and 235 (Uscha. Kritzler and Publik lost south of Honsfeld; Mk IV 613 and 615 (Uscha. Fremdling and Rttf. Kasparek; lost north of Büllingen on the road to Wirtzfeld), Mk IV 715 (Scharf. Rempel lost south of Büllingen), Panther 152 (Ustuf. Fischer in Ligneuville), Panther 115 (Ustuf. Richartz, Stavelot) and Panther 131 (Oscha. Thomas, Cheneux). A number of other tanks had been temporarily disabled by mechanical troubles or mines, but all were later returned to operational condition.

16 In Wanne, Klingelhöfer had exchanged tanks with Rttf. Walter Eichorst who took over the ailing Nr. 701. Ehrhardt and Klingelhofer continued in Eichhorst's Panzer IV. NA, RG-549, Case 6-24, Card for Walter Eichhorst, Records of USAREUR, Card Index to Defendants in the Malmédy Case, No date.

17 De Meyer et al., *op. cit., p. 14*. The tanks in the Stoumont attack: Panthers Nr. 002 (Hstuf. Hans Gruhle), 151 (Stubaf. Werner Poetschke) and the entire available strength of *2. Panzer Kompanie*: 201 (Christ), 202 (Uscha. Hans Friedrich), 211 (Ustuf. Hubert Kaufmann), 214 (Uscha. Rech), 215 (Uscha. Horst Krüger), 221 (Hscha. Heinz Knappich), 222 (Oscha. Walter Ropeter), 225 (Rttf. Franz Prahm), 231 (Ustuf. Helmuth Koch), 232 (Uscha. Herbert Brauschke), 234 (Uscha. Herzog). Following behind as a second echelon, three to five Mk IVs of the following from *6. Panzer Kompanie*: 601 (Ostuf. Benoni Junker), 611 (Uscha. Walter Wrabetz), 611 (Ustuf. Hans Steiniger), 625 (Oscha. Hubert Huber), 631 (possibly Wrabetz), 624 (Rttf. Georg Eberhardt) and one Flakpanzer IV.

18 The little supply column had gone from Kaiserbaracke to Recht, Logbiermé and Wanne before crossing the Amblève river at the Petit Spai bridge. Jean Paul Pallud, *The Battle of the Bulge: Then and Now*, After the Battle, London, 1984, p. 152.

19 Lehmann, The Leibstandarte, *op. cit., vol.* III, p. 389.

20 According to table, moving a 1944 SS panzer regiment would equate to 5,800 gallons (16 cubic meters) of gasoline for the battle group to travel 100 km in the Ardennes' rough terrain. Had Peiper taken the bridge at Trois Ponts, the distance to the Meuse River at Huy was approximately 60 km. Considering the state of fuel when Peiper approached that bridge, his tank columns could have likely reach Nandrin about 10 km short of the river. Reconnaissance elements might have made the distance, but would likely have encountered stout resistance as the strategic bridge at Huy was well understood as a key strategic point.

21 Left behind in La Gleize: Panthers Nr. 101 (Kremser), 102 (Pidun/Richartz), 111 (Hennecke), 114 (Briesemeister), 123 (Strelow), 125 (Drechsler), 131 (Thomas), 13? (Skotz), 124(Mayer). Panther Nr. 111 which had originally been the mount of Hans Hennecke and was knocked out before the bridge in Stavelot was repaired on the 18th by its driver SS Rttf. Willi Bahnes then driven through Stavelot on the night of the 18th to break down once more near Petit Spai north of the bridge. Bahnes eventually repaired the tank once more, but did not reach La Gleize until the night of December 20th when he arrived as the final reinforcement for *Kampfgruppe Peiper*. Timm Haasler et al., Duel in the Mist, Vol. 3, *op. cit.*, 2014, pp. 220-227.

22 Stefan De Meyer, Timm Haasler, Roddy MacDougal, Simon Vosters and Hans Weber, *Duel in the Mist: The Leibstandarte during the Ardennes Offensive, Vol. 1, Kampfgruppe Peiper, Stoumont, December 19, 1944, AFV Modeler*, Newcastle upon Tyne, 2007, pp. 13-14. In particular, for this chapter, I am indebted to Timm Haasler and Hans Weber for ready information and assistance for preparing this chapter.

23 See folder on Friederich Christ, NA, RG-549, Box 47. Born in Munich, Christ had been a member of the Nazi party since 1938.

24 Hans Gruhle was not with his command tank (002) during the assault on Stoumont. According to radio operator Rttf. Georg Ebeling, 'Our tank was the tank of the adjutant of the Regiment. Normally, the adjutant, Hstuf. Gruhle, should have been riding with us, but he was at the time not with us. For reasons unknown to me, he was in the rear with supply.' This was only true early in the offensive. Gruhle caught

up to the advance by the time the attack on Stoumont began. 'Statement of Georg Ebeling,' 26 December 1945, NA, RG-549, Case 6-24, Box 33.

25 Important extended handwritten statement of Erich Rumpf, no date but 1946, transcribed and translated by Helmut Thiess. NA, RG-549, Case 6-24, Box 32.

26 'Statement of Georg Ebeling,' 26 December 1945, NA, RG-549, Case 6-24, Box 33. Also, author's interview with Arndt Fischer, 15 May 1997. 'Peiper's relationship with Gruhle was not so good … their sympathies were not the same.'

27 'Screening Results 15—24 Nov. 1945,' IC #1, Ellis Papers. Jansen may have been Stm. Hinrich Janssen who claimed to have overheard a radio communication between Reinhard Maier and Werner Poetschke on 17 December as what to do with the prisoners at Baugnez.

28 Statement of Rolf Roland Reiser, 3 January 1946, NA, RG-549, Case 6-24, Box 37. 'The same morning, the recon battalion went back to Stavelot because the town had been reconquered in the meantime by American troops.'

29 Maj. Martin S. Hayden, 'AAA Units in Ardennes Battle,' Combat Interview, GL-194, NA, RG-407, 218.2-1, XVIII Corps G-2, January, 1945, Box 24039.

30 Affidavit of Heinz Friedrichs, 21 March 1946, NA, RG-549, Case 6-24, Box 37. The 4th Platoon would return to the *Château Froidcour* at daybreak, remounting their SPWs and driving to Stoumont to join the attack, already in progress at 9 AM. According to Friedrich's affidavit, as the Uscha. Gerhard Schumacher's 3rd squad of the platoon was preparing to join the advance, a German paratrooper came down the road escorting seven American prisoners of war. Inquiring, Schumacher learned that the paratrooper had orders to 'transport them to the rear.' Schumacher: 'Oh, I am going to transport them to the rear myself.' The paratrooper was happy to hand them over and walked back down the road toward Stoumont. Schumacher dismounted his SPW and ordered the others to do so with weapons while the Americans were moved into a pasture about 700 meters west of the *Château Froidcour* along the road. Friedrichs, the driver stayed with the SPW until Schumacher called out 'That means the driver too!' As the American were assembled in the field with raised hands, the armed platoon drew behind them only 6 meters away. 'Now, the prisoners are going to be bumped off. 'We received an order from Schumacher to shoot these prisoners and we had to execute it. I myself shot at two of these American soldiers firing seven or eight shots from my machine pistol. The others who shot were, Schumacher with his machine pistol, [Willi] Braun with a rifle and [Edmund] Tomzack and [Alois] Weis with pistols … They had their hands raised and made no attempt to escape … I am sure that the two Americans I shot were killed … This shooting took place at about 0930 hours on 19 December … Schumacher had us mount the SPW immediately … I knew it was wrong to shoot prisoners of war. I participated in the shooting because I had an order to do so by Uscha. Schumacher and I also knew that he was acting in accordance with the orders that had been given by our Company Commander, Ostuf. Tomhardt the day before the offensive began. The original statement in German with a diagram of the incident is found in Box 9, NA, RG-549, Case 6-24. Friedrichs retracted his Schwäbisch Hall statement on 2 April 1948 (along with others co-ordinated by lawyer Rudolf Aschenauser), claiming he wrote a dictated statement overseen by Harry Thon. It is significant, however, that Strm. Willi Braun essentially corroborated Friedrich's statement in his own describing how he shot prisoners with a Belgian F.N. pistol firing all eight rounds in the magazine. 'First I shot at one prisoner aiming for the head and saw him falling to the ground dead and he didn't move anymore. When that happened, I saw another hit and still moving and lying on the ground. Obviously this man had been only wounded and out of pity to him, I then gave him a mercy shot.' 14 April 1946, NA, RG-549, Case 6-24, Box 9. Moreover, in a plea for mercy on sentencing on 11 July 1946, Heinz Friedrichs obliquely acknowledged shooting of the prisoners, blaming his superiors. 'In order to not sacrifice his life unnecessarily, everyone was obliged to obey all orders,' while farm boy, Braun, on the other hand acknowledged his participation in the incident. 'I would have been shot already if I had refused orders I received from superiors.' Like Friedrichs, he had been only 18 years old at the time of the offensive. U.S. v. Bersin, *op. cit.*, pp. 3209-3217. Friedrichs and Braun were given early clemency in the War Crimes Modification Board, when it reported in May 1951 citing a young age and superior orders. 'Accused Heinz Friedrichs, Review of the War Crimes Branch, 7 May 1951, NA, RG-549, Case 6-24, Box 52. Whether, this war crime actually happened remains a matter of conjecture as most of the evidence for it comes from statement at Schwäbisch Hall by very young enlisted SS men concerned for their welfare. Graves registration made no mention of finding seven dead Americans in a suggestive line of execution.

31 Peiper wondered who had gotten Kuhlmann and Poetschke to agree in Normandy to a mid-morning advance under clear, August skies.

32 Clear evidence, both on the German and on the American side, indicates that the assault on Stoumont started 2-3 hours earlier than Peiper claimed in his trial testimony. It must be pointed out that Peiper made this contention based on an effort to cast dispersion on the pre-trial statement of Hans Hillig that implicated him in the shooting of a lone American prisoner soon after Stoumont was assaulted on the morning of the 19th.

33 U.S. v. Bersin, *op. cit.*, Peiper at the Malmédy trial, 21 June 1946, pp. 1885-2045.

34 Jochen Peiper, 'Kommentar zum Buch *Massacre at Malmédy* von Charles Whiting,' September 1971.

35 'I was one of the first men to reach the entrance to the village of Stoumont on 19 December 1944. The day was dawning. Shortly before the curve in the road, which led to the village, I ordered a halt because I heard the sound of tanks. At the curve, on the left side of the road, there was a burned passenger car. We suspected a minefield for this reason. Some engineers came to the scene and after a short while, we suffered casualties from hand grenades. It grew light in the meantime, and SS Stubaf. Peiper issued the order to attack Stoumont dismounted.' Statement of Lothar Bergmann, 25 September 1947, NA, RG-153, Case 6-24, Box 80.

36 'An Interview with Obst. Joachim Peiper,' ETHINT-10, 7 September 1945, Freising, NA, RG-338, Foreign Military Studies.

37 As only a single tank, that of Prahm, knocked out in Stoumont, must be the German vehicle Kos is referring to.

38 Walter Kos to author, 25 August 1995.

39 Walter Kos to author, 7 August 1995. Kos received the Silver Star for his part in this action.

40 Kos was convinced the officer who prevented his men from being shot was Peiper himself.

41 *Duel in the Mist, op. cit.*, Haasler interview with Strm. Hans-Georg Hübler, the gunner in Prahm's tank. Thanks to Haasler for permission to use the interview.

42 Hayden, 'AAA Units in the Ardennes Battle,' *op. cit.* Contrary to the American account, more than one crew member survived. Strm. Hans-George Hübler (gunner) was able to escape, as did his loader, Strm. Werner Zander. However, the driver and radio operator were killed while bailing out and Rttf. Prahm was severely wounded and dying before reaching La Gleize. Kampfgruppe Peiper's advanced tank was destroyed by a gun from C, 143 AAA Gun Battalion.

43 Testimony of Horst Vollprecht, *U.S. v. Berin*, pp. 2731-32. *Brahm* in original corrected to Prahm. Vollprecht's testimony reinforces the author's conclusion that Al Darago hit Prahm's tank with a bazooka after it had first been halted by anti-tank gun fire. After, Ostuf. Christ came on the radio directing Krüger's tank in the field to the right to avoid the American anti-tank guns.

44 Fifth verse of *Die Panzerlied*.

45 'Declaration of Werner Zander,' 6 October 1947, NA, RG-549, Case 6-24, Box 47. For corroborating testimony, see 'Affidavit of Hans Georg Hübler,' 6 May 1946, NA, RG-549, Case 6-24, Box 21, although Hübler the gunner located the first hits against their tank from the direction of the church and not the source of the final shots that set the tank aflame. Neither man could recall the name of the killed radio operator. Zander had only joined the 2. *Panzer Kompanie* since June 1944 and Hübler had only joined in December just before that attack.

46 Testimony of Heinz Hoffmann, 15 March 1945; Arnold Mikolaschek, 3 April 1946, Erich Werner, 4 April 1946. Hoffmann has been with the LAH since June 1943 and had 150 combat days in action. Other witnesses in nearby Panther Nr. 232, Erwin Szyperski, 8 March 1946 and Rolf Ritzer, 13 March 1946 (NA, RG-549, Case 6-24, Box 9) corroborated the guilt of the crew of Knappich's tank. Also Walter Köbler (RG 153, Box 82), the loader of Nr. 221. The testimony of young SS men confessing to the incident was likely warped by eager prosecutors at Schwäbisch Hall promising preferential treatment for enlisted men to help incriminate Friederich Christ and other SS officers. Indeed, the three statements above for Hoffmann, Mikolaschek and Werner are suspiciously similar—each describing an otherwise mundane incident regarding the company commander, Christ, that would otherwise be unlikely to be remembered by a 19 year old SS enlisted men recalling an incident over a year earlier. The most likely description of the events came from Hans-Georg Hübler, with original text, who had just escaped with Werner Zander from Prahm's stricken tank. In testimony on 5 June 1946, Hübler claimed to have seen several American prisoners shot after escaping from their stricken tank. 'When we arrived at the entrance of Stoumont early in the morning I was in the leading tank, Number 222 [sic, 225] It was very quiet with the exception of some firing coming out of the house. Our commander gave orders to the radioman to return the fire and shoot into the building. After that a Sergeant and two other men went into the building and took about 13 Americans out. The prisoners were taken to the left of our tank. And I could not observe anything further. Later on, we were knocked out … the driver and the radioman jumped out of the vehicle. The radioman was shot and fell. The driver fell as well. The assistant gunner jumped out ahead of me and I jumped out and I sought cover in a little ditch … At the back of me, 2nd Company tanks were standing. I saw how the radio man of Knappich's tank was shooting at the prisoners who were there on the side of the street. There was a great deal of fighting going on … I could see how two of these prisoners were falling down. I did not see anything further and I returned to La Gleize.' Testimony of Hans Huebler, U.S. v. Bersin, pp. 1318-1336. However, rather than claiming to have seen a dozen Americans shot, Huebler recalled only seeing two men fall and described an incident that was much more like a battlefield combat incident than pre-meditated murder. In writing Werner Zander after the trial on 19 September 1946, Hübler still showed emotional scars. He had incriminated Friedrich Christ and Arnold Mikolaschek, the latter for having shot at American prisoners

after he had escaped their stricken tank: 'Yes, Werner, we have a difficult time behind us, have we not? When I tell you that I do not like to think at all about everything, you can believe me. That was something when we met in the cell again. It was a good thing, Werner, that you stuck with things. For me it was otherwise … Werner, I do not like to talk about that, life is serious enough and enough comrades are dead or died in action.' NA, RG-153, Case 6-24, Box 80. Later in a statement on 6 May 1948, Hübler would accuse Morris Ellowitz and Joseph Kirschbaum as having manipulated his testimony at the Malmédy trial. RG-549, Case 6-24, Box 21. In a statement on 20 January 1948, Rolf Ritzer accused Ellowitz and Kirschbaum of having beaten him and other men at Schwäbisch Hall until he agreed to give a misleading statement that incriminated Christ. (Box 63).

47 The author's investigation revealed the shootings described by Knappich's crew on the 19th was likely a battlefield incident within violent fighting rather than a pre-meditated execution Numerous reasons:

- *Lack of physical evidence*: no finding of a concentration of 12-15 American bodies by the Robinson house.
- *No reports of concentrated casualties* in the fighting from the 119th Regiment. For instance, the 3rd Battalion only reported eight killed, and thirty wounded for the entire days fighting. Even counting attached units, the total American casualties in Stoumont were not much greater.
- *Lack of combat witnesses*: Although present during part of this action, Albert Darago never mentioned anything to the author about seeing bodies. Also, when American prisoners from the 3rd Battalion were marched back under German guard to La Gleize later that afternoon, they would certainly have walked by the Robinson house. There was no mention of seeing a concentration of bodies in one location:
- *Civilian witnesses*: Dr Natalis was in a position to observe the place of the mass execution in his encounter with Werner Poetschke outside the Robinson house after the fighting was over. However, in interviews and letters Natalis never mentioned such.
- *Escaped witnesses:* If Knappich's panzer had shot at 12-15 prisoners, some scattering and survivors would be inevitable. Even in a stationary, pre-meditated shooting as with Baugnez, where 49 of 127 men in the massacre incident survived (39%).
- *No reports:* If 5-7 of the group of 12-15 Americans escaped in the direction of La Gleize, as maintained by Rolf Ritzer (consistent with the preceding point), they would certainly have reported being shot at as prisoners when they were liberated on Christmas Eve. There are no such reports.
- *Improbable crossfire:* Ritzer described how the shot down prisoners were watched by three German guards, who would have been dangerously exposed to fire had Prahm's panzer actually shot into prisoners with machine guns.
- Hans-Georg Huebler's testimony at the Malmédy trial seems most believable. His description: there was shooting at a group of Americans looking to surrender as they emerged from a house during the fighting, but Huebler only saw two fall (who could have been wounded) and the description of the incident sounded like the chaos of house-to-house combat.
- The Schwäbisch Hall statements of Arnold Mikolaschek and Rolf Ritzer were suspiciously alike—going so far as emphasize Christ's remark that they could obtain new shoes from prisoners. While if such a remark may have been recalled by each, it seems doubtful they would have been repeated almost verbaitum. At best, the earlier statement of Ritzer (13 March 46) was given to Mikolaschek (3 April 46) who effectively copied it—hardly acceptable in any legal sense.
- Two of the main confessions came from very young SS enlisted men—Werner and Mikolaschek who may have been enticed to satisfy their interrogators who were intent on incriminating Freiderich Christ. Heinz Hoffmann, who was a 20-year-old Rottenführer claimed he was interrogated on several occasions using coercive methods and confronted with his guilt by Mikolaschek and Werner. Statement of Heinz Hoffmann, 11 December 1947, NA, RG-549, Case 6-24, Box 80.

Promises may have been made to elicit fabricated confessions. 'Hübler had to stay there [Schwäbisch Hall] because of the speech in the Blankenheim Forest, as well as Ritzer and some others. Now, in order to secure themselves a better life there, maybe seconds of food, or a pack of tobacco, for that some comrades had to become victims. Such a victim I did become, as Hübler and Ritzer brought to life something which never happened and which neither myself nor any other members of my company were involved.' Heinz Hoffmann to Karl Ehninger, 5 August 1946, NA, RG-549, Case 6-24, Box 44.

48 Interview of Otto Lessau by Thomas Fischer, 22 January 2010. Courtesy Timm Haasler. The fact that the advance past Stoumont station was not more aggressively pursued in the mid-afternoon of 19 December from 2-4 p.m. suggests Poetschke's absence during his movement back and forth between Peiper's headquarters at *Froidcour* and Stoumont station.

49 The losses were two destroyed SPWs of *12. Kompanie, III. SS Pz Gren Rgt. 2.* Rttf. Eduard Moser in the lead vehicle was killed and the following SPW was destroyed too, although all members of its crew survived under Uscha.Anton Motzheim.

50 Statement of Anton Motzheim, 28 February 1946, NA, RG-549, Case 6-24, Box 8 (both handwritten and transcribed and translated statement). Hscha. Jochen Thiele was Motzheim's company commander who

had told his men on the first day of the attack, 'Prisoners won't be taken in this attack. All will be bumped off. Do you understand?' In his confession, Motzheim admitted to having shot an American trying to surrender at Honsfeld on the morning 17 December. It is important to note that Motzheim requested the opportunity to defend himself at the Malmédy trial—a decision that spectacularly backfired in his testimony on 28 June 1946. Even after being convicted, as with all the defendants, he repudiated his earlier confession in a affidavit dated 20 January 1948 where he claimed to have been beaten at Schwäbisch Hall. However, during the courtroom proceedings, Oscha. Wilhelm Pluschke admitted that later in December, while playing cards with other comrades at Petit Thier, that Motzheim described to him how he had killed an American in Honsfeld. U.S. vs. Bersin, *op. cit.*, pp. 888-890.

51 Peiper's testimony at the Malmédy trial, U.S. v. Bersin et al., *op. cit.*, p. 2008.

52 Tanks sent across the dairy pastures north of Stoumont towards Rouat: Nr. 222 (Ropeter), 232 (Brauschke), 231 (Koch) and 234 (Herzog).

53 Detailed account of Rolf Ehrhardt to Gerd Cuppens, undated, p. 2.

54 Testimony of Fritz Willecke, U.S. v. Bersin, *op. cit.*, pp. 2750-2757.

55 Statement of Gerhard Nueske, 31 January 1948, NA, RG-549, Case 6-24, Box 51. The timing in the statement of Nueske was calculated to have Peiper leave the scene of the Robinson house soon after the initial encounter as Hans Hillig so as to not have been available to approve the execution of an American prisoner near that position. Ostuf. Rudi Mäule was later killed in action 24 December 1944. Nueske: 'I went to the U.S. anti-aircraft gun emplacement near the house, together with Peiper and armored artillery officer Ostuf. Rudi Meule [sic, Mäule; the chief of the Stabs Kp.] as Peiper wanted to find out if the gun could still be used. The gun was still in firing condition, but munition was lacking and the sighting mechanism was missing.'

56 Interview with Alice Robinson, courtesy Marie France Gregoire, no date.

57 That Poetschke was present exactly when the fighting surged around the Robinson house complete with the Fallschirmjäger that Natalis recalled, is vividly depicted in a series of photographs made by the *SS Kriegsberichter* on the morning of 19 December 1944. See Jean Paul Pallud, *Battle of the Bulge: Then and Now,* After the Battle, London, UK, 1984, p. 165. In the original interview notes with Natalis by John S. D. Eisenhower, Natalis says, 'a German officer' and does not positively identify Peiper. Both Eisenhower and Natalis understandably speculated that the SS officer was Peiper. However, Natalis was present after the war at the Dachau trial from 20—25 May 1946 and had a chance to see Peiper in the courtroom but made no mention in his trial notes that he recognized Peiper from the 19th of December (Natalis's handwritten notes from Dachau, May 1946, courtesy Paul Natalis). After the war, in reviewing the book of Charles Whiting where Natalis's story is recounted (p. 105), Peiper denied ever having met the professor: 'The Natalis Story is absurd. I neither saw nor talked to a civilian in Stoumont at that time. The story about the aircraft, too, is new to me. Also, it was not necessary for me to give orders to spare the civilians. That was, for us, a routine matter.' Jochen Peiper, 'Kommentar zum Buch *Massacre at Malmédy* von Charles Whiting,' September 1971; courtesy James Weingartner. Of course, Peiper's denial cannot be considered definitive. Considering the Ebeling statement (which preceded any published account), the balance of the evidence would indicate that Peiper was, in fact, the officer who spoke to Natalis, as its description fits closely both with the recollection of Therese Natalis as well as Ernest Natalis himself.

58 The conversation with the SS officer is taken from the handwritten interview notes of Natalis by Eisenhower, 10 October 1966.

59 Interview with Madame Therese Natalis, Stavelot, 27 March 1996. Fourteen-year-old Therese was present for a short time during the argument between her father and the SS officer. 'When we got there, Professor Natalis and Peiper were already in a conversation. He was furious. That was my impression; he was very angry … I heard him say, 'All the people here are terrorists!'

60 Of Stoumont's civilians: 140 were placed in the church, some 40 others at the Robinson house and 200 women and children at the Sanatorium. Fontaine, *op. cit.*, p. 14.

61 Statement of Georg Ebeling, 27 December 1945. NA, RG-549, Case 6-24, Box 33. Concerning the statement about blowing up the church: 'I did not consider this remark an order, but just a remark to show he was in a bad mood.'

62 De Meyer et al., *op. cit.*, p. 268.

63 Essay of Alphonse Prince, Stoumont, December 1946, courtesy of Paul Natalis.

64 After some hours had passed, a young SS trooper from the Alsace descended the steps. 'I need three young women to cook for German officers!' he yelled in accented French. Two young girls volunteered, lest all come to harm. They found precious little food in the kitchen, being lucky that the SS men understood their limitations. Interview with Edith Gregoire, courtesy Marie France Gregoire. Edith and Fanny Hendrick were forced to cook for the SS officers in town on 20 December. However, reaching the place where they were to cook, they found only a little ham, a few eggs and some coffee and blue kettle. The food they prepared was voraciously devoured, but the coffee was a disaster—someone had stored soap in the enamelled kettle.

65 Interview with Therese Natalis, *op. cit.*

Chapter 24 – Strike for the Meuse

1 The contemporary Belgian spelling for Rouat is Roua, but we use the period historical spelling from 1944. For the 743rd at Stoumont: William B. Folkestad, *The View from the Turret: The 743rd Tank Battalion During World War II,* White Mane Publishing Co, Shippensburg, PA, 1996, pp. 73-75.

2 'G-3 Journal, 30th Infantry Division,' 0725, 19 December, NARA, RG-407, 30th Infantry Division, 330-3.2, Box 7634.

3 Extended account from Lt David F. Knox, of the Ardennes fighting of Company L written in May 1945; Letter Knox: 2 October 1984, courtesy Gen. Michael Reynolds.

4 The artillery support upon which U.S. infantry was trained to rely was not set up until the night of December 19th with the self-propelled howitzers of the 400th Artillery Battalion arrived in Chession—too late to help with the debacle in town earlier that day.

5 Lt David F. Knox, of Company L written in May 1945; Letter Knox: 2 October 1984.

6 Peiper, 'Kommentar zum Buch,' *op. cit.*

7 'The beaten enemy was followed for approximately 5 kilometers and then we had to stop because we didn't have a drop of gasoline left. At this time, I tried to take up communication with my division to ask them what steps had been taken as far as Stavelot was concerned and when I could figure on supplies coming up to me.' Peiper's testimony at the Malmédy trial in June 1946, as read from his long interrogation at Freising in August 1945; U.S. v. Valentin Bersin et al., p. 2010.

8 *Mit dem 7. Kompanie Panzer Regiment LSSAH im Einsatz in den Ardennen, Berichte von Rolf Ehrhardt,* Copy provided to author by Wolf Mauder.

9 After the battle, villagers in Stoumont counted only four German tanks and three half-tracks left in the village proper. Fontaine, *op. cit.,* p. 12. Considering the ferocity of the fighting in the village, the few Belgians killed is near miraculous: Émile Servais was killed in his kitchen by a German tank crew during the initial German assault and Jules Constant was killed by shrapnel while outside his home.

10 For the photo of Diefenthal directing American prisoners eastward in Stoumont, see Jean Paul Pallud, *op. cit.,* p. 166. Ann Shields located the exact spot in Stoumont for the author in early August 2010—just west of the last intersection at the north-western end of town.

11 Interview with Baroness Mme George de Harenne at the *Château Froidcour* with Ann Shields, 10 August 2010.

12 Duel in the Mist, *op. cit.,* p. 93.

13 30th Division G-3 Journal, filed on 201247, NARA, RG-407, 30th Infantry Division, 330-3.2, Box 7634.

14 Henry Klein to Leon Kent, 23 October 1996.

15 Springfield was with Company A, 823rd TD Battalion, NARA, RG-407, AAR 823rd TD Battalion, December 1944.

16 Leon Kent to Henry Klein, 18 September 1996.

17 Duel in the Mist, *op.mcit.,* pp. 99-100. Order of the Panthers advancing on Stoumont Station was likely: 222 (Oscha. Ropeter), 201 (Christ), 231 (Koch), 221 (Knappich) and 215 (Krüger).

18 Strength of the 1st Battalion at commitment was 764 officers and men.

19 Interview of Otto Lessau by Thomas Fischer, 22 January 2010. Courtesy Timm Haasler.

20 Testimony of Jochen Peiper, *U.S. v. Bersin, op. cit.,* pp. 1906–1908.

21 The 3rd Battalion began the fight with 447 officers and men. At the end of the engagement, the effective line strength of the 3rd Battalion: Company I (24), Company K (50-55), Company L (80) and Company M (100). Of the 203 missing, ten would return to duty on the 20th with a further 143 recovered in Stoumont and La Gleize after the Americans liberated these towns. The two platoons of the 823rd TD Battalion lost nine men wounded and 16 missing in action as well as one 76mm gun destroyed and seven captured by the enemy. Battery C of the 143rd AAA Battalion had lost two 90mm guns including one half-track fully loaded with ammunition.

22 'After Battle Report No. VII,' 823rd Tank Destroyer Battalion, December 1944, NA, RG-407, TDBN-823-0.3. All the MIA were later liberated on Christmas Day.

23 G-3 Journal 30th Infantry, *op. cit.,* 0900, 19 December. At 9:40 AM, Hobbs was calling for G Company (Capt. Ickland) to push down the road SW towards Ruy, but be careful not to get cut off … 15 enemy tanks were reported down there.'

24 *Ibid,* messages at 191035. By noon, Gen. Thorson with First Army was grilling the 30th Division commander on the happenings in 119th sector: 'We are having a real battle there,' Hobbs related, 'but it is a little obscure right now.' Thorensen replied that it was vital to stop the enemy from moving north on the trails leading out of Stoumont. 'We have a large gas dump we must protect and that is why we want you to be watchful of those roads to the north—it is not very far from where you are fighting … There are several approaches they could come up.' 'We have directed that they block that place (619051).'

25 This is a most ironic claim, as SS-Uscha. Max Beutner was at the center of those likely guilty in the order for the killings at the Baugnez crossroads. The head of the 1st platoon, Beutner was killed in the fighting in

Stoumont for the Sanatorium on the afternoon of 20 December 1944. The leader of the 2nd platoon, Ustuf. August Seitz was killed in the fighting for the Sanatorium in the early morning hours of 21 December 1944. Sworn Statement of Karl-Heinz Rose, 8 November 1947, NA, RG-549, Case 6-24, Box 49.

26 Statement of Josef Pichler, 22 January 1948, NA, RG-549, Case 6-24, Box 13 (original German in Box 44). Pichler's statement must be taken with a large grain of salt in this statement, as the testimony was clearly intended to provide cover to Franz Sievers, saying he could not have been anywhere other than at the CP at the Sanatorium on the 19th of December when he was alleged to have participated in war crimes. Pichler indicates he, Sievers and others left the Sanatorium on the evening of 21 December, reaching a new location at 'a peasant's house' in La Gleize at just after midnight, 22 December. The rest of the *3. Panzer Pionier Kompanie* took up positions in a series of houses on the road to Borgoumont in La Gleize. Again, in La Gleize, Pichler maintained that Sievers did not leave his CP there, but briefly on the 23rd to confer with Peiper—again to provide an alibi such that he could not have been at the site of claimed war crimes from the testimony of Schäfer. As seen in the narrative, Pichler too, was under suspicion for administering mercy shots to two American soldiers shot earlier by Gustav Sprenger.

27 Sworn Statement of Karl Heinz Rose, 8 November 1947, NA, RG-549, Case 6-24, Box 49.

28 Sievers continued to claim Sprenger had shot prisoners in Stoumont, a contention that sounded like revenge given that the enlisted man had accused the SS officer. 'Franz Sievers Petition for Clemency,' 28 October 1946, NA, Case 6-24, RG-549, Box 14.

29 'Despite the many repudiation of pre-trial statements,' the 1951 War Crimes review board considered, 'the record indicates that ten men of the accused's company were allegedly involved in incidents concerning the shooting of American prisoners of war ... The accused did actually order Schaefer to have prisoners shot in Stoumont ... It is more than coincidence that prosecution witness Jourdain saw five dead American soldiers in a place in Stoumont, where Sprenger indicated he had shot these prisoners.' NA, RG-549, Box 66, 'Accused Franz Sievers,' War Crimes Modification Board, European Command, 28 May 1951.

30 It turned out that important witnesses that had incriminated both Pletz and Christ did not actually see prisoners shot in the incident. See Testimony of Otto Lessau, *U.S. v. Bersin,* 5 June 1946, pp. 1353-1358 and that of Horst Vollprecht, pp. 2706-2750. Later, others such as Rolf Ritzer and Erwin Szyperski would repudiate their earlier incriminating statements citing intimidation by interrogators. An accusation from Erich Werner was based on hearsay rather than Werner's own testimony which was also later repudiated. Statement of Hans Pletz, 28 August 1953, NA, RG-549, Case 6-24, Box 48. Beyond multiple sources of exculpation, it must be added that there was no physical evidence for two dozen American prisoners shot at the center of Stoumont.

31 Statement of Gustav Sprenger, 27 February 1946, NA, RG-549, Case 6-24, Box 7 with detailed drawings and original German.

32 'After entering Stoumont, I first parked my SPW for 5 or 10 minutes near a store located on the main street, but shortly moved it to a spot near a house ... where I joined a group of my comrades. In this group was Ostuf. Sievers, Oscha. Schaefer, Sprenger, Neve and Goldschmidt ... While standing there I saw two American soldiers come down the street ... They were carrying a wounded German soldier with them ... Sievers and Schaefer told us to the load the wounded German on the jeep ... I was standing there when I heard Schaefer tell Sprenger to take these two Americans and 'bump them off ... After Sprenger had received the order, he marched the American prisoners down the street ... The Americans were unarmed, had their hands clasp above and behind their heads in a sign of surrender and were being marched a few steps ahead of Sprenger. I walked down the street with Sprenger part of the way and I walked with him and he borrowed my [machine] pistol ... Sprenger marched these two men into a small lane or alleyway leading off to the right-hand side of the road and shot the two Americans in the alleyway ... Sprenger fired 2 or 3 bursts into these prisoners with his [machine] pistol. I saw the men fall to the ground when he shot them.' Affidavit of Joachim Hoffmann, 6 March 1946, NA, RG-549, Case 6-24, Box 6.

33 Marcel Boltz in Sprenger's SPW described the same event claiming that group leader Uscha. Wolfgang Altkrueger shot three of the prisoners in Stoumont. Strm. Franz Vukissewitz and Strm. Sigmund Koehler were witnesses. Affidavit of Marcel Boltz, 21 March 1946, NA, RG-549, Case 6-24, Box 7.

34 In the eventual Malmédy trial, Sprenger did not deny shooting the prisoners in Stoumont, but claimed, that as a young enlisted SS man refusing orders—even to shoot defenseless prisoners—would be met with his own death. Sprenger painted a picture of German youths growing up on the heartless battlefield in the East. Even short-term survival was unexpected. 'Fighting in Russia was very hard and ruthless,' his plea for clemency read, 'The nameless cruelties the German prisoners of war who were taken by the Russians had to suffer, shocked me deeply. At that time I was only 17 years old.' *U.S. v. Bersin,* pp. 3239-40.

35 Zuffenhausen interrogation of Interrogation card for Sepp Pichler: 'Index to Defendants in the Malmédy Case (No. 6-24: Reference witness statements,' NA, Case 6-24, RG-549, Location: 290/59/18/5.

36 Statement of Willi Schaefer, 8 April 1946, U.S. v. Bersin, pp. 1399-1402.

37 Affidavit of Gustav Neve, 6 March 1946, NA, RG-549, Case 6-24, Box 6, Affidavit of Siegfried Jaekel, 1 March 1946, Box 7.

38 Testimony of Albert Jourdain, 5 June 1946, pp. 1407-1408. Jourdain indicated the bodies of two American soldiers were found by his home in approximately the positions marked on photographs taken by investigators Burton Ellis and Robert Byne during their visit to the battlefield in April 1946.

39 Sprenger's confessions were voluminous all within the eventual court case: RG-549, Case 6-24: 22 January 1946 (Box 38), 23 January 1946 (Box 31), 11 February 1946 (Box 38), 15 February 1946 (Box 38), 27 February 1946 (Box 7), 15 March 1946 (Box 7) and 22 April 1946 (Box 7). It is noteworthy, however, that the complexion of the confessions changed over the course of the Sprenger's writing frenzy at Schwäbisch Hall. While the first confessions mention Sievers associated with the Stoumont shooting, suspiciously, Peiper is not mentioned until Sprenger's long handwritten opus on 27 February. Later the statement of 22 April 1946, supplemented by photographs, identifies the specific houses in Stoumont were Peiper and Sievers supposedly presided over the execution. That the Stoumont incident may have happened seem plausible as pre-trial statements of Joachim Hoffmann, Willi Schaefer and Gustav Neve all corroborated Sprenger's statements—although not placing Peiper on the scene.

40 Testimony of Ernst Goldschmidt, *U.S. v. Bersin*, pp. 2398-2434.

41 Not surprisingly Franz Sievers demanded to take the stand at the Malmédy trial to counter the very damaging accusation made by Gustav Sprenger, Hoffmann and Neve of his having ordered Sprenger to shoot two American prisoners on 19 December. Testimony of Franz Sievers, *U.S. v. Bersin*, pp. 2349-2387. Sprenger's own Schwäbisch Hall statement fundamentally agreed saying that Schaefer's 'order to 'Knock 'em off' was in a loud voice, and Sievers was no more than two meters from Schaefer.' 'Affidavit of Gustav Adolf Sprenger, 22 January 1946, NA, RG-549, Case 6-24, Box 38.

42 'We have captured a map showing boundaries which our people interpret as being the *1st SS Division*,' Brig. Gen. Harrison told Gen. Gerow of V Corps. 'It had Stavelot as the northern boundary and has them heading to a place about 10 miles south-west of Liège.' Telephone conversation with Gen. Gerow and Brig. Gen. Harrison, 1320, 19 December 1944, NARA, RG-407, 30th Infantry Division, 330-3.2, Box 7634.

43 Peiper trial testimony, pp. 1951-1952.

44 Peiper: 'Vorschlagliste Nr. 42 für die Verleihung des Eichenlaubes zum Ritterkreuzes des Eiserner Kreuzes,' *op. cit.*

45 U.S. v. Bersin, p. 1948.

46 At 11:03 AM, Stephens was on the phone with Maj. Thomas of the 120th Infantry Regiment requesting Gerow's 'strong patrols' to be dispatched at once to reach the 7th Armored in the vicinity of Recht. 'Send them out as quickly as possible with radio communication and impress them with the importance of getting word back quickly.'

47 'G-3 Journal, 119th Infantry Regiment, December 1944,' NA, RG-407, 330-INF (119th) 0.7, Box 7697. By 1535, Capt. Stuart reported that 140 remnants of the 3rd Battalion had marched east across the heavily wooded ridge to a blocking position north of Stoumont. Soon afterward, Capt. Gooley reported that Company K in the position had been bolstered by two 90mm guns, a 75mm piece, several machine guns and six bazookas.

48 Interview with Corp. Harland Whitcomb, in Folkestad, *op. cit.*, p. 74.

49 For the story of Gilbert Collard and Ernest Jacot: Gérard Grégoire, *Les Panzer de Peiper face à l'US Army*, J. Chauveheid, Stavelot, 1986, pp. 30-31.

50 One operational mystery relative to *Kampfgruppe Peiper* is why, when stopped at Stoumont Station, Peiper did not double back to cross the Amblève on the secondary road which led from Targnon south to the N645, crossing the Amblève near Xhierfômont. From there, he could have proceeded to Chession-Lorcé to pick up the same route to Liège. The bridge had been seized by Peiper's grenadiers on the morning of 19 December. Civilians from Targnon (Mme. Charles) told after the war of having been approached by several Germans while the battle was raging on 19 December and being asked if there were any significant American forces around Xhierfômont. Fontaine, *op.ncit.*, pp. 28-29. Reasons:

- The best road after crossing the Targnon bridge (N645 today) would have led back to Werbomont which Peiper knew was held by the 82nd Airborne.
- The only route likely to be undefended led to Chession and then Lorcé and was no more than a country trail—likely muddy in December 1944. Worse, the road climbed very steep terrain with sharp turns—promising extra fuel consumption.
- The U.S. 400th Armored Field Artillery with its Priest howitzers was on the road at the top of the hill near Chession on the morning of 19 December and any German sally would have met them head on, quickly drawing Gavin's airborne troops.
- If Peiper decided to go to Lorcé, that would have required holding two bridges—the one at Targnon and the other just down the road crossing the Lienne Creek one km further.

Lastly, and most importantly, Peiper had only enough fuel for a single advance.

51 Testimony of Oskar Mauer, *U.S. v. Bersin*, pp. 2741-49.

52 The 740th Tank Battalion had arrived at Utah Beach in November, and when the Ardennes offensive opened was bivouacked in an apple orchard in Neaufchâteau still waiting for tanks! Yet, at 1245 PM, an order was received from Lt Col. Cox, the Assistant Armored Officer of the First Army to send a single

company to their Ordnance Depot in Sprimont, Belgium. At 2 PM, Capt. Raymond Berry's C Company rushed to the ordnance depot in trucks where Col. George K. Rubel learned that the enemy was only a short distance away. George W. Rubel, *Daredevil Tankers*, Germany, September 1945.

53 Account of C.O. Webster, 740th Tank Battalion, prepared for author, August 1995.

54 30th Division G-3 Journal, 1335, 19 December 1944, NARA, RG-407, 30th Infantry Division, 330-3.2, Box 7634. Conversation between Col. Stephens and Gen. Hobbs, 1335 hrs.

55 'Memories of the Battle of the Bulge,' prepared for author by Harry M. Lane, 30 June 1995.

56 There is controversy over who KOed this German Panther. Macht contended it was destroyed by M4 C10, while the 90mm gun received the official credit. (See Folkestead, p. 75).

57 'Narrative Report of the Tank Destroyer Operations of the 143rd AAA Gun Bn,' 18 December–1 January 1945, NA, RG-407, CADBN-143-0.3.

58 Although damaged, Knappich's Panther (Nr. 221) was not destroyed. Indeed, it moved ahead to rescue wounded crew members from Ropeter's stricken panzer. After rescue, the tank moved back east to deliver the burned panzer men to an aid station in La Gleize. It seems likely that the 90mm gun crew was somehow firing high explosive rather than armored piercing shot which would account for several deflected shots off the frontal armor of Nr. 221.

59 To clarify, it should be noted that the *Gare De Stoumont* is actually much closer to the village of Targnon (1 km west) than it is to Stoumont proper (another 3 km further east).

60 Testimony of Horst Vollprecht, *U.S. v. Bersin*, p. 2737.

61 Testimony of Oskar Mauer, *U.S. v. Bersin*, p. 2749. Mauer was gunner in Panther 231. Strangely, German tanks had no functional fuel gauge so that petrol supply was determined by distance travelled and terrain—a most worrisome combination in the Ardennes. Wolfgang Schneider, *Panzertaktik*, 2000. Also, TM-E 3–451, February 1945.

62 'Statement of Rudolf Rayer, Dachau, 27 October 1947,' NA, RG-549, Case 6-24, Box 38.

63 Rayer, *ibid.*

64 Pvt. D.P. Philips and Charles Scofield were seriously wounded in the action at Stoumont Station and Pvt. Donald Eyanson was killed. The other members of the gun crew included: Lt Donald McGuire, Sgt. Alexander Sarkowski, Cpt. Clement J. Guigar, T/5 Kenneth Moore, Pft. Julius J. Fidram, Pfc. Harry Lane and Pfc. Arthur R. Geisinger.

Chapter 25 – The Final Throw

1 'Obtlt. Kurt Wiehle, *Der Panzerlied*, 1933:*Und lasest uns im Stich einst das teulose Glueck, und kehren wir nicht mehr zur Heimat zurück Trifft uns die Todelkugel, ruft unds das Schicksal ab, dann ist uns der Panzer ein ehrenes Grab.'*

2 30th Division G-3 Journal, 1118, 19 December 1944, NARA, RG-407, 30th Infantry Division, 330-3.2, Box 7634.

3 Peiper had been intending to cross the Amblève at Halte (Naze), cross over to Lorcé and advance on Aywaille. With his limited artillery support, Peiper had briefly shelled that road junction just prior to the final push beyond Stoumont station.

4 Lt Col. Rubel, commander of the 740th Tank Battalion: 'I hated to commit the battalion and my fears were doubled when I saw the 743rd Tank Battalion pulling out more tanks than we were putting in … They just did not have the heart.' Ferris, *op. cit.*

5 Affidavit Josef Dietrich, Landsberg Lech, 15 January 1948, NA, RG-549, Case 6-24, Box 50.

6 Testimony of Horst Vollprecht, Malmédy trial, *U.S. v. Bersin, op. cit.*, p. 2728-2750.

7 G-3 Journal 30th Infantry, *op. cit.*, 1200 and 1255, 19 December.

8 On current maps, the spelling is Monthouet, is along the N606 north of Stoumont toward Spa.

9 'Borgoumont and the Battle of the Bulge,' as told by Dr André Bastin in 1951. Translation by Benno Dedecker, 2005.

10 Fontaine, *op. cit.*, pp. 18-19.

11 'The Battle of the Gas Dump,' By Elmer J. Potzmann, 110th AAA Gun Bn, NARA, RG 498, UD 584, Records of the ETO Historian.

12 Ferris, *op .cit.*

13 'The Battle of the Gas Dump,' By Elmer J. Potzmann, *op. cit.*,110th AAA Gun Bn, Capt. Julius Reiver was the Battery D commander during the Bulge. 'A couple of hours later, we heard some tanks rumbling along. We manned the guns and thought this was finally it. Nothing happened and when it did happen, the tanks were coming down the same road we came down from Spa … When they arrived, it was the U.S. 3rd Armored Division, a most welcome sight.'

14 Telephone conversation with Gen. Hobbs and Gen. Gavin, 19107 December 1944, NARA, RG-407, 30th Infantry Division, 330-3.2, Box 7634.

15 *Ibid*, Telephone conversation between Gerow and Hobbs at 8.20 AM.

16 The position of the Nr. 3 Gun of the 110th AAA Gun Battalion has been erroneously located in one account after another (eg. Ferris Report of claims of it having been east of Zabompre farm) but given very careful evaluation by DeMeyer et al. (*Duel in the Mist, Part 3,) p. 126*) it appears to have been located close by the 1st Battalion line. The author is indebted to the analysis within that book and the assistance of Timm Haasler.

17 Trial testimony of Oskar Guttmann, *U.S. v. Bersin*, pp. 2758-2760. In Panther #215 were Ustuf. Krueger, the tank commander; Rttf. Hans Fritsche and Strm. Hermann Schaefer, gunners, and Strm. Karl Daub who was radio operator. Guttmann, who was the driver.

18 Horst Krüger died from his wounds on 22 December and is buried at the German military cemetery in Recogne.

19 There is another scenario for this action as outlined by veteran Curtis A. Martell of Company C, 1st Battalion. He indicated that at dusk on the 19th—as it may have seemed in the heavy gloom, they called on a tank destroyer to move up to help protect them as two German tanks seemed to be moving towards their position. 'I yelled at the tank commander to be on the alert. Soon the lead German tank came close to the bend and the TD opened fire and knocked him out. A second tank tried to get around the burning tank and our tanker knocked him out.' The tank destroyer could have come from 823rd TD Battalion, but is unidentified. *Duel in the Mist*, p. 146. Thanks to Hans Weber for help in dissecting this confusing matter.

20 Tank C-10 of the 743rd Tank Battalion claimed to have shot down the lead German tank. See 'After Action Report, 743rd Tank Battalion, December 1944,' 1 January 1945. NARA, RG407, 743-TNKBN- 3.3.

21 This confusing action has been investigated in the detail: Stefan De Meyer, Timm Haasler, Roddy MacDougal, Simon Vosters and Hans Weber, *Duel in the Mist (Volume 1): Kampfgruppe Peiper. Stoumont December 19th, 1944,* AFV Modeller, Newcastle upon Tyne, 2007, p. 144. It turns out that the 740th Tank Battalion did likely shoot Krüger's tank, although had been destroyed for some time in an earlier action. However, the tanks of Kaufmann and Brauschke moved up after a two-hour period only to run into the 740th Tank Battalion then moving cautiously forward. The author appreciates the review of Timm Haasler and Hans Weber with updated resources and sources.

22 'Statement of Rudolf Rayer,' 27 October 1947 and 26 April 1947, NA, RG-549, Case 6-24, Box 38 and 68.

23 'Affidavit of Herbert Stock,' 15 March 1946, NA, RG-549, Case 6-24, Box 31. Stock, who had been at Cheneux the day before, arrived at Stoumont rail station at about noon.

24 Testimony of Herbert Stock, 13 March 1946, NA, RG-549, Case 6-24, Box 9. Rttf. Kurt Wittwer was later killed in the fighting in La Gleize on 22 December 1944.

25 In Schwäbisch Hall Peiper learned that Preuss had killed the American flier near Büllingen for his wedding ring and boots rather than in a real fight. Peiper was thoroughly disgusted with Preuss—not because he executed the American, but that he had lied and then had stolen from the man. For Peiper his actions betrayed *Anständigkeit*—(to stay clean with proper, dignified behavior) high on Himmler's desired list of attributes for an SS man.

26 'Extended Handwritten statement of Erich Rumpf', NA, RG-549, Case 6-24, Box 32. Other than Georg Preuss, Erich Rumpf said the following individuals were 'in Peiper's favor': Werner Poetschke, Josef Diefenthal, Friedrich Christ and Franz Sievers.

27 The artillery likely came from mortars of the 1st Battalion, 119th Infantry Regiment on the road west of Stoumont station.

28 'We fired our gun at an enemy tank or tanks, which it was we could not recognize because of the darkness. After a very violent fire battle, we were at least shot down.' Statement of Helmut Nestler, 20 August 1947, NA, RG-153, Case 6-24, Box 81.

29 The Panther was 28 feet long, 11 feet wide and in the hands of a skilled operator could turn a circle in a 33 foot radius. Unfortunately, even the best Ardennes roads in December 1944 were no more than 24 feet across and most, including the N33, were considerably more narrow.

30 Statement of Erwin Szyperski, (handwritten original with detailed maps) 8 March 1946. NA, RG-549, Case 6-24, Box 9. Comparison with the statement of crewmate Rolf Ritzer, made on 13 March 1946 shows portions with suspiciously identical language (Box 9). 'I think I remember that on the dictation of this second statement, Szyperski, the driver of the tank in which I was wireless operator, was also present. With slight variations, Mr. Kirschbaum dictated the same statement to Szyperski. While we were writing these statements, another interpreter, Mr. Thon, came frequently into the room. Naturally we were not willing to write such statements which we were incriminating ourselves and others contrary to the truth. Mr. Thon told me he would act as defense counsel in my trial and that I could write without fear the statement dictated to me … [otherwise] I would be sentenced to death and hanged.' Statement of Rolf Ritzer, 9 September 1953, 21 March 1954, NA, RG-549, Case 6-24, Box 48.

31 Contrary to some accounts, Ustuf. Helmut Kaufmann, leading Panther Nr. 211, was not killed on 19 December 1944, but actually later in the war on the 19th of April 1945 after being wounded with Poetschke in the last battles of the Leibstandarte in Hungary. In his statement after the war Szyperski claimed to have shot at American prisoners. 'As we got near to the place where our tank was stuck, I noticed a group of

ten American prisoners … I was carrying the machine pistol and Brauschke said to me, 'You shoot too.'' Szyperski claimed he too fired into the prisoners at twilight on 19 December, seeing clearly by the light of Untersturmführer Kaufmann's tank still burning brightly in the road. In an effort to satisfy his interrogators, Szyperski may have intentionally muddled the two stories. In his declaration of 21 March 1954, Szyperski alleged physical abuse from William Perl at Schwäbisch Hall, and threats of having his parents' ration cards seized. He claimed the statement was dictated to him in German by Joseph Kirschbaum after also being confronted by Rolf Ritzer. The story of the Americans being shot as they made their way back to their tank was obviously untrue, he said. After dictating the statements, 'I said to myself, that the facts which were dictated to my pen would easily be proved impossible given the military situation … it was obvious to almost anybody, that if our tank led the attack of the front line at [beyond] Stoumont, there could not have been any German soldiers before us guarding American prisoners.' Declaration of Erwin Szyperski, 21 March 1954, NA, RG-549, Case 6-24, Box 48.

32 *Ibid*, 'All the following days, thereafter, I remained in a cellar with other wounded soldiers.' Given the sequence of events, there must be considerable doubt about this part of Szyperski's statement.

33 'Sworn Statement of Georg Bunda,' 22 December 1947, NA, RG-153, Case 6-24, Box 80.

34 This section is largely taken from the Ferris account, *op. cit.*

35 Nestler, *op. cit.* Nestler was in Brauschke's Panther: 'Only in the evening when we had reached a railroad station a few kilometers behind Stoumont, did we fire our cannons at enemy anti-tank guns, tanks or whatever it was; on account of the falling darkness, I was unable to distinguish.'

36 Horst Vollprecht in Panther Nr. 231 of Koch indicated that the group of tanks following up the road towards Lorcé remained in the area of Stoumont Station until 'about a half hour before dark' before proceeding forward. Testimony of Vollprecht, *U.S. v. Bersin*, pp. 2706-2739. 'There were four tanks in front of us. To our left front, the tank of Sgt. Krüger, Brauschke's tank was on the right side of the road, behind Brauschke's tank was one of the tanks in the ditch—where the tank of Ustuf. Kaufmann was standing and by Kaufmann's tank was the tank of Sgt. Herzog also on the right side of the road.'

37 Vollprecht, *op. cit.*, p. 2740.

38 Testimony of Oskar Maurer, U.S. v. Bersin et al., *op. cit.*, p. 2748. 'We received pretty severe artillery, anti-tank and mortar fire. This fire concluded with some smoke grenades; at that time we were exactly in this [road] curve towards the right. 2nd Lt Koch drew my attention to the fact that the Americans would come through the fork on the left side, across the [rail] tracks. I turned my turret to the left some and there saw shadows coming through the fog. It looked like assault troops or something else coming in. Fire had ceased at the moment. Upon that, we fired a fragmentation shell down there. Nothing else moved and later the American fire started again … At about 4:30 PM we retired to the station at Stoumont. Then Lt Koch received the order to move back to Stoumont, which we did.'

39 This account differs substantially from that in *Duel in the Mist*, pp. 171-172 or that in *The Devil's Adjutant*, pp. 148-151, based on further research by Hans Weber: 'The Attack West by 119th RCT,' summary prepared for author November 2010 as well as other sources located by the author.

40 ETHINT-10, *op. cit.*

41 Peiper, '*Kommentar zum Buch*,' *op. cit.* To the author, Peiper's claim seems self-serving, for in his entire military career he had never hesitated to advance where there was any opportunity. On the contrary, he was widely known for often over-extending himself to that end (e.g. Kharkov, *Zitadelle* and numerous behind-enemy-line escapades in the East.) He would display the same immutable *modus operandi* in Hungary at Simontarneo in the winter of 1945.

42 Testimony of Friedrich Christ, interrogated by Dwight Fanton, NA, RG-549, Case 6-24, Box 28. Christ had been wounded three times in Russia and once in Normandy.

43 Members of the 740th Tank Battalion would lay claim—largely bolstered by the Ferris report—of having been responsible for turning the high tide of the battle. It turns out that with the heavy fog covering the battlefield on 19 December, the first German tank the 740th first fired upon (Pz 215 of Krüger) had already been destroyed, but the other two they ran across were moving forward. Kaufmann's Nr. 211 was hit by the 740th in the meeting engagement while the crew of Brauschke's tank abandoned theirs in panic.

44 Jochen Peiper, '*Kommentar zum Buch Massacre at Malmédy* von Charles Whiting,' September 1971.

45 U.S. v. Bersin, *op. cit.*, pp. 1954-1955. Peiper indicates that he decided to give up the attack forward as early as noon on the 19th, whereas we are reasonably certain that Kaufmann's and Brauschke's Panthers were not lost until a meeting engagement with 740th Tank Battalion that took place after 3 PM. The fact that Poetschke departed Stoumont Station with Peiper only to return later that afternoon seems the likely explanation for the renewed effort to move forward.

Chapter 26 – The Sanatorium

1 Goethe, Iphigenie

2 *Ibid*, 30th Division Telephone log for 1035, 20 December 1944.

3 'Report of IPW Information,' 222200 December 1944,' G-2 Records, 30th Infantry Division, NA, RG-407, 3330-2.2, Box 7594.

4 Peiper's testimony, U.S. v. Bersin, *op. cit.*, p. 1955-1956.

5 'This counterattack took place at 2300 hours. I entered the castle [Sanitorium] with my platoon and again took this castle, but I could not take over the main front line, because the Americans were in there solid. The Americans tried to throw me out of the castle again on the 21st and that battle restarted and it was a very hard fight. The Americans were shooting in there with tanks and bazookas. One room after the other was taken away from me and at the last I was the happy owner of the kitchen. All afternoon we were fighting over the kitchen.' Trial testimony of Franz Sievers, U.S. v. Bersin et al., pp. 2362-2363.

6 'Extended Handwritten statement of Erich Rumpf, NA, RG-549, Case 6-24, Box 32.

7 The Americans would later claim their eviction was chiefly due to the superior firepower of the German tanks which had crept in close enough to blast shells into individual rooms.

8 'On the 20th of December, in a castle near Stoumont [the Sanatorium], I have killed with pistol shots an American prisoner of war whose lower part of the body was buried in debris. The American lay in the hallway of the castle ... This American groaned as he was obviously in pain because his lower part of the body was buried. Thereupon, I fired from the immediate distance, two pistol shots at this American; one in the head and one in the heart ... The American was dead after these two shots.' Statement of Max Hammerer, 11 April 1946, NA, RG-549, Case 6-24, Box 9. Trained as a locksmith, Hammerer was not a voluntary SS man, having been transferred from the Luftwaffe at the beginning of April 1943. 'We are soldiers and we have to obey orders,' he emphasized. 'Statement of Max Hammerer, 2 October 1946, NA, RG-153, Case 6-24, Box 82. During the research for the book, I was able to locate and communicate with Max Hammerer who had been involved in the Malmedy massacre event, Honsfeld and the heavy fighting in Stoumont. He told the author he'd become a Christian and still had nightmares of that time. Understandably, he was unwilling to speak about Honsfeld or Malmedy. He did recall the death of Beutner in the ferocious fighting for the Sanatorium. 'And now about the large building in Stoumont. The American soldiers came into the main building from an adjacent building over a passageway. After a tough battle we retreated from the main building and pulled back into the village. Then came the order to take this position. Around 1100 o clock we again took the building and the American soldiers surrendered. The American tank was positioned above the building and advanced on the position. A few shots were fired by a German Panzer after an illumination shell went off. The others moved back. The American soldiers in the adjacent building were overtaken and mistakenly shot by their own Panzers.' Max Hammerer to author, 11 Nov and 24 Nov 2011, Fronthausen, Germany. Hammerer was released from Landsberg prison in 1954.

9 In the Malmédy trial, even the defense attempting to establish guilt admitted that Max Hammerer had shot a badly wounded American during the battle for Stoumont. The defense painted this as a merciful act. 'Evidence clearly indicates that such mercy killings were a practice recognized by German troops.' U.S. v. Bersin, pp. 3081-3099.

10 The 2nd Battalion, of the 119th Regiment had been with the 504th Parachute Infantry Regiment just to the south, given that corps was worried that this flank remained unsecured. Only on 20 December, did it start moving back to the north side of the Amblève to help with the desperate situation in the Stoumont-La Gleize area.

11 'G-3 Journal and File,' 30th Infantry Division, 1212, 20 December 1944, NARA, RG-407, 30th Infantry Division, 330-3.2, Box 7634.

12 'Reference you request for air, everything is on the ground. There isn't much hope they can get up.' Hobbs told V Corps that they had stopped the Germans even without it, 'but we will need air tomorrow.' G-3 Journal *op. cit.*, 20 December 1326–1328.

13 The 119th Regiment, AAR shows the co-ordinates of the minefields at 607040 and 639030.

14 This section taken largely from Ferris, *op. cit.* pp. 35-38.

15 'G-3 Journal, 119th Infantry Regiment,' *op. cit.*

16 'G-3 Journal, 119th Infantry Regiment, December 1944,' NA, RG-407, 330-INF (119th) 0.7, Box 7697.

17 AAR 30th Infantry Division, December 1944, NARA, RG-407, 30th Infantry Division, 330-3.2, Box 7634. Task Force Harrison included 197th FA and 400th Armored FA Battalion, 3rd Armored CCB (less Task Force Lovelady) and Company B of the 105th Combat Engineer Battalion. It was given the mission of taking Stoumont and then La Gleize before closing the gap with the 117th Infantry Regiment at Stavelot. At 2100 hours the combat elements were formally attached as Task Force Harrison. Also, Combat Interview GL-191, *op. cit.*

18 Account of Lt Douglas J. Strand, D Company, 1st Battalion, 119th Infantry, no date, copy courtesy Michael Reynolds. Describing the action on the night of 20—21 December: 'During the night, the Germans counterattacked screaming *"Heil Hitler!"* and recaptured part of the sanatorium in savage hand to hand combat. On the morning of the 21st we had lost four officers and about half of our men in our rifle companies. It looked that all we could do was to try and hold our position.'

19 Thanks for clarification on the timing of the American action to first retake the Sanatorium by Hans Weber. Although Pallud and Reynolds had given a later time for the American action, there is no source and the available 119th Infantry Combat Journal and AAR (*op .cit.*) show that their offensive actions against the Sanatorium ended at 1715 hours.

20 Capt. Smithers of the 119th: 'We lost four tanks of the 740th in the fight; they were the first four in the column. They are stopped at least for now.' Gen. Harrison: 'I am postponing that thing, maybe a couple of hours … I am going to call for plenty of arty support over here.' G-3 Journal *op. cit.*, 21 December 0657—0750.

21 Jochen Peiper, 'Kommentar zum Buch *Massacre at Malmédy von Charles Whiting*,' September 1971.

22 Peiper's testimony, U.S. v. Bersin, *op. cit.*, p. 1955-1956.

23 'Report of IPW Information,' 1945, 20 December 1944,' G-2 Records, 30th Infantry Division, NA, RG-407, 3330-2.2, Box 7593. In actuality, the captured NCOs were on an errand to contact their left flank, consisting of Siever's 3. *Pz Pi. Kp* which was south of the N33 in Stoumont.

24 Statement of Erich Rumpf, 14 November 1948, Landsberg, RG 153, Case 6-24, Box 81.

25 'German Counteroffensive: 3rd Armored Division Combat Interviews,' NA, RG 407, 3rd Armored Division, Entry 427, Box 24090.

26 'Declaration of Rudolf Rayer,' Dachau, 26 April 1947 and 'Statement of Rudolf Rayer,' 27 October 1947, NA, RG-549, Case 6-24, Box 28 & Box 38. On the 24 of December 1944, the Americans took Rayer (who had a fractured pelvis and ribs, and shrapnel wounds to his lungs) and other German wounded to a field hospital in Verviers. Under interrogation: 'Did you talk to anyone about it, who saw American prisoners of war were killed?' 'Yes.' 'By whom?' 'Kurt Kramm. 'What did he talk about?' 'He told me that he saw how prisoners of war were shot at the crossing between Engelsdorf and Malmédy.' 'Where did the conversation take place?' 'In the bunker,' he said referring to Peiper's headquarters.

27 'G-3 Journal,' *ibid*, 1042 AM, 20 December.

28 'G-3 Journal,' *op. cit.* Hobbs to Maj. Singleton, S-3, 117th Infantry.

29 'Road to La Gleize,' by Bob Kaufmann, *op. cit.*

30 'German Counteroffensive: 3rd Armored Division Combat Interviews, Task Force McGeorge,' NA, RG 407, 3rd Armored Division, Entry 427, Box 24090.

31 117th Infantry Regiment Unit Journal, NARA, RG-407, 330-INF (117) 3.2, December 1944.

32 In one engagement, the American in Roanne had seen the SS men coming up the hill through the fields coming from the Moulin Marechal and opened fire from the window of the home of Helene Fontaine. Once the firing began, the entire family tried to reach the cellar, but were caught on the floor of the kitchen behind the cupboard by German machine guns. In the 30-minute gun battle, Helene's mother was mortally wounded. Interview with Helene Fontaine, courtesy Marie France Gregoire.

33 'Borgoumont and the Battle of the Bulge,' as told by Dr André Bastin in 1951.

34 Fontaine, *op. cit.*, pp. 20-21. A patrol led by Sgt. Etherbert Stucky discovered the couple.

35 'Affidavit of Herbert Stock,' 15 March 1946, NA, RG-549, Case 6-24, Box 31. Stock's statements are not entirely believable. While, the executed couple were found dead in their easy chairs, as he had mentioned, the ten executed GIs were not discovered nearby—at least as acknowledged by the graves registration units.

36 'G-3 Journal,' *ibid*, Maj. Singleton at 201514. The 119th Infantry Regiment reverted to 30th Division control at 3 PM. after having been temporarily attached to the 82nd Airborne.

37 'G-3 Journal 30th Infantry Division,' entries for the early morning of 20 December, NARA, RG-407, 30th Infantry Division, 330-3.2, Box 7634.

38 3rd Armored CCB consisted of its headquarters company, 2nd battalion 36th Armored Infantry Regiment, headquarters 33rd Armored Regiment, 1st and 2nd Battalions of the 33rd Armored Regiment, 1st platoon reconnaissance company and 1st and 2nd platoons of Company D of the 23rd Engineer Battalion. 3rd Armored Division, AAR, December 1944, NA, RG-407, Entry 427, 601-3AD-0.3.

39 Task Force Jordan consisted of F Company of the 33rd Armored Regiment (M4 Sherman tanks) along with two M-5 Stuart light tank platoons from A Company of the same regiment. This was reinforced by assault gun and mortar platoons of the 36th Armored Infantry Battalion.

40 Task Force McGeorge was a portion of the 1st Battalion, 33rd Armored Regiment consisting of Company I (M4 Sherman tanks), the assault gun platoon of the 33rd Armored, the 2nd infantry platoon of D Company and the mortar platoon of the 36th Armored Infantry Battalion. There was also an engineer squad from the 23rd Engineer Battalion.

41 Task Force Lovelady consisted of the 2nd Battalion of the 33rd Armored Regiment, B Company of the 36th Armored Infantry Regiment, the recon company of the 33rd Armored Regiment and Platoon B of the 23rd Armored Engineer Battalion.

42 S-2 Records of Combat Command B, 3 Armored Division, 1555 hrs, 20 December 1944, NA, RG 407, 603-CCB-2.2, G-2 Reports, Box 12241.

43 Major Gen. Michael Reynolds (*Devil's Adjutant*, p. 179) correctly asks how a battalion of *Kampfgruppe Sandig* could cross the Petit Spai bridge with one company going to Cheneux while much of the rest reached La Gleize unopposed, at the same time Peiper was desperately seeking to link up with a missing fuel column? He ascribes this shortfall to 'a breakdown in communications and/or confusion at the divisional level.' The elements of battalion crossed along with some elements of the 5th SS Battalion, Panzer 1st Artillery Regiment

44 Al Palfey, 'The Trap that Doomed Kampfgruppe Peiper,' Manuscript prepared for author, 26 October 1992.

45 *Mit dem 7. Kompanie Panzer Regiment LSSAH im Einsatz in den Ardennen, Berichte von Rolf Ehrhardt*, Copy provide to author by Wolf Mauder.

46 Ehrhardt, *op. cit.*

47 While Ehrhardt blamed Ustuf. Handtusch, the leader of Tiger 211, the fact remains that Hstuf. Oskar Klingelhoefer was the ranking commander at the position who could have ordered the engagement of Task Force Lovelady as it passed before their guns.

48 The 3rd Armored had been fighting just west of Düren in the area around Echtz and Geich along the Roer River on 12 December 1944.

49 'OB West: Abendsmedlung und Tagesmeldung vom 20.12.1944,' BA-MA, RH 19/IV-84.

50 *Ibid*, 22 December: 'The bravely fighting *1. SS Panzer Division* 'Leibstandarte Adolf Hitler' successfully fought off 14 heavy enemy attacks supported by tanks at Stavelot and La Gleize.'

51 Peiper, 'Kommentar zum Buch,' *op. cit.*

52 Information courtesy Timm Haasler from interviews with Jupp Steinbüchel (29 September 2001) and Willi Dietrich (21 September 2000). The medium-wave Fu G.12 nominally had a 25 km range for voice, but the hilly terrain with Mt. St. Victor between Peiper and Mohnke, severely limited range.

53 'Telephone Conversations Between Gen. Hobbs and Col. Sutherland,' G-3 Journal 30th Infantry Division, 1750, 20 December, NA, RG-407, 30th Infantry Division, 330-3.2, Box 7634.

54 'This commander, talked a good war on the telephone and since Gen. Hobbs never visited the units during combat, he seemed to largely based his opinions on these optimistic telephone conferences.' Gen. William K. Harrison to John Toland, 22 May 1958, John Toland Papers: *Battle: The Story of the Bulge*, Box 35.

55 'My recommendation to relieve the commander was not based on the Stoumont fight alone, but on my observations over a period of some months. Both Col. Stephens and I had recommended his relief at least a month before … I saw him and his regiment at work and had a different opinion.' Gen. William K. Harrison to John Toland, 15 May 1958, John Toland Papers: *Battle: The Story of the Bulge*, Box 35.

56 Wortmann memories, Cuppens archive, *op. cit.* Wortmann's crew of his Wirbelwind Flakpanzer: Gerhard Hübler (loader), Hannes Grässel (loader), Günther Sträter (radio) and Erich Miechen (driver).

57 'Through intelligence and questions of prisoners of war, I could ascertain that I was surrounded by the 36th Infantry Division [*sic*: 30th], the 3rd Armored Division, and the 82nd Airborne Division. The conditions in Stoumont were particularly difficult because it was no longer possible to fight back the enemy which had broken through, and the enemy was in control of the western part of the town from then on.' U.S. v. Bersin, *op. cit.*, p. 1955-1956. The force Peiper likely later observed was Task Force Lovelady of the 3rd Armored Division.

58 'Headquarters 30th Infantry Division, G-2 Periodic Report,' 20 December 1944, NA, RG 407, 603-CCB-2.2, G-2 Reports, Box 12241. 'The enemy has been stripping our PW s and dead of their dogtags, identification cards and uniforms in preparation of the current large scale attack.'

Chapter 27 – In the Cauldron

1 Order of battle summary taken from Michael Reynold's evaluation: *Devil's Adjutant*, p. 188.

2 The author has written about these tragic episodes, both in the small villages near Stavelot as well as in Wanne. Alas, there is not room in this volume. The interested reader is recommended to the complete coverage by Timo R. Worst, *Schnelle Gruppe Knittel*, Netherlands: Boek, 2022. Tragic civilian killings in Wanne implicate Wilhelm Mohnke, Valentin Bersin as well as members of the 6th and 7th Panzer companies.

3 'HQ 30th Infantry Division,' 202100, orders for the operations on 21 December 1944, NARA, RG-407, 30th Infantry Division, 330-3.2, Box 7634. TF Harrison consisted of the 119th Infantry Regiment, Co. A of the 823rd TD Battalion and 740th Tank Battalion with direct artillery support from the 197th FA Battalion.

4 'Telephone conversation between Col. Akers and Leland Hobbs, 30th Division, 927 AM, 21 December 1944, NARA, RG-407, 30th Infantry Division, 330-3.2, Box 7634.

5 Beco interview, *op. cit.*

6 Story the Sanatorium: Abbé C. Hanlet, *La Tragédie de la Maison St-Edouard à Stoumont et Histoire du Préventorium*, 19-22 December 1944, H. Dessain, Liége, 1945.

7 George Kenneth Rubel, *Daredevil Tankers*, Göttingen, 1945, pp. 62-63.

8 'Telephone Conversation between Maj. Gen. Hobbs and Brig. Gen. Harrison,' 1602, 21 December 1944, NARA, RG-407, 30th Infantry Division, 330-3.2, Box 7634.

9 Account of Karl Wortmann and letter to Gerd Cuppens, 21 December 1982, Cuppens archives, description of the fighting in Stoumont on pp. 30-31. The Flakpanzer of Oscha. Hahn was destroyed in Stoumont on 21 December, with crew members Adolf Macht and Heinz Scholz killed in that action.

10 Message from Gen. Harrision, 30th Division, 1322 and further conversation at 1510, 21 December 1944, NARA, RG-407, 30th Infantry Division, 330-3.2, Box 7634.

11 Arn, *op. cit.*, p. 147.

12 McCown to Toland, *op. cit.*

13 MacKay to author, 27 May 1995.

14 John L. Faris to author, 16 November 1996. 'I didn't hear from him again until he re-joined us on Christmas day.' In his letter to the author on 27 May 1995, Elmer MacKay recalled exactly the same conversation, wondering why McCown would say that: the experienced men in Company E had learned to worry if could they could smell rye bread– an odor common to enemy presence.

15 'G-2 Journal and File,' 1755, 21 December, 30th Division Reports, NA, RG-407, 330-2.2, Box 7593. Lt Babo, G-2, 119th Inf. notes that day: 'Major McCown captured with mapboards and all regimental installations on it.'

16 'Observations of an American Field Officer Who Escaped from the 1st SS Panzer Division 'Adolf Hitler',' RG-407, 330-2.2 G-2 Records 30th Infantry Division Box 7569: 330-2.1, Operations Reports, December 1944, McCown's testimony was first reproduced in Annex 1 of 'Headquarters 30th Infantry Division G-2 Periodic Report,' No. 192, 26 December 1944.

17 Faris, *op. cit.*, all involved, Faris, MacKay and Barefoot heard the German submachine gun fire and surmised that McCown had been killed or captured.

18 Interview with Earl B. Barefoot, 4 July 2009. 'I was a runner for the Company Commander of Company E– a runner goes everywhere. I was a private and our company commanders kept getting killed. The radios didn't work worth a damn. We ran phone wires at night, but shrapnel often cut these. And I had to go and find these people and I was shot at many times. It was mighty dangerous and casualties in our company were terrible– twice we were left with only thirty people of the original 200 in the company that were still around. We had the highest casualty rate of any of the companies in 'Old Hickory.' We also had the most self-inflicted wounds. There were reasons for that …' Barefoot's claim was true; both in August and October 1944, the casualty rate in E Company reached 170 and 150 men, respectively, out of an established strength of 200. The total wartime casualties of the company were over four times its established strength: 865. Very detailed records of the casualties of the company were kept by Harry Schniering, the Company Clerk. These were later summarized by Ron Hall and made available to the author.

19 Barefoot's opinion of Capt. Warne Parker was echoed by fellow E Company soldier, Sgt. Elmer S. McKay who indicated that so bad was the situation, that several members considered how to get rid of their company commander. Several people were hurt by misinformation from Parker and 'we damned near shot up some 2nd Armored guys near Mertzenhausen and would have been wiped out if they had of returned the fire …' In one incident, Parker ordered Barefoot to dig a foxhole under the stairs of a basement in which he was hiding while Holycross was leading the company. MacKay to author, 27 May 1995.

20 Interview with Earl B. Barefoot, 4 July 2009.

21 McCown to Toland, *op. cit.*

22 Fontaine, *op. cit.*, p. 33.

23 Interview and personal tour with Baroness de Harenne at the *Chateau Froidcour* by Ann Shields, 10 August 2010. The Baron's family was kept prisoner in one room of the cellar from 19 -23 December 1944. However, due to the fact that no one came to any harm at the castle, a monument to the Mother Mary was created which is still seen at the castle.

24 Reiser account, Tiemann, Vol. IV/2, *op. cit.*, p. 93.

25 Statement of Gerhard Nueske, 31 January 1948, NA, RG-549, Case 6-24, Box 51.

26 Edward C. Arn and Jerome Mushkat, *Arn's War: Memoirs of a World War II Infantryman, 1940-1946*, University of Akron Press, Akron, OH, 2007, p. 146.

27 Letter David F. Knox, 2 October 1984, including account of the Ardennes fighting written by Knox in May 1945; courtesy Gen. Michael Reynolds.

28 Statement of Hans Hennecke, Tiemann, *op. cit.*, pp. 94-95.

29 Ferris report, *op. cit.*

30 33rd Armored Regiment, Combat Interview GL-191, *op. cit.*

31 Four citizens of Stoumont were killed during Battle of Stoumont, including Florent Laboreux who was buried when his house was hit by American shelling.

32 Story of Jenny Lejeune, Sister Soeur Agnes and Mia Hurlet of Stoumont, courtesy interviews of Marie France Gregoire.

33 Story the Sanatorium: Abbé C. Hanlet, *La Tragédie de la Maison St-Edouard à Stoumont et Histoire du Préventorium*, 19-22 December 1944, H. Dessain, Liége, 1945.

34 *La Tragédie de la Maison St-Edouard, op. cit.*

35 *La Tragédie de la Maison St-Edouard, ibid.*
36 . 'Telephone Conversation between Maj. Gen. Hobbs and Brig. Gen. Harrison,' 0810, 22 December 1944, NARA, RG-407, 30th Infantry Division, 330-3.2, Box 7634.
37 'German Counteroffensive: 3rd Armored Division Combat Interviews, Task Force Jordan,' NA, RG 407, 3rd Armored Division, Entry 427, Box 24090
38 Task Force Jordan Combat Interview, *ibid.* It should be noted that the 3rd Battalion of the 119th Infantry Division did not record the same difficulty in Roua in its after action report.
39 Account of Lt Douglas J. Strand, D Company, 1st Battalion, 119th Infantry, no date, copy courtesy Michael Reynolds.
40 Reynolds, *op. cit.*, p. 194.
41 Fontaine, *op. cit.*, p. 38.
42 'Report of IPW Information,' 222200 December 1944,' G-2 Records, 30th Infantry Division, NA, RG-407, 3330-2.2, Box 7594. 'At the time the company had approximately 70-80 men. The company commander, Lt Sievers, is wounded. The 3rd Company took part in last night's counterattack against the castle. The PW s say that paratroopers and SS infantrymen also participated. The 3rd Company sustained heavy losses due to our artillery … and abandoned the castle last night because everything was completely disorganized.'
43 Interview with Raymond Beco, *op. cit.*
44 Prof. Ernest Natalis: '*La Bataille de Stoumont*,' no date. In Stoumont, 18 homes had been burned, some 30 entirely destroyed and another 85 damaged. Four of its inhabitants had been killed, most buried under debris when their homes were struck by artillery. Also, '*La Tragedie des Ardennes*,' by Octave Pétry, 1 February 1945, local Ardennes publication unknown. Courtesy Paul Natalis. 'It doesn't matter that we have suffered,' one older child said upon seeing the Americans, 'so long as the *Boche* do not return. Stoumont, our beautiful village– we will build it back again.'
45 *La Tragédie de la Maison St-Edouard, op. cit.*, the Sanatorium was eventually rebuilt in 1947.
46 'G-2 Message File and Journal,' 2255 , 22 December, 30th Division Reports, NA, RG-407, 330-2.2, Box 7593.

Chapter 28 – McCown

1 Interviews with Karl Paul Fröhlich 20 May 1996 and 19 May 1997.
2 U.S. v. Bersin, *op. cit.*, Peiper testimony at the trial in June 1946, pp. 1957-1958.
3 Peiper, 'Kommentar zum Buch,' *op. cit.*
4 McCown to John S.D. Eisenshower, 10 March 1966, Abilene, KS, Bitter Woods, Box 2.
5 McCown: 'Observations of an American Officer', *op. cit.*
6 McCown: 'Observations of an American Officer,' *op. cit.*
7 Ehrhardt report, *op. cit.*
8 McCown: 'Observations of an American Officer,'*op. cit.*
9 *823rd* TD Battalion, Unit Report, 222200 Dec. 44, NARA, RG-407, 30th Infantry Division, 330-3.2, Box 7634.
10 Ferris, *op. cit.*, p. 42.
11 S-2 Records Combat Command B, 3 Armored Division, 21 December 1944, NA, RG 407, 603-CCB-2.2, G-2 Reports, Box 12241.
12 Reiser account, Tiemann, *op. cit.*, p. 107.
13 'Task Force Lovelady,' prepared for author by James K. Cullen, 24 May 1995. 'The SS were in Trois Ponts on the 19th and were fired on by the 51st Engineers from across the river and the Krauts then took revenge on the civilians during the early morning of the 20th just before we got there. There, I saw an old woman with the blood still flowing.' Cullen letter 12 June 1995.
14 PRO: DEFE 3/319, HP 9926. The encoded message from Mohnke's headquarters was decrypted and speedily signaled to Allied intelligence within three hours of its receipt at 1400 on 20 December.
15 RG-407, 330-2.2 G-2 Records 30th Infantry Division, 21 December, PW s captured in American uniforms near RC 819023.
16 'German Deception,' U.S. First Army G-2 Report No. 193, 20 December 1944, U.S. First Army, NA, RG-407, 101-3.3. Also,'Interrogation of Angelo Acetti,' 22-23 December, U.S. First Army PWI Report, 27 December 1944, NA, RG-407, 101.1- 3.2, M.L.-2125, Box 1497. 'The conspirators are carrying forged identification papers, letters of introduction etc. which should enable them to gain access the general's headquarters.'
17 Skorzeny trial citation, NA, RG-549, War Crimes Cases Tried, Case 6-100, Box 77–79. In fact Skorzeny's Panzer brigade was used as a conventional assault force against the town of halmedy where it was repulsed on 21 and 22 December.
18 'All Paris on Alert for Disguised Foes,' *New York Times*, 23 December 1944.
19 The most famous battlefield relic in the Ardennes, Dollinger's Nr. 213 still survives in La Gleize and for years graced the entrance to Gerard Gregoire's *December 44* museum. Gregoire has since died and the present museum is called 'December 44 Historical Museum,' The map board is still in their possession

20 AAR 30th Infantry Division, December 1944, NARA, RG-407, 30th Infantry Division, 330-3.2, Box 7634. On that day, given the repeated assaults being sustained all along the divisional line, the 30th received another reserve unit when the independent 1st Battalion, 551st Infantry was attached to the division and closed into a reserve position in Ster at 8:15 PM. Meantime, at 1340 Task Force McGeorge reported reaching the road at K668029 and being thwarted by nearby German tanks. S-2 Records Combat Command B, 3 Armored Division, 21 December 1944, NA, RG 407, 603-CCB-2.2, G-2 Reports, Box 12241.
21 'HQ, CCB, 3rd Armored Division,' S-2 Periodic Report, 212200, Combat Command B, 3 Armored Division, 21 December 1944, NA, RG 407, 603-CCB-2.2, G-2 Reports, Box 12241.
22 Oscha. Schäfer and Rottf. Pichler stayed by headquarters until the order to break out from La Gleize. Statement of Josef Pichler, 22 January1948, NA, RG-549, Case 6-24, Box 66.
23 The following Panzer IVs of the *6. Kompanie* were able to follow Peiper to La Gleize and beyond: 601 Benoni Junker, 611 Hans Steininger, 625 Hans Huber, 631 August Tonk.
24 U.S. v. Bersin, *op. cit.*, testimony of Franz Sievers, pp. 2349-2387. Max Hammerer was also wounded in the fighting with 3. Pz. Pi. Kp. in this action.
25 Hammerer to author, 25 July 2011.
26 Interrogation of Willy Schäfer at Landsberg, 6 Feb.1947, Ellis Papers, in author's possession. Werner Wendt: Unpublished manuscript of s. SS-Pz.Abt. 101/501, p. 79. I am grateful for the assistance of Timm Haasler and Hans Weber in sorting out this confusing action.
27 'German Counteroffensive: 3rd Armored Division Combat Interviews, Task Force McGeorge,' NA, RG 407, 3rd Armored Division, Entry 427, Box 24090.
28 'Road to La Gleize,' *op. cit.*
29 Eventually, Klingelhofer's Pz IV, Hantusch's Tiger and the Pumas would take up positions with the other panzer stronghold at Werimont farm.
30 Account of M. Etienne Gregoire Lambert of their experiences in La Gleize 18—24 December 1944, no date, copy courtesy Will Cavanagh.
31 Fontaine, *op. cit.*, p. 40.
32 Account of Eugen Zimmermann, Tiemann, Vol. IV/2, *op. cit.*, pp. 93-94.
33 Not all were so lucky. Jules Legros and his wife Marie, abandoned the shelled ruins of their home in La Gleize on the 22nd to flee with their children to La Venne only to have their father seriously wounded on the road by shrapnel.
34 *Ibid*, p. 2042.
35 Reiser account, Tiemann, Vol. 2/IV, p. 104.
36 Account of Rolf Reiser, Tiemann, Vol. IV/2, *op. cit.*, pp. 97.
37 Bob Hall to author, 9 September 1995 and follow-up telephone conversation on 16 September 1995. Hall recalled moving from one location to the next as prisoner. 'I was in a large cellar for four days and then moved to another cellar which was hit during the night by artillery. It caught on fire, but they got us out of there ... We were treated as well as possible while we were prisoners ... We got out of there and moved to a church in La Gleize. In the church there were about twenty of us and a young German soldier guarding us with a rifle. During the night [of 23rd December] there was heavy shelling by our artillery. I knew our people were very close. Then, the German soldier put down his gun. It was the morning of December 24th, and our troops released us.'
38 Interview with Bob Hall, 16 September 1995.
39 McCown: 'Observations of an American Officer', *op. cit.*
40 McCown to John Toland, 5 April 1958, John S.D. Eisenhower Papers, Abilene, KS, Bitter Woods, Box 3.
41 The 7.5 cm KwK 42 (L/70) gun on the Mk V Panther could easily destroy a Sherman tank at a range of 2,000 meters. Moreover, at a range of 1000 meters the precision optics and rudimentary range finding equipment on the Panther could allow a trained gunner to achieve a 90% hit rate at a range of 1000 meters. A Sherman needed to be considerably closer to be assured of a hit and not head-on (broadside or rear shot) to penetrate the thick armor on the Mark V Ausf G.
42 The 3rd Battalion and the attached Task Force Jordan had held their position from 20-21 December before an enemy roadblock at K63035.
43 Rouat current spelling 'Roua' was not completely cleared until dark on the 22nd after house-to-house fighting. Task Force Jordan spent the night of 22 December in the village.
44 Knox account, *op. cit.*
45 'CCB S-2 Journal,' 1600 22 December 1944, NA, RG 407, 603-CCB-2.2, G-2 Reports, Box 12241.
46 'Annex No. 4 to S-2 Periodic Report,' 22 December 1944, NA, RG 407, 603-CCB-2.2, G-2 Reports, Box 12241. Location of dropped parachutists: K699867.
47 MacKay to author, 27 May 1995.
48 AAR 30th Infantry Division, December 1944, NARA, RG-407, 30th Infantry Division, 330-3.2, Box 7634.
49 'Borgoumont and the Battle of the Bulge,' Dr André Bastin, *op. cit.*

50 Transmission from Maj. Singleton, 1407, 21 December 1944, NARA, RG-407, 30th Infantry Division, 330-3.2, Box 7634.

51 Ehrhardt account, *op. cit.* 'Naturally, again and again one closed one's eyes in the most impossible positions and slept for minutes or quarters of hours. All in all, all the comrades, simple soldiers or commanding officers, were over-strained far beyond what one could call the limit of endurance. The faces were marked, unshaven, and unwashed; the eyes inflamed and everybody had a cold. Many were wounded—shocking conditions.'

52 Ferris, *op. cit.*, p. 42.

53 Ehrhardt account, *op. cit.*

54 'Testimony of Rolf Erhardt at Oberursel,' 30 October 1946. RG 549 'English Summaries and Translations of German Documents Related to War Crimes,' 290/59/18/2-5, Box 13.

55 Statement of Rolf Reiser, 20 March 1946. Original handwritten statements and English translation in RG-549, Case 6-24, Box 9. In later statements and the author's personal interviews with Reiser, he would vehemently deny the contents of this statement.

56 Did this shooting happen? NA, RG-549, Case 6-24, Boxes 8 and 9. Statements of Arvid Freimuth [no date], Herbert Stock [9 April 1946], Oswald Siegmund [4 April 1946] and Theo Rauh [5 April 1946] claimed it took place on 22 December.

> 'The shooting of prisoners of war took place on the 22 December 1944 in La Gleize. The following men participated in it: Rottenf. Dutschke, Max [Arvid] Freimuth, Oswald Siegmund, two or three men of the *10. Kompanie* and I. I was near my SPW as Rttf. Theo Dutscke came to me and drew my attention to the fact that seven or eight American prisoners of war had just been brought in. "They have to be bumped off." Dutschke then further added, "*Masche, Masche* [Preuss] is all for it."'

Rauh's statement claimed that the prisoners were shot in a heartless fashion—used for target practice, lined them up with their backs to a hill and shot from a sporting distance:

> 'I watched the shooting of the others and saw that each one of the men shot at the prisoner of war standing in front of him and thereupon the prisoner collapsed. I myself shot as one of the last ones, [Theo] Dutschke said once more to me, "Shoot, now it is your turn." I fired one shot with my 0.08 pistol at the American prisoner standing in front of me from a distance of about 3 meters ... I saw the prisoner hit by me fall forward dead. I had another look at the body and saw that I had hit the back of the head as intended. The American had a hole in the back of his head out of which blood trickled and he was dead.'

Oswald Siegmund claimed to have shot five prisoners on the orders of Preuss at the Froidcour castle on the 21st. He also corroborated Rauh's confessed incident, although careful to describe the idea of killing via target practice as not his own. Perversely, Siegmund's statement mentioned that they had the GIs turn their back to the shooting 'because we didn't want to let them see when we aimed at them because we had pity on them.' In another statement, dated 15 March 1946 [Box 9] Herbert Stock also claimed to have been involved in the shooting of twenty Americans at the church wall in La Gleize on 22 December along with other members of *11. Panzer Gren. Kompanie*: Gren. Karl Hähnel, Strm. Kumpf, Gren. Walter and Sonnenburg. On the other hand, the author has already noted a number of inconsistencies in Stock's confession leading him to question their content. Moreover, it is noteworthy that Freimuth committed suicide at Schwäbisch Hall after claiming that he had 'perjured' himself in his confession—likely with regards to this event. In the eventual Malmedy trial, SS Strm. Siegfried Lott of *11. Panzer Grenadier Kompanie* on 22 December claimed did not he see Oswald Siegmund, Stock or Rauh in the half-track of Rttf. Heinz Schwartz shoot Americans as target practice in La Gleize on the 22nd. Testimony of Siegfried Lott, U.S. v. Bersin, *op. cit.*, pp. 2889-2897. Stock himself, later retracted his confession—citing 'mistreatments and threats' in an affidavit at Landsberg dated 3 April 1948 [Box 54].

57 See statements of Erich Werner [4 April 1946] and Heinz Hoffmann [15 March 1946]. NA, RG-549, Case 6-24, Box 9. Both statements were later retracted.

58 In the Malmedy trial, Herbert Stock, Heinz Goedicke, Willi Richter, Fritz Rau, Fritz Gebauer and Adolf Weiss were accused of having participated in a mass execution in La Gleize of American prisoners before the church wall. One confession was for 18 December; another was for 22nd December. Defense attorney Walters,'The prosecution has totally failed to prove their *prima facie* case concerning the La Gleize incident,' he said, 'as no proof has been submitted of the finding of any dead bodies as a consequence of the alleged act.' There was 'not a shred of evidence' other than their own statements from Schwäbisch Hall. Defense attorney, Lt Col. Grainger Sutton agreed. The incident, he claimed, was a fabrication by the prosecution. 'Why has the Prosecution failed to produce Belgian civilians or records from the U.S. Graves Registration section to prove the death of American personnel? ... There were no deaths and no shooting as alleged by the Prosecution. You have heard the statements of other Belgian civilians, who certainly have no love for

the Germans and especially the SS, but they have in their own statements have admitted that no Americans were shot in the town of La Gleize during the time alleged by the prosecution.' U.S. v. Bersin, *opt. cit., p.* 3100–3127. For the story of Blokian: pp. 2819–2824.

59 Interview of Wilbert Wahler with Alfred Kreutz, 11 June 1946, p. 2825. Interview of Miles Rulien with Maria Gregoire and Armand Baltus 15 June 1946, p. 2826-2827.

60 Statements of having shot two American prisoners attempting to escape: U.S. v. Bersin, Statement of Axel Rodenburg, 25 February 1946, pp. 1455-1456; Rudolf Schwambach, 11 April 1946, pp. 1482-1483. 'My company commander was Jochen Thiele … Late in the evening of 15 December 1944, Thiele assembled the company and gave a short speech … I remember that he said that in the offensive which was to begin the next day, we should shoot down everything. We shall ruthlessly proceed under all circumstances and that no prisoners of war will be taken.' Statement of Günther Weiss, 12 April 1946, pp. 1486-1487.

61 U.S. v. Bersin, *op. cit.*, Testimony of Hal McCown on 20 June 1946, *ibid*, pp.1816-1853.

62 'Concerning treatment of prisoners by the SS, I can state that at no time were the prisoners of this organization mistreated. Food was scarce, but was nearly as good as that used by the Germans themselves. The American prisoners were always given cellar space to protect them from the exceedingly heavy American artillery barrages. I was taken briefly to the main prisoner enclosure which was in a large two-room, well-constructed cellar quite superior to any I saw in La Gleize. The men were considerably overcrowded and allowed the guards to bully them a little. I organized the entire group of 130 into sections, appointed a First Sgt. And laid down a few rules concerning rotation sleeping, urinating, equality and distribution of food and got the German warrant officer in charge of the prisoners settled upon a fairer method of giving water to prisoners and providing ventilation.' McCown: 'Observations of an American Officer.' *op. cit.*

63 U.S. v. Bersin, 'decided to fight to the last man.' p. 3052.

64 U.S. v. Bersin, Testimony of Gerhard Walla, pp. 2865-2876.

65 At Schwäbisch Hall, Hennecke would alter his story such that Peiper ordered a execution detail to be provided by Rumpf to shoot American POWs, rather than a deserter. It is noteworthy that Hennecke later denied the statement provided (see his Landsberg sworn statement of 20 January 1948), claiming that the changes to the story were orchestrated by dictation during his interrogation by Morris Ellowitz after being subjected to a mock trial (while a mock trial was administered, Ellowitz denied any dictation, saying the statements were voluntary; U.S. v. Bersin, p 2245). For his part, while in prison Hennecke reverted back to the previous version where the execution detail was to shoot an SS deserter and not American soldiers. 'Statement of Hans Hennecke,' 13 March 1946. NA, RG-549, Case 6-24. Box 9. Further, this version of the events was recounted by Gerhard Walla at the Malmédy trial who was present when Peiper gave the order to assemble the execution detail. (U.S. v. Bersin, pp. 2867-2869).

66 'Affidavit of Reinhard Maier,' 22 October 1947, NA, RG-549, Case 6-24, Box 63 (both German and English translation). Another statement of radio operator Jürgen Nerst (21 November 1947; same archival location) corroborated Maier's account. However, it must be noted that these statements arranged after Reiser was in Landsberg were subtly altered from the direct testimony of Gerhard Walla who was also there, who said it was Peiper and not Poetschke who said the deserter should be shot—a convenient change since Poetschke was dead while Peiper was still in prison on death row. Moreover, Maier, not so subtly took pains that Reiser was not connected with the decision to have the deserter killed.

67 'On 24 December 1944 at 0100, we abandoned all our vehicles and started walking back … We had to leave over 300 wounded in La Gleize.' Peiper, ETHINT-10, *op. cit.*

68 Heinz von Westernhagen to family, 27 February 1945, von Westernhagen, *op. cit.*, p. 47.

69 'OB West: Abendsmedlung vom 23.12.1944,' BA-MA, RH 19/IV-84. Earlier in the morning report on 23 December, *Heeresgruppe B* reported that *Kampfgruppe Hansen* was in attack in the direction of La Gleize to make connection with the *Kampfgruppe Peiper.*' However, by evening, the same commentary mentioned that Hansen himself was repelling determined attacks.

70 'First Army PWI Report: From the Bulge to the Rhine, Diary of Feldwebel Karl Laun,' 11/12 March 1945, NA, RG-338, U.S. First Army Interrogation Reports, ETO-MIS-Y, Box 64. (290/56/2/3).

71 In the six days of fighting *Kampfgruppe Peiper,* the artillery with the 30th Infantry Division recorded the expenditure of 57,275 rounds fired on Stoumont and La Gleize.

72 Testimony of Hal McCown, 20 June 1946, U.S. v. Bersin, *op. cit.*, pp.1816-1853. McCown of Peiper: 'However, he later told me he consolidated all wounded in the church and he suffered some further wounding of his casualties and a few deaths among both nationalities from both artillery and piece of roofing falling as a result of the artillery.

73 'I remember getting together with 134 or 135 American prisoners a day or before you were released. I had you count off and appointed a 1st sergeant and reminded you that you we were still under Articles of war. I remember telling you that we would probably be set free as the German captors were cut off from their own lines.' Hal McCown to Bob Hall, no date.

74 'Statements by Prisoner SS Standf. Joachim Peiper,' 15 September 1945 to Leroy Vogel, Oberursel, and 30 October 1946 at Landsberg to F.J. Pearson, within 'General Correspondence: 1939-1947, 333.9 Personnel: McCown Hal D., Interrogation of Col. Joachim Peiper, 30 October 1946,' NA, RG 159, Entry 26E, Box 531.

Chapter 29 – La Gleize

1 For the map that hung on the wall the Heeresgruppe B headquarters showing Peiper's encirclement Christmas 1944: BA-MA, Kart RH2 W/631.

2 As of the morning of 23 December, *Kampfgruppe Peiper* was now opposed by a conglomeration of American forces that amounted to the equivalent of a powerful U.S. armored division: a full U.S. infantry regiment (119th Infantry, 30th Division), a parachute infantry regiment (504th Parachute Infantry) and a full U.S. Armored combat command (CCB, 3rd Armored) with over a hundred tanks as well as other special troops. These included some five artillery battalions that were now tied in to the 119th Infantry Regiment as well as the 740 Tank Battalion and portions of the 743rd Tank Battalion and 823 TD Battalion.

3 '*Parole: 'Frohe Weihnachten,''* ('Password Merry Christmas') by Karl Wortmann, *Der Freiwillige 24, Nr.* 12 (December 1978), p. 4-6. 'Those comrades of the combat group who have so far come away unhurt have formed a strong, hedgehog defence in and around the village. Among the other armored vehicles, the Panthers, Panzer IVs, and Königstigers are standing well camouflaged in their positions, but they have no more fuel and hardly any ammunition.'

4 'First Army PWI Report: From the Bulge to the Rhine, Diary of Feldwebel Karl Laun,' 11/12 March 1945, NA, RG-338, U.S. First Army Interrogation Reports, ETO-MIS-Y, Box 64. (290/56/2/3). Entry for 23 December.

5 Ehrhardt account, *op. cit.*

6 Account of M. Etienne Gregoire Lambert of their experiences in La Gleize 18—24 December 1944, no date, copy courtesy Will Cavanagh.

7 At 6 PM that night, the ferocious shelling of La Gleize stopped once more, Lambert and his family used the opportunity to take to the roads in the darkness and make their way to Cheneux and safety. Also, account of Anne Marie Gregoire of La Gleize, courtesy of Marie France Gregoire.

8 Wortmann, *op. cit.*

9 'Observations of an American Field Officer Who Escaped from the 1st SS Panzer Division 'Adolf Hitler',' RG-407, 330-2.2 G-2 Records 30th Infantry Division Box 7569: 330-2.1, Operations Reports, December 1944, McCown's testimony was first reproduced in Annex 1 of 'Headquarters 30th Infantry Division G-2 Periodic Report,' No. 192, 26 December 1944. Afterwards it was widely circulated throughout the U.S. First Army at many command levels. Hereafter cited as McCown account.

10 'I immediately reported any news of that kind to the Führer and no one could have stopped me from doing so. As an example, Obergruppenführer Fegelein told the Chief of the General Staff, Colonel Guderian and Generloberst Jodl of atrocities committed by the SS Brigade Kaminski in Warsaw … Ten minutes later, I reported this fact to the Führer and he immediately ordered the dissolution of this brigade.' 'Testimony of Alfred Jodl,' Trial of Major War Criminals, International War Tribunal, Nuremberg, 1948, Vol. XV, p. 298.

11 'Screening Results 15- 24 November 1945,' SS Rttf. Gerhard Ellhof, 2nd Kp, Panzer Signals Battalion , LAH, Ellis Papers.

12 On the evening of 23 December, the 30th Infantry Division reported the capture of 41 wounded German prisoners at the *Chateau Froidcourr*, including NCOs and enlisted men from *SS Panzer Regiment 1* and *2 Battalion, Panzer Grenadier Regiment 2*. There were also three prisoners from *12 Kompanie, Parachute Regiment z.b.V.* There was also at least one member of the *6 Kompanie, 8. Regiment, 3rd FJ Division* who had become separated from his unit on 17 December, ended up with *Kampfgruppe Peiper* in Stoumont, and was captured in Targnon at 10 AM on 21 December. 'Report of IPW Information,' 22200, 21 December, 23 December 2200, 30th Infantry Division, G-2 Records, NA, RG-407, 330-2.2, Box 7593 and 7594.

13 'Consolidated Report from PW s from 1SS Panzer Division,' U.S. First Army PWI Report, 27 December 1944, NA, RG-407, 101.1- 3.2, M.L.-2125, Box 1497.

14 Testimony of Jochen Peiper, 21 June 1946, U.S. v. Valentine Bersin, Case 6-24, *op. cit.*, pp. 1960-1961.

15 Major Hans Ulrich Rudel, was arguably the most legendary Stuka pilot with the Luftwaffe during the war. Flying more than 2500 missions in spite of being shot down 30 times and losing a leg, he was credited with destroying 519 enemy tanks, countless vehicles and even a warship in his Ju87G. Rudel's exploits were so extraordinary that Hitler created a special medal just for him. However, contrary to what divisional headquarters told Peiper, Rudel and *Schlachtgeschwader 2* were in the East and not the Western Front. However, *SG-4* with its anti-tank rocket firing Focke Wulf 190 F-8s were available from *Luftflotte 3* out of Köln-Wahn, but could not operate in the soupy weather on 21-22 December.

16 'Report by Rolf Ehrhardt, 7th Panzer Kp., 1 Panzer Regiment, LSSAH Ardennes Offensive, 16 Dec. to 25 Dec. 1944,' composed in 1981, provided to author by Wolf Mauder translation by Helmut Thiess. (hereafter: Ehrhardt report).

17 Interview with Ralf Tiemann, *op. cit.*, 1995.

18 Interview with Walter Wiegand, 18 May 1999. 'We only had 35 tanks working after the Ardennes Offensive.'

19 'ULTRA: Sunset Daily Intelligence Reports, December 1944—January 1945,' NA, RG-457, SRS-1869, Pt. V, Sunset 782-784, 20-22 December 1944. 'Supply of 1 SS Pz Div in area five miles west of Stavelot envisaged for night of 21/22 December, but later cancelled due to bad weather.' *Sonderstaffel Einhorn* was a specialist FW-190G heavy bombing unit earmarked to attack enemy headquarters, bridges and high-value targets. The previous day, ULTRA intercepts had overheard the *1.SS Panzer Division* urgently request air attacks on all roads leading into Stoumont and La Gleize. PRO: DEFE (Defense Ministry) 3/320, BT 20, 21 December 1944. Meanwhile the war diary of *III.SG-4* (courtesy Jean Louis Roba) revealed that eleven FW-190s at Köln-Wahn had their armament changed to *Panzerblitz* mounts, on the 17–19th of December, but that heavy ground fog resulted in cancellation of missions on succeeding days.

20 '*Morgenmeldung vom 22.12.1944, Heeresgruppe B*,' OKW/WFSt/O.(H)/West,' Ia Report, *OB West Tagemeldungen*, BA-MA, RH 19 IV/84 D. In the same report, Model hopefully mentions the *SS Panzer Grenadier Regiment 1* was attacking west of Trois Ponts trying to reach Peiper against strong resistance from enemy tanks. At the end of the same day, *Heeresgruppe B* described the 'bravely fighting Leibstandarte Adolf Hitler' as having repulsed a total of 14 separate attacks from La Gleize to Stavelot.

21 '*Morgenmeldung vom 22.12.1944, Heeresgruppe B*,' OKW/WFSt/O.(H)/West,' Ia Report, *OB West Tagemeldungen*, BA-MA, RH 19 IV/84 D. In the same report, Model hopefully mentions the *SS Panzer Grenadier Regiment 1* was attacking west of Trois Ponts trying to reach Peiper against strong resistance from enemy tanks.

22 MacDonald interview with Karl Wortmann, 16 October 1982. Charles B. MacDonald Papers, USAMHI, Folder, '1st SS Panzer Division: Leibstandarte Adolf Hitler.'

23 Account of Karl Wortmann and letter to Gerd Cuppens, 21 December 1982, Cuppens archives, description of the fighting in Stoumont on pp. 31-32.

24 As with von der Heydte's paratroopers, the canisters were scattered. Three parachute bundles full of 88mm ammunition landed in Xheirfomont (610026) in the zone of 504th Parachute Infantry, a km south-west of Targnon and over 4 km from La Gleize. 'G-Journal,' 1500, 23 December 1944, NA, RG-407-382-2.2, Box 10414. The Germans intended to confuse the American forces with parachute drops, for a claim in the night of December 23rd by the 508th PIR and also V Corps at Camp Elsenborn of having been assaulted by enemy parachutists turned out to consist of 'dummies.'

25 'First Army PWI Report: From the Bulge to the Rhine, Diary of Feldwebel Karl Laun,' 11/12 March 1945, NA, RG-338, U.S. First Army Interrogation Reports, ETO-MIS-Y, Box 64. (290/56/2/3).

26 Jochen Peiper to John Toland, 22 February 1959, John Toland Papers: Battle, LOC, Box 108.

27 Jean Paul Pallud to author, 24 February 1987. Only about a dozen parachute containers were found in the 'Kessel' after the Germans abandoned La Gleize.

28 Hermann Priess, 'Commitment of the I SS Panzer Corps During the Ardennes Offensive,' NA, RG-238, Foreign Military Studies, MS #A-877. Priess recalled Peiper reporting he had been supplied with only 1.5 cubic meters of gasoline (~ 1500 Liters) from the failed resupply mission.

29 Interview with Bruce W. Tate, Jr., 5 December 1995. 'That additional day was the day we got out—Christmas Day … it was a pretty damned good Christmas present.'

30 *History of the 120th Infantry Regiment*, Infantry Journal Press, Washington D.C., 1947, p.132 'During the evening hours every man did his utmost in the face of totally unnecessary catastrophe; the wretched town, once so picturesque and lovely was now a beehive of half-angry, half dazed, but very busy men.'

31 'Telephone conversation of Gen. Hobbs with Gen. Harrison,' 1802 hrs, 23 December 1944, 30th Infantry Division G-3 Journal, NA, RG-407, 330-3.2, Box 8814.

32 'Telephone conversation of Gen. Hobbs with Col. Hill,' 1027, 25 December 1944, NA, RG-407, 330-3.2, 30th Infantry Division G-3 Records, Box 7635.

33 'Diary and Log of Medical Department, 30th Infantry Division,' T/4 Wilson E. Rice, 17 December 1944, NA, RG-407, 30th Infantry Division, Medical Detachment, 330-3.9. When the air force again bombed Malmedy over succeeding days, Rice could only rail at the incompetence. 'Nice going air force!' he entered sarcastically in his diary, 'There is a saying going around. 'When the Germans bomb, the Allies dig in. When the British bomb, the Germans dig in and when the Americans bomb, everybody digs in.'

34 For details, see Col. David Pergrin, First Across the Rhine, Zenith Press, St. Paul, MN, 1989, pp. 172-174. For photos of the Malmedy after the bombing, see Wolfgang Trees, *Schlachtfeld zwischen Maas und Rhein, Trian*gel Verlag, Aachen, 1995, pp. 164-168. For the telephone call to Corps headquarters from Maj. Thomas with 120th Infantry Regiment: 'G-3 Journal, 30th Infantry Division, *op. cit.*, 24 does 'December' go here? 1430 hrs. At 1519, Maj. Thomas phoned that 'We urgently need fire-fighting equipment … The equipment we had here is damaged.' At 1610: 'There are a lot of GIs buried in the debris, K and L Kitchen Companies and two mortar sections.' Fire consumed many buildings and whole blocks had been reduced to rubble.

35 Gen. William B. Kean, Hodges's chief of staff, assured Hobbs they would 'keep them far away. 'Telephone conversation of Gen. Hobbs with Gen. Kean,' 1645 hrs, 24 December 1944, 30th Infantry Division G-3 Journal, NA, RG-407, 330-3.2, Box 7634.

36 After the incident, an investigation was undertaken by the IX Bombardment Division. The weather had been good with good visibility, no flak and little in the way of distraction from enemy aircraft. In spite of many suggested explanations (a map from *Stars & Stripes* had erroneously shown the Germans to be in Malmedy), these were untrue: 'Six aircraft hit the town of Malmedy in friendly territory,' went the report for 23 December, 'due to misidentification of target … reason: bombardier misidentified target.' Royce L. Thompson, 'Malmedy, Belgium Mistaken Bombing, 23 and 25 December 1944,' OCMH, 5 June 1952, Washington D.C.

37 Between June and December 1944, the 30th Infantry Division was struck repeatedly by the U.S. Air Force—so often that after the debacles of 24 and 25 July 1944 its commander, Gen. Leland Hobbs, insisted on a wide margin between the location of his forces and the bomb line. During these two days, 93 were killed in action with a further 530 men wounded with sixty missing. The most infamous casualty of mistaken bombing attacks came on 25 July 1944 when Lt Gen. Lesley J. McNair was killed by an off-target carpet bombing on the 30th Division during preparations for *Operation Cobra.* He was the highest ranking American officer killed in action in World War II.

38 Jochen Peiper, 7 April 1946. 'Brief Review and Reflections about the Battle in the Russian Theater of Operations,' Burton Ellis Archives, original handwritten account and translation in author's possession. Also, 'An Interview with Obstgrf. Sepp Dietrich: Sixth Pz Army in the Ardennes Offensive,' Oberursel, 8-9 August 1945, ETHINT-15, NA, RG-238, Foreign Military Studies, p. 23. Sepp Dietrich to Hermann Göring: 'Your Luftwaffe is not worth a pfennig.'

39 Interview with Ralf Tiemann, 21 October 1995.

40 The chief of staff (Ia) with the Leibstandardte, SS-Stubf. Ralf Tiemann, would claim in composing the division chronicle that all the post war stories of the conditions placed on Peiper to break out were 'nonsensical.' Tiemann, *op. cit.*, p. 109. It is entirely possible that these were deliberately embellished by Peiper himself.

41 After the war, Rudolf Lehman recalled the message received from Peiper at 10 AM morning on 23 December 1944: 'Position considerably worsened; meager supplies of infantry ammunition left. Forced to yield Stoumont and Cheneux during the night. This is the last chance of breaking out.' Rudolf Lehmann, 'The I SS Panzer Corps During the Ardennes Offensive,' 1954, NA, RG-238, Foreign Military Studies, MS #A-779.

42 Peiper to Toland, 22 February 1959, *op. cit.*

43 Peiper's testimony at the Dachau trial, 22 June 1946, *U.S. v. Bersin, op. cit.*, pp. 1987-1988.

44 Rubel claimed he personally chose targets for the rounds fired from the 155mm gun into La Gleize that afternoon. However, in his account, Gen. Michael Reynolds states that from the *Château Froidcour* it was only possible to directly see the area around the church and the *Hôtel de Ville* in La Gleize —the rest being at least partly obscured by trees. (Reynolds, *op. cit.*, p. 227).

45 Gen. Harrison, 30th Division Telephone log, RG-407, 30th Infantry Division, 330-3.2, Box 7634.

46 Account of Lt Douglas J. Strand, D Company, 1st Battalion, 119th Infantry, no date, copy courtesy Michael Reynolds.

47 'German Counteroffensive: 3rd Armored Division Combat Interviews, Task Force Jordan,' NA, RG 407, 3rd Armored Division, Entry 427, Box 24090.

48 Gen. Hobbs to Gen. Harrison, 30th Division Telephone log, 1030, 23 December 1944, NARA, RG-407, 30th Infantry Division, 330-3.2, Box 7634.

49 Handwritten Crissinger account prepared for author, no date, but 1996.

50 'After Action Report No. VII: 823rd Tank Destroyer Battalion,' December 1944, NA, RG-407, TDBN-823-0.3.

51 Crissinger account, *op. cit.*

52 George K. Rubel, *Daredevil Tankers,* U.S. Army, Gottingen, September, 1945, p. 67. Rubel's florid account must be taken with a grain of salt. For instance, he claims erroneously, that Peiper decided to leave La Gleize primarily based on his shelling with his 155mm 'personal weapon.'

53 G-3 Journal 30th Infantry Division, *op. cit.*, conversation between Harrison and Hobbs at 2:32 PM on 23 December. Later, at 1542, Brig. Gen. Harrison received word that an air strike was on the way to hit La Gleize. 'That air strike will be there in a few minutes … make sure your people are ready to go as soon as the strike comes.' Harrison: 'Okay, we are waiting for it.' Yet, the strike never arrived over La Gleize, but instead Malmedy was hit.

54 Letter David Knox, 2 October 1984, courtesy Michael Reynolds.

55 'Combat Interviews with Capt. John W. Herdon and Capt. J.F. Gehman, TF McGeorge, 33rd Armored Regiment,' Ottre, Belgium, no date, NA, RG-407, 3rd Armored Division, Combat Interview, GL-191.

56 Ehrhardt account, *op. cit.*

57 Task Force Lovelady, east of Peiper could not help the other American forces in the attack that day, as it was isolated by the advance of *Kampfgruppe Hansen* over the Petit Spai bridge one km east of Trois Ponts. Even so the Germans could not get armor across to help in the fight; the first 24-ton Jagdpanzer IV self-propelled anti-tank gun that attempted to cross the foot bridge on the morning of 21 December had collapsed the structure and fell into the Amblève river.

58 G-3 Journal 30th Infantry Division, *op. cit.*, conversation between Harrison and Hobbs at 2:32 PM on 23 December.

59 The commander of the 117th Infantry Regiment, Col. Walter Johnson on the orders to pull out Task Force Lovelady at 1945 hrs: 'That will leave me weak, they are pushing into me now and one of my outposts were just shoved back.' Hobbs: 'Can't you replace them?' 'I have nothing to replace them with.' Fortunately, an hour later, Col. Lovelady was on the phone agreeing 'I cannot possibly get out of there before 1000 tomorrow morning. I cannot get a sizeable force out of there until then.' 30th Infantry G-3 Journal, *op .cit.*

60 'Telephone conversation of Gen. Ridgway with Gen. Hobbs,' 2043 Hrs, 23 December 1944, 30th Infantry Division G-3 Journal, *op. cit.*

61 'G-3 Journal,' 241030, XVIII Corps, NA, RG-407, 2.18-3.2, Box 4361.

62 'G-2 Message File and Journal,' *op. cit.*, 1635, 23 December, Box 7594.

63 'Telephone conversation of Gen. Hobbs with Brig. Gen. Boudinet and Col. Eaton,' 2046 and 21012 Hrs, 23 December 1944, 30th Infantry Division G-3 Journal, *op. cit.*

64 Account of Clarence Webster, prepared for author, 30 May 1996. Webster was the bow-gunner and assistant driver of the 105mm M4A3 tank of S/Sgt. Dexter B. Ledbetter. Their vehicle had just been appropriated from a depot in Sprimont two days before. The 740th Tank Battalion lost 40 men killed in combat in the Ardennes fighting.

65 There may have been a plan to erect a temporary bridge across the Salm for the retreating *Kampfgruppe Peiper* as the *Heeregruppe B* evening report of 23 December mentions that '*Kampfgruppe Peiper* repelling enemy successfully. Enemy attacks on La Gleize from the north, west and south … Auxiliary bridge at Trois Ponts to be ready shortly.' OB West KTB, *op. cit.*

66 'Interview with Lt Col. William Lovelady,' 5 January 1945, Harre, NA, RG-407, 3rd Armored Division, Combat Interview GL-191.

67 Preiss, *op. cit.*, *p.* 41.

68 After the death of Lt Albert W. Hope on the afternoon of 20 December, Maj. Stallings assumed command of Company E of Task Force Lovelady which was the 2nd Battalion of the 33rd Armored Regiment, 3rd Armored Division.

69 Letter George Gray to Haynes Dugan, 21 December 1992. 'Col. Stallings had sent me a message to hold at all costs. At that moment, one of my men was shot through the chest and we moved to the cellar of a home to take care of him. Later they threw grenades down the cellar steps and then came after us. They forced us outside and marched us to their company CP. The wounded man, David Conner, was taken to their aid station and that is the last I saw of him. He apparently died there; he is buried at Henri Chapelle. The rest of us were marched through St. Vith and wound up in Hammelburg.'

70 A. Eaton Roberts, 'Five Stars to Victory: The Exploits of Task Force Lovelady,' Atlas Printing, Birmingham, AL, 1949.

71 Letter Al Palfey to author, 2 February 1995. Also, account by Al Palfey: 'The Trap that Doomed Kampfgruppe Peiper,' 26 October 1992. Palfey was a radio operator with TF Lovelady.

72 On the morning of 23 December, E Company of the 120th Infantry Regiment fighting with Task Force Lovelady was pinned by sweeping machine gun fire from a house on the edge of Petit Coo. S/Sgt. Paul L. Bolden charged the house while T/Sgt. Russell L. Snoad covered him with rifle fire from across the street. The SS men in the house responded with a spray of machine gun fire that killed Snoad. Yet, Snoad's ultimate sacrifice allowed Bolden to fling fragmentation and white phosphorous grenades through the building's windows. As they exploded, he rushed to the door, kicked it, in and sprayed the interior with this Thompson submachine gun. Bolden, in turn was struck by four bullets from the SS men surviving and pulled back from the doorway and called for the enemy to surrender. When they did not, Bolden rushed the house again and shot down all who did not give up. Bolden was later awarded the Congressional Medal of Honor on 30 August 1945. Source: Medal of Honor Citation for Sgt. Paul L. Bolden.

73 Bolstered by the infantry of TF Hickory, TF Lovelady's assault resumed on Christmas Eve with a simultaneous infantry assault from both the north and east. Although the infantry suffered severe casualties from heavy weapons and artillery fire from the enemy still defending the forested hills east of Biester, the stubborn SS men south of Petit Coo were overcome by a tank assault. Stallings' besieged team was relieved in place at 11 AM on Christmas Eve morning.

74 Tiemann, *op. cit.*, *p.* 114.

75 These included the Tigers of SS Ustuf. Eduard Kalinowski (Nr 008), Oscha. Werner Wendt (Nr. 133) and SS Ostuf. Jürgen Brandt (Nr. 131).

76 'After Action Report: 30th Division Artillery, December, 1944,' 1 January 1945, NA, RG-407, 330-ART-0.3. The artillery strength of the division consisted of the 113, 118, 197 and 230 Field Artillery Battalions. Also attached during the period were the following: 391st FA,400 Armored Field Artillery (105mm) and the 18th Field Artillery Battalions. All tubes save the 118th FA and 230 FA Battalion were in support of the operation against La Gleize. Since the 19th of December, a provisional artillery battalion, 'Crunch Junior' was created, consisting of the cannon company of the 119th Infantry Regiment, six assault gun tanks of the 740th Tank Battalion and four miscellaneous guns with fire direction from the 197th FA Battalion. They did 'some fine shooting at a time when firepower was needed.' In a letter to the author, Pfc. Thomas Norrie (17 September 1995) described how those firing the Pozit fuze had to make sure there were no artillery observation planes in the area that could adversely trigger the proximity fuze.

77 When Peiper had first returned from Froidcour, he had made his headquarters in the cellar stone house of Mme. Adolphine Boulanger.

78 Ehrhardt report, *op. cit.*

79 Rolf Reiser indicated that Peiper received orders to breakout from division at 2 PM on 23 December. The various commanders were summoned to Peiper's command post and received a briefing on the escape operation. Germans in American uniforms from the *Unternehmen Greif* operation received orders to liquidate an American sentry near the Viaducts south of La Gleize where they expected to march out. Tiemann, *op. cit.*, p. 113.

80 Wortmann, *op. cit.*

81 Ehrhardt report, *op. cit.* Feldwebel Karl Laun had a cynical reaction after narrowly avoiding death under the artillery bombardment: 'Under these conditions and in the fact of the pleasant prospect of an impending bomber attack, which we learn about through interrogation of a captured U.S. major, Peiper decides to beat a retreat (*Absatzmanoeuvre*). But perhaps his prime consideration is his admiring Nazi contemporaries. If he could leave this trap by himself, I don't doubt for a minute that he would gladly leave us in the lurch. 'On the command 'Christmas present' we will fight our way back to the main line of resistance.' Those are the instructions which I get from the Old Man at 2000 hours.' Laun, *op. cit.*

Chapter 30 – 'Password Merry Christmas'

1 Traditional German *Volksweise*; lyrics by Ernst Anschütz, 1824:
O Christmas Tree, O Christmas Tree,
You give us so much pleasure!
How oft at Christmas tide the sight,
O green fir tree, gives us delight!
O Christmas Tree, O Christmas Tree,
You give us so much pleasure!

2 U.S. v. Valentin Bersin, Testimony of Hal McCown, 20 June 1946, pp.1816-1853.

3 Peiper to Toland, 22 February 1959, *op. cit.* Regarding McCown: 'You should not suppress that McCown's gallant testimony resulted in his being indicted for treason. The Chief Prosecutor in the Malmedy case, Lt Col Ellis, in open court claimed that McCown had committed high treason by giving away the array of American troops, and that he had acted as my adjutant during the breakthrough as otherwise it was inconceivable that we could ever have made this return to our lines. He was later court martialed [*sic*] and I, while I was already at Landsberg, was interrogated by a Pentagon Colonel, a very fine old Gentleman, who happened to be a soldier who understood soldiers' problems.'

4 McCown account, *op. cit.*

5 'Experiences of Maj. Hal McCown, December 18—25, 1944,' March 1966, Eisenhower Library, John S.D. Eisenhower Papers, Bitter Woods, Box 2. (hereafter 'McCown Experiences').

6 Peiper's recollection of the meeting with McCown: 'About noon on the 23rd, I received a garbled radio message from division from which I gathered that the combat group that had been sent to my relief was not moving forward anymore and that higher headquarters had the wish that I would return. I called McCown over in order to talk over the matter of prisoners and casualties and made a written statement with him on these subjects. I established that I would leave all prisoners behind except for Maj. McCown. He was to accompany me during the break and the following days I would approach the American lines again with him and at that time, the Americans were to hand over my wounded men, whom I was leaving behind, to me. At the end of this action, McCown was to be sent back to his own unit again. A captain of an anti-tank company who was also captured was to give this written statement to the American troops who would be arriving the next day. He was also put in charge of the prisoners who were remaining behind. I, myself, left a doctor—Dr. Ditmann—behind with the wounded.' Peiper testimony at the Malmedy trial on 21 June 1946, U.S. v. Valentin Bersin, *op. cit.*, pp. 1960-61.

7 Account for author composed by Bruce Crissinger, no date, but 1996. 'I had gone all day without urinating and I was in a bad way. I was able to make my Sergeant friend understand what I wanted to do. Picture

this: the town is burning, shells are falling and exploding and my heroic Nazi superman guard squats down close to the ground and covers his head with his arms while I relieve myself.'

8 These items can all be seen at Gerard Gregoire's *December 44* museum in La Gleize (now under new ownership) where the scene at the home of the Familie George is recreated exactly as Peiper and his men left it before they departed on Christmas Eve 1944. Peiper's map board is still there. http://www.december44.com/en/history_battle_of_the_bulgela_gleize.htm

9 'First Army PWI Report: From the Bulge to the Rhine, Diary of Feldwebel Karl Laun,' 11/12 March 1945, NA, RG-338, U.S. First Army Interrogation Reports, ETO-MIS-Y, Box 64. (290/56/2/3).

10 Rolf Ehrhardt report, *op. cit.*

11 McCown to John Toland, 5 April 1958, John S.D. Eisenhower Papers, Bitter Woods Papers, Box 2.

12 'He told me later that there were a few vehicles he had not destroyed.' McCown account, *op. cit.*

13 McCown: 'Observations of an American Officer,' 26 December 1945, *op. cit.*

14 A group of approximately fifty of Peiper's battlegroup north of La Gleize did not receive the orders to pull back with the rest. These SS men stayed on to fight stubbornly to the death on Christmas Eve 1944, eventually being overwhelmed by the closely supported assault by the 117th Infantry Regiment. Few prisoners were taken.

15 Helmut Naumann, 'Weihnachten 1944 in den Ardennen,' *Volksbund Deutsche Kriegsgräberfürsorge e.V, Pößneck*, 2004.

16 Wortmann interview, *op. cit.*

17 Wortmann, *Der Freiwillige, op. cit.* It should be noted, that the first heavy snow did not come to the region until 30 December 1944. However, on 22 December, light flurries dusted the area around La Gleize and there was thick hoar frost covering the trees and fields. See Gérard Gregoire, *Les Panzer de Peiper Face A L'U.S. Army*, J. Chauveheid, Stavelot, 1986, p. 23. Also, the weather reports from around Liège seen in the John Toland Papers, Battle, Box 137 which show snow flurries and fog on 22 December and clearing on 23 December (High 26, Low 20). The weather was clear and cold on the 24th (High 29, Low 19).

18 These included a number of refugees from La Gleize: Émile Boulanger and Joseph Dewez and their families as well as the Creutze child with them and Jules Delvenne and her baby.

19 Serge Fontaine, *Stoumont- Cheneux—La Gleize, December 1944, CRIBA*, Liège, originally printed in serial form by the Stavelot newspaper *Publicité Idéale* in 1970, pp. 46-47. The eight German parachutists claimed to be the survivors of a group of 40 men who had jumped with the provisions and supplies to Peiper just above Froide Cour during the night of 22 December.

20 The story of Legros, Hakin and Gason is from Fontaine, *op. cit.*, p. 48 and interview of Yvan Hakin by Jean Paul Pallud, 1980 during preparation of *The Battle of the Bulge: Then and Now.*

21 Tragically, young Ernest Gason would later be killed on 24 January 1945 by an unexploded mine on an SPW in the 'orchard of the tanks' in La Gleize where Peiper had left much of the physical material of his self-propelled panzer grenadier battalion.

22 Serge Fontaine, *Stoumont- Cheneux—La Gleize, op. cit.*, pp. 46-47.

23 'G-2 Journal and File,' 2245, 24 December 1944, 30th Infantry Division, NA, RG-407, 330-2.2, Box 7594.

24 Interview with SS Rttf. Hermann Staritz, *13. Infantry Geschutz Kp/ SS Panzer Grenadier Regiment 2*, 12 May 1999.

25 McCown Experiences, 'As he climbed the steep hill south of La Gleize, he took a last look back into the valley. It appeared to be a sea of burning vehicles and exploding ammunition.'

26 Wortmann, *Der Freiwillige, op. cit.*

27 'G-3 Journal, 30th Infantry Division, 24 December 1944,' NA, RG-407, 330-3.2, Box 8814.

28 McCown Experiences, *op. cit.* Also, 'There was no snow,' Peiper said commenting on Charles Whiting's version of this event, 'but the Christmas tree which I showed to McCown was covered by tinsel from American aircraft.' Jochen Peiper, *'Kommentar zum Buch Massacre at Malmedy* von Charles Whiting,' September 1971. The tinsel came from anti-flak radar chaff released by high flying bombers over the Ardennes on December 24th.

29 Interview with SS Rttf. Hermann Staritz, *13. Infantry Geschutz Kp/ SS Panzer Grenadier Regiment 2*, 12 May 1999.

30 This same low flying aircraft was recalled by Yvan Hakin in his interview with Pallud.

31 'After Action Report, 105th Engineer Combat Battalion, December, 1944,' 2 January 1945, NA, RG-407, 105-ENCBN-0.3.

32 Wortmann, *Der Freiwillige, op. cit.*, Ehrhardt report, *op. cit.*

33 Wortmann, *Der Freiwillige, op. cit.*

34 Ehrhardt report, *op. cit.*

35 In his interview with Pallud, Hakin recalled that Peiper ordered everyone to proceed south around 4 PM on Christmas Eve.

36 Staritz interview, *op. cit.*

37 Testimony of Hal McCown, *U.S. v. Valentin Bersin, 20 Ju*ne 1946, NA, RG -153, Case 6-24, pp.1816-1853.

38 Interview with Paul Fröhlich, 20 May 1996. Fröhlich indicated that this conversation was approximately correct in his memory. A similar version, evidently from Charles Whiting's interview with Jochen Peiper appears in *Massacre at Malmedy*, Leo Cooper, 1971, pp. 179-180 which Peiper agreed was true in his review of Whiting Book. Jochen Peiper, *'Kommentar zum Buch Massacre at Malmedy* von Charles Whiting,' September 1971.

39 McCown account, *op. cit.*

40 'Dans La Tourmente: Secteur de Cheneux- La Gleize et Trois Ponts- Wanne,' *Journal des Ardennes*, no date, copy courtesy Paul Natalis.

41 Serge Fontaine, *op. cit.*: Eventually, Hakin and Gason would double back to reach safety and Brume, and eventually La Venne from whence they had come. Meanwhile, as the 30th Division swept through La Gleize that day, at nightfall, the Americans had set up an outpost in La Venne. When the two Belgians returned they found themselves detained and sent up to 30th Division headquarters for interrogation. Yvan Hakin and Laurent Gason were questioned in front of Gen. Harrison of the 30th Infantry Division at the *Chateau de Froid Cour*: 'Where are the Germans going?' 'St. Jacques!' 'How many are there?' 'Two thousand.' 'Two thousand? Do you realize how many men that is?' Hakin and Gason then tried to show the route the escaping Germans had taken on a map. At 11 PM, the two Belgians were freed and driven back by jeep to La Venne. Meantime, the 30th Division alerted the 82nd Airborne Division that there were at least several hundred heavily armed Germans in their rear.

42 Uscha. Vock and four comrades of the artillery regiment also became separated from the main column during the brief clash with American forces. 'The point was engaged and had a short firefight. We also received some small arms fire. Counterfire began with 'Hurrah!' In a short but hard engagement the Americans were thrown back. All of a sudden the battle noise ceased. The enemy had withdrawn. But also our comrades were gone.' Eventually, wandering lost behind American lines, Vock and his comrades were made captive when the house in which the starving men took refuge was surrounded by American forces. Diary of Uscha. Vock in Thomas Fischer, *Von Berlin nach Caen*, Helios Verlags- und Buchvertriebsgesellschaft, Aachen 2004, page 192.

43 Naumann, *op. cit.* Eventually, Helmut Nauman would make his way across the Salm alone to reach a German flak gun position just on the other side of the river. Two unknown German comrades would offer the exhausted and wounded man a ride and two apples. 'Merry Christmas!' they shouted. 'It was my nicest Christmas present of my life,' Naumann recalled.

44 McCown account, *op. cit.*

45 The exact crossing site of the main column is about 1600 meters due east of Bergeval and 1 km north of Rochelinval. This was established by Ann Hamilton Shields in full day cross-country hikes conducted in September 2009, 2010, and 2012. Her journey retraced the steps of *Kampfgruppe Peiper* across muddy forest trails from La Venne circling up Mont St. Victor then to the crossing east of Bergeval. The final descent to the Salm is steep, awkward and hazardous. On the other side, the climb to Wanne is equally steep and taxing, particularly as it would have been in wet uniforms in freezing weather at the end of a starvation diet.

46 'G-2 Journal, 2045, 24 December 44,' G-2 Records of 82nd Airborne Division, NA, RG-407, 382-2.2, Box 10413. 'Well armed with bazookas at 669972, headed East. All infantry; did not fire on challenge.'

47 From the account of Wortmann, it seems that Peiper had not left the group, but in fact had gone up ahead to co-ordinate scouting patrols that would fan out to attempt to find safe passage to the east. 'Unexpectedly I am assigned to the next scouting patrol. With my machine pistol in firing position, I march away with about half a dozen men. After several hundred meters, we come out of the forest. Before us is an open and snow covered meadow … I am standing in the middle of a broad asphalt road and look in all directions. There is nothing to be seen or heard.'

48 After Peiper left the command group in the wee hours of Christmas 1944, the young Captain leader told my two guards: 'If he tries to escape, shoot him!' McCown to author 26 March 1995.

49 McCown account, *op. cit.*

50 In Ehrhardt's recollections, the situation devolved into one of great confusion on the late night of 24 December when no one could find Peiper. He was involved in the later clash with Company I of the 505th Parachute Infantry Regiment which he looked at as wildly fortunate given the chaos within Peiper's splintered column. Ehrhardt report, *op. cit.*

51 McCown experiences, *op. cit.* Also, Testimony of Hal McCown, *U.S. v. Bersin*, 20 June 1946, pp.1816-1853.

52 Report of Peiper's penetration across the Salm is found in the G-2 Journal of the XVIII Corps: 'Force of enemy infantry 50-150 strength armed only with side arms, no transportation, were engaged by 505 Regt. vicinity 669974 about 25100.' 'XVIII G-2,' Message at 430, 25 December, NA, RG-407, 218-2.2, Box 4360.

53 The author is deeply thankful to Ann Hamilton Shields for carefully determining Peiper's escape route on Christmas eve along with interviews of witnesses still recalling the events as children.

54 Staritz interview, *op. cit.*

55 Wortmann, *Der Freiwillige, op. cit.* The firefight that Wortmann describes, likely comprises two engagements, the earlier momentary contact that took place as they attempted to cross the N23 as well as the later confrontation as the column proceeded east of Bergeval. 'The captured American Maj. McCown takes good advantage of the situation. For a moment, his guards take their eyes off him and he takes his chances … Our confusion in the darkness gives him his chance for a dash for freedom. Half an hour after the exchange of fire, we jump across the road in one group. We land in a very deep ditch … The crowd is murmuring; everyone takes a deep breath. Wounded comrades get make shift medical care. The comrade next to me has been shot through his right shoulder. He is groaning in pain. Hardly recovered from shock, we hear a vehicle coming. "It always rains when it pours," someone whispers to me. Although we are not detected from the road, we creep even deeper into the mud … The armored car passes us at low speed, but they don't see us.'

56 An oft repeated opinion of SS veterans (e.g. author's interview with Paul Fröhlich) that Peiper had allowed McCown to escape was emphatically denied by Hal McCown in a letter to the author on 22 March 1996. Instead, McCown indicated that at all times during the trek out with the *Kampfgruppe Peiper*, that he sought an opportunity to escape. 'I believed Peiper's unit would make contact with U.S. combat units in his effort to return to areas of German control and this would give me my best chance for escape.'

57 Interviews with Karl Paul Fröhlich 20 May 1996 and 19 May 1997. In the author's interview with Peiper's motorcycle messenger, Fröhlich indicated, that in spite of postwar legend, he did not purposefully allow Maj. McCown to escape.

58 Serge Fontaine, *Trois Ponts: Decembre 1944, Quand les Ponts Volaient en Eclats,* November 1992. Arthur Deroanne escaped at the same time that McCown did during the clash with Company I of the 505th Parachute Infantry. Deroanne eventually returned to Bergeval.

59 'I was taken successively from their Battalion CP to the 82nd Airborne Division CP to XVIII Corps CP and then back to my own division CP from when I re-joined my unit.' McCown account, *op. cit.*

60 McCown to author, 26 March 1995.

61 'Ardennes Campaign 'The Bulge,' December 1944 & Jan-Feb. 1945,' by William T. Dunfee, 10 October 1985, Columbus World War II Roundtable Collection, Courtesy of Ohio Historical Society, Columbus, OH. 'We would have been content to hold what we had and let Jerry attack. Every time he tried, we cleaned his clock. We were dug-in on the Salm in good position. The one bridge in our area was rigged for demolition. If the enemy tried to get armor across, the first one would have gone airborne … Our withdrawal was reluctant; we hated like hell to give up what we had fought so hard to take … We knew the withdrawal wouldn't be easy either, especially at night. We were very much aware of German presence in our rear and that some of them spoke English and had American uniforms and vehicles.'

62 Communication with Raymond Maikowski, Jr., 9 November 2008. Also, letter William Dunfee to Raymond Maikowski 29 September 2000.

63 Reconnaissance of the approach to the Salm River crossing from Bergeval to Wanne evaluated on foot by Ann Hamilton Shields on 10 August 2010. 'Peiper Route: Salm Crossing, Trois Ponts, Stoumont and Monschau,' document prepared by Ann Shields for author on 14 August 2010.

64 Wortmann, *Der Freiwillige, op. cit.*

65 'First Army PWI Report: From the Bulge to the Rhine, Diary of Feldwebel Karl Laun,' 11/12 March 1945, NA, RG-338, U.S. First Army Interrogation Reports, ETO-MIS-Y, Box 64. (290/56/2/3). 'We start out again at 0200 hours. The once-arrogant SS Kampfgruppe Peiper collects it's sad-looking remnants. In single-file we march over the road bridge south of town. The objective is to regain the main line of resistance at Trois-Ponts. The Tigers, Panther, and a large number of vehicles, self-propelled, and heavy weapons—now become the booty of the Americans, provided they haven't been knocked out by the Yank artillery already. I even forego the destruction of my 2-cm flak pieces, although I have orders to do so. The way leads over cliffs and through swampy bayous, which often look deceptively as if they are frozen. The Panzerfauste load us down. Nobody knows why we drag these bothersome gadgets with us but slyly and cautiously these toys are discarded. A few machine pistols and carbines follow suit. Our password is "Christmas present"—and we get it. When we reach the mountaintop at daybreak, the surprise parcel already awaits us. It comes in the form of a column of troops marching down a newly constructed forest road. At first we don't know whether we have Germans or Yanks in front of us. However, that characteristic U.S. steel helmet soon dispels all doubts. All discipline breaks as everybody scrambles for cover. The danger passes—they don't see us. But the long chain of 700 men has irrevocably been broken. I am fortunate in having my lens-covered compass with me and I take it upon myself to select the escape route for my small group. The lengthy detour around Bodeux appears safer to me than the direct road over the bridges at Trois-Ponts. Noontime finds us exhausted and with empty stomachs. Nobody has a bite to eat with him; orders were to carry along small arms and nothing else. A burning thirst which is caused by the dry cold bothers us most. The men tear ice-covered snow from the trees and suck on it. Others, animal-like, throw themselves over each puddle and drink the muck.

We have to cross one more stretch before we get to Bodeux. In packs of twenty men each, we dash over the road. With our steel helmets in hand, with our ragged camouflage suits, we look more like hobos than soldiers. Dejectedly through a curtain-fog does the sun sink on our antics down here. We stumble along, but then trouble starts multiplying for the circle of *Jabos* above apparently takes interest in us. We perspire profusely in our heavy camouflage suits. At last I get myself to stoop over a murky creek, but my thirst becomes only more painful.

'The forest seems to be without an end. Under the curtain of darkness, we cross a busy highway. In the meantime, 200 men have gathered again and this group tries to reach the German lines in Wanne. Hunger forces me to eat my carefully hoarded chocolate bar. But the thirst becomes insufferable. Our lips are chapped and start cracking. I don't give a damn anymore about the cleanliness of the puddles over which I throw myself, but the mouldy moisture begins to nauseate me.

'The men are becoming more and more exhausted. Here one falls by the roadside and there another breaks formation—probably to stay behind and spend the rest of the war in a prison camp. When we take a five-minute break, some fall asleep on their feet, don't wake up when we resume march, and in the darkness we never see them again. Morale as well as the thermometer seems to be reaching the zero point. We stumble over rocks, get stuck in the moors, tear our hides on the primeval underbrush. At last we reach a good road. We follow it and then find a giant castle. Perhaps it is an abbey. But our dream castle all of the sudden turns into a bastion as only 100 meters away we see parked American vehicles. An American sentry challenges us. Like a bunch of cornered rats, we scatter back into the forest. One of the Greif boys gets orders to approach the sentry. An argument between the real and pseudo American ensues. And the incredible insolence of the Greif man succeeds; he manages to deceive the sentry! But we still have to take the precaution of making a wide circle around the castle …

'So that was my Christmas! A merry Christmas indeed. At dawn, around 0400 hours, we reach the town of Ville du Bois, where we at last see German outposts again … I am overjoyed to be out of this action. To have fought with the SS sure isn't a recommendation for a visit. Perhaps there will soon be a better chance to surrender. But it was just out of the question to get caught with those SS criminals.

'That the long detour we took over Bodeux paid dividends, we learn in the morning. Other groups of stragglers who tried to cross the Salm at Trois-Ponts got entangled with American platoons in which the Kampfgruppe suffered some casualties, among them Peiper, who stopped a bullet with his hand. Oh, hell, why couldn't that Yankee take better aim?'

66 Staritz interview, *op. cit.* 'I think we lost some in the river; some of the men had been afraid of the water.' The road Staritz refers to is the likely now the N68 along the east side of the Salm.

67 Peiper to his father, 2 December 1946, NA, Case 6-24, RG-153, Box 83.

68 Interview with Karl Paul Fröhlich 20 May 1996.

69 'They left as soon as they appeared.' Interview with Karl Paul Fröhlich, 20 May 1996.

70 Wortmann, *Der Freiwillige, op. cit.*

71 Interview with Hans Siptrott, 15 July 2012.

72 Testimony of Werner Löhmann at the Malmedy trial, U.S. v. Bersin, *op. cit.*, p. 548-550. Löhmann was the gunner with Horst Pilarzek's Panzer #734 of the 3rd platoon of the *7. Panzer Kompanie.* He made a virtually identical statement at Schwäbisch Hall on 7 March 1946, NA, RG-549, Case 6-24, Box 32. In that statement he also recalls the briefing given to the platoon by Hans Siptrott just before the attack. 'The enemy must learn to fear us again. Therefore, we will fight in the old SS spirit. There is a new order that no prisoners of war will be taken.'

73 For Brig. Gen. Harrison's planning for the capture of La Gleize: Capt. Franklin Ferris, 'The Defeat of the 1st SS Panzer Division Adolf Hitler,'CI-94 containing GL-225, NA, RG-407, XVIII Corps 218-2.2, Box 24037.

74 Hobbs to Harrision, G-3 Journal, *op. cit.*

75 'From In 119th Infantry. Intercept message indicates that enemy are trying to attempt to break out either from the east or West from La Gleize,' message dated 24 December at 9 AM, 'G-2 Journal, CCB, 3rd Armored Division,' 24 December 1944, NA, 603-CCB-2.2, G-2 Reports, Box 12241.

Chapter 31 – Vanquished

1 BA-MA RH IV/76. *OB West Kriegstagebuch*, 25.12.1944, Frame 158.

2 OB West KTB, BA-MA, RH 19 IV/86, entries for 24 and 25 December 1944.

3 Tiemann, *op. cit., Vol.* IV/2, p. 119.

4 'There was nothing further to be seen of the men, who were allowed to sleep through to the next day.' Manfred Thorn to author, 27 December 2008.

5 Interview with Ralf Tiemann, Untergruppenbach, 21 October 1995.

6 'I myself was slightly wounded while breaking through the American main line of resistance, precisely west of the Salm [River]. I had a violent heart attack and was taken down there unconscious … I did not sleep for nine days during the offensive. In Wanne, I found an aid station of my regiment which had been

established by my regimental surgeon, Dr Sickel. I was bandaged there and slept for a while.' Testimony of Jochen Peiper, 21 June 1946, U.S. v. Valentine Bersin, Case 6-24, *op. cit.*, pp. 1962-1963.

7 'Highlights of Hitler's Speech—New Year's Eve 1944/45: G-2 Periodic Report No. 205, U.S. Third Army G-2,' 2 January 1945, NA, RG-407, 103.2.1.

8 Heinz Guderian, *Panzer Leader,* E.P. Dutton, NY, 1957, pp. 314-316.

9 Hitler at *Adlerhorst* on the night of 29-30 December 1944. See Fragment Nr. 30: Walter Warlimont, *Inside Hitler's Headquarters,* Praeger Publishers, 1964, p. 495-496.

10 Hitler's discussion with Zimmermann about the whereabouts of *Kampfgruppe Peiper* on 10 January 1945 is from transcript No. 19/45—Fragment 33; Helmut Heiber and David M. Glanz, eds. *Hitler and his Generals,* Enigma Books, NY, 2003, pp. 596-597. The original source transcripts captured at Berchtesgaden are at the National Archives in records of the ETO Historian: RG 498, UD 304, Box 1372.

11 The *OB West* maps for the period (BA-MA, RH2W/646, 31.12.44) show on 31 December that the *1.SS Panzer Division* had combat ready 14 Mk IVs, 3 Mk Vs, 14 Mk VIs and 9 Jagdpanzer IV anti-tank guns. In repair: 6 Mk IV, 5 Mk V, 14 Mk VI and 7 Jagdpanzer IV.

12 Christa Schroeder, *Er war mein Chef,* Nation Europa Verlag, GmbH, Coburg, Germany, pp. 150-151. Schroeder's account provide important background and squares with other accounts.

13 Personnel file for Johannes Göhler, NA, BDC Microfilm, RG-242, Roll SSO-A33343-SSO-018A. Also, Investigative Repository Report for Johannes Göhler, NA, RG-319, IRR Report No. XE-084023. Göhler was with the *SS Kavalerie Brigade* for 25 Jun 1941 through 10 November 1943. Hannes Göhler was clearly in Himmler's good graces, being elected to teach SS officer cadets in Bad Tölz for a period in 1942. Later, on 20 August 1944, he was attached to Hitler's headquarters as Hermann Fegelein's adjutant. For the overwhelming case regarding the guilt of the *Kommandostab Reichsfuehrer SS* of which Göhler was a part in 1941, see Martin Cüppers *Wegbereiter der Shoah. Die Waffen-SS, der Kommandostab Reichsführer-SS und die Judenvernichtung 1939-1945,.* Darmstadt 2005.

14 In July 1941 within *SS Kavalerie Brigade,* Göhler was platoon leader *III./ 3. Squadron* under SS Hstuf. Johann Schmid. After the war during war crimes proceedings, Schmid admitted, ordering Göhler to shoot Jews in the summer of 1941, but claimed Himmler's order was '*Wahnsinn*'—insane—a typical postwar alibi. The case was closed by 22 December 1970, since according to new German laws, the court had to prove killings were done 'with pleasure.' Killings by superior order could not be pursued any longer. Even so, Göhler denied, that Schmid ever ordered him to kill Jews. Source: Schmid Statement: Bundesarchiv Ludwigsburg (BArchL), B 162/5531, Verfahren gegen Gustav Lombard u.a., Einstellungsverfügung 22.12.1972.

15 Johannes Göhler to his wife on 21 and 25 December 1944, Microform Ltd. David Irving Collection, *Hitler's War,* Film 97125, Reel 4, Section 15. In several letters exchanged in 1999, Göhler agreed to meet with the author to discuss his memories of late 1944 and some very mysterious happenings at the end of the war in May 1945 at Fischorn castle near Zell-am-See in Austria. However, during review of other correspondence Göhler had with contemporaries (*Nachlasse Hans Schwarz van Berk* in particular at the BA Koblenz), the author learned that Göhler was a vehement Holocaust denier as well as a likely participant in the crimes of extermination of the *SS Kavallerie Brigade* in the summer 1941. For example, on 3 August of that month, the brigade reported that through that date it had liquidated 3,274 partisans and 'Jewish Bolsheviks' without any losses of their own—a telling indicator of the nature of their operation. For the very significant declassified source indicating the Allies knew in the summer of 1941 that the Germans were liquidating Jews on the Russian front: 'Summary of German Police Decodes, 3 July—14 August 1941,' PRO, HW 16/6, Pt. 1, Kew, UK. For a summary of this data: Richard Breitman, *Official Secrets: What the Nazis Planned, What the British and Americans Knew,* Hill and Wang, 1998. Over time, the author learned that Göhler was in close contact both with Walter Harzer as well as Peiper in the 1960s—what looks to have been the inner Waffen SS circle in Stuttgart. The author's communication with Göhler ended abruptly in 2000 when he realized the author did not have the proper sympathies. Göhler denied the Holocaust until his death in February of 2003.

16 In fact, most of the voluminous stenographic notes of many of Hitler's wartime conferences were lost at the end of the war in a plane crash. During the waning days of the war, the Hitler attempted to save valuable documents from falling into the hands of the occupying forces. 'Operation Sergalio' involved using ten Ju52s to spirit away Third Reich insiders to Berchtesgaden along with ten crates stuffed with official archives from the Berlin bunker. Headed to Southern Germany, the flights departed on 22 April 1945. One of the lumbering Junkers transport crashed in East Germany, near the Czech border. Hans Baur, Hitler's personal pilot who was present in the bunker, later recalled that when Hitler heard of this crash he became very upset exclaiming, 'In that plane were all my private archives, that I had intended as a testament to posterity. It is a catastrophe.' James P. O'Donnell, *The Bunker,* Houghton Mifflin, NY, 1978, pp. 116-118. Baur remained totally devoted to Hitler later in life, professing to be disappointed that Hitler himself would not accept his offer of aerial refuge to avoid suicide in Berlin. He had three super-long-range Junkers 390s at Kladow and another at Rechlin. 'Right up to the last day,' he stated proudly after the war, 'I could have flown the Fuhrer anywhere in the world.' Hans Baur, *Ich flog mit den Mächtigen der Erde,* Pröbster, Kempten, 1957, p. 251.

17 'On Christmas Eve I did not get to bed until 0230 hours, on Christmas Day 0300 hours and on the second holiday not until 0430.' 'Typed transcript of shorthand diary kept by Ministerialrat a.T. Karl Thöt, 16 December 1944,' Microform Ltd. David Irving Collection, *Hitler's War*, Film 97125, Reel 4.

18 BDC File on Joachim Peiper, NA RG-242, A 3343-SSO-348A. Vorschlag Nr. 1 für die Verleihung der Schwerter zum Eichenlaub das Ritterkreuzes de E.K, ' 26 December, 1945.

19 Robert E. Merriam, *Dark December*, Ziff-Davis, NY, 1947, p. 194. For the episode with Göring: Parker, *To Win the Winter Sky op. cit.*, pp. 318-319.

20 Operational tank strength for *1.SS Panzer Regiment* on 9 January 1945 assembled in Bras after the final fighting east of Bastogne: 1 Mk IV, 3 Mk VI, 2 Jadgpanzer IV, 2 Flakpanzer IV, NA, RG-238, 'LVIII Panzerkorps,' T-314, Roll 1498.

21 'The Ardennes Offensive was for us no extraordinary undertaking,' Peiper later declared. 'It was relatively benign compared to the Russian theater of operations.' Jochen Peiper, 'Kommentar zum Buch *Massacre at Malmedy* von Charles Whiting,' September 1971.

22 '*Sehr viel höher, zielen wenn man unten treffen will.*' Peiper's recollection of his 1945 conversation with Genflm. Model is from an interview with Peiper in 1974. Transcript from Hans Kettgen and courtesy of Harvey T. Rowe. Peiper had started the offensive with approximately 3,500 men with 117 tanks, 149 SPWs and 800 vehicles, and had returned with only 800 men and the small arms they walked carried. Peiper also admitted leaving upwards to 300 badly wounded men at the *Château Froidcour* and at the church in La Gleize. The strength of the tank regiment alone was 2,300 men. For numbers see Reynolds, *op. cit.*, pp. 48-50; also detailed email to author 'Losses to Kampfgruppe Peiper,' from Timm Haasler, 6 March 2023. Haasler cautions against data presented by Dugdale as much is not sourced and possibly not reliable (Jeff Dugdale, *Panzer Divisions, Panzergrenadier Divisions, Panzer Brigades of the Army and the Waffen SS in the West: Autumn 1944-February 1945, Ardennes and Nordwind, Their Detailed and Precise Strengths and Organizations*, Vol. 1, (Milton Keynes, UK: Military Press, 2000), 36-38.

23 When Peiper was asked how his unit got so far in the Ardennes? Peiper answered: 'No. First, the Americans were so bad. They were not used to such things. They slept at night. And second, we really did not advance that fast. The ones behind us were so slow. They should have come faster. If you ask me, the catastrophe was that the German side did not lead from up front, they all drove behind me. And since we continuously had bridges blown up in front of our noses and had no bridge building equipment with us, we had to look on the map for ways around. Constantly, I got away from main roads to get around bridges through terrain that at that time was soaked soft. The ones behind me just pigheadedly followed our tank tracks. They all got stuck, in the forest and in the mud. While we out front had run out of fuel, munitions, and nothing was following. Things were so congested, that not even wounded personnel could be brought back, not to mention prisoners.' Kettgen interview.

24 'Josef Goebbel's Christmas Eve address to Germany,' intercepted by 12th Army Group Intelligence Services, 2130, 24 December 1944, NA, RG-407, 4th Infantry Division, G-2 Records, 304-2.3, Box 5692.

25 Heinz von Westernhagen to family, 29 December 1944. Copy of original letter graciously provided by Dörte von Westernhagen.

26 Sworn statement of Theo Gernt, 13 April 1948, NA, RG-549, Case 6-24, Box 57. According to SS Oscha. Gernt, the loss to Goltz's Company, which had a strength of 450 men, was 60 killed in action and 240 wounded.

27 Interview with Mme. Juliette Antoine, 19 October 1995. After the SS men left, Mme Antoine evacuated to Stavelot on 27 December. Her husband Morris had fled before the Germans arrived. While hiding at a farm near La Venne he became a witness to Peiper and the column of SS men escaping from La Gleize on Christmas Eve. Morris became very concerned for his wife after learning that many of the people around Stavelot had been killed. On 28 December, Juliette's husband passed through Renardmont and vomited after seeing what the SS men had done to children and infants there. The following day, the couple returned to their home to find a live cow standing in their smashed living room and lowing over the body of a dead SS man.

28 Serge Fontaine, *Stoumont—Cheneux—La Gleize, CRIBA*, 1995, p. 41.

29 George A. Auer (117th Infantry Regiment) to author, 26 August 1995.

30 Tiemann, *op. cit.*, p. 120.

31 Interview with Serge Fontaine, courtesy, Marie France Gregoire, prepared for author in 1995. Julie Marechal, was also at Werimont, returned to find everything torched. 'We were just crying when we saw it,' she remembered. 'We had nothing left.'

32 Peiper's testimony on 21 June 1946: 'The morning of 26 December, I was ordered to my division C.P. The divisional CP was in a little castle about ten kilometers east of Wanne … I had to report what had happened in the operation which had been concluded to my division commander in presence of the commanding officer, General Priess. I was there until noon. From there, I drove to Blanche Fontaine from there and established a command post in the chateau Petit Thier.' U.S. v. Valentin Bersin, *op. cit.*, p. 1963.

33 Peiper's Ritterkreuz commendations, written the day after his disastrous return to Wanne still focused strongly on his old cronies in the SPW *III. Battalion*: 'SS Hstuf. Diefenthal has proven himself to be outstanding in all the field campaigns up till now,' Peiper effused. Mohnke made no effort to deny the mollycoddle , instead letting Peiper take favorites. 'Diefenthal took part in the decisive events related to the penetration in the Ardennes … The Panzer group was positioned on the 18th of December before Stoumont where they experienced dogged resistance in extremely difficult terrain from the Americans blocking their approach. They repulsed a counterattack and then pulled up in the streets and attacked the enemy in the flank … By lightning-fast decisions, Diefenthal immediately followed the heels of the retreating enemy and exploited the resulting panic.' NA, BDC files for Josef Diefenthal (A 3343-SSO. Roll 148) and Georg Preuss (A 3343-SSO. Roll 392A). Strangely Peiper says Diefenthal was instrumental in seizing a bridge beyond Stoumont—likely an exaggeration by Peiper who was by plan, looking to seize the span at Lorcé for his advance over the Meuse.

34 '*Krankenbericht über Herrn Joachim Peiper*,' War Criminal Prison #1, Landsberg/Lech Hospital, 11 December 1954, NA, RG 549, Records Related to Parolees, Box 94, Peiper Medical Files, National Archives.

35 Even within the Waffen SS, Dr Kurt Sickel presented an unsavory character, likely moved into the Leibstandarte because his questionable practice would be acceptable in its ranks. He had been an old-timer in the Nazi movement (born in 1907), his personnel file exposing that he had been politically active since 1923. He had joined the Allgemeine SS in 1931 and was with the Leibstandarte infantry from 19 September—4 November 1939 during the Polish campaign. Afterwards he was with General Inspector of the *SS Totenkopf Standarte* from 20 April 1940 through 30 January 1942 where he worked for Odilo Globocknik. He was later responsible for '*the health of the people*' [author's italics] at concentration camps at Lublin, Lodtz and Maideneck where he was considered indispensable. NA, BDC file for Kurt Sickel, A3343-SSO-134B. When he was interviewed in 1946, his interrogators found him 'a sly, but rather unintelligent bull.' One interrogator told Sickel that they knew everything about his past, 'and he started apologizing about his activity in the extermination camp about which I knew nothing. I let him talk about this and after having spoken about the killings of hundreds of thousands, I incidentally asked about the one killing at Petit-Thier which he admitted right away explaining, 'Here you see, we are not accustomed to highly evaluate a human life.' NA, Case 6-24, RG-549, Box 31. In his own testimony on 9 April 1946 (Case 6-24, RG-549, Box 9) he described his career:

> [S]hortly after the outbreak of the war, I was transferred to the East with the SS Totenkopf Cavalry Division. My duties were supervision of the health of the troops and of Polish Jews, who were constructing a lager for themselves and later were used as slave laborers in the SS works. Later, that is in the years 1942 to 1944, I was garrison surgeon for Lublin, that means I was responsible for the health of the troops and also for the Jews that were brought in from all parts of Europe into the concentration camps in the area of Lublin … I was responsible for these camps for the state of health in the camps from their installation until their dissolution. In these camps, no gassings took place. Executions were occasionally carried out. Now and then, against my will, and on order of my superiors I had to deliver to the *Vernichtungslager* Maideneck, persons who had been working for me in the orthopedic workshops. It was known to me that gassings took place there and that these people got gassed. However, I did not myself, conduct any gassings … On the whole I had to supervise in these camps the health of about 20,000 Jews, men women and children. Continuously new trains arrived from all part of Europe, among them Czech, French and Rumanian Jews. All these camps dissolved one morning in November 1943 by shooting all Jews without me knowing about it. For this purpose these Jews had to build enormous ditches then were lined up in the ditches one close to another and were shot with machine guns and rifles. Then the second shift would go into the ditches and the procedure repeated. The ditches were about 2 ½ meters deep and the Jews were shot in about 4 to 5 layers. Men women and children were shot in the same trenches. According to my estimate, about 20,000 Jews were shot in this manner … Shortly after the extermination of the lagers in the Lublin area, which were under my medical supervision, I got transferred back to the LSSAH to which I belonged already since 1939.

During the eventual trial, the rumor widely circulated among Peiper's men that there were bad things about Sickel and that he was pleased to be in the Malmedy trial rather than one of the more damning tribunals for concentration camp types. Opined Erich Rumpf 'Even if he was never in a battle, but he got the Iron Cross—a fact greatly resented by those who had earned that honor. Some derogatorily referred to him as 'a man of intrigue'—a veiled reference to his shady early-war duties with the concentration camp system. 'He was very disliked,' remembered one officer, 'others made fun of him behind his back referring to the doctor as *Sie Eckel*— 'you bastard.' Source: 'Handwritten testimony of Erich Rumpf,' RG 549, Case 6-24, Box 32. Part of the voluminous notes produced by Erich Rumpf while in captivity, much of it not utilized either by the defense or prosecution. Translated and utilized here for the first time.

36 In his testimony at the Malmedy trial, Peiper estimated that the incident at Petit Thier took place around the 4th or 5th of January. (*op. cit.*, p. 1963). However, this may have been an error as the incident likely took place a week earlier before Peiper moved south to the Bastogne area. Indeed, there are various testimonies about the date it took place. Quite important is the testimony of Otto Wichmann who claimed the incident took place 'in the last few days of the year 1944 or the first four days of 1945.' 'Statement of Otto Wichmann,' NA, RG-549, Case 6-24, Box 9. It is possible, however, that after the fighting around Bastogne that Peiper, Poetschke and the staff of the 1st SS Panzer Regiment all returned to Petit Their before shipping back off to Germany for refitting.

37 'The Truth About Malmedy,' William R. Perl, *Prevent World War III*, September, 1949, William R. Perl Papers, Box 6, George Washington University, Washington D.C. For a contrary statement regarding the Petit Thier incident, see exculpatory testimony of Friederich Ritschel who was Peiper's orderly at his regimental headquarters: 'On or about 10 or 13 January 1945, I was in Peiper's room at the castle or rather the hunting lodge (the only house in the area). Dr Sickel, the former SS Maj. Poetschke and SS LtCol. von Westernhagen were also present. … These officers were just drinking coffee, when the former SS Sgt. Wichmann entered the room with an American prisoner. It was easy to see that the American soldier was very sick, freezing and hungry; he had the sleeves of his field jacket wrapped around his feet and could hardly move. Wichmann told Peiper that he had found this American soldier in the woods … Peiper gave him hot coffee and a cigarette, I think. He asked him his age and how long he had been wandering around the woods. The soldier could hardly speak. Then Dr Sickel said that the soldier was so sick that his brain could no longer function and he could not be cured … Peiper then told Dr Sickel that it was his job as the medical officer to take care of a sick soldier. Dr Sickel then left the commanding officers room accompanied by the soldier and Wichmann.' 'Testimony of Friedrich Ritschel,' Munich 21 January 1948, NA, RG-153, Case 6-24, Box 80. That Wichmann boasted of having shot the American seemed common knowledge for SS men in captivity. 'In Zuffenhausen, SS Oberscharführer von der Heide told me that Unterscharführer Wichmann had shot two persons. He also told von der Heide that he had carried out the shooting upon order. I do not know whose order.' 'Testimony of Rolf Ehrhardt at Oberursel,' 30 October 1946. RG 549 'English Summaries and Translations of German Documents Related to War Crimes,' 290/59/18/2-5, Box 13.

38 'Affidavit of Hans Gruhle,' Landsberg Lech, 14 January 1948, NA, RG-153, Box 83, Case 6-24. Gruhle, who was then also a prisoner at Landsberg with Peiper claimed to have never heard of any regimental order—'no oral order or even unofficial hint' enjoining the shooting of prisoners prior to the offensive. Of course, both Ritschel and Gruhle had real motive in attempting to assist Peiper and keeping the stories straight. Peiper was in deep trouble because of Wichmann's testimony regarding the incident. Both Ritschel and Gruhle repeated that they thought the incident happened 'about 13 January 1945—the date I cannot fix with certainty.' 'Statement of Hans Gruhle,' 18 March 1946, NA, RG-549, Case 6-24, Box 9. Dr Sickel's testimony on Petit Their, 'In the first days of 1945, the exact date which I can no longer remember.' 'Statement of Kurt Sickel,' 9 April 1946, NA, RG-549, Case 6-24, Box 9.

39 'I can still remember that after the prisoner had been led out of the room, we talked about what an immense energy this man must have had, when he could wander around in the woods for 14 days in this weather.' Statement of Joachim Peiper, 26 March 1946, translated from Peiper's handwritten document of 11 pages, Schwabisch Hall, witnessed by Ralph Shumacker and William R. Perl., NA, Case 6-24, War Crimes Cases Tried, RG-549, Box 9.

40 '*Offensive des Ardennes: Note Archives Paroissiale de Petit Thier (Vielsalm)*,' Calthay Cure, Petit Thier, 17 June 1949. Copy courtesy Will Cavanagh. 'They installed themselves in houses which seemed the most comfortable and said they were waiting for new vehicles which never arrived. Their boss was near [Peiper] where later they found American prisoners who had been shot. These are the ones who were suspected of massacres in Stavelot, Trois-Ponts, and Wanne. The German occupation of the village lasted until the 16/17th of January and here are several incidents that occurred during that time. A civilian, Frans Carpentier, was executed on December 24th in the evening. The soldiers declared to the priest that they killed him because he indicated the way leading from St. Hennard to Vielsalm was passable. Further down that way a tank hit a mine and six men were injured. On the 27th the burgomeister, the police chief, the teacher and the priest were interrogated regarding the *Armee Blanche*. None of them came to any harm.'

41 '*Prestation de Serment: Fait á Petit Thier, le 23 mai 48, Camille Gerardy*,' NA RG 549, Entry 143, War Crimes Tried, Box 59. On 27 December some men of the 12th Panzer Grenadier Company relaxed in Petit-Thier over a card game. Anton Motzheim recalled: 'I played cards with several other NCOs of my company and friends of mine and I am certain that the following were there: Uscha. [Wilhelm] Pluscke, Uscha. Kindler, and Uscha. Richter. Everybody was talking about the incidents in the Eifel campaign and I described how I shot an American soldier [in Honsfeld. Statement of Anton Motzheim, 28 February 1946, NA, RG-549, Case 6-24, Box 8. So legally damaging would be Motzheim's description of the Petit Thier card game (he was sentenced to death) that comrade Paul Pötz would issue a sworn statement on 29 May 1947 claiming to have been at the card game and that Motzheim did not make the admission of having shot an American soldier.

42 OB West KTB records that the portions of the division, including what was left of the panzer regiment, moved off from the Vielsalm area to Schimpach on 16.25 PM on 28 December 1944 with most of it arriving east of Bastogne by 21:30 hours the following day. BA-MA, RH 19 IV/86, entries for 28-29 December 1944.
43 Tiemann, *op. cit.*, Vol. IV/2, p. 129.
44 *Heeresgruppe B* maps show *1.SS Pz* operational tank strength on the last day of the year at 14 Mk IVs, 3 Mk Vs, 13 Tigers and 9 Jagdpanzer IVs: BA-MA, RH 2W / 646, 31.12.1944.
45 For an overview of this phase of the battle from the German perspective: Karl Heinz Schulz, *'Die 1.S-Panzer Division 'LAH' im Einsatz in der Ardennes Offensive 1944,' Der Freiwillige,* Heft 4, April 1965.
46 Confirmation of Peiper's medical condition is contained in a report by Dr Kurt Sickel, dated 30 January 1945 in Peiper's BDC files. NA RG 242, A 3343-SSO-348A.
47 Reynolds, *op. cit.*, p. 248.
48 'I dare say I did not sleep at all for nine days … I never even had a chance to shave,' Peiper to Toland, 22 February 1959, *op. cit.*
49 The full excerpt of Hitler's speech to Himmler's generals on 28 December 1944 can be read in *The Battle of the Bulge: The German View: Perspectives from Hitler's High Command,* D.S. Parker (ed.), 1999, Greenhill Books, London, pp. 213-227.
50 Linge diary, *op. cit.*, for 27 and 28 December 1944. Letter to Gerda Bormann on 28 December 1944: H.R. Trevor Roper, *The Bormann Letters,* Weidenfeld & Nichols, London, 1954, pp. 151-152.
51 'Enemy has infiltrated through the north-east of Lutrebois with 20 tanks and have that town.' U.S. 4th Armored Division, HQ CCB, S-3 Journal, 30 December 1944, NA, RG-407, 604-CCB-3.2.
52 Section on Manfred Thorn's experiences from author's interview on 23 March 1996. Also, see account of other German veterans in this action in Ralf Tiemann. *Chronicle of the 7. Panzer-Kompanie 1. SS-Panzer Division,'* Schiffer Military History, Atglen, PA, 1998, pp. 126-135.
53 See Hugh M. Cole, *The Ardennes Campaign: The Battle of the Bulge, OCMH,* U.S. GPO, 1965, pp. 626-627. The ambush that struck down the *7th Panzerkompanie* was likely the 35th Tank Battalion of the 4th Armored Division and its attached 701st Tank Destroyer Battalion.
54 Manfred Thorn, 'Off to War with the Leibstandarte—to Russia, Normandy and Dachau,' Nuremberg, privately printed, copy provided to author, 2010.
55 '1 SS Pz Div. LAH: 2 SS PGR: G-2 Periodic Report, No. 208, HQ U.S. Third Army, G-2, 5 January 1945,' NA, RG-407, 103.2. The I and II Battalion took up positions on the high ground before Lutrebois when the German attack stalled on 30 December. All members of the rearguard in that village were captured on 1 January and the three tanks escorting the grenadiers were also destroyed by air attack on the same day.
56 U.S. 35th Infantry Division, After Action Reports, December, 1944 and Daily Log of Division Historian, NA, RG-407, 335-0.3.0 and 0.7. 'On the last day of December, attempts to relieve the situation of K and L companies, 137th, were in vain. They were finally given up for lost when it was learned from German prisoners that they had either been killed or captured.' Also, 'Combat Interview: 35th Infantry Division, 14 January 1945,' USMHI, CI-107, Carlisle, PA.
57 An indication of the severity of the total tank losses in the Ardennes comes from a report dated 9 January, while the Leibstandarte was nominally part of the LVIII Panzerkorps. This shows total armored strength available to the panzer regiment concentrated around Bras, amounting to a single Mk IV, three Königstiger, two Jagdpanzer IV and no Panthers at all. 'Kriegstagebuch Gen. Kdo LVIII Panzer Korps,' 9 January 1945, NA, RG-338, T-314, Roll 1498. For Peiper's presence at Poetschke's headquarters, author's interview with Rolf Reiser 15 May 1997 and correspondence with Reiser on the particulars of the Bastogne incident: 23 August 2006.
58 See 'The Penalty Platoon, an Institution of SS Divisions,' U.S. III Corps, G-2 Periodic Reports, Daily IPW Report No. 35, 20 January 1945, NA, RG-407, 203-2.2. 'PW was AWOL one day, at a time when the division (LAH) was not under commitment … A court-martial sentenced him to six months in a penalty platoon … When the division is committed, the penalty platoon is attached to some battalion and always selected for particularly dangerous tasks … In Lutremange, the PW began to realize that it was cold-blooded murder to order the German soldiers to attack without artillery or even heavy weapons support.'
59 'Feldgericht der Leibstandarte SS Adolf Hitler: Mißrauch der Disziplinarstrafbefugnis: SS Haupsturmführer Werner Poetschke,' 18 May 1944, BDC File for Werner Poetscheke, NA, BDC A3343-SSO-386A. The action was over harsh treatment of a motorcycle platoon during the actions at Kharkov in January 1943.
60 Interview with Reinhold Kyriss of the *7.Panzerkompanie,* 20 May 1997. Regarding Peiper's quarrel with Poetschke: 'What Peiper meant was that it wasn't useful to kill our men in punishment.' Although the heated argument between Peiper and Poetschke is denied by a number of interviewed officers, the historical record reveals two separate interrogations of Leibstandarte men immediately after the war who corroborated descriptions of the event. All were with the *7.Panzerkompanie.* Interrogation card for SS Unterscharführer Josef Frank, NA, RG 549, Records of U.S. Army Commands, Records of HQ U.S. Army Europe (USAREUR), Index to Defendants in the Malmedy Case (No. 6-24), Defense witness statements. (290/59/18/5).

61 Interview with Hans Siptrott, 15 July 2012.
62 'U.S. Third Army, CG Report: Notes on the Bastogne Operation,' December 1944, NA, RG-407, 103-0.5, Box 2019.
63 George F. Hofmann, *The Super Sixth: History of the 6th Amored Division in World War II,* Sixth Armored Division Association, Louisville, KY. 1975, p. 287.
64 George S. Patton, Jr. *War as I Knew It,* Boston, Houghton Mifflin, 1947, p. 213. Ladislas Farago, *Patton: Ordeal and Triumph,* Dell Publishing Co., NY, 1963, p. 694.
65 'G-2 Periodic Report No. 195, 215 and 222: HQ Third U.S. Army,' 23 December 1945, 12 and 19 January 1945, NA, RG-407, 103-0.5.
66 Genmaj. Ludwig Heilmann, '5th Paratroop Division' 1 December 1945 to 12 January 1945,' MS B-023, NA, RG 338, Foreign Military Studies. Hoecker was commander of the nearby 167th Volksgrenadier Division.
67 "Fernschrift, 11 January 1945," BDC File of Joachim Peiper, op. cit., message signaled from Hitler's headquarters by Johannes Göhler was 2:25 AM and signed by Hitler.
68 Peiper was the only SS officer to be given a commendation for the Ardennes operation in his award on 11 January 1945. Further, the only other leader to achieve the Oak Leaves and Swords was old Genflm. Von Rundstedt himself. The only officer to receive a higher award was Gen. d. Pz Hasso von Manteuffel who had lead the 5th Pz Army within three miles of the Meuse River and received the Diamonds to the Knight's Cross on 18 February.
69 'Erklaerung von Tegernsee zur Larettstadt,' Telegram from Rudolf Brandt, 29 January 1945, NA, T-175, Roll 18. For Peiper's movement in January, we only have the evidence of the movements of the remaining tank elements to the St. Vith area on 10 January and then the dispatch of the division by rail from the Eifel beginning 15 January. (Ralf Tiemann, *Chronicle of the 7. Panzer Kompanie: I. SS-Panzer Division 'Leibstandarte,'* Schiffer Books, Atglen, PA, 1998, pp. 136-137. It is possible, that Peiper stopped off briefly in Triberg, Germany to visit Himmler as this was on the way back to Rottach Egern. For the period issues of the *Tegernee Tal* showing Peiper's promotion in January, I am indebted to Dr Michael Heim.
70 'General d. Art. Warlimont to Reichsführer SS,' z Zt. Gmund a/Teg. Ackerberg, 18 December 1944, T-175, Roll 29, Frame 2536490.
71 'Against a hostile world, I once chose my road, according to my inner call, and strode it, as an unknown and nameless man; often, they reported I was dead and always they wished I were, but in the end I remained victor in spite of all ... Only He can relieve me of this duty Who called me to it. It was in the hand of Providence to snuff me out by the bomb that exploded only one and a half meters from me on 20 July, and thus to terminate my life's work. That the Almighty protected me on that day I consider a renewed affirmation of the task entrusted to me ... We show overcome this calamity too, and this fight, too, will not be won by Central Asia, but by Europe against the East for 1,500 years and shall represent it for all times: our Greater German Reich, the German nation.' For Hitler's speech of 30 January 1945: Nathan Ausubel, ed., *Voices of History 1945-46,* Gramercy, New York, 1946, pp. 46-50.

Chapter 32 – Finis

1 Albert Speer, *Inside the Third Reich,* Macmillian, NY, 1970, p. 538-539.
2 Nicolaus von Below, *At Hitler's Side,* Greenhill Books, London, 2001, p. 223.
3 Edward R. Stettinius was head of the U.S. Department of State: 'American Interests—Germany,' 29 December 1944, NA RG 549, Case 6-24, Box 22. Also, 'U.S. Protests Nazi Massacre of Yank Prisoners,' *Washington Star,* 30 December 1944.
4 Charles Ashman and Robert J. Wagman, *The Nazi Hunters,* Pharos Books, 1988., p. 66.
5 'Information to Establish Prima Facie Case Required by SHAEF Court of Inquiry: Headquarters First U.S. Army to Commanding General 12th Army Group, 27 January 1945, NA, Case 6-24, RG-549, Box 23.
6 The stories of Henri Lejoly and Madame Bodarwe are covered in detail in *Fatal Crossroads, op. cit.,* 208-214.
7 'Report of the Supreme Headquarters Allied Expeditionary Force Court of Inquiry re Shooting of Allied Prisoners of War near Malmédy, Belgium, 17 December 1944,' National Archives, RG 331, Entry 56, Box 127.
8 'German Defends War Brutalities,' *Baltimore Sun,* 10 February 1945.
9 Francis Edwards to author, Petersburg, IL, August 1995.
10 The night before on 30 December, a small 'Combat patrol of Cupboard (120 Inf. Regt) reached Baugnez crossroads at midnight, but captured no enemy. Returned at 0030.' The following night, Pulver would attack with a large combat team. RG-407, 330-2.2 G-2 Records 30th Infantry Division, Box 7595.
11 'History of the 120th Infantry Regiment,' *Infantry Journal Press,* Washington, 1947, p. 137.
12 For quotes from soldiers of the 30th Infantry Division recapturing Baugnez: Hal Boyle, '50 of Massacred U.S. Captives Are Dug from Snow in Belgium,' Associated Press, 15 January 1945. For Inspector General's initial report: 'Information to Establish Prima Facie Case Required by SHAEF Court of Inquiry, Reference Number IG-101,' 27 January 1945, NA RG 153, Case 6-24, Box 70.

13 January 12th: Company L of the 120th Regt reports reaching Baugnez at 0830 AM on the 12th. Left on the edge of town. Snow was 15 inches deep. 37 buzz bombs flew over during the 24 hours period. January 13th: 'To the East in the sector of the 120th Infantry, the 3rd Battalion advanced against mortar, artillery and small arms fire at 0830 when it passed through Geromont and seized the crossroads at Baugnez. Three PWs were taken in Baugnez, 2 from the 3rd Company of the 293rd VGR and one from the 14th company wielding panzerfausts from the same unit. Resistance consisted of small arms, mortar and artillery fire. During this time the 3rd Battalion of the 119th Infantry was still fighting in Hedomont at 0800 and receiving direct fire from a single tank south of the town. At 1130, the battalion was fighting in the town house-to-house. RG-407, 330-2.2 G-2 Records 30th Infantry Division, Box 7597.

14 Killed by machine gun bullets, Pfc. Elmer W. Wald, noted by placard #19, had fallen with his hands over his head only to freeze in this position to be photographed in this position, three weeks after he died.

15 Report for 13-14 Jan: 9th Parachute Regt defended tenaciously at Thirimont. At 1745 on 13 January, they counterattacked with one battalion of infantry, advancing in waves supported by one company of tanks or assault guns. They were driven back by our intense artillery fire … During the attack, two tanks were knocked out. One light counterattack the next day at 1300 moved in with one tank supported by thirty infantry men. Enemy used Thirimont as mutually supported strongpoint and automatic weapons placed in windows made any attempt by our forces to moved, met by strong fire from town … Snow and close-growing trees made movement extremely difficult … Interrogated prisoners still were confident of victory given 'the German fighting spirit and the Führer's infallibility.' Interrogation Report No. 113, 14 January 1945. RG-407, 330-2.2 G-2 Records 30th Infantry Division, Box 7597.

16 This is not to say that there were not indiscretions on the American side. Joseph Peters, an Unteroffizer with the *3. Fallschirmjäger Division,* described a confusing battlefield incident which took place on 29 January 1945. On that date, Peters and a large number of German paratroopers wearing white camouflage snow capes were captured at a farmhouse in the Ardennes border town not far from Losheim. Unfortunately, after surrender a couple of German members suddenly produced weapons and demanded that the half dozen Americans guarding them surrender instead, 'All Americans hands up!' Looking at his comrades, Peters was aghast. 'You must be mad!' Shots rang out and Peters dived into a snow drift. Moments later, while he hid, he heard sustained machine gun fire. 'After about 10 or 15 minutes, we heard English voices. I stood up again and put my hands in the air. We were quickly taken onto the street. At this point there were 10 of us who had been hiding there. Then we were marched in single file to the first house on the village. It must have been the Leuther house which was demolished in 1984. We were taken then and I saw on the ground, 20 or thirty German soldiers were lying on the ground … There was blood coming out of their mouths and blood stains all over the ground. I remember, shouting: "*Die wollen uns ja erschiessen*!—They want to shoot us!" We turned around and we were looking at the muzzles of the American automatic weapons. Shots were heard again. Everybody dropped to the ground again and I started to feel a searing pain on the right side of my body. I automatically fell down and then realized what had happened; that the soldiers lying next to us had been executed. I thought about what had happened and stayed there unmoving until nightfall. I could feel pain on my right side and as the hours passed …

I lay lying there until about 7 or 8 p.m. and it was about -15 °C and very cold. I was so stiffly frozen that I thought that I must risk surrendering again. I did that and walked onto the street. There was a fountain there and I shouted something, but I cannot remember what. I was delirious. Two American soldiers came to the Leuther house and frisked me for the rest of my personal belongings. The two Americans then took me to a house opposite the courtyard of the Leuther house where obviously the command post was set up. There, there was an American officer, a interpreter who asked me where I came from, which unit, name etc. He couldn't tell them anything. All I said, was that I was hurt. The American then told me I was going to the prisoner's assembly area at the school of Holzheim. There was a German medic there who could fix me up. In the classroom there was about 50 German prisoners of war. They were very noisy, because near the school there was a nursing area and there was a lot of red wine there and they had been drinking. The guard had gone to the interpreter who said, "Please be quiet." Then he came again, "Be quiet for the last time … This afternoon we stood thirty men up against the wall, and it won't bother us to if we put another thirty up there." But the noise didn't drop much. About 11—12 hours went by. After that things became peaceful. The interpreter said again, "You will see your buddies early tomorrow morning. You're going to go past there." The next morning, we were taken past the Leuther house and there I saw my comrades piled up on a big heap. I also saw a dead friend with my document bag and my utensils, but did not dare to step out of line to get these things.' Kurt Fagnoul and Hubert Jenniges, ed. *End un Wende im Lande zwischen Venn Schneifel: Augenzeugen berichten von ihren Kriegserlebnissen* 1944/45, ZVS, St. Vith, 1995. Indeed, Holzheim was captured on the afternoon of 28 January 1945 by the 1st Battalion of the 508th Parachute Infantry Battalion. The incident becomes even more controversial since the chronicle of the 508th records that some eighty German troops were captured in Holzheim, but that 'half of these where killed in a failed escape attempt.'

1st Sgt. Leonard A. Funk, Jr. of C Company received the Congressional Medal of Honor for this action (see his Medal of Honor citation in which 21 Germans were killed in the action and another 24 wounded). While there is no question that Funk bravely foiled an enemy escape attempt with his submachine gun, local villagers in Holzheim contend that a number of German soldiers were executed after the failed escape was over. Author's interview with Peter Lenz: 22 March 1996: 'I heard about this [shooting] from the witness in Holzheim who saw it—Morges Christian. They were murdered by the side of his house. It was common knowledge to the locals there.' Funk's buddies with Company C recall him grieving over the death of Company Clerk, Edward C. Wild who was killed in the initial escape attempt. With the medal of honor bestowed by President Harry Truman at the White House in August 1945, Funk became the most decorated U.S. paratrooper of WW II. Gerard M. Devlin, *Paratrooper!*, St Martin's Press, NY, 1979, pp. 542-544.

17 'Interrogation Report for Soldat Gregor Buschhaus, 21 May 1945,' FID IPW Team 223, Report Nr. E 254, NA, RG-338, Records of the Military Intelligence Service Field Interrogation Detachment, 290/56/2/6, Box 83.

18 For Peiper, a nervous wreck in December, 1944: Interview with Gerhard Walla, 10 May 1999. Also, Sigurd Peiper to Hedwig Potthast, 11 December 1944, *Hitler's Warrior, op. cit.*, 111. 'He is totally at the end of his nerves and no longer up to the demands of the front.'Background on the Peiper family residence in Rottach-Egern: Interview with Astrid Nathan and Charlotte Zimmermann, Tegernsee, 17 August 2003.

19 For Peiper's presence at Birkenwald: 'Termine des Reichsführers SS am 4.2.1945,' (NA RG-242, R112, 2637562.

20 Hitler's Warrior, *op. cit.*, 117.

21 'Conversation of Karl Wolff with Lt Klapps,' CSDIC/CMF/X 169, 21 May 1945, TNA, WO 204/12804.

22 For the scene at Birkenwald, *Hitler's Warrior, op. cit.*, 118-119. Also, Hans-Georg Eismann, *Under Himmler's Command*, (West Midlands, UK: Helion, 2010), pp. 34-37. The fate of Hans Kammler at the end of the war has been shrouded in uncertainty for decades. Recently documents have emerged suggesting that Kammler was captured by U.S. intelligence at the end of the war, but without further information regarding his fate. Frank Döbert and Rainer Karlsch, 'Hans Kammler, Hitler's Last Hope, in American Hands,' Wilson Center, Cold War International History Project, Working Paper #91, August 2019.

23 For Peiper's presence on the tour of Berlin, Patrick Agte's statement of Werner Grothmann, 13 May 1998 as cited in Agte, *op. cit.*, p. 510.

24 H.R. Trevor Roper (ed.), *The Bormann Letters*, (London: Weidenfeld & Nichols, 1954, pp. 167-168.

25 Jochen Peiper to Willis Everett, 14 July 1946, Willis Everett Papers. After the war, the story widely circulated of Hitler's 27 April 1945 order for Waffen SS forces to remove their embroidered uniform cuff titles after the surrender of Austria's capital, Vienna. The story of Sepp Dietrich's irreverent response had its origins from Hugh-Trevor Roper (The Last Days of Hitler, Macmillian, 1947). With gallows humor, Dietrich supposedly remarked: "We call our¬selves Panzer¬armee 6 because we have only six panzers left." Nevertheless, it seems that only the members of the 12th SS "Hitler Jugend" Panzer Division actually removed cuff titles. Peiper and the 1st SS Panzer Division, "Leibstandarte Adolf Hitler," did not. See Magnus Pahl, *Fremde Heere Ost: Hitlers militärische Feindaufklärung*, Berlin, Ch. Links Verlag, 2012, pp. 258-259.

INDEX

F

G

H

I

J

K

S

Y

Z